PHILOSOPHY IN THE MIDDLE AGES

The Christian, Islamic, and Jewish Traditions

SECOND EDITION

EDITED BY

Arthur Hyman YESHIVA UNIVERSITY

James J. Walsh COLUMBIA UNIVERSITY

Hackett Publishing Company
Indianapolis

The paper in this book meets the guidelines for permanence and durability of the Committee on Production Guidelines for Book Longevity of the Council on Library Resources.

SECOND EDITION, SECOND PRINTING 1984

Printed in the United States of America

Cover design by Richard L. Listenberger

For further information, please address
Hackett Publishing Company
P.O. Box 44937, Indianapolis, IN 46204

Library of Congress Cataloging in Publication Data
Main entry under title:
Philosophy in the Middle Ages.
Includes bibliographies.
Includes index.
1. Philosophy, Medieval—Addresses, essays, lectures.
I. Hyman, Arthur, 1921– . II. Walsh, James J.
(James Jerome), 1924– .
B720.P5   1983   189   82-23337
ISBN 0–915145–81–2 (cloth)
ISBN 0–915145–80–4 (pbk.)

Contents

Latin Philosophy in the Fourteenth Century 593

Preface to the
Second Edition

WHEN THIS volume was first conceived, we prepared a list of selections based on our experience in teaching medieval philosophy over a number of years. We subsequently circulated our list among teachers at many colleges and universities. Unanimity was not to be expected, but a broad consensus emerged concerning the basic selections. We take responsibility for the final content, but we wish to thank these colleagues for their ready and most helpful responses. Since its appearance in 1967, the volume has found wide acceptance and become a standard work for teaching medieval philosophy in the English-speaking world. We are also grateful for this expression of confidence on the part of our colleagues.

We agreed at the start that this volume would include more than the selections one might expect, especially from the then more neglected areas of Islamic, Jewish and fourteenth-century Latin philosophy. Colleagues who have used the volume have confirmed the soundness of this decision. Because our original publisher specified that the volume could not exceed 750 printed pages, we had to make a number of difficult decisions; one of the most difficult was to conclude the section on Jewish philosophy arbitrarily with Maimonides. Another was to omit all materials pertaining to the medieval background for natural science. In the light of this history, we welcome the opportunity provided by our present publisher for a modest expansion. We have, of course, revised the bibliographies, and we have made the following changes and additions:

In the Islamic section we have added a selection from Algazali's *Tahāfut al-Falāsifah* containing his discussion of causality. This serves to round out the other discussions of causality and has been requested by a number of colleagues. Our major additions have been in the Jewish section. The selection from Gersonides' *Wars of the Lord* deals with God's knowledge and the related problem of His knowledge of contingent beings. The selection is important for its critique of Maimonides and shows that Jewish philosophers addressed a topic that was also of central concern to late medieval Latin philosophers. It also contains a discussion of the view held by Maimonides that essential attributes applied to God must be interpreted as negations, another topic shared with Christian philosophers such as Aquinas. The selection from Crescas' *Light of the Lord* contains part of his critique of Aristotelian philosophers. They had argued that human happiness is achieved by the development

ix

of the human intellect, resulting in the "acquired intellect." Arguing against
this theory on philosophical grounds, Crescas also holds that the love and fear
of God, rather than intellectual speculation, bring about human happiness.
In the section on the Latin thirteenth century, the changes are found in the
Aquinas selections. We have added a discussion of the eternity of the world
which we very reluctantly omitted in the first place, and we have substituted
extensive selections from *On Being and Essence* for those from *Concerning
Spiritual Creatures*. No one needs to be told how central *On Being and Essence* is for an understanding of Aquinas. In the fourteenth-century section
we have added discussions of the nature and cause of motion by Ockham and
Buridan in order at least to suggest the remarkable additions made by recent
scholars to our knowledge of the contribution of medieval philosophy to the
emergence of the new science. We still regret that space limitations forbid
calling parallel attention to discoveries in medieval logic.

In preparing the original volume we received assistance from a number of
people, whom we wish to thank once again: Peter Burmeister, Leon Rosen-
stein, and Frank Emihovich of Columbia College; Sue Muire and Sheila
Farrelly of our office staff; and Astrid Bergundhaugen, who coordinated
operations and maintained morale. Now it is Sheila Farrelly Sheridan who
coordinates and maintains, and Mildred Garcia and Mike Laser who perform staff work. We also wish to express our special thanks to William and
Frances Hackett, whose interest, kindness and intelligence surely go beyond
the obligations undertaken by a publisher.

A. H.

J. J. W.

Introduction

THE EDITORS of this volume hope that it will prove useful for the study of philosophy in the Middle Ages by virtue of the comprehensiveness of its selections. The reader will find here the major representative thinkers of that period and a wide range of topics, including ethics and political theory as well as the more frequently studied epistemology, metaphysics, and natural theology. The reader will also find three groups of philosophers not usually given the scope they have here, and who are historically and philosophically more important than their comparative neglect would indicate. These are the Muslim, Jewish, and fourteenth-century Latin Christian philosophers. Much of this material has only recently been translated, and some is here translated for the first time.

There is little agreement as to just who should be classified as a medieval philosopher. Some scholars, defining medieval philosophy by reference to the effort to resolve the apparent inconsistencies between scriptural revelation and Greek philosophy, look to thinkers of the second century A.D. or even back to Philo of Alexandria in the first century A.D. for their point of departure. Others, seeing a sharp distinction between patristic and scholastic writings, would begin the Middle Ages in Latin Christian philosophy only with Scotus Eriugena in the ninth century or with Anselm of Canterbury in the eleventh. The other boundary is drawn just as variously: some scholars look upon William of Ockham in the fourteenth century as the last medieval philosopher worthy of the name, while others would go on to Nicholas of Cusa in the fifteenth century or to Suarez in the sixteenth. We have here rather arbitrarily begun with Augustine in the fourth century and ended with Buridan in the fourteenth. Muslim philosophy is sometimes regarded as having originated toward the end of the eighth century, when Mu'tazilites (see p. 205) applied Greek philosophical conceptions to the interpretation of Islamic doctrines, although the first formal philosopher is Alkindi, who died some time after 870. Largely because of religious and political developments, the last important Muslim philosopher in the Middles Ages is Averroes, who died at the end of the twelfth century. For the Jews, one can begin

with Philo and end with Spinoza, but it is customary to begin with
Saadia Gaon in the tenth century and end with Albo in the fifteenth. We
have again rather arbitrarily begun with Saadia and ended with Crescas, who
died near the beginning of the fifteenth century.

It is not too long since the very proposal for a work of this kind would
have provoked incredulity. The tradition of serious modern scholarship on
medieval philosophy—Muslim and Jewish as well as Latin—begins in the
mid-nineteenth century with such scholars as Prantl, Hauréau, Renan, and
Munk; and the labor of a hundred years has not eradicated the negative
attitudes toward medieval figures popularized in the satires of Rabelais and
Erasmus on the subtlety and disputatiousness of the schoolmen, and in philosophical treatments such as Francis Bacon's contemptuous rejection of "contentious learning." Indeed, there is a derogatory value judgment implied in
the very labelling of the period as the "middle" ages. Various forms of this
expression were used during the Renaissance (*media tempestas,* 1469; *media
aetas,* 1518; *medium aevum,* 1604), with the sense that this was the age
between the more significant ages of antiquity and modern times. Those two
ages contrast with the middle one in manifesting such civilized virtues as
a sense of beauty, respect for personality, and freedom of thought. Few informed persons today would subscribe to the judgment that medieval cathedrals, illuminated manuscripts, and so forth, are ugly or barbaric, or would
refuse to recognize respect for personality of a high order in the great
medieval saints; but the question of freedom of thought still sometimes
serves as a deterrent to the appreciation of medieval philosophy. It is felt
that since philosophy was the handmaiden of religion during this period, it
must have been servile, its problems raised and decided by theological authority rather than by autonomous reason. In which case, it was hardly
philosophy at all.

There would be little sense in denying the very close relationship of philosophy and religion during the period covered by this anthology. The question
is whether that association really entails such woeful conclusions. To suppose
that it does reflects a considerably oversimplified understanding of medieval
thought. On the assumption of the total authority of scriptural revelation,
one might presume that because of the differences between the three major
religions involved, there would be three independent philosophical traditions
in the Middle Ages. But even superficial examination reveals a large area
of common ground, even in topics sensitive to religious influence. For example, Avicenna the Muslim, Maimonides the Jew, and Thomas Aquinas
the Christian all present the proof for the existence of God which argues to
the being of a necessary existent from the experienced fact of contingent
existences. This philosophical common ground consisted largely in the
philosophical movements of Neoplatonism and Aristotelianism, of which the
former exercised an earlier influence and conditioned the understanding of
the latter. Thus, the initial persisting interpretatons of Latin Christianity
were effected through Neoplatonism, as is abundantly clear in the writings

of Augustine. Among the Jews this neoplatonic movement is evident in Ibn Gabirol. Among the Muslims, although there seems to have been no relatively pure Neoplatonism, the understanding of Aristotle was from the beginning influenced by neoplatonic writings such as the spurious *Theology of Aristotle*. Neoplatonism, with its emphasis on supersensible reality and its conception of the emanation of all being from a single divine unity, lent itself more easily to philosophical interpretation of the religious conceptions of the immortality of the soul and the creation of the world than did Aristotelianism. Indeed, Aristotle's doctrines that the soul is the form of the living body and that the thinking of the divine intellect in some way activates the hierarchy of astronomical and natural processes were reinterpreted along neoplatonic lines, yielding the views that the soul is an independent being bringing life and thought to the body and that the hierarchy of processes emanates from the activity of the divine intellect. Philosophers in all three traditions attempted to recover the true meaning of Aristotle behind such reinterpretations.

The relation of religion to philosophy, then, depends in part upon the philosophy involved. But it also depends upon the religion. All three scripturally derived religions shared problems involving the doctrine of the creation of the world, but they differed in the extent of other stumbling blocks to philosophical reason. The Jews had certain problems about such matters as the election of Israel and the eternity of the Law, and the Muslims were concerned as to whether the Koran as the word of God is created or eternal. But the Christians had a whole series of such problems, eventually classified as "mysteries," of which the doctrine of the Holy Trinity and the sacrament of the Eucharist may be taken as typical. The doctrine of the Trinity is that there is one God with three persons, the Father, Son, and Holy Ghost, which seems to imply that God is one and three at once. The sacrament of the Eucharist involves the conversion of the eucharistic bread and wine into the body and blood of Christ—the process known as transubstantiation. This seems to imply that the very same set of sensible qualities can, without alteration, characterize successively two completely different substances. One can say, then, that in some ways Christianity represents a more formidable challenge to philosophy than do Islam or Judaism.

In the light of these differences: Aristotelianism being less compatible with the scriptural religions than Neoplatonism, and Christianity being less compatible with philosophy than Islam and Judaism, the historical sequence of the interrelations of these movements is quite interesting. Philosophy gained a foothold among Christians through Neoplatonism, and Aristotelianism gained its foothold among Muslims and Jews after having some small impact on Byzantine thought. It was only after Muslim and Jewish thinkers had undertaken judicious interpretations of scriptures and of Aristotle that the two apparently least compatible movements, i.e., Aristotelianism and Latin Christianity, came face to face. The task of a Thomas Aquinas or Duns Scotus was thus in some ways more difficult than that of an Avicenna or

Maimonides, except that the former could make use of the labors of the latter. In all three traditions, it should also be noted, there was philosophically informed criticism of efforts at the synthesis of religion and philosophy. Algazali among the Muslims, Halevi and Crescas among the Jews, and several of the fourteenth-century Latin figures carried out critiques of philosophical pretensions in this area.

Since Judaism, Christianity, and Islam are all practical religions with concern for the goals of human life in this world and the next, and for the function of political organization, ethical and political speculation formed an important part of medieval philosophical thought. Certain complexities parallel to those outlined above should be spelled out for these areas as well. Again we find some common ground; thinkers within the three traditions found it possible to adopt such notions as Aristotle's theory of the moral and intellectual virtues, the Stoic account of law, and neoplatonic doctrine of the ascent of the soul. But further differences seem to have been more pronounced in these areas than in metaphysics or even psychology. For theological and historical reasons, Christian ethical and political doctrines were distinct from those of Judaism and Islam. One difference was determined by different conceptions of man. For Christian thinkers, man was fallen and hence required the grace of God for his salvation. So no matter how much Christian philosophers admired the temporal results of ethical and political doctrines, they considered such doctrines and results insufficient for man's salvation. By contrast, a number of Muslim and Jewish thinkers, especially those of Aristotelian leanings, described the good life as consisting in the development of moral and intellectual virtues, and identified the afterlife with the incorporeal existence of the intellect, whether one for all mankind or many individual intellects. To be sure, Scripture was required and its role was conceived in various ways: for ordaining the proper setting for the intellectual life, for making general laws specific, for making correct opinions available to all men and not merely philosophers, or for providing certain insights not otherwise obtainable. But for Jews and Muslims, the teachings of moral and political philosophy were not too far from those of religion.

Christians differed from Muslims and Jews also in their evaluation of the state. Already the Gospels had distinguished between what is God's and what is Caesar's, and this distinction was to remain fundamental for a good part of medieval Christian thought. Whether Christian philosophers envisaged the state after the Augustinian fashion as merely insuring a limited measure of temporal peace or whether they accepted the more inclusive functional account presented in Aristotle's *Politics,* it was evident that the temporal state was separate from the Church and in some way subordinate to it. Much of medieval political life was marked by controversies concerning the respective powers of the Church and state, and the various opinions on this issue are mirrored in philosophical developments. The distinction between the two realms was further emphasized by the separate development of canon and civil law. Judaism and Islam, on the other hand, were religious laws wedded to a political community. For these religions, the law was brought by a legislative prophet; and the religiously determined state provides the best setting for the attainment of the good life. In such a setting, an explicit and developed distinction between religious and civil law is inapplicable. It is interesting to note that perhaps merely because of historical accident or perhaps because of doctrinal affinity, the central political documents for Jews and Muslims were Plato's *Republic* and *Laws,* whereas after the reception of Aristotle, his *Politics* was the basic work for the Christians. It should also be noted that an exception to this description of the Christian situation can be found in the late medieval movement sometimes described as "political Averroism." Proponents of this position, of whom Marsilius of Padua was the leading representative, set out to develop a philosophy of the state independent of theological teachings, even going so far as to see the clergy in its political role as a functionary of the state.

One more difference between the three traditions is found in their approaches to the problem of the will. Though most thinkers of the three groups (with the possible exception of the Muslim Ash'arites and Crescas the Jew) affirmed the freedom of human acts, Christians emphasized the will more than did Jews and Muslims. For example, the question whether the act of intellect or that of will is more fundamental, which became an important point of difference between Thomists and Scotists, seems to have no precise analogue in Jewish and Muslim thought. In the latter traditions, willing is often viewed simply as the decision-making act of the intellect, rather than as a distinct act of a distinct faculty, as it was among the Latins.

With all these complications, it is little wonder that this very problem of the relation of religion to philosophy was given extensive philosophical attention in the Middle Ages. Thinkers confronted by apparent inconsistencies between revelation or tradition and this or that philosophy did not merely adjust the immediately offending positions. They probed deeper into the very nature of the confrontation itself and conceived a variety of interpretations of it, ranging from the view that religion is simply true philosophy to the view that the two have strictly nothing to do with one another. The attitude that there could be no genuine philosophy as a handmaiden to religion thus reflects only one of the several types of philosophy involved, only one of the several versions of religion, and one of the more extreme solutions to the problem of the possible relationships.

There is another way to approach this issue. As understood by Hegel and others, philosophy as the handmaiden to religion would presumably be theology—the attempt, for example, to interpret the religious dogma about the Eucharist by means of Aristotle's distinction between substance and quality. This kind of thing comes in for attack both from many philosophers and a long tradition among the devout, who cannot see what Athens has to do with Jerusalem, or subtle disputation with simple piety. But these properly theological subjects hardly exhausted the attention of medieval philosophers.

Such subjects stand at one end of a spectrum. Next to them are the problems of what was called natural theology, of which the existence of God is a good example. This problem has been included in the philosophical canon since the days of Xenocrates, and has perhaps never been so thoroughly discussed as in the Middle Ages. We should not suppose that the medievals merely sought more or less ingenious ways to ratify a foregone conclusion; the various proofs were carefully criticized, and the outcome for many critics was that God's existence could not be proved at all by philosophical methods. Next to the topics of natural theology we may place certain issues which, while perhaps not exactly generated by scriptural revelation, certainly were pursued intensively because of it. Typical of these are the immortality of the soul and the freedom of the will, and one can hardly exaggerate the intricacy of medieval treatments of these problems. Then there are the classic or standard philosophical problems concerning being, knowledge, the good, and so forth. Again we should not be misled by an unrealistic picture of the Middle Ages as a time of monolithic harmony. Rationalism and empiricism, teleological and deontological ethical theories, and a great variety of metaphysical positions were developed. And finally, there are subjects such as logic and the natural sciences, which seem to be quite remote from theology. The Middle Ages is one of the great eras in the history of logic, along with antiquity from the rise of the Sophists to the decline of Greek Stoicism, and the modern world from the second half of the nineteenth century. Philosophers in all three traditions wrote summaries or commentaries concerning Aristotle's *Organon,* and a few in the Latin tradition were genuinely creative logicians. As for the natural sciences, one of the great triumphs of modern scholarship is to have uncovered the surprising extent and depth of medieval advances. Once again, then, the view that there could be no genuine philosophy in such a time ignores all but a small segment of the available evidence.

It is true that a characteristic feature of much medieval thought is its architectonic quality, its systematic interconnectedness, so that theological commitments had their impact on philosophical subjects. But it is equally true that positions taken elsewhere on the spectrum outlined above had their impact on theology. Indeed, the complaint of Erasmus and company was not that philosophy had been theologized, but that theology had been made needlessly subtle by its subjection to technical logical analysis and metaphysical refinements. Now that subtlety has once again become an intellectual virtue, perhaps that complaint can be set aside. Even as a handmaiden, then, philosophy had much to say and no mean influence on her mistress.

Erasmus and Rabelais also complained of the contentious character of the philosophy of the schools, a complaint which reached the dignity of a position in Francis Bacon's assumption that the schoolmen aimed merely at victory rather than at truth. This is a serious charge, and should be investigated, for certain features of medieval thought may well be misunderstood in this way. We have here to do with the Latin tradition, for, lacking an analogue to the Renaissance, neither Muslims nor Jews were exposed to this kind of charge. In the Latin tradition, the method of instruction and one of the most prominent vehicles of expression in the Middle Ages was the system of the disputation. A master proposed a problem, often citing authorities on both sides of the issue. A student took his position and stated his arguments, to which the master or another student replied. Further distinctions were drawn and eventually the master resolved the question. This method like most others has its vices; human aggressiveness, for instance, is sorely tempted by debate. But this method produced little literary or personal flourish covering over confusion or fallacy, and gave very little scope to rhetoric. One should not suppose that philosophers trained and expressing themselves in this way were more sophistical or quarrelsome than those working through ways less subject to immediate and public rejoinder. Another point of some relevance to Bacon's accusation has to do with the situation in the later Middle Ages. The intensification of critical rigor at this time led to the demotion of many previously accepted beliefs to the level of probabilities. Furthermore, it was shown that some positions for which philosophical arguments could be constructed were counter to the faith. These positions had then to be maintained as what reason would believe on the natural evidence of the senses if God had not miraculously made things different. There was thus a good deal of philosophical thought about positions which the philosophers could not honestly claim to be true. One may suspect that the sophistication of this situation eluded the critics, who saw in this determination of less than conclusive grounds for belief only sophistry. But to evaluate different kinds of evidence is not to have some end in view other than truth.

There remains one more misconception that should be corrected. This is the view that, regardless of any range of issues discussed, the domination of religion over philosophy during this period was pernicious because it inculcated a habit of relying on authority, whether scriptural or philosophical. As the criticism has been concisely put, medieval thought, including philosophy, was exegetical in character. Certainly when one goes to a typical medieval philosophical work, he finds quotations identified as "authorities." But in the same writing, the philosopher often proves his point "by reason as well as authority." And even if the philosopher seems to be following an authority, he had to find reasons for following this one rather than another. The medievals were aware of this, and the slogan "Authority has a nose of wax" (and hence can be turned wherever one wishes) is attributed to several medieval figures and seems to have been something of a commonplace. One should ask, then, just how these so-called "authorities" function in the actual argument, keeping in mind the difference between using a text to settle an issue, to delineate a problem by presenting representative positions, to serve as a point of departure for finer discriminations, or simply to serve as do many modern footnotes, as a reference to fuller discussions elsewhere. Nor should the reader be unaware of medieval ingenuity in putting a favorable interpretation on a text whose obvious sense one might wish to avoid.

It would indeed be surprising if philosophical work of a high calibre had not been accomplished during the Middle Ages. For hundreds of years in all three traditions self-criticism and development were continuous; and just because of the involvement with theology in a deeply religious period, the finest intellectual talent was drawn into the field. Much of what was done is of genuine philosophical interest to a variety of modern points of view: the existentialist, for instance, may find in the distinction of natures and wills a conception to deepen his concern for the irreducibility of freedom; the metaphysician may find new perspectives in the vast literature on essence and existence and on the problem of individuation; the semanticist should certainly find suggestions in the equally vast literature on universals and on problems of truth and reference. And medieval philosophy must now be accorded an essential place in the history of philosophy. As Wolfson and Gilson have shown for Spinoza and Descartes, humanist antischolasticism may have succeeded in popularizing attitudes of rejection, but it hardly accomplished a genuine hiatus in the history of thought. The commonplaces of medieval philosophy abound in those very philosophers of the seventeenth century who are so forceful in disavowing their immediate past. One of the tasks for future historians will be to trace further the transmission of much-used and much-abused medieval conceptions in such an ungrateful context.

The editors wish to emphasize that this anthology is not intended as a substitute for a full-fledged history of medieval philosophy. Our policy has been to allot space to major figures at the expense of minor ones, and, of course, not everyone will agree with our judgment in this matter. We have also kept the introductions to a minimum so that more space could be given to the selections. For fuller background and interpretation, the reader should consult one or more of the excellent histories of this period; we have provided an introductory bibliography to aid in this further study. We should also add that only the more interesting cross-references have been indicated in the introductions.

Early Medieval Christian Philosophy

 LOOKING BACK at the origins of Christian philosophy from the perspectives of the dialectical subtleties of the twelfth century, or the magisterial syntheses of the thirteenth, or, again, the critical reactions of the fourteenth, it is difficult to realize that when Christian philosophy began, Christians formed a small minority in the pagan world, many theological concepts still required clarification, and the question "what does Athens have to do with Jerusalem?" had not yet been answered. Under these circumstances it became the task of early Christian thinkers to defend the Christian Faith against the arguments of pagans, to give precision to New Testament doctrines and to refute heretical interpretations, and to investigate how Christian teachings are related to philosophic truths. From these rather humble foundations arose the great intellectual edifices of later times.

By necessity, the inquiry into the origins of Christian philosophy must begin with the New Testament itself. Certain philosophic terms occurring in the Pauline writings (e.g., *I Corinthians* 1:24) and the doctrine of the *logos* in the Gospel according to John pose the question whether the canonical writings manifest the influence of Greek philosophic ideas. Some Protestant scholars have answered this question by distinguishing between the pure Christian teachings contained in the synoptic Gospels and later philosophic accretions, while Catholic scholars, though admitting the philosophic sound of certain New Testament terms, have warned against mistaking form for substance.

Speaking for the former group, Adolf Harnack writes:

. . . the most important event which ever happened in the history of Christian doctrines took place at the beginning of the second century, on the day when Christian Apologists laid down the equation: "The Logos is Jesus Christ."

By contrast, Etienne Gilson describes the Catholic view by stating:

> ... *[the] position which is generally held by Catholic historians does not deny the important part played by Greek philosophy in the formulation and interpretation of the Christian dogmas, but it stresses the fact that what was thus formulated and interpreted always remained the authentic teaching of Christ, which has come to us whole through the Catholic theological tradition. In this ... view not a single Greek philosophic notion, taken precisely as philosophical, has ever become a constitutive element of Christian faith as such.**

Whatever the solution to the scriptural problem, it is clear that by the second century—when the so-called Patristic period began—Christian philosophy, or at least its precursor, was on its way. From that century on, Greek and Latin Apologists and Fathers, some of whom had been pagan philosophers before their conversion, wrote in defense of Christianity and in exposition of its doctrine. Though Aristotelian, Stoic, and even materialist doctrines are found in these writings, their prevaling philosophic tenor was Platonic.

To discover whether the saving truths of Christianity are in any way related to the results of philosophic speculations was the most important philosophic issue of this formative period. As was to be expected, Christian thinkers quickly arranged themselves into two groups. Though for both groups the Christian teachings were supreme, there were those who felt that philosophy could be helpful in their exposition, while there were others who saw faith and reason as antagonistic. Among the Greek Apologists of the second century Justin Martyr viewed the study of philosophy positively, holding that "whatever things are rightly said among all men, are the property of us Christians," while his student Tatian, suspicious of philosophy, maintained that whatever was good within philosophy had been borrowed by it from Scripture. During the same period Athenagoras noted an agreement between certain Christian and philosophic teachings, while Hippolytus saw in philosophy the origin of heresies. Hippolytus, together with his teacher Irenaeus, was also active in combatting the teachings of gnostics. Among the Latin Apologists (who include Minucius Felix, Arnobius, and Lactantius), Tertullian is the one who is probably the best known. His much quoted statement "I believe because it is absurd" (*credo quia ineptum*), places him squarely into the antiphilosophic camp.

Christian speculations took a somewhat more substantial form in the writings of the so-called Alexandrines. Clement of Alexandria (*ca.* 150—sometime before 215), who devoted part of his efforts to the persuasion of unbelievers, lauds Greek philosophers for having shown man's need for a spiritual religion, and philosophy, for him, is a good willed by God and communicated by the *logos* to all. Making use primarily of Platonic, but also Aristotelian and Stoic teachings (often as transmitted by Philo), Clement

---

* For both quotations, see E. Gilson, *History of Christian Philosophy in the Middle Ages,* New York, 1955, p. 5.

undertook to transform simple faith into a reasoned belief. In similar fashion, Origen (*ca.* 185—*ca.* 254), who, like Plotinus, had studied under Ammonius Saccas, distinguished between the literal and allegorical sense of Scripture; and he was the first Christian thinker to establish the immateriality of God by means of philosophic arguments. Yet Clement and Origen proposed doctrines whose orthodoxy was challenged later on, such as the eternal creation of the world and (in theology) the subordination of the Son to the Father.

The early fourth century brought a turning point in the fortunes of the Christian Church. Constantine now made Christianity the official religion of the Empire and this recognition helped to produce the political structure of the Church. At the same time, the Council of Nicea (325) fixed the conception of the Trinity by declaring the Son to be consubstantial with the Father—a doctrine which the Arians had denied. The Greek theologians of the fourth century (the so-called Cappadocians) include Eusebius, Gregory of Nazianz, Basil the Great, and Nemesius, but the most important was Gregory of Nyssa. Gregory was the first who tried to find rational arguments for all the teachings of the Church (the mysteries included) and his attempt was repeated later by Anselm of Canterbury and Richard of St. Victor. His kind of Platonism, with its emphasis on the purification of the human soul and man's return to God, influenced the philosophy of John Scotus Eriugena, as well as the mystical theology of Bernard of Clairvaux.

The Latin theologians of the fourth century include Marius Victorinus (the translator of "Platonic" writings) and Ambrose, but they were overshadowed by their "disciple," Augustine (354–430). Interpreting Christian doctrines in the light of neoplatonic teachings, Augustine, in writings often intensely personal and reflecting the heat of intellectual battle, discussed the great themes of truth, God, the human soul, the meaning of history, the state, and salvation, in a manner which made him the greatest Father of the Latin Church. For over a thousand years to come there hardly appeared a Latin theological or philosophic work that did not invoke his authority, and Augustine remains a respected member of the philosophic pantheon of all times.

Though that part of Christian philosophy known as the Patristic Age was to continue after the early fifth century, it was also beginning to draw to a close. Among Greek writers, Pseudo-Dionysius (a writer of the middle of the fifth century whose works were attributed to Dionysius the Areopagite, a disciple of Paul), Maximus the Confessor (*ca.* 580–662), and John of Damascus (eighth century) were to influence later medieval thought, while among the Latins, Boethius (*ca.* 480–524), through his translations of Aristotelian works, his mathematical writings, and his theological treatises, was to become one of the schoolmasters of the later Latin world.

Pseudo-Dionysius became influential through a variety of doctrines. Among them is his notion of a threefold theology according to which God is to be described in positive, negative, and superlative terms. Pseudo-Dionysius views the world as proceeding from God (the supreme good) by way of "illumination," or, alternately, creation is described by him as "theophany" —God revealing Himself. In creating the world, God made use of prototypes, also called divine Ideas, volitions, and predestinations, and the created order possesses a hierarchical structure. Finally, the world not only emanated from God, but also flows back to Him. These great Dionysian themes (together with similar notions of Maximus the Confessor) have their echoes in the later Latin world, and their influence may be gauged from the fact that John Scotus Eriugena, Hugh of St. Victor, Robert Grosseteste, Albertus Magnus, Bonaventure, and Aquinas commented on Dionysian works.

After the sixth century learning declined in the Latin world and Christian philosophy lay dormant until Charles the Great (crowned emperor in 800), who decided that his political conquests should be paralleled by a revival of learning. To further what came to be called the "Carolingian Renaissance" Charles brought foreign scholars to his court, chief among them Alcuin (730–804), an English master. In exaggerated, but, nevertheless, significant fashion, a ninth-century chronicler said of him "Alcuin's teaching was so fruitful that the modern Gauls, or Frenchmen, became the equals of the Ancients of Rome and Athens."

Charlemagne's greatest contribution to the advancement of learning was the establishment of schools. Prior to his time education had been private, but he now decreed that it should be the concern of established schools. In a famous capitulary he proclaimed that

> *. . . in every bishop's see, and in every monastery, instructions shall be given in the psalms, musical notation, chant, the computation of years and seasons, and in grammar. . . .**

The schools resulting from Charlemagne's effort are divisible into three kinds. There was, first of all, the Palatine school connected with the royal court. Its pupils were at first drawn from court circles, but other students were admitted later on. Some modern scholars see the palace school as one of the precursors of the later universities. Then there was the episcopal or cathedral school, which, directed by a bishop or master, was largely for those destined for the priesthood. But by far the most important and enduring was the monastic school, which conducted classes for the younger members of the monastic community as well as for students coming from without. So important were the monastic schools that the two centuries after Charlemagne have been described as the monastic (or Benedictine) centuries.

Important as the revival of learning was, the curriculum of the new schools was modest by later standards. Besides the Bible and the writings of the Fathers (particularly for those who planned to enter the priesthood), the *trivium* (grammar, dialectic, and rhetoric) and the *quadrivium* (arithmetic, geometry, astronomy, and music) formed the major areas of study. However, until about the year 1000, the *quadrivium* was in eclipse and, of the *trivium*,

---

* Cited by David Knowles, *The Evolution of Medieval Thought*, London, 1962, p. 72. Knowles' work contains a fine summary of the state of education during this period.

grammar (which included literature) and rhetoric were the primary disciplines. From the eleventh century on, dialectic became central and exercised considerable influence on theology. No major revision of the curriculum occurred until the introduction of Aristotle's physical and metaphysical works beginning with the late twelfth century.

John Scotus Eriugena (*ca.* 810–*ca.* 877), the major figure of the period sometimes described as prescholastic, fused Christian and neoplatonic teachings into a metaphysical system in the grand manner. But Eriugena was to remain without successors and Christian philosophy after his time developed in an unspectacular fashion. Wars, invasions, the division of the Empire, and the decline of the Carolingian dynasty were not conducive to the advancement of Charlemagne's educational vision. Though learning continued (particularly in the Benedictine monasteries), no major philosopher or theologian was to appear until Anselm of Canterbury (1033–1109) who, following Augustine, defended a Christian neoplatonic position. Anselm wrote on such topics as God, divine attributes, creation, knowledge, and will, but among philosophers, he will probably always be remembered for formulating what Kant later called the "ontological proof" for the existence of God.

Though the eleventh and twelfth centuries manifested varied philosophic and theological interests, there is a sense in which the problem of universals was the major issue of the period. Using as their basic text a passage from Porphyry's *Isagoge,* as transmitted and commented upon by Boethius (see p. 114), philosophers inquired whether genera and species exist only in the mind or in reality; and if the latter, whether they exist in individual substances or in separation from them. In answer to this question a spectrum of positions developed, ranging from Realists who affirmed the independent existence of universals (in the manner of Platonic Ideas) to Nominalists who held that universals were mere names. These dialectical speculations, it should be noted, were not mere logical exercises, but, in the absence of Aristotle's psychological and metaphysical writings, they became the only means for solving an important philosophic question.

The outstanding dialectician, and for that matter, the outstanding philosopher of the twelfth century, was Peter Abailard who, in writings marked by logical subtlety, contributed to the discussion of the problem of universals, to ethics, and to the development of the scholastic method. Abailard's one-time student, John of Salisbury, should also be mentioned in this connection, for to him we are indebted for his vivid account of the opinions of twelfth-century masters.

The twelfth century also saw a vital Platonic movement whose center was the school of Chartres. Characterized by a great admiration for the accomplishments of antiquity, Chartres became a great center of humanistic studies. But Chartres also manifested a marked interest in natural philosophy and science. Plato and Boethius were the major philosophic authorities used, but the writings of Hippocrates, Galen, and of Arabic physical and medical authors were among the works studied. Though Aristotle was considered inferior to Plato, it was at Chartres that the "new logic" (see p. 116) was first received and that Aristotle's physical writings made their first appearance. As was to be expected from the Platonic orientation of the school, its members defended the real existence of universals. Among the masters of Chartres and those who followed the spirit of the school are to be numbered Adelard of Bath, Thierry of Chartres, Clarenbaud of Arras, William of Conches, Gilbert de la Porrée, the previously mentioned John of Salisbury, and, finally, Alan of Lille.

In bringing this review of early medieval Christian philosophy to a close, brief mention should be made of the mystical movement of the twelfth century. Bernard of Clairvaux, rejecting the speculations of Abailard and Gilbert de la Porrée, sought the good life in mystical experience and contemplation, desiring only "to know Jesus and Jesus crucified." At the same time, masters of the school of St. Victor attempted to fuse dialectical and mystical teachings.

Among the following selections, two date from the period of the Fathers. Selections from representative Augustinian writings present his theory of knowledge, aspects of his doctrines of God, the human soul, freedom of the will, his famous discussion of time, and the major themes of his political philosophy. Boethius is represented by his account of the philosophic life and by one of his theological treatises. Though lack of space prevents the presence of selections from the Greek Fathers, an echo of their teachings is found in John Scotus Eriugena, an outline of whose metaphysical teachings is presented here. St. Anselm's "ontological argument" appears in full and with it Gaunilo's attempted refutation, as well as Anselm's reply to Gaunilo. The problem of universals forms the subject of selections from Abailard and John of Salisbury, and, in addition, selections from Abailard's ethics are included.

AUGUSTINE

354-430

AUGUSTINE, the greatest of the Fathers of the Western Church, was the outstanding and most influential Christian Neoplatonist. His teachings dominated Christian thought until the rise of Aristotelianism in the early thirteenth century; he also influenced the Christian Aristotelians, and Augustinianism remained a major intellectual movement throughout the rest of the Middle Ages and beyond. Some of his doctrines had a formative influence on the development of modern philosophy (e.g., Descartes), and his theological views guided the Protestant reformers.

Among philosophers, so Augustine taught, the Neoplatonists had come closest to the truth, but even they had only approximated the ultimate truths found in Christian doctrine. Hence, more theologian than philosopher, Augustine considered philosophy largely as an instrument for understanding the intelligible content of Christianity, rather than as an independent branch of human learning, as did the later Aristotelians. His formula for showing the relation between Christianity and philosophy was "Understand, so that you may believe; believe, so that you may understand." One may well speak of Augustine's philosophy, but its theological setting and employment should always be remembered.

Like his personal life, so Augustine's writings were marked by a passionate quest for certain truth, giving to the theory of knowledge an important place in his thought. Well aware of the skeptical critique of perception, Augustine nevertheless affirms that we have some measure of reliable knowledge about the physical world. Perception for him is not simply the passive reception of sense impressions by bodily organs, but all sensations are combined with rational judgments of some kind. One object is perceived to be more beautiful than another by reference to some absolute standard of beauty, and one line is said to be straighter than another by reference to some absolute standard of straightness. "To sense," Augustine states in language having a Platonic ring, "does not belong to the body, but to the soul through the body." He also said that "the soul gives something of its own substance in forming the images of bodies," a position to which he was committed by his acceptance of the fundamental neoplatonic principle that the lower does not affect the higher.

Far more significant than knowledge of the physical world is knowledge of God and the human soul. "God and the soul," Augustine writes, "that is what I desire to know. Nothing more? Nothing whatever." Man gains knowledge of God and his soul by looking inward, not by examining the outside world. Searching within, man finds that his own existence is a most certain truth. For even if, as the skeptics argue, I may be deceived when I think I know, I still must exist in order to be deceived. This argument influenced Descartes later on. But not only my own existence is certain; it is equally certain that I am alive and that I understand.

Knowledge, in the true sense of the term, is knowledge of immutable Ideas, not knowledge of changing substances within the world. Accepting this Platonic notion, Augustine develops it in his own manner. The Ideas, he holds, do not exist in some "place" or intelligence of their own, but in the mind of God; and they are not known through reminiscence, but by divine illumination. But Augustine did not develop these doctrines fully in his works and, as a result, a variety of interpretations of his illuminationism arose.

No matter which interpretation one is inclined to follow, it is clear that Augustine has in mind knowledge which can be acquired by all men, not some mystical intuition produced by a special act of divine grace. Moreover, it appears that man knows the Ideas as separate from God. That is, it is not the case that man in knowing the Ideas knows the essence of God. Again, it does not seem to follow from Augustine's description that God infuses the Ideas directly into the human mind or that there exists within the mind an Agent Intellect such as Aquinas posits later on. As some historians have suggested, it is perhaps best to let Augustine's metaphor of illumination carry the burden of his argument. As sunlight makes perceptible objects visible to the human eye, so divine illumination makes truths, and especially necessary truths, intelligible to the human mind. Illuminationism, it should be noted, became extremely important in the psychological and epistemological theories of later medieval times.

The search for truth finds its goal in God, who is Truth. As the source of truth, He is the internal teacher who, whenever man understands, teaches him the truth. For Augustine, God is the triune God of Christianity, who is best known through Scripture and the teachings of the Church. At the same time, the world and human nature contain evidence that He exists. Augustine offers a number of arguments for the existence of God, but they are more like guideposts directing the mind to God than demonstrations in the manner of Aristotelian proofs that a prime mover or first cause exists. Augustine uses arguments taken from the order apparent in the world and from "the agreement of all"; but by far his favorite seems to be the argument from truth. It is evident, this argument proceeds, that human beings know some truth. But it is also clear that human truth, being "yours" and "mine," is partial and changeable. Human truth thus points toward a Truth which is total and immutable, and this Truth is God.

God, for Augustine, is the highest being—perfect, eternal, and unchangeable. None of the Aristotelian categories apply to Him, and He is perhaps best described by propositions stating what He is not. But God is not the neoplatonic One causing the emanation of the world through the necessity of its own nature. Instead, He is the God of Scripture who in his infinite goodness freely decided to create a world out of nothing. This world is good, manifesting measure, form, and order; and any evil appearing in it is the privation of some good, not the creation of some independent principle of evil. God created the world according to His wisdom, implanting within its matter "seminal reasons" (an adaptation of the Stoic *logoi spermatikoi* which are germinal principles from which all things develop in the course of time.

The world is arranged according to number, which is the basis for the intelligibility of the natural order. This mathematical understanding of the world became one of the characteristic features of Augustinianism, contributing in some measure to the rise of mathematical science in the seventeenth century. Within the natural world the highest being is man, whom God created as a unitary being. But Augustine frequently uses Platonic language in describing man as an immaterial soul inhering in a body, and he defines the soul as "a special substance, endowed with reason, adapted to rule a body." The man whom God created was endowed by Him with all human perfections, including a free will. No other doctrine is more central to Augustine's moral and political thought than that of human freedom and the concomitant doctrine of love. Rational judgments, to be sure, frequently influence human conduct, but human actions are determined by the free decision of the will and by the objects of love toward which the will is directed. Describing human nature as man's "weight," Augustine writes: "my weight, is my love." There are two primary objects of love for the human will. Man may direct his will toward God, in the possession of whom in love and understanding the greatest human happiness consists, or man may turn in pride toward himself and the world beneath him. In thus falling away from God, he does evil. It is not God who is the author of moral evil, but man himself. To guide man in his moral decisions, God instilled within him by a kind of moral illumination the immutable principles of the eternal law.

However, man existing in the here and now is not the perfect man created by God, but fallen man blemished by original sin. According to the Christian teaching on which Augustine's doctrine rests, Adam, the first man, sinned by disobeying God's command. As a result, his intellect was dimmed by ignorance, his will weakened by concupiscence, and he became subject to death. These blemishes were transmitted by heredity to the descendants of Adam, so that all men born after him were born with a defective nature. But God did not leave all mankind to eternal damnation. In His mercy, expressed in the Incarnation, God freely selected certain men to be saved. These theological doctrines modified Augustine's philosophic account of human freedom. Man, to be sure, retained his freedom of choice even after the Fall; but liberty, the ability not to sin, was gone. Only the grace of God can restore to man his original liberty; and it is the Christian's hope, according to Augustine, that those saved, though free, no longer will be able to sin.

A social nature was among the perfections granted by God to man, and this nature is retained in some measure even after the Fall. Hence, all men live in families and organize states for the attainment of tranquility and peace. But just as natural morality is inadequate for the attainment of ultimate human happiness, so is the temporal political state insufficient for bringing eternal peace. Like happiness, peace can only come through God's grace, even though temporary peace and partial justice can exist even in the pagan state. God's division of mankind into the saved and the damned brings about the existence of two realms or cities. The City of God consists of those who, manifesting love of God, are saved. The City of Man embraces those who, manifesting love of self, are damned. These two cities, it should be noted, are not to be confused with the Church and states existing here and now.

Augustine was born in the small city of Tagaste in the province of Numidia (the modern Tunisia) on November 13, 354. His father, Patricius, was a pagan; his mother, Monica, a Christian. Augustine was reared as a Christian by his devout mother; but, in accordance with the custom of the times, he was not baptized as a child. Having received his early education in his native city and nearby Madaura, he went to study rhetoric at Carthage. This was in 370, the year his father died, having previously become a Christian. Carthage was a metropolitan center, and there Augustine became acquainted with the many intellectual currents abroad. He soon forsook Christian teachings as illogical and barbaric and became a Manichean. Mani (215-279) had taught that the world is governed by the two principles of light or good and darkness or evil. In these teachings Augustine found an answer to the problem of evil which was to trouble him much of his life. At Carthage he took a mistress from whom he had a son named Adeodatus (who appears in the selection from *On the Teacher,* below). Upon completion of his studies, Augustine returned for a short time to Tagaste and then settled in 374 in Carthage, where he opened a school of rhetoric. He immersed himself in the study of Manicheanism, but doubts began to grow in his mind. In 383 a Manichean bishop named Faustus came to Carthage; and when he was unable to resolve those doubts, Augustine began to abandon Manicheanism. Shortly thereafter we find Augustine in Rome, and then in Milan, at that time a more important center than Rome itself. In 384, Augustine was appointed municipal professor of rhetoric there, and was perhaps moving toward still higher office. During this period he finished with Manicheanism and was influenced by the skepticism of the New Academy. But he was not to remain a skeptic for long. In Milan he heard the sermons of Bishop Ambrose and began reading neoplatonic writings (among them some of Plotinus' *Enneads*), newly translated by Marius Victorinus. These studies taught him that true reality is spiritual not material, as the Manicheans taught, and that evil is not an independent principle, but a lack of good. Though he admired the Neoplatonists, their doctrines did not satisfy his spiritual quest. Having read Scripture, especially the writings of Paul, he gained the conviction that not philosophy, but only the grace of God can provide salvation for fallen man, a conviction that was strengthened through conversations with Simplicianus, an old priest, and Pontitianus. Augustine's spiritual crisis came to a head when after the famous scene in the garden when he heard a child's voice chant "take up and read, take up and read" (*Confessions,* VIII, 12), he decided to become a Christian. On Holy Saturday of 386, after a year's retreat at Cassiciacum, he was baptized by Ambrose. He decided to return to Africa, but his mother's death at Ostia delayed the journey. The year 387 found Augustine in Tagaste, where he founded a small religious community with friends. In 391 he was ordained priest; in 395, auxiliary bishop; and in 396, when Valerius, the bishop of Hippo, died, Augustine was chosen to fill his place. Teacher, philosopher, and theologian until then, Augustine now became pastor of his flock, a task calling for the administration of educational and even judicial functions in addition to religious responsibilities. As bishop he also fought incessantly against heretics, denouncing their doctrines in numerous writings and securing their condemnations by church councils. Among these were the dualistic Manicheans, the Pelagians, who placed insufficient emphasis on divine grace in human salvation, and the Donatists, who held that only a priest free of sin was fit to administer the sacraments. Augustine died August 28, 430, while the Vandals were at the gates of Hippo.

Augustine was an unusually productive writer who left behind a veritable library of works. Intensely personal and not at all self-conscious, he wrote out of the depths of his spiritual struggles and the exaltations of his spiritual victories. M. C. D'Arcy put it well when he stated that Augustine had the power "of making what is intensely personal pass into the universal." His writings abound in biblical citations, in references and allusions to Latin literature, and his rhetorical training shines through every page of his works. Even those who do not share his religious fervor respond to his eloquence in his *Confessions,* a work which has become a classic of world literature. Though he did some writing during the teaching years at Carthage, Augustine's literary career began during the retreat at Cassiciacum. During that year (385–386) he wrote his attack on the Academic Skeptics, the *Contra Academicos, On the Happy Life (De beata vita)* and *On Order (De ordine).* Within the short space of two years (386–388) there followed *On the Immortality of the Soul (De immortalitate animae),* the *Soliloquies, On Free Will (Di libero arbitrio),* and *On the Quantity of the Soul (De quantitate animae).* Between his return to Africa and his ordination as priest (388–391) he wrote *On the Teacher (De magistro), On the True Religion (De vera religione),* and he completed *On Music (De musica).* Most of Augustine's major works were written after his ordination as bishop. Between that time and his death he wrote *On Christian Doctrine (De doctrina Christiana), Confessions* (which tells the story of his life until the death of his mother), *On Nature and Grace (De natura et gratia), On the Trinity (De Trinitate), On the Soul and Its Origin (De anima et eius origine), The*

City of God (De civitate Dei), and the *Enchiridion*. Of special interest are his two books of *Retractations (Retractationes)*, which contain Augustine's critical review of his writings and which are important for fixing the chronology of his works. To this impressive list must be added his numerous shorter works, his biblical commentaries, his sermons, and his letters.

The following selections aim at presenting a cross section of Augustine's philosophic views. The first, from *On the Teacher*, contains his account of signification and one of the statements of his doctrine of illumination. The second selection, which is from *On Free Will*, deals with his theory of knowledge and his early doctrine of the will. Of special interest in it are his proof of the existence of God from truth and his account of the relation of divine foreknowledge to the freedom of the human will. This selection is neatly balanced by one from the *Retractations* in which he defends himself against the charge of the Pelagians that the views that he expressed in *On Free Will* put him on their side. The next selection, from *On the Trinity*, contains a brief statement of Augustine's doctrine of the soul. The section which follows, from the *Confessions*, contains a brief account of creation and after that his famous discussion concerning the nature of time. Finally, selections from the *City of God* contain some of the major aspects of his ethical and political doctrines. Marcus Varro (116–27 B.C.), who is mentioned in these selections, composed a now no longer extant *On Philosophy* which Augustine used.

THE TEACHER

A Dialogue Between Augustine and His Son Adeodatus

i, 1. *Augustine.*—What do you suppose is our purpose when we use words? *Adeodatus.*—The answer that occurs to me at the moment is, we want to let people know something, or we want to learn something. *Augustine.*—I agree at once with the former, for it is clear that when we use words we want to let somebody know something. But in what way do we show that we wish to learn? *Adeodatus.*— When we ask questions, of course. *Aug.*—Even then, as I understand it, we want to let somebody know something. Do you ask a question for any other reason than to show the person questioned what you want to know? *Ad.*—No. *Aug.*—You see, then, that when we use words we desire nothing but to let someone know something. *Ad.*—Not quite, perhaps. If speaking means using words, I see that we do so when we sing. Now we often sing when we are alone, with no one present to

From *Augustine: Earlier Writings,* tr. J. H. S. Burleigh, Vol. VI, LCC. Published 1953, The Westminster Press. Used by permission; London: SCM Press, Ltd.

hear us; and then I cannot think we want to tell anyone anything. *Aug.*—And yet I think there is a kind of teaching, and a most important kind, which consists in reminding people of something. I believe this will be made clear as our conversation proceeds. If, however, you do not think that we learn by remembering, or that he who reminds us of something really teaches us, I do not press the point. I assert that there are two reasons for our using words, either to teach, or to remind others or, it may be, ourselves. And we do this also when we sing. Don't you agree?

Ad.—Well, hardly. For I very rarely sing to remind myself of anything, almost always simply to give myself pleasure. *Aug.*—I see what you mean. But don't you notice that what pleases you in singing is the melody? Now this can be added to the words or not added, so that singing is not the same thing as speaking. Flutes and harps make melody. Birds sing. Sometimes we hum a bit of music without words. All these things may be called singing but not speaking. Do you disagree? *Ad.*—No. Not at all.

2. *Aug.*—You agree, then, that there is no other reason for the use of words than either to teach or to call something to mind? *Ad.*—I would agree were I not impressed by the fact that we use words when we pray; and it is not proper to believe that we teach God anything or remind him of anything. *Aug.*—I dare say you do not know that we have been commanded to pray in closed chambers, by which is meant our inmost mind, for no other reason than that God does not seek to be reminded or taught by our speech in order that he may give us what we desire. He who speaks gives by articulate sounds an external sign of what he wants. But God is to be sought and prayed to in the secret place of the rational soul, which is called "the inner man." This he wants to be his temple. Have you not read in the Apostle: "Know ye not that ye are the temple of God, and the Spirit of God dwelleth in you?" (1 Cor. 3:16) and "that Christ may dwell in the inner man" (Eph. 3:17)? Have you not observed in the Prophet: "Commune with your own hearts and be stricken on your beds. Offer the sacrifice of righteousness and hope in the Lord" (Ps. 4:4–5)? Where do you think the sacrifice of righteousness is offered save in the temple of the mind and on the bed of the heart? Where sacrifice is to be offered, there is prayer to be made. Wherefore when we pray there is no need of speech, that is of articulate words, except perhaps as priests use words to give a sign of what is in their minds, not that God may hear, but that men may hear and, being put in remembrance, may with some consent be brought into dependence on God. What do you think? *Ad.*—I entirely agree. *Aug.*—And you are not disturbed by the fact that our great Master, in teaching his disciples to pray, taught them certain words, so that it looks as if he had taught them actually what words to use in prayer? *Ad.*—No. That does not disturb me. For he did not teach them words merely, but by words, by means of which they could keep themselves in constant remembrance, he taught them realities—what they should pray for, and from whom, when they prayed in their inmost mind, as we said. *Aug.*—You have correctly understood the point. And I believe you have also noticed a further point. It might be contended that, though we utter no sound, we nevertheless use words in thinking and therefore use speech within our minds. But such speech is nothing but a calling to remembrance of the realities of which the words are but the signs, for the memory, which retains the words and turns them over and over, causes the realities to come to mind. *Ad.*—I understand and follow.

ii, 3. Aug.—We agree, then, that words are signs. *Ad.*—We do. *Aug.*—That alone can be a sign which signifies something? *Ad.*—Certainly. *Aug.*—How many words are there in this verse?

> Si nihil ex tanta superis placet urbe relinqui
> [If it pleases the gods that nothing be left of so great a city]

Ad.—Eight. *Aug.*—Then there are eight signs? *Ad.*—There are. *Aug.*—I suppose you understand the meaning of the verse. *Ad.*—Yes, I think so. *Aug.*—Tell me what each word signifies. *Ad.*—I know what *si* signifies, but I can think of no other word to explain it. *Aug.*—At least you can explain the state of mind signified by that word. *Ad.*—It seems to me to signify doubt, and doubt is found in the mind. *Aug.*—I accept that in the meantime. Go on to the next word. *Ad.*—*Nihil* signifies simply what is not. *Aug.*—Perhaps you are right. But I am prevented from giving my assent by what you admitted a moment ago. You agreed that only that can be a sign which signifies something. Now, what is not cannot be something. So the second word in the verse is not a sign, because it does not signify something. We were wrong, therefore, in laying it down that all words are signs, or that all signs must signify something. *Ad.*—You press me sore. But surely it is utterly foolish to use a word if we have no meaning to attach to it. When you are speaking with me I believe that you do not utter any merely empty sound, but that in everything that proceeds from your mouth you are giving me a sign by which I may understand something. So you ought not in speaking to pronounce these two syllables unless by them you mean something. If you see that they are necessary to set forth some idea and to teach and remind us of something when they sound in our ears, you assuredly also see what I wish to say but cannot clearly explain. *Aug.*—What then are we to do? Shall we say that the word, *nihil,* signifies a state of mind rather than a thing which is nothing; the state of a mind, I mean, which does not see an object, and discovers or thinks it has discovered nonentity? *Ad.*—Perhaps that was what I was trying to explain. *Aug.*—However it may be, let us go on to the next point lest something most absurd happen to us. *Ad.*—What do you mean? *Aug.*—If "nothing" should detain us, and yet we should suffer delay. *Ad.*—It is indeed ridiculous, and yet somehow I see it can happen and indeed has happened.

4. *Aug.*—At the proper time we shall understand more clearly this kind of difficulty, if God will. Now go back to the verse and do your best to unfold what the other words signify. *Ad.*—The third word is the preposition *ex* for which I think we can substitute *de. Aug.*—But I am not asking you to substitute for one well-known word another equally well-known word which you say means the same thing, if indeed it does mean the same thing. But let that pass meantime. If the poet had written not *ex tanta urbe* but *de tanta urbe,* and I asked what *de* signified, you would say *ex,* since these two words, that is, signs, signify, you think, one and the same thing. But I am looking for the one thing which is signified by these two signs. *Ad.*—I think they mean a separation of a thing A, from a thing, B, in which it had formerly existed. A is said to be "of" or "out of" B. And this in one or other of two ways. Either B does not remain, as in this verse. For Troy has been destroyed but some Trojans could still exist. Or B remains, as when we say that business-men of the City of Rome are in Africa. *Aug.*—I shall concede your point, and not seek to enumerate the many exceptions that can be found to your rule. But you can at least observe that you have been explaining words by means of words, that is, signs by means of signs, well-known words and signs by words and

signs also well-known. But I want you to show me, if you can, what are the things of which these are the signs.

iii, 5. *Ad.*—I am surprised that you do not know, or rather that you pretend not to know, that what you ask cannot be done in conversation, where we cannot answer questions except by means of words. You ask for things which, whatever they may be, are certainly not words, and yet you too use words in asking me. First put your questions without using words, and I shall reply on the same terms. *Aug.*—I admit your challenge is just. But if I were to ask what was signified when these three syllables, *par-i-es,* are pronounced couldn't you point with your finger, so that I should immediately see the thing itself of which that trisyllabic word is the sign? You would be pointing it out without using any words. *Ad.*—I agree that is possible, but only in the case of names signifying corporeal objects, if these objects were at hand. *Aug.*—But surely we do not call a colour a corporeal object? Is it not rather a quality of a corporeal object? *Ad.*—It is so. *Aug.*—Why then can it, too, be pointed out with the finger? Do you include the qualities of corporeal objects among corporeal objects, at least so far as they can be brought to knowledge without words? *Ad.*—When I said corporeal objects I meant all corporeal things to be understood, that is, all the qualities of bodies which are susceptible to sense-perception. *Aug.*—Consider, however, whether some exceptions are to be made. *Ad.*—You do well to warn me. I should have said not all corporeal objects but all visible objects. For I admit that sound, smell, taste, weight, heat, etc., which belong to the other senses, though they cannot be perceived apart from bodies and are therefore corporeal, cannot, nevertheless, be pointed out with the finger. *Aug.*— Have you never seen how men carry on conversation, as it were, with deaf people by means of gesture, and how deaf people, similarly by gesture, ask questions and reply, teach and indicate all their wishes, or at least most of them? Thus not only visible things are pointed out without the use of words, but also sounds, tastes and other such things. Actors, too, in the theatres often unfold and set forth whole stories by dancing simply and without using a single word. *Ad.*—I have no adverse comment to make except that neither I nor your dancing actor will ever be able to point out to you what the preposition, *ex,* signifies without using words.

6. *Aug.*—Perhaps you are right. But suppose he could. You would, I imagine, have no hesitation in saying that whatever movement of his body he used in trying to show me the thing signified by that word, it would still be a sign and not the thing itself. Therefore, though he indeed would not explain a word by a word, he would, none the less, explain a sign by a sign. So that both the monosyllable, *ex,* and his gesture would signify one thing, which was asking to have pointed out to me without a sign, directly. *Ad.*—Pray, how can that possibly be done? *Aug.*— The way a wall does it. *Ad.*—But even a wall, as our reasoning showed, cannot be shown without a pointing finger. The holding out of the finger is not the wall but the sign by means of which the wall is pointed out. So far as I can see there is nothing which can be shown without signs. *Aug.*—Suppose I were to ask you what walking is, and you were to get up and do it, wouldn't you be using the thing itself to show me, not words or any other signs? *Ad.*—Yes, of course. I am ashamed that I did not notice so obvious a fact. Now thousands of examples come to my mind of things which can be demonstrated immediately and without signs, such as eating, drinking, sitting, standing, shouting and other things innumerable. *Aug.*—Well then, tell me this. Supposing I had no idea of the meaning of the word "walking," and I were to ask you when you were walking what "walking"

means, how would you teach me? *Ad.*—I should walk a little more quickly. The change in speed would give notice that I was replying to your question, and I should still be doing what I was asked to demonstrate. *Aug.*—But you know there is a difference between walking and hastening. He who walks does not suddenly hasten, and he who hastens does not necessarily walk. We speak of hastening in writing, reading and very many other things. Consequently, if, after my query, you did what you had been doing, only a little more quickly, I should conclude that walking was the same thing as hastening, for the acceleration was the new feature of your behaviour. So I should be misled. *Ad.*—I admit that a thing cannot be demonstrated without a sign, at any rate if the thing is an action in which we are engaged when we are questioned. If we add nothing new to what we are doing, our questioner will think that we don't want to show him, but are continuing in what we were doing without paying any attention to him. But if his inquiry is about actions which we can perform, and if we are not doing them when he inquires, by doing it after he has inquired we can demonstrate what he asks by the actual thing and not merely by a sign. A special case would arise if, while I was speaking, someone asked me what "speaking" was. In order to let him know I must speak, whatever I actually may say. And I shall continue to show him until I make plain to him what he wants to know, not departing from the actual thing which he wished to have demonstrated to him, and yet not seeking signs apart from the thing itself wherewith to demonstrate it.

iv, 7. *Aug.*—Most acutely stated. Are we, now, agreed that there are two classes of things that can be demonstrated without signs; those which we are not engaged in doing when we are asked and can immediately start doing, and those in which the action consists in simply giving signs? For when we speak we make signs, whence is derived the verb, *to signify*. *Ad.*—Agreed. *Aug.*—When the question concerns signs merely, signs can be demonstrated by signs. But when the question is about things which are not signs, they can be demonstrated by carrying out the action, if possible, after the question has been asked, or by giving signs by means of which the things can be brought to mind. *Ad.*—That is so. *Aug.*—Here, then, we have a threefold classification. Let us first consider, if you please, the case of signs being demonstrated by signs. Words are not the only signs? *Ad.*—No. *Aug.*—It seems to me that in speaking we use words to signify words or other signs, as when we say "gesture" or "letter"; for these two words also signify signs. Or we may express in words something which is not a sign, as for example when we say the word "stone." The word is a sign for it signifies something, but what it signifies is not a sign. But this kind of case where words signify things that are not signs does not concern our present discussion. For we undertook to consider those cases where signs are demonstrated by signs, and we found that they fall into two classes; those in which we teach or call to remembrance by signs similar signs, and those in which we teach or call to remembrance different signs. Do you agree? *Ad.*—Clearly.

8. *Aug.*—Tell me, to what sense do verbal signs pertain? *Ad.*—To the sense of hearing. *Aug.*—And gesture? *Ad.*—To sight. *Aug.*—What about written words? Surely they are words? Or are they better understood as signs of words? A word is a meaningful articulate sound, and sound is perceived by no other sense than hearing. When a word is written, a sign is given to the eyes whereby something that properly belongs to the ears is brought to mind. *Ad.*—I agree entirely. *Aug.*—You will also agree, I imagine, that when we pronounce the word, *nomen* [name],

we signify something. *Ad.*—True. *Aug.*—What, then? *Ad.*—That by which something or somebody is called; for example, Romulus, Rome, Virtue, a River, etc., etc. *Aug.*—These four names signify something. *Ad.*—Indeed they do. *Aug.*—Is there a difference between these names and the things they signify? *Ad.*—A great difference. *Aug.*—I should like you to tell me what is the difference. *Ad.*—In the first place, the names are signs; the things are not. *Aug.*—Shall we call things which can be signified by signs but are not signs "significables," as we call things that can be seen visible? It will simplify our discussion of them. *Ad.*—Very well. *Aug.*—Can these four signs you have just mentioned be signified by no other sign? *Ad.*—I am surprised that you should think I have already forgotten that we found that written words are signs of spoken words, signs, therefore, of signs. *Aug.*—What is the difference? *Ad.*—Written words are visible. Spoken words are audible. Why should we not use the word, audible, if we allow "significable"? *Aug.*—I allow it at once, and am grateful for your suggestion. But I ask again whether these four signs cannot be signified by any other audible sign as well as by the visible signs you have called to mind. *Ad.*—I recall that this too was said recently in our discussion. I said that a name signified some thing and I gave these four examples. I recognize that the word "name" and these four names are all audible when spoken. *Aug.*—What, then, is the difference between an audible sign and other audible signs signified by it? *Ad.*—So far as I can see the difference between the word "name" and the four examples is this; it is the audible sign of audible signs; they are the audible signs not of signs but of things, partly visible, like Romulus, Rome, River, partly intelligible, like Virtue.

9. *Aug.*—I understand and approve. But you know that every articulate sound pronounced with some meaning is called a word. *Ad.*—I do. *Aug.*—A name, therefore, is a word when it is pronounced articulately with a meaning. When we say of a fluent man that he uses good words, we mean also that he uses names. When the slave in Terence said to his aged master, "Good words, I pray you," he used many names. *Ad.*—I agree. *Aug.*—So when we pronounce these two syllables, *ver-bum,* we also signify a name, and the one word is the sign of the other. *Ad.*—I agree. *Aug.*—Here is another question I should like you to answer. You have said that "word" is a sign pointing to "name," and "name" is a sign pointing to "river," and "river" is the sign of a thing which can be seen. Also you have explained the difference between this "thing" and "river," which is its sign, and between "river" and "name," which is the sign of a sign. What do you think is the difference between the sign of a name, that is a word, and the name itself of which it is the sign? *Ad.*—I understand the difference to be this. What is signified by "name" is also signified by "word." A name is a word, and "river" is a word. But everything that has a verbal sign does not have a nominal sign. For *si* at the beginning of the verse you quoted, and *ex,* where this long course of reasoning started, are words but they are not names. And there are many other such words. All names are words, but all words are not names. So the difference between a word and a name is, I think, clear, that is, between the sign of a sign which signifies no other signs, and the sign of a sign that points to other signs. *Aug.*—Every horse is an animal, but every animal is not a horse? *Ad.*—Indubitably. *Aug.*—There is the same difference between "name" and "word" as between horse and animal. Unless perhaps you are prevented from assenting by the fact that we use the word "verb" in a special sense to signify those things which have tenses—I write, I wrote; I read, I have read. Clearly these are not names. *Ad.*—You have mentioned exactly

what caused me to hesitate. *Aug.*—Don't let that trouble you. In all cases where words are employed and something is signified we speak of signs universally and without qualification. On the other hand, we speak of military signs which are properly called signs because words are not used. If I were to say to you that just as every horse is an animal but every animal is not a horse, so every word is a sign but every sign is not a word, you would not hesitate, I believe. *Ad.*—Now I understand and agree that there is the same difference between a word, universally, and a name as between animal and horse.

10. *Aug.*—You know that when we say "animal," that trisyllabic name pronounced by the voice is a different thing from that which it signifies? *Ad.*—We have admitted that is true for all signs and "significables." *Aug.*—Do you think that all signs signify something different from themselves, just as the three syllables of the word "animal" cannot signify the word itself. *Ad.*—Not altogether. For when we say the word "sign" it signifies not only all other signs but also itself. For it is a word, and all words are signs. *Aug.*—Does not the same thing happen when we say the word *verbum*? If that word signifies every meaningful articulate sound, it is itself included in that category. *Ad.*—It is. *Aug.*—Isn't it the same with the word "name"? It signifies names of all categories, and is itself the name of no category. If I were to ask you what part of speech is a name, could you answer correctly except by saying it is a noun? *Ad.*—No, indeed. *Aug.*—There are therefore signs which signify themselves as well as other signs. *Ad.*—There are. *Aug.*—Do you think that the same is true with the quadrisyllabic sign "conjunction" when spoken? *Ad.*—By no means. It is a name, but the things it signifies are not names.

· · ·

ix, 25. *Aug.*—I want you now to understand that things signified are of greater importance than their signs. Whatever exists on account of something else must necessarily be of less value than that on account of which it exists. Do you agree? *Ad.*—It seems to me we must not rashly agree to that statement. The word *caenum* (filth) for example is, I think, far preferable to the thing it signifies. What offends us when it is mentioned has nothing to do with the sound of the word. Change one letter and *caenum* becomes *caelum* (heaven), but what a difference there is between the things signified by these two words! I should not, therefore, attribute to the sign the quality I loathe in the thing signified. We prefer to hear the word to being brought into contact with the thing with our other senses. Accordingly I prefer the sign to the thing signified. *Aug.*—You are most observant. It is false, therefore, that things universally are to be preferred to their signs. *Ad.*—So it seems. *Aug.*—Tell me, then, what you think people wanted to achieve when they bestowed that name on an object so nasty and revolting. Do you approve of what they did or not? *Ad.*—I do not venture to approve or to disapprove, nor do I know what they were trying to do. *Aug.*—But you can know what you intend to do when you mention the word? *Ad.*—Certainly. I want to give a sign to the man with whom I am speaking, by means of which I may let him know what I think he ought to know. *Aug.*—The knowledge, then, conveyed by this word from you to him or from him to you, is more valuable than the word itself? *Ad.*—I agree that the knowledge conveyed by the sign is more important than the sign itself. But this does not mean that the thing signified is better than its sign.

26. *Aug.*—Therefore, though it is false that things universally are to be preferred to their signs, it is nevertheless true that whatever exists on account of something

else is inferior to that on account of which it exists. Knowledge of filth, for example, to convey which knowledge the name was invented, is more important than
the name, while the name is also to be preferred to the thing it designates, as we
have discovered. The knowledge is superior to the sign simply because it is the end
towards which the latter is the means. If some gluttonous man, a worshipper of his
belly, as the Apostle says, were to say that he lived to eat, a temperate man, hearing him, and unable to bear with him, might say: "How much better it would be
if you ate to live." This judgment would proceed from the same rule. What dis-
pleased him would be that the other valued his life so little that he thought less
of it than of the pleasures of gluttony, saying that he lived for banqueting. The
advice to eat in order to live rather than to live in order to eat, is justly praised
simply because it shows understanding of what is means and what is end, that is
to say, of what should be subordinate to what. Similarly you or another man of
discernment, hearing some loquacious lover of verbiage say: "I teach for the sake
of talking," would reply: "My man, why don't you rather talk for the sake of teaching." Now if this is right, as you know it is, you see at once how much less value
we are to attribute to words than to the things on account of which we use words.
The use to which words are put is superior to the words; for words exist to be
used, and used to teach. Just as it is better to teach than to talk, so speech is better
than words. And knowledge is much better than words. I want to hear if you
have any objection to offer.

27. *Ad.*—I agree that knowledge is better than words. But I am not sure that
no objection can be urged against the general rule that everything which is means
to an end is inferior to the end it serves. *Aug.*—We shall have a better opportunity
at another time to discuss that problem more carefully. Meantime what you have
admitted is sufficient for what I am desirous of establishing now. You grant that
the knowledge of things is better than the signs of things. So knowledge of the
things signified by signs is preferable to knowledge of their signs. Is it not? *Ad.*—
Surely I have not granted that the knowledge of things is superior to the knowledge of signs, but not superior to the signs themselves. I am afraid to give my
assent to what you have said. If the word "filth" is better than the thing it signifies,
knowledge of the word would be preferable to knowledge of the thing. And yet
the name itself is inferior to the knowledge. There are four terms here: the name,
the thing, knowledge of the name, knowledge of the thing. Why is not the third
better than the fourth, just as the first is better than the second? And yet surely it
is not to be subordinated?

28. *Aug.*—I see you have a wonderful memory for retaining your admissions
and an excellent way of expounding your views. But take the word "vice" (*vitium*).
When we pronounce the word *vi-ti-um* you know that it is better than the thing it
signifies. And yet mere knowledge of the word is much inferior to knowledge of
the vices. Let us consider your four terms: the name, the thing, knowledge of the
name, knowledge of the thing. We rightly prefer the first to the second. When
Persius used the name in his poem—"This man is stupefied by vice"—he committed no fault of versification, indeed he added an ornament. And yet the thing
signified by the word makes the man in whom it is found necessarily vicious. But
there is not the same relation between your third and fourth terms. The fourth
is obviously better than the third. Knowledge of the word vice is inferior to knowledge of the vices. *Ad.*—Do you think that knowledge is preferable even when it
makes us more miserable? For above all the penalties thought of by the cruelty

of tyrants or calculated by their greed, Persius sets this one penalty which tortures men who are compelled to acknowledge vices which they cannot avoid. *Aug.*—In the same way you could deny that knowledge of the virtues is preferable to knowledge of the word "virtue," for to see and not to possess virtue was the punishment which the satirist wished tyrants to suffer. *Ad.*—May God avert such madness! Now I understand that the knowledge imparted to the mind by a good education is not to be blamed, but those are to be judged most miserable of all who are affected by a disease which no medicine can cure. This, I think, was Persius' view too. *Aug.*—Quite right. But it does not matter to us what Persius thought. In such matters we are not subject to the authority of such as he. It is not easy to explain how one kind of knowledge is preferable to another. It is enough for my present purpose that we agree that knowledge of things signified is better than the signs even if not better than knowledge of the signs. Now let us discuss the greater problem. What kind of things, as we said, can be pointed out by themselves without signs such as speaking, walking, lying, and suchlike? *Ad.*—I remember the problem.

x, 29. *Aug.*—Do you think that all actions which we can perform on being interrogated can be demonstrated without a sign? Or is there any exception? *Ad.*—Considering this whole class of things I find none which can be shown without a sign, except perhaps speaking or possibly teaching. For whatever I do by way of demonstration when someone has asked a question, I see that he cannot learn immediately from the action which he wants to have demonstrated to him. Even if I am doing nothing, or am doing something else, when I am asked what walking is, and if I immediately set about walking, and try to give an answer to the question without a sign, how am I to make sure that "walking" is not taken to mean walking the exact distance that I actually walked. In that case my questioner would be deceived, and would imagine that anyone who walked further or less far than I had walked, had not in fact walked at all. And what I have said of this one action applies to all those which I thought could be demonstrated without a sign, except the two I have mentioned.

30. *Aug.*—I grant that. But now, don't you think speaking and teaching are different things? *Ad.*—Certainly. if they were the same, no one could teach without speaking. Who can doubt there is a difference, seeing that, in fact, we can teach many things with other signs besides words? *Aug.*—Is there any difference between teaching and giving signs? *Ad.*—I think they are the same thing. *Aug.*—So it is correct to say that we give signs in order to teach? *Ad.*—Quite correct. *Aug.*—If anyone says that we teach in order to give signs, he can easily be refuted by the previous sentence? *Ad.*—That is so. *Aug.*—If we give signs in order that we may teach, and do not teach in order that we may give signs, teaching and giving signs are different things. *Ad.*—You are right, and I was wrong when I said they were the same. *Aug.*—Now does he who shows us what teaching is do it by giving signs or otherwise? *Ad.*—I do not see how he can do it otherwise. *Aug.*—So you were wrong in saying a moment ago that, when the question is what teaching is, the true answer can be given without signs. Even this, we see, cannot be done without signs, and you have agreed that giving signs is a different thing from teaching. If, as now appears, they are different, teaching cannot be demonstrated without signs and by itself alone, as you thought. So up to this point we have discovered nothing that can be demonstrated by simply performing the action except speaking, which consists in giving signs. But even speaking is itself a sign, so that

it seems there is absolutely nothing which can be taught without signs. *Ad.*—I have no reason for refusing my assent.

31. *Aug.*—It is established then that: (*a*) nothing is taught without signs, (*b*) knowledge should be more precious to us than the signs by means of which we acquire it; though (*c*) possibly not all things which are signified are better than the signs which indicate them. *Ad.*—So it seems. *Aug.*—Just think what a tiny result has been reached by so long and circuitous a path. Since we began our conversation which has now continued for a long time, we have laboured to find answers to three questions: (*a*) whether anything can be taught without signs, (*b*) whether some signs are to be preferred to the things which they signify, (*c*) whether the knowledge of things is better than the knowledge of their signs. But there is a fourth question to which I should like to hear your answer. Do you think our results now stand beyond all doubt? *Ad.*—I should dearly like to think that after all these turnings and twistings we have indeed reached certainty. But your question makes me anxious, and deters me from answering in the affirmative. For it seems to me that you would not have asked the question unless you had some difficulty in mind. The complexity of our problems does not allow me to examine the whole field or to answer with complete confidence. I am afraid there is something hidden in these complexities, to penetrate to which my mind is not sharp enough. *Aug.*—I am not at all unhappy about your hesitation, for it indicates a cautious mind. And caution is the best guard of tranquillity. It is the most difficult thing in the world not to be upset when opinions which we hold, and to which we have given a too ready and too wilful approval, are shattered by contrary arguments and are, as it were, weapons torn from our hands. It is a good thing to give in calmly to arguments that are well considered and grasped, just as it is dangerous to hold as known what in fact we do not know. We should be on our guard lest, when things are frequently undermined which we assumed would stand firm and abide, we fall into such hatred or fear of reason that we think we cannot trust even the most clearly manifest truth.

32. But come, let us consider expeditiously whether you do right to hesitate about our conclusions. Suppose someone ignorant of how birds are deceived by twigs and birdlime should meet a birdcatcher equipped with his instruments but merely travelling and not actually engaged in his work. Suppose he followed the birdcatcher step by step and wonderingly thought and inquired what could be the purpose of the man's equipment. Suppose the birdcatcher, seeing him all attention, and eager to display his skill, got ready his twigs and tubes and hawk and caught a bird, would he not teach the spectator what he wanted to know by the action itself and without any signs? *Ad.*—I suspect the same trouble would arise as I described in the case of the man who asked what "walking" was. So far as I see the whole art of birdcatching has not been demonstrated. *Aug.*—That trouble can easily be removed by adding a further supposition. Suppose the spectator were sufficiently intelligent to learn the whole art from what he saw. It is sufficient for our present purpose that some men can be taught some, not all, things without a sign. *Ad.*—I can make the same additional supposition in the other case. A man who is sufficiently intelligent will learn the exact meaning of "walking" when the action has been shown by taking a few paces. *Aug.*—I have no objection to your doing so, and indeed I approve. Both of us have now shown that some men can be taught some things without signs, and that our previous view was wrong, that nothing at all can be shown without signs. Hence

not one or two things but thousands of things occur to my mind which can be shown by themselves and without any sign. Why should we doubt it? I need not mention the innumerable spectacles which men exhibit in the theatres, showing them without any sign and just as they are. Think of the sun, the light that suffuses and clothes all things, the moon and the stars, earth and sea, and the innumerable things they bear. Does not God exhibit them in themselves to those who behold them?

33. If we consider this a little more closely, perhaps you will find that nothing is learned even by its appropriate sign. If I am given a sign and I do not know the thing of which it is the sign, it can teach me nothing. If I know the thing, what do I learn from the sign? When I read (Dan. 3:27: LXX Dan. 3:94): "Their *saraballae* were not changed," the word, *saraballae,* does not indicate what it means. If I am told that some covering of the head is so called, would I know what a head is, or a covering, unless I knew already? Knowledge of such things comes to me not when they are named by others but when I actually see them. When these two syllables first struck my ear, *ca-put,* I was as ignorant of what they meant as I was of the meaning of *saraballae* when I first heard or read it. But when the word, *caput,* was frequently repeated, observing when it was said, I discovered it was the name of a thing well known to me from my having seen it. Before I made that discovery the word was merely a sound to me. It became a sign when I had learned the thing of which it was the sign. And this I had learned not from signs but from seeing the actual object. So the sign is learned from knowing the thing, rather than vice versa.

34. To understand this better, suppose we hear the sound, *caput,* for the first time, not knowing whether it is merely a sound or whether it has some meaning. We ask what *caput* is. Remember we want to know not the thing signified but the sign, although we cannot have that knowledge so long as we do not know what it is a sign of. If, then, in answer to our question the thing is pointed out with a finger, we look at it and learn that that was a sign which we had heard but had not known before. In a sign there are two things, sound and meaning. We perceive the sound when it strikes our ear, while the meaning becomes clear when we look at the thing signified. The pointing with the finger can indicate nothing but the object pointed out, and it points not to a sign but to a part of the body which we call *caput.* In that way, accordingly, I cannot learn the thing, because I knew it already, nor can I learn the sign because it is not pointed to. I am not greatly interested in the act of pointing. As a gesture it is a sign of something being pointed out rather than of the object pointed out. It is as when we say, "Lo"; for we are accustomed to use that adverb when we point with the finger in case one sign is not sufficient. What I am really trying to convince you of, if I can, is this. We learn nothing by means of these signs we call words. On the contrary, as I said, we learn the force of the word, that is the meaning which lies in the sound of the word, when we come to know the object signified by the word. Then only do we perceive that the word was a sign conveying that meaning.

35. The same is true of the word "coverings," and all the rest. But even when I have come to know them all, I still do not know what *saraballae* are. If someone points them out, or makes a drawing of them, or shows me something like them, I shall not say that he did not teach me what they were, though I could easily prove that that is true with a little more argument. I

content myself with saying what is obvious; he did not teach me by words. If he saw them when I was present and called my attention to them by saying: "Lo, there are *saraballae*," I should learn something I did not know, not from any words spoken but by looking at the object pointed out to me. In this way I should learn and remember the thing that gives meaning to the word. In learning the thing I did not trust the words of another but my own eyes. I trusted the words simply so far as to direct my attention to what was pointed out, that is, to find my answer by looking at a visible object.

xi, 36. The utmost value I can attribute to words is this. They bid us look for things, but they do not show them to us so that we may know them. He alone teaches me anything who sets before my eyes, or one of my other bodily senses, or my mind, the things which I desire to know. From words we can learn only words. Indeed we can learn only their sound and noise. Even if words, in order to be words really, must also be signs, I do not know that any sound I may hear is a word until I know what it means. Knowledge of words is completed by knowledge of things, and by the hearing of words not even words are learned. We learn nothing new when we know the words already, and when we don't know them we cannot say we have learned anything unless we also learn their meaning. And their meaning we learn not from hearing their sound when they are uttered, but from getting to know the things they signify. It is sound reasoning and truly said that when words are spoken we either know or do not know what they mean. If we know, we do not learn, but are rather reminded of what we know. If we do not know, we are not even reminded, but are perhaps urged to inquire.

37. But you may say: granted we cannot know those headcoverings, the sound of whose name we remember, unless we see them, and that we cannot fully know the name until we know the thing. But what about those young men of whom we have heard (Dan. 3) how they vanquished King Nebuchadnezzar and his fiery furnace by their faithfulness and religion, how they sang praises to God, and won honours from their enemy? Have we learned about them otherwise than by means of words? I reply, Yes. But we already knew the meaning of all these words. I already knew the meaning of "three youths," "furnace," "fire," "king," "unhurt by fire" and so on. But the names, Ananias, Azarias and Misael, are as unknown to me as *saraballae*, and the names did not help me to know them and could not help me. All that we read of in that story happened at that time and was written down, so that I have to confess I must believe rather than know. And the writers whom we believe were not ignorant of the difference. For the prophet says: "Unless ye believe ye shall not know" (Isa. 7:9:LXX). This he would not have said if he had thought there was no difference. What I know I also believe, but I do not know everything that I believe. All that I understand I know, but I do not know all that I believe. And I know how useful it is to believe many things which I do not know, among them this story about the three youths. I know how useful it is to believe many things of which knowledge is not possible.

38. Concerning universals of which we can have knowledge, we do not listen to anyone speaking and making sounds outside ourselves. We listen to Truth which presides over our minds within us, though of course we may be bidden to listen by someone using words. Our real Teacher is he who is so listened to, who is said to dwell in the inner man, namely Christ, that is, the unchangeable

power and eternal wisdom of God. To this wisdom every rational soul gives heed, but to each is given only so much as he is able to receive, according to his own good or evil will. If anyone is ever deceived it is not the fault of Truth, any more than it is the fault of the common light of day that the bodily eyes are often deceived. Confessedly we must pay heed to the light that it may let us discern visible things so far as we are able.

xii, 39. On the one hand we need light that we may see colours, and the elements of this world and sentient bodies that we may perceive things of sense, and the senses themselves which the mind uses as interpreters in its search for sense-knowledge. On the other hand, to know intelligible things with our reason we pay attention to the interior truth. How, then, can it be shown that words teach us anything besides the sound that strikes the ear? Everything we perceive we perceive either by bodily sense or by the mind. The former we call "sensible things," the latter "intelligible things"; or, to use the terminology of our Christian authors, the former we call "carnal things," the latter "spiritual things." When we are asked about the former we reply if they are present to our senses, for example, if we are looking at the new moon and someone asks what it is or where. If our questioner does not see it he believes our words, or perhaps often does not believe them, but he learns nothing unless he himself sees what he is asking about. When he sees he learns not from words uttered but from the objects seen and his sense of sight. Words would have the same sound whether he saw or not. When the question concerns not things which are present to our senses but which once were, we do not speak of the things themselves, but of images derived from them and imprinted on the memory. I do not know how we can call these things true, since what we have in view are only false images, unless it is because we speak of them not as things we see and feel but as things we have seen and felt. So in the halls of memory we bear the images of things once perceived as memorials which we can contemplate mentally and can speak of with a good conscience and without lying. But these memorials belong to us privately. If anyone hears me speak of them, provided he has seen them himself, he does not learn from my words, but recognizes the truth of what I say by the images which he has in his own memory. But if he has not had these sensations, obviously he believes my words rather than learns from them.

40. But when we have to do with things which we behold with the mind, that is, with the intelligence and with reason, we speak of things which we look upon directly in the inner light of truth which illumines the inner man and is inwardly enjoyed. There again if my hearer sees these things himself with his inward eye, he comes to know what I say, not as a result of my words but as a result of his own contemplation. Even when I speak what is true and he sees what is true, it is not I who teach him. He is taught not by my words but by the things themselves which inwardly God has made manifest to him. Accordingly, if asked he can make answer regarding these things. What could be more absurd than that he should suppose that by my speaking I have taught him, when, if asked, he could himself have explained these things before I spoke? It often happens that a man, when asked a question, gives a negative answer, but by further questioning can be brought to answer in the affirmative. The reason lies in his own weakness. He is unable to let

the light illumine the whole problem. Though he cannot behold the whole all at once, yet when he is questioned about the parts which compose the whole, he is induced to bring them one by one into the light. He is so induced by the words of his questioner, words, mark you, which do not make statements, but merely ask such questions as put him who is questioned in a position to learn inwardly. For example, if I were to ask you the question I am at present discussing: "Can nothing be taught by means of words?" it might at first seem to you to be absurd because you cannot visualize the whole problem. So I must put my question in a way suited to your ability to hear the inward Teacher. Then, when you have admitted that what I said was true, that you are certain of it, and assuredly know it, I should say: "Where did you learn that?" You might reply that I had taught you. Then I should say: "If I were to tell you that I had seen a man flying, would my words render you as certain of their truth as if I had said, 'Wise men are better than fools'?" You would certainly say: "No, I don't believe your first statement, or, if I believe it, I certainly do not *know* that it is true; but your second statement I know most certainly to be true." In this way you would realize that neither in the case of your not knowing what I affirmed, nor in the case of your knowing quite well, had you learned anything from my words, because in answer to each question you were able to answer confidently that you did not know this and that you did know that. When you realize that all the parts which constitute the whole are clear and certain, you will then admit what you had denied. You will agree that a man who has heard what we have said must either not know whether it is true, or know that it is false, or know that it is true. In the first case he must either believe it, or suppose it, or doubt it. In the second case he must oppose it and deny it. In the third case he must testify to its truth. In no case, therefore, will he learn. When my words have been spoken both he who does not know whether my words are true, and he who knows they are false, and he who could have given the same answers when asked are proved to have learned nothing from my words.

. . .

ON FREE WILL

BOOK II

. . .

iii, 7. *Augustine.*—Let us discuss these three questions, if you please, and in this order. First, how it is manifest that God exists. Secondly, whether all good things, in so far as they are good, are from him. Lastly, whether free will is to be counted among the good things. When these questions have been answered it will, I think, be evident whether free will has been rightly given to man. First,

From *Augustine: Earlier Writings,* tr. J. H. S. Burleigh, Vol. VI, LCC. Published 1953, The Westminster Press. Used by permission; London: SCM Press, Ltd, then, to begin with what is most obvious, I ask you: "Do you exist?" Are you perhaps afraid to be deceived by that question? But if you did not exist it would be impossible for you to be deceived. *Evodius*—Proceed to your other questions. *Aug.*—Since it is manifest that you exist and that you could not know it unless you were living, it is also manifest that you live. You know these two things are absolutely true. *Ev.*—I do. *Aug.*—Therefore this third fact is likewise manifest, namely, that you have intelligence. *Ev.*—Clearly. *Aug.*—Of these three things which is most excellent? *Ev.*—Intelligence. *Aug.*—Why do you think so? *Ev.*—To exist, to live, and to know are three things. A stone exists but does not live. An animal lives but has not intelligence. But he who has intelligence most certainly both exists and lives. Hence I do not hesitate to judge that that is more excellent, which has all these qualities, than that in which one or both of them is absent. That which lives, thereby exists, but it does not follow that it has also intelligence. That is a life like that of an animal. That which exists does not necessarily have either life or intelligence. Dead bodies must be said to exist but cannot be said to live. Much less can that which has not life have intelligence. *Aug.*—We gather, therefore, that of these three things a dead body lacks two, an animal one, and man none. *Ev.*—That is true. *Aug.*—And of these three things that is most excellent which man has along with the other two, that is intelligence. Having that, it follows that he has both being and life. *Ev.*—I am sure of that.

8. *Aug.*—Tell me now whether you know that you have these common bodily senses—seeing, hearing, smelling, taste, touch. *Ev.*—Yes I know. *Aug.*—What do you think belongs to the sense of sight, that is, what do we sense by seeing? *Ev.*—Corporeal objects. *Aug.*—Do we perceive hardness and softness by seeing? *Ev.*—No. *Aug.*—What then belongs properly to the function of the eyes to perceive? *Ev.*—Colour. *Aug.*—And to the ears? *Ev.*—Sound. *Aug.*—And to the sense of smell? *Ev.*—Odour. *Aug.*—To the sense of taste? *Ev.*—Taste. *Aug.*—To the sense of touch? *Ev.*—The soft and the hard, the smooth and the rough, and many such things. *Aug.*—The forms of corporeal objects, great and small, square and round, and such like qualities we perceive both by sight and touch, and so they cannot be ascribed solely to either sight or touch, but to both. *Ev.*—I understand. *Aug.*—You understand, then, that some things belong to one particular sense whose function it is to convey information about them, while other things belong in this way to several senses? *Ev.*—That also I understand. *Aug.*—Can we by any of the senses decide what belongs to any particular sense, or what belongs to all or several of them together? *Ev.*—By no means. That has to be decided by something else within us. *Aug.*—Perhaps that would be reason, which the beasts lack? For, I suppose, it is by reason that we comprehend sense-data and know that they are as they are. *Ev.*—Rather I think that by reason we comprehend that there is a kind of interior sense to which the ordinary senses refer everything. For in the case of the beast the sense of sight is a different thing from the sense to shun or to seek the things it sees. The former belongs to the eyes, the latter is within the soul itself. For of the things they see or hear or perceive with the other bodily senses, some the animals seek with pleasure and accept, others they avoid as displeasing, and refuse to take. This sense can be called neither sight nor hearing nor smell nor taste nor touch, but must be some other sense which presides over all the others alike. While we comprehend this by reason, as I said, still we cannot call it reason, since clearly the beasts have it too.

9. *Aug.*—I recognize that there is that faculty and I do not hesitate to call it the interior sense. But unless the information conveyed to us by the bodily senses goes beyond that sense it cannot become knowledge. What we know we comprehend by reason. We know that colours are not perceived by hearing nor voices by seeing, to mention these only. When we know this it is not by means of the eyes or the ears or by that interior sense which the beasts also possess. We cannot believe that they know that light is not perceived by the ears nor voices by the eyes, for we do not discern these things without rational observation and thought. *Ev.*—I cannot say that I quite see that. Suppose they do distinguish by the interior sense which you admit the animals have, and realize that colours cannot be perceived by hearing nor voices by seeing? *Aug.*—You do not suppose that they can distinguish between the colour that is seen, the sense that is in the eyes, the interior sense that is in the soul, and the reason by which all these things are defined and enumerated? *Ev.*—Not at all. *Aug.*—Could reason distinguish these four things and define their limits unless the notion of colour were conveyed to it in these various stages? First the sense of sight in the eyes would report to the interior sense which presides over all the external senses, and it would then report direct to reason, that is to say, if there is no intermediate stage. *Ev.*—I see no other way. *Aug.*—The sense of sight perceives colour but is itself perceived by no other sense. Do you see that? You do not see sight with the same sense as you see colour. *Ev.*—Certainly not. *Aug.*—Try to distinguish these two things; for I suppose you do not deny that colour is one thing, and to see colour is another entirely different thing. Moreover, it is another different thing to have the sense that enables us to see colour as if it were before us, even when in actual fact there is no colour before us. *Ev.*—I distinguish these things and admit that they are all different. *Aug.*—Well take these three things. Do you see anything with the eyes except colour? *Ev.*—Nothing else. *Aug.*—Tell me, then, how you see the other two things, for you cannot distinguish between them if you have not seen them. *Ev.*—I know no way. I know it is so, that is all. *Aug.*—So you do not know whether it is by reason or by what we call the interior sense which presides over the bodily senses, or by something else? *Ev.*—I do not know. *Aug.*—And yet you know that they can be defined only by reason, and that reason could not do this unless sense-data were offered for its examination. *Ev.*—That is certain. *Aug.*—Then all in the act of knowing which does not come from sense-perception is provided by reason, to which are reported and referred all external circumstances. And so sense-data can be accepted, but strictly within their own limits, and can be comprehended not by sense only but also by knowledge. *Ev.*—That is so. *Aug.*—Reason distinguishes the senses which are its servants from the data they collect. Likewise it knows the difference between the senses and itself, and is sure that it is much more powerful than they. Does reason comprehend reason by any other means than by reason itself? Would you know that you possess reason otherwise than by reason? *Ev.*—Surely not. *Aug.*—When we see a colour we do not, with the sense of sight, see that we see; when we hear a sound, we do not hear our hearing; when we smell a rose we do not smell our smelling; when we taste anything we do not taste taste in our mouths; and when we touch anything we cannot touch the sense of touch. It is clear, therefore, that none of the five senses can perceive itself, though all in their several ways perceive corporeal objects. *Ev.*—That is quite clear.

iv, 10. *Aug.*—I think it is also clear that the interior sense perceives not only the data passed on to it by the five senses, but also perceives the senses too. A beast would not make the movement necessary for seeking or avoiding anything unless it was conscious of perceiving, which of course it could not be by using the five senses only. I do not suggest that this consciousness in the beast is a step towards knowledge, for that belongs to reason, simply that it is a prerequisite of movement. If there is still some obscurity here an example will elucidate the point. It will be enough to consider the case of one of the senses, say sight. A beast would be quite unable to open its eyes and direct them towards an object it desired to see unless it perceived that it could not see the object so long as its eyes were closed and not directed to the object. If it is conscious of not seeing when it does not see, it must also be conscious of seeing when it does see. The fact that when it sees an object it does not make the movement that would be necessary to bring it into view indicates that it perceives that it sees or does not see. But it is not so clear whether a beast has self-consciousness, as well as consciousness, of perceiving corporeal objects. Possibly it has an inward feeling that every living thing shuns death which is the opposite of life. If so, every living thing which shuns the opposite of life must be conscious of itself as living. But if that is not clear let us omit it, and not strive to establish our position with proofs that are not both certain and self-evident. What is evident is this: corporeal objects are perceived by bodily sense; no bodily sense can perceive itself; the interior sense can perceive both corporeal objects perceived by a bodily sense, and also that bodily sense itself; but reason knows all these things and knows itself, and therefore has knowledge in the strict sense of the term. Don't you think so? *Ev.*—I do indeed. *Aug.*—Come, then, what about the question the answer to which we desired to reach? To reach that answer we have taken all this time and trouble in preparing the way

v, 11. *Ev.*—So far as I remember, of tne three questions we formulated to give the discussion some order, we are now engaged with the first, namely, How is is to be made evident that God exists, a proposition which is most firmly to be accepted in faith. *Aug.*—You are quite right. But I want you to keep firm hold of this too. When I asked you whether you know that you exist, it appeared that you know not only this but two other things as well. *Ev.*—I remember that too. *Aug.*—Now to which of the three do you understand all that impinges on the bodily senses to pertain? I mean, in which class of things would you put all that we perceive by means of the eyes or any other bodily organ? Would you say that all this belongs to the class that merely exists, or to that which also has life, or to that which has intelligence as well? *Ev.*—In that which merely exists. *Aug.* —And where would put the senses? *Ev.*—In that which has life. *Aug.*—And which do you judge to be superior, the senses or their objects? *Ev.*—The senses surely. *Aug.*—Why? *Ev.*—Because that which has life is superior to what merely exists.

12. *Aug.*—What about the interior sense, which we have discovered to be inferior to reason, and possessed by us in common with the beasts? Do you have any hesitation in putting it higher than the senses by means of which we come into contact with corporeal objects, and which you have said are to be reckoned superior to corporeal objects? *Ev.*—I should have no hesitation. *Aug.*—I should like to know why not. You cannot say that the interior sense is to be placed in the category of intelligent things, for it is found in beasts which have no intelli-

gence. This being so, I ask why you put the interior sense higher than the senses which perceive corporeal objects, since both belong to the class of things that have life. You put the bodily senses above corporeal objects just because they belong to the kind of things which merely exist, while it belongs to the kind which also live. So also does the interior sense. Tell me, then, why you think it superior. If you say it is because the interior sense perceives the other senses, I do not believe you will be able to find a rule by which we can establish that every perceiving thing is superior to what it perceives. That would mean that we should be compelled to say that every intelligence is superior to that which it knows. But that is false; for man knows wisdom but is not superior to wisdom. Wherefore consider for what reason you think that the interior sense is superior to the senses by which we perceive corporeal objects. *Ev.*—It is because I recognize that it is in some kind of way a ruler and judge among the other senses. If they failed in their duty it would be like a master demanding a debt from a servant, as we just recently were saying. The eye cannot see whether it has vision or not and therefore it cannot judge where it is defective or where it is sufficient. That is what the interior sense does, as when it teaches a beast to open its eyes and supply what it perceives is lacking. No one doubts that he who judges is superior to that over which he exercises judgment. *Aug.*—You observe, then, that a bodily sense also judges in a manner corporeal objects? Pleasure and pain fall within its jurisdiction, when the body is affected gently or harshly. Just as the interior sense judges whether the sight of the eyes is defective or adequate, so sight judges what is defective or adequate in colours. Just as the interior sense judges of our hearing whether it is sufficient or defective, so the sense of hearing judges voices, whether they flow smoothly or are noisily harsh. We need not go over the other senses. You observe already, I think, what I wish to say. The interior sense judges the bodily senses, approving their integrity and demanding that they do their duty, just as the bodily senses judge corporeal objects approving of gentleness and reproving the opposite. *Ev.*—I see that and agree that it is true.

vi, 13. *Aug.*—Now consider whether reason also judges of the interior sense. I am not asking whether you have any doubts as to its superiority, for I have no doubt that you judge it to be superior. Nor perhaps is it worth inquiring whether reason judges of the interior sense. For about those things which are inferior to reason, that is, about corporeal objects, bodily senses and the interior sense, reason alone tells us how one is superior to another and how reason is more excellent than them all. How could it do so if it were not a judge over them? *Ev.*—That is obvious. *Aug.*—A nature which not only exists but also lives, like that of the beast, though it have not intelligence, is higher than a nature which merely exists and has no life, like an inanimate object. And higher still is a nature which exists and lives and has intelligence, like the rational mind in man. Surely you do not think that in us, that is, in a complete human nature, anything can be found more excellent than that which we have put third among these three levels of being? Obviously we have a body, and life which animates the body. These two things we recognize that beasts also have. But there is a third thing, the head, as it were, or the eye of our soul, or whatever else more fitly describes reason and intelligence, which beasts do not have. Can you, I pray, find anything in human nature higher than reason? *Ev.*—I see nothing at all that could be superior.

14. *Aug.*—If, now, we could find something which you could unhesitatingly

recognize not only as existing but also as superior to our reason, would you have any hesitation in calling it, whatever it may be, God? *Ev.*—Well, I should not without hesitation give the name, God, to anything that I might find better than the best element in my natural composition. I do not wish to say simply that God is that to which my reason is inferior, but that above which there is no superior. *Aug.*—Clearly so, for it is God who has given to your reason to have these true and pious views of him. But, I ask, supposing you find nothing superior to our reason save what is eternal and unchangeable, will you hesitate to call that God? You realize that bodies are mutable; and it is evident that life which animates the body is not without mutability by reason of its varying affections. Even reason is proved to be mutable, for sometimes it strives to reach the truth and sometimes it does not so strive. Sometimes it reaches the truth and sometimes it does not. If without the aid of any bodily organ, neither by touch nor by taste nor by smell, neither by the ears nor the eyes, but by itself alone reason catches sight of that which is eternal and unchangeable, it must confess its own inferiority, and that the eternal and unchangeable is its God. *Ev.*—This I will certainly confess to be God than whom there is nothing superior. *Aug.*—Very well. It will be enough for me to show that there is something of this nature which you will be ready to confess to be God; or if there be something higher still that at least you will allow to be God. However that may be, it will be evident that God exists when with his aid I have demonstrated to you, as I promised, that there is something above reason. *Ev.*—Then proceed with your demonstration as you promise.

vii, 15. *Aug.*—I shall do so. But I first ask you this. Is my bodily sense identical with yours, or is mine mine and yours yours only? If the latter were not the case I should not be able to see anything with my eyes which you also would not see. *Ev.*—I admit that at once, though while each of us has severally the senses of sight, hearing and the rest, your senses and mine belong to the same class of things. For one man can both see and hear what another does not see or hear, and with any of the other senses can perceive what another does not perceive. Hence it is evident that your sense is yours alone and mine mine alone. *Aug.*—Will you make the same reply about the interior sense? *Ev.*—Exactly. My interior sense perceives my perceiving, and yours perceives yours. Often someone who sees something will ask me whether I also see it. The reason for asking simply is that I know whether I see or not, and the questioner does not know. *Aug.*—Has each of us, then, his own particular reason? For it can often happen that I know something when you do not know it, and I know that I know it, but you cannot know that. *Ev.*—Apparently each of us has his own private rational mind.

16. *Aug.*—But you cannot say that each of us has his own private sun or moon or stars or the like, though each of us sees these things with his own particular sense of sight? *Ev.*—No, of course I would not say that. *Aug.*—So, many of us can see one thing simultaneously, though our senses, by which we perceive the object we all see together, are our own. In spite of the fact that my sense and yours are two different things, what we actually see need not be two different things, one of which I see, while you see the other. There is one object for both of us, and both of us see it simultaneously. *Ev.*—Obviously. *Aug.*—We can also hear one voice simultaneously, so that, though my hearing is not your hearing there are not two voices of which you hear one and I another. It is not

as if my hearing caught one part of the sound and yours another. The one sound, and the whole of it, is heard by both of us simultaneously. *Ev.*—That, too, is obvious.

17. *Aug.*—But notice, please, what is to be said about the other senses. It is pertinent to the present discussion to observe that the case with them is not quite the same as with sight and hearing, though it is not entirely different. You and I can breathe the same air and feel its effects by smelling. Likewise we can both partake of one piece of honey, or some other food or drink, and feel its effects by tasting. That is to say, there is one object, but we each have our own senses. You have yours and I have mine. So while we both sense one odour and one taste, you do not sense it with my sense nor I with yours, nor with any sense that we can have in common. My sense is entirely mine and yours yours, even though both of us sense the same odour or the same taste. In this way the senses somewhat resemble sight and hearing. But there is this dissimilarity, which is pertinent to the present problem. We both breathe the same air with our nostrils, and taste one food. And yet I do not breathe in the same particles of air as you do, and I consume a different portion of food from that consumed by you. When I breathe I draw in as much air as is sufficient for me, and when you breathe you draw in as much as is sufficient for you, but both of us use different parts of air. If between us we consume one food, the whole of it is not consumed either by you or by me, as we both hear the whole sound of a word spoken, or see the whole object offered to our sight simultaneously. One part of a drink must pass into your mouth and another into mine. Do you understand? *Ev.*—I admit that is all clear and certain.

18. *Aug.*—Do you think the sense of touch is comparable to the senses of sight and hearing in the fashion we are now discussing? Not only can we both feel one body by touching it, but we can both feel not only the same body but the same part of it. It is not as in the case of food where both of us cannot consume the whole of it when we both eat it. You can touch what I touch and touch the whole of it. We do not touch each one a different part but each of us touches the whole. *Ev.*—So far, I admit that the sense of touch resembles the first two senses, sight and hearing. But I see there is this difference. We can both simultaneously at one and the same time see or hear the whole of what is seen or heard. No doubt we can both touch simultaneously the whole of one object, but in any one moment we can only touch different parts. The same part we can only touch at different times. I cannot touch the part you are touching unless you move away your hand.

19. *Aug.*—You are most vigilant. But here is another thing you ought to notice, since there are some things which both of us can feel, and others which we must feel severally. Our own senses, for example, we must feel each for himself. I cannot feel your sense nor you mine. But in the case of corporeal things, that is, things we perceive with the bodily senses, when we cannot both perceive them together but must do so severally, it is due to the fact that we make them completely ours by consuming them and making them part of ourselves, like food and drink of which you cannot consume the same part as I do. It is true that nurses give infants food which they have chewed, but the part which has been squeezed out and been swallowed, cannot be recalled and used to feed the child. When the palate tastes something pleasant it claims a part, even if only a small part, which it cannot give up, and does with it what is consonant with corporeal

nature. Were this not so no taste would remain in the mouth when what had been chewed was put out. The same can be said of the part of the air which we draw into our nostrils. You may breathe in some of the air which I breathe out, but you cannot breathe that part which has gone to nourish me, for I cannot breathe it out. Physicians sometimes bid us take medicine through our nostrils. I alone feel it when I breathe it in and I cannot put it back again by breathing out, so that you may breathe it in and feel it. All sensible things, which we do not destroy and take into our systems when we sense them, we can perceive, both of us, either at the same time or at different times, one after the other, in such a way that the whole or the part which I perceive can also be perceived by you. I mean such things as light or sound or bodily objects which we do not destroy when we use and perceive them. *Ev.*—I understand. *Aug.*—It is therefore evident that things which we perceive with the bodily senses without causing them to change are by nature quite different from our senses, and consequently are common to us both, because they are not converted and changed into something which is our peculiar and almost private property. *Ev.*—I agree. *Aug.*—By "our peculiar and private property" I mean that which belongs to each of us alone, which each of us perceives by himself alone, which is part of the natural being of each of us severally. By "common and almost public property" I mean that which is perceived by all sentient beings without its being thereby affected and changed. *Ev.*—That is so.

viii, 20. *Aug.*—Now consider carefully, and tell me whether anything can be found which all reasoning beings can see in common, each with his own mind and reason; something which is present for all to see but which is not transformed like food and drink for the use of those for whom it is present; something which remains complete and unchanged, whether they see it or do not see it. Do you perhaps think there is nothing of that kind? *Ev.*—Indeed, I see many such, but it will be sufficient to mention one. The science of numbers is there for all reasoning persons, so that all calculators may try to learn it, each with his own reason and intelligence. One can do it easily, another with difficulty, another cannot do it at all. But the science itself remains the same for everybody who can learn it, nor is it converted into something consumed like food by him who learns it. If anyone makes a mistake in numbers the science itself is not at fault. It remains true and entire. The error of the poor arithmetician is all the greater, the less he knows of the science.

21. *Aug.*—Quite right. I see you are not untaught in these matters, and so have quickly found a reply. But suppose someone said that numbers make their impression on our minds not in their own right but rather as images of visible things, springing from our contacts by bodily sense with corporeal objects, what would you reply? Would you agree? *Ev.*—I could never agree to that. Even if I did perceive numbers with the bodily senses I could not in the same way perceive their divisions and relations. By referring to these mental operations I show anyone to be wrong in his counting who gives a wrong answer when he adds or subtracts. Moreover, all that I contact with a bodily sense, such as this sky and this earth and whatever I perceive to be in them, I do not know how long it will last. But seven and three make ten not only now but always. In no circumstances have seven and three ever made anything else than ten, and they never will. So I maintain that the unchanging science of numbers is common to me and to every reasoning being.

22. *Aug.*—I do not deny that your reply is certainly most true. But you will easily see that numbers are not conveyed to us by our bodily senses if you consider that the value of every number is calculated according to the number of times it contains the number one. For example, twice one is called two; thrice one is called three; ten times one is called ten, and every number receives its name and its value according to the number of times it contains the number one. Whoever thinks with exactitude of unity will certainly discover that it cannot be perceived by the senses. Whatever comes into contact with a bodily sense is proved to be not one but many, for it is corporeal and therefore has innumerable parts. I am not going to speak of parts so minute as to be almost unrealizable; but, however small the object may be, it has at least a right-hand part and a left-hand part, an upper and a lower part, a further and a nearer part, one part at the end and another at the middle. We must admit that these parts exist in any body however small, and accordingly we must agree that no corporeal object is a true and absolute unity. And yet all these parts could not be counted unless we had some notion of unity. When I am seeking unity in the corporeal realm and am at the same time certain that I have not found it, nevertheless I know what I am seeking and failing to find, and I know that I cannot find it, or rather that it does not exist among corporeal things. When I know that no body is a unity, I know what unity is. If I did not know what unity is, I could not count the plurality of parts in a body. However I have come to know unity, I have not learned it from the bodily senses, for by them I can know only corporeal objects, and none of them, as we have proved, is a true unity. Moreover, if we do not perceive unity with any bodily sense, neither do we perceive any number, of the kind at any rate which we discern with the intellect. For there is none of them which is not a multiple of unity, and unity cannot be perceived by the bodily senses. The half of any body, however small, requires the other half to complete the whole, and it itself can be halved. A body can be divided into two parts but they are not simply two. [They may in turn be further sub-divided.] But the number two consists of twice simple unity, so that the half of two, that is, simple unity, cannot be sub-divided by two or three or any other number whatever, because it is true and simple unity.

23. Following the order of the numbers we see that two comes next to one, and is found to be the double of one. The double of two does not immediately follow. Three comes first and then four, which is the double of two. Throughout the numerical series this order extends by a fixed and unchangeable law. After one, which is the first of all numbers, two follows immediately, which is the double of one. After the second number, that is, two, in the second place in order comes the double of two. In the first place after two comes three and in the second place four, the double of two. After the third number, three, in the third place comes its double, for after three four comes first, five second, and in the third place six, which is the double of three. Similarly the fourth number after the fourth is its double; five, six, seven, and in the fourth place eight, which is the double of four. And throughout the numerical series you will find the same rule holds good from first to last. The double of any number is found to be exactly as far from that number as it is from the beginning of the series. How do we find this changeless, firm and unbroken rule persisting throughout the numerical series? No bodily sense makes contact with all numbers, for they are innumerable. How do we know that this rule holds throughout? How can

any phantasy or phantasm yield such certain truth about numbers which are innumerable? We must know this by the inner light, of which bodily sense knows nothing.

24. By many such evidences all disputants to whom God has given ability and who are not clouded by obstinacy, are driven to admit that the science of numbers does not pertain to bodily sense, but stands sure and unchangeable, the common possession of all reasoning beings. Many other things might occur to one that belong to thinkers as their common and, as it were, public property, things which each beholder sees with his own mind and reason, and which abide inviolate and unchangeable. But I am glad that the science of numbers most readily occurred to you when you had to answer my question. For it is not in vain that the holy books conjoin number and wisdom, where it is written, "I turned and [inclined] my heart to know and consider and seek wisdom and number" (Eccl. 7:25).

ix. 25. Now, I ask, what are we to think of wisdom itself? Do you think that individual men have wisdoms of their own? Or is there one wisdom common to all, so that a man is wiser the more he participates in it? *Ev.*—I do not yet know what you mean by wisdom. I observe that men judge variously of what deeds or words are wise. Soldiers think they are acting wisely in following their profession. Those who despise military service and give all their care and labour to agriculture think themselves wise. Those who leave all these things aside or reject all such temporal concerns and devote all their zeal to the search for truth, how they can know themselves and God, judge that this is the chief task of wisdom. Those who are unwilling to give themselves to the life of leisure for the purpose of seeking and contemplating truth, but prefer to accept laborious cares and duties in the service of their fellows and to take part in justly ruling and governing human affairs, they too think themselves to be wise. Moreover, those who do both of these things, who live partly in the contemplation of truth and partly in laborious duties, which they think they owe to human society, those think they hold the palm of wisdom. I do not mention the sects innumerable, of which there is none which does not put its own members above all others and claim that they alone are wise. Since we are now carrying on this discussion on the understanding that we are not to state what we merely believe but what we clearly understand, I can make no answer to your question, unless in addition to believing I also know by contemplation and reason what wisdom is.

26. *Aug.*—Surely you do not suppose that wisdom is anything but the truth in which the chief good is beheld and possessed? All those people whom you have mentioned as following diverse pursuits seek good and shun evil, but they follow different pursuits because they differ as to what they think to be good. Whoever seeks that which ought not to be sought, even though he would not seek it unless it seemed to him to be good, is nevertheless in error. There can be no error when nothing is sought, or when that is sought which ought to be sought. In so far as all men seek the happy life they do not err. But in so far as anyone does not keep to the way that leads to the happy life, even though he professes to desire only to reach happiness, he is in error. Error arises when we follow something which does not lead to that which we wish to reach. The more a man errs in his way of life, the less is he wise, the further he is from the truth in which the chief good is beheld and possessed. Everyone is happy who attains the chief good, which indisputably is the end which we all desire. Just as it is

universally agreed that we wish to be happy, it is similarly agreed that we wish to be wise, because no one is happy without wisdom. For no one is happy except by the possession of the chief good which is beheld and possessed in the truth which we call wisdom. Before we are happy the notion of happiness is stamped upon our minds; that is why we know and can say confidently without any hesitation that we want to be happy. Likewise, even before we are wise we have the notion of wisdom stamped upon our minds. For that reason each of us, if asked whether he wants to be wise, will, without any groping in the dark, answer that, of course, he does.

27. Perhaps we are now agreed as to what wisdom is. You may not be able to express it in words, but if you had no notion in your mind of what it is you would not know that you want to be wise, and that you ought to want to be wise. That, I am sure you will not deny. Suppose, then, that we are agreed as to what wisdom is, please tell me whether you think that wisdom too, like the science of numbers, is common to all reasoning beings. Or, seeing that there are as many minds as there are men, and I cannot observe anything that goes on in your mind, nor you what goes on in mine, do you suppose that there are as many wisdoms as there can be wise men? *Ev.*—If the chief good is one for all men, the truth in which it is seen and possessed, that is, wisdom, must be one and common to all. *Aug.*—Have you any doubt that the chief good, whatever it may be, is one for all men? *Ev.*—I certainly have, because I see that different men rejoice in different things as if they were their chief good. *Aug.*—I wish there were no more doubt about the nature of the chief good than there is about the fact that without it, whatever it may be, no one can become happy. But that is a big question and demands a long discourse, so let us suppose that there are just as many "chief goods" as there are different things sought by different people under the impression that they are "chief goods." Surely it does not follow that wisdom is not one and common to all because the good things which men see in it and choose are manifold and diverse? If you think it does, you might as well doubt whether the light of the sun is one light because there are many diverse things which we see by means of it. Of these each one chooses at will something to enjoy looking at. One man likes to behold a high mountain and rejoices to look at it. Another prefers the plain, another a hollow valley, or green woods, or the wavy expanse of the sea. Some one may like all these or some of them whose united beauty contributes to the pleasure of looking at them. The things which men see by the light of the sun and choose for enjoyment are many and various, but the light is one in which each man sees what he enjoys looking at. So, although there are many diverse good things from among which each may choose what he likes, and seeing and possessing it and enjoying it, may rightly and truly constitute it his own chief good, nevertheless it may be that the light of wisdom in which these things can be seen and possessed is one light common to all wise men. *Ev.*—I admit it may be so, and that there is nothing to prevent there being one wisdom common to all, though there are many various chief goods. But I should like to know whether it is so. To admit that something may be is not exactly the same as to admit that it is. *Aug.*—Meantime we have established that there is such a thing as wisdom, but we have not yet determined whether it is one and common to all, or whether individual wise men have their particular wisdoms just as they have their particular souls or minds. *Ev.*—That is so.

x, 28. *Aug.*—We hold it as settled that there is such a thing as wisdom, or at least that there are wise men, and also that all men want to be happy. But where do we see this? For I have no doubt at all that you see this and that it is true. Do you see this truth in such a way that I cannot know it unless you tell me what you think? Or could I see this truth, just as you understand it, even if you did not tell me? *Ev.*—I do not doubt that you too could see it even if I did not want you to. *Aug.*—Is not one truth which we both see with our different minds common to both of us? *Ev.*—Clearly. *Aug.*—Again, I believe you do not deny that men should strive after wisdom. You admit that that is true? *Ev.*—I have no doubt about that. *Aug.*—Here is another truth which is one and common to all who know it, though each one sees it with his own mind and not with mine or yours or any other man's. Can we deny that, since what is seen can be seen in common by all who see it? *Ev.*—We cannot deny it. *Aug.*—Again, take such propositions as these: Man ought to live justly; the worse ought to be subjected to the better; like is to be compared with like; each man should be given his due. Don't you admit that these statements are absolutely true and stable, to be shared by you and me and all who see them? *Ev.*—I agree. *Aug.*—The same would be true of these statements: The incorrupt is better than the corrupt, the eternal than the temporal, the inviolable than the violable? *Ev.*—Undeniably. *Aug.*—Could anyone claim truths of that kind as his own private truths, seeing they are unchangeably present for all to contemplate who have the capacity to contemplate them? *Ev.*—No one could claim any one of them as his own, for not only are they true but they are equally common property to all. *Aug.*—And again, who denies that the soul ought to be turned from corruption and converted to incorruption, in other words not corruption but incorruption ought to be loved? Who, confessing that that is true, does not also understand that it is unchangeably true and can be understood in commom by all minds which have the capacity to understand it? *Ev.*—Most true. *Aug.*—Will anyone doubt that a life which no adversity can drive from a certain and honourable opinion is better than one which is easily broken and overwhelmed by temporal disadvantages? *Ev.*—Who can doubt it?

29. *Aug.*—I shall ask no more questions of that kind. It is sufficient that you see as I do that these rules and guiding lights of the virtues, as we may call them, are true and unchangeable, and singly or all together they stand open for the common contemplation of those who have the capacity to behold them, each with his own mind and reason. This you admit is quite certain. But I do ask whether you think these truths belong to wisdom. For I am sure you think that he who has acquired wisdom is wise. *Ev.*—I most certainly do. *Aug.*—Could the man who lives justly so live unless he saw how to apply the principles of subordinating the inferior to the superior, joining like to like, and giving to each his due? *Ev.*—He could not. *Aug.*—Would you deny that he who sees this sees wisely? *Ev.*—I would not. *Aug.*—Does not he who lives prudently choose incorruption and perceive that it is preferable to corruption? *Ev.*—Clearly. *Aug.* —If he makes what no one doubts is the right choice as to the goal towards which he should direct his mind, can it be denied that he has made a wise choice? *Ev.*—I could not deny it. *Aug.*—When he directs his mind to what he has wisely chosen, again he does it wisely? *Ev.*—Most certainly. *Aug.*—And if by no terrors or penalties can he be driven from what he has wisely chosen and towards which he has wisely directed his mind, again there is no doubt that he

acts wisely? *Ev.*—There is no doubt. *Aug.*—It is therefore abundantly evident that these rules and guiding lights of virtue, as we have called them, belong to wisdom. The more a man uses them in living his life, and the more closely he follows them, the more wisely does he live and act. Everything that is wisely done cannot rightly be said to be done apart from wisdom. *Ev.*—That is perfectly true. *Aug.*—Just as the rules of numbers are true and unchangeable, and the science of numbers is unchangeably available for all who can learn it, and is common to them all, so the rules of wisdom are true and unchangeable. When you were asked about them one by one you replied that they were true and evident and open to the common contemplation of all who have the capacity to examine them.

xi. 30. *Ev.*—I cannot doubt it. But I should very much like to know whether wisdom and numbers are contained within one class of things. You mentioned that they were linked together in the Holy Scriptures. Or is one of them derived from the other or contained within the other? For example, is number derived from wisdom or is it contained in wisdom? I should not dare to suggest that wisdom is derived from number or is contained in it. For I know many arithmeticians or accountants, or whatever they are to be called, who count perfectly and indeed marvellously, but somehow very few of them have wisdom, perhaps none. So wisdom strikes me as being far more worthy of respect than arithmetic. *Aug.*—You mention a matter which has often made me wonder, too. When I consider in my mind the unchangeable science of numbers and the recondite sanctuary or region, or whatever other name we are to give to the realm and abode of numbers, I find myself far removed from the corporeal sphere. I find possibly some vague idea but no words adequate to express it, and so in order to say something I return wearily to these numbers which are set before our eyes and call them by their wonted names. The same thing happens when I am thinking as carefully and intently as I can about wisdom. And so I greatly marvel that though wisdom and number are alike in being mysteriously and certainly true, and are linked together by the testimony of Scripture which I have quoted, I say I marvel greatly that number is so contemptible to the majority of men, while wisdom is precious. To be sure it may be because they are one and the same thing. On the other hand it is also written in Scripture of Wisdom that "she reaches from one end of the world to the other with full strength and ordereth things graciously" (Wisdom 8:1). Perhaps it is called number from its potency to reach with strength from end to end, and is properly called wisdom because it graciously ordereth all things. For both are functions of wisdom alone.

31. Wisdom has given numbers even to the smallest and most remote of things, and all bodies have their own numbers. But it has not given to bodies the power to be wise, nor even to all souls, but only to rational souls, in which, as it were, it has taken up its abode from whence it ordereth all things, even the smallest to which it has given numbers. Now we have no difficulty in judging corporeal things as things which belong to a lower order, and the numbers they bear stamped upon them we see are also lower than we are. Therefore we hold them in contempt. But when we begin to consider them from another angle we discover that they transcend our minds and abide unchangeably in the truth. And because few can be wise and many fools can count, men admire wisdom and despise numbers. But learned and studious men, the further they are re-

moved from earthly corruption, behold the more clearly in the light of truth both numbers and wisdom, and hold both to be precious. By comparison with truth they prize neither gold nor silver nor the other things over which men strive, indeed they even come to think of themselves as of little account.

32. There is no need to be surprised that men think little of numbers and value wisdom highly, because counting is easier than being wise. You see how they set a higher value on gold than on the light of a candle, compared with which gold is a ridiculous thing. But a vastly inferior thing is more highly honoured because any beggar can light himself a candle, and only a few possess gold. Far be it from me to suggest that compared with numbers wisdom is inferior. Both are the same thing, but wisdom requires an eye fit to see it. From one fire light and heat are felt as if they were "consubstantial," so to speak. They cannot be separated one from the other. And yet the heat reaches those things which are brought near to the fire, while the light is diffused far and wide. So the potency of intellect which indwells wisdom causes things nearer to it to be warm, such as rational souls. Things further away, such as bodies, it does not affect with the warmth of wisdom, but it pours over them the light of numbers. Probably you will find that obscure, but no similitude drawn from visible things can be completely adapted to explain an invisible thing so as to be understood by everybody. Only take note of this which is sufficient for the problem we have in hand, and is clear enough to humbler kinds of mind such as ours. Though it cannot be made crystal-clear to us whether number is part of wisdom or is derived from wisdom or vice versa, or whether both names can be shown to designate one thing, it is at least evident that both are true and unchangeably true.

xii, 33. Accordingly, you will never deny that there is an unchangeable truth which contains everything that is unchangeably true. You will never be able to say that it belongs particularly to you or to me or to any man, for it is available and offers itself to be shared by all who discern things immutably true, as if it were some strange mysterious and yet public light. Who would say that what is available to be shared by all reasoning and intelligent persons can be the private property of any of them? You remember, I dare say, our recent discussion about the bodily senses. Those things with which we both make contact by means of our eyes or ears, colours and sounds which you and I see or hear together, do not belong to our actual eyes or ears, but are common to both of us so that we may alike perceive them. So you would never say that those things which you and I behold in common, each with his own mind, belong to the actual mind of either of us. You would not say that what the eyes of two persons see belongs to the eyes of one or the other of them. It is a third thing towards which both direct their regard. *Ev.*—That is most clear and true.

34. *Aug.*—Do you, then, think that this truth of which we have already spoken so much and in which we behold so many things, is more excellent than our minds, or equal to our minds, or inferior? If it were inferior we should not use it as a standard of judgment, but should rather pass judgment on it, as we do on bodies which are inferior to our minds. For of them we often say not only that it *is* so or is not so, but that it *ought to be* so or not so. Similarly with our minds we know not only that it *is* thus or thus, but often also that it *ought to be* thus or thus. We judge of bodies when

we say this is not so white as it ought to be, or not so square and so on. Of minds we say this one is not so capable as it ought to be, or it is not gentle enough or eager enough, according to our moral standard. All these judgments we make according to those inward rules of truth, which we discern in common. But no man passes any judgment on these rules. One may say the eternal *is* superior to the temporal, or seven and three *are* ten, but no one says these things *ought to be so*. Knowing simply that they are so one does not examine them with a view to their correction but rejoices to have discovered them. If, then, truth were the equal of our minds, it too would be mutable. Our minds sometimes see more sometimes less, and so confess their mutability. But truth abiding steadfast in itself neither advances when we see more, nor falls short when we see less. Abiding whole and uncorrupt it rejoices with its light those who turn to it, and punishes with blindness those who turn from it. We pass judgment on our minds in accordance with truth as our standard, while we cannot in any way pass judgment on truth. For we say of our mind it understands less than it ought, or it understands exactly as it ought; and a mind approaches the proper standard of intelligence as it is brought nearer to unchangeable truth, and becomes able to cleave to it. Hence if truth is neither inferior to nor equal to our mind it must be superior and more excellent.

xiii, 35. I promised, if you remember, to show you something superior to the human mind and reason. There it is, truth itself. Embrace it if you can. Enjoy it. Delight in the Lord and he will grant you the petitions of your heart. What do you ask for more than to be happy? And what is more happy than to enjoy unshakable, unchangeable truth which is excellent above all things? Men exclaim that they are happy when they embrace the beautiful bodies, deeply longed for, of their wives or even of harlots, and shall we doubt that we are happy in the embrace of truth? Men exclaim that they are happy when with throats parched with heat they find a fountain flowing with pure water, or being hungry, find a copious meal all ready prepared, and shall we deny that we are happy when truth is our meat and drink? We are wont to hear the voices of people proclaiming that they are happy if they lie among roses or other flowers and enjoy scented ointments, and shall we hesitate to call ourselves happy when we are inspired by truth? Many place happiness in music, vocal and instrumental, flutes and strings. When they are without music they consider themselves unhappy; when they have it, they are transported with joy. Shall we, when the harmonious and creative silence of truth steals, so to speak, noiselessly over our minds, seek the happy life elsewhere, and fail to enjoy that which is ours now and securely? Men delight in the sheen of gold and silver, gems and colours. They delight in the brightness and pleasantness of visible light as it appears in fire or in the sun, moon and stars. When no trouble or want comes to rob them of that pleasure they think themselves happy, and therefore wish to live for ever. Shall we fear to place the happy life in the light of truth?

36. Nay, since the chief good is recognized to be truth and is possessed when truth is possessed, and truth is wisdom, in wisdom let us discern the chief good and possess it and enjoy it. He is happy indeed who enjoys the chief good. Truth points out all the things that are truly good, and intelligent men, according to their capacity, choose one or more of them in order to enjoy them. People, for example, find pleasure in looking at some object which they are glad to

behold in the light of the sun. Those among them who are endowed with strong healthy eyes love to look at nothing better than at the sun itself, which sheds its light upon the other things which delight weaker eyes. So a strong and vigorous mental vision may behold many true and changeless things with certain reason, but directs its regard to the truth itself whereby all things are made clear, and, cleaving to the truth and forgetting, as it were, all other things, it enjoys them all together in the truth. Whatever is pleasant in other true things is pleasant also in truth itself.

37. Herein is our liberty, when we are subject to truth. And Truth is our God who liberates us from death, that is, from the condition of sin. For the Truth itself, speaking as Man to men, says to those who believe in him: "If ye abide in my word ye are truly my disciples, and ye shall know the truth and the truth shall make you free" (John 8:31–32). No soul enjoys a thing with liberty unless it also enjoys it with security.

xiv. But no one is secure in the possession of goods which he can lose against his will. Truth and wisdom no one can lose unwillingly. From them there can be no spatial separation. What is called separation from truth and wisdom is a perverse will which loves lower things. No one wills anything involuntarily. Here is something which we can all enjoy equally and in common. Here there is no straitness, no deficiency. She receives all her lovers, being grudging to none, shared by all in common but chaste to each. None says to another: "Stand back that I too may approach," or "Remove your hand that I too may touch." All cleave to the same wisdom. All are brought into contact with it. Nothing is consumed as in the case of food, and you cannot drink so as to prevent me from drinking too. From that common store you can convert nothing into your private possession. What you take remains unharmed for me to take also. I do not have to wait for you to breathe out what you have breathed in that I may then breathe it in. Nothing ever belongs to one man or to any group of men as a private possession. The whole is common to all at one and the same time.

38. Truth, therefore, is less like the things we touch or taste or smell, and more like the things we hear and see. For every word is heard as a whole by all who hear it and by each one at the same time. And every sight offered to the eyes is exactly the same for all who see it, and is seen by all at the same time. But though there is similarity there is also a great difference. A whole word is not spoken all at once. It is extended over a period of time, one syllable being pronounced first and another after it. Every visible sight varies with the place from it is seen, and is nowhere seen in its totality. And certainly all these things can be taken from us whether we will or no, and there are difficulties in the way of our enjoying them. Even supposing someone could sing sweetly for ever, those who were eager to hear him would come as rivals. They would get packed closely together, and the more there were of them they would strive for seats, each one anxious to get nearer to the singer. And when they heard him no one would be able to retain permanently what was heard. They would hear nothing but transient fugitive sounds. If I wanted to look at the sun and had the power to do so without being dazzled, nevertheless it would forsake me when it set, or it might be veiled in cloud, and for many other causes I might unwillingly lose my pleasure in seeing the sun. And supposing I had the power and pleasure of eternally seeing the light and hearing music, what great advantage would I have, seeing that even beasts could share it with me? But the beauty

of truth and wisdom, so long as there is a persevering will to enjoy it, does not exclude those who come by any packed crowd of hearers. It does not pass with time or change with locality. It is not interrupted by night or shut off by shadow, and is not subject to the bodily senses. To all who turn to it from the whole world, and love it, it is close at hand, everlasting, bound to no particular spot, never deficient. Externally it suggests, internally it teaches. All who behold it, it changes for the better, and by none is it changed for the worse. No one judges it, and no one without it judges aright. Hence it is evident beyond a doubt that wisdom is better than our minds, for by it alone they are made individually wise, and are made judges, not of it, but by it of all other things whatever.

xv, 39. You admitted for your part that if I could show you something superior to our minds you would confess that it was God, provided nothing existed that was higher still. I accepted your admission and said it would be sufficient if I demonstrated that. If there is anything more excellent than wisdom, doubtless it, rather, is God. But if there is nothing more excellent, then truth itself is God. Whether there is or is not such a higher thing, you cannot deny that God exists, and this was the question set for our discussion. If you are influenced by what we have received in faith from the holy discipline of Christ, that there is the Father of Wisdom, remember that we also received in faith that there is one equal to the eternal Father, namely Wisdom who is begotten of him. Hence there should be no further question, but we should accept it with unshakable faith. God exists and is the truest and fullest being. This I suppose we hold with undoubting faith. Now we attain it with a certain if tenuous form of knowledge. This is sufficient for the question in hand, so that we can go on to explain other pertinent questions; unless you have any opposition to offer. Ev.—I accept what you have said with incredible and inexpressible joy, and I declare it to be absolutely certain. I declare it in my mind where I hope to be heard by the truth itself, and where I hope to cleave to truth. For I confess that it is not only good, but the chief good and the beatific good.

40. Aug.—Indeed you are right, and I too am very glad. But are we already wise and happy, or are we still merely making for the source of wisdom and happiness? Ev.—I think we are rather making for the source. Aug.—Whence then do you derive your comprehension of the certain truths which have made you shout for joy? Has your comprehension got some connection with wisdom? Or can a foolish person know wisdom? Ev.—So long as he remains foolish he cannot. Aug.—Are you then wise already, or do you not yet know wisdom? Ev.—Indeed I am not yet wise, and yet I should not say that I am foolish, for I have some inkling of wisdom. I cannot deny that, since these things which I know are certain, and they belong to wisdom. Aug.—Tell me, pray, wouldn't you admit that he who is not just is unjust; and he who is not prudent is imprudent; and he who is not temperate is intemperate? Is there any doubt about that? Ev.—I admit that *when* a man is not just he is unjust; and I should reply similarly with regard to prudence and temperance. Aug.—Why, then, shouldn't a man be foolish *when* he is not wise? Ev.—I allow that too. *When* anyone is not wise he is foolish. Aug.—Now to which class do you belong? Ev.—Whichever of these epithets you care to apply to me, I do not venture yet to call myself wise. I see that the consequence of my admissions is that I must not hesitate to call myself foolish. Aug.—Then a foolish person knows wisdom.

For as we said, no one would be certain that he wanted to be wise, and that he ought to be wise, unless the notion of wisdom were implanted in his mind. Think how you were able to reply to one question after another in matters which belong to wisdom, and how you rejoiced to know them. *Ev.*—Yes. That is so.

xvi, 41. *Aug.*—What do we do when we are eager to be wise? Don't we with all possible keenness give our whole soul, so to speak, to what is mentally discerned, and keep it steadfastly fixed on that, so that it may not rejoice in any private possession of its own which will implicate it in transient things, but, having put off all affections for things temporal and spatial, it may apprehend what remains ever one and the same? For as the soul is the whole life of the body, so is God the happy life of the soul. While we do as I have just described, so long as we continue, we are in the way [*in via*]. If it is given us to rejoice in these true and certain blessings as they glimmer for us even now on our still darkly shadowed way, perhaps this is what Scripture means when it describes how wisdom deals with the lovers who come to her. For it is written: "In their paths she appeareth unto them graciously, and in every purpose she meeteth them" (Wisdom 6:16). Wherever you turn she speaks to you through certain traces of her operations. When you are falling away to external things she recalls you to return within by the very forms of external things. Whatever delights you in corporeal objects and entices you by appeal to the bodily senses, you may see is governed by number, and when you ask how that is so, you will return to your mind within, and know that you could neither approve nor disapprove things of sense unless you had within you, as it were, laws of beauty by which you judge all beautiful things which you perceive in the world.

42. Behold the heaven, the earth, the sea; all that is bright in them or above them; all that creep or fly or swim; all have forms because all have number. Take away number and they will be nothing. From whom have they their being if not from him who has made number? For they exist only in so far as they have number. The artificers of all corporeal forms work by number and regulate their operations thereby. In working they move their hands and tools until that which is fashioned in the outer world, being referred to the inward light of number, receives such perfection as is possible, and, being reported on by the senses, pleases the internal judge who beholds the supernal ideal numbers. Do you ask who moves the limbs of the artificer? It will be number, for they, too, move by number. Suppose there is no actual work in hand and no intention to make anything, but the motions of the limbs are done for pleasure, that will be dancing. Ask what delights you in dancing and number will reply: "Lo, here am I." Examine the beauty of bodily form, and you will find that everything is in its place by number. Examine the beauty of bodily motion and you will find everything in its due time by number. Examine the art which produces all these things and you never anywhere find in it either space or time, but it is alive with number. It has neither place in space nor length of days. And yet those who want to become artificers, while they accustom themselves to learning their art, move their bodies in space and time, and their minds at least in time. They become more skilled, I mean, with the passing of time. But rise above even the mind of the artificer to behold the eternal realm of number. Then wisdom will shine upon you from its inward seat, from the secret place of truth.

If truth repels you still because you look for it somewhat languidly, direct your mental vision to that path in which "she shows herself graciously." Remember that you have postponed a vision that you will seek again when you have become stronger and sounder.

43. Woe to those who abandon thy leading and wander among things which are but signs of thy working, who love thy nod rather than thyself and are oblivious to what thou teachest thereby, O wisdom, sweetest light of the purified mind. For thou ceasest not to suggest to us what and how great thou art. Thy pleasure is the whole glory of created beings. An artificer somehow suggests to the spectator of his work, through the very beauty of the work itself, not to be wholly content with that beauty alone, but to let his eye so scan the form of the material thing made that he may remember with affection him who made it. Those who love thy creatures in place of thee are like men who, listening to an eloquent sage, pay too much attention to the sweetness of his voice and the aptness of his verbal style and miss the meaning of his sentences, of which the words are but the sound-signals, as it were. Woe to those who turn away from thy light and are happy enough to remain in their own obscurity. It is as if they turned their backs on thee and went on with their carnal labours in their own shadows; yet even so what pleases them is theirs because of thy light shining all round them. But so long as the shadow is loved the mind's eye is made languid and becomes less able to bear to behold thee. So a man becomes more and more shrouded in darkness so long as he pursues willingly what he finds in his weakness is more easy to receive. Then he begins not to be able to see what supremely is, and to consider that to be evil which deceives him because of his lack of foresight, or tempts him because he is in need, or tortures him because he is a slave. All these things he deservedly suffers because he has turned away from truth, and whatever is just cannot be evil.

44. Neither by bodily sense nor by the thinking mind can you find any mutable thing which is not contained in some numerical form. Take away the form and it sinks to nothingness. Nevertheless do not doubt that there is an eternal and immutable form which prevents these mutable things from being reduced to nothingness, and preserves them through their appointed periods of existence in their measured motions and with their distinct varieties of form. That eternal form is neither contained in nor diffused through space, nor does it extend through or vary with changing times. Yet by it all other things can be formed, and, each in its own kind, can occupy spaces and times in which number rules.

xvii, 45. Every mutable thing must also be capable of receiving form. We call that mutable which can be changed, and similarly we call that "formable" which is capable of receiving form. Nothing can "form" itself, because nothing can give itself what it does not have. To be "formed" means precisely to have form. Hence if a thing has form, it does not need to receive what it has. If it has not form it cannot give itself form. So, as we said, nothing can form itself. What more shall we say about the mutability of the body and the mind? We have said enough before. The conclusion is that both body and mind receive form from a form that is unchangeable and eternal. Of this form it is written: "Thou shalt change them and they shall be changed, but thou art the same, and thy years have no end" (Ps. 102:26–27). The prophetic word says "years without end," meaning eternity. Again of this form it is written: "She, remaining in herself, reneweth all things" (Wisdom 7:27). Hence we understand that all things are ruled by providence. If all existing things would cease to be if form were taken from them, the unchangeable form by which all mutable things exist and fulfil their functions in the realm of number is to them a providence. If it were not, they would not be. Therefore he who journeys towards wisdom, beholding and considering the whole created universe, finds wisdom appearing unto him graciously on his way and meeting him in every purpose or providence; and his eagerness to press along that way is all the greater because he sees that the way is rendered beautiful by the wisdom he longs to reach.

46. If you can find any other kind of creature besides these three—that which is but has not life, that which is and has life but not intelligence, and that which is and has life and intelligence—you may then dare to say that there is some good thing which does not owe its existence to God. Now instead of speaking of three kinds of things, we may speak simply of two, body and life. For the life of beasts, which live but have not intelligence, and the life of men, who have intelligence too, are both alike correctly called life. Of course we also speak of the life of the Creator but that is life in a supreme sense. When I speak now about body and life I am thinking only of created things. Well, these two created things, body and life, being "formable" as we said and returning to nothingness when form is completely taken from them, clearly show that they owe their existence to the form which remains always the same. There can be no good things, whether great or small, which do not owe their existence to God. Among created things, what can be greater than intelligent life, and what can be smaller than body? However defective they may become, thereby tending to nothingness, still some form remains in them so that they have some kind of existence. Whatever of form remains in any defective thing derives from that form which cannot be defective, and which does not allow the movement of things up or down the scale of being to transgress the laws of their being. Whatever, therefore, in nature is observed to be praiseworthy, whether it is thought worthy of great or small praise, should point to the exceeding and ineffable praise of the Creator. Have you anything to say to that?

xviii, 47. *Ev.*—I confess I am entirely convinced; and I see also how it can be demonstrated, so far as that is possible in this life and among people like us, that God exists and that all good things come from him. For all things which exist, whether they merely exist or have in addition life and intelligence, all are from God. Now let us look at the third question, which is this. Can it be shown that free will is to be numbered among the things which are good? When this has been demonstrated I shall not hesitate to concede that God has given us free will and has rightly given it to us. *Aug.*—You do well to recall the questions we proposed for our discussion; and you have shown your vigilance in observing that the second of them has been answered. But you ought to have seen that the third also has been solved. You said you thought that we ought not to have been given free will because by it men commit sin. When I urged against your statement that without free choice men could not act rightly, and asserted instead that God gave it to that end, you replied that we should have been given free will just as we have been given justice which can only be used rightly. Your reply compelled us to travel the long circuitous route of discussion in order to prove that all good things, great and small, come from God alone. For that could not be clearly shown unless in the first place our poor reason, such as it is, should, with God's aid on our perilous journey, hit upon some evident answer in so great a matter to the opinions of impious folly such as the fool shows who says in his heart there is no God. These two propositions— that God exists, and that all good things come from him—we already held firmly by faith. But we have so thoroughly discussed them that the third proposition too—that free will is to be numbered among the things which are good— has been made clear.

48. In our previous discussion it was made obvious, and was agreed by us both, that body occupies by nature a lower rank in the scale of being than does soul; and that therefore soul is a greater good than body. If, then, we find among the good things of the body some that a man can abuse, and yet cannot on that account say that they ought not to have been given, since we admit that they are good, it should not be matter for surprise if in the soul too there are some good things which may be abused, but which, because they are good, could only have been given by him from whom all good things come. You see of how much good a body is deprived if it has no hands, and yet a man makes a bad use of his hands who uses them to do cruel or base deeds. If you see a man without feet you will admit that, from the point of view of the wholeness of his body, a very great good is wanting. And yet you would not deny that a man makes a bad use of his feet who uses them to hurt another or to dishonour himself. With the eyes we see the light and distinguish the forms of bodies. Sight is the most splendid possession our bodies have, and for that reason the eyes are set in a place of great dignity. By the use of them we look after our safety and enjoy many other advantages in life. Yet many people use their eyes for many base purposes, compelling them to serve the interests of lust. You see how much good is lost to the human face if it has no eyes. Now who has given us eyes if not God, the bountiful giver of all good things? Just as you approve these good things which the body enjoys, and praise him who has given them, paying no attention to those who make a bad use of them; even so ought you to confess that free will, without which no one can live aright, is a good thing divinely bestowed, and that those are to be condemned who make a bad use of it, rather than to suggest that he who gave it ought not to have done so.

49. Ev.—I should like you first to prove to me that free will is a good thing. Then I shall agree that God gave it, because I admit that all good things come from God. Aug.—Have I not proved this to your satisfaction after all the labour of our previous discussion? You admitted that every corporeal form derives its existence from the supreme form of all, that is, from the truth. And you agreed that every form was good. Truth himself, in the Gospel, tells us that even the hairs of our heads are numbered. Have you forgotten what we said about the supremacy of number, and its power which extends from one end to the other? What perversity it is to number our hairs among the good things though they are small and utterly contemptible, and to attribute their creation to God, the Creator of all good things because all good things, the greatest and the least, come from him from whom is all good; and yet to hesitate to ascribe free will to him, seeing that without it no one can live aright even on the testimony of those who live evil lives. Now tell me, pray, what in us seems to be superior, that without which we *can* live aright, or that without which we *cannot* live aright. Ev.—Now please spare me. I am ashamed of my

blindness. Who can doubt that that is far superior without which there can be no right living? *Aug.*—Will you deny that a one-eyed man can live rightly? *Ev.*—Away with such shocking madness. *Aug.*—You agree that an eye is a good thing, and yet the loss of it does not prevent right living. Can you imagine that free will, without which no one can live aright, is no good thing?

50. Look at justice, of which no one can make a bad use. It is numbered among the best good things which a man can have. So are all the virtues of the soul which constitute the righteous and honourable life. No one makes a bad use of prudence or fortitude or temperance. In all of these, as in justice which you have chosen to mention, right reason prevails, without which there can be no virtues. And no one can make a bad use of right reason. [xix.] These are therefore great good things. But you must remember that there can be no good things, great or small, save from him from whom all good things come, that is, God. So we were persuaded by our previous discussion, in the course of which you so often and so gladly expressed your assent. The virtues then, whereby life is rightly lived, are great goods. But the forms of bodies, without which life can be rightly lived, are the least of good things. And the powers of the soul, without which there can be no righteous life, are intermediate goods. No one makes a bad use of the virtues. But of the other goods, the intermediate and the small, anyone can make not only a good but also a bad use. No one makes a bad use of virtue, just because the function of virtue is the good use of the things of which we can also make a bad use. No one makes a bad use of anything when he uses it well. Wherefore God in his great and lavish goodness affords us not only great goods, but small ones too, and some intermediate between great and small. His goodness is more to be praised for the great goods than for the intermediate ones, and for the intermediate ones more than for the small ones. But for all, his goodness is to be praised more than if he had given only the great goods and not the lesser as well.

51. *Ev.*—I agree, but I still have this difficulty. We see that free will makes use of other things either well or ill. How, then, is it to be numbered among the things we use? *Aug.*—Everything we know scientifically we know by means of reason, and yet reason itself is numbered among the things we know by reason. Have you forgotten that when we were inquiring as to the things we know by reason, you admitted that reason was known by reason? Do not marvel, therefore, if we use other things by free will, and can also use free will by itself. Will, which uses other things, somehow also uses itself, just as reason which knows other things knows itself also. Memory, too, contains not only all the other things which it remembers; but because we do not forget that we have memory, somehow memory remembers itself as well as other things. Or rather by memory we remember other things and memory too.

52. Will is therefore an intermediate good when it cleaves to the unchangeable good as something that is common property and not its own private preserve; of the same nature, that is to say, as truth of which we have spoken a great deal, but nothing worthy of so great a theme; when will cleaves to this good, man attains the happy life. And the happy life, that is, the disposition of soul cleaving to the unchangeable good, is the proper and first good of man. All the virtues are there which no one can use badly. However great and important the virtues may be, we know well enough that they are not common property,

but the property of each individual man. Truth and wisdom are common to all, and all wise men are also happy by cleaving to truth. But one man does not become happy by another's happiness. If one man seeks to attain happiness by imitating another, he seeks his happiness where he sees the other found his, that is to say in unchangeable and common truth. No one is made prudent by the prudence of another, or courageous by his courage, or temperate by his temperance, or just by his justice. A man is made virtuous by regulating his soul according to the rules and guiding lights of the virtues which dwell indestructibly in the truth and wisdom that are the common property of all. For so the virtuous man whom he set before him for imitation has regulated his soul, giving it a fixed objective.

53. The will, therefore, which cleaves to the unchangeable good that is common to all, obtains man's first and best good things though it is itself only an intermediate good. But the will which turns from the unchangeable and common good and turns to its own private good or to anything exterior or inferior, sins. It turns to its private good, when it wills to be governed by its own authority; to what is exterior, when it is eager to know what belongs to others and not to itself; to inferior things, when it loves bodily pleasure. In these ways a man becomes proud, inquisitive, licentious, and is taken captive by another kind of life which, when compared with the life we have just described, is really death. And yet it is still governed and disposed by divine providence, which appoints for all things their proper places, and distributes to each man his due according to his deserts. So it happens that the good things sought by sinners cannot in any way be bad, nor can free will be bad, for we found that it was to be numbered among the intermediate goods. What is bad is its turning away from the unchangeable good and its turning to changeable goods. That "aversion" and "conversion" is voluntary and is not coerced. Therefore it is followed by the deserved and just penalty of unhappiness.

xx, 54. But perhaps you are going to ask what is the cause of the movement of the will when it turns from the immutable to the mutable good. That movement is certainly evil, although free will must be numbered among good things since without it no one can live aright. We cannot doubt that that movement of the will, that turning away from the Lord God, is sin; but surely we cannot say that God is the author of sin? God, then, will not be the cause of that movement; but what will be its cause? If you ask this, and I answer that I do not know, probably you will be saddened. And yet that would be a true answer. That which is nothing cannot be known. Only hold fast to your pious opinion that no good thing can happen to you, to your senses or to your intelligence or to your thought, which does not come from God. Nothing of any kind can happen which is not of God. Do not hesitate to attribute to God as its maker every thing which you see has measure, number and order. When you take these things completely away nothing at all will remain. Wherever measure, number and order are found, there is perfect form. If there is some kind of inchoate form, wanting measure, number and order, you must remove it too, for inchoate form is a kind of material lying to the hand of the artificer to use for perfecting his work. For if the perfection of form is good, the beginning of form is not without some grain of good. Take away all good, and absolutely nothing will remain. All good is from God. Hence there is no natural existence which is not from God. Now that movement of "aversion," which we admit is sin, is a defective movement; and all defect comes from nothing. Observe where it belongs and you will have no doubt that it does not belong to God. Because that defective movement is voluntary, it is placed within our power. If you fear it, all you have to do is simply not to will it. If you do not will it, it will not exist. What can be more secure than to live a life where nothing can happen to you which you do not will? But since man cannot rise of his own free will as he fell by his own will spontaneously, let us hold with steadfast faith the right hand of God stretched out to us from above, even our Lord Jesus Christ. Let us wait for him with certain hope, and long for him with burning charity. If you think that we must still make diligent inquiry for the origin of sin—I myself think that there is no need at all for such inquiry—but if you think so, we must put it off till another discussion. *Ev.*—I bow to your will, but only so far as to postpone to another time the question you have raised. But I will not allow you to imagine that our inquiry has already gone far enough.

Book III

i, 1. *Evodius.*—It is sufficiently evident to me that free will is to be numbered among the good things, and, indeed, not among the least of our good things. We are, therefore, compelled to confess that it has been given us by God, and that he has rightly given it to us. But now, if you think a suitable time has come, I want to learn from you whence arises the movement by which the will itself turns from the unchangeable good, which is the common property of all, to its own interests or to the interests of others or to things beneath it, and so turns to mutable goods. *Augustine.*—Why must you know this? *Ev.*—Because if free will is so given that it has that movement by nature, it turns of necessity to mutable goods; and no blame attaches where nature and necessity prevail. *Aug.*—Do you like or dislike that movement? *Ev.*—I dislike it. *Aug.*—So you find fault with it? *Ev.*—I do. *Aug.*—Then you find fault with a movement of the mind though it is faultless. *Ev.*—No, I do not. But I do not know whether there is any fault in abandoning the unchangeable good and turning towards the mutable goods. *Aug.*—Then you are finding fault with something which you do not know. *Ev.*—Don't insist on a verbal point. I said that I did not know whether there was any fault, but I meant to be understood really as having no doubt about it. Certainly I said I do not know, but obviously I was being ironical in suggesting that there could be any doubt about so clear a matter. *Aug.*—Just consider what is that truth you hold to be so certain that it has caused you so soon to forget what you said a moment ago. If that movement of the will exists by nature or necessity, it is in no way culpable. And yet you are so firmly convinced that it is culpable that you think fit to wax ironical about hesitation over a matter so certain. Why did you think it right to affirm, or at least to say with some hesitation, what you yourself show to be obviously false? You said: "If free will has been given in such fashion that it has that movement by nature, then it turns to mutable things of necessity, and no fault can be found where nature and necessity rule." But you ought to have had no doubt that it was not given in that fashion, since you do not doubt that that movement is culpable. *Ev.*—I said that the movement is culpable, and that therefore it displeases me, and that I cannot doubt that it is reprehensible. But I hold that a soul which is thereby drawn from the unchangeable good to mutable goods is not to be blamed if its nature is such that it is moved by necessity.

2. *Aug.*—To whom belongs the movement which you admit is blameworthy?
Ev.—I see that it is in the soul, but to whom it belongs I know not. *Aug.*—You do
not deny that the soul is moved by that motion? *Ev.*—No. *Aug.*—Do you then
deny that the motion by which a stone is moved is the motion of the stone?
I don't mean the motion that we give to it, or that is given to it by some other
force, when it is thrown upwards, but that by which of its own accord it falls
back to earth. *Ev.*—I do not deny that the motion you refer to, by which it turns
and falls downwards, is the motion of the stone, but it is its natural motion. If
the motion of the soul is like that, it too is natural, and it cannot rightly be
blamed for a motion that is natural. Even if it moves to its own destruction, it is
compelled by the necessity of its own nature. Moreover because we have no doubt
that the soul's motion is culpable we must absolutely deny that it is natural, and
therefore not like the motion of the stone, which is natural motion. *Aug.*—Did
we achieve anything in our two previous discussions? *Ev.*—I am sure we did.
Aug.—No doubt you remember that in the first discussion we discovered that the
mind can become the slave of lust only by its own will. No superior thing and
no equal thing compels it to such dishonour, because that would be unjust. And
no inferior thing has the power. It remains that that must be the mind's own
motion when it turns its will away from enjoyment of the Creator to enjoyment of the creature. If that motion is accounted blameworthy—and you thought
anyone who doubted that deserved to be treated ironically—it is not natural but
voluntary. It is like the motion of the falling stone, in so far as it is a motion of
the soul as the former is the motion of the stone. But it is dissimilar in this, that
it is not in the power of a stone to arrest its downward motion, while if the
soul is not willing it cannot be moved to abandon what is higher and to love
what is lower. Thus the stone's motion is natural, the soul's voluntary. Hence
anyone who says that a stone sins when it is carried downwards by its own
weight is, I will not say more senseless than the stone but, completely mad. But
we charge the soul with sin when we show that it has abandoned the higher
things and prefers to enjoy lower things. What need is there, therefore, to seek
the origin of the movement whereby the will turns from the unchangeable to the
changeable good? We acknowledge that it is a movement of the soul, that it is
voluntary and therefore culpable. And all useful learning in this matter has its
object and value in teaching us to condemn and restrain that movement, and to
convert our wills from falling into temporal delights to the enjoyment of the
eternal good.

3. *Ev.*—I see, and in a sense grasp that what you say is true. There is nothing
that I feel more certainly and more personally than that I have a will, and
that it moves me to enjoy this or that. I know nothing I could call my own if
the will by which I will "yea" or "nay" is not my own. If I use it to do evil, to
whom is the evil to be attributed if not to myself? Since a good God has
made me, and I can do nothing right except by willing, it is clearly evident that
it was to this end that the will has been given to me by God who is good.
Moreover, unless the movement of the will towards this or that object is voluntary and within our power, a man would not be praiseworthy when he turns
to the higher objects nor blameworthy when he turns to lower objects, using
his will like a hinge. There would be no use at all in warning him to pay no
attention to temporal things and to will to obtain the eternal things, or to will
to live aright and to be unwilling to live an evil life. But whoever thinks that

man is not to be so warned ought to be cut off from membership in the human race.

ii, 4. That being so, I have a deep desire to know how it can be that God knows all things beforehand and that, nevertheless, we do not sin by necessity. Whoever says that anything can happen otherwise than as God has foreknown it, is attempting to destroy the divine foreknowledge with the most insensate impiety. If God foreknew that the first man would sin—and that anyone must concede who acknowledges with me that God has foreknowledge of all future events—I do not say that God did not make him, for he made him good, nor that the sin of the creature whom he made good could be prejudicial to God. On the contrary, God showed his goodness in making man, his justice in punishing his sin, and his mercy in delivering him. I do not say, therefore, that God did not make man. But this I say. Since God foreknew that man would sin, that which God foreknew must necessarily come to pass. How then is the will free when there is apparently this unavoidable necessity?

5. *Aug.*—You have knocked vigorously. May God in his mercy grant us his presence and open the door to those who knock. But I verily believe that the vast majority of men are troubled by that question for no other reason than that they do not ask it in a pious fashion. They are swifter to make excuses for their sins than to make confession of them. Some are glad to hold the opinion that there is no divine providence presiding over human affairs. They commit themselves, body and soul, to fortuitous circumstances, and deliver themselves to be carried about and tormented by lusts. They deny that there is any divine judgment, and deceive human judges when they are accused. They imagine that they are driven on by the favour of fortune. In sculpture or painting they are wont to represent Fortune as blind, either because they are better than the goddess by whom they think they are ruled, or because they confess that in their sentiments they are afflicted with that same blindness. In the case of such people it is not absurd to admit that they do everything by chance, seeing that they stumble in all that they do. But against this opinion, so full of foolish and senseless error, we have, I think, sufficiently spoken in our second disputation. Others do not venture to deny that the providence of God presides over human affairs, but they would rather indulge in the wicked error of believing that providence is weak or unjust or evil than confess their sins with suppliant piety. If all these would suffer themselves to be persuaded to believe that the goodness, justice and power of God are greater far, and far superior to any thought they can have of goodness, justice or might, if they would but take thought to themselves, they would know that they owe thanks to God, even if he had willed them to be somewhat lower in the scale of being than they actually are, and with all that is within them they would exclaim with the Psalmist: "I have spoken: Lord have mercy upon me; heal my soul for I have sinned against thee" (Ps. 41:5). So by stages the divine mercy would bring them to wisdom. They would be neither inflated by what they discover, nor rebellious when they fail to find the truth; by learning they would become better prepared to see the truth, and by recognizing their ignorance they would become more patient in seeking it. I am quite sure that these are your views too. Now first answer a few questions I am going to put to you, and you will see how easily I can find a solution to your tremendous problem.

iii, 6. Your trouble is this. You wonder how it can be that these two propositions are not contradictory and incompatible, namely that God has foreknowledge of all future events, and that we sin voluntarily and not by necessity. For if, you say, God foreknows that a man will sin, he must necessarily sin. But if there is necessity there is no voluntary choice in sinning, but rather fixed and unavoidable necessity. You are afraid that by that reasoning the conclusion may be reached either that God's foreknowledge of all future events must be impiously denied, or, if that cannot be denied, that sin is committed not voluntarily but by necessity. Isn't that your difficulty? *Ev.*—Exactly that. *Aug.*—You think, therefore, that all things of which God has foreknowledge happen by necessity and not voluntarily. *Ev.*—Yes. Absolutely. *Aug.*—Try an experiment, and examine yourself a little, and tell me what kind of will you are going to have to-morrow. Will you want to sin or to do right? *Ev.*—I do not know. *Aug.*—Do you think God also does not know? *Ev.*—I could in no wise think that. *Aug.*—If God knows what you are going to will to-morrow, and foresees what all men are going to will in the future, not only those who are at present alive but all who will ever be, much more will he foresee what he is going to do with the just and the impious? *Ev.*—Certainly if I say that God has foreknowledge of my deeds, I should say with even greater confidence that he has foreknowledge of his own acts, and foresees with complete certainty what he is going to do. *Aug.*—Don't you see that you will have to be careful lest someone say to you that, if all things of which God has foreknowledge are done by necessity and not voluntarily, his own future acts will be done not voluntarily but by necessity? *Ev.*—When I said that all future events of which God has foreknowledge happen by necessity, I was having regard only to things which happen within his creation, and not to things which happen in God himself. Indeed, in God nothing happens. Everything is eternal. *Aug.*—God, then, is not active within his creation? *Ev.*—He determined once for all how the order of the universe he created was to go on, and he never changes his mind. *Aug.*—Does he never make anyone happy? *Ev.*—Indeed he does. *Aug.*—He does it precisely at the time when the man in question actually becomes happy. *Ev.*—That is so. *Aug.*—If, then, for example, you yourself are happy one year from now, you will be made happy at that time. *Ev.*—Exactly. *Aug.*—God knows to-day what he is going to do a year hence? *Ev.*—He eternally had that foreknowledge, but I agree that he has it now, if indeed it is to happen so.

7. *Aug.*—Now tell me, are you not God's creature? And will not your becoming happy take place within your experience? *Ev.*—Certainly I am God's creature, and if I become happy it will be within my experience. *Aug.*—If God, then, makes you happy, your happiness will come by necessity and not by the exercise of your will? *Ev.*—God's will is my necessity. *Aug.*—Will you then be happy against your will? *Ev.*—If I had the power to be happy, I should be so at once. For I wish to be happy but am not, because not I but God makes me happy. *Aug.*—The truth simply cries out against you. You could not imagine that "having in our power" means anything else than "being able to do what we will." Therefore there is nothing so much in our power as is the will itself. For as soon as we will [*volumus*] immediately will [*voluntas*] is there. We can say rightly that we do not grow old voluntarily but necessarily, or that we do not die voluntarily but from necessity, and so with other similar things. But who but a raving fool would say that it is not voluntarily that we will? Therefore though God knows how we are going to will in the future, it is not proved that we do not voluntarily will anything. When you said that you did not make yourself happy, you said it as if I had denied it. What I say is that when you become happy in the future it will

take place not against your will but in accordance with your willing. Therefore, though God has foreknowledge of your happiness in the future, and though nothing can happen otherwise than as he has foreknown it (for that would mean that there is no foreknowledeg) we are not thereby compelled to think that you will not be happy voluntarily. That would be absurd and far from true. God's foreknowledge, which is even to-day quite certain that you are to be happy at a future date, does not rob you of your will to happiness when you actually attain happiness. Similarly if ever in the future you have a culpable will, it will be none the less your will because God had foreknowledge of it.

8. Observe, pray, how blind are those who say that if God has foreknowledge of what I am going to will, since nothing can happen otherwise than as he has foreknown it, therefore I must necessarily will what he has foreknown. If so, it must be admitted that I will, not voluntarily but from necessity. Strange folly! Is there, then, no difference between things that happen according to God's foreknowledge where there is no intervention of man's will at all, and things that happen because of a will of which he has foreknowledge? I omit the equally monstrous assertion of the man I mentioned a moment ago, who says I must necessarily so will. By assuming necessity he strives to do away with will altogether. If I must necessarily will, why need I speak of willing at all? But if he puts it in another way, and says that, because he must necessarily so will, his will is not in his own power, he can be countered by the answer you gave me when I asked whether you could become happy against your will. You replied that you would be happy now if the matter were in your power, for you willed to be happy but could not achieve it. And I added that the truth cries out against you; for we cannot say we do not have the power unless we do not have what we will. If we do not have the will, we may think we will but in fact we do not. If we cannot will without willing, those who will have will, and all that is in our power we have by willing. Our will would not be will unless it were in our power. Because it is in our power, it is free. We have nothing that is free which is not in our power, and if we have something it cannot be nothing. Hence it is not necessary to deny that God has foreknowledge of all things, while at the same time our wills are our own. God has foreknowledge of our will, so that of which he has foreknowledge must come to pass. In other words, we shall exercise our wills in the future because he has foreknowledge that we shall do so; and there can be no will or voluntary action unless it be in our power. Hence God has also foreknowledge of our power to will. My power is not taken from me by God's foreknowledge. Indeed I shall be more certainly in possession of my power because he whose foreknowledge is never mistaken, foreknows that I shall have the power. *Ev.*—Now I no longer deny that whatever God has foreknown must necessarily come to pass, nor that he has foreknowledge of our sins, but in such a way that our wills remain free and within our power.

iv, 9. *Aug.*—What further difficulty do you have? Perhaps you have forgotten what we established in our first disputation, and now wish to deny that we sin voluntarily and under no compulsion from anything superior, inferior or equal to us. *Ev.*—I do not venture to deny that at all. But I must confess I do not yet see how God's foreknowledge of our sins and our freedom of will in sinning can be other than mutually contradictory. We must confess that God is just and knows all things beforehand. But I should like to know with what justice he punishes sins which must necessarily be committed; or how they are not necessarily committed when he knows that they will be committed; or how the Creator is to escape having imputed to him anything that happens necessarily in his creature.

10. *Aug.*—Why do you think our free will is opposed to God's foreknowledge? Is it because it is foreknowledge simply, or because it is God's foreknowledge? *Ev.*—In the main because it is God's foreknowledge. *Aug.*—If you knew in advance that such and such a man would sin, there would be no necessity for him to sin. *Ev.*—Indeed there would, for I should have no real foreknowledge unless I knew for certain what was going to happen. *Aug.*—So it is foreknowledge generally and not God's foreknowledge specially that causes the events foreknown to happen by necessity? There would be no such thing as foreknowledge unless there was certain foreknowledge. *Ev.*—I agree. But why these questions? *Aug.*— Unless I am mistaken, you would not directly compel the man to sin, though you knew beforehand that he was going to sin. Nor does your prescience in itself compel him to sin even though he was certainly going to sin, as we must assume if you have real prescience. So there is no contradiction here. Simply you know beforehand what another is going to do with his own will. Similarly God compels no man to sin, though he sees beforehand those who are going to sin by their own will.

11. Why then should he not justly punish sins which, though he had foreknowledge of them, he did not compel the sinner to commit? Just as you apply no compulsion to past events by having them in your memory, so God by his foreknowledge does not use compulsion in the case of future events. Just as you remember your past actions, though all that you remember were not actions of your own, so God has foreknowledge of all his own actions, but is not the agent of all that he foreknows. Of evil actions he is not the agent but the just punisher. From this you may understand with what justice God punishes sins, for he has no responsibility for the future actions of men though he knows them beforehand. If he ought not to award punishment to sinners because he knew beforehand that they would sin, he ought not to reward the righteous, because he knew equally that they would be righteous. Let us confess that it belongs to his foreknowledge to allow no future event to escape his knowledge, and that it belongs to his justice to see that no sin goes unpunished by his judgment. For sin is committed voluntarily and not by any compulsion from his foreknowledge.

v, 12. As to your third question how the Creator is to escape having imputed to him anything that happens necessarily in his creature, it is fitting for us to remember the rule of piety which says that we owe thanks to our Creator. That will provide us with the answer. His lavish goodness should be most justly praised even if he had made us with some lower rank in his creation. Though our soul be soiled with sins it is nevertheless loftier and better than if it were changed into visible light. And yet light is an eminent part of creation, as you can see by considering how much God is praised for it, even by souls wholly given over to bodily sense. Wherefore, though sinful souls are censured, do not let that provoke you to say in your heart that it would have been better if they did not exist. They are censured because they are compared with what they might have been if they had not willed to sin. God, their Maker, is to be gloriously praised for the human faculties with which he has endowed them, not only because he justly subjects them to his order when they sin, but also because he made them such that, even when soiled with sin, they are not surpassed in dignity by corporeal light, for which also God is rightly praised.

13. Possibly you would not go so far as to say that it would have been better if sinful souls did not exist, but take care also not to say that they should have been other than they are. Whatever better argument true reason may suggest to you, know at least that God made them, and that he is author of all good things. For it is not true reason but envious weakness that bids you think that anything ought to have been made better than it is, and that nothing inferior should have been made at all. That is as if you looked at the heavens and concluded that the earth ought not to have been made. That is all wrong. You would be quite right to find fault if you saw that the earth had been made, and no heavens, for then you might say the earth ought to have been made according to your ideal conception of the heavens. But now you see that your ideal earth has been made, only it is called not earth but heaven. I believe that since you have not been defrauded of the better creation you ought not to grudge that there is an inferior creation which we call the earth. In the earth again there is such a variety among its parts that you can think of nothing of an earthly nature which God has not made somewhere in the totality of his work. For the earth contains land of all kinds, passing by gradual stages from the most fruitful and pleasant to the most deceitful and infertile tracts, so that you can only find fault with one kind of land by comparing it with a better kind. So you ascend through all the grades of land with their varying praiseworthy qualities, and when you find the very best land you are glad that there are the other kinds as well. And yet what a difference there is between earth, in all its variety, and heaven! Water and air are interposed. Of these four elements various other forms and species of things are made, innumerable to us but all numbered by God. There may be things in the natural realm which you would never have thought of yourself, but the wholly and purely rational cannot but be. You can think of nothing better in the creation which the Creator did not think of. When the human soul says: "This is better than that," and if it says so truly, it will say so because of its relation to the divine reasons on which it depends. If it understands what it says, it does so likewise because of its relation to these reasons. Let it therefore believe that God has made what true reason knows he must have made, even if it is not evident in created things. If the heavens were invisible, but true reason led to the conclusion that such a thing must have been created, we ought to believe that it has been created though it do not appear to the eye. For thought would have no idea that it ought to have been created if it did not have some relation to the reasons through which all things were created. What does not exist can no more be thought than have true existence.

14. Many err because, beholding the better things with their minds, they look for them also with their eyes in the wrong places. That would be as if someone, who by reason understood perfect rotundity, should be annoyed that he did not observe it in a nut, assuming that he never saw any other round object besides that fruit. So when some people see with true reason that there are better creatures who, though they have free will, have ever adhered to God and have never sinned, they look at the sins of men and lament not that they may cease from sin but simply that men have been created at all. They say: "He did not create us such that we should will ever to enjoy his unchangeable truth and never to sin." Do not let them cry out or be annoyed. He did not compel them to sin by the mere fact that he created them and gave them power to choose good or evil as they would. He made them so far like those angels who never sinned and never will sin. If you delight in a creature which by voluntary perseverance never sins, there

is no doubt you rightly prefer it to a sinful creature. Just as you give it the preference in your thought, so God gives it the preference in his universal order. You may believe that there are such creatures in the loftier regions of the heavens. For if God showed his goodness in creating creatures whom he knew beforehand would sin, he would show his goodness no less in creating creatures whom he knew beforehand would never sin.

15. Those sublime creatures have their happiness perpetually in the eternal enjoyment of their Creator; and their happiness they merit by their perpetual will to hold fast to righteousness. Below them sinful creatures have their proper order. By their sins they have lost happiness, but they have not lost the capacity to recover it. Herein they are superior to those creatures whose will is to remain perpetually in sin. Between these two extremes—those who continue in the will to righteousness and those who continue in the will to sin—there is this middle class who by the humility of repentance recover their exalted rank. But God did not withhold the lavishness of his bounty even from his creatures who he knew beforehand would not only sin but would continue in the will to sin; for he showed it in creating them. An errant horse is better than a stone that cannot err because it has neither motion nor feeling of its own. So a creature which sins by its own free will is more excellent than one which cannot sin because it has no free will. I would praise wine that was good of its kind, and would censure the man who drank it to excess. And yet I would hold the man whom I had censured, even while he was drunk, to be superior to the wine which made him drunk, even though I had praised it. So the corporeal creature is rightly to be praised in its own order, though those are to be censured who use it to excess and are thereby turned away from perception of the truth. And those perverse people, drunkards or the like, are to be preferred to the thing, laudible in its own order, greediness for which made them vain; not indeed because of their vices but because of the dignity of their nature which still remains.

16. Soul is universally superior to body. No soul can fall so far in sinfulness as to be changed into body. Its quality as soul cannot be taken from it, and it cannot in any way lose that which makes it superior to body. Now among corporeal objects light holds the first place. Consequently the worst soul is superior to the first of corporeal things. It is of course possible that some body may be preferable to the body in which a soul resides, but it cannot be preferred to the soul itself. Why, then, should not God be praised with all possible praise, who made souls that were to abide in the laws of righteousness, even if he also made other souls which he knew beforehand would sin or even persevere in sin? For even these are better than things that cannot sin because they have not reason or free choice of will. They are even better than the most splendid brilliance of bodies of any kind, though some people [the Manichees], greatly erring, venerate light as if it were the substance of God most high. In the order of corporeal creatures, from the sidereal choir down to the number of our hairs, the beauty of good things is so perfectly graded that it is a sign of lack of understanding to ask: "What is this?" or "To what purpose is that?" All things are created each in its own order. How much more does it show lack of understanding to ask such questions about any soul whatever? No matter how great a diminution of its glory it may suffer or what defects it may exhibit, nevertheless it will always and without any doubt surpass in dignity every kind of body.

17. Reason has a different standard of judgment from that of utility. Reason

judges by the light of truth, and correctly subordinates lesser things to those that are greater. Utility, guided by experience of convenience, often attributes a higher value to things which reason convinces us are of lesser rank. Reason sets a vast difference in value between celestial and terrestrial bodies, but what carnal man would not prefer that several stars should be wanting in the heavens, than that one shrub should be lacking in his field or one cow from his herd? Older men pay no attention to, or at least are prepared patiently to correct, the judgments of children, who prefer the death of a man (except one of those bound to them by the ties of happy affection), to the death of a favourite sparrow, especially if the man was an object of terror to them, and the sparrow was tuneful and beautiful. So, if there are people, unskilled in judging the values of things, who praise God for his lesser creatures, finding them more easily appreciated by their carnal senses, and do not praise him for his better and superior creatures, or praise him less than they ought, or try to find fault with his creatures and to point out how they might have been better, or even do not believe that he created them, those who have advanced some way towards wisdom either entirely scorn such judgments or hear them with good-natured patience if they cannot correct them or until they are corrected.

vi, 18. Such being the case, it is far from the truth that the sins of the creature must be attributed to the Creator, even though those things must necessarily happen which he has foreknown. So much so that when you say you can find no reason why whatever necessarily happens in the creature should not be attributed to him, I on the contrary find no way, and I assert that none exists or can be found, of attributing to him what is done, necessarily no doubt, but also by the will of the sinner. If anyone says, I should prefer not to exist than to exist in unhappiness, I shall reply: That is a lie; for you are miserable now, and yet you do not wish to die, simply because you wish to exist. You don't want to be miserable but you want to continue in life all the same. Give thanks, therefore, because you exist, as you wish to do, so that the misery you do not wish may be taken from you. You exist as you wish to do, but you are unhappy against your will. If you are ungrateful for your existence you are rightly compelled to be unhappy, which you do not wish. I praise the goodness of the Creator because, even when you are ungrateful, you have what you wish. And I praise the justice of the Orderer of things because for your ingratitude you suffer what you do not wish.

· · ·

RETRACTATIONS

Book i Chapter 9

While we were still staying at Rome, we wished to debate and trace out the cause of evil. Our plan of debate aimed at understanding by means of thorough

From *Saint Augustine, The Problem of Free Choice,* Dom M. Pontifex, trans., Westminster, Md.: The Newman Press, 1955; London: Longmans, Green & Co., Ltd. Used by permission.

rational inquiry—so far as, with God's help, discussion should enable us—what we believed about this question on divine authority. After careful examination of the arguments we agreed that evil occurred only through free choice of will, and so the three books resulting from this discussion were called *The Problem of Free Choice*. I finished the second and third of these books, as well as I could at the time, in Africa, after I was ordained priest at Hippo Regius.

2. In these books we discussed so many problems that some questions arose, which either I could not solve, or which required long consideration before they could be decided, and these we put off. But whatever the answer to these questions, or even if there were many answers, when it was not clear where the truth lay, the conclusion nevertheless came to this, that, whatever the truth, rightly and obviously praise should be given to God. We undertook this discussion because of those who deny that evil is due to free choice of will and who maintain that God, if this is so, deserves blame as the Creator of every kind of thing. Thus they wish in their wicked error—they are the Manichees—to introduce a being, evil in nature, which is unchangeable and coeternal with God. As this was why we raised the problem, these books contain no reference to God's grace, by which He has predestined His elect in such a way that He Himself makes ready the wills of those among them who are now making use of free choice. When there was any occasion for mentioning this grace, it was mentioned in passing, not defended by careful reasoning as if it was the main subject. It is one thing to inquire into the cause of evil, another to inquire how we can return to our former good, or reach one that is greater.

3. Hence the recent Pelagian heretics, who hold a theory of free choice of will which leaves no place for the grace of God, since they hold it is given in accordance with our merits, must not boast of my support. I said much in these books in defence of free choice, which was called for by the purpose of the discussion. In the first book I said indeed that "wrongdoing is punished by God's justice," and added, "it would not be punished justly, unless it were done wilfully" [1.1.1]. Again, when I showed that a good will was so great a good that it was rightly preferred to all bodily and external goods, I said: "I think you now see that it lies in the power of our will whether we enjoy or lack this great and true good. What is so fully in the power of the will as the will itself?" [1.12.26]. And in another place: "Then what reason is there for doubting that, even though we were never wise before, yet by our will we deserve, and spend, a praiseworthy and happy life, and by our will a life that is shameful and unhappy?" [1.13.28]. Again, in another place: "Hence it follows that whoever wishes to live rightly and virtuously, if he wishes so to wish in preference to goods which are but passing, will acquire this great possession with such ease, that to wish for it will be the same as to possess what he wished." [1.13.29]. Again, I said elsewhere: "The eternal law, to the consideration of which it is now time to return, has settled this with unchangeable firmness; it has settled that merit lies in the will, while reward and punishment lie in happiness and misery" [1.14.30]. And in another place: "We have agreed that it lies in the will what each man chooses to seek and attach himself to" [1.16.34]. And in the second book: "Man himself is something good in so far as he is man, for he can live rightly when he so wills" [2.1.2]. In another place I said "that we could not act rightly except by this free choice of will" [2.18.47]. And in the third book: "What need is there to ask the source of that movement by which the will turns from the unchangeable good

to the changeable good? We agree that it belongs only to the soul, and is voluntary and therefore culpable; and the whole value of teaching in this matter consists in its power to make us censure and check this movement, and turn our wills away from temporal things below us to enjoyment of the everlasting good" [3.1.2]. And in another place: "The voice of truth speaks clearly in what you say. You could not be aware of anything in our power, if not of our actions when we will. Nothing is so fully in our power as the will itself, for it is ready at once and without delay to act as we will" [3.3.7]. Again in another place, "If you are praised when you see what you ought to do, though you only see this in Him who is unchangeable truth, how much more should He be praised who has ordered you to will what you ought to do, and has given you the power to carry it out, and has not allowed you to refuse it unpunished!" Then I added, "If everyone owes that which he has received, and if man has been so made that he sins necessarily, then his duty is to sin. Therefore, when he sins, he does what he ought to do. But if it is wicked to say this, then no one is forced by his own nature to sin" [3.16.46]. And again: "Now what could precede the will and be its cause? Either it is the will itself, and nothing else than the will is the root, or it is not the will which is not sinful. Either the will itself is the original cause of sin, or no sin is the original cause of sin. Sin cannot be attributed to anything except to the sinner. It cannot rightly be attributed to anything except to him who wills it" [3.17.49]. And a little later: "No one sins when he cannot guard against it. Yet sin is committed, and therefore we can guard against it" [3.18.50]. Pelagius used this evidence of mine in a book of his. When I answered this book, I chose for the title of my book, *The Problem of Nature and Grace.*

4. In these and similar statements of mine I did not mention God's grace, as this was not the subject I was then dealing with. Hence the Pelagians think, or may think, that I held their views. They are wrong, however, in thinking so. It is the will by which we sin and by which we live rightly, as I explained in these passages. Unless, therefore, the will itself is set free by the grace of God from that slavery by which it has been made *a servant of sin,* and unless it is given help to overcome its vices, mortal men cannot live upright and devout lives. If this gift of God, by which the will is set free, did not precede the act of the will, it would be given in accordance with the will's merits, and would not be grace which is certainly given as a free gift. I have dealt sufficiently with this subject in other small works of mine, in which I have refuted these recent heretics who oppose this view of grace. Yet even in this book, *The Problem of Free Choice,* which was not written against them at all, but against the Manichees, I was not entirely silent about this grace of God, which they attempt with unspeakable wickedness to deny. In fact I said in the second book that, "not to speak of great goods, not even the least can exist except as coming from Him from whom come all good things, that is, from God." And a little later I stated: "The virtues by which we live rightly are great goods, but all kinds of bodily beauty, without which we can live rightly, are the least goods. The powers of the soul, without which we cannot live rightly, are the middle goods. No one uses the virtues wrongly, but anyone can use the other goods, the middle and the least, wrongly as well as rightly. No one uses virtue wrongly, because the work of virtue is the good use of those things which we are capable of using wrongly. No one makes a bad use when he makes a good use. Hence the magnificent abundance of God's goodness has furnished us not only with great goods, but also with the middle and the least. His good-

ness should be praised more highly for great than for middle goods, more for middle than for least, but for all more than if He had not given all" [2.19.50]. And in another place: "Only keep firm your sense of reverence towards God, so that no good may occur either to your senses, your intelligence, or your thoughts in any way, which you do not acknowledge to be from God" [2.20.54]. I also said in another place: "But, though man fell through his own will, he cannot rise through his own will. Therefore let us believe firmly that God's arm, that is, Our Lord Jesus Christ, is stretched out to us from on high" [*ibid.*].

5. In the third book after the words which, as I have mentioned, Pelagius quoted from my works—"No one sins when he cannot guard against it. Yet sin is committed, and therefore we can guard against it"—I added at once: "Nevertheless some actions done in ignorance are judged wrong and in need of correction, as we read in the divine documents. For example, the Apostle says: *I obtained the mercy of God, because I did it ignorantly;* and the Prophet says: *The sins of my youth and my ignorance do not remember.* Actions done of necessity when a man wills to act rightly and cannot, are also judged wrong. Hence the words: *For the good which I will, I do not; but the evil which I will not, that I do;* and, *To will is present with me, but to accomplish that which is good I find not;* and, *The flesh lusteth against the spirit, and the spirit against the flesh; for these are contrary one to another, so that you do not the things that you would.* But all this applies to men as they appear on the scene after the condemnation of death; for if this does not stand for man's punishment, but his natural condition, then there is no question of sin. If man has not lost his natural kind of being, and if he cannot become better, he does what he ought when he acts in this way. But if man would be good if he were constituted differently, and he is not good because he is in his present condition; if he has not the power to become good, whether because he does not see what he ought to be, or because he sees and yet cannot be what he sees he ought to be, then this is surely a punishment. Now every punishment is a punishment for sin, if it is just, and is called a penalty; but if the punishment is unjust, since none doubts it is a punishment, it is imposed on man by an unjust ruler. But it would be folly to doubt the omnipotence and justice of God, and therefore this punishment must be just, and be exacted for some sin. No unjust ruler could have snatched man away from God without His knowledge, or taken him by force against God's will, whether by threat or violence, in order to inflict torture on him as an unjust punishment. No one can frighten God, or struggle with Him. It remains, therefore, that this is a just punishment resulting from man's condemnation" [3.18.50 f.]. And in another place I said: "To approve false for true, so as to err unwillingly, and to be unable to refrain from acts of passion on account of the resistance and pain of the bonds of the flesh, are not natural to man in his orignal state, but are a punishment after his condemnation. When we speak of a will free to act rightly, we speak of the will with which man was created" [3.18.52].

6. Thus, long before the Pelagian heresy arose, we debated as though we were already debating against them. For we stated that all good things come from God—the great, the middle, and the least goods; among the middle goods is found free choice of will since we can use it wrongly, but yet it is such that we cannot live rightly without it. To use it well is at once virtue, and virtue is found among the great goods which no one can use wrongly. Because all good things, as I have said—great, middle, and least—come from God, it follows that from

God comes the good use of free will, which is virtue and is counted among the great goods. Then I spoke of the misery, justly inflicted on sinners, from which the grace of God frees them, because man could fall of his own accord, that is, by his free choice, but could not rise in this way. The misery, to which we are justly condemned, involves ignorance and difficulty, which every man suffers from the moment of his birth, nor is anyone delivered from this evil except by the grace of God. The Pelagians refuse to attribute this misery to a just condemnation, since they deny original sin. Yet, even though ignorance and difficulty were the original and natural state of man, we ought not on this account to blame God, but to praise Him. We argued this in the same third book. This discussion is to be regarded as aimed against the Manichees, who do not recognise as Sacred Scripture the Old Testament, where the story of original sin is told. What we read in the Apostolic Epistles they have the dreadful effrontery to claim is a falsification of Scripture and not the genuine record of the Apostles. But against the Pelagians we have to defend both deposits of Scripture, which Scripture they profess to accept. This work begins with the words, "I should like you to tell me: is not God the cause of evil?"

ON THE TRINITY

BOOK X

CHAPTER 6. *The Opinion Which the Mind Has of Itself Is Deceitful.*

8. But the mind errs, when it so lovingly and intimately connects itself with these images, as even to consider itself to be something of the same kind. For so it is conformed to them to some extent, not by being this, but by thinking it is so: not that it thinks itself to be an image, but outright that very thing itself of which it entertains the image. For there still lives in it the power of distinguishing the corporeal thing which it leaves without, from the image of that corporeal thing which it contains therefrom within itself; except when these images are so projected as if felt without and not thought within, as in the case of people who are asleep, or mad, or in a trance.

CHAPTER 7. *The Opinions of Philosophers Respecting the Substance of the Soul. The Error of Those Who Are of Opinion that the Soul Is Corporeal, Does Not Arise from Defective Knowledge of the Soul, But from Their Adding Thereto Something Foreign to It. What Is Meant by Finding.*

9. When, therefore, it thinks itself to be something of this kind, it thinks itself to be a corporeal thing; and since it is perfectly conscious of its own superiority,

From *History of the Christian Church*, Vol. III: *Nicene and Post-Nicene Fathers*, edited by Philip Schaff, New York: Charles Scribner's Sons, 1884.

by which it rules the body, it has hence come to pass that the question has been raised what part of the body has the greater power in the body; and the opinion has been held that this is the mind, nay, that it is even the whole soul altogether. And some accordingly think it to be the blood, others the brain, others the heart; not as the Scripture says, "I will praise Thee, O Lord, with my whole heart;" and, "Thou shalt love the Lord thy God with all thine heart;" for this word by misapplication or metaphor is transferred from the body to the soul; but they have simply thought it to be that small part itself of the body, which we see when the inward parts are rent asunder. Others, again, have believed the soul to be made up of very minute and individual corpuscules, which they call atoms, meeting in themselves and cohering. Others have said that its substance is air, others fire. Others have been of opinion that it is no substance at all, since they could not think any substance unless it is body, and they did not find that the soul was body; but it was in their opinion the tempering together itself of our body, or the combining together of the elements, by which that flesh is as it were conjoined. And hence all of these have held the soul to be mortal; since, whether it were body, or some combination of body, certainly it could not in either case continue always without death. But they who have held its substance to be some kind of life the reverse of corporeal, since they have found it to be a life that animates and quickens every living body, have by consequence striven also, according as each was able, to prove it immortal, since life cannot be without life.

For as to that fifth kind of body, I know not what, which some have added to the four well-known elements of the world, and have said that the soul was made of this, I do not think we need spend time in discussing it in this place. For either they mean by body what we mean by it, *viz.,* that of which a part is less than the whole in extension of place, and they are to be reckoned among those who have believed the mind to be corporeal: or if they call either all substance, or all changeable substance, body, whereas they know that not all substance is contained in extension of place by any length and breadth and height, we need not contend with them about a question of words.

10. Now, in the case of all these opinions, any one who sees that the nature of the mind is at once substance, and yet not corporeal,—that is, that it does not occupy a less extension of place with a less part of itself, and a greater with a greater, —must needs see at the same time that they who are of opinion that it is corporeal, do not err from defect of knowledge concerning mind, but because they associate with it qualities without which they are not able to conceive any nature at all. For if you bid them conceive of existence that is without corporeal phantasms, they hold it merely nothing. And so the mind would not seek itself, as though wanting to itself. For what is so present to knowledge as that which is present to the mind? Or what is so present to the mind as the mind itself? And hence what is called "invention," if we consider the origin of the word, what else does it mean, unless that to find out (*invenire*) is to "come into" that which is sought? Those things accordingly which come into the mind as it were of themselves, are not usually said to be found out (*inventa*), although they may be said to be known; since we did not endeavor by seeking to come into them, that is, to invent or find them out. And therefore, as the mind itself really seeks those things which are sought by the eyes or by any other sense of the body (for the mind directs even the carnal sense, and then finds out or invents, when that

sense comes to the things which are sought); so, too, it finds out or invents other things which it ought to know, not with the medium of corporeal sense, but through itself, when it "comes into" them; and this, whether in the case of the higher substance that is in God, or of the other parts of the soul; just as it does when it judges of bodily images themselves, for it finds these within, in the soul, impressed through the body.

CHAPTER 8. *How the Soul Inquires into Itself. Whence Comes the Error of the Soul Concerning Itself.*

11. It is then a wonderful question, in what manner the soul seeks and finds itself; at what it aims in order to seek, or whither it comes, that it may come into or find out. For what is so much in the mind as the mind itself? But because it is *in* those things which it thinks of with love, and is wont to be in sensible, that is, in corporeal things with love, it is unable to be in itself without the images of those corporeal things. And hence shameful error arises to block its way, whilst it cannot separate from itself the images of sensible things, so as to see itself alone. For they have marvellously cohered with it by the close adhesion of love. And herein consists its uncleanness; since, while it strives to think of itself alone, it fancies itself to be that, without which it cannot think of itself. When, therefore, it is bidden to become acquainted with itself, let it not seek itself as though it were withdrawn from itself; but let it withdraw that which it has added to itself. For itself lies more deeply within not only than those sensible things, which are clearly without, but also than the images of them; which are indeed in some part of the soul, *viz.*, that which beasts also have, although these want understanding, which is proper to the mind. As therefore the mind is within, it goes forth in some sort from itself, when it exerts the affection of love towards these, as it were, footprints of many acts of attention. And these footprints are, as it were, imprinted on the memory, at the time when the corporeal things which are without are perceived in such way, that even when those corporeal things are absent, yet the images of them are at hand to those who think of them. Therefore let the mind become acquainted with itself, and not seek itself as if it were absent; but fix upon itself the act of [voluntary] attention, by which it was wandering among other things, and let it think of itself. So it will see that at no time did it ever not love itself, at no time did it ever not know itself; but by loving another thing together with itself it has confounded itself with it, and in some sense has grown one with it. And so, while it embraces diverse things, as though they were one, it has come to think those things to be one which are diverse.

CHAPTER 9. *The Mind Knows Itself, by the Very Act of Understanding the Precept to Know Itself.*

12. Let it not therefore seek to discern itself as though absent, but take pains to discern itself as present. Nor let it take knowledge of itself as if it did not know itself, but let it distinguish itself from that which it knows to be another. For how will it take pains to obey that very precept which is given it, "Know thyself," if it knows not either what "know" means or what "thyself" means? But if it knows both, then it knows also itself. Since "know thyself" is not so said to the mind as is "Know the cherubim and the seraphim"; for they are absent, and we

believe concerning them, and according to that belief they are declared to be certain celestial powers. Nor yet again as it is said, Know the will of that man: for this it is not within our reach to perceive at all, either by sense or understanding, unless by corporeal signs actually set forth; and this in such a way that we rather believe than understand. Nor again as it is said to a man, Behold thy own face; which he can only do in a looking-glass. For even our own face itself is out of the reach of our own seeing it; because it is not there where our look can be directed. But when it is said to the mind, Know thyself; then it knows itself by that very act by which it understands the word "thyself"; and this for no other reason than that it is present to itself. But if it does not understand what is said, then certainly it does not do as it is bid to do. And therefore it is bidden to do that thing which it does do, when it understands the very precept that bids it.

CHAPTER 10. *Every Mind Knows Certainly Three Things Concerning Itself— that It Understands, that It Is, and that It Lives.*

13. Let it not then add anything to that which it knows itself to be, when it is bidden to know itself. For it knows, at any rate, that this is said to itself; namely, to the self that is, and that lives, and that understands. But a dead body also is, and cattle live; but neither a dead body nor cattle understand. Therefore it so knows that it so is, and that it so lives, as an understanding is and lives. When, therefore, for example's sake, the mind thinks itself air, it thinks that air understands; it knows, however, that itself understands, but it does not know itself to be air, but only thinks so. Let it separate that which it thinks itself; let it discern that which it knows; let this remain to it, about which not even have they doubted who have thought the mind to be this corporeal thing or that. For certainly every mind does not consider itself to be air; but some think themselves fire, others the brain, and some one kind of corporeal thing, others another, as I have mentioned before; yet all know that they themselves understand, and are, and live; but they refer understanding to that which they understand, but to be, and to live, to themselves. And no one doubts, either that no one understands who does not live, or that no one lives of whom it is not true that he is; and that therefore by consequence that which understands both is and lives; not as a dead body is which does not live, nor as a soul lives which does not understand, but in some proper and more excellent manner. Further, they know that they will, and they equally know that no one can will who is not and who does not live; and they also refer that will itself to something which they will with that will. They know also that they remember; and they know at the same time that nobody could remember, unless he both was and lived; but we refer memory itself also to something, in that we remember those things. Therefore the knowledge and science of many things are contained in two of these three, memory and understanding; but will must be present, that we may enjoy or use them. For we enjoy things known, in which things themselves the will finds delight for their own sake, and so reposes; but we use those things, which we refer to some other thing which we are to enjoy. Neither is the life of man vicious and culpable in any other way, than as wrongly using and wrongly enjoying. But it is no place here to discuss this.

14. But since we treat of the nature of the mind, let us remove from our consideration all knowledge which is received from without, through the senses of the body, and attend more carefully to the position which we have laid down, that

all minds know and are certain concerning themselves. For men certainly have doubted whether the power of living, of remembering, of understanding, of willing, of thinking, of knowing, of judging, be of air, or of fire, or of the brain, or of the blood, or of atoms, or besides the usual four elements of a fifth kind of body, I know not what; or whether the combining or tempering together of this our flesh itself has power to accomplish these things. And one has attempted to establish this, and another to establish that. Yet who ever doubts that he himself lives, and remembers, and understands, and wills, and thinks, and knows, and judges? Seeing that even if he doubts, he lives; if he doubts, he remembers why he doubts; if he doubts, he understands that he doubts; if he doubts, he wishes to be certain; if he doubts, he thinks; if he doubts, he knows that he does not know; if he doubts, he judges that he ought not to assent rashly. Whosoever therefore doubts about anything else, ought not to doubt of all these things; which if they were not, he would not be able to doubt of anything.

15. They who think the mind to be either a body or the combination or tempering of the body, will have all these things to seem to be in a subject, so that the substance is air, or fire, or some other corporeal thing, which they think to be the mind; but that the understanding (*intelligentia*) is *in* this corporeal thing as its quality, so that this corporeal thing is the subject, but the understanding is in the subject: *viz.* that the mind is the subject, which they judge to be a corporeal thing, but the understanding [intelligence], or any other of those things which we have mentioned as certain to us, is in that subject. They also hold nearly the same opinion who deny the mind itself to be body, but think it to be the combination or tempering together of the body; for there is this difference, that the former say that the mind itself is the substance, in which the understanding [intelligence] is, as in a subject; but the latter say that the mind itself is in a subject, *viz.* in the body, of which it is the combination or tempering together. And hence, by consequence, what else can they think, except that the understanding also is in the same body as in a subject?

16. And all these do not perceive that the mind knows itself, even when it seeks for itself, as we have already shown. But nothing is at all rightly said to be known while its substance is not known. And therefore, when the mind knows itself, it knows its own substance; and when it is certain about itself, it is certain about its own substance. But it is certain about itself, as those things which are said above prove convincingly; although it is not at all certain whether itself is air, or fire, or some body, or some function of body. Therefore it is not any of these. And to that whole which is bidden to know itself, belongs this, that it is certain that it is not any of those things of which it is uncertain, and is certain that it is that only, which only it is certain that it is. For it thinks in this way of fire, or air, and whatever else of the body it thinks of. Neither can it in any way be brought to pass that it should so think that which itself is, as it thinks that which itself is not. Since it thinks all these things through an imaginary phantasy, whether fire, or air, or this or that body or that part or combination and tempering together of the body: nor assuredly is it said to be all those things, but some one of them. But if it were any one of them, it would think this one in a different manner from the rest, *viz.* not through an imaginary phantasy, as absent things are thought, which either themselves or some of like kind have been touched by the bodily sense; but by some inward, not feigned, but true presence (for nothing is more present to it than itself); just as it thinks that itself lives, and remembers, and understands,

and wills. For it knows these things in itself, and does not imagine them as though it had touched them by the sense outside itself, as corporeal things are touched. And if it attaches nothing to itself from the thought of these things, so as to think itself to be something of the kind, then whatsoever remains to it from itself, that alone is itself.

CHAPTER 11. *In Memory, Understanding [or Intelligence], and Will, We Have to Note Ability, Learning, and Use. Memory, Understanding, and Will Are One Essentially, and Three Relatively.*

17. Putting aside, then, for a little while all other things, of which the mind is certain concerning itself, let us especially consider and discuss these three—memory, understanding, will. For we may commonly discern in these three the character of the abilities of the young also; since the more tenaciously and easily a boy remembers, and the more acutely he understands, and the more ardently he studies, the more praiseworthy is he in point of ability. But when the question is about any one's learning, then we ask not how solidly and easily he remembers, or how shrewdly he understands; but what it is that he remembers, and what it is that he understands. And because the mind is regarded as praiseworthy, not only as being learned, but also as being good, one gives heed not only to what he remembers and what he understands, but also to what he wills (*velit*); not how ardently he wills, but first, what it is he wills, and then how greatly he wills it. For the mind that loves eagerly is then to be praised, when it loves that which ought to be loved eagerly. Since, then, we speak of these three—ability, knowledge, use—the first of these is to be considered under the three heads, of what a man can do in memory, and understanding, and will. The second of them is to be considered in regard to that which any one has in his memory and in his understanding, which he has attained by a studious will. But the third, *viz.* use, lies in the will, which handles those things that are contained in the memory and understanding, whether it refer them to anything further, or rest satisfied with them as an end. For to use, is to take up something into the power of the will; and to enjoy, is to use with joy, not any longer of hope, but of the actual thing. Accordingly, every one who enjoys, uses; for he takes up something into the power of the will, wherein he also is satisfied as with an end. But not every one who uses, enjoys, if he has sought after that, which he takes up into the power of the will, not on account of the thing itself, but on account of something else.

18. Since, then, these three, memory, understanding, will, are not three lives, but one life; nor three minds, but one mind; it follows certainly that neither are they three substances, but one substance. Since memory, which is called life, and mind, and substance, is so called in respect to itself; but it is called memory, relatively to something. And I should say the same also of understanding and of will, since they are called understanding and will, relatively to something; but each in respect to itself is life, and mind, and essence. And hence these three are one, in that they are one life, one mind, one essence; and whatever else they are severally called in respect to themselves, they are called also together, not plurally, but in the singular number. But they are three, in that wherein they are mutually referred to each other; and if they were not equal, and this not only each to each, but also each to all, they certainly could not mutually contain each other; for not only is each contained by each, but also all by each. For I remember that I have

memory and understanding, and will; and I understand that I understand, and will, and remember; and I will that I will, and remember, and understand; and I remember together my whole memory, and understanding, and will. For that of my memory which I do not remember, is not in my memory; and nothing is so much in the memory as memory itself. Therefore I remember the whole memory. Also, whatever I understand I know that I understand, and I know that I will whatever I will; but whatever I know I remember. Therefore I remember the whole of my understanding, and the whole of my will. Likewise, when I understand these three things, I understand them together as whole. For there is none of things intelligible which I do not understand, except what I do not know; but what I do not know, I neither remember, nor will. Therefore, whatever of things intelligible I do not understand, it follows also that I neither remember nor will. And whatever of things intelligible I remember and will, it follows that I understand. My will also embraces my whole understanding and my whole memory, whilst I use the whole that I understand and remember. And, therefore, while all are mutually comprehended by each, and as wholes, each as a whole is equal to each as a whole, and each as a whole at the same time to all as wholes; and these three are one, one life, one mind, one essence.

CHAPTER 12. *The Mind Is an Image of the Trinity In Its Own Memory, and Understanding, and Will.*

19. Are we, then, now to go upward, with whatever strength of purpose we may, to that chiefest and highest essence, of which the human mind is an inadequate image, yet an image? Or are these same three things to be yet more distinctly made plain in the soul, by means of those things which we receive from without, through the bodily sense, wherein the knowledge of corporeal things is impressed upon us in time? Since we found the mind itself to be such in its own memory, and understanding, and will, that since it was understood always to know and always to will itself, it was understood also at the same time always to remember itself, always to understand and love itself, although not always to think of itself as *separate* from those things which are not itself; and hence its memory of itself, and understanding of itself, are with difficulty discerned in it. For in this case, where these two things are very closely conjoined, and one is not preceded by the other by any time at all, it looks as if they were not two things, but one called by two names; and love itself is not so plainly felt to exist when the sense of need does not disclose it, since what is loved is always at hand. And hence these things may be more lucidly set forth, even to men of duller minds, if such topics are treated of as are brought within reach of the mind in time, and happen to it in time; while it remembers what it did not remember before, and sees what it did not see before, and loves what it did not love before. But this discussion demands now another beginning, by reason of the measure of the present book.

THE CONFESSIONS

Book XI

CHAPTER 3. *The Language of Truth*

(5) Let me hear and understand how "in the beginning" you "made heaven and earth." Moses wrote these words: he wrote them, and he passed away. He passed from this world, from you to you, and he is not now here before me. If he were, I would catch hold of him, and I would ask him, and through you I would beseech him to make these things plain to me. I would lay my body's ears to the sounds breaking forth from his mouth. If he spoke in Hebrew, in vain would his voice strike upon my senses, and none of it would touch my mind. But if he spoke in Latin, I would know what he said.

Yet how would I know whether he spoke the truth? Even if I knew this, would I know it from him? Truly, within me, within the dwelling place of thought, Truth, neither Hebrew nor Greek nor Latin nor barbaric in speech, without mouth or tongue as organ, and without noise of syllables, would say to me, "He speaks the truth." Forthwith I would be certain of it, and I would say confidently to that man, "You speak the truth." Therefore, since I cannot question him who was filled by you, and thus spoke true words, I entreat you O Truth, I entreat you, O my God, "spare my sins." Do you who granted to him, your servant, to speak these true words, grant to me that I may understand them.

CHAPTER 4. *Evidence of Creation*

(6) Lo, heaven and earth exist: they cry out that they have been created, for they are subject to change and variation. Whatever has not been made, and yet exists, has nothing in it which was not previously there, whereas to have what once was not is to change and vary. They also cry out that they did not make themselves: "For this reason, do we exist, because we have been made. Therefore, before we came to be, we did not exist in such wise as to be able to make ourselves."

Self-evidence is the voice with which these things speak. You, therefore, O Lord, who are beautiful, made these things, for they are beautiful; you who are good made them, for they are good; you who are made them, for they are. Yet they are not so good, nor are they so beautiful as you, nor do they even be in such wise as you, their creator. Compared to you, they are neither good, nor beautiful, nor real. We know all this, thanks be to you, but our knowledge compared to your knowledge is ignorance.

CHAPTER 5. *Creator of All Things*

(7) How did you make heaven and earth? What was your engine for doing this mighty work? You did not work as does the human artist, who transforms one body into another according to the purposes of a soul able somehow to imprint forms that it perceives by its inner eye. How could he do this unless you had first created his mind? The artist imprints a form on something already existing and having power to be, such as earth, stone, wood, or gold, or something of that sort. From what source would they be, unless you had decreed them to be? You made the artist's body; you, the soul that gives orders to his members; you, the matter out of which he fashions things; you, the intellect by which he controls his creative imagination and sees within it what he fashions outside himself. You made his bodily senses by which, as through an interpreter, he transfers his work from mind to matter, and then reports back to mind what he has made, so that he may consult therein the truth presiding over him, so as to know whether it was well made.

All these praise you, the creator of all things. But how do you make them? O God, how have you made heaven and earth? Truly, neither in heaven nor upon earth have you made heaven and earth. Nor was it in the air, nor in the waters, for these too belong to heaven and earth. Nor was it in the one wide world that you made that one wide world, for before it was caused to be, there was no place where it could be made. You did not hold in your hand anything out of which to make heaven and earth: whence would you obtain this thing not made by you, out of which you would make a new thing? What exists, for any reason except that you exist? You spoke, therefore, and these things were made, and in your Word you made them.

CHAPTER 6. *God's Voice*

(8) But how did you speak? Was it in the way that the voice came out of the cloud saying, "This is my beloved Son?" That voice went forth and went away; it began and it ceased. The syllables were sounded and they passed away, the second after the first, the third after the second, and the rest in order, until the last one came after all the others, and silence after the last. Whence it is clear and evident that a creature's movement, a temporal movement, uttered that voice in obedience to your eternal will. These words of yours, formed for a certain time, the outer ear reported to the understanding mind, whose interior ear was placed close to your eternal Word. Then the mind compared these words sounding in time with your eternal Word in its silence, and said, "It is far different; it is far different. These words are far beneath me. They do not exist, because they flee and pass away. The Word of my God abides above me forever."

Therefore, if you had said in audible and passing words that heaven and earth should be made, and had so made heaven and earth, then before heaven and earth, there was already some corporeal creature by means of whose temporal movements that voice would run in time. But before heaven and earth, there was no bodily thing. Or if there were one, you surely had made it without using a passing voice by which you would say, "Let heaven and earth be made." Whatsoever that thing might be, from which such a voice could be made, it could not be at all unless it were made by you. By what word, then, did you speak, so that there might be a body from which these words would be uttered?

CHAPTER 7. *The Word of God*

(9) So you call us to understand the Word, God with you, O God, which is spoken eternally, and in which all things are spoken eternally. Nor is it the case that what was spoken is ended and that another thing is said, so that all things may at length be said: all things spoken once and forever. Elsewise, there would already be time and change, and neither true eternity nor true immortality. I know this, my God, and "I give thanks for it." I know this, I confess to you, O Lord God, and together with me whoever is grateful to the sure Truth knows this and blesses you.

We know, O Lord, we know, since in so far as anything which once was now no longer is, and anything which once was not now is, to that extent such a thing dies and takes rise. Therefore, no part of your Word gives place to another or takes the place of another, since it is truly eternal and immortal. Therefore, you say once and forever all that you say by the Word, who is coeternal with you. Whatever you say shall be made, then it is made. But while you do not make anything otherwise than by speaking, yet not all things which you make by speaking are made simultaneously and eternally.

CHAPTER 8. *Christ Our Teacher*

(10) Why, I beseech you, O Lord my God, is this? In a way, I see it, but how I am to express it I do not know, unless it is because whatever begins to be, and then ceases to be, does then begin to be and then cease to be when it is known in your eternal reason, wherein nothing begins or ceases, that it must begin or cease. This is your Word, which is also the beginning because it also speaks to us. Thus in the Gospel he speaks through the flesh, and this word sounded outwardly in the ears of men, so that it might be believed, and sought inwardly, and found in the eternal Truth where the sole good Master teaches all his disciples. There, O Lord, I hear your voice speaking to me, since he who teaches us speaks to us. But a man who does not teach us, even though he speaks, does not speak to us. Who teaches us now, unless it be stable Truth? Even when we are admonished by a changeable creature, we are led to stable Truth, where we truly learn "while we stand and hear him" and "rejoice with joy because of the bridegroom's voice" restoring us to him from whom we are.

Therefore, he is a beginning, for unless he abided when we went astray, he would not be there when we returned. But when we return from error, we truly return by knowing that we do so, and that we may know this, he teaches us, because he is the beginning and he speaks to us.

CHAPTER 9. *Wisdom Itself*

(11) In the beginning, O God, you made heaven and earth in your Word, in your Son, in your Power, in your Wisdom, in your Truth, speaking in a wondrous way and working in a wondrous way. Who shall comprehend it?

Who shall declare it? What is that which shines through me and strikes my heart without injuring it? I both shudder and glow with passion: I shudder, in as much as I am unlike it; I glow with passion in as much as I am like to it.

It is Wisdom, Wisdom itself, which shines through me, cutting through my dark clouds which again cover me over, as I fall down because of that darkness and under the load of my punishments. For thus is my strength weakened in poverty, so that I cannot support my good, until you, O Lord, "who have been gracious to all my iniquities," likewise "heal all my diseases." For you will "redeem my life from corruption," you will "crown me with mercy and compassion," and you will "satisfy my desire with good things," because my "youth shall be renewed like the eagle's." For in hope we are saved, and we wait for your promises through patience.

Let him who can hear you inwardly as you speak to us. I will cry out boldly in words from your oracle: "How great are your works, O Lord; you have made all things in wisdom!" That wisdom is the beginning, and in that beginning you have made heaven and earth.

CHAPTER 10. *A Skeptical Objection*

(12) Lo, are not those men full of their old carnal nature who say to us, "What was God doing before he made heaven and earth?" "For if," they say, "he took his ease and did nothing, why did he not continue in this way henceforth and forever, just as previously he always refrained from work? If any new motion arise in God, or a new will is formed in him, to the end of establishing creation, which he had never established previously, how then would there be true eternity, when a will arises that previously was not there? The will of God is not a creature, but it is before the creature, for nothing would be created unless the creator's will preceded it. Therefore God's will belongs to his very substance. But if anything has appeared in God's substance that previously was not there, then that substance is not truly called eternal. Yet if it were God's sempiternal will for the creature to exist, why is not the creature sempiternal also?"

CHAPTER 11. *Past, Present, and Future*

(13) Men who say such things do not yet understand you, O Wisdom of God, O light of minds. They do not yet understand how those things are made which are made through you and in you. They attempt to grasp eternal things, but their heart flutters among the changing things of past and future, and it is still vain. Who will catch hold of it, and make it fast, so that it stands firm for a little while, and for a little while seize the splendor of that ever stable eternity, and compare it with times that never stand fast, and see that it is incomparable to them, and see that a long time cannot become long except out of many passing movements, which cannot be extended together, that in the eternal nothing can pass away but the whole is present, that no time is wholly present? Who will see that all past time is driven back by the future, that all the future is consequent on the past, and all the past and future are created and take their course from that which is ever present?

Who will hold the heart of man, so that it may stand still and see how steadfast eternity, neither future nor past, decrees times future and those past? Can my hand do this, or does the hand of my mouth by its little words effect so great a thing?

CHAPTER 12. *A Frivolous Answer*

(14) See, I answer the man who says, "What did God do before he made heaven and earth?" I do not give the answer that someone is said to have given, evading by a joke the force of the objection: "He was preparing hell," he said, "for those prying into such deep subjects." It is one thing to see the objection; it is another to make a joke of it. I do not answer in this way. I would rather respond, "I do not know," concerning what I do not know rather than say something for which a man inquiring about such profound matters is laughed at, while the one giving a false answer is praised.

I say that you, our God, are the creator of every creature, and, if by the phrase heaven and earth all creation is understood, I boldly say, "Before God made heaven and earth, he did not make anything." If he made anything, what else did he make except a creature? Would that I knew all I want to know that is for my good in the same way that I know that no creature was made before any creature was made.

CHAPTER 13. *Before All Time*

(15) If any flighty mind wanders among mental pictures of past times, and wonders that you, the all-great, all-creating, and all-sustaining God, maker of heaven and earth, should for countless ages have refrained from doing so great a work before actually doing it, let him awake and realize that he wonders at falsities. How could they pass by, those countless ages, which you had not made, although you are the author and creator of all ages? Or what times would there be, times not been made by you? Or how did they pass by, if they never were? Therefore, since you are the maker of all times, if there was a time before you made heaven and earth, why do they say that you rested from work? You made that very time, and no times could pass by before you made those times. But if there was no time before heaven and earth, why do they ask what you did then? There was no "then," where there was no time.

(16) It is not in time that you precede time: elsewise you would not precede all times. You precede all past times in the sublimity of an ever present eternity, and you surpass all future times, because they are to come, and when they come, they shall be past, "but you are the Selfsame, and your years shall not fail." Your years neither come nor go, but our years come and go, so that all of them may come. Your years stand all at once, because they are steadfast: departing years are not turned away by those that come, because they never pass away. But these years of ours shall all be, when they all shall be no more. Your years are one day, and your day is not each day, but today, because with you today does not give way to tomorrow, nor does it succeed yesterday. With you, today is eternity. Therefore you begot the coeternal, to whom you said, "This day have I begotten you." You have made all times, and you are before all times, and not at any time was there no time.

CHAPTER 14. *What Is Time?*

(17) At no time, therefore, did you do nothing, since you had made time itself. No times are coeternal with you, because you are permanent, whereas if they were permanent, they would not be times. What is time? Who can easily and briefly explain this? Who can comprehend this even in thought, so as to express it in a word? Yet what do we discuss more familiarly and knowingly in conversation than time? Surely we understand it when we talk about it, and also understand it when we hear others talk about it.

What, then, is time? If no one asks me, I know; if I want to explain it to someone who does ask me, I do not know. Yet I state confidently that I know this: if nothing were passing away, there would be no past time, and if nothing were coming, there would be no future time, and if nothing existed, there would be no present time. How, then, can these two kinds of time, the past and the future, be, when the past no longer is and the future as yet does not be? But if the present were always present, and would not pass into the past, it would no longer be time, but eternity. Therefore, if the present, so as to be time, must be so constituted that it passes into the past, how can we say that it is, since the cause of its being is the fact that it will cease to be? Does it not follow that we can truly say that it is time, only because it tends towards non-being?

CHAPTER 15. *Can Time Be Long or Short?*

(18) Yet we say "a long time" and "a short time," and do not say this except of the past or the future. For example, we call a hundred years ago a long time in the past, and a hundred years from now we call a long time in the future. On the contrary, we term ten days ago, let us say, a short time past, and ten days to come, a brief future time. But in what sense is something non-existent either long or short? The past no longer exists, and the future is not yet in being. Therefore we should not say, "It is long," but we should say of the past, "It was long," and of the future, "It will be long." My lord, my light, shall not your truth here also jest at man? That past time which was so long, was it long when it was already past, or before that, when it was still present? It could be long at the time when that existed which could be long. Once past, it did not exist, hence it could not be long, since it in no wise existed. Therefore, let us not say, "Past time was long." We will not find anything which was long, since from the very fact that it is past, it is no more. Let us say, "That time once present was long," because it was long when it was present. It had not yet passed away, so as not to be, and therefore there existed that which could be long. On the other hand, after it passed away, it instantly ceased to be long, because it ceased to be.

(19) Let us see, then, O human soul, whether present time can be long, for it has been granted to you to perceive and to measure tracts of time. What answer do you make me? Are a hundred years, when present, a long time? See first whether a hundred years can be present. If the first of these years is going on, it is present, but the other ninety-nine are still in the future, and therefore as yet are not existent. If the second year is current, one is already past, another is present, and the rest are in the future. So it is if we posit any of the intervening years of the hundred as the present: before it will be past years, and after it, future

years. For this reason, a hundred years cannot be present.

But see, at least, if the year now going on is itself present. If the first month is current, then all the rest are to come; if it is the second, then the first is already past and the others are not yet here. Therefore the current year is not wholly present, and if it is not wholly present, then the year is not present. A year is made up of twelve months, of which any one month, which is current, is the present, and the others are either past or future. However, not even the current month is present, but only a single day. If it is the first day, the others are to come; if the last day, the others are past; if any intervening day, it is between those past and those to come.

(20) See how the present time, which alone we found worthy to be called long, is contracted to hardly the space of a single day. But let us examine it also, because not even a single day is present in its totality. It is completed in twenty-four hours of night and day, and of these the first has the others still to come, the last has them past it, and each of the intervening hours has those before it in the past and those after it in the future. That one hour itself goes on in fleeting moments; whatever part of it has flown away is past, whatever remains is future. If any point of time is conceived that can no longer be divided into even the most minute parts of a moment, that alone it is which may be called the present. It flies with such speed from the future into the past that it cannot be extended by even a trifling amount. For if it is extended, it is divided into past and future. The present has no space.

Where then is the time that we may call long? Is it to come? We do not say of it that it is long, because it does not yet exist, so as to be long. We say that it will be long. When, therefore, will it be? Even then, if it will still be to come, it will not be long, since that which will be long does not yet be. But suppose it will be long, at that time when out of the future, which does not yet be, it will first begin to be and will have become present, so that what may be long can actually exist. Then immediately present time cries out in the words above that it cannot be long.

CHAPTER 16. *Time and Measurement*

(21) Still, O Lord, we perceive intervals of time. We compare them to one another and say that some are longer and some shorter. Also, we measure how much longer or shorter this time may be than that, and answer that this is twice or three times as long as another, or that that one is identical with or just as much as this. But it is passing times that we measure, and we make these measurements in perceiving them. As to past times, which no longer exist, or future, which as yet do not exist, who can measure them, except perhaps a man rash enough to say that he can measure what does not exist? Therefore, as long as time is passing by, it can be perceived and measured, but when it has passed by, it cannot be measured since it does not exist.

CHAPTER 17. *Prophecy and History*

(22) Father, I ask questions; I do not make assertions. My God, govern me and guide me. Who is it that will tell me, not that there are three times, just as we learned as boys and as we have taught to boys, namely, past, present, and future,

but that there is only present time, since the other two do not exist? Or do they too exist, but when the present comes into being from the future, does it proceed from some hidden source, and when past comes out of the present, does it recede into some hidden place? Where did they who foretold things to come see them, if they do not exist? A thing that does not exist cannot be seen. If those who narrate past events did not perceive them by their minds, they would not give true accounts. If such things were nothing at all, they could not be perceived in any way. Therefore, both future and past times have being.

CHAPTER 18. *Induction and Prediction*

(23) Give me leave, "O Lord, my hope" to make further search: do not let my purpose be diverted. If future and past times exist, I wish to know where they are. But if I am not yet able to do this, I still know that wherever they are, they are there neither as future nor as past, but as present. For if they are in that place as future things, they are not yet there, and if they are in that place as past things, they are no longer there. Therefore, wherever they are, and whatever they are, they do not exist except as present things. However, when true accounts of the past are given, it is not the things themselves, which have passed away, that are drawn forth from memory, but words conceived from their images. These images they implanted in the mind like footsteps as they passed through the senses.

My boyhood, indeed, which no longer is, belongs to past time, which no longer is. However, when I recall it and talk about it, I perceive its image at the present time, because it still is in my memory. Whether there may be a like cause of predicting future events as well, namely, that actually existent images of things which as yet do not exist are perceived first, I confess, O my God, I do not know. But this I surely know, that we often premeditate our future actions and such premeditation is present to us, but the action that we premeditate does not yet exist, because it is to be. As soon as we have addressed ourselves to it and have begun to do what we were premeditating, then action will be existent. Then it will not be future, but present.

(24) Howsoever this secret foresight of things to come takes place, nothing can be seen except what is present. But what now is is not future but present. Hence, when future things are said to be seen, it is not the things themselves, which are not yet existent, that is, the things that are to come, but their causes, or perhaps signs of them, which already exist, that are seen. Thus they are not future things, but things already present to the viewers, and from them future things are predicted as conceived in the mind. Again, these conceptions are already existent, and those who predict the future fix their gaze upon things present with them.

Let the vast multitude of such things offer me some example of this. I look at the dawn; I foretell the coming sunrise. What I look at is present; what I foretell is future. It is not the sun that is about to be, for it already exists, but its rising, which as yet is not. Yet if I did not picture within my mind this sunrise, just as when I now speak of it, I would be unable to predict it. Still that dawn, which I see in the sky, is not the sunrise, although it precedes the sunrise, nor is the picture in my mind the sunrise. Both these are perceived as present to me, so that the future sunrise may be foretold. Therefore, future things do not yet exist; if they do not yet exist, they are not; if they are not, they can in no wise be seen.

However, they can be predicted from present things, which already exist and are seen.

CHAPTER 19. *A Prayer for Light*

(25) O you, the ruler of your creation, in what manner do you teach souls those things which are to come? You have taught your prophets. What is that way by which you teach things to come, you to whom nothing is future? Or is it rather that you teach things present concerning what is to come? What does not exist surely cannot be taught. Too distant is this way for my sight. It is too strong for me, and of myself I will not be able to attain it. But with your help I will be able to attain to it, when you will give it to me, you, the sweet light of my hidden eyes.

CHAPTER 20. *Three Kinds of Time*

(26) It is now plain and clear that neither past nor future are existent, and that it is not properly stated that there are three times, past, present, and future. But perhaps it might properly be said that there are three times, the present of things past, the present of things present, and the present of things future. These three are in the soul, but elsewhere I do not see them: the present of things past is in memory; the present of things present is in intuition; the present of things future is in expectation. If we are permitted to say this, then I see three times, and I affirm that there are three times. It may also be said that there are tree times, past, present, and future, as common usage incorrectly puts it. This may be stated. Note that I am not concerned over this, do not object to it, and do not criticize it, as long as we understand what we say, namely, that what is future is not now existent, nor is that which is past. There are few things that we state properly, and many that we speak improperly, but what we mean is understood.

CHAPTER 21. *Measures of Time*

(27) I said just a while ago that we measure passing times, so that we can say that this tract of time is double that single one, or that this one is just as long as the other, and whatever else as to periods of time we can describe by our measurements. Therefore, as I was saying, we measure passing times. If someone says to me, "How do you know this?" I may answer, "I know this because we make such measurements, and we cannot measure things that do not exist, and neither past nor future things exist." Yet how do we measure present time, since it has no extent? Therefore, it is measured as it passes by, but once it has passed by, it is not measured, for what would be measured will no longer exist. But from where, and on what path, and to what place does it pass, as it is measured? From where, except from the future? By what path, except by the present? To what place, except into the past? Therefore, it is from that which does not yet exist, by that which lacks space, and into that which no longer exists.

But what do we measure if time is not in a certain space? We do not say single, or double, or threefold, or equal, or anything else of this sort in the order of time, except with regard to tracts of time. In what space, then, do we measure

passing time? In the future, out of which it passes? But we do not measure what
does not yet exist. Or in the present, by which it passes? We do not measure
what is without space. Or in the past, into which it passes? We do not measure
what no longer exists.

CHAPTER 22. *A New Task*

(28) My mind is on fire to understand this most intricate riddle. O Lord my
God, good Father, I beseech you in the name of Christ, do not shut off, do not
shut off these things, both familiar and yet hidden, from my desire, so that it may
not penetrate into them, but let them grow bright, Lord, with your mercy
bringing the light that lights them up. Of whom shall I inquire concerning them?
To whom shall I more fruitfully confess my ignorance than to you, to whom my
studies, strongly burning for your Scriptures, are not offensive.

Give me what I love, for in truth I love it, and this you have given to me. Give
this to me, Father, for "truly you know how to give good gifts to your children."
Give it to me, for "I studied that I might know this thing; it is a labor in your
sight," until you open it up. I beseech you in the name of Christ, in the name
of him, the saint of saints, let no man interrupt me. "I have believed, therefore
do I speak." This is my hope, for this I live, "that I may contemplate the delight
of the Lord." "Behold, you have made my days old," and they pass away, but how
I do not know. We talk of time and time, of times and times: "How long ago
did he say this?" "How long ago did he do this?" "How long a time since I saw
that?" "This syllable takes twice the time of that short simple syllable." We say
these things, and we hear them, and we are understood, and we understand. They
are most clear and most familiar, but again they are very obscure, and their solution is a new task.

CHAPTER 23. *Bodily Motion as Time*

(29) I have heard from a certain learned man that the movements of the sun,
moon, and stars constitute time, but I did not agree with him. Why should not
rather the movement of all bodies be times? In fact, if the lights of heaven should
stop, while a potter's wheel was kept moving, would there be no time by which
we might measure those rotations? Would we say either that it moved with equal
speeds, or, if it sometimes moved more slowly and sometimes more swiftly, that
some turns were longer and others shorter? Or while we were saying this, would we
not also be speaking in time? Or would there be in our words some long syllables and others short, except for the fact that some were sounded for a longer
and others for a shorter time? Grant to men, O God, that they may see in a little
matter evidence common to things both small and great. The stars and the lights
of heaven are "for signs, and for seasons, and for days, and for years." Truly they
are such. Yet I should not say that the turning of that little wooden wheel constitutes a day, nor under those conditions should that learned man say that there
is no time.

(30) I desire to know the power and the nature of time, by which we measure
bodily movements, and say, for instance, that this movement is twice as long as
that. I put this question: "Since a day is defined not only as the sun's time over
the earth—according to which usage, day is one thing and night another—but

also as its entire circuit from east to east—and accordingly we say 'So many days have passed,' for they are termed 'so many days' with their nights included and are not reckoned as days apart from the night hours—since, then, a day is completed by the sun's movement and its circuit from east to east, I ask whether the movement itself constitutes a day, or the period in which the movement is performed, or both together?"

If the first were a day, then there would be a day even if the sun completed its course in a period of time such as an hour. If the second, then there would not be a day, if from one sunrise to another there were as brief a period as an hour, whereas the sun would have to go around twenty-four times to complete a day. If both, it could not be called a day if the sun ran its entire course in the space of an hour, nor if, while the sun stood still, just so much time passed by as the sun usually takes to complete its entire course from morning to morning.

Therefore, I will not now ask what is it that is called a day, but rather what is time, by which we would measure the sun's circuit and say that it was completed in half the time it usually takes, if it were finished in a period like twelve hours. Comparing both times, we should call the one a single period, the other a double period, even if the sun ran its course from east to east sometimes in the single period and sometimes in the double.

Let no man tell me, then, that movements of the heavenly bodies constitute periods of time. When at the prayer of a certain man, the sun stood still until he could achieve victory in battle, the sun indeed stood still, but time went on. That battle was waged and brought to an end during its own tract of time, which was sufficient for it. Therefore, I see that time is a kind of distention. Yet do I see this, or do I only seem to myself to see it? You, O Light, will show this to me.

CHAPTER 24. *Measures of Movement*

(31) Do you command me to agree with someone who says that time is the movement of a body? You do not command this. I hear that a body is never moved except in time: this you yourself affirm. But I do not hear that the movement of a body constitutes time: this you do not say. When a body is moved, I measure in time how long it is moved, from when it begins to be moved until it ceases. If I did not see when it began, and if it continues to be moved, so that I cannot see when it stops, I am unable to measure it, except perhaps from the time I begin to see it until I stop. If I look at it for long, I can merely report that it is a long time, but not how long. When we say how long, we say so by making a comparison, such as, "This is as long as that," or "Twice as long as that," or something of the sort.

But if we can mark off the distances of the places from which and to which the body that is moved goes—or its parts, if it is moved as on a lathe—then we can say in how much time the movement of that body, or its part, from this place to that, is completed. Since the movement of a body is one thing and that by which we measure how long it takes another, who does not perceive which of the two is better called time? For if a body is sometimes moved in different ways and sometimes stands still, then we measure in time not only its movement but also its standing still. We say, "It stood still just as long as it was moved," or "It stood still twice or three times as long as it was moved," and whatever else our measurements either determine or reckon, more or less, as the saying goes. Time, therefore, is not the movement of a body.

CHAPTER 25. *The Deepening Problem*

(32) I confess to you, O Lord, that I do not yet know what time is, and again I confess to you, O Lord, that I know that I say these things in time, and that I have now spoken at length of time, and that that very length of time is not long except by a period of time. How, then, do I know this, when I do not know what time is? Or perhaps I do not know how to express what I know? Woe is me, who do not even know what I do not know! Behold, O my God, before you I do not lie. As I speak, so is my heart. "You will light my lamp, O Lord, my God, you enlighten my darkness."

CHAPTER 26. *The Definition of Time*

(33) Does not my soul confess to you with a true confession that I measure tracts of time? Yes, O Lord my God, I measure them, and know not what I measure, I measure the motion of a body in time. But again, do I not measure time itself? In fact, could I measure a body's movement, as to how long it is and how long it takes from this place to that, unless I could measure the time in which it is moved? How, then, do I measure time itself? Do we measure a longer time by a shorter one, just as we measure the length of a rod by the length of a cubit? It is thus that we seem to measure the length of a long syllable by the length of a short syllable, and to say that it is twice as long. So also we measure the length of poems by the length of verses, the length of verses by the length of feet, the length of feet by the length of syllables, and the length of long syllables by the length of short ones. This is not as they are on the page—in that manner we measure spaces, not times—but as words pass by when we pronounce them. We say: "It is a long poem for it is composed of so many verses; the verses are long, for they consist of so many feet; the feet are long, for they extend over so many syllables; the syllable is long, for it is double a short one."

But a reliable measure of time is not comprehended in this manner, since it can be that a shorter verse, if pronounced more slowly, may sound for a longer stretch of time than a longer but more hurried verse. So it is for a poem, so for a foot, so for a syllable. For this reason it seemed to me that time is nothing more than distention: but of what thing I know not, and the marvel is, if it is not of the mind itself. For what do I measure, I beseech you, my God, when I say either indefinitely, "This time is longer than that," or even definitely, "This time is twice as long as that?" I measure time, I know. Yet I do not measure the future, because it does not yet exist; I do not measure the present, because it is not extended in space; I do not measure the past, because it no longer exists. What, then, do I measure? Times that pass, but are not yet past? So I have stated.

CHAPTER 27. *Where Time Is Measured*

(34) Be steadfast, O my mind, and attend firmly. "God is our helper." "He made us, and not we ourselves." Look to where truth begins to dawn. See, as an

example, a bodily voice begins to sound, and does sound, and still sounds, and then, see, it stops. There is silence now: that voice is past, and is no longer a voice. Before it sounded, the voice was to come, and could not be measured because it did not yet exist, and now it cannot be measured because it no longer is. Therefore, the time it was sounding, it could be measured, because at that time it existed. Even at that time it was not static, for it was going on and going away. Was it for that reason the more measurable? While passing away it was being extended over some tract of time, wherein it could be measured, for the present has no space. Therefore, if it could be measured at that time, let us suppose that another voice has begun to sound and still sounds on one continuous note without any break. Let us measure it while it is sounding, since when it has ceased to sound, it will be already past and there will be nothing that can be measured. Let us measure it exactly, and let us state how long it is. But it is still sounding, and it cannot be measured except from its beginning, when it begins to sound, up to its end, when it stops. We measure, in fact, the interval from some beginning up to some kind of end. Hence a voice that is never brought to a stop cannot be measured, so that one may say how long or short it is. Nor can it be said to be equal to another, or single or double or anything else with reference to something. But when it will be ended, it will no longer be. In what sense, then, can it be measured? Yet we do measure tracts of time, although not those which as yet are not, not those which no longer are, not those which are prolonged without a break, not those which have no limits. Neither future, nor past, nor present, nor passing times do we measure and still we measure tracts of time.

(35) *Deus creator omnium*—"God, creator of all things"—this verse of eight syllables alternates between short and long syllables. Hence the four short syllables, the first, third, fifth and seventh, are simple with respect to the four long syllables the second, fourth, sixth, and eighth. Each long syllable has a double time with respect to each of the others. This I affirm, this I report, and so it is, in so far as it is plain to sense perception. In so far as sense perception is clear, I measure the long syllable by the short one, and I perceive that it is exactly twice as long. But when one syllable sounds after another, and if the first is short and the second long, how will I retain the short syllable and how will I apply it to the long syllable while measuring it, so as to find that the latter is twice as long? For the long syllable does not begin to sound until the short one has ceased to sound. Do I measure the long syllable itself while it is present, since I do not measure it until it is completed? Yet its completion is its passing away. Therefore, what is it that I measure? Where is the short syllable by which I measure? Where is the long syllable that I measure? Both of them have sounded, have flown off, have passed away, and now they are not. Yet I make measurements, and I answer confidently—in so far as sense activity is relied upon—that this syllable is single and that one double, namely, in length of time. Yet I cannot do this, unless because they have passed away and are ended. Therefore, I do not measure the syllables themselves, which no longer are, but something in my memory that remains fixed there.

(36) It is in you, O my mind, that I measure my times. Do not interrupt me by crying that time is. Do not interrupt yourself with the noisy mobs of your prejudices. It is in you, I say, that I measure tracts of time. The impression that passing things make upon you remains, even after those things have passed. That

present state is what I measure, not the things which pass away so that it be made. That is what I measure when I measure tracts of time. Therefore, either this is time, or I do not measure time.

How is it when we measure stretches of silence, and say that this silence has lasted for as much of time as that discourse lasted? Do we not apply our thought to measurement of the voice, just as though it were sounding, so that we may be able to report about the intervals of silence in a given tract of time? Even though both voice and mouth be silent, in our thought we run through poems and verses, and any discourse, and any other measurements of motion. We report about tracts of time: how great this one may be in relation to that, in the same manner as if we said them audibly.

If someone wished to utter a rather long sound and had determined by previous reflection how long it would be, he has in fact already silently gone through a tract of time. After committing it to memory, he has begun to utter that sound and he voices it until he has brought it to his proposed end. Yes, it has sounded and it will sound. For the part of it that is finished has surely sounded; what remains will sound. So it is carried out, as long as his present intention transfers the future into the past, with the past increasing by a diminution of future, until by the consumption of the future the whole is made past.

CHAPTER 28.   *The Mental Synthesis*

(37) But how is the future, which as yet does not exist, diminished or consumed, or how does the past, which no longer exists, increase, unless there are three things in the mind, which does all this? It looks forward, it considers, it remembers, so that the reality to which it looks forward passes through what it considers into what it remembers. Who, then, denies that future things are not yet existent? Yet there is already in the mind an expectation of things to come. Who denies that past things no longer exist? Yet there is still in the soul the memory of past things. Who denies that present time lacks spatial extent, since it passes away in an instant? Yet attention abides, and through it what shall be present proceeds to become something absent. It is not, then, future time that is long, but a long future is a long expectation of the future. Nor is past time, which is not, long, but a long past is a long memory of the past.

(38) I am about to recite a psalm that I know. Before I begin, my expectation extends over the entire psalm. Once I have begun, my memory extends over as much of it as I shall separate off and assign to the past. The life of this action of mine is distended into memory by reason of the part I have spoken and into forethought by reason of the part I am about to speak. But attention is actually present and that which was to be is borne along by it so as to become past. The more this is done and done again, so much the more is memory lengthened by a shortening of expectation, until the entire expectation is exhausted. When this is done the whole action is completed and passes into memory. What takes place in the whole psalm takes place also in each of its parts and in each of its syllables. The same thing holds for a longer action, of which perhaps the psalm is a small part. The same thing holds for a man's entire life, the parts of which are all the man's actions. The same thing holds throughout the whole age of the sons of men, the parts of which are the lives of all men.

THE CITY OF GOD

Book XIX

III. *Which of the Three Sects that Seek the Supreme Good of Man Does Varro, Following the Doctrine of the Old Academy (on the Authority of Antiochus), Define as Worthy of Choice?*

Which, then, of these three is true and to be pursued he sets out to prove in the following manner. First, since philosophy seeks the supreme good not of a tree, or of a beast, or of God, but of man, he thinks that we must put the question what man himself is. He concludes that in man's nature there are two things, body and soul; and of these two he has no doubt at all that the soul is the better and by far more excellent. But is the soul alone the man, and is the body to him as the horse to the horseman? For the horseman is not a man and a horse, but only a man, and is called a horseman because he bears a certain relation in respect to a horse. Or is the body alone the man, bearing some relation to the soul, like that of the cup to the drink? For it is not the cup and the drink that it contains which are together called the cup, but the cup alone; yet it is so called because it is designed to hold the drink. Or again is it neither the soul alone nor the body alone but both together that constitute the man, of whom the soul and the body are each a part, while the whole man consists of both, as we call two horses yoked together a pair, though we do not call either the near or the off horse, however related to the other, a pair, but only call both together a pair?

Of these three possibilities, Varro chose the third, that man is neither soul alone nor body alone but soul and body together. Therefore, he says, the supreme good of man by which he becomes happy consists in the combination of the goods of each kind of thing, namely soul and body. And he holds accordingly that the primary wants of nature are to be sought for their own sake, and so also virtue, which is implanted by instruction, as being the art of living, which is most outstanding among the goods of the soul. Wherefore this virtue, or art of conducting life, when she has taken over the primary wants of nature, which were there apart from virtue,—nay, were there even when they lacked any instruction whatever,—seeks to satisfy all of them for her own sake and at the same time seeks her own development. She makes use of them and of herself at the same time to the end that she may delight in and enjoy all of them. Her enjoyment may be greater or less as these elements are severally more or less important; still they are all a source of joy, though she may, if that is a necessary condition, slight some ele-

Reprinted by permission of the publishers from Loeb Classical Library, Augustine, *The City of God,* Cambridge, Mass.: Harvard University Press, Copyright, 1960, by the President and Fellows of Harvard College.

ments as less important, in order to win or preserve the more important.

Now of all goods, whether of soul or of body, virtue prefers none at all to herself. For virtue makes good use both of herself and of all the other goods that go to make man happy; but where she is lacking, however many goods a man has, they do him no good, and so must not be called his "goods"; since he uses them ill, they cannot be useful to him. Here, then, is the sort of human life that is termed happy, a life that enjoys virtue and the other goods of soul and body without which virtue cannot exist; a life is called happier, if it enjoys one or more of the goods that virtue can lack and still exist; and happiest, if it enjoys absolutely all goods, so that it lacks not one of the goods either of soul or of body. For life is not identical with virtue, since not every life, but only a wisely conducted life, is virtue; in fact, there can be life of a sort without any virtue, though there can be no virtue without some life. I might say as much of memory and reason and any other such human faculties; these exist before instruction, but without them there can be no instruction, and therefore no virtue, since virtue is in any case imparted by instruction. But swiftness in running, and physical beauty and victories won by unusual strength and the like, can exist without virtue, as virtue without them; yet they are goods, and according to these philosophers, even these are sought by virtue herself for their own sake, and are used and enjoyed by her in her own becoming way.

This happy life, they say, is also social, and loves the good of friends itself for its own sake as being its own good, and wishes for them for their own sakes what it wishes for itself, whether by friends we mean housemates, such as wife or children and others of the household, or neighbours with houses in the same locality, such as fellow citizens of a city, or men anywhere in the whole world, such as nations with whom we are joined by human society, or denizens even of the universe, which is designated by the term heaven and earth, such as those whom they call gods and like to think of as friends of the wise man, whom we more familiarly call angels. About the supreme good and its opposite the supreme evil they deny that there is any room for doubt, and this, they assert, distinguishes them from the New Academy; and they are not at all interested whether any one who practises philosophy, accepting those ends which they deem to be true, wears the Cynic dress and eats the Cynic food or some other. Finally, of those three kinds of life, the inactive, the active and the composite, they state that they prefer the third. That the Old Academy held and taught these doctrines Varro asserts on the authority of Antiochus, Cicero's master and his own, although Cicero would have it that on a good many points he appeared to be a Stoic rather than an Old Academic. But what does that matter to us, who ought rather to base our judgement on the bare facts than to set store on knowing what opinion each man held about them?

iv. *What View the Christians Hold About the Supreme Good and the Supreme Evil, as Against the Philosophers Who Have Maintained that for Them the Supreme Good Is in Themselves.*

If, then, we are asked what the City of God replies when asked about these several matters, and first what its opinion is about the ultimate good and the ultimate evil, it will reply that the ulimate good is eternal life, and that the ultimate evil is eternal death, and that in order to obtain the one and escape the other we must live rightly. Wherefore it is written: "The just man lives by faith." For neither do we see as yet our good, and therefore must seek it by believing, nor is it in our power of ourselves to live rightly unless he who has given us faith to believe that we must seek help from him shall help us, as we believe in and pray to him. But those who have supposed that the ultimate good and evil are to be found in the present life, placing the ultimate good either in the body or in the soul or in both, or, to speak more explicitly, either in pleasure or in virtue or in both, in repose or in virtue or in both, in pleasure combined with repose or in virtue or in both, in the primary wants of nature or in virtue or in both, all these persons have sought, with a surprising vanity, to be happy in this life and to get happiness by their own efforts. Truth laughed at these men through the words of the prophet: "The Lord knows the thoughts of men," or, as the apostle Paul has set forth this passage: "The Lord knows the thoughts of the wise, that they are vain."

For who, no matter how great his torrent of eloquence, can avail to enumerate the miseries of this life? Cicero lamented them, as best he could, in the *Consolation* on the death of his daughter; but how inadequate was his best! For when, where, how can the so-called primary wants of nature be on such a good footing in this life that they are not tossed about at the mercy of blind accidents? Why, what pain is there, the opposite of pleasure, what turbulence is there, the opposite of repose, that may not assail the wise man's frame? Surely the amputation or weakening of a man's limbs forces his freedom from physical defects to capitulate, ugliness his beauty, illness his health, weariness his strength, sleepiness or sluggishness his agility; now, which of these may not invade the flesh of the wise man? Fitting and harmonious attitudes and movements of the body are also reckoned among the primary wants of nature; but what if some disease makes the limbs quake and tremble? What if a man's spine be so bent that he puts his hands on the ground, which makes of him a quadruped, so to speak? Will not this ruin all beauty and grace whether of bodily pose or of movement?

What of the so-called primary goods of the mind itself, of which the two that are rated first, as means to the grasping and observing of truth, are sensation and intelligence? But how much sensation remains, and of what value, if a man becomes deaf and blind, to say nothing of other defects? And whither will reason and intelligence withdraw, where will they slumber, if a man is crazed by some disease? When the insane say or do many absurd things that are for the most part alien to their own aims and characters,—nay, even opposed to their good aims and characters,—whether we use our imaginations or have them before our eyes, if we reflect on their case as it deserves, we can scarce hold back our tears, or it may be even that we cannot. What shall I say of those who are afflicted by attacks of demons? In what hidden or submerged places do their intellects lurk, when the evil spirit is using their souls and bodies according to its own will? And who is quite sure that this evil cannot befall the wise man in this life? Then what sort of observation of truth is there in this flesh, or how great is it, when, as we read in the truthful book of Wisdom: "The corruptible body weighs down the soul, and the earthly frame lies heavy on a mind that ponders many things"? Furthermore, drive or impulse to act,—if either is the correct Latin word for what the Greeks call *hormē*, for that, too, is included among the primary goods of nature,—is not impulse also responsible for those pitiable movements and acts of the insane that shock us, when sensation is distraught and reason is asleep?

Finally, as to virtue itself, which is not among the primary wants of nature, since it is a later addition ushered in by instruction, although it claims the highest place among human goods, what is its activity here but perpetual war with vices, not external vices but internal, not alien but clearly our very own, a war waged especially by that virtue called in Greek *sōphrosynē* and in Latin temperance, which bridles the lusts of the flesh lest they win the consent of the mind and drag it into crimes of every sort? For it is not the case that there is no vice when, as the Apostle says: "The flesh lusts against the spirit." For to this vice there is an opposing virtue, when, as the same Apostle says: "The spirit lusts against the flesh. These two," he says, "are opposed one to the other, so that you do not what you would." But what is it that we would do, when we wish to be made perfect by the ultimate good, unless it be that the flesh should not lust against the spirit, and that there should be in us no such vice for the spirit to lust against it? But since we cannot bring that to pass in the present life, however much we may desire it, we can at least with God's help so act that we do not yield to the lust of the flesh against the spirit by failure of the spirit, and we are not dragged with our own consent to the perpetration of sin. Far be it from us, then, so long as we are engaged in this internal war, to hold it true that we have already attained to that happiness which is the goal that we would gain by victory. And who is so wise that he has no battle at all to wage against his lusts?

What of that virtue which is called prudence? Does she not devote all her vigilance to the discrimination of good and evil, so that in pursuing the one and shunning the other no error may creep in? Thus she bears witness herself that we are among evils, that is, that evils are in us; for she teaches us herself that it is an evil to yield to a lust for sin, and a good not to yield to a lust for sin. But that evil to which prudence teaches and temperance causes us not to yield, is neither by prudence nor by temperance banished from this life. What of justice, whose function it is to assign to each man his due, whereby there is located in man himself a certain right order of nature, so that soul is subordinated to God, and flesh to soul, and therefore both soul and flesh to God? Does not justice thereby demonstrate that she is still labouring in her task rather than resting already at the goal of her labours? For the less the soul keeps God clearly in mind in all its activity, the less it is subordinate to God; and the more the flesh lusts against the spirit, the less it is subordinate to the soul. So long, then, as we have in us this weakness, this sickness, this torpor, how shall we dare say that we are already saved, and if not saved, how already blest with that ultimate bliss? Then truly that virtue called fortitude, though combined with however great wisdom, bears witness most convincingly to human ills, for they are what she is required to endure with patience.

Now I am amazed that the Stoic philosophers have the face to argue that these ills are no ills, though they admit that, if they should be so great that the wise man cannot or ought not to endure them, he is compelled to inflict death on himself and depart from this life. But such is the stupid pride of these men who suppose that the supreme good is to be found in this life, and that they can be the agents of their own happiness, that their wise man,—I mean the man whom they describe as such with astounding inanity,—whom, even if he be blinded and grow deaf and dumb, lose the use of his limbs, be tortured with pain, and visited by every other evil of the sort that tongue can utter or fancy conceive, whereby he is driven to inflict death on himself, they do not scruple to call happy. What a happy life, that seeks the help of death to end it! If it be happy, let a man stay in it. How can those things not be evil that vanquish the good that is fortitude, and compel it not only to give way to them but so to rave that it calls the same life happy from which it advises us to escape? Who is so blind as not to perceive that, if it were happy, it would not be a life to escape from? Why, the word "escape" is an unconcealed admission of weakness in their argument! What ground have they now to keep them, with stiff-necked pride broken, from admitting that it is even a wretched life? Was it not through lack of fortitude, rather than through fortitude, that the famous Cato took his life? For he would not have done it, had he not lacked the fortitude to bear the victory of Caesar. Where, then, is his fortitude? It yielded, it succumbed, it was so far vanquished that he gave up, forsook, escaped from this happy life. Or was it no longer happy? Then it was wretched. How, then, were those not evils that made life wretched and a thing to be escaped from?

And therefore those who admitted that these are evils, as did the Peripatetics and the Old Academics, the sect that Varro defends, speak in a more tolerable manner; but they, too, are sponsors of a surprising error, in that they maintain that amid these evils, even if they be so grave that he who suffers them is obliged to escape by seeking his own death, life is nevertheless happy. "Among evils," says Varro, "are pains and anguish of body, and their evil is the greater in proportion to their severity; and to avoid them one should escape from this life." What life, pray? "This life," he says, "that is beset by so great evils." So it is definitely happy, then, amid those very evils because of which you say that one must escape from it? Or do you call it happy because you have freedom to escape from these evils by death? What, then, if by some divine judgement you were held among them and were not permitted either to die or ever to be free of them? Then, no doubt, at any rate, you would say that such a life is wretched. So it is not unwretched merely because it is soon abandoned, inasmuch as, if it were everlasting, even you yourself would pronounce it to be wretched. And so it ought not to be judged free from all wretchedness because the wretchedness is brief; or, still more absurdly, because the wretchedness is brief, on that account be even called a state of bliss.

Mighty is the power in these evils that compel a man, and according to these philosophers compel even a wise man, to deprive himself of his own existence as a man; although they say, and say truly, that the first and greatest commandment of nature is that a man should be brought into harmony with himself and therefore instinctively avoid death, and that he be his own friend in such wise as to be vigorously determined and eager to keep the breath of life and to live on in this union of body and soul. Mighty is the power in these evils that overcome the natural feeling we hear of, by whose working we use every means and bend all our strength and all our endeavours to avoid death, and so completely defeat nature that what was avoided is now longed for, pursued, and, if it may not arrive from some other quarter, inflicted on a man by himself. Mighty is the power in these evils that make fortitude a homicide, if indeed she should still be called fortitude who is overcome by these evils so completely that she not only cannot by her endurance safeguard the man whom, as virtue, she has undertaken to govern and protect but is herself compelled to go to the length of killing him. The wise man ought, to be sure, to endure even death with firmness, but death that befalls him from an external source. If, then, he is compelled, according to these philosophers, to inflict it on himself, surely they must admit not only that those are evils but that they are in fact intolerable evils that compel him to perpetrate this crime.

The life, then, that is oppressed by the weight of such great and grievous evils or exposed to the chance of them would by no means be termed happy if the men who use that term,—men who, when they are defeated by the increasing pressure of their ills, in the act of inflicting death upon themselves, surrender to misfortune,—would with equal condescension, when they are defeated by sound logic in the attempt to discover a happy life, surrender to the truth, instead of supposing that the enjoyment of the supreme good is a goal to be attained in the mortal state of which they speak. For our very virtues, which are surely the best and most useful attributes of a man, bear trustworthy witness to life's miseries so much the more, the more strongly they support us against life's dangers, toils and sorrows. For if our virtues are genuine,—and genuine virtues can exist only in those who are endowed with true piety,—they do not lay claim to such powers as to say that men in whom they reside will suffer no miseries (for true virtues are not so fraudulent in their claims); but they do say that our human life, though it is compelled by all the great evils of this age to be wretched, is happy in the expectation of a future life in so far as it enjoys the expectation of salvation too. For how can a life be happy, if it has no salvation yet? So the apostle Paul, speaking not of men who lacked prudence, patience, temperance and justice, but of men who lived in accordance with true piety, and whose virtues were therefore genuine, says: "Now we are saved by hope. But hope that is seen is not hope. For how should a man hope for what he sees? But if we hope for that which we do not see, then we look forward with endurance." As, therefore, we are saved by hope, so it is by hope that we have been made happy; and as we have no hold on a present salvation, but look for salvation in the future, so we look forward to happiness, and a happiness to be won "by endurance." For we are among evils, which we ought patiently to endure until we arrive among those goods where nothing will be lacking to provide us ineffable delight, nor will there now be anything that we are obliged to endure. Such is the salvation which in the life to come will itself be also the ultimate bliss. But those philosophers, not believing in this blessedness because they do not see it, strive to manufacture for themselves in this life an utterly counterfeit happiness by drawing on a virtue whose fraudulence matches its arrogance.

v. *About Social Life, Which, Though Very Greatly to Be Desired, Is Often Upset by Many Distresses.*

But in that they believe that the life of the wise man must be social, we approve much more fully. For how could the City of God, about which we are already engaged in writing the nineteenth book, begin at the start or progress in its course or reach its appointed goal, if the life of the saints were not social? But who could reckon up the number and the magnitude of the woes with which human society overflows amid the worries of this our mortal state? Who could be equal to the task of assessing them? Let them give ear to a man in one of their own comedies, who says what every man concurs in: "I have taken a wife; what misery I have known therewith! Children were born; another responsibility." What of the ills that love breeds, as enumerated by that same Terence: "Slights, suspicions, enmities, war, then peace again"? Have they not everywhere made up the tale of human events? Do they not usually occur even when friends are united in a noble love? The history of man is in every cranny infested with them; in this list we count the slights, suspicions, enmities and war, as certainly evil; while peace is but a doubtful good, since we do not know the hearts of those with whom we choose to be at peace, and even if we could know them today, in any case we know not what they may be like tomorrow. Who, moreover, are wont to be more friendly, or at least ought to be, than those who dwell together in the same home? And yet who is free from doubt in such relations, seeing that from the hidden treachery of such persons great woes have often arisen,—woes the more bitter, as the peace was sweeter that was counted real when it was most cleverly feigned?

That is why the words of Cicero so touch all men's hearts that we lament perforce: "No ambushed foes are harder to detect than those who mask their aim with a counterfeit loyalty or under the guise of some close tie. For against an open adversary you would be on your guard, and so easily escape him; but this hidden evil, being internal and domestic, not only arises but even crushes you before you have a chance to observe and investigate it." That is why the divine word has also been spoken: "A man's foes are even those of his own household," words that are heard with great sorrow of heart. For even if any man is strong enough to bear them with equanimity, or alert enough to guard with prudent foresight against the designs of a pretended friend, nevertheless, if he is himself a good man, he must needs feel grievous pain when he finds by experience that they are utterly base, whether they were always evil and feigned goodness or whether they underwent a change from goodwill to the evil mind that he finds in them. If, then, the home, our common refuge amid the ills of this human life, is not safe, what of the city? The larger it is, the more does its forum teem with lawsuits both civil and criminal, even though its calm be not disturbed by the turbulence, or more often the bloodshed, of sedition and civil wars. Cities are indeed free at times from such events, but never from the threat of them.

vi. *About the Error of Human Judgement, When the Truth Is Hidden.*

What of those judgements pronounced by men on their fellow men, which are indispensable in cities however deep the peace that reigns in them? How sad, how lamentable we find them, since those who pronounce them cannot look into the consciences of those whom they judge. Therefore they are often compelled to seek the truth by torturing innocent witnesses though the case does not concern them. What shall I say of torture inflicted on the accused man himself? The question is whether he is guilty; yet he is tortured even if he is innocent, and for a doubtful crime he suffers a punishment that is not doubtful at all, not because it is discovered that he committed it but because it is not known that he did not commit it. Thus the ignorance of the judge generally results in the calamity of the innocent. And what is still more intolerable, and still more to be deplored and, were it possible, purged by floods of tears, is that the judge, in the act of torturing the accused for the express purpose of avoiding the unwitting execution of an innocent man, through pitiable ignorance puts to death, both tortured and innocent, the very man whom he has tortured in order not to execute him if innocent.

For if he has chosen, applying the wisdom of the philosophers mentioned above, to escape from this life rather than endure those torments any longer, he pleads guilty to a crime that he did not commit. And after he has been condemned and put to death, the judge still does not know whether it was a guilty or an innocent man whom he put to death and whom he tortured that he might not unwittingly execute an innocent man; so he has both tortured an innocent man in order to learn the truth and put him to death without learning it. Since there are such dark places in political life, will a wise judge sit on the bench, or will he not dare to do so? Clearly he will; for the claim of society constrains and draws him until he consents to serve; for to desert his duty to society he counts abominable.

For he does not think it abominable that innocent witnesses are tortured in other men's cases; or that the accused are often overcome by the pain of torture and so make false confessions and are punished, though innocent; or that, although not condemned to death, they often die under torture or as a consequence of torture; or that the accusers, perhaps moved by a desire to benefit society by seeing that crimes do not go unpunished, are themselves condemned by an ignorant judge, if both the evidence of witnesses is false and the defendant with fierce resistance to torture makes no admission of guilt, so that they have no way to prove the truth of their allegations, although those allegations are true. These many great evils he does not count as sins; for the wise judge does not commit them because of any will to do harm but because his action is determined by his ignorance, being also, however, determined by the binding claim of society that requires him to sit in judgement. Here, then, is a clear proof of man's miserable lot, of which I speak, even though we may not accuse the judge of evil intent. But if by ignorance and by office he is constrained to torture and punish the innocent, is it not enough that we acquit him of guilt? Must he be happy as well? How much more creditable is it for his powers of reflection and for his worth as a human being when he acknowledges our pitiable condition in that our acts are determined in spite of us, and loathes his own part in it, sending up, if he is wise as a religious man, a cry to God: "From my necessities deliver thou me!"

VII. *About the Diversity of Languages by Which Human Society Is Divided; and About the Misery of Wars, Even of Those Called Just.*

After the state or city comes the world, to which they assign the third level of human society; they begin with the household, then progressively arrive at the city, and then at the world. And this, like a confluence of waters, is the fuller of dangers as it is the larger. In the first place, the diversity of languages separates one man from another. For if two men, each ignorant of the other's language, meet and are compelled by some necessity not to pass on but to remain together, then it is easier for dumb animals, even of different kinds, to associate together than for them, though both are human beings. For where they cannot communicate their views to one another, merely because they speak different languages, so little good does it do them to be alike by endowment of nature, so far as social unity is concerned, that a man would rather have his dog for company than a foreigner. But the imperial city has taken pains to impose on conquered peoples, as a bond of peace, not only her yoke but her language, so that there has been far from a lack, but rather a superfluity, of interpreters. True; but at what a cost has this unity been achieved, all those great wars, all that human slaughter and bloodshed!

These wars are past; yet the miseries of these evils are not ended. For though foreign foes have not been, and are not, lacking, against whom wars have always been waged and are being waged, nevertheless the very extent of the empire has begotten wars of a worse kind; I mean social and civil wars, by which the human race is more wretchedly shaken, whether while they are actually being waged for the sake of calm at last or while they are a source of fear lest a new storm arise. If it were to attempt to do verbal justice to the many and manifold disasters, to the hard and harsh necessities, though I could not possibly deal with them adequately, where would my long-drawn argument end? But the wise man, they say, will wage just wars. As if he would not all the more, if he remembers his humanity, deplore his being compelled to engage in just wars; for if they were not just, he would not have to wage them, and so a wise man would have no wars. For it is the injustice of the opposing side that imposes on the wise man the necessity of waging just wars; and this injustice, even if no necessity of waging war were to arise from it, must still be deplored by a human being, since human beings perpetrate it. Let every man, then, reflect with sorrow upon all these great evils, so horrible and so cruel, and confess his misery. But if any man has no sorrow in his heart either when he suffers himself or when he imagines such suffering, his case is certainly far more miserable, for he thinks himself happy precisely because he has lost all human feeling to boot.

VIII. *That the Friendship of Good Men Can Not Be Free from Anxiety, So Long as It Is Necessary to Worry About the Dangers of this Life.*

If we escape from a kind of ignorance, akin to madness, that often befalls men in the wretched condition of this life, and that leads them to mistake a foe for a friend or a friend for a foe, what consolation have we in this human society, full of mistakes and distresses, save the unfeigned faith and mutual affection of true and good friends? But the more friends we have, and the more widely scattered they are, the further and more widely spread are our fears lest some evil may befall them among the accumulated evils of this age. For we are anxious not only for fear lest they may be afflicted by hunger, warfare, disease, captivity and the unimaginable sufferings of slavery, but also with far more bitter fear lest friendship be changed into perfidy, malice and villainy. And when these contingencies do occur, more frequently as our friends are the more numerous, and the tidings come to our knowledge, who, save the man who experiences them, can conceive of the pain that consumes our hearts? Indeed, we would rather hear that they were dead, although this, too, we could not hear without sorrow.

For if their lives delighted us with the comforts of friendship, how could it be that their death should bring us no sadness? He who would forbid such sadness must forbid, if he can, all friendly conversation, must interdict or intercept all friendly affection, must break with harsh brutality the bonds of all human relationships, or else lay down the law that they must be so indulged that no pleasure may be derived from them. But if this is utterly impossible, how can it be that a man's death shall not be bitter to us if his life be sweet to us? For hence it is that the sorrow of a heart not devoid of human feeling is like some wound or sore for whose healing we use as salve our kindly messages of comfort. Nor must it be supposed that there is nothing to be healed merely because healing is the easier and the more rapid the finer a man's spirit is. Since, then, the life of mortals is afflicted now more gently, again more harshly, by the death of those very dear to us, and especially of those whose performance of public duties is needful for human society, nevertheless we would rather hear of or behold the death of those whom we love than perceive that they have fallen from faith or virtue, that is, that the soul itself has suffered death. The earth is full of this vast store of evils; wherefore it is written: "Is man's life on earth anything but temptation?" And therefore the Lord himself says: "Woe to the world because of offences"; and again: "Because iniquity shall abound, the love of many shall wax cold." The result is that we feel thankful at the death of good men among our friends, and that, though their death brings sorrow, it is the more surely mitigated in that they have been spared those evils by which in this life even good men are crushed or contaminated or at least are in danger of either fate.

IX. *About the Friendship of the Holy Angels, Which Can Not Be Manifest to Man in this Life Because of the Deceitfulness of the Demons into Whose Power Have Fallen Those Who Judged It Proper to Worship Many Gods.*

On the other hand, the society of the holy angels, which those philosophers who held that the gods are our friends placed at a fourth level as it were (passing from the earth to the universe in order thereby in a way to embrace heaven itself), we have no fear lest such friends bring us grief by their death or deterioration. But because they do not mingle with us with the familiarity of men (which in itself is also one of the distresses of this life), and because, as we read, Satan sometimes takes the form of an angel of light in order to tempt men who are in need of the discipline so provided, or deserve to be deceived, there is great need of God's mercy lest some one, when he thinks that he enjoys the friendship of good angels, be enjoying the feigned friendship of evil demons and suffering from their enmity, which is the more harmful the more shrewd and deceitful they are. Indeed, who is in need of this mercy of God if not men in their great misery, which is so weighed down by ignorance as easily to be deceived by such masquerades? And indeed it is most certain that those philosophers in the sacrilegious city who said that the gods were their friends have fallen into the company of the malignant demons to whom that city itself is altogether subject and with whom it will suffer everlasting punishment. The truth is sufficiently revealed by those beings who are worshipped by them, in the sacred, or rather sacrilegious, rites, and in the most filthy shows in which their crimes are celebrated; it is those same demons on whose authority and demand the worshippers supposed that shows so full of such vile indecencies were required as propitiation.

x. *What Reward Is Begotten for the Saints of Their Victory over the Temptation of this Life.*

But not even the saints and the faithful worshippers of the one true and most high God are safe from the deceptions and the manifold temptations of the demons. For in this region of weakness and in these evil days such anxiety is also not without its uses in causing them to seek with a keener longing that place of safety where peace is most complete and assured. For there the gifts of nature, bestowed on our nature by the creator of all natures, shall be not only good but everlasting, not only as regards the spirit, which is healed by wisdom, but also as regards the body, which will be restored by resurrection. There the virtues shall not struggle against any vice or evil whatsoever, but shall hold in possession the reward of victory, an eternal peace that no adversary can disquiet. For this indeed is the final blessedness, the end of perfect attainment that knows no devouring end. Here, to be sure, we are called blessed when we have peace, however small may be the portion which we can possess here in a good life; but this blessedness, when compared to that final blessedness, is found to be downright misery. So when we mortals have such peace as we can enjoy in this mortal estate, if we live rightly, virtue makes the right use of its good things; but when we have it not, virtue makes good use even of the ills from which men suffer. But true virtue is this: to subordinate all the good things that it makes use of, and all that it does in making good use of good and evil things, and also itself, to that end where our peace shall be so excellent and so great that it cannot be improved or increased.

xi. *About the Blessedness of the Everlasting Peace in Which the Saints Find Their End or True Perfection.*

We might say, therefore, of peace, as we have said of the eternal life, that it is the end of all our good, especially since the sacred psalmist says of the city of God, about which our laborious work is written: "Praise the Lord, Jerusalem, praise thy God, O Zion; for he has strengthened the bars of thy gates; he has blessed thy children within thee; he has made thy borders peace." For when the bars of her gates are strengthened, then none shall go in or come out of her; so we must understand that her borders are that peace whose finality it is our purpose to demonstrate. For even the mystic name of the city itself, Jerusalem, as we have said before, means "vision of peace." But since the word "peace" is often applied to the story of our mortal days, where certainly there is no eternal life, we have preferred to call the end of this city, that in which shall be found its supreme good, eternal life rather than peace. And about this end the Apostle says: "But now, being freed from sin, and become servants to God, you have your fruit unto holiness, and the end life everlasting." But, on the other hand, because the life of the wicked may also be held to be eternal life by those who are not familiar with the holy scriptures, either with an eye to the immortality of the soul that is also taught by certain philosophers, or with an eye to our own belief in the endless punishment of the wicked, who surely cannot be tormented forever if they are not also to live forever, it behooves us to say, in order that all may understand our meaning more easily, that the end of this city, whereby it will possess its supreme good, may be put either way, as peace in everlasting life or as everlasting life in peace. For so great a good is peace that even where earthly and mortal affairs are in question no other word is heard with more pleasure, nothing else is desired with greater longing, and finally nothing better can be found. So if we choose to speak about it at a little greater length, we shall not be tedious to our readers, I think, both because our theme is the end of this city and because of the very sweetness of peace, which is dear to all.

XII. *That Even the Fierceness of Those at War and All the Restless Drives of Men Have in Them a Yearning to Attain the End of Peace, a Good that Is Sought by Every Creature.*

Whoever reviews at all, with me, the pattern of human affairs and our common nature observes that just as there is no man who does not wish joy, so there is no man who does not wish peace. For even they who choose warfare desire nothing but victory; it follows that they desire by waging war to arrive at a glorious peace. For what else is victory but the conquest of the other party to the fight? And when this is achieved, there will be peace. Wars also, then, are waged in a struggle for peace, even by those who seek a field of training for prowess in war, whether in command or in personal combat. It follows that peace is the desired end of war. For every man even in the act of waging war is in quest of peace, but no one is in quest of war when he makes peace. For even those who prefer that a state of peace should be upset do so not because they hate peace but because they desire a different state of peace that will meet their wishes. Therefore they do not desire that there shall be no peace, but only that the peace shall be such as they choose. And supposing even that they have separated themselves from other men by sedition, they cannot effect their design without maintaining some sort of peace with their confederates and fellow conspirators. Why, even robbers, in order the more violently and the more safely to attack the peace of other men, choose to maintain peace with their comrades.

Why, even though one man may be so preëminent in strength and so cautious in letting no one know his secrets that he trusts no partner, but lies in wait and triumphs alone, taking his booty after overcoming and slaying such as he can, yet he keeps up some shadow of peace with those whom he cannot kill and from whom he wishes to conceal his deeds. And in his own home he surely strives to be at peace with his wife and children and any other members of the household, since there is no doubt that he is pleased when they are at his beck and call; for if they disobey, he is angry, he rebukes and punishes, and if need be he secures even by cruelty the peace of his home, which, he judges, cannot exist unless all the other members of the same domestic society are subject to one chief; and this chief, in his own home, is himself. So if he were offered the servitude of many, whether of a city or of a nation, on the same terms that he had imposed on his own household, he would no longer keep himself concealed out of sight like a brigand, but would lift his royal head before men's eyes, though the same covetousness and malice were still in him. Thus all men desire to have peace with their own associates, when they wish them to live as they decree. For even those against whom they wage war they wish, if they can, to make their own, and to impose on them after their subjection the laws of their own peace.

But let us imagine a man such as epic and mythical poetry describe, one so unsociable and wild that they have perhaps preferred to call him a semi-man rather than a man. Although, then, his kingdom was the solitude of a dismal cave, and although he himself was so exceedingly bad that his name derived from it (the Greek for "bad" is *kakos*, and Cacus was his name); although he had no wife to exchange fond words with him, no little children to play with, none to command when they were somewhat bigger, no friends to give him the enjoyment of conversation, not even his father Vulcan (whose happiness he much surpassed merely because he begot no monster like himself); although he gave to none, but took what he chose from any one he chose whenever he could; nevertheless in the very solitude of his cave, "the floor of which was always reeking with fresh carnage," as the poet says, all that he desired was peace unmolested by any, a peace whose calm was untroubled by any man's violence or the fear of it. In a word, he longed to be at peace with his own body; and so far as he succeeded in this, all was well with him. His limbs obeyed his commands; and in order to pacify with all possible speed his mortal nature when it rebelled against him through its impoverishment, and incited hunger to wage a civil war that aimed to sever and eject his soul from his body, he ravished, slew and devoured. And yet, cruel and savage though he was, he was providing by his cruelty and savagery for the peace of his life and safety; so if he had been willing to keep the peace with other men as he was content to keep it in his cave and with himself, he would not be called bad or a monster or a semi-man. Or if the ugliness of his body and his belching of murky flames frightened off human companions, perhaps it was not through lust for harm but through the need of keeping alive that he was fierce. But it may be that he never existed, or more likely, that he was not such as he is described with poetic fancy; for Hercules would be underpraised if Cacus were not too much abused. So the existence of such a man, or rather semi-man, as I have said, like many fictions of the poets, is not credited.

For even the most savage beasts, from whom he derived a part of his savagery (for he was in fact called half-wild), preserve their species by a sort of peace: by cohabitation, by begetting, bearing, suckling and rearing their young, although most of them are not gregarious, but solitary; not like sheep, deer, doves, starlings and bees, but like lions, wolves, foxes, eagles and owls. What tigress does not softly purr over her cubs and subdue her fierceness as she caresses them? What kite, however solitary in circling over his prey, does not join a mate, build a nest, hatch the eggs, rear the young birds and maintain with the mother of his brood as peaceful a domestic society as possible? How much more is a man moved by the laws of his nature, so to speak, to enter upon a fellowship with all his fellow men, and to maintain peace with them, so far as he can, since even wicked men wage war to protect the peace of their own fellows, and would make all men their own, if they could, so that all men and all things might serve one master. And how could that be, unless they accepted his peace either through love or through fear? So pride is a perverse imitation of God. For it abhors a society of peers under God, but seeks to impose its own rule, instead of his, on society. In other words, it abhors the just peace of God, and loves its own unjust peace; but peace, of some kind or other, it cannot help loving. For no creature's vice is so completely at odds with nature that it destroys the very last traces of nature.

He, then, who knows enough to prefer right to wrong and the orderly to the perverse, sees that the peace of the unjust, compared with that of the just, does not deserve the name of peace at all. Yet even the perverted must be in, or in dependence upon, or in accord with a part of the whole order of things in which it rests or of which it is made; otherwise it could not exist at all. Just as if a man were to hang with his head downwards, this position of body and limbs is certainly perverted, because the normal attitude of nature is turned topsy-turvy. This perverted position disturbs the peace of the flesh, and is therefore painful; yet the spirit is at peace with its body, and labours for its preservation, and that is why there is one that suffers. But if it is banished from the body by its pains, then so long as the framework of the limbs remains, there is still a sort of peace among them, and that is why there is still some one to hang there. And because the earthly body presses earthwards, and pulls against the bond by which it is suspended, it tends toward its proper peace, and by the plea of its weight, so to speak, demands a place of rest; and now, though lifeless and without sensation, it does not depart from the peace natural to its rank, whether while possessed of it or while tending toward it. For if preservative and treatment are applied to prevent the form of the corpse from dissolution and disintegration, a sort of peace still unites the several parts, and keeps the whole mass attached to its fitting and therefore its peaceable place in the earth.

But if no treatment for embalming is given, and nature is left to take its course, for a time the body is jarred by warring exhalations, offensive to our senses (for that is what we smell in case of putrefaction), until the body joins company with the elements of the world, and little by little, particle by particle, it departs to enter into their peace. And yet in this process not a whit is abated from the laws of the most high Creator and Ruler by whom the peace of the universe is administered. For although tiny animals breed in the carcass of a larger animal, by the same law of the Creator all these little creatures serve in salutary peace their own little spirits. And although the flesh of dead animals be devoured by other animals, no matter where it is transported, no matter what other things it is mixed with, no matter what transformation or permutation it undergoes, it still finds itself among the same laws that are everywhere diffused for the preservation of every mortal species, and act as peacemakers in that they match the parts that belong together.

XIII.   *About the Universal Peace, Which Amid All Disturbances Whatsoever Is Preserved by a Law of Nature, While Every One Under the Decree of the Just Judge Attains to the Ordered State that He Has Earned by His Free Will.*

The peace of the body, therefore, is an ordered proportionment of its components; the peace of the irrational soul is an ordered repose of the appetites; the peace of the rational soul is the ordered agreement of knowledge and action. The peace of body and soul is the ordered life and health of a living creature; peace between mortal man and God is an ordered obedience in the faith under an everlasting law; peace between men is an ordered agreement of mind; domestic peace is an ordered agreement among those who dwell together concerning command and obedience; the peace of the heavenly city is a perfectly ordered and fully concordant fellowship in the enjoyment of God and in mutual enjoyment by union with God; the peace of all things is a tranquillity of order. Order is the classification of things equal and unequal that assigns to each its proper position.

Therefore the wretched,—for, in so far as they are wretched, they certainly are not in a state of peace,—lack the tranquillity of order, in which there is no tumultuous activity; nevertheless, because they are deservedly and justly wretched, in that very wretchedness of theirs they are still unable to escape from the realm of order. Though they are not indeed united with the blessed, yet it is by a law of order that they are separated from them. And when they are free from tumultuous activity, they are adjusted to their condition, no matter how slightly. Hence there is among them some tranquillity of order, and therefore there is among them some peace. But they are wretched because, although they are to some degree free from anxiety and suffering, they are not in such a case as could justify their being free from anxiety and suffering. Still more wretched are they, however, if they are not at peace with the law by which the natural order is administered. But when they suffer, their peace is embroiled in the part that suffers; but in the part where there is no torment of pain and the frame of nature is not dissolved, peace still abides. Just as there can be life, then, without pain, while there can be no pain without life, so, too, there can be peace without any war, but no war without some sort of peace. This does not follow from the nature of war, but because war is waged by or within persons who have some natural being, for they could not exist if there were not some sort of peace to hold them together.

Therefore there is a nature in which there is no evil, nay, in which no evil can even exist; but there cannot be a nature in which there is no good. Hence not even the nature of the devil himself is evil, so far as it is nature; but perversity makes it evil. So he did not stand steadfast in the truth, yet did not escape the judgement of the truth; he did not remain in the tranquillity of order, yet did not thereby flee from the power of the ordainer. The goodness of God, imparted to his nature, does not remove him from the justice of God, which ordains his punishment; nor does God thereby punish the good that he has created, but the evil that the devil has committed. Nor does God take away all that he gave to his nature; but something he takes, and something he leaves, so that there should be something remaining to feel pain at the loss.

And this very pain is evidence of the good that was taken and the good that was left. For had good not been left, he could not feel pain for the good lost. For a sinner is worse if he rejoices in the loss of righteousness; but he who is tormented, though he may gain no good thereby, yet grieves for the loss of salvation. And since both righteousness and salvation are good, and the loss of any good is cause for grief rather than for joy (at least where there is no compensation in the form of a better good, as righteousness of soul is better than bodily health), surely it is more fitting for an unjust man to grieve in punishment than to rejoice in sin. So even as the rejoicing of a sinner because he has abandoned what is good is evidence of a bad will, so his grief is punishment, because of the good that he has lost, is evidence of a good nature. For he who mourns the lost peace of his nature does so by his possession of some remnants of that peace, by reason of which his nature is friendly to itself. Now it is right that in the last punishment the wicked and impious should weep in their torments for the loss of the good that was in their natures, being aware that he who deprived them is an altogether just God whom they scorned when he was the altogether kindly distributor of bounty.

God, then, the most wise creator and most just ordainer of all natures, who has set upon the earth as its greatest adornment the mortal human race, has bestowed on men certain good things that befit this life; to wit, temporal peace, so far as it can be enjoyed in the little span of a mortal life in terms of personal health and preservation and fellowship with one's kind, and all things necessary to safeguard or recover this peace (such as the objects that are suitably and conveniently available for our senses: light, speech, air to breathe and water to drink, and whatever befits the body, to feed and cover it, to heal and adorn it); all this under the most just condition that every mortal who rightly uses such goods, that are designed to contribute to the peace of mortals, shall receive larger and better goods, that is, the peace of immortality, and the glory and honour appropriate to it in an everlasting life spent in the enjoyment of God and of one's neighbour in union with God; while he who uses the goods of this life perversely shall lose them, and shall not receive those of the everlasting life.

XIV. *About Order and Law, Whether Earthly or Heavenly, by Which Human Society Is Both the Concern of Those Who Rule and Served by Their Concern.*

Therefore every use of temporal things is related to the enjoyment of earthly peace in the earthly city, while in the heavenly city it is related to the enjoyment of everlasting peace. Wherefore, if we were irrational animals, we should seek nothing beyond the ordered proportionment of the components of the body and the assuagement of the appetites; nothing, that is, beyond repose of the flesh and good store of pleasures, so that the peace of the body might further serve the peace of the soul. For if bodily peace be wanting, the peace of the irrational soul is also impaired, because it cannot achieve the assuagement of its appetites. But the two together serve the mutual peace of soul and body, the peace of an ordered life and of health. For just as animals, by avoiding pain, show that they love bodily peace, and by pursuing pleasure in order to satisfy the wants of their appetites show that they love peace of soul, so by their shunning death they give a sufficient indication how great is their love of the peace that harmonizes soul and body.

But because man has a rational soul, he subordinates all that he has in common with the beasts to the peace of the rational soul in order that he may exercise his mind in contemplation and may act in accordance with it, and in order that he may thus enjoy that ordered agreement of knowledge and action which we called the peace of the rational soul. It is for this end that he ought to prefer to be annoyed by no pain, moved by no desire, and dissipated by no death, namely, that he may discover some profitable knowledge and may shape his life and character in accordance with such knowledge. But lest by his very eagerness for knowledge he should fall, through the weakness of the human mind, into some fatal infection of error, he needs divine instruction that he may follow with assurance, and divine assistance that he may follow it as a freeman. And since, so long as he is in this mortal body, he wanders on alien soil far from God, he walks by faith, not by sight, and therefore he subordinates all peace, of body or of soul or of both, to that peace which exists between mortal man and the immortal God, that he may show an ordered obedience in faith under the everlasting law.

Now since the divine instructor teaches two chief precepts, love of God and love of one's neighbour, and since in them man finds three objects of love, God, himself, and his neighbour, and he who loves God does not err in loving himself, it follows that he is concerned also for his neighbour that he should love God, since he is bidden to love his neighbour as himself. He is thus concerned for his wife, his children, his household and for other men so far as he can be; and he would wish his neighbour to be so concerned for him, should he perchance stand in need of it. Therefore he will be at peace, so far as in him lies, with all men in that human peace, or ordered agreement, of which the pattern is this: first, to do harm to no man, and, secondly, to help every man that he can. In the first place, then, he has the care of his own household, inasmuch as the order of nature or of human society provides him with a readier and easier access to them for seeking their interest. Wherefore the Apostle says: "Whosoever does not provide for his own, and especially for those of his household, he denies the faith, and is worse than an infidel." So at this point begins domestic peace, the ordered agreement among those who dwell together, concerning command and obedience. For those who are concerned for others give commands, the husband to his wife, the parents to their children, the masters to their servants; while those who are objects of concern obey; for example, the women obey their husbands, the children their parents, the servants their masters. But in the home of the just man who lives by faith and who is still a pilgrim in exile from the celestial city, even those who give commands serve those whom they seem to command. For they command not through lust for rule but through dutiful concern for others, not with pride in exercising princely rule but with mercy in providing for others.

xv. *About the Freedom Natural to Man, and About the Servitude of Which the Prime Cause Is Sin, Because a Man Whose Will Is Evil, Even Though He Is Not the Property of Another Man, Is the Slave of His Own Lust.*

This is the prescription of the order of nature, and thus has God created man. For, he says: "Let him have dominion over the fish of the sea, and over the birds that fly in the heavens, and over every creeping thing that creeps upon the earth." For he did not wish a rational creature, made in his own image, to have dominion save over irrational creatures: not man over man, but man over the beasts. So it was that the first just men were established as shepherds of flocks, rather than as kings of men, so that even so God might indirectly point out what is required by the principle of gradation among his creatures, and what the guilt of sinners demands; for of course it is understood that the condition of slavery is justly imposed on the sinner. Wherefore we do not read of a slave anywhere in the Scriptures until the just man Noah branded his son's sin with this word; so he earned this name by his fault, not by nature. The origin of the Latin word for "slave" is believed to be derived from the fact that those who by the law of war might have been put to death, when preserved by their victors, became slaves, so named from their preservation. But even this could not have occurred were it not for the wages of sin; for even when a just war is waged, the enemy fights to defend his sin, and every victory, even when won by wicked men, humbles the vanquished through a divine judgement, correcting or punishing their sins. Witness the man of God, Daniel, who in captivity confesses to God his own sins and those of his people, and in pious sorrow recognizes in them the cause of his captivity. The prime cause of slavery, then, is sin, so that man was put under man in a state of bondage; and this can be only by a judgement of God, in whom there is no unrighteousness, and who knows how to assign divers punishments according to the deserts of the sinners.

But as our Lord in heaven says: "Every man who sins is the slave of his sins," so many wicked masters, though they have religious men as their slaves, yet are not on that account themselves free; "For by whom a man is vanquished, to him is he also bound as a slave." And surely it is a happier lot to be slave to a man than to a lust; for the most cruel overlord that desolates men's hearts, to mention no other, is this very lust for overlordship. Moreover, in a peaceful order in which some men are subjected to others, humility is as beneficial to servants as pride is harmful to masters. But by nature, in which God first created man, no man is the slave either of another man or of sin. Yet slavery as a punishment is also ordained by that law which bids us to preserve the natural order and forbids us to disturb it; for if nothing had been done contrary to that law, there would have been nothing requiring the check of punishment by slavery. For this reason too the Apostle admonishes slaves to be subject to their masters, and to serve them heartily and with good will, so that if they cannot be freed by their masters they may themselves make their very slavery in some sense free, by serving not in crafty fear but in faithful affection, until all wickedness pass away and all lordship and human authority be done away with and God be all in all.

XVI.　*About Equitable Rule of Masters over Slaves.*

Therefore even if our righteous fathers had slaves, they so administered domestic peace as to distinguish the lot of children from the condition of slaves in regard to these temporal goods; yet in regard to the worship of God, in whom we should find our hope of everlasting goods, they took thought with an equal affection for all the members of their households. And this the order of nature prescribes, so that from it the name of *paterfamilias* arose, and has been so widely used that even those who rule unjustly are glad to be called by it. But those who are true fathers of their households take thought for all in their households just as for their children, to see that they worship and win God's favour, desiring and praying that they may reach the heavenly home where the duty of commanding men will not be necessary, because there will be no duty of taking thought for those who are already happy in that immortal state; but until they arrive there the fathers are more obligated to maintain their position as masters than the slaves to keep their place as servants.

So if any one in the household by disobedience breaks the domestic peace, he is rebuked by a word or a blow or some other kind of just and legitimate punishment, to the extent permitted by human fellowship, for the sake of the offender, so that he may be closely joined to the peace from which he broke away. For just as it is no kindness to help a man at the cost of his losing a greater good, so it is not blameless behaviour to spare a man at the cost of his falling into a graver sin. Hence blamelessness involves the obligation not only to do evil to no man but also to restrain a man from sinning or to punish him if he has sinned, so that either the man himself who is chastised may be reformed by his experience or others may be deterred by his example. Since, then, a man's house ought to be the beginning or least part of the city, and every beginning ministers to some end of its own kind and every part to the integrity of the whole of which it is a part, it follows clearly enough that domestic peace ministers to civic peace, that is, that the ordered agreement concerning command and obedience among those who dwell together in a household ministers to the ordered agreement concerning command and obedience among citizens. Thus we see that the father of a family ought to draw his precepts from the law of the city, and so rule his houseshold that it shall be in harmony with the peace of the city.

XVII. *About the Origin of Peace and of Discord Between the Heavenly and the Earthly Societies.*

But a household of human beings whose life is not governed by faith pursues an earthly peace by means of the good things and the conveniences of this temporal life, while a household of those who live by faith looks to the everlasting blessings that are promised for the future, using like one in a strange land any earthly and temporal things, not letting them entrap him or divert him from the path that leads to God, but making them a means to brace his efforts to ease the burden and by no means to aggravate the load imposed by the corruptible body, which weighs down the soul. Therefore both kinds of human groups and of households use alike the things that are necessary for this mortal life; but each has its own very different end in using them. So, too, the earthly city, that lives not by faith, seeks an earthly peace, and its end in aiming at agreement concerning command and obedience on the part of citizens is limited to a sort of merging of human wills in regard to the things that are useful for this mortal life. Whereas the heavenly city, or rather the part of it that goes its pilgrim way in this mortal life and lives by faith, needs must make use of this peace too, though only until this mortal lot which has need of it shall pass away. Therefore, so long as it leads its life in captivity, as it were, being a stranger in the earthly city, although it has already received the promise of redemption, and the gift of the spirit as a pledge of it, it does not hesitate to obey the laws of the earthly city whereby matters that minister to the support of mortal life are administered to the end that since this mortal life is common to both, a harmony may be preserved between both cities with regard to the things that belong to it.

But because the earthly city has had certain philosophers of its own, whose doctrine is rejected by the divine teaching, and who followed their own surmise or were deceived by demons, and so believed that there are many gods to be won over to support human interests, and that different provinces belong to different responsibilities of theirs, so that the body is the province of one, the soul of another; and in the body, one governs the head, another the neck, and so forth with each of the several members; likewise in the soul, one presides over the natural intelligence, another over education, another over anger, still another over lust; and in the adjuncts of life, one god cares for flocks, other gods severally for grain, wine, oil, woods, money, navigation, wars and victories, marriage, birth, fecundity and so forth; and because the heavenly city, on the other hand, knew only one

God to be worshipped and believed with faithful piety that he is to be served with that service which in Greek is called *latreia,* and should be rendered only to God, it has come to pass that the heavenly city could not have common laws of religion with the earthly city, and on this point must dissent and become a tiresome burden to those who thought differently, and must undergo their anger and hatred and persecutions, except that at length it shook the hostile intent of its adversaries with fear of its own numbers and with evidence of the ever-present divine aid.

While this heavenly city, therefore, goes its way as a stranger on earth, it summons citizens from all peoples, and gathers an alien society of all languages, caring naught what difference may be in manners, laws and institutions, by which earthly peace is gained or maintained, abolishing and destroying nothing of the sort, nay rather preserving and following them (for however different they may be among different nations, they aim at one and the same end, earthly peace), provided that there is no hinderance to the religion that teaches the obligation to worship one most high and true God. Even the heavenly city, therefore, in this its pilgrimage makes use of the earthly peace, and guards and seeks the merging of human wills in regard to the things that are useful for man's mortal nature, so far as sound piety and religion permit, and makes the earthly peace minister to the heavenly peace, which is so truly peace that it must be deemed and called the only peace, at least of a rational creature, being, as it is, the best ordered and most harmonious fellowship in the enjoyment of God and on one another in God. And when we arrive thither, there shall be no mortal life, but a life indeed; no animal body to burden the soul with its corruption, but a spiritual body that wants nothing and is subdued in every part to the will. This peace the heavenly city during its pilgrimage enjoys by faith, and by this faith it lives justly when it makes the attainment of that peace the goal of every good action in which it engages for the service of God and one's neighbour; for the life of a city is certainly a social life.

XVIII. *How Different the Uncertainty of the New Academy Is from the Certainty of the Christian Faith.*

As to that peculiarity which Varro alleges to be a characteristic of the New Academy, the uncertainty of everything, the city of God utterly denounces such doubt, as madness. About matters that its mind and reason apprehend it has most certain knowledge, even though it is slight because of the corruptible body that weighs down the spirit; for, as the Apostle says: "We know in part." It also trusts in all matters the evidence of the senses, which the mind uses through the agency of the body; for wretchedly deceived indeed is he who supposes that they should never be trusted. It believes, too, in the holy Scriptures, old and new, that we call canonical, whence comes the very faith by which the just man lives; by this faith we walk without doubting, so long as we are exiled from the Lord on our pilgrimage. Provided that this faith is sound and certain, we may without just reproach feel doubt about some matters that neither sense nor reason have perceived, and that have not been revealed to us by the canonical Scriptures, and that have not come to our knowledge through witnesses whom it is absurd not to trust.

xxiv. *What Definition of a People and of a State Must Be Accepted If Not Only the Romans but Other Kingdoms Are to Claim These Titles.*

But if a people be defined not in this but in some other manner, for example, in this way: "A people is a large gathering of rational beings united in fellowship by their agreement about the objects of their love," then surely, in order to perceive the character of each people, we must inspect the objects of its love. Yet whatever it loves, if it is a large gathering, not of cattle but of rational beings, and is united in fellowship by common agreement about the objects of its love, then there is no absurdity in using the term "people" of it; and surely the better the objects of its united love, the better the people, and the worse the objects of its love, the worse the people. According to this definition of ours, the Roman people is a people, and its estate is without doubt a state. But what this people loved in its early and in subsequent times, and by what moral decline it passed into bloody sedition and then into social and civil warfare, and disrupted and corrupted that very unity of heart, which is, so to speak, the health of a people, history bears witness, and I have dealt with it at length in the preceding books. And yet I shall not on this account say either that there is no people or that the people's estate is not a state, so long as there remains, however slight, a gathering of rational beings united in fellowship by a common agreement about the objects of its love. But what I have said about this people and about this state let me be understood to have said and meant about those of the Athenians, those of any other Greeks, of the Egyptians, of that earlier Babylon of the Assyrians and of any other nation whatsoever, when they maintained in their states an imperial sway, whether small or great. For in general a city of the impious, not governed by God, since it is disobedient to the command of God that sacrifice be not offered save to himself only, whereby in that city the soul should exercise righteous and faithful rule over the body and reason over the vices, has no true justice.

xxv. *That There Can Be No True Virtues Where There Is No True Religion.*

For however praiseworthy may seem to be the rule of the soul over the body and of the reason over the vices, if the soul and the reason do not serve God as God has commanded that he should be served, then in no wise do they rightly rule the body and the vices. For what kind of mistress over the body and the vices can a mind be that knows not the true God, and that instead of being subject to his command is prostituted to the corrupting power of the most vicious demons? Accordingly, the very virtues that it thinks it possesses, and by means of which it rules the body and the vices in order to obtain or keep any object whatsoever, if it does not subordinate them to God, are themselves vices rather than virtues. For although some suppose that virtues are true and honourable when they are made subject to themselves and are sought for no further end, even then they are puffed up and proud, and so must be reckoned as vices rather than as virtues. For as it is not something that comes from the flesh that makes the flesh live, but something above it, so it is not something that comes from man but something above man that makes him live a blessed life; and this is true not only of man but of every heavenly domination and power.

xxvi. *About the Peace of a People that Is Alienated from God, and the Use
       Made of It for Pious Ends by the People of God During Their Pilgrimage
       in the World.*

Wherefore, as the life of the flesh is the soul, so the blessed life of man is God,
of whom the sacred scriptures of the Hebrews declare: "Blessed is the people
whose God is the Lord." Wretched, therefore, is the people that is alienated
from that God. Yet even this people loves a peace of its own, which must not be
rejected; but it will not possess it in the end, because it does not make good use
of it before the end. But that it should possess this peace meanwhile in this life
is important for us, too, since so long as the two cities are intermingled we also
profit by the peace of Babylon; and the people of God is by faith so freed from
it as meanwhile to be but strangers passing through. For this reason the Apostle
too admonished the church to pray for its kings and other high persons, adding
these words: "That we may live a quiet and tranquil life with all piety and love."
And the prophet Jeremiah, in predicting the captivity that was to befall the
ancient people of God, and in bidding them by divine inspiration to go obediently
to Babylon and by their very patience to do God service, added his own admonition that they should pray for Babylon, saying: "Because in her peace is your
peace"; that is, of course, the temporal peace of the present that is common to
the good and the evil alike.

xxvii. *About the Peace of the Servants of God, a Peace Whose Perfect Tran-
        quillity Can Not Be Apprehended in this Temporal Life.*

But the peace that is ours we even now enjoy with God by faith, and we shall
enjoy it with him forever by sight. But peace in this life, whether that common
to all men or our own special possession, is such as must be called rather a
solace of our wretchedness than a positive enjoyment of blessedness. Our very
justice, too, though true, thanks to the true final good to which it is subordinated,
is nevertheless in this life only such as consists rather in the remission of sins
than in the perfection of virtues. Witness the prayer of the whole city of God
that is exiled on earth, when it cries out to God through all its members: "Forgive us our debts, as we forgive our debtors." And this prayer is not efficacious
for those whose faith is without works, and dead, but only for those whose faith
brings forth works through love. It is because the reason, though subjected to
God, in this mortal condition and in the corruptible body, which weighs down
the soul, does not perfectly rule the vices, that just men need such a prayer. For
even though the reason exercises command over the vices, surely it is not without
a struggle on their part. And even if we fight the good fight or rule as master,
after foes of that sort have been defeated and subdued, still in this realm of weakness something creeps in, so that sin is found, if not in quick-acting performance,
at least in some tripping utterance or some fitting dalliance of thought.

Hence there is no complete peace so long as mastery is exercised over the vices,
because on the one hand the battle is precarious as long as the war continues
against such vices as resist, while those that have been defeated do not yet permit
a triumph of carefree ease, but are held down under a sway that is still full of
anxiety. Among all these temptations, therefore, about which it has been briefly

said in the divine oracles: "Is man's life on earth anything but temptation?", who will dare assume that his life is such that he need not say to God: "Forgive us our debts," unless it be a proud man, one not truly great, but puffed up and bloated, who is justly resisted by him who gives grace in abundance to the humble? Wherefore it is written: "God resists the proud, but to the humble he gives grace." In this life, accordingly, justice for the individual means that God rules and man obeys, the soul rules over the body and reason rules over the vices even when they are rebellious, whether by subjugating or by withstanding them, and that from God himself we seek to obtain favour for our well-deserving deeds and forgiveness for our sins, and that we offer our service of thanksgiving for the benefits received. But in that final peace to which this justice should be subordinated and for the sake of winning which it should be maintained, since our nature will be healed of its sickness by immortality and incorruption and will have no vices, and since nothing either in ourselves or in another will be at war with any one of us, the reason will not need to rule the vices, since they will be no more; but God will rule man, and soul the body, and we shall find in obeying a pleasure and facility as great as the felicity of our living and reigning. And there, for all and for every one, this state will be everlasting, and its everlastingness will be certain; and therefore the peace of this blessedness, and the blessedness of this peace, will be the highest good.

XXVIII.   *What End Awaits the Wicked.*

But, on the other hand, those who do not belong to that city of God will receive everlasting wretchedness, which is called also the second death, because neither the soul that is alienated from God's life can be said to live there, nor the body, which will be subjected to everlasting torments; and this second death will be all the harder to bear in that it cannot find an end in death. But since, just as wretchedness is the opposite of blessedness, and death of life, so war is the opposite of peace, the question is properly raised what or what sort of war can be understood as present in the final state of the wicked, to correspond to the peace that is heralded and lauded in the final state of the righteous. But let the questioner note what is harmful or destructive in warfare, and he will see that it is nothing but the mutual opposition and conflict of things. Now what war can he imagine more grievous and bitter than one in which the will is so opposed to passion and passion to the will that their enmities can be ended by the victory of neither, and in which the power of pain so contends with the very nature of the body that neither yields to the other? For in this life, when such a conflict arises, either pain conquers, and death takes away feeling, or nature conquers, and health removes the pain. But in the life beyond, pain remains, on the one hand, to torment, and nature lasts, on the other, to feel it; neither ceases to be, lest the punishment also should cease.

But since these are the ultimate limits of good and evil, of which we should seek to win the former and escape the latter, and since there is a judgement through which good men will pass to the former and bad men to the latter, I will, so far as God may grant, deal with this judgement in the following book.

SELECTED BIBLIOGRAPHY

BIBLIOGRAPHIES

Andresen, C., *Bibliographia Augustiniana*, 2nd ed., Darmstadt, 1973.

Augustine Bibliography, Institute des Études Augustiniennes, several volumes, Boston, 1972.

van Bavel, J., *Répertoire bibliographique de saint Augustin, 1950–60*, The Hague, 1963.

TRANSLATIONS

Benjamin, A. and L. Hackstaff, trans., *On Free Choice of the Will*, Indianapolis, 1964.

Brown, R., trans., *S. Aureli Augustini De beata vita*, Washington, D.C., 1944.

Burleigh, J., trans., *Augustine, Earlier Writings*, Philadelphia, 1953.

Deferrari, R., *et al.*, eds. and trans., *Fathers of the Church*, Washington, D.C., 1960–.

Dods, M., ed., *The Works of Aurelius Augustinus*, 15 vols., Edinburgh, 1872–1876.

Garvey, M., trans., *Against the Academicians (Contra Academicos)*, Milwaukee, 1957.

MacCracken, G. and W. Greene, trans., *The City of God*, 3 vols., Cambridge, Mass., 1957–1963.

McKeon, R., ed. and trans., *Selections from Medieval Philosophers, I: Augustine to Albert the Great*, New York, 1929.

Oates, W., ed., *Basic Writings of Saint Augustine*, 2 vols., New York, 1948.

O'Meara, J., ed., *An Augustine Reader*, New York, 1973.

Outler, A., ed. and trans., *Confessions and Enchiridion*, Philadelphia, 1955.

Pusey, E., trans., *The Confessions of St. Augustine*, New York, 1949.

Quasten, J., *et al.*, ed. and trans., *Ancient Christian Writers*, Westminster, Md., 1946–.

Robertson, D., trans., *On Christian Doctrine*, Indianapolis, 1958.

Ryan, J., trans., *The Confessions of St. Augustine*, Garden City, N.Y., 1960.

Schaff, P., *A Select Library of Nicene and Post-Nicene Fathers of the Christian Church*, New York, 1890–1908.

Warner, R., trans., *Confessions*, New York, 1963.

Watts, W., trans., *St. Augustine's Confessions*, Cambridge, Mass., 1919.

STUDIES

Armstrong, A., *St. Augustine and Christian Platonism*, Villanova, 1967.

Arquillière, H., *L'Augustinisme politique; essai sur la formation des théories politiques du moyen-âge*, 2. éd. revue et augmentée, Paris, 1955.

Battenhouse, R., ed., *A Companion to the Study of St. Augustine*, New York, 1955.

Bonner, G., *St. Augustine of Hippo: Life and Controversies*, Philadelphia, 1963.

Bourke, V., *Augustine's Quest for Wisdom*, Milwaukee, 1945.

Bourke, V., *Augustine's View of Reality*, Villanova, Pa., 1964.

Boyer, C., *Essays ancien et nouveaux sur la doctrine de Saint Augustine*, Milano, 1970.

Boyer, C., *L'idée de verité dans la philosophie de saint Augustin*, Paris, 1921.

Brown, P., *Augustine of Hippo*, Berkeley and Los Angeles, 1967.

Bubacz, B., "Saint Augustine's Theory of Perception, *visio corporis* and *visio spiritualis*," *The Modern Schoolman*, LVII (1980), 313–337.

Bubacz, B., "St. Augustine's 'Si fallor, sum,'" *Augustinian Studies*, IX (1978), 35–44.

Burleigh, J., *The City of God, a Study of St. Augustine's Philosophy*, London, 1949.

Callahan, J., *Augustine and the Greek Philosophers*, Villanova, 1967.

Combès, G., *La doctrine politique de saint Augustin*, Paris, 1927.

D'Arcy, M., *et al.*, *Saint Augustine*, New York, 1957.

Deane, H., *The Political and Social Ideas of St. Augustine*, New York, 1963.

Fay, T., " 'Imago Dei'. Augustine's metaphysics of man," *Antonianum*, XLIX (1974), 173–197.

Figgis, J., *The Political Aspects of St. Augustine's City of God*, London, 1921.

Fortin, E., *Political Idealism and Christianity in the Thought of St. Augustine*, Villanova, 1972.

Gilson, E., *The Christian Philosophy of Saint Augustine*, New York, 1960.

Guitton, J., *Le temps et l'éternité chez Plotin et s. Augustin*, 3. éd., Paris, 1959.

Hessen, J., *Augustins Metaphysik der Erkenntnis*, 2. neubearbeitete Auflage, Leiden, 1960.

Hessen, J., *Die Begründung der Erkenntnis nach dem hl. Augustinus*, Münster, 1916. (*Beiträge zur Geschichte der Philosophie des Mittelalters*, XIX, 2.)

Hopkins, J., "Augustine on Foreknowledge and Free Will," *International Journal of the Philosophy of Religion*, VII (1977), 111–126.

Jolivet, R., *Dieu soleil des esprits; ou la doctrine augustinienne de l'illumination*, Paris, 1934.

Lacey, H., "Empiricism and Augustine's Problems about Time," *The Review of Metaphysics*, XXII (1968–1969), 219–245.

Markus, R., ed., *Augustine: A Collection of Critical Essays*, Garden City, 1972.

Markus, R., *Saeculum: History and Society in the Theology of St. Augustine*, London-New York, 1970.

Marrou, H., *Saint Augustin et la fin de la culture antique*, 4. ed., Paris, 1958.

Marrou, H., *St. Augustine and His Influence through the Ages*, New York, 1957.

Mausbach, J., *Die Ethik des heiligen Augustinus*, 2 vols., Freiburg, 1929.

Mourant, J., *Augustine on Immortality*, Villanova, 1969.

Nash, R., "Some Philosophic Sources of Augustine's Illumination Theory," *Augustinian Studies*, II (1971), 47–66.

Nash, R., *The Light of the Mind: St. Augustine's Theory of Knowledge*, Lexington, 1969.

O'Connell, R., *Saint Augustine's Confessions: The Odyssey of the Soul*, Cambridge, Mass., 1969.

O'Connell, R., *Saint Augustine's Early Theory of Man, A.D. 386–391*, Cambridge, Mass., 1968.

Pope, H., *Saint Augustine of Hippo*, Westminster, Md., 1949.

Portalié, E., *A Guide to the Thought of St. Augustine*, Chicago, 1960.

Roberts, L., "Augustine's Version of the Ontological Argument and Platonism," *Augustinian Studies*, IX (1978), 93–101.

Roland-Gosselin, B., *La morale de saint Augustin*, Paris, 1925.

Sirridge, M., "Augustine: every Word is a Name," *The New Scholasticism*, L (1976), 183–192.

BOETHIUS

ca. 4 8 0 – 5 2 4

"THE LAST of the Roman philosophers, and the first of the scholastic theologians" (as he has been described), Boethius was, next to Augustine, the most decisive formative influence on pre-thirteenth century Christian thought. Even after the reintroduction of the complete Aristotelian *corpus* diminished his importance, scholastics continued to study his works and comment on them.

Boethius' contributions to medieval thought were many. In philosophy, thinkers of the eleventh and twelfth centuries gained from him most of the knowledge of Aristotle they possessed; and his translations of Aristotelian logical works, his commentaries on them, and his independent treatises formed the foundations of their logical doctrines. In theology, his use of technical philosophic terms for the solution of theological issues, his rigorous demonstrations, and his distinction between faith and reason contributed to what was to become the scholastic method. Moreover, his contention that each science has its own principles made of theology an autonomous science. His example helped to make the commentary a standard form for teaching and writing, his logical and mathematical works became integral parts of the curriculum of medieval schools, and his *Consolation* provided a noble vision of the philosophic life which, at the same time, was compatible with Christian teachings.

Varied as these contributions are, much of Boethius' fame in modern times rests on his role in the early medieval discussion of universals. Almost as old as philosophy itself, the question "what kind of being do universals have?" had been discussed extensively by Plato, Aristotle, and their followers. But the decisive Platonic and Aristotelian writings were not extant in early medieval times and, in their absence, a passage from Porphyry's *Isagoge* (Introduction to Aristotle's *Categories*) together with Boethius' commentary on it became the fundamental texts on which much of the controversy between Nominalists and Realists rested (see p. 164).

Prior to discussing what genera and species are, Porphyry, in his *Isagoge*, inquires concerning the ontological status of these notions. Do genera and species subsist in themselves or do they exist only in the mind? If they subsist in themselves are they corporeal or incorporeal? If they are incorporeal, do they exist in separation from sensible substances or in conjunction with them? But having raised these questions, Porphyry considers it inappropriate to answer them in an introductory work on logic.

Ever the responsible commentator, Boethius undertakes to answer the questions which Porphyry had left unanswered. Weighing the alternatives proposed, Boethius finds that genera and species subsist not solely in themselves nor do they exist only in the mind. For if genera and species subsist only in themselves, it is difficult to see how they can be common to many individuals. And if they exist only in the mind—not in reality—would it not follow that in thinking them the mind thinks nothing?

Turning to Alexander of Aphrodisias, Boethius finds a solution intermediate between these two extremes. Genera and species, he concludes, exist in things in one respect, in the mind in another. As he puts it in a classical formulation: "they subsist in sensible things, but they are understood apart from bodies."

This solution, as Boethius is well aware, is that of Aristotle, and in a commentary on an Aristotelian work it is the one to be set down. But this solution, as he tells us, is at variance with that of Plato who holds that genera and species are substances existing apart from sensible things. There exists evidence that, for himself, Boethius follows the Platonic solution. For in a passage in the *Consolation*, in which he describes in typical Platonic fashion the mind's ascent from sensation to understanding, he concludes that the understanding "beholds with the clear eye of the mind that simple form itself."

One of Boethius' many incisive statements gave rise to another distinction much discussed by later medievals. Commenting on the difference between God and creatures, he states that in beings other than God, "being" (*esse*) and "that which is" (*id quod est*) are different. In making this distinction Boethius has in mind that while individual substances are composed of various parts, none of these parts make a substance to be what it is. Its determinate characteristic is provided by a unifying and determining principle—its being (*esse*). Though, for Boethius, this distinction serves only to describe the relation between a substance and that principle which makes it to be what it is, Aquinas finds in it a supporting text for his own distinction between "essence" and "existence."

Boethius' numerous definitions became commonplaces in scholastic thought. Two in particular became important for their bearing on theological speculations concerning the Trinity—that of person and that of nature. According to Boethius' definitions, "a person is an individual substance having a rational nature," and "nature is the specific difference that gives form to anything."

Anicius Manlius Severinus Boethius was born about 480 into a prominent senatorial family. Through his studies at Athens he gained the knowledge that later enabled him to translate Greek philosophic writings into Latin.

Following the family tradition, he entered upon a distinguished political career. He soon came to the attention of Theodoric, the Ostrogoth; and, after having served in a number of advisory capacities, he was appointed consul in 510 and "Master of Offices," a position requiring his regular attendance at court, in 522. But his political fortune soon changed. In 523, for reasons still unknown, he was accused of treason and condemned; and after a year spent in prison he was executed.

Early in life, Boethius set himself the monumental task of translating all the works of Plato and Aristotle, showing at the same time that on fundamental philosophic issues the two philosophers agreed. Though Boethius never completed this ambitious undertaking, he succeeded in translating Aristotle's *Organon* and Porphyry's *Isagoge* and in commenting on many of these works. His translations of the *Isagoge*, the *Categories*, and *On Interpretation* together with his various commentaries on these works helped to make up the "old logic" (*logica vetus*), while his translations of the *Prior* and *Posterior Analytics, Topics,* and *On Sophistical Refutation*— unknown until the middle of the twelfth century—formed a part of the then emerging "new logic" (*logica nova*). He composed two commentaries each on the *Isagoge* and *On Interpretation* and one on the *Categories*. However, the status of his commentaries on the remainder of the *Organon* still requires clarification. He commented on Cicero's *Topics* and wrote independent works on categorical and hypothetical syllogisms, on division, and on topical differences.

Boethius' masterwork, however, was his *Consolation of Philosophy* which he wrote during his imprisonment. Gibbon calls it "a golden volume, not unworthy of the leisure of Plato or of Tully." Drawing for his imagery, style, and philosophic notions upon his extensive classical learning, Boethius (in alternating rhyme and prose sections) relates how Lady Philosophy visited him in prison to offer him her consolation and to cure him of his grief. Be not overcome by your misfortunes, she counsels, for the gifts of fortune are fleeting and happiness is not to be found in temporal goods. Only by being like God, who is the highest good, can lasting happiness come to man. But the *Consolation* is not merely an exhortatory work. In it Boethius undertakes to solve the cluster of problems arising from the attempt to justify God's ways to man. Why does evil exist? What are providence, fate, and chance? How can divine predestination and knowledge be reconciled with the freedom of the human will? Though the general tenor of the work is neoplatonic, Boethius freely draws upon Aristotelian and Stoic teachings. Direct references to the Bible or any of the Christian writings are lacking from the work. The *Consolation* was the recipient of many glosses and commentaries and it was translated early into the various European tongues. It became one of the most popular books of medieval times.

In his theological treatises, the titles of which indicate their content, Boethius undertakes to solve a number of theological issues in a precise and rigorous manner. Among these treatises are: *On the Holy Trinity (De sancta Trinitate); Whether Father, and Son, and Holy Spirit May Be Substantially Predicated of Divinity (Utrum Pater et Filius et Spiritus Sanctus de divinitate substantialiter praedicentur); On Person and Two Natures in Christ (De persona et duabus naturis in Christo);* and the treatise appearing below. Boethius explains many Aristotelian terms in these treatises and they found many commentators, Thomas Aquinas among them.

Finally, Boethius composed mathematical treatises which became part of the *quadrivium* (a term which he is said to have coined). He wrote a work on arithmetic (*Institutio arithmetica*), one on music (*Institutio musica*), and possibly a work on geometry.

The first of the following selections is taken from the third book of the *Consolation* where it appears after a section in which Boethius describes the transitory nature of temporal goods. A passage showing that God is the highest good (p. 120) is of special interest for its affinity to Anselm's ontological argument for the existence of God (see p. 150). The second selection, consisting of the complete treatise *How Substances can Be Good in Virtue of their Existence without Being Absolute Goods (Quomodo substantiae in eo quod sint bonae sint cum non substantialia bona)*, provides an excellent illustration of Boethius' method. The treatise is addressed to John, the deacon.

THE CONSOLATION OF PHILOSOPHY

IX

"Let it suffice that we have hitherto discovered the form of false felicity, which if thou hast plainly seen, order now requireth that we show thee in what true happiness consisteth." "I see," quoth I, "that neither sufficiency by riches, nor power by kingdoms, nor respect by dignities, nor renown by glory, nor joy can be gotten by pleasures." "Hast thou also understood the causes why it is so?" "Methink I have a little glimpse of them, but I had rather thou wouldst declare them more plainly."

"The reason is manifest, for that which is simple and undivided of itself, is divided by men's error, and is translated from true and perfect to false and unperfect. Thinkest thou that which needeth nothing, to stand in need of power?" "No," quoth I. "Thou sayest well, for if any power in any respect be weak, in this it must necessarily stand in need of the help of others." "It is true," quoth I. "Wherefore sufficiency and power have one and the same nature." "So it seemeth." "Now thinkest thou, that which is of this sort ought to be despised, or rather that it is worthy to be respected above all other things?" "There can be no doubt of

Reprinted by permission of the publishers from "I. T.," trans. and revised by H. F. Stewart, Boethius, *The Consolation of Philosophy*. Cambridge, Mass.: Harvard University Press, 1936.

this," quoth I. "Let us add respect then to sufficiency and power, so that we judge these three to be one." "We must add it if we confess the truth."

"What now," quoth she, "thinkest thou this to be obscure and base, or rather most excellent and famous? Consider whether that which thou hast granted to want nothing, to be most potent, and most worthy of honour, may seem to want fame, which it cannot yield itself, and for that cause be in some respect more abject." "I must needs confess," quoth I, "that, being what it is, this is also most famous." "Consequently then we must acknowledge that fame differeth nothing from the former three." "We must so," quoth I. "Wherefore that which wanteth nothing, which can perform all things by its own power, which is famous and respected, is it not manifest that it is also most pleasant?" To which I answered: "How such a man should fall into any grief, I can by no means imagine. Wherefore if that which we have said hitherto be true, we must needs confess that he is most joyful and content." "And by the same reason it followeth that sufficiency, power, fame, respect, pleasure have indeed divers names, but differ not in substance." "It followeth indeed," quoth I. "This then, which is one and simple by nature, man's wickedness divideth, and while he endeavoureth to obtain part of that which hath no parts, he neither getteth a part, which is none, nor the whole, which he seeketh not after." "How is this?" quoth I. "He who seeketh after riches," quoth she, "to avoid want, taketh no thought for power, he had rather be base and obscure, he depriveth himself even of many natural pleasures that he may not lose the money which he hath gotten. But by this means he attaineth not to sufficiency, whom power forsaketh, whom trouble molesteth, whom baseness maketh abject, whom obscurity overwhelmeth. Again, he that only desireth power, consumeth wealth, despiseth pleasures, and setteth light by honour or glory, which is not potent. But thou seest how many things are wanting to this man also. For sometimes he wanteth necessaries, and is perplexed with anxieties, and being not able to rid himself, ceaseth to be powerful, which was the only thing he aimed at. The like discourse may be made of honours, glory, pleasures. For since every one of these things is the same with the rest, whosoever seeketh for any of them without the rest obtaineth not that which he desireth." "What then?" quoth I. "If one should desire to have them all together, he should wish for the sum of happiness, but shall he find it in these things which we have showed cannot perform what they promise?" "No," quoth I. "Wherefore we must by no means seek for happiness in these things which are thought to afford the several portions of that which is to be desired." "I confess it," quoth I, "and nothing can be more true than this." "Now then," quoth she, "thou hast both the form and causes of false felicity; cast but the eyes of thy mind on the contrary, and thou shalt presently espy true happiness, which we promised to show thee." "This," quoth I, "is evident, even to him that is blind, and thou showedst it a little before, while thou endeavouredst to lay open the causes of the false. For, if I be not deceived, that is true and perfect happiness which maketh a man sufficient, potent, respected, famous, joyful. And that thou mayest know that I understood thee aright, that which can truly perform any one of these because they are all one, I acknowledge to be full and perfect happiness." "O my scholar, I think thee happy by having this opinion, if thou addest this also." "What?" quoth I. "Dost thou imagine that there is any mortal or frail thing which can cause this happy estate?" "I do not," quoth I, "and that hath been so proved by thee, that more cannot be desired." "Wherefore these things seem to afford men the images of the true good, or certain unperfect goods, but they cannot give them the true and perfect good itself." "I am of the same mind," quoth I. "Now then, since thou knowest wherein true happiness consisteth, and what have only a false show of it, it remaineth that thou shouldst learn where thou mayest seek for this which is true." "This is that," quoth I, "which I have long earnestly expected." "But since, as Plato teacheth (in Timaeus), we must implore God's assistance even in our least affairs, what, thinkest thou, must we do now, that we may deserve to find the seat of that sovereign good?" "We must," quoth I, "invocate the Father of all things, without whose remembrance no beginning hath a good foundation." "Thou sayest rightly," quoth she, and withal sung in this sort.

IX

O Thou, that dost the world in lasting order guide,
Father of heaven and earth, Who makest time
swiftly slide,
And, standing still Thyself, yet fram'st all moving
laws,
Who to Thy work wert moved by no external cause:
But by a sweet desire, where envy hath no
place,
Thy goodness moving Thee to give each thing his
grace,
Thou dost all creatures' forms from highest patterns
take,
From Thy fair mind the world fair like Thyself
doth make.
Thus Thou perfect the whole perfect each part
dost frame.
Thou temp'rest elements, making cold mixed with
flame
And dry things join with moist, lest fire away
should fly,
Or earth, opprest with weight, buried too low
should lie.
Thou in consenting parts fitly disposed hast
Th' all-moving soul in midst of threefold nature
placed,
Which, cut in several parts that run a different race,
Into itself returns, and circling doth embrace
The highest mind, and heaven with like proportion
drives.
Thou with like cause dost make the souls and lesser
lives,
Fix them in chariots swift, and widely scatterest
O'er heaven and earth; then at Thy fatherly
behest
They stream, like fire returning, back to Thee,
their God.
Dear Father, let my mind Thy hallowed seat
ascend,

Let me behold the spring of grace and find Thy
    light,
That I on Thee may fix my soul's well cleared sight.
Cast off the earthly weight wherewith I am opprest,
Shine as Thou art most bright, Thou only calm and
    rest
To pious men whose end is to behold Thy ray,
Who their beginning art, their guide, their bound,
    and way.

X

Wherefore since thou hast seen what is the form of perfect and imperfect
good, now I think we must show in what this perfection of happiness is placed.
And inquire first whether there can be any such good extant in the world, as
thou has defined; lest, contrary to truth, we be deceived with an empty show
of thought. But it cannot be denied that there is some such thing extant which
is as it were the fountain of all goodness. For all that is said to be imperfect is
so termed for the want it hath of perfection. Whence it followeth that if in any
kind we find something imperfect, there must needs be something perfect also
in the same kind. For if we take away perfection we cannot so much as devise
how there should be any imperfection. For the nature of things began not from
that which is defective and not complete, but, proceeding from entire and
absolute, falleth into that which is extreme and enfeebled. But *if*, as we showed
before, there be a certain imperfect felicity of frail goods, it cannot be doubted
but that there is some solid and perfect happiness also." "Thou hast," quoth I,
"concluded most firmly and most truly." "Now where this good dwelleth,"
quoth she, "consider this. The common conceit of men's minds proveth that
God the Prince of all things is good. For, since nothing can be imagined better
than God, who doubteth but that is good than which is nothing better? And
reason doth in such sort demonstrate God to be good that it convinceth Him
to be perfectly good. For unless He were so, He could not be the chief of all
things. For there would be something better than He, having perfect goodness, which could seem to be of greater antiquity and eminence than He.
For it is already manifest that perfect things were before the imperfect. Wherefore, lest our reasoning should have no end, we must confess that the Sovereign
God is most full of sovereign and perfect goodness. But we have concluded
that perfect goodness is true happiness, wherefore true blessedness must necessarily be placed in the most high God." "I agree," quoth I, "neither can this
be any way contradicted." "But I pray thee," quoth she, "see how boldly
and inviolably thou approvest that which we said, that the Sovereign God
is most full of sovereign goodness." "How?" quoth I. "That thou presumest
not that this Father of all things hath either received from others that sovereign good with which He is said to be replenished, or hath it naturally in
such sort that thou shouldst think that the substance of the blessedness which
is had, and of God who hath it, were diverse. For if thou thinkest that He had
it from others, thou mayest also infer that he who gave it was better than
the receiver. But we most worthily confess that He is the most excellent of all
things. And if He hath it by nature, but as a diverse thing, since we speak of
God the Prince of all things, let him that can, invent who united these diverse

things. Finally, that which is different from anything, is not that from which it is understood to differ. Wherefore that which is naturally different from the sovereign good, is not the sovereign good itself. Which it were impious to think of God, than whom, we know certainly, nothing is better. For doubtless the nature of nothing can be better than the beginning of it. Wherefore I may most truly conclude that which is the beginning of all things to be also in His own substance the chiefest good." "Most rightly," quoth I. "But it is granted that the chiefest good is blessedness?" "It is," quoth I. "Wherefore," quoth she, "we must needs confess that blessedness itself is God." "I can neither contradict," quoth I, "thy former propositions, and I see this illation followeth from them."

"Consider," saith she, "if the same be not more firmly proved hence, because there cannot be two chief goods, the one different from the other. For it is manifest that of those goods which differ, the one is not the other, wherefore neither of them can be perfect, wanting the other. But manifestly that which is not perfect, is not the chiefest, wherefore the chief goods cannot be diverse. Now we have proved that both blessedness and God are the chiefest good, wherefore that must needs be the highest blessedness which is the highest divinity." "There can be nothing," quoth I, "concluded more truly than this, nor more firmly in arguing, nor more worthy God himself." "Upon this then," quoth she, "as the geometricians are wont, out of their propositions which they have demonstrated, to infer something which they call *porismata* (deductions) so will I give thee as it were a *corollarium*. For since that men are made blessed by the obtaining of blessedness, and blessedness is nothing else but divinity, it is manifest that men are made blessed by the obtaining of divinity. And as men are made just by the obtaining of justice, and wise by the obtaining of wisdom, so they who obtain divinity must needs in like manner become gods. Wherefore everyone that is blessed is a god, but by nature there is only one God; but there may be many by participation." "This is," quoth I, "an excellent and precious *porisma* or *corollarium*." "But there is nothing more excellent than that which reason persuades us to add." "What?" quoth I.

"Since," quoth she, "blessedness seemeth to contain many things, whether do they all concur as divers parts to the composition of one entire body of blessedness, or doth some one of them form the substance of blessedness to which the rest are to be referred?" "I desire," quoth I, "that thou wouldst declare this point, by the enumeration of the particulars." "Do we not think," quoth she, "that blessedness is good?" "Yea, the chiefest good," quoth I. "Thou mayest," quoth she, "add this to them all. For blessedness is accounted the chiefest sufficiency, the chiefest power, respect, fame, and pleasure. What then? Are all these—sufficiency, power, and the rest—the good in the sense that they are members of it, or rather are they referred to good as to the head?" "I understand," quoth I, "what thou proposest, but I desire to hear what thou concludest." "This is the decision of this matter. If all these were members of blessedness, they should differ one from another. For this is the nature of parts, that being divers they compose one body. But we have proved that all these are one and the same thing. Wherefore they are no members, otherwise blessedness should be compacted of one member, which cannot be." "There is no doubt of this," quoth I, "but I expect that which is behind." "It is manifest that the rest are to be referred to goodness; for sufficiency is desired, because it is esteemed good, and likewise power, because that likewise is thought to be good. And we may conjecture the same of respect, fame, and pleasure. Wherefore goodness is the sum and cause of all that is desired. For that which is neither good indeed, nor beareth any show of goodness, can by no means be sought after. And contrariwise those things which are not good of their own nature, yet, if they seem such, are desired as if they were truly good. So that the sum, origin, and cause of all that is sought after is rightly thought to be goodness. And that on account of which a thing is sought, seemeth to be the chief object of desire. As if one would ride for his health, he doth not so much desire the motion of riding, as the effect of health. Wherefore, since all things are desired in respect of goodness, they are not so much wished for as goodness itself. But we granted that to be blessedness for which other things are desired, wherefore in like manner only blessedness is sought after; by which it plainly appeareth, that goodness and blessedness have one and the self-same substance." "I see not how any man can dissent." "But we have showed that God and true blessedness are one and the self-same thing." "It is so," quoth I. "We may then securely conclude that the substance of God consisteth in nothing else but in goodness."

X

Come hither, all you that are bound,
Whose base and earthly minds are drowned
By lust which doth them tie in cruel chains:
Here is a seat for men opprest,
Here is a port of pleasant rest;
Here may a wretch have refuge from his pains.
No gold, which Tagus' sands bestow,
Nor which on Hermus' banks doth flow,
Nor precious stones which scorchéd Indians get,
Can clear the sharpness of the mind,
But rather make it far more blind,
And in the farther depth of darkness set.
For this that sets our souls on work
Buried in caves of earth doth lurk.
But heaven is guided by another light,
Which causeth us to shun the dark,
And who this light doth truly mark,
Must needs deny that Phoebus' beams are bright.

XI

"I consent," quoth I, "for all is grounded upon most firm reasons." "But what account wilt thou make," quoth she, "to know what goodness itself is?" "I will esteem it infinitely," quoth I, "because by this means I shall come to know God also, who is nothing else but goodness." "I will conclude this," quoth she, "most certainly, if those things be not denied which I have already proved." "They shall not," quoth I. "Have we not proved," quoth she, "that those things which are desired of many, are not true and perfect goods, because they differ one from another and, being separated, cannot cause complete and absolute goodness, which is only found when they are united as it were into one form and causality, that the same may be sufficiency, power, respect, fame, and pleasure? And except they be all one and the same thing, that they have nothing worth the desiring?" "It hath been proved," quoth I, "neither can it be any way doubted of." "Those things, then, which, when they differ, are not good and when they are one, become good, are they not made good by obtaining unity?" "So methink," quoth I. "But dost thou grant that all that is good is good by partaking goodness?" "It is so." "Thou must grant then likewise that unity and goodness are the same. For those things have the same substance, which naturally have not diverse effects." "I cannot deny it," quoth I. "Knowest thou then," quoth she, "that everything that is doth so long remain and subsist as it is one, and perisheth and is dissolved so soon as it ceaseth to be one?" "How?" "As in living creatures," quoth she, "so long as the body and soul remain united, the living creature remaineth. But when this unity is dissolved by their separation, it is manifest that it perisheth, and is no longer a living creature. The body also itself, so long as it remaineth in one form by the conjunction of the parts, appeareth the likeness of a man. But if the members of the body, being separated and sundered, have lost their unity, it is no longer the same. And in like manner it will be manifest to him that will descend to other particulars, that everything continueth so long as it is one, and perisheth when it loseth unity." "Considering more particulars, I find it to be no otherwise." "Is there anything," quoth she, "that in the course of nature, leaving the desire of being, seeketh to come to destruction and corruption?" "If," quoth I, "I consider living creatures which have any nature to will and nill, I find nothing that without extern compulsion forsake the intention to remain, and of their own accord hasten to destruction. For every living creature laboureth to preserve his health, and escheweth death and detriment. But what I should think of herbs, and trees, and of all things without life, I am altogether doubtful."

"But there is no cause why thou shouldst doubt of this, if thou considerest first that herbs and trees grow in places agreeable to their nature, where, so much as their constitution permitteth, they cannot soon wither and perish. For some grow in fields, other upon hills, some in fenny, other in stony places, and the barren sands are fertile for some, which if thou wouldst transplant into other places they die. But nature giveth every one that which is fitting, and striveth to keep them from decaying so long as they can remain. What should I tell thee, if all of them, as it were thrusting their head into the ground, draw nourishment by their roots, and convey substance and bark by the inward pith? What, that always the softest, as the pith, is placed within, and is covered without by the strength of the wood, and last of all the bark is exposed to the weather, as being best able to bear it off? And how great is the diligence of nature that all things may continue by the multiplication of seed; all which who knoweth not to be, as it were, certain engines, not only to remain for a time, but successively in a manner to endure for ever? Those things also which are thought to be without all life, doth not every one in like manner desire that which appertaineth to their own good? For why doth levity lift up flames, or heaviness weigh down the earth, but because these places and motions are convenient for them? And that which is agreeable to everything conserveth it, as that which is opposite causeth corruption. Likewise those things which are hard, as stones, stick most firmly to their parts, and make great resistance to any dissolution. And liquid things, as air and water, are indeed easily divided, but do easily also join again. And fire flieth all division. Neither do we now treat of the voluntary motions of the understanding soul, but only of natural operations. Of which sort is, to digest that which we have eaten, without thinking of it, to breathe in our sleep not thinking what we do. For even in living creatures the love of life proceedeth not from the will of the soul, but from the principles of nature. For the will many times embraceth death upon urgent occasions, which nature abhorreth; and contrariwise the act of generation, by which alone the continuance of mortal things is maintained, is sometimes bridled by the will, though nature doth always desire it. So true it is that this self-love proceedeth not from any voluntary motion, but from natural intention. For providence gave to her creatures this as the greatest cause of continuance, that they naturally desire to continue so long as they may, wherefore there is no cause why thou shouldst any way doubt that all things which are desire naturally stability of remaining, and eschew corruption."

"I confess," quoth I, "that I now see undoubtedly that which before seemed very doubtful." "Now that," quoth she, "which desireth to continue and remain seeketh to have unity. For if this be taken away, being itself cannot remain." "It is true," quoth I. "All things then," quoth she, "desire unity." I granted it to be so. "But we have showed that unity is the same as goodness." "You have indeed." "All things then desire goodness, which thou mayest define thus: Goodness is that which is desired of all things." "There can be nothing imagined more true. For either all things have reference to no one principle and, being destitute as it were of one head, shall be in confusion without any ruler: or if there be anything to which all things hasten, that must be the chiefest of all goods." "I rejoice greatly O scholar," quoth she, "for thou hast fixed in thy mind the very mark of verity. But in this thou hast discovered that which a little before thou saidest thou wert ignorant of." "What is that?" quoth I. "What the end of all things is," quoth she. "For certainly it is that which is desired of all things, which since we have concluded to be goodness, we must also confess that goodness is the end of all things.

XI

He that would seek the truth with thoughts profound
And would not stray in ways that are not right,
He to himself must turn his inward sight,
And guide his motions in a circled round,
Teaching his mind that ever she design
Herself in her own treasures to possess:
So that which late lay hidden in cloudiness
More bright and clear than Phoebus' beams shall shine.
Flesh hath not quenchéd all the spirit's light,
Though this oblivion's lump holds her opprest.
Some seed of truth remaineth in our breast,
Which skilful learning eas'ly doth excite.
For being askt how can we answer true
Unless that grace within our hearts did dwell?
If Plato's heavenly muse the truth us tell,
We learning things remember them anew.

XII

Then I said that I did very well like of Plato's doctrine, for she had brought these things to my remembrance now the second time, first, because I lost their memory by the contagion of my body, and after when I was oppressed with the burden of grief. "If," quoth she, "thou reflectest upon that which heretofore hath been granted, thou wilt not be far from remembering that which in the beginning thou confessedst thyself to be ignorant of." "What?" quoth I. "By what government," quoth she, "the world is ruled." "I remember," quoth I, "that I did confess my ignorance, but though I foresee what thou wilt say, yet I desire to hear it more plainly from thyself." "Thou thoughtest a little before that it was not to be doubted that this world is governed by God." "Neither do I think now," quoth I, "neither will I ever think, that it is to be doubted of, and I will briefly explicate the reasons which move me to think so. This world could never have been compacted of so many divers and contrary parts, unless there were One that doth unite these so different things; and this disagreeing diversity of natures being united would separate and divide this concord, unless there were One that holdeth together that which He united. Neither would the course of nature continue so certain, nor would the different parts hold so well-ordered motions in due places, times, causality, spaces and qualities, unless there were One who, Himself remaining quiet, disposeth and ordereth this variety of motions. This, whatsoever it be, by which things created continue and are moved, I call God, a name which all men use."

"Since," quoth she, "thou art of this mind, I think with little labour thou mayest be capable of felicity, and return to thy country in safety. But let us consider what we proposed. Have we not placed sufficiency in happiness, and granted that God is blessedness itself?" "Yes truly." "Wherefore," quoth she, "He will need no outward helps to govern the world, otherwise, if He needed anything, He had not full sufficiency." "That," quoth I, "must necessarily be so." "Wherefore He disposeth all things by Himself." "No doubt He doth," quoth I. "But it hath been proved that God is goodness itself." "I remember it very well," quoth I. "Then He disposeth all things by goodness: since He governeth all things by Himself, whom we have granted to be goodness. And this is as it were the helm and rudder by which the frame of the world is kept steadfast and uncorrupted." "I most willingly agree," quoth I, "and I foresaw a little before, though only with a slender guess, that thou wouldst conclude this." "I believe thee," quoth she, "for now I suppose thou lookest more watchfully about thee to discern the truth. But that which I shall say is no less manifest." "What?" quoth I. "Since that God is deservedly thought to govern all things with the helm of goodness, and all these things likewise, as I have showed, hasten to goodness with their natural contention, can there be any doubt made but that they are governed willingly, and that they frame themselves of their own accord to their disposer's beck, as agreeable and conformable to their ruler?" "It must needs be so," quoth I, "neither would it seem an happy government, if it were an imposed yoke, not a desired health." "There is nothing then which, following nature, endeavoureth to resist God." "Nothing," quoth I. "What if anything doth endeavour," quoth she, "can anything prevail against Him, whom we have granted to be most powerful by reason of His blessedness?" "No doubt," quoth I, "nothing could prevail." "Wherefore there is nothing which either will or can resist this sovereign goodness." "I think not," quoth I. "It is then the sovereign goodness which governeth all things strongly, and disposeth them sweetly." "How much," quoth I, "doth not only the reason which thou allegest, but much more the very words which thou usest, delight me, that folly which so much vexed me may at length be ashamed of herself."

"Thou hast heard in the poets' fables," quoth she, "how the giants provoked heaven, but this benign fortitude put them also down, as they deserved. But wilt thou have our arguments contend together? Perhaps by this clash there will fly out some beautiful spark of truth." "As it pleaseth thee," quoth I. "No man can doubt," quoth she, "but that God is almighty." "No man," quoth I, "that is well in his wits." "But," quoth she, "there is nothing that He who is almighty cannot do." "Nothing," quoth I. "Can God do evil?" "No," quoth I. "Wherefore," quoth she, "evil is nothing, since He cannot do it who can do anything." "Dost thou mock me," quoth I, "making with thy reasons an inextricable labyrinth, because thou dost now go in where thou meanest to go out again, and after go out, where thou camest in, or dost thou frame a wonderful circle of the simplicity of God? For a little before taking thy beginning from blessedness, thou affirmedst that to be the chiefest good which thou saidst was placed in God, and likewise thou provedst, that God Himself is the chiefest good and full happiness, out of which thou madest me a present of that inference, that no man shall be happy unless he be also a God. Again thou toldest me that the form of goodness is the substance of God and of blessedness, and that unity is the same with goodness, because it is desired by the nature of all things; thou didst also dispute that God governeth the whole world with the helm of goodness, and that all things obey willingly, and that there is no nature of evil, and thou didst explicate all these things with no foreign or far-fetched proofs, but with those which were proper and drawn from inward principles, the one confirming the other."

"We neither play nor mock," quoth she, "and we have finished the greatest matter that can be by the assistance of God, whose aid we implored in the beginning. For such is the form of the Divine substance that it is neither divided into outward things, nor receiveth any such into itself, but as Parmenides saith of it:

> In a body like a sphere well-rounded on all sides,

it doth roll about the moving orb of things, while it keepeth itself unmovable. And if we have used no far-fetched reasons, but such as were placed within the compass of the matter we handled, thou hast no cause to marvel, since thou hast learned in Plato's school that our speeches must be like and as it were akin to the things we speak of.

XII

Happy is he that can behold
The well-spring whence all good doth rise,
Happy is he that can unfold
The bands with which the earth him ties.
The Thracian poet whose sweet song
Performed his wife's sad obsequies,

And forced the woods to run along
When he his mournful tunes did play,
Whose powerful music was so strong
That it could make the rivers stay;
The fearful hinds not daunted were,
But with the lions took their way,
Nor did the hare behold with fear
The dog whom these sweet notes appease.
When force of grief drew yet more near,
And on his heart did burning seize,
Nor tunes which all in quiet bound
Could any jot their master ease,
The gods above too hard he found,
And Pluto's palace visiting.
He mixed sweet verses with the sound
Of his loud harp's delightful string,
All that he drank with thirsty draught
From his high mother's chiefest spring,
All that is restless grief him taught,
And love which gives grief double aid,
With this even hell itself was caught,
Whither he went, and pardon prayed
For his dear spouse (unheard request).
The three-head porter was dismayed,
Ravished with his unwonted guest,
The Furies, which in tortures keep
The guilty souls with pains opprest,
Moved with his song began to weep.
Ixion's wheel now standing still
Turns not his head with motions steep.
Though Tantalus might drink at will,
To quench his thirst he would forbear.
The vulture full with music shrill
Doth not poor Tityus' liver tear.
'We by his verses conquered are,'
Saith the great King whom spirits fear.
'Let us not then from him debar
His wife whom he with songs doth gain.
Yet lest our gift should stretch too far,
We will it with this law restrain,
That when from hell he takes his flight,
He shall from looking back refrain.'
Who can for lovers laws indite?
Love hath no law but her own will.
Orpheus, seeing on the verge of night
Eurydice, doth lose and kill
Her and himself with foolish love.
But you this feigned tale fulfil,
Who think unto the day above
To bring with speed your darksome mind.
For if, your eye conquered, you move
Backward to Pluto left behind,
All the rich prey which thence you took,
You lose while back to hell you look.

HOW SUBSTANCES CAN BE GOOD IN VIRTUE OF THEIR EXISTENCE WITHOUT BEING ABSOLUTE GOODS

You ask me to state and explain somewhat more clearly that obscure question in my *Hebdomads* concerning the manner in which substances can be good in virtue of existence without being absolute goods. You urge that this demonstration is necessary because the method of this kind of treatise is not clear to all. I can bear witness with what eagerness you have already attacked the subject. But I confess I like to expound my *Hebdomads* to myself, and would rather bury my speculations in my own memory than share them with any of those pert and frivolous persons who will not tolerate an argument unless it is made amusing. Wherefore do not you take objection to the obscurity that waits on brevity; for obscurity is the sure treasure-house of secret doctrine and has the further advantage that it speaks a language understood only of those who deserve to understand. I have therefore followed the example of the mathematical and cognate sciences and laid down bounds and rules according to which I shall develop all that follows.

I. A common conception is a statement generally accepted as soon as it is made. Of these there are two kinds. One is universally intelligible; as, for instance, "if equals be taken from equals the remainders are equal." Nobody who grasps that proposition will deny it. The other kind is intelligible only to the learned, but it is derived from the same class of common conceptions; as "Incorporeals cannot occupy space," and the like. This is obvious to the learned but not to the common herd.

II. Being (*esse*) and the thing that is (*id quod est*) are different. Simple Being awaits manifestation, but a thing is and exists as soon as it has received the form which gives it Being.

III. A thing that exists can participate in something else; but absolute Being can in no wise participate in anything. For participation is effected when a thing already is; but it is something after it has acquired Being.

IV. That which exists can possess something besides itself. But absolute Being has no admixture of aught besides Itself.

V. Merely to be something and to be something absolutely are different; the former implies accidents, the latter connotes a substance.

VI. Everything that is participates in absolute Being through the fact that it exists. In order to be something it participates in something else. Hence that which exists participates in absolute Being through the fact that it exists, but it exists in order to participate in something else.

VII. Every simple thing possesses as a unity its absolute and its particular Being.

Reprinted by permission of the publishers from Loeb Classical Library, H. F. Stewart and E. K. Rand, trans., Boethius, *The Theological Tractates* and *The Consolation of Philosophy*, Cambridge, Mass.: Harvard University Press, 1936.

VIII.   In every composite thing absolute and individual Being are not one and the same.

IX.   Diversity repels; likeness attracts. That which seeks something outside itself is demonstrably of the same nature as that which it seeks.

These preliminaries are enough then for our purpose. The intelligent interpreter of the discussion will supply the arguments appropriate to each point.

Now the problem is this. Things which are, are good. For all the learned are agreed that every existing thing tends to good and everything tends to its like. Therefore things which tend to good are good. We must, however, inquire how they are good—by participation or by substance. If by participation, they are in no wise good in themselves; for a thing which is white by participation in whiteness is not white in itself by virtue of absolute Being. So with all other qualities. If then they are good by participation, they are not good in themselves; therefore they do not tend to good. But we have agreed that they do. Therefore they are good not by participation but by substance. But those things whose substance is good are substantially good. But they owe their actual Being to absolute Being. Their absolute Being therefore is good; therefore the absolute Being of all things is good. But if their Being is good, things which exist are good through the fact that they exist and their absolute Being is the same as that of the Good. Therefore they are substantial goods, since they do not merely participate in goodness. But if their absolute Being is good, there is no doubt but that, since they are substantial goods, they are like the First Good and therefore they will have to be that Good. For nothing is like It save Itself. Hence all things that are, are God—an impious assertion. Wherefore things are not substantial goods, and so the essence of the Good does not reside in them. Therefore they are not good through the fact that they exist. But neither do they receive good by participation, for they would in no wise tend to good. Therefore they are in no wise good.

This problem admits of the following solution. There are many things which can be separated by a mental process, though they cannot be separated in fact. No one, for instance, can actually separate a triangle or other mathematical figure from the underlying matter; but mentally one can consider a triangle and its properties apart from matter. Let us, therefore, abstract mentally for a moment the presence of the Prime Good, whose Being is admitted by the universal consensus of learned and unlearned opinion and can be deduced from the religious beliefs of savage races. The Prime Good having been thus for a moment abstracted, let us postulate as good all things that are, and let us consider how they could possibly be good if they did not derive from the Prime Good. This process leads me to perceive that their Goodness and their existence are two different things. For let me suppose that one and the same substance is good, white, heavy, and round. Then it must be admitted that its substance, roundness, colour, and goodness are all different things. For if each of these qualities were the same as its substance, weight would be the same thing as colour or goodness, and goodness would be the same as colour; which is contrary to nature. Their Being then in that case would be one thing, their quality another, and they would be good, but they would not have their absolute Being good. Therefore if they really existed at all, they would not be from good nor good, they would not be the same as good, but Being and Goodness would be for them two different things. But if they were nothing else but good substances, and were neither heavy, nor coloured, and possessed neither spatial dimension nor quality, beyond that of goodness, they (or rather it) would seem to be not things but the principle of things. For there is one thing alone that is by nature good to the exclusion of every other quality. But since they are not simple, they could not even exist at all unless that which is the one sole Good willed them to be. They are called good simply because their Being is derived from the Will of the Good. For the Prime Good is essentially good in virtue of Being; the secondary good is in its turn good because it derives from the good whose absolute Being is good. But the absolute Being of all things derives from the Prime Good which is such that of It Being and Goodness are rightly predicated as identical. Their absolute Being therefore is good; for thereby it resides in Him.

Thereby the problem is solved. For though things be good through the fact that they exist, they are not like the Prime Good, for the simple reason that their absolute Being is not good under all circumstances, but that things can have no absolute Being unless it derive from the Prime Being, that is, the Prime Good; their substance, therefore, is good, and yet it is not like that from which it comes. For the Prime Good is good through the fact that it exists, irrespective of all conditions, for it is nothing else than good; but the second good if it derived from any other source might be good, but could not be good through the fact that it exists. For in that case it might possibly participate in good, but their substantial Being, not deriving from the Prime Good, could not have the element of good. Therefore when we have mentally abstracted the Prime Good, these things, though they might be good, would not be good through the fact that they exist, and since they could not actually exist unless the true good had produced them, therefore their Being is good, and yet that which springs from the substantial Good is not like its source which produces it. And unless they had derived from it, though they were good yet they could not be good through the fact that they exist because they were apart from good and not derived from good, since that very good is the Prime Good and is substantial Being and substantial Good and essential Goodness. But we need not say that white things are white through the fact that they exist; for they drew their existence from the will of God, but not their whiteness. For to be is one thing; to be white is another; and that because He who gave them Being is good, but not white. It is therefore in accordance with the will of the Good that they should be good through the fact that they exist; but it is not in accordance with the will of one who is not white that a thing have a certain property making it white in virtue of its Being; for it was not the will of One who is white that gave them Being. And so they are white simply because One who was not white willed them to be white; but they are good through the fact that they exist because One who was good willed them to be good. Ought, then, by parity of reason, all things to be just because He is just who willed them to be? That is not so either. For to be good involves Being, to be just involves an act. For Him being and action are identical; to be good and to be just are one and the same for Him. But being and action are not identical for us, for we are not simple. For us, then, goodness is not the same thing as justice, but we all have the same sort of Being in virtue of our existence. Therefore all things are good, but all things are not just. Finally, good is a general, but just is a species, and this species does not apply to all. Wherefore some things are just, others are something else, but all things are good.

SELECTED BIBLIOGRAPHY

TRANSLATIONS

Edman, I., ed., *Boethius, The Consolation of Philosophy*, New York, 1943.

Greene, R., trans., *The Consolation of Philosophy*, New York, 1962.

McKeon, R., ed. and trans., *Selections from Medieval Philosophers, I: Augustine to Albert the Great*, New York, 1929.

Shapiro, H., ed., *Medieval Philosophy*, New York, 1964.

Stewart, H. and E. Rand, trans., *Boethius, The Theological Tractates* and *The Consolation of Philosophy*, rev. ed., rev. trans. of the *Tractates* by S. Tester, with a new English trans. of the *Consolation* by S. Tester, 2 vols. in 1, London, 1973.

Stump, E., trans., *Boethius's De topicis differentiis*, Ithaca, 1978.

Watts, V., trans., *Boethius, The Consolation of Philosophy*, Baltimore, 1969.

STUDIES

Barrett, H., *Boethius: Some Aspects of his Times and Work*, Cambridge, 1940.

Courcelle, P., *La Consolation de Philosophie dans la tradition littéraire, antécédents et postérité de Boèce*, Paris, 1967.

Dürr, K., *The Propositional Logic of Boethius*, Amsterdam, 1951.

Patch, H., *The Tradition of Boethius; a Study of his Importance in Medieval Culture*, New York, 1935.

Rand, E., *Founders of the Middle Ages*, Cambridge, Mass., 1941.

JOHN SCOTUS ERIUGENA

ca. 8 1 0 – ca. 8 7 7

J OHN SCOTUS ERIUGENA was a rather singular figure within medieval Christian thought. Possessed of an original philosophic gift and able to use the writings of the theologians of the Eastern Church (Gregory of Nazianz, Gregory of Nyssa, Pseudo-Dionysius, and Maximus the Confessor), he formulated a metaphysical system in which he sought to fuse Christian and neoplatonic teachings. His writings appear to have been read in his own time and he had some influence on later thinkers, but there is a sense in which he was outside the main stream of medieval Christian thought.

The interpretation of Eriugena's teachings is not an easy task. On the one hand, he cites Scripture and the writings of the Greek and Latin Fathers and expresses himself in the language of orthodox Christian thought. On the other, many passages in his work have a pantheistic ring. Probably he was an orthodox Christian expressing himself in language theologically difficult at times, but it can be seen why he is sometimes considered a pantheist in Christian guise. His discussion of how faith and reason are related reflects a certain ambiguity of expression, if not of thought. Using an Augustinian notion, he affirms that belief must precede all understanding; but he interprets many scriptural passages as metaphors needing to be translated into philosophical terms, and he holds that when faith and reason conflict, the teachings of reason must prevail.

"Nature" is the fundamental concept of Eriugena's thought. Identifying nature with being or reality, he defines it as the totality of "those things which are and those which are not." This most general description of nature includes even God, though it does not seem to follow that Eriugena considered God as a part of nature or that, for him, God and nature are identical.

Distinguishing between creating and created beings and using these terms and their negations in all possible combinations, Eriugena divides nature into four species. There is, first of all, nature which creates, but is not created.

Then there is nature which is created and creates. Thereafter comes nature which is created, but does not create and, finally, there is nature which neither creates nor is created. Having made these logical distinctions, Eriugena proceeds to interpret them ontologically.

Nature which creates but is not created is identical with God, who is the uncaused cause who created all things out of nothing. Viewed in this manner God is the transcendent God described in Scripture. But, at the same time, God is said to be the essence of all things, their beginning, middle and end, and a being appearing in all things. According to this description, God is immanent.

Though God's essence is unknowable in itself, man can attain a certain measure of knowledge about God. To describe what man can know of God, Eriugena makes use of the threefold theology of the Greek Fathers. According to this doctrine, God is described negatively by denying of Him all things which are, positively by affirming of Him all things which are, and superlatively by saying that attributes applied to Him and creatures exist in a superior manner in Him. The ten Aristotelian categories, Eriugena states (developing an Augustinian point), are inapplicable to God.

From God, who is uncreated but creates, proceeds that nature which is created and creates. Eriugena identifies this nature with the primordial causes, Ideas, predestinations, or prototypes of earlier thinkers (see p. 12). The primordial causes are the exemplary causes of all things and they were implanted by God, the Father, within the Divine Word, the Son. But since, in God, there is no making in time, Eriugena affirms, in language later criticized by theologians, that the primordial causes are co-eternal with God, though, as he adds by way of modification, "not completely co-eternal."

From the primordial causes flows that nature which is created but does not create. This is the world of angels, men, and bodies. To describe the creation of the world, Eriugena uses a variety of metaphors, all analogies for emanation. For example, the world is said to come from God as water from a fountain. Then again, the world is said to be related to God as the radii of a circle to its center. In still another way, Eriugena describes creation as the self-manifestation or revelation of God (theophany). In line with this description, he affirms that God, in making the world, makes Himself. However, in somewhat more orthodox language, creation is said to result from the influence of the Holy Spirit on the primordial causes.

The fourth division of nature (that which neither creates nor is created) refers once again to God. But whereas in the earlier description God was considered as the source of all beings, He is now understood as the final goal to which all things return. Described as "deification," this return does not bring about the obliteration of all distinctions between God and creatures. Though mutable matter will disappear, neither man nor the world will become identical with God. Once again using theological language, Eriugena describes man's return as the redemption of fallen man by the Incarnate Logos.

John Scotus Eriugena was born in Ireland *ca.* 810 and was educated in a monastery there. Since, in the ninth century, Greek was still taught in the Irish schools, Eriugena gained a knowledge of that language as part of his education. In the 840s he went to France where Charles the Bald appointed him head of the palace school. Eriugena became involved in the controversy between Hincmar, the bishop of Rheims, and Gottschalk, a monk, concerning divine predestination. At the request of Hincmar, Eriugena wrote his *Concerning Predestination* (*De praedestinatione*) but the work did not find favor with either party to the dispute and it soon came under suspicion of heresy. Eriugena's general position was condemned by councils of Valence (855) and Langres (859). It appears that he died *ca.* 877.

Besides composing independent works, Eriugena translated and commented on the writings of theologians of the Eastern Church. He translated Gregory of Nyssa's. *On the Making of Man,* and works by Pseudo-Dionysius and Maximus the Confessor. His most important work was *On the Division of Nature* (*De divisione naturae*) which contains the metaphysical system outlined above. In addition, a commentary on Boethius' *Consolation,* glosses on Boethius' theological writings, and glosses on the Gospel according to John are attributed to him.

The following selections are all taken from the first book of the *On the Division of Nature.* The first contains Eriugena's definition of nature and the four species into which it is divided. But, since nature is the totality of those things which are and those which are not, there follows a description of five ways in which things are said to be and not to be.

In the second selection, Eriugena undertakes to clarify a patristic statement affirming that God not only creates, but also is created in things. This passage provides not only a glimpse of his doctrine of creation, but it is an excellent illustration of his dialectical method. The final selection contains his account of the threefold manner in which Divine attributes are to be understood.

ON THE DIVISION OF NATURE

BOOK I

Magister. "While considering, and, as diligently as (my) powers allow, inquiring into the first and highest division of all things, which can be perceived by the soul, or which surpass its reach, into those things which are, and those which are not, a general verbal designation of all these occurred to me, which in greek is called *physis,* in latin, *natura.* Or does it seem otherwise to you?

Translated by C. Schwarz. Reprinted by permission of the translator.

Disciple. No indeed, I agree; for even I, although I am (only) entering on the way of reasoning find these to be so.

Magister. Therefore nature is the general name, as we have said, of all things which are and which are not.

Disciple. It is indeed; for nothing in the universe can occur to our thoughts which could lack such a designation.

Magister. Since therefore we agree concerning the generality of this designation, I should like you to discourse on the principle (*ratio*) of its division through differentiae into species: or if it pleases you, I shall first attempt the dividing, but it will be your task to judge of the divisions.

Disciple. Begin, I beg you, for I am impatient, wanting to hear from you the true principle (*ratio*) of these things.

1. *Magister.* It seems to me that the division of nature receives four species through four differentiae: of which the first is into that which creates and is not created; second into that which is created and creates; third into that which is created and does not create; fourth into that which neither creates nor is created. Of these four there are two pairs of opposites; for the third division is opposed to the first, the fourth to the second; but the fourth is placed with the impossible, whose differentia is not-being-able-to-be. Does such a division seem right to your or not?

Disciple. Right indeed: but I should like you to go over it again so that the opposition of the aforesaid forms may shine forth more clearly.

Magister. You see, unless I am mistaken, the opposition of the third species to the first. For the first creates and is not created; to which that which is created and does not create is opposed *ex contrario*. The second, moreover, to the fourth; inasmuch as the second is both created and creates, which the fourth, which neither creates nor is created, contradicts universally.

Disciple. I see clearly. But the fourth species which has been adjoined by you disturbs me very much. For in no way should I dare to hesitate concerning the other three, since the first is understood, as I judge, in the cause of all those things, which are and which are not; but the second is understood in the primordial causes; the third is understood in those things of which we become aware in generation in times and places. And therefore it is necessary to argue each of them more subtly, as I see.

Magister. You think rightly. But by what order of reasoning the course is to be held, that is, what species of nature should be discussed first, I commit to your judgment.

Disciple. It seems right to me, to say of the first before the others whatever the light of minds has bestowed.

2. *Magister.* So be it. But first I think that we ought to speak briefly of the highest and principal division of all things, as we have said, into those things which are and those which are not.

Disciple. Rightly and prudently. For I see that reasoning should begin from no other starting point: not only because it is the first differentia of all things, but because it both seems to be and is more obscure than the others.

Magister. Consequently this primordial discretive (class producing) differentia of all things requires certain modes of interpretation.

3. The first of these modes seems to be that, through which reason (*ratio*) induces us to say, that all things which are susceptible to corporeal sense or to the perception of intelligence can reasonably be said to be; but those things, which through the excellence of their nature elude not only the material, (*hylion*) that is, every sensitive power, but also the intellect and reason (*ratio*), seem rightly not to be. Which latter things are not rightly understood except in God alone, and in matter, and in the reasons (*rationes*) and essences of all things which are constituted by Him. And not without cause; for He who alone truly is, is the essence of all things, as Dionysius the Areopagite says: *The being,* he says, *of all things is superbeing Divinity.* Gregory the Theologian also with many reasons (*rationes*) confirms that no substance or essence, whether of a visible or invisible creature can be comprehended as to what it is (*quid sit*) by the intellect or by reason (*ratio*). For just as God himself in himself as beyond every creature is comprehended by no intellect, so also the *ousia* (essence) considered in the most secret recesses of the creature made by him and existing in him, is incomprehensible. For whatever in any creature is perceived by the corporeal sense, or considered by the intellect is nothing else than a certain accident incomprehensible per se of each essence, as has been said. For the essence which is known through quality, quantity, form, matter, or a certain differentia, place or time, is not the what (*quid*), but the that (*quia*). This therefore is the first and highest mode of the division of the things which are said to be and not to be; because the mode, which seems admissible in a certain way, (namely) the mode consisting in the privations of relations with respect to substances, such as sight and blindness with respect to the eyes; should not be admitted at all, as I judge. For I do not see how that which entirely is not, nor is able to be, nor surpasses the intellect because of the excellence of its existence, can be received into the divisions of things, unless by chance someone might say that absences and privations of things which are, are not entirely nothing, but that they are supported by a certain marvelous natural power of those things of which they are the privations or absences or oppositions, so that in a certain way they are.

4. Therefore let the second mode of being and of not being be that, which is considered in the orders and differentiae of the natures of creatures, which beginning from the most pre-eminent intellectual power placed closest to God descends as far as the extremity of the rational and irrational creature; that is, to speak more plainly, from the most sublime angel down to the extreme part of the rational and irrational soul, namely the nutritive and augmentative life. That general part of the soul which nourishes and augments the body is the lowest. Whence each order including the very last one looking downwards, which is (the order) of bodies, and in which the whole division is terminated, can in a marvelous manner of understanding be said to be and not to be. For affirmation of the inferior is a negation of the superior. And again negation of the inferior is an affirmation of the superior. And in the same way affirmation of the superior is a negation of the inferior. Negation indeed of the superior will be an affirmation of the inferior. The affirmation, certainly, of man, I mean insofar as mortal, is the negation of the angel. Negation indeed of man is an affirmation of the angel: and on the contrary. For if man is a rational animal, mortal and visible, an angel in fact is neither a rational animal, nor mortal, nor visible. Likewise if an angel is an essential intellectual motion regarding God

and the causes of things, man in fact is not an essential intellectual motion regarding God and the causes of things. And the same law can be observed in all celestial essences, until the highest order of all things is reached; but the highest order is terminated in a supreme negation upward. For its negation asserts no creature superior to itself. Now there are three orders, which they call *homotageis* (of the same order); of which the first are Cherubim, Seraphim, and Thrones; the second Virtues, Powers, Dominations; the third Principles, Archangels, Angels. But downwards the lowest (order) of bodies only negates or affirms (what is) superior to itself, because it has nothing below itself, to either deny or affirm, because it is preceded by all things superior to itself, but it precedes no thing inferior to itself. For this reason (*ratio*) likewise every order of the rational and intellectual creature is said to be and not to be. For *it is* insofar as it is known by superiors or by itself, and *it is not*, insofar as it does not permit itself to be comprehended by inferiors.

5. The third mode is observed not unfittingly in those things, by which the plenitude of this visible world is perfected, and in their preceding causes in the most secret recesses of nature. For whichever of these causes is formed matter is known through generation in times and places, is said to be, by a curious human habit (of speech). But moreover whatever is contained in the very recesses of nature, and does not appear in formed matter either in place or time or in the other accidents, is said not to be by the same aforesaid habit (of speech). Examples of this mode appear widely, and most of all in human nature. For since God has constituted all men simultaneously in that first and one man, whom he made to his image, but did not produce them at once in this visible world, rather at certain times and in certain places bringing the nature, which he had founded simultaneously, into visible being (*essentiam*), according to a certain series, as he himself knew it (from the beginning), these who already appear visibly in the world and have appeared are said to be; those who are latent thus far, but nevertheless are to be, are said not to be. There is this difference between the first and third mode. The first mode is generally in all things, which have been made simultaneously and once in causes and effects. The third specially in those things which are partly latent thus far in their causes, and partly apparent in their effects, out of which the fabric of this world is properly woven. To this mode pertains that reason (*ratio*) which considers the power of seeds, whether in animals, or in trees, or in herbs. For the power of seeds, at that time when it is quietly at rest in the secrets of nature, because it does not yet appear, is said not to be; but as soon as it has appeared in the birth and growth of animals or in the flowers or the fruits of trees and herbs, it is said to be.

6. The fourth mode is that mode which says according to the philosophers (and) not improbably, that those things only truly are, which are comprehended by the intellect alone; but things which through generation are varied, united, separated by additions or subtractions of matter, also by intervals of places and by motions of time, are truly said not to be, as are all bodies, which can come to be and can be corrupted.

7. The fifth mode is that which reason (*ratio*) observes in human nature alone. Which (human nature) when it has deserted by sinning the dignity of the

divine image in which it properly subsists, has deservedly lost its being, and therefore it is said not to be. But when human nature, restored by the grace of the only begotten son of God is led back to the pristine state of its substance, in which it has been made according to the image of God, it begins to be, and begins to live in him who was made according to the image of God. What the Apostle says seems to pertain to this mode; *And he calls those things that are not, as those that are;* that is, those who have been lost in the first man, and who have fallen to a certain insubsistence, God the Father calls through faith in his Son, so that they may be, just as they, who have already been born again in Christ. And yet this could be understood also of those persons whom God calls daily from the secret recesses of nature, where they are estimated not to be, that they may appear visibly in form, and in matter, and in other ways, in which hidden things can appear, and whatever a more searching mind (*ratio*) can find beyond these modes. But as I judge, enough has been said concerning these things for the present, unless it seems otherwise to you.

Disciple. Enough indeed, unless what seems to be said by Saint Augustine in his Exemeron should disturb me for a short time; that is, that *the angelic nature was made before every creature in dignity, not in time;* and through this also considered the primordial causes of everything except itself, that is, the angelic nature considered the principal exemplars, which the Greeks name *prōtotypa,* first in God, then in itself, then considered the creatures themselves in their effects.

. . .

11. *Magister.* And so of the aforesaid divisions of Nature the first differentia seen by us is into that which creates and is not created. Not unreasonably, because such a species of Nature is predicated rightly of God alone, who alone is understood as the *anarchos,* i.e., without a beginning, creating all things, because the principal cause of all things, which have been made from him and through him, alone is, and by this he is also the end of all things which are from him. For all things desire him. Therefore he is the beginning, middle and end. The beginning, because all things which participate (in) essence are from him; but the middle because they subsist and are moved in him and through him; the end, indeed, because they are moved to him seeking the quiet of their motion and the stability of their perfection.

Disciple. I believe most firmly, and, insofar as it is given, I understand that this is predicated rightly only of the divine cause of all things, because it (cause) alone creates all things, which are from it, and is created from nothing superior as though preceding it. For it itself is the highest and sole cause of all things, which subsist from it and in it.

12. Nevertheless I should like to know, what your opinion is concerning this thing. For it disturbs me not a little that most often in the books of the holy Fathers, who attempted to argue about divine nature, I find that it not only creates all things, which are, but also is created. Inasmuch as they say it makes them and is made, and creates and is created. Therefore if this is so, I do not easily find how our reasoning could stand. For we say that it (divine nature) alone creates, but is created by nothing.

Magister. You are disturbed with cause; for I both wonder much concerning this, and I should have wished to have known through you how these things which seem to be contrary, could fail to be opposed to each other, and how true reason (*ratio*) is to be consulted about this.

Disciple. I pray, begin; for I am awaiting your opinion and your way of reasoning concerning such things, not mine.

Magister. Accordingly, I judge that we should consider first, if it seems appropriate, concerning the name itself, which is most used in sacred Scripture, which is God. For although divine nature is denominated by many names, as it is Goodness, Being, Truth, and others of this kind, nevertheless Scripture most frequently uses that divine name.

Disciple. That is plainly seen.

Magister. And thus the etymology of this name has been assumed from the Greeks. For it is derived either from the verb, which is *theōrō*, that is, I see; or from the verb *theō*, that is, I run; or what is more probable it is said rightly to be derived from both, because one and the same meaning is present. For when *theos* (God) is deduced from the verb *theōrō* (I see), he is interpreted as seeing. For he himself sees in himself all things which are, while he looks upon nothing outside himself, because there is nothing outside himself. But when from the verb *theō* (I run), *theos* (God) is rightly understood as running. For he himself runs in all things, and rests in no way, but fills all things by running; as it is written: *his speech runs swiftly*. Nevertheless he is moved in no way: inasmuch as restful motion and mobile rest are said most truly of God. For he rests incommutably in himself, never deserting his natural immobility. But he moves himself through all things, that they may be those things, which subsist essentially from himself; for all things are made by his motion. And through this it is one and the same meaning in the two interpretations of his name, which is God. For to run through all things is not other to God than to see all things; but just as by seeing, and so also by running all things are made.

Disciple. It has been persuaded sufficiently and probably concerning the etymology of the name. But I do not see sufficiently, whither he may move himself, who is everywhere, without whom nothing can be, and outside of whom nothing is extended; for he is the place and the limit of all things.

Magister. I have said that God is moved not outside himself, but by himself, in himself, to himself. For no other motion ought to be believed (to be) in him, beyond the appetite of his will, by which he wills that all things be made; just as his rest is understood not as if it came to rest after motion, but as the incommutably proposed object of his same will, by which he defines the permanence of all things in the incommutable stability of their ratios. For rest or motion is not properly said (to be) in him. For these two seem to be opposite to each other: but true reason (*ratio*) prohibits that opposites be thought or understood in him, particularly since rest is properly the end of motion. But God does not begin to be moved in order to arrive at a certain state. Therefore these names, just as also many similar (names) are referred from the creature to the Creator through a certain divine metaphor. Nor unreasonably, since he is the cause of all things, which are in rest and in motion. For by him they begin to run, that they may be, since he is the principle of all things, and through him they are brought to him by a natural motion, that they may rest eternally and incommutably in him, since he is the end and the quiet of all things. For they desire nothing beyond him. For in him they find the beginning and end of their motion. Therefore God is said (to be) running, not because he runs outside of himself, who always stands

immutably in himself, who fills all things; but because he makes everything run
from things non-existing into things existing.

Disciple. Return to what was proposed (for investigation) for these things
do not seem to be said unreasonably.

Magister. Tell me, I beg you, what proposal do you seek. For when we attempt to say something about incidental questions, we most often forget the
principal question.

Disciple. Have we not proposed this, that we should investigate in proportion
to our powers, by what reason (*ratio*) those who argue concerning the divine
nature say that it both creates and is created? For that it (divine nature) creates
all things, no one of intelligence assuredly doubts; but in what way it is said
to be created has seemed to us not to be passed over perfunctorily.

Magister. In fact so. But, as I judge, from these things which have been said
before, not a slight entrance to the solving of this question has been opened?
For it was deduced by us, that nothing else is to be understood by the motion
of the divine nature than the proposal of divine will to the founding of those
things, which are to be made. Divine nature, which is nothing else than divine
will, therefore is said to be made in all things. For being and willing are not
distinct in it, but one and the same willing and being (is) in establishing all
things which were seen to be made. For example, if one said, that the motion
of the divine will is brought about for this, that those things, which are, might
be: therefore it creates all things, which it brings out of nothing, that they may
be in being from non-being; but it is created, because nothing besides itself is
essentially; for it is the essence of all things. For just as there is no natural good
besides itself, but everything which is said to be good, is good from participation of
the one highest good: so everything which is said to exist, does not exist in itself,
but exists truly by a participation of the existing nature (divine nature). And
not only as it has been considered, in those things, which have been said before,
is the divine nature said to be made, as well as in those who are reformed by
faith, hope and charity and the other virtues, the Word of God is born in a
marvelous and ineffable way, as the Apostle says speaking of Christ: *Who has
been made in us wisdom from God, and justification, and redemption;* but also
it is not unfittingly said to have been made, because it, which is invisible per se,
appears in all the things, which are. For our intellect too, before it arrived at
thought and memory, is not unreasonably said to be; for it is invisible per se, and
is known by no one except by God and by ourselves. But as soon as it has arrived
at thought, and receives a form from certain phantasms, it is said not without
cause to be made. For it (intellect) which was unformed before it arrived at
memory is made in memory, receiving certain forms of things, or of words, or of
colours and of the other sensibles; then it receives as it were a second forming,
when by certain signs of forms, or of words, that is letters, which are signs of
words, and figures, which are signs of forms, it is formed by the mathematical, or
the other sensible indices, through which it can be insinuated to the senses of those
experiencing (these signs). By this similitude, although it is remote from the divine nature, nevertheless I judge that it can be persuaded, how it (divine nature),
while it creates everything, and cannot be created by anything, is created in a marvelous way, in all things which are from it; so just as the intelligence of the mind,
or the design, or counsel, or in whatever way this our innermost and first motion

can be spoken of, when, as we have said, it has arrived at thought, and has received certain forms of phantasms, and then has proceeded in the sign of words, or in the indices of sensible motions, is not unfittingly said to be made; for it becomes formed in phantasms, which per se is without every sensible form: thus the divine essence, which subsisting per se surpasses every intellect, is rightly said to be created, in these things, which have been made from it and through it and in it and for it, that it may be known in them whether by the intellect, if they are intellectual only, or if they are sensitive by sense, by those, i.e., who investigate it (divine essence) by right study.*

Disciple. Enough has been said about these things, as I judge.

. . .

13. . . . . *Disciple.* Already I see the response of the aforesaid Theologian entirely supported by the truth. For the name of the relation, whether in divine or in human nature, cannot be understood in substance or essence, as has been persuaded. Nevertheless I should like to know plainly and briefly through you, whether all the categories, since they are ten in number, can be predicated truly and properly of the one highest essence of divine goodness in three substances, and of the three substances in the same one essence.

Magister. Concerning this difficulty, I do not know who can say briefly and plainly. For either one should be silent once and for all concerning a cause of this kind, and leave it to the simplicity of orthodox faith; for it surpasses every intellect, as it is written: *Who alone has immortality and inhabits inaccessible light;* or if anyone should have begun to argue about it, necessarily he will persuade in the likeness of truth in many ways and by many arguments, using the two principle parts of Theology, namely affirmative (*affirmativa*), which is called *katafatikē* by the Greeks, and negative (*abnegativa*), which is called *apofatikē* (deprivative). Indeed one, *apofatikē* (the negative), denies that the divine essence or substance is something of those things which are, that is, which can be said or understood; but the other, *katafatikē* (affirmative), predicates of it all things which are, and therefore is said (to be) affirmative, not that it confirms something to be of those things which are, but it would persuade that all things, which are from it, can be predicated of it. For it can be reasonably signified causally through the things of which it is the cause. For it says that it is truth, goodness, essence, light, justice, sun, star, spirit, water, lion, city, worm and other innumerable things. And it not only teaches it (cause) from those things which are according to nature, but from those contrary to nature, when it says it is inebriated and is foolish and is insane. But concerning these things it is not our intention to treat now, for enough has been said concerning such things by holy Dionysius the Areopagite in symbolic Theology. And therefore we should return to that which has been sought by you. For you had sought whether all the categories are properly to be predicated of God or some of them.

Disciple. Assuredly we should return. But first it is to be considered, as I judge, why the aforesaid most holy father and Theologian should have pronounced that the aforesaid names, I mean, essence, goodness, truth, justice, wisdom, and others of that kind, which seem to signify not only divine, but even most divine things, and nothing else than that very divine substance or essence, are to be taken metaphorically, that is, transferred from creature to creator. For

* As the intellect is formed in the phantasms, so God is formed in the creation.

we should not think that he said such things without a certain mystic and secret reason (*ratio*).

Magister. You are very watchful; for I see that this also is not to be passed over inconsiderately. And I should like you to respond through answering this question, whether you understand anything as opposed to God or as co-understood with him. I mean by opposed either through privation, or through contrariety, or through relation, or through absence: but by co-understood, that is, understood eternally simultaneously with him, nevertheless not coessential with him.

Disciple. I see clearly what you would like and through this I dare to say neither something opposed to him, nor (something) co-understood to him *heterousion* (diverse essences), that is, that which is of another essence than he is. For opposite things are always opposed to each other through a relation in such a way, that they both begin to develop simultaneously, and they cease to be simultaneously, as long as they are of the same nature, as the simple to the double, subsesquialter to the sesquialter; either through negation, as (for example) it is, it is not; or through natural qualities; through absence, as light and darkness; or according to privation, as death and life; or through a contrary, as sanity and imbecility, speech and silence. But these are attributed by right reason (*ratio*) to those things, which are accessible to intellect and sense, and through this they are not in God. Certainly those things, which differ from each other, cannot be eternal. For if they were eternal, they would not differ from each other. For eternity is similar to itself, and is whole through everything, one simple and individual it subsists in itself. And indeed it is the one principle and the one end of all things, differing in nothing from itself.

14. I do not know who would dare to affirm (that) that which is not co-essential with him, is by the same reason (*ratio*) coeternal with God. For if this can be thought or found, it necessarily follows, that there is not one principle of all things, but two distinct (ones) or many, widely different from each other. Which true reason (*ratio*) is accustomed to reject without any hesitation. From one all things properly begin to be, but from two or many nothing (begins to be).

Magister. You determine rightly, as I think. If therefore the aforesaid divine names refer to other names directly opposed to themselves, necessarily also the things, which are properly signified by them, are understood to possess contrarieties opposite to each other, and through this they cannot properly be predicated of God, to whom nothing (is) opposed, or with whom nothing is observed differing coeternally in nature. For of the aforesaid names and of others similar to it, true reason (*ratio*) can discover no one for which there cannot be discovered some other name differing from it either in some opposed division or in the same genus with it. And that which we know in names it is necessary that we should know in those things, which are signified by them. But although the divine significations, which are predicated of God in sacred Scripture transferred from the creature to the Creator—if indeed it is rightly said that anything can be predicated of God, which is to be considered in another place—are innumerable and by the parvity of our reasoning can neither be discovered nor simultaneously tied together, nevertheless a few divine designations should be proposed for the sake of example. God then is called essence, but properly he is not essence, to whom nothing is opposed; therefore he is *hyperousios*, that is, superessential. Likewise he is called goodness, but properly he is not goodness; for evil is opposed to goodness; therefore *hyperagathos* (supergood), more than good, and *hyperagathotēs* (supergoodness), that is, more than goodness. He is said to be Deus, but he is not properly Deus; for blindness is opposed to vision, and not seeing to seeing: therefore *hypertheos* (superseeing), more than seeing, if *theos* is interpreted as he who sees. But if you should turn back to another origin of this name, so that you may understand *theon,* God, to be derived, not from the verb *theōrō,* I see, but from the verb *theō,* that is, I run, the same reasoning (*ratio*) is similarly against you. For not running is opposed to running, as slowness to quickness. Therefore he will be *hypertheos* (superrunning), that is, more than running, as it is written: *his speech runs swiftly.* For we understand this of God the Word, that he runs ineffably through all things, which are, that they may be. We are obliged to understand in the same way concerning (the name) truth. For falsity is opposed to truth, and for this reason properly he is not truth; therefore he is *hyperalēthēs,* and *hyperalētheia,* more than true, and more than truth. The same reason (*ratio*) is to be observed in all divine names. For he is not properly called eternity, since temporality is opposed to eternity; therefore he is *hyperaiōnios,* and *hyperaiōnia,* more than eternal, and more than eternity. Of wisdom also the same reason (*ratio*) presents itself and therefore it is not to be judged to be predicated properly of God, since foolish and foolishness oppose wisdom and wise; hence he is rightly and truly said to be *hypersofos* (superwise), that is, more than wise, and *hypersofia* (superwisdom), more than wisdom. Similarly he is more than life, inasmuch as death is opposed to life. In the same way it is to be understood concerning light; for darkness stands against light. Thus far, as I judge, we have said enough concerning these things.

Disciple. By all means it (is) to be allowed that enough has been said. For of those things (granted that) whatever ones are necessary to be brought forth for the sake of matters to be argued in the present affair, (nevertheless) what we have proposed for our discussion does not admit them at the present time. Therefore return, if you will, to the consideration of the tenfold number of categories.

Magister. I admire the sharpness of your purpose, which has seemed very watchful thus far.

Disciple. What evidence, I ask, do you have for saying that?

Magister. Have we not said that the ineffable nature can be properly signified by no word, no name, that is, by any sensible sound, (and) by no thing signified? And you have granted this. For he is called essence, truth, wisdom and other things of this kind not properly but translatively; but he is called superessential, more than truth, more than wisdom, and similar things. But do not even these seem to be almost, as it were, certain proper names, if he is not properly called the essence, but properly superessential? Similarly if he is not named truth or wisdom properly, but is properly called more than truth, and more than wisdom? Therefore he is not without proper names; for these names, although they are not pronounced among Latins with a single accent dominating a single harmony of composition (single word) as is customary, with the exception of the name superessential, nevertheless (these words) are pronounced by the Greeks as a single composite word. For never or scarcely ever will you find that supergood (*superbonum*) or supereternal (*superaeternum*) and other similar words are pronounced as a single word.

Disciple. And I myself greatly wonder whither I was tending, when I had completely omitted this important inquiry. And therefore I request it to be investigated thoroughly by you. For so long as divine substance is properly expressed in whatever way either by simple or composite parts of speech, or by phrases (breaking one word into many in translation), in Greek or Latin, it will not seem to be ineffable. For what can be said in a certain manner is not ineffable.

Magister. Now you are vigilant, I see.

Disciple. Indeed I am vigilant, but I see nothing thus far concerning this interposed question.

Magister. Return therefore to those things, which have been concluded between us a little before. For indeed, unless I am mistaken, we have said that there are two most sublime parts of theology; and accepting this not from ourselves, but from the authority of S. Dionysius the Areopagite, who most plainly, as has been said, asserts that Theology has two parts, that is, *katafatikēn* (affirmative), and *apofatikēn* (deprivative or negative), which Cicero translates as *attraction (intentio) and repulsion (repulsionem)*, but we, in order that the force of the words be made more abundantly clear, have chosen to translate (them) by affirmation and negation.

Disciple. I seem to recall these things, as I judge. But what would be useful to these things, which we wish to consider now, I do not yet recognize.

Magister. Do you not see, that these two, namely affirmation and negation, are opposed to each other?

Disciple. I see enough, and I judge that nothing can be more contrary.

Magister. Therefore direct (your thoughts) more diligently. For when you will have arrived at a sight of perfect reasoning, you will consider clearly enough, that these two, which seem to be contrary to each other are opposed to each other in no way, when they refer to divine nature, but are consistent with each other through all things in all things. And in order that this become more plain we shall use a few examples. For example *katafatikē* (affirmative or positive Theology) says, he is truth; *apofatikē* (negative Theology) contradicts, he is not truth. This seems a certain form of contradiction; but when it is looked into more intently, no controversy is discovered. For (by) those things which it (affirmative Theology) says, saying that it (divine essence) is truth, it (affirmative Theology) does not affirm that divine substance is properly truth, but can be called by such a name through a metaphor from the creature to the Creator; it clothes divine essence with such designations although it is naked and untouched by every proper signification. But those things which it says, saying that it is not truth, rightly and clearly knowing the incomprehensible and ineffable divine nature, does not deny that it is, but that properly it is neither said to be, nor is, truth. For *apofatikē* (negative Theology) is unable to despoil the Divinity of all the significations, with which *katafatikē* (positive Theology) clothes it. For one (positive Theology) says that it is wisdom, thereby clothing it (divine essence), the other, says it is not wisdom, thereby unclothing the same thing. Therefore the one says it can be called this, but does not say it properly is this; the other says he is not this, although he can be called from this.

Disciple. I see these things most plainly, unless I am mistaken, and those things which thus far seemed to me to be opposed to each other, are now disclosed more clearly than light to convene with each other, and to contradict each other in nothing, so long as they are considered concerning God. But how they may attain to the solution of the present question, I do not yet profess to know.

Magister. Therefore attend more watchfully and show forth as much as you can to which part of Theology, whether affirmative or negative, those significations, which have been added first, I mean superessential, more than truth, more than wisdom, and others similar, are to be applied.

Disciple. I do not dare sufficiently to decide this by myself. For when I consider that the aforesaid significations are without a negative particle, which is *non*, I become afraid to join them to the negative part of Theology. But if I shall have joined the same (ones) to the affirmative part, I become aware that their meaning does not agree with me. For when it is said, it (divine essence) is superessential, nothing other is given to me to be understood than a negation of essence. For he who says that it is superessential, plainly denies that it is essential. And through this, although the negation does not appear in the pronouncement of the words, nevertheless its meaning is not concealed in secret from those considering well. Then, as I think, I am forced to acknowledge, that those aforesaid significations, which seem to lack a negation, convene more to the negative part of Theology, than to the affirmative, insofar as it is given to understand.

Magister. I see you have responded most cautiously and watchfully, and I approve very much of the way in which you have seen into the meaning of the negative most subtly in the enunciation of the affirmative part. Therefore if it is pleasing, let the solution of this present question be made in this way, that all these things, which are predicated of God by the addition of the particles *super* or *more than*, as (for example that) he is superessential, more than truth, more than wisdom and similar things, are most fully comprehended in se in the two aforesaid parts of Theology (taken together); so that they may obtain the form of the affirmative in enunciation, but the power of the abdicative in meaning. And let us conclude with this brief example. He is essence, affirmation; he is not essence, abdication; he is superessential, simultaneously affirmation and abdication. For on the surface it is without negation; in meaning it has negative force. For he who says, He is superessential, does not say what He is, but what He is not; for he says that He is not essence, but more than essence. But what that is which is more than essence, he does not express, asserting that God is not anything of those (things) which are, but is more than those things which are: but what that being may be, he defines in no way.

Disciple. We should not linger any longer on this question, as I think, and now, if it seems proper, let us consider the nature of the categories.

• • •

SELECTED BIBLIOGRAPHY

BIBLIOGRAPHY

Brennan, M., "A Bibliography of Publications in the Field of Eriugenian Studies, 1800–1975," *Studia medievalia*, XVIII (1977), 401–447.

TRANSLATIONS

McKeon, R., ed. and trans., *Selections from Medieval Philosophers, I: Augustine to Albert the Great,* New York, 1929.

Schwartz, C., trans., *On the Division of Nature,* Book I, Annapolis, 1940.

Shapiro, H., ed., *Medieval Philosophy,* New York, 1964.

Sheldon-Williams, I. and L. Bieler, eds. and trans., *Johannis Scotti Eriugenae Periphyseon (De Divisione Naturae),* 2 vols., Dublin, 1968–72.

Uhlfelder, M., trans., *Joannes Scotus Erigena, Periphyseon. On the Division of Nature,* with summaries by J. Potter, Indianapolis, 1976.

STUDIES

Bett, H., *Johannes Scotus Eriugena, a Study in Medieval Philosophy,* Cambridge, 1925.

Cappuyns, M., *Jean Scot Erigène, sa vie, son oeuvre, sa pensée,* Paris, 1933.

Gracia, J., "Ontological Characterizations of the Relation between Man and Created Nature in Eriugena," *Journal of the History of Philosophy,* XVI (1978), 155–166.

Huber, J., *Johannes Scotus Erigena; ein Beitrag zur Geschichte der Philosophie and Theologie im Mittelalter,* Munich, 1861. (Reprinted, Hildesheim, 1960?)

Jean Scot Érigène et l'histoire de la philosophie, Paris, 1977.

Kristeller, P., "The Historical Position of Johannes Scottus Eriugena," *Latin Script and Letters. Festschrift Bieler,* Leiden, 1976, 156–164.

O'Meara, J. *Eriugena,* Cork, 1969–.

O'Meara, J., and L. Bieler, eds., *The Mind of Eriugena,* Dublin, 1973.

Schneider, A., *Die Erkenntnislehre des Johannes Eriugena im Rahmen ihrer metaphysischen und anthropologischen Voraussetzungen,* 2 vols. Berlin, 1921–1923.

Seul, W., *Die Gotteserkenntnis bei Johannes Skotus Eriugena unter Berücksichtigung ihrer neuplatonischen und augustinischen Elemente,* Bonn, 1932.

Stock, B., "The Philosophical Anthropology of Johannes Scottus Eriugena," *Studia Medievalia,* IV (1963), 75–91.

ANSELM
OF CANTERBURY

1033–1109

ANSELM was sometimes called "the second Augustine," because of his professed unwillingness to say anything inconsistent with Augustine's writings. Like Augustine, he sought "necessary reasons" and thought of their elaboration as a partial fulfillment of religious faith, a position nicely epitomized in his prayer to be granted some degree of understanding of that which he loves and believes. As opposed to those who would remove the faith from logical considerations, Anselm offered his necessary reasons even for the Incarnation and the Holy Trinity—topics reserved as mysteries for most later theologians. From this point of view, he constitutes the highwater mark of reason in the great controversy between faith and reason. But it is not utterly clear just what he interprets as a "necessary reason"; and from another point of view, his position is not nearly so extreme. He sometimes seems to suppose that the discernment of those reasons depends on a divine illumination to be sought in prayer, and even this leaves unsolved the mystery as to *how* the reasons are necessary. If Anselm is the proponent of reason, then, it is hardly the "natural reason" of later structurings of the problem which he represents; and some scholars have even wondered whether he thought of his arguments as philosophical at all. Perhaps it is best to conclude that, bringing to his reflections upon Augustine the rigors of the Boethian and Aristotelian dialectic, his importance lies primarily in his lucid demarkation of problems. Although he is known chiefly for his proofs for the existence of God, Anselm wrote penetratingly on other topics of philosophical interest, expressing a Christian Platonism with painstaking carefulness. He developed a conception of ontological truth, "the truth of things" which is their fulfillment of the relevant standard or ideal, and compared this with the more usual conception of truth as limited to signification. From this he arrives at a single conception of truth as rightness perceptible to the mind alone, with God as the ultimate truth. His further explorations of some of the more subtle problems of signification have recently attracted interest. He also followed Augustine in elaborating a number of distinctions pertaining to the concept of ability and its relation to the problem of free will.

Anselm was born at Aosta, in the Italian Alps, in 1033. Like most saints, he is said to have given early evidence of a religious vocation; and again like many, he met with opposition from his father. He took up the life of a wandering scholar and eventually settled at the Norman monastery of Bec. There he was the disciple of the prior, Lanfranc, who engaged in controversies over the propriety and extent of the use of dialectic in religious matters. Anselm became a monk in 1060; by 1063 he was himself a prior, and in 1078, an abbot. From 1063 to 1093 he was thus the administrator and teacher of one of the model abbeys, and the practice of dialectic in the quiet of Bec must have been subtly different from its later practice in the noisy schools of Paris. It is worth noting that Anselm was an unusually humane medieval teacher, who objected to the popular assumption that frequent beatings have pedagogical value. During these years he wrote his celebrated works dealing with the existence of God, the *Monologion* and *Proslogion;* a semantical work, *On "Literate" (De grammatico);* and studies of the nature of truth and of free choice, *On Truth (De veritate)* and *On Freedom of Choice (Le libertate arbitrii).* In 1093 he was literally dragged into the office of Archbishop of Canterbury, in which role he engaged in the investiture controversy with Kings William II and Henry I of England. Anselm persistently maintained the position that on clerical matters he must obey the pope, and his trials for what he called "the liberty of the Church" were long and wearisome. In spite of pastoral duties, journeys, and exiles, he wrote the *Why God Became Man (Cur deus homo),* a number of theological treatises, and left unfinished a logical work which has been titled *On Power and Powerlessness, Possibility and Impossibility, Necessity and Liberty (De potestate et impotentia, possibilitate et impossibilitate, necessitate et libertate).* The character of the man can perhaps be seen in his reply to the report that he would soon die: "If it is His will I shall gladly obey, but if He should prefer me to stay with you just long enough to solve the question of the origin of the soul which I have been turning over in my mind, I would gratefully accept the chance, for I doubt whether anybody else will solve it when I am gone."* He was canonized in 1494.

The selections which follow include Anselm's initial statement of what since Kant has been called "the ontological argument," followed by the criticisms of a contemporary monk named Gaunilo, and Anselm's reply. Despite Anselm's statement that he was searching for a single self-contained proof, there has been controversy over the alleged difference between the arguments of chapters II and III of the *Proslogion.* One view is that the second simply restates the first; another is that it is distinct from and more cogent than the first; still another is that it gives the ontological explanation for the cogency of the first, in that the necessity of that argument expresses the necessity of God's mode of existence. It can also be asked

---

* Quoted from M. Charlesworth, *St. Anselm's Proslogion,* Oxford, 1965, p. 21.

whether the Platonism of the *Monologion,* where it is argued that all lesser goods exist through the single supreme good, is present in or required by the *Proslogion.* For this, his reply to Gaunilo's claim that he can only nominally conceive of God is of special interest. On the assumption that a Christian Platonism is integral to the proof, including an assumption of divine illumination and even perhaps a scriptural conception of God, it has been claimed that Anselm was not offering such a proof as would be intended to convince skeptics, but merely an elucidation of a belief already held, or perhaps even a kind of map of a mystical journey of the mind to God. But as a straightforward philosophical proof, Anselm's argument has excited discussion in almost every generation since he set it forth; and to judge from recent treatments, its career is far from over.

PROSLOGION

CHAPTER I. *A Rousing of the Mind to the Contemplation of God*

Come now, insignificant man, fly for a moment from your affairs, escape for a little while from the tumult of your thoughts. Put aside now your weighty cares and leave your wearisome toils. Abandon yourself for a little to God and rest for a little in Him. Enter into the inner chamber of your soul, shut out everything save God and what can be of help in your quest for Him and having locked the door seek Him out [Matt. vi. 6]. Speak now, my whole heart, speak now to God: 'I seek Your countenance, O Lord, Your countenance I seek' [Ps. xxvi. 8].

Come, then, Lord my God, teach my heart where and how to seek You, where and how to find You. Lord, if You are not present here, where, since You are absent, shall I look for You? On the other hand, if You are everywhere why then, since You are present, do I not see You? But surely You dwell in 'light inaccessible' [1 Tim. vi. 16]. And where is this inaccessible light, or how can I approach the inaccessible light? Or who shall lead me and take me into it that I may see You in it? Again, by what signs, under what aspect, shall I seek You? Never have I seen You, Lord my God, I do not know Your face. What shall he do, most high Lord, what shall this exile do, far away from You as he is? What shall Your servant do, tormented by love of You and yet cast off 'far from Your face' [Ps. i. 13]? He yearns to see You and Your countenance is too far away from him. He desires to come close to You, and Your dwelling place is inaccessible; he longs to find You and does not know where You are; he is eager to seek You out and he does not know Your countenance. Lord, You are my God and my Lord, and never have I seen You. You have created me and re-created me

From M. J. Charlesworth, trans., *St. Anselm's Proslogion with a Reply on Behalf of the Fool by Gaunilo and the Author's Reply to Gaunilo,* Oxford: The Clarendon Press, 1965. Reprinted by permission of the Clarendon Press, Oxford.

and You have given me all the good things I possess, and still I do not know You. In fine, I was made in order to see You, and I have not yet accomplished what I was made for.

.   .   .

I acknowledge, Lord, and I give thanks that You have created Your image in me, so that I may remember You, think of You, love You. But this image is so effaced and worn away by vice, so darkened by the smoke of sin, that it cannot do what it was made to do unless You renew it and reform it. I do not try, Lord, to attain Your lofty heights, because my understanding is in no way equal to it. But I do desire to understand Your truth a little, that truth that my heart believes and loves. For I do not seek to understand so that I may believe; but I believe so that I may understand. For I believe this also, that 'unless I believe, I shall not understand' [Is. vii. 9].

CHAPTER II.   *That God Truly Exists*

Well then, Lord, You who give understanding to faith, grant me that I may understand, as much as You see fit, that You exist as we believe You to exist, and that You are what we believe You to be. Now we believe that You are something than which nothing greater can be thought. Or can it be that a thing of such a nature does not exist, since 'the Fool has said in his heart, there is no God' [Ps. xiii. 1, lii. 1]? But surely, when this same Fool hears what I am speaking about, namely, 'something-than-which-nothing-greater-can-be-thought', he understands what he hears, and what he understands is in his mind, even if he does not understand that it actually exists. For it is one thing for an object to exist in the mind, and another thing to understand that an object actually exists. Thus, when a painter plans beforehand what he is going to execute, he has [the picture] in his mind, but he does not yet think that it actually exists because he has not yet executed it. However, when he has actually painted it, then he both has it in his mind and understands that it exists because he has now made it. Even the Fool, then, is forced to agree that something-than-which-nothing-greater-can-be-thought exists in the mind, since he understands this when he hears it, and whatever is understood is in the mind. And surely that-than-which-a-greater-cannot-be-thought cannot exist in the mind alone. For if it exists solely in the mind even, it can be thought to exist in reality also, which is greater. If then that-than-which-a-greater-cannot-be-thought exists in the mind alone, this same that-than-which-a-greater-*cannot*-be-thought is that-than-which-a-greater-*can*-be-thought. But this is obviously impossible. Therefore there is absolutely no doubt that something-than-which-a-greater-cannot-be-thought exists both in the mind and in reality.

CHAPTER III.   *That God Cannot Be Thought Not to Exist*

And certainly this being so truly exists that it cannot be even thought not to exist. For something can be thought to exist that cannot be thought not to exist, and this is greater than that which can be thought not to exist. Hence, if that-than-which-a-greater-cannot-be-thought can be thought not to exist, then that-than-which-a-greater-cannot-be-thought is not the same as that-than-which-a-greater-cannot-be-thought, which is absurd. Something-than-which-a-greater-cannot-be-thought exists so truly then, that it cannot be even thought not to exist.

And You, Lord our God, are this being. You exist so truly, Lord my God, that

You cannot even be thought not to exist. And this is as it should be, for if some intelligence could think of something better than You, the creature would be above its creator and would judge its creator—and that is completely absurd. In fact, everything else there is, except You alone, can be thought of as not existing. You alone, then, of all things most truly exist and therefore of all things possess existence to the highest degree; for anything else does not exist as truly, and so possesses existence to a lesser degree. Why then did 'the Fool say in his heart, there is no God' [Ps. xiii. 1, lii. 1] when it is so evident to any rational mind that You of all things exist to the highest degree? Why indeed, unless because he was stupid and a fool?

CHAPTER IV. *How 'the Fool Said in his Heart' What Cannot Be Thought*

How indeed has he 'said in his heart' what he could not think; or how could he not think what he 'said in his heart', since to 'say in one's heart' and to 'think' are the same? But if he really (indeed, since he really) both thought because he 'said in his heart' and did not 'say in his heart' because he could not think, there is not only one sense in which something is 'said in one's heart' or thought. For in one sense a thing is thought when the word signifying it is thought; in another sense when the very object which the thing is is understood. In the first sense, then, God can be thought not to exist, but not at all in the second sense. No one, indeed, understanding what God is can think that God does not exist, even though he may say these words in his heart either without any [objective] signification or with some peculiar signification. For God is that-than-which-nothing-greater-can-be-thought. Whoever really understands this understands clearly that this same being so exists that not even in thought can it not exist. Thus whoever understands that God exists in such a way cannot think of Him as not existing.

I give thanks, good Lord, I give thanks to You, since what I believed before through Your free gift I now so understand through Your illumination, that if I did not want to *believe* that You existed, I should nevertheless be unable not to *understand* it.

A REPLY TO THE FOREGOING BY A CERTAIN WRITER ON BEHALF OF THE FOOL

{By Gaunilo}

[1.] To one doubting whether there is, or denying that there is, something of such a nature than which nothing greater can be thought, it is said here [in the *Proslogion*] that its existence is proved, first because the very one who denies or doubts it already has it in his mind, since when he hears it spoken of he understands what is said; and further, because what he understands is necessarily such that it exists not only in the mind but also in reality. And this is proved by the fact that it is greater to exist both in the mind and in reality than in the mind alone. For if this same being exists in the mind alone, anything that existed also in reality would be greater than this being, and thus that which is greater than everything would be less than some thing and would not be greater than everything, which is obviously contradictory. Therefore, it is necessarily the case that that which is greater than everything, being already proved to exist in the mind, should exist not only in the mind but also in reality, since otherwise it would not be greater than everything.

[2.] But he [the Fool] can perhaps reply that this thing is said already to exist in the mind only in the sense that I understand what is said. For could I not say that all kinds of unreal things, not existing in themselves in any way at all, are equally in the mind since if anyone speaks about them I understand whatever he says? Unless perhaps it is manifest that this being is such that it can be entertained in the mind in a different way from unreal or doubtfully real things, so that I am not said to think of or have in thought what is heard, but to understand and have it in mind, in that I cannot really think of this being in any other way save by understanding it, that is to say, by grasping by certain knowledge that the thing itself actually exists. But if this is the case, first, there will be no difference between having an object in mind (taken as preceding in time), and understanding that the object actually exists (taken as following in time), as in the case of the picture which exists first in the mind of the painter and then in the completed work. And thus it would be scarcely conceivable that, when this object had been spoken of and heard, it could not be thought not to exist in the same way in which God can [be thought] not to exist. For if He cannot, why put forward this whole argument against anyone denying or doubting that there is something of this kind? Finally, that it is such a thing that, as soon as it is thought of, it cannot but be certainly perceived by the mind as indubitably existing, must be proved to me by some indisputable argument and not by that proposed, namely, that it must already be in my mind when I understand what I hear. For this is in my view like [arguing that] any things doubtfully real or even unreal are capable of existing if these things are mentioned by someone whose spoken words I might understand, and, even more, that [they exist] if, though deceived about them as often happens, I should believe them [to exist]—which argument I still do not believe!

[3.] Hence, the example of the painter having the picture he is about to make already in his mind cannot support this argument. For this picture, before it is actually made, is contained in the very art of the painter and such a thing in the art of any artist is nothing but a certain part of his very understanding, since as St. Augustine says [*In Iohannem*, tract. 1, n. 16], 'when the artisan is about actually to make a box he has it beforehand in his art. The box which is actually made is not a living thing, but the box which is in his art is a living thing since the soul of the artist, in which these things exist before their actual realization, is a living thing'. Now how are these things living in the living soul of the artist unless they are identical with the knowledge or understanding of the soul itself? But, apart from those things which are known to belong to the very nature of the mind itself, in the case of any truth perceived by the mind by being either heard or understood, then it cannot be doubted that this truth is one thing and that the understanding which grasps it is another. Therefore even if it were true that there was something than which nothing greater could be thought, this thing, heard and understood, would not, however, be the same as the not-yet-made picture is in the mind of the painter.

[4.] To this we may add something that has already been mentioned, namely, that upon hearing it spoken of I can so little think of or entertain in my mind this being (that which is greater than all those others that are able to be thought of, and which it is said can be none other than God Himself) in terms of an object known to me either by species or genus, as I can think of God Himself, whom indeed for this very reason I can even think does not exist. For neither do I know the reality itself, nor can I form an idea from some other things like it since, as you say yourself, it is such that nothing could be like it. For if I heard something said about a man who was completely unknown to me so that I did not even know whether he existed, I could nevertheless think about him in his very reality as a man by means of that specific or generic notion by which I know what a man is or men are. However, it could happen that, because of a falsehood on the part of the speaker, the man I thought of did not actually exist, although I thought of him nevertheless as a truly existing object—not this particular man but any man in general. It is not, then, in the way that I have this unreal thing in thought or in mind that I can have that object in my mind when I hear 'God' or 'something greater than everything' spoken of. For while I was able to think of the former in terms of a truly existing thing which was known to me, I know nothing at all of the latter save for the verbal formula, and on the basis of this alone one can scarcely or never think of any truth. For when one thinks in this way, one thinks not so much of the word itself, which is indeed a real thing (that is to say, the sound of the letters or syllables), as of the meaning of the word which is heard. However, it [that which is greater than everything] is not thought of in the way of one who knows what is meant by that expression—thought of, that is, in terms of the thing [signified] or as true in thought alone. It is rather in the way of one who does not really know this object but thinks of it in terms of an affection of his mind produced by hearing the spoken words, and who tries to imagine what the words he has heard might mean. However, it would be astonishing if he could ever [attain to] the truth of the thing. Therefore, when I hear and understand someone saying that there is something greater than everything that can be thought of, it is agreed that it is in this latter sense that it is in my mind and not in any other sense. So much for the claim that that supreme nature exists already in my mind.

[5.] That, however, [this nature] necessarily exists in reality is demonstrated to me from the fact that, unless it existed, whatever exists in reality would be greater than it and consequently it would not be that which is greater than everything that undoubtedly had already been proved to exist in the mind. To this I reply as follows: if something that cannot even be thought in the true and real sense must be said to exist in the mind, then I do not deny that this also exists in my mind in the same way. But since from this one cannot in any way conclude that it exists also in reality, I certainly do not yet concede that it actually exists, until this is proved to me by an indubitable argument.

For he who claims that it actually exists because otherwise it would not be that which is greater than everything does not consider carefully enough whom he is addressing. For I certainly do not yet admit this greater [than everything] to be any truly existing thing; indeed I doubt or even deny it. And I do not concede that it exists in a different way from that—if one ought to speak of 'existence' here—when the mind tries to imagine a completely unknown thing on the basis of the spoken words alone. How then can it be proved to me on that basis that that which is greater than everything truly exists in reality (because it is evident that it is greater than all others) if I keep on denying and also doubting that this is evident and do not admit that this greater [than everything] is either in my mind or thought, not even in the sense in which many doubtfully real and unreal things are? It must first of all be proved to me then that this same greater than everything truly exists in reality somewhere, and then only will the fact that it is greater than everything make it clear that it also subsists in itself.

[6.] For example: they say that there is in the ocean somewhere an island which, because of the difficulty (or rather the impossibility) of finding that which does not exist, some have called the 'Lost Island'. And the story goes that it is blessed with all manner of priceless riches and delights in abundance, much more even than the Happy Isles, and, having no owner or inhabitant, it is superior everywhere in abundance of riches to all those other lands that men inhabit. Now, if anyone tell me that it is like this, I shall easily understand what is said, since nothing is difficult about it. But if he should then go on to say, as though it were a logical consequence of this: You cannot any more doubt that this island that is more excellent than all other lands truly exists somewhere in reality than you can doubt that it is in your mind; and since it is more excellent to exist not only in the mind alone but also in reality, therefore it must needs be that it exists. For if it did not exist, any other land existing in reality would be more excellent than it, and so this island, already conceived by you to be more excellent than others, will not be more excellent. If, I say, someone wishes thus to persuade me that this island really exists beyond all doubt, I should either think that he was joking, or I should find it hard to decide which of us I ought to judge the bigger fool—I, if I agreed with him, or he, if he thought that he had proved the existence of this island with any certainty, unless he had first convinced me that its very excellence exists in my mind precisely as a thing existing truly and indubitably and not just as something unreal or doubtfully real.

[7.] Thus first of all might the Fool reply to objections. And if then someone should assert that this greater [than everything] is such that it cannot be thought not to exist (again without any other proof than that otherwise it would not be greater than everything), then he could make this same reply and say: When have I said that there truly existed some being that is 'greater than everything', such that from this it could be proved to me that this same being really existed to such a degree that it could not be thought not to exist? That is why it must first be conclusively proved by argument that there is some higher nature, namely that which is greater and better than all the things that are, so that from this we can also infer everything else which necessarily cannot be wanting to what is greater and better than everything.

When, however, it is said that this supreme being cannot be *thought* not to exist, it would perhaps be better to say that it cannot be *understood* not to exist nor even to be able not to exist. For, strictly speaking, unreal things cannot be *understood*, though certainly they can be *thought* of in the same way as the Fool *thought* that God does not exist. I know with complete certainty that I exist, but I also know at the same time nevertheless that I can not-exist. And I *understand* without any doubt that that which exists to the highest degree, namely God, both exists and cannot not exist. I do not know, however, whether I can *think* of myself as not existing while I know with absolute certainty that I do exist; but if I can, why cannot [I do the same] with regard to anything else I know with the same certainty? If however I cannot, this will not be the distinguishing characteristic of God [namely, to be such that He cannot be thought not to exist].

[8.] The other parts of this tract are argued so truly, so brilliantly and so splendidly, and are also of so much worth and instinct with so fragrant a perfume of devout and holy feeling, that in no way should they be rejected because of those things at the beginning (rightly intuited, but less surely argued out). Rather the latter should be demonstrated more firmly and so everything received with very great respect and praise.

A REPLY TO THE FOREGOING BY THE AUTHOR OF THE BOOK IN QUESTION

Since it is not the Fool, against whom I spoke in my tract, who takes me up, but one who, though speaking on the Fool's behalf, is an orthodox Christian and no fool, it will suffice if I reply to the Christian.

[I.] You say then—you, whoever you are, who claim that the Fool can say these things—that the being than-which-a-greater-cannot-be-thought is not in the mind except as what cannot be thought of, in the true sense, at all. And [you claim], moreover, that what I say does not follow, namely, that 'that-than-which-a-greater-cannot-be-thought' exists in reality from the fact that it exists in the mind, any more than that the Lost Island most certainly exists from the fact that, when it is described in words, he who hears it described has no doubt that it exists in his mind. I reply as follows: If 'that-than-which-a-greater-cannot-be-thought' is neither understood nor thought of, and is neither in the mind nor in thought, then it is evident that *either* God is not that-than-which-a-greater-cannot-be-thought *or* is not understood nor thought of, and is not in the mind nor in thought. Now my strongest argument that this is false is to appeal to your faith and to your conscience. Therefore 'that-than-which-a-greater-cannot-be-thought' is truly understood and thought and is in the mind and in thought. For this reason, [the arguments] by which you attempt to prove the contrary are either not true, or what you believe follows from them does not in fact follow.

Moreover, you maintain that, from the fact that that-than-which-a-greater-cannot-be-thought is understood, it does not follow that it is in the mind, nor that, if it is in the mind, it therefore exists in reality. I insist, however, that simply if it can be thought it is necessary that it exists. For 'that-than-which-a-greater-cannot-be-thought' cannot be thought save as being without a beginning. But whatever can be thought as existing and does not actually exist can be thought as having a beginning of its existence. Consequently, 'that-than-which-a-greater-cannot-be-thought' cannot be thought as existing and yet not actually exist. If, therefore, it can be thought as existing, it exists of necessity.

Further: even if it can be thought of, then certainly it necessarily exists. For no one who denies or doubts that there is something-than-which-a-greater-cannot-be-thought, denies or doubts that, if this being were to exist, it would not be capable of not-existing either actually or in the mind—otherwise it would not be that-than-which-a-greater-cannot-be-thought. But, whatever can be thought as existing and does not actually exist, could, if it were to exist, possibly not exist either actually or in the mind. For this reason, if it can merely be thought, 'that-than-which-a-greater-cannot-be-thought' cannot not exist. However, let us suppose that it does not exist even though it can be thought. Now, whatever can be thought and does not actually exist would not be, if it should exist, 'that-than-which-a-greater-cannot-be-thought'. If, therefore, it were 'that-than-which-a-greater-cannot-be-thought' it would not be that-than-which-a-greater-cannot-be-thought, which is completely absurd. It is, then, false that something-than-which-a-greater-cannot-be-thought does not exist if it can merely be thought; and it is all the more false if it can be understood and be in the mind.

I will go further: It cannot be doubted that whatever does not exist in any one place or at any one time, even though it does exist in some place or at some time, can however be thought to exist at no place and at no time, just as it does not exist in some place or at some time. For what did not exist yesterday and today exists can thus, as it is understood not to have existed yesterday, be supposed not to exist at any time. And that which does not exist here in this place, and does exist elsewhere can, in the same way as it does not exist here, be thought not to exist anywhere. Similarly with a thing some of whose particular parts do not exist in the place and at the time its other parts exist—all of its parts, and therefore the whole thing itself, can be thought to exist at no time and in no place. For even if it be said that time always exists and that the world is everywhere, the former does not, however, always exist as a whole, nor is the other as a whole everywhere; and as certain particular parts of time do not exist when other parts do exist, therefore they can be even thought not to exist at any time. Again, as certain particular parts of the world do not exist in the same place where other parts do exist, they can thus be supposed not to exist anywhere. Moreover, what is made up of parts can be broken up in thought and can possibly not exist. Thus it is that whatever does not exist as a whole at a certain place and time can be thought not to exist, even if it does actually exist. But 'that-than-which-a-greater-cannot-be-thought' cannot be thought not to exist if it does actually exist; otherwise, if it exists it is not that-than-which-a-greater-cannot-be-thought, which is absurd. In no way, then, does this being not exist as a whole in any particular place or at any particular time; but it exists as a whole at every time and in every place.

Do you not consider then that that about which we understand these things can to some extent be thought or understood, or can exist in thought or in the mind? For if it cannot, we could not understand these things about it. And if you say that, because it is not completely understood, it cannot be understood at all and cannot be in the mind, then you must say [equally] that one who cannot see the purest light of the sun directly does not see daylight, which is the same thing as the light of the sun. Surely then 'that-than-which-a-greater-cannot-be-thought' is understood and is in the mind to the extent that we understand these things about it.

[II.] I said, then, in the argument that you criticize, that when the Fool hears 'that-than-which-a-greater-cannot-be-thought' spoken of he understands what he hears. Obviously if it is spoken of in a known language and he does not understand it, then either he has no intelligence at all, or a completely obtuse one.

Next I said that, if it is understood it is in the mind; or does what has been proved to exist necessarily in actual reality not exist in any mind? But you will say that, even if it is in the mind, yet it does not follow that it is understood. Observe then that, from the fact that it is understood, it does follow that it is in the mind. For, just as what is thought is thought by means of a thought, and what is thought by a thought is thus, as thought, *in* thought, so also, what is understood is understood by the mind, and what is understood by the mind is thus, as understood, *in* the mind. What could be more obvious than this?

I said further that if a thing exists even in the mind alone, it can be thought to exist also in reality, which is greater. If, then, it (namely, 'that-than-which-a-greater-cannot-be-thought') exists in the mind alone, it is something than which a greater *can* be thought. What, I ask you, could be more logical? For if it exists even in the mind alone, cannot it be thought to exist also in reality? And if it can [be so thought], is it not the case that he who thinks this thinks of something greater than it, if it exists in the mind alone? What, then, could follow more logically than that, if 'that-than-which-a-greater-*cannot*-be-thought' exists in the mind alone, it is the same as that-than-which-a-greater-*can*-be-thought? But surely 'that-than-which-a-greater-*can*-be-thought' is not for any mind [the same as] 'that-than-which-a-greater-*cannot*-be-thought'. Does it not follow, then, that 'that-than-which-a-greater-*cannot*-be-thought', if it exists in anyone's mind, does not exist in the mind alone? For if it exists in the mind alone, it is that-than-which-a-greater-*can*-be-thought, which is absurd.

[III.] You claim, however, that this is as though someone asserted that it cannot be doubted that a certain island in the ocean (which is more fertile than all other lands and which, because of the difficulty or even the impossibility of discovering what does not exist, is called the 'Lost Island') truly exists in reality since anyone easily understands it when it is described in words. Now, I truly promise that if anyone should discover for me something existing either in reality or in the mind alone—except 'that-than-which-a-greater-cannot-be-thought'—to which the logic of my argument would apply, then I shall find that Lost Island and give it, never more to be lost, to that person. It has already been clearly seen, however, that 'that-than-which-a-greater-cannot-be-thought' cannot be thought not to exist, because it exists as a matter of such certain truth. Otherwise it would not exist at all. In short, if anyone says that he thinks that this being does not exist, I reply that, when he thinks of this, either he thinks of something than which a greater cannot be thought, or he does not think of it. If he does not think of it, then he does not think that what he does not think of does not exist. If, however, he does think of it, then indeed he thinks of something which cannot be even thought not to exist. For if it could be thought not to exist, it could be thought to have a beginning and an end—but this cannot be. Thus, he who thinks of it thinks of something that cannot be thought not to exist; indeed, he who thinks of this does not think of it as not existing, otherwise he would think what cannot be thought. Therefore 'that-than-which-a-greater-cannot-be-thought' cannot be thought not to exist.

[IV.]   You say, moreover, that when it is said that this supreme reality cannot be *thought* not to exist, it would perhaps be better to say that it cannot be *understood* not to exist or even to be able not to exist. However, it must rather be said that it cannot be *thought*. For if I had said that the thing in question could not be *understood* not to exist, perhaps you yourself (who claim that we cannot understand—if this word is to be taken strictly—things that are unreal) would object that nothing that exists can be understood not to exist. For it is false [to say that] what exists does not exist, so that it is not the distinguishing characteristic of God not to be able to be understood not to exist. But, if any of those things which exist with absolute certainty can be understood not to exist, in the same way other things that certainly exist can be understood not to exist. But, if the matter is carefully considered, this objection cannot be made apropos [the term] 'thought'. For even if none of those things that exist can be *understood* not to exist, all however can be *thought* as not existing, save that which exists to a supreme degree. For in fact all those things (and they alone) that have a beginning or end or are made up of parts and, as I have already said, all those things that do not exist as a whole in a particular place or at a particular time can be thought as not existing. Only that being in which there is neither beginning nor end nor conjunction of parts, and that thought does not discern save as a whole in every place and at every time, cannot be thought as not existing.

Know then that you can think of yourself as not existing while yet you are absolutely sure that you exist. I am astonished that you have said that you do not know this. For we think of many things that we know to exist, as not existing; and [we think of] many things that we know not to exist, as existing—not judging that it is really as we think but imagining it to be so. We *can*, in fact, think of something as not existing while knowing that it does exist, since we can [think of] the one and know the other at the same time. And we *cannot* think of something as not existing if yet we know that it does exist, since we cannot think of it as existing and not existing at the same time. He, therefore, who distinguishes these two senses of this assertion will understand that [in one sense] nothing can be thought as not existing while yet it is known to exist, and that [in another sense] whatever exists, save that-than-which-a-greater-cannot-be-thought, can be thought of as not existing even when we know that it does exist. Thus it is that, on the one hand, it is the distinguishing characteristic of God that He cannot be thought of as not existing, and that, on the other hand, many things, the while they do exist, cannot be thought of as not existing. In what sense, however, one can say that God can be thought of as not existing I think I have adequately explained in my tract.

[V.] As for the other objections you make against me on behalf of the Fool, it is quite easy to meet them, even for one weak in the head, and so I considered it a waste of time to show this. But since I hear that they appear to certain readers to have some force against me, I will deal briefly with them.

First, you often reiterate that I say that that which is greater than everything exists in the mind, and that if it is in the mind, it exists also in reality, for otherwise that which is greater than everything would not be that which is greater than everything. However, nowhere in all that I have said will you find such an argument. For 'that which is greater than everything' and 'that-than-which-a-greater-cannot-be-thought' are not equivalent for the purpose of proving the real existence of the thing spoken of. Thus, if anyone should say that 'that-than-which-a-greater-cannot-be-thought' is not something that actually exists, or that it can possibly not exist, or even can be thought of as not existing, he can easily be refuted. For what does not exist can possibly not exist, and what can not exist can be thought of as not existing. However, whatever can be thought of as not existing, if it actually exists, is not that-than-which-a-greater-cannot-be-thought. But if it does not exist, indeed even if it should exist, it would not be that-than-which-a-greater-cannot-be-thought. But it cannot be asserted that 'that-than-which-a-greater-cannot-be-thought' is not, if it exists that-than-which-a-greater-cannot-be-thought, or that, if it should exist, it would not be that-than-which-a-greater-cannot-be-thought. It is evident, then, that it neither does not exist nor can not exist or be thought of as not existing. For if it does exist in another way it is not what it is said to be, and if it should exist [in another way] it would not be [what it was said to be].

However it seems that it is not as easy to prove this in respect of what is said to be greater than everything. For it is not as evident that that which can be thought of as not existing is not that which is greater than everything, as that it is not that-than-which-a-greater-cannot-be-thought. And, in the same way, neither is it indubitable that, if there is something which is 'greater than everything', it is identical with 'that-than-which-a-greater-cannot-be-thought'; nor, if there were [such a being], that no other like it might exist—as this is certain in respect of what is said to be 'that-than-which-a-greater-cannot-be-thought'. For what if someone should say that something that is greater than everything actually exists, and yet that this same being can be thought of as not existing, and that something greater than it can be thought, even if this does not exist? In this case can it be inferred as evidently that [this being] is therefore not that which is greater than everything, as it would quite evidently be said in the other case that it is therefore not that-than-which-a-greater-cannot-be-thought? The former [inference] needs, in fact, a premiss in addition to this which is said to be 'greater than everything'; but the latter needs nothing save this utterance itself, namely, 'that-than-which-a-greater-cannot-be-thought'. Therefore, if what 'that-than-which-a-greater-cannot-be-thought' of itself proves concerning itself cannot be proved in the same way in respect of what is said to be 'greater than everything', you criticize me unjustly for having said what I did not say, since it differs so much from what I did say.

If, however, it can [be proved] by means of another argument, you should not have criticized me for having asserted what can be proved. Whether it can [be proved], however, is easily appreciated by one who understands that it can [in respect of] 'that-than-which-a-greater-cannot-be-thought'. For one cannot in any way understand 'that-than-which-a-greater-cannot-be-thought' without [understanding that it is] that which alone is greater than everything. As, therefore, 'that-than-which-a-greater-cannot-be-thought' is understood and is in the mind, and is consequently judged to exist in true reality, so also that which is greater than everything is said to be understood and to exist in the mind, and so is necessarily inferred to exist in reality itself. You see, then, how right you were to compare me with that stupid person who wished to maintain that the Lost Island existed from the sole fact that being described it was understood.

[VI.] You object, moreover, that any unreal or doubtfully real things at all can equally be understood and exist in the mind in the same way as the being I was speaking of. I am astonished that you urge this [objection] against me, for I was concerned to prove something which was in doubt, and for me it was sufficient that I should first show that it was understood and existed in the mind *in some way or other*, leaving it to be determined subsequently whether it was in the mind alone as unreal things are, or in reality also as true things are. For, if unreal or doubtfully real things are understood and exist in the mind in the sense that, when they are spoken of, he who hears them understands what the speaker means, nothing prevents what I have spoken of being understood and existing in the mind. But how are these [assertions] consistent, that is, when you assert that if someone speaks of unreal things you would understand whatever he says, and that, in the case of a thing which is not entertained in thought in the same way as even unreal things are, you do not say that you think of it or have it in thought upon hearing it spoken of, but rather that you understand it and have it in mind since, precisely, you cannot think of it save by understanding it, that is, knowing certainly that the thing exists in reality itself? How, I say, are both [assertions] consistent, namely that unreal things are understood, and that 'to understand' means knowing with certainty that something actually exists? You should have seen that nothing [of this applies] to me. But if unreal things are, in a sense, understood (this definition applying not to every kind of understanding but to a certain kind) then I ought not to be criticized for having said that 'that-than-which-a-greater-cannot-be-thought' is understood and is in the mind, even before it was certain that it existed in reality itself.

[VII.] Next, you say that it can hardly be believed that when this [that-than-which-a-greater-cannot-be-thought] has been spoken of and heard, it cannot be thought not to exist, as even it can be thought that God does not exist. Now those who have attained even a little expertise in disputation and argument could reply to that on my behalf. For is it reasonable that someone should therefore deny what he understands because it is said to be [the same as] that which he denies since he does not understand it? Or if that is denied [to exist] which is understood only to some extent and is the same as what is not understood at all, is not what is in doubt more easily proved from the fact that it is in some mind than from the fact that it is in no mind at all? For this reason it cannot be believed that anyone should deny 'that-than-which-a-greater-cannot-be-thought' (which, being heard, he understands to some extent), on the ground that he denies God whose meaning he does not think of in any way at all. On the other hand, if it is denied on the ground that it is not understood completely, even so is not that which is understood in some way easier to prove than that which is not understood in any way? It was therefore not wholly without reason that, to prove against the Fool that God exists, I proposed 'that-than-which-a-greater-cannot-be-thought', since he would understand this in some way, [whereas] he would understand the former [God] in no way at all.

[VIII.] In fact, your painstaking argument that 'that-than-which-a-greater-cannot-be-thought' is not like the not-yet-realized painting in the mind of the painter is beside the point. For I did not propose [the example] of the fore-known picture because I wanted to assert that what was at issue was in the same case, but rather that so I could show that something not understood as existing exists in the mind.

Again, you say that upon hearing of 'that-than-which-a-greater-cannot-be-thought' you cannot think of it as a real object known either generically or specifically or have it in your mind, on the grounds that you neither know the thing itself nor can you form an idea of it from other things similar to it. But obviously this is not so. For since everything that is less good is similar in so far as it is good to that which is more good, it is evident to every rational mind that, mounting from the less good to the more good we can from those things than which something greater can be thought conjecture a great deal about that-than-which-a-greater-cannot-be-thought. Who, for example, cannot think of this (even if he does not believe that what he thinks of actually exists) namely, that if something that has a beginning and end is good, that which, although it has had a beginning, does not, however, have an end, is much better? And just as this latter is better than the former, so also that which has neither beginning nor end is better again than this, even if it passes always from the past through the present to the future. Again, whether something of this kind actually exists or not, that which does not lack anything at all, nor is forced to change or move, is very much better still. Cannot this be thought? Or can we think of something greater than this? Or is not this precisely to form an idea of that-than-which-a-greater-cannot-be-thought from those things than which a greater can be thought? There is, then, a way by which one can form an idea of 'that-than-which-a-greater-cannot-be-thought'. In this way, therefore, the Fool who does not accept the sacred authority [of Revelation] can easily be refuted if he denies that he can form an idea from other things of 'that-than-which-a-greater-cannot-be-thought'. But if any orthodox Christian should deny this let him remember that 'the invisible things of God from the creation of the world are clearly seen through the things that have been made, even his eternal power and Godhead' [Rom. i. 20].

[IX.] But even if it were true that [the object] that-than-which-a-greater-cannot-be-thought cannot be thought of nor understood, it would not, however, be false that [the formula] 'that-than-which-a-greater-cannot-be-thought' could be thought of and understood. For just as nothing prevents one from saying 'ineffable' although one cannot specify what is said to be ineffable; and just as one can think of the inconceivable—although one cannot think of what 'inconceivable' applies to—so also, when 'that-than-which-a-greater-cannot-be-thought' is spoken of, there is no doubt at all that what is heard can be thought of and understood even if the thing itself cannot be thought of and understood. For if someone is so witless as to say that there is not something than-which-a-greater-cannot-be-thought, yet he will not be so shameless as to say that he is not able to understand and think of what he was speaking about. Or if such a one is to be found, not only should his assertion be condemned, but he himself contemned. Whoever, then, denies that there is something than-which-a-greater-cannot-be-thought, at any rate understands and thinks of the denial he makes, and this denial cannot be understood and thought about apart from its elements. Now, one element [of the denial] is 'that-than-which-a-greater-cannot-be-thought'. Whoever, therefore, denies this understands and thinks of 'that-than-which-a-greater-cannot-be-thought'. It is evident, moreover, that in the same way one can think of and understand that which cannot not exist. And one who thinks of this thinks of something greater than one who thinks of what can not exist. When, therefore, one thinks of that-than-which-a-greater-cannot-be-thought, if one thinks of what can not exist, one does not think of that-than-which-a-greater-cannot-be-thought. Now the same thing cannot at the same time be thought of and not thought of. For this reason he who thinks of that-than-which-a-greater-cannot-be-thought does not think of something that can not exist but something that cannot not exist. Therefore what he thinks of exists necessarily, since whatever can not exist is not what he thinks of.

[X.] I think now that I have shown that I have proved in the above tract, not by a weak argumentation but by a sufficiently necessary one, that something-than-which-a-greater-cannot-be-thought exists in reality itself, and that this proof has not been weakened by the force of any objection. For the import of this proof is in itself of such force that what is spoken of is proved (as a necessary consequence of the fact that it is understood or thought of) both to exist in actual reality and to be itself whatever must be believed about the Divine Being. For we believe of the Divine Being whatever it can, absolutely speaking, be thought better to be than not to be. For example, it is better to be eternal than not eternal, good than not good, indeed goodness-itself than not goodness-itself. However, nothing of this kind cannot but be that-than-which-a-greater-cannot-be-thought. It is, then, necessary that 'that-than-which-a-greater-cannot-be-thought' should be whatever must be believed about the Divine Nature.

I thank you for your kindness both in criticizing and praising my tract. For since you praised so fulsomely those parts that appeared to you to be worthy of acceptance, it is quite clear that you have criticized those parts that seemed to you to be weak, not from any malice but from good will.

SELECTED BIBLIOGRAPHY

TRANSLATIONS

Charlesworth, M., *St. Anselm's Proslogion with a Reply on Behalf of the Fool by Gaunilo and the Author's Reply to Gaunilo*, trans. with introduction and philosophical commentary, Oxford, 1965.

Colleran, J., trans., *Anselm of Canterbury, Why*

God Became Man and The Virgin Conception and Original Sin, Albany, 1969.

Fairweather, E., trans., "Proslogion and Why God Became Man," in *A Scholastic Miscellany: Anselm to Ockham*, Philadelphia, 1956.

Henry, D., *The De Grammatico of St. Anselm: The Theory of Paronymy*, Notre Dame, Ind., 1964.

Hopkins, J. and H. Richardson, eds. and trans., *Anselm of Canterbury, Works*, I–IV, Toronto-New York, 1976.

Hopkins, J. and H. Richardson, eds. and trans., *Anselm of Canterbury, Trinity, Incarnation, and Redemption: Theological Treatises*, New York, 1970.

Hopkins, J. and H. Richardson, eds. and trans., *Anselm of Canterbury, Truth, Freedom, and Evil: Three Philosophical Dialogues*, New York, 1967.

McKeon, R., ed. and trans., *Selections from Medieval Philosophers, I: Augustine to Albert the Great*, New York, 1929.

STUDIES

Adams, M., "Was Anselm a Realist? The *Monologium*," *Franciscan Studies*, XXXII (1972), 5–14.

Adams, R., "The Logical Structure of Anselm's Arguments," *The Philosophical Review*, LXXX (1971), 28–54.

Barth, K., *Anselm: Fides Quaerens Intellectum*, trans., I. Robinson, Cleveland, 1962.

Clayton, J., *Saint Anselm: a Critical Biography*, Milwaukee, 1933.

Courtenay, W., "Necessity and Freedom in Anselm's Conception of God," *Analecta Anselmiana*, IV, 2, 36–64.

Evans, G., *Anselm and Talking about God*, Oxford, 1978.

Filliatre, C., *La philosophie de saint Anselme*, Paris, 1920.

Gilson, E., "Sens et nature de l'argument de saint Anselme," *Archives d'histoire doctrinale et littéraire du moyen âge*, IX (1934), 5–51.

Hartshorne, C., *Anselm's Discovery: A Re-examination of the Ontological Proof for God's Existence*, La Salle, 1966.

Henry, D., *The Logic of Saint Anselm*, Oxford, 1967.

Henry, D., "St. Anselm on the Varieties of 'Doing.'" *Theoria*, XIX (1953), 178–183.

Henry, D., "The Proslogion Proofs," *The Philo-sophical Quarterly*, V (1955), 147–151.

Henry, D., "The Scope of the Logic of St. Anselm," in *L'homme et son destin d'après les penseurs du moyen âge*, Louvain, 1960.

Hopkins, J., *A Companion to the Study of Saint Anselm*, Minneapolis, 1972.

Hopkins, J., "On Understanding and Preunderstanding St. Anselm," *The New Scholasticism*, LII (1978), 243–260.

Kohlenberger, H., ed., *Saint Anselme, ses précurseurs et ses contemporains*, Frankfurt a.M., 1976.

Koyré, A., *L'idée de Dieu dans la philosophie de saint Anselme*, Paris, 1923.

La Croix, *Proslogion II and III*, Leiden, 1972.

Lewis, D., "Anselm and Activity," *Noûs*, IV (1970), 175–188.

Malcolm, N., "Anselm's Ontological Arguments," *The Philosophical Review*, LXIX (1960), 41–62.

Plantinga, A., ed., *The Ontological Argument*, Garden City, 1965.

Southern, R., *St. Anselm and His Biographer*, Cambridge, 1963.

Stearns, J., "Anselm and the Two-Argument Hypothesis," *The Monist*, LIV (1970), 221–233.

PETER ABAILARD

1079–1142

and

JOHN OF SALISBURY

1120–1180

F

ROM THE REVIVAL of the schools until the assimilation of Aristotle's non-logical works, the medieval curriculum consisted of the *trivium* and the *quadrivium*. The *trivium* included grammar, dialectic, and rhetoric; the *quadrivium*, arithmetic, music, geometry, and astronomy. Emphasis was placed on the *trivium*, which dialectic came more and more to dominate. But early medieval dialectic was very much affected by its association with the other arts of speech, and was known as the *scientia sermocinalis* or the *ars disserendi*: the science of disputation or the art of discussion or discourse. This period has been aptly termed "The Boethian Era," in that Boethius' translations and logical treatises were the leading manuals of instruction and also because his effort to apply dialectic to religious concepts was intensively cultivated. In such a context it is understandable that philosophical problems attendant upon dialectic should have theological repercussions and take on added significance from this. The most prominent such problem concerned the ontological status of universals: whether genera and species exist only in the mind or also in reality, and if the latter, whether they exist in individual things or also apart from them. Realism, the doctrine that universals are not merely mental, fitted into the Neoplatonism of both Augustine and Pseudo-Dionysius, and had been employed in interpreting the dogmas of the Holy Trinity, transubstantiation, and even original sin. Thus Anselm of Canterbury said of the nominalist Roscelin that he who does not understand how several individual men are specifically one man can hardly understand how several divine Persons are one God.

The outstanding figure of this era of dialectic and theology, and indeed the one who is credited with giving "theology" its modern sense, is Peter

164

Abailard. He was called "the Socrates of Gaul," and, like Socrates, his greatest contribution is found less in any doctrine than in the rigor of his method and in his raising the standards of philosophy. To judge from recent estimates of his work he was a gifted logician. Although precise derivations are unknown, it is obvious that the so-called "terminist logic" of later centuries owed much to him. In theology the derivations are known: Abailard's work is ancestral to Peter Lombard's *Four Books of Sentences,* the point of departure for later systematic theology. It was not very clear just what Abailard was trying to accomplish with such exercises as a dialectical analysis of the types of similarity and difference present in the Holy Trinity—or perhaps only in a "similitude" of the Trinity. Sometimes he denounced the pseudo-dialecticians who would accept nothing not comprehensible by their little reasons. But his more characteristic pronouncement was that man is created in the image of the divine Logos by his reason, and he went so far as to credit the ancient philosophers with awareness of the Trinity. This kind of thing provoked Bernard of Clairvaux to say that while Abailard sweated to prove Plato a Christian, he only proved himself a heretic. But Abailard himself wrote to Heloise that he did not want to be a philosopher to contradict Paul, nor an Aristotle to be cut off from Christ.

His life was spectacular, and ended in a sort of Socratic martyrdom. He was born in 1079 at Le Pallet in Brittany and gave up the life of a knight to "follow the tourney-grounds of dialectic." He studied under many masters; just which, is a matter for speculation. We can be sure that about 1094 he heard the nominalist Roscelin and that later he heard the realist William of Champeaux. By about 1105 he had his own school; but about 1113 he turned to theology, studying at Laon. Abailard always attacked and abandoned his teachers, and he soon returned to Paris, where he apparently directed the cathedral school and became famous. Soon there unfolded the tragic romance with Heloise; by 1118 Heloise had been sent to a convent, their son had been sent to Abailard's sister, and Abailard had become a monk at the royal abbey of St. Denys. Before 1120 he had produced several short logical glosses and the more elaborate glosses known from the opening words as the *Logica ingredientibus.* About 1120 he wrote *Treatise on the Divine Unity and Trinity (Tractatus de unitate et trinitate divina),* which was promptly condemned at Soissons in 1121. After confinement he was returned to St. Denys, where he made the discovery that the patron saint was not the Areopagite and had to flee the patriotic wrath of the monks. He tried rural solitude, but students sought him out and he entered into a fruitful period of teaching and writing. During the next few years he produced *Yes and No (Sic et non), Christian Theology (Theologia christiana),* part of *Introduction to Theology (Introductio ad theologiam),* and a logical work known as *Logica nostrorum petitioni.* About 1126 he undertook the role of reforming abbot at a wild Breton monastery, a role which he gave up by about 1132, after an attempt on his life. This is as far as his *History of*

My Adversities (Historia calamitatum mearum) carries us; but we know
that by 1136 he was teaching again at Paris. In this period he must have written the remainder of his *Introduction* and the ethical work *Know Thyself
(Scito teipsum)*. His gift for making enemies never rested, and by 1140
he had found the most dangerous of all, Bernard of Clairvaux. They met at
Sens in what Abailard thought was to be a debate and Bernard had turned
into a trial. Abailard appealed to Rome, but the great Cistercian's influence
was there before him, and he was condemned. He retired to the monastery
of Cluny and was sent to a daughter house for his health. During these last
years he produced a revised edition of *Dialectic (Dialectica)* and the unfinished *Dialogue between a Philosopher, a Jew, and a Christian (Dialogus
inter philosophum, Judaeum et Christianum)*. In the course of his career he
also produced several devotional and exegetical works, as well as his part of
the celebrated correspondence with Heloise. At his death in 1142, the Abbot
of Cluny struck the right note by calling him, not only the Socrates of
Gaul, but also "a genius versatile, subtle, and sharp."

John of Salisbury was for a time the student of Abailard, but he had the
suspicion of a man of letters for obsessive rigor and abstract issues. He
was born at Salisbury before 1120, and studied at Paris and Chartres. He
served at the papal court and in 1154 became secretary to the Archbishop
of Canterbury. By 1159 he produced the *Policraticus,* a work on politics, and
the *Metalogicon,* a discussion of the value of the *trivium* and especially of
logic. He was the adviser of Thomas Becket and witnessed his murder in
1170. In 1176 he became Bishop of Chartres. He died in 1180, a respected
master of the humanistic culture of the tradition of Chartres. He wrote
historical and biographical works and a much-admired correspondence. The
Metalogicon is a mine of information about doctrines and masters of the
twelfth century.

In the following selections, Abailard's treatment of universals is prefaced by
a brief outline of the spectrum of positions on this problem by John of Salisbury. If Nominalism is taken loosely as anti-Realism, Abailard is clearly a
nominalist, as John of Salisbury says. But if finer lines are drawn and
Nominalism is taken to be the doctrine that universals are merely *names,*
then Abailard should rather be considered a conceptualist, for his general
position is that a universal must be capable of predication and no thing,
whether a universal substance or a particular name-sound can be predicated. These selections on universals are followed by excerpts from *Know
Thyself,* where he argues that consent alone, and neither desire nor the
act performed, constitutes sin.

JOHN OF SALISBURY

THE METALOGICON

BOOK II

CHAPTER 17. *In What a Pernicious Manner Logic Is Sometimes Taught; and the Ideas of Moderns About [the Nature of] Genera and Species.*

To show off their knowledge, our contemporaries dispense their instruction in such a way that their listeners are at a loss to understand them. They seem to have the impression that every letter of the alphabet is pregnant with the secrets of Minerva. They analyze and press upon tender ears everything that anyone has ever said or done. Falling into the error condemned by Cicero, they frequently come to be unintelligible to their hearers more because of the multiplicity than the profundity of their statements. "It is indeed useful and advantageous for disputants," as Aristotle observes, "to take cognizance of several opinions on a topic." From the mutual disagreement thus brought into relief, what is seen to be poorly stated may be disproved or modified. Instruction in elementary logic does not, however, constitute the proper occasion for such procedure. Simplicity, brevity, and easy subject matter are, so far as is possible, appropriate in introductory studies. This is so true that it is permissible to expound many difficult points in a simpler way than their nature strictly requires. Thus, much that we have learned in our youth must later be amended in more advanced philosophical studies. Nevertheless, at present, all are here [in introductory logical studies] declaiming on the nature of universals, and attempting to explain, contrary to the intention of the author, what is really a most profound question, and a matter [that should be reserved] for more advanced studies. One holds that universals are merely word sounds, although this opinion, along with its author Roscelin, has already almost completely passed into oblivion. Another maintains that universals are word concepts, and twists to support his thesis everything that he can remember to have ever been written on the subject. Our Peripatetic of Pallet, Abelard, was ensnared in this opinion. He left many, and still has, to this day, some followers and proponents of his doctrine. They are friends of mine, although they often so torture the helpless letter that even the hardest heart is filled with compassion for the latter. They hold that it is preposterous to predicate a thing concerning a thing, although Aristotle is author of this monstrosity. For Aristotle frequently asserts that a thing is predicated concerning a thing, as is evident to anyone who is really familiar with his teaching. Another is wrapped up in a consideration of acts of the [intuitive] understanding, and says that genera and species are nothing more than the latter. Proponents of this view take their cue from Cicero and

From Daniel D. McGarry, trans., *The Metalogicon of John of Salisbury,* Berkeley: University of California Press, 1955. Reprinted by permission.

Boethius, who cite Aristotle as saying that universals should be regarded as and called "notions." "A notion," they tell us, "is the cognition of something, derived from its previously perceived form, and in need of unravelment." Or again [they say]: "A notion is an act of the [intuitive] understanding, a simple mental comprehension." They accordingly distort everything written, with an eye to making acts of [intuitive] understanding or "notions" include the universality of universals. Those who adhere to the view that universals are things, have various and sundry opinions. One, reasoning from the fact that everything which exists is singular in number, concludes that either the universal is numerically one, or it is non-existent. But since it is impossible for things that are substantial to be non-existent, if those things for which they are substantial exist, they further conclude that universals must be essentially one with particular things. Accordingly, following Walter of Mortagne, they distinguish [various] states [of existence], and say that Plato is an individual in so far as he is Plato; a species in so far as he is a man; a genus of a subaltern [subordinate] kind in so far as he is an animal; and a most general genus in so far as he is a substance. Although this opinion formerly had some proponents, it has been a long time since anyone has asserted it. Walter now upholds [the doctrine of] ideas, emulating Plato and imitating Bernard of Chartres, and maintains that genus and species are nothing more nor less than these, namely, ideas. "An idea," according to Seneca's definition, "is an eternal exemplar of those things which come to be as a result of nature." And since universals are not subject to corruption, and are not altered by the changes that transform particular things and cause them to come and go, succeeding one another almost momentarily, ideas are properly and correctly called "universals." Indeed, particular things are deemed incapable of supporting the substantive verb, [i.e., of being said "to be"], since they are not at all stable, and disappear without even waiting to receive names. For they vary so much in their qualities, time, location, and numerous different properties, that their whole existence seems to be more a mutable transition than a stable status. In contrast, Boethius declares: "We say things 'are' when they may neither be increased nor diminished, but always continue as they are, firmly sustained by the foundations of their own nature." These [foundations] include their quantities, qualities, relations, places, times, conditions, and whatever is found in a way united with bodies. Although these adjuncts of bodies may seem to be changed, they remain immutable in their own nature. In like manner, although individuals [of species] may change, species remain the same. The waves of a stream wash on, yet the same flow of water continues, and we refer to the stream as the same river. Whence the statement of Seneca, which, in fact, he has borrowed from another: "In one sense it is true that we may descend twice into the same river, although in another sense this is not so." These "ideas," or "exemplary forms," are the original plans of all things. They may neither be decreased nor augmented; and they are so permanent and perpetual, that even if the whole world were to come to an end, they could not perish. They include all things, and, as Augustine seems to maintain in his book *On Free Will*, their number neither increases nor diminishes, because the ideas always continue on, even when it happens that [particular] temporal things cease to exist. What these men promise is wonderful, and familiar to philosophers who rise to the contemplation of higher things. But, as Boethius and numerous other authors testify, it is utterly foreign to the mind of Aristotle. For Aristotle very frequently opposes this view, as is clear from his books. Bernard of Chartres and his followers labored strenuously to compose the differences between Aristotle and Plato. But I opine that they arrived on the scene too late, so that their efforts to reconcile two dead men, who disagreed as long as they were alive and could do so, were in vain. Still another, in his endeavor to explain Aristotle, places universality in "native forms," as does Gilbert, Bishop of Poitiers, who labors to prove that "native forms" and universals are identical. A "native form" is an example of an original [exemplar]. It [the native form, unlike the original] inheres in created things, instead of subsisting in the divine mind. In Greek it is called the *idos,* since it stands in relation to the idea as the example does to its exemplar. The native form is sensible in things that are perceptible by the senses; but insensible as conceived in the mind. It is singular in individuals, but universal in all [of a kind]. Another, with Joscelin, Bishop of Soissons, attributes universality to collections of things, while denying it to things as individuals. When Joscelin tries to explain the authorities, he has his troubles and is hard put, for in many places he cannot bear the gaping astonishment of the indignant letter. Still another takes refuge in a new tongue, since he does not have sufficient command of Latin. When he hears the words "genus" and "species," at one time he says they should be understood as universals, and at another that they refer to the *maneries* of things. I know not in which of the authors he has found this term or this distinction, unless perhaps he has dug it out of lists of abstruse and obsolete words, or it is an item of jargon [in the baggage] of present-day doctors. I am further at a loss to see what it can mean here, unless it refers to collections of things, which would be the same as Joscelin's view, or to a universal thing, which, however, could hardly be called a *maneries.* For a *maneries* may be interpreted as referring to both [collections and universals], since a number of things, or the status in which a thing of such and such a type continues to exist may be called a *maneries.* Finally, there are some who fix their attention on the status of things, and say that genera and species consist in the latter.

PETER ABAILARD

THE GLOSSES OF PETER ABAILARD ON PORPHYRY

We may open our introduction to logic by examining something of the characteristic property of logic in its genus which is *philosophy.* Boethius says that not any knowledge whatever is philosophy, but only that which consists in the greatest things; for we do not call all wise men philosophers, but only these whose intelligence penetrates subtle matters. Moreover, Boethius distinguishes three species

Reprinted with the permission of Charles Scribner's Sons from *Selections from Medieval Philosophers,* Vol. I, pages 218–258, edited and translated by Richard McKeon. Copyright 1929 Charles Scribner's Sons; renewal copyright © 1957.

of philosophy, *speculative*, which is concerned with speculation on the nature of things, *moral*, for the consideration of the honorableness of life, *rational*, for compounding the relation of arguments, which the greeks call logic. However, some writers separated logic from philosophy and did not call it, according to Boethius, a part of philosophy but an instrument, because obviously the other parts work in logic in a manner, when they use its arguments to prove their own questions. As, if a question should arise in natural or moral speculation, arguments are derived from logic. Boethius himself holds, against them, that there is nothing to prevent the same thing from being both an instrument and a part of a single thing, as the hand is both a part and an instrument of the human body. Logic moreover seems itself often its own instrument when it demonstrates a question pertaining to itself by its own arguments, as for example: *man is the species of animal*. It is none the less logic, however, because it is the instrument of logic. So too it is none the less philosophy because it is the instrument of philosophy. Moreover, Boethius distinguishes it from the other two species of philosophy by its proper end, which consists in compounding arguments. For although the physicist compounds arguments, it is not physics but only logic which instructs him in that.

He noted too in regard to logic that it was composed of and reduced to certain rules of argumentation for this reason, namely, lest it lead inconstant minds into error by false inferences, since it seems to construct by its reasons what is not found in the nature of things, and since it seems often to infer things contrary in their conditions, in the following manner: *Socrates is body, but body is white, therefore Socrates is white*. On the other hand: *Socrates is body, but body is black, therefore Socrates is black*.

• • •

At present concerning genera. He states definitely what those more lofty questions are, although he does not resolve them. And the cause is stated for both actions, namely, that he should pass over inquiring into them and nevertheless should make mention of them. For he does not treat of them for this reason, because the uncultivated reader is not able to inquire into them or perceive them. But on the other hand he mentions them lest he make the reader negligent. For if he had ignored them entirely, the reader, thinking there was absolutely nothing more to be inquired concerning them, would disdain altogether the inquiry into them. There are then three questions, as Boethius says, secret and very useful and tried by not a few philosophers, but solved by few. The *first* is as follows, namely, whether genera and species subsist or are placed in the naked understandings alone, etc., as if he were to say: whether they have true being or whether they consist in opinion alone. The *second* is, if they are conceded to be truly, whether they are corporeal essences or incorporeal, and the *third* is whether they are separated from sensibles or are placed in them. For the species of incorporeal beings are two, in that some incorporeal beings, such as God and the soul, can subsist in their incorporeality apart from sensibles, and others are in nowise able to be beyond the sensible objects in which they are, as line cannot be found except in a body. These questions, however, he passes over in this fashion, saying: *At present I shall refuse to say concerning genera and species this, whether they subsist, etc., or whether subsisting they are corporeal or incorporeal, or whether, when they are said to be incorporeal, they should be separated from sensibles, etc., and in accord with them.* This last can be taken in different ways.

For it can be taken this way, as if to say: I will refuse to make the three assertions stated above concerning them and certain other statements in accord with these, that is, these three questions. In the same way, other questions which are difficult can be brought up concerning them, such as, the question of the common cause of the imposition of universal nouns, namely, what is that cause in virtue of which different things agree, or again the question of the understanding of universal nouns, in which no particular thing seems to be conceived, nor does the universal word seem to deal with any such particular thing, and many other difficult questions. We are able so to expound the words, *and in accord with them* that we may add a fourth question, namely, whether genera and species, so long as they are genera and species, must have some thing subject to them by nomination, —*name* or whether, if the things named were destroyed, the universal could still consist of the meaning only of the conception, as this noun *rose* when there is not a single rose to which it is common. But we shall investigate these questions more carefully later.

Now, however, let us follow the introduction literally. Note that when Porphyry says: *at present,* that is, in the present treatise, he intimates in a way that the reader may expect these questions to be solved elsewhere. *Most exalted business.* He states the reason for which he abstains here from these questions, namely, because to treat them is very exalted with respect to the reader who may not be able to attain to them in order to determine this business now. *And requiring greater diligence of inquiry,* for although the author is able to solve it, the reader is not able to inquire into it. Greater diligence of inquiry, I say, than yours. *This, however.* Having stated these things concerning which he is silent, he states those which he does treat of, namely, that which *the ancients,* not in age but in comprehension, *concluded probably,* that is, with verisimilitude, that is in which all have agreed and there was no dissension, *concerning these things,* to wit, genus and species *and of the* other three *things mentioned.* For in resolving the aforesaid questions some are of one opinion and others of another. Wherefore Boethius records that Aristotle held that genera and species subsist only in sensibles but are understood outside them, whereas Plato held not only that they were understood without sensibles but that they actually were separate. *And of these the ancients,* I say, and *most of all the peripatetics,* that is, part of these ancients; he calls dialecticians or a kind of argumentators the peripatetics.

Plato vs. + Aristotle

Note likewise that the functions which are proper to introductions can be distinguished in this introduction. For Boethius says *on the Topics of Cicero: Every introduction which is intended to compose the reader, as is said in the* Rhetoric, *seizes on benevolence or prepares attention or produces docility.* For it is proper that any one of the three or several at the same time be present in every introduction; but two are to be noted in this introduction, docility when he sets forth the material, which is those five predicables, and attention when he commends the treatise for a fourfold utility in that which the ancients advanced as the doctrine of these, or when he promises the style of an introduction. But benevolence is not necessary here where there is no knowledge hateful to one who seeks the treatment of it by Porphyry.

Let us return now, as we promised, to the above stated questions, and inquire carefully into them, and solve them. And since it is known that genera and species are universals and in them Porphyry touches on the nature of all universals generally, let us inquire here into the common nature of universals by studying these two [genus and species], and let us inquire also whether they apply only to *words* or to *things* as well.

In the *On Interpretation* Aristotle defines the universal as *that which is formed naturally apt to be predicated of many;* Porphyry moreover defines the particular, that is, the individual as *that which is predicated of only one.* Authority seems to ascribe the universal as much to things as to words; Aristotle himself ascribes it to things since he asserted immediately before the definition of universal: *However, since of things some are universals, and others are singulars, I call that universal which is formed to be predicated of many, and that singular which is not,* etc. Likewise Porphyry himself, when he said species are made of genus and difference, located them in the nature of things. From which it is manifest that things themselves are contained in the universal noun.

Nouns too are called universals. Where Aristotle says: *Genus determines quality with respect to substance; for it signifies how each thing is.* And Boethius in the book *on Divisions* says: *It is, however, extremely useful to know this, that the genus is in a certain manner the single likeness of many species, and that likeness displays the substantial agreement of them all.* Yet *to signify* or *to display* pertains to words; but *to be signified* applies to things. And again he says: *The designation of a noun is predicated of many nouns, and is in a certain manner a species containing under itself individuals.* However, it is not properly called species since a noun is not substantial but accidental, but it is decidedly a universal since the definition of the universal applies to it. Hence it follows that words are universals whose function it is to be predicates of propositions.

Since it would seem, then, that things as well as words are called universal, it must be inquired how the universal definition can be applied to things. For it seems that no thing, nor any collection of things, is predicated of many things taken one by one, which [predication] is required as the characteristic of the universal. For although this people or this house or Socrates may be predicated of all their parts at the same time, still no one says that they are universals, since the predication of them does not apply to each of the several individuals or parts. And one thing is predicated of many much less properly than a collection of things. Let us hear therefore how either one thing or a collection of things is called universal, and let us state all the opinions of all thinkers.

Certain philosophers, indeed, take the universal thing thus: in things different from each other in form they set up a substance essentially the same; this is the material essence of the individuals in which it is, and it is one in itself and diverse only through the forms of its inferiors. If these forms should happen to be taken away, there would be absolutely no difference of things, which are separated from each other only by a diversity of forms, since the matter is in essence absolutely the same. For example, in individual men, different in number, [i.e. in the different individuals of the species man] there is the same substance of man, which here is made Plato through these accidents, there Socrates through those. To these doctrines Porphyry seems to assent entirely when he says: *By participation in the species many men are one but in particulars the one and common is many.* And again he says: *Individuals are defined as follows, that each one of them consists of properties the collection of which is not in another.* Similarly, too, they place in the several animals different in species one and essentially the same substance of animal, which they make into diverse species by taking on diverse differences, as if from this wax I should first make the statue of a man, then the statue of a cow, by accommodating the diverse forms to the essence which persists wholly the same. This however is of importance, that the same wax does not constitute the statues at the same time, as is possible in the case of the universal, namely, that the universal is common, Boethius says, in such a way that the same universal is at the same time entirely in the different things of which it constitutes the substance materially; and although it is universal in itself, the same universal is individual through forms advening, without which it subsists naturally in itself; and apart from them it in no sense exists actually; for it is universal in nature but individual in actuality, and it is understood incorporeal and not subject to sense in the simplicity of its universality, but the same universal subsists in actuality, corporeal and sensible through accidents: and according to the same authority, Boethius, individuals subsist and universals are understood.

This is one of two opinions. Although authorities seem to agree very much upon it, physics is in every manner opposed to it. For if what is the same essentially, although occupied by diverse forms, exists in individual things, it is necessary that one thing which is affected by certain forms be another thing which is occupied by other forms, so that the animal formed by rationality is the animal formed by irrationality, and so the rational animal is the irrational, and thus contraries would be placed in the same thing at the same time; but they are in no wise contrary when they come together in the same essence, just as whiteness and blackness would not be contrary if they occurred at the same time in this one thing, although the thing itself were white from one source and black from another, just as it is white from one source and hard from another, that is, from whiteness and from hardness. For things that are diverse by contrariety can not be inherent at the same time in the same thing, like relatives and most others. Wherefore Aristotle in his chapter on *Relativity* [in the *Categories*] demonstrates that great and small, which he shows to be present at the same time in the same thing in diverse respects, can not be contraries because they are present in the same thing at the same time.

But perhaps it will be said according to that opinion that rationality and irrationality are no less contrary because they are found thus in the same thing, namely, in the same genus or in the same species, unless, that is, they be joined in the same individual. That too is shown thus: rationality and irrationality are truly in the same individual because they are in Socrates. But since they are in Socrates at the same time, it is proved that they are in Socrates and in an ass at the same time. But Socrates and the ass are Socrates. And Socrates and the ass are indeed Socrates, because Socrates is Socrates and the ass, since obviously Socrates is Socrates and Socrates is the ass. That Socrates is the ass is shown as follows according to this opinion: whatsoever is in Socrates other than the forms of Socrates, is that which is in the ass other than the forms of the ass. But whatever is in the ass other than the forms of the ass, is the ass. Whatever is in Socrates other than the forms of Socrates, is the ass. But if this is so, since Socrates is himself that which is other than the forms of Socrates, then Socrates is himself the ass. The truth of what we assumed above, namely, that whatever is in the ass other than the forms of the ass is the ass, we may indicate as follows, for neither are the forms of the ass the ass, since then accidents would be substance, nor are the matter and the forms of the ass taken together the ass, since then it would be necessary to say that body and not body were body.

There are those who, seeking an escape from this position, criticize only the words of the proposition, *the rational animal is the irrational animal,* but not the opinion, saying that the animal is both, but that that is not shown properly by these words *the rational animal is the irrational animal,* because clearly although it is one and the same thing, it is called rational for one reason and irrational for another, that is, from opposite forms. But surely, then, there is no opposition in those forms which would adhere absolutely in these things at the same time, nor do critics criticize the following propositions, *the rational animal is the mortal animal* or *the white animal is the walking animal,* because the animal is not mortal in that it is rational, nor does it walk in that it is white, but these propositions they hold as entirely true because the same animal has both forms at the same time although under a different aspect. Otherwise they would say that no animal is man since nothing is man in that it is animal.

Furthermore according to the position of the above-stated doctrine there are only ten essences of all things, that is, the ten generalissima, because in each one of the categories only one essence is found, and that is diversified only through the forms of subordinated classes, as has been said, and without them the essence would have no variety. Therefore, just as all substances are the same at bottom, so all qualities are the same, and quantities, etc. through the categories. Since, therefore, Socrates and Plato have in themselves things of each of the categories, and since these things are at bottom the same, all the forms of the one are forms of the other, which are not essentially different in themselves, just as the substances in which they inhere are not different, so that, for example, the quality of the one is the quality of the other for both are quality. They are therefore no more different because of the nature of qualities than because of the nature of substance, because the essence of their substance is one as is likewise that of qualities. For the same reason quantity, since it is the same, does not make a difference nor do the other categories. For which reason there can be no difference because of forms, which are not different from each other, exactly as substances are no different from each other.

Moreover, how should we explain the plurality of things under substance if the only diversity were of forms while the subject substance remained at bottom the same? For we do not call Socrates many in number because of the imposition of many forms.

That position can not stand, moreover, by which it is held that individuals are made up by the accidents of themselves. For if individuals draw their being from accidents, obviously the accidents are prior naturally to the individuals, as differences are prior to the species they draw into being. For as man is made distinct by the formation of difference, so they speak of Socrates from the imposition of accidents. Whence Socrates can not be without accidents, nor man without differences. Therefore, Socrates is not the basis of accidents as man is not the basis of differences. If, however, accidents are not in individual substances as in subjects, surely they are not in universals. For whatever things are in second substances as in subjects, he shows are likewise universally in first substances as in subjects. Whence, consequently, it is manifest that the opinion in which it is held that absolutely the same essence subsists at the same time in diverse things, lacks reason utterly.

Therefore others are of another opinion concerning universality, and approaching the truth more closely they say that individual things are not only different from each other in forms, but are discrete personally in their essences, nor is that which is in one in any way to be found in another whether it be matter of form; nor even when the forms have been removed can things subsist less discrete in their essences because their personal discreteness (according to which of course this is not that) is not determined by forms but is the diversity itself of essence, just as the forms themselves are diverse one from the other in themselves; otherwise the diversity of forms would proceed *in infinitum,* so that it would be necessary that still other forms be made the basis of the diversity of any forms. Porphyry noted such a difference between the most comprehensive genus and the ultimate species, saying: *Further, species would never become the highest genus and genus would never become the ultimate species,* as if he were to say: this is the difference between them, that the essence of the one is not the essence of the other. So too the distinction of categories is not effected through some forms which make it, but through the diversification of their very essence. But since they hold all things are so diverse from each other that none of them participates with another in either the same matter essentially or the same form essentially, and yet, they cling to the universality of things, they reconcile these positions by saying that things which are discrete are one and the same not *essentially* but *indifferently,* as they say individual men, who are discrete in themselves, are the same in man, that is, they do not differ in the nature of humanity, and the same things which they call individual according to discreteness, they call universal according to *indifference* and the agreement of similitude.

But here too there is disagreement. For some hold that the universal thing is only in a collection of many. They in no manner call Socrates and Plato species in themselves, but they say that all men collected together are that species which is man, and all animals taken together that genus which is animal, and thus with the others. Boethius seems to agree with them in this. *Species must be considered to be nothing other than the thought collected from the substantial likeness of individuals, and genus from the likeness of species.* For since he says the *collected likeness* he indicates a collecting of many. Otherwise they would not have in the universal thing a predication of many things or a content of many things, nor would universals be fewer than individuals.

There are others, moreover, who say that the species is not only men brought together, but also the individuals in that they are men, and when they say that the thing which is Socrates is predicated of many, it is to be taken figuratively as if they were to say: many are the same as he, that is, agree with him, or else he agrees with many. According to the number of things they posit as many species as there are individuals and as many genera, but according to the likeness of natures they assign a smaller number of universals than individuals. Certainly all men are at one time many in themselves by personal discreteness and one by the similitude of humanity; and with respect to discreteness and with respect to likeness the same are judged to be different from themselves, as Socrates, in that he is a man, is divided from himself in that he is Socrates. Otherwise the same thing could not be its own genus or species unless it should have some difference of its own from itself, since things that are relatives must at least in some one respect be opposed one to the other.

Now, however, let us first invalidate the opinion which was set down above concerning collection, and let us inquire how the whole collection of men together, which is called one species, has to be predicated of many that it may be universal, although the whole collection is not predicated of each. But if it be conceded that the whole is predicated of different things by parts, in that, namely, its individual parts are accommodated to themselves, that has nothing to do with the community of the universal, all of which, as Boethius says, must be in each individual, and it is in this point that the universal is distinguished from the type of community which is common by its parts, as for example a field of which the different parts belong to different men. Further, Socrates would in the same way be predicated of many because of his many different parts, so that he would himself be a universal. Even more, it would be proper that any group of many men taken together be called universal, and the definition of the universal or even of the species would be adapted to them in the same way, so that the whole collection of men would then include many species. In the same way we should call any collection of bodies or spirits one universal substance with the result that, since the whole collection of substances is one generalissimum, if any one substance be removed and the others remain, we should have to maintain that there are many generalissima in substances. But perhaps it should be said that no collection which is included in the generalissimum, is generalissimum. But I still object that when one substance has been taken from substances, if the residual collection is not the generalissimum and nevertheless remains universal substance, it is necessary that this be a species of substance and have a coequal species under the same genus. But what can be opposite to it, since either the species of substance is contained entirely in it, or else it shares the same individuals with it, as rational animal, mortal animal? Even more. Every universal is naturally prior to its own individuals. But a collection of many things is an integral whole to the individuals of which it is composed and is naturally posterior to the things from which it is composed. Further. Between the integer and the universal Boethius sets up this difference in the *on Divisions,* that the part is not the same as the whole, but the species is always the same as the genus. But how will the whole collection of men be able to be the multitude of animals?

It remains for us now to attack those who call single individuals, in that they agree with others, universal, and who grant that the same individuals are predicated of many things, not as they may be the many essentially, but because the many agree with them. But if it is the same to be predicated of many as to agree with many, how do we say that an individual is predicated of only one, since clearly there is no thing which agrees with only one thing? How too is a difference made between universal and particular by *being predicated of many,* since in exactly the same way in which man agrees with many, Socrates too agrees with many? Surely man, in so far as he is man and Socrates in so far as he is man agree with others. But neither man, in so far as he is Socrates nor Socrates in so far as he is Socrates agrees with others. Therefore, that which man has, Socrates has and in the same way.

Further, since the thing is granted to be absolutely the same, namely, the man which is in Socrates and Socrates himself, there is no difference of the one from the other. For no thing is itself different from itself at the same time because it has whatsoever it has in itself and in absolutely the same manner. Whence Socrates, at once white and a grammarian, although he has different things in himself, is not nevertheless by that fact different from himself since he has the same two and in absolutely the same manner. Indeed he is not a grammarian in another manner from himself nor white in another manner, just as white is not other than himself nor grammarian other than himself. Moreover how can this, which they

say, be understood, that Socrates agrees with Plato in man, since it is known
that all men differ from each other as well in matter as in form? For if Socrates
agrees with Plato in the thing which is man, but no other thing is man except
Socrates himself or another, it is necessary that he agree with Plato either in himself or in another. But in himself he is rather different from him; with respect to
another it is concluded likewise that he is not another. There are, however, those
who take *agree in man* negatively, as if it were said: Socrates does not differ from
Plato in man. But this likewise can be said, that he does not differ from him in
stone, since neither of them is stone. And so no greater agreement between them
is noted in man than in stone, unless perchance some proposition precede it, as if
it were stated thus: They are man because they do not differ in man. But this can
not stand either, since it is utterly false that they do not differ in man. For if
Socrates does not differ from Plato in the thing which is man, he does not differ
from him in himself. For if he differs in himself from Plato, but he is himself the
thing which is man, certainly he differs from him also in the thing which is man.

Now, however, that reasons have been given why things can not be called
universals, taken either singly or collectively, because they are not predicated of
many, *it remains to ascribe universality of this sort to words alone.* Just as, therefore, certain nouns are called appellative by grammarians and certain nouns
proper, so certain simple words are called by dialecticians *universals,* certain words
particulars, that is, individuals. A *universal* word, however, is one which is apt
by its invention to be predicated singly of many, as this noun *man* which is
conjoinable with the particular names of men according to the nature of the
subject things on which it is imposed. A *particular* word is one which is predicable
of only one, as *Socrates* when it is taken as the name of only one. For if you take
it equivocally, you make it not a word, but many words in signification, because
according to Priscian many nouns obviously may coincide in a single word. When,
therefore, the universal is described to be that which is predicated of many, the
that which, which is used, indicates not only the simplicity of the word as regards
discreteness of expression but also the unity of meaning as regards discreteness
of equivocals.

Having shown, however, what is accomplished by the phrase *that which* above
in the definition of the universal, we should consider carefully two more phrases
which follow, namely, *to be predicated* and *of many.*

To be predicated is to be conjoinable to something truly by the declarative
function of a substantive verb in the present [tense], as *man* can be joined truly
to different things by a substantive verb. Verbs such as *he runs* and *he walks*
likewise when predicated of many have the power of substantive verbs to join as
a copula joins. Whence Aristotle says in the second section of the *on Interpretations: These verbs in which 'is' does not occur, as to run or to walk do the same
when so affirmed as if 'is' were added.* And again he says: *There is no difference
in the expressions, man walks and man is walking.*

That he says, *of many,* however, brings together names according to the
diversity of things named. Otherwise Socrates would be predicated of many when
it is said: *this man is Socrates, this animal is, this white, this musician.* These
names although they are different in the understanding, nevertheless have precisely
the same subject thing.

Note, moreover, that the conjoining involved in *construction* to which *grammarians* direct their attention is one thing, the conjoining of *predication* which

dialecticians consider another: for as far as the power of construction is concerned, *man* and *stone* are properly conjoinable by *is,* and any nominative cases, as *animal* and *man,* in respect to making manifest a meaning but not in respect to showing the status of a thing. The conjoining involved in *construction* consequently is good whenever it reveals a perfect sentence, whether it be so or not. But the conjoining involved in *predication,* which we take up here, pertains to the nature of things and to demonstrating the truth of their status. If any one should say *man is a stone,* he has not made a proper construction of man and stone in respect to the meaning he wished to demonstrate, but there has been no fault of grammar; and although so far as the meaning of the proposition is concerned, this stone is predicated of man, to whom clearly it is construed as predicated (as false categories too have their predicated term), still in the nature of things stone is not predicable of man. We merely note here the great force of this predication while defining the universal.

It seems, then, that the universal is never quite the appellative noun, nor the particular the proper noun, but they are related to each other as that which exceeds and that which is exceeded. For the appellative and proper contain not only the nominative cases but also the oblique cases, which do not have to be predicated, and therefore they are excluded in the definition of the universal by *to be predicated;* these oblique cases, moreover, because they are less necessary to the proposition (which alone, according to Aristotle, is the subject of the present speculation, that is, of dialectic consideration, and assuredly the proposition alone compounds argumentations), are not taken by Aristotle himself in any sense into the nouns, and he himself does not call them nouns but the cases of nouns. But just as it is not necessary that all appellative and proper nouns be called universals or particulars, so also conversely. For the universal includes not only nouns but also verbs and infinite nouns, to which, that is, to infinite nouns, the definition of the appellative which Priscian gives does not seem to apply.

However, now that a definition of universal and of particular has been assigned to words, let us inquire carefully into the property of universal words especially. Questions have been raised concerning these universals, for there are very grave doubts concerning their meaning, since they seem neither to have any subject thing nor to constitute a clear meaning of anything. Universal nouns seemed to be imposed on no things whatsoever, since obviously all things subsisted in themselves discretely and, as has been shown, did not agree in anything, according to the agreement of which thing the universal nouns could be imposed. Consequently, since it is certain that universals are not imposed on things according to the difference of discreteness of things, for they would then be not common, but particular; and again since universals could not name things as they agree in some thing, for there is no thing in which they agree, universals seem to derive no meaning from things, particularly since they constitute no understanding of any thing. Wherefore in the *on Divisions* Boethius says that the word *man* gives rise to doubt of its meaning because when it has been heard, *the understanding of the person hearing is carried off by many changing things and is betrayed into errors. For unless some one define the word, saying 'all men walk' or at least 'certain men,' and should characterize this man if he happens to walk, the understanding of the person hearing does not have anything to understand reasonably.* For since *man* is imposed upon individuals for the same reason, because namely they are rational mortal animals, that very community of imposition is an impediment which prevents any one man being understood in it, as on the contrary in this name *Socrates* the proper person of only one man is understood, and therefore, it is called a particular. But in the common name which is *man,* not Socrates himself nor any other man nor the entire collection of men is reasonably understood from the import of the word, nor is Socrates himself, as certain thinkers hold, specified by that word, even in so far as he is man. For even if Socrates alone be sitting in this house, and if because of him alone this proposition is true: *A man sits in this house,* nevertheless in no wise is the subject transferred by the name of man to Socrates, except in so far as he is also man, otherwise sitting would rationally be understood from the proposition to inhere in him, so that it could be inferred clearly from the fact that a man sits in this house, that Socrates sits in it. In the same way, no other man can be understood in this noun *man,* nor can the whole collection of men since the proposition can be true of only one. Consequently, man or any other universal word seems to signify no one thing since it constitutes the meaning of no thing. But it seems that there can not be a meaning which does not have a subject thing which it conceives. Whence Boethius says in the *Commentary: Every idea is made either from the subject thing, as the thing is constituted or as it is not constituted. For an idea can not be made from no subject.* Wherefore universals seem wholly unrelated to signification.

But this is not so. For they signify in a manner different things by nomination, not however by forming a conception arising from different things but only pertaining to each of them. Just as this word *man* names individual things for a common reason, namely that they are men, because of which it is called universal, and also forms a certain conception which is common, not proper, that is, pertaining to the individuals of which it conceives the common likeness.

But now let us inquire carefully into these things which we have touched upon briefly, namely, *what that common cause by which the universal word is imposed is, and what the conception of the understanding of the common likeness of things is, and whether the word is called common because of a common cause in which the things agree or because of a common conception or because of both at once.*

And first we should consider the *common cause.* Individual men, discrete from each other in that they differ in respect to properties no less in essences than in forms (as we noted above when we were inquiring into the physics of a thing) are united nevertheless in that they are men. I do not say that they are united in man, since no thing is man except a discrete thing, but in being man. But *to be man* is not the same as man nor any thing, if we should consider it very carefully, as *not to be in the subject* is not any thing, nor is it any thing *not to undergo contrariety* or *not to undergo more and less*; in these nevertheless Aristotle says all substances agree. For since, as we have demonstrated above, there can be no agreement in fact, if that by which there is an agreement between any things, be taken in this way, that it is not any thing, so Socrates and Plato are alike in being man as horse and ass are alike in not being man, in which way both horse and ass are called non-man. Consequently for different things to agree is for the individuals to be the same or not to be the same, as to be man or white or not to be man and not to be white. It seems, however, that we must avoid considering the agreement of things according to that which is not any thing (as if we were to unite in nothing things which are) since we say, in fact, that this and that agree in the status of man, that is, in that they are men. But we understand nothing other than that they are men, and in this they do not differ in the least, in this, I say, that they are men, although we appeal to no essence. We call it the status itself of man to be man, which is not a thing and which we also called the common cause of imposition of the word on individuals, according as they themselves agree with each other. Often, however, we call those things too by the name of cause which are not any thing, as when it is said: he was lashed because he does not wish to appear in court. He does not wish to appear in court, which is stated as cause, is no essence. We can also call the status of man those things themselves, established in the nature of man, the common likeness of which he who imposed the word conceived.

Having shown the signification of universals, namely, relative to things by nomination, and having set forth the cause of their common imposition, let us now show *what are the understandings of universals* which they constitute.

And let us first distinguish generally the nature of all understandings.

Although, then, the senses as well as the understandings are of the soul, this is the difference between them, that the senses are exercised only through corporeal instruments and perceive only bodies or what are in bodies, as sight perceives the tower and its visible qualities. The understanding, however, as it does not need a corporeal instrument, so it is not necessary that it have a subject body to which it may be referred, but it is satisfied with the likeness of things which the mind constructs for itself, into which it directs the action of its intelligence. Wherefore if the tower should be destroyed and removed, the sense which acted on it perishes, but the understanding remains in the likeness of the thing preserved in the mind. However, just as the sense is not the thing perceived to which it is directed, so neither is the understanding the form of the thing which it conceives, but the understanding is a certain action of the soul by which it is called intelligent or understanding, but the form to which it is directed is a certain imaginary and fictive thing, which the mind constructs for itself when it wishes and as it wishes, like those imaginary cities which are seen in dreams, or that form of the projected building which the artist conceives as the figure and exemplar of the thing to be formed, which we can call neither substance nor accident.

Nevertheless, there are those who call that form the same as the understanding, as they call the building of the tower, which I conceive while the tower is not there and which I contemplate, lofty and square in the spacious plain, the same as the understanding of the tower. Aristotle seems to agree with them, when he calls, in the *on Interpretation*, those passions of the soul which they call the understandings, the likenesses of things.

We, on the other hand, call the image the likeness of the thing. But there is nothing to prevent the understanding also being called in a sense a likeness, because obviously it conceives that which is properly called the likeness of the thing. But we have said, and well, that it is different from the image. For I ask whether that squareness and the loftiness is the true form of the understanding which is formed to the likeness of the quantity and the composition of the tower. But surely true squareness and true loftiness are present only in bodies, and neither an understanding nor any true essence can be formed from a fictive quality. It remains, therefore, that just as the quality is fictive, a fictive substance is subject to it. Perhaps, moreover, the image in a mirror too, which seems to be the subject of sight, can be said truly to be nothing, since obviously the quality of a contrary color appears often in the white surface of the mirror.

The following question, however, can be raised, when the soul perceives and understands the same thing at the same time, as when it discerns a stone, whether then the understanding too deals with the image of the stone or whether the understanding and the sense at the same time have to do with the stone itself. But it seems more reasonable that the understanding has no need of the image when there is present to it the truth of the substance. If, moreover, any one should say where there is sense there is no understanding, we should not concede that. For it often happens that the mind perceives one thing and understands another, as is apparent to those who study well, who, while they look at the things present to the open eyes, nevertheless think of other things concerning which they write.

Now that the nature of understandings has been examined generally, let us distinguish between the understandings of universals and particulars. These are separated in that that which is of the universal noun, conceives a common and confused image of many things, whereas that which the particular word generates, holds to the proper and as it were the particular form of one thing, that is, restricts itself to only one person. Whence when I hear *man* a certain figure arises in my mind which is so related to individual men that it is common to all and proper to none. When, however, I hear *Socrates* a certain form arises in my mind, which expresses the likeness of a certain person. Whence by this word *Socrates*, which generates in the mind the proper form of one person, a certain thing is specified and determined, but by *man*, the understanding of which rests in the common form of all men, that very community leads to confusion, lest we should not understand any one in particular. Wherefore *man* is rightly said to signify neither Socrates nor any other man, since none is specified by the meaning of the word, although nevertheless it names particulars. *Socrates*, on the other hand, must not only name a certain particular, but also determine the subject thing.

But the question is raised, then, since we said above that according to Boethius every idea has a subject thing, how this applies to the ideas of universals. But it must be noted surely that Boethius introduces this statement in the sophistical argument by which he shows that the idea of universals is vain. Whence there is nothing to prevent that the statement is not proved in truth; whence avoiding falsity he shows the reasons of other writers. We can, moreover, refer to, as the thing subject to the understanding, either the true substance of the thing, as when it is at one with the sense, or else the conceived form of any thing whatsoever, that is, when the thing is absent, whether that form be common as we have said or proper; common, I say, with respect to the likeness of many which it retains although it is still considered in itself as one thing. For thus, to show the nature of all lions, one picture can be made representing what is proper to no one of them, and on the other hand another can be made suitable to distinguish any one of them, which would bring out certain individual characteristics, as if it were painted limping or mutilated or wounded by the spear of Hercules. Just as, therefore, one figure of things is painted common, another particular, so too, are they conceived one common, another proper.

However, with respect to that form to which the understanding is directed, it is a matter of doubt, not unintelligently, whether the word too signifies the form. This seems to be firmly established by authority as well as by reason.

For Priscian in the first book of *Constructions,* after he had stated first the common imposition of universals on individuals, seemed to have a certain other meaning of universals, namely, a meaning of common form, saying: *with respect to the general and special forms of things, those which are constituted in the divine mind intelligibly before they were produced in bodies, are suited to demonstrate the genera or species of the nature of things.* For the question in this place is of God, as of an artist about to compose something, who preconceives in his mind the exemplary form of the thing to be composed; he works to the likeness of this form which is said to go into the body when the true thing is composed in its likeness. This common conception, however, is well ascribed to God, but not to man, because those general works or special states of nature are proper to God, not to the artist; as man, soul, or stone are proper to God, but house or sword to man. Whence the latter, house or sword, are not works of nature, as are the former, nor are words of them of substance, but of accident, and therefore they are neither genera nor are they species. Therefore, conceptions of this sort by abstraction are ascribed well to the divine mind but not to the human mind, because men who learn things only through the senses, scarcely ever or never ascend to simple understanding of this sort, and the exterior sensuality of accidents prevents them from conceiving the natures of things purely. God, however, to whom all things which he created are known through themselves and who knows them before they are, distinguishes the individual states among them, and sense is no impediment to him who alone has only true understanding. Whence it happens that men have, in those things which have not been touched by the sense, opinion rather than understanding as we learn from experience itself. For, when we have thought of some city which we have not seen we discover when we have come to it that we had thought it to be otherwise than it is.

So likewise I think we have opinion of the intrinsic forms which do not come to the senses, such as rationality and mortality, paternity, sitting. Any names of any existent things, on the other hand, generate, so far as is in them, understanding rather than opinion, because their inventor intended that they be imposed according to some natures or properties of things, although even he was not able to think out thoroughly the nature or the property of the thing. Priscian, however, calls these common conceptions general or special, because general or special nouns describe them in one way or another to us. He says that the universals themselves are as proper nouns to these conceptions, which, although they are of confused meaning with respect to the essences named, direct the mind of the auditor to that common conception immediately, just as proper nouns direct the attention to the one thing which they signify. Porphyry, too, when he says that some ideas are constituted from matter and form, and some to the likeness of matter and form, seems to have understood this conception, since he says to the likeness of matter and form, of which more will be said in its proper place. Boethius likewise, when he says that the thought collected from the likeness of many things is genus or species, seems to have understood the same common conception. Some insist that Plato was of this opinion too, namely that he called those common ideas which he places in *nous,* genera or species. In this perhaps Boethius records that he dissented from Aristotle when he says that Plato wanted genera and species and the others not only to be understood universals, but also to be and to subsist without bodies, as if to say that he understood as universals those common conceptions which he set up separated from bodies in *nous*, not perhaps taking the universal as the common predication, as Aristotle does, but rather as the common likeness of many things. For that latter conception seems in no wise to be predicated of many as a noun is which is adapted singly to many.

That he says Plato thinks universals subsist without sensibles, can be resolved in another manner so that there is no disagreement in the opinions of the philosophers. For what Aristotle says to the effect that universals always subsist in sensibles, he said only in regard to actuality, because obviously the nature which is animal which is designated by the universal name and which according to this is called universal by a certain transference, is never found in actuality except in a sensible thing, but Plato thinks that it so subsists in itself naturally that it would retain its being when not subjected to sense, and according to this the natural being is called by the universal name. That, consequently, which Aristotle denies with respect to actuality, Plato, the investigator of physics, assigns to natural aptitude, and thus there is no disagreement between them.

Moreover, now that *authorities* have been advanced who seem to build up by universal words common concepts which are to be called forms, *reason* too seems to assent. For what else is it to conceive forms by nouns than to signify by nouns? But certainly since we make forms diverse from understandings, there arises now besides thing and understanding a third thing which is the signification of nouns. Although authority does not hold this, it is nevertheless not contrary to reason.

Let us, then, set forth what we promised above to define, namely, whether the community of universal words is considered to be because of a common cause of imposition or because of a common conception or because of both. There is nothing to prevent that it be because of both, but the common cause which is taken in accordance with the nature of things seems to have greater force.

Likewise we must define that which we noted above, namely, that *the conceptions of universals are formed by abstraction, and we must indicate how we may speak of them alone, naked and pure but not empty.*

And first concerning *abstraction*. In relation to abstraction it must be known that matter and form always subsist mixed together, but the reason of the mind has this power, that it may now consider matter by itself; it may now turn its attention to form alone; it may now conceive both intermingled. The two first processes, of course, are by abstraction; they abstract something from things conjoined that they may consider its very nature. But the third process is by conjunction. For example, the substance of this man is at once body and animal and man and invested in infinite forms; when I turn my attention to this in the material essence of the substance, after having circumscribed all forms, I have a concept by the process of abstraction. Again, when I consider only corporeity in it, which I join to substance, that concept likewise (although it is by conjunction with respect to the first, which considered only the nature of substance) is formed also by abstraction with respect to other forms than corporeity, none of which I consider, such as animation, sensuality, rationality, whiteness.

Conceptions of this sort through abstraction seemed perhaps false and vain for this reason, that they perceive the thing otherwise than it subsists. For since they are concerned with matter by itself or form separately, and since none the less neither of these subsists separately, they seem obviously to conceive the thing otherwise than it is, and therefore to be empty. But this is not so. For if one understands otherwise than the thing is constituted, in such manner that one considers it manifestly in such a nature and property as it does not have, certainly that understanding is empty. But that is not what is done in abstraction. For, when I consider this man only in the nature of substance or of body, and not also of animal or of man or of grammarian, obviously I understand nothing except what is in that nature, but I do not consider all that it has. And when I say that I consider only this one among the qualities the nature has, the *only* refers to the attention alone, not to the mode of subsisting, otherwise the understanding would be empty. For the thing does not have only it, but it is considered only as having it. And still in a certain sense it is said to be understood otherwise than it is, not in another state than it is, as has been said above, but otherwise, in that the mode of understanding is other than the mode of subsisting. For this thing is understood separately from the other, not separated from it, although it does not, notwithstanding, exist separately; and matter is perceived purely and form simply, although the one is not purely and the other is not simply, so that manifestly that purity or simplicity is reduced to the understanding and not to the subsistence of the thing, so that they are of course modes of understanding and not of subsisting. The senses, moreover, often operate in different ways with composite things, so that if a statue is half of gold and half of silver, I can discern separately the gold and the silver which are joined together, that is, examining now the gold, now the silver by itself, looking separately upon things which are conjoined, but not looking upon them as separated, in that they are not separated. So too the understanding considers separately by abstraction, but does not consider as separated, otherwise it would be empty.

Nevertheless, perhaps such a conception too could be good which considers things which are conjoined, as in one manner separated and in another manner conjoined, and conversely. For the conjunction of things as well as the division can be taken in two ways. For we say that certain things are conjoined to each other by some likeness, as these two men in that they are men or grammarians, and that certain things are conjoined by a kind of apposition and aggregation, as form and matter or wine and water. The conception in question conceives things which are so joined to each other as divided in one manner, in another conjoined. Whence Boethius ascribes the following power to the mind, that it can by its reason both compound that which was disjoined and resolve that which is composite, departing nevertheless in neither from the nature of the thing, but only perceiving that which is in the nature of the thing. Otherwise it would not be reason, but opinion, that is, if the understanding should deviate from the state or the thing.

But the following question arises concerning the *providence* of the artist, whether it is empty when he holds in mind the form of a work still future, seeing that the thing is not yet constituted so. But if we grant that, we are forced to say that likewise the providence of God is empty, which he had before the creation of his work. But if one says this with respect to the effect, namely, that what he foresees would not eventuate actually as he foresees, then it is false that the providence was empty. If on the other hand one says that it was empty for this reason, that it did not yet agree with the future state of the thing, we are disinclined to the evil words but we do not object to the opinion. For it is true that the future state of the world was not yet materially, when he disposed it intelligibly as future still. Nevertheless, we are not accustomed to call empty the thought or the providence of any thing except that which lacks effect, nor do we say that we think in vain except these thoughts which we will not accomplish actually. Consequently, modifying the words we should say that the providence is not empty which does not think in vain, but conceives things which are not yet materially as if they subsisted, which is natural to all providences. Obviously thought concerning future things is called providence; thought concerning past things memory; concerning present things understanding proper. If, however, any one says that he is deceived who thinks of providing for the future state as for the one now existing, he is rather himself deceived in thinking that such an one must be said to be deceived. For, to be sure, he who forsees for the future is not deceived, unless he should think it is already as he forsees. Nor, in fact, does the conception of a non-existent thing lead to deception, but rather the faith added to it. For even though I think of a rational crow, if I do not believe it, I am not deceived. So too the provident person is not deceived, in that he does consider that that which as existing does not now exist thus, but as he thinks of it now he sets it as present in the future. Surely every conception of the mind is as of the present. So if I should consider Socrates in that he was a boy or in that he will be an old man, I join boyhood or old age to him, as it were in the present, because I consider him at present in a past or future property. Nevertheless, no one says that this memory is empty because what it conceives as present it considers in the past. But there will be a fuller investigation of this in relation to the *on Interpretation*.

In the case of God it is decided even more rationally that his substance, which alone is immutable and simple, is varied by no conceptions of things or any other forms. For although the custom of human speech presumes to speak of the creator as of creatures, since of course it calls him either provident or intelligent, still nothing in him should be understood or can be diverse from him, that is, neither his understanding nor any other form. And consequently any question concerning the understanding with respect to God is superfluous. And to speak the truth more expressly, it is nothing other for him to forsee the future than for him, who is true reason in himself, not to be in darkness concerning the future.

Now, however, that many things have been shown concerning the nature of abstraction, let us return to the *conception of universals* which must always be formed by abstraction. For when I hear *man* or *whiteness* or *white* I do not recall from the meaning of the noun all the natures or properties which are in the subject things, but from *man* I have only the conception although confused, not discrete, of animal and rational mortal, but not of the later accidents as well. For the conceptions of individuals, too, are formed by abstraction, when namely, it is said: this substance, this body, this animal, this man, this whiteness, this white. For by *this man* I consider only the nature of man but related to a certain subject, whereas by *man* I consider that same nature simply in itself not related to any one. Wherefore the understanding of universals is rightly spoken of as alone and naked and pure, that is, alone from the senses, because it does not perceive the thing as sensual, and naked in regard to the abstraction of all and of any forms, and pure with respect to discreteness because no thing whether it be

matter or form, is designated in it; in this latter respect we called a conception
of this sort confused above.

Consequently, *having examined these things, let us proceed to the resolution
of the questions concerning genera and species proposed by Porphyry,* which we
can do easily now that the nature of all universals has been shown.

The first question, then, was to this effect, whether genera and species subsist,
that is, signify something truly existent, or are placed in the understanding alone,
etc., that is, are located in empty opinion without the thing, like the following
words, chimera and goat-stag which do not give rise to a rational understanding.
To this it must be replied that in truth they signify by nomination things
truly existent, to wit, the same things as singular nouns, and in no wise are they
located in empty opinion; nevertheless, they consist in a certain sense in the
understanding alone and naked and pure, as has been determined. There is
nothing, however, to prevent one who states the question from taking some words
in one way in inquiry and one who solves it from taking them in another way
in solution, as if he who solves the question were to say: you ask whether they
are placed in the understanding alone, etc. This you can take in the manner
(which is the true one) which we discussed above. And the words can be taken
in absolutely the same sense on both sides, by the resolver and by the inquirer;
and then it is made a single question not by opposition of the prior members of
two dialectical questions, to wit, these: whether they are or are not, and again
whether they are placed in the sole and naked and pure understanding or not.

The same can be said in the second question which is as follows: whether subsisting they are corporeal or incorporeal, that is, when they are conceded to
signify subsistences whether they signify subsistences which are corporeal or
subsistences which are incorporeal. Certainly everything that is, as Boethius says,
is either corporeal, or incorporeal, that is, we take these words corporeal and incorporeal for substantial body and non-body, or for that which can be perceived
by the corporeal sense, such as man, wood, whiteness, or that which can not, such
as soul, justice. Corporeal likewise can be taken for discrete, as if the following
were inquired: since universals signify subsistences, whether they signify them
discrete or not discrete. For he who investigates the truth of the thing well, considers not only what can be said truly, but everything that can be stated in opinion.
Whence even though it be certain to some that nothing subsists except the discrete,
nevertheless because there can be the opinion that there might be other subsistences, it is inquired not without reason concerning them too. And this last meaning of corporeal seems to fall in better with the question; namely, that the question
be raised concerning discrete and non-discrete. But perhaps when Boethius says
that everything that is is either corporeal or incorporeal, the incorporeal seems
superfluous since no existing thing is incorporeal, that is, non-discrete. Nor does
that which comes to mind in relation to the order of the questions seem to afford
any help, unless perhaps in this respect, that as corporeal and incorporeal divide
subsistences in another sense, so too it seems they divide them in this sense, as
if the inquirer were to say: I see that of existing things some are called corporeal
and others incorporeal, which of these shall we say are the things signified by
universals? To which the reply is made: in a certain sense corporeal things, that
is, things discrete in their essence and incorporeal with respect to the designation
of the universal noun because obviously universals do not name discretely and
determinately, but confusedly, as we have set forth sufficiently above. Whence the

universal names themselves are called both corporeal with respect to the nature of things and incorporeal with respect to the manner of signification, because although they name things which are discrete, nevertheless they do not name them discretely and determinately.

The third question, of course, whether they are placed in sensibles, etc., follows from granting that they are incorporeal, because obviously the incorporeal taken in a certain manner is divided by being and by not being in the sensible, as we have also noted above. And universals are said to subsist in sensibles, that is to signify an intrinsic substance existing in a thing which is sensible by its exterior forms, and although they signify this substance which subsists actually in the sensible thing, yet they demonstrate the same substance naturally separated from the sensible thing, as we determind above in relation to Plato. Wherefore Boethius says that genera and species are understood, but are not, outside sensible things, in that obviously the things of genera and species are considered with respect to their nature rationally in themselves beyond all sensuality, because they can truly subsist in themselves even when the exterior forms by which they come to the senses have been removed. For we grant that all genera or species are in sensual things. But because the understanding of them was said to be always apart from sense, they seemed in no wise to be in sensible things. Wherefore it was inquired rightly whether they could ever be in sensibles, and it is replied with respect to some of them that they are, but in such fashion that, as has been said, they continue to be naturally beyond sensuality.

We can however take corporeal and incorporeal in the second question as sensible and insensible, in order that the order of questions may be more appropriate; and since the understanding of universals was said to be only from sense, as has been said, it was asked properly, whether universals were sensible or insensible; and since it is answered that some of them are sensible with respect to the nature of things, and that the same are insensible with respect to the mode of signifying, because obviously they do not designate the sensible things which they name in the same manner as they are perceived, that is as discrete, and sense does not discover them by demonstration of them, it remained a question whether universals named sensible things only or whether they also signified something else; to which it is replied that they signify both sensible things and at the same time that common conception which Priscian ascribes particularly to the divine mind.

And in accord with them. With respect to that which we understand here as the fourth question, as we noted above, the following is the solution, that we in no wise hold that universal nouns are, when, their things having been destroyed, they are not predicable of many things inasmuch as they are not common to any things, as for example the name of the rose when there are no longer roses, but it would still, nevertheless, be significative by the understanding, although it would lack nomination; otherwise there would not be the proposition: there is no rose. *Rose when all gone = understood*

Questions, moreover, were raised properly concerning universal words, but none concerning singular words, because there was no such doubt concerning the meaning of singular words. For their mode of signifying accorded well with the status of things. As things are discrete in themselves, so they are signified by words discretely, and the understanding of them refers to a definite thing, which reference universals do not have. Besides although universals did not signify things as

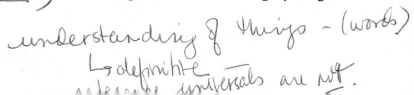
understanding of things — (words)
↳ definite — universals are not.

discrete, they did not seem on the other hand to signify things as agreeing, since, as we have also shown above, there is no thing in which they agree. Consequently, since there was so much doubt concerning universals, Porphyry chose to treat of universals alone, excluding singulars from his intention as clear enough in themselves, although for all that, he sometimes treats of them in passing because of other things.

It must be noted, however, that although the definition of the universal or of the genus or the species includes only words, nevertheless these nouns are often transferred to their things, as when it is said that species is made up of genus and difference, that is, the thing of the species from the thing of the genus. For when the nature of words is examined with respect to signification, it is a question sometimes of words and sometimes of things, and frequently the names of the latter and the former are transferred reciprocally. For this reason most of all, the ambiguous treatment of logic as well as grammar leads many, who do not distinguish clearly the property of the imposition of nouns or the abuse of transference, into error by the transference of nouns.

· · ·

PETER ABAILARD

ETHICS OR KNOW THYSELF

Prologue

In the study of morals we deal with the defects or qualities of the mind which dispose us to bad or good actions. Defects and qualities are not only mental, but also physical. There is bodily weakness; there is also the endurance which we call strength. There is sluggishness or speed; blindness or sight. When we now speak of defects, therefore, we pre-suppose defects of the mind, so as to distinguish them from the physical ones. The defects of the mind are opposed to the qualities; injustice to justice; cowardice to constancy; intemperance to temperance.

CHAPTER I. *The Defect of Mind Bearing upon Conduct*

Certain defects or merits of mind have no connection with morals. They do not make human life a matter of praise or blame. Such are dull wits or quick insight; a good or a bad memory; ignorance or knowledge. Each of these features is found in good and bad alike. They have nothing to do with the system of morals, nor with making life base or honourable. To exclude these we safeguarded above the phrase 'defects of mind' by adding 'which dispose to bad actions,' that is, those defects which incline the will to what least of all either should be done or should be left undone.

From *Abailard's Ethics*, R. McCallum, trans., Oxford: Basil Blackwell, 1935. Reprinted by permission.

CHAPTER II. *How Does Sin Differ from a Disposition to Evil?*

Defect of this mental kind is not the same thing as sin. Sin, too, is not the same as a bad action. For example, to be irascible, that is, prone or easily roused to the agitation of anger is a defect and moves the mind to unpleasantly impetuous and irrational action. This defect, however, is in the mind so that the mind is liable to wrath, even when it is not actually roused to it. Similarly, lameness, by reason of which a man is said to be lame, is in the man himself even when he does not walk and reveal his lameness. For the defect is there though action be lacking. So, also, nature or constitution renders many liable to luxury. Yet they do not sin because they are like this, but from this very fact they have the material of a struggle whereby they may, in the virtue of temperance, triumph over themselves and win the crown. As Solomon says: 'Better a patient than a strong man; and the Lord of his soul than he that taketh a city.' (Prov. xvi, 32.) For religion does not think it degrading to be beaten by man; but it is degrading to be beaten by one's lower self. The former defeat has been the fate of good men. But, in the latter, we fall below ourselves. The Apostle commends victory of this sort; 'No one shall be crowned who has not truly striven.' (2 Tim. ii, 5.) This striving, I repeat, means standing less against men than against myself, so that defects may not lure me into base consent. Though men cease to oppose us, our defects do not cease. The fight with them is the more dangerous because of its repetition. And as it is the more difficult, so victory is the more glorious. Men, however much they prevail over us, do not force baseness upon us, unless by their practice of vice they turn us also to it and overcome us through our own wretched consent. They may dominate our body; but while our mind is free, there is no danger to true freedom. We run no risk of base servitude. Subservience to vice, not to man, is degradation. It is the overlordship of defects and not physical serfdom which debases the soul.

CHAPTER III. *Definition of 'Defect' and of Sin*

Defect, then, is that whereby we are disposed to sin. We are, that is, inclined to consent to what we ought not to do, or to leave undone what we ought to do. Consent of this kind we rightly call sin. Here is the reproach of the soul meriting damnation or being declared guilty by God. What is that consent but to despise God and to violate His laws? God cannot be set at enmity by injury, but by contempt. He is the highest power, and is not diminished by any injury, but He avenges contempt of Himself. Our sin, therefore, is contempt of the Creator. To sin is to despise the Creator; that is, not to do for Him what we believe we should do for Him, or, not to renounce what we think should be renounced on His behalf. We have defined sin negatively by saying that it means not doing or not renouncing what we ought to do or renounce. Clearly, then, we have shown that sin has no reality. It exists rather in *not being* than in *being*. Similarly we could define shadows by saying: The absence of light where light usually is.

Perhaps you object that sin is the desire or will to do an evil deed, and that this will or desire condemns us before God in the same way as the will to do a good deed justifies us. There is as much quality, you suggest, in the good will as there is sin in the evil will; and it is no less 'in being' in the latter than in the former. By willing to do what we believe to be pleasing to God we please Him. Equally,

by willing to do what we believe to be displeasing to God, we displease Him
and seem either to violate or despise His nature.

But diligent attention will show that we must think far otherwise of this
point. We frequently err, and from no evil will at all. Indeed, the evil will itself,
when restrained, though it may not be quenched, procures the palm-wreath for
those who resist it. It provides, not merely the materials for combat, but also
the crown of glory. It should be spoken of rather as a certain inevitable weakness
than as sin. Take, for example, the case of an innocent servant whose harsh master
is moved with fury against him. He pursues the servant, drawing his sword
with intent to kill him. For a while the servant flies and avoids death as best he
can. At last, forced all unwillingly to it, he kills his master so as not to be killed
by him. Let anyone say what sort of evil will there was in this deed. His will was
only to flee from death and preserve his own life. Was this an evil will? You
reply: 'I do not think this was an evil will. But the will that he had to kill the
master who was pursuing him was evil.' Your answer would be admirable and
acute if you could show that the servant really willed what you say that he did.
But, as I insisted, he was unwillingly forced to his deed. He protracted his master's
life as long as he could, knowing that danger also threatened his own life from
such a crime. How, then was a deed done voluntarily by which he incurred danger
to his own life?

Your reply may be that the action was voluntary because the man's will was to
escape death even though it may not have been to kill his master. This charge
might easily be preferred against him. I do not rebut it. Nevertheless, as has been
said, that will by which he sought to evade death, as you urge, and not to kill
his master, cannot at all be condemned as bad. He did, however, fail by consenting,
though driven to it through fear of death, to an unjust murder which he ought
rather to have endured than committed. Of his own will, I mean, he took the
sword. It was not handed to him by authority. The Truth saith: 'Everyone that
taketh the sword shall perish by the sword.' (Matt. xxvi, 52.) By his rashness
he risked the death and damnation of his soul. The servant's wish, then, was
not to kill his master, but to avoid death. Because he *consented,* however, as he
should not have done, to murder, this wrongful consent preceding the crime was
sin.

Someone may interpose: 'But you cannot conclude that he wished to kill his
master because, in order to escape death, he was willing to kill his master. I might
say to a man; I am willing for you to have my cape so that you may give me
five shillings. Or, I am glad for you to have it at this price. But I do not hand it
over because I desire you to have possession of it.' No, and if a man in prison
desired under duress, to put his son there in his place that he might secure his
own ransom, should we therefore admit that he wished to send his son to prison?

It was only with many a tear and groan that he consented to such a course.

The fact is that this kind of will, existing with much internal regret, is not, if
I may so say, *will,* but a passive submission of mind. It is so because the man wills
one thing on account of another. He puts up with *this* because he really desires
that. A patient is said to submit to cautery or lancet that he may obtain health.
Martyrs endured that they might come to Christ; and Christ, too, that we may be
saved by his passion.

Yet we are not bound to admit simply that these people therefore wish for this
mental unease. Such unease can only be where something occurs contrary to

wish. No man suffers so long as he fulfils his wish and does what he likes to experience. The Apostle says: 'I desire to depart and to be with Christ' (Phil. i, 23), that is, to die so that I may attain to him. Elsewhere this apostle says: 'We desire not to be despoiled of our garments, but to be clothed from above, that our mortal part may be swallowed up in life.' This notion, Blessed Augustine reminds us, was contained in the Lord's address to Peter: 'Thou shalt extend thy hands and another shall gird thee, and lead thee whither thou willest not.' (John xxi, 18.) The Lord also spoke to the Father out of the weakness of the human nature which he had taken upon himself: 'If it be possible, let this cup pass from me; nevertheless not as I will, but as thou willest.' (Matt. xxvi, 39.) His spirit naturally trembled before the great terror of death: and he could not speak of what he knew to be punishment as a matter of his own will. When elsewhere it is written of Him: 'He was offered because He himself willed it' (Isaiah liii, 7), it must be understood either of His divine nature, in whose will it was that he should suffer as a man, or 'He himself willed it' must be taken according to the Psalmist's phrase: 'Whatsoever he willed, that he did.' (Ps. cxiii, 3.)

Sin, therefore, is sometimes committed without an evil will. Thus sin cannot be defined as 'will.' True, you will say, when we sin under constraint, but not when we sin willingly, for instance, when we will to do something which we know ought not to be done by us. There the evil will and sin seem to be the same thing. For example a man sees a woman; his concupiscence is aroused; his mind is enticed by fleshly lust and stirred to base desire. This wish, this lascivious longing, what else can it be, you say, than sin?

I reply: What if that wish may be bridled by the power of temperance? What if its nature is never to be entirely extinguished but to persist in struggle and not fully fail even in defeat? For where is the battle if the antagonist is away? Whence the great reward without grave endurance? When the fight is over nothing remains but to reap the reward. Here we strive in contest in order elsewhere to obtain as victors a crown. Now, for a contest, an opponent is needed who will resist, not one who simply submits. This opponent is our evil will over which we triumph when we subjugate it to the divine will. But we do not entirely destroy it. For we needs must ever expect to encounter our enemy. What achievement before God is it if we undergo nothing contrary to our own will, but merely practice what we please? Who will be grateful to us if in what we say we do for him we merely satisfy our own fancy?

You will say, what merit have we with God in acting willingly or unwillingly? Certainly none: I reply. He weighs the intention rather than the deed in his recompense. Nor does the deed, whether it proceed from a good or an evil will, add anything to the merit, as we shall show shortly. But when we set His will before our own so as to follow His and not ours, our merit with God is magnified, in accordance with that perfect word of Truth: 'I came not to do mine own will, but the will of Him that sent me." (John vi, 38.) To this end He exhorts us: 'If anyone comes to me, and does not hate father, and mother . . . yea his own soul also, he is not worthy of me.' (Luke xiv, 26.) That is to say, 'unless a man renounces his parents' influence and his own will and submits himself to my teaching, he is not worthy of me.' Thus we are bidden to hate our father, not to destroy him. Similarly with our own will. We must not be led by it; at the same time, we are not asked to root it out altogether.

When the Scripture says: 'Go not after your own desires' (Eccles. xviii, 30),

and: 'Turn from your own will' (ibid.), it instructs us not to fulfil our desires.
Yet it does not say that we are to be wholly without them. It is vicious to give
in to our desires; but not to have any desires at all is impossible for our weak
nature.

The sin, then, consists not in desiring a woman, but in consent to the desire,
and not the wish for whoredom, but the consent to the wish is damnation.

Let us see how our conclusions about sexual intemperance apply to theft. A
man crosses another's garden. At the sight of the delectable fruit his desire is
aroused. He does not, however, give way to desire so as to take anything by
theft or rapine, although his mind was moved to strong inclination by the thought
of the delight of eating. Where there is desire, there, without doubt, will exists.
The man desires the eating of that fruit wherein he doubts not that there will
be delight. The weakness of nature in this man is compelled to desire the fruit
which, without the master's permission, he has no right to take. He conquers the
desire, but does not extinguish it. Since, however, he is not enticed into consent,
he does not descend to sin.

What, then, of your objection? It should be clear from such instances, that the
wish or desire itself of doing what is not seemly is never to be called sin, but
rather, as we said, the consent is sin. We consent to what is not seemly when we
do not draw ourselves back from such a deed, and are prepared, should opportunity offer, to perform it completely. Whoever is discovered in this intention,
though his guilt has yet to be completed in deed, is already guilty before God in
so far as he strives with all his might to sin, and accomplishes within himself, as
the blessed Augustine reminds us, as much as if he were actually taken in the act.

But while wish is not sin, and, as we have said, we sometimes commit sin unwillingly, there are nevertheless those who assert that every sin is voluntary. In
this respect they discover a certain difference between sin and will. Will is one
thing, they say, but a voluntary act is another. They mean that there is a distinction between will and what is done willingly. If, however, we call sin what we have
already decided that it essentially is, namely, contempt of God or consent to that
which we believe should not, for God's sake, be done how can we say that sin is
voluntary? I mean, how can we say that we wish to despise God? What is sin
but sinking below a standard, or becoming liable to damnation? For although
we desire to do what we know deserves punishment, yet we do not desire to
be punished. Thus plainly we are reprobate. We are willing to do wrong; but
we are unwilling to bear the just punishment of wrong-doing. The punishment
which is just displeases: the deed which is unjust pleases. Often we woo a married
woman because of her charm. Our wish is not so much to commit adultery as a
longing that she were unmarried. On the other hand, many covet the wives of
influential men for the sake of their own fame, and not for the natural attractive-
ness of these ladies. Their wish is for adultery rather than sexual relationship, the
major in preference to the minor excess. Some, too, are ashamed altogether of
being betrayed into any consent to concupiscence or evil will; and thus from the
weakness of the flesh are compelled to wish what they least of all wish to wish.

How, then, a wish which we do not wish to have can be called voluntary, as it
is according to those thinkers I have mentioned, so that all sin becomes a matter
of voluntary action, I assuredly do not understand, unless by voluntary is meant
that no action is determined, since a sin is never a predestined event. Or perhaps
we are to take 'voluntary' to be that which proceeds from some kind of will.

For although the man who slew his master had no will to perform the actual murder, nevertheless he did it from some sort of will, because he certainly wished to escape or defer death.

Some are intensely indignant when they hear us assert that the act of sinning adds nothing to guilt or damnation before God. Their contention is that in this act of sinning a certain delight supervenes, which increases the sin, as in sexual intercourse or indulgence in food which we referred to above. Their statement is absurd unless they can prove that physical delight of this kind is itself sin, and that such pleasure cannot be taken without a sin being thereby committed. If it be as they suppose, then no one is permitted to enjoy physical pleasure. The married do not escape sin when they employ their physical privilege; nor yet the man who eats with relish his own fruits.

Invalids, too, who are treated to more delicate dishes to aid their recovery of strength would likewise be guilty, since they are not able to eat without a sense of delight and should this be lacking, the food does them no good. Finally, God, the Creator of nourishment and of the bodies which receive it, would not be without guilt for having instilled savours which necessarily involve in sin those who ignorantly use them. Yet how should He supply such things for our consumption, or permit them to be consumed, if it were impossible for us to eat them without sin? How, again, can it be said that there is sin in doing what is allowed? In regard to those matters which once were unlawful and forbidden, if they are later allowed and made lawful, they can be done entirely without sin. For instance, the eating of pork and many other things once out of bounds to the Jew are now free to us Christians. When, therefore, we see Jews turned Christian gladly eating food of this sort which the law had prohibited, how can we defend their rectitude except by affirming that this latitude has now been conceded to them by God?

Well, in what was formerly a food restriction and is now food freedom, the concession of freedom excludes sin and eliminates contempt of God. Who then shall say that a man sins in respect of a matter which the divine permission has made lawful for him? If the marriage-bed or the eating of even delicate food was permitted from the first day of our creation, when we lived in Paradise without sin, who can prove that we transgress in these enjoyments, so long as we do not pass the limits of the permission? Another objection is that matrimonial intercourse and the eating of tasty food are only allowed on condition of being taken without pleasure. But, if this is so, then they are allowed to be done in a way in which they never can be done. That concession is not reasonable which concedes that a thing shall be so done as it is certain that it cannot be done. By what reasoning did the law aforetime enforce matrimony so that each might leave his seed to Israel? Or, how did the Apostle oblige wives to fulfil the mutual debt if these acts could not be done without sinning? How can he refer to this debt when already it is of necessity sin? Or how should a man be compelled to do what he will grieve God by doing? Hence, I think that it is plain that no natural physical delight can be set down as sin, nor can it be called guilt for men to delight in what, when it is done, must involve the feeling of delight.

For example, if anyone obliged a monk, bound in chains, to lie among women, and the monk by the softness of the couch and by contact with his fair flatterers is allured into delight, though not into consent, who shall presume to designate guilt the delight which is naturally awakened?

You may urge, with some thinkers, that the carnal pleasure, even in lawful intercourse, involves sin. Thus David says: 'Behold in sin was I conceived.' (Ps. l, 7.) And the Apostle, when he had said: 'Ye return to it again' (1 Cor. vii, 5), adds nevertheless, 'This I say by way of concession, not of command.' (ibid., v, 6.) Yet authority rather than reason, seems to dictate the view that we should allow simple physical delight to be sin. For, assuredly, David was conceived not in fornication, but in matrimony: and concession, that is forgiveness, does not, as this standpoint avers, condone when there is no guilt to forgive. As for what David meant when he says that he had been conceived 'in iniquity' or 'in sin' and does not say 'whose' sin, he referred to the general curse of original sin, wherein from the guilt of our first parents each is subject to damnation, as it is elsewhere stated: 'None are pure of stain, not the infant a day old, if he has life on this earth.' As the blessed Jerome reminds us and as manifest reason teaches, the soul of a young child is without sin. If, then, it is pure of sin, how is it also impure by sinful corruption? We must understand the infant's purity from sin in reference to its personal guilt. But its contact with sinful corruption, its 'stain,' is in reference to penalty owed by mankind because of Adam's sin. He who has not yet perceived by reason what he ought to do cannot be guilty of contempt of God. Yet he is not free from the contamination of the sin of his first parents, from which he contracts the penalty, though not the guilt, and bears in penalty what they committed in guilt. When, therefore, David says that he was conceived in iniquity or sin, he sees himself subject to the general sentence of damnation from the guilt of his racial parents, and he assigns the sins, not to his father and mother but to his first parents.

When the Apostle speaks of indulgence, he must not be understood as some would wish to understand him, to mean permission to be equivalent to pardon for sin. His statement is: 'By way of indulgence not of command.' He might equally have said: 'By permission, not by force.' If husband and wife wish and decide upon mutual agreement they can abstain altogether from intercourse, and may not be compelled to it by command. But should they not so decide they have indulgence, that is, permission to substitute a less perfect for a more perfect rule of life. The Apostle, in this passage, did not therefore refer to pardon for sin, but to the permission of a less strict life for the avoidance of fornication. He meant that this lower level might elude the peaks of sin, and by its inferior standing escape the greater guilt.

We come, then, to this conclusion, that no one who sets out to assert that all fleshly desire is sin may say that the sin itself is increased by the doing of it. For this would mean extending the consent of the soul into the exercise of the action. In short, one would be stained not only by consent to baseness, but also by the mire of the deed, as if what happens externally in the body could possibly soil the soul. Sin is not, therefore, increased by the doing of an action: and nothing mars the soul except what is of its own nature, namely consent. This we affirmed was alone sin, preceding action in will, or subsequent to the performance of action. Although we wish for, or do, what is unseemly, we do not therefore sin. For such deeds not uncommonly occur without there being any sin. On the other hand, there may be consent without the external effects, as we have indicated. There was wish without consent in the case of the man who was attracted by a woman whom he caught sight of, or who was tempted by his neighbour's fruit, but who was not enticed into consent. There was evil consent without evil desire in the servant who unwillingly killed his master.

Certain acts which ought not to be done often are done, and without any sin, when, for instance, they are committed under force or ignorance. No one, I think, ignores this fact. A woman under constraint of violence, lies with another's husband. A man, taken by some trick, sleeps with one whom he supposed to be his wife, or kills a man, in the belief that he himself has the right to be both judge and executioner. Thus to desire the wife of another or actually to lie with her is not sin. But to consent to that desire or to that action is sin. This consent to covetousness the law calls covetousness in saying: 'Thou shalt not covet.' (Deut. v, 21.) Yet that which we cannot avoid ought not to be forbidden, nor that wherein, as we said, we do not sin. But we should be cautioned about the consent to covetousness. So, too, the saying of the Lord must be understood: 'Whosoever shall look upon a woman to desire her.' (Matt. v, 28.) That is, whosoever shall so look upon her as to slip into consent to covetousness, 'has already committed adultery with her in his heart' (Matt. v, 28), even though he may not have committed adultery in deed. He is guilty of sin, though there be no sequel to his intention.

Careful account will reveal that wherever actions are restricted by some precept or prohibition, these refer rather to will and consent than to the deeds themselves. Otherwise nothing relative to a person's moral merit could be included under a precept. Indeed, actions are so much the less worth prescribing as they are less in our power to do. At the same time, many things we are forbidden to do for which there exists in our will both the inclination and the consent.

The Lord God says: 'Thou shalt not kill. Thou shalt not bear false witness.' (Deut. v, 17, 20.) If we accept these cautions as being only about actions, as the words suggest, then guilt is not forbidden, but simply the activity of guilt. For we have seen that actions may be carried out without sin, as that it is not sin to kill a man or to lie with another's wife. And even the man who desires to bear false testimony, and is willing to utter it, so long as he is silent for some reason and does not speak, is innocent before the law, that is, if the prohibition in this matter be accepted literally of the action. It is not said that we should not *wish* to give false witness, or that we should not *consent* in bearing it, but simply that we should not bear false witness.

Similarly, when the law forbids us to marry or have intercourse with our sisters, if this prohibition relates to deed rather than to intention, no one can keep the commandment, for a sister unless we recognize her, is just a woman. If a man, then, marries his sister in error, is he a transgressor for doing what the law forbade? He is not, you will reply, because, in acting ignorantly in what he did, he did not consent to a transgression. Thus a transgressor is not one who *does* what is prohibited. He is one who *consents* to what is prohibited. The prohibition is, therefore, not about action, but about consent. It is as though in saying: 'Do not do this or that,' we meant: 'Do not consent to do this or that, or, 'Do not wittingly do this.'

Blessed Augustine, in his careful view of this question, reduces every sin or command to terms of charity and covetousness, and not to works. 'The law,' he says, 'inculcates nothing but charity, and forbids nothing but covetousness.' The Apostle, also, asserts: 'All the law is contained in one word: thou shalt love thy neighbour as thyself,' (Rom. xiii, 8, 10), and again, 'Love is the fulfilling of the law.' (ibid.)

Whether you actually give alms to a needy person, or charity makes you ready to give, makes no difference to the merit of the deed. The will may be there when the opportunity is not. Nor does it rest entirely with you to deal with every case of need which you encounter. Actions which are right and actions which are far from right are done by good and bad men alike. The intention alone separates the two classes of men.

Augustine reminds us that in the self-same action we find God the Father, the Lord Jesus Christ, and also Judas the betrayer. The betrayal of the Son was accomplished by God the Father, and by the Son, and by the betrayer. For 'the Father delivered up the Son, and the Son Himself' (Rom. viii, 32; Gal. ii, 22) as the Apostle says, and Judas delivered up his Master. The traitor, therefore, did the same thing as God Himself. But did Judas do anything well? No. Good certainly came of his act; but his act was not well done, nor was it destined to benefit him.

God considers not the action, but the spirit of the action. It is the intention, not the deed wherein the merit or praise of the doer consists. Often, indeed, the same action is done from different motives: for justice's sake by one man, for an evil reason by another. Two men, for instance, hang a guilty person. The one does it out of zeal for justice; the other in resentment for an earlier enmity. The action of hanging is the same. Both men do what is good and what justice demands. Yet the diversity of their intentions causes the same deed to be done from different motives, in the one case good, in the other bad.

Everyone knows that the devil himself does nothing without God's permission, when he either punishes a wicked man according to his deserts, or is allowed to afflict a just man for moral cleansing or for an example of endurance. Since, however, in doing what God permits the devil moves at the spur of his own malice, the power which he has may be called good, or even just, while his will is for ever unjust. He receives, that is, the power from God, but his will is of himself.

Who, among the elect, can ever emulate the deeds of hypocrites? Who, for the love of God, ever endures or undertakes so much as they do from thirst for human praise? Who does not agree that sometimes what God forbids may rightly be done, while, contrarily, He may counsel certain things which of all things are least convenient? We note how He forbade certain miracles, whereby He had healed infirmities, to be made public. He set an example of humility lest any man should claim glory for the grace bestowed on him. Nevertheless, the recipients of those benefits did not cease to broadcast them, to the praise of Him who had done such things, and yet had forbidden them to be revealed. Thus we read: 'As much as He bade them not to speak, so much the more did they publish abroad, etc.' Will you judge these men guilty of a fault who acted contrary to the command which they had received, and did so wittingly? Who can acquit them of wrong-doing, unless by finding that they did not act out of contempt for the One who commanded, but decided to do what was to His honour? How, then, did the matter stand? Did Christ command what ought not to have been commanded? Or, did the newly-healed men disobey when they should have obeyed? The command was a good thing; yet it was not good for it to be obeyed.

In the case of Abraham, also, you will accuse God for first enjoining the sacrifice of Abraham's son, and then revoking the command. Has, then, God never *wisely commanded* anything which, if *it had come about*, would not have been good? If good, you will object, why was it afterwards forbidden? But conceive that it was good for the same thing to be prescribed and also to be prohibited. God, we know, permits nothing, and does not himself consent to achieve anything apart from rational cause. Thus it is the pure intention of the command, not the execution of the action which justifies God in wisely commanding what would not in actual fact be good. God did not intend Abraham to sacrifice his son, or command this sacrifice to be put into effect. His aim was to test Abraham's obedience, constancy of faith, and love towards Him, so that these qualities should be left to us as an example. This intention the Lord God plainly asserts afterwards in saying: 'Now know I that thou fearest the Lord.' (Gen. xxii, 12.) It is as if he frankly said: 'I commanded you: you showed yourself ready to obey Me. Both these things were done so that others might know what I had myself known of you from the beginning.' There was a right intention on God's part; but it was not right for it to be put in practice. The prohibition, too, in the case of the miracles of healing was right. The object of this prohibition was not for it to be obeyed, but for an example to be given to our weak spirit in avoiding empty applause. God, in the one case enjoined an action which, if obeyed, would not have been good. In the other case, He forbade what was worth putting into fact, namely, a knowledge of Christ's miracles. The intention excuses Him in the first matter, just as the intention excuses the men who, in the second instance, were healed and did not carry out his injunction. They knew that the precept was not given to be practised, but in order that the aforenamed example of moderation in a successful miracle might be set. In keeping, then, the spirit of the command they showed, by actually disobeying no contempt for Him with whose intention they knew that they were acting.

A scrutiny of the deed rather than of the intention will reveal, then, cases where men frequently not only wish to go against God's bidding, but carry their wish knowingly into effect, and do so without any guilt of sin. An action or a wish must not be called bad because it does not in actual fact fall in with God's command. It may well be that the doer's intention does not at all differ from the will of his divine superior. The intention exonerates Him who gave a practically unseemly command: the intention excuses the man who, out of kindness, disobeyed the command to conceal the miracle.

Briefly to summarize the above argument: Four things were postulated which must be carefully distinguished from one another.

1. Imperfection of soul, making us liable to sin.
2. Sin itself, which we decided is consent to evil or contempt of God.
3. The will or desire of evil.
4. The evil deed.

To wish is not the same thing as to fulfil a wish. Equally, to sin is not the same as to carry out a sin. In the first case, we sin by consent of the soul: the second is a matter of the external effect of an action, namely, when we fulfil in deed that whereunto we have previously consented. When, therefore, temptation is said to proceed through three stages, suggestion, delight, consent, it must be understood that, like our first parents, we are frequently led along these three paths to the commission of sin. The devil's persuasion comes *first* promising from the taste of the forbidden fruit immortality. Delight follows. When the woman sees the beautiful tree, and perceives that the fruit is good, her appetite is whetted by the anticipated pleasure of tasting. This desire she ought to have repressed, so as to obey God's command. But in consenting to it, she was drawn *secondly* into sin. By penitence she should have put right this fault, and obtained pardon. Instead, she *thirdly* consummated the sin by the deed. Eve thus passed through the three stages to the commission of sin.

By the same avenues we also arrive not at sin, but at the action of sin, namely, the doing of an unseemly deed through the suggestion or prompting of something within us. If we already know that such a deed will be pleasant, our imagination is held by anticipatory delight and we are tempted thereby in thought. So long as we give consent to such delight, we sin. Lastly, we pass to the third stage, and actually commit the sin.

It is agreed by some thinkers that carnal suggestion, even though the person causing the suggestion be not present, should be included under sinful suggestion. For example, a man having seen a woman falls into a sensual desire of her. But it seems that this kind of suggestion should simply be called delight. This delight, and other delights of the like kind, arise naturally and, as we said above, they are not sinful. The Apostle calls them 'human temptations.' 'No temptation has taken you yet which was not common to men. God is faithful, and will not suffer you to be tempted above what you are able; but will, with the temptation make a way of escape, that you may be able to bear it.' By temptation is meant, in general, any movement of the soul to do something unseemly, whether in wish or consent. We speak of human temptation without which it is hardly or never possible for human weakness to exist. Such are sexual desire, or the pleasures of the table. From these the Psalmist asks to be delivered when he says: 'Deliver me from my wants, O Lord' (Ps. xxiv, 17); that is, from the temptations of natural and necessary appetites that they may not influence him into sinful consent. Or, he may mean: 'When this life is over, grant me to be without those temptations of which life has been full.'

When the Apostle says: 'No temptation has taken you but what is human,' his statement amounts to this: Even if the soul be stirred by that delight which is, as we said, human temptation, yet God would not lead the soul into that consent wherein sin consists. Someone may object: But by what power of our own are we able to resist those desires? We may reply: 'God is faithful, who will not allow you to be tempted,' as the Scripture says. In other words: We should rather trust him than rely upon ourselves. He promises help, and is true to his promises. He is faithful, so that we should have complete faith in him. Out of pity God diminishes the degree of human temptation, does not suffer us to be tempted above what we are able,' in order that it may not drive us to sin at a pace we cannot endure, when, that is, we strive to resist it. Then, too, God turns the temptation to our advantage: for He trains us thereby so that the recurrence of temptation causes us less care, and we fear less the onset of a foe over whom we have already triumphed, and whom we know how to meet.

Every encounter, not as yet undertaken, is for that reason, to us, a matter of more anxiety and dismay. But when such an encounter comes to those accustomed to victory, its force and terror alike vanish.

. . .

CHAPTER VII. *Why Is God Called 'Inspector Cordis Et Renum,' i.e. Said to Try the Heart and Reins?*

These two desires of the flesh, and of the spirit are, then, distinguished. Now God has been called the 'one who tries the heart and reins.' He scrutinizes, that is to say, intentions and the consents which proceed from them. We on our part cannot discuss and decide these issues of intention, but address our censure to deeds. We punish facts rather than faults. Injury to the soul we do not regard as so much a matter for punishment as injury to others. Our object is to avoid public mischief, rather than to correct personal mistakes. The Lord said to Peter: 'If thy brother sin against thee, correct him between thyself and him.' (Matt. xviii, 15.) 'Sin against thee.' Is the meaning here that we ought to correct and punish injuries done to us and not those done to others, as though 'against thee' meant 'not against another'? By no means. The phrase 'if he sin against thee' means that he acts publicly so as to corrupt you by his example. For if he sins against himself only, his sin, being hidden, involves in guilt merely the man himself. The sin does not, by the sinner's bad example, induce others to indiscretion. Although the evil action has no imitators, or even none who recognize it as wrong, nevertheless, in so far as it is a public act it must, in human society, be chastised more than private guilt, because it can occasion greater mischief, and can be more destructive, by the example it sets, than the hidden failing. Everything which is likely to lead to common loss or to public harm must be punished by a greater requital. Where a sin involves more serious injury the penalty must therefore be heavier. The greater the social stumbling-block, the more stringent must be the social correction, even though the original guilt be relatively light.

Suppose, for example, that someone has, by evil intercourse, corrupted a woman in a church. The people hear of the incident. But they are not roused so much by the violation of a woman, the true temple of God, as by the desecration of the material temple, the church. This is the case even though, admittedly, a wall is of less consequence than a woman, and it is more grievous to harm a human being than a place. Again, the setting fire to houses we punish more severely than fornication. But with God the latter incurs a far greater sentence.

The punishment of public guilt is not so much a debt paid to justice as the exercise of economy. We consult the common interest, as has been said by checking social mischief. Frequently we punish minor misdeeds with major penalties. In doing so, we do not, in a spirit of pure justice ponder what guilt preceded; but, by shrewd foresight, we estimate the damage which may ensue if the deed be lightly dealt with. We reserve, therefore, sins of the soul for the divine judgment. But the effect of these sins, about which we have to determine, we follow up, by our own judgment, employing a certain economy, that is, the rule of prudence referred to above, rather than the precept of equity.

God assigns the penalty of each crime according to the measure of guilt. The degree of contempt displayed by men to God is afterwards proportionately punished, whatever be their condition or calling. Suppose that a monk and a lay-brother both fall into consent to an act of fornication. If the mind of the lay-brother be so inflamed that he would not abstain from shame out of reverence for God, even if he had been a monk, then the lay-brother deserves the same penalty as the monk.

The same notion applies where one man, sinning openly, offends many, and corrupts them by his example; while another man sins in secret, and injures only himself. For the secret sinner, if his intention and his contempt of God are identical with those of the open sinner, rather by accident does not corrupt others. The man who does not restrain himself out of respect for God would hardly refrain, for the same reason from public crime. In God's sight, assuredly, he is committed on a similar charge to that of the open sinner. For, in the recompense of good or evil, God notes the soul alone, not its external effects, and counts what comes from our guilt or good will. It is the soul in its scheme of intention, not in the outward result of its action, that God assesses. There are actions, as we said, common to sinners and saints, all of them in themselves indifferent and only to be called bad or good according to the intention of the agent. Such actions are so described not because it is good or bad for them to be done, but because they are done *well*, or *ill*; that is, they are performed with a seemly, or unseemly intention.

For, as Blessed Augustine reminds us, it is good for a man to be bad since God may use him for a good end, and may not allow him to be otherwise even though his condition be altogether evil.

When, therefore, we call the intention of a man good, and his deed good also, we distinguish two things, intention and deed. Nevertheless, there is only one goodness of intention. It is like speaking of a good man, and the son of a good man. We imagine two men, but not two goodnesses. A man is called good because of his own goodness. But when the son of a good man is spoken of, it is clear that he cannot have good in him just because he is a good man's son. Similarly, everyone's intention is called good in itself. But the deed is not called good in itself, for it only proceeds from a good intention. Thus, there is one goodness, whence both intention and deed are designated good, just as there is one goodness from which a good man and the son of a good man are named; or one goodness by which a good man, and the will of a good man can each be explained.

The objection of some who say that the deed merits equal recompense with the intention, or even an additional recompense, may be proved nonsensical. 'There are two goods,' they exclaim, 'the good intention, and the carrying out of the good intention. Good added to good ought to be worth more than a single good.'

Our reply is: 'Granted that the whole is worth more than the separate parts, must we admit that it merits greater reward?' Not at all. There are many animate and inanimate things which, in large numbers, are useful for more purposes than any one of the number would be alone. Nevertheless, no additional reward is thought to be due to them on that account. For instance, an ox joined to another ox or a horse to a horse; or, again, wood added to wood or iron to iron; these things are good, and a number of them is worth more than each singly. Yet they are not more highly praised when it is seen that two of them put together can do more than one by itself.

True, you say, it is so; but only because these things could never deserve anything, being without reason. Well; but has our deed any reason, so as to be able to deserve praise or blame? None, you say; but our action is said to have merit because it imparts merit to us, making us worthy of reward, or, at any rate, of greater reward. Now it is this very statement which we have denied above. Consider why it is false, apart from what we have already said. Two men set about the same scheme of building poor-houses. One man completes the object to which he devotes himself. The other has the money which he put by stolen forcibly from him, and through no fault of his own—prevented simply by burglary—is not able to conclude what he intended to do. Can the external fact, that the alms-houses are unbuilt, lessen his merit with God, or shall the malice of another make the man who did what he could for God less acceptable to God?

Otherwise, the size of his purse could make a man better and worthier, if property had any bearing upon moral merit or the increase of merit. The richer men were, the better they could be, since from their stock of wealth they would be able to augment their piety by their philanthropy. But it is the height of insanity to assume that wealth can confer true bliss or dignity of the soul, or detract from the merit of poor men. If property cannot make a soul better, then it cannot make the soul dearer to God, nor get any bliss of moral merit.

CHAPTER VIII. *Recompense of Actions*

We do not, however, deny that in this life some recompense should be made for good and bad deeds, so that by means of reward and punishment in the present we may be stirred to good actions or restrained from bad ones. People may also profit by the examples of others in this way. They can copy what is fit and agreeable, and avoid what is not.

CHAPTER XI. *The Good Action Springs from the Good Intention*

We call the intention good which is right in itself, but the action is good, not because it contains within it some good, but because it issues from a good intention. The same act may be done by the same man at different times. According to the diversity of his intention, however, this act may be at one time good, at another bad. So goodness and badness vary. Compare the proposition: 'Socrates sits.' One conceives this statement either truly or falsely according as Socrates actually does sit, or stands. This alteration in truth and falsity, Aristotle affirms, comes about not from any change in the circumstances which compose the true or false situation, but because the subject-matter of the statement (that is, Socrates) moves in itself, I mean changes from sitting to standing or vice versa.

CHAPTER XII. *What Are the Grounds of Good Intention?*

Good or right intention is held by some to be when anyone believes that he acts well, and that what he does pleases God. An example is supplied by those who persecuted the martyrs. About them the Gospel Truth says: 'The hour comes when everyone who kills you will think that he is obedient to God.' (John xvi, 2.) In sympathy with the ignorance of such the Apostle exclaims: 'I bear this testimony on their behalf, that they are zealous for God but not according to knowledge.' That is to say, they are fervently eager to do what they believe pleases God. Since, however, in this desire or keenness of mind they are deceived, their intention is a mistake. The eye of the heart is not so simple as to be capable of seeing clearly and to guard itself from error. For this reason the Lord, when he distinguished works according to right and wrong intention, spoke of the eye of the mind, that is the intention, as either *single*, pure, as it were, from spot, so that it could see clearly, or, on the contrary, as *clouded*. 'If thine eye be single, thy whole body shall be full of light.' This means that, provided the intention was right, all the acts proceeding from the intention which can possibly be foreseen in the manner of mortal affairs, will be worthy of the light; that is to say, good. And, contrarily, from wrong intention arise dark deeds.

The intention, therefore, must not be called good, merely because it seems good, but over and above this, because it is such as it is estimated to be. I mean that, if it thinks to please God in what it aims at its aim therein should not be mistaken. Otherwise the heathen, just like us, could count their good works, since they no less than we believe themselves either to be saved or to please God by their deed.

SELECTED BIBLIOGRAPHY

TRANSLATIONS

Luscombe, D., ed. and trans., *Peter Abelard's Ethics*, New York, 1971.

McCallum, J., trans., *Abailard's Ethics*, Oxford, 1935.

McCallum, J., trans., *Abailard's Christian Theology*, Oxford, 1948.

McGarry, D., trans., *The Metalogicon of John of Salisbury*, Berkeley, 1955.

McKeon, R., ed. and trans., *Selections from Medieval Philosophers, I: Augustine to Albert the Great*, New York, 1929.

Muckle, J., trans., *The Story of Abelard's Adversities*, Toronto, 1954.

Payer, P., trans., Peter Abelard, *A Dialogue of a Philosopher with a Jew and a Christian*, Toronto, 1979.

Pike, J., trans., *Frivolities of Courtiers and Footprints of Philosophers* (from the *Policraticus*), Minneapolis, 1938.

STUDIES

Buytaert, E., ed., *Peter Abelard*, Louvain, 1974.

Cottiaux, J., "La conception de la théologie chez Abélard," *Revue d'histoire ecclésiastique*, XXVIII (1932), 247–295, 523–612, 789–828.

De Rijk, L., "Introduction," *Petrus Abaelardus Dialectica*, Assen, 1956.

De Rijk, L., *Logica Modernorum*: Vol. I, *On the Twelfth Century Theories of Fallacy*, Assen, 1962. Vol. II, *The Origin and Early Development of the Theory of Supposition*, two parts, Assen, 1967.

Freddoso, A., "Abailard and Collective Realism," *Journal of Philosophy*, LXXV (1978), 527–538.

Fumigalli, M., *The Logic of Abelard*, New York, 1970.

Gilson, E., *Heloise and Abelard*, trans. L. Shook, Chicago, 1951.

Grane, L., *Peter Abelard: Philosophy and Christianity in the Middle Ages*, trans. F. and C. Crowley, New York, 1970.

Hendley, B., "John of Salisbury and the Problem of Universals," *Journal of the History of Philosophy*, VIII (1970), 289–302.

Jolivet, J., *Abélard ou la Philosophie dans le langage*, Paris, 1969.

Liebeschütz, H., *Mediaeval Humanism in the Life and Writings of John of Salisbury*, London 1950.

Luscombe, D., *The School of Peter Abelard*, Cambridge, 1969.

Sikes, J., *Peter Abailard*, Cambridge, 1932.

Tweedale, M., "Abailard and Non-Things," *Journal of the History of Philosophy*, V (1967), 329–342.

Tweedale, M., *Abailard on Universals*, Amsterdam, 1976.

Webb, C., *John of Salisbury*, London, 1932.

Islamic Philosophy

ISLAM, like Judaism and Christianity, is a religion of a Book and a Tradition, though it is closer to Judaism in that it is primarily a religion of law. The Book on which Islam rests is the Koran, the *sunnah* (literally, custom), the Tradition. Containing narratives, admonitions, doctrines, moral and ritual precepts, the Koran (according to Muslim belief) is the Word of God, revealed to Mohammed, the last and most important of a series of prophets and apostles which, beginning with Adam, includes Abraham, Moses, and Jesus. Of koranic doctrines, the absolute unity of God and the mission of Mohammed are the most basic. The *sunnah* consists of brief stories recounting deeds and utterances of Mohammed which have as their purpose legal and doctrinal instruction supplementary to that contained in the Koran. The individual story is called a *ḥadīth* (narrative), but this term is also applied to the *sunnah* as a whole. Koran and *sunnah* provide the basis for *fiqh*, the science of jurisprudence and for *sharī'ah*, the Law by which Muslims govern their day to day life.

Whereas Judaism and Christianity began as religions of small groups, Islam, almost from its beginnings, developed as the religion of an expanding empire. Mohammed died in A.D. 632 and in less than a hundred years, military conquests had expanded the Islamic world from India in the east, through North Africa, to Spain in the west. These expansions brought a variety of religious and intellectual communities under Muslim rule and as a result Islam was confronted by the theologies of Judaism, Christianity, and Zoroastrianism; by Indian thought; and by Greek and Hellenistic learning. Theology, apologetics, and philosophy began to flourish. The encounter of Islamic religion and Greek philosophy produced Islamic philosophy, which R. H. Walzer* has felicitously described as

a "productive assimilation" of Greek thought by open-minded and far-sighted representatives of a very different tradition and thus a serious attempt to make this foreign element an integral part of Islamic tradition.

Muslims now used philosophic concepts and arguments for the interpretation of koranic doctrines; they preserved, commented on, criticized, and, developed the teachings of Plato, Aristotle, Neoplatonists, and others; and in general, they inquired about the relation of Islamic doctrines to Greek philosophic notions.

Central to the development of Islamic philosophy were the Arabic translations of works originally written in Greek. Eastern Christians had preserved the Greek philosophic and scientific traditions and at the time of the Muslim conquests there were centers of Greek learning in Mesopotamia, Syria, and Egypt. The translators, most of whom were Nestorian and Jacobite Christians, began their activities during the early Abbasid period (*ca.* 800) and they continued for about two hundred years. Though some of these translations were made directly from the Greek, most of them passed through an intermediate Syriac version. After some pioneering efforts which proved to be sporadic and not completely satisfactory, the translators hit their stride under Al-Ma'mūn (reigned 813–833) and his successors Al-Mu'taṣim (reigned 833–842) and Al-Mutawakkil (reigned 847–861). In 830, Al-Ma'mūn established the "House of Wisdom" (*Bayt al-Ḥikmah*) consisting of a library, an academy, and housing a staff of translators. The most important translators of this period were Ḥunayn ibn Isḥāq (809–873) and his son Isḥāq. Ḥunayn, who knew Greek, carefully collected manuscripts in order to establish from them critical texts. It appears that Ḥunayn translated many works into Syriac and that these, in turn, were translated into Arabic by Isḥāq and other members of his staff. Another school of translators, primarily interested in mathematical and astronomical works, was centered at Ḥarrān. The head of this school of heathen Sabians was Thābit ibn Qurrah (*ca.* 836–901). In the tenth century still another school of translators arose, this time among the Jacobites. Not knowing Greek, these translators worked from earlier Syriac versions and they drew upon the Arabic translations of their predecessors. The best known members of this group were Abū Bishr Mattā, a Nestorian and Yaḥyā ibn 'Adī (893–974), a Jacobite. The Arabic translations were in general very accurate, the translators preferring literalness to elegance of style.

The works translated during this period seem to have been those studied in the late Hellenistic schools. Of the works of Aristotle, all seem to have been translated with the exception of the *Dialogues* and the *Politics*. Together with these works there were translated the writings of his commentators; among them those of Alexander of Aphrodisias, Themistius, and

---

* *Greek into Arabic*, Oxford, 1962, p. 11.

Theophrastus. So much were these commentators part of the Aristotelian tradition, that, at times, their views are cited in the name of Aristotle. Of Platonic works there were translations of the *Timaeus, Republic,* and *Laws* and, in addition, the *Phaedo* and *Crito* were known. It is quite likely that, as our knowledge increases, translations of other dialogues will come to light. Neoplatonism was represented by a number of works, the most famous of which were the *Theology of Aristotle* and the *Liber De Causis.* Though these works were ascribed to Aristotle, the first consisted, in fact, of excerpts from Plotinus' *Enneads,* while the second was taken from Proclus' *Elements of Theology.* The attribution of these works to Aristotle is not too surprising considering that in the Hellenistic schools the teachings of Plato and Aristotle were often considered as being ultimately one—a view which some of the Muslim Aristotelians accepted later on. To this impressive list of philosophic works there must be added translations of works of Galen and of hermetic and pseudo-Empedoclean writings. In this connection it should not be forgotten that the Arabic translations served to transmit Greek learning to the Christian and Jewish worlds.

Though philosophic discussions—primarily about determinism and human freedom—formed part of the controversies among early Islamic sects, Islamic philosophy proper may be said to have had its beginnings with the dialectical theologians, the Mutakallimūn. Divided into groups, of which the Mu'tazilites and the Ash'arites were the most important, the Mutakallimūn were characterized by their use of philosophic arguments for the explication of scriptural notions and for the resolution of difficulties occasioned by apparent inconsistencies in scriptural texts. Hence, more interested in the exegetical uses of philosophic arguments than in the construction of philosophic systems, they drew upon Platonic, Aristotelian, neoplatonic, Stoic, and Epicurean notions as the need arose, as a result of which their philosophic views had an eclectic character.

The Mu'tazilites seem to have had their origin, toward the end of the eighth century, in discussion groups which met in Baṣrah and Bagdad to discover how Greek philosophic thought may be of help in the solution of certain religious problems. Though it was customary at one time to describe them as the "freethinkers of Islam," their position is now understood in more moderate terms. In fact, Mu'tazilite doctrines became the official creed during the reign of Al-Ma'mūn and the affirmation of some of them was required for holding public office. Of the five basic Mu'tazilite doctrines, three were primarily theological, but two—divine unity and justice—were of philosophic interest. Investigations concerning the unity of God were marked by an attempt to show how God can be said to be one and yet be described by many attributes, while inquiries into divine justice had as their goal to show how God can be said to be omnipotent and yet the human will can be held to be free. From their interest in these two issues, the Mu'tazilites were also called "the men of unity and justice." In addition, the Mu'tazilites were known for their proofs of the creation of the world—

proofs for which they were indebted to earlier Christian Neoplatonists. The Mu'tazilites had followers among the Jews, though their influence on Christian thought was indirect.

Like the Mu'tazilites, the Ash'arites sought philosophic clarification of koranic doctrines, though their views were closer to Islamic orthodox thought. Founded by Al-Ash'ari (873–935), who was a Mu'tazilite at one time, they emphasized the omnipotence of God, meaning thereby that God is the direct cause of everything that happens in the world. In accordance with this opinion they denied the existence of secondary causes and the only answer they admitted to the question "Why did this happen?" was "God willed it." Though they were prepared to recognize a certain order and regularity in the phenomena of nature, they refused to ascribe these to necessary laws, holding instead that this apparent regularity is the result of "custom" ('ādah). Similarly, their understanding of divine omnipotence led them to deny the freedom of the human will, though, at the same time, they attempted to develop a doctrine of human responsibility. To accomplish this, they formulated the doctrine of "acquisition" (kasb) according to which, though God determines the outcome of human actions, man can decide to act willingly or with reservation. It is for this mental state that God justly rewards or punishes man. Interesting to note, the Ash'arites did not find any followers among the Jews and their influence on Christian thinkers was, once again, indirect.

Islamic thought became more strictly philosophical in the Platonic-neo-platonic and Aristotelian (falsafah) traditions. Since the Muslims often gained their knowledge of Plato's views through neoplatonic sources, they made no sharp distinction between the views of Plato and those of his neo-platonic followers. Similarly, since the Aristotelian teachings that the Muslims knew were transmitted through the Hellenistic schools, their Aristotelianism was intermingled with neoplatonic teachings. Hence, an inquiry into the degree of neoplatonic influences forms a special problem in the study of Muslim Aristotelianism. Through Platonic-neoplatonic writings of which the *Theology of Aristotle* and the *Liber De Causis* have already been mentioned, Muslims became familiar with such typical doctrines as: that God is best conceived as the One, that He is most properly described by negative attributes, that the world came into being through emanation, that in the emanative process the *logos* serves as intermediary between God and the world, that the soul is a substance, and that the final act of understanding is a kind of "illumination." The latter doctrine became especially important for the philosophic explanation of the experience of the prophets. Platonism was also central to Muslim political thought. In the absence of Aristotle's *Politics* (whether by accident or design), Muslim thinkers based their political doctrines on Plato's *Republic* and *Laws*. The Platonic political tradition yielded the description of the ideal state which came to be identified with the state founded by Islam, the division of the citizens into distinct classes, and the image of the philosopher-king who was identified with the prophet or *imām* (religious leader). Aristotelianism, on the other hand, made its primary contribution through its contention that the world is best studied through a plurality of sciences and through its logical teachings. In logic, Aristotelianism contributed such typical notions as substance and accident, properties, the syllogism in its various forms; in physics: matter and form, the four causes, the various changes, time, place, the prime mover; in psychology: the soul and its faculties, the different intellects; and in metaphysics: being, essence and existence, potentiality and actuality, the incorporeal intelligences, and the description of God. In ethics, there was much common ground between the Platonic and Aristotelian traditions in such doctrines as: that virtue requires control of the passions and that the contemplative life is the highest good for man.

The first Aristotelian is generally held to be Abū Yūsuf Ya'aqūb ibn Isḥāq al-Kindi (*ca.* 800–870). Called the "Philosopher of the Arabs," he was active in Bagdad at the courts of Al-Ma'mūn and Al-Mu'taṣim, having been in fact, the tutor of the latter's son. Over 350 treatises are ascribed to him, but only some 60–70 appear to have survived (see N. Rescher, *Al-Kindi: An Annotated Bibliography*). As an Aristotelian he advocated the independent study of philosophy and he had a major interest in the sciences, though he also wrote on metaphysics and logic. But Mu'tazilite and neoplatonic doctrines also influenced his thought. In psychology, he developed a doctrine of the four intellects—an issue which became a commonplace among the subsequent Aristotelians. However, he deviated from the Aristotelian scheme, coming thereby closer to religious teachings, in holding that the world and with it time and motion had a beginning.

The next significant philosopher was Abū Bakr ibn Muḥammad ibn Zakarīyā al-Rāzi (d. 923 or 932), who was known among the Latins as Razes the great physician. A rather independent spirit, he defended Plato against Aristotle who, to his mind, had corrupted philosophy. He denied that philosophy and religion can be reconciled and he saw no need for prophets, holding that the human intellect, properly used, is quite adequate for all human needs. Philosophy, for him, was not a discipline restricted to a chosen few; all men, so he held, can benefit from philosophic studies. In his physical teachings he was an atomist, but he held with some of the interpreters of the *Timaeus* that the world was created from an eternal, pre-existing matter. He also taught that there are five ultimate substances—not one—which are God, soul, matter, space, and time. It can readily be seen why his views earned him the displeasure of his contemporaries who branded him a heretic.

Aristotelianism in the east continued with Al-Rāzi's contemporary, Alfarabi (870–930) and reached its high point with Avicenna (980–1037). These philosophers, together with Algazali (1058–1111), the great critic of the Aristotelians, will be discussed in later sections. A number of lesser philosophers were at work in the Islamic east, but, though they are interesting in their own right, they have no direct bearing on the contents of this volume. Only the *Sincere Brethren* or *Brethren of Purity* (*Ikhwān al-Ṣafā*) need to be mentioned. Active in the second half of the tenth century, they produced about 50 "Letters" which were an encyclopedia of the philosophical sciences. Their exposition was semipopular and they attempted to strike a middle ground between orthodoxy and the Aristotelians. Though a variety of philosophic influences are at work, the collection has a neoplatonic orientation.

After having reached its highpoint in the east with Avicenna, Islamic philosophy began to shift to Spain and North Africa in the west. In its beginnings in that region, philosophy was heavily neoplatonic, though this Neoplatonism was modified by so-called pseudo-Empedoclean writings. Under the influence of the latter, Ibn Masarrah (883–931), who is said to have introduced philosophy into Spain, modified the typical neoplatonic doctrine of emanation by holding that first matter emanated directly from God and by placing first matter high in the emanationist scheme. This doctrine was accepted by Ibn Gabirol (see 357). Aristotelianism proper developed in the west during the twelfth century, partially because Almohad rulers were generally sympathetic to philosophic speculations. In Spain, it should be noted, the influence of Alfarabi was stronger than that of Avicenna and it became the tendency of Spanish Aristotelianism (especially in the person of Averroes) to cleanse Aristotle's doctrines of their neoplatonic accretions. The first important Aristotelian in the west was Ibn Bājjah (*ca.* 1070–1138), the Avempace of the Latins. His works, most of which are lost, seem to have included commentaries on Aristotle, but among those that have survived (not all complete) there are *The Regimen of the Solitary* and the *Treatise on the Union of the Intellect with Man*. As the title of the former work indicates, Ibn Bājjah was at variance with the general trend of Islamic political philosophy in holding that human happiness is best attained in separation from the state. Ibn Bājjah's doctrine of solitary contemplation influenced Ibn Ṭufayl (1100–1184), the next in the line of Spanish Aristotelians. In his *Ḥayy ibn Yaqzān,* a historical romance, Ibn Ṭufayl tells the story of a child who, having been cast ashore on an uninhabited island, develops a contemplative philosophy of his own as he grows up. When later circumstances make it possible for Ḥayy to return to civilization, he attempts to convert men to the philosophic outlook he has developed. When he is unsuccessful, he returns to his island, spending the rest of his days in contemplation. Islamic Aristotelianism reached its climax in Spain with Ibn Rushd (Averroes), the great commentator on Aristotle's works. But Averroes also marked the virtual end of Aristotelianism in the Islamic world. Deprived of followers among Muslims, he gained expositors and disciples among Jews and Christians. Much of the continuation of Islamic philosophy must be seen in terms of its influence on these two traditions.

In this volume, the Mu'tazilites are represented in the Jewish philosophy section by Saadia Gaon, a Jewish exponent of their views. No separate selection is devoted to the Ash'arites but their views are discussed incidentally by some of the Muslim and Jewish Aristotelians who criticized their position. Neoplatonism is once again represented in the Jewish philosophy section, its exponent being Ibn Gabirol. The prevailing number of the selections in the section on Islamic philosophy are taken from the major Aristotelians—Alfarabi, Avicenna, and Averroes, while Algazali exemplifies the reaction to this movement.

ALFARABI

ca. 8 7 0 – 9 5 0

T HOUGH Muslim Aristotelianism can be said to have begun with Alkindi (see p. 207), Alfarabi was the first major representative of this philosophic group. Known as "the second teacher" (Aristotle was the first), Alfarabi commented on many of Aristotle's works, wrote expositions of Platonic and Aristotelian doctrines, and, in addition, composed a number of independent works. Varied as his philosophic interests were, he was especially praised for his works on logic, and his political theories became perhaps his most distinctive contribution to Muslim and Jewish thought. Among his Muslim successors there was hardly anyone who was not influenced by his teachings, and several Jewish thinkers, Maimonides in particular, held him in high esteem. The Christian world knew him through Latin translations of some of his works, but for it his political writings held little interest and, in general, he was overshadowed by Avicenna and Averroes.

The complexion and intention of Alfarabi's thought is not easily determined. It is clear enough that he was one of those philosophers who believed in the essential unity of Plato and Aristotle (though that this was his real view has recently been challenged), and it is equally clear that in logic, natural philosophy, and ethics he followed Aristotle and his commentators; in politics, Plato; and in metaphysics, Aristotelian and neoplatonic teachings. How exactly these elements serve to make up his thought is less easily determined. Difficulties arise because there are contradictions in his views and because works formerly attributed to him have been shown not to be his. There have been interpreters who have seen in him someone who earnestly attempted to harmonize Islamic doctrines with philosophic teachings, while others have found him to be someone committed to philosophy, but for whom religion had largely a political use.

Two metaphysical doctrines have been ascribed to Alfarabi, but since it is doubtful that he is the author of the two works in which they are primarily set down, it is difficult to determine what role they play in his thought. The first of these is the distinction between possible and necessary existence. When the mind reflects upon existing things, it finds that there are some which can exist or not exist, while there are others which necessarily must exist. From this reflection it becomes clear that all existing things are divisible into those which are possible and those which are necessary. To which it should be added that the series of necessary things comes to an end with a being necessary through itself, and this is God.

A similar examination of existent things reveals that the mind can think their essence without concomitantly thinking that these things exist. Hence existence is different from and superadded to essence, and essence and existence are ontologically distinct. Thus a second metaphysical distinction arises, that between essence and existence. Once again it can be shown that there exists a being in whom essence and existence are identical, and this is God. The two kinds of distinction mentioned are fundamental for Avicenna later on.

One is on more certain ground in describing Alfarabi's account of God. God, for him, is identical with the neoplatonic One and at the same time with Aristotle's divine thought thinking itself. Besides being one, God is knowing, true, and living, but in God all these attributes are identical with His essence. God is incorporeal, pure intellect, and the creator of everything that exists.

To explain the origin of the world, Alfarabi turns to the neoplatonic doctrine of emanation. God contemplates Himself and from this contemplation there issues forth from Him an intellect which is the first emanation. From this intellect there emanate successively nine further intellects, the last of which is the so-called Agent Intellect. To each intellect belongs a celestial sphere, though the intellect exists in separation from its sphere. Invoking neoplatonic cosmological doctrines, Alfarabi identifies each of the first nine spheres with a celestial body. In descending order the spheres are: the first all-encompassing sphere, the sphere of the fixed stars, Saturn, Jupiter, Mars, Sun, Venus, Mercury and the Moon. The Agent Intellect governs the sublunar sphere which is the sphere of generation and corruption. Within the sublunar sphere, intellectual, animate, and natural powers are at work, and everything within it is composed of matter and form. Though it has been held that emanation, for Alfarabi, is voluntary and takes place in time, it seems more likely that emanation, for him, is necessary and eternal.

One of the more fully developed aspects of Alfarabi's philosophy of nature is his doctrine of the intellect. In the third book of the *De Anima* Aristotle had described how the mind knows, but his account was rather enigmatic. The ancient commentators had tried to make Aristotle's teachings more specific and, prior to Alfarabi, Alkindi had written on the intellect. Drawing on these predecessors, Alfarabi gave the Aristotelian doctrines an interpretation of his own. Examining Aristotle and his commentators, he concluded that, in discussing the intellect, Aristotle speaks of it in four senses. First there is that faculty of the human soul which has the ability to think, and this is the intellect in potentiality. It seems that Alfarabi followed Alexander of Aphrodisias in considering this intellect as a power within the body.* When the intellect abstracts the intelligibles from substances within the material world, it becomes an intellect in actuality. The intellect in actuality, in turn, can think the intelligibles within it and, thus, itself; and when it does this, it becomes the acquired intellect. Finally, as any change, thinking requires an efficient cause, and this is the Agent Intellect. As has already been noted, the Agent Intellect is the lowest of the self-existent intellects.

Closely connected with his psychology is Alfarabi's account of prophecy. The prophet is not merely someone arbitrarily selected by God for his prophetic office, but someone possessed of all human perfections. Not only must the prophet possess a healthy constitution, moral virtues, and intellectual perfection, but he must also have a well-developed faculty of imagination. Once these perfections have been attained, the prophet assumes a twofold role. As philosopher, his acquired intellect will be in contact with the Agent Intellect from which it receives a kind of illumination. Alfarabi insists that the prophetic intellect will never become identical with the Agent Intellect, but at the same time he admits that the Agent Intellect is a kind of form for the acquired intellect of the prophet. But besides being an accomplished philosopher, the prophet is also a statesman. As a statesman, he cares for the common good, governing the state in accordance with just laws. Since, as statesman, the prophet must address the masses who can only understand truths presented in metaphorical form, he requires a well-developed imagination in order to be able to persuade them. Maimonides later on was to base his theory of prophecy on Alfarabi's.

Alfarabi's doctrine of the intellect is also important for his account of human immortality. With other Muslim Aristotelians he considered the Koran's physical description of the afterlife as an accommodation to the understanding of the masses, but at the same time he does not seem to have denied human immortality altogether. It appears to have been his view that the acquired intellect of those chosen few who have actualized their intellectual faculty will survive death and that this incorporeal immortality is individual.†

In his political philosophy Alfarabi is the disciple of Plato, though Aristotelian influences are not missing. Man, according to Alfarabi, is political by nature and he attains his happiness within the state. The ideal state, as Plato had taught, consists of the orderly arrangement of its citizens, each one fulfilling the task for which he is best fitted. Men by nature are unequal, but Alfarabi interprets this doctrine in the light of Aristotelian logical distinctions. The intellectual elite which governs the state consists of those who can understand demonstrations, while the masses are those who only understand through various arguments of persuasion. As the world in its totality requires a first principle which is one, so the state requires a single ruler. He is the prophet, also called philosopher, legislator, and *imām*

* Cf. F. Rahman, *Prophecy in Islam*, London, 1958, p. 21.
† Cf. *ibid.*, p. 25.

(leader). Yet having described the ideal state, Alfarabi divides it into three kinds and, in addition, he analyzes a variety of states which are defective.

It is in Alfarabi's political doctrines that philosophy and religion finally meet. For it is the prophet who is the founder of the good state required as a prerequisite for human perfection, and it is the prophet who transmits to the masses philosophic truth in symbolic form. Philosophy contains the final truth, but religion contains its image.

Abū Naṣr al-Fārābī was born *ca.* 870 in the district of the city of Fārāb (Turkestan), of Turkish descent. He studied first in Khurāsān and later in Bagdad where he came in contact with Christian Aristotelians. One of his teachers was the Nestorian Christian Yūḥannā Ibn Haylān, who was versed in the teachings of the school of Alexandria, and another, the translator and commentator Bishr Mattā ibn Yūnus. In 942 he accepted an invitation to the court of Sayf al-Dawlah and he spent most of the remainder of his life at Aleppo. He is said to have lived a modest and ascetic life and to have been a man of mystical inclination. He died about 950.

Over one hundred works have been ascribed to Alfarabi, but many of these are no longer extant. He seems to have commented on many of Aristotle's works, but most of these commentaries are now lost. In addition to a number of logical works, some of which have been edited and translated only recently, there should be mentioned his treatises *Concerning the Intellect* (*Fī al-'Aql*), *The Enumeration of the Sciences* (*Iḥṣā' al-'Ulūm*), *About the Scope of Aristotle's Metaphysics* (*Fī Aghrāḍ Mā Ba'd al-Ṭabī'ah*), *The Harmony between the Views of the Divine Plato and Aristotle* (*Al-Jam' bayan Ra'yay al-Ḥakīmayn Aflāṭūn al-Ilāhī wa-Arisṭūṭālīs*), *On the Vacuum* (*Fī al-Khalā'*), a book in three parts consisting of *The Attainment of Happiness* (*Fī Taḥṣīl al-Sa'ādah*), a political work, and *The Philosophy of Plato* (*Falsafat Aflātun*) and the *Philosophy of Aristotle* (*Falsafat Arisṭūṭālīs*). His political works include *The Political Regime* (*Al-Siyāsat al-Madaniyyah*), *The Opinions of the People of the Virtuous City* (*Fī Ārā' Ahl al-Madīnah al-Fāḍilah*), *Epitome of Plato's Laws,* and *Aphorisms of the Statesman* (*Fuṣūl al-Madanī*). *The Seals of Wisdom* (*Fuṣūṣ al-Ḥikam*) is probably by Avicenna, and it has been questioned whether *The Main Questions* (*'Uyūn al-Masā'il*) is by Alfarabi.

The first of the following selections consists of a portion of *The Letter Concerning the Intellect*. In this work Alfarabi investigates the meaning assigned to the term "intellect" by (1) ordinary people, (2) the Mutakallimūn, (3) Aristotle in his *Posterior Analytics,* (4) Aristotle in the sixth book of his *Ethics,* (5) Aristotle in his *De Anima,* and (6) Aristotle in his *Metaphysics.* The selection consists of the last two sections. The second selection is taken from *The Attainment of Happiness* and deals with aspects of his political philosophy, including his description of the ruler.

THE LETTER CONCERNING THE INTELLECT

• • •

Aristotle set down the intellect which he mentioned in the *De Anima* according to four senses, intellect in potentiality, intellect in actuality, acquired intellect, and agent intellect.

The intellect which is in potentiality is some soul, or part of a soul, or one of the faculties of the soul, or something whose essence is ready and prepared to abstract the quiddities of all existing things and their forms from their matters, so that it makes all of them a form for itself or forms for itself. And those forms which are abstracted from their matters do not become abstracted from their matters in which their existence is unless they become forms for this essence [the intellect in potentiality]. Those forms abstracted from their matters which become forms in this essence are the intelligibles, and this name [intelligibles] is derived for them from the name of that essence which abstracts the forms of existing things, so that they become forms for it. That essence is like matter in which forms come to be. Now, if you imagine some corporeal matter, for example, a piece of wax on which an impression is stamped, and that impression and that form comes to be in its surface and its depth and that form gets possession of all of matter so that the matter in its complete totality becomes that form because the form is spread out in it—then your imagination is close to picturing the manner in which the forms of things come to be in that essence which is like matter and substratum for that form. But [the wax] differs from the other corporeal matters, because the [other] corporeal matters only receive the forms in their surfaces, not in their depths. The essence of this essence [the essence of the intellect in potentiality] does not remain distinguished from the forms of the intelligibles, so that it [the intellect] has a distinct quiddity and the form which is in it has a distinct quiddity, but this essence itself becomes those forms. This is as if you were to imagine the impression and the formation through which a piece of wax is formed cubic or spherical, and this formation sinks into it, spreads through it, and takes possession of all its length, breadth, and depth. Then that wax will have become that very formation without there belonging to it a distinction between its quiddity and the quiddity of that formation.

In accordance with this example you must imagine the coming to be of the forms of existing things in that essence which Aristotle in the *De Anima* calls intellect in potentiality. And as long as there is not within it any of the forms of existing things, it is intellect in potentiality. However, when there come to be in it the forms of existing things, in accordance with the example which we have mentioned, then that essence becomes intellect in actuality. This is

Translated by Arthur Hyman for this volume from Alfarabi, *Risālah fi-'l-'Aql*, ed. M. Bouyges, Beyrouth: Imprimerie Catholique, 1948.

the meaning of intellect in actuality. And when there come to be in it the intelligibles which it abstracts from the matters, then those intelligibles become intelligibles in actuality. Before they were abstracted from their matters they were intelligibles in potentiality, but when they were abstracted, they became intelligibles in actuality, because they became forms for that essence. But that they are intelligibles in actuality and that [the intellect] is an intellect in actuality is the very same thing. The meaning of our statement concerning [the intellect], that it is thinking, is nothing else but that the intelligibles become forms for it, according as it itself becomes those forms. Thus the meaning [of] it is "thinking in actuality," "intellect in actuality," and "intelligible in actuality" is one and the same meaning, indeed one and the same meaning. The intelligibles which are intelligibles in potentiality are, before they become intelligible in actuality, forms in matter outside the soul. But when they become intelligibles in actuality, then their existence, insofar as they are intelligibles in actuality, is not the same as their existence insofar as they are forms in matters. And their existence in themselves [as forms in matters] is not the same as their existence insofar as they are intelligibles in actuality. Now, their existence in themselves [as forms in matters] follows the rest of that which is joined to them, namely sometimes place, sometimes time, sometimes position, at times quantity, at times being qualified by corporeal qualities, at times acting and at times undergoing action. But when these forms become intelligibles in actuality, many of those other categories are removed from them, so that their existence becomes another existence, different from this existence. Then the meanings of these categories or many of them must be understood in some other senses, different from those senses, for example, place when it is considered in regard to the intelligible in actuality. For if you consider the meaning of place in regard to it, either you will not find in it any of the meanings of place at all, or, if you should apply the term "place" it must be understood by you in regard to it in a different meaning, and this meaning according to a different sense.

When [the intelligibles] become intelligibles in actuality, they become, then, one of the things existing in the world, and they are counted, insofar as they are intelligibles, among the totality of existing things. Now, it is the nature of all existing things that they can be thought and that they can become forms for that essence [the intellect in potentiality]. Since this is the case, it is not impossible that the intelligibles insofar as they are intelligibles in actuality, and this is the intellect in actuality, can also be thought. And that which is thought is then nothing but that which is in actuality an intellect. However, that which is in actuality an intellect because some intelligible has become a form for it, is only an intellect in actuality in relation to that form, but it can be an intellect in potentiality in relation to some other intelligible which has not yet come to it in actuality. When the second intelligible comes to it, it becomes an intellect in actuality in respect to the first intelligible and in respect to the second intelligible. And when it becomes an intellect in actuality in relation to all intelligibles and it becomes one of the existing things because it became the intelligibles in actuality, then, when it thinks that existent thing which is an intellect in actuality, it does not think an existing thing outside of itself [or: its essence] but it only thinks itself [or: its essence].

It is clear that if the intellect thinks itself [or: its essence] insofar as it itself [or: its essence] is an intellect in actuality, there does not come to it from that which it thinks of itself [or: its essence], some existing thing whose existence in respect to itself [or: its essence] is different from its existence, namely as an intelligible in actuality; but it thinks of itself [or: its essence] some existing thing whose existence, namely as intelligible, is its existence in itself [or: its essence]. Then this essence becomes an intelligible in actuality, even though it was not, before it was thought, an intelligible in potentiality, but it was an intelligible in actuality. Now it is thought in actuality, insofar as its existence in itself is an intellect in actuality and an intelligible in actuality, which is different from the way in which these things in themselves [the intelligibles] are thought at first. For they were first thought, according as they were abstracted from their matters in which their existence is and according as they are intelligibles in potentiality, but they are thought a second time in such a way that their existence is not that previous existence, but their existence is separate from their matters, according as they are forms which are not in their matters and according as they are intelligibles in actuality. When the intellect in actuality thinks the intelligibles which are forms in it, insofar as they are intelligibles in actuality, then the intellect of which it was first said that it is the intellect in actuality, becomes now the acquired intellect.

If there are existing things which are forms not in matters and which never were forms in matters, then those forms become, when they are thought, an existing thing, namely an intelligible, possessing the same kind of existence which the forms had before they were thought. Now our statement that something is first thought [means] that the forms which exist in matters are abstracted from their matters and there comes to them some other existence, different from their first existence. But if there exist things which are forms which have no matter, it is not at all necessary that this essence [the intellect in potentiality] abstracts them from matters, but it encounters them as abstracted and thinks them just as it encounters itself [or: its essence], insofar as it is an intellect in actuality, as intelligibles which are not in their matters and thinks them. And its existence, insofar as it is an intelligible, becomes a second intellect [and] this is the same existence which belonged to it before it was thought by this intellect. This very same thing must be thought concerning those things which are forms not in matter, namely, that when they are thought, their existence in themselves is their existence, but they are intelligibles for us. And the statement "that which belongs *to us* in actuality as an intellect" and "that which is *in us* in actuality as an intellect" is the very same statement in regard to those forms which are not in matters and which never were in them. For in the same manner in which we say concerning that which belongs to us in actuality as an intellect that it is *in us*, in the same manner must we say concerning those [forms] that they exist *in* the world. However, these forms can only be perfectly thought after all intelligibles or most of them have become thought in actuality, and the acquired intellect has come into being. Now, the acquired intellect is like a form for the intellect which is in actuality, and the intellect in actuality is like a substratum and matter for the acquired intellect, and the intellect which is in actuality is like a form for that essence [the intellect in potentiality] and that essence is like matter. With that, the forms begin to descend to the corporeal, material forms, while before this they ascended little by little until they were separated from matters one after another little by little, in the manner of something which is separated as contending.

If the forms which are not at all in matter, which never were nor ever will be in matter, contend with one another in respect to perfection and immateriality, and they have some order in respect to existence, then, when their order is considered, the more perfect of them will in this way be a form for the less perfect until it comes to the least perfect and this is the acquired intellect. Then it [the form] does not cease descending until it reaches that essence [the intellect in potentiality], and the animate powers which are below it. Then, after that, it reaches nature. Afterwards it does not cease to descend until it reaches the forms of the elements which are the lowest forms in respect to existence, and their substratum is the lowest substratum, and it is prime matter. But if one ascends from prime matter step by step, then one ascends to the nature which is the corporeal forms in hylic matters until one ascends to that essence [the intellect in potentiality], afterwards to that which is above until, when one has reached the acquired intellect, one will have reached that which is like the stars and one will have reached the limit to which those things which are related to hyle and matter ascend. When one ascends from this, then one will have ascended to the first stage of existing things which are immaterial, and the first stage is the stage of the agent intellect.

The agent intellect which Aristotle mentioned in the third treatise of the *De Anima* is a separated form which never existed in matter nor ever will exist in it, and it is in a certain manner an intellect in actuality close in likeness to the acquired intellect. And the agent intellect is that principle which makes that essence which was an intellect in potentiality, an intellect in actuality and which makes the intelligibles which are intelligibles in potentiality, intelligibles in actuality.

The relation of the active intellect to the intellect which is in potentiality is like the relation of the sun to the eye which is sight in potentiality as long as it is in darkness. And sight is sight in potentiality only as long as it is in darkness. The meaning of darkness is transparency in potentiality and the privation of transparency in actuality, and the meaning of transparency is illumination by something opposite which is luminous. When light comes to be in the sight and in the air and in that which is like it, then sight, because of the light which comes to be in it, becomes sight in actuality and colors become visible in actuality. However, we say that sight does not only become sight in actuality because there comes to be in it light and transparency in actuality, but also because, when there comes to be in it transparency in actuality, there comes to be in it the forms of visible things; and with the coming into being of the forms of visible things in the sight, it becomes sight in actuality. And because it was prepared, before that, by the rays of the sun or something else so that it became transparent in actuality, and the air which touches it also became transparent in actuality, that which is visible in potentiality now becomes visible in actuality. Thus the principle through which sight becomes sight in actuality after it was sight in potentiality, and through which visible things which are visible in potentiality become visible in actuality, is the transparency which comes to be in the sight from the sun. And in a similar manner there comes to be in that essence which is an intellect in potentiality something whose relation to it is as the relation of transparency in actuality to sight. But the agent intellect provides this thing which is like transparency for it [the intellect in potentiality] and through it it becomes a principle for which the intelligibles which were in potentiality become intelligibles in actuality. Just as the sun is that which makes the eye sight in actuality and visible things visible in actuality, insofar as it gives [the eye] illumination, so likewise the agent intellect is that which makes the intellect which is in potentiality an intellect in actuality insofar as it gives it of that principle, and through this very same thing the intelligibles become intelligibles in actuality.

The agent intellect is of the species of the acquired intellect. But the forms of immaterial existing things which are above it [and which] are in it do not cease nor will they cease. However, their existence in it [the agent intellect] is according to an order different from the order according to which they exist in the intellect which is in actuality. The reason is that that which is lower in the intellect which is in actuality is ordered mostly so that it is prior to that which is more excellent, because we ascend mostly to the things which are more perfect in existence from the things which are less perfect in existence, as it is explained in the *Posterior Analytics*, [namely] that we ascend from that which is best known to us to that which is unknown, and that which is more perfect in regard to existence in itself is more unknown to us, I intend, that of which our ignorance is greater. Therefore, it is necessary that the order of existent things in the intellect which is in actuality is the opposite of that which is in the agent intellect. And the agent intellect thinks first the most perfect of existing things. The forms which here are forms in matters are in the agent intellect abstract forms, but not such that they at first existed in matter and then were abstracted, but those forms never cease in it in actuality. And it [the agent intellect] is imitated in the realm of first matter and of other matters, because they [the matters] were given in actuality the forms which are in the agent intellect. And the existing things whose coming into being was first intended are, according to our view, those forms, except that, inasmuch as their coming into being here [below] was not possible except in matters, there came into existence these matters.

Those forms are in the agent intellect indivisible, while in first matter they are divisible. And it can not be denied that the agent intellect which is indivisible or whose essence consists of things which are indivisible gives matter a likeness of that which is in its substance, but [matter] does not receive it except as divided. Aristotle also explained this matter in the *De Anima*.

If someone were to ask: Since it is possible that these forms exist without matter, what need is there that they are produced in matters, and how can they descend from the more perfect existence to the less perfect existence? Perhaps someone will answer: It does this so that matters attain a more perfect existence. But it would follow from that [assumption] that those forms came into existence only for the sake of matter, and this contradicts what Aristotle has shown. Or we could answer that all of these [forms] are in the agent intellect in potentiality. But one must not infer from our statement that the agent intellect is in potentiality that the agent intellect is in its potentiality in such a way that it receives these forms, so that they come to be in it insofar as they are received; but we intend that it has a potentiality for producing them in matter as forms and this is the potentiality insofar as it acts in something else and it is that which produces forms in the matters. Afterwards, it undertakes to bring them [the forms in matter] closer to that which is immaterial little by little until there comes to be the acquired intellect and with that the substance of man or man, insofar as he becomes a substance through it, becomes something closer to the agent intellect. This is the ultimate happiness and the afterlife, namely that there comes to man some other thing through which he becomes a substance. And there comes to him his final perfection, namely that there acts some other thing through which he becomes a substance with some other action through which he becomes a substance, and this is the meaning of the afterlife. But its action is not in some other thing outside its essence, and it acts in order that its essence may exist, and its essence, its act, and that it acts, are one and the same thing. Now the acquired intellect does not require for its subsistence a body which is matter for it, nor again does it require for any of its activities that it asks for an activity the help of an animate power in a body, nor that it employ for it any corporeal instrument at all. The least perfect existence of [the intellect's] essence is that it requires for its subsistence, insofar as it is an existent thing, that there is a body which is matter for it and it is a form in a body or a body altogether. Above this is that it does not require for its subsistence that there is the body which is matter for it, but it requires for its activities or for many of them that it employs a corporeal power and that it asks help for its activity, for example, [of] sense and imagination. But the most perfect existence belonging to it is that it attains the state which we have mentioned [that of the acquired intellect].

That the agent intellect exists has been shown in the *De Anima*. And it is clear that the agent intellect does not act always, but it acts at one time, and it does not act at another time. Thus it follows necessarily that [the intermittent action] proceeds from the thing which acts or from that in which it acts according to different relations, that is, it changes from relation to relation. Now, if the agent intellect did not always exist according to its highest perfection, then it would not change from relation to relation at all, but it would change in its essence. Since its ultimate perfection is in its substance, it would be in its substance at one time in potentiality and at another time in actuality; and that which belongs to it in potentiality would be some matter, while that which belongs to it in actuality would not be [some matter]. But we have stated that the agent intellect is separate from every matter. Since it is like this, it always exists in its ultimate perfection and it must necessarily change from relation to relation. Now the defect [namely that it acts at times but not at others], does not come from its essence, but either from the fact that the agent intellect does not always encounter something in which it can act because there does not exist prepared the matter and the substratum in which it can act, or from the fact that it has an impediment from outside of it, so that it ceases, or from both of these things together. From that it is clear that there is not in [the agent intellect] sufficiency through which it is the first principle of all existing things, for it requires that there be ready a matter in which it can act and that it lacks an impediment. Thus, there is not in its essence and in its substance sufficiency for producing the totality of things and there is then in its substance a defect in regard to the production of many existing things. And that in whose existence there is a defect does not have in it sufficiency that its existence is through itself without that its existence is from another than it. And it follows necessarily that there exists for its existence another principle and that there exists another cause which aids it through the production of the matter in which it acts.

It is clear that the substrata in which the agent intellect acts are either bodies or powers in bodies which come to an end and pass away. And it was shown in *De Generatione et Corruptione* that the celestial bodies are the first acting parts [causes] for these bodies and thus they give to the agent intellect the matters and substrata in which it acts.

Every celestial body is moved by a mover which is not a body nor [a force] in a body at all and this mover is the cause for its existence and it is that through which it becomes a substance. And its order in respect to the existence which is its substance is the order of this body. And the mover which is more perfect than it, is more perfect than it in its existence, and the one which is more perfect than it in its existence is the first heaven, and more perfect in its existence than the first heaven is the mover of the first heaven. However, the mover of the first heaven is a principle in which there is the existence of two distinct things. One of these is that through which the first heaven becomes a substance, namely a corporeal or embodied substance, the other is [that through which there comes to be] the mover of the sphere of the fixed stars and this essence is not a body nor [a force] within a body. And it is not possible that the mover of the first heaven produces both of these things together in one respect and through one thing in its essence through which it becomes a substance, but through two natures, one of which is more perfect than the other; for that principle through which it produces that which is more perfect which is something not a body nor a force in a body [that is, the mover of the sphere of the fixed stars] is more perfect than that [principle] through which it produces that which is corporeal and less perfect [namely, the body of the first heaven]. Thus it becomes only a substance through two natures through which its existence is. There is then a principle for its existence to which it can be apportioned that it is the cause through which [the mover of the first heavens] becomes a substance. And it is not possible that the mover of the first heavens is the first principle for all existing things, but it has another principle necessarily. This principle does not have a principle whose existence is more perfect than it. Since the mover of the first heavens is not matter nor in matter, it follows that it is an intellect in its substance and it thinks itself [or: its essence] and the essence of that which is the principle of its existence. And it is clear that that which it thinks of the principle of its existence is more perfect than its two natures which are peculiar to it as the less perfect of them. Since its essence is divided into two natures it does not require anything besides these two.

But that principle which is the principle through which the first heaven becomes a substance is necessarily one in all respects, and it is not possible that there is an existing thing more perfect than it, or that it have a principle. Thus it is the principle of all principles and the first principle of all existing things. And this is the intellect which Aristotle mentioned in letter Lam [book Lambda] of the *Metaphysics*. Each one of these others is also an intellect, but this one is the first intellect and the first existing, the first one, and the first true. The others only become an intellect from it according to order.

But further investigation concerning these matters lies outside that which we intended. Peace.

The Letter concerning the Intellect by Abu Naṣr al-Fārābī is finished.

PHILOSOPHY OF PLATO AND ARISTOTLE

The Attainment of Happiness

II

. . .

37   Therefore the prince occupies his place by nature and not merely by will. Similarly, a subordinate occupies his place primarily by nature and only secondarily by virtue of the will, which perfects his natural equipment. This being the case, the theoretical virtue, the highest deliberative virtue, the highest moral virtue, and the highest practical art are realized in those equipped for them by nature: that is, in those who possess superior natures with very great potentialities.

III

38   After these four things are realized in a certain man, the realization of the particular instances of them in nations and cities still remains; his knowing how to make these particular instances exist in nations and cities remains: he who possesses such a great power ought to possess the capacity of realizing the particular instances of it in nations and cities.

39   There are two primary methods of realizing them: instruction and the formation of character. To instruct is to introduce the theoretical virtues in nations and cities. The formation of character is the method of introducing the moral virtues and practical arts in nations. Instruction proceeds by speech alone. The formation of character proceeds through habituating nations and citizens in doing the acts that issue from the practical states of character by arousing in them the resolution to do these acts; the states of character and the acts issuing from them should come to possess their souls, and they should be as it were enraptured by them. The resolution to do a thing may be aroused by speech or by deed.

40   Instruction in the theoretical sciences should be given either to the *imams* and the princes, or else to those who should preserve the theoretical sciences. The instruction of these two groups proceeds by means of identical approaches. These are the approaches stated above. First, they should know the first premises and the primary knowledge relative to every kind of theoretical science. Then they should know the various states of the premises and their various arrangements as stated before, and be made to pursue the subjects that were mentioned. (Prior to this, their souls must have been set aright through the training befitting the youths whose natures entitle them to this rank in the order of humanity.) They should be habituated to use all the logical methods in all the theoretical sciences. And

they should be made to pursue a course of study and form the habits of character from their childhood until each of them reaches maturity, in accordance with the plan described by Plato. Then the princes among them will be placed in subordinate offices and promoted gradually through the ranks until they are fifty years old. Then they will be placed in the office with the highest authority. This, then, is the way to instruct this group; they are the elect who should not be confined to what is in conformity with unexamined common opinion. Until they acquire the theoretical virtues, they ought to be instructed in things theoretical by means of persuasive methods. They should comprehend many theoretical things by way of imagining them. These are the things—the ultimate principles and the incorporeal principles—that a man cannot perceive by his intellect except after knowing many other things. The vulgar ought to comprehend merely the similitudes of these principles, which should be established in their souls by persuasive arguments. One should draw a distinction between the similitudes that ought to be presented to every nation, and in which all nations and all the citizens of every city should share, and the ones that ought to be presented to a particular nation and not to another, to a particular city and not to one another, or to a particular group among the citizens of a city and not to another. All these [persuasive arguments and similitudes] must be discerned by the deliberative virtue.

41   They [the princes and the *imams*] should be habituated in the acts of the practical virtues and the practical arts by either of two methods. First, by means of persuasive arguments, passionate arguments, and other arguments that establish these acts and states of character in the soul completely so as to arouse the resolution to do the acts willingly. This method is made possible by the practice of the rational arts—to which the mind is naturally inclined—and by the benefits derived from such practice. The other method is compulsion. It is used with the recalcitrant and the obstinate among those citizens of cities and nations who do not rise in favor of what is right willingly and of their own accord or by means of arguments, and also with those who refuse to teach others the theoretical sciences in which they are engaged.

42   Now since the virtue or the art of the prince is exercised by exploiting the acts of those who possess the particular virtues and the arts of those who practice the particular arts, it follows necessarily that the virtuous and the masters of the arts whom he [the prince] employs to form the character of nations and citizens of cities comprise two primary groups: a group employed by him to form the character of whosoever is susceptible of having his character formed willingly, and a group employed by him to form the character of those who are such that their character can be formed only by compulsion. This is analogous to what heads of households and superintendents of children and youths do. For the prince forms the character of nations and instructs them, just as the head of a household forms the character of its members and instructs them, and the superintendent of children and youths forms their character and instructs them. Just as each of the latter two forms the character of some of those who are in his custody by being gentle to them and by persuasion and forms the character of others by compulsion, so does the prince. Indeed it is in virtue of the very same skill that the classes of men who form the character of others and superintend them undertake both the compulsory formation of character and the formation of character received willingly; the skill varies only with respect to its degree and the extent of its power. Thus the power required for forming the character of nations and for superintending

them is greater than the power required for forming the character of children and youths or the power required by heads of households for forming the character of the members of a household. Correspondingly, the power of the princes who are the superintendents of nations and cities and who form their character, and the power of whomever and whatever they employ in performing this function, are greater. The prince needs the most powerful skill for forming the character of others with their consent and the most powerful skill for forming their character by compulsion.

43   The latter is the craft of war: that is, the faculty that enables him to excel in organizing and leading armies and utilizing war implements and warlike people to conquer the nations and cities that do not submit to doing what will procure them that happiness for whose acquisition man is made. For every being is made to achieve the ultimate perfection it is susceptible of achieving according to its specific place in the order of being. Man's specific perfection is called *supreme happiness;* and to each man, according to his rank in the order of humanity, belongs the specific supreme happiness pertaining to his kind of man. The warrior who pursues this purpose is the just warrior, and the art of war that pursues this purpose is the just and virtuous art of war.

44   The other group, employed to form the character of nations and the citizens of cities with their consent, is composed of those who possess the rational virtues and arts. For it is obvious that the prince needs to return to the theoretical, intelligible things whose knowledge was acquired by certain demonstrations, look for the persuasive methods that can be employed for each, and seek out all the persuasive methods that can be employed for it (he can do this because he possesses the power to be persuasive about individual cases). Then he should repair to these very same theoretical things and seize upon their similitudes. He ought to make these similitudes produce images of the theoretical things for all nations jointly, so establish the similitudes that persuasive methods can cause them to be accepted, and exert himself throughout to make both the similitudes and the persuasive methods such that all nations and cities may share in them. Next he needs to enumerate the acts of the particular practical virtues and arts that fulfill the above-mentioned requirements. He should devise methods of political oratory with which to arouse the resolution to such acts in nations and cities. He should employ here (1) arguments that support [the rightness of] his own character; (2) passionate and moral arguments that cause (*a*) the souls of the citizens to grow reverent, submissive, muted, and meek. But with respect to everything contrary to these acts he should employ passionate and moral arguments by which (*b*) the souls of the citizens grow confident, spiteful, insolent, and contemptuous. He should employ these same two kinds of arguments [*a* and *b*], respectively, with the princes who agree with him and with those who oppose him, with the men and the auxiliaries employed by him and with the ones employed by those who oppose him, and with the virtuous and with those who oppose them. Thus with respect to his own position he should employ arguments by which souls grow reverent and submissive. But with respect to his opponents he should employ arguments that cause souls to grow spiteful, insolent, and contemptuous; arguments with which he contradicts, using persuasive methods, those who disagree with his own opinions and acts; and arguments that show the opinions and acts of the opponent as base and make their meanness and notoriety apparent. He should employ

here both classes of arguments: I mean the class that should be employed periodically, daily, and temporarily, and not preserved, kept permanently, or written down; and the other class, which should be preserved and kept permanently, orally and in writing. [The latter should be kept in two Books, a Book of Opinions and a Book of Acts.] He should place in these two Books the opinions and the acts that nations and cities were called upon to embrace, the arguments by which he sought to preserve among them and to establish in them the things they were called upon to embrace so that they will not be forgotten, and the arguments with which he contradicts the opponents of these opinions and acts. Therefore the sciences that form the character of nations and cities will have three ranks of order [the first belongs to the sciences contained in the Book of Opinions, the second to the sciences contained in the Book of Acts, and the third to the unwritten sciences]. Each kind will have a group to preserve it, who should be drawn from among those who possess the faculty that enables them to excel in the discovery of what had not been clearly stated to them with reference to the science they preserve, to defend it, to contradict what contradicts it, and to excel in teaching all of this to others. In all of this they should aim at accomplishing the purpose of the supreme ruler with respect to nations and cities.

45 Then he [the supreme ruler] should inquire next into the different classes of nations by inquiring into every nation and into the human states of character and the acts for which all nations are equipped by that nature which is common to them, until he comes to inquire into all or most nations. He should inquire into that in which all nations share—that is, the *human nature* common to them—and then into all the things that pertain specifically to every group within every nation. He should discern all of these, draw up an actual— if approximate—list of the acts and the states of character with which every nation can be set aright and guided toward happiness, and specify the classes of persuasive argument (regarding both the theoretical and the practical virtues) that ought to be employed among them. He will thus set down what every nation is capable of, having subdivided every nation and inquired whether or not there is a group fit for preserving the theoretical sciences and others who can preserve the popular theoretical sciences or the image-making theoretical sciences.

46 Provided all of these groups exist in nations, four sciences will emerge. First, the theoretical virtue through which the beings become intelligible with certain demonstrations. Next, these same intelligibles acquired by persuasive methods. Subsequently, the science that comprises the similitudes of these intelligibles, accepted by persuasive methods. Finally, the sciences extracted from these three for each nation. There will be as many of these extracted sciences as there are nations, each containing everything by which a particular nation becomes perfect and happy.

47 Therefore he [the supreme ruler] has to find certain groups of men or certain individuals who are to be instructed in what causes the happiness of particular nations, who will preserve what can form the character of a particular nation alone, and who will learn the persuasive methods that should be employed in forming the character of that nation. The knowledge which that nation ought to have must be preserved by a man or a group of men also possessing the faculty that enables them to excel in the discovery of what was not actually given to this man or this group of men but is, nevertheless, of the same kind

for which they act as custodians, enables them to defend it and contradict what opposes it, and to excel in the instruction of that nation. In all of this they should aim at accomplishing what the supreme ruler had in mind for the nation, for whose sake he gave this man or this group of men what was given to them. Such are the men who should be employed to form the character of nations with their consent.

48. The best course is that each member of the groups to which the formation of the character of nations is delegated should possess a warlike virtue and a deliberative virtue for use in case there is need to excel in leading troops in war; thus everyone of them will possess the skill to form the nations' character by both methods. If this combination does not happen to exist in one man, then he [the supreme ruler] should add to the man who forms the character of nations with their consent another who possesses this craft of war. In turn, the one to whom the formation of the character of any nation is delegated should also follow the custom of employing a group of men to form the character of the nation with its consent or by compulsion, by either dividing them into two groups or employing a single group that possesses a skill for doing both. Subsequently, this one group, or the two groups, should be subdivided, and so on, ending in the lowest divisions or the ones with the least power in the formation of character. The ranks within these groups should be established according to the deliberative virtue of each individual: that is, depending on whether his deliberative virtue exploits subordinate ones or is exploited by one superior to it. The former will rule and the latter have a subordinate office according to the power of their respective deliberative virtues. When these two groups are formed in any nation or city, they, in turn, will order the rest.

49 These, then, are the modes and the methods through which the four human things by which supreme happiness is achieved are realized in nations and cities.

IV

50 Foremost among all of these [four] sciences is that which gives an account of the beings as they are perceived by the intellect with certain demonstrations. The others merely take these same beings and employ persuasion about them or represent them with images so as to facilitate the instruction of the multitude of the nations and the citizens of cities. That is because nations and the citizens of cities are composed of some who are the elect and others who are the vulgar. The vulgar confine themselves, or should be confined, to theoretical cognitions that are in conformity with unexamined common opinion. The elect do not confine themselves in any of their theoretical cognitions to what is in conformity with unexamined common opinion but reach their conviction and knowledge on the basis of premises subjected to thorough scrutiny. Therefore whoever thinks that he is not confined to what is in conformity with unexamined common opinion in his inquiries, believes that in them he is of the "elect" and that everybody else is vulgar. Hence the competent practitioner of every art comes to be called one of the "elect" because people know that he does not confine himself, with respect to the objects of his art, to what is in conformity with unexamined common opinion, but exhausts them and scrutinizes them thoroughly. Again, whoever does not hold a political office or does not

possess an art that establishes his claim to a political office, but either possesses no art at all or is enabled by his art to hold only a subordinate office in the city, is said to be "vulgar"; and whoever holds a political office or else possesses an art that enables him to aspire to a political office is of the "elect." Therefore, whoever thinks that he possesses an art that qualifies him for assuming a political office or thinks that his position has the same status as a political office (for instance, men with prominent ancestors and many who possess great wealth), calls himself one of the "elect" and a "statesman."

51 Whoever has a more perfect mastery of the art that qualifies him for assuming an office is more appropriate for inclusion among the elect. Therefore it follows that the most elect of the elect is the supreme ruler. It would appear that this is so because he is the one who does not confine himself in anything at all to what is in conformity with unexamined common opinion. He must hold the office of the supreme ruler and be the most elect of the elect because of his state of character and skill. As for the one who assumes a political office with the intention of accomplishing the purpose of the supreme ruler, he *adheres* to thoroughly scrutinized opinions. However, the opinions that caused him to become an adherent or because of which he was convinced that he should use his art to serve the supreme ruler were based on mere conformity to unexamined common opinions; he conforms to unexamined common opinion in his theoretical cognitions as well. The result is that the supreme ruler and he who possesses the science that encompasses the intelligibles with certain demonstrations belong to the elect. The rest are the vulgar and the multitude. Thus the methods of persuasion and imaginative representation are employed only in the instruction of the vulgar and the multitude of the nations and the cities, while the certain demonstrative methods, by which the beings themselves are made intelligible, are employed in the instruction of those who belong to the elect.

52 This is the superior science and the one with the most perfect [claim to rule or to] authority. The rest of the authoritative sciences are subordinate to this science. By *the rest of the authoritative sciences* I mean the second and the third, and that which is derived from them, since these sciences merely follow the example of that science and are employed to accomplish the purpose of that science, which is supreme happiness and the final perfection to be achieved by man.

53 It is said that this science existed anciently among the Chaldeans, who are the people of al-'Iraq, subsequently reaching the people of Egypt, from there transmitted to the Greeks, where it remained until it was transmitted to the Syrians and then to the Arabs. Everything comprised by this science was expounded in the Greek language, later in Syriac, and finally in Arabic. The Greeks who possessed this science used to call it *true wisdom* and the *highest wisdom*. They called the acquisition of it *science*, and the scientific state of mind *philosophy* (by which they meant the quest and the love for the highest wisdom). They held that potentially it subsumes all the virtues. They called it the *science of sciences*, the *mother of sciences*, the *wisdom of wisdoms*, and the *art of arts* (they meant the art that makes use of all the arts, the virtue that makes use of all the virtues, and the wisdom that makes use of all wisdoms). Now "wisdom" may be used for consummate and extreme competence in any art whatsoever when it leads to performing feats of which most practitioners of that art are

incapable. Here wisdom is used in a qualified sense. Thus he who is extremely competent in an art is said to be "wise" in that art. Similarly, a man with penetrating practical judgment and acumen may be called "wise" in the thing regarding which he has penetrating practical judgment. However, *true* wisdom is this science and state of mind alone.

54   When the theoretical sciences are isolated and their possessor does not have the faculty for exploiting them for the benefit of others, they are defective philosophy. To be a truly perfect philosopher one has to possess both the theoretical sciences and the faculty for exploiting them for the benefit of all others according to their capacity. Were one to consider the case of the true philosopher, he would find no difference between him and the supreme ruler. For he who possesses the faculty for exploiting what is comprised by the theoretical matters for the benefit of all others possesses the faculty for making such matters intelligible as well as for bringing into actual existence those of them that depend on the will. The greater his power to do the latter, the more perfect is his philosophy. Therefore he who is truly perfect possesses with sure insight, first, the theoretical virtues, and subsequently the practical. Moreover, he possesses the capacity for bringing them about in nations and cities in the manner and the measure possible with reference to each. Since it is impossible for him to possess the faculty for bringing them about except by employing certain demonstrations, persuasive methods, as well as methods that represent things through images, and this either with the consent of others or by compulsion, it follows that the true philosopher is himself the supreme ruler.

55   Every instruction is composed of two things: (*a*) making what is being studied comprehensible and causing its idea to be established in the soul and (*b*) causing others to assent to what is comprehended and established in the soul. There are two ways of making a thing comprehensible: first, by causing its essence to be perceived by the intellect, and second, by causing it to be imagined through the similitude that imitates it. Assent, too, is brought about by one of two methods, either the method of certain demonstration or the method of persuasion. Now when one acquires knowledge of the beings or receives instruction in them, if he perceives their ideas themselves with his intellect, and his assent to them is by means of certain demonstration, then the science that comprises these cognitions is *philosophy*. But if they are known by imagining them through similitudes that imitate them, and assent to what is imagined of them is caused by persuasive methods, then the ancients call what comprises these cognitions *religion*. And if those intelligibles themselves are adopted, and *persuasive* methods are used, then the religion comprising them is called *popular, generally accepted,* and *external* philosophy. Therefore, according to the ancients, religion is an imitation of philosophy. Both comprise the same subjects and both give an account of the ultimate principles of the beings. For both supply knowledge about the first principle and cause of the beings, and both give an account of the ultimate end for the sake of which man is made—that is, supreme happiness—and the ultimate end of every one of the other beings. In everything of which philosophy gives an account based on intellectual perception or conception, religion gives an account based on imagination. In everything demonstrated by philosophy, religion employs persuasion. Philosophy gives an account of the ultimate principles (that is, the essence of the first principle and the essences of the incorporeal second principles), as they

are perceived by the intellect. Religion sets forth their images by means of similitudes of them taken from corporeal principles and imitates them by their likenesses among political offices. It imitates the divine acts by means of the functions of political offices. It imitates the actions of natural powers and principles by their likenesses among the faculties, states, and arts that have to do with the will, just as Plato does in the *Timaeus*. It imitates the intelligibles by their likenesses among the sensibles: for instance, some imitate *matter* by *abyss* or *darkness* or *water*, and *nothingness* by *darkness*. It imitates the classes of supreme happiness—that is, the ends of the acts of the human virtues—by their likenesses among the goods that are believed to be the ends. It imitates the classes of true happiness by means of the ones that are believed to be happiness. It imitates the ranks of the beings by their likenesses among spatial and temporal ranks. And it attempts to bring the similitudes of these things as close as possible to their essences. Also, in everything of which philosophy gives an account that is demonstrative and certain, religion gives an account based on persuasive arguments. Finally, philosophy is prior to religion in time.

56 Again, it is evident that when one seeks to bring into actual existence the intelligibles of the things depending on the will supplied by practical philosophy, he ought to prescribe the conditions that render possible their actual existence. Once the conditions that render their actual existence possible are prescribed, the voluntary intelligibles are embodied in laws. Therefore the legislator is he who, by the excellence of his deliberation, has the capacity to find the conditions required for the actual existence of voluntary intelligibles in such a way as to lead to the achievement of supreme happiness. It is also evident that only after perceiving them by his intellect should the legislator seek to discover their conditions, and he cannot find their conditions that enable him to guide others toward supreme happiness without having perceived supreme happiness with his intellect. Nor can these things become intelligible (and the legislative craft thereby hold the supreme office) without his having beforehand acquired philosophy. Therefore, if he intends to possess a craft that is authoritative rather than subservient, the legislator must be a philosopher. Similarly, if the philosopher who has acquired the theoretical virtues does not have the capacity for bringing them about in all others according to their capacities, then what he has acquired from them has no validity. Yet he cannot find the states and the conditions by which the voluntary intelligibles assume actual existence, if he does not possess the deliberative virtue; and the deliberative virtue cannot exist in him without the practical virtue. Moreover, he cannot bring them about in all others according to their capacities except by a faculty that enables him to excel in persuasion and in representing things through images.

57 It follows, then, that the idea of *Imam,* Philosopher, and Legislator is a single idea. However, the name *philosopher* signifies primarily theoretical virtue. But if it be determined that the theoretical virtue reach its ultimate perfection in every respect, it follows necessarily that he must possess all the other faculties as well. *Legislator* signifies excellence of knowledge concerning the conditions of practical intelligibles, the faculty for finding them, and the faculty for bringing them about in nations and cities. When it is determined that they be brought into existence on the basis of knowledge, it will follow that the theoretical virtue must precede the others—the existence of the inferior presupposes the existence of the higher. The name *prince* signifies sovereignty and ability. To be com-

pletely able, one has to possess the power of the greatest ability. His ability to do a thing must not result only from external things; he himself must possess great ability because his art, skill, and virtue are of exceedingly great power. This is not possible except by great power of knowledge, great power of deliberation, and great power of [moral] virtue and art. Otherwise he is not truly able nor sovereign. For if his ability stops short of this, it is still imperfect. Similarly, if his ability is restricted to goods inferior to supreme happiness, his ability is incomplete and he is not perfect. Therefore the true prince is the same as the philosopher-legislator. As to the idea of *Imam* in the Arabic language, it signifies merely the one whose example is followed and who is well received: that is, either his perfection is well received or his purpose is well received. If he is not well received in all the infinite activities, virtues, and arts, then he is not truly well received. Only when all other arts, virtues, and activities seek to realize *his* purpose and no other, will his art be the most powerful art, his [moral] virtue the most powerful virtue, his deliberation the most powerful deliberation, and his science the most powerful science. For with all of these powers he will be exploiting the powers of others so as to accomplish his own purpose. This is not possible without the theoretical sciences, without the greatest of all deliberative virtues, and without the rest of those things that are in the philosopher.

58 So let it be clear to you that the idea of the Philosopher, Supreme Ruler, Prince, Legislator, and *Imam* is but a single idea. No matter which one of these words you take, if you proceed to look at what each of them signifies among the majority of those who speak our language, you will find that they all finally agree by signifying one and the same idea.

59 Once the images representing the theoretical things demonstrated in the theoretical sciences are produced in the souls of the multitude and they are made to assent to their images, and once the practical things (together with the conditons of the possibility of their existence) take hold of their souls and dominate them so that they are unable to resolve to do anything else, then the theoretical and practical things are realized. Now these things are *philosophy* when they are in the soul of the legislator. They are *religion* when they are in the souls of the multitude. For when the legislator knows these things, they are evident to him by sure insight, whereas what is established in the souls of the multitude is through an image and a persuasive argument. Although it is the legislator who also represents these things through images, neither the images nor the persuasive arguments are intended for himself. As far as he is concerned, they are certain. He is the one who invents the images and the persuasive arguments, but not for the sake of establishing these things in his own soul as a religion for himself. No, the images and the persuasive arguments are intended for others, whereas, so far as he is concerned, these things are certain. They are a religion for others, whereas, so far as he is concerned, they are philosophy. Such, then, is true philosophy and the true philosopher.

60 As for mutilated philosophy: the counterfeit philosopher, the vain philosopher, or the false philosopher is the one who sets out to study the sciences without being prepared for them. For he who sets out to inquire ought to be innately equipped for the theoretical sciences—that is, to fulfill the conditions prescribed by Plato in the *Republic*: he should excel in comprehending and conceiving that which is essential. Moreover, he should have good memory and be able to endure the toil of study. He should love truthfulness and truthful

people, and justice and just people; and not be headstrong or a wrangler about what he desires. He should not be gluttonous for food and drink, and should by natural disposition disdain the appetites, the *dirhem*, the *dinar*, and the like. He should be high-minded and avoid what is disgraceful in people. He should be pious, yield easily to goodness and justice, and be stubborn in yielding to evil and injustice. And he should be strongly determined in favor of the right thing. Moreover, he should be brought up according to laws and habits that resemble his innate disposition. He should have sound conviction about the opinions of the religion in which he is reared, hold fast to the virtuous acts in his religion, and not forsake all or most of them. Furthermore, he should hold fast to the generally accepted virtues and not forsake the generally accepted noble acts. For if a youth is such, and then sets out to study philosophy and learns it, it is possible that he will not become a counterfeit or a vain or a false philosopher.

61   The false philosopher is he who acquires the theoretical sciences without achieving the utmost perfection so as to be able to introduce others to what he knows insofar as their capacity permits. The vain philosopher is he who learns the theoretical sciences, but without going any further and without being habituated to doing the acts considered virtuous by a certain religion or the generally accepted noble acts. Instead he follows his own inclination and appetites in everything, whatever they may happen to be. The counterfeit philosopher is he who studies the theoretical sciences without being naturally equipped for them. Therefore, although the counterfeit and the vain may complete the study of the theoretical sciences, in the end their possession of them diminishes little by little. By the time they reach the age at which a man should become perfect in the virtues, their knowledge will have been completely extinguished, even more so than the extinction of the fire [sun] of Heraclitus mentioned by Plato. For the natural dispositions of the former and the habit of the latter overpower what they might have remembered in their youth and make it burdensome for them to retain what they had patiently toiled for. They neglect it, and what they retain begins to diminish little by little until its fire becomes ineffective and extinguished, and they gather no fruit from it. As for the false philosopher, he is the one who is not yet aware of the purpose for which philosophy is pursued. He acquires the theoretical sciences, or only some portion thereof, and holds the opinion that the purpose of the measure he has acquired consists in certain kinds of happiness that are believed to be so or are considered by the multitude to be good things. Therefore he rests there to enjoy that happiness, aspiring to achieve this purpose with his knowledge. He may achieve his purpose and settle for it, or else find his purpose difficult to achieve and so hold the opinion that the knowledge he has is superfluous. Such is the false philosopher.

62   The true philosopher is the one mentioned before. If after reaching this stage no use is made of him, the fact that he is of no use to others is not his fault but the fault of those who either do not listen or are not of the opinion that they should listen to him. Therefore the prince or the *imam* is prince and *imam* by virtue of his skill and art, regardless of whether or not anyone acknowledges him, whether or not he is obeyed, whether or not he is supported in his purpose by any group; just as the physician is physician by virtue of his skill and his ability to heal the sick, whether or not there are sick men for him to heal, whether or not he finds tools to use in his activity, whether he is prosperous or poor—not having any of these things does not do away with his physicianship.

Similarly, neither the *imamate* of the *imam*, the philosophy of the philosopher, nor the princeship of the prince is done away with by his not having tools to use in his activities or men to employ in reaching his purpose.

63   The philosophy that answers to this description was handed down to us by the Greeks from Plato and Aristotle only. Both have given us an account of philosophy, but not without giving us also an account of the ways to it and of the ways to re-establish it when it becomes confused or extinct. We shall begin by expounding first the philosophy of Plato and the ranks of order of his philosophy. We shall begin with the first part of the philosophy of Plato, and then order one part of his philosophy after another until we reach its end. We shall do the same with the philosophy presented to us by Aristotle, beginning with the first part of his philosophy.

64   So let it be clear to you that, in what they presented, their purpose is the same, and that they intended to offer one and the same philosophy.

SELECTED BIBLIOGRAPHY

TRANSLATIONS

Note: English translations of a number of Alfarabi's shorter logical works have appeared in journals. For a convenient listing, see N. Rescher, *Al-Fārābī*.

Dunlop, D., ed. and trans., *Al-Fārābī, Fuṣūl al-Madanī* (Aphorisms of the Statesman), Cambridge, 1961.
Lerner, R., and M. Mahdi, eds., *Medieval Political Philosophy*, New York, 1963.
Lugal, N., and A. Sayili, ed. and trans., *Fārābī's*

Article on Vacuum, Ankara, 1951. (*Türk Tarih Kurumu Yayinlarindan*, XV, Suppl.).
Mahdi, M., trans., *Alfarabi's Philosophy of Plato and Aristotle*, New York, 1962.
Rescher, N., trans., *Alfarabi's Short Commentary on Aristotle's Prior Analytics*, Pittsburgh, 1963.
Zimmerman, F., trans., *Al-Farabi's Commentary and Short Treatise on Aristotle's De Interpretatione*, London, 1981.

STUDIES

Arnaldez, R., "L'âme et le monde dans le système philosophique de Fārābī," *Studia Islamica*, XLIII (1976), 53–63.
Arnaldez, R., "Pensée et langage dans la philosophie de Fārābī (à propos du Kitāb al-Ḥurūf), *Studia Islamica*, XLV (1977), 57–63.
Davidson, H., "Alfarabi and Avicenna on the Active Intellect," *Viator*, III (1972), 109–178.
Fackenheim, E., "The Possibility of the Universe in al-Fārābī, Ibn Sinā, and Maimonides," *Proceedings of the American Academy for Jewish Research*, XVI (1946–1947), 39–70.
Finnegan, J., S.J., "Al-Farabi et le *Peri Nou* d'Alexandre d'Aphrodise," *Mélanges Louis*

Massignon, Damascus, 1957, II, 133–152.
Galston, M., "A Re-examination of al-Fārābī's Neoplatonism," *Journal of the History of Philosophy*, XV (1977), 13–32.
Gyekye, K., "Al-Farabi on the Problem of Future Contingency," *Second Order: an African Journal of Philosophy*, VI, i (1977), 31–54.
Madkour, I., *La Place d'al Fārābī dans l'École Philosophique Musulmane*, Paris, 1934.
Mahdi, M., "Alfarabi on Philosophy and Religion," *Philosophical Forum*, IV (1972), 5–25.
Mahdi, M., "Remarks on Alfarabi's *Attainment of Happiness*," *Essays on Islamic Philosophy and Science*, ed. G. Hourani, Albany, 1975, 47–66.

Mahdi, M., "Science, Philosophy, and Religion in Alfarabi's *Enumeration of the Sciences*," *The Cultural Context of Medieval Learning*, ed. M. Murdoch and E. Sylla, Dordrecht-Boston, 1973, 47–66.

Pines, S., "Ibn Sina et l'Auteur de la Risalat al-Fusus fi'l-Hikma," *Revue des Études Islamiques*, XIX (1951), 121–126.

Rachid, A., "Dieu et l'être selon Al-Fārābī. Le chapitre de 'l'être' dans le Livres des Lettres," *Dieu et l'être*, Paris, 1978, 179–190.

Rescher, N., *Al-Fārābī, An Annotated Bibliography*, Pittsburgh, 1962.

Rosenthal, E., "The Place of Politics in the Philosophy of al-Fārābī," *Islamic Culture*, XXIX (1955), 157–178.

Salman, D., "The Medieval Latin Translations of Alfārābī's Works," *The New Scholasticism*, XIII (1939), 245–261.

Steinschneider, M., *Al-Farabi (Mémoires de l'Académie Imperiale des Sciences de Saint-Pétersbourg*, VII, 13. 4), St. Petersburgh, 1869.

Strauss, L., "Farabi's Plato," *Louis Ginzberg Jubilee Volumes*, American Academy for Jewish Research, New York: 1945, 357–393.

Strauss, L., "How Farabi Read Plato's Laws," *Mélanges Louis Massignon*, Damascus, 1957, III, 319–344.

AVICENNA

980–1037

O F THE Aristotelians in the Islamic east Avicenna was easily the most important, and even in the Islamic west only Averroes was his equal. Physician, scientist, man of affairs, and philosopher, he formulated a distinctive kind of Aristotelianism which is characterized by a strong reliance on neoplatonic notions. A number of his most important doctrines have a naturalistic coloring, but at the same time a certain religious feeling—possibly even mystical inclination—is not lacking from his thought. Algazali (see p. 264) branded a number of his doctrines as incompatible with Islamic beliefs, while Averroes (see p. 293) charged him with having surrendered to theological considerations on certain crucial philosophic points. The Islamic west came to prefer a more rigorous, less neoplatonic, kind of Aristotelianism, but in the Islamic east Avicenna remained the favorite well into the seventeenth century. In the Christian world his teachings were well known. Etienne Gilson has argued that they provided the decisive philosophic influence during the first half of the thirteenth century and, according to the same scholar, they were blended with Augustinian notions to yield an "Avicennizing Augustinianism." Albertus Magnus, Roger Bacon, Thomas Aquinas, and Duns Scotus were scholastics influenced by him in varying degrees. Jewish philosophers knew and used his teachings, but Maimonides considered them inferior to those of Alfarabi, and in the post-Maimonidean period Averroes became, next to Maimonides, the decisive philosophic influence.

Avicenna wrote on all the branches of Aristotelian philosophy, but in a sense he was first and foremost a metaphysician. Describing his particular kind of metaphysics, Afnan writes: "If it be said that the central element of Platonic metaphysics is the theory of Ideas, and that of the Aristotelian is the doctrine of potentiality and actuality, that of the Avicennian metaphysics is the study of being as being."* "Being," according to Avicenna, is the first concept acquired by the mind and, though the world provides a clue to it, introspection is quite adequate for its discovery. The famous argument of the "flying man" is among those advanced for this view. Let us imagine,

* S. M. Afnan, *Avicenna, His Life and Works,* London, 1958, p. 108.

this argument proceeds, a grown man, created suddenly, possessing all his powers. Let us imagine further that his eyes are covered, that he is suspended in empty space, and that his limbs are separated so that they do not touch each other. A man of this description would have no sensory experience of the world, nor of his body and its parts, but he would know that he exists. It follows then, that, given a thinking mind, knowledge of "being" and (important for psychology) awareness of "self" are given concurrently with it. Avicenna's "flying man" found an echo in Descartes' statement "I think, therefore I am."

The knowledge of "being" is immediate and no other notion is prior to it. Hence "being" is not a species which can be defined, nor is it a genus. Yet, certain distinctions are given concomitant with it. One such is that between essence and existence. Examining the world, the mind discovers substances in which essence and existence are combined, but, at the same time, it can think essences without having the simultaneous judgment that these essences exist other than in it. In fact, the mind can think essences which do not now exist and even essences which can never exist. The question "what is it?" differs from "does it exist?" and it follows that essence and existence are ontologically distinct. Existence, according to Avicenna, is superadded to essence or, in alternate language, it is its accident. Whether Avicenna derived this and the following distinction from Alfarabi (see p. 211) or from an even earlier source—they became associated with his name.

Another distinction concurrent with "being" is that between necessary and possible existence. Something is said to be necessary if from the assumption of its non-existence an impossibility will follow, while something is said to be possible if no impossibility will follow, whether it is assumed to exist or not to exist. Necessary being is subdivided into what is necessary through itself and what is necessary through another. Something possible requires a necessary cause for its existence and so does what is necessary through another. Only something necessary through itself exists without a cause. These metaphysical distinctions lead to Avicenna's famous proof for the existence of God according to which the possible beings in the world ultimately require, in order to exist, a being necessary through itself. Maimonides and Aquinas (see p. 526) accepted this Avicennian proof, while Averroes rejected it.

In his description of the attributes of God Avicenna is generally considered the champion of negative attribution. But, as H. A. Wolfson has shown, his position is more complex. Certain attributes, such as "substance," "one," are to be interpreted as negations; others, such as "first," "powerful," "living" as relations in the sense of actions; and still others, such as "willing," "generous" as both negations and relations. In His relation to the world God is its creator. Following Alfarabi, Avicenna identifies creation with the neoplatonic notion of emanation. Possessed of fullness of being, God, thinking Himself, produces a first intelligence. Considered in itself, this intelligence is possible; considered in respect to God, it is necessary. In God, thinker, thinking, and thought are one, while in the first intelligence they are distinct. From the first intelligence there emanates a second intelligence together with the soul and body of the all-encompassing sphere which this intelligence controls. When the first intelligence thinks of God, its necessary source, the second intelligence proceeds from it; when it thinks of itself as necessary through its cause, it produces the soul of the all-encompassing sphere; and when it thinks of itself as possible, it gives rise to the body of that sphere. In similar fashion there arise successively the intelligences, souls, and bodies of the remaining eight celestial spheres, the process coming to an end with the tenth intelligence which governs the sublunar sphere. As "Giver of Forms," this intelligence provides sublunar matter with its forms, while as "Agent Intellect" it produces knowledge in the human mind. Creation, then, is the bestowing of existence on a possible world by God, its necessary cause. God, according to Avicenna, is contemporaneous with the world and He produces it out of the necessity of His own nature. There seems to be little doubt that Avicenna considered this doctrine as a legitimate interpretation of the koranic notion of creation. However, Algazali rejected it as contrary to koranic teachings, while Averroes saw in it a concesssion to theological considerations. Avicenna's account of creation as the bestowing of existence yields a distinction between two kinds of efficient causes. One of these is a metaphysical efficient cause which, synchronous with what it causes, bestows existence; the other is a physical efficient cause which, temporally prior to what it causes, produces change and motion.

Avicenna describes the world in Aristotelian terms, but at the same time he introduces modifications of his own. Among typical Avicennian doctrines are his definition of the "corporeal form" as a form having a predisposition for receiving the three dimensions and his contention that the celestial substances are composed of a soul inhering in the celestial body and an intelligence existing in separation from it. Both of these doctrines were criticized by Averroes (see p. 294) later on. It also appears that Avicenna subscribed to the doctrine of the "multiplicity of forms" according to which lower forms remain in the presence of forms which are higher.

In his conception of the human soul Avicenna combined Aristotelian with Platonic notions. With the Aristotelians he held that the soul comes into being with its body and that, in respect to its operations, it is the body's form; but with the Platonists he affirmed the substantiality of the individual soul. Immortality, for him, consists of the continuous existence of the actualized human mind, and immortality is individual. He interprets the koranic notion of the resurrection of the body figuratively, considering it an accommodation to the understanding of the masses. His theory of knowledge is that of the Muslim Aristotelians, modified by a kind of doctrine of "illumination." Human knowledge begins with the perception of the senses, proceeds from there to the imagination, then to the faculty of estimation, and, through the causal action of the Agent Intellect, is acquired by the mind. Within the mind four stages of intellection or four kinds of mind may be discerned. As a faculty capable of receiving knowledge, the human mind is the "material" or "possible intellect"; as possessing knowledge which is not actually thought it is the "habitual intellect"; as thinking in actuality it is the "actual intellect"; and as receiving forms from the Agent Intellect it is the "acquired intellect." Though, according to this scheme, knowledge has its origin in sense perception, all the stages of cognition prior to the "acquired intellect" are only preparatory, true knowledge consisting of the radiation of forms by the Agent Intellect into the human mind. Most men acquire knowledge in the manner described, but there are singular individuals who can gain the influence of the Agent Intellect intuitively without much preparation. This intuition becomes important for Avicenna's doctrine of prophetic inspiration. For though he agrees with other Muslim philosophers in considering the prophet as legislator and governor of men (see p. 213), he emphasizes the importance of the knowledge gained by prophetic intuition. In some of his later works, Avicenna turns to a description of mystical teachings, analyzing the stages of the mystic's path and the journey of the soul toward God. It is clear that he is primarily interested in mystical speculation rather than in ascetic and devotional practices. However, interpreters disagree about the relation of these mystical doctrines to the remainder of his thought.

Abū 'Ali al-Ḥusayn ibn Sīnā was born in 980 in Afshana, a village in the Kharmaithan district of Bukhāra (modern southern Russia). His father was the governor of the district, but while Avicenna was still a child the family moved to Bukhāra. There he received his education and spent the first period of his life. His studies began with the Koran and Arabic literature, continued with Islamic law, logic, mathematics, and then turned to the natural sciences and metaphysics. Unusually gifted, Avicenna quickly surpassed his teachers and gained much of this knowledge on his own. Next he taught himself medicine, becoming an accomplished physician by the time he was sixteen. During the next eighteen months he reviewed and expanded his knowledge of philosophy, being so zealous in his studies that he did not get a full night's sleep during all this time. Though by now he was an accomplished philosopher, the content of Aristotle's *Metaphysics* still escaped him. He read the work forty times, but not until a book seller provided him with a copy of Alfarabi's *On the Objects of Metaphysics* did the content of the work become clear. When Avicenna's medical skills helped to cure Nūḥ ibn Manṣūr, the Sāmānid sultan of Bukhāra, that ruler enrolled him in his service and made available to him his rich library containing many works that Avicenna had never seen.

His patron died in 997 and with the end of the Sāmānid dynasty in 999 Avicenna's fortune began to change. For reasons possibly religious he was forced to leave Bukhāra, and he spent the remainder of his life at the courts of various provincial rulers in the eastern part of the Caliphate of Bagdad, becoming involved in their politics and their wars. After prolonged wanderings he settled at Raiy where he entered the service of the Buyid rulers Al-Saiyida and her son Majd al-Dawlah. Becoming involved in the conflicts of the dynasty he shifted his allegiance to Shams al-Dawlah, Majd al-Dawlah's brother, and from about 1015 to 1022 he was at his court at Hamadhan. During this period Shams al-Dawlah twice appointed him as his vizier. When Shams al-Dawlah died during a military campaign, his son Tāj al-Mulk wanted to continue Avicenna in his office, but Avicenna declined, entering into secret negotiations with 'Alā al-Dawlah, the ruler of Isfahan. When Avicenna's plans became known he was imprisoned, but he finally succeeded in fleeing to Isfahan. There he spent the remainder of his life, declining a political post that he was offered. He died in 1037.

Though busy with professional duties, Avicenna was an extremely productive author. Over two hundred works have been attributed to him, and of these probably about one hundred are his. His most important medical work was the *Canon (al-Qanūn)* which in its Latin translation became the standard medical work in Europe until the seventeenth century. In philosophy, his major work was *The Healing (al-Shifā')*, a magisterial *summa* of logic, physics, mathematics, and metaphysics. In this work Avicenna set down the parts of those sciences which he believed to be sound without disputing with opponents. Through Latin translations of portions of his work Avicenna's views became known to the Christian world. Christian philosophers also knew his teachings through Algazali's summary in his *The Opinions of the Philosophers* (see p. 264). An abbreviated version of the *Healing* is contained in his *Deliverance (al-Najāt)*. Among his other works are: *On Definitions (Fī al-Ḥudūd)*, *Instructions and Remarks (al-Ishārāt wa-al-Tanbīhāt)*, *On Love (Fī al-'Ishq)*, *On Prayer (Fī al-Salāt)*, *Ḥayy ibn Yaqẓān*, and the *Logic of the Orientals (Mantiq al-Mashriqīyīn)*. We have a biography, part of which Avicenna dictated to his disciple al-Jūzjānī and which the disciple completed on his own. Though most of Avicenna's works were written in Arabic, he is also the author of works in Persian.

In reading the following selections it should be kept in mind that Avicenna is a skillful dialectician who, with great subtlety, investigates the implications of certain fundamental notions and who, at the same time, probes their relation to related notions. In the metaphysical selections his arguments sound rather verbal at times and he appears to be primarily interested in logical distinctions, but these distinctions, it must be recalled, are, for him, metaphysical. Characteristic of his method is the use of hypothetical, disjunctive arguments. Since his arguments in the first two selections are sometimes difficult to follow, a brief outline is presented as an aid to the reader. In the selections, numbers and letters in brackets indicate the structure of arguments.

The first selection, taken from *Healing,* Metaphysics, I, is devoted to the famous distinction between necessary and possible existence. Having described these modes of existence and having enumerated the issues he plans to discuss, Avicenna first shows that that whose existence is necessary through itself does not have a cause and that it can not be necessary through itself and simultaneously necessary through another. By contrast, that whose existence is possible in respect to itself has both its existence and its non-existence through a cause. If it exists, its existence proceeds from a cause which is an existent cause; if it does not exist, its non-existence proceeds from a cause which is the absence of a cause. Furthermore, that whose existence is possible must be necessary in respect to its cause. Next Avicenna shows that there cannot be two beings necessary through themselves —that is, that which is necessary through itself is unique. For if two such beings were possible, each one, considered in itself, must be either necessary through itself or possible through itself. Considering each of these two beings in accordance with the possible relations that it could have to the other, Avicenna shows that each of these assumptions is impossible, so that it follows that there can be only one being which is necessary through itself. Then he shows that something necessary through itself cannot be composed of parts, that is, it must be simple. For if it is assumed that something necessary is composed of parts it must possess some principle of differentiation which divides it into parts. This principle is either different from the essence of the thing or it is part of it. If it differs from the essence it must be a non-essential consequence or accident.* But something necessary through itself cannot possess accidents of this kind. Similarly, something necessary can not have a principle of differentiation which is part of the essence. After having shown this proposition in a general way, Avicenna demonstrates that such a principle could not divide something necessary through itself in the manner in which a differentia divides a genus into species nor can it divide in the manner in which a species is divided. After offering other arguments for the simplicity of that which is necessary through itself, Avicenna turns once again to that which is possible through itself. Something of this kind must be necessary through a cause and this cause may act either always, as in the case of the separate intelligences and the celestial bodies, or it may act during a limited time, as in the case of the substances which are subject to generation and corruption. In the latter case there must be a matter which is temporally prior to the cause. Avicenna concludes by affirming that all beings other than that which is necessary through itself are composite. The metaphysical distinctions of this selection readily apply to God as He is in Himself and as He is related to the world.

The second selection, taken from *Healing,* Metaphysics, VI, is devoted to a discussion of causality. Enumerating the four Aristotelian causes—form, matter, agent, and purpose, Avicenna distinguishes carefully between a metaphysical agent cause which bestows existence and a natural agent cause which produces motion. Two of the causes, the form and the matter, enter the subsistence of that of which they are causes, while two others, the purpose and the agent, do not. In addition, matter, considered as substratum, does not enter the subsistence of that of which it is a cause. If matter is

* For a ready discussion of this term, see *ibid.,* pp. 117–119.

distinguished from the substratum, the causes are five; if the two are considered as one, the causes are four. Strictly speaking, matter is the principle of that which is composed of matter and form and so is form. The form is the formal cause of the composite, not of matter.

The metaphysical agent is ontologically distinct from that which it causes and even if the two happen to exist in the same substratum, such as the nature of wood in wood, the distinction is maintained. An agent can be such that it bestows existence only at some time, and in that case the agent requires some other cause which makes it to be an agent. Now, when an agent produces something, three aspects of this process can be distinguished. There is the "existence" that comes to be, there is the "non-existence" which preceded, and there is the attribute of "existing after non-existence." Of these three properties only "existence" comes from a cause. "Non-existence" is the result of the absence of a cause, while "existence after non-existence" cannot come from a cause at all. Developing his notion of causality further, Avicenna shows next that something not only requires a cause in order to receive existence, but also in order to continue in existence. For if it would not require a cause for the continuation of its existence, then the existence which it receives must be either necessary existence or possible existence. In the latter case, the necessity of its continued existence belongs to it either through a condition which is its coming into being, or an attribute of the quiddity which comes into being, or some attribute separate from it. Each one of these alternatives is shown to be false, and hence continuation of existence requires a cause. Next Avicenna shows once again that only the existence of something has a cause, not the fact that it "exists after it did not exist." Hence the bestowing of existence does not necessarily take place in time. Since ordinary people are unaware of the distinction between a metaphysical and a physical acting cause, they believe that the action of every agent must take place in time. But acting in time is only accidental to an agent.

Avicenna now turns to a difficulty occasioned by the observation that something produced by an agent continues to exist after the agent has ceased to act. From this observation it again seems to follow that something caused does not require an agent for the continuation of its existence. However, a careful analysis shows that the agent which ceases to act is not the real agent, but there exists an agent which continues to act even after the apparent agent ceases. For example, the builder is not the real cause for the production of the building, but rather the nature of the building materials which makes them stay together. This nature is produced by the "Giver of Forms." Now causes are divisible into supporting and preparatory causes, which are accidental, and causes which are essential. The series of accidental causes must be infinite, the series of essential causes finite. An infinite series of accidental causes is possible because of motion. Of the essential causes, that which exists eternally and bestows existence eternally, thereby preventing non-existence, is the best. This cause is God, and His eternally bestowing existence is creation. If the term "coming into being" is applied in the sense that the cause is simultaneous with that which it causes, then everything other than God comes into being. However, if the term is limited to temporal coming into being, then coming into being must be distinguished from being caused. Avicenna concludes by affirming that an agent which acts only accidentally requires a matter in which it acts and that an agent acts at times through itself, at times through a power.

The third selection, taken from *Deliverance,* Psychology, VI, deals with aspects of the Avicennian doctrine of the soul. Avicenna first shows that the soul which is the substratum for the intelligibles is not corporeal, then that it comes into being with the body, and, finally, that it is immortal.

THE HEALING, METAPHYSICS

FIRST TREATISE

CHAPTER 6. *The Beginning of the Discourse Concerning that Whose Existence Is Necessary and that Whose Existence Is Possible; that that Whose Existence Is Necessary Does Not Have a Cause, While that Whose Existence Is Possible Is Caused; that that Whose Existence Is Necessary Is Not Co-equal with Something Else in Respect to Existence, and Is Not Dependent on Something Else for [Its Existence].*

Let us return to our subject. We say: Each one, that whose existence is necessary as well as that whose existence is possible, has [certain] properties. We say: Things which are included in existence can be divided in the mind into two [kinds]. One of these is that which, when it is considered in itself, does not have its existence by necessity. And it is clear that its existence is also not impossible, for if its existence were impossible, it would not be included in existence. This thing is in the domain of possibility. The other of these is that which, when it is considered in itself, has its existence by necessity.

We say: That whose existence is necessary through itself does not have a cause, while that whose existence is possible through itself does have a cause. Further, that whose existence is necessary through itself is necessary in respect to existence in all of its aspects. Again, it is not possible that the existence of that whose existence is necessary is co-equal with another existence so that each of them is equal with the other in respect to the necessity of existence and [so that] both necessarily accompany each other. Moreover, it is not possible that the existence of that whose existence is necessary be composed of a multitude at all. Finally, it is not possible that the true nature which that whose existence is necessary possesses is shared in any way whatsoever. Thus, from what we have asserted it follows necessarily

Translated by Arthur Hyman for this volume from Ibn Sīnā, *Al-Shifā', al-Ilāhiyyāt,* ed. G. C. Anawati and Sa'id Zayed, Cairo: Organisation Générale des Imprimeries Gouvernementales, 1960.

that that whose existence is necessary is not relative, not changeable, not multiple, not sharing in respect to the existence which is peculiar to it.

That that whose existence is necessary does not have a cause is clear. For if that whose existence is necessary were to have a cause for its existence, its existence would be through [that cause]. Now, everything whose existence is through some [other] thing does not have existence by necessity when it is considered in itself apart from that other. And everything which does not have existence by necessity when it is considered in itself apart from the other, is not necessary in respect to existence through itself. Hence it is evident that if that whose existence is necessary through itself were to have a cause, it would not be something whose existence is necessary through itself. It is clear then that that whose existence is necessary does not have a cause. From that it is [also] clear that it is not possible that something is necessary in respect to existence through itself and [simultaneously] necessary in respect to existence through another. For if its existence is necessary through another, it can not exist without that other. And whenever [something] can not exist without another, it is impossible that its existence is necessary through itself. For if it were necessary through itself, it would [already] exist. And that other does not provide its existence for that which is necessary [through itself], [for] that for which something else provides its existence, can not be necessary in regard to its existence through itself.

Furthermore, everything whose existence is possible has, when it is considered in respect to itself, both its existence and its non-existence from a cause. For if it exists, existence as distinguished from non-existence has come to it, and if it does not exist, non-existence as distinguished from existence has come to it. Now each of these two attributes [existence and non-existence] must come to it from something else or not from something else. If it [existence] comes from something else, that other is the cause. If it does not come from something else—but it is evident that everything which does not exist at first and then exists, is determined by something other than itself.

It is similar in the case of non-existence. [All] this is so because either the quiddity of the thing is sufficient for this determination [for existence or non-existence] or the quiddity is not sufficient for it. Now if its quiddity is sufficient for one of these two attributes [existence and non-existence], so that this attribute comes [to it], that thing is something whose quiddity is necessary through itself. But it was assumed that it is not necessary. [Hence] this is a contradiction. If, however, the existence of its quiddity is not sufficient for its existence, but something else bestows its existence upon it, then its existence proceeds from the existence of some other thing different from it and this is necessarily its cause and [thus] the thing has a cause. In sum, one of these two attributes becomes necessary for it, not through itself, but through a cause.

The attribute of existence comes from a cause which is an existing cause, while the attribute of non-existence comes from a cause which is the absence of a cause for the attribute of existence, as you know.

We say: It is necessary that [that whose existence is possible] becomes necessary through a cause and in relation to it. For if it were not necessary, then, with the existence of this cause and in relation to it, it would also be possible. And it would be possible that it exists or that it does not exist without being determined by one of these two attributes [existence and non-existence]. But [something of] this [kind] requires from the beginning, together with the existence of that cause, the existence of some third thing through which there is determined for it existence rather than non-existence, or non-existence rather than existence. And that [third thing] would be another cause, and the discussion [concerning the series of causes] would go on to infinity. If it would go to infinity, then it would not be, with that, that its existence is determined for it, so that it would not be that existence comes to it. This is absurd. [And this is absurd] not only because [the discussion] about the causes would go to infinity (for the state of this problem is still doubtful in this place), but also because that through which it is determined [that is, the cause] would not yet exist. But it was assumed that [the cause] exists. It is clear then that everything whose existence is possible will not exist unless it is necessary in relation to its cause.

We say: It is not possible that that whose existence is necessary is co-equal with another whose existence is necessary, so that the first exists with the second and the second exists with the first, and [so that] one of them is not the cause of the other, but both are co-equal in regard to the necessity of [their] existence. For, if one considers the essence of one of them in itself apart from the other, it must be [I] that it is either necessary through itself or [II] that it is not necessary through itself. Now, if [I] it is necessary through itself, it must be that [since the two are co-equal] [Ia] it also possesses necessity when it is considered together with the second [that is, it is necessary through itself and necessary through another]. Thus something would exist whose existence is necessary through itself and whose existence is necessary because of another. But this is absurd, as has previously been shown. Or [Ib] it is the case that [when that whose existence is necessary through itself is considered together with that which is co-equal with it] it possesses no necessity in respect to the other [that is, it is necessary through itself, possible through another]. In that case, it would not be necessary that its existence would follow from the existence of the other. But it would be necessary for it that its existence does not have a relation to the other, so that it can only exist when the other exists. [Thus one could exist without the other which is against the assumption that they are co-equal.]

Now should it be the case [II] that [the first] is not necessary through itself, it would follow [IIa] that, considered in respect to itself, it would be something whose existence is possible, while, considered in respect to the other, it would be something whose existence is necessary. Then it must be [IIa1] that the second is like the first [that is, it is possible in respect to itself, necessary in respect to another], or [IIa2] the second is not [like the first]. Now, [IIa1] if the second is like the first [that is, it is possible in respect to itself, necessary in respect to another], it again must be that necessity of existence comes to the first from the second either [IIa1a] insofar as the second is in the category of something whose existence is possible, or [IIa1b] insofar as it is in the category of something whose existence is necessary. Now [IIa1b] if necessity of existence comes to the first from the second, while the second is in the category of something whose existence is necessary—yet not necessary through itself or through some third thing which precedes it (as was stated previously)—but necessary through that which proceeds from it [that is, the second must necessarily come from the first], the necessary existence of the first would [then] be a condition in which there is contained a necessary existence which comes after the necessity of its own existence. In that case necessary existence would not come to [the first principle] at all [from the second, since it already possesses it].

But [IIaɪa] if necessary existence comes to the first from the second, while the second is in the category of something [whose existence is] possible, then necessary existence comes to the first from the essence of the second, while the second is in the category of something possible. And it would be the case that the essence of the second, which is in the category of something possible, would impart to the first necessary existence, without there having been imparted to the second the category of the possible from the first, but [the first would have imparted to the second the category of] the necessary. As a result, the cause of the first would be the possible existence of the second, while the first would not be the cause for the possible existence of the second. Thus the two would not be co-equal; I have in mind, that which is its cause essentially and that which is caused essentially.

Then there occurs another difficulty [concerning the proposition that necessary existence comes to the first from the second, while the second is in the category of that whose existence is possible]. It is: If the possible existence of the second is the cause of the necessary existence of the first, then the existence of the first would not depend on the necessity of the second, but on its possibility. It would follow then that the existence of the first is possible with the non-existence of the second. But we have assumed that the two are co-equal [that is, if one exists the other must also exist]. Hence this is a contradiction.

. . .

CHAPTER 7. *That that Whose Existence Is Necessary Is One.*

We say further: That whose existence is necessary must necessarily be one essence. For if it were not, it would be a multitude each one of whose [parts] would be something whose existence is necessary. It would follow then, that each one of these [parts] would not at all differ from another in regard to the notion which is its true nature, or that [one part] would differ from another. Now, if one [part] would not differ from another in regard to the notion which belongs to its essence essentially (yet one [part] differs from another in that it is not the other and this is undoubtedly a difference), then one [part] will differ from another in regard to some other notion. The reason is that the notion [of the essence] which exists in the [different parts] is not differentiated [insofar as it is an essence], but [insofar as] there is adjoined to it something through which it comes to be this [particular part] or in this [particular part], or [insofar as] there is adjoined to it [the determination] that it is this [particular part] or in this [particular part] [that is, it is this particular part or in this particular part through something within itself]. And that which is adjoined to the essence [in one part] is not adjoined to it in the other [part], but [there is adjoined to the other part] that through which the other [part] becomes that other or [the determination] that the other [part] is that other. This [adjoined notion] is a principle of particularization which is adjoined to this notion [that is, the essence] and through it the two [parts] are differentiated.

Now each one of these parts is differentiated from the other through this [principle], while it is not differentiated from the other through the notion itself [that is, the essence], but it is differentiated from the other through some other notion.

The things which are other than the notion [of the essence] and which are adjoined to the notion [of the essence] are the accidents and the consequences which are not essential. Now these consequences occur to the existence of something [I] insofar as it is this [particular] existence and in this case it is necessary that the whole thing agrees in [this consequence]. But it was assumed that the whole is differentiated in respect to [the consequence]. Hence this is absurd. Or [II] [these consequences] occur to it from external causes not from its own quiddity. In that case, if that cause does not exist, [the consequence] will not occur. Hence if that cause does not exist, the thing will not be differentiated. Further, if that cause does not exist, the essences [of the parts] will be one, or they will not be. Again, if this cause does not exist, one [part] will not be, in its pecularity, something whose existence is necessary nor would the other [part] be, in its peculiarity, something whose existence is necessary, [that is] something whose existence is necessary not through its [own] existence, but through accidents. Thus the necessity of existence of each one [of the parts] which is proper to it and which is peculiar to it would be provided by something other than it. But it was stated that everything whose existence is necessary through another, can not be necessary through itself; but, according to the definition of its essence, it is something whose existence is possible. Thus it would be the case that each one of these [parts], even though it is something whose existence is necessary through itself, is [also] something whose existence is possible according to the definition of its essence. This is absurd.

Let us assume then that one [part] differs from another in some inhering notion after it has agreed with it in the notion [of the essence]. Then it must be that that notion is a condition for the necessity of [the part's] existence, or that it is not. Now, if it is a condition for the necessity of [the part's] existence, it is clear that there necessarily agrees in this [notion] everything whose existence is necessary. [But this can not be, since we assumed that the parts differ in respect to this notion.] If, however, this notion is not a condition for the necessity of [the part's] existence, then necessity of existence is established without it as necessity of existence. In that case, this notion would come to it as an accident and it would be joined to it after that necessity of existence has been actualized. But we have already denied this and shown its absurdity. Therefore it is not possible that one part differs from another in the [inhering] notion.

But we must add to this a proof from a different consideration. It is: If the notion of necessary existence is divided into a multitude, it must be divided in one of [the following] two ways: either it is divided according to the manner of its division by differentiae or according to the manner of its division by accidents. Now it is well known that differentiae do not enter into the definition of that which stands in place of the genus, for they do not provide the genus with its true nature, but they provide it with existence in actuality, as for example [the differentia] "rational." For "rational" does not provide "animal" with the notion of animality, but it provides it with existence in actuality as a determined existing being.

It would further be necessary that the differentiae of necessity of existence, [even] if it is true that they do not bestow necessity of existence for the true nature of necessity of existence, still provide for it existence in actuality. But this is impossible for two reasons. One of these is that the true nature of necessity of existence is nothing but the certainty of [its] existence. And it is not like the true nature of animality which is a notion other than the certainty of [its] existence. For [in the case of animality] existence belong to it as something which accompanies it or which comes upon it [from without], as you know. Thus the providing of existence to necessity of existence is the providing of a condition from its necessary true nature. And it is impossible to admit this, as is clear from [the case of] genus and differentia. The second reason is that it would be necessary that the true nature of necessity of existence would be dependent, in order that it may exist in actuality, on something which gives necessity to it. And the concept through which this thing is something whose existence is necessary must have its existence through something else [since it is added to the true nature]. But our discussion is about necessity of existence through itself. Thus it would be the case that something whose existence is necessary through itself would exist necessarily through another. And we have declared the absurdity of this.

It is clear then that the division of necessity of existence by means of those things which would divide it into parts could not be [like] the division of the notion of genus by means of differentiae. And it is evident in regard to the notion which determines necessity of existence that it can not be a generic nature which is divided by differentiae or accidents. It remains then that it is a specific notion. But we say: It is not possible that its specificity [that is, the specific nature of necessity of existence] is predicated of many things. For since the individuals of a species, as we have shown, do not differ in their essential notion, it is necessary that they differ through accidents. But we have denied the possibility of this in the case of necessity of existence. And we can show this through a kind of summary, the aim being to return to that which we intended.

We say: If necessity of existence is an attribute of something and existent in it, then [I] it is necessary in accordance with this attribute, that is, in accordance with necessity of existence, that that [particular] attribute exists in this [particular] subject. In this case it is impossible that one of the two [the attribute] exists in such a way that it is not the attribute of this [particular subject]. Hence it is impossible that it exists in some other [subject]. It follows therefore that it exists in this [subject] alone. Thus there is nothing else that exists by necessity through itself. Or [II] it is the case that the existence of this attribute in this [subject] is possible, not necessary. Then it is possible that this thing is something whose existence is not necessary through itself and [simultaneously] something whose existence is necessary through itself. This is a contradiction. Therefore necessity of existence can only belong to something that is one.

Someone may object: The existence of [this attribute, that is necessary existence] for one [part] does not prevent its existence as an attribute for another [part], nor does its existence as an attribute for a second [part] nullify the necessity of its existence as an attribute for the first [part]. We answer: Our discussion was concerning the fact that necessity of existence is determined as an attribute for this [particular part] and insofar as it is not considered in some other. Thus it is not an attribute for another in its particular nature, but [at best] something like it, [that is,] the necessity in it [the attribute] is that which necessarily belongs to the other in its particular existence.

In accordance with another consideration we say: Now, if the existence of one of the [parts] as something whose existence is necessary is identical with its existence as this particular thing, then everything whose existence is necessary and it are this particular thing and there is nothing besides it. But if its existence as something whose existence is necessary is other than its existence as this particular thing, then necessity of existence is joined to it. For this particular thing is either something existing through itself or something existing through a cause [namely] a cause producing necessity in something else. Now if [the particular thing] exists through itself and because it is something whose existence is necessary, then everything whose existence is necessary is identical with that particular thing. But if it exists through a cause [namely] a cause producing necessity in something else, then its existence as this particular thing has a cause. Hence the particularity of its separate existence has a cause and it would be caused.

Therefore that whose existence is necessary is one thing in its totality, [and it is] not as species under a genus. It is one in number, [but] not as individuals under a species. But it is something the meaning of whose name belongs to it alone and its existence is not shared with another. We shall add an explanation in another place. These are the properties by which that whose existence is necessary is distinguished.

The property of that whose existence is possible is clear from what has been said. It is that it requires necessarily some other thing which makes it exist in actuality. And everything whose existence is possible is always, when it is considered in respect to itself, something whose existence is possible. But sometimes it happens that its existence is necessary through another. And that [necessity of existence] happens to it always, or necessity of existence from another does not [happen] always, but at one time rather than another. [Something of] this [description] must possess matter whose existence precedes it in time, as we shall explain.

That whose existence is always necessary through another is also not something whose true nature is simple. For that which belongs to it when it is considered in respect to itself, is different from that which belongs to it from another. And it is something whose particularity in regard to existence is determined by both of them together. Hence nothing but that whose existence is necessary is free from being clothed with that which is in potentiality and possibility when it is considered in itself. [That whose existence is necessary] is a unity, while everything else is a composite duality.

SIXTH TREATISE

CHAPTER I. *The Division of Causes and Their Dispositions*

We have spoken about the nature of substances and accidents, and about the relation of priority and posteriority in them, and about the knowledge of the agreement between definitions and the things defined, universal as well as particular. It is fitting that we speak now about cause and that which is caused, since they are also among the consequences which belong to that which exists insofar as it exists.

The causes, as you have heard, are: form, element [matter], agent, and purpose. We say: By the formal cause we have in mind the cause which is part of the subsistence of something, through which the thing is what it is in actuality. By the elemental [cause we have in mind] the cause which is part of the subsistence of something, through which the thing is what it is in potentiality and in which there rests the potentiality of its existence. By the agent [we have in mind] the cause which bestows existence separate from itself, that is, its essence is not, according to the first intention, an underlying subject for that which receives from it the existence of something which is formed by it, so that it is in itself the potentiality of its existence [that is, the existence which it bestows] only accidentally. And with that it is necessary that that existence is not from its [that is, the cause's] disposition insofar as it is an agent [in the sense of a principle of motion], but if [existence] is [from it], it must be according to some other relation. The reason is that the metaphysicians do not intend by the agent the principle of movement only, as do the natural philosophers, but also the principle of existence and that which bestows [existence], such as the creator of the world. But the natural acting cause does not bestow existence as distinguished from movement according to one of the kinds of motion, but that which bestows existence in the case of natural things is the principle of motion. By the final [cause] we intend the cause because of which the existence of something separate from it comes to be.

It is clear that there is no cause besides these. We say: The cause of something must either enter its subsistence and be part of its existence, or it must not. Now if it enters its subsistence and is part of its existence, then it is either that part from whose existence alone it would not follow for this thing that it exists in actuality, but only that it exists in potentiality, and this is called *hyle* [that is, matter]. Or it is the part whose existence makes it exist in actuality, and this is the form. However, if [the cause] is not part of its existence, then it is either that for the sake of which [it exists], or it is not. Now if it is that for the sake of which [the thing exists] then it is the purpose; and if it is not that for the sake of which [the thing exists], then the existence [of the thing] must proceed from it in such a way that it [the cause] exists in it only accidentally, and this is the agent; or its existence must come from it in such a way that it exists in it, and this is also its element or its substratum.

Hence the principles in their totality are in one respect five, and in another respect four. For if you consider the element which is a recipient and which is not part of the thing as different from the element which is a part, then there are five. But if you consider both of them [the substratum and matter] as one thing, inasmuch as they agree in the notion of potentiality and predisposition, then there are four. Now, you must not consider the element in the sense of the recipient which is a part [that is, matter] as a principle for the form, but [as a principle] for the composite. The recipient is a principle only accidentally, since it is first constituted in actuality by the form; however, its essence considered in respect to itself alone, exists in potentiality. And something which exists in potentiality insofar as it exists in potentiality, can by no means be a principle. But it is only a principle by accident. Now an accident requires that there exists something in actuality which is a subject for it [and] then it becomes the cause for its subsistence, whether the accident is inseparable (and in that case [the subject] is prior according to essence), or whether it is separable (and in that case it is prior according to essence and according to time). These are the kinds of causes. If the substratum is the cause for an accident which it establishes, then it is not a cause in the same manner in which the substratum is a cause for the composite, but in some other manner.

Now if the form is the cause for the matter which it establishes, then it is not [a cause] in the same manner in which the form is a cause for the composite, even though both agree in that each one of them is the cause for something whose essence is not separate from it. For even if they agree in that, still in one of the two cases the cause [the form] does not bestow upon the other its existence, but something else bestows existence, but it exists in it. However, in the second case, the cause existing in it is the proximate principle for bestowing upon that which is caused its existence in actuality, yet not by itself alone, but only with a partner and a cause which makes this cause, I have in mind, the form, to exist and it causes the other to exist through it. And [the form] together with its partner is an intermediate [cause] for bestowing upon that its existence in actuality. Thus the form is for matter as an acting principle [such that] if it exists in actuality, it would come from it alone. And it appears that the form is part of the acting cause, such as one of the two movers of a ship, as will be explained later. As for the form, it is a formal cause for that which is composed of it and of matter, and the form is the form of matter, but it is not the formal cause of matter.

The agent bestows upon some other thing an existence which does not belong to the other through itself. And that existence proceeds from that which is the agent insofar as the essence of this agent is not the recipient for the form of that existence and [insofar] as it is not united with it as something united which enters into it. But each one of these two essences [the cause and that which is caused] exists apart from the other and there does not exist in one of them a potentiality for receiving the other. Yet it is not farfetched that the agent brings into existence that which is caused [in the place] where it [the agent] is and insofar as it is joined to its essence. Thus the nature which is in the wood is a principle which is an agent for motion, for the motion comes to be in the matter in which the nature exists and where its essence is. However, the two are not combined in such a way that one of them is part of the existence of the other or that it is matter for it, but the two essences are distinguished according to their true natures, even though they have a common subject. And it happens to an agent that it is not an agent at some time and that that which it causes is not caused, but that that which is caused by it does not exist. Hence there occur to the agent causes through which it becomes an agent in actuality. (We have spoken of this in what preceded.) Thus it becomes an agent and there comes to be from it the existence of the thing after it did not exist. Now "existence" belongs to that thing and "that it did not exist" belongs to that thing. However, "that it did not exist" does not belong to it from an agent, nor "that it exists after it did not exist"; only its existence belongs to it from an agent. Hence if non-existence would belong to the thing through its essence, it would follow that its existence would come to be "after it did not exist" and it would become "existing after it did not exist."

Now existence is that which comes to the thing itself through the agent. But the existence which belongs to the thing belongs to it only because some other thing exists in its plenitude, from which [plenitude] it follows necessarily that the other has existence from the existence which it [the cause] has essentially. However, "that it did not exist" does not come from a cause which produces it. For its being non-existent goes back to some cause which is the non-existence of its cause. Further, its "coming into existence after non-existence" is something which does not come from a cause, since it is absolutely impossible that its existence comes to be except after non-existence. But that which is impossible does not have a cause. Thus it is possible that its existence occurs or that it does not occur, and hence its existence has a cause. And it is possible that its non-existence occurs or does not occur, and hence its non-existence can have a cause. However, its "coming into existence after it did not exist" does not have a cause.

Someone may object: It is likewise possible that its "existence after its non-existence" can occur or can not occur [and hence this can also have a cause]. We answer: If you have in mind its existence insofar as it is its existence, then non-existence does not enter it, for its very existence is not necessary, that is, it is possible, and hence it is not not-necessary insofar as "it is after non-existence." But as for the not-necessary, its existence is that which happens now and which [previously] did not exist. However, if you have in mind its existence insofar as it is considered as "existing after it did not exist," then its existence is considered "after it did not exist." In that case its existence is considered "after non-existence" and its existence is considered not as existing simply, even though it exists after it did not exist and came to be after it did not exist. Existence in this sense does not have a cause, nor is there a cause for its "coming into existence after it did not exist," even if there exists a cause for the existence which it has after non-existence, insofar as it is its existence. And it is true that its existence can occur or not occur after actual non-existence. But it is not true that its "existence after non-existence" insofar as it is "existence after non-existence" can be "existence after non-existence" or can not be "existence after non-existence." Indeed, unless it does not exist at all, it exists in relation to existence.

Perhaps someone is of the opinion that the agent and the cause are only required in order that something has existence after it did not exist and that, once the thing exists and the cause is missing, the thing exists as selfsufficient. And he who is of this opinion thinks that something only needs a cause for its coming into being and that, once it has come into being and exists, it can do without the cause. According to this opinion, causes are causes for coming into being only, and they exist prior to the thing, not simultaneously with it. But he who holds this opinion thinks something absurd. For the existence after coming into being must be either [I] necessary existence or [II] not necessary existence. Now if it is [I] necessary existence, then [Ia] its necessity belongs to that quiddity (to the essence of that quiddity) in such a way that that quiddity requires necessary existence and in that case it is impossible that it comes to be. Or [Ib] necessity belongs to it through a condition and that condition is either [Ib1] coming into being, or [Ib2] one of the attributes of that quiddity, or [Ib3] something separate. Now [Ib1] the necessity of its existence can not come from its coming into being since the existence of coming into being itself is not necessary through itself. How then can the existence of something else be necessary through it? Further, coming into being ceases and how can there be with its non-existence a cause for the necessary existence of something else? Unless one were to say that coming into being is not the cause, but the cause is the existence of something to which coming into being has occurred. But this would be one of the attributes which belong to the thing which has come into being. Thus necessity falls under the second group of the divisions [namely, that it occurs through an attribute].

We say: [Ib2a] These attributes must belong to the quiddity insofar as it is a quiddity, not insofar as it came into being. It follows then that that which necessarily belongs to it, necessarily belongs to the quiddity. And necessary existence belongs necessarily to the quiddity. Or [Ib2b] these attributes come into being together with the existence [of the quiddity]. In this case the statement concerning the necessity of its existence is like the statement concerning the first case [that is, something necessary can not come into being]. Now if there exists an unlimited number of attributes, all of them possessing this attribute, then all of them would be things whose existence is possible, not necessary through themselves. Or they lead to an attribute which is necessary through some separate thing. The first division establishes that all the attributes are things whose existence is possible through themselves. Now it is clear that that whose existence is possible through itself, exists through another and hence the totality of the attributes is necessary through something else existing apart. The second division requires that the existence of that which comes into being only remains as existence through a cause from the outside and this is the cause.

You already know that "coming into being" has no meaning except "existence after it did not exist." Thus there is here "existence" and "existence after it did not exist." Now the cause which brings something into being has no influence and effect insofar as the thing does not exist, but its influence and effect extends only insofar as existence proceeds from it. Then it is accidental that it is that thing at that time, "after it did not exist." And the accident which occurs in the production of something, has no entrance into the subsistence of the thing and, hence, the preceding non-existence has no entrance insofar as the existence which comes into being has a cause, but that kind of existence, insofar as it belongs to that kind of quiddities, requires that it has a cause, even if it continues and remains. Because of this you can not say: Something produces the existence of the thing insofar as it "exists after it did not exist," for this is not within its province; but in the case of some of the things which exist it is absolutely necessary that they do not exist after non-existence, while in the case of others it is absolutely necessary that they exist after non-existence.

Now existence insofar as it is the existence of this quiddity can be from a cause, while the attribute of this existence, namely that it "exists after it did not exist," can not be from a cause. And insofar as its existence comes into being, that is, insofar as the existence which belongs to it is described as one which "exists after non-existence," the thing does not, in truth, have a cause. But it has a cause insofar as existence belongs to the quiddity. And the case is the reverse of what they [the Mutakallimūn] think, but the cause belongs to the existence alone. If it happens that non-existence precedes it, then the thing comes into being, but if it does not happen that [non-existence precedes it], then it does not come into being, [even though it is caused].

The agent which [ordinary] people call an agent is not truly a cause insofar as they posit it as an agent. For they posit it as an agent insofar as it must be affirmed concerning it that it was not [previously] an agent. However, it is not an agent insofar as it is a cause; but insofar as it is a cause something is necessary with it. It is an agent insofar as it is considered in respect to that which it produces and concurrently in respect to that which it does not produce. Thus if the cause is considered in respect to that which is bestowed by it concurrently with that which is not bestowed by it, then it is called an agent. Therefore everything which [ordinary people] call an agent has as its condition that it is necessarily at some time not an agent. In that case there is an act of will or a compulsion or there occurs to it some state which did not exist [previously]. When this additional thing is joined to it, then its essence together with that which is adjoined becomes a cause in actuality, after it had been devoid of that. Hence, according to their opinion, it is an agent insofar as it is a cause in actuality after it had been a cause in potentiality, not insofar as it is a cause in actuality in an absolute manner.

Everything which they call an agent must also be something which they call passive. They do not free the agent from there being attached to it something of the state of coming into being, because of which there proceeds from it its existence after it did not exist. It is clear then that the existence of the quiddity depends on something else insofar as it is the existence of that quiddity, not insofar as it exists after it did not exist. And that existence is caused in this manner as long as it exists. Likewise it is caused as dependent on something else. Thus it is clear that that which is caused requires something which bestows existence to it because of existence itself essentially. But that it comes into being and that which is like it, are things which happen to it accidentally. That which is caused requires something which bestows existence upon it continuously, as long as it continues as existing.

CHAPTER 2. *The Solution of the Question Which Arises Concerning the Opinion of the True Philosophers [Who Maintain] that Every Cause Exists Simultaneously with That Which Is Caused by It, and the Verification of the Discourse Concerning the Acting Cause.*

The question of the opponents arises from the fact that the son remains after the father, and the building remains after the builder, and the heat remains after the fire. The reason for this question is the confusion which results from the ignorance of what a cause really is. For the builder, and the father, and the fire are not really causes for the subsistence of the things which they cause. The builder who produces that [building] is not the cause of the subsistence of that building, [he is] not even [the cause] for its existence.

Now the motion of the builder is the cause of some other motion. Thereafter his rest, and his ceasing from motion or the non-existence of his motion, and his moving away after that motion are the cause for the end of that motion. And that very moving away and the end of that motion are the cause of some coming together [namely the coming together of the materials], and that coming together is the cause of a certain shape [namely, the shape of the building]. Each one of these is a cause and it and that which is caused by it exist simultaneously.

[Likewise] the father is the cause of the movement of the semen. And when the motion of the semen comes to an end in the manner mentioned, it [the cessation of motion] is the cause of [the semen's] arrival in its proper place. Then its arrival in its proper place is the cause of the thing. However, that the semen receives the form "animal" and that it remains an animal has some other cause. Since this is so, every cause exists simultaneously with that which is caused by it.

Similarly, fire is a cause for the heating of the element water. And heating is the cause of the destruction of the predisposition which water possesses in actuality for the reception or preservation of the form "water." This or some other thing is the cause of the coming to be of the perfect predisposition (according to a similar state) for the reception of its contrary, namely the form "fire." But the causes which provide for the elements their form are the cause of the form "fire." These are the incorporeal [substances].

Hence causes which are truly causes exist simultaneously with the things caused. But causes which precede the things caused are causes either accidentally or as supporting. Because of this it must be believed that the cause of the shape of the building is the coming together [of its materials] and [that] the cause of that is the natures of the things which come together and their remaining together as they were put together. The cause of that [in turn] is the incorporeal cause which produces the natures. [Similarly,] the cause of the child is the coming together of its form with its matter through the cause which bestows the forms. [Likewise] the cause of fire is the cause which bestows the forms and simultaneously the cessation of the perfect predisposition for that which is contrary to those forms. Thus we find that causes are simultaneous with the things caused.

If we shall show in our discussion which follows that the causes are finite, we ascribe this only to these causes [that is those which are truly causes, namely

acts through itself, at times through a power. That which acts through itself is like heat which would act if it would exist as separated. In that case there would proceed from it what proceeds because it is heat alone. But that which acts through a power is like fire which acts through its heat. We have enumerated the kinds of potentialities in another place.

THE DELIVERANCE, PSYCHOLOGY

SIXTH TREATISE

CHAPTER IX. *The Substratum of Rational Concepts Is Immaterial*

We further maintain that the substance which is the substratum of the intelligibles is neither itself a body nor does it subsist in a body in such a way as to be in any sense a faculty residing in, or a form of, that body. If the substratum of the intelligibles were a body or a magnitude of some kind, then that body which is the substratum of the forms would be either indivisible or divisible. Let us first examine whether such a substratum can have a part that is not further divisible. I think this is absurd, since a point is some sort of a limit and its position cannot be distinguished from the line or the magnitude of which it is the limit. Thus if anything were to be imprinted on it, it must be imprinted on a part of that line. If, however, the point does not exist separately but is an essential part of what is in itself a quantity, one can say that, in some sense, anything which inheres in that quantity (i.e. the line) of which the point is the limit, must also inhere in that point and thus become accidentally quantified by it. When this happens it also remains accidentally limited by that point. If the point were separate and could receive something, it would be an independent self-subsisting entity and would have two sides: one side contiguous with the line from which it is distinguished and another side opposite to it. It would then be separate from the line which would have a limit other than the point touching it. Then that point and not this one would be the limit of the line, and we should have the same problem repeated *ad infinitum*. It would follow from this that the finite or infinite repetition of points produces a line, a view which we have elsewhere shown to be absurd. It is clear, therefore, that the points are not synthesized into a line by being put together. It is also clear that the point has no particular and distinct position. We might, however, allude to a part of the arguments already given to show the absurdity of this view, and say: either

(1) A certain given point which is in the middle of two other points separates them, so that they do not meet. If so, then with primary rational intuition it follows that each of the two is particularized by a special part of the middle point which it touches, and thus the middle point would be divided. This is absurd. Or

(2) The middle part does not prevent the two side-points from touching. The

Reprinted from F. Rahman, trans., *Avicenna's Psychology*, London: Oxford University Press, 1952, by permission of the Clarendon Press, Oxford.

rational form would then inhere in all the points at once, and all the points (inter-penetrating as they are, on this supposition) would be like one single point. But we have already supposed this point to be separate from the line, and therefore the line being separate from it has a limit other than the point by which limit it is separated from the point in question. Thus that point (which separates the line from the point in question) would have a different position from this point. But we have already supposed that all the points have one common position. This is a contradiction. The view that the substratum of the intelligibles is some indivisible part of the body is therefore false.

The remaining solution is that the substratum of the intelligibles (if their substratum is a body) is something divisible. Let us suppose an intelligible form in something divisible. A form thus supposed to subsist in something somehow divisible would itself be accidentally divisible. Then the two parts of the form would be either similar or dissimilar. If they are similar, then why is their synthesis something different from them? For the whole, as such, is different from the part. For if the parts are exactly similar, the only difference their totality would make is an increase in quantity or in number and not in form. But if so, then the intelligible form would be a certain shape or number. No intelligible form, how-ever, has shape or number, otherwise the form would be representational and not intelligible. The following is a still clearer argument. It is not possible to say that the concept of each of the two parts is exactly the same as that of the whole, for, if the second part does not enter into the concept of the whole, it is necessary that at the outset we should reserve the concept of the whole for the first part only and not for both. But if it enters into the concept of the whole, it is obvious that either of these two parts alone cannot indicate exactly the concept of the com-plete whole.

If, on the other hand, the two parts of the form are dissimilar, let us see in what sense an intelligible form can have such parts. These dissimilar parts can only be the parts of definition, viz. genera and differentiae. From this many absurdities would necessarily follow; for example, every part of the body is also potentially divisible *ad infinitum,* so that the genera and differentiae must also be potentially infinite. But it has been established that the genera and essential differentiae of a single thing are not potentially infinite. Furthermore, it is not the supposition of division which produces distinction between the genus and the differentiae; if there were a genus and a differentia necessitating a distinction in the substratum, the division would certainly not depend on supposition. It would necessarily follow that the genera and differentiae would be actually infinite, too. It has been established that the genera and differentiae and parts of definition of a single thing are, in all respects, finite. If they were actually infinite, they could not have come together in the body in this form, for it would necessarily entail a single body being actually divisible *ad infinitum.*

Again, let us suppose that the division takes place in a certain way and has placed genus on one side and differentia on the other. If this manner of division is changed it would place half-genus plus half-differentia on the one side and the other halves on the other. Or genus and differentia would exchange places, so that in our supposition or imagination the position of genus and differentia would revolve, and each of them would move in any direction according to the will of an external person. But this is not the end, for we can go on introducing a new division within a division *ad infinitum.*

Again, not every intelligible is divisible into simpler intelligibles, for certain intelligibles are the simplest and serve as principles for other compound ones. They have no genera and differentiae, nor are they divisible in quantity or concept. It is not possible, then, that the supposed parts of the form should be dissimilar in such a way that each one of them is, in concept, different from the whole and the whole is made up of their aggregate.

If, then, the intelligible form is indivisible, and it does not inhere in an indivisible part of a magnitude, and, at the same time, there must be something in us which receives it, it is clear that the substratum of the intelligibles is a substance which is not a body, nor a bodily faculty such as might be subject to the accidents of the body, e.g. division with all the absurdities it involves.

ANOTHER ARGUMENT

We can prove this in another way by saying that it is the rational faculty itself which abstracts the intelligibles from a definite quantity, place, position, and all the other categories. Let us examine this form itself which is abstracted from position and ask how this has been effected. Is this abstraction with reference to the knowing subject? i.e. is this intelligible abstracted from position in its external existence or in its conceptual existence in the intelligent? It is absurd that it should be so in its external existence, so that the only alternative is that it is abstracted from position and place in its existence in the intellect. Thus, when the intelligible form comes to exist in the intellect, it does not possess a position whereby it might be indicated and so divided or subjected to similar processes; therefore it cannot be in a body. Again, when the unitary, indivisible forms of things which are conceptually indivisible are imprinted on a divisible matter having dimensions, then either none of the supposed parts has any relation to the unitary intelligible which is indivisible and abstract from matter, or each and every one of the supposed parts has relation to it, or some parts have such a relation while others do not. If none of the parts has relation to it, then the whole (composed as it is of the parts) cannot possibly have any relation to it either. If some parts have a relation to it, and the others do not, then the parts which have no relation to this intelligible do not enter into its concept at all. But if every supposed part has some relation to it, then either it is related to the intelligible as a whole or to a part of it. If every supposed part of the matter in which the intelligible inheres has a relation to the whole of the intelligible, then the parts are not parts of the intelligible, but each is independently an intelligible itself; indeed, it would be the intelligible itself. In this case the intelligible would be actually intelligible an infinite number of times in a single moment. If every part has a different relation to this entity, then the entity as an intelligible must be conceptually divisible. This is a contradiction, for we have already supposed it to be indivisible. If the relation of each part is to a different part of the intelligible entity, its divisibility is all the more obvious, except that it is inconceivable. It is clear from this that the forms imprinted on matter are only the exterior forms of particular divisible entities and every part of the former is actually or potentially related to every part of the latter. Also, even a thing which is multiple as regards its parts of definition is a unity when regarded as a whole. This unity is indivisible. So how can this unity, as such, be imprinted on something divisible? Otherwise, the absurdity we have mentioned in the case of the indivisible intelligible would arise.

Again, we have established that the supposed intelligibles which it is the function of the rational faculty actually to know one by one are potentially infinite. It is also certain that the substratum of something which can encompass infinite things cannot be a body nor a faculty in a body. This has been demonstrated in Aristotle's *Physics*. It is quite impossible, then, that the entity which receives intelligibles should be inherent in a body, or that its action should be in a body or through a body.

CHAPTER XII. *Concerning the Temporal Origin of the Soul*

We say that human souls are of the same species and concept. If they existed before the body, they would either be multiple entities or one single entity. But it is impossible for them to be either the one or the other, as will be shown later, therefore it is impossible for them to exist before the body. We now begin with the explanation of the impossibility of its numerical multiplicity and say that the mutual difference of the souls before [their attachment to] bodies is either due to their quiddity and form; or to the element and matter which is multiple in space, a particular part of which each matter occupies; or to the various times peculiar to every soul when it becomes existent in its matter; or to the causes which divide their matter. But their difference is not due to their quiddity or form, since their form is one, therefore their difference is due to the recipient of the quiddity or to the body to which the quiddity is specifically related. Before its attachment to the body the soul is quiddity pure and simple; thus it is impossible for one soul to be numerically different from another, or for the quiddity to admit of essential differentiation. This holds absolutely true in all cases; for the multiplicity of the species of those things whose essences are pure concepts is only due to the substrata which receive them and to what is affected by them, or due only to their times. But when they are absolutely separate, i.e. when the categories we have enumerated are not applicable to them, they cannot be diverse. It is therefore impossible for them to have any kind of diversity or multiplicity among them. Thus it is untrue that before they enter bodies souls have numerically different essences.

I say that it is also impossible for souls to have numerically one essence, for when two bodies come into existence two souls also come into existence in them. Then either—

(1) these two souls are two parts of the same single soul, in which case one single thing which does not possess any magnitude and bulk would be potentially divisible. This is manifestly absurd according to the principles established in physics. Or—
(2) a soul which is numerically one would be in two bodies. This also does not require much effort to refute.

It is thus proved that the soul comes into existence whenever a body does so fit to be used by it. The body which thus comes into being is the kingdom and instrument of the soul. In the very disposition of the substance of the soul which comes into existence together with a certain body—a body, that is to say, with the appropriate qualities to make it suitable to receive the soul which takes its origin from the first principles—there is a natural yearning to occupy itself with that body, to use it, control it, and be attracted by it. This yearning binds the soul specially to this body, and turns it away from other bodies different from it in nature so that the soul does not contact them except through it. Thus when the principle of its individualization, namely, its peculiar dispositions, occurs to it, it becomes an individual. These dispositions determine its attachment to that particular body and form the relationship of their mutual suitability, although this relationship and its condition may be obscure to us. The soul achieves its first entelechy through the body; its subsequent development, however, does not depend on the body but on its own nature.

But after their separation from their bodies the souls remain individual owing to the different matters in which they had been, and owing to the times of their birth and their different dispositions due to their bodies which necessarily differ because of their peculiar conditions.

CHAPTER XIII. *The Soul Does Not Die with the Death of the Body; It Is Incorruptible.*

We say that the soul does not die with the death of the body and is absolutely incorruptible. As for the former proposition, this is because everything which is corrupted with the corruption of something else is in some way attached to it. And anything which in some way is attached to something else is either coexistent with it or posterior to it in existence or prior to it, this priority being essential and not temporal. If, then, the soul is so attached to the body that it is coexistent with it, and this is not accidental but pertains to its essence, then they are essentially interdependent. Then neither the soul nor the body would be a substance; but in fact they are substances. And if this is an accidental and not an essential attachment, then, with the corruption of the one term only the accidental relationship of the other term will be annulled, but its being will not be corrupted with its corruption. If the soul is so attached to the body that it is posterior to it in existence, then, in that case, the body will be the cause of the soul's existence. Now the causes are four; so either the body is the efficient cause of the soul and gives it existence, or it is its receptive and material cause—maybe by way of composition as the elements are for the body or by way of simplicity as bronze is for the statue —or the body is the soul's formal or final cause. But the body cannot be the soul's efficient cause, for body, as such, does not act; it acts only through its faculties. If it were to act through its essence, not through its faculties, every body would act in the same way. Again, the bodily faculties are all of them either accidents or material forms, and it is impossible that either accidents or forms subsisting in matter should produce the being of a self-subsisting entity independent of matter or that of an absolute substance. Nor is it possible that the body should be the receptive and material cause of the soul, for we have clearly shown and proved that the soul is in no way imprinted in the body. The body, then, is not 'informed' with the form of the soul, either by way of simplicity or composition so that certain parts of the body are composed and mixed together in a certain way and then the soul is imprinted in them. It is also impossible that the body should be the formal or the final cause of the soul, for the reverse is the more plausible case.

Thus the attachment of the soul to the body is not the attachment of an effect to a necessary cause. The truth is that the body and the temperament are an accidental cause of the soul, for when the matter of a body suitable to become the instrument of the soul and its proper subject comes into existence, the separate causes bring into being the individual soul, and that is how the soul originates from them. This is because it is impossible to bring arbitrarily into being different souls without any specific cause. Besides, the soul does not admit of numerical multiplicity, as we have shown. Again, whenever a new thing comes into being, it must be preceded by a matter which is prepared to receive it or to have a relationship with it, as has been shown in the other sciences. Again, if an individual soul were to come into being without an instrument through which it acts and attains perfection, its being would be purposeless; but there is nothing purposeless in nature. In truth, when the suitability and preparation for such a relationship exist in the instrument, it becomes necessary that such a thing as a soul should originate from the separate causes.

But if the existence of one thing necessitates the existence of another, the corruption of the former does not necessarily entail that of the latter. This happens only where its very being subsists through or in that thing. Many things originating from other things survive the latter's corruption; when their being does not subsist in them, and especially when they owe their existence to something other than what was merely preparatory for the emanation of their being. And the being of the soul does in fact emanate from something different from the body and bodily functions, as we have shown; its source of emanation must be something different from the body. Thus when the soul owes its being to that other thing and only the time of its realization to the body, its being would be independent of the body which is only its accidental cause; it cannot then be said that they have a mutual relationship which would necessitate the body preceding the soul as its necessary cause.

Let us turn to the third division which we mentioned in the beginning, namely, that the attachment of the soul to the body might be in the sense that the soul is prior to the body in existence. Now in that case the priority will be either temporal as well as essential, and so the soul's being could not possibly be attached to the body since it precedes the body in time, or the priority will be only essential and not temporal, for in time the soul will not be separate from the body. This sort of priority means that when the prior entity comes into existence, the being of the posterior entity must follow from it. Then the prior entity cannot exist, if the posterior is supposed to be non-existent. I do not say that the supposition of the non-existence of the posterior necessitates the non-existence of the prior, but that the posterior cannot be non-existent except when first something has naturally happened to the prior which has made it non-existent, too. Thus it is not the supposition of the non-existence of the posterior entity which necessitates the non-existence of the prior, but the supposition of the non-existence of the prior itself, for the posterior can be supposed to be non-existent only after the prior itself has ceased to exist. This being so, it follows that the cause of non-existence must occur in the substance of the soul necessitating the body's corruption along with it, and that the body cannot be corrupted through a cause special to itself. But in fact the corruption of the body does take place through a cause special to itself, namely, through changes in its composition and its temperament. Thus it is false to hold that the soul is attached to the body as essentially prior to it, and that at the same time the body is indeed corrupted through a cause in itself; so no such relationship subsists between the two.

This being so, all the forms of attachment between the body and the soul have proved to be false and it only remains that the soul, in its being, has no relationship with the body but is related with other principles which are not subject to change or corruption.

As for the proposition that the soul does not admit of corruption at all, I say that there is another conclusive reason for the immortality of the soul. Everything which might be corrupted through some cause has in itself the potentiality of corruption and, before corruption, has the actuality of persistence. But it is absurd that a single thing in the same sense should possess both, the potentiality of corruption and the actuality of persistence; its potentiality of corruption cannot be due to its actual persistence, for the concept of potentiality is contrary to that of actuality. Also, the relation of this potentiality is opposed to the relation of this actuality, for the one is related with corruption, the other with persistence. These two concepts, then, are attributable to two different factors in the concrete thing. Hence we say that the actuality of persistence and the potentiality of corruption may be combined in composite things and in such simple things as subsist in composite ones. But these two concepts cannot come together in simple things whose essence is separate. I say in another absolute sense that these two concepts cannot exist together in a simple thing whose essence is unitary. This is because everything which persists and has the potentiality of corruption also has the potentiality of persistence, since its persistence is not necessary. When it is not necessary, it is possible; and possibility is of the nature of potentiality. Thus the potentiality of persistence is in its very substance. But, of course, it is clear that the actuality of persistence of a thing is not the same as its potentiality of persistence. Thus its actuality of persistence is a fact which happens to the body which has the potentiality of persistence. Therefore that potentiality does not belong to something actual but to something of which actual existence is only an accident and does not constitute its real essence. From this it necessarily follows that its being is composed of a factor the possession of which gives actual existence to it (this factor is the form in every concrete existent), and another factor which attains this actual existence but which in itself has only the potentiality of existence (and this factor is the matter in the concrete existent).

So if the soul is absolutely simple and is not divisible into matter and form, it will not admit of corruption. But if it is composite, let us leave the composite and consider only the substance which is its matter. We say: either that matter will continue to be divisible and so the same analysis will go on being applied to it and we shall then have a regress *ad infinitum*, which is absurd; or this substance and base will never cease to exist. But if so, then our present discourse is devoted to this factor which is the base and origin (i.e. the substance) and not to the composite thing which is composed of this factor and some other. So it is clear that everything which is simple and not composite, or which is the origin and base (i.e. the substance) of the composite thing, cannot in itself possess both the actuality of persistence and the potentiality of corruption. If it has the potentiality of corruption, it cannot possibly have the actuality of persistence, and if it has the actuality of persistence and existence, it cannot have the potentiality of corruption. Obviously, then, the substance of the soul does not have the potentiality of corruption. Of those things which come to be and are corrupted, the corruptible is only the concrete composite. The potentiality of corruption and of persistence at the same time does not belong to something which gives unity to the composite, but to the matter which potentially admits of both contraries. So the corruptible composite as such possesses neither the potentiality of persistence nor that of corruption, let alone both. As to the matter itself, it either has persistence not due to any potentiality, which gives it the capacity for persistence—as some people think—

or it has persistence through a potentiality which gives it persistence, but does not have the potentiality of corruption; this latter being something which it acquires. The potentiality of corruption of simple entities which subsist in matter is due to matter and is not in their own substance. The argument which proves that everything which comes to exist passes away on account of the finitude of the potentialities of persistence and corruption is relevant only to those whose being is composed of matter and form. Matter has the potentiality that this form may persist in it, and at the same time the potentiality that this form may cease to exist in it. It is then obvious that the soul is absolutely incorruptible. This is the point which we wanted to make, and this is what we wanted to prove.

SELECTED BIBLIOGRAPHY

TRANSLATIONS

Note: There exist French and German translations of some of Avicenna's works, of which those of G. Anawati, A. Goichon and M. Horten should be mentioned.

Arberry, A., *Avicenna on Theology*, London, 1951.

Dahiyat, I., ed. and trans., *Avicenna's Commentary on the Poetics of Aristotle*, Leiden, 1974.

Fackenheim, E., "A Treatise on Love by Avicenna," *Mediaeval Studies*, VII (1945), 208–228.

Gohlman, W., trans., *The Life of Ibn Sina*, Albany, 1974.

Lerner, R., and M. Mahdi, eds., *Medieval Political Philosophy*, New York, 1963.

Morewedge, P., trans. and comm., *The Metaphysica of Avicenna (Ibn Sina)*, New York, 1973.

Rahman, F., trans., *Avicenna's Psychology; An English Translation of Kitāb al-Najāt*, Book II, chap. VI, London, 1952.

Shehaby, N., trans., *The Propositional Logic of Avicenna*, Dordrecht-Boston, 1973.

Zabech, F., ed. and trans., *Avicenna's Treatise on Logic*, The Hague, 1971.

STUDIES

Afnan, S., *Avicenna, His Life and Works*, London, 1958.

Amid, M., *Essai sur la psychologie d'Avicenne*, Geneva, 1940.

Brown, S., "Avicenna and the Unity of the Concept of Being," *Franciscan Studies*, XXV (1965), 117–150.

Carra de Vaux, B., *Avicenne*, Paris, 1900.

Chahine, O., *Ontologie et théologie chez Avicenne*, Paris, 1962.

Corbin, H., *Avicenna and the Visionary Recital*, trans. from the French by W. Trask, New York, 1960 (contains some translations).

Courtois, V., ed., *Avicenna Commemoration Volume*, Calcutta, 1956.

Davidson, H., "Avicenna's Proof of the Existence of God as a Necessarily Existent Being," *Islamic Philosophical Theology*, ed. P. Morewedge, Albany, 1979, 167–187.

Galston, M., "Realism and Idealism in Avicenna's Political Philosophy," *Review of Politics* XLI (1979), 561–577.

Gardet, L., *La pensée religieuse d'Avicenne (Ibn Sīnā)*, Paris, 1951.

Gilson, E., "Avicenne en Occident au Moyen Age," *Archives d'histoire doctrinale et littéraire du Moyen Age*, 1969, 89–121.

Goichon, A., *La distinction de l'essence et de l'existence d'après Ibn Sinā (Avicenne)*, Paris, 1937.

Goichon, A., *La philosophie d'Avicenne et son influence en Europe médiévale*, 2. éd., rev. et corr., Paris, 1951.

Goichon, A., *The Philosophy of Avicenna and its Influence on Medieval Europe*, trans. by M. Khan, Delhi, 1969.

Hourani, G., "Ibn Sīnā on Necessary and Possible Existence," *Philosophical Forum*, IV

headings and then goes on to counter each one with arguments of his own. It is noteworthy that Algazali is not a radical occasionalist who holds that God can do anything he pleases. In fact, in the selection, he attacks certain Mutakallimūn for defending this view, maintaining instead that God cannot do anything that is logically impossible. He further holds that God governs the world according to a certain order, but this order is not necessary and God can circumvent it whenever He wishes. Somewhat more technically, it seems to be his view that possibility and necessary causality are incompatible and that something possible can only become actual through a voluntary cause. Necessity is limited to logical relations.

DELIVERANCE FROM ERROR

III. *The Classes of Seekers*

When God by His grace and abundant generosity cured me of this disease [skepticism], I came to regard the various seekers (*sc*. after truth) as comprising four groups:—

(1) the *Theologians* (*mutakallimūn*), who claim that they are the exponents of thought and intellectual speculation;

(2) the *Bāṭinīyah,* who consider that they, as the party of 'authoritative instruction' (*ta'līm*), alone derive truth from the infallible *imam*;

(3) the *Philosophers,* who regard themselves as the exponents of logic and demonstration;

(4) the *Sufis or Mystics,* who claim that they alone enter into the 'presence' (*sc*. of God), and possess vision and intuitive understanding.

I said within myself: 'The truth cannot lie outside these four classes. These are the people who tread the paths of the quest for truth. If the truth is not with them, no point remains in trying to apprehend the truth. There is certainly no point in trying to return to the level of the naive and derivative belief (*taqlīd*) once it has been left, since a condition of being at such a level is that one should not know one is there; when a man comes to know that, the glass of his naive beliefs is broken. This is a breakage which cannot be mended, a breakage not to be repaired by patching or by assembling of fragments. The glass must be melted once again in the furnace for a new start, and out of it another fresh vessel formed.'

I now hastened to follow out these four ways and investigate what these groups had achieved, commencing with the science of theology and then taking the way of philosophy, the 'authoritative instruction' of the Bāṭinīyah, and the way of mysticism, in that order.

I. THE SCIENCE OF THEOLOGY: ITS AIMS AND ACHIEVEMENTS

I commenced, then, with the science of Theology (*'ilm al-kalām*), and obtained a thorough grasp of it. I read the books of sound theologians and myself wrote some books on the subject. But it was a science, I found, which, though attaining

From *The Faith and Practice of al-Ghazāli,* W. M. Watt, trans., London: George Allen and Unwin, Ltd., 1951. Reprinted by permission.

its own aim, did not attain mine. Its aim was merely to preserve the creed of orthodoxy and to defend it against the deviations of heretics.

Now God sent to His servants by the mouth of His messenger, in the Qur'an and Traditions, a creed which is the truth and whose contents are the basis of man's welfare in both religious and secular affairs. But Satan too sent, in the suggestions of heretics, things contrary to orthodoxy; men tended to accept his suggestions and almost corrupted the true creed for its adherents. So God brought into being the class of theologians, and moved them to support traditional orthodoxy with the weapon of systematic argument by laying bare the confused doctrines invented by the heretics at variance with traditional orthodoxy. This is the origin of theology and theologians.

In due course a group of theologians performed the task to which God invited them; they successfully preserved orthodoxy, defended the creed received from the prophetic source and rectified heretical innovations. Nevertheless in so doing they based their arguments on premises which they took from their opponents and which they were compelled to admit by naïve belief (*taqlīd*), or the consensus of the community, or bare acceptance of Qur'an and Traditions. For the most part their efforts were devoted to making explicit the contradictions of their opponents and criticizing them in respect of the logical consequences of what they admitted.

This was of little use in the case of one who admitted nothing at all save logically necessary truths. Theology was not adequate to my case and was unable to cure the malady of which I complained. It is true that, when theology appeared as a recognized discipline and much effort had been expended in it over a considerable period of time, the theologians, becoming very earnest in their endeavours to defend orthodoxy by the study of what things really are, embarked on a study of substances and accidents with their nature and properties. But, since that was not the aim of their science, they did not deal with the question thoroughly in their thinking and consequently did not arrive at results sufficient to dispel universally the darkness of confusion due to the different views of men. I do not exclude the possibility that for others than myself these results have been sufficient; indeed, I do not doubt that this has been so for quite a number. But these results were mingled with naïve belief in certain matters which are not included among first principles.

My purpose here, however, is to describe my own case, not to disparage those who sought a remedy thereby, for the healing drugs vary with the disease. How often one sick man's medicine proves to be another's poison!

2. PHILOSOPHY

After I had done with theology I started on philosophy. I was convinced that a man cannot grasp what is defective in any of the sciences unless he has so complete a grasp of the science in question that he equals its most learned exponents in the appreciation of its fundamental principles, and even goes beyond and surpasses them, probing into some of the tangles and profundities which the very professors of the science have neglected. Then and only then is it possible that what he has to assert about its defects is true.

So far as I could see none of the doctors of Islam had devoted thought and attention to philosophy. In their writings none of the theologians engaged in polemic against the philosophers, apart from obscure and scattered utterances so plainly erroneous and inconsistent that no person of ordinary intelligence would be likely to be deceived, far less one versed in the sciences.

I realized that to refute a system before understanding it and becoming acquainted with its depths is to act blindly. I therefore set out in all earnestness to acquire a knowledge of philosophy from books, by private study without the help of an instructor. I made progress towards this aim during my hours of free time after teaching in the religious sciences and writing, for at this period I was burdened with the teaching and instruction of three hundred students in Baghdad. By my solitary reading during the hours thus snatched God brought me in less than two years to a complete understanding of the sciences of the philosophers. Thereafter I continued to reflect assiduously for nearly a year on what I had assimilated, going over it in my mind again and again and probing its tangled depths, until I comprehended surely and certainly how far it was deceitful and confusing and how far true and a representation of reality.

Hear now an account of this discipline and of the achievement of the sciences it comprises. There are various schools of philosophers, I perceived, and their sciences are divided into various branches, but throughout their numerous schools they suffer from the defect of being infidels and irreligious men, even although of the different groups of philosophers—older and most ancient, earlier and more recent—some are much closer to the truth than others.

A. *The schools of philosophers, and how the defect of unbelief affects them all.* The many philosophical sects and systems constitute three main groups: the Materialists (*Dahriyūn*), the Naturalists (*Tabī'iyūn*), and the Theists (*Ilāhiyūn*). The first group, the *Materialists,* are among the earliest philosophers. They deny the Creator and Disposer of the world, omniscient and omnipotent, and consider that the world has everlastingly existed just as it is, of itself and without a creator, and that everlastingly animals have come from seed and seed from animals; thus it was and thus it ever will be. These are the Zanādiqah or irreligious people.

The second group, the *Naturalists,* are a body of philosophers who have engaged in manifold researches into the world of nature and the marvels of animals and plants and have expended much effort in the science of dissecting the organs of animals. They see there sufficient of the wonders of God's creation and the inventions of His wisdom to compel them to acknowledge a wise Creator Who is aware of the aims and purposes of things. No one can make a careful study of anatomy and the wonderful uses of the members and organs without attaining to the necessary knowledge that there is a perfection in the order which the frame gave to the animal frame, and especially to that of man.

Yet these philosophers, immersed in their researches into nature, take the view that the equal balance of the temperament has great influence in constituting the powers of animals. They hold that even the intellectual power in man is dependent on the temperament, so that as the temperament is corrupted, intellect also is corrupted and ceases to exist. Further, when a thing ceases to exist, it is unthinkable in their opinion that the non-existent should return to existence. Thus it is their view that the soul dies and does not return to life, and they deny the future life—heaven, hell, resurrection and judgement; there does not remain, they hold, any reward for obedience or any punishment for sin. With the curb removed they give way to a bestial indulgence of their appetites.

These are also irreligious for the basis of faith is faith in God and in the Last Day, and these, though believing in God and His attributes, deny the Last Day.

The third group, the *Theists*, are the more modern philosophers and include Socrates, his pupil Plato, and the latter's pupil Aristotle. It was Aristotle who systematized logic for them and organized the sciences, securing a higher degree of accuracy and bringing them to maturity.

The Theists in general attacked the two previous groups, the Materialists and the Naturalists, and exposed their defects so effectively that others were relieved of the task. 'And God relieved the believers of fighting' (Q. 33, 25) through their mutual combat. Aristotle, moreover, attacked his predecessors among the Theistic philosophers, especially Plato and Socrates, and went so far in his criticisms that he separated himself from them all. Yet he too retained a residue of their unbelief and heresy from which he did not manage to free himself. We must therefore reckon as unbelievers both these philosophers themselves and their followers among the Islamic philosophers, such as Ibn Sīnā, al-Fārābī and others; in transmitting the philosophy of Aristotle, however, none of the Islamic philosophers has accomplished anything comparable to the achievements of the two men named. The translations of others are marked by disorder and confusion, which so perplex the understanding of the student that he fails to comprehend; and if a thing is not comprehended how can it be either refuted or accepted?

All that, in our view, genuinely is part of the philosophy of Aristotle, as these men have transmitted it, falls under three heads: (1) what must be counted as unbelief; (2) what must be counted as heresy; (3) what is not to be denied at all. Let us proceed, then, to the details.

B. *The Various Philosophical Sciences.* For our present purpose the philosophical sciences are six in number: mathematics, logic, natural science, theology, politics, ethics.

1. Mathematics. This embraces arithmetic, plane geometry and solid geometry. None of its results are connected with religious matters, either to deny or to affirm them. They are matters of demonstration which it is impossible to deny once they have been understood and apprehended. Nevertheless there are two drawbacks which arise from mathematics.

(a) The first is that every student of mathematics admires its precision and the clarity of its demonstration. This leads him to believe in the philosophers and to think that all their sciences resemble this one in clarity and demonstrative cogency. Further, he has already heard the accounts on everyone's lips of their unbelief, their denial of God's attributes, and their contempt for revealed truth; he becomes an unbeliever merely by accepting them as authorities (*bi'l-taqlīd al-mahd*), and says to himself, 'If religion were true, it would not have escaped the notice of these men since they are so precise in this science'. Thus, after becoming acquainted by hearsay with their unbelief and denial of religion, he draws the conclusion that the truth is the denial and rejection of religion. How many have I seen who err from the truth because of this high opinion of the philosophers and without any other basis!

Against them one may argue: 'The man who excels in one art does not necessarily excel in every art. It is not necessary that the man who excels in law and theology should excel in medicine, nor that the man who is ignorant of intellectual speculations should be ignorant of grammar. Rather, every art has people who have obtained excellence and preeminence in it, even though stupidity and ignorance may characterize them in other arts. The arguments in elementary matters of mathematics are demonstrative whereas those in theology (or metaphysics) are based on conjecture. This point is familiar only to those who have studied the matter deeply for themselves'.

If such a person is fixed in this belief which he has chosen out of respect for authority (taqlīd), he is not moved by this argument but is carried by strength of passion, love of vanity and the desire to be thought clever to persist in his good opinion of the philosophers with regard to all the sciences.

This is a great drawback, and because of it those who devote themselves eagerly to the mathematical sciences ought to be restrained. Even if their subject-matter is not relevant to religion, yet, since they belong to the foundations of the philosophical sciences, the student is infected with the evil and corruption of the philosophers. Few there are who devote themselves to this study without being stripped of religion and having the bridle of godly fear removed from their heads.

(b) The second drawback arises from the man who is loyal to Islam but ignorant. He thinks that religion must be defended by rejecting every science connected with the philosophers, and so rejects all their sciences and accuses them of ignorance therein. He even rejects their theory of the eclipse of sun and moon, considering that what they say is contrary to revelation. When that view is thus attacked, someone hears who has knowledge of such matters by apodeictic demonstration. He does not doubt his demonstration, but, believing that Islam is based on ignorance and the denial of apodeictic proof, grows in love for philosophy and hatred for Islam.

A grievous crime indeed against religion has been committed by the man who imagines that Islam is defended by the denial of the mathematical sciences, seeing that there is nothing in revealed truth opposed to these sciences by way of either negation or affirmation, and nothing in these sciences opposed to the truths of religion. Muhammad (peace be upon him) said, 'The sun and the moon are two of the signs of God; they are not eclipsed for anyone's death nor for his life; if you see such an event, take refuge in the recollection of God (most high) and in prayer'. There is nothing here obliging us to deny the science of arithmetic which informs us specifically of the orbits of sun and moon, and their conjunction and opposition. (The further saying of Muhammad (peace be upon him), 'When God manifests Himself to a thing, it submits to Him', is an addition which does not occur at all in the collections of sound Traditions.)

This is the character of mathematics and its drawbacks.

2. Logic. Nothing in logic is relevant to religion by way of denial or affirmation. Logic is the study of the methods of demonstration and of forming syllogisms, of the conditions for the premises of proofs, of the manner of combining the premises, of the conditions for sound definition and the manner of

ordering it. Knowledge comprises (a) the concept (*taṣawwur*), which is apprehended by definition, and (b) the assertion or judgement (*taṣdīq*), which is apprehended by proof. There is nothing here which requires to be denied. Matters of this kind are actually mentioned by the theologians and speculative thinkers in connection with the topic of demonstrations. The philosophers differ from these only in the expressions and technical terms they employ and in their greater elaboration of the explanations and classifications. An example of this is their proposition, 'If it is true that all A is B, then it follows that some B is A', that is, 'If it is true that all men are animals, then it follows that some animals are men'. They express this by saying that 'the universal affirmative proposition has as its converse a particular affirmative proposition'. What connection has this with the essentials of religion, that it should be denied or rejected? If such a denial is made, the only effect upon the logicians is to impair their belief in the intelligence of the man who made the denial and, what is worse, in his religion inasmuch as he considers that it rests on such denials.

Moreover, there is a type of mistake into which students of logic are liable to fall. They draw up a list of the conditions to be fulfilled by demonstration, which are known without fail to produce certainty. When, however, they come at length to treat of religious questions, not merely are they unable to satisfy these conditions, but they admit an extreme degree of relaxation (*sc.* of their standards of proof). Frequently, too, the student who admires logic and sees its clarity, imagines that the infidel doctrines attributed to the philosophers are supported by similar demonstrations, and hastens into unbelief before reaching the theological (or metaphysical) sciences. Thus this drawback too leads to unbelief.

3. Natural Science or Physics. This is the investigation of the sphere of the heavens together with the heavenly bodies, and of what is beneath the heavens, both simple bodies like water, air, earth, fire, and composite bodies like animals, plants and minerals, and also of the causes of their changes, transformations and combinations. This is similar to the investigation by medicine of the human body with its principal and subordinate organs, and of the causes of the changes of temperament. Just as it is not a condition of religion to reject medical science, so likewise the rejection of natural science is not one of its conditions, except with regard to particular points which I enumerate in my book, *The Incoherence of the Philosophers*. Any other points on which a different view has to be taken from the philosophers are shown by reflection to be implied in those mentioned. The basis of all these objections is the recognition that nature is in subjection to God most high, not acting of itself but serving as an instrument in the hands of its Creator. Sun and moon, stars and elements, are in subjection to His command. There is none of them whose activity is produced by or proceeds from its own essence.

4. Theology or Metaphysics. Here occur most of the errors of the philosophers. They are unable to satisfy the conditions of proof they lay down in logic, and consequently differ much from one another here. The views of Aristotle, as expounded by al-Fārābī and Ibn Sīnā, are close to those of the Islamic writers. All their errors are comprised under twenty heads, on three of which they must be reckoned infidels and on seventeen heretics. It was to show the falsity of

their views on these twenty points that I composed *The Incoherence of the Philosophers*. The three points in which they differ from all the Muslims are as follows:

(a) They say that for bodies there is no resurrection; it is bare spirits which are rewarded or punished; and the rewards and punishments are spiritual, not bodily. They certainly speak truth in affirming the spiritual ones, since these do exist as well; but they speak falsely in denying the bodily ones and in their pronouncements disbelieve the Divine law.

(b) They say that God knows universals but not particulars. This too is plain unbelief. The truth is that 'there does not escape Him the weight of an atom in the heavens or in the earth' (Q. 34, 3).

(c) They say that the world is everlasting, without beginning or end. But no Muslim has adopted any such view on this question.

On the further points—their denial of the attributes of God, their doctrine that God knows by His essence and not by a knowledge which is over and above His essence, and the like—their position approximates to that of the Mu'tazilah; and the Mu'tazilah must not be accounted infidels because of such matters. In my book, *The Decisive Criterion for Distinguishing Islam from Heresy,* I have presented the grounds for regarding as corrupt the opinion of those who hastily pronounce a man an infidel if he deviates from their own system of doctrine.

5. Politics. All their discussion of this is based on considerations of worldly and governmental advantage. These they borrow from the Divine scriptures revealed through the prophets and from the maxims handed down from the saints of old.

6. Ethics. Their whole discussion of ethics consists in defining the characteristics and moral constitution of the soul and enumerating the various types of soul and the method of moderating and controlling them. This they borrow from the teaching of the mystics, those men of piety whose chief occupation is to meditate upon God, to oppose the passions, and to walk in the way leading to God by withdrawing from worldly pleasure. In their spiritual warfare they have learnt about the virtues and vices of the soul and the defects in its actions, and what they have learned they have clearly expressed. The philosophers have taken over this teaching and mingled it with their own disquisitions, furtively using this embellishment to sell their rubbishy wares more readily. Assuredly there was in the age of the philosophers, as indeed there is in every age, a group of those godly men, of whom God never denudes the world. They are the pillars of the earth, and by their blessings mercy comes down on the people of the earth, as we read in the Tradition where Muhammad (peace be upon him) says: 'Through them you receive rain, through them you receive sustenance; of their number were the men of the Cave'. And these, as the Qur'an declares, existed in early times (cp. Surah 18).

From this practice of the philosophers of incorporating in their books conceptions drawn from the prophets and mystics, there arise two evil tendencies, one in their partisans and one in their opponents.

(a) The evil tendency in the case of the opponent is serious. A crowd of men of slight intellect imagines that, since those ethical conceptions occur in the books of the philosophers mixed with their own rubbish, all reference to them must be avoided, and indeed any person mentioning them must be considered a liar. They imagine this because they heard of the conceptions in the first place only from the philosophers, and their weak intellects have concluded that, since their author is a falsifier, they must be false.

This is like a man who hears a Christian assert, 'There is no god but God, and Jesus is the Messenger of God'. The man rejects this, saying, 'This is a Christian conception', and does not pause to ask himself whether the Christian is an infidel in respect of this assertion or in respect of his denial of the prophethood of Muhammad (peace be upon him). If he is an infidel only in respect to his denial of Muhammad, then he need not be contradicted in other assertions, true in themselves and not connected with his unbelief, even though these are also true in his eyes.

It is customary with weaker intellects thus to take the men as criterion of the truth and not the truth as criterion of the men. The intelligent man follows 'Alī (may God be pleased with him) when he said, 'Do not know the truth by the men, but know the truth, and then you will know who are truthful'. The intelligent man knows the truth; then he examines the particular assertion. If it is true, he accepts it, whether the speaker is a truthful person or not. Indeed he is often anxious to separate out the truth from the discourses of those who are in error, for he knows that gold is found mixed in gravel with dross. The money-changer suffers no harm if he puts his hand into the counterfeiter's purse; relying on his skill he picks the true gold from among the spurious and counterfeit coins. It is only the simple villager, not the experienced money-changer, who is made to abstain from dealings with the counterfeiter. It is not the strong swimmer who is kept back from the shore, but the clumsy tiro; not the accomplished snake-charmer who is barred from touching the snake, but the ignorant boy.

The majority of men, I maintain, are dominated by a high opinion of their own skill and accomplishments, especially the perfection of their intellects for distinguishing true from false and sure guidance from misleading suggestion. It is therefore necessary, I maintain, to shut the gate so as to keep the general public from reading the books of the misguided as far as possible. The public are not free from the infection of the second bad tendency we are about to discuss, even if they are uninfected by the one just mentioned.

To some of the statements made in our published works on the principles of the religious sciences an objection has been raised by a group of men whose understanding has not fully grasped the sciences and whose insight has not penetrated to the fundamentals of the systems. They think that these statements are taken from the works of the ancient philosophers, whereas the fact is that some of them are the product of reflections which occurred to me independently—it is not improbable that one shoe should fall on another shoe-mark—while others come from the revealed Scriptures, and in the case of the majority the sense though perhaps not the actual words is found in the works of the mystics.

Suppose, however, that the statements are found only in the philosophers' books. If they are reasonable in themselves and supported by proof, and if they do not contradict the Book and the Sunnah (the example of Muhammad), then it is not necessary to abstain from using them. If we open this door, if we adopt the attitude of abstaining from every truth that the mind of a heretic has apprehended before us, we should be obliged to abstain from much that is true. We should be obliged to leave aside a great number of the verses of the Qur'an and the Traditions of the Messenger and the accounts of the early Muslims, and all the sayings of the philosophers and the mystics. The reason for that is that the author of the book of the 'Brethren of Purity' has cited them in his work. He argues from them, and by means of them he has gradually enticed men of weaker understanding to accept his falsehoods; he goes on making those claims until the heretics wrest truth from our hands by thus depositing it in their writings.

The lowest degree of education is to distinguish oneself from the ignorant ordinary man. The educated man does not loathe honey even if he finds it in the surgeon's cupping-glass; he realizes that the cupping-glass does not essentially alter the honey. The natural aversion from it in such a case rests on popular ignorance arising from the fact that the cupping-glass is made only for impure blood. Men imagine that the blood is impure because it is in the cupping-glass, and are not aware that the impurity is due to a property of the blood itself. Since this property is absent from the honey, the fact that the honey is in such a container does not produce this property in it. Impurity, therefore, should not be attributed to the honey. To do so is fanciful and false.

Yet this is the prevalent idea among the majority of men. Wherever one ascribes a statement to an author of whom they approve, they accept it, even although it is false; wherever one ascribes it to an author of whom they disapprove, they reject it even although it is true. They always make the man the criterion of truth and not truth the criterion of the man; and that is erroneous in the extreme.

This is the wrong tendency towards rejection of the ethics of the philosophers.

(b) There is also a wrong tendency towards accepting it. When a man looks into their books, such as the 'Brethren of Purity' and others, and sees how, mingled with their teaching, are maxims of the prophets and utterances of the mystics, he often approves of these, and accepts them and forms a high opinion of them. Next, however, he readily accepts the falsehood they mix with that, because of the good opinion resulting from what he noticed and approved. That is a way of gradually slipping into falsehood.

Because of this tendency it is necessary to abstain from reading their books on account of the deception and danger in them. Just as the poor swimmer must be kept from the slippery banks, so must mankind be kept from reading these books; just as the boy must be kept from touching the snake, so must the ears be kept from receiving such utterances. Indeed, just as the snake-charmer must refrain from touching the snake in front of his small boy, because he knows that the boy imagines he is like his father and will imitate him, and must even caution the boy by himself showing caution in front of him, so the first-rate scholar too must act in similar fashion. And just as the good snake-charmer on receiving a snake distinguishes between the antidote and the poison, and extracts the antidote while destroying the poison, and would not withhold the antidote from any in need; and just as the acute and experienced money-changer, after putting his hand into the bag of the counterfeiter and extracting from it the pure gold and throwing away the spurious and counterfeit coins, would not withhold the good and acceptable money from one in need; even so does the scholar act.

Again, when a man has been bitten by a snake and needs the antidote, his being turns from it in loathing because he learns it is extracted from the snake, the source of the poison, and he requires to be shown the value of the antidote despite its source. Likewise, a poor man in need of money, who shrinks from receiving the gold taken out of the bag of the counterfeiter, ought to have it brought to his notice that his shrinking is pure ignorance and is the cause of his missing the bene-fit he seeks; he ought to be informed that the proximity between the counterfeit and the good coin does not make the good coin counterfeit nor the counterfeit good. In the same way the proximity between truth and falsehood does not make truth falsehood nor falsehood truth.

This much we wanted to say about the baneful and mischievous influence of philosophy.

. . .

4. THE WAYS OF MYSTICISM

When I had finished with these sciences, I next turned with set purpose to the method of mysticism (or Sufism). I knew that the complete mystic 'way' includes both intellectual belief and practical activity; the latter consists in getting rid of the obstacles in the self and in stripping off its base characteristics and vicious morals, so that the heart may attain to freedom from what is not God and to constant recollection of Him.

The intellectual belief was easier to me than the practical activity. I began to acquaint myself with their belief by reading their books, such as *The Food of the Hearts* by Abū Ṭālib al-Makkī (God have mercy upon him), the works of al-Ḥārith al-Muḥāsibī, the various anecdotes about al-Junayd, ash-Shiblī and Abū Yazīd al-Bisṭāmī (may God sanctify their spirits), and other discourses of their leading men. I thus comprehended their fundamental teachings on the intellectual side, and progressed, as far as is possible by study and oral instruction, in the knowledge of mysticism. It became clear to me, however, that what is most dis-tinctive of mysticism is something which cannot be apprehended by study, but only by immediate experience (*dhawq*—literally 'tasting'), by ecstasy and by a moral change. What a difference there is between *knowing* the definition of health and satiety, together with their causes and presuppositions, and *being* healthy and satisfied! What a difference between being acquainted with the definition of drunkenness—namely, that it designates a state arising from the domination of the seat of the intellect by vapours arising from the stomach—and being drunk! Indeed, the drunken man while in that condition does not know the definition of drunkenness nor the scientific account of it; he has not the very least scientific knowledge of it. The sober man, on the other hand, knows the definition of drunk-enness and its basis, yet he is not drunk in the very least. Again the doctor, when he is himself ill, knows the definition and causes of health and the remedies which restore it, and yet is lacking in health. Similarly there is a difference between knowing the true nature and causes and conditions of the ascetic life and actually leading such a life and forsaking the world.

I apprehended clearly that the mystics were men who had real experiences, not men of words, and that I had already progressed as far as was possible by way of intellectual apprehension. What remained for me was not to be attained by oral instruction and study but only by immediate experience and by walking in the mystic way.

Now from the sciences I had laboured at and the paths I had traversed in my investigation of the revelational and rational sciences (that is, presumably, theology and philosophy), there had come to me a sure faith in God most high, in prophet-hood (or revelation), and in the Last Day. These three credal principles were firmly rooted in my being, not through any carefully argued proofs, but by reason of various causes, coincidences and experiences which are not capable of being stated in detail.

It had already become clear to me that I had no hope of the bliss of the world to come save through a God-fearing life and the withdrawal of myself from vain desire. It was clear to me too that the key to all this was to sever the attachment of the heart to worldly things by leaving the mansion of deception and returning to that of eternity, and to advance towards God most high with all earnestness. It was also clear that this was only to be achieved by turning away from wealth and position and fleeing from all time-consuming entanglements.

Next I considered the circumstances of my life, and realized that I was caught in a veritable thicket of attachments. I also considered my activities, of which the best was my teaching and lecturing, and realized that in them I was dealing with sciences that were unimportant and contributed nothing to the attainment of eternal life.

After that I examined my motive in my work of teaching, and realized that it was not a pure desire for the things of God, but that the impulse moving me was the desire for an influential position and public recognition. I saw for certain that I was on the brink of a crumbling bank of sand and in imminent danger of hell-fire unless I set about to mend my ways.

I reflected on this continuously for a time, while the choice still remained open to me. One day I would form the resolution to quit Baghdad and get rid of these adverse circumstances; the next day I would abandon my resolution. I put one foot forward and drew the other back. If in the morning I had a genuine longing to seek eternal life, by the evening the attack of a whole host of desires had reduced it to impotence. Worldly desires were striving to keep me by their chains just where I was, while the voice of faith was calling, 'To the road! to the road! What is left of life is but little and the journey before you is long. All that keeps you busy, both intellectually and practically, is but hypocrisy and delusion. If you do not prepare *now* for eternal life, when will you prepare? If you do not now sever these attachments, when will you sever them?' On hearing that, the impulse would be stirred and the resolution made to take to flight.

Soon, however, Satan would return. 'This is a passing mood', he would say; 'do not yield to it, for it will quickly disappear; if you comply with it and leave this influential position, these comfortable and dignified circumstances where you are free from troubles and disturbances, this state of safety and security where you are untouched by the contentions of your adversaries, then you will probably come to yourself again and will not find it easy to return to all this'.

For nearly six months beginning with Rajab 488 A.H. (= July 1095 A.D.), I was continuously tossed about between the attractions of worldly desires and the impulses towards eternal life. In that month the matter ceased to be one of choice and became one of compulsion. God caused my tongue to dry up so that I was prevented from lecturing. One particular day I would make an effort to lecture in order to gratify the hearts of my following, but my tongue would not utter a single word nor could I accomplish anything at all.

This impediment in my speech produced grief in my heart, and at the same time my power to digest and assimilate food and drink was impaired; I could hardly swallow or digest a single mouthful of food. My powers became so weakened that the doctors gave up all hope of successful treatment. 'This trouble arises from the heart', they said, 'and from there it has spread through the constitution; the only method of treatment is that the anxiety which has come over the heart should be allayed'.

Thereupon, perceiving my impotence and having altogether lost my power of choice, I sought refuge with God most high as one who is driven to Him, because he is without further resources of his own. He answered me, He who 'answers him who is driven (to Him by affliction) when he calls upon Him' (Qur'an 27, 63). He made it easy for my heart to turn away from position and wealth, from children and friends. I openly professed that I had resolved to set out for Mecca, while privately I made arrangements to travel to Syria. I took this precaution in case the Caliph and all my friends should oppose my resolve to make my residence in Syria. This stratagem for my departure from Baghdad I gracefully executed, and had it in my mind never to return there. There was much talk about me among all the religious leaders of 'Iraq, since none of them would allow that withdrawal from such a state of life as I was in could have a religious cause, for they looked upon that as the culmination of a religious career; that was the sum of their knowledge.

Much confusion now came into people's minds as they tried to account for my conduct. Those at a distance from 'Iraq supposed that it was due to some apprehension I had of action by the government. On the other hand those who were close to the governing circles and had witnessed how eagerly and assiduously they sought me and how I withdrew from them and showed no great regard for what they said, would say, 'This is a supernatural affair; it must be an evil influence which has befallen the people of Islam and especially the circle of the learned'.

I left Baghdad, then. I distributed what wealth I had, retaining only as much as would suffice myself and provide sustenance for my children. This I could easily manage, as the wealth of 'Iraq was available for good works, since it constitutes a trust fund for the benefit of the Muslims. Nowhere in the world have I seen better financial arrangements to assist a scholar to provide for his children.

In due course I entered Damascus, and there I remained for nearly two years with no other occupation than the cultivation of retirement and solitude, together with religious and ascetic exercises, as I busied myself purifying my soul, improving my character and cleansing my heart for the constant recollection of God most high, as I had learnt from my study of mysticism. I used to go into retreat for a period in the mosque of Damascus, going up the minaret of the mosque for the whole day and shutting myself in so as to be alone.

At length I made my way from Damascus to the Holy House (that is Jerusalem). There I used to enter into the precinct of the Rock every day and shut myself in.

Next there arose in me a prompting to fulfil the duty of the Pilgrimage, gain the blessings of Mecca and Medina, and perform the visitation of the Messenger of God most high (peace be upon him), after first performing the visitation of al-Khalil, the Friend of God (God bless him).* I therefore made the journey to the Hijaz. Before long, however, various concerns, together with the entreaties of my children, drew me back to my home (country); and so I came to it again, though at one time no one had seemed less likely than myself to return to it.

---

* That is, Abraham, who is buried in the cave of Machpelah under the mosque at Hebron, which is called 'al-Khalil', in Arabic; similarly the visitation of the Messenger is the formal visit to his tomb at Medina.

Here, too, I sought retirement, still longing for solitude and the purification of the heart for the recollection (of God). The events of the interval, the anxieties about my family, and the necessities of my livelihood altered the aspect of my purpose and impaired the quality of my solitude, for I experienced pure ecstasy only occasionally, although I did not cease to hope for that; obstacles would hold me back, yet I always returned to it.

I continued at this stage for the space of ten years, and during these periods of solitude there were revealed to me things innumerable and unfathomable. This much I shall say about that in order that others may be helped: I learnt with certainty that it is above all the mystics who walk on the road of God; their life is the best life, their method the soundest method, their character the purest character; indeed, were the intellect of the intellectuals and the learning of the learned and the scholarship of the scholars, who are versed in the profundities of revealed truth, brought together in the attempt to improve the life and character of the mystics, they would find no way of doing so; for to the mystics all movement and all rest, whether external or internal, brings illumination from the light of the lamp of prophetic revelation; and behind the light of prophetic revelation there is no other light on the face of the earth from which illumination may be received.

In general, then, how is a mystic 'way' (*tarīqah*) described? The purity which is the first condition of it (*sc.* as bodily purity is the prior condition of formal Worship for Muslims) is the purification of the heart completely from what is other than God most high; the key to it, which corresponds to the opening act of adoration in prayer, is the sinking of the heart completely in the recollection of God; and the end of it is complete absorption (*fanā'*) in God. At least this is its end relatively to those first steps which almost come within the sphere of choice and personal responsibility; but in reality in the actual mystic 'way' it is the first step, what comes before it being, as it were, the antechamber for those who are journeying towards it.

With this first stage of the 'way' there begin the revelations and visions. The mystics in their waking state now behold angels and the spirits of the prophets; they hear these speaking to them and are instructed by them. Later, a higher state is reached; instead of beholding forms and figures, they come to stages in the 'way' which it is hard to describe in language; if a man attempts to express these, his words inevitably contain what is clearly erroneous.

In general what they manage to achieve is nearness to God; some, however, would conceive of this as 'inherence' (*ḥulūl*), some as 'union' (*ittiḥād*), and some as 'connection' (*wuṣūl*). All that is erroneous. In my book, *The Noblest Aim*, I have explained the nature of the error here. Yet he who has attained the mystic 'state' need do no more than say:

> Of the things I do not remember, what was, was;
> Think it good; do not ask an account of it. (Ibn al-Mu'tazz).

In general the man to whom He has granted no immediate experience at all, apprehends no more of what prophetic revelation really is than the name. The miraculous graces given to the saints are in truth the beginnings of the prophets; and that was the first 'state' of the Messenger of God (peace be upon him) when he went out to Mount Ḥirā', and was given up entirely to his Lord, and worshipped, so that the bedouin said, 'Muhammad loves his Lord passionately'.

Now this is a mystical 'state' which is realized in immediate experience by those who walk in the way leading to it. Those to whom it is not granted to have immediate experience can become assured of it by trial (*sc.* contact with mystics or observation of them) and by hearsay, if they have sufficiently numerous opportunities of associating with mystics to understand that (*sc.* ecstasy) with certainty by means of what accompanies the 'states'. Whoever sits in their company derives from them this faith; and none who sits in their company is pained.

Those to whom it is not even granted to have contacts with mystics may know with certainty the possibility of ecstasy by the evidence of demonstration, as I have remarked in the section entitled *The Wonders of the Heart* of my *Revival of the Religious Sciences*.

Certainty reached by demonstration is *knowledge* (*'ilm*); actual acquaintance with that 'state' is *immediate experience* (*dhawq*); the acceptance of it as probable from hearsay and trial (or observation) is *faith* (*īmān*). These are three degrees. 'God will raise those of you who have faith and those who have been given knowledge in degrees (*sc.* of honour)' (Q. 58, 12).

Behind the mystics, however, there is a crowd of ignorant people. They deny this fundamentally, they are astonished at this line of thought, they listen and mock. 'Amazing', they say. 'What nonsense they talk'! About such people God most high has said: 'Some of them listen to you, until, upon going out from you, they say to those to whom knowledge has been given, 'What did he say just now'? These are the people on whose hearts God sets a seal and they follow their passions' (Q. 47, 18). He makes them deaf, and blinds their sight.

Among the things that necessarily became clear to me from my practice of the mystic 'way' was the true nature and special characteristics of prophetic revelation. The basis of that must undoubtedly be indicated in view of the urgent need for it.

IV. *The True Nature of Prophecy and the Compelling Need of All Creation for It*

You must know that the substance of man in his original condition was created in bareness and simplicity without any information about the worlds of God most high. These worlds are many, not to be reckoned save by God most high Himself. As He said, 'None knows the hosts of thy Lord save He' (Q. 74, 34). Man's information about the world is by means of perception; and every perception of perceptibles is created so that thereby man may have some acquaintance with a world (or sphere) from among existents. By 'worlds (or spheres)' we simply mean 'classes of existents'.

The first thing created in man was the sense of *touch*, and by it he perceives certain classes of existents, such as heat and cold, moisture and dryness, smoothness and roughness. Touch is completely unable to apprehend colours and noises. These might be non-existent so far as concerns touch.

Next there is created in him the sense of *sight*, and by it he apprehends colours and shapes. This is the most extensive of the worlds of sensibles. Next *hearing* is implanted in him, so that he hears sounds of various kinds. After that *taste* is created in him; and so on until he has completed the world of sensibles.

Next, when he is about seven years old, there is created in him *discernment* (or the power of distinguishing—*tamyīz*). This is a fresh stage in his development. He now apprehends more than the world of sensibles; and none of these additional factors (*sc.* relations, etc.) exists in the world of sense.

From this he ascends to another stage, and *intellect* (or reason) (*'aql*) is created in him. He apprehends things necessary, possible, impossible, things which do not occur in the previous stages.

Beyond intellect there is yet another stage. In this another eye is opened, by which he beholds the unseen, what is to be in the future, and other things which are beyond the ken of intellect in the same way as the objects of intellect are beyond the ken of the faculty of discernment and the objects of discernment are beyond the ken of sense. Moreover, just as the man at the stage of discernment would reject and disregard the objects of intellect were these to be presented to him, so some intellectuals reject and disregard the objects of prophetic revelation. That is sheer ignorance. They have no ground for their view except that this is a stage which they have not reached and which for them does not exist; yet they suppose that it is non-existent in itself. When a man blind from birth, who has not learnt about colours and shapes by listening to people's talk, is told about these things for the first time, he does not understand them nor admit their existence.

God most high, however, has favoured His creatures by giving them something analogous to the special faculty of prophecy, namely dreams. In the dream-state a man apprehends what is to be in the future, which is something of the unseen; he does so either explicitly or else clothed in a symbolic form whose interpretation is disclosed.

Suppose a man has not experienced this himself, and suppose that he is told how some people fall into a dead faint, in which hearing, sight and the other senses no longer function, and in this condition perceive the unseen. He would deny that this is so and demonstrate its impossibility. 'The sensible powers', he would say, 'are the causes of perception (or apprehension); if a man does not perceive things (*sc.* the unseen) when these powers are actively present, much less will he do so when the senses are not functioning'. This is a form of analogy which is shown to be false by what actually occurs and is observed. Just as intellect is one of the stages of human development in which there is an 'eye' which sees the various types of intelligible objects, which are beyond the ken of the senses, so prophecy also is the description of a stage in which there is an eye endowed with light such that in that light the unseen and other supra-intellectual objects become visible.

Doubt about prophetic revelation is either (a) doubt of its possibility in general, or (b) doubt of its actual occurrence, or (c) doubt of the attainment of it by a specific individual.

The proof of the possibility of there being prophecy and the proof that there has been prophecy is that there is knowledge in the world the attainment of which by reason is inconceivable; for example, in medical science and astronomy. Whoever researches in such matters knows of necessity that this knowledge is attained only by Divine inspiration and by assistance from God most high. It cannot be reached by observation. For instance there are some astronomical laws based on phenomena which occur only once in a thousand years; how can these be arrived at by personal observation? It is the same with the properties of drugs.

This argument shows that it is possible for there to be a way of apprehending these matters which are not apprehended by the intellect. This is the meaning of prophetic revelation. That is not to say that prophecy is merely an expression for such knowledge. Rather, the apprehending of this class of extra-intellectual objects is *one* of the properties of prophecy; but it has many other properties as well. The said property is but a drop in the ocean of prophecy. It has been singled out for mention because you have something analogous to it in what you apprehend in dreaming, and because you have medical and astronomical knowledge belonging to the same class, namely, the miracles of the prophets, for the intellectuals cannot arrive at these at all by any intellectual efforts.

The other properties of prophetic revelation are apprehended only by immediate experience (*dhawq*) from the practice of the mystic way, but this property of prophecy you can understand by an analogy granted you, namely, the dream-state. If it were not for the latter you would not believe in that. If the prophet possessed a faculty to which you had nothing analogous and which you did not understand, how could you believe in it? Believing presupposes understanding. Now that analogous experience comes to a man in the early stages of the mystic way. Thereby he attains to a kind of immediate experience, extending as far as that to which he has attained, and by analogy to a kind of belief (or assent) in respect of that to which he has not attained. Thus this single property is a sufficient basis for one's faith in the principle of prophecy.

If you come to doubt whether a specific person is a prophet or not, certainty can only be reached by acquaintance with his conduct, either by personal observation, or by hearsay as a matter of common knowledge. For example, if you are familiar with medicine and law, you can recognise lawyers and doctors by observing what they are, or, where observation is impossible, by hearing what they have to say. Thus you are not unable to recognise that al-Shāfi'ī (God have mercy upon him) is a lawyer and Galen a doctor; and your recognition is based on the facts and not on the judgement of someone else. Indeed, just because you have some knowledge of law and medicine, and examine their books and writings, you arrive at a necessary knowledge of what these men are.

Similarly, if you understand what it is to be a prophet, and have devoted much time to the study of the Qur'an and the Traditions, you will arrive at a necessary knowledge of the fact that Muhammad (God bless and preserve him) is in the highest grades of the prophetic calling. Convince yourself of that by trying out what he said about the influence of devotional practices on the purification of the heart—how truly he asserted that 'whoever lives out what he knows will receive from God what he does not know'; how truly he asserted that 'if anyone aids an evildoer, God will give that man power over him'; how truly he asserted that 'if a man rises up in the morning with but a single care (*sc.* to please God), God most high will preserve him from all cares in this world and the next'. When you have made trial of these in a thousand or several thousand instances, you will arrive at a necessary knowledge beyond all doubt.

By this method, then, seek certainty about the prophetic office, and not from the transformation of a rod into a serpent or the cleaving of the moon. For if you consider such an event by itself, without taking account of the numerous circumstances accompanying it—circumstances readily eluding the grasp of the intellect —then you might perhaps suppose that it was magic and deception and that it came from God to lead men astray; for 'He leads astray whom He will, and guides whom He will'. Thus the topic of miracles will be thrown back upon you; for if your faith is based on a reasoned argument involving the probative force of the miracle, then your faith is destroyed by an ordered argument showing the difficulty and ambiguity of the miracle.

Admit, then, that wonders of this sort are one of the proofs and accompanying circumstances out of the totality of your thought on the matter; and that you attain necessary knowledge and yet are unable to say specifically on what it is based. The case is similar to that of a man who receives from a multitude of people a piece of information which is a matter of common belief . . . He is unable to say that the certainty is derived from the remark of a single specific person; rather, its source is unknown to him; it is neither from outside the whole, nor is it from specific individuals. This is strong, intellectual faith. Immediate experience, on the other hand, is like actually witnessing a thing and taking it in one's hand. It is only found in the way of mysticism.

This is a sufficient discussion of the nature of prophetic revelation for my present purpose. I proceed to speak of the need for it.

THE INCOHERENCE OF THE PHILOSOPHERS

Concerning the Natural Sciences

. . .

FIRST QUESTION

The connection between what is customarily believed to be a cause and what is believed to be an effect is not necessary, according to our opinion; but each of the two [namely, cause and effect] is independent of the other.[1] The affirmation of one does not imply the affirmation of the other, nor does the denial of one imply the denial of the other; the existence of one does not necessitate the existence of the other, nor does the non-existence of one necessitate the non-existence of the other. [Take] for example: quenching thirst and drinking, satisfying hunger and eating, burning and contact with fire, light and sunrise, death and decapitation, healing and drinking medicine, relaxing the bowels and taking a purgative and so forth for all the things which are observed to be connected in medicine, astronomy, the arts, and the crafts—indeed the connection of these occurs because the decree of God preceded their being created in this sequence, not because the existence [of this connection] is necessary in itself, not receptive of separation. On the contrary, it is within the power [of God] to create satisfying hunger without eating, to create death without decapitation, to let life continue even if decapitation occurs, and so forth for all connections. The philosophers, however, deny the possibility of this and affirm its impossibility.

Since the investigation of these limitless cases would take too long, let us consider one example, namely, the burning of cotton when it is in contact with fire. We consider it possible that there should be contact between the two without burning and we [also] consider it possible that cotton should be turned into ashes without [having] contact with fire. [The philosophers] deny the possibility of this.

The discussion of this question has three points:

Translated by Arthur Hyman for this volume from Algazel, *Tahāfot al-Falāsifat*, ed. M. Bouyges, S. J., Beyrouth: Imprimerie Catholique, 1927.

1. Literally, this is not that and that not this.

The first point: The opponent asserts that the acting cause of burning is fire exclusively and that fire acts by nature not by choice, so that fire, when brought in contact with a subject receptive of it, cannot refrain from acting according to its nature.

This is what we deny. On the contrary, we say that it is God Who, either through the intermediation of angels or without any intermediation, is the acting cause of burning by creating blackness in the cotton, dividing it into its parts, making it burn, or [turning it into] ashes. Fire, however, is inanimate and does not have any action.

What is the proof [of the opponent] that fire is the acting cause? He has no other proof except the observation that burning occurs when there is contact with fire. However, observation only proves that one occurs together with the other, but it does not prove that one occurs through [the agency of] the other. Indeed, there is no other cause but [God]. There is no disagreement [between us and the philosophers[2] concerning the fact] that the introduction of the spirit and of the apprehensive and motive faculties into the semen of animals does not proceed from the natures contained [in the qualities of] heat, cold, moisture, and dryness, or that the father is not the acting cause of his son by depositing the semen into the womb, or that the father is not the acting cause of the son's life, sight, hearing and any of the other faculties which the son has. While it is well known that [these faculties] exist in the father, we do not say that they exist in the son through [the agency] of the father. On the contrary, their existence comes from the First One [God] either without any intermediation or through the intermediation of the angels that are appointed over the things that come to be. This is the argument that the philosophers who speak about the Artisan [God] are unable to answer; and our discussion is with them. It is clear then that the existence [of one thing] together with another does not prove that the existence [of the second] is through [the agency of the first].

We shall make this clear by means of an example. [Let us suppose that] there is a blind man whose eyes are covered by a membrane and who has never heard from anyone about the difference between night and day. If now the membrane is removed from his eyes while it is day, his eyelids are open, and he sees colors, he will think that the opening of his sight is the acting cause of the perception of the forms of colors that has occurred to his eyes. And he will think [further] that as long as his sight is sound and open, the obstruction removed, and the colored object present, it will undoubtedly be necessary that he sees. He will not understand that he cannot see [under these conditions] until the sun sets and the air is dark. Then he will know that the light of the sun is the cause of the impression of colors on his sight. On what evidence does [our] opponent believe that there exist causes in the principles of existence[3] from which there proceed these events when there is contact between them, unless it is that [these events] are constant, not non-existent, and that they are not bodies in motion that disappear? It [these events] would cease to exist or disappear, we would apprehend that they are separable and we would under-

2. Algazali now invokes an argument of the philosophers in order to undermine their position. The philosophers, whose primary spokesman, for Algazali, is Avicenna, had maintained that the causal interaction of inanimate bodies does not require extraneous acting causes, but that the introduction of the various faculties into animals does. These extraneous causes, according to the philosophers, are the incorporeal intelligences whom they identified with the angels of Scripture. The lowest of these intelligences, the Agent Intellect, was, according to Avicenna, the "Giver of Forms." The incorporeal intelligences ultimately depend on God.

3. In the principles of natural substances.

stand that there is a cause beyond our observation. There is no exception to this according to the arguments based on the principles [of the philosophers].[4]

For this reason the true philosophers agreed that these accidents and things which come to be, that occur when there is contact between bodies and, in general, when there is a change in their relation, proceed from the Giver of Forms, who is an angel or angels, so that they say that the impression of the forms of colors on the eye occurs through the Giver of Forms, and that sunrise, a sound pupil, and the colored body are only preparatory and preliminary for the subject's reception of these forms. They applied this [explanation] to everything that comes to be. Through this argument is refuted the claim of those who assert that fire is the acting cause of burning, bread the acting cause of satisfying hunger, medicine the acting cause of health, and so forth for other causes.

The second point: There is [an opponent] who admits that the things that come to be proceed from the principles of the things that come to be,[5] but that the predisposition [in the affected subject] for receiving the forms occurs through causes that are observed and present. They hold, however, that the principles from which proceed the things that come to be act by necessity and nature, not by way of deliberation and choice, as, for example, the procession of light from the sun. The subjects [which receive these forms] differ in respect to receptivity in accordance with the differences in their predispositions. [For example,] a polished body receives the rays of the sun and reflects them, so that another place is illumined by them, while an opaque body does not receive them [in such a manner]. Air does not prevent the penetration of sunlight, while a stone does. Some things become soft through the sun, while others become hard. Some things, like the fuller's garment, become white, others, like the fuller's face, become black. [In all these cases] the principle is one, but the effects are different because of a difference in the subject's predispositions. Thus there is no obstacle or incapacity in the principles of existence with respect to that which proceeds from them, but any shortcoming comes from the recipient subjects. If this is the case, and we posit fire and its properties and we [also] posit two similar pieces of cotton that are in contact with the fire in the same way, how can we conceive that one will burn, while the other will not? There is no choice [in this situation]. From this perspective [the proponents of this view] deny that Abraham was thrown into the fire without being burned, while the fire remained fire. They hold that this [occurrence] would only be possible if heat would be denied of fire, in which case fire would cease being fire, or through a change in the essence of Abraham [through which] his body would be changed into stone or into something on which fire has no effect. Neither of these alternatives is possible.

The answer to this opinion is *twofold:*

First: we say that we do not admit that [these] principles[6] do not act by choice, nor that God does not act by will. We have already refuted their claim concerning this in the question on the creation of the world.[7] If it is affirmed that the acting

---

4. By holding that the incorporeal intelligences, particularly the Giver of Forms, are acting causes in the sublunar world, the philosophers are forced to admit that, in the case of sublunar substances, there is no necessary connection between cause and effect. While the drift of the passage is clear, its final section is somewhat obscure.

5. That is, the incorporeal intelligences, particularly the Giver of Forms. The Abrahamic miracle mentioned further on is recorded in the Koran.

6. The principles of existence.

7. The first question of the *Incoherence* is devoted to a discussion of the creation of the world.

cause [God] creates burning through His will, when cotton and fire are in contact, then it is possible, according to reason, that He may not create burning when contact [between cotton and fire] exists.

[The opponent] could reply: this opinion leads to the perpetration of aboninable impossibilities. For if you deny the necessary connection between effects and causes and attribute [the effects] to the will of their Creator, and [maintain] that the will does not have a particular well-defined pattern, but that it is possible that it may vary and change, each one of us would have to consider it possible that there might be in his presence wild beasts, raging fires, high mountains, armed enemies, which he will not see, since God did not create sight in him. And someone who has left a book in his house might find, upon returning home, that [the book] has been changed into a handsome, intelligent, and efficient young slave or into an animal. Or if he left a young slave at home, he might find that he was changed into a dog, or having left ashes he might find them changed into musk, or a stone changed into gold, or gold into a stone. If he were asked about any of these things, he could properly answer: I do not know what is now in my house. The only thing I know is that I left a book in my house, but perhaps by now it has turned into a horse which dirties my library with its urine and excrement, and I have left in my house a jar of water which, perhaps, has changed into an apple tree. For God has power over everything. It is not necessary that a horse should be created from semen, nor is it necessary that a tree should be created from a seed. On the contrary, it is not necessary that it should be created from anything. Perhaps [God] created things which never existed before. Indeed, if someone sees a man whom he has never seen until now and he is asked: "has this man been born?" he might hesitate and answer: "perhaps he was one of the fruits in the market which was changed into a man and he is that man. God has the power over everything that is possible and [the occurrence of] this is possible. There is no escape from hesitation concerning this." One can go to any length in conceiving [objections] of this kind, but this much [discussion] is sufficient.

In answer to this argument we say: if it could be shown that the existence of the possible [implies] that knowledge of its non-existence cannot be created for man, these absurdities will necessarily follow. But we are not in doubt about the cases that you have described. Indeed, God has created within us knowledge that he will not bring about everything that is possible and we do not assert that everything possible will necessarily come to be. On the contrary, [we have asserted that] they are possible [whereby we mean that] they may happen or they may not happen. But if something happens habitually time after time, its [habitual] course will be firmly rooted in our minds in accordance with the habitual past occurrence in such a way that it cannot be removed from [the mind]. However, it is possible that a certain prophet may know, in the manner mentioned by [the philosophers],[8] that someone will not return from his journey tomorrow. Even though his return is possible, [the prophet] knows that this possibility will not be realized. Even if you consider an ordinary man and you are aware that he does not know any of these strange things nor can he apprehend the intelligible unless he is taught them, yet it cannot be denied that his soul and estimative faculties have the ability to apprehend what the prophets apprehend, insofar as [the prophets] are aware of the possibility of this event, know-

8. Algazali reports in the section preceding this selection that the philosophers admit that fore-knowledge of the future is possible.

ing at the same time that this possibility will not be realized. If God interrupts the habitual occurrence by producing [this unusual event], then at the time when the habitual occurrence is interrupted, He removes the knowledge [of the habitual occurrence] from [their] hearts and He does not create it. Nothing prevents us from affirming that, while something is possible for God's power, He knows through His eternal knowledge that He will not do it, even though it is possible at a certain time, and that He will create for us the knowledge that He will not do it at that time. And the statement of the philosophers is nothing but pure abomination.

The *second answer* [to the objection of the opponents] in which there is found an escape from the abominations [of the philosophers]: We admit that fire is created [by God] in such a manner that it will burn two similar pieces of cotton brought in contact with it, and [fire] does not differentiate between them if they are similar in every respect. Yet in spite of this, we consider it possible that a prophet is thrown into fire, yet is not burned, either because the property of fire is altered or because the property of the prophet is altered. [We explain this by affirming] that there comes to be from God or the angels a property in the fire which limits the heat of the fire to its own body, so that it will not pass over [to the body of the prophet]. Heat remains with the fire and fire retains its own form and true nature, yet its heat and effect do not pass over [to something else]. Or there comes to be in the body of the person [the prophet], a property which, while not keeping the body from being flesh and bone, keeps it from the effect of fire. [For example,] we see that someone covers himself with talc, sits down in a flaming oven, yet is not affected by it. Whoever has not observed this will deny it. The denial of the opponent that it is in [God's] power to confer a certain property upon fire or upon [a person's] body which prevents burning, is like the denial of someone who has not observed talc and its effect. In God's power there are strange and wondrous things, not all of which we have observed. How is it proper that we should deny their possibility or affirm their impossibility?

Similarly, the resurrection of the dead and the changing of a staff into a serpent[9] are possible in this way [as can be seen from the fact] that matter can receive every form,[10] so that earth and the other elements can be changed into a plant, a plant, when eaten by an animal, is changed into blood, blood is changed into semen; and semen, when ejaculated in the womb, creates an animal. This, according to the order of habitual occurrences, takes place over a long period of time. But why does [our] opponent deny that it is within God's power that matter should pass through these stages in a period of time shorter than usual? And if a shorter period of time is allowed, there is nothing that keeps it from being the shortest. As a result these powers are speeded up in their actions and through this the miracle of the prophet comes to be.

[Suppose] someone were to ask: does [the miracle] proceed from the soul of the prophet or from some other principles through the instigation of the prophet?[11]

9. This is an allusion to Moses' miracle which is reported in the Koran.

10. Literally, every thing.

11. In the section preceding this selection, Algazali reported that the philosophers accepted limited miracles. From the observation that the human soul can produce bodily effects, such as salivation when one thinks of something sweet, they go on to argue that the soul of the prophet can produce effects on other corporeal substances as well. For example, through the power of his soul he can produce rain, thunder, and earthquakes. However, these miracles are limited to ordinary natural occurrences, not to such things as turning a staff into a serpent.

We answer: when you admit that the downfall of rain, thunder, and earthquake occur through the power of the soul of the prophet, does this [miracle] occur through the soul of the prophet or through some other principle? What we say concerning our example is like what you say concerning yours.[12] According to us as well as according to you, it is best to attribute this to God, either without inter-mediation or with the intermediation of angels. When the time appropriate for the occurrence of the miracle has arrived, the mind of the prophet turns toward it. The order of the good becomes clear through its appearance, [and the miracle occurs] to preserve the order of the Law. [This need] determines its existence. In itself [the miracle] is possible, but [God's] generosity is the principle through which it comes to be. However, [the miracle] only proceeds from God when necessity determines its existence and good appears in it. And the good only appears in it when the prophet needs it to establish his prophetic office, in order to promulgate the good.[13]

All this is in agreement with what [the philosophers] have said and they must necessarily admit it, inasmuch as they have opened the gate by allowing the prophet a special property which distinguishes him from the customary run of people.[14] The mind cannot grasp the extent of the special property's possibility. There is no need to consider it false if it rests on [reliable] tradition and its truth is verified by the Law. In general, only the semen receives the form of the animal, and the animal faculties come upon it from the angels, who, according to the opinion [of the phi-losophers], are the principles of existing things; man is created only from the semen of a man and a horse only from the semen of a horse, inasmuch as its coming to be from a horse determines the preponderance of the form of a horse over other forms and it receives the preponderant form only in this way. Likewise barley does not come from wheat, nor an apple from the seed of a pear. We further see kinds of animals, such as worms, which are generated from dust, and these do not generate other animals at all. Then there are other animals, such as the mouse, the snake, and the scorpion, which are both not generated and generated from other animals, since they can [also] be generated from dust. The predispositions for receiving forms varies through causes hidden from us, and it is not within the power of flesh to know them. Since, according to the opinion [of the philosophers], these forms do not proceed from the angels through desire and through conjecture,[15] but they proceed upon every subject only insofar as there exists a receptivity [for these forms] through the existence of a predisposition in this subject. The predispositions differ, and their principles, according to [the opinion of the philosophers], are the configurations of the stars, and the different relations that the upper [celestial] bodies have in their motions. Through this theory the possibility is opened that there may be strange and wondrous things in the principles of these predispositions, so that those who master talismans can use their knowledge of particular properties of mineral

12. Literally, what we say concerning this is like what you say concerning that.

13. The points of this rather involuted passage are: God produces miracles through His gen-erosity; miracles occur only when they are necessary; miracles occur to authenticate the prophet and confirm the Law.

14. The following argument is designed to show that since the philosophers admit that the prophet can produce "ordinary" miracles, such as rainfall, thunder, and earthquakes, they are obligated to admit that he can also produce such "extraordinary" miracles as the staff's turning into a snake.

15. The forms proceed by necessity, but variations in their effects are determined by a difference in the predispositions of the subjects that receive them.

substances and their knowledge of the stars to combine celestial powers with particular properties of mineral substances.[16] And they select the figures of these earthly things and by seeking particular celestial powers for them, they can bring about strange things in the world. Sometimes they drive away snakes and scorpions from the city and [sometimes] bugs, and they bring about other things known to them through the science of the talisman.

Since the principles of these predispositions are not firm and we cannot discover their quantity and we have no way of knowing their limit, how can we know that it is impossible that some bodies should have predispositions, such that these bodies can pass through the phases of the transformation in a shorter time, as a result of which such a body would be disposed to receive a form, for the reception of which it was not predisposed before? This is considered a miracle. The denial of this only betrays a lack of understanding and an unfamiliarity with the upper [celestial] beings and an unawareness of the secrets of God in the created world and in nature. He who has studied the wonders of the sciences will not in any way consider it impossible for the power of God to bring about any of the things which are related concerning prophetic miracles.

If[17] [an opponent] were to say: we agree with you that everything possible is within the power of God and you agree [with us] that everything impossible is not within His power. [We further agree] that there are some things that are known to be impossible, some things that are known to be possible, and some things concerning which the intellect is undecided, affirming neither their impossibility nor their possibility. What, according to [your opinion], is the definition of the impossible? If it is the simultaneous·denial and affirmation of the same thing, then say of two things that one is independent of the other,[18] and that the existence of one does not require the existence of the other. And say [further], that God has the power to create will without knowledge of that which is willed and that He can create knowledge without life. [God also] has the power to move the hand of a dead man, make him sit, write volumes with his hand, engage in the sciences, while his eyes are open and his sight is directed toward what is in front of him, even though he does not see, is not alive, does not have any power. [The dead man writes], because God created these ordered actions when he moved his hand; and the motion comes from God. By regarding this as possible the distinction between a voluntary motion and trembling [an involuntary motion] is nullified, and a prudent act will not indicate the knowledge and power of the acting cause. It would be proper to affirm that God has the power to change genera, to change a substance into an accident, to change knowledge into power, blackness into whiteness, and sound into smell; just as He has the power to change a mineral into an animal, a stone into gold. From [your opinion] there would necessarily follow impossibilities without limit.

The answer: No one [not even God] has power over the impossible.[19] The impossible is: The simultaneous affirmation and denial of something; or the simul-

---

16. In the section preceding this selection, Algazali lists the talismanic art as one of the subsidiary natural sciences. He defines it as "the art of combining celestial powers with the powers of some earthly bodies to produce through this combination a power which can effect unusual things in the earthly [sublunar] world."

17. The section does not have any superscription, but it contains a discussion of the third point (see above, P. 283, bottom).

18. See above, note 1.

19. No one can do what is impossible.

taneous affirmation of the particular and the denial of the universal; or the simultaneous affirmation of two things and the denial of one of them.[20] Whatever does not fall under these [three cases] is not impossible, and what is not impossible, can be done. The co-existence of blackness and whiteness is impossible, since from the affirmation that the form of blackness exists in the subject, we understand the denial that the form of whiteness exists in the same subject and the existence of blackness. If the denial of whiteness is understood from the affirmation of blackness, then the simultaneous affirmation and denial of whiteness is impossible. It is [also] impossible that a certain person should be in two places [at the same time], since we understand from his being in the house that he cannot be outside the house; it is impossible that he should be simultaneously outside the house and in the house, since [his being in the house] is understood from the denial that he is outside the house. Likewise, we understand by will the seeking of something known. Now if seeking is supposed, but not knowledge, there cannot be will; for this supposition would contain the denial of what we have understood [by will]. Further, it is impossible that knowledge be created in a mineral, since we understand by mineral that which does not apprehend. If apprehension were created in it, it would be impossible to call it a mineral in the sense in which we understand [this term]; but if [the mineral] would not apprehend, it would be impossible to call the newly created property knowledge, inasmuch as its subject does not apprehend anything through it. This is the reason [why the creation of knowledge in minerals] is impossible.

Some of the Mutakallimūn maintain that God has the power to change genera.

We reply that it is unintelligible that something be changed into something else. If, for example, blackness is changed into power, blackness would remain or not remain. If it ceases to exist [that is, if it does not remain], it would not be changed, but it would not exist anymore, and something else would exist. If it would exist together with power, it would not be changed, but some other property would be joined to it. If blackness would remain and power would not exist, then [blackness] has not changed [at all], but it remains as it is. But if we say that blood is changed into semen, we mean thereby, that one and the same matter divested itself of one form and has taken on another form. As a result, one form ceases to exist while another form comes to be; but the matter remains the same for the two forms that succeed each other in it. When we say that water, when heated, is changed into air, we mean thereby that the matter which had received the form of water divests itself of this form and has received another form; the matter remains common, but the property [form] has been altered. The case is similar, when we say that the staff is changed into a serpent and dust into an animal. [By contrast,] there is no common matter for accident and substance, nor for blackness and power, nor is there a common matter for other genera. For this reason it is impossible that they should be changed into one another.

As for God's moving the hand of the dead man and raising him up in the form of a living [man] who sits, writes in such a way that through the motion of his hand an ordered script comes to be, this is not impossible in itself as long as we ascribe these events to the will of someone who acts by choice; they are only denied because the habitual course [of events] is denied by its rejection. But your assertion that our explanation will lead to the denial that a prudential act indicates the wisdom of the agent is incorrect, since in this case God is the acting cause, and He is prudent as

20. The three types of impossibilities are: (1) X is Y, X is not Y; (2) some X is Y, no X is Y; (3) X is both Y and Z, X is not Y (or Z).

well as the acting cause. To your objection that there would not remain any distinction between trembling [, an involuntary motion,] and a voluntary motion, we reply that we apprehend this distinction through ourselves, since we observe through ourselves a distinction between these two states and we affirm that the distinction between them comes to be through power. We know that one of these two possibles [namely, trembling and voluntary motion] occurs in one state, the other in another state, that is, in one state the movement is produced with power, in another state without power. Now, when we observe someone else and we see many ordered motions, we attain knowledge of the power behind them. God creates these [kinds] of knowledge by means of the habitual course [of events], through which becomes known the existence of one class of possibles. However, the impossibility of the second class is not proved thereby, as has been shown previously.

SELECTED BIBLIOGRAPHY

TRANSLATIONS

Abu Zayd, Abdu-r-Rahman, trans., *Al-Ghazālī on Divine Predicates and their Properties*, Lahore, 1970.

Bagley, F., trans., *Ghazāli's Book of the Counsel for Kings (Naṣīḥat al-Mulūk)*, New York, 1964.

Brewster, D., trans., *The Just Balance (Al-Qisṭas al-Mustaqim)*, Lahore, 1978.

Calverly, E., trans., *Worship in Islam: being a translation with commentary of the Ihyā on the worship*. Madras, 1925.

Faris, N., trans., *The Book of Knowledge*, Lahore, 1962.

Gairdner, W., trans., *Al-Ghazzālī's Mishkāt al-Anwār (The Niche for Lights)*, London, 1924.

Kamali, S., trans., *Tahafūt al Falāsifa*, Lahore, 1963. (A large portion of the work appears also in: S. Van den Bergh, trans., *Averroes' Tahafut al-Tahafut*, Vol. I, London, 1954.)

McCarthy, R., trans., *Freedom and Fulfillment*. An annotated translation of al-Ghazālī's *al-Munqidh min al-Dalāl* and other relevant works of al-Ghazālī, Boston, 1980.

Scherer, G., trans., *Al-Ghazali's Ayyuha 'l-Walad*, Beirut, 1933.

Watt, W., trans., *The Faith and Practice of al-Ghazali*, London, 1953.

STUDIES

Alon, I., "Al-Ghazālī on Causality," *Journal of the American Oriental Society*, C (1980), 397–405.

Bousquet, G., *Ghazali, Ih'ya 'ouloum ed-dīn, ou vivification des sciences de la foi; analyse et index*, Paris, 1955.

Bouyges, M., *Essai de chronologie des oeuvres de al-Ghazali (Algazel)*, Beyrouth, 1959.

Carra de Vaux, B., *Gazali*, Paris, 1902.

Gardner, W., *An Account of al-Ghazālī's Life and Works*, Madras, 1919.

Goodman, L., "Did al Ghazālī Deny Causality," *Studia Islamica*, XLVII (1978), 83–120.

Goodman, L., "Ghazālī's Argument from Creation," *Journal of Middle East Studies*, II (1971), 67–85, 168–188.

Gyekye, K., "Al-Ghazālī on Causation," *Second Order; an African Journal of Philosophy*, II (1973), 31–39.

Hourani, G., "Ghazālī on the Ethics of Action," *Journal of the American Oriental Society*, XCVI (1976), 69–88.

Jabre, F., *La notion de certitude selon Ghazali dans ses origines psychologiques et historiques*, Paris, 1958.

Jabre, F., *La notion de la Ma'rifa chez Ghazali*, Beirut, 1958.

Laoust, H., *La politique de Ghazali*, Paris, 1970.

L'Hopital, J.-Y., "Le point de vue de Ghazālī sur la condition de l'homme," *Arabica*, XXVI (1979), 274–297.

MacDonald, D., "The Life of al-Ghazzālī with

Special Reference to his Religious Experience and Opinions," *Journal of the American Oriental Society*, XX (1899), 71–132.

Marmura, M., "Ghazālī and Demonstrative Science," *Journal of the History of Philosophy*, III (1965), 183–204.

Marmura, M., "Ghazali's Attitude to the Secular Sciences and Logic," *Essays on Islamic Philosophy and Science*, ed., G. Hourani, Albany, 1975, pp. 100–111.

Marzouki, A., *Le concept de causalité chez Gazali*, Tunis, 1978.

Obermann, J., *Der philosophische und religiöse Subjektivismus Ghazālīs; ein Beitrag zum Problem der Religion*, Wien, 1921.

Sawwaf, A.-F., *Al-Ghazzali, études de la réforme ghazzalienne dans l'histoire de son developpement*, Fribourg, 1962.

Shanab, R., "Ghazālī and Aquinas on Causation," *Monist*, LVIII (1974), 140–150.

Shehadi, F., *Ghazali's Unknowable God*, Leiden, 1964.

Sherif, M., *Ghazali's Theory of Virtue*, Albany, 1975.

Smith, M., *Al-Ghazālī, the Mystic*, London, 1944.

Umaruddin, M., *The Ethical Philosophy of Al-Ghazali*, Aligarh, 1962.

Watt, W., *Muslim Intellectual; a Study of al-Ghazali*, Edinburgh, 1963.

Wensinck, A., *La pensée de Ghazzālī*, Paris, 1940.

Wolfson, H., "Nicolaus of Autrecourt and Ghazali's Arguments against Causality," *Speculum*, LXIV (1969), 234–238.

AVERROES

1126–1198

VERROES marked the climax of Muslim Aristotelianism and, at the same time, its virtual end. Historic circumstances deprived him of followers among his own people, but through translations of his works into Latin and Hebrew he found attentive students as well as faithful disciples among Christians and Jews. His incisive commentaries on most of Aristotle's works earned him the title "The Commentator" and his particular kind of Aristotelianism became a well-defined strand in the fabric of later medieval thought.

First and foremost Averroes was a commentator on Aristotle's works. As such he considered it his primary task to cleanse Aristotle's teachings of the impurities which had resulted from the erroneous interpretation of earlier commentators. His polemic was directed in particular against Avicenna who, so he thought, had capitulated to theological interests on certain crucial points. Then again, there appeared to be lacunae in Aristotle's works. Averroes had no doubts that the missing portions had been discussed by Aristotle in works no longer extant, but in his own days what was missing had to be supplied by judicious interpretation. Still further, the dialectical theologians had dealt with philosophic issues in faulty ways and their mistakes had to be corrected. And finally, Algazali (see p. 264) had launched a grand attack on Aristotelianism as a whole and this attack had to be repulsed.

Averroes' position is perhaps best characterized by his critique of a certain Avicennian point. Analyzing substances existing within the world, Avicenna had distinguished between their essence and existence, affirming at the same time that essence is ontologically prior to existence and that existence is something added to essence (see p. 235). Rejecting this Avicennian distinction, Averroes held that individual substances exist primarily and, though the mind can distinguish between essence and existence in them, ontologically speaking, the two are one. Thus, while for Avicenna essences were primary, for Averroes primacy belonged to individual substances.

In his physical teachings Averroes accepted the Aristotelian picture of the universe with its distinction between a sublunar and translunar world.

The sublunar world is subject to generation and corruption and substances within it are ultimately reducible to the four elements. The four elements, in turn, are composed of first matter and a substantial or elemental form. The translunar world, on the other hand, is eternal, and it consists of celestial spheres each of which is composed of a celestial body and an immaterial mover. Yet, upon this general scheme Averroes imposed modifications of his own. An example is provided by his doctrine of the corporeal form. To bridge the gap between Aristotle's prime matter (which is a rather enigmatic notion) and the elemental form, interpreters had posited a corporeal form. This form was common to all bodies and, according to some, it was related in some way to the property of dimensionality. Avicenna had defined the corporeal form as a form having a predisposition for receiving the three dimensions, insisting, however, that this form must differ from three-dimensionality, since form must be in the category of substance, while dimensionality must be in the category of quantity. For reasons which will appear in a selection below, Averroes accepted the alternative rejected by Avicenna, defining the corporeal form as being identical with indeterminate three-dimensionality. Similarly, Averroes differed from Avicenna in his description of the celestial movers. Invoking an analogy between man and the celestial spheres, both philosophers agreed that the celestial movers consist of soul and intellect. But whereas for Avicenna the celestial soul inhered within the celestial body while the celestial intelligence existed in separation from it, for Averroes soul and intelligence were but two aspects of the same immaterial celestial mover.

As in physics so in metaphysics, Averroes offered interpretations of his own. Avicenna had maintained that metaphysics not only investigates whatever can be known about God but also demonstrates that He exists. In support of this position he had formulated his famous proof of the existence of God, known as the proof from necessity and contingency (see p. 235). Taking issue with Avicenna, Averroes maintained that physics establishes the existence of the subject matter of metaphysics and that, moreover, Avicenna's proof is invalid. Avicenna's proof, he argued, requires that there exist beings possible through themselves and necessary through another; and it can be shown that such beings do not exist. Hence, for Averroes, only physical proofs, that is those which establish the existence of a prime mover, are valid for demonstrating that God exists.

In describing God and His relation to the world Averroes turned from the neoplatonic One to Aristotle's divine thought thinking itself. In thinking himself, God also thinks things and events within the world, and this is what is meant by providence. There is evidence that, according to Averroes, God thinks the things within the world as particulars. But God's knowledge, as he points out, is completely different from that of man. Averroes similarly turns from neoplatonic teachings in his account of creation. For Neoplatonists and their Muslim followers the major issue was to explain how a multiple world could come to be from an ultimate principle that was unique and

simple. The world, they held, came into being through successive emana-
tions such that each principle emanated from one above it in the scale of
being. The problem of the one principle and its many effects held little
interest for Averroes and, hence, he rejected the doctrine of emanation.
Creation, for him, meant the causal structure of the world, not its emanation
from a first principle. If things within the world are said to come from a first
principle at all, they all must come from that principle without the aid of
intermediary beings. To illustrate this point Averroes compares the world
to an army which is directed by a leader. With the rejection of emanation,
Averroes also denied Avicenna's "Giver of Forms," which is the Agent
Intellect insofar as it provides forms for sublunar beings. Creation does not
take place in time.

His doctrine of the intellect became one of those teachings for which Averroes was best known. Like earlier Muslims, he tried to give precision to the
various intellects of which Aristotle had spoken in his *De Anima* or which
the commentators had found implied in Aristotle's words. Averroes agreed
with other Muslims in identifying the Agent Intellect, required as an efficient
cause for thinking, with the lowest of the intelligences, namely that which
governs the sublunar sphere (see p. 212). But in describing the material intellect he formulated a doctrine of his own. Reviewing earlier opinions, he rejected that of Alexander of Aphrodisias who had identified this intellect with a
bodily predisposition, as well as that of Themistius and others who had identified it with an individual spiritual substance. Averroes held that the material
intellect, like any intellectual principle, must be immaterial and universal, that
is, it must be common to all men. This is Averroes' much-to-be-debated doctrine
of the unity of the intellect. It follows from Averroes' description that when
the material intellect becomes actualized, it remains one for all men and that
immortality, therefore, is general, not particular. Knowledge becomes particular through phantasms which accompany it in the imagination of everyone who
knows. Averroes identified Aristotle's passive intellect with the imagination.

In addition to commenting on Aristotle, Averroes also wrote on politics
and religion, following in the footsteps of Alfarabi and other Muslim
Aristotelians. Here his orientation was Platonic. With other Muslim
Aristotelians, he accepted Plato's notion of an ideal state to which he (as
they) added that it comes into being through a prophet-legislator. The state
is composed of different classes and the prophetic law must speak to all.
Averroes undertook to give a more specific description of the classes within
the state. Invoking Aristotelian logical principles, he divided the citizens into
the rulers who can follow demonstrations, the masses who are persuaded by
rhetorical arguments, and, between them, the dialectical theologians who can
understand dialectical discussions (see p. 301). But whereas Alfarabi advocated a refinement of popular religious beliefs, Averroes insisted that each
of the three classes must be taught on its own level. General philosophical
enlightenment, according to him, is proscribed. From this exposition it
follows that truth appears in three forms—demonstrative, dialectical, rhetori-

cal—the last two being primarily the province of religion. Whether Averroes finally saw all three forms of truth or only the first as productive of ultimate human happiness, has been debated by interpreters.

Abū al-Walīd Muhammad Ibn Aḥmad Ibn Rushd was born in 1126 in Cordova, son of a distinguished family of jurists. Though it is not known who his teachers were, it is evident from his works that he received thorough training in Islamic law as well as in the philosophical sciences. In 1153 he was in Marrakesh where he was in contact with the first Almohad ruler 'Abd al-Mu'min, perhaps in connection with a school which the ruler had founded at that time. Of the next period nothing is known but that he composed a book on medicine. In 1168 he was in Marrakesh once again and at this time Ibn Ṭufayl, vizier and court physician, introduced him to Abū Ya-'qūb Yūsuf, the son who had succeeded 'Abd al-Mu'min as ruler. According to one account, the ruler, at a meeting, asked Averroes what the Aristotelians think about the eternity of the world. Afraid, Averroes claimed to be not conversant with their teachings. But when the ruler, in conversation with Ibn Ṭufayl, showed that he was acquainted with philosophy and sympathetic to it, Averroes no longer hesitated to speak. Somewhat later Ibn Ṭufayl transmitted to Averroes the ruler's invitation to comment on Aristotle's works which he had found rather obscure. In 1169, Averroes was appointed judge in Seville and in that year his first commentary on Aristotle appeared. In 1171, he returned to Cordova where he probably also filled the office of judge. In 1182, when Ibn Ṭufayl retired, he took his place as court physician to Abū Ya'qūb Yūsuf. When in 1184 the ruler died and his son Abū Yūsuf Ya'qūb took his place, Averroes retained his post. In 1195, for reasons which are not too clear, Averroes fell in disgrace and all his works except those of a purely scientific nature were burned. Having been exiled to Lucenna (near Cordova) for a short time, he was restored to grace. He lived in retirement in Marrakesh until his death in 1198.

The majority of Averroes' works were commentaries on Aristotle's writings. These commentaries appeared in three forms—epitomes, intermediate commentaries, and long commentaries. Altogether he wrote thirty-eight commentaries of the various kinds. Of these only twenty-eight are still extant in the original Arabic, thirty-six in Hebrew translations, and thirty-four in Latin translations dating from various times. Besides a number of opuscula dealing with a variety of philosophic issues, among them *De Substantia Orbis,* he wrote a refutation of Algazali, *The Incoherence of the Incoherence (Tahāfut al-Tahāfut).* Algazali (see p. 264) had written a work entitled *The Incoherence of the Philosophers (Tahāfut al-Falāsifah)* in which he attacked the opinions of the Muslim Aristotelians, in particular those of Avicenna. Averroes' *Tahāfut* was his reply. In addition there must be mentioned his work on medicine *Kullīyāt (Colliget),* his *Commentary on Plato's Republic,* and his treatises on religion, chief among them *The Decisive Treatise Determining the Nature of the Connection between Religion and Philosophy (Faṣl al-Maqāl).*

It should be added that the Latin world knew Averroes primarily as interpreter of Aristotle and his works on religion were either not known at all or were known very late. Small wonder then that Averroes, for the Latin world, was a naturalistic Aristotelian who advocated the doctrines of the eternity of the world, absence of individual providence, and collective immortality—all doctrines contradictory to principles of Christian faith. It can readily be seen why Christian philosophers saw in him the father of the theory of the double truth, according to which philosophy and religion can stand in contradiction, although, in fact, he never subscribed to this view.

The first selection is the *Decisive Treatise*. It should be noted that this work is written in the form of a legal *responsum* designed to show that koranic law requires the study of philosophy for those who are fit for it. It should be added that Abū Naṣr is Alfarabi, Ibn Sīnā is Avicenna, and Abū Ḥāmid is Algazali. For a description of the Mu'tazilites and the Ash-'arites the reader is referred to the introduction to the Islamic section. The translator divided the work into chapters and the superscriptions are his. The second selection consists of the first chapter of the *De Substantia Orbis*. It deals with two aspects of Averroes' physical theories and it contains his polemic against Avicenna on these two points. At the beginning of the selection he discusses the nature of the corporeal form, and thereafter the nature of the heavens and the celestial movers. The final selection is taken from the *Long Commentary on the De Anima* and it contains Averroes' account of the material intellect.

THE DECISIVE TREATISE DETERMINING THE NATURE OF THE CONNECTION BETWEEN RELIGION AND PHILOSOPHY

What is the attitude of the Law to philosophy?

Thus spoke the lawyer, *imām,* judge, and unique scholar, Abul Walīd Muḥammad Ibn Aḥmad Ibn Rushd:

Praise be to God with all due praise, and a prayer for Muḥammad His chosen servant and apostle. The purpose of this treatise is to examine, from the standpoint of the study of the Law, whether the study of philosophy and logic is allowed by the Law, or prohibited, or commanded—either by way of recommendation or as obligatory.

From *Averroes on the Harmony of Religion and Philosophy,* G. F. Hourani, trans., London: Luzac & Co., Ltd., 1961. Reprinted by permission of the Gibb Memorial Trust.

CHAPTER ONE. *The Law Makes Philosophic Studies Obligatory.*

If teleological study of the world is philosophy, and if the Law commands such a study, then the Law commands philosophy.

We say: If the activity of 'philosophy' is nothing more than study of existing beings and reflection on them as indications of the Artisan, i.e. inasmuch as they are products of art (for beings only indicate the Artisan through our knowledge of the art in them, and the more perfect this knowledge is, the more perfect the knowledge of the Artisan becomes), and if the Law has encouraged and urged reflection on beings, then it is clear that what this name signifies is either obligatory or recommended by the Law.

The Law commands such a study.

That the Law summons to reflection on beings, and the pursuit of knowledge about them, by the intellect is clear from several verses of the Book of God, Blessed and Exalted, such as the saying of the Exalted, 'Reflect, you have vision' (Koran, LIX, 2): this is textual authority for the obligation to use intellectual reasoning, or a combination of intellectual and legal reasoning (VII, 185). Another example is His saying, 'Have they not studied the kingdom of the heavens and the earth, and whatever things God has created?': this is a text urging the study of the totality of beings. Again, God the Exalted has taught that one of those whom He singularly honoured by this knowledge was Abraham, peace on him, for the Exalted said (VI, 75), 'So we made Abraham see the kingdom of the heavens and the earth, that he might be' [and so on to the end of the verse]. The Exalted also said (LXXXVIII, 17-18), 'Do they not observe the camels, how they have been created, and the sky, how it has been raised up?' and He said (III, 191), 'and they give thought to the creation of the heavens and the earth', and so on in countless other verses.

This study must be conducted in the best manner, by demonstrative reasoning.

Since it has now been established that the Law has rendered obligatory the study of beings by the intellect, and reflection on them, and since reflection is nothing more than inference and drawing out of the unknown from the known, and since this is reasoning or at any rate done by reasoning, therefore we are under an obligation to carry on our study of beings by intellectual reasoning. It is further evident that this manner of study, to which the Law summons and urges, is the most perfect kind of study using the most perfect kind of reasoning; and this is the kind called 'demonstration'.

To master this instrument the religious thinker must make a preliminary study of logic, just as the lawyer must study legal reasoning. This is no more heretical in the one case than in the other. And logic must be learned from the ancient masters, regardless of the fact that they were not Muslims.

The Law, then, has urged us to have demonstrative knowledge of God the Exalted and all the beings of His creation. But it is preferable and even necessary for anyone, who wants to understand God the Exalted and the other beings demonstratively, to have first understood the kinds of demonstration and their conditions [of validity], and in what respects demonstrative reasoning differs from dialectical, rhetorical and fallacious reasoning. But this is not possible unless he has previously learned what reasoning as such is, and how many kinds it has, and which of them are valid and which invalid. This in turn is not possible unless he has previously learned the parts of reasoning, of which it is composed, i.e. the premisses and their kinds. Therefore he who believes in the Law, and obeys its command to study beings, ought prior to his study to gain a knowledge of these things, which have the same place in theoretical studies as instruments have in practical activities.

For just as the lawyer infers from the Divine command to him to acquire knowledge of the legal categories that he is under obligation to know the various kinds of legal syllogisms, and which are valid and which invalid, in the same way he who would know [God] ought to infer from the command to study beings that he is under obligation to acquire a knowledge of intellectual reasoning and its kinds. Indeed it is more fitting for him to do so, for if the lawyer infers from the saying of the Exalted, 'Reflect, you who have vision', the obligation to acquire a knowledge of legal reasoning, how much more fitting and proper that he who would know God should infer from it the obligation to acquire a knowledge of intellectual reasoning!

It cannot be objected: 'This kind of study of intellectual reasoning is a heretical innovation since it did not exist among the first believers.' For the study of legal reasoning and its kinds is also something which has been discovered since the first believers, yet it is not considered to be a heretical innovation. So the objector should believe the same about the study of intellectual reasoning. (For this there is a reason, which it is not the place to mention here.) But most [masters] of this religion support intellectual reasoning, except a small group of gross literalists, who can be refuted by [sacred] texts.

Since it has now been established that there is an obligation of the Law to study intellectual reasoning and its kinds, just as there is an obligation to study legal reasoning, it is clear that, if none of our predecessors had formerly examined intellectual reasoning and its kinds, we should be obliged to undertake such an examination from the beginning, and that each succeeding scholar would have to seek help in that task from his predecessor in order that knowledge of the subject might be completed. For it is difficult or impossible for one man to find out by himself and from the beginning all that he needs of that subject, as it is difficult for one man to discover all the knowledge that he needs of the kinds of legal reasoning; indeed this is even truer of knowledge of intellectual reasoning.

But if someone other than ourselves has already examined that subject, it is clear that we ought to seek help towards our goal from what has been said by such a predecessor on the subject, regardless of whether this other one shares our religion or not. For when a valid sacrifice is performed with a certain instrument, no account is taken, in judging the validity of the sacrifice, of whether the instrument belongs to one who shares our religion or to one who does not, so long as it fulfils the conditions for validity. By 'those who do not share our religion' I refer to those ancients who studied these matters before Islam. So if such is the case, and everything that is required in the study of the subject of intellectual syllogisms has already been examined in the most perfect manner by the ancients, presumably we ought to lay hands on their books in order to study what they said about that subject; and if it is all correct we should accept it from them, while if there is anything incorrect in it, we should draw attention to that.

After logic we must proceed to philosophy proper. Here too we have to learn from our predecessors, just as in mathematics and law. Thus it is wrong to forbid the study of ancient philosophy. Harm from it is accidental, like harm from taking medicine, drinking water, or studying law.

When we have finished with this sort of study and acquired the instruments by whose aid we are able to reflect on beings and the indications of art in them (for he who does not understand the art does not understand the product of art, and he who does not understand the product of art does not understand the Artisan), then we ought to begin the examination of beings in the order and manner we have learned from the art of demonstrative syllogisms.

And again it is clear that in the study of beings this aim can be fulfilled by us perfectly only through successive examinations of them by one man after another, the later ones seeking the help of the earlier in that task, on the model of what has happened in the mathematical sciences. For if we suppose that the art of geometry did not exist in this age of ours, and likewise the art of astronomy, and a single person wanted to ascertain by himself the sizes of the heavenly bodies, their shapes, and their distances from each other, that would not be possible for him—e.g. to know the proportion of the sun to the earth or other facts about the sizes of the stars—even though he were the most intelligent of men by nature, unless by a revelation or something resembling revelation. Indeed if he were told that the sun is about 150 or 160 times as great as the earth, he would think this statement madness on the part of the speaker, although this is a fact which has been demonstrated in astronomy so surely that no one who has mastered that science doubts it.

But what calls even more strongly for comparison with the art of mathematics in this respect is the art of the principles of law; and the study of law itself was completed only over a long period of time. And if someone today wanted to find out by himself all the arguments which have been discovered by the theorists of the legal schools on controversial questions, about which debate has taken place between them in most countries of Islam (except the West), he would deserve to be ridiculed, because such a task is impossible for him, apart from the fact that the work has been done already. Moreover, this is a situation that is self-evident not in the scientific arts alone but also in the practical arts; for there is not one of them which a single man can construct by himself. Then how can he do it with the art of arts, philosophy? If this is so, then whenever we find in the works of our predecessors of former nations a theory about beings and a reflection on them conforming to what the conditions of demonstration require, we ought to study what they said about the matter and what they affirmed in their books. And we should accept from them gladly and gratefully whatever in these books accords with the truth, and draw attention to and warn against what does not accord with the truth, at the same time excusing them.

From this it is evident that the study of the books of the ancients is obligatory by Law, since their aim and purpose in their books is just the purpose to which the Law has urged us, and that whoever forbids the study of them to anyone who is fit to study them, i.e. anyone who unites two qualities, (1) natural intelligence and (2) religious integrity and moral virtue, is blocking people from the door by which the Law summons them to knowledge of God, the door of theoretical study which leads to the truest knowledge of Him; and such an act is the extreme of ignorance and estrangement from God the Exalted.

And if someone errs or stumbles in the study of these books owing to a deficiency in his natural capacity, or bad organization of his study of them, or being dominated by his passions, or not finding a teacher to guide him to an understanding of their contents, or a combination of all or more than one of these causes, it does not follow that one should forbid them to anyone who is qualified to study them. For this manner of harm which arises owing to them is something that is attached to them by accident, not by essence; and when a thing is beneficial by its nature and essence, it ought not to be shunned because of something harmful contained in it by accident. This was the thought of the Prophet, peace on him, on the occasion when he ordered a man to give his brother honey to drink for his diarrhoea, and the diarrhoea increased after he had given him the honey: when the man complained to him about it, he said, 'God spoke the truth; it was your brother's stomach that lied.' We can even say that a man who prevents a qualified person from studying books of philosophy, because some of the most vicious people may be thought to have gone astray through their study of them, is like a man who prevents a thirsty person from drinking cool, fresh water until he dies of thirst, because some people have choked to death on it. For death from water by choking is an accidental matter, but death by thirst is essential and necessary.

Moreover, this accidental effect of this art is a thing which may also occur accidentally from the other arts. To how many lawyers has law been a cause of lack of piety and immersion in this world! Indeed we find most lawyers in this state, although their art by its essence calls for nothing but practical virtue. Thus it is not strange if the same thing that occurs accidentally in the art which calls for practical virtue should occur accidentally in the art which calls for intellectual virtue.

For every Muslim the Law has provided a way to truth suitable to his nature, through demonstrative, dialectical or rhetorical methods.

Since all this is now established, and since we, the Muslim community, hold that this divine religion of ours is true, and that it is this religion which incites and summons us to the happiness that consists in the knowledge of God, Mighty and Majestic, and of His creation, that [end] is appointed for every Muslim by the method of assent which his temperament and nature require. For the natures of men are on different levels with respect to [their paths to] assent. One of them comes to assent through demonstration; another comes to assent through dialectical arguments, just as firmly as the demonstrative man through demonstration, since his nature does not contain any greater capacity; while another comes to assent through rhetorical arguments, again just as firmly as the demonstrative man through demonstrative arguments.

Thus since this divine religion of ours has summoned people by these three methods, assent to it has extended to everyone, except him who stubbornly denies it with his tongue or him for whom no method of summons to God the Exalted has been appointed in religion owing to his own neglect of such matters. It was for this purpose that the Prophet, peace on him, was sent with a special mission to 'the white man and the black man' alike; I mean because his religion embraces all the methods of summons to God the Exalted. This is clearly expressed in the saying of God the Exalted (XVI, 125), 'Summon to the way of your Lord by wisdom and by good preaching, and debate with them in the most effective manner'.

CHAPTER TWO. *Philosophy Contains Nothing Opposed to Islam*

Demonstrative truth and scriptural truth cannot conflict.

Now since this religion is true and summons to the study which leads to knowledge of the Truth, we the Muslim community know definitely that demonstrative study does not lead to [conclusions] conflicting with what Scripture has given us; for truth does not oppose truth but accords with it and bears witness to it.

If the apparent meaning of Scripture conflicts with demonstrative conclusions it must be interpreted allegorically, i.e. metaphorically.

This being so, whenever demonstrative study leads to any manner of knowledge about any being, that being is inevitably either unmentioned or mentioned in Scripture. If it is unmentioned there is no contradiction, and it is in the same case as an act whose category is unmentioned, so that the lawyer has to infer it by reasoning from Scripture. If Scripture speaks about it, the apparent meaning of the words inevitably either accords or conflicts with the conclusions of demonstration about it. If this [apparent meaning] accords there is no argument. If it conflicts there is a call for allegorical interpretation of it. The meaning of 'allegorical interpretation' is: extension of the significance of an expression from real to metaphorical significance, without forsaking therein the standard metaphorical practices of Arabic, such as calling a thing by the name of something resembling it or a cause or consequence or accompaniment of it, or other things such as are enumerated in accounts of the kinds of metaphorical speech.

If the lawyer can do this, the religious thinker certainly can. Indeed these allegorical interpretations always receive confirmation from the apparent meaning of other passages of Scripture.

Now if the lawyer does this in many decisions of religious law, with how much more right is it done by the possessor of demonstrative knowledge! For the lawyer has at his disposition only reasoning based on opinion, while he who would know [God] [has at his disposition] reasoning based on certainty. So we affirm definitely that whenever the conclusion of a demonstration is in conflict with the apparent meaning of Scripture, that apparent meaning admits of allegorical interpretation according to the rules for such interpretation in Arabic. This proposition is questioned by no Muslim and doubted by no believer. But its certainty is immensely increased for those who have had close dealings with this idea and put it to the test, and made it their aim to reconcile the assertions of intellect and tradition. Indeed we may say that whenever a statement in Scripture conflicts in its apparent meaning with a conclusion of demonstration, if Scripture is considered carefully, and the rest of its contents searched page by page, there will invariably be found among the expressions of Scripture something which in its apparent meaning bears witness to that allegorical interpretation or comes close to bearing witness.

All Muslims accept the principle of allegorical interpretation; they only disagree about the extent of its application.

In the light of this idea the Muslims are unanimous in holding that it is not obligatory either to take all the expressions of Scripture in their apparent meaning or to extend them all from their apparent meaning by allegorical interpretation. They disagree [only] over which of them should and which should not be so interpreted: the Ash'arites for instance give an allegorical interpretation to the verse about God's directing Himself and the Tradition about His descent, while the Hanbalites take them in their apparent meaning.

The double meaning has been given to suit people's diverse intelligence. The apparent contradictions are meant to stimulate the learned to deeper study.

The reason why we have received a Scripture with both an apparent and an inner meaning lies in the diversity of people's natural capacities and the difference of their innate dispositions with regard to assent. The reason why we have received in Scripture texts whose apparent meanings contradict each other is in order to draw the attention of those who are well grounded in science to the interpretation which reconciles them. This is the idea referred to in the words received from the Exalted (III, 7), 'He it is who has sent down to you the Book, containing certain verses clear and definite' [and so on] down to the words 'those who are well grounded in science'.

In interpreting texts allegorically we must never violate Islamic consensus, when it is certain. But to establish it with certainty with regard to theoretical texts is impossible, because there have always been scholars who would not divulge their interpretation of such texts.

It may be objected: 'There are some things in Scripture which the Muslims have unanimously agreed to take in their apparent meaning, others [which they have agreed] to interpret allegorically, and others about which they have disagreed; is it permissible, then, that demonstration should lead to interpreting allegorically what they have agreed to take in its apparent meaning, or to taking in its apparent meaning what they have agreed to interpret allegorically?' We reply: If unanimous agreement is established by a method which is certain, such [a result] is not sound; but if [the existence of] agreement on those things is a matter of opinion, then it may be sound. This is why Abū Hāmid, Abul-Ma'ālī, and other leaders of thought said that no one should be definitely called an unbeliever for violating unanimity on a point of interpretation in matters like these.

That unanimity on theoretical matters is never determined with certainty, as it can be on practical matters, may be shown to you by the fact that it is not possible for unanimity to be determined on any question at any period unless that period is strictly limited by us, and all the scholars existing in that period are known to us (i.e. known as individuals and in their total number), and the doctrine of each of them on the question has been handed down to us on unassailable authority, and, in addition to all this, unless we are sure that the scholars existing at the time were in agreement that there is not both an apparent and an inner meaning in Scripture, that knowledge of any question ought not to be kept secret from anyone, and that there is only one way for people to understand Scripture. But it is recorded in Tradition that many of the first believers used to hold that Scripture has both an apparent and an inner meaning, and that the inner meaning ought not to be learned by anyone who is not a man of learning in this field and who is incapable of understanding it. Thus, for example, Bukhārī reports a saying of 'Alī Ibn Abī Tālib, may God be pleased with him, 'Speak to people about what they know. Do you want God and His Prophet to be accused of lying?' Other examples of the same kind are reported about a group of early believers. So how can it possibly be conceived that a unanimous agreement can have been handed down to us about a single theoretical question, when we know definitely that not a single period has been without scholars who held that there are things in Scripture whose true meaning should not be learned by all people?

The situation is different in practical matters: everyone holds that the truth about these should be disclosed to all people alike, and to establish the occurrence of unanimity about them we consider it sufficient that the question [at issue] should have been widely discussed and that no report of controversy about it should have been handed down to us. This is enough to establish the occurrence of unanimity on matters of practice, but on matters of doctrine the case is different.

Ghazālī's charge of unbelief against Fārābī and Ibn Sīnā, for asserting the world's eternity and God's ignorance of particulars and denying bodily resurrection, is only tentative, not definite.

You may object: 'If we ought not to call a man an unbeliever for violating unanimity in cases of allegorical interpretation, because no unanimity is conceivable in such cases, what do you say about the Muslim philosophers, like Abū Naṣr and Ibn Sīnā? For Abū Ḥāmid called them both definitely unbelievers in the book of his known as *The disintegration* [*The Incoherence of the Philosophers*], on three counts: their assertions of the pre-eternity of the world and that God the Exalted does not know particulars' (may He be Exalted far above that [ignorance]!), 'and their allegorical interpretation of the passages concerning the resurrection of bodies and states of existence in the next life.'

We answer: It is apparent from what he said on the subject that his calling them both unbelievers on these counts was not definite, since he made it clear in *The book of distinction* that calling people unbelievers for violating unanimity can only be tentative.

Such a charge cannot be definite, because there has never been a consensus against allegorical interpretation. The *Qur'ān* itself indicates that it has inner meanings which it is the special function of the demonstrative class to understand.

Moreover, it is evident from what we have said that a unanimous agreement cannot be established in questions of this kind, because of the reports that many of the early believers of the first generation, as well as others, have said that there are allegorical interpretations which ought not to be expressed except to those who are qualified to receive allegories. These are 'those who are well grounded in science'; for we prefer to place the stop after the words of God the Exalted (III, 7) 'and those who are well grounded in science', because if the scholars did not understand allegorical interpretation, there would be no superiority in their assent which would oblige them to a belief in Him not found among the unlearned. God has described them as those who believe in Him, and this can only be taken to refer to the belief which is based on demonstration; and this [belief] only occurs together with the science of allegorical interpretation. For the unlearned believers are those whose belief in Him is not based on demonstration; and if this belief which God has attributed to the scholars is peculiar to them, it must come through demonstration, and if it comes through demonstration it only occurs together with the science of allegorical interpretation. For God the Exalted has informed us that those [verses] have an allegorical interpretation which is the truth, and demonstration can only be of the truth. That being the case, it is not possible for general unanimity to be established about allegorical interpretations, which God has made peculiar to scholars. This is self-evident to any fair-minded person.

Besides, Ghazālī was mistaken in ascribing to the Peripatetics the opinion that God does not know particulars. Their view is that His knowledge of both particulars and universals differs from ours, in being the cause, not an effect, of the object known. They even hold that God sends premonitions in dreams of particular events.

In addition to all this we hold that Abū Ḥāmid was mistaken about the Peripatetic philosophers, in ascribing to them the assertion that God, Holy and Exalted, does not know particulars at all. In reality they hold that God the Exalted knows them in a way which is not of the same kind as our way of knowing them. For our knowledge of them is an effect of the object known, originated when it comes into existence and changing when it changes; whereas Glorious God's Knowledge of existence is the opposite of this: it is the cause of the object known, which is existent being. Thus to suppose the two kinds of knowledge similar to each other is to identify the essences and properties of opposite things, and that is the extreme of ignorance. And if the name of 'knowledge' is predicated of both originated and eternal knowledge, it is predicated by sheer homonymy, as many names are predicated of opposite things: e.g. *jalal* of great and small, *ṣarīm* of light and darkness. Thus there exists no definition embracing both kinds of knowledge at once, as the theologians of our time imagine. We have devoted a separate essay to this question, impelled by one of our friends.

But how can anyone imagine that the Peripatetics say that God the Glorious does not know particulars with His eternal Knowledge, when they hold that true visions include premonitions of particular events due to occur in future time, and that this warning foreknowledge comes to people in their sleep from the eternal Knowledge which orders and rules the universe? Moreover, it is not only particulars which they say God does not know in the manner in which we know them, but universals as well; for the universals known to us are also effects of the nature of existent being, while with His Knowledge the reverse is true. Thus the conclusion to which demonstration leads is that His Knowledge transcends qualification as 'universal' or 'particular'. Consequently there is no point in disputing about this question, i.e. whether to call them unbelievers or not.

On the question of the world, the ancient philosophers agree with the Ash'arites that it is originated and coeval with time. The Peripatetics only disagree with the Ash'arites and the Platonists in holding that past time is infinite. This difference is insufficient to justify a charge of unbelief.

Concerning the question whether the world is pre-eternal or came into existence, the disagreement between the Ash'arite theologians and the ancient philosophers is in my view almost resolvable into a disagreement about naming, especially in the case of certain of the ancients. For they agree that there are three classes of beings: two extremes and one intermediate between the extremes. They agree also about naming the extremes; but they disagree about the intermediate class.

[1] One extreme is a being which is brought into existence from something other than itself and by something, i.e. by an efficient cause and from some matter; and it, i.e. its existence, is preceded by time. This is the status of bodies whose generation is apprehended by sense, e.g. the generation of water, air, earth, animals, plants, and so on. All alike, ancients and Ash'arites, agree in naming this class of beings 'originated'. [2] The opposite extreme to this is a being which is not made from or by anything and not preceded by time; and here too all members of both schools agree in naming it 'pre-eternal'. This being is

apprehended by demonstration; it is God, Blessed and Exalted, Who is the Maker, Giver of being and Sustainer of the universe; may He be praised and His Power exalted!

[3] The class of being which is between these two extremes is that which is not made from anything and not preceded by time, but which is brought into existence by something, i.e. by an agent. This is the world as a whole. Now they all agree on the presence of these three characters in the world. For the theologians admit that time does not precede it, or rather this is a necessary consequence for them since time according to them is something which accompanies motion and bodies. They also agree with the ancients in the view that future time is infinite and likewise future being. They only disagree about past time and past being: the theologians hold that it is finite (this is the doctrine of Plato and his followers), while Aristotle and his school hold that it is infinite, as is the case with future time.

Thus it is clear that [3] this last being bears a resemblance both to [1] the being which is really generated and to [2] the pre-eternal Being. So those who are more impressed with its resemblance to the pre-eternal than its resemblance to the originated name it 'pre-eternal', while those who are more impressed with its resemblance to the originated name it 'originated'. But in truth it is neither really originated nor really pre-eternal, since the really originated is necessarily perishable and the really pre-eternal has no cause. Some—Plato and his followers—name it 'originated and coeval with time', because time according to them is finite in the past.

Thus the doctrines about the world are not so very far apart from each other that some of them should be called irreligious and others not. For this to happen, opinions must be divergent in the extreme, i.e. contraries such as the theologians suppose to exist on this question; i.e. [they hold] that the names 'pre-eternity' and 'coming into existence' as applied to the world as a whole are contraries. But it is now clear from what we have said that this is not the case.

Anyhow, the apparent meaning of Scripture is that there was a being and time before God created the present being and time. Thus the theologians' interpretation is allegorical and does not command unanimous agreement.

Over and above all this, these opinions about the world do not conform to the apparent meaning of Scripture. For if the apparent meaning of Scripture is searched, it will be evident from the verses which give us information about the bringing into existence of the world that its form really is originated, but that being itself and time extend continuously at both extremes, i.e. without interruption. Thus the words of God the Exalted (XI, 7) 'He it is Who created the heavens and the earth in six days, and His throne was on the water', taken in their apparent meaning imply that there was a being before this present being, namely the throne and the water, and a time before this time, i.e. the one which is joined to the form of this being, namely the number of the movement of the celestial sphere. And the words of the Exalted (XIV, 48), 'On the day when the earth shall be changed into other than earth, and the heavens as well,' also in their apparent meaning imply that there will be a second being after this being. And the words of the Exalted (XLI, 11), 'Then He directed Himself towards the sky, and it was smoke', in their apparent meaning imply that the heavens were created from something.

Thus the theologians too in their statements about the world do not conform to the apparent meaning of Scripture but interpret it allegorically. For it is not stated in Scripture that God was existing with absolutely nothing else: a text to this effect is nowhere to be found. Then how is it conceivable that the theologians' allegorical interpretation of these verses could meet with unanimous agreement, when the apparent meaning of Scripture which we have mentioned about the existence of the world has been accepted by a school of philosophers!

On such difficult questions, error committed by a qualified judge of his subject is excused by God, while error by an unqualified person is not excused.

It seems that those who disagree on the interpretation of these difficult questions earn merit if they are in the right and will be excused [by God] if they are in error. For assent to a thing as a result of an indication [of it] arising in the soul is something compulsory, not voluntary: i.e. it is not for us [to choose] not to assent or to assent, as it is to stand up or not to stand up. And since free choice is a condition of obligation, a man who assents to an error as a result of a consideration that has occurred to him is excused, if he is a scholar. This is why the Prophet, peace on him, said, 'If the judge after exerting his mind makes a right decision, he will have a double reward; and if he makes a wrong decision he will [still] have a single reward.' And what judge is more important than he who makes judgements about being, that it is thus or not thus? These judges are the scholars, specially chosen by God for [the task of] allegorical interpretation, and this error which is forgivable according to the Law is only such error as proceeds from scholars when they study the difficult matters which the Law obliges them to study.

But error proceeding from any other class of people is sheer sin, equally whether it relates to theoretical or to practical matters. For just as the judge who is ignorant of the [Prophet's] way of life is not excused if he makes an error in judgement, so he who makes judgements about beings without having the proper qualifications for [such] judgements is not excused but is either a sinner or an unbeliever. And if he who would judge what is allowed and forbidden is required to combine in himself the qualifications for exercise of personal judgement, namely knowledge of the principles [of law] and knowledge of how to draw inferences from those principles by reasoning, how much more properly is he who would make judgements about beings required to be qualified, i.e. to know the primary intellectual principle and the way to draw inferences from them!

Texts of Scripture fall into three kinds with respect to the excusability of error. [1] Texts which must be taken in their apparent meaning by everyone. Since the meaning can be understood plainly by demonstrative, dialectical and rhetorical methods alike, no one is excused for the error of interpreting these texts allegorically. [2] Texts which must be taken in their apparent meaning by the lower classes and interpreted allegorically by the demonstrative class. It is inexcusable for the lower classes to interpret them allegorically or for the demonstrative class to take them in their apparent meaning. [3] Texts whose classification under the previous headings is uncertain. Error in this matter by the demonstrative class is excused.

In general, error about Scripture is of two types: either error which is excused to one who is a qualified student of that matter in which the error occurs (as the skilful doctor is excused if he commits an error in the art of medicine and the skilful judge if he gives an erroneous judgement), but not excused to one who is not qualified in that subject; or error which is not excused to any person whatever, and which is unbelief if it concerns the principles of religion, or heresy if it concerns something subordinate to the principles.

This [latter] error is that which occurs about [1] matters, knowledge of which is provided by all the different methods of indication, so that knowledge of the matter in question is in this way possible for everyone. Examples are acknowledgement of God, Blessed and Exalted, of the prophetic missions, and of happiness and misery in the next life; for these three principles are attainable by the three classes of indication, by which everyone without exception can come to assent to what he is obliged to know: I mean the rhetorical, dialectical and demonstrative indications. So whoever denies such a thing, when it is one of the principles of the Law, is an unbeliever, who persists in defiance with his tongue though not with his heart, or neglects to expose himself to learning the indication of its truth. For if he belongs to the demonstrative class of men, a way has been provided for him to assent to it, by demonstration; if he belongs to the dialectical class, the way is by dialectic; and if he belongs to the class [which is convinced] by preaching, the way for him is by preaching. With this in view the Prophet, peace on him, said, 'I have been ordered to fight people until they say "There is no god but God" and believe in me'; he means, by any of the three methods of attaining belief that suits them.

[2] With regard to things which by reason of their recondite character are only knowable by demonstration, God has been gracious to those of His servants who have no access to demonstration, on account of their natures, habits or lack of facilities for education: He has coined for them images and likenesses of these things, and summoned them to assent to those images, since it is possible for assent to those images to come about through the indications common to all men, i.e. the dialectical and rhetorical indications. This is the reason why Scripture is divided into apparent and inner meanings: the apparent meaning consists of those images which are coined to stand for those ideas, while the inner meaning is those ideas [themselves], which are clear only to the demonstrative class. These are the four or five classes of beings mentioned by Abū Ḥāmid in *The book of the distinction*.

[1] But when it happens, as we said, that we know the thing itself by the three methods, we do not need to coin images of it, and it remains true in its apparent meaning, not admitting allegorical interpretation. If an apparent text of this kind refers to principles, anyone who interprets it allegorically is an unbeliever, e.g. anyone who thinks that there is no happiness or misery in the next life, and that the only purpose of this teaching is that men should be safeguarded from each other in their bodily and sensible lives, that it is but a practical device, and that man has no other goal than his sensible existence.

If this is established, it will have become clear to you from what we have said that there are [1] apparent texts of Scripture which it is not permitted to interpret allegorically; to do so on fundamentals is unbelief, on subordinate matters, heresy. There are also [2] apparent texts which have to be interpreted allegorically by men of the demonstrative class; for such men to take them in their apparent meaning is unbelief, while for those who are not of the demonstrative class to interpret them allegorically and take them out of their apparent meaning is unbelief or heresy on their part.

Of this [latter] class are the verse about God's directing Himself and the Tradition about His descent. That is why the Prophet, peace on him, said in the case of the black woman, when she told him that God was in the sky, 'Free her, for she is a believer'. This was because she was not of the demonstrative class; and the reason for his decision was that the class of people to whom assent comes only through the imagination, i.e. who do not assent to a thing except in so far as they can imagine it, find it difficult to assent to the existence of a being which is unrelated to any imaginable thing. This applies as well to those who understand from the relation stated merely [that God has] a place; these are people who have advanced a little in their thought beyond the position of the first class, [by rejecting] belief in corporeality. Thus the [proper] answer to them with regard to such passages is that they belong to the ambiguous texts, and that the stop is to be placed after the words of God the Exalted (III, 7) 'And no one knows the interpretation thereof except God'. The demonstrative class, while agreeing unanimously that this class of text must be interpreted allegorically, may disagree about the interpretation, according to the level of each one's knowledge of demonstration.

There is also [3] a third class of Scriptural texts falling uncertainly between the other two classes, on which there is doubt. One group of those who devote themselves to theoretical study attach them to the apparent texts which it is not permitted to interpret allegorically, others attach them to the texts with inner meanings which scholars are not permitted to take in their apparent meanings. This [divergence of opinions] is due to the difficulty and ambiguity of this class of text. Anyone who commits an error about this class is excused, I mean any scholar.

The texts about the future life fall into [3], since demonstrative scholars do not agree whether to take them in their apparent meaning or interpret them allegorically. Either is permissible. But it is inexcusable to deny the fact of a future life altogether.

If it is asked, 'Since it is clear that scriptural texts in this respect fall into three grades, to which of these three grades, according to you, do the descriptions of the future life and its states belong?', we reply: The position clearly is that this matter belongs to the class [3] about which there is disagreement. For we find a group of those who claim an affinity with demonstration saying that it is obligatory to take these passages in their apparent meaning, because there is no demonstration leading to the impossibility of the apparent meaning in them —this is the view of the Ash'arites; while another group of those who devote themselves to demonstration interpret these passages allegorically, and these people give the most diverse interpretations of them. In this class must be counted Abū Ḥāmid and many of the Sūfīs; some of them combine the two interpretations of the passages, as Abū Ḥāmid does in some of his books.

So it is likely that a scholar who commits an error in this matter is excused, while one who is correct receives thanks or a reward: that is, if he acknowledges the existence [of a future life] and merely gives a certain sort of allegorical interpretation, i.e. of the mode of the future life not of its existence, provided that the interpretation given does not lead to denial of its existence. In this matter only the negation of existence is unbelief, because it concerns one of the principles of religion and one of those points to which assent is attainable through the three methods common to 'the white man and the black man'.

The unlearned classes must take such texts in their apparent meaning. It is unbelief for the learned to set down allegorical interpretations in popular writings. By doing this Ghazālī caused confusion among the people. Demonstrative books should be banned to the unqualified, but not to the learned.

But anyone who is not a man of learning is obliged to take these passages in their apparent meaning, and allegorical interpretation of them is for him unbelief because it *leads* to unbelief. That is why we hold that, for anyone whose duty it is to believe in the apparent meaning, allegorical interpretation is unbelief, because it leads to unbelief. Anyone of the interpretative class who discloses such [an interpretation] to him is summoning him to unbelief, and he who summons to unbelief is an unbeliever.

Therefore allegorical interpretations ought to be set down only in demonstrative books because if they are in demonstrative books they are encountered by no one but men of the demonstrative class. But if they are set down in other than demonstrative books and one deals with them by poetical, rhetorical or dialectical methods, as Abū Ḥāmid does, then he commits an offence against the Law and against philosophy, even though the fellow intended nothing but good. For by this procedure he wanted to increase the number of learned men, but in fact he increased the number of the corrupted not of the learned! As a result, one group came to slander philosophy, another to slander religion, and another to reconcile the [first] two [groups]. It seems that this [last] was one of his objects in his books; an indication that he wanted by this [procedure] to arouse minds is that he adhered to no one doctrine in his books but was an Ashʿarite with the Ashʿarites, a Ṣūfī with the Ṣūfīs and a philosopher with the philosophers, so that he was like the man in the verse:

> 'One day a Yamanī, if I meet a man of Yaman,
>   And if I meet a Maʿaddī, I'm an ʿAdnānī.'

The *imāms* of the Muslims ought to forbid those of his books which contain learned matter to all save the learned, just as they ought to forbid demonstrative books to those who are not capable of understanding them. But the damage done to people by demonstrative books is lighter, because for the most part only persons of superior natural intelligence become acquainted with demonstrative books, and this class of persons is only misled through lack of practical virtue, unorganized reading, and tackling them without a teacher. On the other hand their total prohibition obstructs the purpose to which the Law summons, because it is a wrong to the best class of people and the best class of beings. For to do justice to the best class of beings demands that they should be known profoundly, by persons equipped to know them profoundly, and these are the best class of people; and the greater the value of the being, the greater is the injury towards it, which consists of ignorance of it. Thus the Exalted has said (XXXI, 13). 'Associating [other gods] with God is indeed a great wrong.'

We have only discussed these questions in a popular work because they were already being publicly discussed.

This is as much as we see fit to affirm in this field of study, i.e. the correspondence between religion and philosophy and the rules for allegorical interpretation in religion. If it were not for the publicity given to the matter and to these questions which we have discussed, we should not have permitted ourselves to write a word on the subject; and we should not have had to make excuses for doing so to the interpretative scholars, because the proper place to discuss these questions is in demonstrative books. God is the Guide and helps us to follow the right course!

CHAPTER THREE   *Philosophical Interpretations of Scripture Should Not Be Taught to the Majority. The Law Provides Other Methods of Instructing Them.*

The purpose of Scripture is to teach true theoretical and practical science and right practice and attitudes.

You ought to know that the purpose of Scripture is simply to teach true science and right practice. True science is knowledge of God, Blessed and Exalted, and the other beings as they really are, and especially of noble beings, and knowledge of happiness and misery in the next life. Right practice consists in performing the acts which bring happiness and avoiding the acts which bring misery; and it is knowledge of these acts that is called 'practical science'. They fall into two divisions: (1) outward bodily acts; the science of these is called 'jurisprudence'; and (2) acts of the soul such as gratitude, patience and other moral attitudes which the Law enjoins or forbids; the science of these is called 'asceticism' or 'the sciences of the future life'. To these Abū Ḥāmid turned his attention in his book: as people had given up this sort [of act] and become immersed in the other sort, and as this sort [2] involves the greater fear of God, which is the cause of happiness, he called his book *'The revival of the sciences of religion'*. But we have digressed from our subject, so let us return to it.

Scripture teaches concepts both directly and by symbols, and uses demonstrative, dialectical and rhetorical arguments. Dialectical and rhetorical arguments are prevalent because the main aim of Scripture is to teach the majority. In these arguments concepts are indicated directly or by symbols, in various combinations in premises and conclusion.

We say: The purpose of Scripture is to teach true science and right practice; and teaching is of two classes, [of] concepts and [of] judgements, as the logicians have shown. Now the methods available to men of [arriving at] judgements are three: demonstrative, dialectical and rhetorical; and the methods of forming concepts are two: either [conceiving] the object itself or [conceiving] a symbol of it. But not everyone has the natural ability to take in demonstrations, or [even] dialectical arguments, let alone demonstrative arguments which are so hard to learn and need so much time [even] for those who are qualified to learn them. Therefore, since it is the purpose of Scriptures simply to teach everyone, Scripture has to contain every method of [bringing about] judgements of assent and every method of forming concepts.

Now some of the methods of assent comprehend the majority of people, i.e. the occurrence of assent as a result of them [is comprehensive]: these are the rhetorical and the dialectical [methods]—and the rhetorical is more comprehensive than the dialectical. Another method is peculiar to a smaller number of people: this is the demonstrative. Therefore, since the primary purpose of Scripture is to take care of the majority (without neglecting to arouse the élite), the prevailing methods of expression in religion are the common methods by which the majority comes to form concepts and judgements.

These [common] methods in religion are of four classes:

One of them occurs where the method is common, yet specialized in two respects: i.e. where it is certain in its concepts and judgements, in spite of being rhetorical or dialectical. These syllogisms are those whose premisses, in spite of being based on accepted ideas or on opinions, are accidentally certain, and whose conclusions are accidentally to be taken in their direct meaning without symbolization. Scriptural texts of this class have no allegorical interpretations, and anyone who denies them or interprets them allegorically is an unbeliever.

The second class occurs where the premisses, in spite of being based on accepted ideas or on opinions, are certain, and where the conclusions are symbols for the things which it was intended to conclude. [Texts of] this [class], i.e. their conclusions, admit of allegorical interpretation.

The third is the reverse of this: it occurs where the conclusions are the very things which it was intended to conclude, while the premisses are based on accepted ideas or on opinions without being accidentally certain. [Texts of] this [class] also, i.e. their conclusions, do not admit of allegorical interpretation, but their premisses may do so.

The fourth [class] occurs where the premisses are based on accepted ideas or opinions, without being accidentally certain, and where the conclusions are symbols for what it was intended to conclude. In these cases the duty of the élite is to interpret them allegorically, while the duty of the masses is to take them in their apparent meaning.

Where symbols are used, each class of men, demonstrative, dialectical and rhetorical, must try to understand the inner meaning symbolized or rest content with the apparent meaning, according to their capacities.

In general, everything in these [texts] which admits of allegorical interpretation can only be understood by demonstration. The duty of the élite here is to apply such interpretation; while the duty of the masses is to take them in their apparent meaning in both respects, i.e. in concept and judgement, since their natural capacity does not allow more than that.

But there may occur to students of Scripture allegorical interpretations due to the superiority of one of the common methods over another in [bringing about] assent, i.e. when the indication contained in the allegorical interpretation is more persuasive than the indication contained in the apparent meaning. Such interpretations are popular; and [the making of them] is possibly a duty for those powers of theoretical understanding have attained the dialectical level. To this sort belong some of the interpretations of the Ash'arites and Mu'tazilites— though the Mu'tazilites are generally sounder in their statements. The masses on the other hand, who are incapable of more than rhetorical arguments, have the duty of taking these [texts] in their apparent meaning, and they are not permitted to know such interpretations at all.

Thus people in relation to Scripture fall into three classes:

One class is these who are not people of interpretation at all: these are the rhetorical class. They are the overwhelming mass, for no man of sound intellect is exempted from this kind of assent.

Another class is the people of dialectical interpretation: these are the dialecticians, either by nature alone or by nature and habit.

Another class is the people of certain interpretation: these are the demonstrative class, by nature and training, i.e. in the art of philosophy. This interpretation ought not to be expressed to the dialectical class, let alone to the masses.

To explain the inner meaning to people unable to understand it is to destroy their belief in the apparent meaning without putting anything in its place. The result is unbelief in learners and teachers. It is best for the learned to profess ignorance, quoting the *Qur'ān* on the limitation of man's understanding.

When something of these allegorical interpretations is expressed to anyone unfit to receive them—especially demonstrative interpretations because of their remoteness from common knowledge—both he who expresses it and he to whom it is expressed are led into unbelief. The reason for that [in the case of the latter] is that allegorical interpretation comprises two things, rejection of the apparent meaning and affirmation of the allegorical one; so that if the apparent meaning is rejected in the mind of someone who can only grasp apparent meanings, without the allegorical meaning being affirmed in his mind, the result is unbelief, if it [the text in question] concerns the principles of religion.

Allegorical interpretations, then, ought not to be expressed to the masses nor set down in rhetorical or dialectical books, i.e. books containing arguments of these two sorts, as was done by Abū Ḥāmid. They should [not] be expressed to this class; and with regard to an apparent text, when there is a [self-evident] doubt whether it is apparent to everyone and whether knowledge of its interpretation is impossible for them, they should be told that it is ambiguous and [its meaning] known by no one except God; and that the stop should be put here in the sentence of the Exalted (III, 7), 'And no one knows the interpretation thereof except God'. The same kind of answer should also be given to a question about abstruse matters, which there is no way for the masses to understand; just as the Exalted has answered in His saying (XVII, 85), 'And they will ask you about the Spirit. Say, "The Spirit is by the command of my Lord; you have been given only a little knowledge" '.

Certain people have injured the masses particularly, by giving them allegorical interpretations which are false. These people are exactly analogous to bad medical advisers. The true doctor is related to bodily health in the same way as the Legislator to spiritual health, which the *Qur'ān* teaches us to pursue. The true allegory is "the deposit" mentioned in the *Qur'ān*.

As for the man who expresses these allegories to unqualified persons, he is an unbeliever on account of his summoning people to unbelief. This is contrary to the summons of the Legislator, especially when they are false allegories concerning the principles of religion, as has happened in the case of a group of people of our time. For we have seen some of them thinking that they were being philosophic and that they perceived, with their remarkable wisdom, things which conflict with Scripture in every respect, i.e. [in passages] which do not admit of allegorical interpretation; and that it was obligatory to express these things to the masses. But by expressing those false beliefs to the masses they have been a cause of perdition to the masses and themselves, in this world and the next.

The relation between the aim of these people and the aim of the Legislator [can be illustrated by] a parable of a man who goes to a skilful doctor. [This doctor's] aim is to preserve the health and cure the diseases of all the people, by prescribing for them rules which can be commonly accepted, about the necessity of using the things which will preserve their health and cure their diseases, and avoiding the opposite things. He is unable to make them all doctors, because a doctor is one who knows by demonstrative methods the things which preserve health and cure disease. Now this [man whom we have mentioned] goes out to the people and tells them, 'These methods prescribed by this doctor for you are not right'; and he sets out to discredit them, so that they are rejected by the people. Or he says, 'They have allegorical interpretations'; but the people neither understand these nor assent to them in practice. Well, do you think that people in this condition will do any of the things which are useful for preserving health and curing disease, or that this man who has persuaded them to reject what they formerly believed in will now be able to use those [things] with them, I mean for preserving health? No, he will be unable to use those [things] with them, nor will they use them, and so they will all perish.

This [is what will happen] if he expresses to them true allegories about those matters, because of their inability to understand them; let alone if he expresses to them false allegories, because this will lead them to think that there are no such things as health which ought to be preserved and disease which ought to be cured—let alone that there are things which preserve health and cure disease. It is the same when someone expresses allegories to the masses, and to those who are not qualified to understand them, in the sphere of Scripture; thus he makes it appear false and turns people away from it; and he who turns people away from Scripture is an unbeliever.

Indeed this comparison is certain, not poetic as one might suppose. It presents a true analogy, in that the relation of the doctor to the health of bodies is [the same as] the relation of the Legislator to the health of souls; i.e. the doctor is he who seeks to preserve the health of bodies when it exists and to restore it when it is lost, while the Legislator is he who desires this [end] for the health of souls. This health is what is called 'fear of God'. The precious Book has told us to seek it by acts conformable to the Law, in several verses. Thus the Exalted has said (XXII, 37), 'Fasting has been prescribed for you, as it was prescribed for those who were before you; perhaps you will fear God.' Again the Exalted has said (XXII, 37), 'Their flesh and their blood shall not touch God, but your fear shall touch him'; (XXIX, 45) 'Prayer prevents immorality and transgression'; and other verses to the same effect contained in the precious Book. Through knowledge of Scripture and practice according to Scripture the Legislator aims solely at this health; and it is from this health that happiness in the future life follows, just as misery in the future life follows from its opposite.

From this it will be clear to you that true allegories ought not to be set down in popular books, let alone false ones. The true allegory is the deposit which man was charged to hold and which he held, and from which all beings shied away, i.e. that which is mentioned in the words of the Exalted (XXXIII, 72), 'We offered the deposit to the heavens, the earth and the mountains', [and so on to the end of] the verse.

It was due to the wrong use of allegorical interpretation by the Mu'tazilites and Ash-'arites that hostile sects arose in Islam.

It was due to allegorical interpretations—especially the false ones—and the supposition that such interpretations of Scripture ought to be expressed to everyone, that the sects of Islam arose, with the result that each one accused the others of unbelief or heresy. Thus the Mu'tazilites interpreted many verses and Traditions allegorically, and expressed their interpretations to the masses, and the Ash'arites did the same, although they used such interpretations less frequently. In consequence they threw people into hatred, mutual detestation and wars, tore the Scriptures to shreds, and completely divided people.

In addition to all this, in the methods which they followed to establish their interpretations they neither went along with the masses nor with the élite: not with the masses, because their methods were [more] obscure than the methods common to the majority, and not with the élite, because if these methods are inspected they are found deficient in the conditions [required] for demonstrations, as will be understood after the slightest inspection by anyone acquainted with the conditions of demonstration. Further, many of the principles on which the Ash'arites based their knowledge are sophistical, for they deny many necessary truths such as the permanence of accidents, the action of things on other things, the existence of necessary causes for effects, of substantial forms, and of secondary causes.

And their theorists wronged the Muslims in this sense, that a sect of Ash'arites called an unbeliever anyone who did not attain knowledge of the existence of the Glorious Creator by the methods laid down by them in their books for attaining this knowledge. But in truth it is they who are the unbelievers and in error! From this point they proceeded to disagree, one group saying 'The primary obligation is theoretical study', another group saying 'It is belief'; i.e. [this happened] because they did not know which are the methods common to everyone, through whose doors the Law has summoned all people [to enter]; they supposed that there was only one method. Thus they mistook the aim of the Legislator, and were both themselves in error and led others into error.

The proper methods for teaching the people are indicated in the *Qur'ān*, as the early Muslims knew. The popular portions of the Book are miraculous in providing for the needs of every class of mind. We intend to make a study of its teachings at the apparent level, and thus help to remedy the grievous harm done by ignorant partisans of philosophy and religion.

It may be asked: 'If these methods followed by the Ash'arites and other theorists are not the common methods by which the Legislator has aimed to teach the masses, and by which alone it is possible to teach them, then what are those [common] methods in this religion of ours'? We reply: They are exclusively the methods set down in the precious Book. For if the precious Book is inspected, there will be found in it the three methods that are available for all the people, [namely] the common methods for the instruction of the majority of the people and the special method. And if their merits are inspected, it becomes apparent that no better common methods for the instruction of the masses can be found than the methods mentioned in it.

Thus whoever tampers with them, by making an allegorical interpretation not apparent in itself, or [at least] not more apparent to everyone than they are (and that [greater apparency] is something non-existent), is rejecting their wisdom and rejecting their intended effects in procuring human happiness. This is very apparent from [a comparison of] the condition of the first believers with the condition of those who came after them. For the first believers arrived at perfect virtue and fear of God only by using these sayings [of Scripture] without interpreting them allegorically; and anyone of them who did find out an allegorical interpretation did not think fit to express it [to others]. But when those who came after them used allegorical interpretation, their fear of God grew less, their dissensions increased, their love for one another was removed, and they became divided into sects.

So whoever wishes to remove this heresy from religion should direct his attention to the precious Book, and glean from it the indications present [in it] concerning everything in turn that it obliges us to believe, and exercise his judgement in looking at its apparent meaning as well as he is able, without interpreting any of it allegorically, except where the allegorical meaning is apparent in itself, i.e. commonly apparent to everyone. For if the sayings set down in Scripture for the instruction of the people are inspected, it seems that in mastering their meaning one arrives at a point, beyond which none but a man of the demonstrative class can extract from their apparent wording a meaning which is not apparent in them. This property is not found in any other sayings.

For those religious sayings in the precious Book which are expressed to everyone have three properties that indicate their miraculous character: (1) There exist none more completely persuasive and convincing to everyone than they. (2) Their meaning admits naturally of mastery, up to a point beyond which their allegorical interpretation (when they are of a kind to have such an interpretation) can only be found out by the demonstrative class. (3) They contain means of drawing the attention of the people of truth to the true allegorical meaning. This [character] is not found in the doctrines of the Ash'arites nor in those of the Mu'tazilites, i.e. their interpretations do not admit of mastery nor contain [means of] drawing attention to the truth, nor are they true; and this is why heresies have multiplied.

It is our desire to devote our time to this object and achieve it effectively, and if God grants us a respite of life we shall work steadily towards it in so far as this is made possible for us; and it may be that that work will serve as a starting point for our successors. For our soul is in the utmost sorrow and pain by reason of the evil fancies and perverted beliefs which have infiltrated this religion, and particularly such [afflictions] as have happened to it at the hands of people who claim an affinity with philosophy. For injuries from a friend are more severe than injuries from an enemy. I refer to the fact that philosophy is the friend and milk-sister of religion; thus injuries from people related to philosophy are the severest injuries [to religion]—apart from the enmity, hatred and quarrels which such [injuries] stir up between the two, which are companions by nature and lovers by essence and instinct. It has also been injured by a host of ignorant friends who claim an affinity with it: these are the sects which exist within it. But God directs all men aright and helps everyone to love Him; He unites their hearts in the fear of Him, and removes from them hatred and loathing by His grace and His mercy!

Indeed God has already removed many of these ills, ignorant ideas and misleading practices, by means of this triumphant rule. By it He has opened a way to many benefits, especially to the class of persons who have trodden the path of study and sought to know the truth. This [He has done] by summoning the masses to a middle way of knowing God the Glorious, [a way] which is raised above the low level of the followers of authority but is below the turbulence of the theologians; and by drawing the attention of the élite to their obligation to make a thorough study of the principles of religion. God is the Giver of success and the Guide by His Goodness.

A TREATISE CONCERNING THE SUBSTANCE
OF THE CELESTIAL SPHERE

CHAPTER ONE

In this treatise we intend to investigate concerning the nature of the things of which the celestial body is composed. That the celestial body is composed of two natures in the same manner as are the transient bodies has already been demonstrated, except that in the case of the latter bodies it is clear that these two natures exist on account of the existence of generation and corruption in them, while in the case of the celestial bodies it is evident that they exist on account of the existence of locomotion in them. The proof thereof is as follows: It has been shown concerning the celestial bodies that they have locomotion in virtue of themselves. Now, it is obvious in the case of something moved in virtue of itself that it is composed of two natures, one undergoing motion and the other producing it, for clearly everything moved has a mover, and something can not be mover and moved in the same respect. Thus it is clear that the celestial bodies are composed of two natures.

Therefore we want to investigate in this treatise concerning these two natures of which the celestial body is composed whether they are like the two natures of which the transient bodies are composed, one of which is called "form" the other "matter," that is to say, we want to investigate whether matter and form here below are the same in species with matter and form up above, or whether they differ in species, or whether they differ according to more and less? Now, if the celestial and terrestrial natures differ in species, then the term "corporeity" is predicated of them either according to equivocation or according to a sort of priority and posteriority.

That, however, these two natures which exist in these respective bodies do not agree in species becomes self-evident once it has been laid down that the celestial body is neither generated nor corruptible, whereas the bodies which are with us here below are generated and corruptible, for it is impossible that the causes of the transient and of the eternal should be the same in species. This being the case, it only remains for us to investigate in what respect those two natures which are in the celestial body differ from the two natures which are in the transient body.

The starting point of the investigation is what we have gathered from Aristotle concerning these matters. For concerning things existent [in nature] no opinion has reached us from the ancients which is truer than his, or less subject to doubt, or presented in better order. Therefore we take his opinion to be that human opinion which man may attain by nature, that is, it is the most advanced of those opinions which man, insofar as he is man, may by his own knowledge and intel-

Translated by Arthur Hyman from his unpublished edition of the Hebrew text of Averroes, *De Substantia Orbis* (*Ma'amar be-'Eṣem ha-Galgal*). The Latin text is found in *Aristotelis omnia opera*, Venice; Apud Junctas, 1562–1574, Vol. IX, pp. 3r–5v. Reprinted, Frankfurt: Minerva, 1962.

lect attain. Thus, as Alexander puts it, "Aristotle is the one on whom we are to rely in the sciences." We shall begin by recalling Aristotle's opinion concerning the nature of the bodies which are with us here below, what he lays down about their being composed matter and form, and what he asserts about the nature of the matter and form existing in them. From these things we shall proceed to an inquiry into the nature of the celestial bodies, analogous to those inquiries we have made in regard to the nature of the transient bodies, that is to say, we want to find out in what respect they agree and in what respect they differ.

And we say that when Aristotle observed that each one of the individuals existing in virtue of themselves here below, called substances, passes from one descriptive predicate to another, he found that this change takes place according to two kinds. One kind is a change in descriptive predicates existing apart from the essences of the substances existing in virtue of themselves. This kind does not require a change in the individuals underlying, as subjects, these descriptive predicates, neither in the term by which they are called nor in their definition. Examples of such descriptive predicates are those called qualities, quantities and the other categories called accidents. The other kind is a change of descriptive predicates such that it demands a change in the individuals underlying, as subjects, these predicates, both in respect to the terms by which they are called and in respect to the definition by which their essence is indicated. This latter kind of change is called generation and corruption.

When Aristotle reflected on these two kinds of change he found in each one of them things which are common to both and things which are peculiar to each. Concerning the common things which he found in both kinds of change, he noticed that they both have a subject which is the recipient of the change, inasmuch as change and motion would be impossible for them without a subject. He also discovered that in both kinds of change the precedence of non-existence is a requisite for the existence of that which comes to be, for only that which does not exist can come to be. Furthermore, the prior existence of a possibility in the subject is a requisite for the existence of each of the two kinds of change, inasmuch as that which is impossible can not come to be. He also found among the requisites of these two kinds of change that that from which the change proceeds and that towards which it goes are either contraries or that which is between contraries. And these contraries belong to the same genus and they are reducible to the primary contraries, namely privation and form.

But concerning those things in which the two kinds of change differ, he found that the change which individuals undergo in respect to their substances requires that the subject should not be something existing in actuality and that it should not have a form in virtue of which it would become a substance. For if it had a form through which it becomes a substance, it could not receive the other forms except by destruction of this first form, for one form can only have one subject. And if the subject were also a simple substance existing in actuality, it could not be passive and not receptive, for that which is actual can not, insofar as it is actual, be the recipient of something else actual. Therefore, the nature of that subject which receives the substantial forms, that is to say, the subject called prime matter, is the nature of the potential, that is to say, being potential is the essential differentia of prime matter [as a subject]. Therefore, prime matter has no proper form nor does it have a nature existing in actuality, but its essence is to be only potential. It is for this reason that it can receive all forms.

But the difference which there is between the potentiality through which this subject becomes a substance and between the nature of the subject which becomes a substance through this potentiality consists in this, namely, that the term potentiality is predicated only in relation to form [and hence this subject should belong to the category of relation], while the subject is one of those beings which exist in virtue of themselves, the substances whereof exist in potentiality [and hence this subject should belong to the category of substance]. Therefore, [since the nature of prime matter is to be only potential,] it is difficult to conceive of it except in relation to something else, as Aristotle has already pointed out.

When Aristotle observed that the substantial forms are divisible in virtue of the divisibility of this subject—and divisibility belongs to this subject only insofar as it possesses quantity—he understood that the three dimensions, called "body," are the first thing existing in this subject. And when he found that all forms have these three dimensions in common, while each form is distinguished by having a determinate quantity of them, he knew that the indeterminate dimensions become determinate and the ultimate dimensions in actuality only after the substantial forms become inherent in the subject, the case being the same as that of the other accidents which exist in actuality. For Aristotle also observed that the respective subjects of all accidents are individual substances existing in actuality, namely they are those actual individual substances concerning whose nature it is clear that they are composed of forms and of a subject existing in potentiality.

From the fact that the subject receives transitory accidents Aristotle also adduced proof that the subject is not a simple thing, for if it were actually simple, it would be impossible for it to receive accidents. For passivity towards the reception of something is contrary to the actual possession of it. And as regards the existence of the indeterminate dimensions, which all forms have in common, he understood that prime matter is never divested of these indeterminate dimensions, for if prime matter were ever divested of them, then body would come from non-body and dimension from non-dimension and the corporeal form would change from one contrary state to another and it would come upon the subject in successive and changing stages, as is the case with the substantial forms.

All this is in agreement with what appears through sense perception. Thus, by way of an example, when the calefactory form operates in water, water undergoes an increase in its dimensions and these dimensions approach the dimensions of air. Now, when water has reached the greatest quantity of dimensions which may exist in water, the subject strips itself of the form of water and of the maximum quantity of dimensions proper to water and it receives the form of air and the quantity of dimensions proper to the reception of the form of air. The reverse takes place when the frigorific form operates in air, that is, the dimensions of air do not cease shrinking until the subject has stripped itself of the form of air, and the form of water has come to be. But as for the absolute dimensions, and those are the dimensions to which we apply the term "body" in its absolute sense, prime matter never strips itself of them, as it never strips itself of the rest of the accidents common to all of those bodies which change into their contrary, or to two or more of them, an example of the latter case being the property of transparency which fire and air have in common.

Inasmuch as the form of the indeterminate three dimensions is the first form residing in prime matter and [one substantial form] comes upon it in succession to another [only] as a result of change—seeing that it is not possible for this quantitatively indeterminate matter to receive two of the four substantial forms [simultaneously] in one and the same abode of determinate quantity, nor is it possible that both, the substantial form which is being destroyed and its contrary, the successive substantial form which is destroying, should be without prime matter as their subject, nor is it possible that the form which comes to be as a successor to the one which is destroyed should be generated in the subject except through an agent which brings it from potentiality to actuality—it follows from these considerations that the substantial forms must be contraries so that each one of them at some time destroys its contrary, the result being that the subject receives a form similar to the one bringing about the destruction. Thus, the forms of the elements are contraries and they reside in a single subject. Therefore we say that things undergoing change are in some respect contrary and in some respect similar. It will follow as a corollary that if there exist simple bodies whose forms have no contraries, it will necessarily be true in regard to these forms that they are not generable or corruptible and that they do not possess a common subject.

All this being as we have described, it should be clear to you that the cause of the destruction and the generation of existing things is the contrariety belonging to their forms. As for the common subject, it has no proper form, but it is potentially receptive of enumeration which is applicable to forms differing in species, and also of enumeration which is applicable to forms differing in number or which is according to the distinction between great and small.

The reason for all this is that this subject first receives the indeterminate three dimensions which are susceptible of division, and that it is potentially many. For if the subject would not possess the indeterminate dimensions, it could not receive simultaneously, that is, in different parts of itself, either those forms which differ in number or those forms which differ in species, but there would exist in it only one form at a given time. On the other hand, if matter, despite being one in number, were not potentially many, then it would never have been denuded of that form of which it happened to be the recipient and that form would have been in the very essence of that underlying matter, so that it would be impossible that that underlying matter should be completely denuded of its form or that it should lose this form and obtain another.

Inasmuch as this subject receives many forms simultaneously only in virtue of having received the three dimensions first, it is clear that if this subject were to possess only one form continuously, it would be numerically one in an absolute manner and no multiplicity could be in it at all, either potentially or actually. Furthermore, this subject would not be divisible by a form, nor would that one form which has been assumed to reside in it, be divisible by the division of the subject. The reason for all these conclusions would be that the subject does not receive the indeterminate quantity prior to receiving the form. For if the subject were to receive this indeterminate quantity first, it would be divisible by the substantial form and the substantial form, in turn, would be divisible by its division, that is to say, by the division of the subject, and the activities of this form would be finite in accordance with the finiteness of the quantity proper to it, and the form would be capable of receiving the distinction of great and small and part and whole.

Now, if there would exist here below a form which does not receive the distinction of great and small and which is not divisible by division of its sub-

ject and of which the subject is not divisible by division of that form—wherein by
the expression "division of form" I mean the diversification of it—it is evident that
the primary dimensions would not settle upon the subject belonging to this form
nor would these primary dimensions exist in it until after the form has settled
upon it, and when I use the term "after" I have in mind posteriority in respect
to existence not posteriority in respect to time. The case of the primary dimensions
would then be like the case of all the accidents existing in prime matter, that is,
the primary dimensions would exist in prime matter only insofar as prime matter
possesses a form existing in actuality.

For this reason Avicenna thought that the case of the three dimensions which
exist in matter absolutely, that is to say, the three indeterminate dimensions, is
the same as the case of the determinate dimensions in it. And he asserts that it is
impossible but that a primary form settle upon the primary matter prior to the
settlement upon it of the primary dimensions. And many absurdities follow
from this view. Among them: that the substantial forms would not be divisible
by the division of the primary matter, that the forms would not receive the
attributes of great and small, that they would be eternal not divisibly by division
of the subject, and that they would not have a contrary diverse from them in
subject. Finally, if what has been assumed were true, then matter would not
receive any other form apart from that one form which would be proper to it.

Aristotle gave an account of those properties which belong to generated beings
in virtue of their subject and in virtue of their forms, these properties being the
ones through which generation and corruption comes to these beings, that is,
to the individuals which exist in virtue of themselves. He showed, in addition, that
the celestial bodies are neither generable nor corruptible. As a result of this he
denied that the celestial bodies possess a subject which is receptible to enumeration and division in virtue of the fact that the absolute dimensions settle upon
it before the form is settled upon it, thereby also denying that the celestial bodies
are many in potentiality though one in number. Furthermore, Aristotle denied
regarding the forms of the celestial bodies that they are divisible by division of
their subject and that their activities are finite in virtue of their own finitude,
for in the case of forms divisible by the division of their subject, the potentiality
of the whole is greater than the potentiality of a part.

Inasmuch as Aristotle found that the activities of the celestial forms are infinite,
he concluded that those forms do not settle upon their subject by means of the
indeterminate three dimensions, that is to say, since the forms do not exist by
means of the indeterminate dimensions, they are not forces in bodies. And from
the difference between the force of the whole and that of a part in the case of the
forms divisible in virtue of the division of their subject, he demonstrated apodic-
tically, that it is impossible that a power producing an infinite activity should
exist in a finite body or that an infinite power should exist in a finite body.

After these premises were set down by Aristotle and after he found that the
celestial forces act with an infinite activity he drew the following conclusions:
the celestial forces do not inhere in a subject at all, they do not have a matter
which receives them by means of the indeterminate dimensions, they do not
have a matter in virtue of which they are potentially many, they are not recipients
of the attributes of great and small, and they do not have a contrary. All these
conclusions follow from the fact that these forms act with an infinite activity.
And all this is discussed in the *Physics*.

When Aristotle also investigated concerning the nature of the celestial bodies in the first book of the *De Caelo* he demonstrated that they are simple, since their motion is simple, and that their nature is a nature which is neither heavy nor light, that is, they are not ordinarily described by the terms of heaviness or lightness. Since it became clear to him that heavy and light bodies are contraries because their motions are contrary to each other and since it also became clear to him that the motions of the celestial bodies do not possess contraries or contrariety, he concluded from this that the celestial bodies are neither generated nor corruptible, and that they do not have a subject which receives the dimensions first, [and then the forms], and hence that their forms are divisible by the division of their subject. This is the meaning of his statement in the first book of the *De Caelo,* that "these celestial bodies have no contrary in their forms nor have they a subject." In like manner he deduced the very same thing from the fact that their motions, which proceed from principles existing in them, are infinite motions.

Inasmuch as it is apparent in regard to the celestial bodies that they receive dimensions, and that it is impossible for them to receive the determinate dimensions except in virtue of their forms, and also that they do not receive their forms by means of the indeterminate dimension, as is the case with the transient forms, it follows that the celestial bodies receive the dimensions in a manner which does not require that their forms are transient, that is, their matter receives the dimensions first by means of its forms. And the matter does not receive its forms by means of the dimensions, that is, the indeterminate dimensions, which exist in it potentially, the latter being the case with those dimensions which exist in prime matter together with the form of that matter. But the dimensions which exist in the celestial element are one of its properties.

Since it became clear to Aristotle concerning the celestial bodies that their forms settle upon their subjects in such a manner that they are not divisible by the division of their subjects, and the reason for that is that they do not settle upon the subjects insofar as they are divisible, it followed that these forms do not subsist in the subject, but they are separated from the subject in respect to existence. For, since these forms settle upon the whole subject yet are not divisible in virtue of its division, they have no subsistence in the subject, for they do not settle upon the subject, not in the whole, nor in part of it and generally not in something divisible nor in something indivisible.

This being so, it also follows that the form by which the celestial body is moved is the same as that toward which it is moved, for in the case of the forms which subsist in their subject, the form by which the body is moved is not the same as that toward which it is moved. And similarly the form subsisting in a subject which moves that subject to another form by virtue of its existing in the subject, is itself moved in order to attain perfection through another form. The motion of that subsisting form is therefore finite inasmuch as it produces motion in the subject only while it itself is moved. And this is also one of the arguments which moved Aristotle to believe that the forms of the celestial bodies do not subsist in their subjects, for if they did, their motions would be finite.

And an opponent [Averroes has in mind Avicenna] should not say that the forms by which the celestial bodies are moved are different from those toward which they are moved and that those forms which must be absolutely without matter and without position are those forms toward which the spheres are moved and not those by which they are moved, inasmuch as those by which they are moved are forms in matters even though they are not divisible by the division of their matters. For if this what the opponents would say were true, the forms by which the celestial bodies are moved would be subsisting in their subjects and, hence, moved by the motion or their subjects. But if this were so, they would be divisible by the division of their subject, for with regard to that which is moved, if it is moved essentially, that is, in the case of a body, it is divisible essentially and if it is moved accidentally it is divided accidentally. Therefore, there is nothing in the celestial body whereby the form by which the motion takes place differs from that toward which the motion tends, but they are one and the same form differing only in disposition. Furthermore, were the opponent correct in his contention that the form toward which the celestial body is moved is different from that by which it is moved, then the latter in causing motion would itself be moved and consequently the motion would be finite, for that which is moved while producing motion can not be a principle for eternal motion. This is in accordance with what Aristotle has already stated. Furthermore, in opposition to the opponent's view it can be shown by the analogous fact that the intellect and the intelligible in the celestial body are one and the same thing that the form toward which the sphere is moved and the form by which it is moved are one and the same. All this concerning the intellect and the intelligible has already been explained in other places.

And the heavens are said to possess a soul only in virtue of a desire existing in them and in virtue of possessing locomotion. Now, the desire which belongs to the celestial body exists only insofar as this body has life in virtue of itself and desire in virtue of itself, and not in virtue of a force existing in it which is divisible by the division of this body, for, if the latter were the case, the celestial body would be generated and destructible. And the celestial body is said to undergo motion on account of a principle which exists in it as something separate from it, and not on account of a principle which exists in it as something which is a part of it, and in the same manner it is said to be living and thinking. Now if it would be thinking by means of a part of itself, it would not be thinking in virtue of itself and the celestial body would be thinking like man, for a man is thinking by means of a part of himself and in like manner it is through part of himself that he is living, desiring and moving in place. And generally, since it is clear that the activity of this body is eternal, it is also clear concerning the nature of its form that it does not subsist in a subject, and that its subject is simple, not composed of matter and form, for if the latter were the case, the celestial body would be generated and corruptible.

Some of those who philosophize have said that the souls of the celestial bodies are forms in their respective matters which can not subsist apart from a subject and that they acquire eternal existence from forms which do exist apart from matter. This statement is devoid of any meaning. For if it were true, it would follow that something which according to its nature can not be eternal acquires eternal existence from something else. All this is absurd, since a nature which is generated and corruptible can not receive eternal existence from something else. All this is clear to him who is familiar with the fundamental principles of Aristotle.

It has been proved then in this treatise what the substance of the heavens is according to the knowledge of the substances of their forms and matters. Not everything we have said was found explained in those books of the sayings of Aristotle which have reached us, but some of these things were found explained in his writings and some of them follow from what he has proved in the books which have reached us. However, it appears from his words that he has explained all of these matters in books of his which have not come down to us. And God is He who guideth one into the right path. This treatise is called "A Discourse Concerning the Substance of the Celestial Sphere." It is more worthy of his name than the treatise of Avicenna bearing this title (?). This great and useful treatise has been completed. Praise be to God; in Him we trust.

LONG COMMENTARY ON *DE ANIMA*

Book III

Text 4. It is necessary, therefore, that, if [the intellect] understands all things, it be not mixed, as Anaxagoras has said, in order that it may dominate, that is in order that it may understand. For if [something] were to appear in it, that which appears would prevent something foreign [from appearing in it], since it is something other.

Commentary. After [Aristotle] has set down that the material, receiving intellect must belong to the genus of passive powers, and, that in spite of this, it is not altered by the reception [of that which it receives], for it is neither a body nor a power within a body, he provides a demonstration for this [opinion]. And he says: *It is necessary, therefore, that, if the intellect understands,* etc. That is, it is necessary, therefore, that, if [the intellect] understands all those things which exist outside the soul, it be described—prior to its understanding— as belonging to the genus of passive, not active, powers, and [it is necessary] that it be not mixed with bodies, that is, that it be neither a body nor a power within a body, be it a natural or animate [power], as Anaxagoras has said. Thereafter [Aristotle] says: *in order that it may understand* etc. That is, it is necessary that it be not mixed, in order that it may understand all things and receive them. For if it were mixed, then it would be either a body or a power within a body, and if it were one of these, it would have a form proper to itself, which form would prevent it from receiving some foreign form.

This is what he has in mind when he says: *For if something were to appear in it* etc. That is, if [the passive intellect] were to have a form proper to itself, then that form would prevent it from receiving the various external forms, which are different from it. Thus, one must inquire into those propositions by means of which Aristotle shows these two things about the intellect, namely [1] that it belongs to the genus of passive powers, and [2] that it is not alterable, since it

Translated by Arthur Hyman for this volume from *Averrois Cordubensis Commentarium Magnum in Aristotelis De Anima Libros,* ed. F. S. Crawford, Cambridge, Mass.: The Medieval Academy of America, 1953.

is neither a body nor a power within a body. For these two [propositions] are the starting point of all those things which are said about the intellect. As Plato said, the most extensive discussion must take place in the beginning; for the slightest error in the beginning is the cause of the greatest error in the end, as Aristotle says.

We say: That conception by the intellect belongs in some way to a passive power, just as in the case of a sensory power [perception by a sense belongs to a passive power], becomes clear through the following [considerations]. Now, the passive powers are moveable by that to which they are related (*attribuuntur*), while active powers move that to which they are related (*attribuuntur*). And since it is the case that something moves something else only insofar as it exists in actuality and [something] is moved insofar as it exists in potentiality, it follows necessarily, that since the forms of things exist in actuality outside the soul, they move the rational soul insofar as it understands them, just as in the case of sensible things it is necessary that they move the senses insofar as they are things existing in actuality and that the senses are moved by them. Therefore, the rational soul must consider the forms (*intentiones*) which are in the imaginative faculty, just as the senses must inspect sensible things. And since it appears that the forms of external things move this power in such a way that the mind abstracts these forms from material things and thereby makes them the first intelligibles in actuality, after they had been intelligibles in potentiality—it appears from this that this soul [the intellect] is [also] active, not [only] passive. For insofar as the intelligibles move [the intellect], it is passive, but insofar as they are moved by it, it is active. For this reason Aristotle states subsequently that it is necessary to posit in the rational soul the following two distinct [powers], namely, an active power and a passive power. And he states clearly that each one of [the rational soul's] parts is neither generable nor corruptible. In the present discussion, however, he begins to describe the nature (*substantiam*) of this passive power, to the extent to which it is necessary in this exposition. Therefore he states that this distinct [power], namely, that which is passive and receptive, exists in the rational faculty.

That the substance which receives these forms can not be a body or a power in a body, becomes clear from the propositions of which Aristotle makes use in this discussion. One of these is that this substance [the material intellect] receives all material forms, and this is [something well] known about this intellect. The other is that everything which receives something else must necessarily be devoid of the nature of that which it receives and that its essence (*substantiam*) is not the same in species as the essence (*substantiam*) of that which it receives. For, if that which receives is of the same nature as that which is received, then something would receive itself and that which moves would be the same as that which is moved. Wherefore it is necessary that the sense which receives color lacks color and the sense which receives sound lacks sound. And this proposition is necessarily [true] and there is no doubt about it. From these two propositions it follows that the substance which is called the material intellect does not have any of the material forms in its nature. And since the material forms are either a body or forms in a body, it is evident that the substance which is called the material intellect is not a body or a form in a body. For this reason it is not mixed with matter in any way at all. And you should know that what he states is necessarily [so], [namely] that, since it [the

material intellect] is a substance, and since it receives the forms of material
things or material [forms], it does not have in itself a material form, that is
[it is not] composed of matter and form. Nor is it some one of the material
forms, for the material forms are not separable [from bodies]. Nor, again, is it
one of the first simple forms since these are separable [from bodies], but it
[the material intellect] does not . . . receive forms except as differentiated and
insofar as they are intelligible in potentiality, not in actuality [that is, it must
be related to the body in some way]. Therefore it is something different from
form and from matter and from that which is composed of these. But whether
this substance [the material intellect] has a proper form which is different in
its being from the material forms has not yet been explained in this discussion.
For the proposition which states that that which receives must be devoid of the
nature of that which it receives is understood as referring to the nature of the
species, not to the nature of its genus, and even less to [the nature of] something remote, and still less to [the nature of] something which is predicated
according to equivocation. Thus we say that in the sense of touch there exists
something intermediate between the two contraries which it perceives, for
contraries differ in species from intermediate things. Since this is the disposition of the material intellect, namely, that it is some existing thing, and
that it is a power separate from body, and that it has no material form, it is
clear that it is not passive [in the sense of being alterable] (for passive things,
that is things which are alterable, are like material forms), and that it is simple,
and separable from body, as Aristotle says. The nature of the material intellect is
understood by Aristotle in this manner. We shall speak subsequently about the
questions which he raised.

Text 5. And thus [the material intellect] has no other nature but that which
is possible. Therefore that [part] of the soul which is called intellect (and I
call intellect that [part] by means of which we distinguish and think) is not
something existing in actuality before it thinks.

Commentary. After [Aristotle] has shown that the material intellect does not
possess any of the forms of material things, he begins to define it in the following manner. And he says that it has no nature but the nature of the possibility
for receiving the material intelligible forms. And he states: *And thus [the
material intellect] has no other nature,* etc. That is, that [part] of the soul which
is called the material intellect has no nature and essence through which it exists
(*constituatur*) insofar as it is material but the nature of possibility, for it is
devoid of all material and intelligible forms.

Thereafter he says: *and I call intellect,* etc. That is, and I intend by *intellect*
that faculty of the soul which is truly called intellect, not that faculty which
is called intellect in a general sense, that is, the imaginative faculty (in the
Greek language), but [I intend] that faculty by means of which we distinguish
speculative things and by means of which we think about things to be done
in the future. Thereafter he says: *it is not something existing in actuality before
it thinks.* That is, it is the definition of the material intellect that it is that
which is in potentiality all the concepts (*intentiones*) of the universal material
forms and it is not something in actuality before it understands them.

Since this is the definition of the material intellect, it is clear that it differs
in respect to itself from prime matter in that it is in potentiality all the concepts

(*intentiones*) of the universal material forms, while prime matter is in potentiality all these sensible forms, not [as] knowing and comprehending. And the reason why this nature, that is, the material intellect, distinguishes and knows, while prime matter does not distinguish or know, is that prime matter receives differentiated, that is, individual and particular forms, while [the material intellect] receives universal forms. And from this it is clear that this nature, [that is, the material intellect] is not some individual thing, either a body or a power in a body, for if it were, it would receive the forms insofar as they are differentiated and particular, and if this were the case, then the forms existing in [the material intellect] would be intelligible in potentiality and thus [this intellect] would not distinguish the nature of the forms insofar as they are forms, and the case would be the same as that of a disposition for individual forms, whether they are spiritual or corporeal. Therefore, if this nature, which is called intellect, receives forms, it is necessary that it receives [these] forms in a manner of reception different from that according to which these matters receive the forms whose determination in prime matter is the determination of prime matter in respect to them. Therefore it is not necessary that there belong to the genus of those matters by which the form is determined as particular anything but prime matter. For if there were other matters in this genus, then the reception of forms in these [matters] would be of the same genus, for diversity in the nature of the receptacle produces a diversity in the nature of that which is received. This consideration moved Aristotle to affirm that this nature, that is, the material intellect, differs from the nature of matter and from the nature of form and from the nature of the composite.

. . .

All these things being as they are, it seems to me proper to write down what appears to me [to be correct] concerning this subject. And if that which appears to me [to be correct] will not be complete, let it be the starting point for something which can be completed. Now, I beg those brethren who see what has been written, that they write down their questions and perhaps in this way that which is true about this subject will be discovered, if I should not have discovered it. But should I have discovered [what is true], as I think I have, then [this truth] will become clear through these questions. For truth, as Aristotle says, agrees with itself and bears witness to itself in every way.

As for the question stating: in what way are the speculative intelligibles generable and corruptible, while [the intellect] producing them and that receiving them are eternal (and what need would there be to posit an agent intellect and a receiving [intellect] were there not something that is generated)—this question would not arise would there not exist something which is the cause of the generation of the speculative intelligibles. But what has been said concerning the fact that these [speculative] intelligibles consists of two [principles], one of which is generated, the other of which is not generated is according to the course of nature. For, since conception by the intellect, as Aristotle says, is like perception by the senses—but perception by a sense is accomplished through two principles, one of which is that object through which sense perception becomes true (and this is the sensible outside the soul), and the other is that subject through which sense perception is an existing form (and this is the first actuality of the sense organ), it is likewise necessary that the intelligibles in actuality have two principles, one of which is the object (*subiectum*) through which they are true, namely, the forms which are the true images, the other one of which is that subject (*subiectum*) through which the intelligibles are one of the things existing in the world, and this is the material intellect. But there is no difference between sense and intellect except that the object through which sense-perception is true exists outside the soul, while the object through which conception by the intellect is true exists within the soul. As will be seen subsequently, this is what was said by Aristotle about this intellect.

. . .

This similarity exists in an even more perfect manner between the visible object which moves the sense of sight and the intelligible object which moves the intellect. For just as the visible object, which is color, moves the sense of sight only when through the presence of light it was made color in actuality after it had been [color] in potentiality, so also the imaginative forms (*intentiones*) move the material intellect only when they are made intelligibles in actuality after they had been [intelligibles] in potentiality. And for this reason (as will be seen later) it was necessary for Aristotle to posit an agent intellect, and this is the intellect which brings the imaginative forms from potentiality into actuality. Thus, just as the color which exists in potentiality is not the first actuality of that color which is the perceived form (*intentio*), while the subject which is actualized by this color is the sense of sight, so also the subject which is actualized by the intelligible object is not the imaginative forms (*intentiones*) which are intelligible in potentiality, but the material intellect is that subject which is actualized by the intelligibles. And the relation of the intelligible forms to the material intellect is as the relation of the form (*intentio*) of color to the faculty of sight.

All these matters being as we have related, it is only necessary that the intelligibles in actuality, that is the speculative intelligibles, are generable according to the object through which they are true, that is according to the imaginative forms, but not according to that subject through which they are one of the existing things, that is, according to the material intellect.

But the second question which states: in what way is the material intellect numerically one in all individual human beings, not generable nor corruptible, while the intelligibles existing in it in actuality (and this is the speculative intellect) are numbered according to the numeration of individual human beings, and generable and corruptible through the generation and corruption of individual [human beings]—this question is extremely difficult and one that has the greatest ambiguity.

If we posit that this material intellect is numbered according to the numeration of individual human beings, it follows that it is some individual thing, either a body or a power in a body. And if it were some individual thing, it would be the intelligible form (*intentio*) in potentiality. But the intelligible form in potentiality is an object which moves the receiving intellect, not a subject which is moved. For, if the receiving subject were assumed to be some individual thing, it would follow, as we have said, that something receives itself, and this is impossible.

[Even] if we were to admit that it receives itself, it would necessarily follow that it receives itself insofar as it is diverse. And thus the intellectual faculty would be the same as the sensory faculty, and there would be no distinction between the existence of the form outside the soul and in the soul. For this individual matter receives the forms only as particulars and individuals. And this is one of the arguments which provide evidence that Aristotle was of the opinion that the [material] intellect is not an individual form (*intentio*).

[On the other hand], were we to assert that [the material intellect] is not numbered according to the numeration of individual [human beings], it would follow that its relation to all individual human beings who possess its ultimate perfection through generation would be the same. Whence it would be necessary that if one of these individual [human beings] acquires some knowledge, this knowledge would be acquired by all of them. For, if the conjunction (*continuatio*) of these individual human beings [with what is known] occurs because of the conjunction (*propter continuationem*) of the material intellect with them, just as the conjunction of a human being with the sensory form (*intentione*) occurs because of the conjunction of the first perfection of the sense organ with him who receives the sensory form (but the conjunction of the material intellect with all human beings who exist in actuality in their ultimate perfection at some given time must be one and the same conjunction, for there is nothing which would produce any difference in the relation of conjunction between the two who are conjoined)—if, I say, this is the case, it is necessary that if you acquire some knowledge, I will acquire the same knowledge, which is absurd.

And regardless whether you assert that the ultimate perfection which is generated in some individual [human being]—that is, that perfection through which the material intellect is joined [to human beings] and through which it is as a form separable from the subject to which it is joined—inheres in the intellect, if something like that should be the case, or whether you assert that this perfection belongs to one of the faculties of the soul or to one of the faculties of the body, each of these assumptions leads to an absurd conclusion.

Therefore* one must be of the opinion that if there exist some beings having a soul whose first perfection is a substance existing in separation from their subjects, as it is thought about the celestial bodies, it is impossible that there exist in each of their species more than one individual. For if there would exist in these, that is, in each of their species more than one individual, for example, in the body moved by the same mover, then the existence of these individuals would be unnecessary and superfluous, since their motion would result from the form (*intentio*) which is one in number. For example, it is unnecessary that one sailor [captain] should have more than one ship at the same time, and it is likewise unnecessary that one artisan should have more than one instrument of the same kind.

This is the meaning of what was said in the first book of *De Caelo*, namely that, if there existed another world, there would have to exist another celestial body [corresponding to a celestial body in this world]. And if there existed another celestial body, it would have to have a motive force numerically different from the motive force of this celestial body [that is, the one existing in this world]. If this were the case, then the motive force of the celestial body would be material and numbered through the numeration of the celestial bodies, since it is impossible that a motive force which is one in number should belong to two bodies which

* The following argument contains an objection to Averroes' thesis that the intellect *in habitu* is one in all men. For if this were the case, it would follow that, since this intellect exists in separation from bodies, it could only have one body not many. This is absurd.

are different in number. Therefore, a craftsman does not use more than one instrument when only one action proceeds from him. And it is generally thought that necessarily absurd conclusions will follow from the assertion we have made, namely, that the intellect *in habitu* is one in number. Avempace enumerated most of these absurd conclusions in his Letter which he called *The Conjunction of the Intellect with Man*. Since this is so, of what sort is the road toward the solution of this difficult question?

We say that it is evident that a man is thinking in actuality only because of the conjunction of the intelligible in actuality with him. It is also evident that matter and form are joined to one another in such a way that something which is composed of them is a unitary thing and this is especially evident in the case of the conjunction of the material intellect and the intelligible form (*intentio*) in actuality. For that which is composed of these [the material intellect and the intelligible form] is not some third thing different from them as is the case in respect to other beings composed of matter and form. Hence the conjunction of the intelligible with man is only possible through the conjunction of one of these two parts with him, namely that part which belongs to it [the intelligible] as matter or that part which belongs to it (namely, the intelligible) as form.

Since it is clear from the previously mentioned difficulties that it is impossible that the intelligible be joined to each individual human being and that it be numbered according their numeration through that part which is to it as matter, that is, through the material intellect, it remains that the conjunction of the intelligibles with us human beings takes place through the conjunction of the intelligible forms (and they are the imaginative forms) with us, that is, through that part which is in us in respect to them in some way like a form. And therefore the statement that a boy is potentially thinking can be understood in two ways. One of these is insofar as the imaginative forms which exist in him are intelligible in potentiality; the other is insofar as the material intellect, to whose nature it belongs to receive the concept of this imaginative form, is receptive in potentiality and joined to us in potentiality.

It is clear, therefore, that the first perfection of the intellect differs from the first perfection of the other faculties of the soul and that the term *perfection* is predicated of them in an equivocal fashion, and this is the opposite of what Alexander [of Aphrodisias] thought. For this reason Aristotle said in his definition of the soul that the soul is the first perfection of a natural organic body, for it is not yet clear whether a body is perfected by all faculties in the same way, or whether there is among them some faculty by which a body is not perfected, or, if it is perfected by it, it will be perfected in some other way.

Now the predisposition of the intelligibles which exists in the imaginative faculty is similar to the predispositions which exist in the other faculties of the soul, namely, the predisposition for the first perfections of the other faculties of the soul, insofar as each of these predispositions is generated through the generation of the individual [in which it exists] and destroyed through the destruction of this individual and, generally, this predisposition is numbered according to the numeration of that individual.

But the two kinds of predisposition differ in that the first kind, namely, the predisposition which exists in the imaginative forms, is a predisposition in a moving principle, while the second kind, namely that predisposition which exists for the first perfections of the other parts of the soul, is a predisposition in a recipient.

Because of the similiarity between these two kinds of predispositions Avempace thought that the only predisposition for the production of the intelligible concept is the predisposition existing in the imaginative forms. But these two predispositions differ as earth and heaven. For one of them is a predisposition in a moving principle insofar as it is a moving principle, while the other is a predisposition in something moved insofar as it is moved and is a recipient.

Thus one should hold the opinion which has already become clear to us from Aristotle's discussion, [namely] that there are two kinds of intellect in the soul. One of these is the receiving intellect whose existence has been shown here, the other is the agent intellect and this is the one which causes the forms which are in the imaginative faculty to move the material intellect in actuality, after they had only moved [it] potentially, as will be clear further on from Aristotle's discussion. And these two kinds [of intellect] are not generable or corruptible. And the agent intellect is to the receiving intellect as form to matter, as will be shown later on.

Now Themistius was of the opinion that we are the agent intellect, and that the speculative intellect is nothing but the conjunction of the agent intellect with the material intellect. And it is not as he thought, but one must be of the opinion that there are three kinds of intellect in the soul. One of these is the receiving intellect, the second is the producing [agent] intellect, and the third is the produced [speculative] intellect. Two of these intellects are eternal, namely the agent and receiving intellects, the third, however, is generable and corruptible in one way, eternal in another way.

Since as a result of this discussion we are of the opinion that the material intellect is a single one for all human beings and since we are also of the opinion that the human species is eternal, as has been shown in other places, it follows that the material intellect is never devoid of the natural principles which are common to the whole human species, namely, the first propositions and individual concepts which are common to all. For these intelligibles are one according to the recipient [the material intellect], and many according to the received form [the imaginative form].

Hence according to the manner in which they are one, they are necessarily eternal, for existence does not depart from the received object, namely the moving principle which is the form (*intentio*) of the imaginative forms, and there is nothing on part of the recipient which prevents [its reception]. For generation and corruption belongs to them only according to the multitude which befalls them, not according to the manner according to which they are one. Therefore, when in respect to some individual human being, some knowledge of the things first known is destroyed through the destruction of the object through which it is joined to us and through which it is true, that is the imaginative form, it does not follow that this knowledge is destroyed absolutely, but it is [only] destroyed in respect to some individual human being. Because of this we can say that the speculative intellect is one in all [human beings].

If one considers these intelligibles insofar as they exist absolutely, not in respect to some individual [human being], they are truly said to be eternal, and [it is not the case] that they are known at one time and not known at another time, but they are known always. And that existence belongs to them as intermediate between absence of existence and permanent existence. For in accordance with the quantitative difference [literally: according to the increase and decrease] which comes to the intelligibles from the ultimate perfection [of human beings] they are generable and corruptible, while insofar as they are one in number they are eternal.

This will be the case if it is not set down that the disposition in respect to the ultimate perfection in man is as the disposition in respect to the intelligibles which are common to all [men], that is, that the world [literally: worldly existence] is not devoid of such an individual existence. That this should be impossible is not obvious, but someone who affirms this must have an adequate reason and one that puts the mind at rest. For if knowledge belongs in some proper fashion to human beings, just as the various kinds of crafts belong in some proper fashions to human beings, one should think that it is impossible that philosophy should be without any abode, just as one must be of the opinion that its is impossible that all the natural crafts should be without any abode. For if some part [of the earth] lacks them, that is, these crafts, for example, the northern quarter of the earth, the other quarters will not lack them, since it is clear that they can have an abode in the southern part, just as in the northern.

Thus, perhaps, philosophy comes to be in the major portion of the subject at all times, just as man comes to be from man and horse from horse. According to this mode of existence the speculative intellect is neither generable nor corruptible.

In general, the case of the agent intellect which produces the intelligibles is the same as the case of the intellect which distinguishes and receives [the intelligibles]. For just as the agent intellect never ceases from generating and producing [intelligibles] in an absolute manner, even though some particular subject may be removed from this generation, so is it with the intellect that distinguishes.

Aristotle indicated this in the first treatise of this book [*De Anima*] when he said: *Conception and consideration by the intellect are differentiated, so that within the intellect something other is destroyed, while the intellect itself is not subject to destruction.* Aristotle intends by *something other* the human imaginative [forms]. And he intends by *conception by the intellect* the reception which exists always in the material intellect, about which he intends to raise questions in the present treatise as well as in the former when he says: [*And when it (the intellect) is set free*] . . . *we do not remember, since this intellect is not passive, but the passive intellect is corruptible, and without it nothing thinks.*

And by the *passive intellect* he intends the imaginative faculty, as will be shown later. Generally, this meaning seems to be remote, namely, that the soul, that is the speculative intellect, should be immortal.

For this reason Plato said that the universals are neither generable nor corruptible and that they exist outside the mind. This statement is true in the sense that the intelligibles inhering in the speculative intellect are immortal, but false according to the sound of his words (and this is the sense which Aristotle labored to destroy in the *Metaphysics*). In general, in regard of the nature (*intentio*) of the soul, there is something true in the probable propositions which attribute to the soul both kinds of existence, namely mortal and immortal, since it is impossible that probable propositions should be completely false. The Ancients give an account of this and all the religious laws agree in this account.

The third question (namely, in what way is the material intellect some existing thing, while it is not one of the material forms nor prime matter) is answered as follows. One should be of the opinion that there are four kinds of existence. For just as sensible being is divided into form and matter, so also must intelligible being be divided into principles similar to these, that is into something similar to form and something similar to matter. This distinction is necessary for every incorporeal intellect which understands another, for if this distinction did not apply there would be no multiplicity in regard to the incorporeal forms. It has been shown in *First Philosophy* [that is in the *Metaphysics*] that there exists no form absolutely free from potentiality except the first form which does not think anything outside itself, but its existence (*essentia*) is its quiddity, but other forms are differentiated in respect to quiddity and existence (*essentia*) in some way. Were there not this genus of beings which we know in the science of the soul, we could not think of multiplicity in the case of incorporeal beings, just as we would not know that incorporeal motive forces must be intellects, if we would not know the nature of the intellect.

This escaped many modern philosophers, so that they deny what Aristotle said in the eleventh treatise of the *First Philosophy,* namely, that it is necessary, that the incorporeal forms which move the celestial bodies are [numbered] according to the number of the celestial bodies. Therefore, knowledge about the soul is necessary for the knowledge of First Philosophy. It is necessary that the receiving intellect knows the intellect which exists in actuality. For if [this intellect] understands the material forms, it is more fitting that it understands immaterial forms, and that which it knows of the incorporeal forms, for example, of the agent intellect, does not hinder it from knowing the material forms.

But the proposition which states that a recipient must not have anything in actuality insofar as it receives is not said in an absolute fashion, but with the provision, that it is not necessary that the receiving intellect be not anything whatsoever in actuality, but [only] that it is not something in actuality in respect to that which it receives, as we have stated previously. Indeed, you should know that the relation of the agent intellect to the receiving intellect is as the relation of light to the transparent medium, and that the relation of the material forms to the receiving intellect is as the relation of color to the transparent medium. For just as light is the perfection of the transparent medium, so is the agent intellect the perfection of the material [intellect]. And just as the transparent medium is only moved by color and receives it when it is illuminated, so also the [material] intellect only receives the intelligibles which exist in it when the material intellect is perfected by the agent intellect and illuminated by it. And just as light makes color in potentiality exist in actuality, as a result of which it [color] can move the transparent medium, so also the agent intellect makes the intelligible forms in potentiality exist in actuality, as a result of which the material intellect receives them. In this manner one must understand about the material and agent intellect.

When the material intellect becomes joined insofar as it is perfected through the agent intellect, then we are joined with the agent intellect. And this disposition is called *acquisition (adeptio)* and *acquired intellect (intellectus adeptus)*, as will be seen later. The manner in which we have described the essence of the material intellect answers all the questions arising about our statement that this intellect is one and many. For if something which is known by me and by you were one in all respects, it would follow that, if I know something, you would also know it, and many other absurdities [would also follow]. And if we were to assert that the material intellect is many, it would follow that something known by me and by you is one in respect to species and two in respect to individual, and thus something known would possess something else known and this would go on to infinity. Thus it will be impossible that a student learns from a teacher if the knowledge which exists in the teacher is not a force generating and producing the knowledge which is in the student, in the same manner as one fire produces another fire alike to it in species, which is absurd. The fact that something known by the teacher and the student is the same in this manner made Plato believe that learning is remembering. But if we assert that something known by me and by you is many in respect to that object (*in subiecto*) according to which it is true, that is in respect to the imaginative forms, and one in respect to the subject through which it is an existing intellect (and this is the material intellect), these questions are resolved completely.

• • •

SELECTED BIBLIOGRAPHY

TRANSLATIONS

Blumberg, H., trans., *Averroes' Epitome of Parva Naturalia,* Cambridge, Mass., 1961.

Butterworth, C., ed. and trans., *Averroes' Three Short Commentaries on Aristotle's 'Topics,' 'Rhetoric,' and 'Poetics,'* Albany, 1977.

Davidson, H., trans., *Averroes' Middle Commentary on Porphyry's Isagoge and on Aristotle's Categories,* Cambridge, Mass., 1969.

Hourani, G., trans., *On the Harmony of Religion and Philosophy,* London, 1961.

Kurland, S., trans., *Averroes on Aristotle's De Generatione et Corruptione, Middle Commentary and Epitome,* Cambridge, Mass.,

1958.

Lerner, R., trans., *Averroes on Plato's Republic,* Ithaca, 1974.

Lerner, R., and M. Mahdi, eds., *Medieval Political Philosophy: A Sourcebook,* New York, 1963.

Rosenthal, E., ed. and trans., *Averroes' Commentary on Plato's Republic,* Cambridge, 1966.

van den Bergh, S., trans., *Averroes' Tahafut al-Tahafut (The Incoherence of the Incoherence),* 2 vols., London, 1954.

STUDIES

L'Averroismo in Italia (Academia nazionale dei Lincei), Rome, 1979.

Butterworth, C., "New Light on the Political Philosophy of Averroes," *Essays on Islamic Philosophy and Science,* ed. G. Hourani, Albany, 1975, 118–127.

Christ, P., *The Psychology of the Active Intellect of Averroes,* Philadelphia, 1926.

Fakhry, M., *Islamic Occasionalism and its Critique by Averroes and Aquinas,* London, 1958.

Gauthier, L., *La theorie d'Ibn Rochd (Averroès) sur les rapports de la religion et de la philosophie,* Paris, 1909.

Gauthier, L., *Ibn Rochd (Averroès),* Paris, 1948.

Hourani, G., "Averroes on Good and Evil," *Studia Islamica,* XVI (1962), 13–40.

Hyman, A., "Aristotle's Theory of the Intellect and its Interpretation by Averroes," in *Studies in Aristotle,* ed. D. O'Meara, Washington, 1981, 161–191.

Ivry, A., "Averroes on Causation," *Studies in Jewish Religious and Intellectual History,* presented to Alexander Altmann, ed. S. Stein and R. Loewe, University, Alabama, 1979, 143–156.

Ivry, A., "Averroes on Intellection and Conjunction," *Journal of the American Oriental Society,* LXXXVI (1966), 76–85.

Ivry, A., "Toward a Unified View of Averroes' Philosophy," *Philosophical Forum,* IV (1972), 87–113.

Leaman, O., "Ibn Rushd on Happiness and Philosophy," *Studia Islamica* LII (1981), 167–181.

Manser, G., "Die göttliche Erkenntnis der Einzeldinge und die Vorsehung bei Averroës," *Jahrbuch für Philosophie und spekulative Theologie*, XXIII (1909), 1–29.

Manser, G., "Das Verhältniss von Glaube und Wissen bei Averroës," *Jahrbuch für Philosophie und spekulative Theologie*, XXIV (1910), 398–408; XXV (1911), 9–34, 163–179, 250–277.

Mehren, A., "Études sur la philosophie d'Averroès concernant ses rapports avec celle d'Avicenne et Gazzali," *Muséon*, VII (1888), 613–627; VIII (1889), 5–20.

Multiple Averroès. Actes du colloque international organisé à l'occasion du 850e anniversaire de la naissance d'Averroès, Paris, 20–23 Septembre, 1976, Paris, 1978.

Renan, E., *Averroès et l'Averroisme: essai historique*, 3rd ed., Paris, 1866 (reprinted, 1948).

Salman, D., "Note sur la première influence d'Averroès," *Revue néoscolastique de philosophie*, XL (1937), 203–212.

Tornay, S., "Averroes' Doctrine of the Mind," *Philosophic Review*, LII (1943), 270–282.

Vajda, G., "A propos de l'averroïsme juif," *Sefarad*, XII (1952), 3–29.

de Vaux, R., "La première entrée d'Averroès chez les Latins," *Revue des sciences philosophiques et théologiques*, XXII (1933), 193–245.

Wolfson, H., "Averroes' Lost Treatise on the Prime Mover," *Hebrew Union College Annual*, XXIII, I (1950–1951), 683–710.

Wolfson, H., "The Plurality of Immovable Movers in Aristotle and Averroes," *Harvard Studies in Classical Philology*, LXIII (1958), 233–253.

Wolfson, H., "The Twice-Revealed Averroes," *Speculum*, XXXVI, No. 3 (1961), 373–393.

Wolfson, H., "Revised Plan for the Publication of a *Corpus Commentariorum Averrois in Aristotelem*," *Speculum*, XXXVII (1963), 88–104. (Reprinted, *Studies in the History of Religion*, ed. I. Twersky and G. Williams, vol. I, Cambridge, Mass., 1973, 430–454.)

Zedler, B., "Averroes on the Possible Intellect," *Proceedings of the American Catholic Philosophical Association*, XXV (1951), 164–178.

Jewish Philosophy

 MEDIEVAL JEWISH philosophy may be described as the explication of Jewish beliefs and practices by means of philosophic concepts and norms. Somewhat more rigorously, its subject matter is divisible into three parts. As interpretation of Jewish tradition, medieval Jewish philosophy manifests a special interest in such indigenously Jewish doctrines as the election of Israel, the prophecy of Moses, the Law (*Torah*) and its eternity, and Jewish conceptions of the Messiah and the afterlife. As religious philosophy, it investigates those philosophic notions which have a special bearing on issues common to Judaism, Christianity, and Islam, such as the existence of God, His attributes, creation, providence, prophecy, and general principles of human conduct. Finally, as philosophy, it studies topics which are primarily of philosophic interest, such as the structure of logical arguments, the division of being, and the constitution of the world. Because of these varied interests, medieval Jewish philosophy must be seen as part of the history of philosophy at large, no less than as a development of the biblical-rabbinic tradition on which Judaism rests.

Whereas the biblical and rabbinic writings developed within the Jewish community, Jewish philosophy flourished whenever Jewish thinkers participated in the philosophic speculations of an outside culture. Jewish philosophy arose for the first time in the Diaspora community of the Hellenistic world, where, from the second century B.C. until the middle of the first century A.D., Jewish thinkers produced a philosophic literature in Greek. The foremost member of this group was Philo Judaeus (*ca.* 25 B.C.–*ca.* 40 A.D.) who in a series of works, largely commentaries on biblical topics, undertook to harmonize Jewish with Platonic and Stoic teachings. H. A. Wolfson, the eminent historian of medieval thought, considers Philo the founder of religious philosophy in Judaism, Christianity, and Islam.

Though Philo influenced Fathers of the Christian Church, he found no direct successors among the Jews. Jewish philosophy lay dormant until it flourished once again as part of a general cultural revival in the Islamic east (see p. 204). From the early tenth century until the early thirteenth, Jewish philosophers, living in Muslim lands, produced a varied philosophic literature in Arabic.

Saadia Gaon (882–942), head of the rabbinical academy at Sura (near Bagdad), was the first major Jewish philosopher on the Islamic scene. Using and adapting the teachings of the Mu'tazilite branch of the Muslim dialectical theologians, the Mutakallimūn (see p. 205), Saadia fashioned what has been called a Jewish Kalām. In true Kalāmic fashion, he selected Divine unity and justice as the two major subjects of his *Book of Doctrines and Beliefs,* and Kalāmic proofs for the creation of the world have a prominent place within the work. As the Muslim Mutakallimūn, he has a greater interest in the philosophic solutions of scriptural difficulties than in independent philosophic speculations.

Kalāmic teachings influenced later Jewish philosophers, but Saadia was to remain the major representative of this school of thought. Already in his own days Jewish philosophy turned in a neoplatonic direction. Under the influence of such works as the *Theology of Aristotle* (see p. 205), Jewish Neoplatonists investigated how the world emanated from God, and how man, through philosophic speculations, can return to Him. But in accordance with their religious beliefs, Jewish Neoplatonists described God as a being having attributes of personality who created the world by an act of will, rather than as an impersonal principle who produced the world out of the necessity of its own nature.

The first Jewish Neoplatonist was Isaac ben Solomon Israeli (*ca.* 855–*ca.* 955), Saadia's somewhat older contemporary. Author of medical treatises and philosophic works, Israeli was known among philosophers for his *Book of Definitions* and his *Book of Elements.* In their Latin translations, these two works were cited by Christian philosophers from the twelfth century on. But by far the most important Jewish Neoplatonist was Solomon Ibn Gabirol (*ca.* 1022–*ca.* 1051 or 1070), who in the Latin world was known as Avicebrol, Avicebron, and Avencebrol. With him, the setting of Jewish philosophy became Spain in the Islamic west. In his *Fountain of Life* Gabirol defended the distinctive doctrine that spiritual as well as corporeal substances are composed of matter and form. In the thirteenth and fourteenth centuries this principle was widely debated by Christian scholastics who possessed a complete Latin translation of Gabirol's work.

The eleventh and twelfth centuries produced two Jewish philosophers who, virtually unknown in the outside world, enjoyed great popularity among their own people for the less technical and more pietistic nature of their views. Baḥya Ibn Paḳuda of Saragossa (end of the eleventh century) wrote a much-read ethical work, *Guidebook to the Duties of the Heart,* in which he describes ten spiritual qualities, presenting at the same time directions for how they may be attained. Judah Halevi (*ca.* 1085–*ca.* 1141), who in his antiphilosophic views shows some similarity to Algazali (see p. 264), composed his *Kuzari* as an *apologia* for the Jewish faith. Abraham bar Ḥiyya, the first to write philosophy in Hebrew, and Joseph Ibn Zaddik, a Neoplatonist (both early twelfth century) are two additional philosophers that should be mentioned.

In the second half of the twelfth century, Jewish philosophy, under the influence of Alfarabi, Avicenna (Ibn Sīnā), and Avempace (Ibn Bājjah) (see p. 208), entered its Aristotelian phase. Medieval Jewish Aristotelianism began with Abraham Ibn Daud (*ca.* 1110–*ca.* 1180 or 1190), whose *Exalted Faith*— a work containing an extensive critique of Gabirol's views—discussed a number of Aristotelian physical and metaphysical topics and their relation to Jewish religious thought. But Jewish Aristotelianism reached its climax with Moses Maimonides (1135–1204) who became the overtowering figure of medieval Jewish thought. Maimonides first presented a more popular exposition of his philosophic views within his various legal works, proceeding to a more technical account in his *Guide of the Perplexed*. Addressing students of philosophy who had become vexed by the literal sense of certain scriptural passages, Maimonides shows that scriptural teachings, properly interpreted, are in harmony with philosophic truths. In a Latin translation, Maimonides' *Guide* was read and cited by Christian scholastics of the thirteenth and fourteenth centuries.

After Maimonides the setting of Jewish philosophy shifted to Christian lands—Christian Spain, southern France, and Italy becoming the new centers. As a result, the knowledge of Arabic among the Jews declined and Hebrew became the language of Jewish philosophy. Works originally written in Arabic were now translated into Hebrew. Among the newly translated works, the commentaries of Averroes (1126–1198) (see p. 293) were of great importance, for, under their influence, Jewish philosophy turned into a more rigorously Aristotelian direction. At the same time, divergences between the strict Aristotelianism of Averroes and the more moderate views of Maimonides formed the subject matter of new investigations. Maimonides' *Guide* gave rise to many commentaries, the most important commentators being Shem Tob Falkera (d. 1290), Joseph Kaspi (1279–*ca.* 1340), and Moses of Narbonne (d. after 1362). During the second half of the thirteenth century, Hillel of Verona used Thomistic arguments to attack the Averroistic doctrine of the unity of the intellect in his *Rewards of the Soul,* while, by contrast, Isaac Albalag developed a doctrine of the double truth.

The most important post-Maimonidean Jewish Aristotelian was Levi ben Gerson—also called Gersonides—astronomer, biblical exegete, and commentator on Averroes. In his major work, *The Wars of the Lord,* he investigated, in true scholastic fashion, problems which Maimonides had not discussed sufficiently or which he had not resolved to Gersonides' satisfaction. When Maimonides and Averroes differ, Gersonides often sides with the latter philosopher. Gersonides differs from Maimonides in holding that God is thought thinking itself, that He can be described by positive attributes, that creation can be demonstrated, and that the world was created out of an eternally existing unformed matter. Moreover, Gersonides' stricter Aristotelianism came to the fore when he taught that God knows the world only insofar as it is subject to general laws and that miracles are caused by the Active Intellect rather than by God Himself.

As Aristotelianism spread among the Jews, opposition to it did not lag far behind. But not until Ḥasdai Crescas (*ca.* 1340–1410) wrote his *Light of the Lord* did someone undertake a systematic critique of the Aristotelian physical and metaphysical teachings. Denying the Aristotelian principle that an infinite can only exist in potentiality, Crescas affirms the actual existence of infinite magnitude, of infinite space, and of an infinite series of causes and effects. The affirmation of the latter principle brought Crescas to reject the Aristotelian proofs for the existence of God as first mover and first cause, since these proofs rest on the proposition that it is impossible that an actually . infinite series of causes and effects should exist. However, Crescas retained the proof which shows that God is a being necessary through Himself. Crescas also took issue with the Aristotelians in holding that goodness rather than wisdom is the primary attribute of God and in emphasizing that God created the world through love and will. The primacy of love became decisive in Crescas' philosophy of man. For man attains his ultimate happiness by loving God rather than by speculating about Him.

Though Crescas was to remain the last major Jewish philosopher of the Middle Ages, philosophic speculations among Jews continued after his time. In Spain, Jewish philosophers were at work until the expulsion of the Jews in 1492, while in Italy Jewish philosophy continued into the sixteenth century. Among Jewish philosophers of late medieval times, Simon ben Zemaḥ Duran (1361–1444), Joseph Albo (d. 1444), Isaac Abrabanel (1437–1509), and Elijah Delmedigo (*ca.* 1460–1493) should be mentioned.

In the selections that follow, Saadia serves as a representative of the MutaKallimūn, Ibn Gabirol stands for the neoPlatonist, Maimonides and Gersonides exemplify two kinds of Aristotelianism, and Crescas illustrates the critique of Aristotelianism.

SAADIA

882–942

$\mathfrak{S}$AADIA BEN JOSEPH is generally considered the father of medieval Jewish philosophy and his *Book of Doctrines and Beliefs* (*Kitāb al-'Amānāt wa-al-I'tiqādāt, Sefer ha-Emunot we-ha-De'ot*) the first major medieval philosophic work written by a Jew. In his philosophic teachings Saadia bases himself on the doctrines of the Muslim dialectical theologians, the Mutakallimūn, in particular on the doctrines of their rationalist branch, the Mu'tazilites (see p. 205). Adopting, modifying, and supplementing Mu'tazilite teachings and basing himself on Hebrew rather than Islamic Scripture and tradition, he fashioned what has been called a Jewish Kalām.

As the Mutakallimūn in general and the Mu'tazilites in particular, Saadia occupied himself with the philosophical analysis of certain scriptural problems rather than with the construction of a philosophical or theological system in the manner of the Neoplatonists and Aristotelians. To accomplish this task, he drew freely on Platonic, Aristotelian, Stoic, and neoplatonic teachings and this method imposed a certain eclectic character on his work.

Saadia was indebted to the Mu'tazilites not only for a number of their doctrines, but also for the structure of his book. Following them, he divided his *Book of Doctrines and Beliefs* into two major sections, one devoted to a discussion of divine unity, the other devoted to an account of divine justice. Moreover, in true Mu'tazilite fashion, Saadia begins his book with what has become one of the distinctive Kalāmic contributions to medieval philosophy at large—proofs for the creation of the world.

In the Islamic east of Saadia's time, Jews, Christians, Muslims, and Zoroastrians, as well as the members of a variety of philosophic schools freely taught their doctrines, attempting at the same time to refute opinions that were at variance with their own. This diversity of teachings produced, according to Saadia's own testimony, false opinions, doubts, and even outright skepticism among his fellow Jews. To remove the confusions of his contemporaries and to transform them from men who believed on the basis of scriptural authority alone into men who could support their beliefs with philosophical arguments, became the twofold goal of Saadia's major work.

Taking account of the skeptical temper of his times, Saadia begins his

Book of Doctrines and Beliefs with an "Introduction" in which he investigates the sources of doubt and what knowledge is worthy of belief. Reproducing the standard arguments of the skeptics taken from the unreliability of sense perception and the uncertainty of human knowledge, he shows that correct observation, careful analysis, and proper logical method can produce knowledge that can be trusted. Having met the objections of the skeptics, he defines "belief" and then discusses three sources of truth which make it possible to distinguish true from false beliefs. According to him, these sources are: sense perception, self-evident first principles, and inferential knowledge. To these three sources, Saadia adds "reliable tradition" as a fourth. Based on historical evidence, "reliable tradition" guarantees the veracity of Scripture and of the rabbinic teachings.

Saadia begins the book proper with four proofs designed to demonstrate the creation of the world. In setting down these proofs, he differs from later philosophers, such as Maimonides and Aquinas, who hold that to demonstrate creation lies outside the competence of the human mind. According to Saadia, an adequate doctrine of creation affirms: creation in time, the difference between the creator and the world that He created, and creation out of nothing. Since proofs for creation lead to the existence of the creator, they are, at the same time, proofs for the existence of God.

In his treatise on creation, Saadia exhibits his erudition and breadth of learning by presenting and attempting to refute twelve cosmogonic and cosmological theories which are at variance with his own. All of these theories seem to have been defended by contemporaries, and they range from doctrines that accept creation but deny that the world was created out of nothing to outright skeptical doctrines which deny the validity of all knowledge, sense perception included.

The central section of the discussion of God is a treatise devoted to Divine unity. In it Saadia investigates how God can be said to be one, both in the sense of being unique and simple, and how, at the same time, a multitude of attributes can be ascribed to Him. Saadia attributes the multiplicity of attributes to the shortcomings of human language, not to any multiplicity within God Himself. It is the nature of human language, he explains, to use a multiplicity of terms to describe a being who, ontologically, is really one. Whether Saadia's teachings imply that he considered Divine attributes to be negative terms or whether he accepted a doctrine of positive predication has been debated by his interpreters. Saadia's attempts to refute dualistic and trinitarian conceptions of God form interesting sections of his discussions of Divine unity.

In the final treatise of the section on Divine unity, Saadia turns to prophecy as God's communication with man, presenting, as part of his discussion, his philosophy of law. Once again using Mu'tazilite distinctions, he divides the commandments of the Law, (*Torah*) into "rational commandments" which, though recorded in the Law, can also be discovered by human reason, and "traditional commandments" which are solely products of the Divine will.

Saadia's division of commandments became a major issue in later medieval Jewish thought, some philosophers accepting the distinction, and others (Maimonides in particular) rejecting it.

In the second portion of the *Book of Doctrines and Beliefs* Saadia, as has been noted, turns to a discussion of Divine justice, the central problem being how God's omnipotence and omniscience are compatible with the freedom of human choice. Accepting the freedom of human acts, both as a believing Jew and as a philosopher, Saadia marshals the classical arguments of libertarians to support his view. Man feels himself to be free, he states, and without a belief in human freedom no adequate doctrine of responsibility can be developed. Yet the affirmation of freedom of choice does not require the denial of God's omnipotence and omniscience. God, making use of His infinite power, willed that man should be free and though God foreknows what man will do, this knowledge is not a causal factor in the production of human acts.

In other treatises of the section on Divine justice, Saadia discusses the classification of human action and the nature of the soul. The final treatises contain what is probably one of the most extensive philosophical accounts of Jewish eschatological teachings—the resurrection of the dead, the Messiah, the redemption of Israel, and the afterlife.

Saadia was the outstanding Jewish scholar and communal leader of his day. Born in 882 in Egypt, he received his early training in his native land and he pursued further studies in Palestine. In 921, when a controversy concerning a matter of the Jewish calendar broke out between the Palestinian and Babylonian authorities (in reality a controversy about who should exercise religious authority in Jewish life), Saadia sided with the Babylonians and his view prevailed. In 928, he was appointed head (Gaon) of the declining rabbinical academy of Sura (near Bagdad) and under his leadership the academy rose to new heights. When, in 930, he refused to endorse a judgment of the Exilarch's court, the Exilarch, who was the secular head of Babylonian Jewry, removed him from his post. Saadia spent seven years in exile in Bagdad before he was reinstated. During a major portion of his life he waged a ceaseless battle against the sectarian Karaites (who accepted the Bible but not the teachings of the rabbis) and he, as much as anyone, is responsible for their ultimate decline. He died in 942.

Saadia was a prolific writer who contributed to all branches of Jewish learning. He translated the Bible into Arabic, commenting at the same time on a number of its books. He composed works on Jewish law, the liturgy, and Hebrew grammar. As polemicist, he wrote against Ḥiwi al-Balkhi, who had attacked the Bible, and against the Karaites. His commentary on the mystical *Sefer Yezirah* contains matters of philosophic interest.

Saadia is included in this volume not only as an outstanding Jewish philosopher, but also as a representative of Mu'tazilite Kalām at large. The two selections appearing here are both taken from his *Book of Doctrines and Beliefs*. The first contains his doctrine of creation with its characteristic four proofs. The second selection is devoted to his philosophy of law. As part of it, there appears the division of the commandments of the Law into those which are rational (*'aqliyyāt, sikliyot*) and those which are traditional (*sam-'iyyāt, shim'iyot*).

BOOK OF DOCTRINES AND BELIEFS

CHAPTER I. Creatio Ex Nihilo

I. THE NATURE OF THE PROBLEM

The problem dealt with in this chapter is one on which we have no data from actual observation or from sense perception, but conclusions which can be derived only from postulates of the pure Reason. We mean the problem of the origin of the world. The ultimate proposition which we seek to establish is of a very subtle nature. It cannot be grasped by the senses, and one can only endeavour to comprehend it by thought. This being the nature of the subject, one who inquires into it must necessarily expect to arrive at results of a corresponding nature, and one ought not to reject such results, or try to obtain results of a different character. It is quite certain that the origin of things is a matter concerning which no human being was ever able to give evidence as an eye-witness. But we all seek to probe this distant and profound matter which is beyond the grasp of our senses, and regarding which it has been said by the wise king, 'That which was is far off, and exceeding deep; who can find it out?' (Eccl. 7.24). Should, therefore, our inquiry lead us to the conclusion that all things were created *ex nihilo*—a thing the like of which was never experienced by sense perception—we have no right to reject it out of hand on the ground that we never experience the like of it, so how can we believe it; for what we tried to find from the very outset of our inquiry was precisely something the like of which we never experienced. We must welcome this solution and rejoice in it, since it presents a success on our part in attaining the object of our inquiry.

I thought it necessary to make the above introductory remark in order to warn the reader of this book not to expect me to demonstrate the *creatio ex nihilo* by way of sense perception. I have made it clear in my Introduction that if this were possible there would be no need for argument or speculation or logical inferences. Furthermore, there would be agreement between us and all other people in regard to its truth, and opinions would not be divided on any point connected with this problem. But in fact we do depend on speculation to reveal to us the truth of the matter, and on arguments to clarify it, since it in no way comes within the domain of experience or sense perception.

From Saadya Gaon, *Book of Doctrines and Beliefs,* ed. and trans. Alexander Altmann, London: East and West Library, 1946. Also reprinted in Hans Lewy, Alexander Altmann, and Isaak Heinemann, *Three Jewish Philosophers,* New York: Harper Torchbooks, 1966. Reprinted by permission.

We are, in fact, not the only ones who have agreed to accept a cosmological theory which has no basis in sense perception. All those who discuss this problem and seek a solution are agreed on this point. Those, for instance, who believe in the eternity of the world seek to prove the existence of something which has neither beginning nor end. Surely, they never came across a thing which they perceived with their senses to be without beginning or end, but they seek to establish their theory by means of postulates of Reason. Likewise, the Dualists exert themselves to prove the co-existence of two separate and opposing principles, the mixture of which caused the world to come into being. Surely they never witnessed two separate and opposing principles, nor the assumed process of mixture, but they try to produce arguments derived from the pure Reason in favour of their theory. In a similar way, those who believe in an eternal Matter regard it as a *Hyle,* i.e. something in which there is originally no quality of hot or cold, moist or dry, but which becomes transformed by a certain force and thus produces those four qualities. Surely their senses never perceived a thing which is lacking in all those four qualities, nor did they ever perceive a process of transformation and the generation of the four qualities such as is suggested. But they seek to prove their theory by means of arguments drawn from the pure Reason. And so it is with all other opinions, as I shall explain later. This being so, it is clear that all have agreed to accept some view concerning the origin of the world which has no basis in sense perception. If, therefore, our treatment of the subject produces something similar, namely, the doctrine of the *creatio ex nihilo,* let the reader of this book who inquires into this problem not be hasty in rejecting our theory, since from the very outset of his inquiry he was virtually asking for some result similar to this, and every student of this problem is asking for such a result. But the reader may be assured that our arguments are stronger than theirs, and that, moreover, we are in a position to disprove their arguments, whatever their school of thought. We have, too, the advantage of being supported in our doctrine by the signs and miracles of Scripture which were intended to confirm our belief. I would ask the reader to bear in mind these three facts which will meet him in every part of this book, namely, (1) that our arguments are stronger than theirs; (2) that we are able to disprove the arguments of our opponents; and (3) that we have in the bargain the testimony of the miracles narrated in Scripture.

2. FOUR ARGUMENTS FOR CREATION

From these introductory remarks I go on to affirm that our Lord (be He Exalted) has informed us that all things were created in time, and that He created them *ex nihilo,* as it is said, 'In the beginning God created the heaven and the earth' (Gen. 1.1), and as it is further said, 'I am the Lord that maketh all things; that stretched forth the heavens alone; that spread abroad the earth by Myself' (Isa. 44.24). He verified this truth for us by signs and miracles, and we have accepted it. I probed further into this matter with the object of finding out whether it could be verified by speculation as it had been verified by prophecy. I found that this was the case for a number of reasons, from which, for the sake of brevity, I select the following four.

(1) The first proof is based on the finite character of the universe. It is clear that heaven and earth are finite in magnitude, since the earth occupies the centre and the heaven revolves round it. From this it follows that the force residing in them is finite in magnitude. For it is impossible for an infinite force to reside in a

body which is finite in magnitude. This would be contradictory to the dictates of Reason. Since, therefore, the force which preserves heaven and earth is finite, it necessarily follows that the world has a beginning and an end. Being struck by the force of this argument, I subjected it to a close examination, taking good care not to be hasty in drawing definite conclusions before having scrutinized it. I, therefore, asked myself: Perhaps the earth is infinite in length, breadth and depth? I answered: If this were the case, the sun could not encompass it and complete his revolution once every day and night, rising again in the place in which he rose the day before, and setting again in the place in which he set the day before; and so with the moon and the stars. Then I asked myself: Perhaps the heaven is infinite? To this I answered: How could this be the case seeing that all celestial bodies are moving and continually revolving round the earth? For it cannot be supposed that only the sphere that is next to us performs this rotation, whereas the others are too large to perform any movement. For by 'heaven' we understand the body which revolves, and we are not aware of anything else beyond it, far less do we believe it to be the heaven and not revolving. Then I explored further and asked: Perhaps there exists a plurality of earths and heavens, each heaven revolving round its earth. This would involve the assumption of the co-existence of an infinite number of worlds, a thing in its nature impossible. For it is inconceivable that, nature being what it is, some earth should exist above the fire, or that air should be found beneath the water. For both fire and air are light, and both earth and water are heavy. I cannot doubt that if there were a clod of earth outside our earth, it would break through all air and fire until it reached the dust of our earth. The same would happen if there were a mass of water outside the waters of our oceans. It would cut through air and fire until it met our waters. It is, therefore, perfectly clear to me that there exists no heaven apart from our heaven, and no earth except our earth; moreover, that this heaven and this earth are finite, and that in the same way as their bodies are limited, their respective force, too, is limited and ceases to exist once it reaches its limit. It is impossible that heaven and earth should continue to exist after their force is spent, and that they should have existed before their force came into being. I found that Scripture testifies to the finite character of the world by saying, 'From the one end of the earth, even unto the other end of the earth' (Deut. 13.8), and, 'From the one end of heaven unto the other' (Deut. 4.32). It further testifies that the sun revolves round the earth and completes its circle every day by saying, 'The sun also ariseth, and the sun goeth down, and hasteneth to his place where he ariseth' (Eccl. 1.5).

(2) The second proof is derived from the union of parts and the composition of segments. I saw that bodies consist of combined parts and segments fitted together. This clearly indicated to me that they are the skilful work of a skilful artisan and creator. Then I asked myself: Perhaps these unions and combinations are peculiar to the small bodies only, that is to say the bodies of the animals and plants. I, therefore, extended my observation to the earth, and found the same was true of her. For she is a union of soil and stone and sand, and the like. Then I turned by mental gaze to the heavens and found that in them there are many layers of spheres, one within another, and that there are in them also groups of luminaries called stars which are distinguished from one another by being great or small, and by being more luminous or less luminous, and these luminaries are set in those spheres. Having noted these clear signs of the union and composition which has been created in the body of the heaven and the other bodies, I

believe also, on the strength of this proof, that the heaven and all it contains are created. I found that Scripture also declares that the separateness of the parts of the organisms and their combination prove that they are created. In regard to man it is said, 'Thy hands have made me and fashioned me' (Ps. 119.73); in regard to the earth it is said, 'He is God, that formed the earth and made it, He established it' (Isa. 45.18); in regard to the heaven it is said, 'When I behold Thy heavens, the work of Thy fingers, the moon and the stars, which Thou hast established' (Ps. 8.4).

(3) The third proof is based on the nature of the accidents. I found that no bodies are devoid of accidents which affect them either directly or indirectly. Animals, e.g. are generated, grow until they reach their maturity, then waste away and decompose. I then said to myself: Perhaps the earth as a whole is free from these accidents? On reflection, however, I found that the earth is inseparable from plants and animals which themselves are created, and it is well known that whatsoever is inseparable from things created must likewise be created. Then I asked myself: Perhaps the heavens are free from such accidents? But, going into the matter, I found that this was not the case. The first and principal accident affecting them is their intrinsic movement which goes on without pause. There are, however, many different kinds of movement. If you compare them, you will find that some planets move slowly, others quickly. And another kind of accident is the transmission of light from one celestial body to another one, which becomes illumined by it, like the moon. The colours of the various stars also differ. Some are whitish, some reddish, others yellowish and greenish. Having thus established that these bodies are affected by accidents which are coeval with them, I firmly believe that everything which has accidents coeval with it must be created like the accident, since the accident enters into its definition. Scripture also uses the accidents of heaven and earth as argument for their beginning in time by saying, 'I, even I, have made the earth and created man upon it; I, even My hands, have stretched out the heavens, and all their hosts have I commanded' (Isa. 45.12).

(4) The fourth proof is based on the nature of Time. I know that time is threefold: past, present and future. Although the present is smaller than any instant, I take the instant as one takes a point and say: If a man should try in his thought to ascend from that point in time to the uppermost point, it would be impossible for him to do so, inasmuch as time is now assumed to be infinite and it is impossible for thought to penetrate to the furthest point of that which is infinite. The same reason will also make it impossible that the process of generation should traverse an infinite period down to the lowest point so as ultimately to reach us. Yet if the process of generation did not reach us, we would not be generated, from which it necessarily follows that we, the multitude of generated beings, would not be generated and the beings now existent would not be existent. And since I find myself existent, I know that the process of generation has traversed time until it has reached us, and that if time were not finite, the process of generation would not have traversed it. I profess unhesitatingly the same belief with regard to future time as with regard to past time. I find that Scripture speaks in similar terms of the far distant time by saying, 'All men have looked thereon; man beholdeth it afar off' (Job 36.25); and the faithful one says, 'I will fetch my knowledge from afar' (Job 36.3).

It has come to my notice that a certain heretic in conversation with one of the Believers in the Unity (of God) objected to this proof. He said: 'It is possible for a man to traverse that which has an infinite number of parts by walking. For if we consider any distance which a man walks, be it a mile, or an ell, we shall find that it can be divided into an infinite number of parts.' To answer this argument some thinkers resorted to the doctrine of the indivisible atom. Others spoke of *tafra* (the leap). Others again asserted that all the parts (in space) are covered by corresponding parts (in time). Having carefully examined the objection raised I found it to be a sophism for this reason: the infinite divisibility of a thing is only a matter of imagination, but not a matter of reality. It is too subtle to be a matter of reality, and no such division occurs. Now if the process of generation had traversed the past in the imagination, and not in reality, then, by my life, the objection raised would be valid. But seeing that the process of generation has traversed the real time and reached us, the argument cannot invalidate our proof, because infinite divisibility exists only in the imagination.

In addition to these four proofs, there are some more, part of which I have adduced in my Commentary on Genesis, others in my Commentary on Hilkōt Yeṣīrah, and in my Refutation of Ḥiwi al-Balkhi, in addition to more details which the reader will find in other books of mine. Moreover, the arguments employed by me in the present chapter in refutation of the various opponents of our belief, are all sources of this belief, and strengthen and confirm it.

3. THE TRANSCENDENCE OF THE CREATOR; ARGUMENTS FOR THE CREATIO EX NIHILO

Having made it perfectly clear to myself that all things are created, I considered the question whether it was possible that they had created themelves, or whether the only possible assumption is that they were created by someone external to them. In my view it is impossible that they should have created themselves, for a number of reasons of which I shall mention three. The first reason is this: Let us assume that an existing body has produced itself. It stands to reason that after having brought itself into existence that particular body should be stronger and more capable of producing its like than before. For if it was able to produce itself when it was in a relatively weak state, it should all the more be able to produce its like now that it is relatively strong. But seeing that it is incapable of creating its like now when it is relatively strong, it is absurd to think that it created itself when it was relatively weak. The second reason is: If we imagine that a thing has created itself, we shall find that the question of the time when it did so presents an insuperable difficulty. For if we say that the thing created itself before it came into being, then we assume that it was non-existent at the time when it created itself, and obviously something non-existent cannot create a thing. If, on the other hand, we say that it created itself after it had come into being, the obvious comment is that after a thing has come into existence there is no need for it to create itself. There is no third instant between 'before' and 'after' except the present which, however, has no duration in which an action can take place. The third reason is: If we assume that a body is able to create itself, we must necessarily admit that at the same time it is likewise capable of abstaining from the act of self-creation. Under this assumption we shall find that the body is both existent and non-existent at the same time. For in speaking of the body as *capable,* we take it to be existent, but in going on to speak of it as being capable of abstaining from the act of self-creation, we assume it to be non-existent. Obviously, to attribute existence and non-existence to the same thing at the same time is utterly absurd. I found that Scripture had already anticipated the refutation of this belief, namely, that things created themselves, by saying, 'It is He that hath made us, not we' (Ps. 100.3), and by rebuking the one who said, 'My river is mine own, and I have made it for myself' (Ez. 39.3).

Having proved by these arguments that things can on no account have created themselves, and that they must necessarily be regarded as created by a Creator who is external to them, I tried to reason out an answer to the question whether the Creator made them from something (*prima materia*) or from nothing (*ex nihilo*) as revealed in the Scriptures. I found that it is wrong to assume that things were created from something already existent. Such a view is self-contradictory, because the term *creation* implies that the substance of the thing is created and has a beginning in time, whilst the qualifying statement, 'From something' implies that its substance was eternal, uncreated and without beginning in time. If we assume that things were created *ex nihilo,* there is no self-contradiction.

Someone may raise the following objection: 'You have affirmed as a conclusion acceptable to Reason that things have a Creator because in the realm of sense perception you have witnessed that nothing is made without a maker. But you likewise find in the realm of sense perception that nothing comes from nothing. Why, then, have you made use of the proposition that nothing is made except by a maker, and have ignored the proposition that everything comes from something already existent, seeing that the two propositions are equally valid?' My answer is: The problem which forms the object of my inquiry, and to the solution of which my arguments are directed, is the question whether or not the world is created *ex nihilo.* Obviously it is inadmissible that a proposition which is under examination should be adduced as evidence in favour of itself against an alternative proposition. We must seek evidence on its behalf from elsewhere; and since the principle that nothing is made except by a maker has a bearing on the subject-matter of our inquiry, I applied this to the solution of our problem, and it led to the conclusion that the world is created *ex nihilo.* I followed this procedure although I found that in certain cases it is permissible to use a proposition in this way as evidence; but this is a subtle matter which lies outside the province of this book. I, therefore, decided to leave it alone and to follow the plain course.

Another point which I made clear to myself is this: Whatever we imagine to be the thing from which the existent beings were created, it must necessarily be assumed to have existed from all eternity. But if it were pre-existent, it would be equal to the Creator in regard to its eternity. From this it follows that God would not have had the power to create things out of it, since it would not have accepted His command, nor allowed itself to be affected according to His wish and shaped according to His design, except if we were to imagine, in addition to these two, the existence of a third cause which intervened between the two with the result that the one of the two became the Maker, and the other the thing made. But such a view would postulate the existence of something which does not exist; for we have never found anything except a maker and the thing made.

I remembered further that the principal object of our inquiry was to find out who created the substance of things. Now it is well known to us that the maker must necessarily be prior to the thing made by him, and that, by virtue of his being prior to the substance of the thing, the thing becomes one that is created in time. Should we, however, believe the substance to be eternal, the maker would not be prior to the thing created by him, and neither of the two could claim priority so as to be the cause of the other's existence, which is completely absurd.

There is another point which I remembered: The assertion that God created the world from something already existent must inevitably lead to the conclusion that He created nothing at all. For the reason which causes us to think that the world originated from something (*prima materia*) is the fact that such is the way we find the objects of sense perception come into being. Now it is common ground that the objects of sense perception are also found to exist in Space and Time, in shape and form, in measured quantity, in a fixed position and mutual relation, and other similar conditions. All of these experiences are on the same footing as the experience that everything comes from something. Now if we are going to allow all these experiences their full weight and say that things were created from something which existed in Time, Space, form, quantity, position, relation, etc., all this would have to be considered as eternal, and nothing would remain to be created. Creation would become meaningless altogether.

I went still further, arguing that if we fail to admit the existence of something which has nothing prior to it, it is impossible for us to accept the fact that there exists anything at all. For if we consider in our mind that one thing comes from another thing, we have to predicate the same thing of the second as of the first, and say that it could only have come into being from a third thing; the same predicate again must be made of the third thing, namely that it could only have come into being from a fourth thing, and so *ad infinitum*. Since, however, an infinite series cannot be completed, it follows that we are not in existence. But, behold, we are in existence, and unless the things which preceded us were finite (in number), they could not have been completed so as to reach us.

What we have deduced from the postulates of Reason, has also been intimated in the Books of the Prophets, namely, that material bodies originate from the design of the Creator, as is said, 'Before the mountains were brought forth, or ever Thou hadst formed the earth and the world, even from everlasting to everlasting, Thou art God' (Ps. 90.2).

Having thus succeeded in demonstrating by argument these three principles, viz. that the things are created, that their Creator is external to them, and that He created them *ex nihilo,* as it has been verified by the Tradition of the Prophets and by miracles, and this opinion being the first one discussed in this chapter (which is devoted to a speculation on the origin of things) I will now proceed to deal, in the following, with twelve opinions which are held by those who disagree with us in regard to this doctrine. Thus there are altogether thirteen opinions. I shall explain both the arguments put forward by the advocates of these opinions, and their refutation. Whenever their opinion seems to find support in Scripture, I shall elucidate the Scriptural passages concerned, with the help of God.

CHAPTER III.　Commandment and Prohibition

I. LAW AND GRACE

It is desirable that I should preface this chapter by the following remarks. Since it has been established that the Creator (be He exalted and glorified) is eternal, and that there was nothing co-existent with Him, His creation of the world testifies to His goodness and grace, as we mentioned at the end of Chapter I in speaking of the reason for the creation of things, and according to what we find in the Scriptures as well, namely, that He is good and doeth good, as is said,

'The Lord is good to all; and His tender mercies are over all His works' (Ps. 145.9).

The first of His acts of kindness towards His creatures was the gift of existence, i.e. His act of calling them into existence after they had been non-existent, as He said to the men of distinction among them, 'Everyone that is called by My name, and whom I have created for My glory' (Isa. 43.7). Thereafter He offered them a gift by means of which they are able to obtain complete happiness and perfect bliss, as is said, 'Thou makest me to know the path of life; in Thy presence is fullness of joy, in Thy right hand bliss for evermore (Ps. 16.11). This gift consists of the commandments and prohibitions which He gave them.

When faced with this statement, the first impulse of Reason will be to object that God should have been able to bestow upon men perfect bliss and to grant them everlasting happiness without imposing upon them commandments and prohibitions. Moreover, it would seem that in this way His goodness would have been more beneficial to them, seeing that they would have been free from the necessity of making any laborious effort. My answer to this objection is that, on the contrary, the order instituted by God, whereby everlasting happiness is achieved by man's labours in fulfilment of the Law, is preferable. For Reason judges that one who obtains some good in return for work which he has accomplished enjoys a double portion of happiness in comparison with one who has not done any work and receives what he receives as a gift of grace. Reason does not deem it right to place both on the same level. This being so, our Creator has chosen for us the more abundant portion, namely, to bestow welfare on us in the shape of reward, thus making it double the benefit which we could expect without an effort on our part, as is said, 'Behold, the Lord God will come as a Mighty One, and His arm will rule for Him; behold, His reward is with Him, and His recompense before Him' (Isa. 40.10).

2. THE TWO CLASSES OF LAW: LAWS OF REASON AND LAWS OF REVELATION

After these introductory remarks, I now come to the subject proper. I declare that our Lord (be He exalted and glorified) has informed us through the words of His prophets that He wishes us to lead a religious life by following the religion which He instituted for us. This religion contains laws, which He has prescribed for us, and which it is our duty to keep and to fulfill in sincerity, as is said, 'This day the Lord thy God commanded thee to do these statutes and ordinances; thou shalt, therefore, observe and do them with all thy heart and with all thy soul' (Deut. 26.16). His messengers established these laws for us by wondrous signs and miracles, and we commenced to keep and fulfill them forthwith. Later we found that speculation confirms the necessity of the Law for us. It would, however, not have been appropriate to leave us to our own devices.

It is desirable that I should explain which matters and aspects (of the Divine Law) speculation confirms as necessary. (1) I maintain that Reason bids us respond to every benefactor either by returning his kindness if he is in need of it, or by offering thanks if he is not in need of recompense. Now since this is a dictate of Reason itself, it would not have been fitting for the Creator (be He exalted and glorified) to waive this right in respect of Himself, but it was necessary that He should command his creatures to worship Him and to render thanks unto Him for having created them. (2) Reason further lays down that the wise man should not permit himself to be vilified and treated with contempt. It is similarly necessary that the Creator should forbid His servants to treat Him in this way. (3) Reason further prescribes that human beings should be forbidden to trespass upon one another's rights by any sort of aggression. It is likewise necessary that the Wise should not permit them to act in such a way. (4) Reason, furthermore, permits a wise man to employ a workman for any kind of work and pay him his wages for the sole purpose of allowing him to earn something; since this is a matter which results in benefit to the workman and causes no harm to the employer.

If we put together these four points, their total is tantamount to a summary of the laws which our Lord has commanded us. That is to say, he imposed upon us the duty of knowing and serving Him with a sincere heart, as the prophet said, 'And thou, Solomon, my son, know thou the God of thy father, and serve Him with a whole heart and with a willing mind' (1 Chron. 28.9). Then he forbade us to hurl at Him insult and abuse although it causes Him no harm, seeing that it would not be consonant with wisdom to permit it. Thus it is said, 'Whosoever curseth his God, shall bear his sin' (Lev. 24.15). He did not permit us to trespass upon one another's rights nor to defraud one another, as it said, 'Ye shall not steal; neither shall ye deal falsely, nor lie one to another' (Lev. 19.11). These three groups of laws and their subdivisions form the first of the Two Classes of Law. The first group of the three includes humbleness before God, worship, standing up in His presence, etc. All this is written in the Law. The second group includes the prohibition of idolatry, swearing falsely by His name, describing Him by derogatory attributes, etc. All this is written in the Law. To the third group belongs the practice of justice, truth-telling, equity, and impartiality, the avoidance of homicide, adultery, theft, tale-bearing, and trickery against one's fellowman; also the command that the Believer should love his neighbour as he loves himself, and whatever is involved in these precepts. All this is written in the Law.

In regard to all the things which He commands us to do, He has implanted approval of them in our Reason; and in regard to all the things which He forbids us to do, He has implanted disapproval of them in our Reason, as is said in the Book of Wisdom—wisdom being identical with Reason—'For my mouth shall utter truth, and wickedness is an abomination to my lips' (Prov. 8.7).

The Second Class of Law consists of matters regarding which Reason passes no judgment in the way either of approval or disapproval so far as their essence is concerned. But our Lord has given us an abundance of such commandments and prohibitions in order to increase our reward and happiness through them, as is said, 'The Lord was pleased, for His righteousness' sake, to make the Law great and glorious' (Isa. 42.21). That which belongs to the things commanded by God assumes the character of 'good', and that which belongs to the things forbidden by Him assumes the character of 'evil' on account of the Service thereby performed. Thus the Second (Class of Law) is in fact joined to the First Class. In spite of this one cannot fail, upon closer examination, to find in it some slender moral benefits and rational basis to act against the greater moral benefits and firmer rational basis attached to the First Class (of Law).

It is proper that I should first and foremost discuss the rational laws. Wisdom lays down that bloodshed must be prevented among human beings, for if it were allowed people would annihilate each other. That would mean, apart from the pain suffered, a frustration of the purpose which the Wise (God) intended to achieve through them. Homicide cuts them off from the attainment of any purpose He created and employs them for.

Wisdom further imposes the prohibition of adultery; for, otherwise, human beings would become similar to the animals. No person would be able to know and honour his father in return for the education he received at his hands. Nor would a father be able to bequeath to his son his means of livelihood though the son inherited his existence from him; nor would one know one's other relatives such as paternal and maternal uncles; nor would one be able to show them the kindness due to relatives.

Wisdom further imposes the prohibition of theft; for if it were permitted some people would rely on their ability to steal some other people's property, and would not do any productive work nor amass wealth. But if everyone relied on this sort of subsistence, theft itself would be rendered impossible by the abolition of property since nothing at all would be found to steal.

Wisdom further lays down, and this is perhaps its first principle, that one should speak the truth and abstain from falsehood, for truth is a statement which accords with facts and actual conditions, whereas a lie is a statement which does not accord with facts and actual conditions. When the senses perceive an object in a certain state, and the soul ascribes to it another state, then the two statements conflict in the soul, and from their contradiction the soul knows that there is something blamable.

I will furthermore say this: I have met certain people who think that our selection of these four things as objects of reprobation is wrong. In their opinion that is to be reprobated which causes them pain and grief, and the good, in their opinion, is that which causes them pleasure and rest. To this proposition I reply at length in Chapter 4 on the subject of Justice. I will here mention only part of the reply. I say that one who holds this opinion has ignored all the arguments which I have adduced, and one who ignores this is a fool with whom we need not trouble ourselves. Nevertheless, I shall not be content until I have compelled him to admit that his view is self-contradictory and impossible. I declare that the killing of an enemy whilst pleasing to the killer causes pain to the killed; that the seizure of any property or married woman whilst pleasing to the person who commits this act causes pain to the person who suffers it. According to the opinion of those who hold this theory it would necessarily follow from their premise that each of these acts is both wisdom and folly at the same time. Wisdom because it affords pleasure to the person who commits murder, robbery and rape, and folly because it causes pain to his victim. But every theory which involves a self-contradiction is invalid. The contradictory qualities may also appear combined in relation to one person as in the case of honey into which poison has been dropped. In this case the same person eats something which affords pleasure and causes death at the same time. Surely this compels them to admit that (according to their theory) wisdom and folly will exist together.

The Second Class of Law concerns such matters as are of a neutral character from the point of view of Reason, but which the Law has made the objects of commandment in some cases, and of prohibition in others, leaving the rest in their neutral state. Instances are the distinguishing from ordinary days of Sabbath and Festivals; the selection of certain individuals to be Prophets and Leaders; the prohibition to eat certain foodstuffs; the avoidance of sexual intercourse with certain people; the abstention enforced during periods of impurity. The great motive for the observance of these principles and the laws derived and branching out from them is, of course, the command of our Lord and the promotion of our happiness resulting from it, but I find for most of them also some minor and partial motives of a useful character. I wish to point out and to discuss some of them, realizing as I do that God's wisdom (be He blessed and exalted) is above all this.

The distinction conferred upon certain times has these advantages: In the first place, it enables us to desist from our work at certain times and obtain a rest from our many travails; furthermore, to enjoy the pleasures of learned pursuits, and to have the benefit of additional prayer; there is also the advantage that people will be free to meet at gatherings and discuss matters concerning their religion and proclaim them in public, etc.

The distinction conferred upon a certain person has these advantages: it enables the public to receive reliable instruction from him, to ask his intercession; and it enables him to inspire people with a desire for godliness that they may attain something like his own rank, and to devote his efforts to promoting piety amongst men, since he is worthy of that; and similar activities.

The prohibition not to eat certain animals has this advantage: it makes it impossible to liken any of the animals to the Creator; since it is unthinkable that one should permit oneself either to eat or to declare as impure what one likens to God; also it prevents people from worshipping any of the animals, since it is unthinkable that one should worship either what serves for food or what one declares as impure.

The prohibition of sexual intercourse with certain categories of women has this advantage: in the case of a married woman, I have already stated the reason before. As to one's mother, sister and daughter, the reason is this: the necessities of daily life foster intimacy between the members of a family. Consequently, if marriage between them were permitted, they would indulge in sexual licence. Another purpose is to prevent men from being attracted only by those women who are of beautiful appearance and rejecting those who are not, when they see that their own relatives do not desire them.

The laws of defilement and purity have this advantage: they teach men humility and reverence; they strengthen in them (the desire) to pray once more after a period of neglect; they make people more conscious of the dignity of the Holy Place after they have abstained from entering it for a period; and they turn their minds to the fear of God.

If one examines most of these revelational laws in the above fashion, one will find for them a great number of partial motives and reasons of usefulness. But the wisdom of the Creator and His knowledge is above everything human beings can attain, as is said, 'For the heavens are higher than the earth, so are My ways higher than your ways' (Isa. 55.9).

3. THE NECESSITY OF REVELATION

Having distinguished in the preceding chapter the Two Classes of Law, namely, the rational and the revelational laws, it is now desirable that I should explain the necessity of prophetic Revelation. For I have heard that there are people who contend that men do not need prophets, and that their Reason is sufficient to guide them aright according to their innate cognition of good and evil. I, therefore, subjected this view to the test of true reasoning, and it showed me that if things were as they make out, God would know it better and would not have sent us prophets, for He does not do things which have no purpose. Then I reflected still more deeply and found that mankind is fundamentally in need of the prophets, not solely on account of the revelational laws, which had to be announced, but also on account of the rational laws, because their practice cannot be complete unless the prophets show us how to perform them. Thus, for instance, Reason commands gratitude towards God for the blessings received from Him, but does not specify the form, time, and posture appropriate to the expression of such gratitude. So we are in need of prophets. They gave it a form which is called 'Prayer'; they fixed its times, its special formulae, its special modes and the special direction which one is to face when praying. Another instance: Reason disapproves of adultery, but gives no definition of the way in which a woman can be acquired by a man so as to become his legal wife; whether this is effected merely by a form of words, or merely by means of money, or by her and her father's consent, or by the witness of two or ten people, or in the presence of the whole population of a town, or by a symbolic act, or by impressing a sign upon her. So the prophets laid down the rules of dowry, contract and witness. Another instance: Reason disapproves of theft, but gives no definition of the way in which some object of value becomes a man's property; whether by means of labour, or by way of commerce, or by inheritance, or by the appropriation of unowned articles as in the case of a hunter in the desert or on the seas; whether the purchase becomes valid by the payment of the price, or by the act of taking possession of the purchased article, or merely by repeating a form of words; and so with many other questions which arise in the wide and extensive field covered by this subject. So the prophets presented us with an equitable decision on every single point relating to these matters. Another instance is the measure of punishment for crimes. Reason deems it right that every crime be punished according to its measure, but does not define its measure; whether punishment should be in the nature of a reprimand only, or should include the defamation of the evildoer, or include, in addition, corporal punishment by stripes, and if so, to what extent, which question applies likewise to defamation and reprimand; or whether nothing short of capital punishment would suffice; and whether the punishment of every offender should be one and the same, or whether one punishment should be different from another. So the prophets prescribed a measure of punishment for each crime according to its nature; they did not lay down the same rule for all, fixing for some a fine in money. And because of these matters which we have enumerated, and other similar ones, we are in need of prophetic Revelation. If we had had to rely on our own judgment in these matters, we should have opposed each other and never agreed on anything; moreover, prophetic Revelation was necessary on account of the revelational laws, as I have already explained.

SELECTED BIBLIOGRAPHY

TRANSLATIONS

Altmann, A., trans., Saadya Gaon, *The Book of Doctrines and Beliefs,* Abridged edition, Oxford: East and West Library, 1946. (Reprinted in *Three Jewish Philosophers,* New York, 1966.)

Rosenblatt, S., trans., Saadia Gaon, *The Book of Beliefs and Opinions,* New Haven, 1948.

STUDIES

Altmann, A., "Saadya's Conception of the Law," *Bulletin of the John Rylands Library,* XXVIII (1944), 320–339.

Altmann, A., "Saadya's Theory of Revelation," *Saadya Studies,* E. Rosenthal, ed., Manchester, 1943, 4–25.

Davidson, H., "John Philoponus as a Source of Medieval Islamic and Jewish Proofs of Creation," *Journal of the American Oriental Society,* LXXXIX (1969), 357–391.

Diesendruck, Z., "Saadya's Formulation of the Time Argument for Creation," *Jewish Studies in Memory of G. A. Kohut,* New York, 1935, 145–158.

Efros, I.,"Saadya's Second Theory of Creation in its Relation to Pythagoreanism and Platonism," *Louis Ginzberg Jubilee Volume,* English Section, New York, 1945, 133–142.

Efros, I., "Saadya's Theory of Knowledge," *Jewish Quarterly Review,* N.S., XXXIII (1942–1943), 133–170.

Efros, I., "The Philosophy of Saadia Gaon," *Studies in Medieval Jewish Philosophy,* New York-London, 1974, 1–137.

Fox, M., "On the Rational Commandments in Saadia's Philosophy, a Re-Examination," *Modern Jewish Ethics: Theory and Practice,* ed. M. Fox, Columbus, 1975, 174–187.

Guttmann, Jacob, *Die Religionsphilosophie des Saadia,* Göttingen, 1882.

Heschel, A., "The Quest for Certainty in Saadia's Philosophy," *Jewish Quarterly Review,* N.S. XXXIII (1942–1943), 213–264.

Heschel, A., "Reason and Revelation in Saadia's Philosophy," *Jewish Quarterly Review,* N.S., XXXIV (1944), 391–408.

Horovitz, S., "Über die Bekanntschaft Saadias mit der griechischen Skepsis," *Judaica, Festschrift zu Hermann Cohens 70. Geburtstag,* Berlin, 1912, 235–252.

Malter, Henry, *Saadia Gaon: His Life and Works,* Philadelphia, 1921.

Rau, David, "Die Ethik R. Saadja's," *Monatsschrift für Geschichte und Wissenschaft des Judentums,* LV (1911); LVI (1912).

Rawidowitz, S., "Saadya's Purification of the Idea of God," *Saadya Studies,* E. Rosenthal, ed., Manchester, 1943, 139–165.

Vajda, G., "Autour de la théorie de la connaissance chez Saadia," *Revue des Études Juives,* CXXVI (1967), 135–189, 373–395.

Ventura, M., *La philosophie de Saadia Gaon,* Paris, 1934.

Wolfson, H., "Arabic and Hebrew Terms for Matter and Element with Especial Reference to Saadia," *Jewish Quarterly Review,* N.S., XXXVIII (1947), 47–61.

Wolfson, H., "Atomism in Saadia," *Jewish Quarterly Review,* N.S., XXXVII (1946), 107–124.

Wolfson, H., "The Jewish Kalam," *The Seventy-Fifth Anniversary Volume of the Jewish Quarterly Review,* Philadelphia, 1967, 544–573.

Wolfson, H., "The Kalam Argument for Creation in Saadya, Averroes, Maimonides, and St. Thomas," *Saadya Anniversary Volume,* New York, 1943. Vol. II, 197–245.

Wolfson, H., "The Kalam Problem of Nonexistence and Saadia's Second Theory of Creation," *Jewish Quarterly Review,* N.S., XXXVII (1946), 371–391.

Wolfson, H., *Repercussions of the Kalam in Jewish Philosophy,* Cambridge, Mass., 1979.

SOLOMON IBN GABIROL

ca. 1022–*ca.* 1051 or *ca.* 1070

Solomon Ibn Gabirol was the outstanding Jewish Neoplatonist of the Middle Ages. A pure philosopher rather than one interested in theological speculations, he devoted his efforts to the construction of an ontological system. This system is outlined in his *Fountain of Life* (*Meḳor Ḥayyim, Fons Vitae*), though the work is primarily devoted to his account of matter and form.

The ultimate principle in Gabirol's ontology is the first essence, also called God and the first maker. From the first essence emanated the Divine Will, and from the Divine Will, substances composed of matter and form. The latter substances, in turn, are divided into spiritual substances intelligible to the mind and corporeal substances perceptible to the senses.

Gabirol describes the first essence in typical neoplatonic fashion. Existing above all beings, the first essence is infinite and eternal. Only its existence, not its essence, can be known. It is one in all respects and its attributes are identical with its essence.

To bridge the gap between the first essence which is one and the world of matter and form which is many, Gabirol posits the Divine Will as an intermediary principle. However, Gabirol's doctrine of the Divine Will is not completely clear. There are passages in which he considers the Will as an attribute or power identical with God, while there are other passages in which he describes it as a hypostasis existing in separation from God. Since the Divine Will is the primary agent in the production of the world, it is also called the Acting *Logos*. The Will can only be known through a kind of intuition which may occur once the created order has been understood. It appears that Gabirol, in positing Will as the intermediary principle, desires to emphasize the voluntary character of creation.

Within the created order, all beings, spiritual as well as corporeal, are composed of matter and form. The highest principles within the world are universal matter and universal form, these two principles being said to have

357

emanated respectively from the first essence and the Divine Will. The rest of the created order comes to be through the successive determinations of universal matter and universal form, much in the same manner as a species comes to be through the determination of a genus by a differentia. In the procession of matters and forms the higher matters and forms appear in the lower ones. This doctrine is said to make Gabirol a proponent of the doctrine of the multiplicity of forms—a doctrine stating that several substantial forms exist within a given substance.

Invoking the analogy between man, the microcosm, and the world, the macrocosm, Gabirol posits three spiritual substances. Just as intelligence, soul, and nature are formal principles within man, so a universal intelligence, a universal soul, and a universal nature are formal principles within the world. These spiritual substances, it should be emphasized once again, are composed of matter and form.

Within the corporeal world, body is the highest substance. It is composed of the form of corporeality and of a matter which marks the transition from the spiritual to the corporeal world. The corporeal world consists of celestial bodies, human beings, animals, plants, and the four elements.

Little is known of Gabirol's life. He was born *ca.* 1022 in Malaga, reared and educated in Saragossa. A marked poetic gift came early to the fore and we have poems he composed at the age of sixteen. He was in touch with many of the Jewish notables of his day, as poems about them show, but his relations with them were not always amiable. According to some authorities he died *ca.* 1051, according to others *ca.* 1070.

Whereas in the world at large Gabirol became known for his philosophic work, among his own people he was celebrated for his magnificent Hebrew poems. He composed over three hundred secular and religious poems, some of the latter becoming a fixed part of the liturgy of Spanish Jews. Of these poems, a poetic version of his cosmology, entitled "The Royal Crown" (*Keter Malkut*), possesses philosophic interest. In his *Fountain of Life* Gabirol mentions that he had written a book on the Divine Will, but this work is not extant. He also wrote two popular ethical treatises, *The Improvement of the Qualities of the Soul* and *The Choice of Pearls.*

Gabirol's *Fountain of Life* suffered a rather curious fate. Written in Arabic, the total work has been preserved only in a Latin translation made by Johannes Hispanus and Dominicus Gundissalinus in the middle of the twelfth century. This translation was well known to Christian scholastics who variously called its author Avicebrol, Avicebron, or Avencebrol. Because of the total absence of all biblical and rabbinic quotations from the work, some scholastics considered its author a Muslim, while others, possibly because of the hypostasized Will, considered him a Christian Arab. Not until the middle of the nineteenth century, when Solomon Munk discovered and published a Hebrew florilegium made by Shem Tob Falḳera (1225–1290), was it established that Ibn Gabirol and Avicebrol are one and the same author.

William of Auvergne, Albertus Magnus, Alexander Hales, Bonaventure,

Thomas Aquinas, and Duns Scotus were among the scholastics who cited Gabirol. He was known among them primarily for his doctrine that spiritual beings—the angels of the scholastics—are composed of matter and form. Franciscan thinkers accepted Gabirol's doctrine, while Dominicans rejected it. In Jewish circles Gabirol's influence was slight. His views were adopted by some later Neoplatonists and some of his doctrines had an influence on medieval Jewish mysticism.

The following two selections from the *Fountain of Life* deal with two aspects of Gabirol's doctrine of matter and form. The first consists of one of his derivations of the existence of universal matter and universal form—that described by him as being "according to the universal way." The second selection contains a series of arguments designed to show that spiritual substances are composed of matter and form and that, in spite of this, they are simple.

In reading these selections it should be kept in mind that Gabirol is a dialectician. He relies heavily on images and analogies and often uses many arguments to prove the same point. Moreover, depending on the context, he uses the same philosophic term in different senses. Gabirol's method makes it difficult at times to find the exact meaning of what he says.

The Aristotelian notions of matter and form are used by Gabirol in two distinct ways. In certain passages they are considered as principles of change, matter being the principle of potentiality, form the principle of actuality. In other passages, matter and form are considered as component principles of all substances. According to this usage (which is the one prevalent in the selections), matter is the unifying underlying substratum which determines the nature of a substance by giving it its name and essence, while form inheres in matter as a principle of multiplicity and action. Gabirol frequently invokes the neoplatonic principle that if an inferior being emanated from a superior one, the properties of the superior are found in the inferior.

THE FOUNTAIN OF LIFE

FIRST TREATISE

. . .

Pupil. I understand about the soul what is possible for me to understand, even though I have not attained the ultimate knowledge which I should have about it. Nevertheless, let us now begin to inquire about universal matter and

Translated by Arthur Hyman for this volume from *Avencebrolis (Ibn Gebirol) Fons Vitae*, ed. C. Baeumker (*Beiträge zur Geschichte und Philosophie des Mittelalters*, I), Münster, 1892–1895.

universal form. I wish, however, that you begin by first enumerating the chapter headings of the subjects about which we must inquire during the investigation in which we are engaged and that you divide the treatises of the investigation in a reasonable manner, in order that I may have everything [readily] at hand.

Master. Since it is our purpose to inquire about universal matter and universal form, we must say that everything composed of matter and form is divided into two [kinds]: composite corporeal substance, and simple spiritual substance. Corporeal substance [in turn] is likewise divided into two [kinds]: corporeal matter which underlies the form of qualities, and spiritual matter which underlies the corporeal form. Because of the latter distinction there must be in this work two treatises, to which we must direct our attention. The first of these is devoted to those matters which must first be set down in order to describe universal matter and universal form, to investigate the science of matter and form existing in sensible substances, and to speak of the corporeal matter which underlies qualities. The second treatise is devoted to a discussion of the spiritual matter which underlies the corporeal form. Now, since the spiritual substance requires proofs through which existence is attributed to it and demonstrations through which [its existence] is ascertained (for the existence of spiritual substance is not self-evident by means of necessary knowledge), there must also be a third treatise devoted to a discussion of proofs for the existence of simple substances. There must, furthermore, be a fourth treatise devoted to the discussion of the inquiry into the knowledge which exists concerning the matter and form of simple substances. When the investigation contained in these four treatises will have been completed, we must then inquire about universal matter and form as they are in themselves. Hence there will be a fifth treatise which is appropriate for the investigation of this subject. Everything which we must investigate concerning matter and form will be contained in the five treatises which we have delineated and this is everything this book contains.

Pupil. Since you have well divided the treatises of our inquiry concerning matter and form, let us begin then to investigate that which we intended to investigate about these two principles.

Master. The existence of universal matter and universal form is known in more than one way.

Pupil. Make clear to me these ways.

Master. The ways by which the existence of universal matter and universal form can be known are, at first thought, two: the universal, general [way], and the particular, specific [way].

Pupil. How can the existence of matter and form be known according to the universal way?

Master. Every object of investigation [the existence of] which we want to know through its characteristics, can only be investigated through those properties which are inseparable from it. When it has been understood that these properties exist and what they are, then the existence of that thing whose properties they are will be known.

Pupil. Give me an example of what you have said concerning this investigation.

Master. If there exists a universal matter of all things, the following properties must belong to it: it must exist in virtue of itself, it must have one essence, it must be a subject underlying diversity, it must give its essence and name to all things.

Pupil. What is the proof that these properties must belong to universal matter and must be united with it?

Master. If universal matter exists, it must have these properties.

Pupil. How is this?

Master. [Universal] matter must have existence, for something which does not exist can not serve as matter for something which exists. [Universal matter] must be said to exist in virtue of itself, for if it did not exist in virtue of itself [it would exists in some other matter and this matter in still another], so that the series [of matters] would go on to infinity; [but the existence of an infinite series is impossible]. [Universal matter] must possess one essence, for we seek only one matter of all existing things. [Universal matter] must be a subject underlying diversity, for diversity exists only as the result of forms, and forms do not exists in virtue of themselves. [Universal matter] gives its essence and name to all things, for since it underlies as subject all things, it must necessarily exist in all things, and since it exists in all things, it must give its essence and name to all things.

Pupil. It is clear now that universal matter must possess these properties.

Master. Therefore, seek these properties in all existing things and when you will have found them in all existing things, you will have found first matter.

Pupil. How shall I investigate this?

Master. By means of rational analysis, that is, by removing from what exists one form after another and by proceeding from that which is manifest to that which is hidden until you will come to a form after which there is no other form. This is the form which precedes all other forms in the matter which underlies it.

Pupil. Give me an example of this.

Master. An example of this is the heavens, of whose forms color is the first which appears. Thereafter comes figure, then corporeity, then substantiality, then the other forms, namely the spiritual intelligences, until you will come to the notion of something created existing in virtue of itself which underlies as subject all these forms. Then you will have found that principle which is described by the previously mentioned properties, and you will have found that this is the hidden principle beyond which there is no other principle except one, namely the creator, whose name is exalted.

Pupil. In accordance with your instructions I have removed the forms of that which exists one after another and I have proceeded from that which is manifest to that which is hidden until I have reached the hidden principle beyond which there is no other principle.

Master. Now [reverse the process and] proceed again from the hidden principle to one that is manifest and from one that is manifest to another principle that is more manifest until you will reach the point from which you began. You will find that the properties of the hidden principle [that is, universal matter] will accompany you and go with you from the hidden principle to the manifest one.

Pupil. I have looked for these properties in all existing things, until I came to an individual substance which can no longer be divided and I have found them to be infused in all existing things and spread out through them from the highest being to the lowest, and yet I did not see that it is necessary because of this that there should exist a universal matter which underlies all things and which is different from them.

Master. Did you not admit that it is one of the properties of universal matter to give to all things its substance and name? From where then would all existing things have these properties, if there would not exist a universal matter which gives these properties to them?

Pupil. It is as you have said. But in what way is this matter different from the things which exist?

Master. It is not possible that the essence of matter should differ from the essence of existing things. However, existing things are made to differ from matter by the forms which come upon matter, that is, by differences which divide matter. Whence the manifest difference among existing things comes to be only through manifest forms and, likewise, the hidden difference among existing things comes to be only through the hidden forms. Thus diversity comes to be only through the forms of existing things. But the hidden essence which receives the forms is the one first universal matter which has no diversity [in itself].

Pupil. Give me an example of this.

Master. Consider golden armbands [and] necklaces made of gold [Falkera's translation: a nosering, an armband, and a sealring made of gold] and put them in place of all existing things. You will find them to be different through [their] forms, while you will find the matter which underlies them to be one. And the essence of their matter will not be different from their own essence. From this [example] you can understand that existent things are different through their form, while the matter which underlies them is one and the essence of this matter is not different from the essence of these things.

Pupil. You have done well in making me discover universal matter, for I found its properties in all existing things. Make me discover universal form in a manner similar to this.

Master. Consider in like manner the properties of universal form. They are: to inhere in a subject which differs from it, to actualize the essence of that subject in which it inheres, and to confer existence upon this subject. If you will find these properties in the forms of existing things, you will have found the universal form.

Pupil. What argument do you adduce [to show] that these properties belong to the universal form?

Master. The [universal] form must necessarily inhere in a subject, for if it did not inhere in a subject, it would be a subject and in that case form would be matter and it would have the characteristic of matter. To actualize the essence of the subject in which it inheres and to confer existence upon it belongs also to the form, inasmuch as something has the kind of being it has only through the form.

Pupil. Did we not say previously that matter also has existence?

Master. We said that matter has existence only when we had conferred upon it a spiritual form. In itself, however, matter does not have the kind of existence it has when a form is joined to it, the latter kind of existence being existence in actuality. Otherwise, when we say that matter has existence, we have in mind that it has existence only in potentiality.

Pupil. I have investigated these properties and find them to accompany all the forms of existing things. But from whence can I say that there exists a universal form from which is derived the existence and perfection of all forms?

Master. Refrain from this question now and do not hurry so much, for the answer to it will follow later.

. . .

FOURTH TREATISE

. . .

Master. From what has been said previously it will have become clear to you that matter and form exist in composite substances. Likewise also, in the treatise which precedes this one it has been demonstrated to you by means of necessary proofs that simple substances exist. If you now desire to know that matter and form exist in simple substances, remember those things which were said concerning composite substances, since the way of deriving the knowledge of matter and form is the same in both kinds of [substances].

Pupil. How is this?

Master. If something inferior emanated from something superior, then everything existing in the inferior must also exist in the superior.

Pupil. You seem to suggest that the corporeal spheres [substances] are in the likeness of the spiritual spheres [substances] and that the former emanated from the latter.

Master. I want nothing but this.

Pupil. Does it seem to you that if the corporeal spheres possess matter and form, so likewise do the spiritual spheres?

Master. It can not be otherwise.

Pupil. What is the proof of this?

Master. The proof that the spiritual substances are the same in their matter, but different in their forms is this: Since the effects produced by the spiritual substances are different, there can be no doubt that their forms are different. But it is not possible that the matters of these substances are different, since all of these substances are simple and spiritual. And difference proceeds only from the form, and simple matter has no form in itself.

Pupil. What would you answer, were I to say that [in the case of spiritual substances] the substance of soul is matter and the substance of intellect form?

Master. It is impossible that the substance of soul be matter, since soul is composite, and since intellect is above it, and since it is an agent [and because of these reasons it must possess a form]. Similarly, it is also not possible that the substance of intellect be form, for intellect is also composite [and hence it possesses matter]. The proof [that soul can not be only matter and intellect only form] is the agreement of these two substances with other spiritual substances in respect to substantiality [as a result of which all spiritual substances possess matter] and the difference between them in respect to knowledge and perfection [as a result of which all spiritual substances possess form].

Pupil. What would you say, were I to maintain that the [spiritual] substances are only matter?

Master. If these substances were only matter, they would not be differentiated and they would indeed be one and they would not act on anything. For the matter of something is one, not differentiated in itself, and actions proceed from forms not from matters, as is evident in the case of the sensible substances.

Pupil. Perhaps these substances are only forms?

Master. How is it possible that forms should inhere in an underlying subject without there being a subject in which they inhere?

Pupil. Why not? For indeed the forms are substances.

Master. If these simple substances are one form, how do they become differentiated?

Pupil. Perhaps they are differentiated through themselves?

Master. Were they differentiated through themselves, they would never have anything in common.

Pupil. Thus they differ in respect to perfection and imperfection.

Master. If they were to differ in respect to perfection and imperfection, there would have to exist some subject which underlies perfection and which underlies imperfection.

Pupil. That which underlies perfection is the form and that which underlies imperfection is likewise the form.

Master. Hence the forms are matters, since they are subjects which underlie something. [But that form should be matter is impossible.]

Pupil. From what has been stated I understand that simple substances are composed of matter and form. But add [further] explanation in support of this principle.

Master. It is also not possible that the intelligible substance be only one thing. It is likewise not possible that [the intelligible substance be composed of] two matters or two forms. It follows, therefore, that [the intelligible substance is composed of] matter and form only.

Pupil. How is it possible that the spiritual substance is composite if it is spiritual?

Master. Since it is necessary that the concept of spirituality is different from the concept of corporeity, and it is necessary that this concept inheres in something other than it which describes it, hence spiritual substance is composed in the same way. [This passage may be rendered more freely: Since it is necessary that the form of spirituality is above the form of corporeity, and since it is necessary that the latter form inheres in a subject other than it which gives it its description, (and since corporeal substances are similar to spiritual substances inasmuch as they have emanated from them), it follows that spiritual substance is composed of matter and form in the same way as corporeal substance.] And likewise the division of spiritual substance into intellect and soul and the distinction between intellect and soul in bodies and the separation of these one from the other provides proof for the distinction between matter and form [in spiritual substances]. Therefore, the relation of each of these simple substances in its distinction from the spiritual substance is like the relation of simple matter and form in their distinction from corporeal substance. And also the fact that one spiritual substance is simpler and more perfect than another provides proof that above the spirituality that comes after body there is another spirituality more perfect than it.

Pupil. Indeed, were it the case that spirituality is a cause which prevents division, it would not be possible that soul is separate from intellect or that one spiritual substance should be more spiritual than another. Hence the distinction between soul and intellect is proof that spirituality is not one and since it is not one, it is subject to division, and diversification comes upon it.

Master.. .I add a [further] explanation about this by saying that, just as it is necessary that some body is simpler than another, and that there exist in these bodies matter and form which are closer to spirituality and which possess greater simplicity, so is it similarly necessary that some spiritual substance is simpler than another and that spiritual substances possess matter and form of greater simplicity and greater spirituality.

Pupil. It is very difficult for me to imagine that these simple substances are composed of matter and form and to imagine that there exist diversity and difference among them, inasmuch as all are spiritual and simple.

Master. Since it is difficult for you to imagine that spiritual substances are composed of two [principles, namely matter and form], consider their difference from composite substances and their difference among themselves. Then you will be forced to admit that there are differences by means of which spiritual substances differ from composite substances and by means of which spiritual substances differ among themselves, and [the causes of these differences] are the forms inhering in them.

Pupil. Even though it must be admitted that there exist differences among spiritual substances because of the forms which belong to them, why must it be admitted that there exist differences between these forms, since these forms exist in a state of highest spirituality?

Master. You must watch yourself at this point, since the error [which occurs here] is not small. You must imagine the following about the spiritual forms, namely, that they all are one form and that there exists no diversity in them in respect to themselves, since they are pure spiritual [beings]. Diversity only befalls them because of the matter which underlies them as subject. For if [the underlying matter] is close to perfection it will be subtle and the form which inheres in it will be in the highest state of simplicity and spirituality, and the contrary will be the case if the underlying matter is gross. Take the light of the sun as an example of this. For this light in itself is one, but when it encounters subtle, clear air it will penetrate it, and it will appear in a different manner in subtle, clear air and in thick, unclear air. Something similar must be said about the [spiritual] form.

Pupil. What would you answer were I to say that one spiritual substance does not differ from another because of a substantial form, but because there comes upon it an affection (*passio*) resulting from a difference in the bodies which receive its action? Thus the difference between spiritual forms is the result of their action not of the substance itself?

Master. I did not think that you would raise objections of this kind after the previous proofs accounting for the differences among simple substances. [It is] as if it were not certain to you that the form of nature differs from the vegetative soul, and the form of the vegetative soul differs from the form of the sensory soul, and that the form of the sensory soul differs from the form of the rational soul, and that the form of the rational soul differs from the form of the intellect.

Pupil. The difference among simple substances is now clear to me. But perhaps at some other time there will arise some other doubt concerning these matters. How can you satisfy me concerning the difference among spiritual substances, seeing that my desire for this knowledge is very strong?

Master. If this sort of doubt will befall you, recall some of the excellent and noble spiritual accidents existing in the substance of the soul. You will find then those accidents which will change the soul from that which it was and through which it becomes something which it was not. [And this change] is the result of the arrival of this subtle, accidental form in the soul. If this notion will arise in your imagination, you will resist by means of it the notion which made you doubt, and the former notion will expel the latter and will establish its opposite.

Pupil. Much doubt has so far befallen me concerning the division of simple substances into matter and form and concerning the difference of these spiritual substances one from the other, inasmuch as I deny that it is possible that something spiritual is divisible. Set down a discussion sufficient to remove this doubt.

Master. As argument against the first doubt [namely that spiritual substances are composed of matter and form] set down the difference between spiritual substances and corporeal substances and the difference of spiritual substances one from another. As argument against the second doubt [namely that spiritual substances differ from one another] set down the difference of the substance of the soul in itself which results from the accidents which come to be in it. Furthermore, consider that in the case of everything which you perceive by means of sense or intellect, you perceive only its form which actualizes its essence. Hence that form has a subject which underlies it and of which it is the form. When you will have understood by means of your intellect the form [of spiritual substance], that is, when you will have understood the nature of that form as a result of which the spiritual substance is what it is, then you will conclude that the spiritual substance possesses a matter which underlies its form.

Pupil. From the arguments which you have previously set down it is now clear to me that the spiritual substance consists of matter and form. But is there another argument which throws further light on this?

Master. Another argument showing that the simple substances which are above the composite substances are composed of matter and form is one that I have often set down previously. It is that the inferior proceeds from the superior and that the inferior is an example for the superior. For if the inferior comes to be from the superior, it is necessary that the order of corporeal substances is in the likeness of the order of spiritual substances. For just as the corporeal substances are arranged in a three-fold order, namely, gross body, subtle body, and the matter and form of which the corporeal substances consist, so similarly, is the spiritual substance arranged in a three-fold order, namely, first, the spiritual substance which comes after the corporeal substance, then, the spiritual substance which is more spiritual than it and, finally, the matter and form of which the spiritual substances are composed.

Pupil. Make clear to me that the superior exists in the inferior by means of a clear demonstration which establishes this notion.

Master. The proof that all spiritual substances and forms, that is, their essences and action, exist in corporeal substances is that everything that is common to the properties of things exists in the corporeal substances. Since the superior property exists in the inferior, does it not follow necessarily that whatsoever exists in the inferior must also exist in the superior? Indeed, what has been stated in the logical sciences, namely that the higher beings [the genera for example], give their name and definition to the lower being [the species], also shows this.

Pupil. This is certainly so.

Master. The fact that the intellect abstracts forms from bodies also shows this and in this there is proof that the form of the intellect is in agreement with all forms, just as it is clear from the proofs which we previously set down, that the forms which inhere in composite substances emanate from the simple substances.

Pupil. You have already shown that it is not possible that spiritual substances are only matter or only form. But in what way shall I conceive them to be simple, if they are composed of matter and form?

Master. This should be clear to you from what has been said previously. However, I shall add further explanation. I say, that, since it is not impossible that something composite should be simple, so also is it not impossible that something simple should be composite. For something composite is simple in respect to something which is below it, and something simple is composite in respect to that which is above it.

Pupil. Since the matter in simple substances differs from the form existing in them, consider whether the matter, inasmuch as it differs from the form and is opposed to it in its essence, can exist without the form even for an instant, or whether the matter can not exist without the form even for an instant? For how can the distinction between matter and form become clear, if neither of these principles can exist without the other even for an instant?

Master. Wait a while, do not rush in asking until we shall have spoken about universal matter in itself and universal form in itself.

Pupil. About what have we spoken then until now?

Master. Was your inquiry not about the principle that in the intelligible being there exists nothing besides matter and form, just as in the sensible being there exist no principles besides these? And I demonstrated that the intelligible substances consist of matter and form, because they differ in one respect and agree in another. I showed you the same principle also in other ways, and I showed you that it is false that they are only matter or only form. Through these demonstrations you gained knowledge concerning the question whether matter and form exist in simple substances. Later on we shall describe what each one of these principles is [in itself] and we shall investigate how one principle differs from the other. Then you will have gained knowledge of whether they exist, what they are, and in what manner they are. But an answer to the question why they are you will derive from the quality of universal matter and universal form. For in this discussion we did not inquire about universal matter and universal form, for we intended to investigate only concerning the matters of spiritual substances. And we take the matter of the particular intellect and its form as an example for attributing matter and form to each one of the spiritual substances. And I set this down as a rule for describing the substance of the universal intelligence and of the universal substances which are below it.

Pupil. How is this?

Master. Since the particular intellect is composed of matter and form, it necessarily follows that the universal intellect is composed of matter and form. In this way we infer [from the composition of] the particular intellect [the composition of] the universal intellect, just as we infer the existence of the universal intellect from the existence of the particular intellect.

. . .

SELECTED BIBLIOGRAPHY

TRANSLATIONS

Cohen, A., trans., *Solomon Ibn Gabirol's Choice of Pearls*, New York, 1925.

Lewis, B., trans., *The Kingly Crown*, London, 1961.

Wedeck, H., trans., Solomon ibn Gabirol, *The*

Fountain of Life (Abridged), New York, 1962.

Wise, S., trans., *The Improvement of the Moral Qualities*, New York, 1901.

STUDIES

Bieler, M., *Der göttliche Wille (Logosbegriff) bei Gabirol*, Breslau, 1933.

Brunner, F., "La doctrine de la matière chez Avicebron," *Revue de Théologie et de Philosophie*, III (1956), 261–279.

Brunner, F., "Études sur le sense et la structure des systèmes réalistes," *Cahiers de Civilisation Médiévale*, I (1958), 295–317.

Brunner, F., *Platonisme et Aristotélisme: la critique d'Ibn Gabirol par Saint Thomas D'Aquin*, Louvain, 1965.

Brunner, F., "Sur la philosophie d'Ibn Gabirol, à propos d'un ouvrage récent," *Revue des Études Juives*, CXXVII (1969), 317–337.

Dreyer, K., *Die Religiöse Gedankenwelt des Salomo ibn Gabirol*, Leipsig, 1930.

Guttmann, Jacob, *Die Philosophie des Solomon ibn Gabirol*, Göttingen, 1889.

Heschel, A., "Das Wesen der Dinge nach der Lehre Gabirols," *Hebrew Union College Annual*, XIV (1939), 359–385.

Heschel, A., "Der Begriff der Einheit in der Philosophie Gabirols," *Monatsschrift für*

Geschichte und Wissenschaft des Judentums, LXXXII (1938), 89–111.

Heschel, A., "Der Begriff des Seins in der Philosophie Gabirols," *Festschrift Jakob Freimann*, Berlin, 1937, 68–77.

Joel, M., "Ibn Gebirols (Avicebrons) Bedeutung für die Geschichte der Philosophie," *Monatsschrift für Geschichte und Wissenschaft des Judentums*, VI (1857); VII (1858).

Kaufmann, D., *Studien über Salomon ibn Gabirol*, Budapest, 1899.

Munk, S., *Mélanges de philosophie juive et arabe*, Paris, 1859. (Reprinted Paris, 1955).

Rudavsky, T., "Conflicting Motifs in Ibn Gabirol's Discussion of Matter," *New Scholasticism*, LII (1978), 54ff.

Schlanger, J., *La philosophie de Salomon Ibn Gabirol*, Leiden, 1968.

Wittmann, M., *Die Stellung des hl. Thomas von Aquin zu Avencebrol*, Münster, 1900.

Wittmann, M., *Zur Stellung Avencebrols im Entwicklungsgang der arabischen Philosophie*, Münster, 1905.

MOSES MAIMONIDES

1135–1204

OSES MAIMONIDES was by far the best known Jewish philosopher of the Middle Ages and his *Guide of the Perplexed* (*Dalālat al-Ḥā'irīn*) is easily the most important medieval Jewish philosophic work. For Jewish thinkers, Rabbi Moses ben Maimon's *Moreh Nebukim* determined the course of philosophy from the early thirteenth century on, and there appeared hardly any work for the remainder of the Middle Ages that did not cite Maimonides' views and comment on them. For Christian scholastics of the thirteenth and fourteenth centuries, Rabbi Moses' *Doctor Perplexorum* formed a respected part of the philosophic literature of the day.

In his philosophic views Maimonides was an Aristotelian and it was he who put medieval Jewish philosophy on a firm Aristotelian basis. As philosopher, Maimonides followed the teachings of Aristotle as interpreted by the ancient commentators (Alexander of Aphrodisias in particular) and as expounded by the Muslim Aristotelians al-Fārābī, Ibn Sīnā (Avicenna), and Ibn Bājjah (Avempace). The writings of his older contemporary Ibn Rushd (Averroes) became known to Maimonides in his later years, but they did not seem to have had a formative influence on his thought.

Though Maimonides considered himself in continuity with the Muslim Aristotelians, adapting and developing their teachings in accordance with his own views, he differed from them in the works which he produced. Unlike the Muslims, he wrote no commentary on any of Aristotle's works, collected no *summa* of the philosophical sciences, nor composed any independent philosophic treatises, an early work on logic excepted. Holding that the available philosophic literature was adequate for all needs, Maimonides investigated how the Aristotelian teachings can be related to the beliefs and practices of Jewish tradition.

Maimonides' *Guide* is a rather enigmatic book. Instead of being a work of straightforward philosophic or theological exposition, it takes the form of a personal communication to Joseph ben Judah, a former pupil. Moreover, though the topics of the work are clear enough, their arrangement does not always follow an easily discernible order. Still further, Maimonides himself informs his reader that he makes use of methods of indirection and that views set down in one part of the *Guide* at times contradict opinions expressed in another part. It is not surprising that this method produced divergent interpretations of Maimonides' views. There are scholars who see in him a moderate Aristotelian who made a sincere effort to harmonize scriptural and philosophic teachings, while there are others who consider him a rigorous Aristotelian who, by innuendo, subscribes to such doctrines as the eternity of the world and the determination of the human will.

The enigmatic nature of the *Guide* resulted from design. For both the religious and the philosophic traditions within which Maimonides worked maintained that speculative teachings are esoteric and that they are not to be communicated indiscriminately to the masses. Thus, Maimonides' rabbinic sources record as binding law that Ma'aseh Merkabah (The account of the Divine Chariot) and Ma'aseh Bereshit (the account of the creation of the world)—rabbinic doctrines which Maimonides unhesitatingly identified with Aristotelian metaphysics and physics—may only be taught to select, properly qualified students. This rabbinic injunction was in agreement with the principle of philosophic prudence that philosophic truths should not be communicated to the masses.

In view of Maimonides' method and the rather unusual arrangement of his *Guide,* it may be well to review the purpose and contents of the work. According to his own testimony, Maimonides wrote his *Guide* for someone who believed in the validity of the Law, who had studied the philosophical sciences and who had become perplexed by the literal meaning of certain biblical terms and parables. Hence, the work is not addressed to the simple believer who has no philosophic interest, nor to the philosopher for whom religion has, at best, a utilitarian function. The proper subject of the *Guide* may thus be said to be the philosophic exegesis of the Law or, as Maimonides himself puts it, an account of "the science of the Law in its true sense" or of the "secrets of the Law."

Since his addressee is vexed by the literal meaning of certain biblical terms and parables, in particular by anthropomorphisms and anthropopathisms applied to God, Maimonides begins, after a preface setting down the purposes and method of the work, with chapters devoted to biblical exegesis. Citing a large number of difficult terms, he shows that even in the biblical text these terms have, besides a physical, also a spiritual meaning. Having disposed of this philological task, Maimonides proceeds to a philosophic account of Divine attributes. Accepting the Avicennian distinction between essence and existence as a real distinction, Maimonides concludes that no positive attributes may be predicated of God. Of the various attributes by which God is described, accidental attributes must be understood as attributes of action, while essential attributes are to be understood as negations. The doctrine of "negative attributes" became a characteristic part of Maimonides' philosophic views. This doctrine was later attacked by, among others, Thomas Aquinas.

Having shown how Divine attributes are to be understood, Maimonides proceeds to formal demonstrations of the existence, unity, and incorporeality of God, and to a discussion of the creation of the world. Prior to Maimonides, these doctrines had been discussed by Muslim and Jewish Mutakallimūn (see p. 205). But the Kalāmic demonstrations, according to Maimonides, were false, for they were based on categories of the imagination rather than on categories of reason. Hence, Maimonides considered it necessary to refute the arguments of the Mutakallimūn prior to setting down his own demonstrations. The latter chapters of the first part of the *Guide* are devoted to the exposition and refutation of the Kalāmic views.

Maimonides opens the second section of the *Guide* with his own demonstrations of the existence, unity, and incorporeality of God. His proofs are preceded by twenty-five physical and metaphysical propositions which he considers as having been demonstrated in the philosophic literature of his day. To these propositions he adds (as Thomas later on) the premise that the world is eternal. However, this premise is set down as a hypothesis required to demonstrate that God exists, not as a proposition which Maimonides accepts as true.

Generally speaking, Maimonides' proofs of the existence of God are those familiar from the philosophic literature of the Middle Ages. All of his proofs, it appears, are physical, that demonstrating the existence of God as the prime mover being his major proof. As one of the four proofs that he presents, Maimonides accepts that of Avicenna, known as the proof from necessity and contingency. Yet, unlike Avicenna, Maimonides seems to consider this proof as physical rather than metaphysical. His proofs for the unity and incorporeality of God follow the conventional pattern.

Once Maimonides had completed his philosophic discussion of the existence, unity, and incorporeality of God (and the intelligences), he turned to problems of a more religious nature, the first being the creation of the world. Whereas for Aristotle the question whether the world is eternal or created formed a rather minor point in his discussion of the heavens, for Maimonides, as for other religious philosophers, it became a major issue. In solving this problem Maimonides shows a good deal of ingenuity and his solution was accepted by Aquinas later on. Attempting to show on textual as well as philosophic grounds, that Aristotle never claimed to have demonstrated the eternity of the world, Maimonides concludes that Aristotle's view is only a likely opinion, not a decisive demonstration. Moreover, Maimonides argues, demonstrations of the eternity or creation of the world lie outside the competence of the human mind. At best, the human mind can offer likely arguments for either view. In the absence of apodictic demonstrations, Maimonides affirms that the arguments for the creation of the world are more convincing than those against it and, in addition, creation is supported by scriptural teachings. Once Maimonides had accepted the creation of the world, it became easier for him to account for miracles and prophecy.

It is to an analysis of the latter problem that Maimonides turns next. In his account, he strikes a balance between the pietistic view which sees prophecy solely as an arbitrary gift of God and the philosophic view which considers prophecy exclusively as a fulfillment of natural human powers. To be sure, the prophet, according to Maimonides, must be someone healthy in his constitution and possessed of a well developed intellect and imagination; but at the same time God has a role in prophetic inspiration, be it to prevent someone who is qualified from prophesying, or be it to provide an emanation productive of prophecy. The prophet gains certain cognitions which the philosopher does not have, but by far his most important function is political. In the case of Moses, he is someone who brings the Law, while in the case of the other Hebrew prophets he is someone who admonishes about the Law.

After expounding certain metaphysical doctrines in explanation of passages from Ezekiel, Maimonides, in the third part of the *Guide,* proceeds to a discussion of evil and providence. Moral evil is due to human choice, while natural evil is considered as a privation of good. God's providence for the world is generally manifest through the orderly laws of nature, but in the case of man it is individual, the degree of providence being determined by the development of the intellectual faculties of a person.

In the final section of the *Guide,* Maimonides turns to an explanation of the precepts of the Law. For him, the Law is the result of Divine wisdom rather than the product of arbitrary Divine will. Hence, for all the laws, with the exception of certain particular norms, there exist reasons—at least for God—and many of these reasons can be discovered by the human mind. The general purposes of the Law are two: to instil correct opinions and to regulate men's political relations. Correct opinions lead to the intellectual virtues on which, according to Maimonides, human immortality depends. Maimonides sees a number of the ritual laws as reactions to pagan practices current in ancient times.

Moses ben Maimon was born in Cordova on March 30, 1135. From his father Maimon and other teachers he received a thorough training in biblical and rabbinic learning and in philosophy and the sciences. When, in 1148, the fanatic Almohads conquered Cordova, Maimon and his family were forced to flee. Though little is known about the subsequent period, it seems that the family wandered at first in Spain, finally settling in Fez in North Africa. But since North Africa was also under Almohad rule, the family, after a brief stay in Palestine, settled in Egypt in 1165. At first, the family was supported by Maimonides' older brother, David, but after the brother's tragic death, Maimonides turned to the practice of medicine. He gained renown as a physician and was appointed court physician to the vizier of Saladin.

Within the Jewish community Maimonides became known and respected for his unparalleled rabbinic learning. Jews from all over the world addressed inquiries to him and he was appointed head (Nagid) of all Egyptian Jews. He died on December 13, 1204 and he was buried in Tiberias. Of him it was said: "from Moses (the prophet) to Moses (ben Maimon) there had arisen no one like unto him."

Maimonides was one of the greatest Jewish legal scholars of all times. At the age of twenty-three he had begun his first major work the *Book of Il-lumination (Kitāb al-Sirāj, Sefer ha-Ma'or)*, a commentary on the Mishnah, the basic rabbinic text. This work was completed ten years later, in 1168.

Though its subject matter is primarily legal, Maimonides' commentary contains two "Introductions" (really monographs) of special philosophic and theological interest. The introduction to the "Sayings of the Fathers," known as the "Eight Chapters," contains a summary of his psychological views, while the introduction to the tenth chapter of the tractate Sanhedrin contains an account of his eschatological views and of his famous thirteen principles of Jewish belief. The commentary was written in Arabic and later translated into Hebrew.

The *Mishneh Torah,* his great code, was Maimonides' second major work. In this book he undertook to codify the totality of Jewish law, a task which no one had attempted before. Most of this work is taken up with practical matters of law, but, in line with his conviction that all believers must possess a rudiment of correct theological and philosophic opinions, Maimonides began the work with a "Book of Knowledge" (Sefer ha-Madda') containing a popular exposition of physical and metaphysical topics. The *Mishneh Torah* was his only major work written in Hebrew.

Maimonides' third major work was his *Guide of the Perplexed.* Written in Arabic, the work was first translated into Hebrew by Maimonides' contemporary Samuel Ibn Tibbon and a second time by Judah al-Ḥarizi. The medieval Latin translation was based on Ḥarizi's text. Maimonides also composed a number of medical treatises and among his other writings, the previously mentioned *Treatise on Logic* is of special philosophic interest.

The following selections, all taken from the *Guide,* deal with four basic aspects of Maimonides' thought. The first selection is devoted to a detailed account of his doctrine of Divine attributes. Within this section chapters fifty-nine and sixty are of special interest, for in them he shows what kind of knowledge of God negative attributes supply. In these chapters he anticipates the objections of later philosophers who hold that negative attributes provide no satisfactory knowledge of God. The second selection contains the major aspects of his doctrine of creation, and the third discusses prophecy. In the final selection, Maimonides develops certain aspects of his philosophy of law. In it is found his critique of the Kalāmic division of laws into those which are rational and those which are traditional (see p. 344).

THE GUIDE OF THE PERPLEXED

BOOK I

CHAPTER 51

There are many things in existence that are clear and manifest: primary intelligibles and things perceived by the senses and, in addition, the things that

Reprinted from *Guide of the Perplexed,* by S. Pines, trans., by permission of The University of Chicago Press. Copyright 1963 by The University of Chicago Press.

come near to these in respect to their clarity. If man had been left as he [naturally] is, he would not have needed a proof of them—for instance, for the existence of motion, the existence of man's ability to act, the manifestations of generation and corruption, the natures of the things that are apparent to the senses, like the hotness of fire, the coldness of water, and many other things of this kind. Yet since strange opinions have arisen due either to people who committed errors or to people who acted with some end in view, so that professing such opinions they ran counter to the nature of existence and denied a sensibly perceived thing or wished to suggest to the estimative faculty the existence of a nonexistent thing, the men of science have had to resort to proving those manifest things and to disproving the existence of things that are only thought to exist. Thus we find that Aristotle establishes the fact of motion, as it had been denied, and demonstrates the nonexistence of atoms, as their existence had been asserted. To this category belongs the denial of essential attributes to God, may He be exalted. For that denial is a primary intelligible, inasmuch as an attribute is not the essence of the thing of which it is predicated, but is a certain mode of the essence and hence an accident. If, however, the attribute were the essence of the thing of which it is predicated, the attribute would be either a tautology— as if you were saying that man is man—or the attribute would be a mere explanation of a term—as if you said that man is a rational living being. For being a rational animal is the essence and true reality of man, and there does not exist in this case a third notion, apart from those of animal and of rational, that constitutes man. For man is the being of which life and rationality are predicated. Thus those attributes merely signify an explanation of a term and nothing else. It is as if you said that the thing denoted by the term "man" is the thing composed of life and rationality. It is then clear that an attribute may be only one of two things. It is either the essence of the thing of which it is predicated, in which case it is an explanation of a term. We, in this respect, do not consider it impossible to predicate such an attribute of God, but do consider it impossible in another respect, as shall be made clear. Or the attribute is different from the thing of which it is predicated, being a notion superadded to that thing. This would lead to the conclusion that that attribute is an accident belonging to that essence.

Now by denying the assertion that terms denoting accidents are attributes of the Creator, one does not deny the notion of accident. For every notion superadded to an essence is an adjunct to it and does not perfect its essence, and this is the meaning of accident. This should be considered in addition to the circumstances that there would be many eternal things if there were many attributes. For there is no oneness at all except in believing that there is one simple essence in which there is no complexity or multiplication of notions, but one notion only; so that from whatever angle you regard it and from whatever point of view you consider it, you will find that it is one, not divided in any way and by any cause into two notions; and you will not find therein any multiplicity either in the thing as it is outside of the mind or as it is in the mind, as shall be demonstrated in this Treatise.

In discussing this subject, some people engaged in speculation have ended by saying that His attributes, may He be exalted, are neither His essence nor a thing external to His essence. This is similar to what others say, namely, that the modes—by which term they mean the universals—are neither existent nor nonexistent, and, again similar to what others say, that the atom is not in a place, but occupies a locality, and that there is no act of a man but that there may be an acquisition of an act by him. These are things that are merely said; and accordingly they subsist only in words, not in the mind; all the more, they have no existence outside of the mind. But as you know and as everyone knows who does not deceive himself, these assertions are defended by means of many words and falsifying parables and are proved correct by shouting defamatory polemics and various complicated kinds of dialectic arguments and sophistries. Should, however, the man who proclaims these things and attempts to establish them in the ways indicated, reflect upon his belief, he would find nothing but confusion and incapacity. For he wants to make exist something that does not exist and to create a mean between two contraries that have no mean. Or is there a mean between that which exists and that which does not exist, or in the case of two things is there a mean between one of them being identical with the other or being something else? What forces him to this is, as we have said, the wish to preserve the conceptions of the imagination and the fact that all existent bodies are always represented to oneself as certain essences. Now every such essence is of necessity endowed with attributes, for we do not ever find an essence of a body that while existing is divested of everything and is without an attribute. This imagination being pursued, it was thought that He, may He be exalted, is similarly composed of various notions, namely, His essence and the notions that are superadded to His essence. Several groups of people pursued the likening of God to other beings and believed Him to be a body endowed with attributes. Another group raised themselves above this consequence and denied His being a body, but preserved the attributes. All this was rendered necessary by their keeping to the external sense of the revealed books as I shall make clear in later chapters that will deal with these notions.

CHAPTER 52

An attribute predicated of any thing, of which thing it is accordingly said that it is such and such, must necessarily belong to one of the following five groups:

The first group is characterized by the thing having its definition predicated of it—as when it is predicated of man that he is a rational living being. This attribute, which indicates the essence and true reality of a thing, is, as we have already made clear, merely the explanation of a term and nothing else. This kind of attribute should be denied to God according to everybody. For He, may He be exalted, has no causes anterior to Him that are the cause of His existence and by which, in consequence, He is defined. For this reason it is well known among all people engaged in speculation, who understand what they say, that God cannot be defined.

The second group is characterized by the thing having part of its definition predicated of it—as when it is predicated of man that he is a living being or a rational being. This attribute signifies an inseparable connection. For our saying, every man is rational, signifies that reason must be found in every being in whom humanity is found. This kind of attribute should be denied to God, may He be exalted, according to everybody. For if He has a part of an essence, His essence must be composite. The absurdity of divine attributes belonging to this group is like the absurdity recognized with regard to the first group.

The third group consists of attributes predicated of a thing that go beyond its true reality and its essence so that the attribute in question is not a thing through which the essence is perfected and constituted. Consequently that attribute is a certain quality with respect to the thing of which it is predicated. Now quality, considered one of the supreme genera, is regarded as one of the accidents. Thus if an attribute belonging to this group would subsist in Him, may He be exalted, He would be a substratum of accidents. This is sufficient to show how far from His true reality and essence this is, I mean the supposition that He is endowed with quality. It is, however, strange that those who proclaim the existence of attributes, deny with reference to Him, may He be exalted, the possibility of likening Him to something else and of qualifying Him. For what is the meaning of their saying that He may not be qualified unless it be that He is not endowed with quality? Now every attribute that is affirmed of a certain essence as pertaining to it essentially either constitutes the essence, in which case it is identical with the latter, or is a quality of that essence.

Now there are, as you know, four genera of qualities. I will accordingly give you examples in the way of attributes of every one of these genera, in order that the impossibility of the subsistence of attributes of this kind in God, may He be exalted, be made clear to you. The first example is as follows. You predicate of a man one of his speculative or moral habits or one of the dispositions subsisting in him qua an animate being, as when you say someone is a carpenter or chaste or ill. There is no difference between your saying a carpenter or your saying a learned man or a sage, all of these being dispositions subsisting in the soul. There is also no difference between your saying a chaste man and your saying a merciful man. For all arts, sciences, and settled moral characters are dispositions subsisting in the soul. All this is clear to whoever has occupied himself even to the slightest extent with the art of logic. The second example is as follows. You predicate of a thing a natural faculty that is in it or the absence of a natural faculty, as when you say soft or hard. And there is no difference between your saying soft and hard and your saying strong and weak, all these being natural dispositions. The third example is as follows. You predicate of a man a passive quality or an affection, as when you say someone is irascible, irritable, timid, or merciful, in cases in which this character is not firmly established. Your predicating a color, a taste, a smell, warmth, coldness, dryness, and humidity of a certain thing also belongs to this kind. The fourth example is as follows. You predicate of a thing that which pertains to it in respect of quantity considered as such, as when you say long, short, crooked, and straight and other similar things. Now when you consider all these attributes and what is akin to them, you will find that it is impossible to ascribe them to God. For He does not possess quantity so that there might pertain to Him a quality pertaining to quantity as such. Nor does He receive impressions and affections so that there might pertain to Him a quality belonging to the affections. Nor does He have dispositions so that there might be faculties and similar things pertaining to Him. Nor is He, may He be exalted, endowed with a soul, so that He might have a habitus pertaining to Him—such as clemency, modesty, and similar things—or have pertain to Him that which pertains to animate beings as such—for instance, health and illness. It is accordingly clear to you that no attribute that may be brought under the supreme genus of quality can subsist in Him, may He be exalted.

With regard to those three groups of attributes—which are the attributes indicative of the essence or of a part of the essence or of a certain quality subsisting in the essence—it has already been made clear that they are impossible with reference to Him, may He be exalted, for all of them are indicative of composition, and the impossibility of composition in respect to the deity we shall make clear by demonstration.

The fourth group of attributes is as follows. It is predicated of a thing that it has a relation to something other than itself. For instance, it is related to a time or to a place or to another individual, as for instance when you predicate of Zayd that he is the father of a certain individual or the partner of a certain individual or an inhabitant of a certain place or one who was at a certain time. Now this kind of attribute does not necessarily entail either multiplicity or change in the essence of the thing of which it is predicated. For the Zayd who is referred to may be the partner of Umar, the father of Bakr, the master of Khālid, a friend of Zayd, an inhabitant of such and such dwelling place, and one who was born in such and such a year. Those notions of relation are not the essence of the thing or something subsisting in its essence, as do the qualities. At first thought it seems that it is permissible to predicate of God, may He be exalted, attributes of this kind. However, when one knows true reality and achieves greater exactness in speculation, the fact that this is impossible becomes clear. There is no relation between God, may He be exalted, and time and place; and this is quite clear. For time is an accident attached to motion, when the notion of priority and posterity is considered in the latter and when motion becomes numbered, as is made clear in the passages especially dealing with this subject. Motion, on the other hand, is one of the things attached to bodies, whereas God, may He be exalted, is not a body. Accordingly there is no relation between Him and time, and in the same way there is no relation between Him and place. The subject of investigation and speculation is therefore the question whether there is between Him, may He be exalted, and any of the substances created by Him a true relation of some kind so that this relation might be predicated of Him. It is clear at the first glance that there is no correlation between Him and the things created by Him. For one of the properties of two correlated things is the possibility of inverting the statement concerning them while preserving their respective relations. Now He, may He be exalted, has a necessary existence while that which is other than He has a possible existence, as we shall make clear. There accordingly can be no correlation between them. As for the view that there is some relation between them, it is deemed correct, but this is not correct. For it is impossible to represent oneself that a relation subsists between the intellect and color although, according to our school, both of them are comprised by the same "existence." How then can a relation be represented between Him and what is other than He when there is no notion comprising in any respect both of the two, inasmuch as existence is, in our opinion, affirmed of Him, may He be exalted, and of what is other than He merely by way of absolute equivocation. There is, in truth, no relation in any respect between Him and any of His creatures. For relation is always found between two things falling under the same—necessarily proximate

—species, whereas there is no relation between the two tnings if they merely fall under the same genus. On this account one does not say that this red is more intense than this green or less or equally so, though both fall under the same genus, namely, color. If, however, two things fall under two different genera, there is no relation between them in any respect whatever, not even according to the inchoate notions of common opinion; this holds even for cases in which the two things fall in the last resort under one higher genus. For instance, there is no relation between a hundred cubits and the heat that is in pepper inasmuch as the latter belongs to the genus quality and the former to the genus quantity. There is no relation either between knowledge and sweetness or between clemency and bitterness, though all of them fall under the supreme genus quality. How then could there subsist a relation between Him, may He be exalted, and any of the things created by Him, given the immense difference between them with regard to the true reality of their existence, than which there is no greater difference? If a relation subsisted between them, it would necessarily follow that the accident of relation must be attached to God. Even if it is not an accident with regard to His essence, may He be exalted, nevertheless it is, generally speaking, some sort of accident. There is accordingly no way of escape offering the possibility of affirming that He has an attribute, not even with regard to relation, if one has knowledge of true reality. However, relation is an attribute with regard to which it is more appropriate than with regard to the others that indulgence should be exercised if it is predicated of God. For it does not entail the positing of a multiplicity of eternal things or the positing of alteration taking place in His essence, may He be exalted, as a consequence of an alteration of the things related to Him.

The fifth group of the affirmative attributes is as follows. A thing has its action predicated of it. I do not intend to signify by the words, his action, the habitus of an art that belongs to him who is described—as when you say a carpenter or a smith—inasmuch as this belongs to the species of quality, as we have mentioned. But I intend to signify by the words, his action, the action that he who is described has performed—as when you say Zayd is the one who carpentered this door, built that particular wall, or wove this garment. Now this kind of attribute is remote from the essence of the thing of which it is predicated. For this reason it is permitted that this kind should be predicated of God, may He be exalted, after you have—as shall be made clear—come to know that the acts in question need not be carried out by means of differing notions subsisting within the essence of the agent, but that all His different acts, may He be exalted, are all of them carried out by means of His essence, and not, as we have made clear, by means of a superadded notion.

A summary of the contents of the present chapter would be as follows: He, may He be exalted, is one in all respects; no multiplicity should be posited in Him; there is no notion that is superadded to His essence; the numerous attributes possessing diverse notions that figure in the Scriptures and that are indicative of Him, may He be exalted, are mentioned in reference to the multiplicity of His actions and not because of a multiplicity subsisting in His essence, and some of them, as we have made clear, also with a view to indicating His perfection according to what we consider as perfection. As for the question whether it is possible that one simple essence in which no multiplicity is posited should perform diverse actions, the answer shall be made clear by means of examples.

CHAPTER 53

The reasons that led those who believe in the existence of attributes belonging to the Creator to this belief are akin to those that led those who believe in the doctrine of His corporeality to that belief. For he who believes in this doctrine was not led to it by intellectual speculation; he merely followed the external sense of the texts of the Scriptures. This is also the case with regard to the attributes. For inasmuch as the books of the prophets and the revealed books existed, which predicated attributive qualifications of Him, may He be exalted, these were taken in their literal sense; and He was believed to possess attributes. The people in question have, as it were, divested God of corporeality but not of the modes of corporeality, namely, the accidents—I mean the aptitudes of the soul, all of which are qualities. For with regard to every attribute that the believer in attributes considers to be essential in respect to God, may He be exalted, you will find that the notion of it is that of a quality, even if these people do not state it clearly; for they in fact liken the attribute in question to what they meet with in the various states of all bodies endowed with an animal soul. Of all this it is said: *The Torah speaketh in the language of the sons of man.* The purpose for which all these attributes are used is to predicate perfection of Him, but not the particular notion that is a perfection with respect to creatures possessing a soul. Most of these attributes are attributes pertaining to His diverse actions. Now there need not be a diversity in the notions subsisting in an agent because of the diversity of his various actions. Of this I shall give you an instance taken from things that are to be found with us—I mean an example of the fact that though an agent is one, diverse actions may proceed from him, even if he does not possess will and all the more if he acts through will. An instance of this is fire: it melts some things, makes others hard, cooks and burns, bleaches and blackens. Thus if some man would predicate of fire that it is that which bleaches and blackens, which burns and cooks, which makes hard and which melts, he would say the truth. Accordingly he who does not know the nature of fire thinks that there subsist in it six diverse notions, by means of one of which it blackens, whereas it bleaches by means of another, cooks by means of a third, burns by means of a fourth, melts by means of a fifth, and makes hard by means of a sixth—all these actions being opposed to one another, for the meaning of any one of them is different from that of any other. However, he who knows the nature of fire, knows that it performs all these actions by virtue of one active quality, namely, heat. If, however, such a state of affairs exists with respect to a thing acting by virtue of its nature, it exists all the more with respect to one who acts through will, and again all the more with respect to Him, may He be exalted, who is above every attributive qualification. We have grasped with regard to Him relations having corresponding diverse notions— for the notion of knowledge is in us other than the notion of power, and the latter other than the notion of will. Yet how can we regard as a necessary consequence of this the subsistence in Him of diverse notions that are essential to Him, so that there would subsist in Him something by virtue of which He knows as well as something by virtue of which He wills and something by virtue of which He has power, for this is the meaning of the attributes whose existence is asserted by the people in question? Some of them state this clearly, enumerating the notions that are superadded to the essence. Others belonging to them do not state this clearly; however it is quite clear in their belief, even if it is not expressed in comprehensible language. This is the case when some of them assert that He possesses power because of His essence, possesses knowledge because of His essence, is living because of His essence, possesses will because of His essence.

I shall illustrate this by the example of the rational faculty subsisting in man. It is one faculty with regard to which no multiplicity is posited. Through it he acquires the sciences and the arts; through the same faculty he sews, carpenters, weaves, builds, has a knowledge of geometry, and governs the city. Those very different actions, however, proceed from one simple faculty in which no multiplicity is posited. Now these actions are very different, and their number is almost infinite—I mean the number of the arts brought forth by the rational faculty. It accordingly should not be regarded as inadmissible in reference to God, may He be magnified and honored, that the diverse actions proceed from one simple essence in which no multiplicity is posited and to which no notion is superadded. Every attribute that is found in the books of the deity, may He be exalted, is therefore an attribute of His action and not an attribute of His essence, or it is indicative of absolute perfection. There accordingly is not, as these people believe, an essence composed of diverse notions. For the fact that they do not use the term "composition" does not abolish the notion of composition with regard to the essence possessing attributes. However, there exists a point of doubt that led them to this doctrine. This is the one I am going to explain to you. For those who believe in attributes do not do so because of the multiplicity of His actions. Rather do they say: Yes, the One Essence performs diverse actions, but the attributes that are essential to Him, may He be exalted, do not belong to His actions. For it is not permissible to imagine that God has created His own essence. They differ with respect to those attributes that they call essential, I mean with regard to their number, inasmuch as all of them follow the text of some book. We shall mention that as to which all of them agree and consider to be cognized by the intellect and in which case there is no need to follow the text of the word of a prophet. There are four such attributes: living, possessing power, possessing knowledge, possessing will. They say that these are distinct notions and such perfections that it would be impossible for the deity to be deprived of any of them. It is not permissible to suppose that they belong to His actions. This is a summary of their opinion.

Now you know that the notion of knowledge in reference to Him, may He be exalted, is identical with the notion of life, for everyone who apprehends his own essence possesses both life and knowledge by virtue of the same thing. For we wished to signify by "knowledge" the apprehension of one's own essence. Now the essence that apprehends is undoubtedly the same as the essence that is apprehended. For in our opinion He is not composed of two things, the thing that apprehends and another thing that does not apprehend, as man is composed of a soul that apprehends and of a body that does not apprehend. Accordingly, inasmuch as our saying "possessing knowledge" is intended to signify "he who apprehends his own essence," life and knowledge form in this case one notion. However, the people in question do not consider this notion but consider rather His apprehension of His creatures. Similarly, without any doubt, neither power nor will exists in, and belongs to, the Creator in respect to His own essence;

for He does not exercise His power on His own essence, nor can it be predicated of Him that He wills His own essence. And nobody represents this to himself. Rather have these attributes been thought of in reference to the diverse relations that may obtain between God, may He be exalted, and the things created by Him. For He possesses the power to create what He created, and possesses the power to bring into being that which exists in the manner in which He has brought it into being, and also possesses the knowledge of what He has brought into being. Thus it has become clear to you that these attributes too are not to be considered in reference to His essence, but in reference to the things that are created. For this reason, we, the community of those who profess the Unity by virtue of a knowledge of the truth—just as we do not say that there is in His essence a superadded notion by virtue of which He has created the heavens, and another one by virtue of which He has created the elements, and a third one by virtue of which He has created the intellects—so we do not say that there is in Him a superadded notion by virtue of which He possesses power, and another by virtue of which He possesses will, and a third one by virtue of which He knows the things created by Him. His essence is, on the contrary, one and simple, having no notion that is superadded to it in any respect. This essence has created everything that it has created and knows it, but absolutely not by virtue of a superadded notion. It makes no difference whether these diverse attributes correspond to His actions or to diverse relations between Him and the things produced by the actions, in conformity with what we have likewise explained regarding the truth of relation and its being merely something that is in thought. This is what ought to be believed with regard to the attributes mentioned in the books of the prophets; or, as we shall make clear, it may be believed with regard to some of them that they are attributes indicative of a perfection likened to our perfections, which are understood by us.

CHAPTER 58

More obscure than what preceded. Know that the description of God, may He be cherished and exalted, by means of negations is the correct description—a description that it not affected by an indulgence in facile language and does not imply any deficiency with respect to God in general or in any particular mode. On the other hand, if one describes Him by means of affirmations, one implies, as we have made clear, that He is associated with that which is not He and implies a defiency in Him. I must make it clear to you in the first place how negations are in a certain respect attributes and how they differ from the affirmative attributes. After that I shall make it clear to you that we have no way of describing Him unless it be through negations and not otherwise.

I shall say accordingly that an attribute does not particularize any object of which it is predicated in such a way that it is not associated by virtue of that particular attribute with other things. On the contrary, the attribute is sometimes attributed to the object of which it is predicated in spite of the fact that the latter has it in common with other things and is not particularized through it. For instance, if you would see a man at some distance and if you would ask: What is this thing that is seen? and were told: This is a living being—this affirmation would indubitably be an attribute predicated of the thing seen though it does not particularize the latter, distinguishing it from everything else. However, a certain particularization is achieved through it; namely, it may be learnt from it that the thing seen is not a body belonging to the species of plants or to that of the minerals. Similarly if there were a man in this house and you knew that some body is in it without knowing what it is and would ask, saying: What is in this house? and the one who answered you would say: There is no mineral in it and no body of a plant—a certain particularization would be achieved and you would know that a living being is in the house though you would not know which animal. Thus the attributes of negation have in this respect something in common with the attributes of affirmation, for the former undoubtedly bring about some particularization even if the particularization due to them only exists in the exclusion of what has been negated from the sum total of things that we had thought of as not being negated. Now as to the respect in which the attributes of negation differ from the attributes of affirmation: The attributes of affirmation, even if they do not particularize, indicate a part of the thing the knowledge of which is sought, that part being either a part of its substance or one of its accidents; whereas the attributes of negation do not give us knowledge in any respect whatever of the essence the knowledge of which is sought, unless this happens by accident as in the example we have given.

After this preface, I shall say that it has already been demonstrated that God, may He be honored and magnified, is existent of necessity and that there is no composition in Him, as we shall demonstrate, and that we are only able to apprehend the fact that He is and cannot apprehend His quiddity. It is consequently impossible that He should have affirmative attributes. For he has no "That" outside of His "What," and hence an attribute cannot be indicative of one of the two; all the more His "What" is not compound so that an attribute cannot be indicative of its two parts; and all the more, He cannot have accidents so that an attribute cannot be indicative of them. Accordingly He cannot have an affirmative attribute in any respect.

As for the negative attributes, they are those that must be used in order to conduct the mind toward that which must be believed with regard to Him, may He be exalted, for no notion of multiplicity can attach to Him in any respect on account of them; and, moreover, they conduct the mind toward the utmost reach that man may attain in the apprehension of Him, may He be exalted. For instance, it has been demonstrated to us that it is necessary that something exists other than those essences apprehended by means of the senses and whose knowledge is encompassed by means of the intellect. Of this thing we say that it exists, the meaning being that its nonexistence is impossible. We apprehend further that this being is not like the being of the elements, for example, which are dead bodies. We say accordingly that this being is living, the meaning being that He, may He be exalted, is not dead. We apprehend further that this being is not like the being of the heaven, which is a living body. We say accordingly that He is not a body. We apprehend further that this being is not like the being of the intellect, which is neither a body nor dead, but is caused. We say accordingly that He, may He be exalted, is eternal, the meaning being that He has no cause that has brought Him into existence. We apprehend further that the existence of this being, which is its essence, suffices not only for His being existent, but also for many other existents flowing from it, and that this overflow—unlike that of heat from fire and unlike the proceeding of light from the sun—is an overflow that, as we shall make clear, constantly procures for those existents duration and order by means of wisely contrived governance. Accordingly we say of Him, because of these notions, that He is powerful and knowing and willing. The intention in ascribing these attributes to Him is to signify that He is neither powerless nor ignorant nor inattentive nor negligent. Now the meaning of our saying that He is not powerless is to signify that His existence suffices for the bringing into existence of things other than He. The meaning of our saying that He is not ignorant is to signify that He apprehends—that is, is living, for every apprehending thing is living. And the meaning of our saying that He is not inattentive or negligent is to signify that all the existent things in question proceed from their cause according to a certain order and governance—not in a neglected way so as to be generated as chance would have it, but rather as all the things are generated that a willing being governs by means of purpose and will. We apprehend further that no other thing is like that being. Accordingly our saying that He is one signifies the denial of multiplicity.

It has thus become clear to you that every attribute that we predicate of Him is an attribute of action or, if the attribute is intended for the apprehension of His essence and not of His action, it signifies the negation of the privation of the attribute in question. Moreover, even those negations are not used with reference to or applied to Him, may He be exalted, except from the following point of view, which you know: one sometimes denies with reference to a thing something that cannot fittingly exist in it. Thus we say of a wall that it is not endowed with sight. Now you who read this Treatise with speculative intent know that whereas this heaven is a moving body of which we have measured the cubits and inches and in regard to which we have moreover achieved knowledge of the dimension of certain of its parts and of most of its movements, our intellects are quite incapable of apprehending its quiddity. And this, in spite of our knowing that it has of necessity matter and form, for its matter is not like that which is in us. For this reason we are unable to predicate of it any attributes except in terms whose meaning is not completely understood, but not by means of affirmations that are completely understood. Accordingly we say that the heavens are neither light nor heavy nor acted upon and consequently not receptive to external impressions, that they have no taste and no smell; and we make other negations of this kind. All this is due to our ignorance with regard to that matter.

What then should be the state of our intellects when they aspire to apprehend Him who is without matter and is simple to the utmost degree of simplicity, Him whose existence is necessary, Him who has no cause and to whom no notion attaches that is superadded to His essence, which is perfect—the meaning of its perfection being, as we have made clear, that all deficiences are negated with respect to it—we who only apprehend the fact that He is? There is accordingly an existent whom none of the existent things that He has brought into existence resembles, and who has nothing in common with them in any respect; in reference to whom there is no multiplicity or incapacity to bring into existence things other than He; whose relation to the world is that of a captain to his ship. Even this is not the true relation and a correct likeness, for this likeness has been used in order to lead the mind toward the view that He, may He be exalted, governs the existent things, the meaning of this being that He procures their existence and watches over their order as it ought to be watched over. This notion will be made clear more completely than it is here.

Glory then to Him who is such that when the intellects contemplate His essence, their apprehension turns into incapacity; and when they contemplate the proceeding of His actions from His will, their knowledge turns into ignorance; and when the tongues aspire to magnify Him by means of attributive qualifications, all eloquence turns into weariness and incapacity!

CHAPTER 59

Someone may ask and say: If there is no device leading to the apprehension of the true reality of His essence and if demonstration proves that it can only be apprehended that He exists and that it is impossible, as has been demonstrated, to ascribe to Him affirmative attributes, in what respect can there be superiority or inferiority between those who apprehend Him? If, however, there is none, *Moses our Master* and *Solomon* did not apprehend anything different from what a single individual among the pupils apprehends, and there can be no increase in this knowledge.

Now it is generally accepted by the men of the Law, nay even by the philosophers, that there exist numerous differences of degree in this respect. Know, therefore, that this is indeed so and that the differences of degree between those who apprehend are very great indeed. For the thing of which attributes are predicated becomes more particularized with every increase in attributes that are predicated of it, and he who predicates these attributes accordingly comes nearer to the apprehension of the true reality of the thing in question. In a similar way, you come nearer to the apprehension of Him, may He be exalted, with every increase in the negations regarding Him; and you come nearer to that apprehension than he who does not negate with regard to Him that which, according to what has been demonstrated to you, must be negated. For this reason a man sometimes labors for many years in order to understand some science and to gain true knowledge of its premises so that he should have certainty with regard to this science, whereas the only conclusion from this science in its entirety consists in our negating with reference to God some notion of which it has been learnt by means of a demonstration that it cannot possibly be ascribed to God. To someone else who falls short in his knowledge of speculation, this demonstration will not be clear; and he will consider it doubtful whether or not this notion exists with reference to God. Again another one belonging to those who are struck with intellectual blindness ascribes to Him that notion which has been demonstrated should rather be negated with reference to Him. For instance, I shall demonstrate that He is not a body, whereas another man will doubt and not know whether or not He is a body, and a third one will categorically decide that He is a body and will seek to approach God by means of this belief. How great is the difference between the three individuals! The first is undoubtedly nearer to God, while the second is far away from Him, and the third still farther away. Similarly if we may suppose a fourth one to whom the impossibility of affections in Him, may He be exalted, has become clear by demonstration—whereas this was not the case with regard to the first one who denied His corporeality—this fourth individual would undoubtedly be nearer to God than the first. And so on always; so that if an individual exists to whom it has been made clear by demonstration that many things, whose existence with reference to Him or whose proceeding from Him we hold possible, are, on the contrary, impossible with reference to Him, may He be exalted—and this applies of course all the more if we believe that these things are necessarily attached to Him—that individual will undoubtedly be more perfect than we.

It has accordingly become manifest to you that in every case in which the demonstration that a certain thing should be negated with reference to Him becomes clear to you, you become more perfect, and that in every case in which you affirm of Him an additional thing, you become one who likens Him to other things and you get further away from the knowledge of His true reality. It is from this point of view that one ought to come nearer to an apprehension of Him by means of investigation and research: namely, in order that one should know the impossibility of everything that is impossible with reference to Him—not in order that one should make an affirmation ascribing to Him a thing as being a notion superadded to His essence or because the notion in question is held to be a perfection with reference to Him, since one finds it a perfection with reference to us. For all perfections are habitus, and not every habitus can exist in every being possessing habitus. Know that when you make an affirmation ascribing another thing to Him, you become more remote from Him in two respects: one of them is that everything you affirm is a perfection only with reference to us, and the other is that He does not possess a thing other than His essence, which, as we have made clear, is identical with His perfections.

As everyone is aware that it is not possible, except through negation, to achieve an apprehension of that which is in our power to apprehend and that, on the other hand, negation does not give knowledge in any respect of the true reality of the thing with regard to which the particular matter in question has been negated —all men, those of the past and those of the future, affirm clearly that God, may He be exalted, cannot be apprehended by the intellects, and that none but He Himself can apprehend what He is, and that apprehension of Him consists in the inability to attain the ultimate term in apprehending Him. Thus all the philosophers say: We are dazzled by His beauty, and He is hidden from us because of the intensity with which He becomes manifest, just as the sun is hidden to eyes that are too weak to apprehend it. This has been expatiated upon in words that it would serve no useful purpose to repeat here. The most apt phrase concerning this subject is the dictum occurring in the *Psalms* (65:2), *Silence is praise to Thee*, which interpreted signifies: silence with regard to You is praise. This is a most perfectly put phrase regarding this matter. For of whatever we say intending to magnify and exalt, on the one hand we find that it can have some application to Him, may He be exalted, and on the other we perceive in it some deficiency. Accordingly, silence and limiting oneself to the apprehensions of the intellects are more appropriate—just as the perfect ones have enjoined when they said (Ps. 4:5): *Commune with your own heart upon your bed, and be still. Selah.*

You also know their famous dictum—would that all dicta were like it. I shall quote it to you textually, even though it is well remembered, so as to draw your attention to the various significations it expresses. They have said (B.T., Berakhot, 33b): *Someone who came into the presence of Rabbi Ḥaninah said [in prayer]: God the Great, the Valiant, the Terrible, the Mighty, the Strong, the Tremendous, the Powerful. Thereupon [Rabbi Ḥaninah] said to him: Have you finished all the praises of your Master? Even as regards the first three epithets [used by you] we could not have uttered them if Moses our Master had not pronounced them in the Law and if the men of the Great Synagogue had not [subsequently] come and established [their use] in prayer. And you come and say all this. What does this resemble? It is as if a mortal king who had millions of gold pieces were praised for possessing silver. Would this not be an offense to him?* Here ends the dictum of this perfect one. Consider in the first place his reluctance and unwillingness to multiply the affirmative attributes. Consider also that he has stated clearly that if we were left only to our intellects we should never have mentioned these attributes or stated a thing appertaining to them. Yet the necessity to address men in such terms as would make them achieve some representation—in accordance with the dictum of the Sages: *The Torah speaks in the language of the sons of man*—obliged resort to predicating of God their own perfections when speaking to them. It must then be our purpose to draw a line at using these expressions and not to apply them to Him except only in reading the *Torah.* However, as the *men of the Great Synagogue,* who were prophets, appeared in their turn and inserted the mention of these attributes in the prayer, it is our purpose to pronounce only these attributes when saying our prayers. According to the spirit, this dictum makes its clear that, as it happened, two necessary obligations determined our naming these attributes in our prayers: one of them is that they occur in the *Torah,* and the other is that the prophets in question used them in the prayer they composed. Accordingly, we should not have mentioned these attributes at all but for the first necessary obligation; and but for the second necessity, we should not have taken them out of their context and should not have had recourse to them in our prayers. As you continue to consider the attributes, it will become clear to you from this statement that we are not permitted in our prayers to use and to cite all the attributes ascribed to God in the books of the prophets. For [Rabbi Ḥaninah] not only says: *If Moses our Master had not pronounced them, we could not have uttered them,* but poses a second condition: *And if the men of the Great Synagogue had not [subsequently] come and established [their use] in prayer*—whereupon we are permitted to use them in our prayers.

Thus what we do is not like what is done by the truly ignorant who spoke at great length and spent great efforts on prayers that they composed and on sermons that they compiled and through which they, in their opinion, came nearer to God. In these prayers and sermons they predicate of God qualificative attributions that, if predicated of a human individual, would designate a deficiency in him. For they do not understand those sublime notions that are too strange for the intellects of the vulgar and accordingly took God, may He be magnified and glorified, for an object of study for their tongues; they predicated attributes of Him and addressed Him in all the terms that they thought permitted and expatiated at such length in this way that in their thoughts they made Him move on account of an affection. They did this especially when they found the text of a prophet's speech regarding these terms. Thereupon they had full license to bring forward texts that ought to be interpreted in every respect, and to take them according to their external meaning, to derive from them inferences and secondary conclusions, and to found upon them various kinds of discourses. This kind of license is frequently taken by poets and preachers or such as think that what they speak is poetry, so that the utterances of some of them constitute an absolute denial of faith, while other utterances contain such rubbish and such perverse imaginings as to make men laugh when they hear them, on account of the nature of these utterances, and to make them weep when they consider that these utterances are applied to God, may He be magnified and glorified. If I were not unwilling to set out the deficiencies of those who make these utterances, I should have quoted to you something of the latter in order that you should give heed to the points in which they may be impugned. However, the deficiencies in these utterances are most manifest to him who understands. It also behooves you to consider and say that in view of the fact that *speaking ill* and *defamation* are acts of great disobedience, how much all the more so is the loosening of the tongue with regard to God, may He be exalted, and the predicating of Him qualificative attributions above which He is exalted. But I shall not say that this is an act of disobedience, but rather that it constitutes *unintended obloquy and vituperation* on the part of the multitude who listen to these utterances and on the part of the ignoramus who pronounces them. As for him who apprehends the deficiency of those speeches and yet uses those speeches, he belongs in my opinion to the category of people of whom it is said (II Kings 17:9), *And the children of Israel did impute things that were not right unto the Lord their God,* and is said elsewhere, (Isa. 32:6), *And to utter error against the Lord.* Accordingly if you are one *who has regard for the honor of his Creator,* you ought not to listen in any way to these utterances, let alone give expression to them and still less make up others like them. For you know the extent of the sin of him who *makes vituperative utterances against what is above.* You accordingly ought not to set forth in any respect the attributes of God in an affirmative way—with a view, as you think, to magnifying Him—and ought not to go beyond that which has been inserted in the prayers and *benedictions* by the *men of the Great Synagogue.* For this is sufficient from the point of view of necessity; in fact, as *Rabbi Ḥaninah* said, it is amply sufficient. But regarding the other attributes that occur in the books of the prophets and are recited during the perusal of these books, it is believed, as we have made clear, that they are attributes of action or that they indicate the negation of their nonexistence in God. This notion concerning them also should not be divulged to the vulgar. For this kind of speculation is more suitable for the elite who consider that the magnification of God does not consist in their saying improper things but in their understanding properly.

Hereupon I shall return to completing the indications concerning the dictum of *Rabbi Ḥaninah* and to giving it correct interpretation. He does not say, for example: *What does this resemble? It is as if a mortal king who had millions of gold pieces were praised for possessing one hundred pieces.* For this example would have indicated that the perfections of Him, may He be exalted, while more perfect than the perfections that are ascribed to Him, still belong to the same species as the latter. As we have demonstrated, this is not so. But the wisdom manifest in this parable lies in his saying: *gold pieces and were praised for possessing silver.* He says this in order to indicate that in God, may He be exalted, there is nothing belonging to the same species as the attributes that are regarded by us as perfections, but that all these attributes are deficiencies with regard to God, just as he made clear in this parable when he said: *Would this not be an offense to Him?* I have then already made it known to you that everything in these attributes that you regard as a perfection is a deficiency with regard to Him, may He be exalted, as it belongs to a species to which the things that are with us belong. *Solomon,* peace be on him, has rightly directed us with regard to this subject, in words that should be sufficient for us, when he said (Eccles. 5:1): *For God is in heaven and thou upon the earth; therefore let thy words be few.*

CHAPTER 60

I wish to tell you in this chapter parables by means of which you will be able to add to your representation of the necessity to multiply His attributes by means of negations and also to add to your shrinking from the belief in positive attributes regarding Him, may He be exalted.

Assume that a man has acquired true knowledge regarding the existence of a ship, but does not know to what it is that this term is applied: namely, whether it is applied to a substance or to an accident. Then it became clear to some other individual that a ship is not an accident; afterwards it became clear to yet another individual that it is not a mineral; then it became clear to someone else that it is not a living being; then it became clear to someone else that it is not a plant forming a continuum with the earth; then it became clear to someone else that it is not one body naturally forming a continuum; then it became clear to someone else that it does not possess a simple shape as do tables and doors; then it became clear to someone else that it is not a sphere, and to another individual that it is not conical, and to yet another individual that it is not spherical and not possessed of equal sides, and to someone else again that it is not solid all through. Now it is clear that the last individual has nearly achieved, by means of these negative attributes, the representation of the ship as it is. He has, as it were, attained equality with one who has represented the ship as being a body consisting of timber, a body that is hollow, oblong, and composed of a number of pieces of timber; that is, he has attained equality with one who has represented the ship by means of affirmative attributes. As for those whom we have cited in the parable as being prior to him, every one of them is more remote from representing the ship to himself than the one who comes after him; thus the first one figuring in our parable knows nothing but the bare term alone. Accordingly the negative attributes make you come nearer in a similar way to the cognition and apprehension of God, may He be exalted. Desire then wholeheartedly that you should know by demonstration some additional thing to be negated, but do not desire to negate merely in words. For on every occasion on which it becomes clear to you by means of a demonstration that a thing whose existence is thought to pertain to Him, may He be exalted, should rather be negated with reference to Him, you undoubtedly come nearer to Him by one degree. In this respect there are people who are very near to Him, whereas others are extremely far away from Him— not that there is in this matter a local nearness so that one may come nearer or get farther away from Him, as is thought by those whose mental eyes are blind. Understand this well and know it and rejoice therein. For the way has become clear to you by walking in which you may come near to Him, may He be exalted. Walk accordingly therein if you so wish.

On the other hand, the predication of affirmative attributes of Him, may He be exalted, is very dangerous. For it has been already demonstrated that anything that we think of as a perfection—even if it existed as pertaining to Him—in accordance with the opinion of those who believe in the attributes, nevertheless would not belong to the species of perfection that we think of, save only by equivocation, just as we have made clear. Accordingly you must of necessity go over to the notion of negation. For if you say that, with one knowledge and with this changeless knowledge that has no multiplictiy in it, He knows the multiple and changeable things that are constantly being renewed without any renewal of knowledge in Him, and that His knowledge of a thing before it has come into being and after it has acquired reality as existent and after it has ceased to exist is one and the same knowledge in which there is no change, you have clearly stated that He knows with a knowledge that is not like our knowledge. Similarly it follows necessarily that He exists, but not according to the notion of that existence which is in us. Consequently you resort to negations. Accordingly you have not arrived at a knowledge of the true reality of an essential attribute, but you have arrived at multiplicity. For you believe that He is a certain essence possessing unknown attributes. Now with regard to the attributes that, as you deem, should be affirmed with reference to Him, if you deny that they have a likeness to the attributes known to us, it follows that they do not belong to the same species as the latter. Accordingly the matter of affirmation of attributes has, as it were, withdrawn from you; for if you say God, may He be exalted, is a certain substratum bearing certain things as adjuncts and that this substratum is not like these adjuncts, the utmost of our apprehension would be, on the basis of this belief, polytheism and nothing else. For every substratum bearing things is undoubtedly, according to its definition, a duality, even if it be one in its existence. For the notion of the substratum is different from that of the adjunct borne by it. Now the demonstration of the impossibility of composition in Him, may He be exalted, and, to go even further, the demonstration of His absolute simplicity, which is extreme and ultimate, will be made clear to you in certain chapters of this Treatise.

I shall not say that he who affirms that God, may He be exalted, has positive attributes either falls short of apprehending Him or is an associator or has an apprehension of Him that is different from what He really is, but I shall say that he has abolished his belief in the existence of the deity without being aware of it. To make this clear: he who falls short of the apprehension of the true reality of some matter is one who apprehends part of it and is ignorant of another part—for instance, someone who apprehends in the notion of man the necessary concomitants of animality and does not apprehend in it the necessary concomitants of rationality. Now there is no multiplicity in the true reality of the existence of God, may He be exalted, so that one thing pertaining to Him might be understood while another remains unknown. In a similar way an associator with reference to a certain thing is one who represents to himself the true reality of a certain essence as this essence veritably is and affirms of another essence that its true reality is like that of the first essence. Now in the opinion of those who think that the attributes in question exist, these attributes are not the essence of the deity, but rather notions superadded to the essence. Furthermore, one who has an apprehension of a thing that is different from what that thing really is, must yet necessarily apprehend something of it as it really is. However, I shall not say of him who represents to himself that taste is a quantity, that his representation of the thing is different from what the latter really is; rather I shall say that he is ignorant of the being of taste and does not know to what the term applies. This is a very subtle speculation; understand it.

In accordance with this elucidation you shall know that he is incapable of apprehending the deity and is far removed from knowledge of Him who has no clear understanding of the necessity of negating with respect to God a notion negated by someone else on the basis of a demonstration. And, as we have made clear in the beginning of this chapter, the fewer negations there are on his part, the more his apprehension falls short.

As for one who affirms an attribute of Him without knowing a thing about it except the mere term, it may be considered that the object to which he imagines the term applies is a nonexistent notion—an invention that is false; for he has, as it were, applied this term to a notion lacking existence, as nothing in existence is like that notion. An example is that of a man who has heard the term elephant and knows that it is an animal and demands to know its shape and true reality. Thereupon one who is himself mistaken or who misleads others tells him that it is animal possessing one leg and three wings, inhabiting the depths of the sea, having a transparent body and a broad face like that of man in its form and shape, talking like a man, and sometimes flying in the air, while at other times swimming like a fish. I will not say that this representation of the elephant differs from what the latter really is, nor that the man in question falls short in his apprehension of the elephant. But I shall say that the thing that he has imagined as having these attributes is merely an invention and is false and that there is nothing in existence like that, but that it is a thing lacking existence to which a term signifying an existent thing has been applied—a thing like "anqā mughrib" [a fabulous bird] or a centaur and other imaginary forms of this kind to which a term simple or compound, signifying some existent thing, has been applied. In the present case the matter is similar and of the same kind. For God, may His praise be magnified, is an existent whose existence has been demonstrated to be necessary. And, as I shall demonstrate, from His being the necessarily existent there necessarily follows His absolute simplicity.

As for thinking that this simple essence—whose existence, as has been said, is necessary—is endowed with attributes and with other notions accompanying it: the thing thus imagined cannot, as has been demonstrated, be existent in any respect. Accordingly, if we say that this essence, which for the sake of example shall be called deity, is an essence in which subsist many notions that are predicated of it, we apply this term to absolute nonexistence. Consider accordingly how great is the danger in affirming with reference to Him [positive] attributes. Accordingly it behooves us to believe with regard to the attributes figuring in the revealed books or the books of the prophets that all of them are mentioned only to direct the mind toward nothing but His perfection, may He be exalted, or that they are attributes referring to actions proceeding from Him, as we have made clear.

BOOK II

CHAPTER 13

There are three opinions of human beings, namely, of all those who believe that there is an existent deity, with regard to the eternity of the world or its production in time.

The first opinion, which is the opinion of all who believe in the Law of *Moses our Master, peace be on him,* is that the world as a whole—I mean to say, every existent other than God, may He be exalted—was brought into existence by God after having been purely and absolutely nonexistent, and that God, may He be exalted, had existed alone, and nothing else—neither an angel nor a sphere nor what subsists within the sphere. Afterwards, through His will and His volition, He brought into existence out of nothing all the beings as they are, time itself being one of the created things. For time is consequent upon motion, and motion is an accident in what is moved. Furthermore, what is moved—that is, that upon the motion of which time is consequent—is itself created in time and came to be after not having been. Accordingly one's saying: God "was" before He created the world—where the word "was" is indicative of time—and similarly all the thoughts that are carried along in the mind regarding the infinite duration of His existence before the creation of the world, are all of them due to a supposition regarding time or to an imagining of time and not due to the true reality of time. For time is indubitably an accident. According to us it is one of the created accidents, as are blackness and whiteness. And though it does not belong to the species of quality, it is nevertheless, generally stated, an accident necessarily following upon motion, as is made clear to whoever has understood the discourse of Aristotle on the elucidation of time and on the true reality of its existence.

We shall expound here a notion that, though it does not belong to the purpose that we pursue, is useful with regard to it. This notion is as follows. What caused the nature of time to be hidden from the majority of the men of knowledge so that that notion perplexed them—like Galen and others—and made them wonder whether or not time had a true reality in that which exists, is the fact that time is an accident subsisting in an accident. For the accidents that have a primary existence in bodies, as for instance colors and tastes, can be understood at the outset and a mental representation can be had of their notions. But the nature of the accidents whose substrata are other accidents, as for instance the glint of a color and the curve and circularity of a line, is most hidden—more particularly if, in addition, the accident that serves as a substratum has no permanent state, but passes from one state to another. For in consequence the matter becomes even more hidden. In time both characteristics are conjoined. For it is an accident concomitant with motion, the latter being an accident in that which is moved. Moreover, motion has not the status of blackness and whiteness, which constitute a permanent state. For the true reality and substance of motion consist in its not remaining in the same state even for the duration of the twinkling of an eye. This accordingly is what has rendered it necessary for the nature of time to be hidden. The purpose however is that, according to us, time is a created and generated thing as are the other accidents and the substances serving as substrata to these accidents. Hence God's bringing the world into existence does not have a temporal beginning, for time is one of the created things. Consider this matter thoroughly. For thus you will not be necessarily attached to objections from which there is no escape for him who does not know it. For if you affirm as true the existence of time prior to the world, you are necessarily bound to believe in the eternity [of the world]. For time is an accident which necessarily must have a substratum. Accordingly it follows necessarily that there existed some thing prior to the existence of this world existing now. But this notion must be avoided.

This is one of the opinions. And it is undoubtedly a basis of the Law of *Moses our Master*, peace be on him. And it is second to the basis that is the belief in the unity [of God]. Nothing other than this should come to your mind. It was *Abraham our Father, peace be on him*, who began to proclaim in public this opinion to which speculation had led him. For this reason, he made his proclamation (Gen. 21:33) *in the Name of the Lord, God of the world;* he had also explicity stated this opinion in saying (Gen. 14:22): *Maker of heaven and earth.*

The second opinion is that of all the philosophers of whom we have heard reports and whose discourses we have seen. They say that it is absurd that God would bring a thing into existence out of nothing. Furthermore, according to them, it is likewise not possible that a thing should pass away into nothing; I mean to say that it is not possible that a certain being, endowed with matter and form, should be generated out of the absolute nonexistence of that matter, that it should pass away into the absolute nonexistence of that matter. To predicate of God that He is able to do this is, according to them, like predicating of Him that He is able to bring together two contraries in one instant of time, or that He is able to create something that is like Himself, may He be exalted, or to make Himself corporeal, or to create a square whose diagonal is equal to its side, and similar impossibilities. What may be understood from their discourse is that they say that just as His not bringing impossible things into existence does not argue a lack of power on His part—since what is impossible has a firmly established nature that is not produced by an agent and that consequently cannot be changed —it likewise is not due to lack of power on His part that He is not able to bring into existence a thing out of nothing, for this belongs to the class of all the impossible things. Hence they believe that there exists a certain matter that is eternal as the deity is eternal; and that He does not exist without it, nor does it exist without Him. They do not believe that it has the same rank in what exists as He, may He be exalted, but that He is the cause of its existence; and that it has the same relation toward Him as, for instance, clay has toward a potter or iron toward a smith; and that He creates in it whatever He wishes. Thus He sometimes forms out of it a heaven and an earth, and sometimes He forms out of it something else. The people holding this opinion believe that the heaven too is subject to generation and passing-away, but that it is not generated out of nothing and does not pass away into nothing. For it is generated and passes away just as the individuals that are animals are generated from existent matter and pass away into existent matter. The generation and passing-away of the heaven is thus similar to that of all the other existents that are below it.

The people belonging to this sect are in their turn divided into several sects. But it is useless to mention their various sects and opinions in this Treatise. However, the universal principle held by this sect is identical with what I have told you. This is also the belief of Plato. For you will find that Aristotle in the "Physics" (VIII, 1) relates of him that he, I mean Plato, believed that the heaven is subject to generation and passing-away. And you likewise will find his doctrine plainly set forth in his book to Timaeus. But he does not believe what we believe, as is thought by him who does not examine opinions and is not precise in speculation; he [the interpreter] imagines that our opinion and his [Plato's] opinion are identical. But this is not so. For as for us, we believe that the heaven was generated out of nothing after a state of absolute nonexistence, whereas he believes that it has come into existence and has been generated from some other thing. This then is the second opinion.

The third opinion is that of Aristotle, his followers, and the commentators of his books. He asserts what also is asserted by the people belonging to the sect that has just been mentioned, namely, that something endowed with matter can by no means be brought into existence out of that which has no matter. He goes beyond this by saying that the heaven is in no way subject to generation and passing-away. His opinion on this point may be summed up as follows. He thinks that this being as a whole, such as it is, has never ceased to be and will never do so; that the permanent thing not subject to generation and passing-away, namely, the heaven, likewise does not cease to be; that time and motion are perpetual and everlasting and not subject to generation and passing-away; and also that the thing subject to generation and passing-away, namely, that which is beneath the sphere of the moon, does not cease to be. I mean to say that its first matter is not subject in its essence to generation and passing-away, but that various forms succeed each other in it in such a way that it divests itself of one form and assumes another. He thinks furthermore that this whole higher and lower order cannot be corrupted and abolished, that no innovation can take place in it that is not according to its nature, and that no occurrence that deviates from what is analogous to it can happen in it in any way. He asserts—though he does not do so textually, but this is what his opinion comes to—that in his opinion it would be an impossibility that will should change in God or a new volition arise in Him; and that all that exists has been brought into existence, in the state in which it is at present, by God through His volition; but that it was not produced after having been in a state of nonexistence. He thinks that just as it is impossible that the deity should become nonexistent or that His essence should undergo a change, it is impossible that a volition should undergo a change in Him or a new will arise in Him. Accordingly it follows necessarily that this being as a whole has never ceased to be as it is at present and will be as it is in the future eternity.

This is a summary and the truth of these opinions. They are the opinions of those according to whom the existence of the deity for this world has been demonstrated. Those who have no knowledge of the existence of the deity, may He be held sublime and honored, but think that things are subject to generation and passing-away through conjunction and separation due to chance and that there is no one who governs and orders being, are Epicurus, his following, and those like him, as is related by Alexander [of Aphrodisias]. It is useless for us to mention these sects. For the existence of the deity has already been demonstrated, and there can be no utility in our mentioning the opinions of groups of people who built their doctrine upon a foundation the reverse of which has been demonstrated as true. Similarly it is useless for us to wish to prove as true the assertion of the people holding the second opinion, I mean that according to which the heaven is subject to generation and passing-away. For they believe in eternity; and there is, in our opinion, no difference between those who believe that heaven must of necessity be generated from a thing and pass away into a thing or the belief of Aristotle who believed that it is not subject to generation and corruption. For the purpose of every follower of the Law of *Moses and Abraham our Father* or of those who go the way of these two is to believe that there is nothing eternal in any way at all existing simultaneously with God; to believe also that the bringing into existence of a being out of nonexistence is for the deity not an impossibility, but rather an obligation, as is deemed likewise by some of the men of speculation.

After we have expounded those opinions, I shall begin to explain and summarize the proofs of Aristotle in favor of his opinion and the motive that incited him to adopt it.

CHAPTER 16

This is a chapter in which I shall explain to you what I believe with regard to this question. After that I shall give proofs for what we desire to maintain. I say then with regard to all that is affirmed by those Mutakallimūn who think that they have demonstrated the newness of the world, that I approve of nothing in those proofs and that I do not deceive myself by designating methods productive of errors as demonstrations. If a man claims that he sets out to demonstrate a certain point by means of sophistical arguments, he does not, in my opinion, strengthen assent to the point he intends to prove, but rather weakens it and opens the way for attacks against it. For when it becomes clear that those proofs are not valid, the soul weakens in its assent to what is being proved. It is preferable that a point for which there is no demonstration remain a problem or that one of the two contradictory propositions simply be accepted. I have already set forth for your benefit the methods of the Mutakallimūn in establishing the newness of the world, and I have drawn your attention to the points with regard to which they may be attacked. Similarly all that Aristotle and his followers have set forth in the way of proof of the eternity of the world does not constitute in my opinion a cogent demonstration, but rather arguments subject to grave doubts, as you shall hear. What I myself desire to make clear is that the world's being created in time, according to the opinion of our Law—an opinion that I have already explained—is not impossible and that all those philosophic proofs from which it seems that the matter is different from what we have stated, all those arguments have a certain point through which they may be invalidated and the inference drawn from them against us shown to be incorrect. Now inasmuch as this is true in my opinion and inasmuch as this question—I mean to say that of the eternity of the world or its creation in time—becomes an open question, it should in my opinion be accepted without proof because of prophecy, which explains things to which it is not in the power of speculation to accede. For as we shall make clear, prophecy is not set at nought even in the opinion of those who believe in the eternity of the world.

After I have made it clear that what we maintain is possible, I shall begin to make it prevail likewise, by means of speculative proof, over any other affirmations; I refer to my making prevail the assertion of creation in time over the assertion of eternity. I shall make it clear that just as a certain disgrace attaches to us because of the belief in the creation in time, an even greater disgrace attaches to the belief in eternity. I shall now start to bring into being a method that shall render void the proofs of all those who prove by inference the eternity of the world.

CHAPTER 23

Know that when one compares the doubts attaching to a certain opinion with those attaching to the contrary opinion and has to decide which of them arouses fewer doubts, one should not take into account the number of the doubts but rather consider how great is their incongruity and what is their disagreement with what exists. Sometimes a single doubt is more powerful than a thousand other doubts. Furthermore this comparison can be correctly made only by someone for whom the two contraries are equal. But whoever prefers one of the two opinions because of his upbringing or for some advantage, is blind to the truth. While one who entertains an unfounded predilection cannot make himself oppose a matter susceptible of demonstration, in matters like those under discussion such an opposition is often possible. Sometimes, if you wish it, you can rid yourself of an unfounded predilection, free yourself of what is habitual, rely solely on speculation, and prefer the opinion that you ought to prefer. However, to do this you must fulfill several conditions. The first of them is that you should know how good your mind is and that your inborn disposition is sound. This becomes clear to you through training in all the mathematical sciences and through grasp of the rules of logic. The second condition is to have knowledge of the natural sciences and to apprehend their truth so that you should know your doubts in their true reality. The third condition concerns your morals. For whenever a man finds himself inclining—and to our mind it makes no difference if this happens because of his natural disposition or because of an acquired characteristic—toward lusts and pleasures or preferring anger and fury, giving the upper hand to his irascible faculty and letting go its reins, he shall be at fault and stumble wherever he goes. For he shall seek opinions that will help him in that toward which his nature inclines. I have drawn your attention to this in order that you should not be deceived. For someone may some day lead you into vain imaginings through setting forth a doubt concerning the creation of the world in time, and you may be very quick to let yourself be deceived. For in this opinion is contained the destruction of the foundation of the Law and a presumptuous assertion with regard to the deity. Be therefore always suspicious in your mind as to this point and accept the authority of the two prophets [i.e., Abraham and Moses] who are the pillars of the well-being of the human species with regard to its beliefs and its associations. Do not turn away from the opinion according to which the world is new, except because of a demonstration. Now such a demonstration does not exist in nature.

Furthermore, the student of this Treatise should not engage in criticism because of my using this rhetorical mode of speech in order to support the affirmation of the newness of the world. For Aristotle, the prince of the philosophers, in his main writings has likewise used rhetorical speeches in support of his opinion that the world is eternal. In such cases it may truly be said (B.T., Baba Bathra, 116a): *Shall not our perfect Torah be [worth as much] as their frivolous talk?* If he refers in support of his opinion to the ravings of the Sabians, how can we but refer in support of our opinion to the words of *Moses* and *Abraham* and to everything that follows therefrom?

I have promised you a chapter in which I shall expound to you the grave doubts that would affect whoever thinks that man has acquired knowledge as to the arrangement of the motions of the sphere and as to their being natural things going on according to the law of necessity, things whose order and arrangement are clear. I shall now explain this to you.

CHAPTER 24

You know of astronomical matters what you have read under my guidance and understood from the contents of the "Almagest." But there was not enough time to begin another speculative study with you. What you know already is that as far as the action of ordering the motions and making the course of the stars conform to what is seen is concerned, everything depends on two principles: either that of the epicycles or that of the eccentric spheres or on both of them. Now I shall draw your attention to the fact that both those principles are entirely outside the bounds of reasoning and opposed to all that has been made clear in natural science. In the first place, if one affirms as true the existence of an epicycle revolving round a certain sphere, positing at the same time that that revolution is not around the center of the sphere carrying the epicycles—and this has been supposed with regard to the moon and to the five planets—it follows necessarily that there is rolling, that is, that the epicycle rolls and changes its place completely. Now this is the impossibility that was to to be avoided, namely, the assumption that there should be something in the heavens that changes its place. For this reason Abū Bakr Ibn al-Sā'igh [i.e., Ibn Bājja] states in his extant discourse on astronomy that the existence of epicycles is impossible. He points out the necessary inference already mentioned. In addition to this impossibility necessarily following from the assumption of the existence of epicycles, he sets forth there other impossibilities that also follow from that assumption. I shall explain them to you now.

The revolution of the epicycles is not around the center of the world. Now it is a fundamental principle of this world that there are three motions: a motion from the midmost point of the world, a motion toward that point, and a motion around that point. But if an epicycle existed, its motion would be neither from that point nor toward it nor around it.

Furthermore, it is one of the preliminary assumptions of Aristotle in natural science that there must necessarily be some immobile thing around which circular motion takes place. Hence it is necessary that the earth should be immobile. Now if epicycles exist, theirs would be a circular motion that would not revolve round an immobile thing. I have heard that Abū Bakr has stated that he had invented an astronomical system in which no epicycles figured, but only eccentric circles. However, I have not heard this from his pupils. And even if this were truly accomplished by him, he would not gain much thereby. For eccentricity also necessitates going outside the limits posed by the principles established by Aristotle, those principles to which nothing can be added. It was by me that attention was drawn to this point. In the case of eccentricity, we likewise find that the circular motion of the spheres does not take place around the midmost point of the world, but around an imaginary point that is other than the center of the world. Accordingly, that motion is likewise not a motion taking place around an immobile thing. If, however, someone having no knowledge of astronomy thinks that eccentricity with respect to these imaginary points may be considered—when these points are situated inside the sphere of the moon, as they appear to be at the outset—as equivalent to motion round the midmost point of the world, we would agree to concede this to him if that motion took place round a point in the zone of fire or of air, though in that case that motion would not be around an immobile thing. We will, however, make it clear to him that the measures of eccentricity have been demonstrated in the "Almagest" according to what is assumed there. And the latter-day scientists have given a correct demonstration, regarding which there is no doubt, of how great the measure of these eccentricities is compared with half the diameter of the earth, just as they have set forth all the other distances and dimensions. It has consequently become clear that the eccentric point around which the sun revolves must of necessity be outside the concavity of the sphere of the moon and beneath the convexity of the sphere of Mercury. Similarly the point around which Mars revolves, I mean to say the center of its eccentric sphere, is outside the concavity of the sphere of Mercury and beneath the convexity of the sphere of Venus. Again the center of the eccentric sphere of Jupiter is at the same distance —I mean between the sphere of Mercury and Venus. As for Saturn, the center of its eccentric sphere is between the spheres of Mars and Jupiter. See now how all these things are remote from natural speculation! All this will become clear to you if you consider the distances and dimensions, known to you, of every sphere and star, as well as the evaluation of all of them by means of half the diameter of the earth so that everything is calculated according to one and the same proportion and the eccentricity of every sphere is not evaluated in relation to the sphere itself.

Even more incongruous and dubious is the fact that in all cases in which one of two spheres is inside the other and adheres to it on every side, while the centers of the two are different, the smaller sphere can move inside the bigger one without the latter being in motion, whereas the bigger sphere cannot move upon any axis whatever without the smaller one being in motion. For whenever the bigger sphere moves, it necessarily, by means of its movement, sets the smaller one in motion, except in the case in which its motion is on axis passing through the two centers. From this demonstrative premise and from the demonstrated fact that vacuum does not exist and from the assumptions regarding eccentricity, it follows necessarily that when the higher sphere is in motion it must move the sphere beneath it with the same motion and around its own center. Now we do not find that this is so. We find rather that neither of the two spheres, the containing and the contained, is set in motion by the movement of the other nor does it move around the other's center or poles, but that each of them has its own particular motion. Hence necessity obliges the belief that between every two spheres there are bodies other than those of the spheres. Now if this be so, how many obscure points remain? Where will you suppose the centers of those bodies existing between every two spheres to be? And those bodies should likewise have their own particular motion. Thābit has explained this in a treatise of his and has demonstrated what we have said, namely, that there must be the body of a sphere between every two spheres. All this I did not explain to you when you read under my guidance, for fear of confusing you with regard to that which it was my purpose to make you understand.

As for the inclination and deviation that are spoken of regarding the latitude of Venus and Mercury, I have explained to you by word of mouth and I have shown you that it is impossible to conceive their existence in those bodies. For the rest Ptolemy has said explicitly, as you have seen, that one was unable to do this, stating literally: No one should think that these principles and those similar to them may only be put into effect with difficulty, if his reason for doing this be that he regards that which we have set forth as he would regard things obtained by artifice and the subtlety of art and which may only be realized with difficulty. For human matters should not be compared to those that are divine. This is, as you know, the text of his statement. I have indicated to you the passages from which the true reality of everything I have mentioned to you becomes manifest, except for what I have told you regarding the examination of where the points lie that are the centers of the eccentric circles. For I have never come across anybody who has paid attention to this. However this shall become clear to you through the knowledge of the measure of the diameter of every sphere and what the distance is between the two centers as compared with half the diameter of the earth, according to what has been demonstrated by al-Qabīsī in the "Epistle Concerning the Distances." If you examine those distances, the truth of the point to which I have drawn your attention will become clear to you.

Consider now how great these difficulties are. If what Aristotle has stated with regard to natural science is true, there are no epicycles or eccentric circles and everything revolves round the center of the earth. But in that case how can the various motions of the stars come about? Is it in any way possible that motion should be on the one hand circular, uniform, and perfect, and that on the other hand the things that are observable should be observed in consequence of it, unless this be accounted for by making use of one of the two principles or of both of them? This consideration is all the stronger because of the fact that if one accepts everything stated by Ptolemy concerning the epicycle of the moon and its deviation toward a point outside the center of the world and also outside the center of the eccentric circle, it will be found that what is calculated on the hypothesis of the two principles is not at fault by even a minute. The truth of this is attested by the correctness of the calculations—always made on the basis of these principles—concerning the eclipses and the exact determination of their times as well as of the moment when it begins to be dark and of the length of time of the darkness. Furthermore, how can one conceive the retrogradation of a star, together with its other motions, without assuming the existence of an epicycle? On the other hand, how can one imagine a rolling motion in the heavens or a motion around a center that is not immobile? This is the true perplexity.

However, I have already explained to you by word of mouth that all this does not affect the astronomer. For his purpose is not to tell us in which way the spheres truly are, but to posit an astronomical system in which it would be possible for the motions to be circular and uniform and to correspond to what is apprehended through sight, regardless of whether or not things are thus in fact. You know already that in speaking of natural science, Abū Bakr Ibn al-Ṣā'igh [i.e., Ibn Bājja] expresses a doubt whether Aristotle knew about the eccentricity of the sun and passed over it in silence—treating of what necessarily follows from the sun's inclination, inasmuch as the effect of eccentricity is not distinguishable from that of inclination—or whether he was not aware of eccentricity. Now the truth is that he was not aware of it and had never heard about it, for in his time mathematics had not been brought to perfection. If, however, he had heard about it, he would have violently rejected it; and if it were to his mind established as true, he would have become most perplexed about all his assumptions on the subject. I shall repeat here what I have said before. All that Aristotle states about that which is beneath the sphere of the moon is in accordance with reasoning; these are things that have a known cause, that follow one upon the other, and concerning which it is clear and manifest at what points wisdom and natural providence are effective. However, regarding all that is in the heavens, man grasps nothing but a small measure of what is mathematical; and you know what is in it. I shall accordingly say in the manner of poetical preciousness (Ps. 115:16): *The heavens are the heavens of the Lord, but the earth hath He given to the sons of man.* I mean thereby that the deity alone fully knows the true reality, the nature, the substance, the form, the motions, and the causes of the heavens. But He has enabled man to have knowledge of what is beneath the heavens, for that is his world and his dwelling-place in which he has been placed and of which he himself is a part. This is the truth. For it is impossible for us to accede to the points starting from which conclusions may be drawn about the heavens; for the latter are too far away from us and too high in place and in rank. And even the general conclusion that may be drawn from them, namely, that they prove the existence of their Mover, is a matter the knowledge of which cannot be reached by human intellects. And to fatigue the minds with notions that cannot be grasped by them and for the grasp of which they have no instrument, is a defect in one's inborn disposition or some sort of temptation. Let us then stop at a point that is within our capacity, and let us give over the things that cannot be grasped by reasoning to him who was reached by the mighty divine overflow so that it could be fittingly said of him (Num. 12:8): *With him do I speak mouth to mouth.* That is the end of what I have to say about this question. It is possible that someone else may find a demonstration by means of which the true reality of what is obscure for me will become clear to him. The extreme predilection that I have for investigating the truth is evidenced by the fact that I have explicitly stated and reported my perplexity regarding these matters as well as by the fact that I have not heard nor do I know a demonstration as to anything concerning them.

CHAPTER 25

Know that our shunning the affirmation of the eternity of the world is not due to a text figuring in the *Torah* according to which the world has been produced in time. For the texts indicating that the world has been produced in time are not more numerous than those indicating that the deity is a body. Nor are the gates of figurative interpretation shut in our faces or impossible of access to us regarding the subject of the creation of the world in time. For we could interpret them as figurative, as we have done when denying His corporeality. Perhaps this would even be much easier to do: we should be very well able to give a figurative interpretation of those texts and to affirm as true the eternity of the world, just as we have given a figurative interpretation of those other texts and have denied that He, may He be exalted, is a body.

Two causes are responsible for our not doing this or believing it. One of them is as follows. That the deity is not a body has been demonstrated; from this it follows necessarily that everything that in its external meaning disagrees with this demonstration must be interpreted figuratively, for it is known that such texts are of necessity fit for figurative interpretation. However, the eternity of the world has not been demonstrated. Consequently in this case the texts ought not to be rejected and figuratively interpreted in order to make prevail an opinion whose contrary can be made to prevail by means of various sorts of arguments. This is one cause.

The second cause is as follows. Our belief that the deity is not a body destroys for us none of the foundations of the Law and does not give the lie to the claims of any prophet. The only objection to it is constituted by the fact that the ignorant think that this belief is contrary to the text; yet it is not contrary to it, as we have explained, but is intended by the text. On the other hand, the belief in eternity the way Aristotle sees it—that is, the belief according to which the world exists in virtue of necessity, that no nature changes at all, and that the customary course of events cannot be modified with regard to anything—destroys the Law in its principle, necessarily gives the lie to every miracle, and reduces to inanity all the hopes and threats that the Law has held out, unless—by God!—one interprets the miracles figuratively also, as was done by the Islamic internalists; this, however, would result in some sort of crazy imaginings.

If, however, one believed in eternity according to the second opinion we have explained—which is the opinion of Plato—according to which the heavens too are subject to generation and corruption, this opinion would not destroy the foundations of the Law and would be followed not by the lie being given to miracles, but by their becoming admissible. It would also be possible to interpret figuratively the texts in accordance with this opinion. And many obscure passages can be found in the texts of the *Torah* and others with which this opinion could be connected or rather by means of which it could be proved. However, no necessity could impel us to do this unless this opinion were demonstrated. In view of the fact that it has not been demonstrated, we shall not favor this opinion, nor shall we at all heed that other opinion, but rather shall take the texts according to their external sense and shall say: The Law has given us knowledge of a matter the grasp of which is not within our power, and the miracle attests to the correctness of our claims.

Know that with a belief in the creation of the world in time, all the miracles become possible and the Law becomes possible, and all questions that may be asked on this subject, vanish. Thus it might be said: Why did God give prophetic revelation to this one and not to that? Why did God give this Law to this particular nation, and why did He not legislate to the others? Why did He legislate at this particular time, and why did He not legislate before it or after? Why did He impose these commandments and these prohibitions? Why did He privilege the prophet with the miracles mentioned in relation to him and not with some others? What was God's aim in giving this Law? Why did He not, if such was His purpose, put the accomplishment of the commandments and the nontransgression of the prohibitions into our nature? If this were said, the answer to all these questions would be said: He wanted it this way; or His wisdom required it this way. And just as He brought the world into existence, having the form it has, when He wanted to, without our knowing His will with regard to this or in what respect there was wisdom in His particularizing the forms of the world and the time of its creation—in the same way we do not know His will or the exigency of His wisdom that caused all the matters, about which questions have been posed above, to be particularized. If, however, someone says that the world is as it is in virtue of necessity, it would be a necessary obligation to ask all those questions; and there would be no way out of them except through a recourse to unseemly answers in which there would be combined the giving the lie to, and the annulment of, all the external meanings of the Law with regard to which no intelligent man has any doubt that they are to be taken in their external meanings. It is then because of this that this opinion is shunned and that the lives of virtuous men have been and will be spent in investigating this question. For if creation in time were demonstrated—if only as Plato understands creation—all the overhasty claims made to us on this point by the philosophers would become void. In the same way, if the philosophers would succeed in demonstrating eternity as Aristotle understands it, the Law as a whole would become void, and a shift to other opinions would take place. I have thus explained to you that everything is bound up with this problem. Know this.

CHAPTER 32

The opinions of people concerning prophecy are like their opinions concerning the eternity of the world or its creation in time. I mean by this that just as the people to whose mind the existence of the deity is firmly established, have, as we have set forth, three opinions concerning the eternity of the world or its creation in time, so are there also three opinions concerning prophecy. I shall not pay attention to the opinion of Epicurus, for he does not believe in the existence of a deity and all the more does he not believe in prophecy. I only aim to set forth the opinions of those who believe in the deity.

The first opinion—that of the multitude of those among the Pagans who considered prophecy as true and also believed by some of the common people professing our Law—is that God, may He be exalted, chooses whom He wishes from among men, turns him into a prophet, and sends him with a mission. According to them it makes no difference whether this individual is a man of knowledge or ignorant, aged or young. However, they also posit as a condition his having a certain goodness and sound morality. For up to now people have not gone so far as to say that God sometimes turns a wicked man into a prophet unless He has first, according to this opinion, turned him into a good man.

The second opinion is that of the philosophers. It affirms that prophecy is a certain perfection in the nature of man. This perfection is not achieved in any individual from among men except after a training that makes that which exists in the potentiality of the species pass into actuality, provided an obstacle due to temperament or to some external cause does not hinder this, as is the case with regard to every perfection whose existence is possible in a certain species. For the existence of that perfection in its extreme and ultimate form in every individual of that species is not possible. It must, however, exist necessarily in at least one particular individual; if, in order to be achieved, this perfection requires something that actualizes it, that something necessarily exists. According to this opinion it is not possible that an ignoramus should turn into a prophet; nor can a man not be a prophet on a certain evening and be a prophet on the following morning, as though he had made some find. Things are rather as follows: When, in the case of a superior individual who is perfect with respect to his rational and moral qualities, his imaginative faculty is in its most perfect state and when he has been prepared in the way that you will hear, he will necessarily become a prophet, inasmuch as this is a perfection that belongs to us by nature. According to this opinion it is not possible that an individual should be fit for prophecy and prepared for it and not become a prophet, except to the extent to which it is possible that an individual having a healthy temperament should be nourished with excellent food, without sound blood and similar things being generated from that food.

The third opinion is the opinion of our Law and the foundation of our doctrine. It is identical with the philosophic opinion except in one thing. For we believe that it may happen that one who is fit for prophecy and prepared for it should not become a prophet, namely, on account of the divine will. To my mind this is like all the miracles and takes the same course as they. For it is a natural thing that everyone who according to his natural disposition is fit for prophecy and who has been trained in his education and study should become a prophet. He who is prevented from it is like him who has been prevented, like *Jeroboam* (I Kings 13:4), from moving his hand, or, like the *King of Aram's* army going to seek out *Elisha* (II Kings 6:18), from seeing. As for its being fundamental with us that the prophet must possess preparation and perfection in the moral and rational qualities, it is indubitably the opinion expressed in their dictum (B.T., Shabbat, 92a): *Prophecy only rests upon a wise, strong, and rich man.* We have explained this in our Commentary on the *Mishnah* (Introduction to Seder Zera'im) and in our great compilation (*Mishneh Torah*, Yesodei ha-Torah, VII), and we have set forth that the *disciples of the prophets* were always engaged in preparation. As for the fact that one who prepares is sometimes prevented from becoming a prophet, you may know it from the history of *Baruch, son of Neriah.* For he followed *Jeremiah,* who trained, taught, and prepared him. And he set himself the goal of becoming a prophet, but was prevented; as he says (Jer. 45:3): *I am weary with my groaning, and I find no rest.* Thereupon he was told through *Jeremiah* (Jer. 45:4-5): *Thus shalt thou say unto him: Thus saith the Lord, and so on. And seekest thou great things for thyself? Seek them not.* It is possible to say that this is a clear statement that prophecy is too *great a thing* for *Baruch.* Similarly it may be said, as we shall explain, that in the passage (Lam. 2:9), *Yea, her prophets find no vision from the Lord,* this was the case because they were in *Exile.* However, we shall find many texts, some of them scriptural and some of them dicta of the *Sages,* all of which maintain this fundamental principle that God turns whom He wills, whenever He wills it, into a prophet—but only someone perfect and superior to the utmost degree. But with regard to one of the ignorant among the common people, this is not possible according to us—I mean, that He should turn one of them into a prophet—except as it is possible that He should turn an ass or a frog into a prophet. It is our fundamental principle that there must be training and perfection, whereupon the possibility arises to which the power of the deity becomes attached. You should not be led astray by His saying (Jer. 1:5): *Before I formed thee in the belly I knew thee, and before thou camest forth from the womb I sanctified thee.* For this is the state of every prophet: he must have a natural preparedness in his original natural disposition, as shall be explained. As for his saying (Jer. 1:6), *For I am young [na^car],* you know that in the Hebrew language *Joseph the righteous* was called *young [na^car]* though he was thirty years old, and that *Joshua* was called *young [na^car]* though he was near his sixtieth year. For it says with reference to the time of *the doings* concerning *the calf* (Exod. 33:11): *But his servant Joshua, son of Nun, a young man, departed not, and so on.* Now *Moses our Master* was at that time eighty-one years old, and his whole life lasted one hundred and twenty years. *Joshua* lived after him fourteen years, and the life of *Joshua* lasted one hundred and ten years. Accordingly it is clear that *Joshua* was at that time at least fifty-seven years old, and was nevertheless called *young [naᶜar]*. Again you should not be led astray by His dictum figuring in the promises (Joel 3:1): *I will pour out My spirit upon all flesh, and your sons and your daughters shall prophesy,* for He interprets this and lets us know what kind of prophecy is meant, for He says (Joel 3:1): *Your old men shall dream dreams, your young men shall see visions.* For everyone who communicates knowledge as to something secret, whether this be with the help of soothsaying and divination or with the help of a veridical dream, is likewise called a *prophet.* For this reason *prophets of Baal* and *prophets of Asherah* are called *prophets.* Do you not see that He, may He be exalted, says (Deut. 13:2): *If there arise among you a prophet or a dreamer of dreams?* As for the *Gathering at Mount Sinai,* though through a miracle all the people saw the great fire and heard the frightening and terrifying voices, only those who were fit for it achieved the rank of prophecy, and even those in various degrees. Do you not see that He says (Exod. 24:1): *Come up unto the Lord, thou and Aaron, Nadab and Abihu, and seventy of the elders of Israel.* He, peace be upon him, had the highest rank, as He said (Exod. 21:2): *And Moses alone shall come near unto the Lord; but they shall not come near. Aaron* was below him; *Nabad and Abihu* below *Aaron;* the *seventy elders* below *Nadab and Abihu;* and the other people below the latter according to their degrees of perfection. A text of the *Sages, may their memory be blessed,* reads (Mekhilta on Exod. 19:24): *Moses is an enclosure apart, and Aaron an enclosure apart.*

As we have come to speak of the *Gathering at Mount Sinai,* we shall give indications, in a separate chapter, concerning what becomes clear regarding that *Gathering* as it was, from the scriptural texts, if they are well examined, and fr)m the dicta of the *Sages.*

CHAPTER 36

Know that the true reality and quiddity of prophecy consist in its being an overflow overflowing from God, may He be cherished and honored, through the intermediation of the Active Intellect, toward the rational faculty in the first place and thereafter toward the imaginative faculty. This is the highest degree of man and the ultimate term of perfection that can exist for his species; and this state is the ultimate term of perfection for the imaginative faculty. This is something that cannot by any means exist in every man. And it is not something that may be attained solely through perfection in the speculative sciences and through improvement of moral habits, even if all of them have become as fine and good as can be. There still is needed in addition the highest possible degree of perfection of the imaginative faculty in respect of its original natural disposition. Now you know the perfection of the bodily faculties, to which the imaginative faculty belongs, is consequent upon the best possible temperament, the best possible size, and the purest possible matter, of the part of the body that is the substratum for the faculty in question. It is not a thing whose lack could be made good or whose deficiency could be remedied in any way by means of a regimen. For with regard to a part of the body whose temperament was bad in the original natural disposition, the utmost that the corrective regimen can achieve is to keep it in some sort of health; it cannot restor it to its best possible condition. If, however, its defect derives from its size, position, or substance, I mean the substance of the matter from which it is generated, there is no device that can help. You know all this; it is therefore useless to explain it at length.

You know too, the actions of the imaginative faculty that are in its nature, such as retaining things perceived by the senses, combining these things, and imitating them. And you know that its greatest and noblest action takes place only when the senses rest and do not perform their actions. It is then that a certain overflow overflows to this faculty according to its disposition, and it is the cause of the veridical dreams. This same overflow is the cause of the prophecy. There is only a difference in degree, not in kind. You know that [the Sages] have said time and again (B.T. Berakhot, 57b): *A dream is the sixtieth part of prophecy.* No proportion, however, can be established between two things differing in their species. One is not allowed to say, for instance, that the perfection of a man is a certain number of times greater than the perfection of a horse. They reiterated this point in *Bereshith Rabbah* (XVIII and XLIV), saying: *Dream is the unripe fruit [nobeleth] of prophecy.* This is an extraordinary comparison. For *unripe fruit [nobeleth]* is the individual *fruit* itself, but one that has fallen before it was perfect and before it had matured. Similarly the action of the imaginative faculty in the state of sleep is also its action in the state of prophecy; there is, however, a deficiency in it and it does not reach its ultimate term. Why should we teach you by means of the dicta of [the Sages], *may their memory be blessed,* and leave aside the texts of the *Torah? If there be a prophet among you, I the Lord do make Myself known unto him in a vision, I do speak with him in a dream* (Num. 12:6). Thus He, may He be exalted, has informed us of the true reality and quiddity of prophecy and has let us know that it is a perfection that comes in a *dream* or in a *vision [mar'eh]*. The word *mar'eh [vision]* derives from the verb *ra'oh [to see]*. This signifies that the imaginative faculty achieves so great a perfection of action that it sees the thing as if it were outside, and that the thing whose origin is due to it appears to have come to it by the way of external sensation. In these two groups, I mean *vision* and *dream,* all the degrees of prophecy are included, as shall be explained. It is known that a matter that occupies a man greatly—he being bent upon it and desirous of it —while he is awake and while his senses function, is the one with regard to which the imaginative faculty acts while he is asleep when receiving an overflow of the intellect corresponding to its disposition. It would be superfluous to quote examples of this and to expatiate on it as this is a manifest matter that everyone knows. It is similar to the apprehension of the senses with regard to which no one whose natural disposition is healthy disagrees.

After these preliminary propositions, you should know that the case to be taken into consideration is that of a human individual the substance of whose brain at the origin of his natural disposition is extremely well proportioned because of the purity of its matter and of the particular temperament of each of its [that is, the brain's] parts and because of its size and position, and is not affected by hindrances due to temperament, which derive from another part of the body. Thereupon that individual would obtain knowledge and wisdom until he passes from potentiality to actuality and acquires a perfect and accomplished human intellect and pure and well-tempered human moral habits. Then all his desires will be directed to acquiring the science of the secrets of what exists and knowledge of its causes. His thought will always go toward noble matters, and he will be interested only in the knowledge of the deity and in reflection on His works and on what ought to be believed with regard to that. By then, he will have detached his thought from, and abolished his desire for, bestial things—I mean the preference for the pleasures of eating, drinking, sexual intercourse, and, in general, of the sense of touch, with regard to which Aristotle gave a clear explanation in the "Ethics" (III, 10), saying that this sense is a disgrace to us. How fine is what he said, and how true it is that it is a disgrace! For we have it in so far as we are animals like the other beasts, and nothing that belongs to the notion of humanity pertains to it. As for the other sensual pleasures—those, for instance, that derive from the sense of smell, from hearing, and from seeing—there may be found in them sometimes, though they are corporeal, pleasure for man as man, as Aristotle has explained. We have been led to speak of things that are not to the purpose, but there was need for it. For most of the thoughts of those who are outstanding among the men of knowledge are preoccupied with the pleasures of this sense, are desirous of them. And then they wonder how it is that they do not become prophets, if prophecy is something natural. It is likewise necessary that the thought of that individual should be detached from the spurious kinds of rulership and that his desire for them should be abolished—I mean the wish to dominate or to be held great by the common people and to obtain from them honor and obedience for its own sake. He should rather regard all people according to their various states with respect to which they are undubitably either like domestic animals or like beasts of prey. If the perfect man who lives in solitude thinks of them at all, he does so only with a view to saving himself from the harm that may be caused by those among them who are harmful if he happens to associate with them, or to obtaining an advantage that may be obtained from them if he is forced to it by some of his needs. Now there is no doubt that whenever—in an individual of this description—his imaginative faculty, which is as perfect as possible, acts and receives from the intellect an overflow corresponding to his speculative perfection, this individual will only apprehend divine and most extraordinary matters, will see only God and His angels, and will only be aware and achieve knowledge of matters that constitute true opinions and general directives for the well-being of men in their relations with one another. It is known that with regard to these three aims set forth by us—namely, the perfection of the rational faculty through study, the perfection of the imaginative faculty through natural disposition, and the perfection of moral habit through the turning-away of thought from all bodily pleasures and the putting an end to the desire for the various kinds of ignorant and evil glorification—there are among those who are perfect very many differences in rank; and on the differences in rank with regard to these aims there depend the differences in rank that subsist between the degrees of all the prophets.

You know that every bodily faculty sometimes grows tired, is weakened, and is troubled, and at other times is in a healthy state. Now the imaginative faculty is indubitably a bodily faculty. Accordingly you will find that the prophecy of the prophets ceases when they are sad or angry, or in a mood similar to one of these two. You know their saying (B.T. Shabbath, 30b), that *prophecy does not descend [during a mood of] sadness or of languor;* that prophetic revelation did not come to *Jacob our Father* during the time of his mourning because of the fact that his imaginative faculty was preoccupied with the loss of *Joseph* (Chapter of Rabbi Eliezer, XXXVIII); and that prophetic revelation did not come to *Moses,* peace be on him, after the disastrous incident of the *spies* and until the whole *generation* of *the desert* perished, in the way that revelation used to come before (B.T. Ta'anith,

30), because—seeing the enormity of their crime—he suffered greatly because of this matter. This was so even though the imaginative faculty did not enter into his prophecy, peace be on him, as the intellect overflowed toward him without its inter-mediation. For, as we have mentioned several times, he did not prophesy like the other prophets by means of parables. This will be made clear later on, for it is not the purpose of this chapter. Similarly you will find that several prophets prophesied during a certain time and that afterwards prophecy was taken from them and could not be permanent because of an accident that had supervened. This is in-dubitably the essential and proximate cause of the fact that prophecy was taken away during the time of the *Exile*. For what *languor* or *sadness* can befall a man in any state that would be stronger than that due to his being a thrall slave in bondage to the ignorant who commit great sins and in whom the privation of true reason is united to the perfection of the lusts of the beasts? *And there shall be no might in thine hand* (Deut. 28:32). This was with what we have been threatened. And this was what it meant by saying (Amos 8:12): *They shall run to and fro to seek the word of the Lord, and shall not find it.* And it also says (Lam. 2:9): *Her king and her princes are among the nations, the Law is no more; yea, her prophets find no vision from the Lord.* This is true, and the cause thereof is clear. For the instrument has ceased to function. This also will be the cause for prophecy being restored to us in its habitual form, as has been promised *in the days of the Messiah, may he be revealed soon.*

CHAPTER 37

It is fitting that your attention be aroused to the nature of that which exists in the divine overflow coming toward us, through which we have intellectual cogni-tion and through which there is a difference of rank between our intellects. For sometimes something comes from it to a certain individual, the measure of that something being such that it renders him perfect, but has no other effect. Some-times, on the other hand, the measure of what comes to the individual overflows from rendering him perfect toward rendering others perfect. This is what happens to all beings: some of them achieve perfection to an extent that enables them to govern others, whereas others achieve perfection only in a measure that allows them to be governed by others, as we have explained.

After this, you should know that the case in which the intellectual overflow overflows only toward the rational faculty and does not overflow at all toward the imaginative faculty—either because of the scantiness of what overflows or because of some deficiency existing in the imaginative faculty in its natural disposition, a deficiency that makes it impossible for it to receive the overflow of the intellect—is characteristic of the class of men of science engaged in speculation. If, on the other hand, this overflow reaches both faculties—I mean both the rational and the im-aginative—as we and others among the philosophers have explained, and if the imaginative faculty is in a state of ultimate perfection owing to its natural dis-position, this is characteristic of the class of prophets. If again the overflow only reaches the imaginative faculty, the defect of the rational faculty deriving either from its original natural disposition or from insufficiency of training, this is char-acteristic of the class of those who govern cities, while being the legislators, the soothsayers, the augurs, and the dreamers of veridical dreams. All those who do extraordinary things by means of strange devices and secret arts and withal are not men of science belong likewise to this third class. You ought to obtain knowledge of the true reality, which is that some people belonging to this third class have—even while they are awake—extraordinary imaginings, dreams, and amazed states, which are like the *vision of prophecy* so that they think about themselves that they are prophets. And they are very much pleased with what they apprehend in these imaginings and think that they acquired sciences without instruction; and they bring great confusion into speculative matters of great import, true notions being strangely mixed up in their minds with imaginary ones. All this is due to the imaginative faculty, to the weakness of the rational faculty, and to its not having obtained anything—I mean thereby that it has not passed into actuality.

It is known that in each of these three classes there are very many differences of degree and that each of the first two classes is divided into two parts, as we have explained. For the measure of the overflow that comes to each of these two is either such as only to render the individual who receives it perfect and to have no other effect, or such that from that individual's perfection there is something left over that suffices to make others perfect. With regard to the first class—that of the men of science—the measure of the overflow that reaches the rational faculty of the individual is sometimes such that it makes him into a man who inquires and is endowed with understanding, who knows and discerns, but is not moved to teach others or to compose works, neither finding in himself a desire for this nor having the ability to do it. And sometimes the measure of the overflow is such that it moves him of necessity to compose works and to teach. The same holds good for the second class. Sometimes the prophetic revelation that comes to a prophet only renders him perfect and has no other effect. And sometimes the prophetic revelation that comes to him compels him to address a call to the people, teach them, and let his own perfection overflow toward them.

It has already become clear to you that, were it not for this additional perfection, sciences would not be set forth in books and prophets would not call upon the people to obtain knowledge of the truth. For a man endowed with knowledge does not set anything down for himself in order to teach himself what he already knows. But the nature of that intellect is such that it always overflows and is transmitted from one who receives that overflow to another one who receives it after him until it reaches an individual beyond whom this overflow cannot go and whom it merely renders perfect, as we have set out in a parable in one of the chapters of this Treatise. The nature of this matter makes it necessary for someone to whom this additional measure of overflow has come, to address a call to people, regardless of whether that call is listened to or not, and even if he as a result thereof is harmed in his body. We even find that prophets addressed a call to people until they were killed—this divine overflow moving them and by no means letting them rest and be quiet, even if they met with great misfortunes. For this reason you will find that *Jeremiah,* peace be on him, explicitly stated that because of the contempt he met with at the hand of the disobedient and unbelieving people who lived in his time, he wished to conceal his prophecy and not to address to them a call to the truth, which they rejected, but he was not able to do it. He says (Jer. 20:8–9): *Because the word of the Lord is made a reproach unto me, and a derision, all the day. And if I say: I will not make mention of him, nor speak anymore in His name; then there is in my heart as it were a burning fire shut up in my bones, and I weary myself to hold it in, but cannot.* This is also the meaning of the words of the other prophet (Amos 3:8): *The Lord God hath spoken, who shall not prophesy?* Know this.

CHAPTER 38

Know that in every man there is necessarily the faculty of courage. Were this not so, he would not be moved in his thought to ward off that which harms him. Among the faculties of the soul, this faculty is to my mind similar to the faculty of repulsion among the natural faculties. This faculty of courage varies in strength and weakness, as do other faculties, so that you may find among people some who will advance upon a lion, while others flee from a mouse. You will find someone who will advance against an army and fight it, and will find another who will tremble and fear if a woman shouts at him. There also must necessarily exist a temperamental preparation in the original natural disposition, which may increase through the passage of that which is potential into actuality—a passage effected in consequence of an effort made with a view to it and in accordance with a certain opinion. It may also diminish through a deficiency of exercise and in accordance with a certain opinion. The abundance or the weakness of this faculty in the young is made clear to you from their infancy.

Similarly the faculty of divination exists in all people, but varies in degree. It exists especially with regard to things with which a man is greatly concerned and about which his thought turns. Thus you will find in your soul that so and so spoke or acted in such and such a manner in such and such an episode, and the thing is really so. You will find among people a man whose conjecturing and divination are very strong and habitually hit the mark, so that he hardly imagines that a thing comes to pass without its happening wholly or in part as he imagined it. The causes of this are many—they are various anterior, posterior, and present circumstances. But in virtue of the strength of this divination, the mind goes over all these premises and draws from them conclusions in the shortest time, so that it is thought to happen in no time at all. In virtue of this faculty, certain people give warnings concerning great future events.

These two faculties must necessarily be very strong in prophets, I mean the faculty of courage and that of divination. And when the intellect overflows toward them, these two faculties become very greatly strengthened so that this may finally reach the point you know: namely, the lone individual, having only his staff, went boldly to the great king in order to save a religious community from the burden of slavery, and had no fear or dread, because it was said to him (Exod. 3:12): *I will be with thee.* This too is a state that varies in them, but it is indispensable for them. Thus it was said to *Jeremiah* (Jer. 1:8, 17, 18): *Be not afraid and so on. Be not dismayed at them, and so on. For, behold, I have made thee this day a fortified city, and so on.* And it was said to *Ezekiel* (Ezek. 2:6): *Be not afraid of them or of their words.* Similarly you will find all of them, peace be on them, to be endowed with great courage. Also, because of the abundance of the faculty of divination in them, they give information regarding future events in the shortest time. This faculty likewise varies in them as you know.

Know that the true prophets indubitably grasp speculative matters; by means of his speculation alone, man is unable to grasp the causes from which what a prophet has come to know necessarily follows. This has a counterpart in their giving information regarding matters with respect to which man, using only common conjecture and divination, is unable to give information. For the very overflow that affects the imaginative faculty—with a result of rendering it perfect so that its act brings about its giving information about what will happen and its apprehending those future events as if they were things that had been perceived by the senses and had reached the imaginative faculty from the senses—is also the overflow that renders perfect the act of the rational faculty, so that its act brings about its knowing things that are real in their existence, and it achieves this apprehension as if it had apprehended it by starting from speculative premises. This is the truth that is believed by whoever chooses to be equitable toward himself. For all things bear witness to one another and indicate one another. This should be even more fitting for the rational faculty. For the overflow of the Active Intellect goes in its true reality only to it [that is, to the rational faculty], causing it to pass from potentiality to actuality. It is from the rational faculty that that overflow comes to the imaginative faculty. How then can the imaginative faculty be perfected in so great a measure as to apprehend what does not come to it from the senses, without the rational faculty being affected in a similar way so as to apprehend without having apprehended by way of premises, inference, and reflection?

This is the true reality of the notion of prophecy, and these are the opinions that are peculiar to the prophetic teaching. In my exposition I have put in the proviso that it refers to true prophets only. This was in order to exclude from it the people belonging to the third class, who have no rational conceptions at all and no knowledge, but only imaginings and whims. Perhaps they—I mean what these people apprehend—are merely opinions that they once had had and of which traces have remained impressed upon their imaginings together with everything else that subsist in their imaginative faculty. Accordingly when they void and annul many of their imaginings, the traces of these opinions remain alone and become apparent to them; whereupon they think that these are things that have unexpectedly occurred to them and have come from outside. To my mind they may be compared to a man who had with him in his house thousands of individual animals. Then all of them except one individual, which was one of those that were there, went out of that house. When the man remained alone with that individual, he thought that it had just now entered the house and joined him, whereas that was not the case, that individual being the one among that multitude that did not go out. This is one of the points that lead astray and cause perdition. How many among those who have aspired to obtain discernment have perished through this! Hence you will find that certain groups of people establish the truth of their opinions with the help of dreams that they have seen, thinking that what they have seen in sleep is something else than the opinion that they believe in or that they had heard while awake. Therefore one ought not to pay attention to one whose rational faculty has not become perfect and who has not attained the ultimate term of speculative perfection. For only one who achieves speculative perfection is able to apprehend other objects of knowledge when there is an overflow of the divine intellect toward him. It is he who is in true reality a prophet. This is explicitly stated (Ps. 90:12): *And the prophet [possesseth] a heart of wisdom.* It says here that one who is a prophet in true reality has *a heart of wisdom.* This too ought to be known.

CHAPTER 39

After we have spoken of the quiddity of prophecy, have made known its true reality, and have made it clear that the prophecy of *Moses our Master* is different from that of the others, we shall say that the call to the Law followed necessarily from that apprehension alone. For nothing similar to the call addressed to us by *Moses our Master* has been made before him by any one of those we know who lived in the time between *Adam* and him; nor was a call similar to that one made by one of our prophets after him. Correspondingly it is a fundamental principle of our Law that there will never be another Law. Hence, according to our opinion, there never has been a Law and there never will be a Law except the one that is the Law of *Moses our Master*. The explanation of this, according to what is literally stated in the prophetic books and is found in the tradition, is as follows. Not one of the prophets—such as the *Patriarchs, Shem, Eber, Noah, Methuselah,* and *Enoch*—who came before *Moses our Master,* has ever said to a class of people: God has sent me to you and has commanded me to say to you such and such things; He has forbidden you to do such and such things and has commanded you to do such and such things. This is a thing that is not attested to by any text of the *Torah* and that does not figure in any true tradition. These men only received prophetic relevation from God according to what we have set forth. He who received a great overflow, as for instance *Abraham,* assembled the people and called them by the way of teaching and instruction to adhere to the truth that he had grasped. Thus *Abraham* taught the people and explained to them by means of speculative proofs that the world has but one deity, that He has created all the things that are other than Himself, and that none of the forms and no created thing in general ought to be worshipped. This is what he instructed the people in, attracting them by means of eloquent speeches and by means of the benefits he conferred upon them. But he never said: God has sent me to you and has given me commandments and prohibitions. Even when the commandment of circumcision was laid upon him, his sons, and those who belonged to him, he circumcised them alone and did not use the form of a prophetic call to exhort the people to do this. Do you not see the text of the *Torah* referring to him that reads (Gen. 18:19): *For I have known him, and so on.* Thus it is made clear that he acted only through injunction. *Isaac, Jacob, Levi, Kohat,* and *Amram* also addressed their call to the people in this way. You will find likewise that the *Sages* say (Genesis Rabbah, XLIII) with reference to the prophets who came before him: *the court of justice of Eber, the court of justice of Methuselah, the school of Methuselah.* For all of them, peace be on them, were prophets who taught the people through being instructors, teachers, and guides, but did not say: *The Lord said to me: Speak to the sons of so and so.* Things were like that before *Moses our Master.* As for *Moses,* you know what was said to him, what he said, and what all the people said to him (Deut. 5:21): *This day we have seen that God doth speak, and so on.* As for the prophets from among us who came after *Moses our Master,* you know the text of all their stories and the fact that their function was that of preachers who called upon the people to obey the Law of *Moses,* threatened those who rejected it, and held out promises to those who were firm in observing it. We likewise believe that things will always be this way. As it says (Deut. 30:12, 29:28): *It is not in heaven, and so on; for us and for our children for ever.* And that is as it ought to be; for when a thing is as perfect as it is possible to be within its species, it is impossible that within that species there should be found another thing that does not fall short of that perfection either because of excess or deficiency. Thus in comparison with a temperament whose composition is of the greatest equibalance possible in the species in question, all other temperaments are not composed in accordance with this equibalance because of either deficiency or excess. Things are similar with regard to this Law, as is clear from its equibalance. For it says (Deut. 4:8): *Just statutes and judgments;* now you know that the meaning of *just* is equibalanced. For these are manners of worship in which there is no burden and excess—such as monastic life and pilgrimage and similar things—nor a deficiency necessarily leading to greed and being engrossed in the indulgence of appetites, so that in consequence the perfection of man is diminished with respect to his moral habits and to his speculation—this being the case with regard to all the other nomoi of the religious communities of the past. When we shall speak in this Treatise about the reasons accounting for the commandments, their equibalance and wisdom will be made clear to you in so far as this is necessary. For this reason it is said with reference to them (Ps. 19:8): *The Law of the Lord is perfect.* As for those who deem that its burdens are grievous, heavy, and difficult to bear—all of this is due to an error in considering them. I shall explain later on how easy they are in true reality according to the opinion of the perfect. For this reason it says (Deut. 10:12): *What doth the Lord thy God require of thee, and so on.* And it says (Jer. 2:31): *Have I been a wilderness unto Israel, and so on.* However, all this refers to the virtuous, whereas in the opinion of those who are unjust, violent, and tyrannical, the existence of a judge who renders tyranny impossible is a most harmful and grievous thing. As for the greedy and the vile, the most grievous thing in their opinion is that which hinders their abandoning themselves to debauchery and punishes those who indulge in it. Similarly everyone who is deficient in any respect considers that a hindrance in the way of the vice that he prefers because of his moral corruption is a great burden. Accordingly the facility or difficulty of the Law should not be estimated with reference to the passions of all the wicked, vile, morally corrupt men, but should be considered with reference to the man who is perfect among the people. For it is the aim of this Law that everyone should be such a man. Only that Law is called by us divine Law, whereas the other political regiments—such as the nomoi of the Greeks and the ravings of the Sabians and of others—are due, as I have explained several times, to the action of groups of rulers who were not prophets.

CHAPTER 40

It has been explained with utmost clarity that man is political by nature and that it is his nature to live in society. He is not like the other animals for which society is not a necessity. Because of the manifold composition of this species— for, as you know, it is the last one to have been composed—there are many differences between the individuals belonging to it, so that you can hardly find two individuals who are in any accord with respect to one of the species of moral habits, except in a way similar to that in which their visible forms may be in accord with one another. The cause of this is the difference of the mixtures, owing to which the various kinds of matter differ, and also the accidents consequent to the form in question. For every natural form has certain accidents proper and consequent to it, those accidents being other than those that are consequent to matter. Nothing like this great difference between the various individuals is found among the other species of animals, in which the difference between individuals belonging to the same species is small, man being in this respect an exception. For you may find among us two individuals who seem, with regard to every moral habit, to belong to two different species. Thus you may find in an individual cruelty that reaches a point at which he kills the youngest of his sons in his great anger, whereas another individual is full of pity at the killing of a bug or any other insect, his soul being too tender for this. The same holds good for most accidents.

Now as the nature of the human species requires that there be those differences among the individuals belonging to it and as in addition society is a necessity for this nature, it is by no means possible that his society should be perfected except—and this is necessarily so—through a ruler who gauges the actions of the individuals, perfecting that which is deficient and reducing that which is excessive, and who prescribes actions and moral habits that all of them must always practice in the same way, so that the natural diversity is hidden through the multiple points of conventional accord and so that the community becomes well ordered. Therefore I say that the Law, although it is not natural, enters into what is natural. It is a part of the wisdom of the deity with regard to the permanence of this species of which He has willed the existence, that He put it into its nature that individuals belonging to it should have the faculty of ruling. Among them there is the one to whom the regimen mentioned has been revealed by prophecy directly; he is the prophet or the bringer of the nomos. Among them there are also those who have the faculty to compel people to accomplish, observe, and actualize that which has been established by those two. They are a sovereign who adopts the nomos in question, and someone claiming to be a prophet who adopts the Law of the prophet—either the whole of it or a portion. His adopting a portion and abandoning another portion may be due either to this being easier for him or to his wishing out of jealousy to make people fancy that those matters came to him through a prophetic revelation and that with regard to them he does not follow somebody else. For among the people there are men who admire a certain perfection, take pleasure in it, have a passion for it, and wish that people should imagine that this perfection belongs to them, though they know that they possess no perfection. Thus you see that there are many who lay claim to, and give out as their own, the poetry of someone else. This has also been done with regard to certain works of men of science and to particular points of many sciences. For an envious and lazy individual sometimes comes upon a thing invented by somebody else and claims that it was he who invented it. This has also happened with regard to the prophetic perfection. For we find people who laid a claim to prophecy and said things with regard to which there had never been at anytime a prophetic revelation coming from God; thus, for instance, *Zedekiah, son of Chenaanah* (Cf. I Kings 22:11 and 24). And we find other people who laid a claim to prophecy and said things that God has indubitably said—I mean things that had come through a prophetic revelation, but a prophetic revelation addressed to other people; thus, for instance, *Hananiah, son of Azzur* (Cf. Jer. 28:1ff). Accordingly these men give out as their own the prophetic revelation in question and adorn themselves with it. The knowledge and discernment of all this are very clear. I shall explain this to you in order that the matter should not be obscure to you and so that you should have a criterion by means of which you will be able to distinguish between the regimens of nomoi that have been laid down, the regimens of the divine Law, and the regimens of those who took over something from the dicta of the prophets, raised a claim to it, and give it out as their own.

Concerning the nomoi with respect to which those who have laid them down have stated clearly that these are nomoi that they have laid down by following their own thoughts, there is no need to adduce proofs for this, for with its being recognized by the adversary, no further evidence is needed. Accordingly I only want to give you knowledge concerning the regimens with regard to which the claim is made that they are prophetic; some of them are truly prophetic—I mean divine—while others are nomoi, and others again are plagiarisms.

Accordingly if you find a Law the whole end of which and the whole purpose of the chief thereof, who determined the actions required by it, are directed exclusively toward the ordering of the city and of its circumstances and the abolition in it of injustice and oppression; and if in that Law attention is not at all directed toward speculative matters, no heed is given to the perfecting of the rational faculty, and no regard is accorded to opinions being correct or faulty—the whole purpose of that Law being, on the contrary, the arrangement, in whatever way this may be brought about, of the circumstances of people in their relations with one another and provision for their obtaining, in accordance with the opinion of that chief, a certain something deemed to be happiness—you must know that that Law is a nomos and that the man who laid it down belongs, as we have mentioned, to the third class, I mean to say to those who are perfect only in their imaginative faculty.

If, on the other hand, you find a Law all of whose ordinances are due to attention being paid, as was stated before, to the soundness of the circumstances pertaining to the body and also to the soundness of belief—a Law that takes pains to inculcate correct opinions with regard to God, may He be exalted in the first place, and with regard to the angels, and that desires to make man wise, to give him understanding, and to awaken his attention, so that he should know the whole of that which exists in its true form—you must know that this guidance comes from Him, may He be exalted, and that this Law is divine.

It remains for you to know whether he who lays claim to such a guidance is a perfect man to whom a prophetic revelation of that guidance has been vouchsafed, or whether he is an individual who lays claim to these dicta, having plagiarized them. The way of putting this to a test is to consider the perfection of that individual, carefully to examine his actions, and to study his way of life. The strongest of the indications you should pay attention to is constituted by his renunciation of, and contempt for, the bodily pleasures, for this is the first of the degrees of the people of science and, all the more, of the prophets. In particular this holds good with regard to the sense that is a disgrace to us—as Aristotle has set forth—and especially in what belongs to it with regard to the foulness of copulation. For this reason God has stigmatized through it everyone who lays a claim to prophecy, so that the truth should be made clear to those who seek it and they should not go astray and fall into error. Do you not see how *Zedekiah, son of Maaseiah, and Ahab, son of Kolaiah,* claimed prophecy, were followed by the people, and gave forth dicta deriving from a revelation that had come to others; and how they were plunged into the vileness of the pleasure of sexual intercourse so that they fornicated with the wives of their companions and followers so that

God made them notorious, just as He disgraced others, and *the King of Babylon* burned them. As *Jeremiah* has set forth, saying (Jer. 29:22–23): *And of them shall be taken up a curse by all the exiles of Judah that are in Babylon, saying: The Lord make thee like Zedekiah and like Ahab, whom the King of Babylon roasted in the fire; because they have wrought vile deeds in Israel, and have committed adultery with their neighbors' wives, and have spoken words in My name falsely, which I commanded them not; but I am He that knoweth and am witness, saith the Lord.* Understand this intention.

BOOK III

CHAPTER 26

Just as there is disagreement among the men of speculation among the adherents of Law whether His works, may He be exalted, are consequent upon wisdom or upon the will alone without being intended toward any end at all, there is also the same disagreement among them regarding our Laws, which He has given to us. Thus there are people who do not seek for them any cause at all, saying that all Laws are consequent upon the will alone. There are also people who say that every commandment and prohibition in these Laws is consequent upon wisdom and aims at some end, and that all Laws have causes and were given in view of some utility. It is, however, the doctrine of all of us—both of the multitude and of the elite—that all the Laws have a cause, though we ignore the causes for some of them and we do not know the manner in which they conform to wisdom. With regard to this the texts of the Book are clear (Deut. 4:8, Ps. 19:10): *righteous statutes [huqqim] and judgments; The judgments of the Lord are true, they are righteous altogether.*

About the statutes designated a *huqqim*—for instance those concerning the *mingled stuff, meat in milk,* and *the sending of the goat* (Cf. Deut. 22:11, Exod. 23:19, Lev. 16:10 and 21)—[the Sages], *May their memory be blessed,* make literally the following statement (B.T., Yoma, 67b): *Things which I have prescribed for you, about which you have not the permission to think, which are criticized by Satan and refuted by the Gentiles.* They are not believed by the multitude of the *Sages* to be things for which there is no cause at all and for which one must not seek an end. For this would lead, according to what we have explained, to their being considered as frivolous actions. On the contrary, the multitude of the *Sages* believe that there indubitably is a cause for them—I mean to say a useful end—but that it is hidden from us either because of the incapacity of our intellects or the deficiency of our knowledge. Consequently there is, in their opinion, a cause for all the *commandments;* I mean to say that any particular commandment or prohibition has a useful end. In the case of some of them, it is clear to us in what way they are useful—as in the case of the prohibition of killing and stealing. In the case of others, their utility is not clear—as in the case of the interdiction of the *first products* [of trees] (Cf. Lev. 19:23) and of [sowing] *the vineyard with diverse seeds* (Cf. Deut. 22:9). Those commandments whose utility is clear to the multitude are called *mishpatim [judgments]*, and those whose utility is not clear to the multitude are called *huqqim [statutes]*. They always say with regard to the verse (Deut. 32:47): *For it is no vain thing —And if it is vain, it is because of you* (J.T., Pe'ah I; J.T., Kethuboth, VIII);

meaning that this legislation is not a vain matter without a useful end and that if it seems to you that this is the case with regard to some of the *commandments,* the deficiency resides in your apprehension. You already know the tradition that is widespread among us according to which the causes for all the *commandments,* with the exception of that concerning the *red heifer,* were known to *Solomon* (Cf. Midrash Qoheleth, 7:23); and also their dictum (Cf. B.T., Sanhedrin, 21b) that God hid the causes for the *commandments* in order that they should not be held in little esteem, as happened to *Solomon* with regard to the three *commandments* whose causes are made clear.

All their dicta proceed according to this principle, and the texts of the [scriptural] books indicate it. However, I found in *Bereshith Rabbah* a text of the *Sages, may their memory be blessed,* from which it appears when one first reflects on it that some of the *commandments* have no other cause than merely to prescribe a law, without there having been in view in them any other end or any real utility. This is their dictum in that passage (Genesis Rabbah, XLIV): *What does it matter to the Holy One, blessed be He, that animals are slaughtered by cutting their neck in front or in the back? Say therefore that the commandments were only given in order to purify the people. For it is said* (Ps. 18:31): *The word of the Lord is purified.* Though this dictum is very strange and has no parallel in their other dicta, I have interpreted it, as you will hear, in such a manner that we shall not abandon the views of all their dicta and we shall not disagree with a universally agreed upon principle, namely, that one should seek in all the Laws an end that is useful in regard to being (Deut. 32:47): *For it is no vain thing.* He says (Isa. 45:19): *I said not unto the seed of Jacob: Seek ye Me for nothing; I the Lord speak righteousness, I declare things that are right.*

What everyone endowed with a sound intellect ought to believe on this subject is what I shall set forth to you: The generalities of the *commandments* necessarily have a cause and have been given because of a certain utility; their details are that in regard to which it was said of the commandments that they were given merely for the sake of commanding something. For instance the killing of animals because of the necessity of having good food is manifestly useful, as we shall make clear. But the prescription that they should be killed through having the upper and not the lower part of their throat cut, and having their esophagus and windpipe severed at one particular place is, like other prescriptions of the same kind, imposed with a view *to purifying the people.* The same thing is made clear to you through their example: *Slaughtered by cutting their neck in front or in the back.* I have mentioned this example to you merely because one finds in their text, *may their memory be blessed: Slaughtered by cutting their neck in front or in the back.* However, if one studies the truth of the matter, one finds it to be as follows: As necessity occasions the eating of animals, the commandment was intended to bring about the easiest death in an easy manner. For beheading would only be possible with the help of a sword or something similar, whereas a throat can be cut with anything. In order that death should come about more easily, the condition was imposed that the knife should be sharp. The true reality of particulars of commandments is illustrated by the sacrifices. The offering of sacrifices has in itself a great and manifest utility, as I shall make clear. But no cause will ever be found for the fact that one particular sacrifice consists in a *lamb* and another in a *ram* and that the number of the victims should be one particular number. Accordingly, in my opinion, all those who occupy themselves with finding causes for something of these particulars are stricken with a prolonged madness in the course of which they do not put an end to an incongruity, but rather increase the number of incongruities. Those who imagine that a cause may be found for suchlike things are as far from truth as those who imagine that the generalities of a *commandment* are not designed with a view to some real utility.

Know that wisdom rendered it necessary—or, if you will, say that necessity occasioned—that there should be particulars for which no cause can be found; it was, as it were, impossible in regard to the Law that there should be nothing of this class in it. In such a case the impossibility is due to the circumstances that when you ask why a *lamb* should be prescribed and not a *ram,* the same question would have to be asked if a *ram* had been prescribed instead of a *lamb.* But one particular species had necessarily to be chosen. The same holds for your asking why *seven lambs* and not *eight* have been prescribed. For a similar question would have been put if *eight* or *ten* or *twenty* had been prescribed. However, one particular number had necessarily to be chosen. This resembles the nature of the possible, for it is certain that one of the possibilities will come to pass. And no question should be put why one particular possibility and not another comes to pass, for a similar question would become necessary if another possibility instead of this particular one had come to pass. Know this notion and grasp it. The constant statements of [the Sages] to the effect that there are causes for all the commandments, as well as the opinion that the causes were known to *Solomon,* have in view the utility of a given *commandment* in a general way, not an examination of its particulars.

This being so, I have seen fit to divide the *six hundred and thirteen commandments* into a number of classes, every one of which comprises a number of *commandments* belonging to one kind or akin in meaning. I shall inform you of the cause of every one of these classes, and I shall show their utility about which there can be no doubt and to which there can be no objection. Then I shall return to each of the *commandments* comprised in the class in question and I shall explain to you the cause of it, so that only very few *commandments* will remain whose cause has not been clear to me up to now. Some of the particulars of, and conditions for, some of the *commandments* have also become clear to me, and it is possible to give their causes. You will hear all this. However, I shall not be able to clarify to you all this giving of causes before I set before you, as a preliminary, a number of chapters in which I will include premises that are useful as an introduction for the purpose I have in mind. These are the chapters with which I will begin now.

CHAPTER 27

The Law as a whole aims at two things: the welfare of the soul and the welfare of the body. As for the welfare of the soul, it consists in the multitude's acquiring correct opinions corresponding to their respective capacity. Therefore some of them [namely, the opinions] are set forth explicitly and some of them are set forth in parables. For it is not within the nature of the common multitude that its capacity should suffice for apprehending that subject matter as it is. As for the welfare of the body, it comes about by the improvement of their ways of living one with another. This is achieved through two things. One of them is the abolition of their wronging each other. This is tantamount to every individual among the people not being permitted to act according to his will and up to the limits of his power, but being forced to do that which is useful to the whole. The second thing consists in the acquisition by every human individual of moral qualities that are useful for life in society so that the affairs of the city may be ordered. Know that as between these two aims, one is indubitably greater in nobility, namely, the welfare of the soul—I mean the procuring of correct opinions—while the second aim—I mean the welfare of the body—is prior in nature and time. The latter aim consists in the governance of the city and the well-being of the states of all its people according to their capacity. This second aim is the more certain one, and it is the one regarding which every effort has been made precisely to expound it and all its particulars. For the first aim can only be achieved after achieving this second one. For it has already been demonstrated that man has two perfections: a first perfection, which is the perfection of the body, and an ultimate perfection, which is the perfection of the soul. The first perfection consists in being healthy and in the very best bodily state, and this is only possible through his finding the things necessary for him whenever he seeks them. These are his food and all the other things needed for the governance of his body, such as a shelter, bathing, and so forth. This cannot be achieved in any way by one isolated individual. For an individual can only attain all this through a poltical association, it being already known that man is political by nature. His ultimate perfection is to become rational in actu, I mean to have an intellect in actu; this would consist in his knowing everything concerning all the beings that it is within the capacity of man to know in accordance with his ultimate perfection. It is clear that to this ultimate perfection there do not belong either actions or moral qualities and that 'it consists only of opinions toward which speculation has led and that investigation has rendered compulsory. It is also clear that this noble and ultimate perfection can only be achieved after the first perfection has been achieved. For a man cannot represent to himself an intelligible even when taught to understand it and all the more cannot become aware of it of his own accord, if he is in pain or is very hungry or is thirsty or is hot or is very cold. But once the first perfection has been achieved it is possible to achieve the ultimate, which is indubitably more noble and is the only cause of permanent preservation.

The true Law then, which as we have already made clear is unique—namely, the Law of *Moses our Master*—has come to bring us both perfections, I mean the welfare of the states of people in their relations with one another through the abolition of reciprocal wrongdoing and through the acquisition of a noble and excellent character. In this way the preservation of the population of the country and their permanent existence in the same order become possible, so that every one of them achieves his first perfection; I mean also the soundness of the beliefs and the giving of correct opinions through which ultimate perfection is achieved. The letter of the *Torah* speaks of both perfections and informs us that the end of this Law in its entirety is the achievement of these two perfections. For He, may He be exalted, says (Deut. 6:24): *And the Lord commanded us to do all these statutes [ḥuqqim], to fear the Lord our God, for our good always, that He might preserve us alive, as it is at this day.* Here He puts the ultimate perfection first because of its nobility; for, as we have explained, it is the ultimate end. It is referred to in the dictum: *For our good always.* You know already what [the Sages], *may their memory be blessed,* have said interpreting His dictum, may He be exalted (Deut. 22:7): *That it may be well with thee, and that thou mayest prolong they days.* They said (B.T., Qiddushin, 39b): *That it may be well with thee in a world in which everything is well and that thou mayest prolong thy days in a world the whole of which is long.* Similarly the intention of His dictum here, *For our good always,* is this same notion: I mean the attainment of *a world in which everything is well and [the whole of which is] long.* And this is perpetual preservation. On the other hand, His dictum, *That He might preserve us alive, as it is at this day,* refers to the first and corporeal preservation, which lasts for a certain duration and which can only be well ordered through political association, as we have explained.

CHAPTER 28

Among the things to which your attention ought to be directed is that you should know that in regard to the correct opinions through which the ultimate perfection may be obtained, the Law has communicated only their end and made a call to believe in them in a summary way—that is, to believe in the existence of the deity, may He be exalted, His unity, His knowledge, His power, His will, and His eternity. All these points are ultimate ends, which can be made clear in detail and through definitions only after one knows many opinions. In the same way the Law also makes a call to adopt certain beliefs, belief in which is necessary for the sake of political welfare. Such, for instance, is our belief that He, may He be exalted, is violently angry with those who disobey Him and that it is therefore necessary to fear Him and to dread Him and to take care not to disobey. With regard to all the other correct opinions concerning the whole of being—opinions that constitute the numerous kinds of all the theoretical sciences through which the opinions forming the ultimate end are validated— the Law, albeit it does not make a call to direct attention toward them in detail as it does with regard to [the opinions forming ultimate ends], does do this in summary fashion by saying (Deut. 11:13): *To love the Lord.* You know how this is confirmed in the dictum regarding *love; With all thy heart, and with all thy soul, and with all thy might* (Deut. 6:5). We have already explained in *Mishneh Torah* (Yesodei ha-Torah, II, 2 f.) that this *love* becomes valid only through the apprehension of the whole of being as it is and through the consideration of His wisdom as it is manifested in it. We have also mentioned there the fact that the *Sages, may their memory be blessed,* call attention to this notion.

What results from what we have now stated as a premise regarding this subject is that whenever a *commandment,* be it a prescription or a prohibition, requires abolishing reciprocal wrongdoing, or urging to a noble moral quality leading to a good social relationship, or communicating a correct opinion that ought to be believed either on account of itself or because it is necessary for the abolition of reciprocal wrongdoing or for the acquisition of a noble moral quality, such a *commandment* has a clear cause and is of a manifest utility. No question concerning the end need be posed with regard to such *commandments.* For no one was ever so perplexed for a day as to ask why we were commanded by the Law that God is one, or why we were forbidden to kill and to steal, or why we were forbidden to exercise vengeance and retaliation, or why we were ordered to love each other. The matters about which people are perplexed and opinions disagree—so that some say that there is no utility in them at all except the fact of mere command, whereas others say that there is a utility in them that is hidden from us—are the *commandments* from whose external meaning it does not appear that they are useful according to one of the three notions we have mentioned: I mean to say that they neither communicate an opinion nor inculcate a noble quality nor abolish reciprocal wrongdoing. Apparently these *commandments* are not related to the welfare of the soul, as they do not communicate a belief, or to the welfare of the body, as they do not communicate rules useful for the governance of the city or for the governance of the household. Such, for instance, are the prohibitions of the *mingled stuff,* of the *mingling* [of diverse species], and of *meat in milk* (Cf. Deut. 22:11, Lev. 19:19, Exod. 23:19), and the commandment *concerning the covering of blood, the heifer whose neck was broken,* and the *firstling of an ass* (Cf. Lev. 17:13, Deut. 21:19, Exod. 13:13), and others of the same kind. However, you will hear my explanation for all of them and my exposition of the correct and demonstrated causes for them all with the sole exception—as I have mentioned to you—of details and particular *commandments.* I shall explain that all these and others of the same kind are indubitably related to one of the three notions referred to—either to the welfare of a belief or to the welfare of the conditions of the city, which is achieved through two things: abolition of reciprocal wrongdoing and acquisition of excellent characters.

Sum up what we have said concerning beliefs as follows: In some cases a *commandment* communicates a correct belief, which is the one and only thing aimed at—as, for instance, the belief in the unity and eternity of the deity and in His not being a body. In other cases the belief is necessary for the abolition of reciprocal wrongdoing or for the acquisition of a noble moral quality—as, for instance, the belief that He, may He be exalted, has a violent anger against those who do injustice, according to what is aid (Exod. 22:23): *And My wrath shall wax hot, and I will kill, and so on,* and as the belief that He, may He be exalted, responds instantaneously to the prayer of someone wronged or deceived (Exod. 22:26):*And it shall come to pass, when he crieth unto Me, that I will hear; for I am gracious.*

SELECTED BIBLIOGRAPHY

TRANSLATIONS

Efros, I., ed. and trans., *Maimonides' Treatise on Logic,* New York, 1938.

Friedländer, M., trans., *The Guide for the Perplexed,* 2nd ed., New York, 1936 (reprinted as paperback: New York, 1956).

Goodman, L., ed. and trans., *Rambam: Readings in the Philosophy of Moses Maimonides,* New York, 1977.

Gorfinkle, I., ed. and trans., *The Eight Chapters of Maimonides on Ethics (Shemonah Perakim), a Psychological and Ethical Treatise,* New York, 1912. (Reprinted, New York, 1966.)

Halkin, A., ed., B. Cohen, trans., *Epistle to Yemen,* New York, 1952.

Hyamson, M., ed. and trans., *Mishneh Torah, The Book of Knowledge,* New York, 1937 (Reprinted, Jerusalem, 1962).

Pines, S., trans., *The Guide of the Perplexed,* Chicago, 1963.

Rabin, C., trans., *Guide for the Perplexed,* abridged and introduced by Julius Guttmann, London, 1952.

Twersky, I., ed., *A Maimonides Reader,* New York, 1972.

Weiss, R. and C. Butterworth, trans., *Ethical Writings of Maimonides,* New York, 1975.

STUDIES

Altmann, A., "Das Verhältniss Maimunis zur jüdischen Mystik," *Monatsschrift für Geschichte und Wissenschaft des Judentums,* LXXX (1936), 305–330.

Altmann, A., "Essence and Existence in Maimonides," *Bulletin of the John Rylands Library,* XXXV (1953), 294–315.

Altmann, A., "Maimonides and Thomas Aquinas: Natural or Divine Prophecy," *AJS Review (Association for Jewish Studies Review),* III (1978), 1–19.

Altmann, A., "Maimonides' 'Four Perfections'," *Israel Oriental Studies,* II (1972), 15–24.

Bacher, W., M. Brann, and others, *Moses ben Maimon, sein Leben, seine Werke, und sein Einfluss,* 2 vols., Leipzig, 1908, 1914.

Bamberger, F., *Das System des Maimonides: eine Analyse des More Newuchim vom Gottesbegriff aus,* Berlin, 1935.

Berman, L., "A Reexamination of Maimonides' Statement on Political Science," *Journal of the American Oriental Society,* LXXXIX (1969), 106–111.

Berman, L., "Maimonides, the Disciple of Alfarabi," *Israel Oriental Studies,* IV (1974), 154–178.

Broadie, A., "Maimonides on Negative Attribution," *Transactions of Glasgow University Oriental Society,* Glasgow, XXV (1976), 1–17.

Buijs, J., "Comments on Maimonides' Negative Theology," *New Scholasticism,* XLIX (1975), 87–93.

Buijs, J., "The Philosophical Character of Maimonides' *Guide,"* *Judaism,* XXVII (1978), 448–457.

Davidson, H., "Maimonides' Secret Position on Creation," *Studies in Medieval Jewish History and Literature,* ed. I. Twersky, Cambridge, Mass.-London, 1979, 16–40.

Davidson, H., "Maimonides' *Shemonah Peraqim* and Alfarabi's *Fusūl al-Madanī,"* *Proceedings of the American Academy for Jewish Research,* XXXI (1963), 33–50. (Reprinted in *Essays in Medieval Jewish and Islamic Philosophy,* ed. A. Hyman, New York, 1977, 116–133.)

Davidson, H., *The Philosophy of Abraham Shalom: a Fifteenth Century Exposition and Defense of Maimonides,* Berkeley-Los Angeles, 1964.

Diesendruck, Z., "Die Teleologie bei Maimonides," *Hebrew Union College Annual,* V (1928), 415–534.

Diesendruck, Z., "Maimonides' Lehre von der Prophetie," *Jewish Studies in Memory of Israel Abrahams,* New York, 1927, 74–134.

Dienstag, J., ed., *Studies in Maimonides and*

St. *Thomas Aquinas,* New York, 1975.

Fox, M., "Maimonides and Aquinas on Natural Law," *Dine Yisra'el,* III (1972), V–XXXVI (reprinted in *Studies in Maimonides and St. Thomas Aquinas,* ed. J. Dienstag, 75–106).

Fox, M., "Prolegomenon," in A. Cohen, *The Teachings of Maimonides,* New York, 1968.

Galston, M., "The Purpose of the Law according to Maimonides," *Jewish Quarterly Review,* LXIX (1978), 27–51.

Hartman, D., *Maimonides: Torah and Philosophic Quest,* Philadelphia, 1977.

Heinemann, I., "Maimuni und die Arabischen Einheitslehrer," *Monatsschrift für Geschichte und Wissenschaft des Judentums,* LXXIX (1935), 102–148.

Hyman, A., "A Note on Maimonides' Classification of Law," *Jubilee Volume, American Academy for Jewish Research,* ed. S. Baron and I. Barzilay, Jerusalem, 1980, 323–343.

Hyman, A., "Maimonides' Thirteen Principles," *Jewish Medieval and Renaissance Studies,* A. Altmann, ed., Cambridge, Mass., 1967, 119–144.

Hyman, A., "Some Aspects of Maimonides' Philosophy of Nature," *La filosofia della natura nel Medioevo,* Milan, 1966, 209–218.

Kellner, M., "Maimonides and Gersonides on Mosaic Prophecy," *Speculum,* LII (1977), 62–97.

Lerner, R., "Maimonides' Letter on Astrology," *History of Religions,* VIII (1968), 143–158.

Miller, C., "Maimonides and Aquinas on Naming God," *Journal of Jewish Studies,* XXVIII (1977), 65–71.

Neuberger, C., *Das Wesen des Gesetzes in der Philosophie des Maimonides,* Danzig, 1933.

Pines, S., "The Limitations of Human Knowledge according to Al-Farabi, ibn Bajja, and Maimonides," *Studies in Medieval Jewish History and Literature,* ed. I. Twersky, Cambridge, Mass.-London, 1979, 82–109.

Rawidowicz, S., "Philosophy as Duty," *Moses Maimonides,* I. Epstein, ed., London, 1935, 179–188.

Reines, A., *Maimonides and Abrabanel on Prophecy,* Cincinnati, 1970.

Reines, A. J., "Maimonides' Concept of Providence and Theodicy," *Hebrew Union College Annual,* XLIII (1972), 169–206.

Rosenthal, E., "Maimonides' Conception of State and Society," *Moses Maimonides,* I. Epstein, ed., London, 1935, 191–206.

Rosin, D., *Die Ethik Maimonides,* Breslau, 1876.

Roth, Leon, *The Guide for the Perplexed,* London, 1948.

Roth, Leon, *Spinoza, Descartes, and Maimoni-*

des, New York, 1963.

Sarachek, J., *Faith and Reason: The Conflict over the Rationalism of Maimonides*, Williamsport, Pa., 1935.

Scheyer, S., *Das psychologische System des Maimonides*, Frankfurt a.M., 1845.

Schwarzschild, S., "Moral Radicalism and the Ethic of Middlingness in the Ethics of Maimonides," *Studies in Medieval Culture*, XI (1977), 65–94.

Silver, D., *Maimonidean Criticism and Maimonidean Controversy 1180–1240*, Leiden, 1965.

Strauss, L., "Der Ort der Vorsehungslehre nach der Ansicht Maimonides," *Monatsschrift für Geschichte und Wissenschaft des Judentums*, LXXXI (1937), 93–105.

Strauss, Leo, "The Literary Character of *The Guide for the Perplexed*," *Essays on Maimonides*, S. Baron, ed., New York, 1941, 37–91. (Reprinted in L. Strauss, *Persecution and the Art of Writing*.)

Strauss, L., "Maimonides' Statement on Political Science," *Proceedings of the American Academy for Jewish Research*, XXII (1953), 115–130.

Strauss, L., "Notes on Maimonides' Book of Knowledge," *Studies in Mysticism and Religion Presented to Gershom Scholem*, eds. E. Urbach and others, Jerusalem, 269–285.

Strauss L., "On the Plan of the *Guide of the Perplexed*," *Harry Austryn Wolfson Jubilee Volumes*, English Section, Jerusalem, 1965, 775–792. (Appears also in S. Pines, trans., *The Guide of the Perplexed*.)

Strauss, L., *Philosophie und Gesetz*, Berlin, 1935.

Twersky, I., *Introduction to the Code of Maimonides (Mishneh Torah)*, New Haven-London, 1980, esp. 356–514.

Vajda, G., "La pensée religieuse de Moise Maimonides: unité ou dualité?" *Cahiers de Civilisation Médiévale*, IX (1966), 29–49.

Wolfson, H., "The Aristotelian Predicables and Maimonides' Division of Attributes," *Essays and Studies in Memory of Linda R. Miller*, I. Davidson, ed., New York, 1938, 201–234. (Reprinted in H. Wolfson, *Studies in the History and Philosophy of Religion*, II, 161–194.)

Wolfson, H., "Halevi and Maimonides on Design, Chance, and Necessity," *Proceedings of the American Academy for Jewish Research*, XI (1941), 105–163. (Reprinted in *Essays in Medieval Jewish and Islamic Philosophy*, ed. A. Hyman, New York, 1977, 34–59.)

Wolfson, H., "Halevi and Maimonides on Prophecy," *Jewish Quarterly Review*, N.S., XXXII (1942), 345–370; XXXIII (1942), 49–82. (Reprinted in H. Wolfson, *Studies in the History of Philosophy and Religion*, II, 60–119.)

Wolfson, H., "Maimonides and Gersonides on Divine Attributes as Ambiguous Terms," *Mordecai M. Kaplan Jubilee Volume*, New York, 1953, 515–530. (Reprinted in H. Wolfson, *Studies in the History of Philosophy and Religion*, II, 231–246.)

Wolfson, H., "Maimonides and Halevi: A Study in Typical Attitudes towards Greek Philosophy in the Middle Ages," *Jewish Quarterly Review*, N.S., II (1912), 297–339. (Reprinted in H. Wolfson, *Studies in the History of Philosophy and Religion*, ed. I. Twersky and G. Williams, 2 vols., Cambridge, Mass., 1973 and 1977, II, 120–160.)

Wolfson, H., "Maimonides on Negative Attributes," *Louis Ginzberg Jubilee Volume*, English Section, New York, 1945, 411–446. (Reprinted in *Essays in Medieval Jewish and Islamic Philosophy*, ed. A. Hyman, 180–215.)

Wolfson, H., "Maimonides on the Internal Senses," *Jewish Quarterly Review*, XXV (1935), 441–467. (Reprinted in H. Wolfson, *Studies in the History of Philosophy and Religion*, I, 344–370.)

Wolfson, H., "Note on Maimonides' Classification of the Sciences," *Jewish Quarterly Review*, N.S., XXVI (1936), 369–377. (Reprinted in H. Wolfson, *Studies in the History of Philosophy and Religion*, I, 551–560.)

LEVI BEN GERSON

1288 – 1344

WHEN, IN THE thirteenth century, the setting of Jewish philosophy shifted from Muslim to Christian lands, knowledge of Arabic declined among Jews, and Hebrew became the language of their philosophic works. The translation of a large portion of the philosophic literature composed by Jews and Muslims during the earlier period was one of the first products of the changed linguistic situation. The new translations stimulated philosophic speculations among Jews and, for some three hundred years, Jewish philosophers wrote commentaries on earlier works and summaries of them as well as independent treatises and books.

The intellectual climate of the period was determined by the Hebrew translations of Maimonides' *Guide of the Perplexed* and of a large number of Averroes' commentaries on Aristotle's works. The tenor of philosophic speculations was an Averroean kind of Aristotelianism (Aristotle, after all, was the Philosopher and Averroes his Commentator), but it was by no means monolithic. Commentators and independent authors weighed and evaluated their predecessors' views, accepting only those that they considered philosophically sound. The positions that developed ranged from that of naturalistic Aristotelians who accepted the eternity of the universe, the collective immortality of mankind, and the identity of divine providence and the necessary laws of nature to that of harmonists who, accepting the teachings of the Torah in more literal fashion, believed in creation, individual immortality, and the role of God's will in providence.

Of the post-Maimonidean Aristotelians, Levi ben Gerson (Gershom), also known as Gersonides, was the most important. A man of wide intellectual interests, Gersonides presented his philosophic views in still unpublished supercommentaries on Averroean works, in Biblical commentaries, and in his major work, *The Wars of the Lord (Milḥamot Adonai)*. Addressing advanced students trained in mathematics, physics and metaphysics, Gersonides wrote his work to "wage the Lord's war against the false opinions found among [his] predecessors" and to present the opinions he considered correct. Demonstrating independence of mind, he did not hesitate to criticize Maimonides whom he treated with respect, just as he did not hesitate to take issue with Averroes when he considered him wrong. Thus, for example, he differed from Averroes in defending individual human immortality and from Maimonides in holding that the creation of the world can be demonstrated by philosophic proofs.

In his *Wars* Gersonides employs what has been called the scholastic method, that is, he shows the technical rigour and attention to detail that is often associated with the late medievals. In his exposition he reviews significant opinions of predecessors, offers arguments in their support, refutes those arguments he considers false, and concludes with his own opinions and their supporting arguments. Throughout the work he takes care to show that his conclusions are identical or, at least, compatible with the views of the Torah.

Agreeing with the Aristotelians that the acquisition of the intellectual virtues is the final goal of human life, Gersonides states that it is the purpose of his work "to investigate very precious and obscure questions on which depend the great fundamental principles which bring man to scientific [intellectual] happiness." Foregoing the synoptic presentation of his views, Gersonides addresses six topics concerning which his predecessors had erred or concerning which their exposition had been inadequate: (1) immortality of the soul (intellect), (2) prediction of the future in dreams, divination and prophecy, (3) divine knowledge of particulars, (4) divine providence, (5) celestial bodies, their movers, the arrangement of these movers, and their relation to God, and (6) creation. One treatise of the *Wars* is devoted to each of these topics. The fifth treatise contains a long, as yet unpublished, astronomical section. It should be noted that while Gersonides draws primarily upon the Jewish and Islamic philosophic traditions, there is evidence that he had some acquaintance with Christian scholastic thought. Since it appears that he did not know Latin, he must have received his information through personal contacts with Christian scholars.

Levi ben Gerson (Gershom), known in Latin as Magister Leo de Baneolis, Leo de Bagnolo, Magister Leo Hebraeus, was born in 1288 and died in 1344. He was active in the Provençal towns of Bagnol (possibly his place of birth), Orange, and, for a short time, in Avignon, but little else is known about his life. A prolific author, Gersonides demonstrated his knowledge of the Bible in commentaries on many of its books, chief among them his commentaries on the Pentateuch and on the book of Job. His commentaries became standard parts of the Jewish exegetical literature and their importance may be gathered from the facts that the commentary on the Pentateuch was one of the first printed Hebrew books (Mantua, before 1480) and that his Biblical commentaries were printed many times. Unlike some Jewish philosophers, he was well versed in rabbinic learning as is attested by a no longer extant commentary on the Talmudic Treatise *Berakhot* and two extant responsa. Three liturgical poems by him are also extant.

Gersonides' supercommentaries on Averroean works have already been mentioned and they cover Averroes' commentaries on Aristotle's logical, physical, psychological and metaphysical writings as well as some of Averroes' *quaestiones*. In *The Book of the Correct Syllogism (Sefer ha-Hekkesh ha-*

Yashar), Gersonides undertakes to correct errors in Aristotle's account of the syllogism in the *Prior Analytics*. A Latin translation of the work is extant in manuscript and some of Gersonides' other logical writings appear, in Latin translation, in some of the 16th century editions of Aristotle's works.

Gersonides' scientific contributions were largely in mathematics, particularly astronomy. In the already mentioned first part of book five of the *Wars* and in other works he wrote on arithmetic and geometry as contained in Euclid's *Elements,* on trigonometry, and on astronomic theories of Ptolemy and Al-Bitrūji of which he was critical. He invented an astronomical instrument known as "Jacob's Staff," and he composed astronomical tables based on his own observations. For Phillip of Vitry, bishop of Meaux, he wrote, in 1343, a treatise on harmonic numbers. Some of Gersonides' scientific writings were translated into Latin.

Taken from the third treatise of the *Wars of the Lord,* the selection that follows is devoted to God's knowledge. For Gersonides the basic question was: can God know contingent particulars and, if He can, what kind of knowledge of them does He possess? Gersonides is critical of the views of Aristotle and his followers and of Maimonides and arrives at an intermediate position of his own.

The Aristotelians, notes Gersonides, are divided into two groups: (1) those who deny that God knows contigent particulars both according to their essence and according to their particularity, and (2) those who, while denying that God knows them according to their particularity, affirm that He can know them according to their essence. God, the second group holds, knows contingent particulars according to their eternal and immutable essences as well as according to the unchanging order of the universe and the necessary laws of nature.

Maimonides, by contrast, affirmed that God's perfection requires that He know particulars not only according to their essence, but according to their particularity as well. However, since God's knowledge is eternal and immutable, He knows them simultaneously and from eternity. God, then, has knowledge of of future contingents and knows them before they exist. To the question "how is God's foreknowledge compatible with the existence of contingency and, especially, freedom of human choice?" Maimonides answers that, since God's knowledge is unlike ours, God can foreknow without changing the nature of contingency or human choice.

Holding that God's knowledge is totally different from that of man, Maimonides (*Guide of the Perplexed,* III, 20) lists five characteristics that distinguish God's knowledge from ours: (1) God is one, yet can know things belonging to various species, (2) He can know something that is non-existent, (3) He can know something infinite, (4) His knowledge is unchanging even with regard to things existing in time, and (5) His knowledge does not require that one of two possibilities must necessarily come to be. In his critique (for part of it, see below, pp. 429, 433) Gersonides takes issue with all these points.

According to Gersonides' own view God knows contingent particulars in one respect, but is ignorant of them in another. Since knowledge, correctly speaking, can only be of immutable essences and the unchangeable laws of nature, Gersonides agrees with the Aristotelians that God can know them only in that way—in his terminology, God knows them insofar as they are ordered and determinate. But at the same time, God knows that they are contingent, though He does not know which of the possibilities will come to be. God's ignorance of the particularity of contingent things is no defect in God, for not to know what is unknowable, is not a defect. Gersonides' view makes for a rather strong defense of the freedom of the human will.

As part of his discussion of God's knowledge, Gersonides inquires how the term 'knowledge' is predicated of God and man. Maimonides had maintained that the unlikeness of God and man requires that the term is predicated according to complete equivocation and must signify by way of negation (see above, pp. 381 ff.). Against this view, Gersonides argues that, in spite of differences between God and man, there must be some similarity in the two usages of the term. 'Knowledge', he holds, is predicated according to priority and posteriority, that is, God possesses knowledge in a more perfect way than man. For a similar critique of Maimonides by Thomas Aquinas, see below, pp. 527 ff.

In the selection the term 'sages of the Torah' refers to those philosophers, especially Maimonides, who interpreted the Torah philosophically. The phrases "May He be blessed" (applied to God) and "of blessed memory" have been omitted from the translation by the editor.

THE WARS OF THE LORD

Book III

The Nature of Divine Knowledge

CHAPTER I

It is appropriate to examine whether or not God knows individual, contingent things in the sub-lunar world; and if He does know them, [there is still the question], how He knows them. Since the philosophers and the sages [i.e. philosophers] who adhere to our Torah have differed with respect to this problem, it is proper that we first examine their views. Whatever truth we find in them we shall accept; and in whatever falsity we find, we shall indicate the truth that is to be found in refuting it.

There are two main views on this topic amongst the ancients that are worthy of discussion: (1) the view of Aristotle and his followers, and (2) the view of the great sages of the Torah. Aristotle [*Metaphysics* XII: 9] maintained that God does

From Levi ben Gerson, *The Wars of the Lord,* trans. and comm. S. Feldman, Philadelphia: The Jewish Publication Society of America, forthcoming. By permission of the Jewish Publication Society of America.

not know the individual things in the sub-lunar world. Those who followed him
are divided into two camps on this question, the first group maintaining that
Aristotle believed that God has no knowledge of things in the sub-lunar world,
either generally or individually. For if He had either general or individual knowledge, there would be multiplicity in His knowledge and hence in His essence. In
short, His essence would be divided into a more perfect part and a less perfect part.
This is similar to the case of things with definitions; some part of the definition is
the perfection of the other part of the definition.[1] The second camp holds that
Aristotle's view is that God knows the things in the sub-lunar world with respect to
their general natures, i.e. their essences, but not in so far as they are particulars, i.e.
contingents. Nor is there any multiplicity in His essence on this view, since He
knows only Himself and in this knowledge He knows all things with respect to
their general natures; for He is the principle of law, order and regularity in the
universe. But God, [according to this view,] does not know particulars; hence there
is no order to them, inasmuch as He does not know them as particulars, although
they do exhibit some order and regularity in so far as God knows them [generally].
It shall be demonstrated (with God's help) in Book V [part 3, Chap. 3] of this
treatise that this is the authentic view of Aristotle.

However, the great sages of our Torah, such as the outstanding philosopher
Maimonides and others of the sages of our Torah who have followed him, maintain
that God does know all particular and contingent things in so far as they are particular. Indeed, they believe that in one piece of knowledge He knows all these
things, which in fact are infinite. This is indeed the view of Maimonides who in
chapter 20 of part three of his great book *The Guide of the Perplexed,* says the
following: "Similarly we say that the various things that occur are known to Him
before they take place and that He doesn't cease knowing them. Hence, no new
knowledge accrues to Him at all. For example, He knows that a particular person
is now non-existent but will exist at some later date, and will continue to exist for
some time and then will be non-existent. Now when this person actually does exist
according to [God's] prior knowledge of him, there is no addition to His knowledge
and no new piece of information has arisen which was not already known to Him.
But something has in fact taken place that previously was known would take place
and exactly in the same way [as He knew it would]. This belief implies that
[God's] knowledge refers to the non-existent and encompasses the infinite. We
accept this belief, and we say that [God] has knowledge of that which is now non-
existent but which He can foresee and bring about." It is clear from this that Maimonides maintains that God knows individual, contingent things in so far as they
are particular.

CHAPTER 2

After having mentioned these opinions of [our] predecessors on this matter, let
us now examine them to see which is the true one. It will be necessary to examine
the arguments in behalf of each of these views as well as those that purport to
refute them.

Aristotle's thesis that God does not know contingent particulars has been thought
to be quite plausible. Firstly, a particular is not apprehended except by means of a

---

1. In the definition of 'man' as 'rational animal', rationality completes or perfects the generic
property animality.

corporeal faculty, such as the senses or the imagination. But it is obvious that God has no corporeal faculty. Hence, God does not know particulars. The following syllogism can be constructed: God has no corporeal faculty; anything that apprehends a particular possesses a corporeal faculty; hence, God cannot apprehend particulars.

Secondly, particulars are temporal phenomena, i.e. their existence is in some portion of time. But someone who cannot be described as in motion or at rest cannot apprehend temporal phenomena. Now God cannot be described as in motion or at rest; hence He cannot apprehend particulars. The following syllogism can be constructed: God cannot be described as in motion or at rest; anyone who cannot be described as in motion or at rest cannot apprehend temporal phenomena; hence, God cannot apprehend temporal phenomena. To this conclusion we add a self-evident premise in order to get the desired result: particulars are temporal phenomena. From this it follows that God cannot apprehend particulars. . . .

Sixthly, if it were alleged that God knows things that are generated, the following dilemma ensues: either He knows them *before* they occur, or He knows them only *simultaneously* with their occurrence, not beforehand. Now, if we assume that He knows them before their occurrence, His knowledge would refer to non-being. But this is absurd; for knowledge is necessarily [the cognition] of an existent, apprehended thing. Moreover, this divine foreknowledge of contingent things before they occur implies the following dilemma. If He knows them as genuine contingents, then His knowledge that one of these contingencies is to occur is compatible with the occurrence of the alternative. If, on the other hand, He knows precisely *which* of the two alternative states of affairs will occur, its alternative will not be genuinely possible. Now, if we assume that God has knowledge of these events as genuine contingencies [the first horn of this dilemma], His foreknowedge of these events would change when they actually occur; for prior to their occurrence they could or could not have happened, but after their occurrence this possibility has been removed. And since the intellect is constituted by what it knows, God would be continually changing—but this is utterly absurd. If, on the other hand, God knows *precisely* which of these contingencies will occur [the second horn of this dilemma], it follows that there is no genuine contingency at all; hence everything would be necessary. But this too is absurd and repugnant. It is clear, then, that it is false to say that God has knowledge of these generated events before they occur. But if we say that He has knowledge of them simultaneously with their occurrence [the second horn of the original dilemma], new knowledge would continually arise in Him. And since the intellect is constituted by what it knows, the divine essence would be continually changing—which is utterly impossible.

Seventhly, if God has knowledge of particulars, the following trilemma ensues: Either He guides and orders them in a good and perfect manner; or He is incapable of ordering them and has no power over them; or He has the power to order them properly but He neglects and forgets them either because they are despicable, lowly, and trivial in His eyes or because He is jealous. Now the latter two of those three alternatives are obviously false. It is evident that God can do whatever He pleases and that He does not refrain from giving perfection to each existent as much as is possible. This is clearly and marvelously exhibited by the wisdom evident in the creation of animals, and the great power God has in bringing about the greatest possible perfection in them, so that it is impossible for them to be any more perfect than they are. Hence, only the first of these alternatives remains; i.e.

God orders these particulars in a perfect and complete way if He knows them at all. But this is contrary to what we in fact observe of these particulars. They exhibit frequently evil and disorder, so that many evils befall the righteous whereas many goods befall the sinners. Indeed, this is the strongest argument in the eyes of those who deny divine knowledge of particulars. It seems that it was this argument that led Aristotle to say that God does not know particulars. This is evident from what he says in the *Metaphysics* [XII: 9–10]. [In sum,] these are the arguments that we have been able to extract from the words of the philosophers explicitly or implicitly in support of the thesis that God does not know particulars. . . .

Nevertheless, the view of our sages of the Torah, that God does know particulars is not implausible. Firstly, since it is admitted by all who philosophize that God is the most perfect being, it is improper to attribute to Him the defect of ignorance i.e. that He lacks knowledge of anything; for ignorance is one of the greatest defects. Someone who chooses to attribute to Him ignorance of particulars rather than to ascribe to Him the inability to arrange these particulars in an orderly manner escapes from one evil and falls into something worse. For it could be the case that the recipient [that is, matter] cannot receive more perfection than it actually does; and this is not a defect with respect to God.

Secondly, it is not proper to ascribe to the agent who produces something ignorance of his product; rather, his knowledge of the product is more perfect than that possessed by someone else. For he knows through one cognition everything that will derive from the produced thing by virtue of the disposition [i.e. structure] according to which he made it. Someone else, however, acquires his knowledge of it from the product; and when he observes that the object exhibits some new property resulting from the nature with which it has been endowed, he acquires new knowledge of that new property. And so new properties of a thing give rise to successive cognitions in the observer; and it is possible that the observer will never obtain a complete knowledge of the properties that accrue to this object, [especially] if the properties that accrue to this object are quite numerous. Thus, since God is the creator of the whole world, He has a complete knowledge of what shall happen to that which He has made, a knowledge that cannot be compared to our knowledge. For He knows in one cognition everything that will happen with respect to the world according to the nature with which He has endowed it; whereas we know these things only as they occur. Hence, it is not proper to compare our knowledge and His knowledge, saying that if God were to have this knowledge, He would have many cognitions, and hence His essence would be subject to plurality. What we know by many cognitions is known to God in one cognition, as we have seen. Indeed, God knows through one cognition these particulars, of which we can have knowledge [only] by means of a plurality of cognitions; for our knowledge does not encompass the many things that are generated in the world according to the nature with which God has endowed the world.

These two arguments are given by Maimonides in part III of his celebrated book *The Guide of the Perplex*ed [chaps. 20–21] in behalf of the claim that God knows all these particulars. It is clear that the second argument, in addition to proving that God knows all the things that happen, refutes some of the arguments of the philosophers against the view that God does know particulars. On the other hand, some of the philosophers have countered the first argument in behalf of divine knowledge of all particulars by saying that the denial of this claim does not entail any defect in God. For not every privation is a defect; it is a defect only when the thing is able to have the characteristic in question, not when it cannot have this characteristic. For example, motion is a perfection of animate creatures; when we deny motion of God, however, it is not a defect in Him but a perfection. Similarly, they say that in claiming that God does not know particulars, no imperfection in Him results, only perfection; for His knowledge concerns superior things, not these trivial matters. And so Aristotle says in Book XII of the *Metaphysics* [1074b 25–34] that it is better not to see some things than to see them.

Maimonides countered all those difficulties that have been believed to entail the rejection of divine knowledge of particulars by means of his dictum that it is not appropriate to compare divine cognition with human cognition. For to the extent that His being is greater than ours, so too is His knowledge greater than ours; and this is a necessary truth, since His knowledge is identical with Himself as the philosophers [Aristotle, *Metaphysics* XII, 1072b 19–23] have explained. Accordingly, Maimonides frequently rebukes the philosophers for comparing divine knowledge with human knowledge, and inferring therefrom that God does not know particulars. They themselves have shown us in some sense that the term 'knowledge' when applied both to God and men is equivocal. And it is obvious that with respect to things having equivocal predicates inferences from one to the other cannot be made. By means of this argument Maimonides claimed that it is not impossible, despite the arguments of the philosophers, for God to know all particulars. And when it has been shown that there is no impossibility in this supposition, it is clearly proper then to ascribe this power to Him in order to remove the defect of ignorance from Him.

There are five factors, admitted by Maimonides, by virtue of which God's knowledge differs from our knowledge; i.e. each one of these factors that is present in divine cognition cannot obtain in human cognition. I shall explain this in discussing these five factors. . . .

The second of these factors that differentiate divine cognition from human cognition is, according to Maimonides, that divine knowledge refers to things that are non-existent. It should be realized that Maimonides had to introduce this difference between divine and human cognition because he had already assumed that God knows *all* particulars and hence knows those that are now non-existent but will exist at some other time and will not exist at another time. Accordingly, His knowledge of this event that is non-existent now is actually present, whereas the object of knowledge to which this knowledge refers is non-existent. This kind of cognition cannot be at all attributed to our cognition; for, since the object of knowledge and the act of knowledge are numerically one, when the former is absent so is the latter. Hence, in our cognition, if there is a cognitive act, the object of cognition to which it refers must also be present. . . .

CHAPTER 3

It is proper that we determine whether Maimonides' efforts to counter all the possible objections of the philosophers who differ from him are adequate, before we examine the truth or falsity of these arguments and the validity of the conclusions inferred from them, if the latter are true. For if Maimonides' arguments against these objections are adequate, there will be no need for us to examine them by means of another method.

We claim that the first thing to do is to examine whether the term 'knowledge' is equivocal with respect to divine and human knowledge, such that the difference between them is as Maimonides thought—i.e. that divine knowledge is the opposite of our knowledge, so that what we consider to be opinion, error or confusion is with respect to God knowledge—or whether the equivocation involved here is such that this difference cannot be such [as Maimonides claimed]. It seems to us that Maimonides' position on this question of divine cognition is not entailed by any philosophical principles; indeed, reason denies this view, as I shall show. It seems rather that theological considerations[2] have forced him to this view. The question whether the Torah requires this doctrine shall be considered after our philosophical analysis of this problem.

That philosophical argument rules out Maimonides' position on this topic will be demonstrated as follows. It would seem that the term 'knowledge' is equivocal with respect to God and man in the sense of prior and posterior predication, i.e. the term 'knowledge' is predicated of God according to priority and of other beings according to posteriority. For in God knowledge is identical with His essence, whereas in anyone else knowledge is the effect of God's knowledge. In such a case the term is applied to God in a prior sense and to other things in a posterior sense. The same is true with respect to such terms as 'exists', 'one', 'essence', and the like, i.e. they are predicated of God primarily [i.e. according to priority] and of other things secondarily [i.e. according to posteriority]. For His existence, unity, and essence belong to Him essentially, whereas the existence, unity and essence of every [other] existent thing emanate from Him. Now when something is of this kind, the predicate applies to it in a prior sense; whereas the predicate applies in a posterior sense to the other things that are called by this predicate in so far as they are given this property directly by the substance that has the property in the prior sense. All of this is obvious to the reader of this treatise and it shall be discussed in detail in Book V [part 3, chap. 12]. Hence, it seems that the difference between divine and human cognition is a difference in terms of greater perfection; for this is prior and posterior predication. Now if what we have said is true, and since it is obvious that the most perfect knowledge is the most true with respect to specificity and determinateness, it would follow that God's knowledge is more true with respect to specificity and determinateness. Hence, it cannot be that what is considered knowledge with respect to God can be called with respect to us 'belief', 'error' or 'confusion'.

We can show in another way that the difference between divine and human cognition is not as Maimonides thought. It is evident that we proceed to affirm attributes of God from that with which we are familiar. That is, we say that God knows, because of the knowledge found in us. For example, since we apprehend that the knowledge belonging to our intellect is a perfection of our intellect—without which the latter could not be an intellect in act [i.e. perfect]—we predicate of God that He knows by virtue of the fact, which we have demonstrated concerning Him, that God is indubitably an intellect in act. It is self-evident that when a predicate is affirmed of some object because it is true of some other thing, it is not predicated of both things in an absolutely equivocal sense; for between things that are absolutely equivocal there is no analogy. For example, just as it would be impossible to infer that man is intelligent from the fact that body is a continuous magnitude, so too would it be obviously impossible to infer this if we were to

2. Literally, the Torah

introduce [arbitrarily] a term that is predictable of both 'intelligent' and 'continuous' in an absolutely equivocal sense. Hence, it is clear that the term 'knowledge' is not completely equivocal when applied to God and man. Since this term also cannot be applied univocally with respect to God and man, it must be predicated in the sense of priority and posteriority. The same holds for other attributes that are predicated of both God and us. Thus, the difference between divine and human knowledge is one of greater perfection, albeit exceedingly so; and this type of knowledge is more precise and clear. In general, the kind of equivocation with respect to divine and human knowledge is analogous to the equivocation involved in the attribute of substance in God and in the acquired intellect amongst men, since the knowledge and the knower are numerically identical (as has been previously explained); and just as God's substantiality is more perfect than the substantiality of the acquired intellect in us, so too is His knowledge more perfect than our knowledge. . . .

Indeed, it can be verified that the attributes of God are predicated of Him primarily but of other things secondarily, even though it be conceded that there is no similarity between God and His creatures. There are several predicates that are predicated of some things primarily and others secondarily in this way [i.e. even though these things are not similar]. For example, the term 'existent' is predicated of a substance primarily but secondarily of accidents, as has been shown in the *Metaphysics* [IV: 2, 1003b 6–9; VII: 1, 1028a 10–30]; yet it is evident that there is no similarity between substance and its accidents. It is important to realize that there are attributes that *must* be attributed to God, e.g. that He is a substance. The term 'substance', however, is not predicated of God and other beings univocally, but [of God] primarily and [of everything else] secondarily. For that which makes all [other] things that are described by some attribute in such a way that they are [truly] describable by that attribute—because they acquire this attribute from it essentially and primarily—is more appropriately describable by that attribute. Now God makes all other things in such a way that they are substances, for He endows them with their substantiality; accordingly, He is more appropriately describable as 'substance'. Moreover, the divine substance is self-subsistent, whereas all other substances derive their existence from something else; and whatever is self-subsistent is more appropriately described as 'substance' than something whose existence derives from another thing. . . .

On the basis of this entire discussion it is now evident that reason shows that the term 'knowledge' is predicated of God primarily and of creatures secondarily, not absolutely equivocally, and that the principles [of religious language] adopted by Maimonides in order to remove the objections of the philosophers concerning the problem of divine knowledge are not acceptable.

CHAPTER 4

. . . Now, when we consider these arguments that have been brought forth in favor of divine knowledge of particulars and the arguments adduced by the philosophers against this thesis, there is no alternative but to say that God knows particulars in one respect but does not know them in another respect. But what these respects are, would that I know!

It has been previously shown [Book II, chap. 2] that these particulars are ordered and determinate in one sense, yet contingent in another sense. Accordingly, it is evident that the sense in which God knows these particulars is the sense in which they are ordered and determinate, as is the case with the Agent Intellect, according to the results previously established. For from this aspect it is possible to have knowledge of them. On the other hand, the sense in which God does not know particulars is the sense in which they are not ordered, i.e. the sense in which they are contingent. For in the latter sense knowledge of them is not possible. However, God does know from this aspect that the events may not occur because of the freedom [of choice], with which He has endowed man to compensate for the deficiencies in the supervision coming from the heavenly bodies, as has been explained in Book II [chap. 2]. But He does not know which of the contradictory outcomes will be realized in so far as they are [genuinely] contingent affairs; for if He did, there would not be any contingency at all. [Nevertheless,] the fact that God does not have the knowledge of which possible outcome will be realized does not imply any defect in God, for perfect knowledge of some thing is the knowledge of what that thing is in reality; when the thing is not apprehended as it is, this is error, not knowledge. Hence, God knows all these things in the best manner possible; for He knows them in so far as they are ordered in a determinate and certain way, and He knows in addition that these events are contingent, in so far as they fall within the domain of human choice, [and as such He knows them] truly as contingent. Thus, God, by means of the Prophets, commands men who are about to suffer evil fortune that they mend their ways so that they will avert this punishment, as in the case of King Zedekiah who was commanded to make peace with the King of Babylonia [*Jeremiah* 38: 17–18]. Now this indicates that what God knows of future events is known by him as not necessarily occurring; however, He knows them in the sense that they are part of the general order and also as possibly not occurring in so far as they are contingent. . . .

Nor do Maimonides' arguments establish the claim that God knows more than what we have maintained and that He knows *all* particulars. The first argument maintains that God knows sub-lunar phenomena; for otherwise He would be ignorant. It is clear that on our theory there is no defect in God's knowledge of contingents; indeed, He knows them just as they are, [i.e. as contingents]. Concerning his second argument [i.e. the analogy with the artisan], we pointed out, while we were discussing this argument, that God's knowledge of particulars is the knowledge of their intelligible order from which they emanate, and no more; and this is what we have maintained here concerning this topic.

And when this point is appreciated, we shall show that none of the aforementioned arguments of the philosophers against divine knowledge of particulars is valid against our theory.

The first of these arguments of the philosophers—since God has no corporeal faculties, He has no knowledge of particulars—does not prove that God has no knowledge of the intelligible order inherent in them and in terms of which they are ordered and determinate. This argument implies only that He does not know them as particulars and as individuals. This is evident. Similarly, the second argument—God has no knowledge of particulars because they are temporal phenomena—does not refute our theory. For we have not claimed that His knowledge encompasses their temporal aspects; rather we have claimed that it is concerned with the intelligible order in terms of which they are ordered, and from this aspect they are not temporally specified. . . .

The sixth argument maintains that God cannot know generated events [i.e.

particular events]; for if He did, He would know them either *before* their occurrence or only *simultaneously* with their occurrence. If he knows them before their occurrence, His knowledge would refer to non-existents. Moreover, if this is indeed the case, either He knows them as they really are, i.e. as contingents, and then the contradictory of what He predicted will occur is still possible; or He knows definitely which alternative of two contradictory states of affairs will occur such that the other alternative is not possible. If we say that He knows them as genuine contingents, His foreknowledge of these events would be subject to change when the event in question has occurred; for prior to its occurrence the event could or could not have occurred, whereas after its occurrence this possibility has disappeared. And since the intellect is constituted by its knowledge, God's essence would be continually subject to change, which is absurd. On the other hand, if we say that He knows definitely which of two contradictory events will occur, no contingency would exist. Finally, if we say that God knows particulars only as they occur, His knowledge would always be generated and His essence subject to change. Since all of these suppositions are absurd, it follows that God does not know particulars at all.

Nevertheless, this argument does not invalidate our version of the thesis that God knows particulars. In saying that God knows particulars in so far as they are ordered and that He knows them as contingent in so far as human choice is involved, we are not subject to any of the above-mentioned absurdities. [In the first place], His knowledge does not refer to non-existents, since we maintain that His knowledge of particulars is grounded in the intelligible order pertaining to them as it is present in His mind, but not in these particulars themselves. [In the second place], it doesn't follow that His knowledge is subject to change when any of these events has occurred, for we have not claimed that His knowledge is based upon any of these events; rather it is grounded in their intelligible order in His mind. And this order is eternally in His mind and never changes. [In the third place], it doesn't follow from our hypothesis that there is no contingency [merely because] we maintain that God has foreknowledge of which of two contradictory events will occur. On our theory God knows that a particular event *should* occur given the ordering of phenomena [in the intelligible order of things], but not that it *must absolutely* occur; for God recognizes that by virtue of human choice this event might not occur, and this is the sense in which these things are contingent.

The seventh argument claims that if God had knowledge of particulars, He would have arranged them equitably and perfectly; but this is contrary to what we observe of these things, since they exhibit much injustice and disorder. This argument will be refuted when we show that the order obtaining amongst contingent affairs and the contingency exhibited in them manifests the best order and perfection possible. We have already demonstrated this in our commentary on *Job* and we shall, with God's help, prove it in Book IV [chap. 2] of this treatise. . . .

CHAPTER 5

One of the evident advantages of our theory of divine knowledge of particulars is that none of the absurdities that ensue from Maimonides' account of divine knowledge is applicable to it; i.e. the difficulties deriving from the five features that allegedly differentiate divine knowledge from human knowledge. . . .

The second feature—i.e. divine knowledge refers to the non-existent—does not follow from our account of this kind of knowledge. For we have claimed that God's knowledge of particulars as ordered is based upon the intelligible order pertaining to them which is eternally inherent in His intellect, and is not based upon these contingent things. For God does not acquire His knowledge from them; rather they acquire their existence from His knowledge of them, since their existence is an effect of the intelligible order pertaining to them inherent in the divine intellect. Hence, it doesn't follow from this that divine knowledge is grounded in non-existence; rather it is grounded in something that eternally and immutably exists. . . .

CHAPTER 6

It is now incumbent upon us to show that the theory we have established by philosophical argument is identical with the view of our Torah. It is a fundamental and pivotal belief of the Torah that there are contingent events in the world. Accordingly, the Torah commands us to perform certain things and prohibits other things. It is a fundamental principle implicit in all the Prophets that God informs them of these contingent events before they actually occur; as it is said [*Amos* 3:17], "God will not do anything without revealing His secret to His servants, the Prophets." Yet it is not necessary that any evil predicted by them must occur; as it is said [*Joel* 2:13], "God is gracious and repents of the evil." These principles are reconcilable only on the hypothesis that [firstly] these contingent events are in some sense ordered, and it is in this respect that knowledge of them is possible, but in another sense not ordered, and it is in the latter sense that they are contingent; and [secondly] that God knows all future contingents in so far as they are ordered and [in addition] knows them as contingent. It is therefore clear that the view of our Torah is identical with the theory that philosophical argument has proven with respect to divine knowledge. Moreover, it can be shown that the view of the Torah is that God knows these things in a general manner, not as particulars; for it is said [*Psalms* 33:15] "He that fashioneth the hearts of them *all,* that considered *all* their doings." That is, God created the hearts and thoughts of men *at the same time* in so far as He endowed the heavenly bodies with those patterns from which [these thoughts] are in their entirety derived. In this way God considers *all* their deeds, i.e. simultaneously, not in the sense that His knowledge refers to the particular as particular. This shows that [according to the Torah] God understands all human affairs in a general way. . . .

In short, there is nothing in the words of the Prophets that implies anything incompatible with the theory we have developed by means of philosophy. Hence, it is incumbent upon us to follow philosophy in this matter. For, when the Torah, interpreted literally, seems to conflict with doctrines that have been proven by reason, it is proper to interpret those passages according to philosophical understanding, so long as none of the fundamental principles of the Torah will be destroyed. Maimonides too followed this practice in many cases, as his famous book *The Guide of the Perplexed* shows. It is even more proper that we not disagree with philosophy when the Torah itself does not disagree with it. Maimonides relates further in Chapter 20 of Part 3 of the celebrated *Guide of the Perplexed* that some thinkers have been inclined to say that God's knowledge refers to the species and *uniformly* encompasses all members of the species and that every believer in a revealed religion and follower of reason should accept this view. This shows that Maimonides believed that this view [God knows particulars only generally] agrees with the view of the Torah. It seems too that the sage Abraham ibn Ezra was of this opinion; for in his *Commentary to the Torah* he says: "The truth is that He knows every particular generally, not as a particular." The agreement between our philosophically established theory of divine knowledge and the Torah will be more fully appreciated after we have examined the question of divine providence in the Torah, which will be treated in the next book.

SELECTED BIBLIOGRAPHY

TRANSLATIONS

Bleich, J., *Providence in the Philosophy of Gersonides*, New York, 1973.
Lassen, A., trans., *The Commentary of Levi ben Gerson (Gersonides) on the Book of Job*, New York, 1946.
Levi ben Gerson, *The Wars of the Lord*, trans.
and comm. S. Feldman, Philadelphia: The Jewish Publication Society of America, forthcoming.
Samuelson, N., trans., *The Wars of the Lord. Treatise Three: On God's Knowledge*, Toronto, 1977.

STUDIES

Feldman, S., "Gersonides on the Possibility of Conjunction with the Agent Intellect," *Association for Jewish Studies Review*, III (1978), 99–120.
Feldman, S., "Gersonides' Proofs for the Creation of the Universe," *Proceedings of the American Academy for Jewish Research*, XXXV (1967), 113–137. (Reprinted, A. Hyman, ed., *Essays in Medieval Jewish and Islamic Philosophy*, New York, 1977, 219–243.)
Feldman, S., "Platonic Themes in Gersonides' Cosmology," *S. W. Baron Jubilee Volume*, Jerusalem, 1975, 383–406.
Goldstein, B., "Astronomical and Astrological Themes in the Philosophical Works of Levi ben Gerson," *Archives Internationales d'Histoire des Sciences*, XXVI (1976), 221–224.
Kellner, M., "Gersonides and his Cultured Despisers: Arama and Abravanel," *Journal of Medieval and Renaissance Studies*, VI (1976), 269–296.
Kellner, M., "Gersonides, Providence and the Rabbinic Tradition," *Journal of the American Academy of Religion*, XLII (1974), 673–685.
Kellner, M., "R. Levi ben Gerson: A Bibliographical Essay," *Studies in Bibliography and Booklore*, XII (1979), 13–23.
Kellner, M., "Maimonides and Gersonides on Mosaic Prophecy," *Speculum*, LII (1977), 62–79.
Pines, S., *Scholasticism after Thomas Aquinas and the Teachings of Hasdai Crescas and his Predecessors*, Jerusalem, 1966, *passim* (Proceedings of the Israel Academy of Sciences and Humanities, I, 10).
Samuelson, N., "Gersonides' Account of God's Knowledge of Particulars," *Journal of the History of Philosophy*, X (1972), 399–416.
Samuelson, N., "On Knowing God: Maimonides, Gersonides, and the Philosophy of Religion," *Judaism Magazine*, XVIII (1969), 64–77.
Samuelson, N., "Philosophic and Religious Authority in the Thought of Maimonides and Gersonides," *Central Conference of American Rabbis Journal*, XVI (1969), 31–43.
Samuelson, N., "The Problem of Free Will in Maimonides, Gersonides, and Aquinas," *Central Conference of American Rabbis Journal*, XVII (1970), 2–20.
Samuelson, N., "The Problem of Future Contingents in Medieval Jewish Philosophy," *Studies in Medieval Culture*, VI–VII (1976), 71–82.
Silverman, D., "Dreams, Divination and Prophecy: Gersonides and the Problem of Precognition," *The Samuel Friedland Lectures: 1967–1974*, New York, 99–120.
Touati, C., *La pensée philosophique et théologique de Gersonide*, Paris, 1973.
Wolfson, H., "Maimonides and Gersonides on Divine Attributes as Ambiguous Terms," *Mordecai M. Kaplan Jubilee Volume*, ed. M. Davis, New York, 1953, 515–530.

ḤASDAI CRESCAS

d. ca. 1412

ᚹHEN, UNDER the influence of Maimonides' *Guide of the Perplexed* and the Hebrew translations of Averroes' commentaries on Aristotle's works, Aristotelianism spread in Jewish circles, the reaction to the study of philosophy was not far behind. While there were fideists who opposed the study of philosophy on the ground that it undermined religious beliefs and practices and while, in certain of its phases, the controversy was marked by excommunications and counter-excommunications, there were others who invoked reasoned arguments to show that philosophy's claim to have attained truth and certainty had not been made good. The most important of the philosophic critics was Ḥasdai Crescas who, in his *Light of the Lord (Or Adonai)*, presented arguments against some fundamental Aristotelian notions and went on to develop a philosophy of his own.

The literary structure of the *Light of Lord* was determined by a debate that had been initiated by Maimonides and had gone on since his days. Maimonides, in his commentary on the Mishnah (see above pp. 372–373,) had set down thirteen principles of Jewish belief and had demanded that belief in them was obligatory for every Jew. These principles were: existence of God, His unity, His incorporeality, His eternity, that only God is to be worshiped, prophecy, the superiority of Moses' prophecy to that of other prophets, divine origin of the Torah, eternity of the Torah, God's knowledge of human deeds, reward and punishment, days of the Messiah, and resurrection of the dead. While there had been predecessors who had investigated Jewish beliefs, Maimonides was the first who had attempted to formulate a set of authoritative and binding beliefs. Because of Maimonides' standing in the Jewish community, his bold innovation could not be ignored and his thirteen principles gave rise to a lively debate. There were those who accepted Maimonides' notion that there are authoritative beliefs, but differed from him concerning their content, structure, and number, and there were others who rejected the notion of beliefs altogether, holding that Judaism knows only of the commandments of the Torah.

Crescas was among those who accepted the notion that there are Jewish beliefs, but, differing with Maimonides, he presented his own version in the four books *(ma'amarim)* of the *Light of the Lord*. There are, first of all, basic principles or roots *(shorashim)* of all scriptural beliefs and they are: existence,

436

unity, and incorporeality of God (book I). These are followed by six scriptural principles *(pinnot toriyyot)* on which the validity of the Torah depends and they are: God's knowledge of existent things, providence, divine omnipotence, prophecy, human freedom, and purpose of the Torah (book II). Next come true beliefs *(emunot amitiyyot)* which every adherent of the Torah must accept and the denial of which constitutes heresy. These are divided into those that do not depend on any specific commandment and those that do. The former category consists of: creation of the world, immortality of the soul, reward and punishment, resurrection of the dead, eternity of the Torah, superiority of the prophecy of Moses, the efficacy of the Urim and Thumim worn by the High Priest (Exodus 28:30) in predicting the future, and the coming of the Messiah; the latter consists of such beliefs as the efficacy of prayer and of repentance (book III). The *Light of the Lord* concludes with thirteen questions *(de'cot u-sebarot)* ranging from whether there exists more than one world to the existence of demons (book IV). In his exposition Crescas exhibits mastery of the biblical-rabbinic tradition, the Islamic and Jewish philosophic literature, and some familiarity with late medieval Christian thought. There are also some kabbalistic influences in his work.

Of special philosophic interest is Crescas' critique of certain Aristotelian physical and metaphysical notions which Maimonides had presented (*Guide* II, Introduction) in twenty-five propositions on which he based his proofs of the existence, unity, and incorporeality of God. The Aristotelians had defined place as the inner surface of a surrounding body; Crescas spoke of space, which he identified with dimensionality. The Aristotelians had denied the existence of a vacuum; Crescas affirmed its existence. The Aristotelians had argued for the existence of one world; Crescas envisaged the existence of many. The Aristotelians had denied that an actual infinite, be it of space, number, magnitude, or time, can exist; Crescas argued for its existence.

Crescas' opinion that an actual infinite can exist put into question the Aristotelians' proofs of the existence of God. These proofs depended on the validity of the principle that an infinite regress, such as that of motions or causes and effects, is impossible; but this was the very principle that Crescas denied. However, Crescas did not reject altogether the possibility of proving the existence of God, since the proof from necessity and contingency (see below, p. 526) is independent of the contested principle and, hence, valid. Against Maimonides (see above, pp. 381 ff.), Crescas affirmed that positive attributes can be predicated of God.

One of the more enigmatic discussions is Crescas' account of human freedom. While Maimonides and Gersonides had, each in his own way, safeguarded the voluntary character of human actions, Crescas was more deterministic. Affirming that every event in the universe is the result of prior causes and is necessitated by divine omniscience, Crescas also held that human actions are produced by a decision of the will. However, this decision is determined by prior causes. Crescas tried to mitigate this determinism by listing the commandments of the Torah, training, and similar factors as causes determining the will. More formally, Crescas expressed his opinion by holding that, while the will is determined with respect to its causes, it is contingent in its nature. In his philosophy of man, Crescas held that the soul rather then the acquired intellect is immortal and that human happiness and immortality come to be through love and fear of God rather than through intellectual speculation.

Some of Crescas' ideas influenced Renaissance and early modern philosophy. Giovanni Francesco Pico della Mirandola, in his *Examen Doctrinae Vanitatis Gentium,* drew upon Crescas for his discussion of such topics as vacuum, place, motion and time, and it is possible that Giordano Bruno was influenced by Crescas in some of his critique of Aristotle. Spinoza explicitly mentions Crescas' proof of the existence of God (Letter XII) and his discussion of the infinite and other notions was influenced by Crescas.

Born in Barcelona, Ḥasdai Crescas was active in Spain during the second half of the fourteenth century and the first decade of the fifteenth. His times were marked by persecutions of the Jews and by false charges against them. In 1367, Crescas, then a merchant and communal leader in Barcelona, was imprisoned with others on the made-up charge of desecrating the Host; but he was soon released. In 1383 he was a member of a delegation that negotiated the renewal of Jewish privileges with Pedro IV, king of Aragon. With the accession of Juan I to the throne of Aragon, in 1387, Crescas became closely associated with the court and received the title "member of the royal household." Shortly thereafter he moved from Barcelona to Saragossa, where he became the rabbi of the community. Through royal decree he received the right to invoke the ban of excommunication and to prosecute and punish informers against Jews. Reports that he became chief-rabbi of Aragon are not confirmed by documentary evidence.

The year 1391 was marked by widespread anti-Jewish riots, massacres, and the destruction of Jewish communities throughout Spain. While Crescas, because of his connection with the court, was safe, his only son suffered a martyr's death in Barcelona. The queen and Crescas had sent letters to the authorities in Barcelona asking for the protection of Crescas' family, but the letters arrived too late. Crescas described the events of 1391 and his son's death in a letter to the Jewish community of Avignon. After the persecutions ceased, Crescas occupied himself with reconstructing the Jewish communities of Spain, having received royal permission to collect funds and resettle the communities of Barcelona and Valencia. He also undertook to reform the administrative structure of the Jewish community of Saragossa. Crescas' influence can be seen from the fact that he was consulted by the chief-rabbinate of France (1391) and of Navarre. Crescas died ca. 1412.

Possibly because of his many responsibilities, Crecas' literary output was rather modest. To counteract the missionizing efforts of Christians he wrote, in Catalan, "Refutation of the Dogmas of the Christians;" but the work has only been preserved in a Hebrew translation. Another polemical work against Christianity is cited by a later author, but this work is no longer extant.

Crescas had planned to write a comprehensive work entitled *Lamp of God (Ner Elohim)* as a kind of counterpart to Maimonides' *Mishneh Torah* and *Guide of the Perplexed* (see above, p. 373). The first part, *Lamp of the Commandment (Ner Miṣvah)*, which was to deal with legal matters, never came to be; the second part is *Light of the Lord*.

In the chapter of the *Light of the Lord* from which the following selection is taken, Crescas investigates the true, that is, the ultimate purpose of the Torah. Convinced that there can be only one such purpose, he considers four possibilities: (a) moral perfection, (b) bodily perfection, (c) intellectual perfection, and (d) perfection of the soul (cf. Maimonides, *Guide of the Perplexed,* III, 27 and 54). In the section preceding the selection, Crescas discusses the first two of these perfections, coming to the conclusion that they cannot be the ultimate purpose of the Torah. For the Torah seeks to bring about eternal perfection, that is, immortality, while moral and bodily perfections are temporal. In this preliminary discussion, he similarly rules out intellectual perfection as the ultimate goal, since the intellect, while it is joined to the body, thinks intermittently, so that it is temporal as well.

The selection begins with the possibility that the perfection of opinions, that is, intellectual perfection, may be the ultimate purpose of the Torah. This, in fact, had been the view of such Aristotelians as Maimonides and Gersonides, and this is the view which Crescas combats. Drawing upon the psychological theories of Aristotle and his commentators, the Jewish (as well as the Islamic) Aristotelians had maintained that the human intellect begins as the material intellect and can become, through philosophic speculation, the acquired intellect, an incorporeal substance. While there were various interpretations of this general scheme, particularly of the nature of the material intellect, Aristotelians were generally agreed that ultimate human happiness, and with it immortality, comes to be through the acquired intellect.

This general theory, Crescas reports, had two interpretations: (a) that of Gersonides, according to which the intellectual apprehension of material and immaterial substances brings about happiness and immortality, and (b) that of Maimonides, according to which only the intellectual apprehension of God and incorporeal intelligences brings about man's ultimate state. Invoking biblical verses, rabbinic sayings, as well as philosophic arguments, Crescas sets out to show that both versions of the contested theory undermine the fundamental principles of Torah and Tradition. More than that, he argues that the Aristotelian theory of the acquired intellect is philosophically untenable. Crescas' arguments against the Aristotelians are subtle and complex. Here it should only be noted that Crescas holds that, of the varying interpretations of the material intellect, that of Themistius is normative for all Aristotelians. According to this, the material intellect is an incorporeal substance. In fact, Averroes had rejected this interpretation in favor of his own, and Crescas found it possible to use some of Averroes' arguments against Themistius for his own purposes. Similarly, Crescas, while combatting the overall positions of Maimonides and Gersonides, finds some of their arguments useful for his own needs.

Having completed his refutation of the Aristotelians' theory that the perfection of opinions is the ultimate purpose of the Torah, Crescas goes on to present his own view. According to Crescas, the perfection of the soul is the ultimate purpose of the Torah and this perfection is brought about by love and fear of God, not by intellectual apprehension. Once again, he supports his opinion by biblical verses, rabbinic sayings, and philosophic arguments. Crescas bases his position on four propositions (see below, pp. 444–445), explaining each one at length.

Crescas' condensed and technical exposition, which, at times, reads like lecture notes, makes the translation of the *Light of the Lord* quite difficult. As an aid to the reader of this volume, the translation is somewhat paraphrastic. It is based on the more literal translation of W. Harvey.

THE LIGHT OF THE LORD

Book II, Part 6, Chapter 1
The Explanation of the True Purpose of the Torah

The perfection of opinions might be considered more essential for this purpose [namely, the true purpose of the Torah which is to lead man to happiness and immortality]. We must elaborate on this statement since, it appears to us, some of the philosophers of our nation have stumbled on it. [Through this investigation] we shall be directed aright to understand the true purpose of the Torah.

We say that it is agreed among [these philosophers] that the intellect becomes a substance through the intelligibles it apprehends and that from them an acquired intellect, which is not intermingled with the material intellect, comes to be. [And] since this intellect is immaterial, it survives eternally, in spite of the fact that it is generated and comes to be; for this intellect has no cause for corruption. For, as is made clear in the *Metaphysics,* matter is the cause of corruption and evil. Accordingly, eternal happiness consists in the apprehension of the acquired intelligibles; and the more [intelligible] concepts one apprehends, the greater in quality will be his happiness. The happiness will be still greater when the [intelligible] concepts are more precious in themselves.[1]

They are also agreed that whoever attains [this kind of] happiness will rejoice and delight after death in what he has apprehended. From the pleasure we attain in this life when we apprehend the intelligibles, they estimate that the pleasure must be even greater after death, when we understand the intelligibles simultaneously and continuously.[2] [From this extrapolation] it follows that there is no

Based on text and translation in: W. Harvey, *Crescas' Critique of the Theory of the Acquired Intellect* (Doctoral Dissertation, Columbia University, 1973). By permission of the author.

1. Apprehension of God and other incorporeal substances produces greater happiness than apprehension of corporeal substances.

2. In this life we apprehend the intelligibles sequentially and intermittently, in the next life simultaneously and continuously.

relation[3] between the pleasure derived from the lesser intelligibles and that derived from the noble intelligibles, for pleasure in the apprehension of the intelligibles in this life differs exceedingly from that in the afterlife.

This is the general opinion that they share and on which they agree, but we have found that they differ [in their particular interpretations]:[4]

[Version I] Some think that this happiness will be greater the more numerous the [intelligible] concepts [apprehended], regardless of whether they are [intelligible concepts] of material or immaterial existent things. They hold this because they think that the order of all existent things is contained in the Agent Intellect, so that whoever comes closer to the Agent Intellect through the apprehension of intelligibles, [be they of material or immaterial things,] will attain a higher degree [of happiness].

[Version II] Others think that only that survives which is apprehended truly by the human intellect concerning the existence of God and His angels, and the more one apprehends, the greater his degree [of happiness]. It appears that [this interpretation is based on the view] that the intellect becomes a substance only through the apprehension of immaterial beings and that it becomes eternal [only through this kind of apprehension]. The more [the intellect] apprehends of these immaterial beings, the greater will be its happiness.

These two opinions not only destroy the Torah and uproot the principles of Tradition, but they can also be disproved by philosophic speculation.

That they destroy the principles of the Torah and Tradition can be seen from the following arguments:

(1) It is one of the principles of the Torah and Tradition that man attains eternal life by performing the commandments. The Mishnah (Kiddushin, I:10) teaches this explicitly when it states that "good will be done to him, who observes one commandment" and the Gemara explains this to mean that this good is "the good reserved for the righteous" [namely, eternal life]. According to the opinions of the philosophers, by contrast, the practical commandments are only prerequisites for [the apprehension of] the intelligibles and once the intellect has become a substance through [the apprehension of] the intelligibles, there is no longer any benefit in performing the commandments. . . .[5]

That these opinions are false from the point of view of philosophic speculation can also be seen from the following arguments:

(1) According to these opinions, the Torah's purpose for man would be addressed to another species:[6]

(1a) According to these opinions, the acquired intellect which remains [after death] is immaterial and not intermingled with man. Hence, it is neither his form

3. I.e., comparison.

4. The first of the versions that follows seems to be that of Gersonides, the second that of Maimonides.

5. Here follow other arguments from the Torah and Tradition designed to show that the afterlife is contingent upon the performance of the commandments, not upon the apprehension of the intelligibles.

6. The meaning of this rather enigmatic statement is as follows: the happiness intended by the Torah is for man, a material substance composed of soul and body; yet according to the philosophers, it is for the acquired intellect, an immaterial substance. Now, since material and immaterial substances differ in species, it would follow that the Torah is intended for the acquired intellect, not for man as he exists in the here and now. This is absurd. There now follow arguments to show the absurdity of the opinion of the philosophers.

nor an accident conjoined with him. This is the case, because this intellect has been posited as immaterial and as becoming a substance through the intelligibles.[7]

(1b) Since it has been laid down that [the acquired intellect] survives death, the corruption of man may be conceived without the corruption of this intellect. If [of two things,] the corruption of one is possible without the corruption of the other, and [the first] is not intermingled [with the second], [the first] is necessarily a different individual [from the second]. And if [of two things,] one is a different individual from the other and is not joined with it, the former cannot be the form of the latter.

(1c) The corruption of the immaterial [intellect] may surely be conceived without the corruption of man.

Since, then, it has been shown to be true that [the acquired intellect] is not the form of man, it has been shown thereby that the purpose which [according to the opinions of the philosophers] the Torah has for man, namely the immortality of the intellect is for something else [that is, another species].

That the immortality of the intellect would be for a species other than man can easily be demonstrated from the nature of each one. For man by his nature goes toward corruption, so that it is impossible that an individual man should be eternal. By contrast, the acquired intellect is posited to be eternal according to its nature, so that its corruption is impossible by its very essence. And corruptible and eternal things differ in species.

(2) It is far-fetched as far as divine justice is concerned that reward and punishment be for someone other than the one who serves God or rebels against Him.[8]

(3) The proposition that the intellect becomes a substance through its [intelligible] concepts, as a result of which it comes to exist separate from the material intellect is clearly false for the following reasons:

(3a) Since [the acquired intellect] has been posited as immaterial, it does not possess matter as an underlying substratum and as something from which it comes to be. But since it has [also] been posited that [this intellect] is generated, it follows that it must come to be from nothing. But this conclusion is clearly false, since it is impossible that something comes to be out of nothing, and this principle has no exception.[9] The only alternative that remains is that the acquired intellect comes to be by way of a miracle from the absolute power of God.[10]

(3b) This proposition is self-contradictory. For when it is laid down that "the intellect becomes a substance through its [intelligible] concepts," the intellect to which this proposition refers cannot be the material intellect. For it has already been assumed that this intellect [namely, the one that becomes a substance through its intelligible concepts] is separate from the material intellect. But should the proposition refer to the acquired intellect, then, when we say that [this intellect] becomes a substance through its [intelligible] concepts, we have [in fact] affirmed that it exists before it comes to be. By God, this is equivalent to saying that something brings itself into existence. This is obviously false and absurd.

(3c) That the intellect should become a substance through its [intelligible]

---

7. The implied conclusion is that since the acquired intellect is neither the form of man nor one of his accidents, but an immaterial substance, it must be a different species.

8. Hence reward and punishment cannot be contingent upon intellectual apprehension.

9. Literally, and this is one of the impossibles that have a fixed nature.

10. This cannot be the case since the acquired intellect comes to be through a natural process, not a miracle.

concepts is clearly false, for there is no escape from the following disjunction: either (3c1) intellectual apprehension, which is the act of apprehending the intelligible, is identical with the intelligible itself, as the philosophers agree [when they hold that] the intellect, the one who apprehends the intelligibles, and the intelligibles are identical,[11] or (3c2) [these three] are not identical.

If (3c1) intellectual apprehension and the intelligible are identical, one of the following two absurdities would necessarily follow:

Either (3c1a) one intelligible is identical with any other intelligible, from which it would follow that all intelligibles are identical. In that case, intellectual apprehension would be one and undifferentiated for all intelligibles. This is clearly absurd, since, in that case, someone who apprehends many intelligibles would have no advantage or preeminence over someone who apprehends only one intelligible.

Or (3c1b) one intelligible is not identical with another intelligible and the act of apprehending one intelligible differs from the act of apprehending another intelligible. From [this assumption] it follows necessarily that when this intellect has become a substance through one intelligible and afterwards apprehends another intelligible, [it becomes another substance, and] there will be as many substances [that is, intellects] as there are intelligibles. Or, alternately, [this intellect remains the same, but] one intelligible is changed into another and becomes a substance through another. As a result, it becomes another substance different in species from the previous one. This is completely absurd. In addition, since [on this assumption] the essential form of man would continuously be produced anew, it would follow that a given man would change and alter from essence to essence. This is completely absurd and false. . . .

From all these arguments the absurdity of these [two] opinions[12] can clearly be seen. However, the first opinion is more reprehensible in one respect, the second in another:

[Version I] According to the first opinion, immortality depends on the apprehension of the intelligibles which belong to philosophy. As a result, the fundamental principles of the Torah would be derivatives[13] of philosophy. It would follow then that if someone apprehends one of the intelligibles belonging to geometry, he would live eternally, inasmuch as these intelligibles exist in the Agent Intellect. But this is fantasy and invention, lacking any sense.

[Version II] According to the second opinion, the intellectual apprehension of the essence of the incorporeal substances is not through affirmation, but through negation, as Maimonides has explained at length.[14] From this it follows that the apprehension [of the incorporeal substances] is imperfect and, even more, that [the intelligible] would not be in the intellect as [its object] is outside the intellect.[15] I wish that I knew, how this imperfect intelligible which does not exist outside the soul [that is, the intellect] as it exists within it, can become a substance.[16]

11. Cf. Maimonides, *Guide of the Perplexed*, I, 68.

12. The two versions of the opinions of the philosophers.

13. Literally, conclusions

14. See above, pp. 381 ff.

15. In the case of corporeal substances the intelligible in the mind corresponds exactly to the form of the substance outside the mind, since the intelligible signifies positively. In the case of the intelligibles of incorporeal substances, there is no such exact correspondence, since these intelligibles signify through negation.

16. The point of this somewhat awkward phrase is that the intellect cannot become a substance through an imperfect intelligible.

But the philosophers made up these opinions as if the nature of truth had compelled them to believe in the immortality of the souls [that is, the intellects] and they conceived thoughts and multiplied words that multiply vanity[17] and some of the philosophers of our nation strayed after them, and they did not perceive nor did it enter their mind how they were razing thereby the wall of the edifice of the Torah and breaching its hedges, even though this theory [namely, that of the philosophers] is groundless.

Since then it has been shown that that purpose [namely, human happiness and immortality] is not consequent upon the perfection of opinions, as the philosophers had laid down, and since it has also been shown that the other perfections [namely, bodily perfection and the moral virtues] are only prerequisites for [the acquisition of] the intelligibles, it follows that the purpose [of the Torah] is not primarily and essentially consequent upon either opinions or actions. But since this purpose [namely, human happiness and immortality] is consequent upon the Torah, as Tradition teaches, it follows necessarily that this purpose is consequent primarily and essentially upon that part [of the Torah] which is not concerned with opinions alone, or with actions alone. When we examined the Torah and its parts, we found in it a part, small in quantity [but] large in quality, which is not concerned with opinions alone or with actions alone, namely, [that concerned with] the love of God and true fear of Him. And I affirm that this is [the part of the Torah] which necessarily brings about this purpose according to every supporting argument, be it according to Torah and Tradition or according to philosophic speculation.

[That love and fear of God bring about human happiness and immortality is clear] from the Torah when it states explicitly (Deut. 10:12): "And now, Israel, what doth the Lord thy God require of thee, but to fear the Lord thy God, to walk in all His ways, and to love Him, and to serve the Lord thy God with all thy heart and with all thy soul." . . .[18]

[From these verses] it is apparent that the [ultimate] purpose sought by the Torah consists of obeying God, by performing his commandments with great ardor and by not transgressing his prohibition by exercising great care—all this with joy and gladness. [This kind of conduct] is the secret of worship, love, and true fear of God, as is stated frequently in biblical verses and in the sayings of the Rabbis. Since [this kind of conduct] is the [ultimate] purpose sought by the Torah and since it is evident that happiness and immortality are consequent upon it, it is also clear, according to Torah and Tradition, that this purpose [that is, this kind of conduct] will bring about happiness and immortality.

[That love and fear of God produce happiness and immortality can also be demonstrated] through philosophic speculation itself, once we have laid down three propositions, concerning whose truth there is no doubt:

(1) First proposition: the soul of man, which is his form, is a spiritual substance disposed toward intellectual apprehension, [but] not intellectually apprehending in actuality in virtue of itself.

(2) Second proposition: someone who is perfect, owing to his essence, loves good and perfection and desires it. And love and pleasure in desire are according to the [degree of] perfection.

(3) Third proposition: Love and pleasure in desire differ from intellectual apprehension.

17. Cf. Eccles. 6:11

18. Here follow other biblical verses showing that love and fear of God bring about human happiness and immortality.

We shall add a fourth proposition which is self-evident, namely (4) perfection of the soul and the soul's adhesion to God bring about this goal [namely, human happiness and immortality].

How these propositions are shown to be true, I shall now state:

(1) First proposition:[19]

(1a) We began by stating that the soul of man is "his form." This is self-evident, for when the soul is separated from the body, man ceases to exist in such a way that the definition [of man] can no longer be truly predicated of him.[20]

(1b) Then we stated that the soul is "a substance." This is something that has been demonstrated in the first book of the *Physics* where it has been shown that the term "substance" applies primarily to form rather than to matter.

(1c) We stated next that the soul is "spiritual." This is clear, since the soul possesses faculties that it uses through an exercise of will apart from any of the senses, such as imagination, memory and intellect.[21]

(1d) Finally we stated that the soul is "disposed toward intellectual apprehension." This is clear since it has been shown that the soul is a substratum for the rational faculty, inasmuch as this faculty inheres in the body through the intermediacy of the soul. For it is inescapable that the substratum of this disposition [that is, the rational faculty] be either (1) an intellect, (2) a soul or (3) a body, since there is no fourth kind of existence here on earth.[22]

That this substratum cannot be (1) an intellect, as some of the commentators on Aristotle's works have thought,[23] is clear from the following arguments:

(1a) First, if the substratum of this disposition were an intellect, this disposition would be intermingled with an intellectual form. As a result, it would be incapable of apprehending all forms, for something can only receive all things if it is devoid of all of them. But, since we have laid down that the intellect is a substratum for this disposition [that is, the rational faculty], it would be the case that, when this intellect receives the intelligibles, it would become a substance through them by receiving them as intermingled. But this is impossible, since [according to the original assumption] this intellect is not devoid of all forms.[24]

By contrast, when we posit the soul as the substratum of this [intellectual] disposition, we posit the soul as a condition for the existence of this disposition, but we do not say that the soul is affected [that is, it becomes a substance] by the reception of the intelligibles. The reason is that the substrata of a disposition to receive

19. Crescas now goes on to explain the parts of the first proposition.

20. While a living man and a corpse may share the shape of man, the definition of man applies only to a living human being.

21. Sense perception is involuntary and totally corporeal; imagining, remembering and thinking are voluntary and not totally dependent on the body. This is what Crescas has in mind when he says that the soul is "spiritual."

22. Crescas now proceeds by a kind of *reductio ad absurdum* proof. Envisaging the possibilities that intellect, soul, or body could be the substratum for the intellectual faculty, he disproves that intellect or body can be that substratum. Hence it must be soul. The numbers that follow, (1), (2), (3), refer to these three possibilities.

23. The commentators on Aristotle disagreed concerning the nature of the material intellect (see above, p. 295) which is here considered as the substratum of the rational faculty. Crescas identifies the interpretation of Themistius, that the material intellect is an immaterial substance, with the general opinion of the commentators on Aristotle.

24. This argument is a variation of an argument used by Averroes to disprove Themistius' conception of the material intellect. The point of the argument is that, were the substratum of this disposition an intellect, it would possess an intellectual form of its own. But since a substance can only have one form, the substratum cannot receive the intelligibles.

things vary greatly. In the case of some, the substratum is affected in some way by the species of that which it apprehends, as is the case with the sense of touch. In the case of others, the substratum receives [its objects] in such a way that it is not affected by the species of that which it apprehends, as is the case when the sense of sight receives colors. For in the case of sight, [the eye] does not receive the shade of the perceived color, yet it is affected by it in some fashion, so that after [the eye] has a strong sensation, it will not have a weak sensation. The common sense is affected by the objects it apprehends even less, for its apprehension is spiritual. The imagination is still more spiritual, and for this reason the imagination is consequent upon our will. And finally, the intellectual disposition [is so spiritual that it] receives its objects [namely the intelligibles] in such a manner that its substratum is not affected by them at all. Thus it is possible that the intellectual disposition receives all the forms, when it is posited that [its] substratum is the soul.

However, if it is posited that the intellect [is the substratum of the intellectual disposition], it would be impossible to affirm of it [that it receives all forms]. For if we were to suppose that the [intellectual] disposition receives the intelligibles in such a way that they are not intermingled with the substratum [that is, the intellect],[25] the following disjunction is unavoidable: either (a) the substratum would be intellectually apprehending, or (b) [the substratum] would not be intellectually apprehending. Now it is false [by definition] that the intellect is not intellectually apprehending, so [that the only alternative that remains is] that it is intellectually apprehending. But if we posit some intelligible which the disposition receives, it would necessarily follow that this intelligible would be in the intellect simultaneously in potentiality and in actuality, and this is false. Unless, by God, one were to concoct that there can be an intelligible which has no relation or connection with the intelligibles which the [intellectual] disposition receives. And this is clearly ludicrous and absurd. Hence, it is clear that the intellect cannot be the substratum of this disposition.

(1b) Second,[26] if the substratum for this disposition were an intellect, it would be inescapable, that it be either(1b1) generated or (1b2) not generated.

If (1b1) it were generated, it would, in turn, be inescapable that it be generated either (1b1a) from some other substratum, or (1b1b) out of nothing.

If (1b1a) [the intellect as substratum for the disposition were generated] from some other substratum, it would necessarily follow that this other substratum is subject to change, in order that the substratum [of the disposition] may come to be from it. But, since it has been shown that everything subject to change must be a body, it follows necessarily that [the prior substratum] must be a body. Now, since it is self-evident that something incorporeal cannot come from something corporeal, it would necessarily follow that the substratum [of the disposition] would also be corporeal. But this conclusion contradicts the assumption that the substratum [of the disposition] is an intellect [namely, that it is incorporeal]. Since this contradiction follows from the assumption that [the substratum of the disposition] is generated, it is the conclusion of this argument that [the substratum] cannot be generated.

25. Having disposed of the possibility that, if the material intellect is the substratum of the intelligibles, it receives these intelligibles as intermingled with it, Crescas now considers the possibility that this intellect (as substratum) receives the intelligibles as existing in separation from it.

26. Here follow further arguments that the substratum of the intellectual disposition cannot be an intellect.

If then, the substratum of the disposition is not generated [see above, 1b2], it must be either (1b2a) immaterial or (1b2b) material:[27]

If (1b2b) it is material,[28] it follows necessarily that the intellect of a given man must have been hidden and concealed in matter before he came to be. And since the intellect of [this] man from which that matter came to be became apparent in him, it would be necessary that there is another intellect in him. Furthermore this must also be the case with respect to the matter out of which that matter was generated, and so on to infinity. And it would necessarily follow that all generated and corruptible matters would possess an infinite number of intellects. By God, the only other alternative would be that the intellect is transferred from without when matter comes to be and it would be hidden in matter until its actions appeared. And this is absurd and ludicrous.[29]

If, on the other hand, we assume (1b2a) that the substratum of the disposition is immaterial, then the intellect of Ruben differs from that of Simon in such a way that either (1b2a1) their forms are different or (1b2a2) [the intellects of the two] do not differ in this fashion.

If (1b2a1) we suppose that the two intellects differ, then they must necessarily differ in species, for it is inconceivable in the case of immaterial beings that they should agree in species, but differ as individuals—as has been demonstrated in its place. But it is also false that the two intellects differ in species, since in that case the individuals belonging to the same species would differ in species. If then the intellect of Ruben and the intellect of Simon differ neither in species nor as individuals, then the forms of individuals belonging to the same species would be one in number[30] and an individual member of a species would be identical with another member of that species and vice versa. In addition, this one intellect would be simultaneously in potentiality and actuality, inasmuch as the intelligibles which Ruben has in potentiality, Simon can have in actuality. Furthermore, individual members of the species would not require sense perception in order to acquire the intelligibles, as long as one member of the species would employ his senses in order to acquire these intelligibles.

It is evident then that many absurdities would follow were we to posit that the substratum of this disposition is an intellect. It necessarily follows then that the substratum must be either (3) a body, or (2) a soul.[31]

If we assume that this substratum is a body, it is clear that this substratum could not receive [this disposition] without some intermediary. For it is inconceivable that a body should lack those forms which a body by its very nature receives without an intermediary. For this reason it would follow that were a body to receive this disposition without an intermediary,[32] all bodies would possess an intellect. [This is absurd.] On the other hand, if we posit (2) that the substratum [of this disposition] is a soul, it is clear that [this soul] is not the substratum of [the disposition] in virtue of

27. Literally, it must be something immaterial (or incorporeal) or not immaterial (or incorporeal).

28. Literally, not immaterial (or incorporeal).

29. This argument is obscure.

30. If the intellects of Ruben and Simon etc. would differ neither in species nor as individuals, there would be only one intellect for all men.

31. Crescas now returns to the remaining two alternatives. See above, p. 445 (1d).

32. If a body would receive the intellectual disposition without an intermediary, this disposition would be a form belonging to a body in virtue of itself, and, hence, all bodies would possess an intellect.

itself, for it is not the nature of forms, that some forms are the substratum of other forms, unless it be through the intermediacy of matter.[33] From all this it is clear that the substratum of this disposition is a soul through the intermediacy of the body.

In this manner we have verified our expression that "the soul of man is a substance disposed toward intellectual apprehension."

We said "disposed" since the faculty of disposition inheres in the soul.

We said "not intellectually apprehending in virtue of itself," even though our saying "disposed" would indicate that it is not [apprehending] in actuality. For this additional phrase indicates that the underlying substance [that is the soul] does not become constituted as a substance through intellectual apprehension. And the feet of some of our predecessors stumbled on this phrase. For they thought that the substratum of the disposition is a substance outside the soul.[34] But if this assumed external substance were to become a substance through intellectual apprehension, it would change from one essence to another. And the assertion that the acquired intelligibles become a substance apart from the substratum and that a separate intellect [that is, the acquired intellect] comes to be from them is groundless, as is clear from our previous discussion.

This is sufficient, in keeping with brevity, for establishing the truth of the first proposition.

(2) The second proposition[35] is demonstrated as follows: It is well known that God is the source and fountain of all perfections and that God in virtue of His perfection, which is His essence, loves the good. This is apparent from his actions in bringing the universe in its entirety into existence, from His preserving it, and from His continuous recreation of it—and all this by virtue of his simple will. From this it follows necessarily that love of good is an essential property of perfection. It also follows from this that the greater the perfection, the greater is the love and the pleasure in desire. This agrees very well with what is related in the Torah, for when it mentions the Patriarchs' love for God it uses the term *ahabah* (love) as in the phrase (Isaiah 41:8) "Abraham *ohabi* (who loves me)" and in the commandments it also uses *ahabah* (love). But when the Torah mentions God's love for the Patriarchs it uses the term *ḥesheq* (passionate love) which indicates the strength of the love, saying (Deut. 10:15) "yet the Lord passionately loved *(ḥashaq)* your fathers." Now this is among the things that point to the truth of what we have said. For it appears that the love is proportionate to the good that is loved, and that the greater the good, the greater the love. But if the good is infinite in greatness, it is appropriate that the love is also infinite. This might bring one to think that man's love for God should be infinitely great and that consequently [the Torah] should have applied the term *ḥesheq* (passionate love) in describing the Patriarchs' love for God and the term *ahabah* (love) in describing His love for them. Yet, since love is an essential property of perfection and since God's perfection is infinitely great, God's love for the good is greater [than that of man], even though the good He loves is of a very low degree. This is sufficient for the second proposition.

(3) The third proposition is self-evident from the definition of its terms. For *will*

33. If the soul were a form by itself it could not receive the intellectual disposition, another form. But since the soul belongs to a body, it can receive the intellectual disposition.

34. The Aristotelians held, according to Crescas, that the material intellect that is the substratum of the disposition is an incorporeal substance. (See above, p. 439.) It would then be the case that the material intellect and the acquired intellect would be distinct substances, while it should be the case that the acquired intellect is, in some sense, the actualized material intellect.

35. See above, p. 444.

is nothing other than the aggregate and the interrelation of the appetitive and imaginative faculties, namely, the agreement concerning things desired, and the pleasure of desire is going to be proportionate to the interrelation. Intellectual apprehension, however, consists of conception and judgment,[36] both of which belong to the rational faculty. All of this has been demonstrated in the *De Anima*. Since the rational faculty differs from the appetitive and imaginative faculties, it has been shown to be true that love and pleasure in desire differ from intellectual apprehension. This is the third proposition.

These propositions having been verified, I say that, since it has been demonstrated in the first proposition that the soul of man is a spiritual substance, immortality after separation [from the body] is possible for it. The reason is that since the soul is immaterial, it has none of the causes of corruption. And existence in separation [from the body] is possible for it, since it is a rational substance. And we observe that this substance exercises intellectual apprehension with additional power when the corporeal organs are weak. This is one of the observations indicating that the soul can exist by itself and that it does not pass away as other forms do. [For these forms pass away] when the things of which they are the forms pass away. Since, then the soul can exist by itself and since it can exist in separation from the thing of which it is the form [namely, the body], it necessarily has eternal existence according to its nature. For the soul is devoid of materiality which is the cause of corruption, inasmuch as passive faculties do not acquiesce to the active faculties, as has been explained in its place.

Since it has been shown in the second proposition that the love of the good and pleasure in it is proportionate to the perfection [of the lover], it has become clear that the perfection [of the lover] will be proportionate to the degree of the good loved. From this it follows that [man's] love of God, Who is infinite good, is necessary for the greatest conceivable perfection of the soul.

Since it has been shown in the third proposition that love and pleasure in it differ from intellectual apprehension, what is essential for the perfection of the soul is something other than intellectual apprehension, namely, love. Now it is evident that love will bring about adhesion to God, for even in the case of natural things it is clear that love and mutual attraction are the cause of their perfection and unity. Indeed, one of the ancients [Empedocles] thought that love is the principle of generation and combination, while hatred is the principle of corruption and separation. [If this is the case for natural things,] how much more will it be the case for spiritual things that love and agreement among them will give rise to adhesion and unity. And since it has previously been demonstrated and will be further demonstrated in book three, God willing, that God's love for the good is immense, it is evident that the greater the love between God and man, the greater and stronger will be the adhesion.

Since it has been established in the fourth proposition that the perfection of the soul and its adhesion to God must bring about this purpose [namely human happiness and immortality], it is undoubtedly clear that philosophic speculation itself agrees with what has been set down clearly according to the Torah and Tradition, namely, that true love brings about this [ultimate] purpose, which is the eternal survival [of the soul]. This principle has been accepted by the [Jewish] nation. We were reared on it and the Torah has enlightened us concerning it. It also agrees with philosophic speculation and does not contradict it. . . .

36. These are the first two activities of the intellect.

SELECTED BIBLIOGRAPHY

TRANSLATION

Wolfson, H., *Crescas' Critique of Aristotle: Problems of Aristotle's Physics in Jewish and* *Arabic Philosophy*, Cambridge, Mass., 1929.

STUDIES

Bloch, P., *Die Willensfreiheit von Chasdai Kreskas*, Munich, 1879.

Guttmann, J., "Chasdai Creskas als Kritiker der Aristotelischen Physik," *Festschrift zum 70. Geburtstag Jacob Guttmanns*, Leipzig, 1915, 23–54.

Guttmann, J., "Das Problem der Willensfreiheit bei Hasdai Crescas und den islamischen Aristotelikern," *Jewish Studies in Memory of George A. Kohut*, New York, 1935, 326–349.

Harvey, W., *Crescas' Critique of the Theory of the Acquired Intellect* (Doctoral Dissertation, Columbia University), 1973.

Joel, M., *Don Chasdai Creskas religionsphilosophische Lehren*, Breslau, 1866.

Pines, S., *Scholasticism after Thomas Aquinas and the Teachings of Ḥasdai Crescas and his Predecessors, Proceedings of the Israel Academy of Sciences and Humanities*, I, 10, 1967.

Rabinovitch, N. L., "Rabbi Ḥasdai Crescas (1340–1410) on Numerical Infinites," *Isis*, LXI (1970), 224–230.

Waxman, M., *The Philosophy of Don Ḥasdai Crescas*, New York, 1920 (Reprint, A.M.S., 1966).

Wolfson, H., "Crescas on the Problem of Divine Attributes," *Jewish Quarterly Review* n. s., VII (1916), 1–44, 175–221.

Wolfson, H., "Notes on Crescas' Definition of Time," *Jewish Quarterly Review* n. s., X (1919), 1–17.

Wolfson, H., "Studies in Crescas," *Proceedings of the American Academy for Jewish Research*, V (1933–34), 155–175. (Reprinted in: A. Hyman, ed., *Essays in Medieval Jewish and Islamic Philosophy*, New York, 1977.)

Latin Philosophy in the Thirteenth Century

THE THIRTEENTH CENTURY is often regarded as "The Golden Age of Scholastic Philosophy." It was the age of the *summae,* magisterial and comprehensive syntheses ranging over a wide domain of theology and philosophy. Two movements stemming from the later twelfth century provided foundations for these intellectual monuments, so often compared to the great cathedrals built during the same period. One is the rise of the universities and the other is the reception of Aristotle. A third factor, more imponderable in its effect, was the creation of the mendicant, or begging orders of friars, especially the Dominicans and Franciscans. Their prominence may have given to theology a somewhat greater sway over philosophical developments than would otherwise have been the case.

The universities provided institutional regularity and *esprit de corps* for one of the most demanding intellectual methods in the history of philosophy. The last half of the twelfth century saw the emergence of a few major centers of learning out of the scattered monastic and cathedral schools, along with the formation by masters and students of typical guild associations, or, as they came to be called, universities. Although the student-dominated Italian universities were somewhat earlier, most relevant to the career of philosophy was the University of Paris, which received royal and papal protection during the first two decades of the thirteenth century, at about the same time that Oxford also won its charters. What was at stake in this movement was, as against local secular authority, the right to autonomous clerical jurisdiction and the regulation of living conditions. As against local clerical authority what was gained was the right to license teachers, to regulate the curriculum, and to regulate educational conditions. Within this framework, students participated in two types of instruction. The lecture or exposition was a preliminary reading-through of a prescribed text with some explication of obscure passages. More important was the "question" or disputation, in which difficult problems were debated in set form by students and masters, and then resolved by the master. Public disputations sponsored by the university were held on some feast days, and twice a year there were "open" or "quodlibetal" disputations in which burning issues were aired. But the student engaged in many more than these—indeed, practice disputations were a favorite form of entertainment. This popularity of the disputation expresses the triumph of dialectic over the other branches of the *trivium,* and gives to much medieval philosophy the atmosphere of the logic exercise which contrasts so noticeably with the more rhetorical or confessional vehicles of other eras. It should be remembered, however, that the medieval *quaestio* is one of the few philosophical formats which insures that at least some of the objections to a position will be taken into account.

Concurrent with the rise of the universities was the reception of Aristotle, whose works reached the Latin West through two channels. From the twelfth century on, scholars in Spain and Italy, where Christians were in contact with Muslim learning, prepared Latin translations of the Arabic texts of Aristotle which, at an earlier time, had been translated from the Greek and Syriac (see p. 204). In the first half of the thirteenth century, when the often better Byzantine texts became available to the West, new and often more accurate translations were made from the original Greek. After varying periods of dissemination, this new learning appeared at the universities. Until the 1240s, the leading interpreter of Aristotle was Avicenna; thereafter this role was assumed by Averroes. The study of Aristotle eventually replaced most of the older curriculum and was a necessary prerequisite to theology. In that discipline the curriculum was based on the Bible and the *Four Books of Sentences* by Peter Lombard, a collection of patristic texts organized by the *Sic et Non* method brought from law into theology by Abailard. Many of the philosophical discussions of the thirteenth and fourteenth centuries are found in the commentaries on that work required of every master in theology.

Just why so many thinkers of the west were so eager to find the new learning is an interesting question, since it seems not to have been welcome to many prelates and theologians. But Aristotle was so ambiguous and provided such a flexible battery of concepts that he could be understood in many ways, and even the rejection of his positions could be formulated in his own terminology. He could be held to have taught the creation of the world as well as its eternity, the necessity of events as well as their contingency, the derivation of human knowledge from perception as well as its dependence on some form of activation by a superior mind; and these and other issues could be argued in terms of form and matter, substance and accident, potentiality and actuality, the four causes, and so forth. The situation was further complicated by the fact that the understanding of Aristotle which was received was to a greater or lesser extent influenced by neoplatonic conceptions, especially emanation and the independence of the soul from the body. This influence was stronger in Avicenna than in Averroes, and so a spectrum of alignments was possible: one could simply adhere to the already regnant authority of Augustine; one could express Augustine's views in Aristotelian terminology; one could find enough affinity between Avicenna and Augustine to justify adopting the views of the former; one could turn from Avicenna to Averroes in understanding Aristotle; one could try to come at Aristotle comparatively free from Muslim interpretations; one could give various types of assent to the Aristotle one comprehended, and so on. Some scholars seek out characteristic families of positions and classify them as "Augustinian," "Avicennizing Augustinian," "Averroist," and so on. Thus Augustinianism is allegedly revealed by such doctrines as that divine illumination is essential to human knowledge, that since the soul is independent of the body, there must be several forms in the human composite, and that the will is not limited by the intellect. But other scholars think this approach makes too little of individual ingenuity and suggest that because a man may be "Augustinian" on some issues does not imply that he will not be "Averroist," for example, on others.

Despite the salutary good sense of such a caution, the following selections were chosen with an eye to representativeness as well as intrinsic merit. Bonaventure must stand here for the Augustinian reaction to Aristotle, even if he does use Aristotle's language. With him there should be grouped his master Alexander of Hales, his compatriot John Peckham, and many others, including Mathew of Aquasparta, Robert Kilwardby, and Henry of Ghent. Robert Grosseteste and Roger Bacon present an attitude prominent in England, influenced by the neoplatonic element in the new learning and deeply interested in its possibilities for natural science. Siger of Brabant must represent those arts masters more interested in philosophy than theology, and who were perhaps jeeringly called "Averroists" in the succeeding era. Included with Siger in this tradition are Boethius of Dacia, John of Jandun, and a long line of Italian masters reaching into the seventeenth century. Thomas Aquinas here stands for the theological exploitation of Aristotle, a position requiring a fresh understanding of him. Thomas was preceded in this by his master Albert the Great, and his work was carried on by Giles of Rome among other followers.

It would be overdramatic to say that this period in which the central problems were posed by Aristotle's philosophy came to an end in 1277 with the condemnation of many positions propounded by his partisans, for such problems were discussed long thereafter. But the effort after synthesis came to be overshadowed by a spirit of criticism; and in that sense the Condemnation marks an ending of a sort to the enterprise begun when the translations opened a new world to Latin Christianity.

BONAVENTURE

1221–1274

For all that he is known as a leading theologian of love and seems to have been a man of the utmost personal charity, Bonaventure's career was dominated by controversies. Within his own religious order, he was caught up in the struggle between those who wished to fulfill the primitive vision of St. Francis of Assisi and those who wished to make accommodations; and in the intellectual world, he took a leading role in checking what he took to be a dangerously uncritical acceptance of Aristotelianism. Scholars debate whether he should be classified as an "Augustinian" who occasionally used Aristotelian terminology like all the schoolmen of the time, or as an eclectic with no special animus against Aristotle in philosophy, so long as his doctrines did not invade theology. Against the latter there is the claim that it depends on a conception of philosophy and indeed, of nature, as autonomous, which Bonaventure rejected. Regardless of how the nuances of interpretation are to be settled, there is little doubt that, especially in his later years, Bonaventure opposed not only the so-called "Averroists" whom Thomas Aquinas also opposed, but also the more moderate efforts of Aquinas himself. Bonaventure placed special emphasis on exemplarism, the Christian version of Plato's theory of Ideas. It is Aristotle's rejection of the Ideas, he said, that leads to the pernicious errors of the eternity of the world, the unity of the intellect for all men, and the necessity of all that happens.

Consonant with his adherence to exemplarism, Bonaventure developed the illumination theory of knowledge into an elaborate system of types of illumination and degrees of the traces of God in the world. He was deeply influenced by twelfth-century figures such as Bernard of Clairvaux and Hugh of St. Victor, and in the style of the earlier period was given to brief encyclopedic compendia. But he could explore an issue in depth when he wished and was unusually sensitive to the systematic implications of individual positions. He maintained that the world can be proved not to be eternal, that there is a kind of spiritual matter, that there are several substantial forms in man, forming a hierarchy perfected by the intellective soul, and so on—a catalogue of positions certainly owing something to Augustine. But of more importance than any group of positions is his effort to orient philosophy toward theology, and theology toward the mystical union. Without such an effort, philosophy is merely an outgrowth of worldly curiosity, placing man on "the infinite precipice." In following the controversies of the thirteenth century it is important to remember that for men such as Bonaventure, the price of philosophical error is not merely confusion; it is also the ultimate disaster of damnation.

Bonaventure was born at Bagnorea, not far from Viterbo, in Italy, in 1221. His name was John of Fidanza, and his father may have been a doctor. When the father could not cure him of a childhood disease, the invocation (one tradition says the presence) of St. Francis did, and the second name of "Bonaventure" may have something to do with this event. He entered the Franciscan Order, perhaps as early as 1238 or as late as 1243, and for a period after 1243, studied at Paris under Alexander of Hales, a theologian of Augustinian loyalties who had joined the Franciscan Order in the wave of enthusiasm which brought many academics into it. From 1250 to perhaps 1253, Bonaventure delivered his *Commentary on the Sentences (Commentarius in quatuor libros Sententiarum Petri Lombardi)* and perhaps during this period he also wrote *Retracing the Arts to Theology (De reductione artium ad theologiam)*. Along with Brother Thomas Aquinas of the Dominicans, he was a target of the University's struggle to bring the mendicant orders under university discipline, and it took papal directives to allow him the mastership. But before he could exercise it, he was called to a different and more poignant responsibility. The general of the Franciscan Order resigned and suggested Bonaventure as his successor; and on February 2, 1257, he was elected. This is not the place to present the background of the Spiritualist controversy, nor an estimation of the relative importance in it of the wish to be true to the man who proclaimed himself God's simpleton as against the wish to fulfill the condemned apocalyptic theory of history of Joachim of Flora. Bonaventure was firm against the Joachimites, to the extent even of imprisoning the very former general who had nominated him. He tried to be true intellectually to St. Francis by emphasizing the mystical tradition and maintaining the attitude toward worldly learning outlined above. But the cry of a companion of St. Francis, "Paris, Paris, thou that destroyest Assisi," may be a comment on the very concept of a Franciscan theologian. There is a wry contrast between the way with a book of the founder and his disciple: Francis is said once to have found a part of the New Testament and taken it apart for distribution, so that each might have a share of the precious story. Bonaventure's regulations for Franciscan libraries prohibited the lending of books, which would come back dirty and torn, if at all.

For the rest of his life, Bonaventure moved about on the business of his Order and the wider Church. In 1259 he stayed at Monte Alvernia, where Francis had received the stigmata, and wrote the *Journey of the Mind to God (Itinerarium mentis in Deum)*, placing an elaborate interpretation on Francis' vision, an interpretation calling upon Dionysius the (Pseudo)

Areopagite for its structure. In 1265 he was named Archbishop of York, but managed to be excused. The controversy over Aristotelianism was mounting at Paris, and in 1266 he began the practice of public disputations by Franciscan students at the meetings of the Order. At Paris, the Franciscan theologian John Peckham attacked the theses of Thomas Aquinas, and there is little doubt that he was backed in this by his general. Finally, in April and May of 1273, Bonaventure himself conducted a series of *Conferences on the Hexaemeron* (*Collationes in Hexaemeron*) which are described as containing the seeds of the Condemnation of 1277. Also in 1273, he was made a cardinal by the man whom he had suggested as Pope in 1271. This time he could not escape. After taking an active part in the General Council of the Church at Lyons, he died there July 15, 1274. He was canonized April 14, 1482, and declared a Doctor of the Church in 1587. Needless to say, he wrote a great deal on Franciscan and other religious subjects which has not been mentioned here.

The selections which follow begin with two brief excerpts from the *Conferences on the Hexaemeron*. In the first of these Bonaventure lists the major errors of Aristotle and attributes them to a rejection of Plato's theory of Ideas, and hence, exemplarism. In the second, he presents the proper order of studies, placing philosophy in relation to the theological *summas,* the writings of the saints, and the Bible. These are followed by the entire *Retracing the Arts to Theology,* whose title is self-explanatory.

CONFERENCES ON THE HEXAEMERON

Vision III, Discussion VII

Introduction to the Fourth Vision or, Concerning the Study of Science, Sanctity, and Wisdom

Now one should go on to the fourth vision, namely, of understanding through elevated contemplation. But since that vision is indeed great and the cognition of a great deal of the truth is included in it, before we treat it we set forth a transition from the aforesaid three visions, preparatory to the fourth.

It should be noted, then, that to go forth from Egypt, that is, from the darkness of curiosity, from vanity, from transitory and changeable things, to the land of promise and the recognition of truth, is not for the Egyptians, but rather, for the sons of Israel. But the opposite movement, namely, from light to dark-

Translated by James J. Walsh for this volume from *S. Bonaventurae Collationes in Hexaëmeron,* ed. R. Delorme, Florence: Ad Claras Aquas, 1934. The biblical references are given in the Douay version, in which the numbering of certain Psalms differs from the King James version.

ness, etc., is for the sons of perdition. Lucifer first began this movement, and those of his party imitated him: "I said, I will ascend into the heaven, I will exalt my throne above the stars of God, I will be like the most High. But yet thou shalt be brought down to hell" (Isaiah. 14, 13–15). He is imitated who dismissed the "tree of life," clinging to and savoring of the "tree of the knowledge of good and evil" (Genesis. 2, 9). He hides himself from God after he sees himself naked and removed from all good habits, since he neglected the principal fruits, which are wisdom and charity, to which vanity is directly contrary. Solomon is imitated, who, after he had instructed the people in Proverbs, after he had shown in Ecclesiastes that everything transitory is vain and despicable, and had hastened to the true wisdom given in the Canticles, yet became curious and vain and, wishing to know everything, forgot himself. It is patently obvious through this that there is no sure passage to wisdom through science.

Some wish to be all-wise and all-knowing, but it happens to them just as to the woman: "And the woman saw that the tree was good to eat, and fair to the eyes" (Genesis. 3, 6). They see the beauty of transitory science and being delighted, they linger, they savor, and they are received. We do not belong to the party of their companions, the disciples of Solomon, but to that of David his father, who preferred the study of sanctity and wisdom to that of science. "Teach me goodness and discipline and knowledge," he said (Psalms. 118, 66). I wish to taste "how the Lord is sweet" (Psalms. 33, 9). But he came to this through discipline or science, but to wisdom through the exercise of science, but this with the help of the Most High. Hence, beginning with the principal prayer for the highest, he goes on to the accessories; he does not prefer the last to the first. It is a bad merchant who prefers tin to gold.

The good angels watch over the first movement, according to Augustine in *The City of God*. Hence they are called angels since they are messengers, and since they are humble, they are glorified for this. The bad angels watch over the second movement, those who are called "quasi-knowing," since they teach one to prefer the study of science to that of sanctity. The demons achieve this many times through science, since unless it is watched very carefully, there is easy ruin in science. These demons are called "quasi-knowing" because they turned to a natural though depraved ruin. Bernard said, "The first vice is curiosity," and through it Lucifer and Adam fell, and many today are ruined. We should desire to know nothing unless we become more holy and go forward in the wisdom which takes us toward God. Otherwise, time is wasted in the instruction. "I have had understanding above the ancients: because I have sought thy commandments" (Psalms. 118, 100). The desire for science should be altered, then, lest we know more than one should.

It is therefore necessary to pay heed to how these things contemplated in science and sanctity should be studied. "For the labor of fools shall afflict them that know not how to go to the city" (Ecclesiastes. 10, 15), that is, to make progress in wisdom and the Scriptures and sanctity. Seneca said, "I have found many exercising the body, few the mind." Hugh says almost the same in the *Didascalion*: "Many are students, but few are wise." Proverbs: "I passed by the field of the slothful man," etc. (24, 30). When he who has a good disposition neglects to study, he will be confused when touched by a word. Whence, "Diligently tend thy ground" (Proverbs. 24, 27). Thus the manner of studying has four conditions, which are, order, assiduity, enjoyableness, and measure.

Order is given in many ways among diverse subjects, but, omitting the others, it is necessary to have the order whereby the prior does not become posterior nor vice versa. But there are four types of writings which are studied: first, the books of the Holy Scriptures, twenty-two in the Old Testament, eight in the New Testament; second, there are the books of the originals, namely, the saints; and the *summas* of the masters are the third writings; fourth, there are the writings of worldly learning. Thus, let him who wishes to learn, seek science at its source, namely, in Holy Scripture, since "the knowledge of salvation given for the remission of our sins" (Luke. 1, 77) is not found among the philosophers, nor among the *summas* of the masters, since they draw from the originals of the saints. But certain science cannot be taken from the originals beyond what the saints draw from Holy Scripture, since the saints could be deceived.

But the disciple of Christ ought first to study Holy Scripture, in which there is no error, just as boys first learn the letters, namely, ABC, afterwards, the syllables, then to read, then what the part and the construction signify, and then they understand. For he who refuses to learn the alphabet will never be proficient in grammar. Likewise for Holy Scripture: first one must study its letters and the text, and just as on the lute a certain string is necessary for harmony, so the entire Scripture is a kind of lute, and so one must have the entire text of the Holy Scripture at hand. Otherwise, one will never be a ready expositor of Holy Scripture.

. . .

One can only come to the understanding of the letter through those (writings) in which the Holy Spirit has revealed it, as are the original (writings) of the saints. This is obvious in the book of Augustine, *Against Faustus,* where he allegorizes elegantly what he takes from others. Consider also his other books, destructive of error and constructive of truth. One must, then, have recourse to the originals of the saints, but they are also most difficult; some studying them have fallen into many errors and heresies. Hence there are the *summas* of the masters, in which those difficulties are elucidated; but beware of the multitude of writers. And then since these writings make use of the words of many philosophers, the student of Holy Scripture must hear and learn or add this.

Thus there is danger in descending to the originals; there is more danger in descending to the *summas* of the masters; but the greatest danger lies in descending to philosophy. This is because the words of the originals are pretty and can be too attractive; but Holy Scripture does not have pretty words like that. Augustine would not take it for good if I should prefer him to Christ because of the beauty of his words, just as Paul reproached those who wished to be baptized in the name of Paul. In the course of study, then, caution must be exercised in descending from careful attention in reading Scripture to the originals. There should be a similar warning about descending to the *summas* of the masters, for the masters sometimes do not understand the saints, as the Master of the *Sentences*, great as he was, did not understand Augustine in some places. Whence the *summas* of the masters are like the introductions of boys to the text of Aristotle. Let the student beware, then, lest he depart from the common way.

Likewise, the greatest danger is in the descent to philosophy. "Forasmuch as this people hath cast away the waters of Siloe, that go with silence, and hath rather taken Rasin, and the sons of Romelia: Therefore behold the Lord will bring upon them the waters of the river strong and many" (Isaiah. 8, 6–7). Whence there is no going back into Egypt for such things.

Take note of how Jerome was scourged for such a descent, as he wrote in the letter *To Eustochius*; after the study of Cicero, he did not find relish in sacred letters. This was done to him for our sake. Hence the masters and doctors of Scripture ought not prize the writings of philosophers, making themselves disciples in the example of those who cast away the waters of Siloe, in which there is the highest perfection, and go to philosophy, in which there is dangerous deception.

Take note of Gideon, whom the Lord commanded to test the people by the waters; and those who lapped were chosen, that is, those who drink moderately from philosophy. They were given vessels, trumpets, and torches in the battle-line, through which they conquered Madian. Those three hundred chosen for the battle are the preachers of Scripture, sounding the trumpet in preaching; the torches are miracles, the vessels are their bodies exposed for the truth. These terrify and subdue the enemy. The others who drank while lying down are those who give themselves entirely to philosophy, and they are not worthy to stand up in the battle-line, but they are bent over in submission to infinite errors, (treating) the sayings of certain philosophers as though they were the life-giving ferment of Scripture.

Again, take note of the sultan to whom the blessed Francis replied, when he wished to dispute with him about the faith, that faith is above reason and is proved only by the authority of Scripture and the divine power, which is manifested in miracles; hence he made the fire which he wished to enter into their presence. For the water of philosophical science is not to be mingled with the wine of Holy Scripture merely so that the wine is transmitted into water, which is indeed a bad sign and contrary to the primitive church, when recently converted clerics such as Dionysius dismissed the books of the philosophers and took up the books of Holy Scripture. But in modern times the wine is changed into water and the bread into stone, just the reverse of the miracles of Christ.

The order thus is that first of all the letter and spirit of Holy Scripture is studied, and then the originals are read, and they are subordinated to Scripture. Likewise in passing over to the study of the writings of the philosophers; but the contrary is always done, since the professors, even if not openly, secretly read, copy, and conceal the quartos of the philosophers as though they were idols, like Rachel concealing the stolen idols of her father. (Genesis. 31, 19 ff.). Our waters, therefore, ought not go into the Dead Sea, but return to the sea as in the drying up of the Jordan. There is, then, this kind of order in study.

. . .

Vision I, Discussion III

On God, the Causal Exemplar of Everything, and on the Four Cardinal Virtues Exemplified There and Their Three Degrees

"And God saw the light that it was good" (Genesis. 1, 4). This text was chosen because of the first vision of understanding given through nature. "God saw the light," that is, he made the light to be seen. This was mentioned above in the two Discussions of scientific consideration and how the light radiates as the truth of things, of words, and of manners, concerning which there are nine partial instructions and three principal rays.

Again, "God saw the light," that is, he made (it) be seen through wisdom's contemplation by illuminating the soul in itself, in reflection, and in understanding. And this last illumination in understanding is distinguished by six conditions which that light impresses in the mind; for it is the first simple cause, etc., and in creatures there are opposed conditions. The soul raises itself to that understanding by reason, experience, and understanding of the simple. From all of which, every perfection is given in the soul in those six conditions, since it has substance, power, operation, etc.

To all these the understanding given through nature reaches, and hence the philosophers have come to them; and so in them just as in the angels, "Light is divided from darkness" (Genesis. 1, 4). Thus they knew that light as it is great in the quiddity of things, clear in the pronunciation of words, best in the ordering of manners.

But there was a difference as to whether in that light there is the characteristic of being the exemplar of everything, some saying that it knows itself alone, as in Book XI of the *Metaphysics*, the last chapter: "And it moves through being loved and desired." These do not posit any exemplar at all. The first of these is Aristotle, who attacked eternal reasons and Ideas, as well as their defender, Plato. The commentator on Book I of the *Ethics*, where Aristotle proves that the highest good is not an Idea, replies to his arguments.

From this there follows a second error, namely, that the truth of divine providence and foreknowledge is put aside, if everything is not distinct in it. Whence they say that God knows nothing as a particular and that there is no truth of the future except by necessity, and so foreknowledge is removed and one must maintain that everything happens by chance. Hence fate is necessarily brought in, as the Arabs maintain, that is, the error that the substances moving the world are the causes of everything. And from this there follows the unsuitable position that the disposition of the world is beyond punishment and glory. For if those substances do not err in moving, neither hell nor demon is posited; whence Aristotle did not posit demons nor more angels than celestial spheres.

Most of all, then, the truth of divine providence and the disposition of the world is put aside in this way. And thus in the putting aside of the truth there is given the error of the eternity of the world, as even Aristotle himself seems to sense, according to the doctors who impute this to him, namely, Gregory of Nazianzus and Gregory of Nyssa. From this there follows the unity of the intellect or its transmigration into another body or what is corporeal; and since it is not proper to posit an infinite number of intellects, he thought to posit one for all. All these follow if it is held that the world is eternal. And further, it follows that after this life there is neither punishment nor glory.

Those holding such views, therefore, fall into these errors, the understanding of which is closed by the key to the bottomless pit from which a great fog arises. It is more circumspect, then, to say that Aristotle did not feel that the world is eternal, whether he felt so or not, since he was so great that everyone followed him and was devoted to saying the same things; thus all the light determined in his predecessors was extinguished. But we follow him where he spoke well, not where he was in the dark, not on those matters of which he was ignorant or which he concealed. From doing that, men in this life are on the infinite precipice.

RETRACING THE ARTS TO THEOLOGY
OR
SACRED THEOLOGY
THE MISTRESS AMONG THE SCIENCES

1. *Every best gift and every perfect gift is from above, coming down from the Father of lights,* James in the first chapter of his Epistle. These words of Sacred Scripture not only reveal the source of all illumination but they likewise point out the generous flow of manifold rays which issue from that Fount of light. Notwithstanding the fact that every illumination of knowledge is within, still, we can with propriety distinguish what we may call the *external* light, or the light of mechanical skill; the *lower* light, or the light of sense perception; the *inner* light, or the light of philosophical knowledge; and the *higher* light, or the light of grace and of Sacred Scripture. The first light illumines in the consideration of the *arts and crafts;* the second, in regard to *natural form;* the third, in regard to *intellectual truth;* the fourth and last, in regard to *saving truth.*

2. The first light, then, since it enlightens the mind for an appreciation of the *arts and crafts,* which are, as it were, exterior to man and intended to supply the needs of the body, is called the light of *mechanical skill.* Being, in a certain sense, servile and of a lower nature than philosophical knowledge, this light can rightly be termed *external.* It has seven divisions corresponding to the seven mechanical arts enumerated by Hugh in his *Didascalion,* namely, weaving, armour-making, agriculture, hunting, navigation, medicine, and the dramatic art. That the above mentioned arts *suffice* for all the needs of mankind is shown in the following way: every mechanical art is intended for man's *consolation* or his *comfort;* its purpose, therefore, is to banish either *sorrow* or *want;* it either *benefits* or *delights,* according to the words of Horace:

> Either to serve or to please is the wish of the poets.

And again:

> He hath gained universal applause who hath combined
> the profitable with the pleasing.

If its aim is to afford *consolation* and amusement, it is *dramatic art,* or the art of exhibiting plays, which embraces every form of entertainment, be it song, music, drama, or pantomime. If, however, it is intended for the *comfort* or betterment of the exterior man, it can accomplish its purpose by providing either *covering* or *food,* or by *serving as an aid in the acquision of either.* In the matter of *covering,* if it provides a soft and light material, it is weaving; if, a strong and hard material, it is *armour-making* or metal-working, an art which extends to

From *De Reductione Artium ad Theologiam,* Sister Emma Thérèse Healy, trans., St. Bonaventure, N.Y.: St. Bonaventure College, 1955. Reprinted by permission of the translator.

every tool or implement fashioned of iron or of any metal whatsoever, of stone, or of wood.

In the matter of *food*, mechanical skill may benefit in two ways, for we derive our sustenance from *vegetables* and from *flesh meats*. If it supplies us with *vegetables,* it is *farming;* if it provides us with *flesh meats,* it is *hunting.* Or, again, as regards *food,* mechanical skill has a twofold advantage: either it aids in the *production* and multiplication of crops, in which case it is agriculture, or in the various ways of *preparing* food under which aspect it is hunting, an art which extends to every conceivable way of preparing foods, drinks, and delicacies—a task with which bakers, cooks, and innkeepers are concerned. The term "hunting" (*venatio*), however, is derived from one single aspect of the trade, undoubtedly, on account of the excellent nature of game and the popularity of the chase at court.

Furthermore, as an aid in the *acquisition of each of these necessities,* the mechanical arts contribute to the welfare of man in two ways: either by *supplying a want,* and in this case it is *navigation*, which includes all commerce of articles of covering or of food; or by *removing impediments* and ills of the body, under which aspect it is *medicine*, whether it is concerned with the preparation of drugs, potions, or ointments, with the healing of wounds or with the amputation of members, in which latter case it is called surgery. Dramatic art, on the other hand, is in a class by itself. Considered in this light, the classification of the mechanical arts seems adequate.

3. The second light, which enables us to discern *natural forms,* is the light of *sense perception*. Rightly is it called the *lower* light because sense perception begins with a material object and takes place by the aid of corporeal light. It has five divisions corresponding to the five senses. In his third book on Genesis, St. Augustine, in the following way bases the *adequacy* of the senses on the nature of the light present in the elements: if the light or brightness, which makes possible the discernment of things corporeal, exists in a *high degree of its own property* and in a certain purity, it is the sense of *sight; commingled with the air,* it is *hearing; with vapor,* it is smell; *with a fluid* of the body, it is *taste; with a solid earthy substance,* it is *touch*. Now the sensitive life of the body partakes of the nature of light for which reason it thrives in the nerves which are naturally unobstructed and capable of transmitting impressions, and in these five senses it possesses more or less vigor according to the greater or less soundness of the nerves. Therefore, since there are in the world five simple substances, namely, the four elements and the fifth essence, man has for the perception of all these corporeal forms five senses well adapted to these substances, because, on account of the well-defined nature of each sense, apprehension can take place only when there is a certain conformity and rapport between the faculty and the object. There is another way of determining the adequacy of the senses, but St. Augustine sanctions this method and it seems reasonable since corresponding elements on the part of the faculty, the medium, and the object lend joint support to the proof.

4. The third light which guides man in the investigation of *intelligible truths* is the light of *philosophical knowledge*. It is called *inner* because it inquires into inner and hidden causes through principles of knowledge and natural truth, which are inherent in man. It is a threefold light diffusing itself over the three divisions of philosophy: *rational, natural,* and *moral,* a classification which seems suitable,

since there is truth of *speech*, truth of *things*, and truth of *morals*. *Rational* philosophy considers the truth of *speech; natural* philosophy, the truth of *things;* and *moral* philosophy, the truth of *conduct*. Or considering it in a different light: just as we believe that the principle of the efficient, the formal or exemplary, and the final cause exists in the Most High God, since "He is the Cause of being, the Principle of knowledge, and the Pattern of human life", so do we believe that it is contained in the illumination of philosophy which enlightens the mind to discern the *causes of being* in which case it is physics; or to understand *principles of reasoning* in which case it is *logic*; or to learn the *right way of living* in which case it is *moral* or practical philosophy. Considering it under its third aspect: the light of philosophical knowledge illumines the intellect itself and this enlightenment may be threefold: if it governs the *motive*, it is *moral* philosophy; if it sways the *reason,* it is *natural* philosophy; if it directs the *interpretation*, it is *discursive* philosophy. As a result, man is enlightened as regards the truth of life, the truth of knowledge, and the truth of doctrine.

And since one may, through the medium of *speech*, give expression to his thoughts with a threefold purpose in view: namely, to communicate his ideas, to propose something for belief, or to arouse love or hatred, for this reason, *discursive* or rational philosophy has three subdivisions: *grammar, logic*, and *rhetoric*. Of these sciences the first aims to express; the second, to teach; the third, to persuade. The first considers the mind as *apprehending*; the second, as *judging*; the third, as *motivating*, and since the mind apprehends by means of *correct* speech, judges by means of *true* speech, and persuades by means of *embellished* speech, with good reason does this triple science consider these three qualities in speech.

Again, since our intellect must be guided in its judgment by fixed principles, these principles, likewise, must be considered under three aspects: when they pertain to *matter*, they are termed *formal causes*; when they pertain to the *mind*, they are termed *intellectual causes*; and when they pertain to *Divine Wisdom*, they are called *ideal causes*. Natural philosophy, therefore, is subdivided into *physics properly so-called,* into *mathematics,* and *metaphysics*. Physics, accordingly, treats of the generation and corruption of matter by natural powers and seminal causes; *mathematics* considers abstract forms through intellectual causes; *metaphysics* treats of the knowledge of all entities, which leads back to one ultimate Principle from which they proceeded according to ideal causes, that is, to God since He is the *Beginning*, the *End*, and the *Exemplar*. Concerning these ideal causes, however, there has been some controversy among metaphysicists.

Finally, since there are three standards of ethical principles, namely, those governing the *individual*, the *family,* and the *state,* so are there three corresponding divisions of moral philosophy: namely, *ethical, economic,* and *political*, the content of each being clearly indicated by its name.

5. Now the fourth light, which illumines the mind for the understanding of *saving truth*, is the light of *Sacred Scripture*. This light is called *higher* because it leads to things above by the manifestation of truths which are beyond reason and also because it is not acquired by human research, but comes down by inspiration from the *"Father of lights"*. Although in its literal sense, it is *one*, still, in its spiritual and mystical sense, it is *threefold*, for in all the books of Sacred Scripture, in addition to the *literal* meaning which the words clearly express, there is implied a threefold *spiritual* meaning: namely, the *allegorical*,

by which we are taught what to believe concerning the Divinity and humanity; the *moral* by which we are taught how to live; and the *anagogical* by which we are taught how to keep close to God. Hence all of Sacred Scripture teaches these three truths: namely, the eternal generation and Incarnation of Christ, the pattern of human life, and the union of the soul with God. The first regards *faith*; the second, *morals*; the third, the *purpose of both*. To the study of the first, the doctors should devote themselves; on that of the second, the preachers should concentrate; and to the attainment of the third, the contemplatives should aspire. Augustine is the chief exponent of the first class; Gregory, of the second; Dionysius, of the third. Anselm follows Augustine; Bernard follows Gregory; Richard (of St. Victor) follows Dionysius, for Anselm excels in reasoning, Bernard in preaching, Richard in contemplation, but Hugh, in all three.

6. From the foregoing statements, it is evident that although, according to our first classification, the light coming down from above is *fourfold*, still, it admits of *six* modifications: namely, the light of *Sacred Scripture*, the light of *sense perception,* the light of *mechanical knowledge,* the light of *rational philosophy*, the light of *natural philosophy*, and the light of *moral philosophy*. And for that reason there are in this life six illuminations and they have their twilight, for all science will be destroyed; for that reason, too, there follows a seventh day of rest, a day which knows no evening, *the illumination of glory*.

7. Wherefore, very fittingly may these six illuminations be compared to the six days of creation or illumination in which the world was made, the knowledge of Sacred Scriptures corresponding to the creation of the first day, that is, to the creation of light and so on one after the other in order. Moreover, just as all those creations had their origin in one light, so, too, are all these branches of knowledge ordained for the knowledge of Sacred Scripture; they are contained in it; they are perfected by it; and by means of it they are ordained for eternal illumination. Wherefore, all our knowledge should have its foundation in the knowledge of Sacred Scripture and especially is this true of the *anagogical* knowledge through which the light is reflected back to God whence it came. And so there the cycle ends; the six are complete and, consequently, there is rest.

8. Let us see, therefore, how the other illuminations of knowledge are to be reduced to the light of Sacred Scripture. First of all, let us consider the illumination of *sense* perception, which is concerned exclusively with the cognition of sensible objects, a process in which three phases are to be considered: namely, the *medium* of perception, the *exercise* of perception, and the *delight* of perception. If we consider the *medium* of perception, we shall see therein the Word begotten from all eternity and made man in time. Indeed, a sensible object can make an impression upon a cognitive faculty only through the medium of a likeness which proceeds from the object as an offspring from its parent, and in every sensation, this likeness must be present either generically, specifically, or symbolically. That likeness, however, results in actual sensation only if it is brought into contact with the organ and the faculty, and once that contact is established, there results a new percept, an expressed image by means of which the mind reverts to the object. And even though the object is not always present to the senses, still, the fact remains that perception in its finished form begets an image. In like manner, know that from the mind of the Most High, Who is knowable by the interior senses of the mind, from all eternity there emanated a Likeness, an Image, and an Offspring; and afterwards, when "the fulness of time had come" He was united

to a mind and body and assumed the form of man which He had never been before, and through Him all our minds, which bear the likeness of the Father through faith in our hearts, are brought back to God.

9. To be sure, if we consider the *exercise* of sense perception, we shall see therein the pattern of human life, for each sense applies itself to its own object, shrinks from what may harm it, and does not appropriate the object of any other sense. In like manner, the *spiritual sense* operates in an orderly way, for while applied to its proper object, it opposes *negligence;* while refraining from what is harmful, it combats *concupiscence;* and while respecting the rights of other, it acts in opposition to *pride.* Of a truth, every irregularity springs from negligence, from concupiscence, or from pride. Surely, then, he who lives a prudent, temperate, and submissive life leads a well-ordered life, for thereby he avoids negligence in his duties, concupiscence in his appetites, and pride in his excellence.

10. Furthermore, if we consider the *delight,* we shall see therein the union of the soul with God. Indeed, every sense seeks its proper sensible with longing, finds it with delight, and seeks it again without ceasing, because "the eye is not filled with seeing, neither is the ear filled with hearing." In the same way, our spiritual senses must seek longingly, find joyfully, and seek again without ceasing the beautiful, the harmonious, the fragrant, the sweet, or the delightful to the touch. Behold how the Divine Wisdom lies hidden in sense perception and how wonderful is the contemplation of the five spiritual senses in the light of their conformity to the senses of the body.

11. By the same process of reasoning is Divine Wisdom to be found in the illumination of the mechanical arts, the sole purpose of which is the *production of works of art.* In this illumination we can see the *eternal generation and Incarnation of the Word,* the *pattern of human life,* and the *union of the soul with God.* And this is true if we consider the *production,* the *effect,* and the *advantage* of the work, or if we consider the *skill of the artist,* the *quality of the effect produced,* and the *utility of the advantage to be derived therefrom.*

12. If we consider the *production,* we shall see that the work of art proceeds from the artificer according to a model existing in his mind; this pattern or model the artificer studies carefully before he produces and then he produces as he has predetermined. The artificer, moreover, produces an exterior work bearing the closest possible resemblance to the interior model, and if it were in his power to produce an effect which would know and love him, this he would assuredly do; and if that creature could know its maker, it would be by means of a likeness according to which it came from the hands of the artificer; and if the eyes of the understanding were so darkened that the creature could not be elevated to things above, in order to bring it to a knowledge of its maker, it would be necessary for the likeness according to which the effect was produced to lower itself even to that nature which the creature could grasp and know. In like manner, understand that no creature has proceeded from the Most High Creator except through the Eternal Word, "in Whom He ordered all things", and by which Word He produced creatures bearing not only the nature of His *vestige* but also of His *image* so that through knowledge and love, they might be united to Him. And since by sin the rational creature had dimmed the eye of contemplation, it was most fitting that the Eternal and Invisible should become visible and take flesh that He might lead us back to the Father and, indeed, this is what is related in the fourteenth chapter of St. John: "No man cometh to the Father but by Me"; and in the

eleventh chapter of St. Matthew: "Neither knoweth any man the Father save the Son, and he to whomsoever the Son will reveal Him." For that reason, then, it is said, "the Word was made flesh". Therefore, considering the illumination of mechanical skill as regards the production of the work, we shall see therein the Word begotten and made incarnate, that is, the Divinity and the Humanity and the integrity of all faith.

13. If we consider the *effect,* we shall see therein the *pattern of human life,* for every artificer, indeed, aims to produce a work that is beautiful, useful, and enduring, and only when it possesses these three qualities is the work highly valued and acceptable. Corresponding to the above-mentioned qualities, in the pattern of life there must be found three elements: "knowledge, will, and unaltering and persevering toil". *Knowledge* renders the work beautiful; the *will* renders it useful; *perseverance* renders it lasting. The first resides in the rational, the second in the concupiscible, and the third in the irascible appetite.

14. If we consider the *advantage,* we shall find the union of the soul with God, for every artificer who fashions a work does so that he may derive *praise, benefit,* or *delight* therefrom—a threefold purpose which corresponds to the three formal objects of the appetites: namely, a *noble* good, a *useful* good, and an *agreeable* good. It was for this same threefold reason that God made the soul rational, namely, that of its own accord, it might *praise* Him, *serve* Him, *find delight* in Him, and be at rest; and this takes place through charity. "He that abideth in it, abideth in God and God in him"; in such a way that there is found therein a kind of wondrous union and from that union comes a wondrous delight, for in the Book of Proverbs it is written, "My delights were to be with the children of men". Behold how the illumination of mechanical knowledge is the path to the illumination of Sacred Scripture. There is nothing therein which does not bespeak true wisdom and for this reason Sacred Scripture quite rightly makes frequent use of such similitudes.

15. In the same way is Divine Wisdom to be found in the illumination of *rational philosophy,* the main purpose of which is concerned with *speech.* Here are to be considered three elements corresponding to the threefold consideration of speech itself: namely, as regards the *person speaking,* the *delivery* of the speech, and its final purpose or its effect upon the *hearer.*

16. Considering speech in the light of the *speaker,* we see that all speech is the expression of a *mental concept.* That inner concept is the word of the mind and its offspring which is known to the person conceiving it, but that it may become known to the hearer, it assumes the nature of the voice and clothed in that form, the intelligible word becomes sensible and is heard without; it is received into the ear of the person listening and, still, it does not depart from the mind of the person uttering it. Practically the same procedure is seen in the begetting of the Eternal Word, because the Father conceived Him, begetting Him from all eternity, as it is written in the eighth chapter of the Book of Proverbs, "The depths were not as yet, and I was already conceived". But that He might be known by man who is endowed with senses, He assumed the nature of flesh, and "the Word was made flesh and dwelt amongst us," and yet He remained "in the bosom of His Father".

17. Considering speech in the light of its *delivery,* we shall see therein the *pattern of human life,* for three essential qualities work together for the perfection of speech: namely, *propriety, truth,* and *ornament.* Corresponding to these three qualities, every act of ours should be characterized by *measure, form,* and

order so that it may be *restrained* by propriety in its outward accomplishment, *rendered beautiful* by purity of affection, *regulated* and adorned by uprightness of intention. For then, truly, does one live a correct and well-ordered life when his intention is upright, his affection pure, and his deeds unassuming.

18. Considering speech in the light of its *purpose,* we find that it aims to *express,* to *instruct,* and to *persuade;* but it never *expresses* except by means of a likeness; it never *teaches* except by means of a clear light; and it never *persuades* except by power, and it is evident that these effects are accomplished only by means of an inherent likeness, light, and power intrinsically united to the soul. Therefore, St. Augustine concludes that he alone is a true teacher who can imprint a likeness, shed light, and grant power to the heart of his hearer. Hence it is that "He that teaches within hearts has His throne in heaven". Now, as perfection of speech requires the union of power, light, and a likeness within the soul, so, too, for the instruction of the soul in the knowledge of God by interior conversation with Him, there is required a union with Him who is "the brightness of glory and the figure of His substance, upholding all things by the word of His power". Hence we see how wondrous is this contemplation by which St. Augustine in his many writings leads souls to Divine Wisdom.

19. By the same mode of reasoning is the Wisdom of God to be found in the illumination of *natural philosophy,* which is concerned chiefly with the *formal causes* in *matter,* in the *mind,* and in *Divine Wisdom.* These formal causes it is fitting to consider under three aspects: namely, as regards the *nature of their relationship,* the *effect of causality,* and their *medium of union,* and these three considerations have their analogies in the three branches of natural philosophy already mentioned.

20. Considering the formal causes according to the nature of their relationship, we shall see therein the *Word Eternal* and the *Word Incarnate.* The intellectual and abstract causes are, as it were, midway between the *seminal* and the *ideal* causes. But *seminal* causes cannot exist in *matter* without the generation and production of form; neither can *intellectual* causes exist in the *mind* without the generation of the word in the mind. Therefore, *ideal* causes cannot exist in God without the generation of the Word from the Father in due likeness. Truly, this is a mark of dignity and, if it is becoming to the creature, how much more so to the Creator. It was for this reason that St. Augustine said that the Son of God is the "art of the Father". Again, the sensitive appetite is so related to intellectual causes that the generation can in no way be perfect unless the rational mind be united to the material substance. By similar reasoning, therefore, we come to the conclusion that the highest and noblest perfection cannot exist in this world except in the nature in which seminal, intellectual, and ideal causes are combined, all functioning conjointly in one person, as was the case in the Incarnation of the Son of God. Therefore, all the branches of natural philosophy by reason of the nature of their relationship predicate the Word of God begotten and become Incarnate so that He is the *Alpha* and *Omega,* that is, He was begotten in the beginning and before all time but became Incarnate in the fulness of time.

21. Now if we consider these causes according to the *effect of causality,* we shall be contemplating the *pattern of human life,* since generation by seminal causes can take place in generative and corruptible matter only by the beneficent light of the heavenly bodies which are far removed from generation and corruption, that is, by the light of the *sun,* the *moon,* and the *stars.* So, too, the soul

can perform no living works, unless it receive from the sun, that is, from Christ, the aid of His gratuitous light; unless it seek the protection of the moon, that is, of the Virgin Mary, Mother of Christ; and unless it imitate the example of the other saints. Under these conditions there is accomplished in the soul a living and perfect work: therefore, the right order of living depends upon this threefold co-operation.

22. Moreover, if we consider these formal causes as regards their *medium of union,* we shall understand how *union of the soul* with God takes place, for the corporeal nature cannot be united to the soul except through the medium of moisture, air, and warmth—three conditions which dispose the body to receive life from the soul. So, too, we may understand that God does not preserve the life of the soul and He is not united to it unless it be *moist* with tears of compunction and filial love, *made spiritual* by contempt of earthly possessions, and *enkindled* with the desire of its heavenly home and its own Beloved. Behold how in natural philosophy lies hidden the Wisdom of God.

23. In the same way is the light of *Sacred Scripture* to be found in the illumination of *moral philosophy.* Since moral philosophy is concerned principally with rectitude, it treats of general justice which St. Anselm calls the "rectitude of the will". The term "right" has a threefold signification and, accordingly, in the consideration of rectitude are revealed the three truths of Sacred Scripture previously mentioned. In one sense of the word, that is called "right or straight the middle of which is not out of line with its extreme points". If, then, God is perfect rectitude and that by His very nature since He is the Beginning and the End of all things, it follows that in God there must be an intermediary *of His own nature* so that there may be one Person who only produces, another who is only produced, but an intermediary who both produces and is produced. There is likewise need of an intermediary in the *going forth* and in the *return* of things; in the *going forth,* an intermediary which will prevail over the one producing, but in the *return,* one which will prevail over the one returning. Therefore, as creatures went forth from God by the Word of God, so for a perfect return, it was necessary that the Mediator between God and man be not only God but also man so that He might lead men back to God.

24. In another sense, that is called "right" which is conformable to rule. Accordingly, in the consideration of rectitude man beholds a *rule of life,* for he, indeed, lives rightly who is guided by the regulations of the Divine law, as is the case when the will of man accepts necessary *precepts,* salutary *warnings,* and *counsels* of perfection that he may thereby prove the good, the acceptable, and the perfect will of God. And then is the rule of life right when no obliquity can be found therein.

25. In a third sense, that is called "right" or "upright" the summit of which is raised upward, as, for instance, we say that man has an upright stature. And in this sense, in the consideration of rectitude there is manifested the *union of the soul with God;* for since God is above, it follows that the highest faculty of man's soul must necessarily be raised aloft. And, indeed, this is what actually happens when his *rational* nature seeks the Source of truth for His own sake and above all things, when his *irascible* nature strives after the Highest Bounty, and when his *concupiscible* nature clings to the Greatest Good. He who in this way keeps close to God *is one in spirit with Him.*

26. And thus it is clear how the *manifold Wisdom of God,* which is clearly

revealed in Sacred Scripture, lies hidden in all knowledge and in all nature. It is clear also how all divisions of knowledge are handmaids of theology and it is for this very reason that theology makes use of illustrations and terms pertaining to every branch of knowledge. It is likewise evident how wide is the luminous way and how in everything which is perceived or known, God Himself lies hidden within. And this is the advantage of all sciences, that in all faith is strengthened, *God is honored,* character is formed, and consolation is derived from union of the spouse with her beloved, a union which takes place through charity, to the attainment of which the whole purpose of sacred Scripture, and, consequently, every illumination descending from above, is directed—a union without which all knowledge is vain because no one comes to the Son except through the Holy Ghost who teaches us *all truth, who is blessed forever and ever. Amen.*

SELECTED BIBLIOGRAPHY

BIBLIOGRAPHY

Bougerol, G. *et al.,* eds., *Bibliographia Bonaventuriana,* vol. V of *S. Bonaventura* (1274–1974), Grottaferrata, 1974.

TRANSLATIONS

Boas, G., trans., *Saint Bonaventura, The Mind's Road to God,* New York, 1953.

Boehner, P., trans., *Itinerarium mentis in Deum. With an Introduction, Translation and Commentary,* St. Bonaventure, N.Y., 1956.

de Vinck, J., trans., *The Works of Bonaventure; I, Mystical Opuscula; II, The Breviloquium,* Paterson, N.J., 1960, 1963.

Healy, Sister E., trans., *St. Bonaventure's De reductione artium ad theologiam. A Commentary with an Introduction and Translation,* St. Bonaventure, N.Y., 1939.

McKeon, R., ed. and trans., *Selections from Medieval Philosophers, II: Roger Bacon to William of Ockham,* New York, 1930.

Vollert, C., L. Kendzierski, and P. Byrne, trans., *St. Thomas Aquinas, Siger of Brabant, St. Bonaventure: On the Eternity of the World,* Milwaukee, 1964.

STUDIES

Aquinas and Bonaventure (d. 1274), Norman, 1974.

Bonansea, B., "The Question of an Eternal World in the Teaching of St. Bonaventura," *Franciscan Studies,* XXXIV (1974), 7–32.

Bougerol, J., *Introduction to the Works of Bonaventure,* Brady, 1975.

Bougerol, J., *Lexique Saint Bonaventure,* Paris, 1969.

Bougerol, J., ed., *S. Bonaventura* (1274–1974), Grottaferrata, 1973.

Cousins, E., *Bonaventure and the Coincidence of Opposites,* Chicago, 1978.

Cousins, E., "St. Bonaventure, St. Thomas, and the Movement of Thought in the 13th Century," *International Philosophical Quarterly,* XIV (1974), 393–409.

Doyle, J., "Saint Bonaventure and the Ontological Argument," *The Modern Schoolman,* LII (1974–75), 27–48.

Gilson, E., *The Philosophy of St. Bonaventure,* trans., I. Trethowan and F. Sheed, London, 1938.

Klubertanz, G., "*Esse* and *Existere* in the Philosophy of St. Bonaventure," *Mediaeval Studies,* VIII (1946), 169–188.

Mathias, T., "Bonaventurian Ways to God through Reason," *Franciscan Studies,* XXXVI (1976), 192–232.

O'Leary, C., *The Substantial Composition of Man According to St. Bonaventure,* Washington, D.C., 1931.

Pegis, A., "St. Bonaventure, St. Francis and Philosophy," *Mediaeval Studies,* XV (1953), 1–13.

Pegis, A., "The Bonaventurean Way to God," *Mediaeval Studies,* XXIX (1967), 206–242.

Quinn, J., *The Historical Constitution of St. Bonaventure's Philosophy,* Toronto, 1973.

Shahan, R. and F. Kovack, eds., *Bonaventure and Aquinas,* Norman, 1976.

Thomas and Bonaventure, A Septicenary Commemoration, Proceedings of the American Catholic Philosophical Association, XLVIII (1974).

Tracy, D., ed., *Celebrating the Medieval Heritage. A Colloquy on the Thought of Aquinas and Bonaventure,* Chicago, 1978.

ROBERT GROSSETESTE

ca. 1168–1253

and

ROGER BACON

ca. 1214 – *ca.* 1292

SOME SCHOLARS suggest that the movement of thought at thirteenth-century Oxford was significantly different from that at Paris. At Oxford an older Augustinian tradition prevailed comparatively unchallenged, and the primary interest in the new Greek and Arabic materials was scientific rather than metaphysical in character. Thirteenth-century Oxford is not nearly so thoroughly studied as Paris, but if this suggestion is sound, it testifies to the influence of one of the most respected men of the time, Robert Grosseteste, Bishop of Lincoln. A few scholars would credit him with the role often accorded to Roger Bacon, that of pioneering in the West the advancement of what we now call natural science. Bacon was critical of the intellectual fashions around him and emphasized the importance of mathematics and "experimental science." Because of this, and because he mentions gunpowder and lenses and made such remarkable proposals as horseless carriages and flying machines, he has often been regarded as a lonely prophet of the modern world, a martyr out of his time for science and freedom of thought. But Bacon himself gives much of the credit for his scientific outlook, if not for the flying machines, to Grosseteste. In this he seems to have been correct.

Grosseteste's thought for the most part fits the classification by the eminent historian Etienne Gilson as "Avicennizing Augustianism." The Augustinianism owes much to Anselm of Canterbury and is most obvious in a doctrine of ontological truth and an adherence to the illumination theory of knowledge. The most important impress of Avicenna is found in Grosseteste's discussion of induction in his commentary on the *Posterior Analytics*. The heart of this discussion is the claim that mere collection of similar data in the memory must be supplemented by experiment in which care has been taken to isolate relevant factors. Since this became the standard commentary, these remarks must have been read by undergraduates for over a hundred years. The examples used show that Grosseteste here draws upon Avicenna's medical methodology. Unlike Avicenna, however, Grosseteste refused the effort to reconcile Aristotle and revelation. Echoing Bernard of Clairvaux's remark about Abailard and Plato, he said that moderns who try to make Aristotle a Catholic only make themselves heretics. He denied, for instance, that any interpretations based on the actual texts would allow Aristotle to teach the beginning of the world, and produced a refutation of his arguments, based on a distinction between thinking of time by imagination and by reason. He could support such a claim as this, for unlike most who were trying to cope with Aristotle at this time, he learned Greek.

None of this except learning Greek is so very remarkable, and fails to convey the genius which made him so respected and so influential. We may find a glimpse of this in his theory of light. Putting together the preoccupation with light in the neoplatonic tradition both of Augustine and the Pseudo-Dionysius, and Ibn Gabirol's analogy of light and the propagation of causal influences, Grosseteste said that the very nature or form of body itself is light. He elaborated this in a cosmology in which, as he said, "the usefulness of considering lines, angles, and figures is the greatest." This may be compared to such later justifications of mathematics as the view that God ever geometrizes. Grosseteste's theory gave a special importance to optics, a science to which he and later medieval thinkers contributed greatly, and the success of geometry in optics may have served as a model for other sciences.

Robert Grosseteste may be one of the few prominent medieval figures to come from a peasant background. He was born at Stradbroke in Suffolk, probably before 1168. By 1189, he is described as a "master," and probably studied at Oxford. He had a reputation in medicine, and after service with the Bishop of Hereford, he probably returned to teach at Oxford. One of the side-effects of King John's difficulties was the closing of the schools from 1209 to 1214, and it is presumed that Grosseteste studied theology at Paris during those years. When the schools reopened, he returned to Oxford and soon was perhaps the first Chancellor of the University. In 1224, the Franciscans came to Oxford, and he became their teacher, acting as their official master from about 1229, when he was made Archdeacon of Leicester, until 1235, when he became Bishop of Lincoln. As bishop, he was an energetic inspector of clerical institutions and defender of papal authority at the same time that he protested abuses and confusions stemming from the papal wars. He maintained the pastoral commitment prominent in his theological teaching, writing a treatise on kingship and one on agriculture, and through his friendship with Simon de Montfort, perhaps having some distant impact on the political turmoils surrounding King Henry III. He died in 1253, one of the most constructive men of the English Middle Ages.

The chronology of his works is obscure. He may have written the commentary on the *Posterior Analytics* before 1209. He also commented upon the *Sophisticis Elenchis* and, some time between 1230 and 1235, the *Physics*. Between 1215 and 1235 he composed several works on optics and astronomy, including *On Light* (*De luce*). As a relaxation from his labors as bishop he either translated or supervised the translation of the *Nicomachean Ethics* and its Greek commentaries. He may have been at work on a kind of *summa* based on the *Sentences* of Peter Lombard, and he may have composed a *De Anima*. There are a number of other treatises of philosophical interest and a number of exegetical works. He also translated several theological works, including those by the Pseudo-Dionysius and John Damascene. This last may account for the prominence of Damascene in the writings of William of Ockham.

Roger Bacon often professed his admiration for Grosseteste, and may possibly have been his student. Bacon also professed admiration for Avicenna, and may have been deeply influenced by an apocryphal work, *The Secret of Secrets,* a supposed letter from Aristotle to Alexander the Great. The dominating conceptions which Bacon derived from his various inspirations are that wisdom is a unity embracing all knowledge, that all science was revealed to the patriarchs but lost thereafter, and that science is preeminently practical. He dreamed of a unified Christendom guided by a recovered wisdom. On the more standard topics of the era, Bacon is a rather commonplace Augustinian, maintaining an illuminationism similar to that of Grosseteste, the hylemorphism of the soul, the plurality of substantial forms, and even holding that Aristotle believed that the world had a beginning. On the topics more distinctive of him, it should be noted that his justification for mathematics in science is not merely substantive—indeed, there is some doubt as to whether he subscribed to Grosseteste's theory of light or, instead, to the older theory that the transmission of causal influences is only analogous to the transmission of light. He also offers the methodological justification that mathematics is clear and its demonstrations cogent, and hence it can be used by other sciences to clarify problems and regulate conclusions. This gives to mathematics a role usually reserved for logic. A question should be raised about his celebrated espousal of *scientia experimentalis.* It is not clear from what he says whether he has in mind experimentation or merely careful observation, and whether he means to assign to this the decision between theories or merely the production of belief.

Roger Bacon was born about 1214, possibly near Ilchester, in the county of Somerset. He may have been at Oxford in 1230, and thus could have heard Grosseteste; but the earmarks of Grosseteste's influence do not appear until much later, nor is he ever mentioned by Grosseteste. He seems to have been in Paris by 1236, and may have been one of the first to teach the previously prohibited *Physics* and *Metaphysics.* He composed a set of *Questions* on each. At some time, he glossed *The Secret of Secrets.* Perhaps around 1247, his scientific interests were awakened, and he says that he spent a very large sum on equipment and secret books. He came to know men like Pierre de Maricourt, experimenters, engineers, astrologers—"wise men," as he calls them—and no doubt it is from them that many of his remarkable proposals were drawn. He may have gone back for a while to Oxford and, strange to say, he became a Franciscan, perhaps because he had discovered the work of Grosseteste and supposed the Franciscan Order would support his researches. He certainly had little of the humility and sweetness of the founder, and his unbridled criticism may be one reason for his subsequent troubles. In 1260 the Franciscans imposed internal censorship, and the next thing we know of Roger Bacon is that he is under some kind of house arrest at Paris, complaining of menial chores, discipline by hunger, and constant surveillance. Nonetheless, he apparently managed to write, for several works, including the *Metaphysics,* are assigned to this period. In 1266, Pope Clement VI requested a copy of his works regardless of Franciscan regulations. Bacon had nothing suitable ready, but despite surveillance, composed the *Greater Work (Opus majus),* the *Lesser Work (Opus minus),* and the *Third Work (Opus tertium).* In 1268 one, and possibly all three, were sent to the Pope, who died before anything could come of the project. By 1272, Bacon had written an incomplete *Compendium of Philosophy (Compendium studii philosophiae).* There is a tradition that he was released and returned to England, only to be imprisoned again in the aftermath of the Condemnation of 1277. He was charged with "suspected novelties," which may refer to astrology, to Joachimism, or to general troublesomeness, but, considering the respect accorded to such scientifically minded figures as Grosseteste and Albert the Great, hardly to scientific interests. Bacon was released in 1289 or 1292, and his last work was a *Compendium of Theology (Compendium studii theologiae).* Tradition has it that he died soon thereafter. He was ignored for some time, but by the end of the fourteenth century his reputation, both for science and magic, began to grow. In the fifteenth century he was quoted in disputations and is mentioned as contributing to the fame of Oxford.

The selections which follow include Grosseteste's *On Light* in its entirety, and excerpts from Bacon's *Greater Work* dealing with the scientific role of mathematics and "experiment."

ROBERT GROSSETESTE

ON LIGHT

The first bodily form (*forma*), which some call corporeity, I judge to be light. For light (*lux*) of itself diffuses itself in every direction, so that a sphere of light as great as you please is engendered instantaneously (*subito*) from a point of light,

Reprinted by permission from *On Light, or The Incoming of Forms,* C. G. Wallis, trans., St. John's Bookstore, Annapolis, 1939. Reprinted by permission of the Estate of C. G. Wallis.

unless something opaque stands in the way. But corporeity is that upon which of necessity there follows the extension of matter into three dimensions, although nevertheless each of them, namely corporeity and matter, is a substance which in itself is simple and has no dimensions at all. But it was impossible for form which in itself is simple and without dimensions to bring in everywhere dimensions into matter which is similarly simple and without dimensions, except by plurifying itself and by diffusing itself instantaneously' in every direction and, in its diffusion of itself, extending matter, since form cannot abandon matter, because it (form) is not separable, and because matter cannot be emptied of form. Still, I have put forward light as being that which of itself has this operation, namely to plurify itself and to diffuse itself instantaneously in every direction. Therefore whatever does this work either is light itself or is a doer of this work insofar as it participates in light, which does this of itself. Therefore corporeity either is light itself or is the doer of the said work and the bringer of dimensions into matter, insofar as it (corporeity) participates in light itself and acts through the virtue of the light itself. But it is impossible for the first form to bring dimensions into matter through the virtue of a form which follows upon it (the first form). Therefore light is not a form which follows upon corporeity, but is corporeity itself.

Further: men of good sense judge that the first bodily form is more worthy than all the later forms and of a more excellent and noble essence and more like the forms which stand separate. But light is of a more worthy and more noble and more excellent essence than all bodily things; and it is more like the forms which stand separate—and they are the intelligences—than all bodies are. Therefore light is the first bodily form.

Therefore as light, which is the first form created in first matter and which of itself plurifies itself everywhere infinitely and stretches out equally in every direction, could not abandon matter, it drew out matter, along with itself, into a mass as great as the world-machine (*machina mundi*) and in the beginning of time extended matter. Nor could the extension of matter occur through a finite plurification of light, because a simple which is plurified a finite number of times does not engender a quantum (*simplex finities replicatum quantum non generat*), as Aristotle shows in the DE COELO ET MUNDO. But if a simple is plurified an infinite number of times, it necessarily engenders a finite quantum, because the product of the infinite plurification of something exceeds infinitely that by the plurification of which it was produced. Yet a simple is not exceeded infinitely by a simple, but a finite quantum alone exceeds a simple (thing) infinitely. For an infinite quantum exceeds a simple (thing) infinitely an infinite number of times. Therefore, if light, which in itself is simple, is plurified an infinite number of times, it necessarily extends matter, which is similarly simple, into dimensions of finite magnitude.

But it is possible that an infinite sum of number be related to an infinite sum (of number) in every numeric ratio and also in every non-numeric ratio. And there are infinities which are greater (*plura*) than other infinities; and infinities which are smaller (*pauciora*) than other infinities. For the sum of all numbers both even and odd is infinite; and so it is greater than the sum of all even numbers, which nevertheless is infinite. For (the sum of the even and odd) exceeds the sum of the even by the sum of all the odd numbers. Moreover the sum of the numbers doubled continuously from unity is infinite; and similarly the sum of all the halves corresponding to these doubles is infinite. And the sum of these halves is necessarily half of the sum of their doubles. Similarly the sum of all numbers tripled from unity is three times the sum of all the thirds corresponding to the triples. And the same thing is clear in all species of numeric ratio, since the infinite can be proportioned to the infinite in any of these ratios.

But if there are posited the infinite sum of all the doubles continuously from unity and the infinite sum of all the halves corresponding to those doubles and if unity or any finite number you please be taken away from the sum of the halves; then, after the subtraction has been made, the ratio of two to one will no longer hold between the first sum and the remainder of the second sum. Nor does any numeric ratio hold any longer; because, if, in the case of a numeric ratio after a subtraction has been made from the lesser sum, some other numeric ratio still holds, it is necessary that what has been subtracted be an aliquot part or the aliquot parts of an aliquot part of that from which it has been subtracted. But a finite number cannot be an aliquot part or the aliquot parts of an aliquot part of an infinite number. Therefore, if a number is subtracted from the infinite sum of halves, a numeric ratio no longer holds between the infinite sum of doubles and the remainder of the infinite sum of halves.

Therefore, since this is the case, it is manifest that light, by its infinite plurification, extends matter into lesser finite dimensions and into greater finite dimensions according to any ratios you please, that is, numeric and non-numeric ratios. For if light by an infinite plurification of itself extends matter to a dimension of two cubits, then by twice this same infinite plurification it extends matter to a dimension of four cubits, and by half of that same plurification it extends matter to the dimension of one cubit; and so on according to the other numeric and non-numeric ratios.

This, I presume, was the concept (*intellectus*) of the philosophers who lay down that all things are composed of atoms and who say that bodies are composed of surfaces, and surfaces of lines, and lines of points.—And this opinion does not contradict the one which lays down that magnitude is composed only of magnitudes; because "whole" is said in as many senses as "part" is. For in one sense "half" is said to be "part" of the "whole," because, if taken twice, it gives the whole: and in another sense the side is part of the diameter, not because, if taken an aliquot number of times, it gives the diameter; but because, if taken an aliquot number of times, it is exceeded by the diameter. And in another sense the angle of tangency is said to be part of a right angle, into which it goes an infinite number of times, and nevertheless, if subtracted from it a finite number of times, lessens it; and in still another sense a point is part of a line, into which it goes an infinite number of times, and, if subtracted from it a finite number of times, does not lessen it.

Accordingly, returning to my discourse, I say that by the infinite plurification of itself equally in every direction light extends matter everywhere equally into the form of a sphere; and it follows of necessity that in this extension the outmost parts of matter are more extended and more rarefied than the inmost parts near the center. And since the outmost parts will have been rarefied to the utmost, the inner parts will still be susceptible of greater rarefaction.

Therefore light in the aforesaid way, extending matter into the form of a sphere and rarefying the outmost parts to the utmost, has in the farthest sphere fulfilled the possibility of matter and has not left matter susceptible of any further impression. And so the first body is perfected in the boundary of the sphere and is called the "firmament," having nothing in its composition except first matter and first form. And accordingly it is the most simple body as regards the parts constituting its essence and greatest quantity, and it does not differ from the genus body except that in it (the most simple body) matter has been fulfilled merely by the first form. But the genus body, which is in this and in other bodies and which has first matter and first form in its essence, abstracts from the fulfilment of matter by the first form and from the diminishing of matter by the first form.

And so, when the first body, which is the firmament, has been fulfilled in this way, it spreads out its lumière (*lumen*) from every part of itself to the center of the whole. For since light (*lux*) is the perfection of the first body and plurifies itself from the first body naturally, then of necessity light is diffused to the center of the whole. And since light is the whole which is not separable from matter in the diffusion of itself (light) from the first body, it extends the spirituality of the matter of the first body. And thus there proceeds from the first body "lumière," which is a spiritual body or, as you may prefer to say, bodily spirit. And this lumière in its passage does not divide the body through which it passes; and accordingly it passes instantaneously (*subito*) from the first body of the heavens down to the center. And its passage is not as if you were to understand that something one in number passes instantaneously from the heaven to the center—for that is quite impossible; but its passage occurs through the infinite plurification of itself and the infinite engendering of lumière. Therefore the lumière itself, which has been spread out from the first body to the center and gathered together, has assembled the mass (*molem*) existing within the first body. And since the first body, as being fulfilled and invariable, could not now be diminished, and since no place could become void, it was necessary in the very assembling that the outmost parts of the mass should be extended and dispersed. And thus a greater density came about in the inmost parts of the said mass, and the rarity was increased in the outmost parts. And the power of the lumière which was doing the assembling and the power of the lumière which in the very assembling was doing the separating were so great that they subtilized and rarefied to the utmost the outmost parts of the mass contained within the first body. And so there came to be in the outmost parts of the said mass "the second sphere," which is fulfilled and not receptive of any further impression. And thus there is the fulfillment and perfection of the second sphere: for lumière is engendered from the first sphere, and light, which in the first sphere is simple, is twofold in the second sphere.

But just as the lumière engendered by the first body has fulfilled the second sphere and within the second sphere has left the mass denser, so the lumière engendered from the second sphere has perfected the "third sphere" and within the third sphere has left the mass still denser by the assembling. And this assembling which disperses (*congregatio disgregans*) proceeded in this order, until the "nine celestial spheres" were fulfilled, and until the most dense mass—which was matter for the four elements, was assembled within the ninth and lowest sphere. But the lowest sphere, which is the sphere of the "moon," also engenders lumière from itself, and by its lumière it has assembled the mass contained within itself, and by this assembling it has subtilized and dispersed its outmost parts. Nevertheless the power of this lumière was not so great that by its assembling it dispersed its outmost parts to the utmost. On that account imperfection and the possibility of the reception of assembling and dispersal has remained in every part of this mass. And the highest part of this mass was not dispersed to the utmost but by its dispersal was made to be fire, and it still remained matter for the elements. And this element, engendering lumière from itself and assembling the mass contained within itself, has dispersed its outmost parts, but with a smaller dispersal of the fire itself; and thus it has brought forth "fire." But fire, engendering lumière from itself and assembling the mass contained within, has dispersed its outmost parts, but with a smaller dispersal of itself. And thus it has brought forth air. Air also, engendering from itself a spiritual body or bodily spirit and assembling that which is contained within itself and by this assembling dispersing its outer parts, has brought forth "water" and "earth." But because more of this assembling virtue than of the dispersing has remained in water, the water together with the earth has remained weighty.

So in this way the thirteen spheres of this sensible world were brought into being; namely the nine celestial, which cannot be altered, increased, generated, or corrupted, because fulfilled; and the four spheres which exist in the contrary manner and can be altered, increased, generated, and corrupted, because unfulfilled. And that is clear, since every higher body by reason of the lumière engendered from itself is the form (*species*) and perfection of the body following. And just as unity is potentially every number which follows, so the first body by the plurification of its own lumière is every body which follows.

The earth however is all the higher bodies because the higher lumières are summed up in itself; on that account the earth is called Pan by the poets—that is, All; and it is named Cybele, as if *cubile*, from the cube, that is, from solidity; because the earth is the most greatly compressed of all bodies, that is, Cybele the mother of all the gods; because, though the higher lumières are gathered together in the earth, nevertheless they are not arisen in the earth by their own operations, but it is possible for the lumière of any sphere you please to be drawn forth from the earth into act and operation; and so whatever god you wish will be born of the earth as if of some mother. But the middle bodies have two relations. For indeed they are related to the lower bodies as the first heaven is to all the remaining; and to the higher bodies, as the earth is to all the other bodies. And thus in some certain modes all the remaining bodies are in any one of them.

And the form (*species*) and perfection of all bodies is light (*lux*): but the light of the higher bodies is more spiritual and simple, while the light of the lower bodies is more bodily and plurified. Nor are all bodies of the same form or species, though they have originated from a simple or plurified light; just as all numbers are not of the same form or species, though nevertheless they are produced by the greater or lesser plurification from unity.

And in this discourse it is quite clear what the meaning is of those who say, "all things are one by the perfection of one light," and the meaning of those who say, "those things which are many are many by the diverse plurification of the very light."

But since the lower bodies participate in the form (*formam*) of the higher bodies, the lower bodies, by their participation in the same form as the higher body, are receptive of movement from the same bodiless motor virtue, by which motor virtue the higher body is moved. Wherefore the bodiless virtue of intelligence or soul, which moves the first and highest sphere by the daily movement, moves all the lower celestial spheres by the same daily movement. But insofar as they are lower, they receive this movement more weakly, because insofar as a sphere is lower, the first and bodily light in it is less pure and more weak.

But though the elements do participate in the form of the first heaven, nevertheless they are not moved in a daily movement by the mover of the first heaven. Although they participate in that first light, nevertheless they do not yield to the first motor virtue, since they have that light as impure, weak, and distant from its purity in the first body, and since they have density of matter too, which is the beginning (*principium*) of resistance and unyieldingness. Nevertheless some think that the sphere of fire wheels around in the daily movements, and they take the wheeling around of comets as a sign of that, and they say moreover that this movement continues as far as the waters of the sea, so that the tides of the sea may come from it. But nevertheless all who rightly philosophize say that the earth is exempt from this movement.

Moreover, in the same way because the spheres after the second sphere— usually named the eighth in the upward reckoning—participate in its form, all share in its movement which they have as their own in addition to the daily movement.

But because the celestial spheres are fulfilled and are not receptive of rarefaction or condensation, the light in them does not bend the parts of matter away from the center, in order to rarefy them, or toward the center, in order to condense them. And on that account the celestial spheres themselves are not receptive of movement upward or downward, but only of circular movement from the intellectual motor virtue, which turns back its glance toward itself in a bodily fashion (*in sese aspectum corporaliter reverberans*) and makes the spheres themselves resolve in a circular bodily movement. But because the elements themselves are unfulfilled, rarefiable, and condensable, the lumière which is in them either bends away from the center, in order to rarefy them, or toward the center in order to condense them. And on that account they are naturally movable either upward or downward.

But in the highest body, which is the most simple of bodies, there are four things to be found, namely, form, matter, composition, and the composite. Now the form, as being most simple, has the place of unity. But on account of the twofold power of the matter, namely its ability to receive impressions and to retain them, and also on account of density, which has its roots in matter—and this twofold power belongs first principally to the number two—matter is duly allotted the nature of the number two. But the composition holds the number three in itself, because in the composition there are evident the formed matter and the materialized form and the thing about the composition which is its very own (*proprietos*) and found in any composite whatever as a third thing other than the matter and the form. And that which besides these three is properly the composite is comprehended under the number four. Therefore the number four is in the first body, wherein all the other bodies are virtually; and accordingly at the roots (*radicaliter*) the number of the other bodies is not found to be beyond ten. For when the number one of the form, and the number two of the matter and the number three of the composition and the number four of the composite are added together, they make up the number ten. On this account ten is the number of the bodies of the spheres of the world, because, although the sphere of the elements is divided into four, nevertheless it is one by participation in the terrestrial and corruptible nature.

From this it is clear that ten is the full number of the universe, because every whole and perfect thing has something in itself like form and unity, and something like matter and the number two and something like composition and the number three, and something like the composite and the number four. And it is not possible to add a fifth beyond these four. Wherefore every whole and perfect thing is a ten.

But from this it is evident that only the five ratios found between the four numbers one, two, three, and four, are fitted to the composition and to the concord which makes every composite steadfast. Wherefore only those five concordant ratios exist in musical measures, in dances, and in rhythmic times.

ROGER BACON

THE OPUS MAJUS

Part Four of this Plea

In Which Is Shown the Power of Mathematics in the Sciences and in the Affairs and Occupations of this World

FIRST DISTINCTION, IN THREE CHAPTERS:

CHAPTER I.

After making it clear that many famous roots of knowledge depend on the mastery of the languages through which there is an entrance into knowledge on the part of the Latins, I now wish to consider the foundations of this same knowledge as regards the great sciences, in which there is a special power in respect to the other sciences and the affairs of this world. There are four great sciences, without which the other sciences cannot be known nor a knowledge of things secured. If these are known any one can make glorious progress in the power of knowledge without difficulty and labor, not only in human sciences, but in that which is divine. The virtue of each of these sciences will be touched upon not only on account of knowledge itself, but in respect to the other matters aforesaid. Of these sciences the gate and key is mathematics, which the saints discovered at the beginning of the world, as I shall show, and which has always been used by all the saints and sages more than all other sciences. Neglect of this branch now for thirty or forty years has destroyed the whole system of study of the Latins. Since he who is ignorant of this cannot know the other sciences nor the affairs of this world, as I shall prove. And what is worse men ignorant of this do not perceive their own ignorance, and therefore do not seek a remedy.

From *The Opus Majus of Roger Bacon,* 2 vols., R. B. Burke, trans., Philadelphia: University of Pennsylvania Press, 1928. Reprinted by permission of the publisher.

And on the contrary the knowledge of this science prepares the mind and
elevates it to a certain knowledge of all things, so that if one learns the roots
of knowledge placed about it and rightly applies them to the knowledge of the
other sciences and matters, he will then be able to know all that follows without
error and doubt, easily and effectually. For without these neither what precedes
nor what follows can be known; whence they perfect what precedes and regulate
it, even as the end perfects those things pertaining to it, and they arrange and
open the way to what follows. This I now intend to intimate through authority
and reason; and in the first place I intend to do so in the human sciences and
in the matters of this world, and then in divine knowledge, and lastly according
as they are related to the Church and the other three purposes.

CHAPTER III.

What has been shown as regards mathematics as a whole through authority,
can now be shown likewise by reason. And I make this statement in the first
place, because other sciences use mathematical examples, but examples are given
to make clear the subjects treated by the sciences; wherefore ignorance of the
examples involves an ignorance of the subjects for the understanding of which
the examples are adduced. For since change in natural objects is not found without
some augmentation and diminution nor do these latter take place without change,
Aristotle was not able to make clear without complications the difference between augmentation and change by any natural example, because augmentation
and diminution go together always with change in some way; wherefore he gave
the mathematical example of the rectangle which augmented by a gnomon
increases in magnitude and is not altered in shape. This example cannot be understood before the twenty-second proposition of the sixth book of the *Elements*.
For in that proposition of the sixth book it is proved that a smaller rectangle is
similar in every particular to a larger one and therefore a smaller one is not
altered in shape, although it becomes larger by the addition of the gnomon.
Secondly, because comprehension of mathematical truths is innate, as it were,
in us. For a small boy, as Tullius states in the first book of the *Tusculan Disputations,* when questioned by Socrates on geometrical truths, replied as though
he had learned geometry. And this experiment has been tried in many cases,
and does not hold in other sciences, as will appear more clearly from what
follows. Wherefore since this knowledge is almost innate, and as it were
precedes discovery and learning, or at least is less in need of them than other
sciences, it will be first among sciences and will precede others disposing us
toward them; since what is innate or almost so disposes toward what is acquired.
Thirdly, because this science of all the parts of philosophy was the earliest
discovered. For this was first discovered at the beginning of the human race.
Since it was discovered before the flood and then later by the sons of Adam, and
by Noah and his sons, as is clear from the prologue to the *Construction of the
Astrolabe* according to Ptolemy, and from Albumazar in the larger introduction
to astronomy, and from the first book of the *Antiquities,* and this is true as
regards all its parts, geometry, arithmetic, music, astronomy. But this would not
have been the case except for the fact that this science is earlier than the others
and naturally precedes them. Hence it is clear that it should be studied first, that
through it we may advance to all the later sciences.

Fourthly, because the natural road for us is from what is easy to that which is more difficult. But this science is the easiest. This is clearly proved by the fact that mathematics is not beyond the intellectual grasp of any one. For the people at large and those wholly illiterate know how to draw figures and compute and sing, all of which are mathematical operations. But we must begin first with what is common to the laity and to the educated; and it is not only hurtful to the clergy, but disgraceful and abominable that they are ignorant of what the laity knows well and profitably. Fifthly, we see that the clergy, even the most ignorant, are able to grasp mathematical truths, although they are unable to attain to the other sciences. Besides, a man by listening once or twice can learn more about this science with certainty and reality without error, than he can by listening ten times about the other parts of philosophy, as is clear to one making the experiment. Sixthly, since the natural road for us is to begin with things which befit the state and nature of childhood, because children begin with facts that are better known by us and that must be acquired first. But of this nature is mathematics, since children are first taught to sing, and in the same way they can learn the method of making figures and of counting, and it would be far easier and more necessary for them to know about numbers before singing, because in the relations of numbers in music the whole theory of numbers is set forth by example, just as the authors on music teach, both in ecclesiastical music and in philosophy. But the theory of numbers depends on figures, since numbers relating to lines, surfaces, solids, squares, cubes, pentagons, hexagons, and other figures, are known from lines, figures, and angles. For it has been found that children learn mathematical truths better and more quickly, as is clear in singing, and we also know by experience that children learn and acquire mathematical truths better than the other parts of philosophy. For Aristotle says in the sixth book of the *Ethics* that youths are able to grasp mathematical truths quickly, not so matters pertaining to nature, metaphysics, and morals. Wherefore the mind must be trained first through the former rather than through these latter sciences. Seventhly, where the same things are not known to us and to nature, there the natural road for us is from the things better known to us to those better known to nature, or known more simply; and more easily do we grasp what is better known to ourselves, and with great difficulty we arrive at a knowledge of those things which are better known to nature. And the things known to nature are erroneously and imperfectly known by us, because our intellect bears the same relation to what is so clear to nature, as the eye of the bat to the light of the sun, as Aristotle maintains in the second book of the *Metaphysics;* such, for example, are especially God and the angels, and future life and heavenly things, and creatures nobler than others, because the nobler they are the less known are they to us. And these are called things known to nature and known simply. Therefore, on the contrary, where the same things are known both to us and to nature, we make much progress in regard to what is known to nature and in regard to all that is there included, and we are able to attain a perfect knowledge of them. But in mathematics only, as Averroës says in the first book of the *Physics* and in the seventh of the *Metaphysics* and in his commentary on the third book of the *Heavens and the World,* are the same things known to us and to nature or simply. Therefore as in mathematics we touch upon what is known fully to us, so also do we touch upon what is known to nature and known simply. Therefore we are able to reach directly an intimate knowledge of that science.

Since, therefore, we have not this ability in other sciences, clearly mathematics is better known. Therefore the acquistion of this subject is the beginning of our knowledge.

Likewise, eighthly, because every doubt gives place to certainty and every error is cleared away by unshaken truth. But in mathematics we are able to arrive at the full truth without error, and at a certainty of all points involved without doubt, since in this subject demonstration by means of a proper and necessary cause can be given. Demonstration causes the truth to be known. And likewise in this subject it is possible to have for all things an example that may be perceived by the senses, and a test perceptible to the senses in drawing figures and in counting, so that all may be clear to the sense. For this reason there can be no doubt in this science. But in other sciences, the assistance of mathematics being excluded, there are so many doubts, so many opinions, so many errors on the part of man, that these sciences cannot be unfolded, as is clear since demonstration by means of a proper and necessary cause does not exist in them from their own nature because in natural phenomena, owing to the genesis and destruction of their proper causes as well as of the effects, there is no such thing as necessity. In metaphysics there can be no demonstration except through effect, since spiritual facts are discovered through corporeal effects and the creator through the creature, as is clear in that science. In morals there cannot be demonstrations from proper causes, as Aristotle teaches. And likewise neither in matters pertaining to logic nor in grammar, as is clear, can there be very convincing demonstrations because of the weak nature of the material concerning which those sciences treat. And therefore in mathematics alone are there demonstrations of the most convincing kind through a necessary cause. And therefore here alone can a man arrive at the truth from the nature of this science. Likewise in the other sciences there are doubts and opinions and contradictions on our part, so that we scarcely agree on the most trifling question or in a single sophism; for in these sciences there are from their nature no processes of drawing figures and of reckonings, by which all things must be proved true. And therefore in mathematics alone is there certainty without doubt.

Wherefore it is evident that if in other sciences we should arrive at certainty without doubt and truth without error, it behooves us to place the foundations of knowledge in mathematics, in so far as disposed through it we are able to reach certainty in other sciences and truth by the exclusion of error. This reasoning can be made clearer by comparison, and the principle is stated in the ninth book of Euclid. The same holds true here as in the relation of the knowledge of the conclusion to the knowledge of the premises, so that if there is error and doubt in these, the truth cannot be arrived at through these premises in regard to the conclusion, nor can there be certainty, because doubt is not verified by doubt, nor is truth proved by falsehood, although it is possible for us to reason from false premises, our reasoning in that case drawing in inference and not furnishing a proof; the same is true with respect to sciences as a whole; those in which there are strong and numerous doubts and opinions and errors, I say at least on our part, should have doubts of this kind and false statements cleared away by some science definitely known to us, and in which we have neither doubts nor errors. For since the conclusions and principles belonging to them are parts of the sciences as a whole, just as part is related to part, as conclusion to premises, so is science related to science, so that a science which is full of doubts and besprinkled with opinions and obscurities, cannot be rendered certain, nor made clear, nor verified except by some other science known and verified, certain and plain to us, as in the case of a conclusion reached through premises. But mathematics alone, as was shown above, remains fixed and verified for us with the utmost certainty and verification. Therefore by means of this science all other sciences must be known and verified.

Since we have now shown by the peculiar property of that science that mathematics is prior to other sciences, and is useful and necessary to them, we now proceed to show this by considerations taken from its subject matter. And in the first place we so conclude, because the natural road for us is from sense perception to the intellect, since if sense perception is lacking, the knowledge related to that sense perception is lacking also, according to the statement in the first book of the *Posterior Analytics,* since as sense perception proceeds so does the human intellect. But quantity is especially a matter of sense perception, because it pertains to the common sense and is perceived by the other senses, and nothing can be perceived without quantity, wherefore the intellect is especially able to make progress as respects quantity. In the second place, because the very act of intelligence in itself is not completed without continuous quantity, since Aristotle states in his book on *Memory and Recollection* that our whole intellect is associated with continuity and time. Hence we grasp quantities and bodies by a direct perception of the intellect, because their forms are present in the intellect. But the forms of incorporeal things are not so perceived by our intellect; or if such forms are produced in it, according to Avicenna's statement in the third book of the *Metaphysics,* we, however, do not perceive this fact owing to the more vigorous occupation of our intellect in respect to bodies and quantities. And therefore by means of argumentation and attention to corporeal things and quantities we investigate the idea of incorporeal things, as Aristotle does in the eleventh book of the *Metaphysics.* Wherefore the intellect will make progress especially as regards quantity itself for this reason, that quantities and bodies as far as they are such belong peculiarly to the human intellect as respects the common condition of understanding. Each and every thing exists as an antecedent for some result, and this is true in higher degree of that which has just been stated.

Moreover, for full confirmation the last reason can be drawn from the experience of men of science; for all scientists in ancient times labored in mathematics, in order that they might know all things, just as we have seen in the case of men of our own times, and have heard in the case of others who by means of mathematics, of which they had an excellent knowledge, have learned all science. For very illustrious men have been found, like Bishop Robert of Lincoln and Friar Adam de Marisco, and many others, who by the power of mathematics have learned to explain the causes of all things, and expound adequately things human and divine. Moreover, the sure proof of this matter is found in the writings of those men, as, for example, on impressions such as the rainbow, comets, generation of heat, investigation of localities on the earth and other matters, of which both theology and philosophy make use. Wherefore it is clear that mathematics is absolutely necessary and useful to other sciences.

These reasons are general ones, but in particular this point can be shown by a survey of all the parts of philosophy disclosing how all things are known by the application of mathematics. This amounts to showing that other sciences are not to be known by means of dialectical and sophistical argument as commonly introduced, but by means of mathematical demonstrations entering into the truths and activities of other sciences and regulating them, without which they cannot be understood, nor made clear, nor taught, nor learned. If any one in particular should proceed by applying the power of mathematics to the separate sciences, he would see that nothing of supreme moment can be known in them without mathematics. But this simply amounts to establishing definite methods of dealing with all sciences, and by means of mathematics verifying all things necessary to the other sciences. But this matter does not come within the limits of the present survey.

· · ·

Part Six of this Plea

It Is Also the Sixth Part of the Opus Majus, on Experimental Science

CHAPTER I.

Having laid down fundamental principles of the wisdom of the Latins so far as they are found in language, mathematics, and optics, I now wish to unfold the principles of experimental science, since without experience nothing can be sufficiently known. For there are two modes of acquiring knowledge, namely, by reasoning and experience. Reasoning draws a conclusion and makes us grant the conclusion, but does not make the conclusion certain, nor does it remove doubt so that the mind may rest on the intuition of truth, unless the mind discovers it by the path of experience; since many have the arguments relating to what can be known, but because they lack experience they neglect the arguments, and neither avoid what is harmful nor follow what is good. For if a man who has never seen fire should prove by adequate reasoning that fire burns and injures things and destroys them, his mind would not be satisfied thereby, nor would he avoid fire, until he placed his hand or some combustible substance in the fire, so that he might prove by experience that which reasoning taught. But when he has had actual experience of combustion his mind is made certain and rests in the full light of truth. Therefore reasoning does not suffice, but experience does.

This is also evident in mathematics, where proof is most convincing. But the mind of one who has the most convincing proof in regard to the equilateral triangle will never cleave to the conclusion without experience, nor will he heed it, but will disregard it until experience is offered him by the intersection of two circles, from either intersection of which two lines may be drawn to the extremities of the given line; but then the man accepts the conclusion without any question. Aristotle's statement, then, that proof is reasoning that causes us to know is to be understood with the proviso that the proof is accompanied by its appropriate experience, and is not to be understood of the bare proof. His statement also in the first book of the *Metaphysics* that those who understand the reason and the cause are wiser than those who have empiric knowledge of a fact, is spoken of such as know only the bare truth without the cause. But I am here speaking of the man who knows the reason and the cause through experience.

These men are perfect in their wisdom, as Aristotle maintains in the sixth book of the *Ethics,* whose simple statements must be accepted as if they offered proof, as he states in the same place.

He therefore who wishes to rejoice without doubt in regard to the truths underlying phenomena must know how to devote himself to experiment. For authors write many statements, and people believe them through reasoning which they formulate without experience. Their reasoning is wholly false. For it is generally believed that the diamond cannot be broken except by goat's blood, and philosophers and theologians misuse this idea. But fracture by means of blood of this kind has never been verified, although the effort has been made; and without that blood it can be broken easily. For I have seen this with my own eyes, and this is necessary, because gems cannot be carved except by fragments of this stone. Similarly it is generally believed that the castors employed by physicians are the testicles of the male animal. But this is not true, because the beaver has these under its breast, and both the male and female produce testicles of this kind. Besides these castors the male beaver has its testicles in their natural place; and therefore what is subjoined is a dreadful lie, namely, that when the hunters pursue the beaver, he himself knowing what they are seeking cuts out with his teeth these glands. Moreover, it is generally believed that hot water freezes more quickly than cold water in vessels, and the argument in support of this is advanced that contrary is excited by contrary, just like enemies meeting each other. But it is certain that cold water freezes more quickly for any one who makes the experiment. People attribute this to Aristotle in the second book of the *Meteorologics;* but he certainly does not make this statement, but he does make one like it, by which they have been deceived, namely, that if cold water and hot water are poured on a cold place, as upon ice, the hot water freezes more quickly, and this is true. But if hot water and cold are placed in two vessels, the cold will freeze more quickly. Therefore all things must be verified by experience.

But experience is of two kinds; one is gained through our external senses, and in this way we gain our experience of those things that are in the heavens by instruments made for this purpose, and of those things here below by means attested by our vision. Things that do not belong in our part of the world we know through other scientists who have had experience of them. As, for example, Aristotle on the authority of Alexander sent two thousand men through different parts of the world to gain experimental knowledge of all things that are on the surface of the earth, as Pliny bears witness in his *Natural History.* This experience is both human and philosophical, as far as man can act in accordance with the grace given him; but this experience does not suffice him, because it does not give full attestation in regard to things corporeal owing to its difficulty, and does not touch at all on things spiritual. It is necessary, therefore, that the intellect of man should be otherwise aided, and for this reason the holy patriarchs and prophets, who first gave sciences to the world, received illumination within and were not dependent on sense alone. The same is true of many believers since the time of Christ. For the grace of faith illuminates greatly, as also do divine inspirations, not only in things spiritual, but in things corporeal and in the sciences of philosophy; as Ptolemy states in the *Centilogium,* namely, that there are two roads by which we arrive at the knowledge of facts, one through the experience of philosophy, the other through divine inspiration, which is far the better way, as he says.

Moreover, there are seven stages of this internal knowledge, the first of which is reached through illuminations relating purely to the sciences. The second consists in the virtues. For the evil man is ignorant, as Aristotle says in the second book of the *Ethics*. Moreover, Algazel says in his *Logic* that the soul disfigured by sins is like a rusty mirror, in which the species of objects cannot be seen clearly; but the soul adorned with virtues is like a well-polished mirror, in which the forms of objects are clearly seen. For this reason true philosophers have labored more in morals for the honor of virtue, concluding in their own case that they cannot perceive the causes of things unless they have souls free from sins. Such is the statement of Augustine in regard to Socrates in the eighth book of the *City of God,* chapter III. Wherefore the Scripture says, "in a malevolent soul, etc." For it is not possible that the soul should rest in the light of truth while it is stained with sins, but like a parrot or magpie it will repeat the words of another which it has learned by long practice. The proof of this is that the beauty of truth known in its splendor attracts men to the love of it, but the proof of love is the display of a work of love. Therefore he who acts contrary to the truth must necessarily be ignorant of it, although he may know how to compose very elegant phrases, and quote the opinions of other people, like an animal that imitates the words of human beings, and like an ape that relies on the aid of men to perform its part, although it does not understand their reason. Virtue, therefore, clarifies the mind, so that a man comprehends more easily not only moral but scientific truths. I have proved this carefully in the case of many pure young men, who because of innocency of soul have attained greater proficiency than can be stated, when they have had sane advice in regard to their study. Of this number is the bearer of this present treatise, whose fundamental knowledge very few of the Latins have acquired. For since he is quite young, about twenty years of age, and very poor, nor has he been able to have teachers, nor has he spent one year in learning his great store of knowledge, nor is he a man of great genius nor of a very retentive memory, there can be no other cause except the grace of God, which owing to the purity of his soul has granted to him those things that it has as a rule refused to show to all other students. For as a spotless virgin he has departed from me, nor have I found in him any kind of mortal sin, although I have examined him carefully, and he has, therefore, a soul so bright and clear that with very little instruction he has learned more than can be estimated. And I have striven to aid in bringing it about that these two young men should be useful vessels in God's Church, to the end that they may reform by the grace of God the whole course of study of the Latins.

The third stage consists in the seven gifts of the Holy Spirit, which Isaiah enumerates. The fourth consists in the beatitudes, which the Lord defines in the Gospels. The fifth consists in the spiritual senses. The sixth consists in fruits, of which is the peace of God which passes all understanding. The seventh consists in raptures and their states according to the different ways in which people are caught up to see many things of which it is not lawful for a man to speak. And he who has had diligent training in these experiences or in several of them is able to assure himself and others not only in regard to things spiritual, but also in regard to all human sciences. Therefore since all the divisions of speculative

philosophy proceed by arguments, which are either based on a point from authority or on the other points of argumentation except this division which I am now
examining, we find necessary the science that is called experimental. I wish to
explain it, as it is useful not only to philosophy, but to the knowledge of God,
and for the direction of the whole world; just as in the preceding divisions I
showed the relationship of the languages and sciences to their end, which is the
divine wisdom by which all things are disposed.

CHAPTER II

Since this Experimental Science is wholly unknown to the rank and file of
students, I am therefore unable to convince people of its utility unless at the same
time I disclose its excellence and its proper signification. This science alone, therefore, knows how to test perfectly what can be done by nature, what by the effort
of art, what by trickery, what the incantations, conjurations, invocations, depreca-
tions, sacrifices, that belong to magic, mean and dream of, and what is in them,
so that all falsity may be removed and the truth alone of art and nature may be
retained. This science alone teaches us how to view the mad acts of magicians,
that they may be not ratified but shunned, just as logic considers sophistical
reasoning.

This science has three leading characteristics with respect to other sciences. The
first is that it investigates by experiment the notable conclusions of all those
sciences. For the other sciences know how to discover their principles by experiments, but their conclusions are reached by reasoning drawn from the principles
discovered. But if they should have a particular and complete experience of their
own conclusions, they must have it with the aid of this noble science. For it is
true that mathematics has general experiments as regards its conclusions in its
figures and calculations, which also are applied to all sciences and to this kind of
experiment, because no science can be known without mathematics. But if we
give our attention to particular and complete experiments and such as are attested
wholly by the proper method, we must employ the principles of this science
which is called experimental. I give as an example the rainbow and phenomena
connected with it, of which nature are the circle around the sun and the stars,
the streak (*virga*) also lying at the side of the sun or of a star, which is apparent
to the eye in a straight line, and is called by Aristotle in the third book of the
Meteorologics a perpendicular, but by Seneca a streak, and the circle is called a
corona, phenomena which frequently have the colors of the rainbow. The natural
philosopher discusses these phenomena, and the writer on Perspective has much
to add pertaining to the mode of vision that is necessary in this case. But neither
Aristotle nor Avicenna in their Natural Histories has given us a knowledge of

phenomena of this kind, nor has Seneca, who composed a special book on them.
But Experimental Science attests them.

SELECTED BIBLIOGRAPHY

TRANSLATIONS

Burke, R., trans., *The Opus Majus of Roger Bacon*, 2 vols., Philadelphia, 1928.

Lerner, R., and M. Mahdi, eds., *Medieval Political Philosophy: A Sourcebook*, New York, 1963.

McKeon, R., ed. and trans., *Selections from Medieval Philosophers, I: Augustine to Albert the Great, II: Roger Bacon to William of Ockham*, New York, 1929, 1930.

Riedl, C., trans., Robert Grosseteste, *On Light or the Beginning of Forms*, Milwaukee, 1942.

STUDIES

Baur, L., "Die Philosophie des Robert Grosseteste," *Beiträge zur Geschichte der Philosophie des Mittelalters*, XVIII (1917), fasc. 4–6.

Callus, D., "Robert Grosseteste's Place in the History of Philosophy," *Actes du XIe Congrès international de philosophie*, XII, 161–165.

Callus, D., "The Oxford Career of R. Grosseteste," *Oxoniensia*, X (1945), 42–72.

Callus, D., ed., *Robert Grosseteste, Scholar and Bishop*, Oxford, 1955.

Carton, R., *L'expérience physique chez Roger Bacon*, Paris, 1924.

Carton, R., *La synthèse doctrinale de Roger Bacon*, Paris, 1924.

Crombie, A., *Robert Grosseteste and the Origins of Experimental Science*, Oxford, 1953.

Crowley, T., *Roger Bacon, The Problem of the Soul in his Philosophical Commentaries*, Louvain, 1950.

Dunbabin, J., "Robert Grosseteste as Translator, Transmitter, and Commentator: the Nicomachean Ethics," *Traditio*, XXVIII (1972), 460–472.

Easton, S., *Roger Bacon and his Search for a Universal Science*, Oxford, 1952.

Eastwood, B., "Mediaeval Empiricism: The Case of Grosseteste's Optics," *Speculum*, XLIII (1968), 306–321.

Little, A., ed., *Roger Bacon Essays*, Oxford, 1914.

Lynch, L., "The Doctrine of Divine Ideas and Illumination in Robert Grosseteste," *Mediaeval Studies*, III (1941), 161–173.

Palma, R., "Grosseteste's Ordering of *scientia*," *The New Scholasticism*, L (1976), 447–463.

Serene, E., "Robert Grosseteste on Induction and Demonstrative Science," *Synthèse*, XL (1979), 97–115.

Sharp, D., *Franciscan Philosophy at Oxford in the Thirteenth Century*, Oxford, 1930.

Thomson, S., *The Writings of Robert Grosseteste, Bishop of Lincoln*, 1235–1253, Cambridge, 1940.

SIGER OF BRABANT

ca. 1240 – *ca.* 1284

ITH THE introduction of Aristotle's physical and metaphysical writings together with the commentaries of Muslim interpreters, two types of Aristotelians arose within the Christian world. There were those (such as Albertus Magnus and Thomas Aquinas) who, being theologians, undertook to harmonize Christian and Aristotelian teachings, while there were others who interpreted Aristotle in a purely philosophic fashion. Often called "Latin Averroists," these interpreters are perhaps better described as "secular Aristotelians" ("integral," "radical," "heterodox" Aristotelians are other terms used by modern scholars), for though they accepted a number of Averroistic doctrines, they also used the teachings of other philosophers.

The secular Aristotelians, many of whom seem to have been members of the Faculty of Arts at Paris, pursued philosophic studies without regard to Christian theological teachings. As philosophers, they taught such doctrines as the eternity of the world, the unity of the passive intellect in all men, and the resultant doctrines of collective immortality, determinism within the world, and the absence of free will in man. Since doctrines such as these clearly contradicted orthodox Christian teachings, small wonder that the views of secular Aristotelians were attacked by theologians and that the theses taught by them were publicly condemned. There is hardly a major theologian after the middle of the thirteenth century who did not write against the Averroistic doctrine of the unity of the intellect, and this response culminated in Etienne Tempier's publication of lists of condemned theses, first in 1270 and then again in 1277 (see p. 582).

Being Christians, or at least living within the Christian community, the secular Aristotelians, no less than the theologians, had to solve the problem of faith and reason. In the light of their commitment to pure philosophic speculation they developed what has been called a theory of the "double truth." The exact nature of this theory is not easily determined, though it is clear that it rests on the admission that philosophic and Christian teachings can contradict one another. How this contradiction is to be understood has been formulated by modern scholars in three ways. According to the first of these formulations, proponents of the theory affirm that a person can accept two contradictory propositions at the same time. Thus, for example, he can affirm as philosopher that the world is eternal, while as a Christian he maintains that the world has been created. It is questionable that anyone ever accepted the theory in accordance with this formulation. According to another formulation, proponents of the theory hold that they are merely explaining what Aristotle had taught, not expressing their own views. This is the view that was described (possibly by Aquinas) in a sermon at the University of Paris which says: "Among those who labor in philosophy, some say things that are not true according to faith, and when told that what they say goes against faith, they answer that it is the Philosopher who says so; as to themselves they do not affirm it, they are only repeating the Philosopher's words."* In still another formulation, the contradiction is explained by saying that the conclusions of philosophy are only the discoveries of the human mind, while the truths of faith are the products of supernatural revelation. Hence, in the case of conflict, the teachings of revelation are to be accepted.

It can easily be seen that doctrines such as these give rise to questions about the sincerity of their proponents. Were the secular Aristotelians believing Christians who, as philosophers, taught theologically difficult propositions, or were they philosophers who, for reason of expediency, assumed the guise of orthodox Christians? Put in this manner, there is no general answer to the question. Probably both kinds of persons were found among the secular Aristotelians. Only the detailed examination of a given philosopher's work can provide a description of his position, but even then one can not always be certain where he stands.

It is generally admitted that Siger of Brabant was the most prominent of the secular Aristotelians. At the same time, however, his teachings have been subject to varying interpretations, depending on how the chronology of his writings is fixed and how his professions of orthodox Christian beliefs are understood. These interpretations have ranged from that of Mandonnet and his followers who find in Siger an "Averroist" who embraces Christian teachings because it is expedient, to that of Van Steenberghen who finds no need to question Siger's sincerity, and sees him as moving from an "integral Aristotelianism" to a position approximating that of Aquinas.

Whatever one's solution of this question, it is clear that at least during a part of his life, Siger accepted some of the typical propositions of the secular Aristotelians: the truths of religion and philosophy can conflict, creation out of nothing is untenable philosophically, the intellectual soul in all men is one, and the human will is determined. But it would be false to see in Siger merely a proponent of certain unorthodox views. He was a serious philosopher who addressed himself to a variety of philosophic issues current in his day. Thus, for example, he sided with Averroes against Avicenna in maintaining that the existence of God is demonstrated in physics rather than

---

* Quoted by Étienne Gilson, *History of Christian Philosophy in the Middle Ages*, New York, 1955, p. 398.

in metaphysics, and that existence is not an attribute superadded to essence. Again, in formulating a doctrine of creation he inquires what "Aristotle, Avicenna, faith, and Proclus have in mind [when they say] that there exists one efficient cause of all things." In his question *On the Soul* he pays tribute to "two leading men in philosophy, Albertus and Thomas," though he does not share their views.

Brief mention must be made of a problem that is related to the interpretation of Siger's thought. Dante in his *Divine Comedy* (*Paradiso* X, 133–137) places Siger within Paradise, having him praised by none other than Thomas Aquinas. The interpretation of this passage is not easy. If Siger inclined toward Thomas' teachings (as Van Steenberghen thinks), his role can readily be understood. But if, as it is more frequently held, Dante was a Thomist while Siger was a secular Aristotelian, how could Dante place Siger within Paradise? Modern scholars have proposed three solutions to this question. Mandonnet holds that Dante was not acquainted with Siger's teachings; Gilson, that Siger is a symbol for philosophy and not the historical Siger; and Nardi, that Dante was not an orthodox Thomist, but made use of the doctrines of other philosophers.

Siger was born *ca.* 1240. He studied at Paris where by 1266, when he is first mentioned, he had become a master in the faculty of arts. For the next eleven years Siger together with his followers was the center of controversies at Paris. Bonaventure attacked Siger's teachings at conferences in 1267 and 1268 (see p. 456) and Etienne Tempier, as has been noted, condemned some of his theses publicly in 1270. It appears that after this condemnation Siger became more moderate in his language, though it is questionable that he changed his basic views. In 1277, the year of Tempier's second condemnation, Siger was summoned by Simon du Val, the Chief Inquisitor of France. But by that time Siger had left Paris, probably for Rome, perhaps because he felt that his case would fare better at the more lenient papal Curia. Siger was acquitted of heresy by Pope Nicholas III, but kept under house arrest. Sometime between 1281 and 1284 he was murdered at Orvieto by his demented secretary.

The discovery and publication of Siger's works during the past seventy years has been one of the major events in the study of medieval philosophy. For now medieval philosophy can no longer be viewed exclusively as the work of theologians, and room has had to be found for its secular branch. Among the works published are: *On the Intellective Soul* (*De anima intellectiva*), *On the Eternity of the World* (*De aeternitate mundi*), *On the Necessity and Contingency of Causes* (*De necessitate et contingentia causarum*), a number of logical, physical, psychological, and metaphysical Questions, six *Impossibilia,* and fragments of *On the Intellect* (*De intellectu*) and the *Book on Happiness* (*Liber de felicitate*).

The following selection consists of one of Siger's complete works, the *Question on the Eternity of the World*. Writing with great philosophic rigor and constructing his arguments carefully, Siger investigates in this work in what manner the human species (and the species of other beings subject to generation and corruption) was caused. But since the discussion rests on statements concerning the mode of existence of universals and the relation of potency to actuality, sections of the work are devoted to these two topics. Siger's characteristic statement "we say these things as the opinion of the Philosopher [Aristotle], although not asserting them as true," (see p. 500) is to be noted.

QUESTION ON THE
ETERNITY OF THE WORLD

The first question is whether the human species and in general the species of all individuals began to exist only by way of the propagation of generable and corruptible things when it had no previous existence whatsoever; and it seems that this is so.

That species of which any individual began to exist when it had had no previous existence at all is new and began to have existence since it universally and entirely had had no previous existence. The human species is such, and in general the species of all individuals generable and corruptible, because every individual of this type of species began to exist when it had had no previous existence. And, therefore, any species of such things is also new and began, since in all cases it had not previously existed. The major is stated thus: because the species does not have being nor is caused except in singulars and in causing singulars. If, therefore, any individual of some species has been created when it had not existed before, the species of those beings will be such a kind.

Secondly, this same conclusion is also able to be reached in a different manner thus: universals, just as they do not have existence in singulars, so neither are they caused. Every being is caused by God. Therefore, if man has been caused by God, since he is some being of the world, it is necessary that he come to exist in a certain determined individual; just as the heaven and whatever else has been caused by God. Because, if man does not have an individual eternity, as has the sensible heaven according to philosophers, then the human species will have been caused by God so that it began to exist when it had not existed before.

To prove this one must consider, in the first place how the human species was caused, and in general any other universals of generable and corruptible things; and in this way an answer should be made to the question and the forementioned argument.

Secondly, since the foregoing argument admits that universals exist in singulars, one must seek or consider how this may be true.

From C. Vollert, L. Kendzierski, and P. M. Byrne, ed. and trans., *St. Thomas Aquinas, Siger of Brabant, St. Bonaventure: On the Eternity of the World,* Milwaukee: Marquette University Press, 1964. This Question was translated by L. Kendzierski. Reprinted by permission.

Thirdly, because some species began to exist when it had surely not existed before, and because it follows that potentiality precedes act in duration, it should be seen which of these preceded the other in duration. For, this presents a difficulty within itself.

Concerning the first, therefore, we should know that the human species has not been caused, according to philosophers, except through generation. Now, because in general the being of all things is in matter which is in potency to form, they are made by a generation which is either essential or accidental. From this, however, that the human species has been made by God through generation, it follows that it does not proceed directly from Him. The human species, however, and in general the species of all things which are in matter, since it is made through generation, is not generated essentially but accidentally. It is not generated essentially, because if any one were to study those things which are made universally, then every thing which is made is made from this determined and individual matter. For, although arguments and knowledge are concerned with universals, yet operations are regarding singulars. Now, however, determined matter does not pertain to the meaning of species, and therefore is not generated essentially; and this is held by Aristotle in VII *Metaphysicae*. The same reason why form is not generated is also the reason why the composite which is species is not generated. And I call the species a composite, just as Callias in his own nature is this soul in this body, so also animal is soul in body. The common nature of form and species that they are not generated essentially is because individuated matter pertains to the consideration or reasoning of neither of the things from which generation essentially comes, through the transmutation of the thing from non-being to being, or from privation to form. The human species, however, although not generated essentially has nevertheless been generated accidentally, because it thus happens if man, just as he has been abstracted in thought from individual matter and from the individual, so he might be abstracted in existence. Then, just as he is not generated essentially, it might be thought that he is also not generated accidentally; but, because man in his being is this man, Socrates or Plato, then Socrates is also a man, as Aristotle says in VII *Metaphysicae,* that generating a brass sphere generates a sphere because a brass sphere is a sphere. And since just as Socrates is a man, so is Plato, and so with the others. Hence it is that man is generated through the generation of any individual, and not only of one determined individual.

Now, from the explanation it is clear in what way the human species is considered by philosophers eternal and caused. For, it is not to be thought of as eternal and caused as if it existed abstracted from individuals. Nor is it eternally caused in the sense that it exists in an eternally caused individual, as the species of heaven or an intelligence; but rather because in the individuals of the human species one is generated before the other eternally, and the species has to be and to be caused through an individual's existing and being caused. Hence it is that the human species always exists and that it did not begin to be after previous non-existence. For, to say that it began to be after it had not existed before is to say that there began to be a certain individual before whom no other individual of that species had existed. And since the human species has not been caused otherwise than generated through the generation of individual before individual, the human species or that which is called by the name of man begins to exist because universally everything generated begins to exist; begins, nevertheless, to exist when it existed and had previously existed. For, man begins to be through the generation of Socrates who is generated, he exists, nevertheless, through the existence of Plato of the previous generation. Those things are not contradictory about the universal; just as there is nothing repugnant for a man to run and not to run. Indeed, man runs in the person of Socrates, and man does not run in the person of Plato. From the fact, nevertheless, that Socrates runs, it is not true to say that man universally and entirely does not run. So also, in the fact that Socrates is generated man begins to be, is not to say that man begins to be in such a way that he had not in any wise previously existed.

From the previous discourse the solution to the forementioned argument is clear.

And first, it must be said that this argument as just stated, namely, that that species is new and began to exist when it had not previously existed, must be denied. Any individual of this kind began to be when it did not previously exist because even though it be true that no individual man began to be after not existing, yet no individual of this kind begins to be unless another one had previously existed. Species does not have existence so much through the existence of one of its individuals as another, and so the human species does not begin to be when it had not existed before. For, to admit that the species is such is to say that not only a certain individual of it began to be when he had not been before, but any individual of it began to be when neither he nor another individual of that species had existed before.

And the given reason is similar to the reasoning by which Aristotle speculates in IV *Physicorum* whether past time is finite. All past time whether near or remote is a certain *then,* and the certain *then* has a measured distance to the present *now;* therefore all past time is finite. And each of the forementioned propositions is clear from the meaning of that *then* which Aristotle speaks of in IV *Physicorum.* The solution of this reasoning, according to Aristotle, is that although every second is finite, nevertheless since in time there is a *then* before the *then* to infinity, therefore not all past time is finite. For, what is composed of things finite in quantity yet infinite in number has to be infinite. So also, although there is no individual man but that he has begun to exist when he had not existed before, yet there is an individual before the individual to infinity; it is thus that man does not begin to be when he had in no wise existed before, and neither does time. And the case is similar—just as past time has to be through a certain *then,* so also species have to be through the existence of any one of its individuals.

Finally, as regards the form of the reasoning as proposed in the second way, it must be said that the universal does not have existence nor is caused except in singulars; since it is also said that all being has been caused by God, it must be conceded that man also exists as a being of the world and caused by God. But, since it is brought in the discussion and inferred that man has come into existence in some determined individual, it must be said that this conclusion is in no wise to be drawn from the premises; indeed, that reasoning is a hindrance to itself. For, it is accepted in the first place, that man does not have existence except in singulars nor is caused except in singulars; and it is clear that according to this reasoning he has existence and is created through one or through another. For this reason, therefore, it must be concluded that it is reasonable that man has come into existence in some determined individual. Indeed, the human species comes and came into being accidentally by the generation of individual before individual to infinity. This is not to say, however, that it (the human species) comes into existence only in some determined individual and when it had not existed before. Whence we should wonder about those arguing thus since they want to argue that the human species had begun through its being made; and yet that it was not made essentially but rather by the making of the individual, as they confess. To show their intention they ought to show that individual has not been generated before individual to infinity. This, however, they do not show but they propose one false theory, that the human species is not able to have been made eternal by God unless it had been created in some determined and eternal individual, just as the species of heaven was made eternal; and when they find no eternal being among the individuals of man, they think that they have demonstrated that the whole species began to exist when it had not been at all before.

II

    The second question is whether universals are in particulars, and it is clear that they are not since Aristotle says in II *De Anima,* that universals in themselves exist in the mind. And Themistius in a similar book, says that concepts are similar things which are universals, which the mind collects and stores within itself. And the same Themistius, in *super principium De Anima,* says that genus is a certain concept gathered from the slight similitude of the singulars; the concepts however are in the conceiving mind, and universals, since they are concepts, are also in the mind.

    But on the other hand, universals are universal things for otherwise they might not be said of particulars; and for this reason universals are not within the mind.

    Moreover, the thing itself, which is the subject for universality, the man or the stone, is not in the mind. Also, the intention of universality must consist in its being called and denominated universal; and hence man and stone since they are called universals, the intention of universality is in these. Either both, the thing and the intention, or neither is in the mind. Because, if man and stone in respect to the fact that they are, are not in the mind, it seems that neither are they there in respect to the fact that they are universals.

    The solution. The universal, because it is a universal, is not a substance, as Aristotle states in VII *Metaphysicae.* And so this is clear. The universal, in that it is a universal, is different from any singular. If, therefore, the universal, in that it is universal, would be a substance, then it would be differing in substance from any of the singulars, and each (singular) would be a substance in act, both singular and universal; the act however would be distinguished. Therefore universals would be distinct substances and separated from particulars; on this account with Aristotle it amounts to the same thing to say that universals are substances as to say that they are separated from particulars. And if the universal, in that it is universal, is not a substance, then it is evident that there are two things in the universal, namely, the thing which is denominated universal, the man or stone, which is not in the mind, and the intention itself of universality, and this is in the mind; so that the universal in that it is universal does not exist except in the mind, as is evident in this way. For, nothing is called a universal because it exists of its own nature commonly and abstractly from particulars, or by the work of the intellect in the nature of things; because if in its own nature, in its very being, it were to exist abstracted from particulars, it would not be spoken of them since it would be separated from them and we would not need an active intellect. Moreover, the active intellect does not give things any abstraction in existence from individual matter or from particulars, but gives to them an abstraction according to intellection by producing an abstract intellection of those things. If, therefore, the man or stone are universals, it is not except that these things are known universally and abstractly from individual matter. These things do not exist thus in the nature of things because if understood, those things, the man and the stone, do not have existence except in the mind. Since the abstract comprehension of these things is not in things, then those things, because they are universals, are in the mind. And this can also be seen in like cases.

A certain thing is said to be known because there is a knowledge of it and it happens that it is understood. The thing itself, however, with respect to what it is, although it be outside the mind, yet in respect to its being understood, that is, in so far as there is understanding of it, exists only in the mind. Because, if universals are universals, and they are understood as such, namely, abstract and common to particulars, then the universals as universals do not exist except in the mind. And this is what Averroes says in *super Illum De Anima,* that universals as universals are entirely intelligibles; not as beings but as intelligibles. The intelligible, however, as intelligible, that is, in so far as there is an understanding of it, is entirely in the soul. Thus also Themistius says that universals are concepts.

But it must be observed that the abstract and common understanding of any nature, although it be something common, as a common understanding of particulars, yet is not common according to its being predicated of particulars in that it has to be abstracted from particulars; but that which is abstractly and commonly understood and of consequence is so signified, is spoken concerning particulars. For this reason—because that very nature which is spoken of and comprehended as a general thing is in things and is therefore spoken concerning particulars. Although those things are known and understood abstractly and commonly, they do not exist as such; therefore things of this kind are not predicated of particulars according to the ideas of genus and species.

And one must also consider that it is not necessary that the universal exist in actuality before it may be known because the universal in actuality is intelligible in actuality. Now, it is one and the same actuality whether of the intelligible in actuality or of the intellect in actuality; just as it is one motion whether of the active or of the passive, although they be different. But the intelligible in potency certainly precedes the understanding of it; however, such a thing is not universal also except in potency, and so it is not necessary that the universal have to be universal except in potency before it is understood.

Nevertheless, some have held the contrary in this discussion because the very activity of understanding precedes in the natural order the object causing that act. Now, however, the universal, in that it is universal, moves the intellect and is the object which causes the act of understanding; on this account it seems to them that the universal is not universal in that it is so understood, indeed, because the universal in the natural order is universal before it is so understood and is the cause of that understanding of it.

But the solution of this is that that nature by which is caused the act of the intelligible and of the intellect, which is the intellect in act, is the active intellect and also the phantasm which naturally precede that act. In what manner, however, those two concur to cause the act of understanding must be sought in *super IIIum De Anima*. But this must be said that the universal is not a universal before the concept and the act of understanding, as at least that act is of the active intellect. For, the understanding of the thing which is in the possible intellect, since it is possible as regards the subject, belongs to the active intellect as efficient. Thus the universal does not have formally that which is universal from the nature which causes the act of understanding. Indeed, as has been mentioned before, it is the concept and the actuality from which the universal receives its universality. Therefore universals, in that they are universals, are entirely in the mind. On this account they are not generated by nature inasmuch as they are universals, neither essentially nor accidentally. For, the nature which is stated and understood universally is in particular things and is generated accidentally.

To the first objection it must be said that the fact that universals are universal things can be understood in two ways; either because they exist universally or because they are understood universally. Universals, however, are not universal things in the first manner as if they existed universally in the nature of things, for they then would not be concepts of the mind. But universals are universal things in a second manner, that is, they are understood universally and abstractly; in this way universals, in so far as they are universals and since they are concepts, cannot be spoken of particulars as such. For, the idea of genus or species is not said of them, but the very nature which is thus understood as that which is itself included, is not in the mind, and is said of particulars.

In regard to another point, it must be said that things are rightly named after something which does not exist in reality. For, a thing understood is named from the understanding of it which is not in it but in the mind; and so also the universal is named from the universal and abstract understanding of it which is not in it but in the mind.

III

Consequently we must investigate the third question. Although act precedes potency in thought, for potentiality is defined through act, as we say the builder is able to build, potency nevertheless is prior to act in substance and in perfection in a thing which proceeds from potency to act because the things which are later in generation are, in substance and perfection, prior, since generation proceeds from the imperfect to the perfect and from potentiality to act. Act is also before potentiality in substance and perfection in the respect that potentiality and act are looked at in different ways; because eternal things are prior to corruptible things in substance and perfection. But nothing eternal, in respect that it is such a thing, is in potentiality. In corruptible beings, however, there is an admixture of potency.

The question is whether act precedes potentiality in time or potentiality the act.

And it seems that the act does not precede potentiality in time because in eternal beings one is not before the other in time. But when the act of a certain species and the potentiality to that act are looked upon according to the species, they are both eternal. For, man is always in act and is always able to be man.

Therefore the act thought of in relation to the species does not precede potentiality in time.

Moreover, in this matter in which one is to come from the other in a cycle to infinity, there is none which is first in time. But the seed is from the man and the man from the seed to infinity. Therefore, in those things the one does not precede the other in time. Just as in the case of the seed from which a man is generated there is another generating man previously existing, so also previous to that generating man, since he himself was generated, there must have been a seed from which he was generated.

What is first in the order of generation is first in the order of time. But potentiality is prior to act in the order of generation since generation proceeds from potentiality to act, and therefore it is prior in the order of time.

Moreover, there is no reason why act should precede potentiality in time except that by a power a being is made in act through some agent of its own kind existing in act. But, although from this it follows that the act of the agent precedes in time the act and perfection of the generated thing by that agent, nevertheless, it does not seem to happen that the act of the one generating precedes in time that which is in potentiality to the act of generation. Nor from this also does act simply precede potentiality in time, although some act precedes some potentiality to that act. For, just as being in potentiality comes into actuality through something of its own species in act, so also the thing existing in act in that species is generated from something existing in potentiality to the act of that species. For, just as that which is in potentiality, namely a man, is brought into act by a man in act, so also the man generating is generated from the previous seed and from a man in potency; and so in that reasoning the hen has preceded the egg in time and the egg the hen, as people argue.

On the other side is Aristotle in IX *Metaphysicae*. For, he holds that although what proceeds from potentiality to act is the same in number, yet potentiality precedes the act in time, nevertheless, the same being in relation to species and existing in act precedes potentiality.

Moreover, everything existing in potentiality is brought into actuality through something existing in act and at length is brought into the order of moving things by a mover existing completely in act who did not previously have in his power to be anything except in act. Therefore, according to this, act is seen simply to precede potency in time.

To prove this we must first consider that something numerically the same which has existence at some time in potentiality and some time in act is able to be prior in time than it is. But because this potency is preceded by act in another, since every being in potentiality comes into actuality by that which is in some way of its species, therefore it is not proper to say simply that potentiality precedes act in time.

Secondly, one must consider that if the whole universe of caused beings were at some time not being, as certain poets, theologians and natural philosophers claimed, Aristotle says in XII *Metaphysicae,* then potentiality would precede act simply. And also if some entire species of being, as the human species, would begin to exist when it had never existed before, just as some think they have demonstrated, the potentiality for the actuality of that species would simply precede the act. But each of these is impossible, as is evident from the first consideration.

For, if the whole universe of beings at some time had been in potentiality, so that none of the beings would be totally in act—always an agent in act and the mover—then the beings and the world would not now be except in potentiality, and matter of itself would come into act, which is impossible. Thus Aristotle says in XII *Metaphysicae,* and so does his Commentator, that for things to be at rest in an infinite time and afterwards to be in motion is the same as for matter to be self-moving.

From the second question it is evident that this is impossible. For, since the prime mover and agent is always in act, and something in potency is not prior to something in act, it follows that it always moves and acts and makes anything or does anything without an intermediate movement. From this, however, that it is always moving and so acting, it follows that no species of being proceeds to actuality, but that it has proceeded before, so that the same species which were, return in a cycle; and so also opinions and laws and religions and all other things so that the lower circle around from the circling of the higher, although because of the antiquity there is no memory of the cycle of these. We say these things as the opinion of the Philosopher, although not asserting them as true. One, nevertheless, should notice that a certain species of being is able to go into act when it did not exist except in potentiality, although at another time it also was in act, as is evident. For, it happens in the heavens that a certain spectacle and constellation appear in the heavens previously not existing, the effect of which is properly another species of being here below, which is then caused and which yet previously existed.

Thirdly, it must be considered that when it is taken that the potency to an act and the act educing that potency are of the same kind in the generator and thing generated, it is not said in so taking them that act precedes potentiality simply nor potentiality act, unless the act is taken according to the species and the proper potentiality is taken according to the individual. For, a man in act, and a certain man in act, inasmuch as he is generating, precedes in time that which is being in potency, namely, man generated. But because in this order, just as being in potency proceeds into act through something existing in act, and so act precedes any given potentiality, so also everything existing in act in this species goes from potentiality to act, and so potentiality in this species precedes any given act. Therefore neither simply precedes the other in time, but one comes before the other to infinity, as was stated.

In the fourth question we must consider that in a certain order of moving and acting beings it is necesary that that thing which proceeds from potentiality to act come to some act that educes that potentiality to actuality, and this act does not have to go from potentiality to act. Therefore, since every being in potentiality goes to actuality through some being of its own species in act, not all being, however, in actuality and generating proceeds from potentiality to act. Hence it is that in any given being in potentiality to some act, the act of the species in a certain way, although not entirely for the same reason, precedes that potentiality in time; not however in any given being in act does potentiality from which it proceeds to act, precede. And, therefore, the act is simply said to precede potentiality in time, as has been explained, namely, because the first mover leading into act all being in potentiality does not precede in time the being in potentiality, since the being in potentiality is regarded in the rank of prime matter. For, just as God always exists, according to Aristotle, so also does the potential man, since he is regarded as in prime matter. Moreover, the prime mover does not precede in time the being in potentiality, since it is looked upon as in matter properly considered in relation to species, as man is in the seed. For, it is never true, according to Aristotle, to say that God existed, unless potential man existed or had existed, as in the seed. But in a third manner from what has been said, act simply precedes potentiality in time because in any being in potentiality, as given in proper matter, the act of that potentiality having to educe the potency to act, precedes in time. It is not thus with any given being in act that the potentiality to that act precedes it in time, as is evident in prime movers educing to actuality all beings in potentiality. In the afore-mentioned we utilize, as also does Aristotle, prime movers as species of things which are educed from potentiality to actuality by them; and unless they were the beings of a certain kind in act which do not proceed from potentiality to actuality, the act would not simply precede the potentiality in time, as Aristotle has said in IX *Metaphysicae,* saying that act precedes potentiality in time, adding the reason, because one act is always taken as before another up to the one which is always the prime mover.

From this the solution of the reasoning of those opposed is clear.

To the first problem, therefore, it must be said that being in potentiality is not eternal unless when it is regarded as in prime matter. For, when taken as in its proper matter, according to which anything is said to exist properly in potentiality, as is said in IX *Metaphysicae,* it is new, unless it were taken according to species. For, just as nothing generated is corruptible in infinite time, so also nothing generable is not generated in infinite time since the generable has been taken as in proper matter and in a position near to generation, as the Commentator says in *super Ium Caeli et Mundi.*

To the second problem it must be said, as has been mentioned, that in the order of things generating existing in act which also proceed from potentiality to act, there is no being in act before the being in potentiality, but one there is always before the other to infinity. Because every being in potentiality in the essential order of moving and acting beings at length comes to some being existing in act which does not go from potentiality to act, hence it is that on account of that order the act is said simply to precede that potency.

To the third problem it must be said that it is well established that in a being which is the same in number proceeding from potency to act, potency precedes act; but that, nevertheless, before the being in potency there is another of the same species in act, educing it from potency to act.

To the last problem we must say that it is truly spoken that the act precedes potentiality, because all being in potentiality goes into actuality through something existing in act. Nor do those two things which are contradictory hinder one another. In the first place, this is not so because the being in act educing that which is in potentiality into act precedes in time not only the act in the being generated, but also the potentiality proper to the actuality of the being generated because of the fact that not only is the act of the generated being from the one generating, but also the being in potentiality to the act of the generated being is also from the one generating, as the seed from the man. And universally, proper matters are from the prime mover educing each thing from potentiality to act. In the second place, what is opposed does not hinder, as is evident from what has been said above. Although in the order of moving beings, on the basis of which the argument is made, it is necessary to admit that before being in act, there is a being in potency from which it proceeds into act, so also before being in potency there is a being in act which educes itself from potentiality to act; nevertheless, in another order of moving things it is necessary to hold that there is a being in act which educes into act what is in potency, since the being in potency from which it is made does not precede it, as is evident.

SELECTED BIBLIOGRAPHY

TRANSLATIONS

Shapiro, H., ed., *Medieval Philosophy: Selected Readings from Augustine to Buridan*, New York, 1964.

Vollert, C., L. Kendzierski, and P. Byrne, ed. and trans., *St. Thomas Aquinas, Siger of Brabant, St. Bonaventure: On the Eternity of the World*, Milwaukee, 1964.

STUDIES

Baeumker, C., *Die Impossibilia des Siger von Brabant; eine philosophische Streitschrift aus dem XIII. Jahrhundert*, Münster, 1898. (*Beiträge zur Geschichte der Philosophie des Mittelalters*, II, 4.)

Bazán, B., "Le dialogue philosophique entre Siger de Brabant et Thomas d'Aquin," *Revue philosophique de Louvain*, LXXII (1974), 53–155.

Bruckmüller, F., *Untersuchungen über Sigers De anima intellectiva*, Munich, 1908.

Bukowski, T., "The eternity of the world according to Siger of Brabant: probable or demonstrative?" *Recherches de théologie ancienne et médiévale*, XXXVI (1969), 225–229.

Duin, J., *La doctrine de la providence dans les écrits de Siger de Brabant; textes et étude*, Louvain, 1954.

Grabmann, M., *Der Lateinische Averroismus des 13. Jahrhunderts und seine Stellung zur Christlichen Weltanschauung; Mitteilungen aus ungedruckten Ethikkommentaren*, Munich, 1931. (Sitzungsberichte der Bayerischen Akademie der Wissenschaften; Philosophische-philologische und historische Klasse, 1931, Heft 2.)

Hissette, R., "Substance et création selon Siger de Brabant. A propos de l'interpretation d'Étienne Gilson," *Recherches de théologie ancienne et médiévale*, XLVI (1979), 221–224.

Kuksewicz, Z., *De Siger de Brabant à Jacques de Plaisance. La théorie de l'Intellect chez les Averroists latins des XIIIe et XIVe siècles*, Wroclaw, 1968.

Lefèvre, C., "Siger de Brabant a-t-il influencé Saint Thomas? Propos sur la cohérence de l'anthropologie thomiste," *Mélánges de science religieuse* (Lille), LXXIV (1974), 203–215.

MacClintock, S., "Heresy and Epithet: An Approach to the Problem of Latin Averroism," *The Review of Metaphysics*, VIII (1954–1955), 176–199, 342–356, 526–545.

MacClintock, S., *Perversity and Error; Studies on the "Averroist" John of Jandun*, Bloomington, 1956.

Mahoney, E., "Saint Thomas and Siger of Brabant Revisited," *The Review of Metaphysics*, XXVII (1974), 531–553.

Mandonnet, P., *Siger de Brabant et l'Averroism latin au XIIIme siècle*, Deuxième éd., revue et augmentée, 2 vols., Louvain, 1908–1911. (Les philosophes belges. Textes et études. Vols. 6–7.)

Maurer, A., "*Esse* and *Essentia* in the Metaphysics of Siger of Brabant," *Mediaeval Studies*, VIII (1946), 68–86.

Renan, E., *Averroès et l'Averroism*, 3rd ed., Paris, 1866. (Reprinted, 1948.)

Van Steenberghen, F., *Les oeuvres et la doctrine de Siger de Brabant*, Bruxelles, 1938.

Van Steenberghen, F., *Maître Siger de Brabant*, Louvain-Paris, 1977.

Van Steenberghen, F., *Siger de Brabant d'après ses oeuvres inédites*, 2 vols., Louvain, 1931–1942.

Van Steenberghen, F., "Siger de Brabant et la condamnation de l'Aristotelism hétérodoxe la 7 mars 1277," *Bulletin de l'Académie Royal de Belgique* (Lettres), LXIV (1978), 63–74.

Van Steenberghen, F., *Thomas Aquinas and Radical Aristotelianism*, Washington, 1980.

THOMAS AQUINAS

1225–1274

I N 1879, Pope Leo XIII issued the encyclical *Aeterni Patris,* in which he said, "we exhort you, venerable brethren, in all earnestness to restore the golden wisdom of St. Thomas, and to spread it far and wide for the defense and beauty of the Catholic faith, for the good of society, and for the advantage of all the sciences. . . . Let carefully selected teachers endeavor to implant the doctrine of Thomas Aquinas in the minds of students, and set forth clearly his solidity and excellence over others. Let the universities already founded or to be founded by you illustrate and defend this doctrine, and use it for the refutation of prevailing errors."* This only climaxed a long series of papal commendations of Aquinas. Thomism thus has the status of a kind of official doctrine in modern times, and this leads one to suppose that it must have been equally important in the thirteenth century. When one learns that several of his positions were condemned shortly after his death, it may well be wondered whether the reputation of Aquinas as the master voice of the golden age of scholastic philosophy may not owe more to modern intellectual politics than to authentic history. But when one looks to authentic history, it is clear that Thomas Aquinas was an important thinker in his own day and was controversial just because of that. He became Preacher General of his Order, he taught at the papal court, and, in an extremely unusual assignment, he served a second term as regent master of theology at Paris. His early canonization confirms this impression of a central significance.

Some of the reasons for this are not difficult to discover. The major controversies of the time were based upon the philosophy of Aristotle and his Muslim interpreters. In the early years of the thirteenth century it was forbidden to teach his physical and metaphysical works. But the culminating prohibition of 1231 was to hold only until those works had been purged of errors. The commission appointed for this did little, the prohibition was gradually ignored, and in the 1240s, Aristotle was taught in full at Paris as elsewhere. The bearing of his philosophy on theology thus became an unavoidable issue, intensifying the need to finish the task of "purging Aristotle." Aquinas can be seen as doing just this—in the words of his teacher

* Paragraph 31, quoted from J. Maritain, *St. Thomas Aquinas,* New York, 1958, p. 208.

Albert the Great, "making Aristotle intelligible to the Latins." To accomplish this, Aquinas had the advantage of new and accurate translations from the Greek made by his fellow Dominican, William of Moerbecke; he also was not as docile in accepting previous interpretations as authentic Aristotle as were some of his contemporaries. Aquinas thus could be said to do for Aristotle what he said Augustine did for Plato: "whenever he found in his teaching anything consistent with the faith he adopted it; and those things which he found contrary to faith he amended."

But to regard Aquinas merely as the Catholic Aristotle is to miss features of his thought of which much has been made by his followers. We must remember that the objections to Aristotle were theologically grounded. Bonaventure, for instance, thought the Aristotelian assumption of the self-sufficiency of nature was not as expressive of the dependence of creation on the Creator as the Platonic denigration of the sensible world in favor of ideal Forms. Piecemeal censorship could hardly cope with such encompassing objections; without comparable theological considerations there would be little reason to undertake a purgation at all. Aquinas' response is given in two equally fundamental positions: to detract from creatures is to detract from their Creator, and, grace perfects but does not destroy nature. The world of nature thus takes on a dignity which helps to legitimize the philosophical naturalism of Aristotle. The sensible world is not to be taken merely as a deficient symbol of a more purely spiritual realm, but as one of the levels of divine creation, with its own genuinely operative causes and powers. Such powers include man's natural reason, which is adequate for the knowledge of natural essences and certain truths deducible from them, such as the existence of God. But what of the problems which prompted the prohibitions of Aristotle in the first place? What, for instance, of his proof that the world is eternal, which contradicts the divine revelation that it is created? The problems are accentuated for Aquinas by his further principle that since truths knowable by natural reason and truths revealed in sacred Scriptures are parts of a single divine science, they can not be mutually contradictory. Furthermore, revealed truths must be regulative, since for the most part they concern matters which lie beyond the competence of natural reason. Aquinas must sift the claims of the philosophers, pointing out not only where their reasoning sometimes errs, but more interestingly, also where their assumptions can not be naturally validated. Some questions, including this one of the eternity of the world, are thus undecideable by natural reason.

It has also been urged that he does more than provide Aristotle with theological inspection and justification. Guided by revelation, he is held to have effected a properly philosophical transformation of certain Aristotelian positions—or, as it has been put, he makes Aristotle say things the Stagirite might not recognize. A good example of this is the doctrine of being. Aristotle's primary metaphysical distinction was between potentiality and actuality, and for him, being is ultimately actuality. Such a doctrine

could not be the last word for a theologian reflecting on creation and on the
statement in Exodus 3:14, "I am, that I am," which seems to say that God
is Being. Aquinas took up the distinction between essence and existence
already employed by the Muslims and used it to deepen Aristotle's conception. Existence he did not construe as an accident accruing to essence,
as Avicenna had it, but rather, as the very act of existing of the essence. In
God, essence and this act are identical, but creatures are ontologically complex. In natural creatures, the essence includes both form and matter, so there
is not only the actualization in form of the potentialities of matter, but also
the realization in existence of the entire essence. Needless to say, at a time
when the mode of a distinction was often as important as the distinction
itself, controversy soon developed as to whether this Thomistic version of
essence and existence was a distinction between realities or was some other
type of distinction.

One should, then, pay attention not only to the Aristotelianism of
Thomas Aquinas, but also to the theological perspective from which
Aristotle is legitimized and occasionally transformed. Sometimes Aquinas
seems to be aware that he is altering Aristotle, but sometimes he does not.
It is best not to assume that one has understood Aquinas fully merely because one understands the relevant passage from Aristotle, for the sea-
change it undergoes may be crucial.

Thomas Aquinas was born in 1225 at Roccasecca, near Aquino, not far
from Monte Cassino, the great parent abbey of the Benedictines. He was the
seventh son of a noble family; and, perhaps with political intent, perhaps because of a lame leg, or perhaps because of a precocious piety, he
was sent to that abbey as an oblate at the age of five. At fourteen he went
to the University of Naples, where despite resistance from his family he
became interested in the new Dominican Order. He is reported at one
time to have been offered the opportunity to become abbott of Monte Cassino with the privilege of remaining a nominal Dominican; but he persisted,
and in 1244, after the death of his father, he became a real Dominican.
Shortly thereafter he was kidnapped by his brothers and held for over a
year. Perhaps due to papal influence, he was released; and in the autumn
of 1245 was at the University of Paris studying under Albert the Great,
an encyclopedic thinker with a strong interest in Aristotle. By 1248, Aquinas
had his bachelor's degree and went to Cologne with Albert to set up a
Dominican study center. By 1252, he was back at Paris studying theology,
and in 1256 he obtained the master's degree. He had to be given a papal
dispensation to take the degree under age and a royal guard to protect him
from masters and students who were enraged by the freedom from university discipline of the members of the new mendicant orders. For the next
three years he taught theology at Paris. In June of 1259, the young theologian helped propose a program of study in the liberal arts for his Order at
a chapter held at Valenciennes, and in the same year he began a lengthy
sojourn with the papal court, moving from Anagni to Orvieto to Rome to

Viterbo. At Orvieto, both Albert the Great and William of Moerbecke were present. In 1268, Aquinas was sent back to Paris for his second period as regent master in theology. There he was confronted by the "Averroism" or secular Aristotelianism of many of the arts masters, led by Siger of Brabant, and by the "Augustinianism" forcefully expressed by John Peckham of the Franciscans, seconded by his general, Bonaventure. After the controversies of this regency, Aquinas was sent to Naples in 1272 to found a new study center; and there, suddenly, on December 6, 1273, he stopped writing. Such things had been revealed to him, he said, that all he had written seemed as straw. He became ill on his way to a general council of the Church; and on March 7, 1274, he died at the Cistercian monastery of Fossanuova. Controversy over his doctrines continued, and in 1277, certain of his theses were condemned by the Bishop of Paris along with many from so-called "Averroism." His works were adopted by the Dominicans and proscribed by the Franciscans. Under the sympathetic Pope John XXII, he was canonized on July 18, 1323, and the then Bishop of Paris revoked the earlier condemnation of his positions.

Aquinas wrote an enormous amount, even by medieval standards. Only major works which are widely recognized as philosophically important will be mentioned here. For further information, the reader can consult the "Catalogue of St. Thomas' Works" by I. T. Eschmann, O.P., which forms an appendix to E. Gilson, *The Christian Philosophy of St. Thomas Aquinas*. It was presumably between 1254 and shortly after 1256 that he completed his discussion of Peter Lombard's *Sentences* (*Scriptum in IV Libros Sententiarum*) and the very important *On Being and Essence* (*De ente et essentia*). During his first regency he completed some theological commentaries and the disputations appropriate for a teaching master: *Disputed Questions on Truth* (*Quaestiones disputatae de veritate*) and *Quodlibetal Questions* (*Quaestiones quodlibetales*). The greatest of his productions during the early years with the papal court is the *Summa against the Gentiles* (*Summa de veritate fidei Catholicae contra Gentiles*), finished in 1264. Tradition has it that this was written as a guide for Dominican missionaries in Spain. It was followed by the equally important *Summa of Theology* (*Summa Theologiae*), written to provide an ordered synthesis for beginners. The work was probably begun in 1265, and remained unfinished at Aquinas' death. He began at the papal court and finished later at Paris a series of expository commentaries on works of Aristotle, including the *De Interpretatione, De Anima, Nicomachean Ethics, Metaphysics, Physics, Politics* and *Posterior Analytics*. Upon his return to Paris, he engaged in further disputations, including *Disputed Question on the Soul* (*Quaestio disputata de anima*) and *Disputed Questions on Evil* (*Quaestiones disputatae de malo*). He also produced a series of short works on the burning issues of the time: *On the Eternity of the World* (*De aeternitate mundi*), *On the Unity of the Intellect* (*De unitate intellectus*), and *On Separate Substances* (*De substantiis separatis*).

esse = being

The selections which follow begin with the basic ontological doctrine Aquinas set forth in the early *On Being and Essence.* It should be pointed out that the term *esse* is translated here simply as 'being'. Some think that the complexity of Aquinas' thought calls for this to be translated as 'existence' or even 'act of existence'. It should also be noted that a major doctrine of Aquinas is that individuation is through matter in determinate dimensions. He calls this *materia signata,* which is rendered here as 'signate matter'. He also uses *designata,* but since he does not seem to have in mind the semantic relation moderns sometimes term 'designation', this is rendered usually as 'determinate'. However translated, this doctrine has important consequences for his conception of the soul and theory of knowledge, and came in for considerable criticism (see the Condemnation of 1277).

The remaining selections are all drawn from the *Summa of Theology,* where Aquinas intended a conciseness fitted for the introductory student. They begin with the nature of theology, showing how it is distinguished from philosophy, and exploring problems involved in the understanding of religious language. One problem concerns the logical status of predications concerning God and Creature, which Aquinas resolves by holding that such predication is analogical, which contrasts with the view held by Maimonides among others that they are negative, and with Duns Scotus' claim that some such predications must be univocal. The next group of selections is concerned directly for God. In those concerning the demonstrability of the existence of God, the criticism of Anselm's proof should be noted, and the limitations of Aquinas' own proofs. They proceed from facts of nature and the definitions of terms, rather than the knowledge of the divine essence, and such proofs can only show that something exists, not that its existence is adequately explained. They should also be compared with the proofs of Duns Scotus, who seems to regard these as less perfect than more properly metaphysical ones such as his. It should also be noted that the "Rabbi Moses" of the selections on providence is Moses Maimonides. The selections on the eternity of the world can be compared to the treatment by Siger of Brabant, and to that by St. Bonaventure, not included here. The acceptability of an infinite series of accidental efficient causes should also be brought to bear on the treatment of causal series in St. Thomas's proofs for the existence of God.

The next series emphasizes the problem of the soul, inseparable from the problem of knowledge for thirteenth-century thinkers. Aquinas' position is directed against Bonaventure and Averroes as well. The former held that in man there is not just one substantial form, but several, and that the soul has its own "spiritual" matter—a doctrine derived from Ibn Gabirol (see (p. 358). Averroes held that the individual knows by a complex relationship to an intellect common to the human species. Aquinas' account of the adequacy of natural cognitive powers can also be contrasted to the illuminationism of Augustine, and to the critique of the entire epistemology of intelligible species by William of Ockham. The emphasis on the role of the in-

Anselm

tellect in Aquinas' treatment of free will provides an introduction to the selections concerned for ethics, where there is a similar emphasis on the intellect in his treatment of happiness and in his theory of law. Here there are interesting comparisons to be made to Maimonides, Duns Scotus, and William of Ockham. The definition of law from Question 90, article 4, may also be helpful in following this treatment: "Law is nothing else than an ordinance of reason for the common good, promulgated by him who has the care of the community."

Aquinas' position as a major philosopher, both in the medieval and the modern worlds, needs little amplification. There may be room for doubt as to whether he is the most characteristic medieval Christian philosopher, but there is none that he has made the greatest mark in the world.

ON BEING AND ESSENCE

Introduction

A slight error in the beginning is large in the end, according to the Philosopher in *De Caelo et Mundo,* and being and essence are what is first conceived in the intellect, as Avicenna says in the *Metaphysics.* So, lest from ignorance of these error should occur, one should first set out the difficulty regarding them by telling what is signified by the terms 'essence' and 'being', how being and essence are found in various cases, and how they stand with respect to the logical intentions, i.e. genera, species and differentia.

Moreover, as we ought to take knowledge of what is simple from what is complex, and come to what is prior from what is posterior, so learning is helped by beginning with what is easier. Hence we should proceed from the signification of being to the signification of essence.

CHAPTER I

One should be aware that, as the Philosopher remarks in the *Metaphysics,* being just as being has two senses. One is that which is divided through the ten categories; the other is that which signifies the truth of propositions. The difference between these is that in the second sense everything can be called being about which an affirmative proposition can be formed, even if it calls for nothing real; this is the sense in which privations and negations are called beings. For we say that affirmation is opposed to negation, and that blindness is in the eye. But in the first sense it cannot be said that anything is being unless it calls for something real; so that in

Translated by James J. Walsh for this volume from *S. Thomas Aquinatis opusculum De ente et essentia,* ed. C. Boyer, Rome: Gregorian University, 1933. Boyer utilized both the Baur and Roland-Gosselin editions. An excellent annotated translation is by A. Maurer, *On Being and Essence,* Toronto: The Pontifical Institute of Mediaeval Studies, 1949. A more recent translation and interpretation is by J. Bobik, *Aquinas On Being and Essence,* Notre Dame: University of Notre Dame Press, 1965.

the first sense, blindness and such as that are not beings. Thus the term 'essence' is not taken from being in the second sense, for some are called beings in that sense which do not have an essence, as is obvious in the case of privations. But essence is taken from being in the first sense. Whence the Commentator, in the same place, says, "Being in the first sense is what signifies real substance."

And since, as was remarked, being in this sense is divided through the ten categories, it is required that essence signify something common to all natures through which various beings are organized into various species in various genera, as humanity is the essence of man, and so for other cases. And since that through which a thing is constituted into its own genus or species is what we signify through the definition indicating what a thing is, the term 'essence' has been changed by philosophers into the term 'quiddity' (whatness). And this is what the Philosopher often calls "what it was to be," that is, that through which something is *what* it is. It is also called form, in the sense in which the certitude of any thing is signified through form, as Avicenna says in Book II of his *Metaphysics*. By another name it is also called nature, taking nature in the first of the four senses which Boethius gives in his *De Duabis Naturis*. According to this, nature is said to be all that the intellect can grasp in any way, for a thing is only intelligible through its definition and essence. And the Philosopher also says in Book V of the *Metaphysics* that every substance is nature. But the term 'nature' taken in this sense seems to signify the essence of a thing ordered to the proper operation of the thing, since no thing lacks its own operation. But the term 'quiddity' is taken from what is signified through the definition, and it is called essence since through it and in it a thing has being.

CHAPTER II

But since being is primarily and unqualifiedly said of substances, and secondarily in a qualified sense of accidents, essence is truly and properly found in substances, but only in a qualified way in accidents.

Of substances, some are simple and some composite, and there is essence in both; but in a truer and nobler way in simples. . . .

In composite substances, form and matter are characteristic, such as are soul and body in man. But it cannot be said that either of these alone is called essence. It is clear that matter alone is not essence, since a thing is knowable and ordered in species or genus through its essence. But matter is not the basis of knowledge, nor is anything determined to species or genus in accordance with it, but rather only in accordance with that by which it is in act. Nor can form alone be called the essence of composite substance, howevermuch some try to maintain this. From what has been said, it is obvious that essence is what is signified through the definition of a thing, but the definition of natural substances does not contain form alone, but also matter. Otherwise, natural and mathematical definitions would not differ. Nor can it be said that matter is to be taken as a mere addition to essence in the definition of natural substance, as a being outside of its essence. For this manner of definition is more proper to accidents, which do not have perfect essence, and hence take substance or a subject outside of their genus in their definition. Thus it is obvious that essence includes matter and form. But it cannot be said that essence signifies a relation between matter and form or anything over and above them, since this would necessarily be an accident or extraneous to the thing, and the thing would not be known through it, all of which pertains to essence. For matter is brought into a being in act and a definite thing through form, which is the act of matter. So that which is added over and above does not give unqualified being in act to matter, but being in act in a certain way, as accidents do, as whiteness makes something white in act. When a form such as that is taken on, it is not said to be absolutely generated, but qualifiedly.

What remains, therefore, is that the term 'essence' signifies in the case of composite substances that which is compounded from matter and form.... however much it is form alone that in its way is the cause of being of this type. We see the same in other instances which are constituted from several principles. These things are not named from one or another of those principles alone, but from what embraces both. This is clear for flavors: sweetness is caused by the action of heat dissipating the humid, and however much heat is in this way the cause of sweetness, a body is not called sweet from the heat, but from the flavor which embraces heat and the humid. But since the principle of individuation is matter, it might seem to follow from this that the essence, which embraces form as well, is only of the particular and not the universal. From which it would follow that a universal would not have a definition, if essence is what is signified through definition. Hence it should be known that the matter which is the principle of individuation is not matter taken in any and every way, but only signate matter. And I call matter signate which is considered under definite dimensions. This matter is not called for in the definition of man just as man; but it would be called for in the definition of Socrates, if Socrates had a definition. In the definition of man, non-signate matter is called for, for it is not this bone and this flesh which is called for in the definition of man, but just bone and flesh, which are the non-signate matter for man.

CHAPTER III

... The essences of genus and of species also differ with respect to signate and non-signate, however much another manner of determination *(designationis)* might belong to each. For the determination of an individual with respect to a species is through matter determinate in its dimensions, but determination of a species with respect to genus is through a constitutive difference, which is taken from the form of the thing. But this determination or designation which is in the species with respect to the genus is not through anything existing in the essence of the species which is in no way in the essence of the genus. Indeed, whatever is in the species is also in the genus, although not as determinate. . . .

Hence the basis is apparent for the analogy between genus, species, and differentia on the one hand and matter, form, and the composite in nature on the other, even though the latter are not the same as the former. For genus is not matter, but is taken from matter as signifying the whole; nor is the differentia form, but is taken from form as signifying the whole. Whence we say man is the rational animal, but not from animal and rational in the way we say he is from soul and body. He is said to be man from soul and body in the way that a third thing is constituted from two things, neither of which the third thing is. For man is not the soul nor is he the body. But if man is said to be in some way from animal and rational, it will not be as a third thing from two things, but as a third concept *(intellectus)* from two concepts. For the concept of animal lacks the determination of the species-form, and it expresses the nature of the thing through its status as matter with respect to the final perfection. But the concept of the differentia "rational" consists in the determination of the species-form. The concept of the species or definition is constituted from these two concepts. And so, just as a thing constituted from various things does not take the predication of those things from which it is constituted, so neither does a concept take the predication of those concepts from which it is constituted. For we do not say that a definition is the genus or the differentia. . . .

As has been said, the nature of the species is indeterminate with respect to the individual, just as the nature of the genus is with respect to the species. Hence just as the genus, as it is predicated of the species, implies in its signification, however indistinctly, all that is determinately in the species, so the species, as it is predicated of the individual, must signify, though indistinctly, all that is essentially in the individual. In this way the essence of the species is signified by the word 'man', whence man is predicated of Socrates. But if the nature of the species is signified as set apart from the signate matter which is the principle of individuation, it will stand as a part, and the word 'humanity' signifies it in this way. For humanity signifies that whence man is man. But signate matter is not that whence man is man, and so in no way is it contained among those from which man has it that he is man. Since, therefore, the concept of humanity includes only those from which man has it that he is man, it is obvious that signate matter is excluded or set aside from its signification. And because a part is not predicated of the whole, so it is that humanity is predicated neither of man nor of Socrates. And so Avicenna says that the quiddity of a composite is not that very composite, however much the quiddity itself is composite. Thus humanity, even though it is composite, still is not man; rather, it has to be received into signate matter.

But, as was said, the determination of a species with respect to the genus is through forms, and the determination of an individual with respect to the species is through matter. So the term signifying that from which the nature of the genus is taken, setting the determining form completing the species, has to signify that material part of the whole, just as body is the material part of man. But the term signifying that from which the nature of the species is taken, setting aside the signate matter, signifies the formal part, and so humanity is signified as a certain form. And it is called the form of the whole, but not as though it were added on to the essential parts, matter and form, as the form of a house is added to its integral parts. Rather, it is a form which is the whole, embracing both form and matter, while setting aside that through which matter is rendered determinate.

And so it is apparent that the term 'man' and the term 'humanity' each signify the essence of man, but in different ways, as has been said. For the term 'man' signifies it as a whole, in that it does not explicitly involve the determination of matter, but contains that implicitly and indistinctly, just as the genus was said to contain the differentia. Hence the term 'man' is predicated of individuals. But the term 'humanity' signifies the essence as a part, since it only contains in its signification what belongs to man as man, with all determination of matter set aside. As a result it is not predicated of individual men. On account of this, sometimes the term 'essence' is found predicated of a thing (for Socrates is said to be a certain essence) and sometimes it is denied, as when we say the essence of Socrates is not Socrates.

CHAPTER IV

Having seen what is signified by the term 'essence' in composite substances, one should see how it stands with respect to the nature of genus, species, and differentia.

Since that to which the characteristic *(ratio)* of genus, species or differentia pertains is predicated of this designated singular, it is impossible for the characteristic of a universal, namely genus or species to pertain to essence signified as a part, as by the term 'humanity' or 'animality'. Hence Avicenna says that rationality is not the differentia, but the basis for the differentia; for the same reason, humanity is not the species nor is animality the genus. Likewise, it cannot be said that the characteristic of genus or species pertains to essence as a certain thing existing outside of singulars, as the Platonists maintained. For in that way, genus and species would not be predicated of this individual; it cannot be said that Socrates is what is separate from him, nor does what is separate conduce to the knowledge of this singular. What is left, then, is that the characteristic of genus or species pertains to essence as it is signified in the manner of a whole, as by the terms 'man' or 'animal', implicitly and indistinctly containing all that is in the individual.

Nature or essence taken thus can be regarded in two ways. One way is according to its own nature, and this is the absolute consideration of it. In this way, nothing is true to say of it except what pertains to it in just such a way; anything else is falsely attributed to it. For example, to man just as man there pertain rational and animal and whatever else falls into his definition. But white or black or any such not belonging to the nature of humanity does not pertain to man as man. Hence if it is asked whether this very nature can be called one or many, neither should be conceded. For either is outside of the concept of humanity, and either can accrue to it. For if plurality were of its very nature, it could never be one; yet it is one as it is in Socrates. Likewise, if unity belonged to its concept and nature, then there would be one and the same nature of Socrates and Plato, and it could not be pluralized among several instances.

Considered in the other way, essence has being in this one or that, and thus something is predicated as an accident of it by reason of that in which it is. In this way it is said that man is white, since Socrates is white, however much that does not pertain to man as man. But this nature has two-fold being, one in singulars, the other in the soul; and accidents follow upon the said nature in each. Thus in singulars it has multiple being according to the diversity of singulars. Yet for the nature itself, according to its proper, that is, absolute consideration, none of these has to be. For it is false to say that the nature of man, taken thus, has to be in this singular. For if to be in a singular pertained to man just as man, it would not ever be outside this singular. Likewise, if it pertained to man just as man not to be in this singular, it would never be in it. But it is true to say that being in this singular or that or in the soul does not belong to man just as man. It is obvious, then, that the nature of man absolutely considered abstracts from any being whatever, in a way that does not set aside any of them, and this nature so considered is what is predicated of all individuals. Yet it cannot be said that universality pertains to a nature taken thus, since unity and community belong to universality. But neither of those pertains to human nature according to its absolute consideration; for if community belonged to the concept of man, then wherever humanity were found, community would be found, and this is false. For in Socrates there is not found any community; whatever is in him is individuated. Likewise it cannot be said that the status of genus or species attaches to human nature according to the being which it has in individuals, since human nature is not found in individuals according to the unity pertaining to all, which is what the nature of universality requires.

What remains, then, is that the status of a species attaches to human nature according to the being it has in the intellect. For human nature has being in the intellect abstracted from everything individuating. It has a uniform character with regard to all individuals which are outside the soul, as it is equally the image of all and conducive to the knowledge of all insofar as they are men. And from its having such a relation to all individuals, the intellect devises and attributes to it the character of a species. Whence the Commentator says in Book I of the *De Anima* that it is the intellect which makes universality in things. Avicenna also says this in his *Metaphysics*. And however much this nature as known has the character of a universal as compared to the things which are outside the soul, since it is one likeness for all, still, according to the being it has in this or that intellect, it is a certain particular appearance *(species . . . intellecta)*. Hence the mistake of the Commentator in the *De Anima* is obvious. He wished to argue the unity of the intellect from the universality of the form as known. But the universality of that form is not according to the being which it has in the intellect, but according to the way it is referred to things as their likeness, just as if there were a corporeal statue representing many men, surely the image or appearance *(species)* of the statue would have its own singular being in the way it would be in this particular matter; but it would have the character of community as commonly representative of several. . . .

Thus it is clear how essence or nature stands regarding the character of species. This character does not come from those features which pertain to it in its absolute consideration, nor from the accidents such as whiteness or blackness which accrue to it according to the being it has outside the soul; but it comes from the accidents which accrue to it according to the being it has in the intellect. It is also in this way that the character of genus or differentia pertains to it.

CHAPTER V

Now it remains to see how essence is in separate substances, namely, the soul, the intelligences and the First Cause. Howevermuch all philosophers concede the simplicity of the First Cause, still some try to maintain the composition of matter and form in the intelligences and in souls. The author of this position is said to have been Avicebron in the book *Fons Vitae*. But this is contrary to what is usually said by philosophers, since they describe those substances as separate from matter and they argue them to be without matter. The strongest argument is from the power for knowing which is in them. For we only see forms to be actually known as separated from matter and its conditions; and they are made to be actually known only through the power of a knowing substance, as achieved by it and received in it. Whence it is necessary that in any knowing substance whatever, there be every type of immunity from matter; so that it does not have a material component, nor is it even as a form impressed in matter, as are materialized forms.

Nor can anyone claim that it is not every kind of matter that impedes the capacity to be known, but only corporeal matter. For if this were by reason of corporeal matter only, then to impede knowability would require that the matter have a corporeal form, since matter is only called corporeal because it stands under a corporeal form. And this cannot be, since that very corporeal form is actually knowable, as are other forms which are abstracted from matter. So in no way is there composition from matter and form in an intellective soul or an intelligence, with matter taken as it is in corporeal substances. But there is a composition of form and being. Thus in the comment on the ninth proposition of the *Liber de Causis* it is said that an intelligence is one having form and being, and form is taken there as the quiddity itself or the simple nature. And how this is, is plain to see. For whatever things are so disposed that one is the cause for the other to be, the one that has the character of the cause can be without the other, but not the reverse. But such a disposition is found in form and matter that form gives being to matter. So it is impossible for there to be any matter without form, but it is not impossible for there to be some form without matter. For form just as form does not have dependence on matter. If some forms are found which can only be in matter, this happens in that they are distant from the First Principle, which is the first act and pure act. And so those forms which are closest to the First Principle are forms inherently subsisting without matter, for form does not require matter throughout the genus, as was said. Forms of this kind are intelligences, and so it is not required that the essences or quiddities of these substances be other than form itself.

The essences of composite and simple substances differ, then, in that the essence of composite substances embraces not only form, but form and matter; but the essence of simple substances is form alone. And this makes for two other differences. One is that the essence of composite substance can be signified as a whole or a part, which happens because of the determination of matter, as was said. Hence the essence of a composite thing cannot be predicated in just any way of that composite thing, for it cannot be said that man is his quiddity. But the essence of a simple thing, which is its form, can only be signified as a whole, since there is nothing there except form as receiving the form. And so the essence of a simple substance is predicated of it in whichever way it is taken. So Avicenna says that the quiddity of a simple substance is itself simple, since there is not anything to receive it.

The second difference is that from the fact that the essences of composite things received in determinate matter are multiplied according to its division, it happens that some are the same in species but diverse in number. But since the essence of simples is not received in matter, no such multiplication can obtain in that case. Hence it is not required that many individuals of the same species be found for those substances; but there are as many species as there are individuals, as Avicenna explicitly states. Howevermuch such substances are forms without matter, it is not simplicity of every type which is in them, such as are pure acts, but they are mixed with potentiality, in this way: whatever does not belong to the concept of essence or quiddity comes from outside it and makes up a composition with essence, since no essence can be known without the parts of essence. But every essence or quiddity can be known without anything being known concerning its being. For I can know what man is, or a phoenix, and still not know whether or not it has being in reality *(rerum natura)*. Therefore it is obvious that being is other than essence or quiddity, unless perchance there is some thing whose quiddity is its being. There can only be one such being, the First. For it is impossible that there should be pluralization of anything except through the addition of some differentia, the way the nature of a genus is multiplied in species, or through a form being received in diverse matter, the way the nature of a species is multiplied in diverse individuals, or through one being abstracted and another received in something, in the way that if there were some separated heat, from the separation itself it would be other than an unseparated heat. But if there were given some thing which is only being, such that the very being is subsistent, this being would not take the addition of a differentia. For then it would not be being alone, but being and some form outside of that. And much less would it take the addition of matter, since then it would not be a subsisting being but a material one. So what is left is that there can only be one such thing which is its own being, when it is necessary that in any other thing outside of that, its being is other than its quiddity or nature or form. Thus it is necessary that in intelligences, being is outside of form; hence it was said that an intelligence is form and being.

But all that pertains to something is either caused from the principles of its own nature, as is the capacity to laugh in man, or comes to it from some extrinsic principle, as the light in the air from the influence of the sun. But being itself cannot be caused by the form or quiddity of a thing, speaking of the efficient cause, because then a thing would be the cause of itself and would bring itself into being, which is impossible. Therefore it is necessary that every such thing whose being is other than its nature should have its being from another. And since everything which is through something else is reduced to a first cause which is through itself, it is necessary that there be some thing which is the cause of being for all things, in that it is being alone. Otherwise there would be an infinity in causes, since everything which is not being alone has a cause for its being, as has been said. Thus it is apparent that an intelligence is form and being, and that it has its being from a first being which is being alone, and this is the First Cause, which is God.

But everything which receives something from another is in potentiality with respect to that, and what is received in it is its act. Therefore it is necessary that the form or quiddity which is an intelligence be in potentiality with respect to the being which it receives from God, and that the being is received as act. It is in this way that act and potency are found in intelligences, yet not form and matter, except equivocally. And so to undergo, to receive, to be a subject and all such which seem to pertain to things by reason of matter, pertain equivocally to intellectual and to corporeal substances, as the Commentators says in Book III of the *De Anima*. . . .

Distinction among these (separated) substances is thus according to the grade of potentiality and act, so that a superior intelligence which is closer to the First, has more of act and less of potentiality, and so for the others. This is ended in the human soul, which occupies the lowest rung among intellectual substances. Whence the possible intellect is disposed to knowable forms in the way that prime matter, which occupies the lowest rung in sensible being, is to sensible forms, as the Commentator says in Book III of the *De Anima*. So the Philosopher compares it to a blank slate on which nothing is written. And because it has more of potentiality than other substances capable of knowledge, it performs in such proximity to material things that a material thing is drawn to participate in its being. So from soul and body there results one being in one composite, however much that being, as belonging to the soul, is not dependent on the body. And after this form which is the soul, other forms are found having more of potentiality and closer to matter, so much so that they do not have being without matter. In these also is found order and grade, on down to the primary forms of the elements, which are closest to matter, so that they do not have any operation except according to the demands of active and passive qualities and others which dispose matter to form. . . .

THE SUMMA THEOLOGICA
Part One

Question I.   The Nature and Domain of Sacred Doctrine

FIRST ARTICLE.   *Whether, Besides the Philosophical Sciences, any Further Doctrine Is Required?*

We proceed thus to the First Article:—

Objection 1. It seems that, besides the philosophical sciences, we have no need of any further knowledge. For man should not seek to know what is above reason: *Seek not the things that are too high for thee* (*Ecclus.* iii. 22). But whatever is not above reason is sufficiently considered in the philosophical sciences. Therefore any other knowledge besides the philosophical sciences is superfluous.

Obj. 2. Further, knowledge can be concerned only with being, for nothing can be known, save the true, which is convertible with being. But everything that is, is considered in the philosophical sciences—even God Himself; so that there is a part of philosophy called theology, or the divine science, as is clear from Aristotle. Therefore, besides the philosophical sciences, there is no need of any further knowledge.

On the contrary, It is written (2 *Tim.* iii. 16): *All Scripture inspired of God is profitable to teach, to reprove, to correct, to instruct in justice.* Now Scripture, inspired of God, is not a part of the philosophical sciences discovered by human reason. Therefore it is useful that beside the philosophical sciences there should be another science—*i.e.,* inspired of God.

I answer that, It was necessary for man's salvation that there should be a knowledge revealed by God, besides the philosophical sciences investigated by human reason. First, because man is directed to God as to an end that surpasses the grasp of his reason: *The eye hath not seen, O God, besides Thee, what things Thou hast prepared for them that wait for Thee* (*Isa.* lxiv. 4). But the end must first be known by men who are to direct their thoughts and actions to the end. Hence it was necessary for the salvation of man that certain truths which exceed human reason should be made known to him by divine revelation. Even as regards those truths about God which human reason can investigate, it was necessary that man be taught by a divine revelation. For the truth about God, such as reason can know it, would only be known by a few, and that after a long time, and with the admixture of many errors; whereas man's whole salvation, which is in God, depends upon the knowledge of this truth. Therefore, in order that the salvation of men might be brought about more fitly and more surely, it was necessary that they be taught divine truths by divine revelation. It was therefore necessary that, besides the philosophical sciences investigated by reason, there should be a sacred science by way of revelation.

Reply Obj. 1. Although those things which are beyond man's knowledge may not be sought for by man through his reason, nevertheless, what is revealed by God must be accepted through faith. Hence the sacred text continues, *For many things are shown to thee above the understanding of man (Ecclus.* iii. 25). And in such things sacred science consists.

Reply Obj. 2. Sciences are diversified according to the diverse nature of their knowable objects. For the astronomer and the physicist both prove the same conclusion—that the earth, for instance, is round: the astronomer by means of mathematics (*i.e.,* abstracting from matter), but the physicist by means of matter itself. Hence there is no reason why those things which are treated by the philosophical sciences, so far as they can be known by the light of natural reason, may not also be treated by another science so far as they are known by the light of the divine revelation. Hence the theology included in sacred doctrine differs in genus from that theology which is part of philosophy.

SECOND ARTICLE. *Whether Sacred Doctrine Is a Science?*

We proceed thus to the Second Article:—

Objection 1. It seems that sacred doctrine is not a science. For every science proceeds from self-evident principles. But sacred doctrine proceeds from articles of faith which are not self-evident, since their truth is not admitted by all: *For all men have not faith* (2 Thess. iii. 2). Therefore sacred doctrine is not a science.

Obj. 2. Further, science is not of individuals. But sacred doctrine treats of individual facts, such as the deeds of Abraham, Isaac and Jacob, and the like. Therefore sacred doctrine is not a science.

On the contrary, Augustine says that *to this science alone belongs that whereby saving faith is begotten, nourished, protected and strengthened.* But this can be said of no science except sacred doctrine. Therefore sacred doctrine is a science.

I answer that, Sacred doctrine is a science. We must bear in mind that there are two kinds of sciences. There are some which proceed from principles known by the natural light of the intellect, such as arithmetic and geometry and the like. There are also some which proceed from principles known by the light of a higher science: thus the science of optics proceeds from principles established by geometry, and music from principles established by arithmetic. So it is that sacred doctrine is a science because it proceeds from principles made known by the light of a higher science, namely, the science of God and the blessed. Hence, just as music accepts on authority the principles taught by the arithmetician, so, sacred science accepts the principles revealed by God.

Reply Obj. 1. The principles of any science are either in themselves self-evident, or reducible to the knowledge of a higher science; and such, as we have said, are the principles of sacred doctrine.

Reply Obj. 2. Individual facts are not treated in sacred doctrine because it is concerned with them principally; they are rather introduced as examples to be followed in our lives (as in the moral sciences), as well as to establish the authority of those men through whom the divine revelation, on which this sacred scripture or doctrine is based, has come down to us.

THIRD ARTICLE. *Whether Sacred Doctrine Is One Science?*

We proceed thus to the Third Article:—

Objection 1. It seems that sacred doctrine is not one science, for according to the Philosopher *that science is one which treats only of one class of subjects.* But the creator and the creature, both of whom are treated in sacred doctrine, cannot be grouped together under one class of subjects. Therefore sacred doctrine is not one science.

Obj. 2. Further, in sacred doctrine we treat of angels, corporeal creatures and human morality. But these belong to separate philosophical sciences. Therefore sacred doctrine cannot be one science.

On the contrary, Holy Scripture speaks of it as one science: *Wisdom gave him the knowledge* [*scientiam*] *of holy things* (*Wis.* x. 10).

I answer that, Sacred doctrine is one science. The unity of a power or habit is to be gauged by its object, not indeed, in its material aspect, but as regards the formality under which it is an object. For example, man, ass, stone, agree in the one formality of being colored; and color is the formal object of sight. Therefore, because Sacred Scripture (as we have said) considers some things under the formality of being divinely revealed, all things which have been divinely revealed have in common the formality of the object of this science. Hence, they are included under sacred doctrine as under one science.

Reply Obj. 1. Sacred doctrine does not treat of God and creatures equally, but of God primarily, and of creatures only so far as they are referable to God as their beginning or end. Hence the unity of this science is not impaired.

Reply Obj. 2. Nothing prevents inferior powers or habits from being diversified by objects which yet agree with one another in coming together under a higher power or habit; because the higher power or habit regards its own object under a more universal formality. Thus, the object of the *common sense* is the sensible, including, therefore, whatever is visible or audible. Hence the *common sense,* although one power, extends to all the objects of the five senses. Similarly, objects which are the subject-matter of different philosophical sciences can yet be treated by this one single sacred science under one aspect, namely, in so far as they can be included in revelation. So that in this way sacred doctrine bears, as it were, the stamp of the divine science, which is one and simple, yet extends to everything.

FOURTH ARTICLE.   *Whether Sacred Doctrine Is a Practical Science?*

We proceed thus to the Fourth Article:—

Objection 1. It seems that sacred doctrine is a practical science, for a practical science is that which ends in action, according to the Philosopher. But sacred doctrine is ordained to action: *Be ye doers of the word, and not hearers only* (*Jas.* i. 22). Therefore sacred doctrine is a practical science.

Obj. 2. Further, sacred doctrine is divided into the Old and the New Law. But law belongs to moral science, which is a practical science. Therefore sacred doctrine is a practical science.

On the contrary, Every practical science is concerned with the things man can do; as moral science is concerned with human acts, and architecture with buildings. But sacred doctrine is chiefly concerned with God, Who is rather the Maker of man. Therefore it is not a practical but a speculative science.

I answer that, Sacred doctrine, being one, extends to things which belong to the different philosophical sciences, because it considers in each the same formal aspect, namely, so far as they can be known through the divine light. Hence, although among the philosophical sciences some are speculative and others practical, nevertheless sacred doctrine includes both; as God, by one and the same science, knows both Himself and His works.

Still, it is more speculative than practical, because it is more concerned with divine things than with human acts; though even of these acts it treats inasmuch as man is ordained by them to the perfect knowledge of God, in which consists eternal beatitude.

This is a sufficient answer to the Objections.

EIGHTH ARTICLE. *Whether Sacred Doctrine Is Argumentative?*

We proceed thus to the Eighth Article:—

Objection 1. It seems this doctrine is not argumentative. For Ambrose says: *Put arguments aside where faith is sought.* But in this doctrine faith especially is sought: *But these things are written that you may believe* (*Jo.* xx. 31). Therefore sacred doctrine is not argumentative.

Obj. 2. Further, if it is argumentative, the argument is either from authority or from reason. If it is from authority, it seems unbefitting its dignity, for the proof from authority is the weakest form of proof according to Boethius. But if from reason, this is unbefitting its end, because, according to Gregory, *faith has no merit in those things of which human reason brings its own experience.* Therefore sacred doctrine is not argumentative.

On the contrary, The Scripture says that a bishop should *embrace that faithful word which is according to doctrine, that he may be able to exhort in sound doctrine and to convince the gainsayers* (*Tit.* i. 9).

I answer that, As the other sciences do not argue in proof of their principles, but argue from their principles to demonstrate other truths in these sciences, so this doctrine does not argue in proof of its principles, which are the articles of faith, but from them it goes on to prove something else; as the Apostle argues from the resurrection of Christ in proof of the general resurrection (*I Cor.* xv, 12). However, it is to be borne in mind, in regard to the philosophical sciences, that the inferior sciences neither prove their principles nor dispute with those who deny them, but leave this to a higher science; whereas the highest of them, viz., metaphysics, can dispute with one who denies its principles, if only the opponent will make some concession; but if he concedes nothing, it can have no dispute with him, though it can answer his arguments. Hence Sacred Scripture, since it has no science above itself, disputes argumentatively with one who denies its principles only if the opponent admits some at least of the truths obtained through divine revelation. Thus, we can argue with heretics from texts in Holy Scripture, and against those who deny one article of faith we can argue from another. If our opponent believes nothing of divine revelation, there is no longer any means of proving the articles of faith by argument, but only of answering his objections— if he has any—against faith. Since faith rests upon infallible truth, and since the contrary of a truth can never be demonstrated, it is clear that the proofs brought against faith are not demonstrations, but arguments that can be answered.

Reply Obj. 1. Although arguments from human reason cannot avail to prove what belongs to faith, nevertheless, this doctrine argues from articles of faith to other truths.

minister
reason to
faith.

Reply Obj. 2. It is especially proper to this doctrine to argue from authority, inasmuch as its principles are obtained by revelation; and hence we must believe the authority of those to whom the revelation has been made. Nor does this take away from the dignity of this doctrine, for although the argument from authority based on human reason is the weakest, yet the argument from authority based on divine revelation is the strongest. But sacred doctrine also makes use of human reason, not, indeed, to prove faith (for thereby the merit of faith would come to an end), but to make clear other things that are set forth in this doctrine. (Since therefore grace does not destroy nature, but perfects it, natural reason should minister to faith as the natural inclination of the will ministers to charity.) Hence the Apostle says: *Bringing into captivity every understanding unto the obedience of Christ* (2 *Cor.* x. 5). Hence it is that sacred doctrine makes use also of the authority of philosophers in those questions in which they were able to know the truth by natural reason, as Paul quotes a saying of Aratus: *As some also of your own poets said: For we are also His offspring* (*Acts* xvii. 28). Nevertheless, sacred doctrine makes use of these authorities as extrinsic and probable arguments, but properly uses the authority of the canonical Scriptures as a necessary demonstration, and the authority of the doctors of the Church as one that may properly be used, yet merely as probable. For our faith rests upon the revelation made to the apostles and prophets, who wrote the canonical books, and not on the revelations (if any such there are) made to other doctors. Hence Augustine says: *Only those books of Scripture which are called canonical have I learned to hold in such honor as to believe their authors have not erred in any way in writing them. But other authors I so read as not to deem anything in their works to be true, merely because of their having so thought and written, whatever may have been their holiness and learning.*

NINTH ARTICLE.   *Whether Holy Scripture Should Use Metaphors?*

We proceed thus to the Ninth Article:—

Objection 1. It seems that Holy Scripture should not use metaphors. For that which is proper to the lowest science seems not to befit this science, which holds the highest place of all. But to proceed by the aid of various similitudes and figures is proper to poetic, the least of all the sciences. Therefore it is not fitting that this science should make use of such similitudes.

Obj. 2. Further, this doctrine seems to be intended to make truth clear. Hence a reward is held out to those who manifest it: *They that explain me shall have life everlasting* (*Ecclus.* xxiv. 31). But by such similitudes truth is obscured. Therefore to put forward divine truths under the likeness of corporeal things does not befit this doctrine.

Obj. 3. Further, the higher creatures are, the nearer they approach to the divine likeness. If therefore any creature be taken to represent God, this representation ought chiefly to be taken from the higher creatures, and not from the lower; yet this is often found in the Scriptures.

On the contrary, It is written (*Osee* xii. 10): *I have multiplied visions, and I have used similitudes by the ministry of the prophets.* But to put forward anything by means of similitudes is to use metaphors. Therefore sacred doctrine may use metaphors.

I answer that, It is befitting Holy Scripture to put forward divine and spiritual truths by means of comparisons with material things. For God provides for everything according to the capacity of its nature. Now it is natural to man to attain to intellectual truths through sensible things, because all our knowledge originates from sense. Hence in Holy Scripture spiritual truths are fittingly taught under the likeness of material things. This is what Dionysius says: *We cannot be enlightened by the divine rays except they be hidden within the covering of many sacred veils.* It is also befitting Holy Scripture, which is proposed to all without distinction of persons—*To the wise and to the unwise I am a debtor* (*Rom.* i. 14)—that spiritual truths be expounded by means of figures taken from corporeal things, in order that thereby even the simple who are unable by themselves to grasp intellectual things may be able to understand it.

Reply Obj. 1. Poetry makes use of metaphors to produce a representation, for it is natural to man to be pleased with representations. But sacred doctrine makes use of metaphors as both necessary and useful.

Reply Obj. 2. The ray of divine revelation is not extinguished by the sensible imagery wherewith it is veiled, as Dionysius says; and its truth so far remains that it does not allow the minds of those to whom the revelation has been made, to rest in the likenesses, but raises them to the knowledge of intelligible truths; and through those to whom the revelation has been made others also may receive instruction in these matters. Hence those things that are taught metaphorically in one part of Scripture, in other parts are taught more openly. The very hiding of truth in figures is useful for the exercise of thoughtful minds, and as a defense against the ridicule of the unbelievers, according to the words, *Give not that which is holy to dogs* (*Matt.* vii. 6).

Reply Obj. 3. As Dionysius says, it is more fitting that divine truths should be expounded under the figure of less noble than of nobler bodies; and this for three reasons. First, because thereby men's minds are the better freed from error. For then it is clear that these things are not literal descriptions of divine truths, which might have been open to doubt had they been expressed under the figure of nobler bodies, especially in the case of those who could think of nothing nobler than bodies. Second, because this is more befitting the knowledge of God that we have in this life. For what He is not is clearer to us than what He is. Therefore similitudes drawn from things farthest away from God form within us a truer estimate that God is above whatsoever we may say or think of Him. Third, because thereby divine truths are the better hidden from the unworthy.

TENTH ARTICLE.   *Whether in Holy Scripture a Word May Have Several Senses?*

We proceed thus to the Tenth Article:—

Objection 1. It seems that in Holy Scripture a word cannot have several senses, historical or literal, allegorical, tropological or moral, and anagogical. For many different senses in one text produce confusion and deception and destroy all force of argument. Hence no argument, but only fallacies, can be deduced from a multiplicity of propositions. But Holy Scripture ought to be able to state the truth without any fallacy. Therefore in it there cannot be several senses to a word.

Obj. 2. Further, Augustine says that *the Old Testament has a fourfold division: according to history, etiology, analogy, and allegory.* Now these four seem altogether different from the four divisions mentioned in the first objection. Therefore it does not seem fitting to explain the same word of Holy Scripture according to the four different senses mentioned above.

Obj. 3. Further, besides these senses, there is the parabolical, which is not one of these four.

On the contrary, Gregory says: *Holy Scripture by the manner of its speech transcends every science, because in one and the same sentence, while it describes a fact, it reveals a mystery.*

I answer that, The author of Holy Scripture is God, in Whose power it is to signify His meaning, not by words only (as man also can do), but also by things themselves. So, whereas in every other science things are signified by words, this science has the property that the things signified by the words have themselves also a signification. Therefore that first signification whereby words signify things belongs to the first sense, the historical or literal. That signification whereby things signified by words have themselves also a signification is called the spiritual sense, which is based on the literal, and presupposes it. Now this spiritual sense has a threefold division. For as the Apostle says (*Heb.* x. 1) the Old Law is a figure of the New Law, and Dionysius says *the New Law itself is a figure of future glory.* Again, in the New Law, whatever our Head has done is a type of what we ought to do. Therefore, so far as the things of the Old Law signify the things of the New Law, there is the allegorical sense; so far as the things done in Christ, or so far as the things which signify Christ, are signs of what we ought to do, there is the moral sense. But so far as they signify what relates to eternal glory, there is the anagogical sense. Since the literal sense is that which the author intends, and since the author of Holy Scripture is God, Who by one act comprehends all things by His intellect, it is not unfitting, as Augustine says, if, even according to the literal sense, one word in Holy Scripture should have several senses.

Reply Obj. 1. The multiplicity of these senses does not produce equivocation or any other kind of multiplicity, seeing that these senses are not multiplied because one word signifies several things, but because the things signified by the words can be themselves signs of other things. Thus in Holy Scripture no confusion results, for all the senses are founded on one—the literal—from which alone can any argument be drawn, and not from those intended allegorically, as Augustine says. Nevertheless, nothing of Holy Scripture perishes because of this, since nothing necessary to faith is contained under the spiritual sense which is not elsewhere put forward clearly by the Scripture in its literal sense.

Reply Obj. 2. These three—history, etiology, analogy—are grouped under the literal sense. For it is called history, as Augustine expounds, whenever anything is simply related; it is called etiology when its cause is assigned, as when Our Lord gave the reason why Moses allowed the putting away of wives—namely, because of the hardness of men's hearts (*Matt.* xix. 8); it is called analogy whenever the truth of one text of Scripture is shown not to contradict the truth of another. Of these four, allegory alone stands for the three spiritual senses. Thus Hugh of St. Victor includes the anagogical under the allegorical sense, laying down three senses only—the historical, the allegorical and the tropological.

Reply Obj. 3. The parabolical sense is contained in the literal, for by words things are signified properly and figuratively. Nor is the figure itself, but that which is figured, the literal sense. When Scripture speaks of God's arm, the literal sense is not that God has such a member, but only what is signified by this member, namely, operative power. Hence it is plain that nothing false can ever underlie the literal sense of Holy Scripture.

Question II. The Existence of God

FIRST ARTICLE.   *Whether the Existence of God Is Self-Evident?*

We proceed thus to the First Article:—

Objection 1. It seems that the existence of God is self-evident. For those things are said to be self-evident to us the knowledge of which exists naturally in us, as we can see in regard to first principles. But as Damascene says, *the knowledge of God is naturally implanted in all.* Therefore the existence of God is self-evident.

Obj. 2. Further, those things are said to be self-evident which are known as soon as the terms are known, which the Philosopher says is true of the first principles of demonstration. Thus, when the nature of a whole and of a part is known, it is at once recognized that every whole is greater than its part. But as soon as the signification of the name *God* is understood, it is at once seen that God exists. For by this name is signified that thing than which nothing greater can be conceived. But that which exists actually and mentally is greater than that which exists only mentally. Therefore, since as soon as the name *God* is understood it exists mentally, it also follows that it exists actually. Therefore the proposition *God exists* is self-evident.

Obj. 3. Further, the existence of truth is self-evident. For whoever denies the existence of truth grants that truth does not exist: and, if truth does not exist, then the proposition *Truth does not exist* is true: and if there is anything true, there must be truth. But God is truth itself: *I am the way, the truth, and the life (Jo.* xiv. 6). Therefore *God exists* is self-evident.

On the contrary, No one can mentally admit the opposite of what is self-evident, as the Philosopher states concerning the first principles of demonstration. But the opposite of the proposition *God is* can be mentally admitted: *The fool said in his heart, There is no God (Ps.* lii. 1). Therefore, that God exists is not self-evident.

I answer that, A thing can be self-evident in either of two ways: on the one hand, self-evident in itself, though not to us; on the other, self-evident in itself, and to us. A proposition is self-evident because the predicate is included in the essence of the subject: *e.g., Man is an animal,* for animal is contained in the essence of man. If, therefore, the essence of the predicate and subject be known to all, the proposition will be self-evident to all; as is clear with regard to the first principles of demonstration, the terms of which are certain common notions that no one is ignorant of, such as being and non-being, whole and part, and the like. If, however, there are some to whom the essence of the predicate and subject is unknown, the proposition will be self-evident in itself, but not to those who do not know the meaning of the predicate and subject of the proposition. Therefore, it happens, as Boethius says, that there are some notions of the mind which are common and self-evident only to the learned, as that incorporeal substances are not in space. Therefore I say that this proposition, *God exists,* of itself is self-evident, for the predicate is the same as the subject, because God is His own existence as will be hereafter shown. Now because we do not know the essence of God, the proposition is not self-evident to us, but needs to be demonstrated by things that are more known to us, though less known in their nature—namely, by His effects.

Reply Obj. 1. To know that God exists in a general and confused way is implanted in us by nature, inasmuch as God is man's beatitude. For man naturally desires happiness, and what is naturally desired by man is naturally known by him. This, however, is not to know absolutely that God exists; just as to know that someone is approaching is not the same as to know that Peter is approaching, even though it is Peter who is approaching; for there are many who imagine that man's perfect good, which is happiness, consists in riches, and others in pleasures, and others in something else.

Reply Obj. 2. Perhaps not everyone who hears this name *God* understands it to signify something than which nothing greater can be thought, seeing that some have believed God to be a body. Yet, granted that everyone understands that by this name *God* is signified something than which nothing greater can be thought, nevertheless, it does not therefore follow that he understands that what the name signifies exists actually, but only that it exists mentally. Nor can it be argued that it actually exists, unless it be admitted that there actually exists something than which nothing greater can be thought; and this precisely is not admitted by those who hold that God does not exist.

Reply Obj. 3. The existence of truth in general is self-evident, but the existence of a Primal Truth is not self-evident to us.

SECOND ARTICLE.   *Whether It Can Be Demonstrated that God Exists?*

We proceed thus to the Second Article:—

Objection 1. It seems that the existence of God cannot be demonstrated. For it is an article of faith that God exists. But what is of faith cannot be demonstrated, because a demonstration produces scientific knowledge, whereas faith is of the unseen, as is clear from the Apostle (*Heb.* xi. 1). Therefore it cannot be demonstrated that God exists.

Obj. 2. Further, essence is the middle term of demonstration. But we cannot know in what God's essence consists, but solely in what it does not consist, as Damascene says. Therefore we cannot demonstrate that God exists.

Obj. 3. Further, if the existence of God were demonstrated, this could only be from His effects. But His effects are not proportioned to Him, since He is infinite and His effects are finite, and between the finite and infinite there is no proportion. Therefore, since a cause cannot be demonstrated by an effect not proportioned to it, it seems that the existence of God cannot be demonstrated.

On the contrary, The Apostle says: *The invisible things of Him are clearly seen, being understood by the things that are made* (*Rom.* i. 20). But this would not be unless the existence of God could be demonstrated through the things that are made; for the first thing we must know of anything is, whether it exists.

I answer that, Demonstration can be made in two ways: One is through the cause, and is called *propter quid*, and this is to argue from what is prior absolutely. The other is through the effect, and is called a demonstration *quia;* this is to argue from what is prior relatively only to us. When an effect is better known to us than its cause, from the effect we proceed to the knowledge of the cause. And from every effect the existence of its proper cause can be demonstrated, so long as its effects are better known to us; because, since every effect depends upon its cause, if the effect exists, the cause must pre-exist. Hence the existence of God, in so far as it is not self-evident to us, can be demonstrated from those of His effects which are known to us.

Reply Obj. 1. The existence of God and other like truths about God, which can be known by natural reason, are not articles of faith, but are preambles to the articles; for faith presupposes natural knowledge, even as grace presupposes nature and perfection the perfectible. Nevertheless, there is nothing to prevent a man, who cannot grasp a proof, from accepting, as a matter of faith, something which in itself is capable of being scientifically known and demonstrated.

Reply Obj. 2. When the existence of a cause is demonstrated from an effect, this effect takes the place of the definition of the cause in proving the cause's existence. This is especially the case in regard to God, because, in order to prove the existence of anything, it is necessary to accept as a middle term the meaning of the name, and not its essence, for the question of its essence follows on the question of its existence. Now the names given to God are derived from His effects, as will be later shown. Consequently, in demonstrating the existence of God from His effects, we may take for the middle term the meaning of the name *God.*

Reply Obj. 3. From effects not proportioned to the cause no perfect knowledge of that cause can be obtained. Yet from every effect the existence of the cause can be clearly demonstrated, and so we can demonstrate the existence of God from His effects; though from them we cannot know God perfectly as He is in His essence.

THIRD ARTICLE. *Whether God Exists?*

We proceed thus to the Third Article:—

Objection 1. It seems that God does not exist; because if one of two contraries be infinite, the other would be altogether destroyed. But the name *God* means that He is infinite goodness. If, therefore, God existed, there would be no evil discoverable; but there is evil in the world. Therefore God does not exist.

Obj. 2. Further, it is superfluous to suppose that what can be accounted for by a few principles has been produced by many. But it seems that everything we see in the world can be accounted for by other principles, supposing God did not exist. For all natural things can be reduced to one principle, which is nature; and all voluntary things can be reduced to one principle, which is human reason, or will. Therefore there is no need to suppose God's existence.

On the contrary, It is said in the person of God: *I am Who am (Exod.* iii. 14). *I answer that,* The existence of God can be proved in five ways.

The first and more manifest way is the argument from motion. It is certain, and evident to our senses, that in the world some things are in motion. Now whatever is moved is moved by another, for nothing can be moved except it is in potentiality to that towards which it is moved; whereas a thing moves inasmuch as it is in act. For motion is nothing else than the reduction of something from potentiality to actuality. But nothing can be reduced from potentiality to actuality, except by something in a state of actuality. Thus that which is actually hot, as fire, makes wood, which is potentially hot, to be actually hot, and thereby moves and changes it. Now it is not possible that the same thing should be at once in actuality and potentiality in the same respect, but only in different respects. For what is actually hot cannot simultaneously be potentially hot; but it is simultaneously potentially cold. It is therefore impossible that in the same respect and in the same way a thing should be both mover and moved, *i.e.*, that it should move itself. Therefore, whatever is moved must be moved by another. If that by which it is moved be itself moved, then this also must needs be moved by another, and that by another again. But this cannot go on to infinity, because then there would be no first mover, and, consequently, no other mover, seeing that subsequent movers move only inasmuch as they are moved by the first mover; as the staff moves only because it is moved by the hand. Therefore it is necessary to arrive at a first mover, moved by no other; and this everyone understands to be God.

The second way is from the nature of efficient cause. In the world of sensible things we find there is an order of efficient causes. There is no case known (neither is it, indeed, possible) in which a thing is found to be the efficient cause of itself; for so it would be prior to itself, which is impossible. Now in efficient causes it is not possible to go on to infinity, because in all efficient causes following in order, the first is the cause of the intermediate cause, and the intermediate is the cause of the ultimate cause, whether the intermediate cause be several, or one only. Now to take away the cause is to take away the effect. Therefore, if there be no first cause among efficient causes, there will be no ultimate, nor any intermediate, cause. But if in efficient causes it is possible to go on to infinity, there will be no first efficient cause, neither will there be an ultimate effect, nor any intermediate efficient causes; all of which is plainly false. Therefore it is necessary to admit a first efficient cause, to which everyone gives the name of God.

The third way is taken from possibility and necessity, and runs thus. We find in nature things that are possible to be and not to be, since they are found to be generated, and to be corrupted, and consequently, it is possible for them to be and not to be. But it is impossible for these always to exist, for that which can not-be at some time is not. Therefore, if everything can not-be, then at one time there was nothing in existence. Now if this were true, even now there would be nothing in existence, because that which does not exist begins to exist only through something already existing. Therefore, if at one time nothing was in existence, it would have been impossible for anything to have begun to exist; and thus even now nothing would be in existence—which is absurd. Therefore, not all beings are merely possible, but there must exist something the existence of which is necessary. But every necessary thing either has its necessity caused by another, or not. Now it is impossible to go on to infinity in necessary things which have their necessity caused by another, as has been already proved in regard to efficient causes. Therefore we cannot but admit the existence of some being having of itself its own necessity, and not receiving it from another, but rather causing in others their necessity. This all men speak of as God.

The fourth way is taken from the gradation to be found in things. Among beings there are some more and some less good, true, noble, and the like. But *more* and *less* are predicated of different things according as they resemble in their different ways something which is the maximum, as a thing is said to be hotter according as it more nearly resembles that which is hottest; so that there is something which is truest, something best, something noblest, and, consequently, something which is most being, for those things that are greatest in truth are greatest in being, as it is written in *Metaph.* ii. Now the maximum in any genus is the cause of all in that genus, as fire, which is the maximum of heat, is the cause of all hot things, as is said in the same book. Therefore there must also be something which is to all beings the cause of their being, goodness, and every other perfection; and this we call God.

The fifth way is taken from the governance of the world. We see that things which lack knowledge, such as natural bodies, act for an end, and this is evident from their acting always, or nearly always, in the same way, so as to obtain the best result. Hence it is plain that they achieve their end, not fortuitously, but designedly. Now whatever lacks knowledge cannot move towards an end, unless it be directed by some being endowed with knowledge and intelligence; as the arrow is directed by the archer. Therefore some intelligent being exists by whom all natural things are directed to their end; and this being we call God.

Reply Obj. 1. As Augustine says: *Since God is the highest good, He would not allow any evil to exist in His works, unless His omnipotence and goodness were such as to bring good even out of evil.* This is part of the infinite goodness of God, that He should allow evil to exist, and out of it produce good.

Reply Obj. 2. Since nature works for a determinate end under the direction of a higher agent, whatever is done by nature must be traced back to God as to its first cause. So likewise whatever is done voluntarily must be traced back to some higher cause other than human reason and will, since these can change and fail; for all things that are changeable and capable of defect must be traced back to an immovable and self-necessary first principle, as has been shown.

Question XIII. The Names of God

SECOND ARTICLE. *Whether Any Name Can Be Applied to God Substantially?*

We proceed thus to the Second Article:—

Objection 1. It seems that no name can be applied to God substantially. For Damascene says: *Everything said of God must not signify His substance, but rather show forth what He is not; or express some relation, or something following from His nature or operation.*

Obj. 2. Further, Dionysius says: *You will find a chorus of holy doctors addressed to the end of distinguishing clearly and praiseworthily the divine processions in the denominations of God.* This means that the names applied by the holy doctors in praising God are distinguished according to the divine processions themselves. But what expresses the procession of anything does not signify anything pertaining to its essence. Therefore the names said of God are not said of Him substantially.

Obj. 3. Further, a thing is named by us according as we understand it. But in this life God is not understood by us in His substance. Therefore neither is any name we can use applied substantially to God.

On the contrary, Augustine says: *For God to be is to be strong or wise, or whatever else we may say of that simplicity whereby His substance is signified.* Therefore all names of this kind signify the divine substance.

I answer that, Names which are said of God negatively or which signify His relation to creatures manifestly do not at all signify His substance, but rather express the distance of the creature from Him, or His relation to something else, or rather, the relation of creatures to Himself.

But as regards names of God said absolutely and affirmatively, as *good, wise,* and the like, various and many opinions have been held. For some have said that all such names, although they are applied to God affirmatively, nevertheless have been brought into use more to remove something from God than to posit something in Him. Hence they assert that when we say that God lives, we mean that God is not like an inanimate thing; and the same in like manner applies to other names. This was taught by Rabbi Moses. Others say that these names applied to God signify His relationship towards creatures: thus in the words, *God is good,* we mean, God is the cause of goodness in things; and the same interpretation applies to other names.

Both of these opinions, however, seem to be untrue for three reasons. First, because in neither of them could a reason be assigned why some names more than others should be applied to God. For He is assuredly the cause of bodies in the same way as He is the cause of good things; therefore if the words *God is good* signified no more than, *God is the cause of good things,* it might in like manner be said that God is a body, inasmuch as He is the cause of bodies. So also to say that He is a body implies that He is not a mere potentiality, as is primary matter. Secondly, because it would follow that all names applied to God would be said of Him by way of being taken in a secondary sense, as healthy is secondarily said of medicine, because it signifies only the cause of health in the animal which primarily is called healthy. Thirdly, because this is against the intention of those who speak of God. For in saying that God lives, they assuredly mean more than to say that He is the cause of our life, or that He differs from inanimate bodies.

Therefore we must hold a different doctrine—viz., that these names signify the divine substance, and are predicated substantially of God, although they fall short of representing Him. Which is proved thus. For these names express God, so far as our intellects know Him. Now since our intellect knows God from creatures, it knows Him as far as creatures represent Him. But it was shown above that God prepossesses in Himself all the perfections of creatures, being Himself absolutely and universally perfect. Hence every creature represents Him, and is like Him, so far as it possesses some perfection: yet not so far as to represent Him as something of the same species or genus, but as the excelling source of whose form the effects fall short, although they derive some kind of likeness thereto, even as the forms of inferior bodies represent the power of the sun. This was explained above in treating of the divine perfection. Therefore, the aforesaid names signify the divine substance, but in an imperfect manner, even as creatures represent it imperfectly. So when we say, *God is good,* the meaning is not, *God is the cause of goodness,* or, *God is not evil;* but the meaning is, *Whatever good we attribute to creatures pre-exists in God,* and in a higher way. Hence it does not follow that God is good because He causes goodness; but rather, on the contrary, He causes goodness in things because He is good. As Augustine says, *Because He is good, we are.*

Reply Obj. 1. Damascene says that these names do not signify what God is because by none of these names is what He is perfectly expressed; but each one signifies Him in an imperfect manner, even as creatures represent Him imperfectly.

Reply Obj. 2. In the signification of names, that from which the name is derived is different sometimes from what it is intended to signify, as for instance this name *stone* [*lapis*] is imposed from the fact that it hurts the foot [*lædit pedem*]; yet it is not imposed to signify that which hurts the foot, but rather to signify a certain kind of body; otherwise everything that hurts the foot would be a stone. So we must say that such divine names are imposed from the divine processions; for as according to the diverse processions of their perfections, creatures are the representations of God, although in an imperfect manner, so likewise our intellect knows and names God according to each kind of procession. But nevertheless these names are not imposed to signify the processions themselves, as if when we say *God lives,* the sense were, *life proceeds from Him,* but to signify the principle itself of things, in so far as life pre-exists in Him, although it pre-exists in Him in a more eminent way than is understood or signified.

Reply Obj. 3. In this life, we cannot know the essence of God as it is in itself, but we know it according as it is represented in the perfections of creatures; and it is thus that the names imposed by us signify it.

FIFTH ARTICLE.   *Whether What Is Said of God and of Creatures Is Univocally Predicated of Them?*

We proceed thus to the Fifth Article:—

Objection 1. It seems that the things attributed to God and creatures are univocal. For every equivocal term is reduced to the univocal, as many are reduced to one: for if the name *dog* be said equivocally of the barking dog and of the dogfish, it must be said of some univocally—viz., of all barking dogs; otherwise we proceed to infinitude. Now there are some univocal agents which agree with their effects in name and definition, as man generates man; and there are some agents which are equivocal, as the sun which causes heat, although the sun is hot only in an equivocal sense. Therefore it seems that the first agent, to which all other agents are reduced, is a univocal agent: and thus what is said of God and creatures is predicated univocally.

Obj. 2. Further, no likeness is understood through equivocal names. Therefore, as creatures have a certain likeness to God, according to the text of *Genesis* (i. 26), *Let us make man to our image and likeness,* it seems that something can be said of God and creatures univocally.

Obj. 3. Further, measure is homogeneous with the thing measured, as is said in *Metaph.* x. But God is the first measure of all beings. Therefore God is homogeneous with creatures; and thus a name may be applied univocally to God and to creatures.

On the contrary, Whatever is predicated of various things under the same name but not in the same sense is predicated equivocally. But no name belongs to God in the same sense that it belongs to creatures; for instance, wisdom in creatures is a quality, but not in God. Now a change in genus changes an essence, since the genus is part of the definition; and the same applies to other things. Therefore whatever is said of God and of creatures is predicated equivocally.

Further, God is more distant from creatures than any creatures are from each other. But the distance of some creatures makes any univocal predication of them impossible, as in the case of those things which are not in the same genus. Therefore much less can anything be predicated univocally of God and creatures; and so only equivocal predication can be applied to them.

I answer that, Univocal predication is impossible between God and creatures. The reason of this is that every effect which is not a proportioned result of the power of the efficient cause receives the similitude of the agent not in its full degree, but in a measure that falls short; so that what is divided and multiplied in the effects resides in the agent simply, and in an unvaried manner. For example, the sun by the exercise of its one power produces manifold and various forms in these sublunary things. In the same way, as was said above, all perfections existing in creatures divided and multiplied pre-exist in God unitedly. Hence, when any name expressing perfection is applied to a creature, it signifies that perfection as distinct from the others according to the nature of its definition; as, for instance, by this term *wise* applied to a man, we signify some perfection distinct from a man's essence, and distinct from his power and his being, and from all similar things. But when we apply *wise* to God, we do not mean to signify anything distinct from His essence or power or being. And thus when this term *wise* is applied to man, in some degree it circumscribes and comprehends the thing signified; whereas this is not the case when it is applied to God, but it leaves the thing signified as uncomprehended and as exceeding the signification of the name. Hence it is evident that this term *wise* is not applied in the same way to God and to man. The same applies to other terms. Hence, no name is predicated univocally of God and of creatures.

Neither, on the other hand, are names applied to God and creatures in a purely equivocal sense, as some have said. Because if that were so, it follows that from creatures nothing at all could be known or demonstrated about God; for the reasoning would always be exposed to the fallacy of equivocation. Such a view is against the Philosopher, who proves many things about God, and also against what the Apostle says: *The invisible things of God are clearly seen being understood by the things that are made* (*Rom.* i. 20). Therefore it must be said that these names are said of God and creatures in an *analogous* sense, that is, according to proportion.

This can happen in two ways: either according as many things are proportioned to one (thus, for example *healthy* is predicated of medicine and urine in relation and in proportion to health of body, of which the latter is the sign and the former the cause), or according as one thing is proportioned to another (thus, *healthy* is said of medicine and an animal, since medicine is the cause of health in the animal body). And in this way some things are said of God and creatures analogically, and not in a purely equivocal nor in a purely univocal sense. For we can name God only from creatures. Hence, whatever is said of God and creatures is said according as there is some relation of the creature to God as to its principle and cause, wherein all the perfections of things pre-exist excellently. Now this mode of community is a mean between pure equivocation and simple univocation. For in analogies the idea is not, as it is in univocals, one and the same; yet it is not totally diverse as in equivocals; but the name which is thus used in a multiple sense signifies various proportions to some one thing: *e.g.,* *healthy,* applied to urine, signifies the sign of animal health; but applied to medicine, it signifies the cause of the same health.

Reply Obj. 1. Although in predications all equivocals must be reduced to univocals, still in actions the non-univocal agent must precede the univocal agent. For the non-univocal agent is the universal cause of the whole species, as the sun is the cause of the generation of all men. But the univocal agent is not the universal efficient cause of the whole species (otherwise it would be the cause of itself, since it is contained in the species), but is a particular cause of this individual which it places under the species by way of participation. Therefore the universal cause of the whole species is not a univocal agent: and the universal cause comes before the particular cause. But this universal agent, while not univocal, nevertheless is not altogether equivocal (otherwise it could not produce its own likeness); but it can be called an analogical agent, just as in predications all univocal names are reduced to one first non-univocal analogical name, which is *being*.

Reply Obj. 2. The likeness of the creature to God is imperfect, for it does not represent the same thing even generically.

Reply Obj. 3. God is not a measure proportioned to the things measured; hence it is not necessary that God and creatures should be in the same genus.

The arguments adduced in the contrary sense prove indeed that these names are not predicated univocally of God and creatures; yet they do not prove that they are predicated equivocally.

Question XIX. The Will of God

EIGHTH ARTICLE. *Whether the Will of God Imposes Necessity on the Things Willed?*

We proceed thus to the Eighth Article:—

Objection 1. It seems that the will of God imposes necessity on the things willed. For Augustine says: *No one is saved, except whom God has willed to be saved. He must therefore be asked to will it; for if He wills it, it must necessarily be.*

Obj. 2. Further, every cause that cannot be hindered produces its effect necessarily, because, as the Philosopher says, *nature always works in the same way, if there is nothing to hinder it.* But the will of God cannot be hindered. For the Apostle says (*Rom.* ix. 19): *Who resisteth His will?* Therefore the will of God imposes necessity on the things willed.

Obj. 3. Further, whatever is necessary by its antecedent cause is necessary absolutely; it is thus necessary that animals should die, being compounded of contrary elements. Now things created by God are related to the divine will as to an antecedent cause, whereby they have necessity. For this conditional proposition is true: *if God wills a thing, it comes to pass:* and every true conditional proposition is necessary. It follows therefore that all that God wills is necessary absolutely.

On the contrary, All good things that exist God wills to be. If therefore His will imposes necessity on the things willed, it follows that all good happens of necessity; and thus there is an end of free choice, counsel, and all other such things.

I answer that, The divine will imposes necessity on some things willed, but not on all. The reason of this some have chosen to assign to intermediate causes, holding that what God produces by necessary causes is necessary, and what He produces by contingent causes contingent.

This does not seem to be a sufficient explanation, for two reasons. First, because the effect of a first cause is contingent because of the secondary cause, from the fact that the effect of the first cause is hindered by deficiency in the second cause, as the sun's power is hindered by a defect in the plant. But no defect of a secondary cause can hinder God's will from producing its effect. Secondly, because if the distinction between the contingent and the necessary is to be referred only to secondary causes, this must mean that the distinction itself escapes the divine intention and will; which is inadmissible.

It is better therefore to say that this happens because of the efficacy of the divine will. For when a cause is efficacious to act, the effect follows upon the cause, not only as to the thing done, but also as to its manner of being done or of being. Thus from defect of active power in the seed it may happen that a child is born unlike its father in accidental points, which belong to its manner of being. Since then the divine will is perfectly efficacious, it follows not only that things are done, which God wills to be done, but also that they are done in the way that He wills. Now God wills some things to be done necessarily, some contingently, so that there be a right order in things for the perfection of the universe. Therefore to some effects He has attached unfailing necessary causes, from which the effects follow necessarily; but to others defectible and contingent causes, from which effects arise contingently. Hence it is not because the proximate causes are contingent that the effects willed by God happen contingently; but God has prepared contingent causes for them because He has willed that they should happen contingently.

Reply Obj. 1. By the words of Augustine we must understand a necessity in things willed by God that is not absolute, but conditional. For the conditional proposition that *if God wills a thing, it must necessarily be,* is necessarily true.

Reply Obj. 2. From the very fact that nothing resists the divine will, it follows not only that those things happen that God wills to happen, but that they happen necessarily or contingently according to His will.

Reply Obj. 3. Consequents have necessity from their antecedents according to the mode of the antecedents. Hence things effected by the divine will have that kind of necessity that God wills them to have, either absolute or conditional. Not all things, therefore, are necessary absolutely.

Question XXII. The Providence of God

SECOND ARTICLE.   *Whether Everything Is Subject to the Providence of God?*

We proceed thus to the Second Article:—

Objection 1. It seems that not everything is subject to divine providence. For nothing foreseen can happen by chance. If then everything has been foreseen by God, nothing will happen by chance. And thus chance and fortune disappear; which is against common opinion.

Obj. 2. Further, a wise provider excludes any defect or evil, as far as he can, from those over whom he has a care. But we see many evils existing in things. Either, then, God cannot hinder these, and thus is not omnipotent; or else He does not have care for everything.

Obj. 3. Further, whatever happens of necessity does not require providence or prudence. Hence, according to the Philosopher: *Prudence is the right reason of contingent things concerning which there is counsel and choice.* Since, then, many things happen from necessity, everything cannot be subject to providence.

Obj. 4. Further, whatsoever is left to itself cannot be subject to the providence of a governor. But men are left to themselves by God, in accordance with the words: *God made man from the beginning, and left him in the hand of his own counsel (Ecclus.* xv. 14). And particularly in reference to the wicked: *I let them go according to the desires of their heart (Ps.* lxxx. 13). Everything, therefore, cannot be subject to divine providence.

Obj. 5. Further, the Apostle says (*1 Cor.* ix. 9): *God doth not care for oxen;* and we may say the same of other irrational creatures. Thus everything cannot be under the care of divine providence.

On the contrary, It is said of divine wisdom: *She reacheth from end to end mightily, and ordereth all things sweetly (Wis.* viii. 1).

I answer that, Certain persons totally denied the existence of providence, as Democritus and the Epicureans, maintaining that the world was made by chance. Others taught that incorruptible substances only were subject to providence, while corruptible substances were not in their individual being, but only according to their species; for in this respect they are incorruptible. They are represented as saying (*Job* xxii. 14): *The clouds are His covert; and He doth not consider our things; and He walketh about the poles of heaven.* Rabbi Moses, however, excluded men from the generality of corruptible things, because of the excellence of the intellect which they possess, but in reference to all else that suffers corruption he adhered to the opinion of the others.

We must say, however, that all things are subject to divine providence, not only in general, but even in their own individual being. This is made evident thus. For since every agent acts for an end, the ordering of effects towards that end extends as far as the causality of the first agent extends. Whence it happens that in the effects of an agent something takes place which has no reference towards the end, because the effect comes from some other cause outside the intention of the agent. But the causality of God, Who is the first agent, extends to all beings not only as to the constituent principles of species, but also to the individualizing principles; not only of things incorruptible, but also of things corruptible. Hence all things that exist in whatsoever manner are necessarily directed by God towards the end; as the Apostle says: *Those things that are of God are well ordered (Rom.* xiii. 1). Since, therefore, the providence of God is nothing other than the notion of the order of things towards an end, as we have said, it necessarily follows that all things, inasmuch as they participate in being, must to that extent be subject to divine providence. It has also been shown that God knows all things, both universal and particular. And since His knowledge may be compared to the things themselves as the knowledge of art to the objects of art, as was said above, all things must of necessity come under His ordering; as all things wrought by an art are subject to the ordering of that art.

Reply Obj. 1. There is a difference between universal and particular causes. A thing can escape the order of a particular cause, but not the order of a universal cause. For nothing escapes the order of a particular cause, except through the intervention and hindrance of some other particular cause; as, for instance, wood may be prevented from burning by the action of water. Since, then, all particular causes are included under the universal cause, it is impossible that any effect should escape the range of the universal cause. So far then as an effect escapes the order of a particular cause, it is said to be by chance or fortuitous in respect to that cause; but if we regard the universal cause, outside whose range no effect can happen, it is said to be foreseen. Thus, for instance, the meeting of two servants, although to them it appears a chance circumstance, has been fully foreseen by their master, who has purposely sent them to meet at the one place, in such a way that the one has no knowledge of the other.

Reply Obj. 2. It is otherwise with one who is in charge of a particular thing, and one whose providence is universal, because a particular provider excludes all defects from what is subject to his care as far as he can; whereas one who provides universally allows some little defect to remain, lest the good of the whole should be hindered. Hence, corruption and defects in natural things are said to be contrary to some particular nature, yet they are in keeping with the plan of universal nature, inasmuch as the defect in one thing yields to the good of another, or even to the universal good: for the corruption of one is the generation of another, and through this it is that a species is kept in existence. Since God, then, provides universally for all being, it belongs to His providence to permit certain defects in particular effects, that the perfect good of the universe may not be hindered; for if all evil were prevented, much good would be absent from the universe. A lion would cease to live, if there were no slaying of animals; and there would be no patience of martyrs if there were no tyrannical persecution. Thus Augustine says: *Almighty God would in no wise permit evil to exist in His works, unless He were so almighty and so good as to produce good even from evil.* It would appear that it was because of these two arguments to which we have just replied, that some were persuaded to consider corruptible things—*i.e.,* things in which chance and evil are found—as removed from the care of divine providence.

Reply Obj. 3. Man is not the author of nature; but he uses natural things for his own purposes in his works of art and virtue. Hence human providence does not reach to that which takes place in nature from necessity; but divine providence extends thus far, since God is the author of nature. Apparently it was this arugment that moved those who withdrew the course of nature from the care of divine providence, attributing it rather to the necessity of matter as did Democritus, and others of the ancients.

Reply Obj. 4. When it is said that God left man to himself, this does not mean that man is exempt from divine providence, but merely that he has not a prefixed operating power determined to only the one effect; as in the case of natural things, which are only acted upon as though directed by another towards an end: for they do not act of themselves, as if they directed themselves towards an end, like rational creatures, through the possession of free choice, by which these are able to take counsel and make choices. Hence it is significantly said: *In the hand of his own counsel.* But since the very act of free choice is traced to God as to a cause, it necessarily follows that everything happening from the exercise of free choice must be subject to divine providence. For human providence is included under the providence of God as a particular cause under a universal cause. God, however, extends His providence over the just in a certain more excellent way than over the wicked, inasmuch as He prevents anything happening which would impede their final salvation. For *to them that love God, all things work together unto good* (*Rom.* viii. 28). But from the fact that He does not restrain the wicked from the evil of sin, He is said to abandon them. This does not mean that He altogether withdraws His providence from them; otherwise they would return to nothing, if they were not preserved in existence by His providence. This was the reason that had weight with Tully, who withdrew human affairs, concerning which we take counsel, from the care of divine providence.

Reply Obj. 5. Since a rational creature has, through its free choice, control over its actions, as was said above, it is subject to divine providence in an especial manner: something is imputed to it as a fault, or as a merit, and accordingly there is given to it something by way of punishment or reward. In this way the Apostle withdraws oxen from the care of God: not, however, that individual irrational creatures escape the care of divine providence, as was the opinion of the Rabbi Moses.

THIRD ARTICLE. *Whether God Has Immediate Providence over Everything?*

We proceed thus to the Third Article:—

Objection 1. It seems that God has not immediate providence over all things. For whatever pertains to dignity must be attributed to God. But it belongs to the dignity of a king that he should have ministers, through whose mediation he provides for his subjects. Therefore much less has God Himself immediate providence over all things.

Obj. 2. Further, it belongs to providence to order all things to an end. Now the end of everything is its perfection and its good. But it pertains to every cause to bring its effect to good; and therefore every agent cause is a cause of the effect over which it has providence. If therefore God were to have immediate providence over all things, all secondary causes would be withdrawn.

Obj. 3. Further, Augustine says that, *It is better to be ignorant of some things than to know them, for example, ignoble things;* and the Philosopher says the same. But whatever is better must be attributed to God. Therefore He has not immediate providence over ignoble and wicked things.

On the contrary, It is said (*Job* xxxiv. 13): *What other hath He appointed over the earth? or whom hath He set over the world which He made?* On which passage Gregory says: *Himself He ruleth the world which He Himself hath made.*

I answer that, Two things belong to providence—namely, the exemplar of the order of things foreordained towards an end, and the execution of this order, which is called government. As regards the first of these, God has immediate providence over everything, because he has in His intellect the exemplars of everything, even the smallest; and whatsoever causes He assigns to certain effects, He gives them the power to produce those effects. Whence it must be that He has pre-comprehended the order of those effects in His mind. As to the second, there are certain intermediaries of God's providence, for He governs things inferior by superior, not because of any defect in His power, but by reason of the abundance of His goodness; so that the dignity of causality is imparted even to creatures. Thus Plato's opinion, as narrated by Gregory of Nyssa, is removed. He taught a threefold providence. First, one which belongs to the supreme Deity, Who first and foremost has provision over spiritual things, and thus over the whole world as regards genus, species, and universal causes. The second providence, which is over the individuals of all that can be generated and corrupted, he attributed to the divinities who circulate in the heavens; that is, certain separate substances, which move corporeal things in a circular motion. The third providence, which is over human affairs, he assigned to demons, whom the Platonic philosophers placed between us and the gods, as Augustine tells us.

Reply Obj. 1. It pertains to a king's dignity to have ministers who execute his providence. But the fact that he does not know the plans of what is done by them arises from a deficiency in himself. For every operative science is the more perfect, the more it considers the particular things where action takes place.

Reply Obj. 2. God's immediate provision over everything does not exclude the action of secondary causes, which are the executors of His order, as was said above.

Reply Obj. 3. It is better for us not to know evil and ignoble things, insofar as by them we are impeded in our knowledge of what is better and higher (for we cannot understand many things simultaneously), and insofar as the thought of evil sometimes perverts the will towards evil. This does not hold true of God, Who sees everything simultaneously at one glance, and Whose will cannot turn in the direction of evil.

FOURTH ARTICLE. *Whether Providence Imposes any Necessity on What It Foresees?*

We proceed thus to the Fourth Article:—

Objection 1. It seems that divine providence imposes necessity upon what it foresees. For every effect that has an essential cause (present or past) which it necessarily follows, comes to be of necessity; as the Philosopher proves. But the providence of God, since it is eternal, precedes its effect, and the effect flows from it of necessity; for divine providence cannot be frustrated. Therefore divine providence imposes a necessity upon what it foresees.

Obj. 2. Further, every provider makes his work as stable as he can, lest it should fail. But God is most powerful. Therefore He assigns the stability of necessity to things whose providence He is.

Obj. 3. Further, Boethius says: *Fate from the immutable source of providence binds together human acts and fortunes by the indissoluble connexion of causes.* It seems therefore that providence imposes necessity upon what it foresees.

On the contrary, Dionysius says that *to corrupt nature is not the work of providence.* But it is in the nature of some things to be contingent. Divine providence does not therefore impose any necessity upon things so as to destroy their contingency.

I answer that, Divine providence imposes necessity upon some things; not upon all, as some believed. For to providence it belongs to order things towards an end. Now after the divine goodness, which is an extrinsic end to all things, the principal good in things themselves is the perfection of the universe; which would not be, were not all grades of being found in things. Whence it pertains to divine providence to produce every grade of being. And thus for some things it has prepared necessary causes, so that they happen of necessity; for others contingent causes, that they may happen by contingency, according to the disposition of their proximate causes.

Reply Obj. 1. The effect of divine providence is not only that things should happen *somehow;* but that they should happen either by necessity or by contingency. Therefore whatsoever divine providence ordains to happen infallibly and of necessity, happens infallibly and of necessity; and what the divine providence plans to happen contingently, happens contingently.

Reply Obj. 2. The order of divine providence is unchangeable and certain, so far as all things foreseen happen as they have been foreseen, whether from necessity or from contingency.

Reply Obj. 3. The indissolubility and unchangeableness, of which Boethius speaks, pertain to the certainty of providence, which does not fail to produce its effect, and that in the way foreseen; but they do not pertain to the necessity of the effects. We must remember that, properly speaking, *necessary* and *contingent* are consequent upon being as such. Hence the mode both of necessity and of contingency falls under the foresight of God, Who provides universally for all being; not under the foresight of causes that provide only for some particular order of things.

Question XLVI. On the Beginning of the Duration of Creatures

ARTICLE ONE. *Whether the universe of creatures always existed?*

(1) One goes on thus to the first article. It seems that the universe of creatures, which is called by the name of the world, did not begin, but existed from eternity. For it was possible for anything which began to exist that it should exist before it did exist; otherwise it would have been impossible for it to come into existence. Therefore, if the world began to exist, it was possible for it to exist before it began. But what is possible to exist is matter, which stands in potentiality to existence, which is through form, and to non-existence, which is through deprivation. Therefore if the world began to exist, matter existed before the world. But matter cannot exist without form; yet the matter of the world together with form just is the world. Therefore the world existed before it began, which is impossible.

(2) Besides, nothing that has the power to exist always sometimes exists and sometimes not, since how far the power of anything extends, so long does it exist. But everything incorruptible has the power to exist always, for it does not have the power for a limited stretch of time. Therefore nothing incorruptible sometimes exists and sometimes not. But everything which begins to exist sometimes exists and sometimes not. Therefore no incorruptible began to exist. But there are many incorruptibles in the world, such as the celestial bodies and all intellectual substances. Therefore the world did not begin to exist. . . .

(5) Besides, nothing begins to move anew unless the mover or the moveable is differently disposed now than before. But what is differently disposed now than before is moved. Therefore before every movement beginning anew there was some movement. Movement, therefore, always existed; therefore also the moveable, since movement is only in the moveable. . . .

(7) Besides, whatever is always in its beginning and always in its end can neither begin nor cease, since what begins is not in its end, but what ceases is not in its beginning. But time is always in its beginning and end, since nothing belongs to time except *now*, which is the end of the past and the beginning of the future.

Translated by James J. Walsh for this volume from *St. Thomas Aquinas, Summa Theologiae*, vol. 8, ed. T. Gilby, Cambridge: Blackfriars, 1967.

Therefore time can neither begin nor cease, and consequently neither can motion, whose numerical measure time is.

(8) Besides, God is either prior to the world in nature only, or also in time. If in nature only, then since God exists from eternity, the world also exists from eternity. But if He is prior in duration, prior and posterior in duration constituting time, then time existed before the world, which is impossible. . . .

(10) Besides, the effect of that whose action is eternal is also eternal. But the action of God is His substance, which is eternal; therefore the world is also eternal.

But to the contrary is what is said in *John,* "And now glorify thou me, O Father, with thyself, with the glory which I had, before the world was, with thee," and *Proverbs,* "The Lord possessed me in the beginning of his ways, before He made any thing from the beginning."

I reply that nothing outside of God can have existed from eternity. And indeed, to maintain this is not impossible. For it has been shown that the will of God is the cause of things. Therefore it is necessary for anything to exist just as it is necessary for God to will it, since the necessity of the effect depends on the necessity of the cause, as is said in the *Metaphysics.* But it has been shown that, speaking absolutely, it is not necessary for God to will anything except Himself. It is not therefore necessary for God to will that the world should have always existed. But the world exists as much as God wills it to exist, since the existence of the world depends on the will of God as on its cause. Therefore it is not necessary for the world always to exist.

And so neither can it be demonstratively proved. Nor are the arguments Aristotle adduces for this absolutely demonstrative, but only relatively, namely, for contradicting arguments of the older thinkers maintaining in truly impossible ways that the world began. And this is apparent from three cases. First, in the *Physics* as well as the *De Caelo* he sets forth certain opinions, such as those of Anaxagoras and Empedocles and Plato, against which he adduces contradictory arguments. Second, everywhere he speaks of this topic, he brings in the testimony of the older thinkers, which does not pertain to demonstrating, but to persuading with probability. Third, since he says expressly in the *Topics,* Chapter 9, that there are certain dialectical problems for which we do not have arguments, such as "Whether the world is eternal."

To the first, therefore, it should be said that before the world should exist it was possible for the world to exist, not, indeed, according to the passive potency which is matter, but according to the active potency of God. This is also according to what is called absolute possibility, not according to some power, but from the disposition of terms alone which are not mutually contradictory, as the possible is opposed to the impossible by the Philosopher in the *Metaphysics.*

To the second it should be said that what has the power always to exist does not sometimes exist and sometimes not from the fact that it has that power. But before it had that power it did not exist. Whence the argument which Aristotle proposes in the *De Caelo* does not conclude absolutely that incorruptibles did not begin to exist, but that they did not begin to exist in the natural way by which generable and corruptible things begin to exist. . . .

To the fifth it should be said that the first mover was always disposed in the same way, but the first moveable was not always disposed in the same way, in that it began to exist when it had previously not existed. But this was not through alteration, but through creation, which is not alteration, as was said above. Whence it is obvious that this argument, which Aristotle proposes in the *Physics,* goes against those who maintain eternal moveables but non-eternal movement, as is obvious from the views of Anaxagoras and Empedocles. But we maintain that movement has always existed from the time that moveables began. . . .

To the seventh it should be said that just as it says in the *Physics,* prior and posterior pertain to time according as prior and posterior pertain to movement. Whence beginning and end are to be taken in time just as in movement. But on the assumption of the eternity of movement, it is necessary that any moment taken in movement be a beginning and end of movement, which is not required if movement were to begin. And the now of time has the same character. So it is obvious that the characterization of the instant now, that it is always the beginning and end of time, presupposes the eternity of time and movement. Thus Aristotle brings in this argument in the *Physics* against those who maintained the eternity of time but denied the eternity of movement.

To the eighth it should be said that God is prior to the world in duration. But the 'prior' does not indicate priority of time, but of eternity. Or one should say that it indicates the eternity of imagined time, not existing in reality. Just as when it is said, "Beyond the heaven there is nothing," the 'beyond' indicates only an imaginary place, according as it is possible to imagine other dimensions of body added to the dimensions of the heaven. . . .

To the tenth it should be said that with action given, the effect follows according to the requirement of the form which is the principle of the action. But in those acting through the will, what is conceived and delimited in advance is taken as the form which is the principle of action. Therefore from the eternal action of God there does not follow an eternal effect, but such as God wills, namely that it should have existence after nonexistence.

ARTICLE TWO. *Whether it is an article of faith that the world began?*

One goes on thus to the second article. It seems that it is not an article of faith, but a demonstrable conclusion that the world began. For everything made has a beginning of its duration. But it can be demonstrably proved that God is the effective cause of the world, and the more likely philosophers also maintained this. Therefore it can be demonstrably proved that the world began.

(2) Besides, if it is necessary to say that the world was made by God, then either from nothing or from something. But not from something, since in that way the matter of the world would have preceded the world. The arguments of Aristotle maintaining the heaven to have been ungenerated tell against that. Thus one is required to say that the world is made from nothing, and in this way it has existence after non-existence. Therefore it is necessary that it began to exist. . . .

(5) Besides, it is certain that nothing can be equal to God. But if the world had always existed, it would be equal to God in duration. Therefore it is certain that the world did not always exist.

(6) Besides, if the world always existed, infinite days would have gone before this one. But infinity is not traversed; thus it never would have been gone through to this day, which is manifestly false.

(7) Besides, if the world was eternal, and generation was from eternity, then one man is generated from another unto infinity. But the father is the efficient cause of the son, as is said in the *Physics.* Therefore there is an infinite series of efficient causes, which is disproved in the *Metaphysics.*

(8) Besides, if the world and generation always existed, infinite men would have

gone before. But the soul of man is immortal. Therefore infinite human souls would now actually exist, which is impossible. Therefore it can be known by necessity that the world began, and it is held not merely by faith.

But to the contrary: articles of faith cannot be demonstratively proved, since faith is of what is not apparent. But for God to be the creator of the world, so that the world began to exist, is an article of faith. For we say, "I believe in one God, etc." Again, Gregory says that Moses spoke prophetically about the past, saying "In the beginning God created heaven and earth," in which the newness of the world is transmitted. Therefore the newness of the world is had through revelation alone, and hence it cannot be demonstrably proved.

I reply that for the world not always to have existed is held only by faith and cannot be demonstrably proved, as was said above about the mystery of the Trinity. And the reason for this is that the newness of the world cannot be demonstrated on the basis of the world itself. For essence is the basis of demonstration. And anything according to its specific characteristic abstracts from here and now. Because of this it is said that universals are everywhere and always. Whence it cannot be demonstrated that man or sky or stone did not always exist. Likewise, it cannot be demonstrated on the basis of the agent cause, which acts through the will. The will of God cannot be investigated by reason, except for those things it is absolutely necessary for God to will; but they are not what He wills regarding creatures, as was said. But the divine will can be made manifest to man through revelation, on which faith rests. So for the world to have begun is a matter of belief, but it is not demonstrable or knowable. And there is a utility in this, when it is considered that someone presuming to demonstrate what belongs to faith might adduce reasons not necessary, which would give material for laughter to the infidel thinking we believe what belongs to faith because of such reasons.

To the first, thus, should be said what Augustine says, that the opinion of the philosophers maintaining the eternity of the world was two-fold. For some maintained that the substance of the world is not from God, and the error of these is intolerable and is disproved by necessity. But some maintained the world eternal in such a way that they still said the world is made by God. For they want the world not to have a beginning of time, but of its creation, so that in a scarcely intelligible way it is always made. But they found a way that they might understand that, as the same Augustine says, "For just as if a foot should have stood from eternity in the dust, the footprint would always have been beneath, which no one would doubt to be made by the one treading. In such a way the world also always existed, with the one who made it always existing." And for understanding this it should be considered that an efficient cause which acts through motion necessarily precedes its effect in time, since the effect only exists in the termination of the action; and any agent must be the beginning of the action. But if the action is instantaneous and not successive, it is not necessary for the maker to be prior in time to what is made, as is obvious in the case of illumination. Whence they say it does not necessarily follow, if God is the active cause of the world, that He is prior to the world in duration. For the creation by which He produced the world is not a successive alteration, as was said above.

To the second it should be said that those who would maintain the world eternal would hold the world to be made by God from nothing, not made after nothing (according to what we understand by the term 'creation'), but because it is not made of anything. And so some of them do not reject the term 'creation', as is obvious from Avicenna.

To the fifth it should be said that even if the world had always existed, it still would not be on a level with God in eternity, as Boethius says at the end of the *Consolation,* since divine existence is existence entire without succession, but this is not the way it is for the world.

To the sixth it should be said that traversal is always understood from term to term. But whatever past day is meant, from that one up to this one there are finite days which can be gone through. But the objection develops as if given the extreme terms there are infinite intervening ones.

To the seventh it should be said that for efficient causes it is impossible to proceed essentially *(per se)* to infinity, as for instance if the causes which are essentially required for some effect were multiplied to infinity, as if a stone were moved by a stick and the stick by a hand, and so on to infinity. But to proceed accidentally to infinity in agent causes is not deemed impossible, as for instance if all the causes which are multiplied to infinity do not maintain order except as one cause, but their multiplication is accidental, as if a craftsman acts accidentally with many hammers since one after another is broken; thus it is an accident for this hammer that it acts after the action of some other hammer. Likewise it is an accident for this man insofar as he generates that he is generated by another; for he generates in that he is a man, and not in that he is the son of some other man. For all generating men have one grade among efficient causes, namely, the grade of the particular generator. Whence it is not impossible that man should be generated by man unto infinity; but it would be impossible if the generation of this man were to depend on this man, and on a corporeal element, and on the sun, and thus to infinity.

To the eighth it should be said that those maintaining the eternity of the world can avoid this argument in several ways. For some do not deem it impossible for there to be infinite souls in act, as is obvious in the *Metaphysics* of Al Ghazali, saying this to be an accidental infinity. But this was disproved above. Some, moreover, say that the soul is corrupted with the body. Some say that out of all the souls only one remains. And as Augustine says, others on account of this maintain a circuit of souls, so that souls separated from bodies, after a determinate cycle of time, return again to bodies. All these will be treated in what follows. It should yet be considered that this argument is limited, so that one could say that the world was eternal, or at least some such creature as an angel, and not man. But our concern is generally whether any creature existed from eternity.

Question LXXV. On Man Who Is Composed of a Spiritual and a Corporeal Substance; and First, Concerning What Belongs to the Essence of the Soul

SIXTH ARTICLE. *Whether the Human Soul Is Corruptible?*

We proceed thus to the Sixth Article:—

Objection 1. It would seem that the human soul is corruptible. For those things that have a like beginning and process seemingly have a like end. But the beginning, by generation, of men is like that of animals, for they are made from the earth. And the process of life is alike in both; because *all things breathe alike, and man hath nothing more than the beast,* as it is written (*Eccles.* iii. 19). Therefore,

From *Basic Writings of Saint Thomas Aquinas,* edited by Anton C. Pegis. Copyright 1945 by Random House, Inc.; London: Burns and Oates. Reprinted by permission.

as the same text concludes, *the death of man and beast is one, and the condition of both is equal.* But the souls of brute animals are corruptible. Therefore the human soul too is corruptible.

Obj. 2. Further, whatever is out of nothing can return to nothingness, because the end should correspond to the beginning. But as it is written (*Wis.* ii. 2), *We are born of nothing;* and this is true, not only of the body, but also of the soul. Therefore, as is concluded in the same passage, *After this we shall be as if we had not been,* even as to our soul.

Obj. 3. Further, nothing is without its own proper operation. But the operation proper to the soul, which is to understand through a phantasm, cannot be without the body. For the soul understands nothing without a phantasm, and *there is no phantasm without the body,* as the Philosopher says. Therefore the soul cannot survive the dissolution of the body.

On the contrary, Dionysius says that human souls owe to divine goodness that they are *intellectual,* and that they have *an incorruptible substantial life.*

I answer that, We must assert that the intellectual principle which we call the human soul is incorruptible. For a thing may be corrupted in two ways—in itself and accidentally. Now it is impossible for any subsistent being to be generated or corrupted accidentally, that is, by the generation or corruption of something else. For generation and corruption belong to a thing in the same way that being belongs to it, which is acquired by generation and lost by corruption. Therefore, whatever has being in itself cannot be generated or corrupted except in itself; while things which do not subsist, such as accidents and material forms, acquire being or lose it through the generation or corruption of composites. Now it was shown above that the souls of brutes are not self-subsistent, whereas the human soul is, so that the souls of brutes are corrupted, when their bodies are corrupted, while the human soul could not be corrupted unless it were corrupted in itself. This is impossible, not only as regards the human soul, but also as regards anything subsistent that is a form alone. For it is clear that what belongs to a thing by virtue of the thing itself is inseparable from it. But being belongs to a form, which is an act, by virtue of itself. And thus, matter acquires actual being according as it acquires form; while it is corrupted so far as the form is separated from it. But it is impossible for a form to be separated from itself; and therefore it is impossible for a subsistent form to cease to exist.

Granted even that the soul were composed of matter and form, as some pretend, we should nevertheless have to maintain that it is incorruptible. For corruption is found only where there is contrariety, since generation and corruption are from contraries and into contraries. Therefore the heavenly bodies, since they have no matter subject to contrariety, are incorruptible. Now there can be no contrariety in the intellectual soul; for it is a receiving subject according to the manner of its being, and those things which it receives are without contrariety. Thus, the notions even of contraries are not themselves contrary, since contraries belong to the same science. Therefore it is impossible for the intellectual soul to be corruptible.

Moreover we may take a sign of this from the fact that everything naturally aspires to being after its own manner. Now, in things that have knowledge, desire ensues upon knowledge. The senses indeed do not know being, except under the conditions of *here* and *now,* whereas the intellect apprehends being absolutely, and for all time; so that everything that has an intellect naturally desires always to exist. But a natural desire cannot be in vain. Therefore every intellectual substance is incorruptible.

Reply Obj. 1. Solomon reasons thus in the person of the foolish, as expressed in the words of *Wis.* ii. Therefore the saying that man and animals have a like beginning in generation is true of the body; for all animals alike are made of earth. But it is not true of the soul. For while the souls of brutes are produced by some power of the body, the human soul is produced by God. To signify this, it is written of other animals: *Let the earth bring forth the living soul* (*Gen.* i. 24); while of man it is written (*Gen.* ii. 7) that *He breathed into his face the breath of life.* And so in the last chapter of *Ecclesiastes* (xii. 7) it is concluded: *The dust returns into its earth from whence it was; and the spirit returns to God Who gave it.* Again, the process of life is alike as to the body, concerning which it is written (*Eccles.* iii. 19): *All things breathe alike,* and (*Wis.* ii. 2), *The breath in our nostrils is smoke.* But the process is not alike in the case of the soul, for man has understanding whereas animals do not. Hence it is false to say: *Man has nothing more than beasts.* Thus death comes to both alike as to the body, but not as to the soul.

Reply Obj. 2. As a thing can be created, not by reason of a passive potentiality, but only by reason of the active potentiality of the Creator, Who can produce something out of nothing, so when we say that a thing can be reduced to nothing, we do not imply in the creature a potentiality to non-being, but in the Creator the power of ceasing to sustain being. But a thing is said to be corruptible because there is in it a potentiality to non-being.

Reply Obj. 3. To understand through a phantasm is the proper operation of the soul by virtue of its union with the body. After separation from the body, it will have another mode of understanding, similar to other substances separated from bodies, as will appear later on.

Question LXXVI. The Union of Body and Soul

SECOND ARTICLE.   *Whether the Intellectual Principle Is Multiplied According to the Number of Bodies?*

We proceed thus to the Second Article:—

Objection 1. It would seem that the intellectual principle is not multiplied according to the number of bodies, but that there is one intellect in all men. For an immaterial substance is not multiplied numerically within one species. But the human soul is an immaterial substance, since it is not composed of matter and form, as was shown above. Therefore there are not many human souls in one species. But all men are of one species. Therefore there is but one intellect in all men.

Obj. 2. Further, when the cause is removed, the effect is also removed. Therefore, if human souls were multiplied according to the number of bodies, it would follow that if the bodies were removed, the number of souls would not remain, but from all the souls there would be but a single remainder. This is heretical, for it would do away with the distinction of rewards and punishments.

Obj. 3. Further, if my intellect is distinct from your intellect, my intellect is an individual, and so is yours; for individuals are things which differ in number but agree in one species. Now whatever is received into anything must be received according to the condition of the receiver. Therefore the species of things would be received individually into my intellect, and also into yours; which is contrary to the nature of the intellect, which knows universals.

Obj. 4. Further, the thing understood is in the intellect which understands. If, therefore, my intellect is distinct from yours, what is understood by me must be distinct from what is understood by you; and consequently it will be reckoned *as something individual,* and be only *potentially something understood.* Hence, the common intention will have to be abstracted from both, since from things which are diverse something intelligible and common to them may be abstracted. But this is contrary to the nature of the intellect, for then the intellect would not seem to be distinct from the imagination. It seems to follow, therefore, that there is one intellect in all men.

Obj. 5. Further, when the disciple receives knowledge from the teacher, it cannot be said that the teacher's knowledge begets knowledge in the disciple, because then knowledge too would be an active form, such as heat is; which is clearly false. It seems, therefore, that the same individual knowledge which is in the teacher is communicated to the disciple. This cannot be unless there is one intellect in both. Seemingly, therefore, the intellect of the disciple and teacher is but one; and, consequently, the same applies to all men.

Obj. 6. Further, Augustine says: *If I were to say that there are many human souls, I should laugh at myself.* But the soul seems to be one chiefly because of the intellect. Therefore there is one intellect of all men.

On the contrary, The Philosopher says that the relation of universal causes to what is universal is like the relation of particular causes to individuals. But it is impossible that a soul, one in species, should belong to animals of different species. Therefore it is impossible that one individual intellectual soul should belong to several individuals.

I answer that, It is absolutely impossible for one intellect to belong to all men. This is clear if, as Plato maintained, man is the intellect itself. For if Socrates and Plato have one intellect, it would follow that Socrates and Plato are one man, and that they are not distinct from each other, except by something outside the essence of each. The distinction between Socrates and Plato would then not be other than that of one man with a tunic and another with a cloak; which is quite absurd.

It is likewise clear that this is impossible if, according to the opinion of Aristotle, it is supposed that the intellect is a part or a power of the soul which is the form of man. For it is impossible for many distinct individuals to have one form, just as it is impossible for them to have one being. For the form is the principle of being.

Again, this is clearly impossible, whatever one may hold as to the manner of the union of the intellect to this or that man. For it is manifest that, if there is one principal agent, and two instruments, we can say without qualification that there is one agent but several actions; as when one man touches several things with his two hands, there will be one who touches, but two contacts. If, on the contrary, we suppose one instrument and several principal agents, we can say that there are several agents, but one act; for example, if there be many pulling a ship by means of a rope, those who pull will be many, but the pulling will be one. If, however, there is one principal agent, and one instrument, we say that there is one agent and one action; as when the smith strikes with one hammer, there is one striker and one stroke. Now it is clear that no matter how the intellect is united or joined to this or that man, the intellect has the primacy among all the other things which pertain to man, for the sensitive powers obey the intellect, and are at its service. So if we suppose two men to have two intellects and one sense,—for instance, if two men had one eye,—there would be two seers, but one seeing. But if the intellect is held to be one, no matter how diverse may be all those things which the intellect uses as instruments, it is in no way possible to say that Socrates and Plato are more than one understanding man. And if to this we add that to understand, which is the act of the intellect, is not produced by any organ other than the intellect itself, it will further follow that there is but one agent and one action; in other words, all men are but one "understander," and have but one act of understanding,—I mean, of course, in relation to one and the same intelligible object.

Now, it would be possible to distinguish my intellectual action from yours by the distinction of the phantasms—because there is one phantasm of a stone in me, and another in you—if the phantasm itself, according as it is one thing in me and another in you, were a form of the possible intellect. For the same agent produces diverse actions through diverse forms. Thus, through the diverse forms in things in relation to the same eye, there are diverse "seeings." But the phantasm itself is not the form of the possible intellect; the intelligible species abstracted from phantasms is such a form. Now in one intellect, from different phantasms of the same species, only one intelligible species is abstracted; as appears in one man, in whom there may be different phantasms of a stone, and yet from all of them only one intelligible species of a stone is abstracted, by which the intellect of that one man, by one operation, understands the nature of a stone, notwithstanding the diversity of phantasms. Therefore, if there were one intellect for all men, the diversity of phantasms in this man and in that would not cause a diversity of intellectual operation in this man and that man, as the Commentator imagines. It follows, therefore, that it is altogether impossible and inappropriate to posit one intellect for all men.

Reply Obj. 1. Although the intellectual soul, like the angel, has no matter from which it is produced, yet it is the form of a certain matter; in which it is unlike an angel. Therefore, according to the division of matter, there are many souls of one species; while it is quite impossible for many angels to be of one species

Reply Obj. 2. Everything has unity in the same way that it has being, and consequently we must judge of the multiplicity of a thing as we judge of its being. Now it is clear that the intellectual soul is according to its very being united to the body as its form. And yet, after the dissolution of the body, the intellectual soul retains its own being. In like manner, the multiplicity of souls is in proportion to the multiplicity of bodies; and yet, after the dissolution of the bodies, the souls remain multiplied in their being.

Reply Obj. 3. The individuality of the understanding being, or of the species whereby it understands, does not exclude the understanding of universals; or otherwise, since separate intellects are subsistent substances, and consequently individual, they could not understand universals. But it is the materiality of the knower, and of the species whereby he knows, that impedes the knowledge of the universal. For as every action is according to the mode of the form by which the agent acts, as heating is according to the mode of the heat, so knowledge is according to the mode of the species by which the knower knows. Now it is clear that the common nature becomes distinct and multiplied by reason of the individuating principles which come from the matter. Therefore if the form, which is the means of knowledge, is material—that is, not abstracted from material conditions—its likeness to the nature of a species or genus will be according to the distinction and multiplication of that nature by means of individuating principles; so that the knowledge of the nature in its community will be impossible. But if the species be abstracted from the conditions of individual matter, there will be a likeness of the nature without those things which make it distinct and multiplied. And thus there will be knowledge of the universal. Nor does it matter, as to this particular point, whether there be one intellect or many; because, even if there were but one, it would necessarily be an individual intellect, and the species whereby it understands, an individual species.

Reply Obj. 4. Whether the intellect be one or many, what is understood is one. For what is understood is in the intellect, not in itself, but according to its likeness; for *the stone is not in the soul, but its likeness is,* as is said *De Anima* iii. Yet it is the stone which is understood, not the likness of the stone, except by a reflection of the intellect on itself. Otherwise, the objects of sciences would not be things, but only intelligible species. Now it is possible for different things, according to different forms, to be likened to the same thing. And since knowledge is begotten according to the assimilation of the knower to the thing known, it follows that the same thing can be known by several knowers; as is apparent in regard to the senses, for several see the same color by means of diverse likenesses. In the same way several intellects understand one thing. But there is this difference, according to the opinion of Aristotle, between the sense and the intellect— that a thing is perceived by the sense according to that disposition which it has outside the soul—that is, in its individuality; whereas, though the nature of the thing understood is outside the soul, yet its mode of being outside the soul is not the mode of being according to which it is known. For the common nature is understood as apart from the individuating principles; whereas such is not its mode of being outside the soul. (But according to the opinion of Plato, the thing understood exists outside the soul in the same way as it is understood. For Plato supposed that the natures of things exist separate from matter.)

Reply Obj. 5. One knowledge exists in the disciple and another in the teacher. How it is caused will be shown later on.

Reply Obj. 6. Augustine denies such a plurality of souls as would involve a denial of their communication in the one nature of the species.

Question LXXXII. The Will

FIRST ARTICLE. *Whether the Will Desires Something of Necessity?*

We proceed thus to the First Article:—

Objection 1. It would seem that the will desires nothing of necessity. For Augustine says that if anything is necessary, it is not voluntary. But whatever the will desires is voluntary. Therefore nothing that the will desires is desired of necessity.

Obj. 2. Further, *the rational powers,* according to the Philosopher, *extend to opposite things.* But the will is a rational power, because, as he says, *the will is in the reason.* Therefore the will extends to opposite things, and hence is determined to nothing of necessity.

Obj. 3. Further, by the will we are masters of our own actions. But we are not masters of that which is of necessity. Therefore the act of the will cannot be necessitated.

On the contrary, Augustine says that *all desire happiness with one will.* Now if this were not necessary, but contingent, there would at least be a few exceptions. Therefore the will desires something of necessity.

I answer that, The word *necessity* is employed in many ways. For that which must be is necessary. Now that a thing must be may belong to it by an intrinsic principle:—either material, as when we say that everything composed of contraries is of necessity corruptible;—or formal, as when we say that it is necessary for the three angles of a triangle to be equal to two right angles. And this is *natural* and *absolute necessity.* In another way, that a thing must be belongs to it by reason of something extrinsic, which is either the end or the agent. The necessity is imposed on something by the end when without it the end is not to be attained or so well attained: for instance, food is said to be necessary for life, and a horse is necessary for a journey. This is called the *necessity of the end,* and sometimes also *utility.* The necessity is imposed by the agent when someone is forced by some agent, so that he is not able to do the contrary. This is called the *necessity of coercion.*

Now this necessity of coercion is altogether repugnant to the will. For we call *violent* that which is against the inclination of a thing. But the very movement of the will is an inclination to something. Therefore, just as a thing is called *natural* because it is according to the inclination of nature, so a thing is called *voluntary* because it is according to the inclination of the will. Therefore, just as it is impossible for a thing to be at the same time violent and natural, so it is impossible for a thing to be absolutely coerced, or violent, and voluntary.

But the necessity of the end is not repugnant to the will, when the end cannot be attained except in one way; and thus from the will to cross the sea arises in the will the necessity to desire a ship.

In like manner, neither is natural necessity repugnant to the will. Indeed, just as the intellect of necessity adheres to first principles, so the will must of necessity adhere to the last end, which is happiness; for the end is in practical matters what the principle is in speculative matters, as is said in *Physics* ii. For what befits a thing naturally and immovably must be the root and principle of all else pertaining thereto, since the nature of a thing is the first in everything, and every movement arises from something immovable.

Reply Obj. 1. The words of Augustine are to be understood of the necessity of coercion. But natural necessity *does not take away the liberty of the will,* as he himself says in the same work.

Reply Obj. 2. The will, so far as it desires a thing naturally, corresponds rather to the intellect of natural principles than to the reason, which extends to contraries. Hence, in this respect, it is rather an intellectual than a rational power.

Reply Obj. 3. We are masters of our own actions by reason of our being able to choose this or that. But choice regards, not the end, but *the means to the end,* as the Philosopher says. Consequently, the desire of the ultimate end is not among those actions of which we are masters.

SECOND ARTICLE. *Whether the Will Desires of Necessity Whatever It Desires?*

We proceed thus to the Second Article:—

Objection 1. It would seem that the will desires of necessity all that it desires. For Dionysius says that *evil is outside the scope of the will.* Therefore the will tends of necessity to the good which is proposed to it.

Obj. 2. Further, the object of the will is compared to the will as the mover to the movable thing. But the movement of the movable necessarily follows the mover. Therefore it seems that the will's object moves it of necessity.

Obj. 3. Further, just as the thing apprehended by sense is the object of the sensitive appetite, so the thing apprehended by the intellect is the object of the intellectual appetite, which is called the will. But what is apprehended by the sense moves the sensitive appetite of necessity, for Augustine says that *animals are moved by things seen.* Therefore it seems that whatever is apprehended by the intellect moves the will of necessity.

On the contrary, Augustine says that *it is the will by which we sin and live well.* Thus, the will extends to opposites. Therefore it does not desire of necessity all things whatsoever it desires.

I answer that, The will does not desire of necessity whatsoever it desires. In order to make this evident we must observe that, just as the intellect naturally and of necessity adheres to first principles, so the will adheres to the last end, as we have said already. Now there are some intelligible things which have no necessary connection with first principles: *e.g.,* contingent propositions, the denial of which does not involve a denial of first principles. And to such the intellect does not assent of necessity. But there are some propositions which have a necessary connection with first principles, namely, demonstrable conclusions, a denial of which involves a denial of first principles. And to these the intellect assents of necessity, when once it is aware (by demonstration) of the necessary connection of these conclusions with the principles; but it does not assent of necessity until through the demonstration it recognizes the necessity of such a connection.

It is the same with the will. For there are certain particular goods which have not a necessary connection with happiness, because without them a man can be happy; and to such the will does not adhere of necessity. But there are some things which have a necessary connection with happiness, namely, those by means of which man adheres to God, in Whom alone true happiness consists. Nevertheless, until through the certitude produced by seeing God the necessity of such a connection be shown, the will does not adhere to God of necessity, nor to those things which are of God. But the will of the man who sees God in His essence of necessity adheres to God, just as now we desire of necessity to be happy. It is therefore clear that the will does not desire of necessity whatever it desires.

Reply Obj. 1. The will can tend to nothing except under the aspect of good. But because good is of many kinds, for this reason the will is not of necessity determined to one.

Reply Obj. 2. The mover of necessity causes movement in the movable thing only when the power of the mover exceeds the movable thing in such a way that its entire capacity is subject to the mover. But as the capacity of the will is for the universal and perfect good, it is not subjected to any particular good. And therefore it is not of necessity moved by it.

Reply Obj. 3. The sensitive power does not compare different things with each other, as reason does; but it apprehends simply some one thing. Therefore, according to that one thing, it moves the sensitive appetite in a determinate way. But the reason is a power that compares several things together. Therefore the intellectual appetite—that is, the will—may be moved by several things, but not of necessity by one thing.

THIRD ARTICLE. *Whether the Will Is a Higher Power than the Intellect?*

We proceed thus to the Third Article:—

Objection 1. It would seem that the will is a higher power than the intellect. For the object of the will is the good and the end. But the end is the first and highest cause. Therefore the will is the first and highest power.

Obj. 2. Further, in the order of natural things we observe a progress from imperfect things to perfect. And this also appears in the powers of the soul, for sense precedes the intellect, which is more noble. Now the act of the will, according to a natural order, follows the act of the intellect. Therefore the will is a more noble and perfect power than the intellect.

Obj. 3. Further, habits are proportioned to their powers, as perfections to what they make perfect. But the habit which perfects the will—namely, charity—is more noble than the habits which perfect the intellect; for it is written (*1 Cor.* xiii. 2): *If I should know all mysteries, and if I should have all faith, and have not charity, I am nothing.* Therefore the will is a higher power than the intellect.

On the contrary, The Philosopher holds the intellect to be the highest power of the soul.

I answer that, The superiority of one thing over another can be considered in two ways: *absolutely* and *relatively.* Now a thing is considered to be such absolutely when it is considered such in itself; but relatively, when it is such in relation to something else. If therefore the intellect and will be considered with regard to themselves, then the intellect is the higher power. And this is clear if we compare their respective objects to one another. For the object of the intellect is more simple and more absolute than the object of the will. For the object of the intellect is the very notion of the appetible good; and the appetible good, the notion of which is in the intellect, is the object of the will. Now the more simple and the more abstract a thing is, the nobler and higher it is in itself; and therefore the object of the intellect is higher than the object of the will. Therefore, since the proper nature of a power is according to its order to its object, it follows that the intellect, in itself and absolutely, is higher and nobler than the will.

But relatively, and by comparison with something else, we find that the will is sometimes higher than the intellect; and this happens when the object of the will occurs in something higher than that in which occurs the object of the intellect. Thus, for instance, I might say that hearing is relatively nobler than sight, inasmuch as something in which there is sound is nobler than something in which there is color, though color is nobler and simpler than sound. For, as we have said above, the act of the intellect consists in this—that the likeness of the thing understood is in the one who understands; while the act of the will consists in this—that the will is inclined to the thing itself as existing in itself. And therefore the Philosopher says in *Metaph.* vi. that *good and evil,* which are objects of the will, *are in things,* but *truth and error,* which are objects of the intellect, *are in the mind.* When, therefore, the thing in which there is good is nobler than the soul itself, in which is the understood likeness, then, by comparison with such a thing, the will is higher than the intellect. But when the thing which is good is less noble than the soul, then, even in comparison with that thing, the intellect is higher than the will. Hence, the love of God is better than the knowledge of God; but, on the contrary, the knowledge of corporeal things is better than the love of them. Absolutely, however, the intellect is nobler than the will.

Reply Obj. 1. The notion of cause is perceived by comparing one thing to another, and in such a comparison the notion of good is found to be nobler; but truth signifies something more absolutely, and extends to the notion of good itself. Thus, the good is something true. But, again, the true is something good. For the intellect is a given reality, and truth is its end. And among other ends this is the most excellent: just as is the intellect among the other powers.

Reply Obj. 2. What precedes in the order of generation and time is less perfect, for in one and the same thing potentiality precedes act, and imperfection precedes perfection. But what precedes absolutely and in the order of nature is more perfect; for thus act precedes potentiality. And in this way the intellect precedes the will, as the motive power precedes the movable thing, and as the active precedes the passive; for it is the *apprehended* good that moves the will.

Reply Obj. 3. This argument is verified of the will as compared with what is above the soul. For charity is the virtue by which we love God.

Question LXXXIV. How the Soul While United to the Body Understands Corporeal Things Beneath It

FIFTH ARTICLE. *Whether the Intellectual Soul Knows Material Things in the Eternal Exemplars?*

We proceed thus to the Fifth Article:—

Objection 1. It would seem that the intellectual soul does not know material things in the eternal exemplars. For that in which anything is known must itself be known more and antecedently. But the intellectual soul of man, in the present state of life, does not know the eternal exemplars, for it does not know God in Whom the eternal exemplars exist, but is *united to God as to the unknown,* as Dionysius says. Therefore the soul does not know all in the eternal exemplars.

Obj. 2. Further, it is written (*Rom.* i. 20) that *the invisible things of God are clearly seen . . . by the things that are made.* But among the invisible things of God are the eternal exemplars. Therefore the eternal exemplars are known through creatures, and not the converse.

Obj. 3. Further, the eternal exemplars are nothing else but ideas, for Augustine says that *ideas are permanent exemplars existing in the divine mind.* If therefore we say that the intellectual soul knows all things in the eternal exemplars, we come back to the opinion of Plato who said that all knowledge is derived from them.

On the contrary, Augustine says: *If we both see that what you say is true, and if we both see that what I say is true, where do we see this, I pray? Neither do I see it in you, nor do you see it in me; but we both see it in the unchangeable truth which is above our minds.* Now the unchangeable truth is contained in the eternal exemplars. Therefore the intellectual soul knows all truths in the eternal exemplars.

I answer that, As Augustine says: *If those who are called philosophers said by chance anything that was true and consistent with our faith, we must claim it from them as from unjust possessors. For some of the doctrines of the pagans are spurious imitations or superstitious inventions, which we must be careful to avoid when we renounce the society of the pagans.* Consequently whenever Augustine, who was imbued with the doctrines of the Platonists, found in their teaching anything consistent with faith, he adopted it; and those things which he found contrary to faith he amended. Now Plato held, as we have said above, that the forms of things subsist of themselves apart from matter. These he called Ideas, and he said that our intellect knows all things by participation in them; so that just as corporeal matter, by participating in the Idea of a stone, becomes a stone, so our intellect, by participating in the same Idea, has knowledge of a stone. But it seems contrary to faith that the forms of things should subsist of themselves without matter outside the things themselves, as the Platonists held, asserting that *life-in-itself* and *wisdom-in-itself* are certain creative substances, as Dionysius relates. Therefore, in the place of the Ideas defended by Plato, Augustine said that the exemplars of all creatures existed in the divine mind. It is according to these that all things are formed, as well as that the human soul knows all things.

When, therefore, the question is asked: Does the human soul know all things in the eternal exemplars? we must reply that one thing is said to be known in another in two ways. First, as in an object itself known; as one may see in a mirror the images of the things reflected therein. In this way the soul, in the present state of life, cannot see all things in the eternal exemplars; but thus the blessed, who see God and all things in Him, know all things in the eternal exemplars. Secondly, one thing is said to be known in another as in a principle of knowledge; and thus we might say that we see in the sun what we see by the sun. And thus we must needs say that the human soul knows all things in the eternal exemplars, since by participation in these exemplars we know all things. For the intellectual light itself, which is in us, is nothing else than a participated likeness of the uncreated light, in which are contained the eternal exemplars. Whence it is written (*Ps.* iv. 6, 7), *Many say: who showeth us good things?* which question the Psalmist answers, *The light of Thy countenance, O Lord, is signed upon us;* as though to say: By the seal of the divine light in us, all things are made known to us.

But since besides the intellectual light which is in us, intelligible species, which are derived from things, are required in order that we may have knowledge of material things, therefore this knowledge is not due merely to a participation of the eternal exemplars, as the Platonists held, maintaining that the mere participation in the Ideas sufficed for knowledge. Therefore Augustine says: *Although the philosophers prove by convincing arguments that all things occur in time according to the eternal exemplars, were they able to see in the eternal exemplars, or to find out from them, how many kinds of animals there are and the origin of each? Did they not seek for this information from the story of times and places?*

Now that Augustine did not understand all things to be known in their *eternal exemplars* or in *the unchangeable truth,* as though the eternal exemplars themselves were seen, is clear from what he says, viz., that *not each and every rational soul can be said to be worthy of that vision,* namely, of the eternal exemplars, *but only those that are holy and pure,* such as the souls of the blessed.

From what has been said the objections are easily solved.

Question LXXXV. The Mode and Order of Understanding

FIRST ARTICLE. *Whether Our Intellect Understands Corporeal and Material Things by Abstraction from Phantasms?*

We proceea thus to the First Article:—

Objection 1. It would seem that our intellect does not understand corporeal and material things by abstraction from the phantasms. For the intellect is false if it understands a thing otherwise than as it is. Now the forms of material things do not exist in abstraction from the particular things represented by the phantasms. Therefore, if we understand material things by the abstraction of species from phantasms, there will be error in the intellect.

Obj. 2. Further, material things are those natural things which include matter in their definition. But nothing can be understood apart from that which enters into its definition. Therefore material things cannot be understood apart from matter. Now matter is the principle of individuation. Therefore material things cannot be understood by the abstraction of the universal from the particular; and this is to abstract intelligible species from the phantasm.

Obj 3. Further, the Philosopher says that the phantasm is to the intellectual soul what color is to the sight. But seeing is not caused by abstraction of species from color, but by color impressing itself on the sight. Therefore neither does the act of understanding take place by the abstraction of something from the phantasms, but by the phantasms impressing themselves on the intellect.

Obj. 4. Further, the Philosopher says that there are two things in the intellectual soul—the possible intellect and the agent intellect. But it does not belong to the possible intellect to abstract the intelligible species from the phantasm, but to receive them already abstracted. Neither does it seem to be the function of the agent intellect, which is related to phantasms as light is to colors; since light does not abstract anything from colors, but rather acts on them. Therefore in no way do we understand by abstraction from phantasms.

Obj. 5. Further, the Philosopher says that *the intellect understands the species in the phantasms;* and not, therefore, by abstraction.

On the contrary, The Philosopher says that *things are intelligible in proportion as they are separable from matter.* Therefore material things must needs be understood according as they are abstracted from matter and from material images, namely, phantasms.

I answer that, As stated above, the object of knowledge is proportionate to the power of knowledge. Now there are three grades of the cognitive powers. For one cognitive power, namely, the sense, is the act of a corporeal organ. And therefore the object of every sensitive power is a form as existing in corporeal matter; and since such matter is the principle of individuation, therefore every power of the sensitive part can have knowledge only of particulars. There is another grade of cognitive power which is neither the act of a corporeal organ, nor in any way connected with corporeal matter. Such is the angelic intellect, the object of whose cognitive power is therefore a form existing apart from matter; for though angels know material things, yet they do not know them save in something immaterial, namely, either in themselves or in God. But the human intellect holds a middle place; for it is not the act of an organ, and yet it is a power of the soul, which is the form of the body, as is clear from what we have said above. And therefore it is proper to it to know a form existing individually in corporeal matter, but not as existing in this individual matter. But to know what is in individual matter, yet not as existing in such matter, is to abstract the form from individual matter which is represented by the phantasms. Therefore we must needs say that our intellect understands material things by abstracting from phantasms; and that through material things thus considered we acquire some knowledge of immaterial things, just as, on the contrary, angels know material things through the immaterial.

But Plato, considering only the immateriality of the human intellect, and not that it is somehow united to the body, held that the objects of the intellect are separate Ideas, and that we understand, not by abstraction, but rather by participating in abstractions, as was stated above.

Reply Obj. 1. Abstraction may occur in two ways. First, by way of composition and division, and thus we may understand that one thing does not exist in some other, or that it is separate from it. Secondly, by way of a simple and absolute consideration; and thus we understand one thing without considering another. Thus, for the intellect to abstract one from another things which are not really abstract from one another, does, in the first mode of abstraction, imply falsehood. But, in the second mode of abstraction, for the intellect to abstract things which are not really abstract from one another, does not involve falsehood, as clearly appears in the case of the senses. For if we said that color is not in a colored body, or that it is separate from it, there would be error in what we thought or said. But if we consider color and its properties, without reference to the apple which is colored, or if we express in word what we thus understand, there is no error in such an opinion or assertion; for an apple is not essential to color, and therefore color can be understood independently of the apple. In the same way, the things which belong to the species of a material thing, such as a stone, or a man, or a horse, can be thought without the individual principles which do not belong to the notion of the species. This is what we mean by abstracting the universal from the particular, or the intelligible species from the phantasm; in other words, this is to consider the nature of the species apart from its individual principles represented by the phantasms. If, therefore, the intellect is said to be false when it understands a thing otherwise than as it is, that is so, if the word *otherwise* refers to the thing understood; for the intellect is false when it understands a thing to be otherwise than as it is. Hence, the intellect would be false if it abstracted the species of a stone from its matter in such a way as to think that the species did not exist in matter, as Plato held. But it is not so, if the word *otherwise* be taken as referring to the one who understands. For it is quite true that the mode of understanding, in one who understands, is not the same as the mode of a thing in being; since the thing understood is immaterially in the one who understands, according to the mode of the intellect, and not materially, according to the mode of a material thing.

Reply Obj. 2. Some have thought that the species of a natural thing is a form only, and that matter is not part of the species. If that were so, matter would not enter into the definition of natural things. Therefore we must disagree and say that matter is twofold, common and *signate,* or individual: common, such as flesh and bone; individual, such as this flesh and these bones. The intellect therefore abstracts the species of a natural thing from the individual sensible matter, but not from the common sensible matter. For example, it abstracts the species of *man* from *this flesh and these bones,* which do not belong to the species as such, but to the individual, and need not be considered in the species. But the species of man cannot be abstracted by the intellect from *flesh and bones.*

Mathematical species, however, can be abstracted by the intellect not only from individual sensible matter, but also from common sensible matter. But they cannot be abstracted from common intelligible matter, but only from individual intelligible matter. For sensible matter is corporeal matter as subject to sensible qualities, such as being cold or hot, hard or soft, and the like; while intelligible matter is substance as subject to quantity. Now it is manifest that quantity is in substance before sensible qualities are. Hence quantities, such as number, dimension, and figures, which are the terminations of quantity, can be considered apart from sensible qualities, and this is to abstract them from sensible matter. But they cannot be considered without understanding the substance which is subject to the quantity, for that would be to abstract them from common intelligible matter. Yet they can be considered apart from this or that substance, and this is to abstract them from individual intelligible matter.

But some things can be abstracted even from common intelligible matter, such as *being, unity, potency, act,* and the like, all of which can exist without matter, as can be verified in the case of immaterial substances. And because Plato failed to consider the twofold kind of abstraction, as above explained, he held that all those things which we have stated to be abstracted by the intellect, are abstract in reality.

Reply Obj. 3. Colors, as being in individual corporeal matter, have the same mode of being as the power of sight; and therefore they can impress their own image on the eye. But phantasms, since they are images of individuals, and exist in corporeal organs, have not the same mode of being as the human intellect, as is clear from what we have said, and therefore they have not the power of themselves to make an impression on the possible intellect. But through the power of the agent intellect, there results in the possible intellect a certain likeness produced by the turning of the agent intellect toward the phantasms. This likeness represents what is in the phantasms, but includes only the nature of the species. It is thus that the intelligible species is said to be abstracted from the phantasm; not that the identical form which previously was in the phantasm is subsequently in the possible intellect, as a body transferred from one place to another.

Reply Obj. 4. Not only does the agent intellect illumine phantasms, it does more; by its power intelligible species are abstracted from phantasms. It illumines phantasms because, just as the sensitive part acquires a greater power by its conjunction with the intellectual part, so through the power of the agent intellect phantasms are made more fit for the abstraction of intelligible intentions from them. Now the agent intellect abstracts intelligible species from phantasms inasmuch as by its power we are able to take into our consideration the natures of species without individual conditions. It is in accord with their likeness that the possible intellect is informed.

Reply Obj. 5. Our intellect both abstracts the intelligible species *from* phantasms, inasmuch as it considers the natures of things universally, and yet understands these natures *in* the phantasms, since it cannot understand the things, of which it abstracts the species, without turning to phantasms, as we have said above.

SECOND ARTICLE. *Whether the Intelligible Species Abstracted from Phantasms Are Related to Our Intellect as that Which Is Understood?*

We proceed thus to the Second Article:—

Objection 1. It would seem that the intelligible species abstracted from phantasms are related to our intellect as that which is understood. For the understood in act is in the one who understands: since the understood in act is the intellect itself in act. But nothing of what is understood is in the actually understanding intellect save the abstracted intelligible species. Therefore this species is what is actually understood.

Obj. 2. Further, what is actually understood must be in something; or else it would be nothing. But it is not in something outside the soul; for, since what is outside the soul is material, nothing therein can be actually understood. Therefore what is actually understood is in the intellect. Consequently it can be nothing else than the aforesaid intelligible species.

Obj. 3. Further, the Philosopher says that *words are signs of the passions in the soul.* But words signify the things understood, for we express by word what we understand. Therefore these passions of the soul, viz., the intelligible species, are what is actually understood.

On the contrary, The intelligible species is to the intellect what the sensible species is to the sense. But the sensible species is not *what* is perceived, but rather that *by which* the sense perceives. Therefore the intelligible species is not what is actually understood, but that by which the intellect understands.

I answer that, Some have asserted that our intellectual powers know only the impressions made on them; as, for example, that sense is cognizant only of the impression made on its own organ. According to this theory, the intellect understands only its own impressions, namely, the intelligible species which it has received.

This is, however, manifestly false for two reasons. First, because the things we understand are also the objects of science. Therefore, if what we understand is merely the intelligible species in the soul, it would follow that every science would be concerned, not with things outside the soul, but only with the intelligible species within the soul; just as, according to the teaching of the Platonists, all the sciences are about Ideas, which they held to be that which is actually understood. Secondly, it is untrue, because it would lead to the opinion of the ancients who maintained that *whatever seems, is true,* and that consequently contradictories are true simultaneously. For if a power knows only its own impressions, it can judge only of them. Now a thing *seems* according to the impression made on the cognitive power. Consequently the cognitive power will always judge of its own impression as such; and so every judgment will be true. For instance, if taste perceived only its own impression, when anyone with a healthy taste perceives that honey is sweet, he would judge truly, and if anyone with a corrupt taste perceives that honey is bitter, this would be equally true; for each would judge according to the impression on his state. Thus every opinion, in fact, every sort of apprehension, would be equally true.

Therefore it must be said that the intelligible species is related to the intellect, as that by which it understands. Which is proved thus. Now action is twofold, as it is said in *Metaph*. ix: one which remains in the agent (for instance, to see and to understand), and another which passes into an external object (for instance, to heat and to cut). Each of these actions proceeds in virtue of some form. And just as the form from which proceeds an act tending to something external is the likeness of the object of the action, as heat in the heater is a likeness of the thing heated, so the form from which proceeds an action remaining in the agent is a likeness of the object. Hence that by which the sight sees is the likeness of the visible thing; and the likeness of the thing understood, that is, the intelligible species, is the form by which the intellect understands. But since the intellect reflects upon itself, by such reflection it understands both its own act of understanding, and the species by which it understands. Thus the intelligible species is secondarily that which is understood; but that which is primarily understood is the thing, of which the species is the likeness.

This also appears from the opinion of the ancient philosophers, who said that *like is known by like*. For they said that the soul knows the earth outside itself by the earth within itself; and so of the rest. If, therefore, we take the species of the earth instead of the earth, in accord with Aristotle who says *that a stone is not in the soul, but only the likeness of the stone*, it follows that by means of its intelligible species the soul knows the things which are outside it.

Reply Obj. 1. The thing understood is in the knower by its own likeness. It is in this sense that we say that the thing actually understood is the intellect in act, because the likeness of the thing understood is the form of the intellect, just as the likeness of a sensible thing is the form of the sense in act. Hence it does not follow that the abstracted intelligible species is what is actually understood; but rather that it is the likeness thereof.

Reply Obj. 2. In these words *the thing actually understood* there is a double meaning:—the thing which is understood, and the fact that it is understood. In like manner, the words *abstract universal* mean two things, the nature of a thing and its abstraction or universality. Therefore the nature itself which suffers the act of being understood, or the act of being abstracted, or the intention of universality, exists only in individuals; but that it is understood, abstracted or considered as universal is in the intellect. We see something similar to this in the senses. For the sight sees the color of the apple apart from its smell. If therefore it be asked where is the color which is seen apart from the smell, it is quite clear that the color which is seen is only in the apple; but that it be perceived apart from the smell, this is owing to the sight, inasmuch as sight receives the likeness of color and not of smell. In like manner, the humanity which is understood exists only in this or that man; but that humanity be apprehended without the conditions of individuality, that is, that it be abstracted and consequently considered as universal, befalls humanity inasmuch as it is perceived by the intellect, in which there is a likeness of the specific nature, but not of the individual principles.

Reply Obj. 3. There are two operations in the sensitive part. One is limited to immutation, and thus the operation of the senses takes place when the senses are impressed by the sensible. The other is formation, inasmuch as the imagination forms for itself an image of an absent thing, or even of something never seen. Both of these operations are found in the intellect. For in the first place there is the passion of the possible intellect as informed by the intelligible species; and then the possible intellect, as thus informed, then forms a definition, or a division, or a composition, which is expressed by language. And so, the notion signified by a *term* is a definition; and a *proposition* signifies the intellect's division or composition. Words do not therefore signify the intelligible species themselves; but that which the intellect forms for itself for the purpose of judging of external things.

Question LXXXVI. What Our Intellect Knows in Material Things

FIRST ARTICLE. *Whether Our Intellect Knows Singulars?*

We proceed thus to the First Article:—

Objection 1. It would seem that our intellect knows singulars. For whoever knows a composition, knows the terms of composition. But our intellect knows this composition: *Socrates is a man,* for the intellect can form a proposition to this effect. Therefore our intellect knows this singular, *Socrates.*

Obj. 2. Further, the practical intellect directs to action. But action has relation to singular things. Therefore the intellect knows the singular.

Obj. 3. Further, our intellect understands itself. But in itself it is a singular, or otherwise it would have no action of its own; for actions belong to singulars. Therefore our intellect knows singulars.

Obj. 4. Further, a superior power can do whatever is done by an inferior power. But sense knows the singular. Much more, therefore, can the intellect know it.

On the contrary, The Philosopher says that *the universal is known by reason, and the singular is known by sense.*

I answer that, Our intellect cannot know the singular in material things directly and primarily. The reason for this is that the principle of singularity in material things is individual matter; whereas our intellect, as we have said above, understands by abstracting the intelligible species from such matter. Now what is abstracted from individual matter is universal. Hence our intellect knows directly only universals. But indirectly, however, and as it were by a kind of reflexion, it can know the singular, because, as we have said above, even after abstracting the intelligible species, the intellect, in order to understand actually, needs to turn to the phantasms in which it understands the species, as is said in *De Anima* iii. Therefore it understands the universal directly through the intelligible species, and indirectly the singular represented by the phantasm. And thus it forms the proposition, *Socrates is a man.*

Therefore the reply to the first objection is clear.

Reply Obj. 2. The choice of a particular thing to be done is as the conclusion of a syllogism formed by the practical intellect, as is said in *Ethics* vii. But a singular proposition cannot be directly concluded from a universal proposition, except through the medium of a singular proposition. Therefore the universal principle of the practical intellect does not move save through the medium of the particular apprehension of the sensitive part, as is said in *De Anima* iii.

Reply Obj. 3. Intelligibility is incompatible with the singular not as such, but as material; for nothing can be understood otherwise than immaterially. Therefore if there be an immaterial singular such as the intellect, there is no reason why it should not be intelligible.

Reply Obj. 4. The higher power can do what the lower power can, but in a more eminent way. And so, what the sense knows materially and concretely, which is to know the singular directly, the intellect knows immaterially and in the abstract, which is to know the universal.

THE SUMMA THEOLOGICA
First Part of the Second Part

Question II. Of Those Things in Which Man's Happiness Consists

EIGHTH ARTICLE. *Whether Any Created Good Constitutes Man's Happiness?*

We proceed thus to the Eighth Article:—

Objection 1. It would seem that some created good constitutes man's happiness. For Dionysius says that Divine wisdom *unites the ends of first things to the beginnings of second things,* from which we may gather that the summit of a lower nature touches the base of the higher nature. But man's highest good is happiness. Since then the angel is above man in the order of nature, as stated in the First Part, it seems that man's happiness consists in man somehow reaching the angel.

Obj. 2. Further, the last end of each thing is that which, in relation to it, is perfect: hence the part is for the whole, as for its end. But the universe of creatures which is called the macrocosm, is compared to man who is called the microcosm, as perfect to imperfect. Therefore man's happiness consists in the whole universe of creatures.

Obj. 3. Further, man is made happy by that which lulls his natural desire. But man's natural desire does not reach out to a good surpassing his capacity. Since then man's capacity does not include that good which surpasses the limits of all creation, it seems that man can be made happy by some created good. Consequently some created good constitutes man's happiness.

On the contrary, Augustine says: *As the soul is the life of the body, so God is man's life of happiness: of Whom it is written: 'Happy is that people whose God is the Lord'* (Ps. cxliii. 15).

I answer that, It is impossible for any created good to constitute man's happiness. For happiness is the perfect good, which lulls the appetite altogether; else it would not be the last end, if something yet remained to be desired. Now the object of the will, *i.e.,* of man's appetite, is the universal good; just as the object of the intellect is the universal true. Hence it is evident that naught can lull man's will, save the universal good. This is to be found, not in any creature, but in God alone; because every creature has goodness by participation. Wherefore God alone can satisfy the will of man, according to the words of Ps. cii. 5: *Who satisfieth thy desire with good things.* Therefore God alone constitutes man's happiness.

From *The "Summa theologica" of St. Thomas Aquinas,* literally translated by fathers of the English Dominican Province, New York: Benziger Brothers, Inc.; London: Burns Oates & Washbourne, Ltd., 2nd ed., 1927. Reprinted by permission.

Reply Obj. 1. The summit of man does indeed touch the base of the angelic nature, by a kind of likeness; but man does not rest there as in his last end, but reaches out to the universal fount itself of good, which is the common object of happiness of all the blessed, as being the infinite and perfect good.

Reply Obj. 2. If a whole be not the last end, but ordained to a further end, then the last end of a part thereof is not the whole itelf, but something else. Now the universe of creatures, to which man is compared as part to whole, is not the last end, but is ordained to God, as to its last end. Therefore the last end of man is not the good of the universe, but God himself.

Reply Obj. 3. Created good is not less than that good of which man is capable, as of something intrinsic and inherent to him: but it is less than the good of which he is capable, as of an object, and which is infinite. And the participated good which is in an angel, and in the whole universe, is a finite and restricted good.

Question III. What Is Happiness?

FOURTH ARTICLE. *Whether, if Happiness Is in the Intellective Part, It Is an Operation of the Intellect or of the Will?*

We proceed thus to the Fourth Article:—

Objection 1. It would seem that happiness consists in an act of the will. For Augustine says that man's happiness consists in peace; wherefore it is written (Ps. cxlvii. 3): *Who hath placed peace in thy end* (Douay,—*borders*). But peace pertains to the will. Therefore man's happiness is in the will.

Obj. 2. Further, happiness is the supreme good. But good is the object of the will. Therefore happiness consists in an operation of the will.

Obj. 3. Further, the last end corresponds to the first mover: thus the last end of the whole army is victory, which is the end of the general, who moves all the men. But the first mover in regard to operations is the will: because it moves the other powers, as we shall state further on. Therefore happiness regards the will.

Obj. 4. Further, if happiness be an operation, it must needs be man's most excellent operation. But the love of God, which is an act of the will, is a more excellent operation than knowledge, which is an operation of the intellect, as the Apostle declares (1 Cor. xiii.). Therefore it seems that happiness consist in an act of the will.

Obj. 5. Further, Augustine says that *happy is he who has whatever he desires, and desires nothing amiss.* And a little further on he adds: *He is almost happy who desires well, whatever he desires: for good things make a man happy, and such a man already possesses some good—i.e., a good will.* Therefore happiness consists in an act of the will.

On the contrary, Our Lord said (Jo. xvii. 3): *This is eternal life: that they may know Thee, the only true God.* Now eternal life is the last end, as stated above. Therefore man's happiness consists in the knowledge of God, which is an act of the intellect.

I answer that, As stated above two things are needed for happiness: one, which is the essence of happiness: the other, that is, as it were, its proper accident, *i.e.,* the delight connected with it. I say, then, that as to the very essence of happiness, it is impossible for it to consist in an act of the will. For it is evident from what has been said that happiness is the attainment of the last end. But the attainment of the end does not consist in the very act of the will. For the will is directed to the end, both absent, when it desires it; and present, when it is delighted by resting therein. Now it is evident that the desire itself of the end is not the attainment of the end, but is a movement towards the end: while delight comes to the will from the end being present; and not conversely, is a thing made present, by the fact that the will delights in it. Therefore, that the end be present to him who desires it, must be due to something else than an act of the will.

This is evidently the case in regard to sensible ends. For if the acquisition of money were through an act of the will, the covetous man would have it from the very moment that he wished for it. But at that moment it is far from him; and he attains it, by grasping it in his hand, or in some like manner; and then he delights in the money got. And so it is with an intelligible end. For at first we desire to attain an intelligible end; we attain it, through its being made present to us by an act of the intellect; and then the delighted will rests in the end when attained.

So, therefore, the essence of happiness consists in an act of the intellect: but the delight that results from happiness pertains to the will. In this sense Augustine says that happiness is *joy in truth,* because, to wit, joy itself is the consummation of happiness.

Reply Obj. 1. Peace pertains to man's last end, not as though it were the very essence of happiness; but because it is antecedent and consequent thereto: antecedent, in so far as all those things are removed which disturb and hinder man in attaining the last end: consequent, inasmuch as, when man has attained his last end, he remains at peace, his desire being at rest.

Reply Obj. 2. The will's first object is not its act: just as neither is the first object of the sight, vision, but a visible thing. Wherefore, from the very fact that happiness belongs to the will, as the will's first object, it follows that it does not belong to it as its act.

Reply Obj. 3. The intellect apprehends the end before the will does: yet motion towards the end begins in the will. And therefore to the will belongs that which last of all follows the attainment of the end, viz., delight or enjoyment.

Reply Obj. 4. Love ranks above knowledge in moving, but knowledge precedes love in attaining: for *naught is loved save what is known,* as Augustine says. Consequently we first attain an intelligible end by an act of the intellect; just as we first attain a sensible end by an act of sense.

Reply Obj. 5. He who has whatever he desires, is happy, because he has what he desires: and this indeed is by something other than the act of his will. But to desire nothing amiss is needed for happiness, as a necessary disposition thereto. And a good will is reckoned among the good things which make a man happy, forasmuch as it is an inclination of the will: just as a movement is reduced to the genus of its terminus, for instance, *alteration* to the genus *quality.*

FIFTH ARTICLE.   *Whether Happiness Is an Operation of the Speculative, or of the Practical Intellect?*

We proceed thus to the Fifth Article:—

Objection 1. It would seem that happiness is an operation of the practical intellect. For the end of every creature consists in becoming like God. But man is like God, by his practical intellect, which is the cause of things understood, rather than by his speculative intellect, which derives its knowledge from things.

Therefore man's happiness consists in an operation of the practical intellect rather than of the speculative.

Obj. 2. Further, happiness is man's perfect good. But the practical intellect is ordained to the good rather than the speculative intellect, which is ordained to the true. Hence we are said to be good, in reference to the perfection of the practical intellect, but not in reference to the perfection of the speculative intellect, according to which we are said to be knowing or understanding. Therefore man's happiness consists in an act of the practical intellect rather than of the speculative.

Obj. 3. Further, happiness is a good of man himself. But the speculative intellect is more concerned with things outside man; whereas the practical intellect is concerned with things belonging to man himself, viz., his operations and passions. Therefore man's happiness consists in an operation of the practical intellect rather than of the speculative.

On the contrary, Augustine says that *contemplation is promised us, as being the goal of all our actions, and the everlasting perfection of our joys.*

I answer that, Happiness consists in an operation of the speculative rather than of the practical intellect. This is evident for three reasons. First because if man's happiness is an operation, it must needs be man's highest operation. Now man's highest operation is that of his highest power in respect of its highest object: and his highest power is the intellect, whose highest object is the Divine Good, which is the object, not of the practical, but of the speculative intellect. Consequently happiness consists principally in such an operation, viz., in the contemplation of Divine things. And since that *seems to be each man's self, which is best in him,* according to *Ethic.* ix. 8, and x. 7, therefore such an operation is most proper to man and most delightful to him.

Secondly, it is evident from the fact that contemplation is sought principally for its own sake. But the act of the practical intellect is not sought for its own sake but for the sake of action: and these very actions are ordained to some end. Consequently, it is evident that the last end cannot consist in the active life, which pertains to the practical intellect.

Thirdly, it is again evident, from the fact that in the contemplative life man has something in common with things above him, viz., with God and the angels, to whom he is made like by happiness. But in things pertaining to the active life, other animals also have something in common with man, although imperfectly.

Therefore the last and perfect happiness, which we await in the life to come, consists entirely in contemplation. But imperfect happiness, such as can be had here, consists first and principally in contemplation, but secondarily, in an operation of the practical intellect directing human actions and passions, as stated in *Ethic.* x. 7, 8.

Reply Obj. 1. The asserted likeness of the practical intellect to God is one of proportion; that is to say, by reason of its standing in relation to what it knows, as God does to what He knows. But the likeness of the speculative intellect to God is one of union and *information;* which is a much greater likeness.—And yet it may be answered that, in regard to the principal thing known, which is His Essence, God has not practical but merely speculative knowledge.

Reply Obj. 2. The practical intellect is ordained to good which is outside of it: but the speculative intellect has good within it, viz., the contemplation of truth. And if this good be perfect, the whole man is perfected and made good thereby: such a good the practical intellect has not; but it directs man thereto.

Reply Obj. 3. This argument would hold, if man himself were his own last end; for then the consideration and direction of his actions and passions would be his happiness. But since man's last end is something outside of him, to wit, God, to Whom we reach out by an operation of the speculative intellect; therefore man's happiness consists in an operation of the speculative intellect rather than of the practical intellect.

EIGHTH ARTICLE.   *Whether Man's Happiness Consists in the Vision of the Divine Essence?*

We proceed thus to the Eighth Article:—

Objection 1. It would seem that man's happiness does not consist in the vision of the Divine Essence. For Dionysius says that by that which is highest in his intellect, man is united to God as to something altogether unknown. But that which is seen in its essence is not altogether unknown. Therefore the final perfection of the intellect, namely, happiness, does not consist in God being seen in His Essence.

Obj. 2. Further, the higher perfection belongs to the higher nature. But to see His own Essence is the perfection proper to the Divine intellect. Therefore the final perfection of the human intellect does not reach to this, but consists in something less.

On the contrary, It is written (1 Jo. iii. 2): *When He shall appear, we shall be like to Him; and* (Vulg., *because*) *we shall see Him as He is.*

I answer that, Final and perfect happiness can consist in nothing else than the vision of the Divine Essence. To make this clear, two points must be observed. First, that man is not perfectly happy, so long as something remains for him to desire and seek: secondly, that the perfection of any power is determined by the nature of its object. Now the object of the intellect is *what a thing is, i.e.,* the essence of a thing, according to *De Anima* iii. 6. Wherefore the intellect attains perfection, in so far as it knows the essence of a thing. If therefore an intellect knows the essence of some effect, whereby it is not possible to know the essence of the cause, *i.e.,* to know of the cause *what it is;* that intellect cannot be said to reach that cause simply, although it may be able to gather from the effect the knowledge that the cause is. Consequently, when man knows an effect, and knows that it has a cause, there naturally remains in man the desire to know about that cause, *what it is.* And this desire is one of wonder, and causes inquiry, as is stated in the beginning of the *Metaphysics.* For instance, if a man, knowing the eclipse of the sun, considers that it must be due to some cause, and knows not what that cause is, he wonders about it, and from wondering proceeds to inquire. Nor does this inquiry cease until he arrives at a knowledge of the essence of the cause.

If therefore the human intellect, knowing the essence of some created effect, knows no more of God than *that He is;* the perfection of that intellect does not yet reach simply the First Cause, but there remains in it the natural desire to seek the cause. Wherefore it is not yet perfectly happy. Consequently, for perfect happiness the intellect needs to reach the very Essence of the First Cause. And thus it will have its perfection through union with God as with that object, in which alone man's happiness consists, as stated above.

Reply Obj. 1. Dionysius speaks of the knowledge of wayfarers journeying towards happiness.

Reply Obj. 2. As stated above, the end has a twofold acceptation. First, as to the thing itself which is desired: and in this way, the same thing is the end of the higher and of the lower nature, and indeed of all things, as stated above. Secondly, as to the attainment of this thing; and thus the end of the higher nature is different from that of the lower, according to their respective habitudes to that thing. So then the happiness of God, Who, in understanding his Essence, comprehends It, is higher than that of a man or angel who sees It indeed, but comprehends It not.

Question V. Of the Attainment of Happiness

FIFTH ARTICLE. *Whether Man Can Attain Happiness by His Natural Powers?*

We proceed thus to the Fifth Article:—

Objection 1. It would seem that man can attain Happiness by his natural powers. For nature does not fail in necessary things. But nothing is so necessary to man as that by which he attains the last end. Therefore this is not lacking to human nature. Therefore man can attain Happiness by his natural powers.

Obj. 2. Further, since man is more noble than irrational creatures, it seems that he must be better equipped than they. But irrational creatures can attain their end by their natural powers. Much more therefore can man attain Happiness by his natural powers.

Obj. 3. Further, Happiness is a *perfect operation,* according to the Philosopher. Now the beginning of a thing belongs to the same principle as the perfecting thereof. Since, therefore, the imperfect operation, which is as the beginning in human operations, is subject to man's natural power, whereby he is master of his own actions; it seems that he can attain to perfect operation, *i.e.,* Happiness, by his natural powers.

On the contrary, Man is naturally the principle of his action, by his intellect and will. But final Happiness prepared for the saints, surpasses the intellect and will of man; for the Apostle says (1 Cor. ii. 9): *Eye hath not seen, nor ear heard, neither hath it entered into the heart of man, what things God hath prepared for them that love Him.* Therefore man cannot attain Happiness by his natural powers.

I answer that, Imperfect happiness that can be had in this life, can be acquired by man by his natural powers, in the same way as virtue, in whose operation it consists: on this point we shall speak further on. But man's perfect Happiness, as stated above, consists in the vision of the Divine Essence. Now the vision of God's Essence surpasses the nature not only of man, but also of every creature, as was shown in the First Part. For the natural knowledge of every creature is in keeping with the mode of its substance: thus it is said of the intelligence that *it knows things that are above it, and things that are below it, according to the mode of its substance.* But every knowledge that is according to the mode of created substance, falls short of the vision of the Divine Essence, which infinitely surpasses all created substance. Consequently neither man, nor any creature, can attain final Happiness by his natural powers.

Reply Obj. 1. Just as nature does not fail man in necessaries, although it has not provided him with weapons and clothing, as it provided other animals, because it gave him reason and hands, with which he is able to get these things for himself; so neither did it fail man in things necessary, although it gave him not the wherewithal to attain Happiness: since this it could not do. But it did give him free-will, with which he can turn to God, that He may make him happy. *For what we do by means of our friends, is done, in a sense, by ourselves.*

Reply Obj. 2. The nature that can attain perfect good, although it needs help from without in order to attain it, is of more noble condition than a nature which cannot attain perfect good, but attains some imperfect good, although it need no help from without in order to attain it, as the Philosopher says. Thus he is better disposed to health who can attain perfect health, albeit by means of medicine, than he who can attain but imperfect health, without the help of medicine. And therefore the rational creature, which can attain the perfect good of happiness, but needs the Divine assistance for the purpose, is more perfect than the irrational creature, which is not capable of attaining this good, but attains some imperfect good by its natural powers.

Reply Obj. 3. When imperfect and perfect are of the same species, they can be caused by the same power. But this does not follow of necessity, if they be of different species: for not everything, that can cause the disposition of matter, can produce the final perfection. Now the imperfect operation, which is subject to man's natural power, is not of the same species as that perfect operation which is man's happiness: since operation takes its species from its object. Consequently the argument does not prove.

Question LXI. The Cardinal Virtues

FIRST ARTICLE. *Whether the Moral Virtues Should Be Called Cardinal or Principal Virtues?*

We proceed thus to the First Article:—

Objection 1. It would seem that moral virtues should not be called cardinal or principal virtues. For *the opposed members of a division are by nature simultaneous,* so that one is not principal rather than another. Now all the virtues are opposed members of the division of the genus *virtue.* Therefore none of them should be called principal.

Obj. 2. Further, the end is superior to the means. But the theological virtues are about the end, while the moral virtues are about the means. Therefore the theological virtues, rather than the moral virtues, should be called principal or cardinal.

Obj. 3. Further, that which is essentially so is superior to that which is so by participation. But the intellectual virtues belong to that which is essentially rational, whereas the moral virtues belong to that which is rational by participation, as was stated above. Therefore the intellectual virtues are principal, rather than the moral virtues.

On the contrary, Ambrose, in explaining the words *Blessed are the poor in spirit* (*Luke* vi. 20) says: *We know that there are four cardinal virtues, viz., temperance, justice, prudence and fortitude.* But these are moral virtues. Therefore the moral virtues are cardinal virtues.

I answer that, When we speak without qualification of virtue, we are understood to speak of human virtue. Now human virtue, as was stated above, is virtue according to its perfect nature if it requires the rectitude of the appetite; for such a virtue not only confers the ability to do well, but also causes the use of the good work. On the other hand, a virtue is so called according to the imperfect notion of virtue, when it does not require rectitude of the appetite, because it merely confers the ability of doing well without causing the use of the good work. Now it is evident that the perfect is principal as compared to the imperfect; and so those virtues which contain rectitude of the appetite are called principal virtues. Such are the moral virtues, and among the intellectual virtues prudence alone is such, for it is also in a way a moral virtue with respect to its subject matter, as was shown above. Consequently, those virtues which are called principal or cardinal are fittingly found among the moral virtues.

Reply Obj. 1. When a univocal genus is divided into its species, the members of the division are on a par in the point of the generic notion; although considered according to reality, one species may surpass another in rank and perfection, as man surpasses the other animals. But when we divide an analogous notion, which is applied to several things, but to one before it is applied to another, nothing hinders one from ranking before another, even with respect to the common notion; as the notion of being is applied to substance more principally than to accident. Such is the division of virtue into the various genera of virtue, since the good defined by reason is not found in the same way in all things.

Reply Obj. 2. The theological virtues are above man, as was stated above. Hence they should properly be called not human, but *super-human* or divine virtues.

Reply Obj. 3. Although the intellectual virtues, except prudence, rank before the moral virtues, in the point of their subject, they do not rank before them according to the nature of virtue; for a virtue, as such, has reference to the good, which is the object of the appetite.

SECOND ARTICLE.   *Whether There Are Four Cardinal Virtues?*

We proceed thus to the Second Article:—

Objection 1. It would seem that there are not four cardinal virtues. For prudence is the directing principle of the other moral virtues, as is clear from what has been said above. But that which directs others ranks before them. Therefore prudence alone is a principal virtue.

Obj. 2. Further, the principal virtues are, in a way, moral virtues. Now we are directed to moral works both by the practical reason and by a right appetite, as is stated in *Ethics* vi. Therefore there are only two cardinal virtues.

Obj. 3. Further, even among the other virtues one ranks higher than another. But in order that a virtue be principal, it need not rank above all the others, but above some. Therefore it seems that there are many more principal virtues.

On the contrary, Gregory says: *The entire structure of good works is built on four virtues.*

I answer that, Things may be numbered either in respect of their formal principles, or according to the subjects in which they are; and in either way we find that there are four cardinal virtues.

For the formal principle of the virtue of which we speak now is the good as defined by reason. This good can be considered in two ways. First, as existing in the consideration itself of reason, and thus we have one principal virtue called prudence. Secondly, according as the reason puts its order into something else, and this either into operations, and then we have justice, or into passions, and then we need two virtues. For the need of putting the order of reason into the passions is due to their thwarting reason; and this occurs in two ways. First, when the passions incite to something against reason, and then they need a curb, which we thus call *temperance;* secondly, when the passions withdraw us from following the dictate of reason, *e.g.,* through fear of danger or toil, and then man needs to be strengthened for that which reason dictates, lest he turn back, and to this end there is *fortitude.*

In like manner, we find the same number if we consider the subjects of virtue. For there are four subjects of the virtue of which we now speak, viz., the power which is rational in its essence, and this is perfected by *prudence;* and that which is rational by participation, and is threefold, the will, subject of *justice,* the concupiscible power, subject of *temperance,* and the irascible power, subject of *fortitude.*

Reply Obj. 1. Prudence is absolutely the principal of all the virtues. The others are principal, each in its own genus.

Reply Obj. 2. That part of the soul which is rational by participation is threefold, as was stated above.

Reply Obj. 3. All the other virtues, among which one ranks before another, are reducible to the above four, both as to the subject and as to the formal principles.

Question LXII. Of the Theological Virtues

FIRST ARTICLE.   *Whether There Are any Theological Virtues?*

We proceed thus to the First Article:—

Objection 1. It would seem that there are not any theological virtues. For according to *Phys.* vii, text 17, *virtue is the disposition of a perfect thing to that which is best: and by perfect, I mean that which is disposed according to nature.* But that which is Divine is above man's nature. Therefore the theological virtues are not virtues of a man.

Obj. 2. Further, theological virtues are quasi-Divine virtues. But the Divine virtues are exemplars, as stated above, which are not in us but in God. Therefore the theological virtues are not virtues of man.

Obj. 3. Further, the theological virtues are so called because they direct us to God, Who is the first beginning and last end of all things. But by the very nature of his reason and will, man is directed to his first beginning and last end. Therefore there is no need for any habits of theological virtue, to direct the reason and will to God.

On the contrary, The precepts of the Law are about acts of virtue. Now the Divine Law contains precepts about the acts of faith, hope, and charity: for it is written (*Ecclus.* ii. 8, *seqq.*): *Ye that fear the Lord believe Him,* and again, *hope in Him,* and again, *love Him.* Therefore faith, hope, and charity are virtues directing us to God. Therefore they are theological virtues.

I answer that, Man is perfected by virtue, for those actions whereby he is directed to happiness, as was explained above. Now man's happiness is twofold, as was also stated above. One is proportionate to human nature, a happiness, to wit, which man can obtain by means of his natural principles. The other is a happiness surpassing man's nature, and which man can obtain by the power of God alone, by a kind of participation of the Godhead, about which it is written (2 *Pet.* i 4) that by Christ we are made *partakers of the Divine nature.* And because such happiness surpasses the capacity of human nature, man's natural principles which enable him to act well according to his capacity, do not suffice to direct man to this same happiness. Hence it is necessary for man to receive from God some additional principles whereby he may be directed to supernatural happiness, even as he is directed to his connatural end, by means of his natural principles, albeit not without the Divine assistance. Such-like principles are called *theological virtues*: first, because their object is God, inasmuch as they direct us aright to God: secondly, because they are infused in us by God alone: thirdly, because these virtues are not made known to us, save by Divine revelation, contained in Holy Writ.

Reply Obj. 1. A certain nature may be ascribed to a certain thing in two ways. First, essentially: and thus these theological virtues surpass the nature of man. Secondly, by participation, as kindled wood partakes of the nature of fire: and thus, after a fashion, man becomes a partaker of the Divine Nature, as stated above: so that these virtues are proportionate to man in respect of the Nature of which he is made a partaker.

Reply Obj. 2. These virtues are called Divine, not as though God were virtuous by reason of them, but because by them God makes us virtuous, and directs us to Himself. Hence they are not exemplar but exemplate virtues.

Reply. Obj. 3. The reason and will are naturally directed to God, inasmuch as He is the beginning and end of nature, but in proportion to nature. But the reason and will, according to their nature, are not sufficiently directed to Him in so far as He is the object of supernatural happiness.

SECOND ARTICLE. *Whether the Theological Virtues Are Distinct from the Intellectual and Moral Virtues?*

We proceed thus to the Second Article:—

Objection 1. It would seem that the theological virtues are not distinct from the moral and intellectual virtues. For the theological virtues, if they be in a human soul, must needs perfect it, either as to the intellective, or as to the appetitive part. Now the virtues which perfect the intellective part are called intellectual; and the virtues which perfect the appetitive part, are called moral. Therefore, the theological virtues are not distinct from the moral and intellectual virtues.

Obj. 2. Further, the theological virtues are those which direct us to God. Now, among the intellectual virtues there is one which directs us to God: this is wisdom, which is about Divine things, since it considers the highest cause. Therefore the theological virtues are not distinct from the intellectual virtues.

Obj. 3. Further, Augustine shows how the four cardinal virtues are the *order of love.* Now love is charity, which is a theological virtue. Therefore the moral virtues are not distinct from the theological.

On the contrary, That which is above man's nature is distinct from that which is according to his nature. But the theological virtues are above man's nature; while the intellectual and moral virtues are in proportion to his nature, as clearly shown above. Therefore they are distinct from one another.

I answer that, As stated above, habits are specifically distinct from one another in respect of the formal difference of their objects. Now the object of the theological virtues is God Himself, Who is the last end of all, as surpassing the knowledge of our reason. On the other hand, the object of the intellectual and moral virtues is something comprehensible to human reason. Wherefore the theological virtues are specifically distinct from the moral and intellectual virtues.

Reply Obj. 1. The intellectual and moral virtues perfect man's intellect and appetite according to the capacity of human nature: the theological virtues, supernaturally.

Reply Obj. 2. The wisdom which the Philosopher reckons as an intellectual virtue, considers Divine things so far as they are open to the research of human reason. Theological virtue, on the other hand, is about those same things so far as they surpass human reason.

Reply Obj. 3. Though charity is love, yet love is not always charity. When, then, it is stated that every virtue is the order of love, this can be understood either of love in the general sense, or of the love of charity. If it be understood of love, commonly so called, then each virtue is stated to be the order of love, in so far as each cardinal virtue requires ordinate emotions; and love is the root and cause of every emotion, as stated above. If, however, it be understood of the love of charity, it does not mean that every other virtue is charity essentially: but that all other virtues depend on charity in some way, as we shall show further on.

THIRD ARTICLE.   *Whether Faith, Hope, and Charity Are Fittingly Reckoned as Theological Virtues?*

We proceed thus to the Third Article:—

Objection 1. It would seem that faith, hope, and charity are not fittingly reckoned as three theological virtues. For the theological virtues are in relation to Divine happiness, what the natural inclination is in relation to the connatural end. Now among the virtues directed to the connatural end there is but one natural virtue, viz., the understanding of principles. Therefore there should be but one theological virtue.

Obj. 2. Further, the theological virtues are more perfect than the intellectual and moral virtues. Now faith is not reckoned among the intellectual virtues, but is something less than a virtue, since it is imperfect knowledge. Likewise hope is not reckoned among the moral virtues, but is something less than a virtue, since it is a passion. Much less therefore should they be reckoned as theological virtues.

Obj. 3. Further, the theological virtues direct man's soul to God. Now man's soul cannot be directed to God, save through the intellective part, wherein are the intellect and will. Therefore there should be only two theological virtues, one perfecting the intellect, the other, the will.

On the contrary, The Apostle says (1 Cor. xiii. 13): *Now there remains faith, hope, charity, these three.*

I answer that, As stated above, the theological virtues direct man to supernatural happiness in the same way as by the natural inclination man is directed to his connatural end. Now the latter happens in respect of two things. First, in respect of the reason or intellect, in so far as it contains the first universal principles which are known to us by the natural light of the intellect, and which are reason's starting-point, both in speculative and in practical matters. Secondly, through the rectitude of the will which tends naturally to good as defined by reason.

But these two fall short of the order of supernatural happiness, according to 1 Cor. ii. 9: *The eye hath not seen, nor ear heard, neither hath it entered into the heart of man, what things God hath prepared for them that love Him.* Consequently in respect of both the above things man needed to receive in addition something supernatural to direct him to a supernatural end. First, as regards the intellect, man receives certain supernatural principles, which are held by means of a Divine light: these are the articles of faith, about which is faith.— Secondly, the will is directed to this end, both as to the movement of intention, which tends to that end as something attainable,—and this pertains to hope,—and as to a certain spiritual union, whereby the will is, so to speak, transformed into that end,—and this belongs to charity. For the appetite of a thing is moved and tends towards its connatural end naturally; and this movement is due to a certain conformity of the thing with its end.

Reply Obj. 1. The intellect requires intelligible species whereby to understand: consequently there is need of a natural habit in addition to the power. But the very nature of the will suffices for it to be directed naturally to the end, both as to the intention of the end and as to its conformity with the end. But the nature of the power is insufficient in either of these respects, for the will to be directed to things that are above its nature. Consequently there was need for an additional supernatural habit in both respects.

Reply Obj. 2. Faith and hope imply a certain imperfection: since faith is of things unseen, and hope, of things not possessed. Hence faith and hope, in things that are subject to human power, fall short of the notion of virtue. But faith and hope in things which are above the capacity of human nature surpass all virtue that is in proportion to man, according to 1 Cor. i. 25: *The weakness of God is stronger than men.*

Reply Obj. 3. Two things pertain to the appetite, viz., movement to the end, and conformity with the end by means of love. Hence there must needs be two theological virtues in the human appetite, namely, hope and charity.

THE SUMMA THEOLOGICA
First Part of the Second Part

Question XCII. Of the Effects of Law

FIRST ARTICLE. *Whether an Effect of Law Is To Make Men Good?*

We proceed thus to the First Article:—

Objection 1. It seems that it is not an effect of law to make men good. For men are good through virtue, since virtue, as stated in *Ethic.* ii. 6 is *that which makes its subject good.* But virtue is in man from God alone, because He it is Who *works it in us without us,* as we stated above in giving the definition of virtue. Therefore the law does not make men good.

From A. Pegis, ed., *Basic Writings of Saint Thomas Aquinas*, New York: Random House, 1948; London: Burns and Oates. Reprinted by permission.

Obj. 2. Further, Law does not profit a man unless he obeys it. But the very fact that a man obeys a law is due to his being good. Therefore in man goodness is presupposed to the law. Therefore the law does not make men good.

Obj. 3. Further, Law is ordained to the common good, as stated above. But some behave well in things regarding the community, who behave ill in things regarding themselves. Therefore it is not the business of the law to make men good.

Obj. 4. Further, some laws are tyrannical, as the Philosopher says. But a tyrant does not intend the good of his subjects, but considers only his own profit. Therefore law does not make men good.

On the contrary, The Philosopher says that the *intention of every lawgiver is to make good citizens.*

I answer that, As stated above, a law is nothing else than a dictate of reason in the ruler by whom his subjects are governed. Now the virtue of any subordinate thing consists in its being well subordinated to that by which it is regulated: thus we see that the virtue of the irascible and concupiscible faculties consists in their being obedient to reason; and accordingly *the virtue of every subject consists in his being well subjected to his ruler,* as the Philosopher says. But every law aims at being obeyed by those who are subject to it. Consequently it is evident that the proper effect of law is to lead its subjects to their proper virtue: and since virtue is *that which makes its subject good,* it follows that the proper effect of law is to make those to whom it is given, good, either simply or in some particular respect. For if the intention of the lawgiver is fixed on true good, which is the common good regulated according to Divine justice, it follows that the effect of the law is to make men good simply. If, however, the intention of the lawgiver is fixed on that which is not simply good, but useful or pleasurable to himself, or in opposition to Divine justice; then the law does not make men good simply, but in respect to that particular government. In this way good is found even in things that are bad of themselves: thus a man is called a good robber, because he works in a way that is adapted to his end.

Reply Obj. 1. Virtue is twofold, as explained above, viz., acquired and infused. Now the fact of being accustomed to an action contributes to both, but in different ways; for it causes the acquired virtue; while it disposes to infused virtue, and preserves and fosters it when it already exists. And since law is given for the purpose of directing human acts; as far as human acts conduce to virtue, so far does law make men good. Wherefore the Philosopher says in the second book of the *Politics* that *lawgivers make men good by habituating them to good works.*

Reply Obj. 2. It is not always through perfect goodness of virtue that one obeys the law, but sometimes it is through fear of punishment, and sometimes from the mere dictate of reason, which is a beginning of virtue, as stated above.

Reply Obj. 3. The goodness of any part is considered in comparison with the whole; hence Augustine says that *unseemly is the part that harmonizes not with the whole.* Since then every man is a part of the state, it is impossible that a man be good, unless he be well proportionate to the common good: nor can the whole be well consistent unless its parts be proportionate to it. Consequently the common good of the state cannot flourish, unless the citizens be virtuous, at least those whose business it is to govern. But it is enough for the good of the community, that the other citizens be so far virtuous that they obey the commands of their rulers. Hence the Philosopher says that *the virtue of a sovereign is the same as that of a good man, but the virtue of any common citizen is not the same as that of a good man.*

Reply Obj. 4. A tyrannical law, through not being according to reason, is not a law, absolutely speaking, but rather a perversion of law; and yet in so far as it is something in the nature of a law, it aims at the citizens being good. For all it has in the nature of a law consists in its being an ordinance made by a superior to his subjects, and aims at being obeyed by them, which is to make them good, not simply, but with respect to that particular government.

Question XCIV. The Natural Law

FIRST ARTICLE. *Whether the Natural Law Is a Habit?*

We proceed thus to the First Article:—

Objection 1. It would seem that the natural law is a habit. For, as the Philosopher says, *there are three things in the soul, power, habit and passion.* But the natural law is not one of the soul's powers, nor is it one of the passions, as we may see by going through them one by one. Therefore the natural law is a habit.

Obj. 2. Further, Basil says that the *conscience or synderesis is the law of our mind,* which can apply only to the natural law. But *synderesis* is a habit, as was shown in the First Part. Therefore the natural law is a habit.

Obj. 3. Further, the natural law abides in man always, as will be shown further on. But man's reason, which the law regards, does not always think about the natural law. Therefore the natural law is not an act, but a habit.

On the contrary, Augustine says that *a habit is that whereby something is done when necessary.* But such is not the natural law, since it is in infants and in the damned who cannot act by it. Therefore the natural law is not a habit.

I answer that, A thing may be called a habit in two ways. First, properly and essentially, and thus the natural law is not a habit. For it has been stated above that the natural law is something appointed by reason, just as a proposition is a work of reason. Now that which a man does is not the same as that whereby he does it, for he makes a becoming speech by the habit of grammar. Since, then, a habit is that by which we act, a law cannot be a habit properly and essentially.

Secondly, the term habit may be applied to that which we hold by a habit. Thus *faith* may mean *that which we hold by faith.* Accordingly, since the precepts of the natural law are sometimes considered by reason actually, while sometimes they are in the reason only habitually, in this way the natural law may be called a habit. So, too, in speculative matters, the indemonstrable principles are not the habit itself whereby we hold these principles; they are rather the principles of which we possess the habit.

Reply Obj. 1. The Philosopher proposes there to discover the genus of virtue; and since it is evident that virtue is a principle of action, he mentions only those things which are principles of human acts, viz., powers, habits and passions. But there are other things in the soul besides these three: *e.g.,* acts, as *to will* is in the one that wills; again, there are things known in the knower; moreover its own natural properties are in the soul, such as immortality and the like.

Reply Obj. 2. *Synderesis* is said to be the law of our intellect because it is a habit containing the precepts of the natural law, which are the first principles of human actions.

Reply Obj. 3. This argument proves that the natural law is held habitually; and this is granted.

To the argument advanced in the contrary sense we reply that sometimes a man is unable to make use of that which is in him habitually, because of some impediment. Thus, because of sleep, a man is unable to use the habit of science. In like manner, through the deficiency of his age, a child cannot use the habit of the understanding of principles, or the natural law, which is in him habitually.

SECOND ARTICLE. *Whether the Natural Law Contains Several Precepts, or Only One?*

We proceed thus to the Second Article:—

Objection 1. It would seem that the natural law contains, not several precepts, but only one. For law is a kind of precept, as was stated above. If therefore there were many precepts of the natural law, it would follow that there are also many natural laws.

Obj. 2. Further, the natural law is consequent upon human nature. But human nature, as a whole, is one, though, as to its parts, it is manifold. Therefore, either there is but one precept of the law of nature because of the unity of nature as a whole, or there are many by reason of the number of parts of human nature. The result would be that even things relating to the inclination of the concupiscible power would belong to the natural law.

Obj. 3. Further, law is something pertaining to reason, as was stated above. Now reason is but one in man. Therefore there is only one precept of the natural law.

On the contrary, The precepts of the natural law in man stand in relation to operable matters as first principles do to matters of demonstration. But there are several first indemonstrable principles. Therefore there are also several precepts of the natural law.

I answer that, As was stated above, the precepts of the natural law are to the practical reason what the first principles of demonstrations are to the speculative reason, because both are self-evident principles. Now a thing is said to be self-evident in two ways: first, in itself; secondly, in relation to us. Any proposition is said to be self-evident in itself, if its predicate is contained in the notion of the subject; even though it may happen that to one who does not know the definition of the subject, such a proposition is not self-evident. For instance, this proposition, *Man is a rational being*, is, in its very nature, self-evident, since he who says *man* says *a rational being*; and yet to one who does not know what a man is, this proposition is not self-evident. Hence it is that, as Boethius says, certain axioms or propositions are universally self-evident to all; and such are the propositions whose terms are known to all, as, *Every whole is greater than its part*, and, *Things equal to one and the same are equal to one another*. But some propositions are self-evident only to the wise, who understand the meaning of the terms of such propositions. Thus to one who understands that an angel is not a body, it is self-evident that an angel is not circumscriptively in a place. But this is not evident to the unlearned, for they cannot grasp it.

Now a certain order is to be found in those things that are apprehended by men. For that which first falls under apprehension is *being*, the understanding of which is included in all things whatsoever a man apprehends. Therefore the first indemonstrable principle is that *the same thing cannot be affirmed and denied at the same time*, which is based on the notion of *being* and *not-being*: and on this principle all others are based, as is stated in *Metaph.* iv. Now as *being* is the first thing that falls under the apprehension absolutely, so *good* is the first thing that falls under the apprehension of the practical reason, which is directed to action (since every agent acts for an end, which has the nature of good.) Consequently, the first principle in the practical reason is one founded on the nature of good, viz., that *good is that which all things seek after*. Hence this is the first precept of law, that *good is to be done and promoted, and evil is to be avoided*. All other precepts of the natural law are based upon this; so that all the things which the practical reason naturally apprehends as man's good belong to the precepts of the natural law under the form of things to be done or avoided.

Since, however, good has the nature of an end, and evil, the nature of the contrary, hence it is that all those things to which man has a natural inclination are naturally apprehended by reason as being good, and consequently as objects of pursuit, and their contraries as evil, and objects of avoidance. Therefore, the order of the precepts of the natural law is according to the order of natural inclinations. For there is in man, first of all, an inclination to good in accordance with the nature which he has in common with all substances, inasmuch, namely, as every substance seeks the preservation of its own being, according to its nature; and by reason of this inclination, whatever is a means of preserving human life, and of warding off its obstacles, belongs to the natural law. Secondly, there is in man an inclination to things that pertain to him more specially, according to that nature which he has in common with other animals; and in virtue of this inclination, those things are said to belong to the natural law *which nature has taught to all animals*, such as sexual intercourse, the education of offspring and so forth. Thirdly, there is in man an inclination to good according to the nature of his reason, which nature is proper to him. Thus man has a natural inclination to know the truth about God, and to live in society; and in this respect, whatever pertains to this inclination belongs to the natural law: *e.g.*, to shun ignorance, to avoid offending those among whom one has to live, and other such things regarding the above inclination.

Reply Obj. 1. All these precepts of the law of nature have the character of one natural law, inasmuch as they flow from one first precept.

Reply Obj. 2. All the inclinations of any parts whatsoever of human nature, *e.g.*, of the concupiscible and irascible parts, in so far as they are ruled by reason, belong to the natural law, and are reduced to one first precept, as was stated above. And thus the precepts of the natural law are many in themselves, but they are based on one common foundation.

Reply Obj. 3. Although reason is one in itself, yet it directs all things regarding man; so that whatever can be ruled by reason is contained under the law of reason.

FOURTH ARTICLE. *Whether the Natural Law is the Same in All Men?*

We proceed thus to the Fourth Article:—

Objection 1. It would seem that the natural law is not the same in all. For it is stated in the *Decretals* that *the natural law is that which is contained in the Law and the Gospel.* But this is not common to all men, because, as it is written (*Rom.* x. 16), *all do not obey the gospel.* Therefore the natural law is not the same in all men.

Obj. 2. Further, *Things which are according to the law are said to be just,* as is stated in *Ethics* v. But it is stated in the same book that nothing is so just for all as not to be subject to change in regard to some men. Therefore even the natural law is not the same in all men.

Obj. 3. Further, as was stated above, to the natural law belongs everything to which a man is inclined according to his nature. Now different men are naturally inclined to different things,—some to the desire of pleasures, others to the desire of honors, and other men to other things. Therefore, there is not one natural law for all.

On the contrary, Isidore says: *The natural law is common to all nations.*

I answer that, As we have stated above, to the natural law belong those things to which a man is inclined naturally; and among these it is proper to man to be inclined to act according to reason. Now it belongs to the reason to proceed from what is common to what is proper, as is stated in *Physics* i. The speculative reason, however, is differently situated, in this matter, from the practical reason. For, since the speculative reason is concerned chiefly with necessary things, which cannot be otherwise than they are, its proper conclusions, like the universal principles, contain the truth without fail. The practical reason, on the other hand, is concerned with contingent matters, which is the domain of human actions; and, consequently, although there is necessity in the common principles, the more we descend towards the particular, the more frequently we encounter defects. Accordingly, then, in speculative matters truth is the same in all men, both as to principles and as to conclusions; although the truth is not known to all as regards the conclusions, but only as regards the principles which are called *common notions.* But in matters of action, truth or practical rectitude is not the same for all as to what is particular, but only as to the common principles; and where there is the same rectitude in relation to particulars, it is not equally known to all.

It is therefore evident that, as regards the common principles whether of speculative or of practical reason, truth or rectitude is the same for all, and is equally known by all. But as to the proper conclusions of the speculative reason, the truth is the same for all, but it is not equally known to all. Thus, it is true for all that the three angles of a triangle are together equal to two right angles, although it is not known to all. But as to the proper conclusions of the practical reason, neither is the truth or rectitude the same for all, nor, where it is the same, is it equally known by all. Thus, it is right and true for all to act according to reason, and from this principle it follows, as a proper conclusion, that goods entrusted to another should be restored to their owner. Now this is true for the majority of cases. But it may happen in a particular case that it would be injurious, and therefore unreasonable, to restore goods held in trust; for instance, if they are claimed for the purpose of fighting against one's country. And this principle will be found to fail the more, according as we descend further towards the particular, *e.g.,* if one were to say that goods held in trust should be restored with such and such a guarantee, or in such and such a way; because the greater the number of conditions added, the greater the number of ways in which the principle may fail, so that it be not right to restore or not to restore.

Consequently, we must say that the natural law, as to the first common principles, is the same for all, both as to rectitude and as to knowledge. But as to certain more particular aspects, which are conclusions, as it were, of those common principles, it is the same for all in the majority of cases, both as to rectitude and as to knowledge; and yet in some few cases it may fail, both as to rectitude, by reason of certain obstacles (just as natures subject to generation and corruption fail in some few cases because of some obstacle), and as to knowledge, since in some the reason is perverted by passion, or evil habit, or an evil disposition of nature. Thus at one time theft, although it is expressly contrary to the natural law, was not considered wrong among the Germans, as Julius Cæsar relates.

Reply Obj. 1. The meaning of the sentence quoted is not that whatever is contained in the Law and the Gospel belongs to the natural law, since they contain many things that are above nature; but that whatever belongs to the natural law is fully contained in them. Therefore Gratian, after saying that *the natural law is what is contained in the Law and the Gospel*, adds at once, by way of example, *by which everyone is commanded to do to others as he would be done by.*

Reply Obj. 2. The saying of the Philosopher is to be understood of things that are naturally just, not as common principles, but as conclusions drawn from them, having rectitude in the majority of cases, but failing in a few.

Reply Obj. 3. Just as in man reason rules and commands the other powers, so all the natural inclinations belonging to the other powers must needs be directed according to reason. Therefore it is universally right for all men that all their inclinations should be directed according to reason.

FIFTH ARTICLE. *Whether the Natural Law Can Be Changed?*

We proceed thus to the Fifth Article:—

Objection 1. It would seem that the natural law can be changed. For on *Ecclus.* xvii. 9 (*He gave them instructions, and the law of life*) the *Gloss* says: *He wished the law of the letter to be written, in order to correct the law of nature.* But that which is corrected is changed. Therefore the natural law can be changed.

Obj. 2. Further, the slaying of the innocent, adultery and theft are against the natural law. But we find these things changed by God: as when God commanded Abraham to slay his innocent son (*Gen.* xii. 2); and when He ordered the Jews to borrow and purloin the vessels of the Egyptians (*Exod.* xii. 35); and when He commanded Osee to take to himself *a wife of fornications* (*Osee* i. 2). Therefore the natural law can be changed.

Obj. 3. Further, Isidore says that *the possession of all things in common, and universal freedom, are matters of natural law.* But these things are seen to be changed by human laws. Therefore it seems that the natural law is subject to change.

On the contrary, It is said in the *Decretals: The natural law dates from the creation of the rational creature. It does not vary according to time, but remains unchangeable.*

I answer that, A change in the natural law may be understood in two ways. First, by way of addition. In this sense, nothing hinders the natural law from being changed, since many things for the benefit of human life have been added over and above the natural law, both by the divine law and by human laws.

Secondly, a change in the natural law may be understood by way of subtraction, so that what previously was according to the natural law, ceases to be so. In this sense, the natural law is altogether unchangeable in its first principles. But in its secondary principles, which, as we have said, are certain detailed proximate conclusions drawn from the first principles, the natural law is not changed so that what it prescribes be not right in most cases. But it may be changed in some particular cases of rare occurrence, through some special causes hindering the observance of such precepts, as was stated above.

Reply Obj. 1. The written law is said to be given for the correction of the natural law, either because it supplies what was wanting to the natural law, or because the natural law was so perverted in the hearts of some men, as to certain matters, that they esteemed those things good which are naturally evil; which perversion stood in need of correction.

Reply Obj. 2. All men alike, both guilty and innocent, die the death of nature; which death of nature is inflicted by the power of God because of original sin, according to *1 Kings* ii. 6: *The Lord killeth and maketh alive.* Consequently, by the command of God, death can be inflicted on any man, guilty or innocent, without any injustice whatever.—In like manner, adultery is intercourse with another's wife; who is allotted to him by the law emanating from God. Consequently intercourse with any woman, by the command of God, is neither adultery nor fornication.—The same applies to theft, which is the taking of another's property. For whatever is taken by the command of God, to Whom all things belong, is not taken against the will of its owner, whereas it is in this that theft consists.—Nor is it only in human things that whatever is commanded by God is right; but also in natural things, whatever is done by God is, in some way, natural, as was stated in the First Part.

Reply Obj. 3. A thing is said to belong to the natural law in two ways. First, because nature inclines thereto: *e.g.*, that one should not do harm to another. Secondly, because nature did not bring with it the contrary. Thus, we might say that for man to be naked is of the natural law, because nature did not give him clothes, but art invented them. In this sense, *the possession of all things in common and universal freedom* are said to be of the natural law, because, namely, the distinction of possessions and slavery were not brought in by nature, but devised by human reason for the benefit of human life. Accordingly, the law of nature was not changed in this respect, except by addition.

Question XCV.   Human Law

FIRST ARTICLE.   *Whether It Was Useful for Laws To Be Framed by Men?*

We proceed thus to the First Article:—

Objection 1. It would seem that it was not useful for laws to be framed by men. For the purpose of every law is that man be made good thereby, as was stated above. But men are more to be induced to be good willingly by means of admonitions, than against their will, by means of laws. Therefore there was no need to frame laws.

Obj. 2. Further, As the Philosopher says, *men have recourse to a judge as to animate justice.* But animate justice is better than inanimate justice, which is contained in laws. Therefore it would have been better for the execution of justice to be entrusted to the decision of judges than to frame laws in addition.

Obj. 3. Further, every law is framed for the direction of human actions, as is evident from what has been stated above. But since human actions are about singulars, which are infinite in number, matters pertaining to the direction of human actions cannot be taken into sufficient consideration except by a wise man, who looks into each one of them. Therefore it would have been better for human acts to be directed by the judgment of wise men, than by the framing of laws. Therefore there was no need of human laws.

On the contrary, Isidore says: *Laws were made that in fear thereof human audacity might be held in check, that innocence might be safeguarded in the midst of wickedness, and that the dread of punishment might prevent the wicked from doing harm.* But these things are most necessary to mankind. Therefore it was necessary that human laws should be made.

I answer that, As we have stated above, man has a natural aptitude for virtue; but the perfection of virtue must be acquired by man by means of some kind of training. Thus we observe that a man is helped by diligence in his necessities, for instance, in food and clothing. Certain beginnings of these he has from nature, viz., his reason and his hands; but he has not the full complement, as other animals have, to whom nature has given sufficiently of clothing and food. Now it is difficult to see how man could suffice for himself in the matter of this training, since the perfection of virtue consists chiefly in withdrawing man from undue pleasures, to which above all man is inclined, and especially the young, who are more capable of being trained. Consequently a man needs to receive this training from another, whereby to arrive at the perfection of virtue. And as to those young people who are inclined to acts of virtue by their good natural disposition, or by custom, or rather by the gift of God, paternal training suffices, which is by admonitions. But since some are found to be dissolute and prone to vice, and not easily amenable to words, it was necessary for such to be restrained from evil by force and fear, in order that, at least, they might desist from evil-doing, and leave others in peace, and that they themselves, by being habituated in this way, might be brought to do willingly what hitherto they did from fear, and thus become virtuous. Now this kind of training, which compels through fear of punishment, is the discipline of laws. Therefore, in order that man might have peace and virtue, it was necessary for laws to be framed; for, as the Philosopher says, *as man is the most noble of animals if he be perfect in virtue, so he is the lowest of all, if he be severed from law and justice.* For man can use his reason to devise means of satisfying his lusts and evil passions, which other animals are unable to do.

Reply Obj. 1. Men who are well disposed are led willingly to virtue by being admonished better than by coercion; but men whose disposition is evil are not led to virtue unless they are compelled.

Reply Obj. 2. As the Philosopher says, *it is better that all things be regulated by law, than left to be decided by judges.* And this for three reasons. First, because it is easier to find a few wise men competent to frame right laws, than to find the many who would be necessary to judge rightly of each single case.— Secondly, because those who make laws consider long beforehand what laws to make, whereas judgment on each single case has to be pronounced as soon as it arises; and it is easier for man to see what is right, by taking many instances into consideration, than by considering one solitary instance.—Thirdly, because law-givers judge universally and about future events, whereas those who sit in judgment judge of things present, towards which they are affected by love, hatred, or some kind of cupidity; and thus their judgment becomes perverted.

Since, then, the animated justice of the judge is not found in every man, and since it can be bent, therefore it was necessary, whenever possible, for the law to determine how to judge, and for very few matters to be left to the decision of men.

Reply Obj. 3. Certain individual facts which cannot be covered by the law *have necessarily to be committed to judges*, as the Philosopher says in the same passage: *e.g., concerning something that has happened or not happened*, and the like.

SECOND ARTICLE. *Whether Every Human Law Is Derived from the Natural Law?*

We proceed thus to the Second Article:—

Objection 1. It would seem that not every human law is derived from the natural law. For the Philosopher says that *the legal just is that which originally was a matter of indifference*. But those things which arise from the natural law are not matters of indifference. Therefore the enactments of human laws are not all derived from the natural law.

Obj. 2. Further, positive law is divided against natural law, as is stated by Isidore and the Philosopher. But those things which flow as conclusions from the common principles of the natural law belong to the natural law, as was stated above. Therefore that which is established by human law is not derived from the natural law.

Obj. 3. Further, the law of nature is the same for all, since the Philosopher says that *the natural just is that which is equally valid everywhere*. If therefore human laws were derived from the natural law, it would follow that they too are the same for all; which is clearly false.

Obj. 4. Further, it is possible to give a reason for things which are derived from the natural law. But *it is not possible to give the reason for all the legal enactments of the lawgivers*, as the Jurist says. Therefore not all human laws are derived from the natural law.

On the contrary, Tully says: *Things which emanated from nature, and were approved by custom, were sanctioned by fear and reverence for the laws.*

I answer that, As Augustine says, *that which is not just seems to be no law at all*. Hence the force of a law depends on the extent of its justice. Now in human affairs a thing is said to be just from being right, according to the rule of reason. But the first rule of reason is the law of nature, as is clear from what has been stated above. Consequently, every human law has just so much of the nature of law as it is derived from the law of nature. But if in any point it departs from the law of nature, it is no longer a law but a perversion of law.

But it must be noted that something may be derived from the natural law in two ways: first, as a conclusion from principles; secondly, by way of a determination of certain common notions. The first way is like to that by which, in the sciences, demonstrated conclusions are drawn from the principles; while the second is likened to that whereby, in the arts, common forms are determined to some particular. Thus, the craftsman needs to determine the common form of a house to the shape of this or that particular house. Some things are therefore derived from the common principles of the natural law by way of conclusions: *e.g.,* that *one must not kill* may be derived as a conclusion from the principle that *one should do harm to no man;* while some are derived therefrom by way of determination: *e.g.,* the law of nature has it that the evil-doer should be punished, but that he be punished in this or that way is a determination of the law of nature.

Accordingly, both modes of derivation are found in the human law. But those things which are derived in the first way are contained in human law, not as emanating therefrom exclusively, but as having some force from the natural law also. But those things which are derived in the second way have no other force than that of human law.

Reply Obj. 1. The Philosopher is speaking of those enactments which are by way of determination or specification of the precepts of the natural law.

Reply Obj. 2. This argument holds for those things that are derived from the natural law by way of conclusion.

Reply Obj. 3. The common principles of the natural law cannot be applied to all men in the same way because of the great variety of human affairs; and hence arises the diversity of positive laws among various people.

Reply. Obj. 4. These words of the Jurist are to be understood as referring to the decisions of rulers in determining particular points of the natural law; and to these determinations the judgment of expert and prudent men is related as to its principles, in so far, namely, as they see at once what is the best thing to decide. Hence the Philosopher says that, in such matters, *we ought to pay as much attention to the undemonstrated sayings and opinions of persons who surpass us in experience, age and prudence, as to their demonstrations.*

SELECTED BIBLIOGRAPHY

BIBLIOGRAPHIES

The literature on St. Thomas Aquinas is enormous and constantly growing. The following bibliographies may serve as at least partial guides.

Bourke, V., *Thomistic Bibliography,* St. Louis, 1945.

Mandonnet, P., and J. Destrez, *Bibliographie Thomiste,* 2nd ed., Paris, 1960.

Miethe, T. and V. Bourke, *Thomistic Bibliography,* 1940–1978, Westport, Conn. and London, 1980.

Walz, A., *Saint Thomas Aquinas, A. Bibliographical Study,* trans. S. Bullough, Westminster, Md., 1951.

Wyser, P., "Thomas von Aquin," in *Bibliographische Einführungen in das Studium der Philosophie,* 13/14, Bern, 1950.

TRANSLATIONS

Blackwell, R., R. Spath, and W. Thirlkel, trans., *Commentary on Aristotle's Physics,* New Haven, 1963.

Bobik, J., *Aquinas On Being and Essence: A Translation and Interpretation,* Notre Dame, 1965.

The English Dominicans, trans., *The "Summa theologica" of St. Thomas Aquinas,* 2nd ed., 22 vols., London, [1921?]–1932.

Foster, K., and S. Humpfries, trans., *Commentary on the De Anima,* London, 1951.

Gilby, T., and P. Meagher, and T. O'Brien, a new translation of *Summa Theologiae,* London–New York, 1964, sqq.

McKeon, R., ed. and trans., *Selections from Medieval Philosophers, II: Roger Bacon to William of Ockham*, New York, 1930.

Mulligan, R., R. Schmidt, and J. McGlynn, trans., *Truth*, 3 vols., Chicago. 1952–1954.

Pegis, A., ed., *Basic Writings of Saint Thomas Aquinas*, 2 vols., New York, 1948.

Pegis, A., ed., *Introduction to Saint Thomas Aquinas*, New York, 1948.

Pegis, A., J. Anderson, V. Bourke, and C. O'Niel, trans., *On the Truth of the Catholic Faith (Summa Contra Gentiles)*, 5 vols., New York, 1954–1956.

Phelan, G., and I. Eschmann, trans., *On Kingship to the King of Cyprus*, Toronto, 1949.

Rowan, J., trans., *The Soul*, St. Louis, 1949.

Rowan, J., trans., *Commentary on the Metaphysics*, 2 vols., Chicago, 1961.

STUDIES

Aquinas and Bonaventure (d. 1274), Norman, 1974.

Ardagh, D., "Aquinas on Happiness: A Defence," *The New Scholasticism*, LIII (1979), 428–459.

Bukowski, T., "J. Pecham, T. Aquinas *et al.* on the Eternity of the World," *Recherches de théologie ancienne et médiévale*, 1979, 216–221.

Burrell, D., *Aquinas. God and Action*, London, 1974.

Cajetan, *Commentary on Being and Essence (In De Ente et Essentia d. Thomas Aquinitatis)*, trans. L. Kendzierski and F. Wade, Milwaukee, 1964.

Centenary of St. Thomas Aquinas (1274–1974), The Thomist, XXXVIII (1974).

Chenu, M. -D., *Introduction à l'étude de saint Thomas d'Aquin*, Paris, 1950.

Clarke, W., "The Meaning of Participation in St. Thomas," *Proceedings of the American Catholic Philosophical Association*, XXVI (1952), 147–157.

Copleston, F., *Aquinas*, Harmondsworth, 1955.

Cousins, E., "St. Bonaventure, St. Thomas, and the Movement of Thought in the 13th Century," *International Philosophical Quarterly*, XIV (1974), 393–409.

Gilson, E., *The Christian Philosophy of St. Thomas Aquinas*, trans. L. Shook, with a catalogue of Thomas' works by I. T. Eschmann, New York, 1956.

Jordan, M., "Modes of Discourse in Aquinas' Metaphysics," *The New Scholasticism*, LIV (1980), 401–446.

Kenny, A., *Aquinas*, Oxford, 1980.

Kenny, A., ed., *Aquinas*, London, 1969.

Kenny, A., *The Five Ways: St. Thomas Aquinas' Proofs of God's Existence*, New York, 1969.

Klubertanz, G., *St. Thomas Aquinas on Analogy*, Chicago, 1960.

Klubertanz, G., *The Discursive Power: Sources and Doctrine of the Vis Cognitiva According to St. Thomas Aquinas*, St. Louis, 1952.

Knasas, J., "Making Sense of the *Tertia Via*," *The New Scholasticism*, LIV (1980), 476–511.

Lefèvre, C., "Siger de Brabant a-t-il influence Saint Thomas? Propos sur la cohérence de l'anthropologie thomiste," *Mélange de science religeuse* (Lille), LXXIV (1974), 203–215.

Mahoney, E., "Saint Thomas and Siger of Brabant Revisited," *The Review of Metaphysics*, XXVII (1974), 531–553.

Mahoney, E., "Themistius and the Agent Intellect in James of Viterbo and other Thirteenth Century Philosophers (Saint Thomas, Siger of Brabant and Henry Bate)," *Augustiniana*, XXIII (1973), 422–467.

Maritain, J., *St. Thomas Aquinas*, trans. of revised edition by J. Evans and P. O'Reilly, New York, 1958.

Maurer, A. *et al.*, eds. *St. Thomas Aquinas, 1274–1974, Commemorative Studies*, I–II, Toronto, 1974.

Maurer, A., "St. Thomas and Eternal Truths," *Mediaeval Studies*, XXXII (1970), 91–107.

Monist, LVIII (1974) (Aquinas volume).

O'Connor, D., *Aquinas and Natural Law*, New York, 1968.

Owens, J., "Aquinas on Knowing Existence," *The Review of Metaphysics*, XXIX (1975–1976), 670–690.

Owens, J., "Cause of Necessity in Aquinas' Tertia Via," *Mediaeval Studies*, XXXIII (1971), 21–45.

Owens, J., "Judgement and Truth in Aquinas," *Mediaeval Studies*, XXXVI (1970), 138–158.

Paul, A., ed., *Calgary Aquinas Studies*, Toronto, 1978.

Pegis, A., *St. Thomas and the Problem of the Soul in the Thirteenth Century*, Toronto, 1934.

The Review of Metaphysics, A Commemorative Issue: Thomas Aquinas, 1224–1274, XXVII (March, 1974).

Rousseau, M., "Avicenna and Aquinas on Incorruptibility," *The New Scholasticism*, LI (1977), 524–536.

Schmidt, R., *The Domain of Logic according to St. Thomas*, The Hague, 1969.

Sertillanges, A., *Saint Thomas Aquinas and His Work*, trans. G. Anstruther, London, 1933.

Shahan, R. and F. Kovach, eds., *Bonaventure*

and Aquinas, Norman, 1976.

Smith, G., *Natural Theology,* New York, 1951.

Thomas and Bonaventure. A Septicenary Commemoration, Proceedings of the American Catholic Philosophical Association, XLVIII (1974).

Tommaso d'Aquino nel suo Settimo Centenario, 9 vols., Napoli, 1974.

Tracy, D., ed., *Celebrating the Medieval Heritage. A Colloquy on the Thought of Aquinas and Bonaventure,* Chicago, 1978.

Van Steenberghen, F., *Thomas Aquinas and Radical Aristotelianism,* trans. J. O'Meara et al., Washington, D.C., 1980.

Verbeke, G. and D. Vehelst, eds., *Aquinas and Problems of his Time,* Louvain, 1976.

Weber, E., *La controverse de 1270 à l'université de Paris et son retentissement sur la pensée de S. Thomas D'Aquin,* Paris, 1970.

Weisheipl, J., *Friar Thomas D'Aquino,* Garden City, 1974.

Wippel, J., "Aquinas's Route to the Real Distinction: A Note on *De ente et essentia," The Thomist,* XLIII (1979), 279–295.

Yarty, G., "Order and Right Reason in Aquinas' Ethics," *Mediaeval Studies,* XXXVII (1975), 407–418.

THE CONDEMNATION
OF 1277

ALMOST from the beginning of the availability of the physical and metaphysical works of Aristotle and his Muslim interpreters there were Christian theologians and prelates who were profoundly suspicious of those works. William of Auvergne, for instance, whose major writings were completed before 1240, had enough respect for the autonomy of philosophy to recommend referring to philosophers when philosophical matters were at stake. But he criticized many positions held by Aristotle and Avicenna, the major interpreter then available, including the basic assumption that natures have their own power. The power of natures is only that of the creator, he maintained, thus underscoring the difference between the Aristotelian prime mover and the omnipotent Christian creator. In 1210, 1215, and 1231, the teaching of certain Aristotelian works at Paris was prohibited by bishop, cardinal, and pope respectively. The works were read privately, however, and from the 1240s on, the prohibitions seem to have been forgotten. Averroes replaced Avicenna as the major interpreter, and Aristotelian theses inspired much of the controversy of the period. Not all the arts masters who taught the works of Aristotle went on to the theological program or were even theologically oriented, and it has been remarked that in such leading arts masters as Siger of Brabant, the figure of the professional philosopher makes his first medieval appearance. By 1267, Bonaventure was protesting against excessive daring in philosophical investigation; and in 1268, Thomas Aquinas was back in Paris, surely because his superiors thought that the university was undergoing an intellectual emergency. Aquinas himself did not escape criticism in the decade of acrimonious but not easily discernible controversy which ensued.

On December 10, 1270, the hierarchy intervened once more. Etienne Tempier, the Bishop of Paris, condemned thirteen propositions concerning the unity of the intellect, the necessity of events, the eternity of the world, and various limitations on the divine power and knowledge. This move apparently did not make a very deep impression on some of the arts masters, and in 1272 and 1276, the university itself took steps, forbidding masters of arts to deal with theological subjects and forbidding secret teaching. There can be little doubt that, just as in the earlier period, the doctrinal situation at the leading theological center in Christendom was of extreme interest to the papacy, especially to the new Pope, John XXI. He was elected in 1276, and had been a doctor; but before that he had written as Peter of Spain the most widely used logic textbook, after Aristotle, in the Middle Ages. On January 18, 1277, he asked Bishop Tempier for a report on the situation at Paris. It is not known whether such a report was sent or whether the pope authorized the steps then taken. On March 7, 1277, Bishop Tempier condemned 219 propositions in the document excerpted below. On March 18, Archbishop Kilwardby of Canterbury, himself a former Dominican theologian at Paris, condemned 30 related propositions.

Bishop Tempier's list includes many so-called "Averroistic" commonplaces on the role of philosophy, the eternity of the world, the necessity of divine action, and the unity of the intellect in all men. But it also includes a few positions derived from the writings of Thomas Aquinas. In the selections which follow, the propositions stemming from Aquinas are identified by an "A" after the number. The numbering is that of Mandonnet, who attempted to organize the list by major topics. The Thomistic propositions have mostly to do with the theory of individuation through matter and the relation of intellect to will. It is interesting that Aquinas' very controversial thesis that man has but one substantial form was not included. It is often remarked that the list was compiled hurriedly and represents a rather crude version of the doctrines it purports to condemn. Thus, no one seems actually to have taught that there are two types of truth which can be contradictory to one another. Views on this subject seem to have ranged from holding that the offending positions merely represent what Aristotle said to holding that they are what natural reason, based on the senses and ignoring miracles, would have to say. Some distortion may have resulted from quoting or paraphrasing out of context, but many of the propositions seem to be such that distortion or misinterpretation is hardly conceivable.

Most scholars agree that these condemnations had a profound effect on the history of medieval thought, but they disagree as to the nature and significance of that effect. The condemnations have been called a brutal victory for Augustinianism over Aristotelianism, but Aristotle flourished in the schools after as well as before. It has been said that by freeing the later Middle Ages from the domination of a rigid Averroistic Aristotelianism, the way was opened for the development of natural science as the inquiry into nature rather than the dogmatic reiteration of the Aristotelian Corpus. But surely this exaggerates the monolithic character of the acceptance of Aristotle even by masters such as Siger of Brabant, and underestimates the continued influence of Aristotle and Averroes on the development of natural science. A more general and widely accepted view is that with the Condemnation of 1277, the scholastic effort to incorporate and renovate philosophy came to an end. But this surely underestimates the philosophical advances, especially the methodological ones, of the later period. Whatever the wider significance, there can be little doubt of the immediate impact. The reader will discern many echoes of this document in Duns Scotus, especially in the treatments of individuation and the will, and the "Parisian Articles" figure prominently in the writings of other late medieval figures. In 1325, after the canonization of Thomas Aquinas, the condemnation of his positions was revoked by the then Bishop of Paris.

CONDEMNATION OF 219 PROPOSITIONS

Stephen, by divine permission unworthy servant of the church of Paris, sends greetings in the Son of the glorious Virgin to all those who will read this letter.

We have received frequent reports, inspired by zeal for the faith, on the part of important and serious persons to the effect that some students of the arts in Paris are exceeding the boundaries of their own faculty and are presuming to treat and discuss, as if they were debatable in the schools, certain obvious and loathsome errors, or rather *vanities and lying follies* [Ps. 39:5], which are contained in the roll joined to this letter. These students are not hearkening to the admonition of Gregory, "Let him who would speak wisely exercise great care, lest by his speech he disrupt the unity of his listeners," particularly when in support of the aforesaid errors they adduce pagan writings that—shame on their ignorance—they assert to be so convincing that they do not know how to answer them. So as not to appear to be asserting what they thus insinuate, however, they conceal their answers in such a way that, while wishing to avoid Scylla, they fall into Charybdis. For they say that these things are true according to philosophy but not according to the Catholic faith, as if there were two contrary truths and as if the truth of Sacred Scripture were contradicted by the truth in the sayings of the accursed pagans, of whom it is written, *I will destroy the wisdom of the wise* [I Cor. 1:19; cf. Isa. 29:14], inasmuch as true wisdom destroys false wisdom. Would that such students listen to the advice of the wise man when he says: *If you have understanding, answer your neighbor; but if not, let your hand be upon your mouth, lest you be surprised in an unskillful word and be confounded* [Ecclus. 5:14].

Lest, therefore, this unguarded speech lead simple people into error, we, having taken counsel with the doctors of Sacred Scripture and other prudent men, strictly forbid these and like things and totally condemn them. We excommunicate all those who shall have taught the said errors or any one of them, or shall have dared in any way to defend or uphold them, or even to listen to them, unless they choose to reveal themselves to us or to the chancery of Paris within seven days: in addition to which we shall proceed against them by inflicting such other penalties as the law requires according to the nature of the offense.

Translated by E. L. Fortin and P. D. O'Neill from the edition by P. Mandonnet, *Siger de Brabant et l'averroïsme latin au XIIIme siècle, 2me partie, Textes inédites,* 2nd ed., Louvain, 1908, pp. 175–191. Full translation reprinted by permission of·The Free Press from R. Lerner and M. Mahdi, eds., *Medieval Political Philosophy: A Sourcebook.* Copyright © 1963 by The Free Press of Glencoe, a Division of The Macmillan Company.

By this same sentence of ours we also condemn the book *De Amore*, or *De Deo Amoris*, which begins with the words, *Cogit me multum*, and so on, and ends with the words, *Cave, igitur, Galtere, amoris exercere mandata*, and so on, as well as the book of geomancy that begins with the words, *Existimaverunt Indi*, and so on, and ends with the words, *Ratiocinare ergo super eum invenies*, and so on. We likewise condemn the books, scrolls, and leaflets dealing with necromancy, or containing experiments in fortunetelling, invocations of devils or incantations endangering lives, or in which these and similar things evidently contrary to the orthodox faith and good morals are treated. We pronounce the sentence of excommunication against those who shall have taught the said scrolls, books, and leaflets, or listened to them, unless they reveal themselves to us or to the chancery of Paris within seven days in the manner described earlier in this letter; in addition to which we shall proceed to inflict such other penalties as the gravity of the offense demands.

Given in the year of the Lord 1276, on the Sunday on which *Laetare Jerusalem* is sung at the court of Paris.

1. That there is no more excellent state than to study philosophy.

2. That the only wise men in the world are the philosophers.

. . .

4. That one should not hold anything unless it is self-evident or can be manifested from self-evident principles.

5. That man should not be content with authority to have certitude about any question.

6. That there is no rationally disputable question that the philosopher ought not to dispute and determine, because reasons are derived from things. It belongs to philosophy under one or another of its parts to consider all things.

. . .

8. That our intellect by its own natural power can attain to a knowledge of the first cause.—This does not sound well and is erroneous if what is meant is immediate knowledge.

9. That we can know God by His essence in this mortal life.

10. That nothing can be known about God except that He is, or His existence.

. . .

13. That God does not know things other than himself.

14. That God cannot know contingent beings immediately except through their particular and proximate causes.

15. That the first cause does not have science of future contingents. The first reason is that future contingents are not beings. The second is that future contingents are singulars, but God knows by means of an intellectual power, which cannot know singulars. Hence, if there were no senses, the intellect would perhaps not distinguish between Socrates and Plato, although it would distinguish between a man and an ass. The third reason is the relation of cause to effect; for the divine foreknowledge is a necessary cause of the things foreknown. The fourth reason is the relation of science to the known; for even though science is not the cause of the known, it is determined to one of two contradictories by that which is known; and this is true of divine science much more than of ours.

16. That the first cause is the most remote cause of all things.—This is erroneous if so understood as to mean that it is not the most proximate.

17. That what is impossible absolutely speaking cannot be brought about by God or by another agent.—This is erroneous if we mean when is impossible according to nature.

18. That what is self-determined, like God, either always acts or never acts; and that many things are eternal.

. . .

20. That God of necessity makes whatever comes immediately from Him.—This is erroneous whether we are speaking of the necessity of coercion, which destroys liberty, or of the necessity of immutability, which implies the inability to do otherwise.

. . .

22. That God cannot be the cause of a newly-made thing and cannot produce anything new.

23. That God cannot move anything irregularly, that is, in a manner other than that in which He does, because there is no diversity of will in Him.

24. That God is eternal in acting and moving, just as He is eternal in existing; otherwise He would be determined by some other thing that would be prior to Him.

25. That God has infinite power, not because He makes something out of nothing, but because He maintains infinite motion.

26. That God has infinite power in duration, not in action, since there is no such infinity except in an infinite body, if there were such a thing.

27A. That the first cause cannot make more than one world.

28. That from one first agent there cannot proceed a multiplicity of effects.

. . .

30. That the first cause cannot produce something other than itself, because every difference between maker and made is through matter.

. . .

33. That the immediate effect of the first being has to be one only and most like unto the first being.

34. That God is the necessary cause of the first intelligence, which cause being posited, the effect is also posited; and both are equal in duration.

. . .

38. That the intelligences, or separated substances, which they say are eternal, do not have an efficient cause properly speaking, but only metaphorically, in so far as they have a cause conserving them in existence; but they were not newly-made, because then they would be mutable.

39. That all the separated substances are coeternal with the first principle.

40. That everything that does not have matter is eternal, because that which was not made through a change in matter did not exist previously; therefore it is eternal.

. . .

42A. That God cannot multiply individuals of the same species without matter.

43A. That God could not make several intelligences of the same species because intelligences do not have matter.

. . .

50A. That if there were any separated substance that did not move some body in this sensible world, it would not be included in the universe.

. . .

52A. That the separated substances, in so far as they have a single appetite, do not change in their operation.

53A. That an intelligence or an angel or a separated soul is nowhere.

54A. That the separated substances are nowhere according to their substance.—This is erroneous if so understood as to mean that substance is not in a place. If, however, it is so understood as to mean that substance is the reason for being in a place, it is true that they are nowhere according to their substance.

55A. That the separated substances are somewhere by their operation, and that they cannot move from one extreme to another or to the middle except in so far as they can will to operate either in the middle or in the extremes.—This is erroneous if so understood as to mean that without operation a substance is not in a place and that it does not pass from one place to another.

. . .

61. That since an intelligence is full of forms, it impresses these forms on matter by using the heavenly bodies as instruments.

. . .

63. That the higher intelligences impress things on the lower, just as one soul impresses things on another and even on a sensitive soul; and that through such an impression a spellbinder is able to cast a camel into a pitfall just by looking at it.

64. That God is the necessary cause of the motion of the higher bodies and of the union and separation occurring in the stars.

. . .

66. That God could not move the heaven in a straight line, the reason being that He would then leave a vacuum.

67. That the first principle cannot produce generable things immediately because they are new effects and a new effect requires an immediate cause that is capable of being otherwise.

68. That the first principle cannot be the cause of diverse products here below without the mediation of other causes, inasmuch as nothing that transforms, transforms in diverse ways without being itself transformed.

69. That God cannot produce the effect of a secondary cause without the secondary cause itself.

. . .

73. That the heavenly bodies are moved by an intrinsic principle which is the soul, and that they are moved by a soul and an appetitive power, like an animal. For just as an animal is moved by desiring, so also is the heaven.

. . .

76. That the intelligence moving the heaven influences the rational soul, just as the body of the heaven influences the human body.

. . .

79. That if the heaven stood still, fire would not burn flax because God would not exist.

80. That the reasoning of the Philosopher proving that the motion of the heaven is eternal is not sophistic, and that it is surprising that profound men do not perceive this.

. . .

82. That if in some humor by the power of the stars such a proportion could be achieved as is found in the seed of the parents, a man could be generated

from that humor; and thus a man could be adequately generated from putrefaction.

83. That the world, although it was made from nothing, was not newly-made, and, although it passed from nonbeing to being, the nonbeing did not precede being in duration but only in nature.

84. That the world is eternal because that which has a nature by which it is able to exist for the whole future has a nature by which it was able to exist in the whole past.

85. That the world is eternal as regards all the species contained in it, and that time, motion, matter, agent, and receiver are eternal, because the world comes from the infinite power of God and it is impossible that there be something new in the effect without there being something new in the cause.

86. That eternity and time have no existence in reality but only in the mind.

87. That nothing is eternal from the standpoint of its end that is not eternal from the standpoint of its beginning.

* * *

89. That it is impossible to refute the arguments of the Philosopher concerning the eternity of the world unless we say that the will of the first being embraces incompatibles.

* * *

91. That there has already been an infinite number of revolutions of the heaven, which it is impossible for the created intellect but not for the first cause to comprehend.

92. That with all the heavenly bodies coming back to the same point after a period of thirty-six thousand years, the same effects as now exist will reappear.

* * *

96. That beings depart from the order of the first cause considered in itself, although not in relation to the other causes operating in the universe.—This is erroneous because the order of beings to the first cause is more essential and more inseparable than their order to the lower causes.

* * *

99. That there is more than one prime mover.

100. That, among the efficient causes, if the first cause were to cease to act, the secondary cause would not, as long as the secondary cause operates according to its own nature.

101. That no agent is in potency to one or the other of two things; on the contrary, it is determined.

102. That nothing happens by chance, but everything comes about by necessity, and that all the things that will exist in the future will exist by necessity, and those that will not exist are impossible, and that nothing occurs contingently if all causes are considered.—This is erroneous because the concurrence of causes is included in the definition of chance, as Boethius says in his book *On Consolation*.

* * *

110A. That forms are not divided except through matter.—This is erroneous unless one is speaking of forms educed from the potency of matter.

* * *

112. That the elements are eternal. They were nevertheless newly produced in the disposition that they now possess.

• • •

115A. That God could not make several numerically different souls.

116A. That individuals of the same species differ solely by the position of matter, like Socrates and Plato, and that since the human form existing in each is numerically the same, it is not surprising that the same being numerically is in different places.

117. That the intellect is numerically one for all, for although it may be separated from this or that body, it is not separated from every body.

118. That the agent intellect is a certain separated substance superior to the possible intellect, and that it is separated from the body according to its substance, power, and operation and is not the form of the human body.

• • •

122. That from the sensitive and intellectual parts of man there does not result a unity in essence, unless it be a unity such as that of an intelligence and a sphere, that is, a unity in operation.

123. That the intellect is not the form of the body, except in the manner in which a helmsman is the form of a ship, and that it is not an essential perfection of man.

• • •

126. That the intellect, which is man's ultimate perfection, is completely separated.

• • •

129. That the substance of the soul is eternal, and that the agent intellect and the possible intellect are eternal.

• • •

131. That the speculative intellect is simply eternal and incorruptible; with respect to this or that man, however, it is corrupted when the phantasms in him are corrupted.

• • •

133. That the soul is inseparable from the body, and that the soul is corrupted when the harmony of the body is corrupted.

• • •

135. That the separated soul is not alterable, according to philosophy, although according to the faith it is altered.

136. That the intellect can pass from body to body, in such a way that it is successively the mover of different bodies.

• • •

138. That there was no first man, nor will there be a last; indeed, the generation of man from man always was and always will be.

• • •

140. That the agent intellect is not united to our possible intellect, and that the possible intellect is not united to us substantially. And if it were united to us as a form, it would be inseparable.

141. That the possible intellect is nothing in act before it understands, because in the case of an intelligible nature, to be something in act is to be actually understanding.

• • •

143. That a man is said to understand to the same extent that the heaven is said to understand, or to live, or to move of itself, that is, because the agent

performing these actions is united to him as mover to moved and not substantially.

. . .

146A. That the fact that we understand less perfectly or more perfectly comes from the passive intellect, which he says is a sensitive power.—This statement is erroneous because it asserts that there is a single intellect in all men or that all souls are equal.

147A. That it is improper to maintain that some intellects are more noble than others because this diversity has to come from the intelligences, since it cannot come from the bodies; and thus noble and ignoble souls would necessarily belong to different species, like the intelligences.—This is erroneous, for thus the soul of Christ would not be more noble than that of Judas.

. . .

150. That that which by its nature is not determined to being or nonbeing is not determined except by something that is necessary with respect to itself.

151. That the soul wills nothing unless it is moved by another. Hence the following proposition is false: the soul wills by itself.—This is erroneous if what is meant is that the soul is moved by another, namely, by something desirable or an object in such a way that the desirable thing or object is the whole reason for the movement of the will itself.

. . .

154. That our will is subject to the power of the heavenly bodies.

. . .

156. That the effects of the stars upon free choice are hidden.

157. That when two goods are proposed, the stronger moves more strongly.—This is erroneous unless one is speaking from the standpoint of the good that moves.

158. That in all his actions man follows his appetite and always the greater appetite.—This is erroneous if what is meant is the greater in moving power.

159. That the appetite is necessarily moved by a desirable object if all obstacles are removed.—This is erroneous in the case of the intellectual appetite.

160. That it is impossible for the will not to will when it is in the disposition in which it is natural for it to be moved and when that which by nature moves remains so disposed.

161. That in itself the will is undetermined to opposites, like matter, but it is determined by a desirable object as matter is determined by an agent.

162A. That the science of contraries alone is the cause for which the rational soul is in potency to opposites, and that a power that is simply one is not in potency to opposites except accidentally and by reason of something else.

163A. That the will necessarily pursues what is firmly held by reason, and that it cannot abstain from that which reason dictates. This necessitation, however, is not compulsion but the nature of the will.

. . .

165. That after a conclusion has been reached about something to be done, the will does not remain free, and that punishments are provided by law only for the correction of ignorance and in order that the correction may be a source of knowledge for others.

166. That if reason is rectified, the will is also rectified.—This is erroneous because contrary to Augustine's gloss on this verse from the Psalms: *My soul*

hath coveted to long, and so on [Ps. 118:20], and because according to this, grace would not be necessary for the rectitude of the will but only science, which is the error of Pelagius.

167. That there can be no sin in the higher powers of the soul. And thus sin comes from passion and not from the will.

168. That a man acting from passion acts by compulsion.

169A. That as long as passion and particular science are present in act, the will cannot go against them.

. . .

172. That happiness is had in this life and not in another.

. . .

174. That after death man loses every good.

. . .

177. That raptures and visions are caused only by nature.

. . .

180. That the Christian law impedes learning.

181. That there are fables and falsehoods in the Christian law just as in others.

182. That one does not know anything more by the fact that he knows theology.

183. That the teachings of the theologian are based on fables.

. . .

188. That it is not true that something comes from nothing or was made in a first creation.

189. That creation is not possible, even though the contrary must be held according to the faith.

. . .

191. That the natural philosopher has to deny absolutely the newness of the world because he bases himself on natural causes and natural reasons, whereas the faithful can deny the eternity of the world because he bases himself on supernatural causes.

. . .

200. That no other virtues are possible except the acquired or the innate.

. . .

216. That a philosopher must not concede the resurrection to come, because it cannot be investigated by reason.—This is erroneous because even a philosopher must *bring his mind into captivity to the obedience of Christ* [cf. II Cor. 10:5].

. . .

SELECTED BIBLIOGRAPHY

Hissette, R., *Enquête sur les 219 articles condamnés à Paris le 7 mars 1277*. Vol. 22, *Philosophes médiévaux*, Louvain, 1977.

Hissette, R., "Étienne Tempier et ses condamnations," *Recherches de théologie ancienne et médiévale*, XLVII (1980), 231–270.

Van Steenberghen, F., "Siger de Brabant et la condamnation de l' Aristotelism hétérodoxe le 7 mars 1277," *Bulletin de l'Académie Royale de Belgique* (Lettres), LXIV (1978), 63–74.

Wippel, J., "The Condemnations of 1270 and 1277 at Paris," *The Journal of Medieval and Renaissance Studies*, VII (1977), 169–201.

Latin Philosophy in the Fourteenth Century

THE MOST POPULAR way to interpret the movement of philosophy in the fourteenth century is to contrast it with the previous century as a period of disintegration and decline. The division of philosophy into official schools such as Thomism, Scotism, Albertism, and Nominalism is placed in the context of the disruption of Christendom by heresies, schisms, and rampant nationalist monarchies. But heresy, schism, and royal ambition did not first appear on the medieval scene in the fourteenth century, and one could hardly describe the philosophical situation of any medieval period as tranquil. Nor should one obscure the earlier fourteenth century by displacing to it conditions which only later came to the fore. Thomism was the official doctrine of the Dominicans as early as 1278, but as late as the 1350s the leading Nominalists show little sense of membership in a school of their own. There seems, then, to have been no more than the usual disintegration in the intellectual life of the first half of the fourteenth century, and controversy in any event is as much a sign of life as of decay. Another argument for decline is sometimes drawn from the rise of the critical mentality which is strikingly expressed in Duns Scotus and finds technical formulation in the analytic methods of the Nominalists. These critically oriented thinkers found much that had been accepted as demonstrated to be probable at best, often by applying the argument from divine omnipotence, which appealed from the order God *has* ordained to the limits of what He *could* ordain, as the test of necessity. The remarkable vogue of this argument is traced to the wish, stimulated in part by the Condemnation of 1277, to defend the doctrine of divine freedom from any philosophically conceived necessities based on the order of nature. And so it came to be doubted that God could be proved to exist, that the soul could be proved to be immortal, that the world could be proved to have

593

teleological unity, and that many other positions belonging to natural theology could be proved. In the eyes of many, this amounts to the divorce of religion and philosophy, and hence the end of medieval scholasticism.

But divorce or not, mere criticism of assumptions which had made it plausible to attempt the synthesis of Catholic dogma and Aristotelian philosophy is not a decline of philosophy in any very obvious sense. A few scholars see this as the giving up of metaphysical pretensions to knowledge of the super-sensible world, and applaud this critical movement as an anticipation of later empiricism. The issue of decline would thus seem to hinge on the preconceptions of the interpreter, and one may wish to turn to the texts without this distraction. They are difficult texts, and since this period has only been closely studied by a few pioneer scholars, sometimes the bearing of the points being made or even the meaning of the terminology employed is hard to understand. But since recent scholarship in the history of science and logic has shown how misguided Erasmus and Rabelais and other humanists were to ridicule such topics as the intension and remission of forms or the modes of supposition as mere barbaric nonsense, perhaps one may now confront such strange-sounding philosophical topics as the intuitive cognition of non-existents with some faith in their significance, especially since they appear in attenuated guise in Descartes and other seventeenth-century figures. As the wedding of religion and philosophy was carried out through discussions centering around the soul and knowledge as a kind of activity, the divorce was executed through discussions centering around evidence and knowledge as a kind of claim to validity. Both discussions were protracted, acute, and instructive.

By the fifteenth century, the philosophical situation in northern Europe consisted in large measure of a conflict between the *via antiqua,* the "older way" often called Realism, and the *via moderna,* the "modern way" usually called Nominalism. The authorities for the former were Albert the Great, Thomas Aquinas, or Duns Scotus, and for the latter, William of Ockham and John Buridan. Our selections largely reflect this situation, and so we begin with Duns Scotus. He is sometimes linked to the Augustinianism of Bonaventure, but British masters such as Thomas of York and William of Ware also helped form his thought. He left a movement of continental dimensions, some of whose prominent figures are Antonius Andreas, Francis of Meyronnes, William of Alnwick, and John of Ripa. The second figure presented here is William of Ockham, who gave decisive formulation to lines of thought already well advanced by Durand of St. Pourçain, Peter Auriol, and Henry of Harclay, and within the circle of his enormous influence numbered Adam Wodham and Robert Holcot as authentic disciples. Sometimes Gregory of Rimini is brought into this inner circle, but his views on propositional reference seem to preclude this. The position of our next figure, Nicholas of Autrecourt, illustrates the difficulty of the historian in achieving a sense of the structure of the period, for although Autrecourt and his fellow anti-Aristotelian John of Mirecourt were not disciples of Ockham, they are often assimilated to Nominalism merely on the strength of their skeptical conclusions. Marsilius of Padua is included here as an epitome of an entire range of political discussion in which papalist positions were taken by Giles of Rome and James of Viterbo, monarchist positions by Dante and Ockham, and an effort after balance and moderation was made by John of Paris among others. The background to our last figure, John Buridan, can be found in Ockham and to some extent in the scientific movement at Oxford. His tradition was carried into Germany by Albert of Saxony and Marsilius of Inghen, and was carried on at Paris by Nicholas of Oresme. Reviewing this list, one must regret limitations of space that have made it impossible to include such prominent and independent thinkers as Walter Burley and Thomas Bradwardine, and anything from the entire line of German mysticism whose fountainhead was Eckhart. Limitation of space must also stand as the justification for ending with Buridan—that and the fact that the rich field of later medieval thought is as yet only very partially explored.

JOHN DUNS SCOTUS

1 2 6 5 – 1 3 0 8

T HE SUBTLE DOCTOR—and, by the transvaluation of things medieval, the original dunce. Duns Scotus has sustained several interpretations in the career of his difficult and elaborate thought. During the later Middle Ages, when his influence was at its height, he was thought of as the Prince of Realists, standing beside Thomas Aquinas and Albert the Great against the novelties of William of Ockham and other Nominalists. Realism was also called the *via antiqua,* and the folios of "old-fashioned" Scotism were abandoned to the winds in the quads of Reformation Oxford. But even though there are occasional refutations of doctrines similar to those of the Nominalists in his work, Duns Scotus could hardly have defined his thought through any sustained attack on an as yet undeveloped Nominalist movement. Indeed, some scholars look upon him as a transitional figure, working by means of an intense concern for the freedom of the will and for logical nuance toward that very Nominalism whose opponent he was then taken to be. From this point of view he is the exaggerated critic, undermining the stability of the great thirteenth-century syntheses, especially that of Thomas Aquinas. It is natural here to link him with the condemnations of the 1270s, especially through his doctrines of individuation and the will. But it is worth noting that his criticisms do not usually run against Thomas Aquinas. That honor is reserved for Henry of Ghent, an "Augustinian" theologian who may have had a great deal to do with the condemnations by virtue of his advice to Bishop Tempier. No one has produced a more devastating refutation of the "Augustinian" shibboleth of illuminationism than Duns Scotus, and Henry of Ghent was his immediate target.* Etienne Gilson has suggested that Avicenna provides the point of departure for his metaphysics and epistemology; but his very prominent and insistent conception of the will and its role in creation is in direct contrast to Avicenna's necessitarianism. Now it is not unusual for a medieval thinker to sustain a wide range of influences; but the impression received from Duns Scotus is

---

* See the *Oxford Commentary,* Book I, Dist. III, Question 4, edited and translated by R. McKeon in *Selections from Medieval Philosophers II,* New York, 1930, and by A. Wolter in *Duns Scotus, Philosophical Writings,* Indianapolis, 1964.

that of a complex and unresolved doctrine, an impression fortified by a style of writing that is exploratory rather than finished, intended to record Duns Scotus' thought for himself, rather than communicate it to less thorough and critical minds. It should be added that he died before subjecting his work to a comprehensive editing. It should also be noted that until recently, difficulties in textual attribution discouraged and distorted the interpretive study of his writings. There is, then, no widely accepted and monolithic interpretation of the labyrinthine subleties of Duns Scotus.

There are, however, certain emphases that can be indicated. Duns Scotus has often been called a "voluntarist." The term usually epitomizes a philosophy glorifying the will as against reason; but it has been well remarked that Duns Scotus' voluntarism is not at all irrationalist. Which combinations of mutually consistent essences are to be individualized through creation are freely chosen by the divine will. But the essences themselves are not the products of any will, and, of course, the immutability of the divine will guarantees the permanence of contingent regularities. And although the free act of the human will is not totally caused by the intellect's knowledge, neither is it totally caused by any irrational appetite. The celebrated Scotist voluntarism amounts to an insistence that for the will to be free, it must be capable in some sense of choosing other than it does. For this to be true, the act of will must not be determined by the intellect, human or divine. But for that in turn to be true does not require that the will be construed as some kind of antirational power. But it does require that natures and wills be quite distinct kinds of beings. And it enforces an interest in modal propriety, for clearly marking out what is contingent from what is truly necessary. This in turn goes together with an effort to defend the validity of cognitive activities, since an emphasis on contingency can easily lead to skepticism, as the successors of Duns Scotus soon discovered. This effort leads to some of the most characteristic of his doctrines. The reality of common natures, the formal distinction between diverse characteristics of single things, and even perhaps the distinction between the powers man might exercize in his full human nature and those he exercizes in his present condition all owe something to this antiskeptical crusade. Another and closely related Scotist emphasis is upon individuality. He rejects the position that individuation is through matter, and maintains that individuality is intrinsically intelligible, although not, perhaps, by man in his present condition. In line with this, he develops the theory of intuitive cognition, a direct cognition of individual things as present and existing, rather than the indirect knowledge of them through some abstracted universal. But, as the reader will soon find, a catalogue of these themes should not be confused with a genuine perspective on Duns Scotus. Perhaps that could be discovered in an exploration of the Franciscan spirituality which led him to the championing of the Immaculate Conception of the Virgin Mary and the title of the Marian Doctor—certainly he argues more often from confessedly theological considerations than does, for instance, Thomas Aquinas. But such an exploration cannot be undertaken here.

The scholarship concerning his life is only slightly more definitive than the interpretation of his writings. The most recent places his birth in 1265 and his home at Duns, in Scotland. A chronicle says that in 1278 he was taken to the Franciscan friary at Dumfries. In 1281 he took his vows as a friar and in 1291, after an interval for which nothing is known, he was ordained priest. It has been argued that during this interval he studied at Paris and Oxford and perhaps taught at Cambridge. By 1300 he was lecturing on the *Sentences* at Oxford, but by the autumn term of 1302 he had moved to Paris. In 1303, together with other foreign friars who sided with Pope Boniface VIII against King Philip the Fair, he was required to leave France. Where he went is not known. In late 1304 he was back at Paris, completing the series of disputations for the mastership in theology, and he probably incepted as master in 1305. Again we are ignorant of his whereabouts until he was sent to Cologne in 1307, where he died, November 8, 1308. His career was thus extremely short.

Included in the standard Wadding edition of his works are many now claimed to be by other authors, and a new edition is being prepared. Even in the case of works admitted to be Scotist in origin, it is not sure that the version we have is his own and whether all the included material even stems from him. In this brief resume, the views of Gilson and Wolter have been followed.

Tradition has it that certain *Questions* on logical works are youthful works, including those on Porphyry and on Aristotle's *Categories, De Interpretatione,* and *De Sophisticis Elenchis.* The *Speculative Grammar* and *Questions* on the *Analytics* and on the *Physics* are not his. Among the authentic works appropriate to an arts student and thus presumably stemming from that phase of his career are the *Questions on the De Anima* (*Quaestiones in libros Aristotelis De anima*) and the *Most Subtle Questions on the Metaphysics* (*Quaestiones subtilissimae in Metaphysicam Aristotelis*). It should be noted, though, that the former may contain some foreign matter and that the latter seem to have been revised if not composed while he was lecturing on the *Sentences.* The last two books may also be spurious. The main source for the doctrine of Duns Scotus is his commentary on the *Sentences* of Peter Lombard, which we have in a bewildering array of versions. The central version has for a long time been called *The Oxford Commentary* (*Opus Oxoniense*). As edited in the seventeenth century and republished in the nineteenth, this included additional notes and even passages from other works. The original revised edition by Duns Scotus himself is called the *Ordinatio,* and is now in process of reconstruction and publication. This work presumably substantially represents the version given during his stay at Oxford. The version given at Paris is called the *Reportata Parisiensia.* It is briefer, and is called a "*reportata*" because it stems from lecture notes taken by students, rather than the original hand of the master. There are also an unedited *Reportata examinata,* checked by Duns Scotus, and at least two sets of preliminary lecture notes. As a student and master, he engaged in several disputations, several of which have been preserved. The most important are the *Quodlibetal Questions* (*Quaestiones quodlibetales*), sometimes thought to be his most mature work, and certain *Parisian and Oxonian Discussions* (*Collationes Parisienses et Oxonienses*). Two works having similar titles should be carefully distinguished: the *Treatise on the First Principle* (*Tractatus de primo principio*) is authentic, whereas *On the Principle of Things* (*De rerum principio quaestiones XXVI*) is not. And finally, the strange collection of critical notes titled simply *Theorems* (*Theoremata*) is still the center of controversy. Even if it is by Duns Scotus, its purpose, whether to expound doctrine, to raise questions, or to serve as preliminary studies, is not clear.

Before introducing the selections which follow, something should be said regarding the translations. These have all been made from the Wadding edition of the *Oxford Commentary*. This edition was chosen over the new Balic edition because the latter has not yet reached many of the passages chosen and it was thought that a uniform edition should be used. Translating Duns Scotus is more difficult than translating many other medieval philosophers. There is the problem of interminable sentences, advancing by qualifications within qualifications, and there is the problem of the philosophical vocabulary of the times. An effort has been made to break up the sentences, which may not do justice to the protracted continuities of Duns Scotus' arguments. The term "*quidditas*" and its derivatives have simply been anglicized: a "quiddity" is the "whatness" of something, expressed in a real definition, and "whatness" seems scarcely less barbaric than "quiddity." Predication *in quid,* however, has been rendered as "definitional predication." "*Commune*" is occasionally rendered as "general," but more often as "common." "*Passio*" is usually rendered as "attribute," since the note of passivity or emotion attendant on the English "passion" is not really intended in most Scotist uses. "*Proprium*" is usually left as "proper," though "distinctive of" would sometimes convey the sense. Two terms so bothersome that in many translations they are left in the Latin are "*per se*" and "*simpliciter.*" The former is usually "intrinsically" here, and the latter, "unqualified" or "absolute." Finally, "*ratio,*" like its Greek original, "*logos,*" is notoriously the translator's despair. It is translated here as "argument," "character," "characteristic," or "reason" as the context seems to demand. Duns Scotus is laborious reading, and an effort has been made to translate as literally as possible, in part so that the reader may have some sense of what the stylists of the Renaissance were complaining about when they read him, and in part in the hope that where the ambiguity of the Latin is preserved in the English, the reader may succeed where the translator did not in making sense of the text.

The reader should not be put off by the formidable questions which initiate each selection. These are usually theological in character. Their resolution often turns upon philosophical positions, and it is the discussions of these which for the most part have been excerpted. The two first concern the conceivability and existence of God. Duns Scotus criticizes both negative theology and the theory that predication of God and creature is analogical —although whether it is precisely the Thomist version that is criticized can be debated. A remark from the *Most Subtle Questions on the Metaphysics* helps explain the prominence of infinity in these selections. It is said there that the metaphysical concept of God as the first being is more perfect than the physical concept of the first mover, since it calls for the concept of infinite perfection. The proof for the existence of God, then, is a metaphysical proof arguing from possibility to an infinite being. The "coloring" of Anselm's ontological argument is worth noticing, as is the rather frequent citation of Anselm, along with Augustine, Avicenna, and Aristotle, throughout Duns Scotus' work.

In the Question on the object of the human intellect, Duns Scotus rejects both Thomas Aquinas' doctrine that the human mind most naturally understands the essences of material things, and Henry of Ghent's view that God is this object. In the Question, Duns Scotus sets forth some of his doctrine of being and some of his speculations about the difference between human nature in itself and man in his present condition. A brief selection explaining the so-called "formal distinction on the part of the thing" then introduces a series of selections on universals, essences, and individuation. This "formal distinction" is central for Duns Scotus. He uses it to distinguish essence from existence, the parts of the soul, common natures and individualizing differences, and so on. Ockham's rejection of its validity for the natural world defines the parting of the ways of the two great camps of later medieval philosophy. In view of this it is extremely interesting that in the next selection we find Duns Scotus criticizing a position not too remote from the Nominalist position that individuality is so essential to existence that it calls for no special explanation. In this selection one should take care over the distinction Duns Scotus draws between a common nature in things and an actual universal in the mind, since he is usually taken to be the archrealist on this topic. There follows the critique of what must have seemed the standard Aristotelian view of individuation through matter, including the Thomistic version limiting this to *materia signata*, translated here as "demarkated matter." In this selection there is a portentous argument from the claim that miracles do not include contradictions. This anticipates the systematic expansion of the argument from divine omnipotence by Ockham and other fourteenth-century thinkers. The series culminates in Duns Scotus' own doctrine of individuation by what is called *"haecceitas"* ("thisness") in the *Reportata Parisiensia*. As an epilogue there is a short selection on intuitive cognition, another conception to have great influence on Ockham.

The last series of selections takes up the problem of the will, a collection of burning issues for Duns Scotus, and of mounting significance after him.

Behind his treatment of contingency and creation stand not only the old Christian problem of predestination and responsibility, but also the problem of necessity and divine production, which was associated with the Arabians at the time. The subsequent treatment of the human will is directed primarily at the intellectualist tradition in which one finds Thomas Aquinas, but also criticizes the standard doctrine that the will is essentially an appetite. The last selection draws conclusions for the ethics of natural law from the strict conceptions of necessity, contingency, and divine freedom which seemed so important to Duns Scotus. The extension of those conclusions into an ethics of command and obligation will be found in Ockham.

For some two hundred years after his death, Duns Scotus was a towering figure. But considering the extreme difficulty of his thought it is perhaps little wonder that the "formalities" and "thisness" and so on of Scotism should have been ridiculed by some of the more literary figures of the Renaissance. But he has always been found rewarding by those willing to study him closely, and thinkers as diverse as Peirce and Heidegger might agree with the poet Gerard Manley Hopkins in finding him "Of realty the rarest-veinéd unraveller."

THE OXFORD COMMENTARY ON THE
FOUR BOOKS OF THE SENTENCES

Book I, Distinction III

QUESTIONS   *1 and 2*

Whether God is naturally knowable by the wayfarer?
. . .
Whether God is naturally the primary object of knowledge in this present condition?
. . .

In the first question there should be no distinction made as to whether God can be known negatively rather than affirmatively, since negation is only known through affirmation: Book II of the *De Interpretatione* and Book IV of the *Metaphysics*. It is also obvious that we only understand negations concerning God by way of affirmations through which we take away some incompatibilities from those affirmations, as, for instance, we do not remove compositeness unless we attribute simplicity or some such.

Translated by James J. Walsh for this volume from *Joannis Duns Scoti Opus Oxoniense*, T. IX, *Opera Omnia*, ed. L. Wadding, Paris: L. Vives, 1893. A full translation by A. Wolter based on the text of the *Ordinatio* can be found in *Duns Scotus, Philosophical Writings*, Edinburgh: Thomas Nelson and Sons, Ltd., 1962.

Nor do we love negations most of all. Likewise, either negation is conceived in isolation or as said about something. If a negation, such as not-stone, is conceived in isolation, this pertains as much to nothing as it does to God, since a pure negation is said of being and non-being. Thus God is no more understood in this than is nothing, or the chimaera. If not-stone is understood of something, then I ask whether the underlying concept with respect to which this negation is understood to be true is affirmative or negative. If it is affirmative, the proposed position is gained. If negative, I ask as before, whether the negation is conceived in isolation or as said about something. If the former, it pertains as much to nothing as it does to God; if the latter, then once again as before.

And however far we go with negations, either God is no more understood than is nothing, or the series comes to a halt in some affirmative concept, which is primary.

Nor should a distinction be made between the knowledge of *whether a thing is* and *what it is*, since the point is to find a simple concept concerning which being might be known through an act of the intellect compounding and dividing. For I never know of anything *whether it is* unless I have some concept of that which I know to be, and this inquiry is about that concept. . . .

Nor is it worthwhile to distinguish between natural and supernatural concepts, since the inquiry concerns the natural one.

Nor is it worthwhile to distinguish regarding the natural between speaking of nature in the absolute or of nature in this present condition, since the inquiry concerns knowledge in this present condition.

Nor is it worthwhile to distinguish between knowledge of God in a creature and in Himself, since if knowledge is had through a creature, so that discursive cognition begins from the creature, I ask in what term this cognition comes to a halt. If in God in Himself, I have the proposed position, since the inquiry concerns the concept of God in Himself. If it does not come to a halt in God, but in a creature, then the same will be the end and the beginning of the discursive process, and so no knowledge will be had of God.

The sense of the question, then, is this: whether the intellect of the wayfarer can naturally have a simple concept in which God is conceived. . . .

I say first of all that not only can a concept be naturally had in which God is conceived as it were accidentally, as for instance in some attribute, but also in which God is conceived intrinsically and definitionally. I prove this: in conceiving wisdom, a property is conceived (according to Henry of Ghent), or a quasi-property in complete actualization perfecting the nature. Therefore, in understanding wisdom it is required that one pre-understand something as a quasi-subject in which that quasi-property is understood to inhere. And so prior to any concept of an attribute or quasi-attribute one must inquire concerning some definitional concept to which those are understood to be attributed. And that other concept will be definitional of God, since in no other can there be a stopping-point.

Secondly—not making an assertion, since it is not consonant with common opinion—it can be said that God is conceived not only in a concept by analogy with the concept of a creature, which concept is altogether different from that which is said of a creature, but in some concept univocal to Himself and a creature.

And lest there should be a dispute about the name "univocity," I call that a univocal concept whose unity suffices for contradiction when it is affirmed and denied of the same thing. It also suffices as a syllogistic middle term; so that the extremes, united without the fallacy of equivocation in a middle term which is one in this way, may be concluded to be unified among themselves.

And I prove univocity so understood in three ways. First: every intellect certain about one concept and doubtful about different ones has a concept of that of which it is certain which is different from the concepts about which it is doubtful. But the subject includes the predicate, and the intellect of the wayfarer can be certain of something (God) that it is being while at the same time doubting whether that is finite or infinite, created or uncreated being. Therefore, the concept of the being of anything (God) is different from this concept or that one, and so it is neither in itself and is included in both. Therefore, it is univocal. The proof of the major is that since no self-same concept is certain and doubtful, therefore either there is another one, which is the proposed position, or else there is none; and then there will be no certitude concerning any concept. I prove the minor: every philosopher was certain that what he held as first principle is being—for instance, one was certain that fire is being and another that water is being. But he was not certain whether it is created or uncreated being, first or not first. He was not certain that it is first, since then he would have been certain about what is false, and what is false cannot be known. Nor was he certain that it is not the first being, since then he would not have been able to maintain the opposite.

The argument is confirmed, for anyone seeing the philosophers disagree could be certain concerning any of them that he held the first principle to be being, and yet, because of the contrariety of their opinions, he could doubt whether it is this being or that. And such a doubter, if he should make a demonstration affirming or destroying some lower concept, for instance that fire was not the first being, but some being posterior to the first being, that first certain concept which he had of being would not be destroyed, but it would be preserved in that particular concept proved of fire. And through this is proved the proposition assumed in the last consequence of the argument, which was that that certain concept which is of itself neither of the doubtful ones, is preserved in both of them.

But if you do not care for this authority accepted from the diversity of the opinions of the philosophizers, but you say that any one has two neighboring concepts in the intellect which seem to be one concept because of the nearness of the analogy, it seems to be against this that from this evasion there seems to be destroyed every way for proving the unity of any univocal concept. For if you say that man has one concept for Socrates and Plato, it will be denied, and it will be said that they are two, but they seem one because of the great similarity.

I argue the second principal proof thus: No concept of what is real is naturally produced in the intellect of the wayfarer unless by what naturally activates our intellect. But that is a phantasm or an object reflected in the phantasm, as well as the active intellect. Thus no simple concept is now naturally produced in our intellect except what can be produced by virtue of these. But a concept which would not be univocal with an object reflected in a phantasm, but rather would be altogether different from and prior to that to which it has analogy, could not be produced by virtue of the active intellect and a phantasm, as I shall prove. Thus there never will be such a different and analogous concept which is posited as occurring naturally in the intellect of the wayfarer; and in this way no concept of God could ever be naturally possessed, which is false. Proof of the assumption: Any object, whether reflected in a phantasm or in an intelligible species, with the active or possible intellect acting coordinately to the limit of its forces, produces in the intellect as an effect adequate to itself its own concept and every concept essentially or virtually included in it. But that other concept, which is held to be analogous, is neither essentially nor virtually included in this, nor is it this very concept. Therefore, it is not produced by any such activator. . . .

Third: every metaphysical inquiry concerning God proceeds in this way: by considering a formal characteristic of something and by removing from that formal characteristic the imperfection which it has in creatures, and by reserving that formal characteristic and attributing to it completely the highest perfection, and in this way attributing it to God. Take the formal characteristic of wisdom, whether of the intellect or the will; it is considered first of all in itself and according to itself, and from the fact that the characteristic does not include any imperfection nor limitation, those imperfections which accompany it in creatures are removed from it; and reserving the same characteristic of wisdom and of the will, they are attributed to God most perfectly. Thus every inquiry concerning God presupposes that the intellect has the same univocal concept which it takes from creatures. . . .

Thirdly, I say that God is not naturally known by the wayfarer properly and in particular, that is, under the characteristic of this essence *as this* and in itself. . . .

There is thus another argument for this conclusion that God, as this essence in itself, is not naturally knowable by us, because under such a characteristic He is a volitional and not a natural object, except with respect to His intellect alone. And hence He can be naturally known by no created intellect under the characteristic of this essence (as this); nor does any essence naturally knowable by us sufficiently display this essence *as this*, neither through the similarity of univocity nor of imitation. For univocity only pertains to general characteristics, and imitation is lacking because it is imperfect, since creatures imperfectly imitate Him.

But whether there is another reason for this impossibility, namely, because of the characteristic of the primary object of the intellect, which others hold to be the quiddity of a material thing, consult the Question concerning the primary object of the intellect.

Fourthly, I say that we can arrive at many concepts proper to God which do not belong to creatures. Such are concepts of every perfection taken unconditionally in the highest degree, and the most perfect concept through which we know God, as it were under a certain description, is the conception of all the perfections taken unconditionally and in the highest degree; but still, the more perfect and simple concept possible for us is the concept of unqualifiedly infinite being. This is simpler than the concept of good being or true being or others similar to these, since infinity is not, as it were, an attribute of being or of that of which it is said, but predicates an intrinsic mode of that being; so that when I say "infinite being," I do not have, as it were, an accidental concept from a subject and an attribute, but rather, a concept of the subject itself in a certain grade of perfection, namely infinity—just as "intense white" does not predicate an accidental concept such as "visible white." Rather, intensity predicates an intrinsic degree of whiteness in itself. And so the simplicity of this concept "infinite being" is obvious.

The perfection of this concept is proved in many ways. First, because among all the concepts conceivable by us this one includes more virtually. For just as "being" includes "good" and "true" virtually in itself, so "infinite being" includes "infinite truth" and "infinite good" and every unqualified perfection under the characteristic of infinity. And then, because in the demonstration of the fact (of God's existence), existence is finally concluded for infinite being, or infinite existence of some being, as is apparent from Distinction II, Question 1. But those things are more perfect which are finally known by a demonstration of the fact from creatures, since because of their remoteness from creatures it is most difficult to know them from creatures.

But if you say of "highest good" or "highest being" that this expresses an intrinsic mode of being and includes virtually other concepts, I reply that if "highest" is understood comparatively, it is expressed with respect to something external. But "infinite" expresses a concept for itself. But if you understand "highest" as absolute, that is, as that which from the very nature of the thing cannot be exceeded, that perfection is more explicitly conceived in the characteristic of infinite being. For "highest good" does not indicate in itself whether it is finite or infinite. . . .

Fifthly, I say that what is known of God is known through the species of creatures, since whether the more universal and the less universal are known through the same less universal species, or whether each has its own intelligible species, at least that which can impress or cause a less universal species in the intellect can also cause a more universal one. And so creatures which impress their own species in the intellect can also impress the species of the transcendentals, which belong in common both to them and to God. And then the intellect by its own strength can make use of many species at once in order to conceive at once that of which they are the species—for instance, the species of good and of the highest and of act in order to conceive the highest and most actual good, which is apparent from the topic *a minori*. For the imagination can make use of the species of different sensibles in order to imagine something composite, as is obvious in imagining a golden mountain. . . .

• • •

Book I, Dist. II

QUESTIONS *1 and 2*

Whether among beings anything infinite exists in act?
• • •
Whether anything infinite, or God, is intrinsically known to exist?
• • •

I proceed thus regarding the first question because as far as we are concerned, existence cannot be demonstrated of an infinite being by an adequately grounded demonstration, even though the proposition would be demonstrable from an adequate ground by the nature of the terms. But as far as we are concerned, it is demonstrable by a demonstration of fact from creatures. But the properties of infinite being relative to creatures are more immediately disposed to the middle terms in a demonstration of fact than are the absolute properties, so that existence can be more immediately concluded from those relative properties as the middle terms for such a demonstration than from the absolute properties. For from the being of a relative, the being of its correlative immediately follows. Hence I shall first show the existence of certain relative properties of infinite being, namely, primacy and causality. And second, from these I shall show the existence of infinite being, since these relative properties belong to infinite being alone. And so there will be two principal articles.

As to the first article, I say that the relative properties of infinite being to creatures are either the properties of causality or eminence. Of causality there is either efficient or final. The causality of an exemplar, which is added, is not a different kind causality than efficient, since then there would be five types of causes. And so the exemplary cause is some kind of efficient, which acts through the intellect as distinct from acting through nature; concerning it, see elsewhere.

In the first principal article, therefore, I show three principal things:

First, that something among beings is in act which is unqualifiedly first according to efficiency; and something is unqualifiedly first as an end; and something is unqualifiedly first according to eminence.

Second, I show that the same which is first according to one primacy, is also first according to the other primacies.

Third, I show that this three-fold primacy belongs to one nature alone, so that the primacies do not belong to several natures differing in species or definitionally. And in the first article there will be three less principal articles.

The first of these includes three principal conclusions, following the triple primacy; but any of these three conclusions has three from which it depends: first, that it is something thus primary. Second, that it is uncausable. Third, that it exists in act among beings.

Thus in the first article there are nine conclusions, but three principal ones.

The first of these conclusions is this: something causally effective is unconditionally first, so that it cannot be an effect nor is it effective by virtue of something other than itself. I prove it thus: some being can be an effect, and then, either from itself or from nothing or from something else. Not from nothing, since that which is nothing is the cause of nothing. Nor from itself, since no thing makes itself or produces itself—see Augustine, Book I of *On the Trinity*. Therefore, it is from something else. Let that other be A. If A is first in the way set out, I have the proposed position. If it is not first, then it is derivatively effective, since it can be effected by something else or it is effective by virtue of something else; for if a negation is denied, the affirmative is maintained. Let that other be given and let it be B; the same argument applies to it as to A. And so either there is a process to infinity in which anything will be a second with respect to what is prior to it, or the process will come to a halt in something not having anything prior to it. But an ascending infinity is impossible. Therefore, primacy is necessary, since what has nothing prior to it, is posterior to nothing prior to itself, for a circle in causes is not suitable.

Against this argument there are two objections. . . . the second is that it seems to proceed from contingents and so is not a demonstration. The antecedent is proved, since the premises assume the existence of something caused, and everything like that exists contingently. . . .

To the second objection, which says that the argument proceeds from contingents and so is not a demonstration, I reply that it could be argued thus: some nature is effected because some subject is altered, and so the limit of the alteration begins to exist in a subject. And so that limit or composite is produced or effected. Therefore, there is something efficient, by the nature of correlatives. And then the premiss would be according to contingent truth. But still, this is not the argument for proving the first conclusion, but rather one that goes this way: Some nature *can* be effected; therefore some *is* effective. The antecedent is proved, since some subject is alterable, and something among beings is possible, taking "possible" as distinguished over against "necessary," and so one proceeds from necessaries. And then the proof of the first conclusion proceeds or concludes from quidditative being, or from possible being, but not from actual existence. But the actual existence of that whose possibility has now been shown will be proved in the third conclusion. . . .

The third conclusion about the first causally effective being is this: The first causally effective being exists in act, and some nature existing in act is thus effective. Proof: That whose defining characteristic is inconsistent with having its being depend on something else, if it can exist, can exist from itself. But the defining characteristic of the first causally effective being is inconsistent with having its being depend on something else, as is obvious from the second conclusion. And it can exist, as is obvious from the fifth argument given for A, which seems to conclude less, but still concludes this. . . .

Therefore, the unconditionally first causally effective being can exist from itself, and therefore, it does exist from itself. Because what does not exist from itself, cannot exist from itself, since then a non-being would produce something existent, which is impossible; and then the same thing would cause itself, and so it would not be altogether uncausable. This last, namely, the existence of the first causally effective being, is shown in another way, in that it is unsuitable for the universe to be lacking the highest possible grade of existence. Again, in addition to that, take note of a certain corollary which, as it were, contains the three conclusions proved. The corollary is that the first causally effective being is not merely prior to the others, but also that for another to be prior to it includes a contradiction. So insofar as it is first, it exists. This is proved in the same way as the preceding. For what is most of all included in the defining characteristic of the first is that it is uncausable, as was proved from the second conclusion. Therefore, if it can exist, which is not contrary to its being, as was proved from the first conclusion, it follows that it can exist from itself; and so it does exist from itself.

In addition to the three first conclusions concerning the effective cause, I propose three similar conclusions concerning the final cause.

The first conclusion is: Some end is unconditionally first, that is, it can neither be ordered to something else, nor serve as an end in virtue of something else. And this is proved by five arguments similar to those which were given for the first conclusion concerning the first effective cause.

The second conclusion is this: The first end is uncausable. This is proved in that it can have no further end, else it would not be first; and in addition, it cannot, therefore, be effected. This consequence is proved in that everything acting through itself acts for the sake of an end, from Book II of the *Physics*, where the Philosopher wishes this to hold for nature, concerning which it seems less to hold than for an agent acting from a purpose. But that of which there is no intrinsically efficient cause cannot be effected, since in no kind of cause can that which is accidental be primary, as is obvious in what is especially proposed for causes acting accidentally, which are chance and fortune. According to the intention of the Philosopher in Book II of the *Physics,* these are reduced to prior causes necessarily intrinsic, namely, to nature and intellect or purpose. Therefore, that of which there is no intrinsic agent will have no agent at all; but that of which there is no end has no intrinsic agent cause, and so it cannot be effected, and then further, as was shown above concerning the first causally effective being.

The third conclusion is that the first end exists in act, and that this primacy necessarily belongs to some nature necessarily existing in act. It is proved as is the third conclusion concerning the first causally effective being in the first way.

As a corollary, it follows that the first end is first in such a way that it is impossible for anything to be prior to it, and it is proved as the corollary in the previous way concerning the efficient cause.

To the three conclusions regarding each order of extrinsic causality already given, I propose three similar ones concerning the order of eminence.

The first conclusion is this: Some eminent nature is unqualifiedly first according to perfection. This is obvious in the essential order, since according to Aristotle in Book VIII of the *Metaphysics, forms are disposed just as numbers are;* and in this order there is a halt, which is proved by the five arguments which were adduced above concerning the halt in the series of causally effective beings.

The second conclusion is that the supreme nature cannot be caused. This is proved in that it cannot have an end; now what can have an end is excelled in goodness and hence in perfection by the end. Further, it therefore cannot be effected; and further, it is therefore uncausable. These last consequences are proved in the second conclusion concerning the first causally effective being. . . .

The third conclusion is that the supreme nature is something existing in act, which is proved from the preceeding.

A corollary is that for some nature to be more eminent or superior to it includes a contradiction. This is proved as is the corollary concerning the efficient cause.

As to the second article, I say that this three-fold primacy which is briefly proved concerning this quiddity, belongs to the same quiddity, which is shown in the two following conclusions.

The first is that the primary efficient is the ultimate end.

The second is that the primary efficient is the primary eminent. So this article has two conclusions. The first is proved thus: Everything intrinsically efficient acts for the sake of an end, and a prior efficient acts for the sake of a prior end; therefore, the primary efficient acts for the sake of the ultimate end. But it acts principally and ultimately for the sake of nothing other than itself, since nothing other than itself could be its end. Therefore, it acts for the sake of itself as for the sake of the ultimate end, and therefore, the primary efficient is the ultimate end.

The second conclusion of this article is proved thus: The primary efficient is not univocal with respect to the effected natures, but is equivocal; therefore it is more eminent and more noble than they; therefore the primary efficient is most eminent.

As for the third article, I say that this three-fold primacy belongs to the same nature, not merely in such a way that where one is, the others are as well, but also that there is such an identity there that the primary efficient is one according to quiddity and nature.

In order to show this, I show first a preliminary conclusion, and then the principal one.

The preliminary one is that the efficient which is first with this triple primacy necessarily exists from itself. The proof is that it is altogether uncausable, since for anything to be prior to it in the genus of the efficient or final cause includes a contradiction, and consequently, in any type of cause whatsoever. Thus it is altogether uncausable.

From this I argue so: nothing can be non-existing unless something positively or privatively incompatible with it can exist; but there cannot be anything which is positively or privatively incompossible with that which exists of itself and is altogether uncausable. Therefore, etc. The major premiss is obvious, since no being can be destroyed except through what is positively or privatively incompossible with it. The minor is proved, because that incompossible can either exist from itself or from another; if from itself, then it is from itself. Thus there will be two incompossibles at once, or else neither will exist, since each destroys the existence of the other. If from another, the objection is that no cause can destroy any being through repugnance of its effect to that being unless the cause gives to its effect a more perfect and intense existence than is the existence of the one to be destroyed. But no derivative being has from its cause a more noble existence than the existence of what is from itself, since everything caused has dependent existence, but that which is from itself has independent existence.

From this let us go on to the proposed position principally intended in this third article: the unity of the first nature, and for this I adduce three arguments. The first is that if two natures necessarily exist, they are distinguished by certain real characteristics belonging to each. Let these be called A and B. These characteristics are formally necessary for being or they are not. If they are, and outside of this those two are formally necessary through that in which they agree, then each of the two formal characteristics will have necessary existence. This is impossible, because since neither of those characteristics intrinsically includes the other; each of them taken apart would have necessary existence through the other, and so something would have necessary existence through that, in isolation from which, it would no less necessarily exist. Indeed, if neither is formally necessary through those characteristics by which they are formally distinguished, then those characteristics are not formally those for necessarily existing, and so it follows that neither is included in necessary existence, since necessary existence includes nothing which is not necessary existence.

This is proved secondly in that there cannot be two most eminent natures in the universe, and thus neither can there be two first causally effective beings. The proof of the antecedent is that *species are disposed as are numbers,* from Book III of the *Metaphysics*; and consequently, if there cannot be two in the same order, much less can there be two first or most eminent.

This is obvious, thirdly, through an argument from the nature of finality. If there were two ultimate ends, they would have two coordinations of beings to themselves, so that one set of beings would have no order with respect to the other, since they would have no order to the end of the other. For those which are ordered to one ultimate end cannot be ordered to another; it is impossible for there to be two total and perfect causes of the same result in the same order. For then something would be an intrinsic cause in some order, and when that cause were not given, the result would none the less be perfectly caused. Thus those ordered to one end are in no way ordered to the other, nor, consequently, to those which are ordered to the other. And so from these two sets a single universe would not be achieved. . . .

These preliminaries having been shown, I argue for infinity in four ways:

First, by way of efficiency, where the proposed position is proved twice. The first, in that it is the first efficient cause of all.

Second, in that, being efficient, it knows everything that can be produced.

Third, infinity is shown by way of finality.

Fourth, by way of eminence.

The Philosopher touches upon the first way, from efficiency, in Book VIII of the *Physics* and Book XII of the *Metaphysics,* and he argues thus: *the first (cause) moves with an infinite movement.* Therefore, it has infinite power. This argument is colored as to the antecedent thus: the proposed position is just as well established if it (the first cause) *can* move through infinity as if it *does* move through infinity, since it would in both cases be required to exist in act. But that "can" is obvious of the first insofar as it exists from itself. Thus even if the first should not move with an infinite movement as Aristotle proves, still, if the antecedent "Insofar as it exists from itself it *can* so move," is accepted, a true and sufficient basis for inferring the proposed position is had. The consequence is proved thus: if it moves with an infinite movement from itself and not by virtue of something else, then it does not receive (the ability) so to move from something else; but, because it is independent, it has its entire effect at once by virtue of its own activity. But what has an infinite effect at once in its power is infinite. Therefore, etc. . . .

The second way follows. I argue thus from the fact that (the first cause) knows distinctly everything that can be produced or understood: Intelligibles are infinite, and actually so in the intellect understanding everything. Thus the intellect actually knowing all them at once is infinite. Such is the divine intellect, as was proved above in the conclusion of the first, on knowing.

I prove the antecedent and the conseqence of this enthymeme. The antecedent, thus: Whatever is infinite in potency, so that taking one after another they (the members) can have no end, if they are all in act at once, they are an infinite in act. Intelligibles are infinite in potency with respect to the created intellect, which is sufficiently obvious; and in the uncreated intellect all those which are successively intelligible by the created intellect are actually understood at once. Therefore, an actual infinite is there understood. I prove the major of this syllogism thus, although it seems sufficiently evident: taking all such, when they exist all at once, they are either a finite number in act or they are an infinite number in act. If finite, then taking them one after another, they can still all be taken in act; thus if they cannot all be taken in act, if they are in act all at once, then they are an infinite in act. I prove the consequence of the first enthymeme in that wherever plurality requires or establishes a greater perfection than does paucity, an infinite number establishes infinite perfection. . . .

The third way, from finality, is argued thus: Our will is able to love something greater than anything finite, just as our intellect can so understand;

and, what is more, there seems to be a natural inclination toward loving an infinite good in the highest degree. For this natural inclination is argued to be something in the will from the fact that the free will wishes that (infinite good) from itself, spontaneously and with delight, and without a habit. So it seems that we experience an act of loving an infinite good—rather, it does not seem that the will is perfectly stilled by anything else. And if that were opposed to its object, how does the will not naturally hate it, just as it naturally hates non-existence, according to Augustine, chapter II, *On Free Will?* For it seems that if infinity were repugnant to goodness, the will would in no way rest in a good under the characteristic of infinity, nor would it easily tend toward it, just as it does not toward anything repugnant to its object. . . .

The fourth way, from eminence, I argue thus: It is impossible for anything more perfect than the most eminent thing to exist with the most eminent, as was made plain above. But it is not impossible for something more perfect than something finite to exist with it. Wherefore, etc. The minor is proved in that infinity is not repugnant to being and what is infinite is greater than anything finite. Wherefore, etc.

Another argument to the same effect is this: That to which intensively infinite being is not repugnant is not maximally perfected unless it *is* infinite; for if it is finite, it can be exceeded or excelled, if infinite being is not repugnant to it. Infinity is not repugnant to being. Therefore, the most perfect being is infinite. The minor premiss of this consequence, which was also accepted in the preceding argument, does not seem able to be shown or proved a priori. For just as contradictories contradict from their own characteristics, and this cannot be proved from anything more manifest, so non-repugnance is from characteristics and can apparently only be shown by explicating those characteristics. But being is explicated by nothing better known. Infinity we understand through the finite. I expound it popularly thus: The infinite is that which exceeds any given finite according to no finite measure, but rather it goes beyond any such assignable measure. The proposed position can also be persuasively supported thus: Just as anything is to be posited as possible of which the impossibility is not apparent, so also as compossible of which the incompossibility is not apparent. Here there appears no incompossibility, since finitude is not of the very nature of being, nor does it appear from the nature of being that finitude is an attribute convertible with being. And one or the other of these is required for the aforesaid repugnance. And the primary and convertible attributes of being seem to be well enough known.

Another persuasive argument is that the infinite in its way is not repugnant to quantity, that is, taking part after part. Therefore, neither is the infinite in its way repugnant to being, that is, in perfection existing all at once.

Again, if the quantity of a virtue is unqualifiedly more perfect than the quantity of a mass, why should infinity be possible in a mass and not in virtue? But if it is possible, it is also actual, as is obvious from the third conclusion concerning the first causally effective being, given above.

Again, why does the intellect, whose object is being, find no repugnance in understanding something infinite? Rather, that seems to be most perfectly intelligible. But it would be a wonder if such a contradiction concerning its primary object were obvious to no intellect, since discord in sound so easily offends the ear. For if it is unsuitable, it is at once perceived and gives offence. Why, then, does no intellect naturally withdraw from an infinite intelligible as though it were unsuitable, rather, as though it were destructive of its primary object?

In this way the argument of Anselm about the highest thinkable good, in Chapter II of the *Proslogion*, can be colored. His description should be understood thus: God is that which, having been thought without contradiction, a greater cannot be thought without contradiction. And that *without contradiction* should be added is obvious, for that in the thought of which is included a contradiction, is said to be unthinkable. For then there are two opposed things that can be thought in no way making one thing that can be thought, since neither determines the other.

That the aforesaid highest thinkable thing exists in reality without contradiction is proved first for quidditative being, since the intellect comes most of all to rest in such a highest thinkable thing. Therefore, it has in the highest degree the characteristic of the primary object of the intellect, namely, being. And it is further argued that that should be said about the being of existence, since the highest thinkable thing is not merely in the thinking intellect, since then it could exist since it is a possible thinkable, and also it could not exist, in that existence is repugnant to its nature from another cause, as was obvious in the second conclusion about the first causally effective being above. Therefore, that which exists in reality is a greater thinkable thing than that which is merely in the intellect. But this should not be understood so that if something is thought, the same thing is a greater thinkable if it should exist, but rather that anything thinkable which is in reality or exists is greater than what is merely in the intellect.

Or it might be colored differently, thus: That which exists is more thinkable, that is, more perfectly knowable, since it is visible or intelligible by intuitive knowledge. But what does not exist is not intellectually visible, neither in itself nor in what is more noble, to which it adds nothing. What is visible is more perfectly knowable than what is not visible but is merely abstractively intelligible. Therefore, what is most perfectly knowable exists. See Distinction III for the difference between intuitive and abstractive knowledge and how intuitive is more perfect. . . .

From the aforesaid the solution of the question is obvious, for from the first article the position is had, that some being is unqualified first with a threefold primacy, namely, of efficiency, finality, and eminence, and is so unqualifiedly first that it is impossible that anything should be prior; and in this the existence of God is proved with regard to the properties of God with respect to creatures, or insofar as He terminates the respect and dependency of creatures toward and upon Him.

From the second article the position that that first is infinite is had in four ways:

First, since He is the first efficient cause.

Second, since He is the first knower, knowing everything knowable, and because of the second way four conclusions concerning the knowing of the first were offered.

Third, since He is the ultimate end.

Fourth, since He is the most eminent.

Added to the first way, a certain useless way from creation was excluded.

Added to the second, another way from the perfection of the primary object in intelligibility was touched upon.

Added to the fourth, the argument of Anselm from Chapter II of the *Proslogion* was expounded, which stands in this proposition: *That than which a greater cannot be thought, exists.*

Finally, a useless way from immateriality, inferring to infinity, was excluded. And so, I bring together the conclusions of the two principal articles thus: Some being triply first among beings exists in act; this triply first among beings is infinite. Therefore, some infinite being exists in act. And in this the existence of God is proved with regard to that absolute (concept), which is first among all the perfections of God conceivable by us, as is said in Distinction III, Question 1. And consequently, the existence of God is proved with regard to the concept of God most perfect or possible to us.

· · ·

Book I, Dist. III

QUESTION 3. *Whether God Is the Object Naturally Adequate with Respect to the Intellect of the Wayfarer?*

· · ·

In this question there is one opinion which says that the primary object of our intellect is the quiddity of a material thing. The reason presented for this is that a power is proportioned to the object. The cognitive power, however, is three-fold: one is altogether separate from matter, both in being and in operation, as is a separate intellect; another is conjoined to matter both in being and in operation, as is an organic power which perfects matter and only operates by means of an organ from which it is separated neither in operation nor in being; another is conjoined to matter in being, but does not make use of a material organ in operation, as is our intellect. To these there correspond proportionate objects, for to altogether separate powers, such as the first, there ought to correspond a quiddity altogether separate from matter. To the second, an altogether material singular. To the third, therefore, there corresponds the quiddity of a material thing which, even though it exists in matter, is nonetheless known not as in singular matter.

But this cannot be sustained by a theologian, since the intellect, existing as the very same power, knows the quiddity of an immaterial substance, as is obvious for a beatified soul, according to the faith. But a power remaining the same cannot have an act concerning anything which is not contained under its primary object.

But if you say that it will be elevated through the light of glory, so that it may know those immaterial substances, I object that the primary object of a habit is contained under the primary object of the power, or at least does not exceed it. For if a habit is ordered with respect to some object which is not contained under the primary object of the power, but exceeds it, then that would not be the habit of that power, but would constitute it a different power.

The argument is confirmed, since when a power, as a first sign of the nature in which it is a power, has such a primary object, nothing posterior to the nature, and thus presupposing the character of that power, can make it have a different primary object; but every habit naturally presupposes a power.

You might say that this opinion is held by the Philosopher also—for instance, if he should maintain that our intellect, because of its weakness among intellects, and because of its joining with the imagining power in the knowing subject, is ordered directly to images, just as the imagination has a direct order to the common sense. And hence, just as the imaging power is only moved by what is an object of the common sense, even though it may know that same object in a different way, so he might say that our intellect, not merely because of some special condition, but from the very nature of the power, could not understand anything unless it could be abstracted from an image.

There are three arguments against this. The first is that in an intellect knowing an effect there is a natural desire to know the cause, and in one knowing a cause in a universal, there is a natural desire to know it in a particular, and distinctly. But a natural desire is not for what is impossible, from the very nature of desiring, since then it would be for nothing. It is not impossible, therefore, from the fact that the intellect knows the material effect, for the intellect just as intellect to know immaterial substance in particular. And so the primary object of the intellect does not exclude that immaterial substance.

The second argument is that no power can know any object under a characteristic more general than that of its own primary object. This is obvious, first of all, through the characteristic, since then that characteristic of its primary object would not be adequate to it. It is also obvious through an example. Sight does not know anything under a characteristic more general than color or light, nor does the imagination know anything under one more general than the imaginable, which is its primary object. But the intellect knows something under a characteristic more general than that of a material being, since it knows something under the characteristic of being in general; otherwise, metaphysics would not be a science for our intellect.

Besides, thirdly, and this comes almost to the same as the second, whatever is intrinsically known by a cognitive power is either its primary object or is contained under that object. But being, which is more general than what is sensible, is intrinsically understood by our intellect. Otherwise, metaphysics would not be a more transcending science than physics. Nothing, therefore, can be the primary object of our intellect which is more particular than being, because then being in itself would in no way be understood by us. It seems, then, that there is a false supposition in the said opinion about the primary object, and this is speaking about the power from its very nature as a power. . . .

Also, the congruence which is adduced in support of that opinion is nothing. For power and object do not have to be alike in manner of being; they are disposed to one another as mover and moveable, and since this is as act and potency, they are disposed as dissimilars. Still, they are proportionate, since this proportion requires the dissimilarity of what is proportionate, as is commonly said about every proportion and as is obvious about matter and form, part and whole, cause and effect and other proportionals. Therefore, from the manner of being of such a power, a similar manner of being in the object cannot be concluded.

Against this it is objected that although a producing agent can be unlike the object which is passive to it, what is operative in the cognitive operation ought still to be like its object, for that is not a passive object, but is more an agent and assimilator. For all the ancients agree that cognition is accomplished through assimilation. Nor does Aristotle contradict them in this. Thus what is required is not merely proportion, but similarity.

I reply that it is one thing to talk about the manner of being of the power in itself, and another to talk of it in act or in proximate disposition to act, which is different from the very nature of the power. Now it is true that the cognitive power is assimilated to the known object through its act of knowing, which is some kind of likeness to the object, or through the species putting it in proximate readiness for knowing; but to conclude from this that the intellect in itself naturally has a way of being which is similar to that of the object, or vice versa, is to commit the fallacy of accident, and of figure of speech. Thus it does not follow that because bronze is made like Caesar in having a shape imposed on it, the bronze has in itself a manner of being similar to that of Caesar. Or, more to the point, because a seeing eye is assimiliated to an object through the species of the object, it does not follow that sight has a manner of being similar to that of the object. And further, just as certain visible things have matter, which is the cause of decay and incoherence, and certain others such as the celestial bodies lack such matter, so there would be one kind of sight in such matter and another without it, or one such kind of an organ and another not that way. Or, still more to the point: an Idea in the divine mind, which is a likeness of the object, is immaterial; therefore, stone, of which it is the Idea, would also be immaterial. Thus it does not seem suitable merely because of that congruence to restrict the intellect, from the very nature of the power, to a sensible object, so that it would only exceed sense in its way of knowing.

There is another opinion, which holds that God is the primary object of the intellect. Its fundamental arguments were adduced for the principal position in the first part of the question. Because of them, it maintains that God is the primary object of the will, since He is the reason for willing everything else. And the authority of Augustine is adduced, from Book VIII of *On the Trinity*: "Why, therefore, do we love another, etc." And there follows, "whom we believe to be righteous, and do not love that form itself wherein we see what is a righteous mind, that we also may be able to be righteous? Is it that unless we loved that also, we should not love him at all, whom through it we love?"

Against this opinion there is the following argument: The primary natural object of any power has a natural order to that power. God does not have a natural order to our intellect as a mover, unless perhaps under the characteristic of some general attribute as that opinion maintains. Thus He is not the primary object except under the characteristic of that attribute; or, according to the opinion previously maintained (that God is not understood except under the characteristic of being), He will not have a natural order except under such a universal concept. But a particular which is not understood except in something general is not the primary object of the intellect, which is rather, that general. Therefore, etc.

Besides, God certainly does not have the primacy of adequation because of commonness, such that He is predicated of every object intrinsically intelligible to us. Thus if He has any primacy of adequation it will be because of virtuality, since He contains virtually in Himself everything intrinsically intelligible. But

He will not be the primary object adequate to our intellect just because of this, since other beings move our intellect by their own power. It is not that the divine essence moves our intellect first of all to itself and then secondly to the knowledge of everything else knowable. But as was said in the Question on the subject of theology, the divine essence is the primary object of the *divine* intellect, since it alone moves the divine intellect both to know itself and everything else knowable by that intellect. By the same kind of argument it is proved that substance in general cannot be maintained to be the primary object of our intellect merely on the ground of the attribution of all accidents to substance. For accidents have their own power to move the intellect. Thus substance does not move the intellect to itself and to everything else knowable as well.

I reply to the question, therefore, that no natural primary object of our intellect can be given on the ground of such virtual adequation, because of the argument touched upon against the virtual primacy of the object in the case of God or of substance. Either, therefore, no primary object is to be given, or a primary adequate object must be maintained on the ground of commonness. But if being is taken to be equivocal with regard to created and uncreated, substance and accident, then, since all these are intrinsically intelligible to us, it does not seem possible to posit a primary object of our intellect, neither on the ground of virtuality nor of commonness. But in maintaining the position I took in the first Question of this Distinction concerning the univocity of being, the view that something is the primary object of our intellect can be preserved in some way. So that this can be understood, I first of all clarify what the univocity of being is and to what, and from this I go to the proposed position.

As to the first, I say that being is not univocally predicated definitionally of everything intrinsically intelligible, since it is not so of ultimate differentiae, nor of the proper attributes of being itself.

The first, concerning ultimate differentiae, I prove in two ways. First: If differentiae include being univocally predicated of them, and they are not altogether the same, then, with something (remaining) the same, they are diverse beings. . . . Therefore, those ultimate differentiae will be different. Therefore, they will differ through other differentiae. Because those others include being definitionally, the argument will be repeated for them as for the prior ones; and so there will be an infinite regress in differentiae, or else it will come to a halt for some completely excluding being definitionally. This is the proposed position, since only those will be ultimate.

Second: just as a being composite in reality is composed of act and potency in reality, so a composite concept intrinsically one is composed from a potential and actual concept, or from a determinable and determining concept. Thus just as the resolution of composite beings comes ultimately to a halt in what is unqualifiedly simple, namely, in an ultimate act and potency which are primarily diverse in that nothing of the one includes anything of the other (lest the one not be primarily act nor the other primarily potency—for what includes any potentiality is not primarily an act), so in concepts. Every concept not unqualifiedly simple, but still intrinsically one, is resolved into a determinable and a determining concept, so that this resolution comes to a halt in unqualifiedly simple concepts, namely, in a still determinable concept including nothing determining, and a determining concept not including any determinable concept. The still determinable concept is the concept of being, and the determining is the concept of the ultimate differentia. These, therefore, are primarily diverse, so that one includes nothing of the other.

The second, namely, the proposed position concerning the attributes of being, I prove in two ways. . . .

The second way is this: considering what includes it definitionally, being is sufficiently divided into uncreated being, the ten genera, and the essential parts of the ten genera. Whatever belongs to these does not seem to have more definitional divisions not among these. Thus if "one" as "one" should include being definitionally, it would be contained under some of these. But it is not any of the ten genera, nor is it of itself uncreated being, since it pertains to created beings. Therefore, it should be a species in some genus, or the essential principle of some genus. But this is false, since any essential part in any genus whatsoever, and any species of any genus whatsoever, includes limitation; and so any transcendental would be finite of itself, and consequently would be repugnant to infinite being. Nor could it be predicated of infinite being, which is false, since all transcendentals are termed unqualified perfections and belong to God in the highest degree. . . .

As to the second principal article, I say that from these four arguments, and since nothing can be more common than being, and being cannot be predicated univocally, in common, and definitionally of everything intrinsically intelligible since it is not so predicated of ultimate differentiae nor of its own attributes, it follows that nothing is the primary object of our intellect on the ground of the definitional commonness of it to everything intrinsically intelligible. And yet, despite this, I say that being is the primary object of our intellect, since a two-fold primacy concurs in it, namely, the primacies of commonness and virtuality. For everything intrinsically intelligible either essentially includes the characteristic of being or includes it virtually. For all genera and species, as well as individuals, and all the essential parts of genera, and uncreated being, include being definitionally. All ultimate differentiae are included in some of these essentially or definitionally. All attributes of being are included in being, and are included virtually in what is inferior to it. Therefore, those to which being is not definitionally univocal are included in those to which it is thus univocal. And so it is obvious that being has the primacy of commonness to the primary intelligibles, that is, to the definitional concepts of genera, species, individuals, and the essential parts of all these, as well as to uncreated being. And it has the primacy of virtuality to intelligibles included in these primary intelligibles, that is, to the qualificative concepts of the ultimate differentiae and its own attributes.

But what I have supposed concerning the commonness of being definitionally to all the aforesaid definitional concepts is proved for all those by the two arguments offered in the second Question of this Distinction, for proving the commonness of being to created and uncreated being, because, as should be obvious, I treat them equally.

First: concerning any of the aforesaid definitional concepts it happens that the intellect is certain that it is being, while doubting whether the differentia contracting being to such a concept is such a being or not. And so the concept of being, as it belongs to that concept, is different from those lower concepts about which the intellect is doubtful, and is included in each lower concept; for those contracting differentiae presuppose the same common concept of being which they contract.

The second argument I treat so: Just as it is argued that God is not naturally knowable by us unless being is univocal to created and uncreated, so it can be argued concerning substance and accident. For, since substance does not immediately stimulate our intellect to some understanding of it, but rather a sensible accident does so, it follows that we can have no definitional concept of it except such as can be abstracted from the concept of an accident; but no such definitional concept is abstractible from the concept of an accident unless it is the concept of a being. Therefore, etc. The supposition that substance does not immediately stimulate our intellect to an act concerning itself is proved thus: Whatever in its presence stimulates the intellect can be naturally known by the intellect in its absence, when the intellect is not stimulated. So, it appears from Book II of the *De Anima* that sight is perceptive of darkness, when light is not present, and hence when sight is not stimulated by substance. Therefore, let the intellect naturally be immediately stimulated by substance to the act concerning it; it would follow that when substance is not present, it could naturally be known not to be present. And so it could naturally be known that the substance of bread is not in the consecrated host on the altar, which is manifestly false. Therefore, no definitional concept of substance is naturally had by being immediately caused by substance, but only one caused by or abstracted first from an accident; and that requires the concept of being.

The proposed position concerning the essential parts of substance is concluded along the same lines. For if matter does not stimulate the intellect to an act concerning it, and if neither does substantial form, I ask what simple concept is had in the intellect of matter or form? If you say, some relational concept, for instance, that of a part, or an accidental concept, for instance of some property of matter or form, I ask what is the definitional concept to which this accidental or relational concept is attributed? And if no definitional concept is had, there will be nothing to which this accidental concept is attributed. But no definitional concept can be had unless it is impressed by or abstracted from that which moves the intellect, for instance, from an accident; and that will be the concept of being. And so nothing would be known of the essential parts of substance if being were not univocally common to them and to accidents.

These arguments do not establish the univocity of being definitionally to ultimate differentiae and to its attributes. . . .

In a third way it can be replied to the first argument that that concept concerning which there is certainty is different from those concerning which there is doubt; and if that certain concept is preserved in either of those doubtful ones, it truly is univocal, as it is conceived with either of them. But it is not required that it be in each of them definitionally; but it is either that way, or it is univocal to them as determinable to determining, or as denominable and denominating. And so, briefly, being is univocal to all, but to concepts not unqualifiedly simple it is univocal definitionally when said of them; but to unqualifiedly simple ones it is univocal as determinable or as denominable, but not as predicated of them definitionally, since this includes a contradiction.

From these it appears how the two-fold primacy concurs in being, namely, the primacy of definitional commonness to all concepts not unqualifiedly simple, and the primacy of virtuality in itself or in its inferiors to all unqualifiedly simple. And that concurring two-fold primacy suffices for it to be the primary object of the intellect, although it has neither one alone for everything intrinsically intelligible. . . .

These having been seen concerning being, there remains a further doubt, whether any other transcendental could be given as the primary object of our intellect because it seems to have commonness equal to that of being. And it seems so, and that *truth* is the adequate and primary object of our intellect, and not being. This is proved in three ways.

First: distinct powers have distinct formal objects, from Book II of the *De Anima*. But the intellect and the will are distinct powers. Therefore, they have distinct formal objects; and it seems that this cannot be sustained if *being* is given as the primary object of the intellect. But if *truth* is given, the distinct formal objects can be assigned. . . .

But against this conclusion about truth I argue thus: The primary, that is, the adequate object, is adequate according to commonness or according to virtuality or according to this two-fold concurring primacy. But *truth* is adequate to the intellect in none of these ways, whereas being is, as was made obvious. Therefore, etc. The proof of the first part of the minor is this: *Truth* is not predicated definitionally of everything intrinsically intelligible, since it is not predicated definitionally of being, nor of anything intrinsically inferior to being. The second part of the minor is proved together with the third, since those that are inferior to *truth*, although they include it essentially, still do not include everything else intelligible, either virtually or essentially. For this *truth* which is in stone does not include stone essentially or virtually; but, just the reverse, the being which is in stone includes truth, and so for any other beings and their truths.

Again, *truth* is an attribute of being and of whatever is inferior to being. Therefore, in understanding being and whatever is inferior to it, precisely under the characteristic of truth, the understanding is only according to an accident and not according to a definitional characteristic. But the knowledge of anything according to a definitional characteristic is the primary and more perfect knowledge of it, from chapter 1, Book VII of the *Metaphysics*. Therefore, no knowledge of anything precisely under the characteristic of *truth* is the primary knowledge of the object, and so neither is truth the primary characteristic precisely for knowing the object. . . .

I reply to the opposing arguments by turning them in the opposite direction. The first, thus: Just as the will cannot have an act concerning what is unknown, so it cannot have an act concerning an object under a completely unknown formal characteristic. Therefore, every characteristic according to which anything is an object of the will is knowable by the intellect. And so it cannot be that the characteristic of being the primary object of the intellect is distinguished over against the characteristic of being capable of being willed if it is by that that it is such. . . .

To the view which is accepted in the argument about the distinction of objects, I reply that disparate powers are disposed to one another in three ways: either they are altogether disparate or they are subordinated one to another—and then they are either in the same genus, as superior and inferior cognitive powers, or they belong to different genera, as a cognitive to its appetitive power.

In the first way, the disparate powers have altogether disparate objects, since none of them, from the very fact that they are disparate, is intrinsically operative concerning an object about which another is. Such are the exterior senses among themselves, such as sight, hearing, etc.

In the second way, disparate powers have subordinate primary objects, so that the primary object of a superior power contains under itself the primary object of an inferior power. Otherwise, that object would not be adequate to the superior power. Whence the primary object of sight is contained according to its commonness, as an inferior, under the primary object of the common sense.

In the third way, powers are so disposed that if the appetitive were made adequate to the cognitive in operating with regard to any object, there would be the same primary object for each, and under the same formal characteristic of the object. But if the appetitive power had an act with regard to something knowable and also something not, then the object of the appetitive power would be inferior to that of the cognitive power.

In connection with the proposed position, the intellect and will fall under the third heading; and if the will is held to have an act with regard to everything intelligible, both will and intellect are held to have the same object, and under the same formal characteristic. But if the will only has an act with regard to those intelligibles which are ends or beings ordered to an end, and not with regard to what can merely be contemplated, then the object of the will is held to be somewhat more particular than the object of the intellect, but being remains the object of the intellect. . . .

It is thus obvious from what has been said that nothing can be so suitably held to be the primary object of the intellect as being, neither anything virtually primary nor any other transcendental, since the same argument applies to them as to *truth*.

But one doubt remains: If being according to its most common characteristic is the primary object of the intellect, why cannot whatever is contained under being move the intellect naturally, as was argued in the first argument to the first Question in the Prologue? And then it seems that God could be known naturally by us, and all immaterial substances could likewise, which was denied. Rather, it was denied for all substances and all essential parts of substances, since it was said that they are not conceived in any definitional concept unless in the concept of being.

I reply that the primary object of a power is assigned as what is adequate to the power in its characteristic as a power, but not as what is adequate to a power in some special condition. For instance, the primary object of sight is not given as precisely that which is adequate to sight existing in a medium illuminated by the light of a candle, but as what is inherently adequate to sight insofar as it exists from its own nature. But now, as was proved against the first opinion on the Question concerning the primary, that is, the adequate, object of the intellect—which opinion maintained the quiddity of the material thing to be the primary object—nothing can be adequate as a primary object to our intellect from the very nature of the power unless it is most common. But still, *in this present condition*, the quiddity of a sensible thing is adequate to it in the character of its mover; and hence, in this present condition it does not naturally know anything which is not contained under that primary mover.

If it is asked, what is the reason for this condition, I reply that a condition does not seem to exist except as made fast through the stable permanence of the laws of the divine wisdom. But it is established in those laws of wisdom that our intellect should only understand in this present condition those things of which the species are reflected in a phantasm. And whether this is because of the punishment of original sin or because of the natural concordance of the powers of the soul in operating, according to which we see that the superior power operates with regard to the same as does the inferior if each has a perfect operation, as a matter of fact this is the way it is with us, that whatever we understand universally, we have had a singular phantasm of it. But still, this concord, which belongs as a matter of fact to this present condition, does not come from the nature of our intellect, from which it is an intellect, nor even from its being in a body, for then it would necessarily have a similar concord in the glorious body, which is false. Therefore, whatever is the reason for this condition, whether from the mere will of God or from punitive justice or from weakness—which is the cause that Augustine intimates in the last chapter of Book XV of *On the Trinity:* "What is the cause why you cannot see that light with a fixed gaze except weakness? And what makes you be that way except iniquity?"—whether, I say, this is the entire cause or some other, at least the quiddity of a material thing is not the primary object of the intellect as a power; but it is something common to everything intelligible, although the primary object adequate in moving the intellect in this present condition may be the quiddity of a sensible thing.

. . .

Book I, Dist. II

QUESTION 7. *Whether in God There Are Two Productions, and Not Several?*

. . .

One distinction in the intellect is concerned for different ways of conceiving the same formal object, whether grammatically, as "man" and "of man," or logically, as "man" and "humanity." There is another important distinction in the intellect, in conceiving two formal objects in two acts. And these can either correspond to different things, as in understanding man and ass, or one external thing, as in understanding color and its differentia. . . .

Secondly, it is necessary to see what sort of distinction this is which is held to precede every act of the intellect.

I say that in things as well as in the intellect there is a major manifest difference, from which is frequently concluded a lesser difference which is not manifest, just as from the difference of creatures there is concluded a difference of ideas in the divine intellect, as is obvious through Augustine, Question 46, *Eighty-three Questions.*

But in reality there is a manifest distinction of things, and this is two-fold, namely, of subjects and of natures; in the intellect there is a manifest two-fold distinction, namely of modes of conceiving and of formal objects.

From these there is concluded the difference intended here, which is not manifest, and no wonder, since it is the least in its order, that is, between all those which precede the act of understanding. . . .

But is this distinction never called real?

I reply, it is not properly real as actual, taking this as it is commonly said. The real as actual difference is between things in act, and because of the divine simplicity there is not any difference of things in one divine person. And just as this is not a distinction of the real as actual, so it is not of the real as potential, since there is nothing there (in God) in potency which is not also in act. It can be called a difference of reason, as a certain doctor says, but not if "reason" is taken for a difference formed by the intellect, but rather, as taken for the quiddity of a thing as the quiddity is the object of the intellect. Or, in another way, it can be called virtual difference, since that which has such a distinction in itself does not have one thing and another, but it is one thing having as it were virtually or eminently two realities. For to each reality as it is in that thing, there belongs that property which is in such a reality, as if it were a distinct thing. For this reality is distinguished so, and it is not distinguished as if this were one thing and that another.

Or, to speak most carefully, we can discover several degrees of unity.

The first is the minimum unity of a collection.

The second is the unity of order, which adds something over and above the unity of a collection.

The third is the unity of accident, where beyond order there is a being formed, albeit accidentally, as compared with others which are one in this way.

The fourth is the intrinsic unity of that which is a composite from essential principles intrinsically actual and intrinsically potential.

The fifth is the unity of simplicity, which is truly identity. For whatever is there is really the same as whatever else is there, and is not merely one by union as is the case in the other modes. So, beyond all those up to here there is formal identity.

I call identity formal where that which is said to be the same includes that with which it is the same in its formal characteristic, and thus intrinsically in the primary way. But in the proposed position, the (divine) essence does not include the property of a subject in its formal characteristic, nor vice versa, and hence it can be conceded that before any act of the intellect there is the reality of the (divine) essence, which is communicable, and the reality of the (divine) subject, which is not; and before an act of intellect this reality is not formally that, or is not formally the same as that, according to what was said above about what it is to be formally the same as something.

Therefore, ought no distinction be conceded?

I reply that it is better to use the negative formulation, "This is not formally the same," rather than "This is distinct in such and such a way."

But does it not follow that if A and B are not formally the same, then they are formally distinct?

I reply that it does not have to follow, since formality is denied in the antecedent and affirmed in the consequent.

I say briefly, then, omitting the terminology of the distinction of reason and the virtual distinction, not because they are poorly put, but because they are not required, that before the act of the intellect there is in the divine essence the entity A and there is the entity B, and this is not formally that, so that the intellect of the Father, considering A and considering B, has *from the nature of the thing* the wherewithal for the verification of this composite: "A is not formally B," but not just from some act of the *intellect* concerning A and B.

This difference is manifest in an example. If whiteness is taken as a simple species, not having two natures in itself, there still is in whiteness something in reality from which it has the characteristic of color, and something from which it has the characteristic of a differentia, and this reality is not formally that reality, nor vice versa. Rather, one is outside the reality of the other, formally speaking, just as if there were two things, although now through identity these two realities were one thing. Though this example is like the proposed case in this, namely, that real identity does not necessarily establish the formal identity of whatever is in the same subject to anything in it, still the example is not altogether like the proposed case. For there is a certain composition in whiteness, even though it is not the composition of thing and thing, and that is not conceded in God merely because of formal non-identity.

· · ·

Book II, Dist. III

QUESTION I *Whether Material Substance Is Individual or Singular from Itself or Its Own Nature?*

· · ·

It seems so. The Philosopher, in Book VII of the *Metaphysics,* proves against Plato that the substance of any kind of thing is proper to it and is not in something else. Therefore, material substance from its own nature, setting aside anything else, is proper to that in which it is, such that from its own nature it cannot be in something else. Thus it is individual from its own nature.

On the contrary: Whatever is in something intrinsically, from its nature, is in it whatever it is in. Therefore, if the nature of stone is "this" of itself, in whatever there is the nature of stone, that nature would be this stone. The consequent is unsuitable in speaking about determinate singularity, which is what the question is about.

Besides, that to which an opposite belongs of itself is of itself repugnant to the other opposite. Therefore, if a nature were of itself one in number, numerical multitude would be repugnant to it of itself.

Here it is said that just as a nature is formally a nature of itself, so is a singular of itself, so that it is not necessary to seek a cause of singularity other than the cause of the nature, as though a nature were prior in time or that a nature is a nature before it is singular and then it is made singular by something added on which contracts it. Which position is proved by an analogy, since just as a nature has true existence from itself outside the soul, but only has dependent existence in the soul—that is, dependent on the soul itself (and the reason is that true existence belongs to it unqualifiedly, but existence in the soul is derived)— so universality only belongs to a thing as it has dependent existence in the soul. But singularity belongs to a thing according to true existence, and so, from itself and unqualifiedly. What is to be sought, then, is the cause whereby a nature is universal; and the intellect should be given as the cause. But a cause does not have to be sought whereby a nature is singular, other than the nature of a thing —a cause, that is, which would mediate between the nature and its singularity. But the causes of the unity of a thing are also the causes of the singularity of a thing. Therefore, etc.

Against this it is argued thus: An object insofar as it is an object is naturally prior to its act; and according to you, an object as prior is singular of itself, since this always belongs to a nature not taken as dependent, or according to the existence it has in the soul. Therefore, the intellect knowing that object under a universal characteristic, knows it under a characteristic opposed to its own, for as it precedes the act, it is of itself determined to the opposite of that characteristic.

Besides, the real unity proper and sufficient to anything whatsoever is less than numerical unity; it is not of itself one with numerical unity, or it is not of itself "this." But the real unity proper or sufficient to the nature of stone existing in this stone is less than numerical unity. Therefore, etc. The major is obvious of itself, since nothing is of itself one with a unity greater than that sufficient to it. For if the unity which ought to be proper to something of itself is less than numerical unity, numerical unity does not belong to it from the nature and according to itself, lest from its nature alone it should have a greater and lesser unity, which are opposites concerning and according to the same thing. For a multitude opposed to a greater unity can stand together with a lesser unity without contradiction; but that multitude cannot stand together with the greater unity because it is repugnant to it. Therefore, etc. The minor premiss is proved in that if there is no real unity of a nature less than singularity, but every unity other than singular unity is merely the unity of reason, then there will be no real unity less than numerical unity. The consequent is false, which I prove in five or six ways. Therefore, etc. . . .

Besides, secondly, I prove that the consequent is false, because according to the Philosopher in Book VII of the *Physics,* an atom is compared to a species, since it is one in nature, but not to a genus, since a genus does not have such a unity. This true unity is not a unity of reason, since the concept of a genus is just as much one in the intellect as is the concept of a species. Otherwise no concept would be definitionally predicated of many species, and so no concept would be of a genus if as many concepts were predicated of species as there are concepts of species. For then in single predications the same would be predicated of itself. Likewise, whether the unity is of a concept or not of a concept is irrelevant to the intention of the Philosopher, namely, with regard to the comparison. Therefore, the Philosopher intended the specific nature there to be one with the unity of a specific nature, but he did not intend it to be one with numerical unity, since no comparison was made to numerical unity. Therefore, etc. . . .

Again, sixthly, since if every unity is numerical, then every real diversity is numerical. But the consequent is false, since every numerical diversity insofar as it is numerical is equal; and so everything would be equally distinct, and then it follows that the intellect can no more abstract something common from Socrates and Plato than from Socrates and a line, and any universal would be a pure figment. . . .

Again, seventhly, it is not by anything existing in the intellect that fire causes fire and destroys water, and that there is a certain real unity of generator to generated according to form, because of which, generation is univocal. For intellectual consideration does not make generation to be univocal; but it knows it to be univocal.

In reply to the question, therefore, I concede the conclusion of these arguments, and I say that material substance from its own nature is not of itself "this," since then, just as the first argument concluded, the intellect could not understand it under the opposite, unless it understood under a characteristic unsuited for the understanding of such an object. As the second argument also concluded with all its proofs, there is a certain real unity in a thing apart from any operation of the intellect. This unity of a nature in itself is less than numerical unity, or the unity proper to a singular. And since a nature is not of itself one with that unity, it is according to its own proper unity indifferent to the unity of singularity.

This can also be understood through the saying of Avicenna in Book V of the *Metaphysics,* where he says that "horseness is just horseness, of itself neither one nor many, universal nor particular." One should understand that a nature is not of itself one with numerical unity, nor many with a plurality opposed to that unity. Nor is it actually universal, in the way that something is made universal by the intellect; neither is it of itself particular. Although it is never really without some of these, still, of itself it is none of them; but it is naturally prior to all. And according to this natural priority it is "that which is," and is the intrinsic object of the intellect. As such, it is considered by the metaphysician and is expressed through a definition. And propositions true in the primary way are true by reason of a quiddity so accepted, since nothing is predicated in the primary way of a quiddity that is not essentially included in it insofar as it is abstracted from everything naturally posterior to it. Not only is a nature of itself indifferent to existence in the intellect and in a particular, and hence to universal and singular existence, but also, in having existence in the intellect it does not have universality primarily from itself. For although it is understood under universality, as under the mode for understanding it, still, universality is not a part of its primary concept, since that is not a concept of the metaphysician, but rather, of the logician. For according to Avicenna himself, the logician considers second intentions applied to first intentions. Thus the primary understanding is of a nature, without any mode understood with it, neither that which belongs to it in the intellect, nor that which belongs to it outside the intellect, even though the mode of it to the intellect in understanding is universality—but it is not a mode of the intellect. And just as a nature is not of itself universal according to that existence, as though universality accrued to that nature according to its primary characteristic, but rather universality accrues to it as being an object of the intellect; so also in external reality. There, a nature exists with singularity; but the nature is not of itself limited to singularity. It is naturally prior to that characteristic contracting it to that singularity. And insofar as it is naturally prior to what contracts it, it is not repugnant to it to exist without what contracts it. And just as an object in the intellect has true intelligible existence according to that being and universality; so also in things, a nature has true real existence outside the soul according to that being. And according to that being it has a unity proportional to itself which is indifferent to singularity, so that of itself it is not repugnant to that unity, which is given with every unity of singularity.

In this way, therefore, I understand a nature to have a real unity less than numerical unity. And although it does not have numerical unity of itself, so that it would be internal to the characteristic of a nature, since "horseness is just horseness," according to Avicenna in Book V of the *Metaphysics,* still that unity is an attribute proper to a nature according to its primary being. And consequently, it is not of itself internally "this," nor is it necessarily included in a nature according to its own primary being.

But against this there seem to be two objections. One, that it seems to hold that a universal is something real in a thing, which is against the Commentator, Book I of the *De Anima,* comment 8, who says that "the intellect makes universality in things," so that universality only exists through the intellect, and so is merely a being of reason. The proof of the consequence is that this nature, as it is a being in this stone, but still naturally prior to the singularity of this stone, is being said indifferently to this singular and to that. . . .

To the first objection I say that the universal in act is that which has indifferent unity, according to which it is the same in proximate power as said of whatever individual subject, since, according to the First Book of the *Posterior Analytics,* "that is universal which is one in many and of many." For nothing according to whatever unity in a thing is such that according to just that unity it is in a proximate power to whatever subject, as said of whatever subject in a predication saying "this is this." For although to be in a singularity different from that in which it is, is not repugnant to something existing in a thing, still it cannot be truly said of just any inferior that that is it. For this is only possible of an object considered by the intellect in the same indifferent act, which object as understood also has the numerical unity of an object, according to which the same is predicable of every singular, in saying that this is this.

From this appears the disproof of that saying that the agent intellect makes universality in things, through this, that it uncovers the *that which is* existing in a phantasm. For wherever it is, before it has the existence of an object of the possible intellect, whether it is in a thing or in a phantasm, it either has certain existence or is deduced by reason. And if it is not through some illumination, but is always such a nature from itself, to which it is not repugnant to exist in another, still it is not that to which as a proximate power it belongs to be said of whatever you wish, but it is only in proximate power as it is in the possible intellect. In a thing, therefore, it is common, which is not "this" of itself, and consequently to which it is not of itself repugnant not to be "this." But such a common is not a universal in act, because there is lacking to it that differentia according to which a universal is fully universal, namely, according to which the same is predicable by some identity of whatever individual, so that the individual is it. . . .

And through this the reply is obvious to the principal argument in which he disproves that fiction which he imposes upon Plato, namely, that this intrinsically existing man, which is posited as the Idea, cannot intrinsically exist universally in every man. For every intrinsically existing substance is proper to that to which it belongs. That is, it is either from itself or it is proper through something which in contracting, makes it proper, which contracting having been posited, it cannot be in another, although it is not repugnant to it from itself to be in something else.

This gloss is also true speaking of substance as it is taken for the nature. And then it follows that the Idea will not be the substance of Socrates, since it is not the nature of Socrates either. For it is of itself neither proper to nor appropriated to Socrates, as it is merely in him, but it is also in another. But if substance is taken for first substance, then it is true that any substance is proper to that to which it belongs. And then it follows much more that that idea which is posited as substance existing intrinsically in this way cannot be the substance of Socrates or Plato. But the first member suffices for the proposed position.

For the confirmation of the opinion it is obvious that commonness and singularity are not disposed to a nature as existence in the intellect and true existence outside the soul respectively, since commonness as well as singularity belong to a nature outside the intellect. And commonness belongs to a nature of itself, whereas singularity belongs to a nature through something contracting it in the thing. But universality does not belong to a thing of itself, and hence I concede that the cause of universality is to be sought. But the cause of commonness is not to be sought, other than the nature itself. And commonness having been posited in a nature in accordance with its own being and unity, it is necessary to seek the cause of singularity, which adds something to that to which the nature belongs.

Book II, Dist. III

QUESTION 4 *Whether Material Substance Is Individual or Singular Through Quantity?*

· · ·

Here it is said that material substance is singular and individual through quantity, and the reason given is that what primarily and intrinsically belongs to something, belongs to anything else by reason of it. But substance and quantity do not make a one intrinsically, but only accidentally; and consequently, no one property belongs intrinsically to them at once and equally primarily, but rather, to one through the other. But to be divided into parts of the same character is a property which belongs intrinsically to quantity, from Book V of the *Metaphysics*. Thus it belongs to another, namely substance, through the characteristic of quantity. The division of a species into its individuals is of such a sort, since these divided individuals do not formally differ in character as do the species dividing a genus. . . .

Besides, this fire differs from that fire only because form differs from form; and form differs from form only because it is received in a part of matter different from another part. And a part of matter differs from another part only because it is under a part of quantity different from another part. Therefore, the entire distinction of this fire from that fire is reduced to quantity as what is primarily distinct. . . .

I argue against this conclusion in four ways. First, from the identity of numerical character, whether belonging to individuation or singularity. Second, from the order of substance to accident. Third, from the nature of predicational coordination. And these three ways together prove that no accident can be the intrinsic characteristic through which material substance is individuated. The fourth way will be especially against quantity, with regard to the conclusion of the opinion. And fifth, it will be argued especially against the arguments of the opinion.

As to the first way, I first explain what I understand by individuation, whether numerical unity or through singularity: not, indeed, the indeterminate unity according to which anything in a species is called one in number, but a unity demarkated as "this," so that, as was said before, it is impossible for an individual to be divided into subject-parts. And what is sought is the reason for this impossibility. So I say that it is impossible for an individual not to be a "this," demarkated by this singularity; and it is not the cause of singularity in general which is sought, but of this specially demarkated singularity, namely, as it is determinately "this." Understanding singularity thus, there is a two-fold argument from the first way:

First: a substance existing in act and not altered by some substantial transmutation cannot be turned from "this" to "not this," since this singularity (as was just said) cannot be in one thing and another with the same substance remaining the same and not substantially altered. But a substance existing in act with no substantial alteration can without contradiction be under one and another quantity, or any absolute accident. Therefore, this substance is in no such way formally demarkated by this singularity. The minor is obvious, since it is not a contradiction that God should conserve the same substance having this quantity and inform it with another quantity; nor would that substance existing in act be substantially altered because of this, since there would only be an alteration from quantity to quantity. Likewise, if it were altered in any accident without substantial alteration, possible or impossible, it would not on that account be formally "not this."

If you say that this is a miracle and hence is not conclusive against natural reason, my reply is that a miracle does not include contradictories, for which there is no power. But it is a contradiction for the same enduring substance to be two substances without substantial alteration, and this successively as well as simultaneously, which would follow if it were formally this substance through any accident. For then, with accident succeeding accident, the same unaltered substance would successively be two substances. . . .

Perhaps to escape these criticisms, the position that individuation is by quantity is held in this other way, namely, that just as the extension of matter is different from the quantity of that matter and adds nothing to the essence of the matter so demarkated, so the demarkation of matter, which it has causally by way of quantity, is different from the demarkation of its quantity and is naturally prior to the demarkation which it has through quantity. For substance as substance is naturally prior to quantity without any accident whatsoever. And the demarkation of matter is different from the demarkation of quantity, but it is not different from substance, so that just as matter does not have parts through the nature of quantity, since a part of matter is matter, so demarkated substance does not exist without substance. For demarkation only conveys a way of being disposed.

Against this: the position seems to include contradictories twice over. First, since it is impossible for anything naturally posterior and dependent to be the same as what is naturally prior, since then it would be prior and not prior. But substance is naturally prior to quantity. Therefore, nothing caused through quantity or in any way presupposing the nature of quantity can be the same as substance. This demarkation, therefore, is not the same as substance even though it is caused by quantity. The proof of the major is that where there is true and real identity, even though it is not formal, it is impossible for this to exist and that not, since then the same would really exist and not exist. But it is possible for what is naturally prior to exist without what is naturally posterior; consequently, much more without what is determined or caused by what is naturally posterior.

Besides, a necessary condition of a cause cannot have its existence from its result, since then the cause as sufficient for the causing would be caused by the result, and the result would be its own cause. But the singularity or demarkation of substance is a necessary condition for causing quantity in substance, since a singular result requires a singular cause. Therefore, it is impossible for this demarkation to be derived from what is caused by substance, insofar as it is singular.

Besides, I ask what it is to determine quantity or to cause such a mode in substance. If it precedes quantity, then demarkation is in no way through quantity. But if it is anything else, I ask how it is caused by quantity, and by what type of cause? The only type of cause that it seems possible to assign here is the efficient cause, but quantity is not an active form.

. . .

Book II, Dist. III

QUESTION 6   *Whether Material Substance Is Individual Through Some Positive Entity Intrinsically Determining a Nature to Singularity?*

. . .

I reply "yes" to the question. I argue that just as common unity intrinsically accompanies common being, so some kind of unity intrinsically accompanies any being. Thus unqualified unity, which is the unity of an individual often described above as that to which a division into several substantial parts is repugnant and to which it is repugnant not to be a demarkated "this," if, as every opinion supposes, it exists, intrinsically accompanies some being. But it does not intrinsically accompany the being of a nature, since that has its own intrinsically real unity, as was proved in the solution to the first Question. Therefore, it accompanies some other being determining this, and together with the being of the nature making something intrinsically one which is whole and perfect of itself. . . .

This solution can be further clarified by comparing this being by which there is this perfect unity to the being from which specific difference is taken. For specific difference, or the being from which it is taken, can be compared to what is below, above, or beside it. In the first way, it is repugnant to specific difference and that specific being to be intrinsically divided into several which are essentially species or nature, and through this it is repugnant to the whole of which that entity is an intrinsic part. So it is in what is proposed: it is repugnant to this individual entity to be divided primarily into substantial parts of any kind, and through this such a division is repugnant intrinsically to the whole of which that entity is a part. And still there is a difference, in that the unity of a specific nature is less than this unity; and because of this, that unity does not exclude all division according to substantial parts, but only the division into essential parts. But the latter excludes all such division. And from this the proposed position is sufficiently confirmed, since it does not seem probable from the fact that the lesser unity has its own being which accompanies it to deny its own accompanying being to this perfect unity.

In comparison to what is above it, I say that the reality from which specific difference is taken is actual with respect to that from which the genus is taken, so that the one reality is not formally the other. Otherwise, definition would be frivolous, and the genus alone would define sufficiently, since it would indicate the entire being of the defined without the differentia. Sometimes what contracts is different from the form from which the characteristic of the genus is taken, namely, when the species adds something over and above the nature of the genus; but sometimes it is not another thing, but only another formality, or another real concept of the same thing. And following this, some specific difference does not have an irreducibly simple concept, for instance, that which is taken from the formality; some does have an irreducibly simple concept, namely that which is taken from the ultimate abstraction of the form. This distinction between specific differences has been discussed in the third distinction of Book I, where it was said how some specific differences include being, and some not. On one point, individual reality is like specific reality, since it is a sort of act determining the reality of species as though that were possible and potential. But on another point it is dissimilar, since it is never taken from an added form, but precisely from the ultimate reality of the form. On still another point it is dissimilar, since specific reality constitutes a composite in quidditative being, of which it is a part, since it is a kind of quidditative being. But individual being is fundamentally diverse from every quidditative being. This is proved from the fact that in knowing any kind of quidditative being, speaking of limited quidditative being, one does not know whence it is "this." Therefore, that being which is of itself "this" is a different being from quidditative being, and it thus cannot constitute a whole of which it is a part in quidditative being, but rather in being of a different character. . . .

And if you ask, "What is this individual being from which individual difference is taken? Is it not matter, or form, or the composite?"

I reply that every quidditative entity, whether partial or total of any kind, is of itself indifferent, as quidditative entity, to this entity and that one, so that as quidditative entity it is naturally prior to this entity as "this." And as it is naturally prior, just as being "this" does not belong to it, so the opposite is not repugnant to it from its own character. And just as the composite insofar as it is a nature does not include the being by which it is "this," so neither does matter insofar as it is a nature, nor form. Therefore, this being is not matter, nor form, nor the composite, insofar as any of these is a nature; but it is the ultimate reality of the being which is matter, or which is form, or the composite, so that anything common and yet determinable can still be distinguished, however much it is one thing, into several formally distinct realities, of which this is not formally that. But this is formally the being of a singular, and that is formally the being of a nature. And these two realities cannot be as thing and thing, as can the realities from which genus and differentia are taken, from which specific reality is taken; but in the same thing, whether part or whole, they are always formally distinct realities of the same thing. . . .

To the second objection I concede that a singular is intrinsically intelligible on its side. But if it is not intrinsically intelligible to some intellect, for instance, ours, at least this is not an impossibility on the part of the singular, just as it is not on the part of the sun that to see at night is impossible, but rather on the part of the eye.

. . .

Book II, Dist. III

QUESTION 9 *Does an Angel Have a Distinct Natural Knowledge of the Divine Essence?*

. . .

Therefore, I reply differently to the question. First, two types of cognition should be distinguished. For there can be one cognition of an object according to what is abstracted from all actual existence, and there can be another of it according to what is existing, and according to what is present in some actual existence.

This distinction is proved by argument and by analogy. The first (type) is obvious from the fact that we can have awareness of certain quiddities; but science is of an object according to what is abstracted from actual existence. Otherwise, science could sometimes exist and sometimes not, and so it would not be perpetual; but with the thing destroyed, the science of that thing would also be destroyed—which is false. The second (type) is proved, since what there is of perfection in an inferior power seems to exist in a higher way in a superior power of the same kind. But in sense, which is a cognitive power inferior to intellect, there is the perfection of knowing a thing as existing in itself and according to what is present following its existence. Therefore, this is possible in the intellect, which is the supreme cognitive power. Therefore it can have cognition of a thing according to what is present.

And to be brief, I call the first "abstractive," which is of the quiddity as abstracted from actual existence and non-existence. The second, which is of the quiddity of a thing according to its actual existence or of what is present following such existence, I call "intuitive cognition"—not as "intuitive" is distinguished from "discursive," since in this way any abstractive would be intuitive, but unqualifiedly intuitive, in the way in which we speak of intuiting a thing just as it is in itself.

The second member (of the distinction) is through the fact that we do not await the kind of knowledge of God which could be had of Him if he were (as is impossible) non-existent, or not present through His essence; but we await intuitive cognition, which is called face-to-face, just as sensory cognition is face-to-face with a thing as it presently exists.

The second clarification of this distinction is by analogy with the sensory powers. For a particular power or sense knows an object in one way and the imagination, in another. For a particular sense is of an object according to what is through itself or existing in itself; imagination knows the same according to what is present through a species, which species can be an image of it even though it is not existent or present. So imaginative cognition is abstractive in comparison with a particular sense. And since what is dispersed in inferiors is sometimes united in the superior, these two ways of knowing which are dispersed in the sensitive powers because of the organs (for the organ that receives well is not the same as that which retains well) are united in the intellect, which as one power can perform either act.

• • •

Book I, Dist. XXXIX

THE SINGLE QUESTION   *Whether God Has a Determinate Knowledge of Everything, Pertaining to All Conditions of Existence?*

• • •

Concerning these questions, the certitude of the divine science regarding everything, pertaining to all conditions of existence, is maintained on the ground of Ideas which are posited in the divine intellect. And this is because of their perfection in representation, since they represent that whose Ideas they are not only each as a whole in itself, but also according to every characteristic and every situation. And so there is a sufficient reason in the divine intellect, not only for apprehending what has Ideas in an absolute way, but also for apprehending every union of them and their every mode pertaining to their existence.

Against this: the reasons for knowing the terms of some complex do not suffice for the knowledge of that complex unless it is inherently knowable from terms (alone). But a contingent complex is not inherently knowable from terms, since then not only would it be necessary, but it would also be primary and immediate. Therefore, no matter how perfectly the reasons for knowing terms may represent them, they do not suffice for knowing the contingent complex.

Besides, Ideas only represent naturally, and under a natural characteristic. This is proved because Ideas are in the divine intellect before any act of the divine will, so that in no way are they there through an act of the divine will. But whatever naturally precedes the act of will is natural only. I take, then, the Ideas of two extremes which are represented in them, for instance, "man" and "white," and I ask whether these Ideas from themselves represent the composition of those extremes, or their division, or both. If the composition alone, then that divine intellect knows that naturally and so necessarily; and consequently, it does not know the division at all. And the same way if they represent the division alone. If both, then God knows nothing through them, since to know that contradictories are or that they are true is to know nothing.

Besides, there are Ideas of non-future possibilities just as there are of future ones, since this difference between future and non-future possibilities is only through the act of the divine will. Thus the Idea of a future possible no more represents that future to exist than does the Idea of a non-future possible. . . .

The third proposition says that although in a certain respect the divine sciences are necessary, still, it does not follow that there cannot be contingencies with respect to proximate causes. And this is confirmed by Boethius in Book V of the *Consolation*, the last chapter, or section 6, where he speaks thus: "If you say that what God sees will happen, cannot fail to happen; but that what cannot fail to happen comes about by necessity, you bind me to this term 'necessity.' I reply, something future is necessary when it is referred to the divine knowledge, but when the same thing is considered in its own nature, it is utterly free and released from the bonds of necessity." It is also argued for this that imperfection can belong to an effect from a proximate cause, although not from the remote or prior cause, just as deformity is in the act caused by the will, but not insofar as it is from the divine will, and hence the sin is not brought back to God as its cause, but is imputed only to the created will. Thus even if there were a necessity of things on the part of God, who is the remote cause, there could still be contingency in them from their proximate causes.

It was argued against this in the second distinction, where it was proved through the contingency of things that God knows and wills other things to exist contingently, since there can be no contingency in the causation of any cause with respect to its effect unless the first cause is contingently disposed to the cause next to it or to its effect.

This is now briefly proved in that when a cause which moves insofar as it is moved, is necessarily moved, then it moves necessarily. Therefore, any second cause which produces insofar as it is moved by the first, if it is moved necessarily by the first, necessarily moves the one next to it, or produces its effect. Thus the entire order of causes up to the last effect would produce necessarily if the disposition to the first cause to that next to it were necessary. . . .

Besides, whatever is produced by posterior causes can be immediately produced by the first, and then it would have the same being which it has now, and then it would be contingent just as it is now contingent. It therefore has its contingency even now from the first cause, and not from the proximate cause only.

Besides, God produced and produces much immediately, as he created the world and now creates souls, and still, everything (is produced) contingently.

Concerning the solution of these questions, this is the order to be followed: first it is to be seen in what way contingency exists. Second, how the certitude and immutability of the divine science stands concerning it.

As to the first, I say that this disjunction *necessary or possible* is an attribute of being, which is a circumlocution for "attribute convertible with being," as are many others non-limited among beings. But convertible attributes of being, as more common, are immediately predicated of being, since being has an irreducibly simple concept, and hence there can be no connecting link between it and its attribute, since neither has a definition which could serve as such a link. Even if there were some non-primary attribute of being, it is difficult to see through what prior medium it could be deduced from being, since it is not easy to see an order among the attributes of being. Nor if the order were known, would the propositions serving as premises seem much more evident than the conclusions. But in disjunctive attributes, even though the entire disjunction cannot be demonstrated of being, still it is commonly assumed that from the fact that the less noble belongs to some being it can be concluded that the more noble belongs to some other being. Just so, it follows that if some being is finite, then some being is infinite, and if some being is contingent, then some being is necessary. For in such cases the less perfect member could not particularly belong to a being unless the more perfect member belonged to some being on which that one depended.

But it does not seem possible to infer in this way to the less perfect member of such a disjunction, for if the more perfect belongs to some being, it is not necessary that the less perfect should belong to some other being, unless the disjunctive members should be correlative, such as cause and caused. And so this disjunction *necessary or contingent* cannot be shown to belong to being through any prior medium. Nor indeed could that part of the disjunction which is *contingent* be shown to belong to anything on the assumption of some necessary being. And hence this proposition *Some being is contingent* seems to be a primary truth, and not demonstrable from an adequate ground. Whence the Philosopher, in arguing against the necessity of future events, did not deduce to something more impossible than the hypothesis, but to something impossible which is more manifest to us, namely, that it would not be appropriate either to take counsel nor to deliberate. Hence those who deny what is thus manifest need punishment or perception. For, as Avicenna says in Book I of the *Metaphysics, Those who deny the first principle should be flogged or burned until they admit that it is not the same thing to be burned and not burned, or whipped and not whipped.* And so also, those who deny that any being is contingent should be subjected to torments until they concede that it is possible for them not to be tortured.

On this assumption, then, that it is truly manifest that some being is contingent, it should be asked how contingency among beings can be preserved. And, because of the first argument made against the third opinion, which is further explicated in the Question on the existence of God, I say that no causation of any cause can preserve contingency unless, as Catholics maintain, the first cause is held to cause contingently immediately, and with perfect causality. But the first cause causes through intellect and will, and if a third executive power were posited other than these, it would not help toward the proposed position, since if it understood and willed necessarily, it would produce necessarily. Thus it is necessary to seek this contingency in the divine will or in the divine intellect. But it is not in the intellect, as that has a first act before any act of will, since whatever the intellect knows in this way, it knows only naturally and by natural necessity. So there can be no contingency in knowing or understanding anything which it does not know or understand by such a primary act of knowing. It is necessary, then, to seek the first contingency in the divine will; and to see how this should be treated, we should first look at our own will. Here there are three points to be considered: First, with respect to what the freedom of our will might be. Second, how possibility or contingency follows this freedom. And third, regarding the logical distinction of propositions, how possibility or contingency with respect to opposites is expressed.

As to the first, I say that the will in its primary act is free with respect to opposite acts; it is also free by means of them with respect to the opposite objects to which it tends, and further, with respect to the opposite effects which it produces. The first freedom necessarily has some imperfection attached to it because of the passive potentiality and mutability of the will. The third freedom is not the first, since if (as would be impossible) the will should produce no external effect, as a will it could still tend freely to its objects. But the second characteristic of freedom is without imperfection; rather, it is necessary for perfection, since every perfect power can tend to all that which is the inherent object of such a power. Thus the perfect will can tend to all that which is inherently capable of being willed. Therefore, the first freedom without imperfection as freedom is with respect to the opposite objects to which the will tends, through which it produces opposite effects.

On the second point, I say that a manifest power for opposites accompanies this freedom. For although it does not have the power to will and not will at once, since that is nothing, yet there is in it the power to will after not willing, or to will a succession of opposed acts; and this power is also manifest in everything in which the succession of opposites can occur. But there is also another without any succession which is not so manifest. Take a will created such as to have its existence only for a single instant, and which performs a particular volition in that instant. It would not perform this necessarily. The proof is that if in that instant it should perform it necessarily, then, since there is no cause except in the instant in which it causes, the will would cause it unqualifiedly necessarily. For a cause is not contingent only because it exists before the instant in which it causes and as pre-existent could cause or not cause; since just as this particular being, when it exists, is necessary or contingent, so when a cause causes, it does so necessarily or contingently. Therefore, in the instant in which the will causes this act of volition and does not do it necessarily, it does it contingently.

There is thus a power of this cause for the opposite of that which it causes, without succession being involved, and as the power for the first act for opposites, this real power is naturally prior to those which are naturally posterior as pertaining to the second act. For the first act, considered in that instant in which it is naturally prior to the second, contingently causes the second to exist, such that it could just as well cause its opposite to exist. The logical power of the non-repugnance of terms also accompanies this real active power which is naturally prior to what is produced. For to the will as first act, even when it is producing this particular volition, the opposite volition is not repugnant. This is, first, because the cause is contingent with respect to its effect, and so the opposite as effect is not repugnant to it; and second, because as a subject it is contingently disposed to being informed by this act, since the opposite of an accident is not an accident repugnant to a subject. Therefore, the power for successive opposites and for those of the same instant as well, accompanies the freedom of our will. And this power rather than the logical is the real cause of the naturally prior act; but the fourth power, namely, the power for simultaneous opposites, does not accompany it, since there is none.

From this second, a third is obvious, namely a distinction concerning this proposition, "The will willing A can not-will." For in the sense of composition, this is false, as the possibility of this composition would be signified: "The will willing A does not will A." But it is true in the sense of division, as the possibility for successive opposites would be signified. For the will willing A is able not to will B. But if we take a proposition of possibility uniting the extremes for the same instant, for example, this one: "The will not willing anything for (instant) A can will that for (instant) A," this again should be distinguished according to composition and division. In the sense of composition it is false, namely, that it would be possible to be willing for A and not willing for A simultaneously. But in the sense of division it is true, namely, as it would signify that not willing for A can belong to the will willing for A, but not so that the not-willing obtains at the same time, since then that willing would not belong to it.

And in order to understand this second distinction, which is more obscure, I say that in the sense of composition there is a categorical (proposition) whose subject is "The will not willing for A," and whose predicate is "willing for A." And then this predicate is attributed only possibly to this subject to which it is repugnant and consequently would belong to it impossibly, and which is noted as possibly belonging to it. In the sense of division, there are two categorical propositions, enunciating two predicates concerning the will. The one is a proposition of inherence, and in it, this predicate "not willing A" is enunciated concerning the will; and this categorical is understood through implicit composition. But the other is a categorical of possibility, and in it "possibly willing A" is enunciated. And these two propositions are verified for A, since they signify their predicates to be attributed to the subject for the same instant. And this is indeed true, for in the same instant "not willing A" belongs to this will together with the possibility for the opposite, just as this proposition of possibility signifies. . . .

The third objection is that if for some instant there is a power for something whose opposite exists, either this is a power with the act or before the act. Obviously it is not with the act; nor is it before the act, since then it would be for an act for a different instant than that for which that power exists. . . .

To the third objection I say it is the power before the act—not "before" in duration, but "before" in the order of nature. For that which precedes this act naturally can exist together with the opposite of that act. And then it should be denied that every power is either with the act or before the act, understanding "before" for priority in duration. But it is true, understanding "before" for priority in nature.

But it is objected to this that if it can will A for this instant and does not will A for this instant, then it can not-will A for this instant, since that of possibility follows that of inherence. And then it seems to follow that it can will A and not-will A simultaneously, for the same instant.

To this I reply, according to the Philosopher in Book IX of the *Metaphysics,* that this having the power for opposites so acts that in acting it has the power, but not so that it has the power in acting, which would refer the mode to the term of the power but not to the power itself. For I have at once the power for opposites, but not for opposites at once. Then I say that from "It can will this in instant A," and "It can not-will this in A," this does not follow: "Therefore, it can will and not-will in A," since there can be a power for either one of opposites disjunctively for some instant, although not for both at once. For just as there is the possibility for one of them, so there is for the non-existence of the other, and vice versa. It is not, therefore, for the existence of this one and its opposite, since there would only be the possibility for simultaneity if it were for the concurrence of both in the same instant, which is not obtained from the fact that the power is for either of them separately for this instant.

An example of this appears in permanent objects. It does not follow from the fact that a given body can be in a particular place in instant A, and the fact that another body can be in the same place in instant A, that therefore, these two bodies can be in the same place in instant A. For this body can be there because that body can not be there, and vice versa; and hence it does not follow that if the power is for either of them for the same instant or place, then it is for both at once, but fails whenever either of the two excludes the other. It also does not follow that because I can carry a stone which is portable and within the scope of my strength the whole day, and can also carry some other stone for the whole day, therefore, I can carry both at the same time. It does not follow, because in this case either one for which there is the power disjunctively excludes the other. Moreover, simultaneity can never be inferred from the identity of that one instant or place alone, but it is necessary to have the conjunction of the two which are said to be simultaneous with this.

Along with what has been said about our will, certain points should be seen concerning the divine will. And first, with respect to what its freedom pertains. Second, what contingency is with respect to what is willed. Third, regarding the logical distinction of propositions, what is proportionately the same there and here.

As to the first, I say that the divine will is not indifferent with respect to the diverse acts of negative and positive volition, since in my will this was not without imperfection of the will. For our will was free with respect to opposite acts so that it might be free with respect to opposite objects, and this is because of the limitation of each act with respect to its object. Thus given the non-limitation of the same will for diverse objects, it would not be necessary to posit the freedom for opposite acts because of the freedom for opposite objects. The divine will is also free for opposite effects, but this is not the first freedom, just as it is not in ours, either. That freedom remains, then, which is without imperfection and is intrinsically perfect, namely, the freedom for opposed objects; so that just as our will can through diverse volitions tend to diverse objects of volition, so that will can by a single, simple, and unlimited volition tend to any object of volition whatsoever. So that if that will or that volition were only for one such object, and could not be for the opposite (so long as that is still capable of being willed), this would be an imperfection in the will, as was deduced above about our will. And although a distinction can be made regarding our will as it is receptive, operative, and productive, in that it is productive of acts, and is that by which its possessor operates in formally willing, and is receptive of its own volition, yet its freedom seems to belong to it as operative, insofar, that is, as its possessor can formally tend by it to some object. Therefore, it is as the operative power that freedom is posited in the divine will primarily and intrinsically; and so, although it is not receptive nor productive of its own volition, still, a certain freedom can be preserved for it insofar as it is productive. For although production in the being of existence does not necessarily accompany its operation (since its operation is in eternity and production in the being of existence is in time), still, production in the willed being necessarily accompanies its operation. And then that power of the divine will cannot indeed be first as productive, but rather, derivatively, in the willed being, and this production accompanies that power as operative.

As to the second article, I say that the divine will looks necessarily to nothing other than its essence for an object; therefore, it is disposed to anything else contingently, so that it could be (so disposed) to the opposite. And this is considering it as it is naturally prior to the tendency toward that object, not only as the will is naturally prior to its act, but also as it is actually willing. For just as our will as naturally prior to its act so elicits the act that it could elicit the opposite in the same instant, so, insofar as the divine will is volitional, it is natural prior to such a tendency. And it tends toward that object contingently, so that it can tend toward the opposite object in the same instant; and this is as much from the logical power of the non-repugnance of terms, as was said concerning our will, as from the real power which is naturally prior to its act.

Having seen the contingency of things as to existence, considering this with respect to the divine will, the second principal point remains to be seen: how the certitude of the divine science stands with regard to this. This can be given in two ways. In one way, through the fact that the divine intellect sees the determination of the divine will, namely, "That will exist at (instant) A." For the divine will determines that to exist at that time. For the divine intellect knows that will to be immutable and without impediment.

Or, since this way seems to posit a certain discursive process in the divine intellect, as though it comes to the conclusion that this will exist from an intuition of the determination and immutability of the will, it can be given otherwise. It can be held that the divine intellect either offers simples whose union is contingent in reality, or, if it offers a complex, it offers that as neither true nor false, and the will in choosing one part, namely, the conjunction of these for some *now* in reality, makes that to be determinately true. But, this existing as determinately true, the essence is the reason for the divine intellect knowing that truth. And insofar as this is on the part of the essence, it is natural, so that just as it knows all necessary principles naturally, as though before the active of the divine will (since their truth does not depend on that act and they would be known by the divine intellect if, as is impossible, it were not performing an act of will), so the divine essence is the reason for knowing them in that prior instant of the nature. For they are true then, but not because those truths move the divine intellect, nor even because their terms move it to the apprehension of such truth. For then the divine intellect would be debased, since it would be affected by something other than its essence. But just as the divine essence is the reason for knowing simples, so also for such complexes. But then they are not true contingents, since then there is nothing through which they have determinate truth. But given the determination of the divine will they are true for that second instant. And this same will be the reason for the divine intellect knowing these which are true in the second instant and would have been known in the first instant if they had been in the first instant.

An example: just as if there were in my eye from my visual power one act of seeing an object which always stood, then, if something were presented at one moment with this color and at another moment with that, my eye would now see this and now, that. And it would still be through the same vision, however much there is a difference in the priority and posteriority of the seeing because of the object presented earlier and later. And if one color were naturally present and another, freely, there would not be a formal difference in my vision, since on its part, the eye would see both naturally. Yet it could see one naturally and another necessarily, insofar as one were present contingently and the other, necessarily. So the divine intellect is held to know the existence of things in both of these ways. . . .

To the other argument for the third opinion, I say that contingency is not merely a privation or defect of being like the deformity in the second act which is sin. Rather, contingency is a positive mode of being, just as necessity is another mode. And everything positive in an effect is more principally from the prior cause. And hence it is not, like deformity, the result of the second cause rather than the first. Rather, contingency is through the first cause rather than the second, because nothing caused would formally be contingent unless the first cause caused contingently, as has been shown.

· · ·

Book II, Dist. XXV

THE SINGLE QUESTION   *Whether Anything Other than the Will Effectively Causes the Act of Willing in the Will?*

· · ·

I argue for the affirmative: . . .

Again, what is of itself undetermined to one of opposites does not act unless a determining agent concurs, since as undetermined it is no more disposed to the being of an effect than to its non-being. But the will of itself is so disposed to its act; whence another agent must be posited, which seems only to be the object.

On the contrary, Augustine says in Chapter 6, Book XII of the *City of God*, that if two men are equally affected in soul and body, and then they are tempted by the same beauty or object, whence is it that one falls and the other does not? And he says that this is from the will alone. Anselm says the same thing in Chapter VIII, *On the Virgin Birth.*

Again, Augustine says in Book II of *On Free Will* that unless what is voluntary for us were placed in our power, the will should neither be praised nor blamed, nor even admonished; and he who says or feels that the will should not be admonished should himself be exterminated from the number of men. . . .

It is said by a modern doctor that something other than the will is the effective cause of volition in it, and he holds that other to be the phantasm. His principal argument is this: mover and moved must be distinct in subject; but in the intellective part of the soul nothing can be distinct in subject from the will. Therefore, nothing there is the mover of it, and hence that must be something else outside of the intellective part; and that is held to be the phantasm. He proves the first proposition thus: to hold that mover and moved are not distinct in subject is the same as to hold that a thing moves itself, which is impossible. . . .

The second argument is that the material and efficient (causes) do not coincide in what is numerically the same. See Book II of the *Physics.* Thus neither do agent and patient. . . .

There is another opinion, of an older Doctor, which comes to the same conclusion, namely, that the will is moved by something else; but that is held to be the object known or understood. . . . These two opinions agree in that they hold that something other than the will moves it, but they disagree as to the mover, as is obvious.

There are major arguments against the conclusion in itself, and I reply, deducing them thus: A natural agent cannot by itself be the cause of contraries with respect to the same patient (which excludes the example of something melting ice and drying mud); but it is in the power of our will to have negative and positive volition, which are contraries, with respect to a single object. Thus they cannot be produced by an agent naturally, and thus not by the object, which is a natural agent. Let it be, then, that the object is the cause of the positive volition; something else would nonetheless have to be the cause of the negative volition. But that something else other than the will could only be an evil object. But since evil is a privation, it could not be the cause of the posited (positive?) act of such a kind as negative volition. Therefore it must be effectively from the will.

Again, to undergo something is not in the power of what undergoes it, especially when it is by a natural agent. But if the object naturally produces volition, and not the will, then the volition will not be in the power of the will. And if so, then neither would any other act commanded by the will be in its power; and so it would neither be deserving nor blameworthy through volition.

It is said that volition is in the power of the will just so far as the will can determine the intellect to the consideration of this or that, or can avert it from this or that; and so volition is in the power of the will, yet not so far as the first act.

On the contrary: take the first action in the will, caused by the object, whatever it might be that has to be posited, according to you. That action is merely natural, and thus is not in the power of the will. For according to Augustine it is not in our power that we should not be touched by what we see. Therefore, if after this act I can move the intellect to consider this or that, I ask, by what act?—not by this one, since it is not in the power of the will. So it must be by another. About the other I ask, whence is it?—from the will itself, from the object, or from the phantasm? If from the will, I have the proposed position, since then that volition is in its power and is effectively from it; and by the same argument, the first volition. Or it is from something else, namely, the object or phantasm; and if so, then it will be a natural act. And consequently, to command the intellect concerning the consideration of this or that will no longer be in the power of the will, any more than was the first act. . . .

To the first argument for that opinion, which says that mover and moved must necessarily be distinct in subject, I reply that this is only true for corporeal beings. I even believe that in their case it is not necessarily true. At least I say that for spiritual beings it is utterly false. . . .

To the other argument, that the material and efficient (causes) do not coincide, it is said that we can consider two (features) in the will: insofar as it is appetite, or insofar as it is free. As free, it is effective; as appetite, it is receptive—so that there is here a difference of meaning regarding the will, as appetite and as free.

I do not take this well, since the proximate characteristic constituting a species, such as the ultimate differentia, is the proximate characteristic for receiving a distinctive attribute. For man does not receive his ability to laugh by reason of being an animal, but by reason of being rational. But freedom is a more formal characteristic of the will than is appetite, wherefore the characteristic for receiving is freedom, just as the characteristic of freedom is more than for constituting it. . . .

Besides, the material subject does not coincide numerically with the efficient, which is properly spoken of as distinct from an agent. For to be efficient or effective in this way is to pass over into an extrinsic matter, as in producing. But the action of an agent, speaking properly of an agent, does not pass over so; its action is merely internal. . . .

I say then to the question that nothing other than the will is the total cause of volition in the will. One argument outside of the previously mentioned ones is this: something in things happens contingently. And I call that to happen contingently which happens avoidably. Otherwise, if everything happened inevitably, one would not be required to take counsel, nor to deliberate, as Aristotle says in Book I of the *De Interpretatione*. I ask, then, whence or from what cause does that which happens contingently, happen? Not from a determined cause, because for that instant for which it is so determined, the effect cannot happen contingently. Thus, by a cause undetermined to one or another of opposites. Therefore, either that cause can determine itself contingently to one of the opposites (since it cannot do so to both at once, as Aristotle says in Book IX of the *Metaphysics,* concerning rational potency), or it cannot determine itself, but something else determines it to one of them. If it can determine itself to one of them contingently or not inevitably, the proposed position is had. If it is determined to one of them by something else, is this necessarily or contingently? If necessarily, the effect happens inevitably. But what determines to one of them contingently and avoidably, in such a way that it can determine to the other, can only be the will, since every natural active cause is determined to one effect—or if a natural cause is undetermined, it can neither determine itself nor another.

You say that this indetermination is on the part of the intellect, in representing the object to the will as existing or not existing in the future. But the intellect cannot determine the will indifferently to either of contradictories, for instance this existence or non-existence, except by demonstrating one and making a paralogism or sophistical syllogism regarding the other, so that in drawing the conclusion it is deceived. Thus if that contingency by which this can exist or not exist were from the intellect so dictating on the ground of opposite conclusions, then nothing would happen contingently by the will of God, since He does not make paralogisms, nor is He deceived. But this is false and is disproved in Book I, Distinction VIII, the last Question.

Also, the intellect acts in a way which is most of all natural, according to Augustine in Book III of *On the Trinity* and in many other places. Thus he posits the intellect as the appropriated principle with respect to the production of the Son in the Divine persons, Who is produced most naturally. The intellect, thus, is least of all an undetermined cause with respect to any effect; rather, it is determined.

You say that the Philosopher divides nature as against intellect and as against acting from a purpose, and that therefore, he does not understand intellect to be a cause through the mode of nature. I say that intellect can be taken either intrinsically, according to which it is a certain operative power of an operation such that it is distingushed as against the operation of the will. And taken thus, insofar as it is from itself, it acts naturally. Or it can be taken as a practical power with respect to what can be done externally; and in this way, the Philosopher has art, intellect, purpose, choice, and appetite for the same thing. And in taking intellect in this way he distinguishes acting by intellect from acting by nature; and in this second way he frequently speaks about intellect in almost the entire book of the *Ethics,* and in Book IX of the *Metaphysics,* and Book III of the *De Anima,* and Book II of the *Physics* on the rational power. But in the first way, the Philosopher says little about intellect. . . .

To another argument I concede that the will is an active power. And when it is said that an active power is a principle for altering something other (than itself), insofar as it is other, I reply that the definition of the productive power is given there, and I concede that the same thing cannot *produce* itself.

But I speak differently, as Aristotle does in Books V and IX of the *Metaphysics,* where he gives the example of a doctor who cures himself but who still is not different from himself. But he cures as a doctor and is different from himself as being cured; for it is as sick that he is cured, not as a doctor. So in the proposed position I say that the will as an active power which can elicit its volition is formally different in character from the power for receiving its self-perfecting volition. Whence the "insofar as it is other" reduplicates a different formal characteristic when mover and moved are not distinct in subject; but when they are distinct in subject, it repeats a different thing and a different characteristic. . . .

To the other argument concerning the power of contradiction, that it is not in the power of contradiction to determine itself to one of the opposites, I say that there is a certain form of the power of contradiction, such as science, which is of contraries; and this cannot determine itself, since it is diminshed and imperfect insofar as it looks to both contraries. Whence Aristotle, texts 3 and 10, wishes to say that if it should of itself proceed to act, without anything else determining it, it would produce contraries at the same time. But there is another form of the power, which is undetermined when the object is presented to it, and is perfect and not diminished, such as the will. And this can determine itself and also others. Whence in Book IX of the *Metaphysics,* because he had said that science is of contraries and still is unable to determine itself to any of them, he adds what is determinative: "But this I call appetite or choice." Therefore, the perfect rational power such as the will, even though it is of contradictories, with the object having been presented, can determine itself to one of them.

Book III, Dist. XXXVII

THE SINGLE QUESTION   *Whether All the Precepts of the Ten Commandments Belong to the Natural Law?*

. . .

For the negative: In those cases which belong to the law of nature it does not seem that God can make dispensations; but he has made dispensations in certain cases which seem to be against the precepts of the Decalogue. Proof of the major premiss: it is either necessary principles known from their terms or conclusions necessarily following from such principles that belong to the law of nature. But one way or the other, they possess necessary truth. Therefore, God cannot make them to be false. Therefore, He cannot make what they command to be done not to be good, and what they prohibit, not to be evil; and consequently, He cannot make such forbidden cases to be permitted. Proof of the minor premiss: to kill and to steal and to commit adultery are against the Commandments, as is obvious from Exodus, 20; but God seems to have granted dispensations in these cases. This is obvious for homicide in Genesis, 22, concerning the sacrifice of the son of Abraham; for theft, Exodus, 11 and 12, where he ordered the sons of Israel to despoil the Egyptians, and despoliation is taking what belongs to another without his consent, which is the definition of theft; for adultery, Hosea, 1: *Make children of fornications.*

Besides, in Romans, 7, the Apostle says, "I had not known lust, except the law had said, Thou shall not covet." But what is known from the law of nature is known to be avoided or committed even though it is not written, just as what is naturally known in speculative matters would be naturally known even though it were not revealed.

Besides, the law of nature is obligatory in every condition, since it is known in such a nature what is to be done or not; but the Commandments are not obligatory in every condition, for instance, not in the condition of innocence, since then the law of the Decalogue was not given, and before it was given it was not obligatory. . . .

The affirmative position is held in some such way as this: The law of nature is law proceeding from the first principles known for actions; such are certain seminal practical principles known from their terms. The intellect is naturally inclined to their truth from the terms, and the will is naturally inclined to assent to precepts from such principles. But whatever is in the Commandments is directly or indirectly of this kind, for everything commanded there has formal goodness which in itself is ordered to the last end, so that through them man is turned to that end and pursues it. Likewise, everything prohibited there has formal evil turning one aside from the last end. So what is commanded there is good not merely because it is commanded; but it is commanded because it is good in itself. Likewise, what is prohibited there is evil, not merely because it is prohibited, but it is forbidden because it is evil.

And consequently, it seems that the reply to the first argument should be that God is absolutely unable to grant dispensations in such cases, for it does not seem that what is of itself unlawful can be made lawful through any will. As, for instance, if killing is an evil act from the fact that it is directed at such-and-such a recipient, namely, a neighbor, then given that case, it will always be evil. And so no *willing* which is outside of the characteristics of those terms can make it good. And then it is necessary to explain those authoritative texts which seem to say that God has granted dispensations in such cases; and they are explained in one way, that although a dispensation can be granted concerning an act with regard to the type of the act, still, not concerning it insofar as it is prohibited, and so, it cannot be granted against the prohibition.

To put it otherwise, an act remaining unauthorized cannot be made authorized; but insofar as an act is against a prohibition, it is unauthorized. Hence it cannot be subject to dispensation insofar as it is against a prohibition.

But these explanations (which perhaps come down to the same) do not seem to preserve the proposed position. For to grant a dispensation is not to make something against a precept lawful with the precept still standing, but it is to revoke the precept, or to declare how it ought to be understood. For dispensation is two-fold, namely, revocation of the law and clarification of the law.

I ask whether, with all circumstances staying the same in the act of killing a man, with only the circumstance of prohibition and non-prohibition changing, could God make that act, which is prohibited at another time with such other circumstances, be permitted and not prohibited on another occasion? If so, then He can grant dispensations unconditionally, just as he changed the old law as to ceremonials when he gave the new—not, indeed, making it such that with the precept on ceremonials remaining in force it should not be followed, but making it such that with the act remaining the same, one was not bound to that precept as before. So any lawmaker makes dispensations unconditionally when he revokes a precept of the positive law made by him—not, indeed, making it such that with the act prohibited or with the precept remaining as itself, the characteristic of being unlawful is removed and the act made lawful.

But if God cannot make this act which was prohibited with such circumstances not be prohibited with the same circumstances, then he cannot make killing not be prohibited—the opposite of which is manifestly obvious concerning Abraham.

Besides, what is true from terms, whether necessary from terms or consequents from such necessaries, precedes every act of will in truth, or at least they have their truth setting aside (as is impossible) every act of will. Therefore, if the precepts of the Decalogue, or practical propositions which can be formed from them, had such necessity, for instance, if these were necessary: "A neighbor should not be killed," "Theft should not be committed"—so that such complexes would be known by the intellect apprehending them with every act of will set aside—then the divine intellect apprehending them would necessarily apprehend them as true from itself. And then the divine will would necessarily agree with them as apprehended, or it would not be right. And that would be to posit in

God the characteristic of practical science, which was denied above. It would also be to maintain that the divine will is unconditionally necessarily determined with respect to something other than itself which is capable of being willed. The opposite of that was mentioned above, where it was said that divine will tends to nothing other than itself, except contingently. . . .

In reply to the question, therefore, I say that something can be said to belong to the law of nature in two ways: in one way, as a practical first principle, known from terms, or as a conclusion necessarily following from it. And these are said to belong to the law of nature most strictly. And the arguments against the first opinion prove that from these there can be no dispensation, which I concede. But none of the precepts of the second table of the Commandments are of this kind, since the grounds for what is there commanded or forbidden are not unconditionally necessary practical principles nor unconditionally necessary conclusions. For the goodness necessary for the last end, turning one to it, is not found in what is commanded there, nor is the evil necessarily turning one from the last end found in what is prohibited there, since if the good (found there) were not commanded, the last end could be loved and attained, and if that evil were not forbidden, the acquisition of the last end would be consistent with it.

But it is otherwise concerning the precepts of the first table, since they pertain immediately to God as their object. The two first, if they are understood to be merely negative: "Thou shalt not have foreign gods," and "Thou shalt not take the name of thy God in vain," that is, do not be irreverent to your God, belong strictly to the law of nature. For it follows necessarily that if He is God, He should be loved as God, and that nothing else is to be honored as God, nor is irreverence to be committed toward God. And consequently, God will not be able to grant dispensation from these, so that one could lawfully do the opposite of what is thus prohibited. . . .

Some things are said to belong to the law of nature in another way, since a great deal is consonant with that law although it does not necessarily follow from practical principles necessarily known from terms to every apprehending intellect. It is certain that in this way all the precepts of the second table belong to the law of nature, since their rightness is surely consonant with necessarily known practical first principles.

This distinction can be clarified by an example. Given the principle of positive law that life in a community or state ought to be peaceful, it does not follow necessarily from this that therefore, one person ought to have possessions distinct from those of another, for peace in mutual life would be possible even if everything were had in common. Nor is that consequence necessary even on the assumption of the poor character of those living together. But still, that possessions should be distinct for persons of poor character is certainly consonant with peaceful social life, since such people care more for their own goods than for communal, and they wish that communal goods were theirs rather than the community's or its representatives', and thus strife and disorder come about. And so it is for almost all positive laws: although there is some principle which is the basis for establishing other laws or rights, still, positive laws do not follow unconditionally from that principle; but they clarify or explicate that principle with respect to certain particulars. These explications are indeed consonant with the naturally universal principle.

And so, pulling everything together: first, it is denied that all the Commandments of the second table belong to the law of nature, strictly speaking. Second, it is conceded that the first two Commandments of the first table belong to the law of nature, strictly speaking. Third, there is some doubt about the third Commandment of the first table. And fourth, it is conceded that all belong to the law of nature, speaking broadly.

• • •

SELECTED BIBLIOGRAPHY

BIBLIOGRAPHIES

Gieber, S., "Bibliographia Scotistica recentior 1953–1965," *Laurentianum*, VI (1965).

Grajewski, M., "Scotistic Bibliography of the Last Decade (1929–1939)," *Franciscan Studies*, I and II (1941–1942).

Schäfer, O., *Bibliographie de vita, operibus et doctrina Iohannis Duns Scoti Doctoris Subtilis ac Mariani saeculorum XIX–XX*, Romae, 1955.

Schäfer O., "Resenha abreviada da bibliografphia escotista mais recente (1954–1966)," *Revista Portugesa de Filosofia*, XXIII (1967), 338–363.

TRANSLATIONS

Alluntis, F. and Wolter, A., trans., John Duns Scotus, *God and Creatures: The Quodlibetal Questions*, Princeton, 1975.

McKeon, R., ed. and trans., *Selections from Medieval Philosophers, II: Roger Bacon to William of Ockham*, New York, 1930.

Micklem, N., *Reason and Revelation: A Question from Duns Scotus*, Edinburgh, 1953.

Roche, E., ed. and trans., *The De Primo Principio of John Duns Scotus*, St. Bonaventure, N.Y., 1949.

Wolter, A., "Duns Scotus and the Necessity of Revealed Knowledge. Prologue to the *Ordinatio* of John Duns Scotus," *Franciscan Studies*, XI (1951), 231–272. (Reprinted in H. Shapiro, ed., *Medieval Philosophy*, New York, 1964.)

Wolter, A., ed. and trans., *Duns Scotus, Philosophical Writings*, Nelson, 1962. (English translation only in paperback edition, Indianapolis, 1964.)

Wolter, A., ed. and trans., *John Duns Scotus: A Treatise on God as First Principle*, Chicago, 1966.

STUDIES

Bettoni, E., *Duns Scotus: The Basic Principles of his Philosophy*, ed. and trans. B. Bonansea, Washington, D.C., 1961.

Dahlstrom, D., "Significance and Logic: Scotus on Universals from a Logical Point of View," *Vivarium*, XVIII (1980), 81–111.

Day, S., *Intuitive Cognition: A Key to the Significance of the Later Scholastics*, St. Bonaventure, N.Y., 1947.

Effler, R., *John Duns Scotus and the Principle "Omne quod movetur, ab alio movetur,"* St. Bonaventure, N.Y., 1962.

Gilson, E., *Jean Duns Scot. Introduction à ses positions fondamentales*, Paris, 1952.

Grajewski, M., *The Formal Distinction of Duns Scotus*, Washington, D.C., 1944.

Harris, C., *Duns Scotus*, 2 vols., Oxford, 1927. (Occasionally misleading because of credence in the authenticity of the *De rerum principio*.)

Martinich, A., "Scotus and Anselm on the Existence of God," *Franciscan Studies*, XXXVII (1977), 139–152.

The Monist, XLIX, no. 4 (October, 1965). An issue devoted to the philosophy of Duns Scotus.

O'Brien, O., "Duns Scotus' Teaching on the Distinction between Essence and Existence," *The New Scholasticism*, XXXVIII (1964), 61–77.

Prentice, R., *The Basic Quidditative Metaphysics of Duns Scotus as Seen in His De Primo Principio*, Rome, 1970.

Prentice, R., "The Voluntarism of Duns Scotus as Seen in His Comparison of the Intellect and the Will," *Franciscan Studies*,

XXVIII (1968), 63–103.

Rudavsky, T., "The Doctrine of Individuation in Duns Scotus," *Franziskanische Studien,* LIX (1977), 320–377.

Ryan, J., and B. Bonansea, eds., *John Duns Scotus,* 1265–1965, Washington, D.C., 1965.

Sharp, D., *Franciscan Philosophy at Oxford in the Thirteenth Century,* Oxford, 1930.

Shircel, C., *The Univocity of the Concept of Being in the Philosophy of John Duns Scotus,* Washington, D.C., 1942.

Tweedale, M., "Scotus and Ockham on the Infinity of the Most Eminent Being," *Franciscan Studies,* XXIII (1963), 257–267.

Vier, P., *Evidence and its Function According to John Duns Scotus,* St. Bonaventure, N.Y., 1951.

Wolter, A., *The Transcendentals and Their Function in the Metaphysics of Duns Scotus,* St. Bonaventure, N.Y., 1946.

WILLIAM OF OCKHA

ca. 1 2 8 0 – 1 3 4 9

𝕿HE VENERABLE INCEPTOR. An inceptor was a student who had com-pleted most of the requirements for teaching as a master in theology, and Ockham was prevented from exercising the mastership. But an inceptor is also an initiator; and so the title was later taken to refer to Ockham's sup-posed role as the founder of the Nominalist movement, the "modern way" which dominated many universities in the fifteenth century. Ockham him-self seems not to have been conscious of founding a new movement—at least he does not associate himself with those he calls "the moderns." None-theless, he was the one to whom later Nominalists looked for their program. Some care should be taken in interpreting this fact, since if Nominalism is the doctrine that only the name is common to the many things called by that name, then Ockham, like Abailard, ought rather perhaps to be called a con-ceptualist. And it may seem strange that a position on this one issue should generate a movement with distinctive treatments of a great range of prob-lems. It may be of some interest, then, to discover what those who called themselves Nominalists and venerated the great Inceptor thought they stood for. Fortunately, we have a letter which the Nominalist masters of the University of Paris sent to King Louis XI in 1473 or 1474, setting forth the persecution of their movement by erring popes and princes, and offering the following self-characterization:

> *Those doctors are called Nominalists who do not multiply the things prin-cipally signified by terms in accordance with the multiplication of the terms. Realists, however, are those who contend on the contrary that things are multi-plied according to the multiplicity of terms. For example, Nominalists say that divinity and wisdom are one and the same thing altogether, because everything which is in God, is God. But realists say that the divine wisdom is divided from divinity.*
>
> *Again, those are called Nominalists who show diligence and zeal in under-standing all the properties of terms on which the truth and falsity of a sentence depends, and without which the perfect judgment of the truth and falsity of propositions cannot be made. These properties are: supposition, appellation, am-pliation, restriction, exponible distribution. They especially understand obliga-tions and the nature of the insoluble, the true foundation of dialectical arguments*

and of their failure. Being instructed in these things, they easily understand concerning any given argumentation whether it is good or bad. But the realists neglect all these things, and they condemn them, saying, "We proceed to things, we have no concern for terms." Against them Master John Gerson said, "While you proceed to things, neglecting terms, you fall into complete ignorance of things themselves." This is in his treatise on the Magnificat; *and he added that the said Realists involve themselves in inexplicable difficulties, since they seek difficulty where there is none, unless it is logical difficulty.**

This manifesto proposes two criteria for Nominalism: the refusal to multiply entities and the systematic employment of technical devices from the logic of terms. Some of these devices will be explained in the selections below. The first criterion recalls the so-called "Ockham's Razor" and suggests that the refusal to posit *universal* entities, for which Ockham is most famous, is only part of a wider controversy. It has often been pointed out that the Razor, which in one of Ockham's formulations runs, "Plurality is not to be posited without necessity," was common in the Middle Ages, and so is hardly distinctive of Ockham. Indeed, where Ockham employs the Razor against Duns Scotus, Duns Scotus himself employs it against St. Thomas Aquinas.† Realist and Nominalist alike believed that entities should not be posited without necessity—the deeper issues arose over what counts as necessary, and why. In Ockham's case, the controlling conviction was that everything outside the mind is singular; and much of his effort goes to show that with correct logical analysis, entities such as real universals, relational beings, and Scotistic formalities need not be posited.

There is another prominent element of Ockham's method which is difficult to assess with any exactitude. This is a striking concern for the divine omnipotence, grounded in the first article of the Apostles' Creed and the Nicene Creed. This concern is formulated in the distinction between the absolute and ordained power of God. The ordained power governs the system which God has decreed, and the reservation of the absolute power expresses the fact that God is not necessitated or limited by this system—that God *could* decree otherwise than He has. For the most part, this distinction is applied to theological topics such as the order of grace and salvation; but two related principles are employed in more purely philosophical subjects. The first is that God can do anything except that which involves contradiction, and the second is that God can perform directly what He now performs through the activity of created causes. These principles could work together with the Razor to give rise to a highly skeptical critique, as have many other philosophical programs limiting necessity to logical necessity

---

* Translated by James J. Walsh from the text on pp. 322–323 of F. Ehrle, *Der Sentenzenkommentar Peters von Candia*, Münster: Aschendorffsche Verlagsbuchhandlung, 1925. A translation of the entire letter can be found in L. Thorndike, *University Records and Life in the Middle Ages*, New York, 1944, pp. 355–360.

† See Duns Scotus, *The Oxford Commentary*, Book II, Dist. xvi, the Single Question, and William of Ockham, *On the Four Books of the Sentences*, Book II, Question 24. The topic is the reality of the distinction between the powers of the soul.

alone. But there are only occasional manifestations of such a critique in Ockham. Indeed, he says that God employs more means than He requires; and we find in him no effort to denigrate the concepts of substance and causation such as we find in the more radical critique of Nicholas of Autrecourt. We have, then, the Razor, terminist analysis, the reservation of the divine omnipotence, and the master conviction of the singularity of real existents; and none of these can be omitted as fundamental to Ockhamism.

William of Ockham may have been born as early as the 1280s since he was ordained subdeacon in 1306. It is usually supposed that he came from the village of Ockham, not far from London; but there is only the evidence of his name to support this. He apparently joined the Franciscan Order early, and pursued a normal course of study, lecturing on the *Sentences* at Oxford from 1317 to 1319. Ockham was thus a *baccalaureus formatus,* needing only to complete a four-year probationary period of preaching and disputations to become a regent master in theology. During this period, however, one John Lutterell, sometimes described as "an overzealous Thomist," succeeded, after some controversy in the university and some political delay, in accusing Ockham of heresy before Pope John XXII at Avignon. In 1324, Ockham was summoned to the papal court; and shortly thereafter a commission began a lengthy examination of his works. Two lists of suspect theses were compiled, but apparently were not formally condemned. At any event, by 1328, Ockham was involved in affairs of greater urgency. The Franciscan Order and the Pope were engaged in a controversy over the value of poverty which had raged in and around the Order almost since its beginning. A crucial question was whether Jesus and his disciples possessed property. At the request of Michael Cesena, the general of his Order, Ockham investigated the issue. He subscribed to the doctrine of evangelical poverty against the Pope; and on May 26, 1328, escaped with Cesena to Italy, where they later took refuge with another papal opponent, the Emperor Louis of Bavaria. After moving to Munich, Ockham gradually expanded his opposition to include the relation of the papacy to secular authority and various topics concerning the fate of the soul. On evangelical poverty and secular authority he remained in opposition during the reigns of succeeding popes and wrote a series of polemical works. The power of Louis waned, making Ockham's situation difficult; and in 1347, with the death of Louis, Ockham took steps of reconciliation with the papacy. A formula of submission was drawn up, ignoring the theological issues for which he was first summoned to Avignon. He may or may not have subscribed to this formula. His stormy career was soon closed, probably by the Black Death, in 1349.

The chronology of Ockham's works is difficult to ascertain. In this resume of his major nonpolitical writings, the views of Father Boehner, O.F.M. are followed. These are conveniently presented in his introduction to the *Tractatus de Successivis.* The reader may also wish to consult Baudry's *Guillaume d'Occam.* Ockham's chief work is the commentary *On the Four Books of the Sentences (Super 4 libros sententiarum).* The last three books of this commentary are known as the *Reportatio,* since they were not subjected to a final editing by Ockham. The first book is known as the *Ordinatio,* since it was so edited. The *Reportatio* as we have it is older than the *Ordinatio,* and both date from before 1323. Some time after them, but before 1329, he produced the *Summa of Logic (Summa logicae,* or *Summa totius logicae),* and before 1333, the *Seven Quodlibeta (Quodlibeta septem).* After the *Quodlibeta* come the *Questions on the Books of the Physics (Quaestiones in libros Physicorum)* and the *Summulae on the Books of the Physics (Summulae in libros Physicorum).* He also produced several short logical and theological treatises; and various other works have been controversially attributed to him, including the *Treatise on Successives (Tractatus de successivis),* a compilation of his physical doctrines completed before 1350. Among the political works stemming from the period in Germany are the *Work of Ninety Days (Opus nonaginta dierum)* and the *Dialogue on the Power of the Emperor and the Pope (Dialogus de potestate Papae et Imperatoris).* As is the case with most medieval theologians, a great deal that is of philosophical interest is to be found in Ockham's theological works, especially the commentary on the *Sentences.*

The selections which follow begin with the logic of terms. Without familiarity with the terminology of that discipline it is difficult to follow the rest of Ockham's writings, and this portion of medieval logic is of considerable philosophical interest in its own right. There follows the critique for which Ockham is most widely known, of the conception of universals as entities common to their instances and yet really distinct from them. To this there is appended the critique of the more subtle Scotist conception of a formal distinction between the common nature and the individualizing difference. These selections also contain Ockham's theories of definition and science, topics which he says are always put forward by the defenders of Plato. The reader may also find the treatment of a typical *sophisma,* or logical puzzle, of interest, as these *sophismata* were extremely popular in later medieval thought, and contain some of its most advanced logical speculations. With the abandonment of Realism in universals goes the abandonment of the epistemology of intelligible species based on it; the next selection contains Ockham's critique of that epistemology, and his own alternative, based on intuitive and abstractive cognition and substituting habit for species. The precedence of the intuitive cognition of singulars is clearly stated here, and the entire discussion is important for the development of British Empiricism. In this selection there are references to a "first question." This is the preceeding Question, which is: "Whether an angel knows what is other than itself through its essence or through a species?" There follow selections which show the Ockhamist critique at work. The problem of the reality of relations was important in his opposition to Duns Scotus and raised severe problems for him. In the selections on motion, the term *motus* is translated as "motion" or "movement" as the context seems to require. The selections contain an interesting polemic against abstractions, and should be compared with the parallel yet different treatment by John Buridan. The selection on teleological explanation sheds much light on the abandonment of the concept of the final cause in later theories of nature. The last selection concerns ethics. There Ockham clarifies the ontology of the moral act and develops an ethics of obligation based on the divine commands rather than the nature of man. But he still holds that right reason is intrinsic to moral virtue, going so far as to hold that reason must be an object of the moral act. The apparent inconsistency between this authoritarianism and rationalism is resolved by limiting the morality of right reason to the ordained power of God.

It has been justly said that William of Ockham is the most influential of later medieval philosophers; but in granting his influence, one also grants that of Duns Scotus. For Ockham's thought develops largely through critical reflection on his Franciscan predecessor; and if he opposes the Subtle Doctor on much, he also shows great respect for him, and carries his views forward on other topics. The two great Franciscans are in no small measure responsible for the persistent élan of British philosophy.

SUMMA TOTIUS LOGICAE

On Terms [in General]

All those who deal with logic try to establish that arguments are composed of propositions, and propositions of terms. Hence a term is simply one of the parts into which a proposition is directly divided. Aristotle defines 'terms' in the first book of the *Prior Analytics* by saying: 'I call a term that into which a proposition is resolved (viz. the predicate, or that of which something is predicated) when it is affirmed or denied that something *is* or *is not* something'.

Although every term is or can be a part of a proposition, yet not all terms are of the same kind. Hence to obtain a perfect knowledge of them, we must first get acquainted with some distinctions between terms.

According to Boethius in the first book of the *De interpretatione*, language is threefold: written, spoken and conceptual. The last named exists only in the intellect. Correspondingly the term is threefold, viz. the written, the spoken and the conceptual term. A written term is part of a proposition written on some material, and is or can be seen with the bodily eye. A spoken term is part of a proposition uttered with the mouth and able to be heard with the bodily ear. A conceptual term is a mental content or impression which naturally possesses signification or consignification, and which is suited to be part of a mental proposition and to stand for that which it signifies.

Translated by Philotheus Boehner, O.F.M., from William Ockham, *Summa totius logicae*, in *Ockham, Philosophical Writings*, Edinburgh: Thomas Nelson and Sons, Ltd., 1957. Reprinted by permission.

These conceptual terms and the propositions formed by them are those mental words which St Augustine says in the fifteenth book of *De Trinitate* do not belong to any language; they remain only in the mind and cannot be uttered exteriorly. Nevertheless vocal words which are signs subordinated to these can be exteriorly uttered.

I say vocal words are signs subordinated to mental concepts or contents. By this I do not mean that if the word 'sign' is taken in its proper meaning, spoken words are properly and primarily signs of mental concepts; I rather mean that words are applied in order to signify the very same things which are signified by mental concepts. Hence the concept signifies something primarily and naturally, whilst the word signifies the same thing secondarily. This holds to such an extent that a word conventionally signifying an object signified by a mental concept would immediately, and without any new convention, come to signify another object, simply because the concept came to signify another object. This is what is meant by the Philosopher when he says 'Words are signs of the impressions in the soul'. Boethius also has the same in mind when he says that words signify concepts. Generally speaking, all authors who maintain that all words signify, or are signs of, impressions in the mind, only mean that words are signs which signify secondarily what the impressions of the mind import primarily. Nevertheless, some words may also primarily signify impressions of the mind, or concepts; these may in turn signify secondarily other intentions of the mind, as will be shown later.

What has been said about words in regard to impressions or contents or concepts holds likewise analogously for written words in reference to spoken words.

Certain differences are to be found among these [three] sorts of terms. One is the following: A concept or mental impression signifies naturally whatever it does signify; a spoken or written term, on the other hand, does not signify anything except by free convention.

From this follows another difference. We can change the designation of the spoken or written term at will, but the designation of the conceptual term is not to be changed at anybody's will.

For the sake of quibblers, however, it should be noted that 'sign' can assume two meanings. In one sense it means anything which, when apprehended, makes us know something else; but it does not make us know something for the first time, as has been shown elsewhere; it only makes us know something actually which we already know habitually. In this manner, a word is a natural sign, and indeed any effect is a sign at least of its cause. And in this way also a barrel-hoop signifies the wine in the inn. Here, however, I am not speaking of 'sign' in such a general meaning. In another sense, 'sign' means that which makes us know something else, and either is able itself to stand for it, or can be added in a proposition to what is able to stand for something—such are the syncategorematic words and the verbs and other parts of a proposition which have no definite signification—or is such as to be composed of things of this sort, e.g., a sentence. If 'sign' is taken in this sense, then a word is not a natural sign of anything.

. . .

Division into Categorematic and Syncategorematic Terms

There is still another distinction holding both between vocal, and between mental, terms. Some are categorematic, others syncategorematic, terms. Categorematic terms have a definite and fixed signification, as for instance the word 'man' (since it signifies all men) and the word 'animal' (since it signifies all animals), and the word 'whiteness' (since it signifies all occurrences of whiteness). Syncategorematic terms, on the other hand, as 'every', 'none', 'some', 'whole', 'besides', 'only', 'in so far as', and the like, do not have a fixed and definite meaning, nor do they signify things distinct from the things signified by categorematic terms. Rather, just as, in the system of numbers, zero standing alone does not signify anything, but when added to another number gives it a new signification; so likewise a syncategorematic term does not signify anything, properly speaking; but when added to another term, it makes it signify something or makes it stand for some thing or things in a definite manner, or has some other function with regard to a categorematic term. Thus the syncategorematic word 'every' does not signify any fixed thing, but when added to 'man' it makes the term 'man' stand for all men actually, or with confused distributive *suppositio*. When added, however, to 'stone', it makes the term 'stone' stand for all stones; and when added to 'whiteness', it makes it stand for all occurrences of whiteness. As with this syncategorematic word 'every', so with others, although the different syncategorematic words have different tasks, as will be shown further below.

Should some quibbler say that the word 'every' is significant and consequently it signifies something, we answer that it is called significant, not because it signifies something determinately but only because it makes something else signify or represent or stand for something, as we explained before. And just as we say that the noun 'every' does not signify anything in a determinate and limited way, to use Boethius's way of speaking, we must maintain the same of all syncategorematic words and all conjunctions and prepositions.

It is, however, different with some adverbs, because certain of them determinately signify the same things which categorematic words signify, though they do so in a different mode of signification.

On the Difference Between Connotative and Absolute Terms

Having discussed concrete and abstract terms, we must now speak of another division of names frequently used by the teachers of philosophy.

Certain names are purely absolute, others are connotative. Purely absolute names are those which do not signify one thing principally, and another or even the same thing secondarily; but everything alike that is signified by the same absolute name, is signified primarily. For instance, the name 'animal' just signifies oxen, donkeys and also all other animals; it does not signify one thing primarily and another secondarily, in such a way that something has to be expressed in the nominative case and something else in an oblique case; nor is there any need to have nouns in different cases, or participles, in the definitions which express the meaning of 'animal'. On the contrary, properly speaking, such names have no definitions expressing the meaning of the term. For, strictly speaking, a name that has a definition expressing the meaning of the name, has only one such definition, and consequently no two sentences which express the meaning of such terms are so different in their parts that some part in the first sentence signifies something that is not signified by any corresponding part in the second. The meaning of absolute names, however, may be explained in some manner by several sentences, whose respective parts do not signify the same things. Therefore, properly speaking, none of these is a definition explaining the meaning of the name. For instance, 'angel' is a purely absolute name, at least if it means the substance and not the office of an angel. This name has not some one definition expressing the meaning of the term. For someone may explain the signification of the name by saying: 'I understand by "angel" a substance which exists without matter'; another thus: 'An angel is an intellectual and incorruptible substance'; again another thus: 'An angel is a simple substance which does not enter into any composition with anything else'. And what is signified by this name is explained just as well by the one as by the other definition. Nevertheless, not every term in each of these sentences signifies something that is signified in the same manner by a similar term in each of the other sentences. For this reason, none is, strictly speaking, a definition expressing the meaning of the name. And so it is with many names that are purely absolute. Strictly speaking, none of them has a definition expressing the meaning of the names. Names like the following are of this kind: 'man', 'animal', 'goat', 'stone', 'tree', 'fire', 'earth', 'water', 'sky', 'whiteness', 'blackness', 'heat', 'sweetness', 'odour', 'taste', and so on.

A connotative name, however, is that which signifies something primarily and something else secondarily. Such a name has, properly speaking, a definition expressing the meaning of the name. In such a definition it is often necessary to put one of its terms in the nominative case and something else in an oblique case. This holds, for instance, for the name 'white'. For it has a definition expressing the meaning of the name in which one expression is put in the nominative case, and another in an oblique case. When you ask, therefore, 'What does the name "white" signify?' you will answer: 'It signifies the same as the entire phrase "Something that is qualified by whiteness", or "Something that has whiteness".' It is manifest that one part of this phrase is put in the nominative case and another in the oblique case. Sometimes it may happen that a verb appears in the definition expressing the meaning of the name. If, for instance, it is asked 'What does the name "cause" signify?' it can be answered that it means the same as the phrase 'Something whose existence is followed by the existence of something else', or 'Something that can produce something else', or the like.

Such connotative names include all the concrete names of the first kind, mentioned in Chapter V, because such concrete names signify one thing in the nominative case and something else in the oblique case; that is to say, in the definition expressing the meaning of the name, one term signifying one thing must be put in the nominative case, and another term signifying another thing must be put in the oblique case. That becomes evident as regards all such names as 'just', 'white', 'animated', 'human' and the like.

Also to this type belong all relative names. For their definition has to contain distinct parts which either signify the same thing in different ways, or signify distinct things; this is evident as regards the name 'similar'. For if 'similar' is defined, we have to say 'The similar is something that has such a quality as another thing has', or some such definition. However, it does not matter which examples we take.

From this it becomes clear that the common name 'connotative' is a higher genus than the name 'relative', at least if we take the common noun 'connotative' in its broadest sense. For such names include all names pertaining to the genus of quantity, according to those who maintain that quantity is not a different thing from substance and quality. Thus, for them, 'body' has to be considered a connotative name. Hence, according to them, it must be said that a body is nothing else but a thing which has part distant from part in length, breadth and height, and a continuous and permanent quantity is a thing which has part distant from part. This, then, would be a definition expressing the meaning of the name. In consequence, these people have also to maintain that 'figure' or 'shape', 'curvature', 'straightness', 'length', 'height', and the like are connotative names. Further, those who maintain that everything is either a substance or a quality, have to suppose also that all terms contained in the categories other than substance and quality are connotative names, and also some of the genus quality are connotative names, as will be shown later on.

To this group of names belong also such terms as 'true', 'good', 'one', 'potency', 'act', 'intellect', 'intelligible', 'will', 'willable' and the like. The word 'intellect', for instance, has the meaning: 'Intellect is soul able to understand'. Thus the soul is signified by the nominative case and the act of understanding by the rest of the phrase. The name 'intelligible' is also a connotative term. It signifies the intellect, both in the nominative and in the oblique case, since its definition is this: 'The intelligible is something that can be apprehended by the intellect'. In this definition the intellect is signified by the name 'something', and also by the oblique case 'by the intellect'. The same must be said of 'true' and 'good'; for 'true', which is convertible or co-extensive with 'being', signifies the same as 'intelligible'. Likewise 'good', which is co-extensive with 'being', signifies the same as the phrase 'Something which can be willed and loved according to right reason'.

On Names of First and Second Imposition

We have thus given the divisions that apply both to terms which signify naturally and to those which are made by convention; we have now to say something about certain divisions which concern only terms made by convention.

A first division is this: Some of the conventional names are names of first imposition and some are names of second imposition. Names of second imposition are names which are applied to signify conventional signs, and also what goes with such signs, but only as long as they are signs.

But the general term 'name of second imposition' can be taken in two senses; one broad, the other strict. In a broad sense a name of second imposition is one that signifies utterances conventionally used, but only as long as they have this conventional use, whether or not such a name be also shared by mental contents, which are natural signs. Such names are 'noun', 'pronoun', 'verb', 'conjunction', 'case', 'number', 'tense' and the like, when used as the grammarian understands them. These names are called names of names, because they are applied only to signify parts of speech, and only as long as these are significative. For names which are predicated of words both when they are significant and when they are not, are not called names of second imposition. Hence such names as 'quality', 'spoken', 'utterance' and the like, are not names of second imposition, though they signify conventional utterances, since they would signify them even if they were not significant as they now are. But 'noun' is a name of second imposition, since neither the word 'man' nor any other word was a noun before it was employed to signify. Likewise 'man's' was of no case, before it was used to signify what it does. The same holds good for the other words of this kind.

In the strict sense, however, 'name of the second imposition' is that which signifies only a conventional sign, and therefore does not refer to mental contents, which are natural signs. Such names are 'figure', 'conjugation' and the like. All other names that are not names of second imposition in one or the other way, are called names of first imposition.

'Name of first imposition', however, can be taken in two senses. In a broad sense all names not of second imposition are names of first imposition. Thus all such syncategorematic signs as 'every', 'none', 'some', 'any' and the like, are names of first imposition. In a strict sense, however, only categorematic names not of second imposition are called names of first imposition, and not syncategorematic names.

Names of first imposition, in the strict sense, are of two classes. Some are names of first intention, others of second intention. Names of second intention are those nouns which are used precisely to signify mental concepts, which are natural signs, and also other conventional signs, or what goes with such signs. All the following are of this kind: 'genus', 'species', 'universal', 'predicable' and the like. For such names signify only mental contents, which are natural signs, or conventional signs.

Hence it can be said that this common term, 'name of second intention', can be taken strictly or broadly. Broadly speaking, that is said to be a name of second intention which signifies mental contents that are natural signs, whether or not it also signifies conventional signs for just such time as they function as signs. In this sense some names of first imposition and second intention are also names of second imposition. Strictly speaking, however, that only is called a name of second intention which precisely signifies mental contents that are natural signs. In this sense no name of second intention is a name of first imposition.

Names of first intention, on the other hand, are all names that differ from the former; that is, they signify some things which neither are signs nor go with such signs as for instance, 'man', 'animal', 'Socrates', 'Plato', 'whiteness', 'white', 'true', 'good' and the like. Some signify precisely things that are not signs able to stand for other things; some signify such signs and other things as well.

From all this it may be gathered that certain names precisely signify conventional signs, but only as long as they are signs; some signify both natural and conventional signs; some, however, signify only those things which are not such signs, which are parts of propositions; some indifferently signify both things which are not parts of propositions or speech, and also such signs; of this kind are the following names: 'thing', 'being', 'something', 'one' and the like.

'Suppositio' of Terms [in General]

Up to now we have been speaking about the signification of terms. It remains now to discuss *suppositio*, which is a property belonging to a term, but only when used in a proposition.

We have to know first that *suppositio* is taken in two meanings. In a broad sense, it is not contrasted with appellation; appellation is rather a subclass of *suppositio*. In a strict sense, *suppositio* is contrasted with appellation. However, I do not intend to speak about *suppositio* in this sense, but only in the former. Thus, both subject and predicate have *suppositio*. Generally speaking, whatever can be subject or predicate in a proposition has *suppositio*.

'*Suppositio*' means taking the position, as it were, of something else. Thus, if a term stands in a proposition instead of something, in such a way (*a*) that we use the term for the thing, and (*b*) that the term (or its nominative case, if it occurs in an oblique case) is true of the thing (or of a demonstrative pronoun which points to the thing), then we say that the term has *suppositio* for the thing. This is true, at least, when the term with *suppositio* is taken in its significative function. Hence, in general, when a term with *suppositio* is the subject of a proposition, then the thing for which the term has *suppositio,* or a demonstrative pronoun pointing to this, is that of which the proposition denotes that the predicate is predicated. But where the term with *suppositio* is predicate, the thing or pronoun is the one of which the proposition, if formulated, denotes that the subject is a subject. For instance, the proposition 'Man is an animal' denotes that Socrates is truly an animal, so that the proposition 'This is an animal' would be true, if it were formulated while pointing at Socrates. The proposition ' "Man" is a noun', however, denotes that the vocal sound 'man', is a noun. Therefore in this proposition 'man' stands for this vocal sound. Likewise, the proposition 'A white thing is an animal' denotes that this thing which is white is an animal, so that this proposition would be true: 'This'—pointing at that thing which is white—'is an animal'. Hence the subject stands for that thing. Much the same must be said as regards the predicate. For the proposition 'Socrates is white' denotes that Socrates is *that* thing, which has whiteness; and for that reason the predicate stands for *that* thing, which has whiteness. And if no other thing had whiteness but Socrates, then the predicate would stand for Socrates alone.

There is a general rule, namely that in any proposition a term never stands for something of which it is not truly predicated, at least if the term is taken in its significative function. From this it follows that it is false to say, as some ignorant people do, that the concrete term as a predicate stands for a form—for instance to say that in the proposition 'Socrates is white' the term 'white' stands for whiteness. For whichever *suppositio* the terms may have, the proposition 'Whiteness is white' is simply false. Therefore, according to the teaching of Aristotle, a concrete term of this kind never stands for such a form as is signified by the corresponding abstract term. But in regard to other concrete terms of which we have spoken before, this is quite possible. In the same way in this proposition 'A man is God', 'man' truly stands for the Son of God, because He is truly man.

The Division of 'Suppositio'

We have to know that '*suppositio*' is primarily divided into personal, simple and material *suppositio*.

Generally speaking, we have personal *suppositio* when a term stands for the objects it signifies, whether the latter be things outside the mind, or vocal sounds, or mental concepts, or writing, or anything else imaginable. Whenever the subject or the predicate of a proposition stands for the object signified, so that it is taken in its significative function, we always have personal *suppositio*.

An example of the first would be 'Every man is an animal', where 'man' stands for the objects it signifies, since 'man' is a conventional sign meant to signify *these* men and nothing else; for properly speaking it does not signify something common to them, but, as St John Damascene says, these very men themselves. An example of the second would be to say 'Every vocal noun is a part of speech'. In this case 'noun' stands only for vocal signs; therefore its *suppositio* is personal. An example of the third would be to say 'Every species is universal', or 'Every mental content is in the mind'. In either case the subject has personal *suppositio*, since it stands for what it conventionally signifies. An example of the fourth would be to say 'Every written expression is an expression'. Here the subject stands only for the thing it signifies, namely for written signs. Hence it has personal *suppositio*.

From this it is clear that personal *suppositio* is not adequately described by those who say that personal *suppositio* occurs when a term stands for a thing. But the definition is this: 'Personal *suppositio* obtains when a term stands for what it signifies and is used in its significative function'.

Simple *suppositio* is that in which the term stands for a mental content, but is not used in its significative function. For instance 'Man is a species'. The term 'man' stands for a mental content, because this content is the species; nevertheless, properly speaking, the term 'man' does not signify that mental content. Instead, this vocal sign and this mental content are only signs, one subordinate to the other, which signify the same thing, in the manner explained elsewhere. This shows the falsity of the opinion held by those who say (as is commonly accepted) that simple *suppositio* occurs when a term stands for the object it signifies. For simple *suppositio* obtains when a term stands for a mental content, which is not properly speaking the object signified by the term, because the term signifies real things and not mental contents.

Material *suppositio* occurs when a term does not stand for what it signifies, but stands for a vocal or written sign, as ' "Man" is a noun'. Here, 'man' stands for itself; and yet it does not signify itself. Likewise in the proposition ' "Man" is written', we can have material *suppositio,* since the term stands for that which is written.

As the three sorts of *suppositio* apply to a spoken sign, so also they can be applied to a written sign. Hence, if the following four propositions are written, 'Man is an animal', 'Man is a species', ' "Man" is a monosyllabic word', ' "Man" is a written word', each one of these could be true, but each one for a different object. For that which is an animal is by no means a species, nor a monosyllabic word, nor a written word. Likewise, that which is a species is not an animal nor a monosyllabic sign. And so with the others. Yet in the two latter propositions the term has material *suppositio*.

Material *suppositio* could be subdivided according as the subject stands for a spoken sign or for a written sign. If we had terms for them, we could distinguish *suppositiones* for a spoken sign, and for a written sign, just as we distinguish *suppositio* for the object signified and *suppositio* for a mental content, calling one 'personal' and the other 'simple' *suppositio*. However, we have no such names.

As such a difference of *suppositio* can apply to a vocal and written term, so also it can apply to a mental term. For a mental content may stand for that which it signifies, or for itself, or for a spoken or written sign.

It should be noted, however, that personal *suppositio* is not called 'personal' because a term stands for a person, nor is simple *suppositio* so called because a term stands for a simple thing, nor is material *suppositio* so called because a term stands for matter; but only for the reasons mentioned. Therefore the terms 'material', 'personal' and 'simple' are being used in an equivocal meaning in logic and in other sciences. In logic, however, they are not used frequently except in conjunction with the term '*suppositio*'.

What Is Requisite to the Truth of a Singular Proposition?

... Let us first speak of singular propositions of inherence in the present tense [and not determined by a modality], which have both the predicate and the subject in the nominative case, and are not equivalent to a hypothetical proposition. For the truth of such a singular proposition, which is not equivalent to many propositions, it is not required that the subject and the predicate be really the same, nor that the predicate be really in the subject, or really inhere in the subject, nor that it be really united with the subject outside the mind. For instance, for the truth of the proposition 'This is an angel' it is not required that this common term 'angel' be really the same with that which has the position of subject in this proposition, or that it be really in it, or anything of the sort; but it is sufficient and necessary that subject and predicate should stand for the same thing. If, therefore, in the proposition 'This is an angel' subject and predicate stand for the same thing, the proposition is true. Hence it is not denoted, by this proposition, that this [individual] has 'angelity', or that 'angelity' is in him, or something of that kind, but it is denoted that this [individual] is truly an angel. Not indeed that he is this predicate ['angel'], but that he is that for which the predicate stands. In like manner also the propositions 'Socrates is a man', 'Socrates is an animal', do not denote that Socrates has humanity or animality, nor that humanity or animality is in Socrates, nor that man or animal is in Socrates, nor that man or animal belongs to the essence or quiddity of Socrates or to the quidditative concept of Socrates. They rather denote that Socrates is truly a man and that he is truly an animal; not that Socrates is the predicate 'man' or the predicate 'animal', but that he is something that the predicate 'man' and the predicate 'animal' stand for or represent; for each of these predicates stands for Socrates.

From this it becomes clear that all the following propositions are false in their literal meaning: 'Man belongs to the quiddity of Socrates', 'Man is of the essence of Socrates', 'Humanity is in Socrates', 'Socrates has humanity', 'Socrates is a man by his humanity', and many such propositions, which almost everyone concedes. The falsity of such propositions is clear; I take one of them, viz. 'Humanity is in Socrates', and I ask: For what does 'humanity' stand? Either for a thing, or for a mental content; that is, such a proposition denotes either that a real thing outside the mind is in Socrates, or that a mental content is in Socrates. If 'humanity' stands for a thing, then I ask, For which thing? Either for Socrates, or for a part of Socrates, or for a thing that is neither Socrates nor a part of Socrates. If it stands for Socrates, then the proposition is false. For no thing that is Socrates is in Socrates, because Socrates is not in Socrates, although Socrates is Socrates. And likewise humanity is not in Socrates, but is Socrates, if 'humanity' stands for a thing that is Socrates. If, however, 'humanity' stands for a thing that is part of Socrates, then, again, the proposition is false, because every thing which is part of Socrates is either matter, or form, or a composite of matter and form (only one human substantial form, not any other such form, is in question), or else an integral part of Socrates. But none of these parts is humanity, as can be shown case by case. For the intellective soul is not humanity; because then true humanity would have remained in Christ during the three days after his death, and consequently humanity would have been truly united with the divine Word during this time, and therefore the Word would then have been truly a man, which is false. Likewise, matter is not humanity, nor is the body of Socrates humanity, nor the foot nor the head, nor any of the other parts of Socrates, because no part of Socrates is humanity, but only a part of humanity. Consequently, 'humanity' cannot stand for a part of Socrates. If, however, it stands for a thing which is neither Socrates nor a part of Socrates, such a thing is only an accident or some other thing which is not Socrates; and therefore 'humanity' in this case would stand for an accident or for some other thing which is neither Socrates nor a part of Socrates. This is manifestly false. If, however, 'humanity' stands for a content of the mind, then also our proposition is manifestly false, since a content of the mind is not Socrates. It is clear then that the proposition 'Humanity is in Socrates' is utterly false.

COMMENTARY ON THE SENTENCES

Book I (*Ordinatio*), Distinction II

QUESTION 4

Concerning the identity and distinction of God and creatures, it should be asked: *Whether there is anything common to God and creature which is univocally and essentially predicable of each?* Because this question and much that has been said and should be said in the following questions depends on the knowledge of the nature of the univocal and universal, to make what has and will be said evident, I first ask certain questions concerning the nature of the universal and the univocal. Concerning which I first ask, whether that which is immediately and proximately denominated by a universal and univocal intention is any true thing outside the mind, intrinsic and essential to those to which it is common and univocal, and really distinct from them.

First, there is a true thing essential and intrinsic to those to which it is common, since according to the Commentator, Book V of the *Metaphysics,* comment 7, these two men, namely, universal and particular, to which univocation befalls, are essentially one. But that which is essentially one with some real being outside the soul is a true thing and essential to some thing. Therefore, universal man is a true thing outside the soul and is essential to those to which it is common. Secondly, that it is a real and distinct thing seems to be so in that it is impossible for the same thing to be corruptible and incorruptible. But universals are incorruptible, and those to which they are common are corruptible. Therefore, they are not the same thing as singulars.

For the opposite: The Commentator, Book XII of the *Metaphysics,* comment 22: One and being are from universal things which do not have being outside the soul. Thus, according to him, universals do not have being outside the soul.

Translated by James J. Walsh for this volume from Guillelmus De Occam, O.F.M., *Super 4 Libros Sententiarum,* Vol. III, *Opera Plurima,* Lyon, 1494–1496, *Réimpression en fac-similé,* London: The Gregg Press Limited, 1962.

But nothing which does not have being outside the soul is really the same as a being outside the soul. Therefore, etc.

On this question there is an opinion that any univocal universal is a certain thing really existing outside the soul in some singular, and that the essence of any singular is really distinct from the singular and from any other universal. So the universal man is a true thing outside the soul, really existing in any man and really distinguished from any man and from the universal animal and the universal substance, and thus for every genus and species whether subalternate or not. And so, according to this opinion, as many universals as there are predicable intrinsically, essentially, and primarily of any singular, there are that many universals really distinct within it, of which each is really distinct from the others and from that singular. And all these things which are in any individual of the same species are in no way multiplied as the singulars are multiplied.

There are several arguments for this opinion. The first is that definition is primarily of substance and secondarily of accidents, according to the Philosopher in Book VII of the *Metaphysics*. But according to that same (text), definition is not primarily of singular substance. Therefore it is another substance than the singular which is primarily definable. But that is not separate from singulars, since such is not definable, according to the Philosopher in the same place. Therefore it is of the essence of the singular. This I confirm in that something in the genus of substance is definable according to everyone. But an individual is not definable. . . .

This opinion is simply false and absurd. I first argue against it thus: No thing which is one in number, not varied nor multiplied, is in many supposita or singulars, nor in whatever individuals are created at once. But such a thing if posited would be one in number; therefore it would not be in many singulars nor belong to their essence. The major is manifest in that it is proper to the divine essence alone that without any division and multiplication it is in many really distinct supposita. . . .

A third argument is this: an individual of any species can be created afresh, however much other previously created or produced individuals of the same species persist. But creation is absolutely from nothing, so that nothing essential or intrinsic to the thing precedes it in real being. Therefore, no non-varied thing pre-existing in any individual belongs to the essence of this freshly created individual, since if anything essential to this thing preceded it, then it would not be created. Therefore, there is no universal thing belonging to the essence of these individuals, since if there were, it would exist prior to every individual after the first one produced. In consequence, all produced after the first would not be created, since they would not be from nothing. Besides, every singular thing can be annihilated without the annihilation or destruction of another singular thing on which it in no way depends. Therefore, this man can be annihilated by God without any other man being annihilated or destroyed. But in annihilation what is intrinsic to the thing remains neither in itself nor in anything else in real being. Therefore, there is no such thing common to each, since then that would be annihilated; and consequently, no other man would remain in accordance with his essence. . . .

Hence, I reply otherwise to the question, that no thing really distinct from singular things and intrinsic to them is universal or common to them. For such a thing should not be posited except to preserve the essential predication of one of another, or else to preserve the science and the definitions of things, which everyone arguing for the opinion of Plato puts forward. But the first is not valid, in that what is there posited as intrinsic to and really distinct from the singular thing would have to be a part of the thing. But a part cannot be predicated essentially of a thing, just as neither matter nor form is predicated essentially of the composite. Therefore, if it is predicated essentially of a thing it must not supposit for itself, but for the singular thing. But such supposition can be preserved by maintaining that the something predicated is neither the entire thing nor a part of the thing. Therefore, in order to preserve such predication one does not have to posit that what is predicated in some other thing which still is intrinsic to the thing. For example, this proposition "Man is animal," or "Socrates is animal," is essential, intrinsic in the primary way, and generic. This can just as well be preserved by maintaining that the predicate is in reality neither the subject nor a part of the subject, as by maintaining that the predicate is an essential part of the subject. For if it is maintained that the predicate is an essential part of the subject, I ask what is denoted through the affirmation. It is either that the subject is essentially that predicate; and this is impossible, since a whole is never essentially nor really its part. Or else it is denoted that that which is truly man is something which is truly animal—that is to say, that that for which "man" supposits is the same as that for which "animal" supposits. Whatever predicate it is that supposits, it is not that for which it supposits in that proposition. But this all can just as well be preserved by maintaining that the predicate is not the subject nor part of it, as by maintaining that it is a part of it, since it is just as possible for something extrinsic to a thing to supposit for it as for a part of it to supposit for it. Therefore, in order to preserve this predication one does not have to maintain that a predicable common to anything is intrinsic to it.

This is confirmed in that in this proposition, "Man is animal," either the terms supposit for themselves, or not. If so, then the proposition would be false, since these terms are distinct, and one is not the other. This is both according to the opinion given above and according to the truth. If they do not supposit for themselves, then for something other than themselves; and so it is suitable for something extrinsic to supposit for what is other than itself, just as what is intrinsic. Therefore, etc. . . .

I reply to the first argument for the other opinion, in which it is assumed that definition is primarily of substance: I say that for a definition to be primarily of something can be understood in two ways. One concerns that of which the definition is primarily and adequately predicated, so that the definition and what is defined are convertible; and in this way, definition is not primarily of substance, since a definition is primarily and adequately predicated of no substance. But in this way, definition is primarily of some universal term convertible with the definition, however much the term is not in reality that definition. . . . For a definition to be primarily of something can be understood otherwise, namely, that the something is that whose parts are primarily expressed through such a definition. And this can be understood in two ways. . . . If in the first way, I still say that definition is primarily of nothing, since nothing is primarily definable, since the parts of nothing require to be expressed, except the parts of some singular. And the parts of one singular are no more primarily expressed through a definition than are those of another. In the second way, I say that definition is primarily of substance, since the parts of substance are primarily expressed through definition.

When it is urged that definition is not primarily of singular substance, I reply that this is true in the first way, since a definition is primarily or adequately predicated of no singular substance. Still, in this last way I say that definition is primarily of singular substance, since its parts are primarily expressed through definition, and such a definition is not predicated intrinsically of any other suppositum. For example, this is a definition: "rational animal." This definition is primarily of this term "man," since it is primarily and adequately predicated of this term. For it is predicated of nothing except of what this term "man" is predicated. And of everything of which this term "man" is predicated when it has personal supposition, this definition is truly predicated if it has personal supposition, and hence this definition and what is defined are convertible. For this is to be convertible with something: that of whatever the one is predicated, the rest is also, and vice versa, if they have personal supposition. . . . So, therefore, this definition "rational animal" is primarily of this term "man," but its parts are not expressed through the definition. In a second way, this definition is primarily of nothing, since the only parts expressed through this definition are the parts of Socrates and Plato; for just as nothing is a rational animal except Socrates or Plato, and so for other singulars, so the parts of nothing else are expressed through this definition. And yet the parts of Socrates are no more expressed than those of Plato, nor vice versa. Therefore the parts of nothing are primarily expressed in such a way, namely, that the parts of something are more primarily expressed than the parts of anything else. In a third way, the parts of Socrates are primarily expressed through this definition, and likewise the parts of Plato, since the parts of no other are more primarily expressed. And hence in understanding what is thus first defined, I say that Socrates is first defined, and likewise Plato, and so for any man, since this definition is truly predicated of any such. Nor is it truly predicated of anything else suppositing for itself, but of those which supposit for singular men. Whence, if in this proposition, "Man is the rational animal," "man" should supposit for anything else than for a singular man, this would be simply false. And nothing imaginable is a rational animal unless it is this man or that, and so for other singulars. And consequently, by the same argument, the real parts of this man and that and so for other singulars. . . .

To the second principal argument I reply that real science is not always of things, as of those which are immediately known, but it is of others suppositing for things. For the understanding of this, and much said previously and yet to be said, and for the sake of some who are unskilled in logic, it should be known that any science, whether real or rational, is of propositions as what is known, since only propositions are known. But according to Boethius on the First of the *Perihermenias,* a proposition has a threefold being, namely mental, vocal, and written. That is to say, some propositions are merely conceived and understood, some are uttered, and some are written; and if there were other signs instituted for signifying as sounds and letters are, propositions would be in them as in these. And so, just as an uttered proposition is truly composed of sounds and a written, of script, so a proposition merely conceived is composed merely of understandings or concepts or intentions of the soul. And moreover, just as every sound can be a part of a vocal proposition, so every understanding can be a part of a mental proposition, according to one opinion—or every concept, according to another opinion. But a sound which is a part of an uttered proposition can have multiple supposition, namely material and personal and simple. This is obvious in those propositions which are uttered and are heard with the ears, for instance, " 'Man' is a two-syllable sound," in which that sound is taken materially, since there that sound, according to which the proposition is true, stands and supposits for itself. Likewise, "Man runs." There it stands personally, since it supposits for men themselves, not for a sound, since a sound cannot run. But in this one, "Man is a species," the sound has simple supposition for something common. The same holds for a similar proposition in the mind, setting aside any sound; since if it belongs to no language at all (as Augustine says in Book III of the *De Trinitate* that there is a certain word which belongs to no language), insofar as it is a part of such a proposition, it can have personal supposition. And then it stands and supposits for the things signified, if it should signify things. Or else it can have simple supposition, and then it stands and supposits for itself. Through this argument I say that this uttered proposition "Every man is capable of laughing," is known—for as it is true, so it is truly known, since everything that is true can be known. And no one but a madman can deny that some uttered propositions are true and some false; for who would say that he had never heard a lie with his own bodily ears? Nothing can be heard with the ears except sound, just as nothing can be seen with the bodily eyes except color or light. Therefore, some propositions composed precisely of sounds are true, such as these: "Every man is an animal," "Every man is capable of laughing," "A species is predicated of many differing in number in what is intrinsic," "A genus is predicated of many differing in species," and so for others which can be known. But now, the science of some such uttered propositions is real, and (that of) some is rational; and still, what are known and all their parts are truly sounds, since when the parts of some supposit and stand, not for the sounds themselves, but for external things, for example, for a subject, then the science of those propositions is called real. But other parts of other propositions stand for concepts of the mind. Hence the science of those can be called rational or logical. And the science of these uttered propositions, " 'Man' is a two-syllable word," " 'Animal' is a three-syllable word," can be called grammatical. And still all such propositions and their parts are vocal, and are only said to pertain to diverse sciences because the parts of the said propositions have diverse suppositio1s, in that some supposit for things, some for concepts in the mind, and some for sounds. Therefore it is the same proportionally for propositions in the mind, which can truly be known by us in our present condition, since all the terms of those propositions are concepts and are not external substance itself. For the terms of some propositions stand and supposit personally, that is, for external things, as in such propositions as these: "Any moveable is partly in the limit from which, etc.," "Any man is capable of laughing," or "Any triangle has three, etc.," and so for others. Hence, real science is said to be of such propositions. But the terms of other propositions have simple supposition, namely, for concepts themselves, as in these: "Any demonstration is from true first principles, etc.," "Man is a species," and so for others. Hence the science of such is said to be rational. Therefore, it does not pertain to real science that the terms known are things outside the soul or that they are in the soul, as long as they stand and supposit for external things. And so it is not necessary because of real science to posit such universal things really distinct from singular things.

Through this, I say to the form of the argument that for science to be of things can be understood in three ways. One is that the thing itself is known, and in this way no science is of substantial things, mostly because nothing is known except complexes. But a complex is not outside the soul, unless perhaps in a sound or similar sign. Another way is that things are parts of that which is known, and in this way it is not necessary for real science to be of external things. The third way is that things are that for which the parts known supposit; and in this way real science is of things, but not of universal things, since supposition is not made for them. For in this proposition in the mind, "Every body is composed of matter and a singular form," no supposition is made for any universal body, since no such body exists; and even if it did, it would not be composed of matter and a singular form. But science in this way is of singular things, since the terms supposit for singulars themselves. And it is not in this way that the Philosopher denied that science is of singulars, but in the second way, since the terms of propositions known are not singular things, but they are universals. And science is of them in the second way, in that universals are the terms of the propositions known. And if science is sometimes found to be of universal things, one ought to understand that it is of universals predicable of things. Briefly, therefore, for the intention of the Philosopher it should be known that real science is not distinguished from rational science in that real science is of things in such a way that those very things are the propositions known or parts of those propositions known, and that rational science is not of things in this way. But rather, they are distinguished in that the parts, that is the terms, of the propositions known in real science stand and supposit for things. But the terms of propositions known in rational science are not so; those terms stand and supposit for something else.

And what if, with regard to this and other things previously said, the question is raised that this is true: "Someone promises to another that he will give some horse to him," and then it is asked whether he promises to give to the other some singular thing, or a universal, or a concept? It is not a singular thing, since it is no more one thing than another; and so he promises no horse, and can fulfill the promise in giving no horse. Or else he promises any horse without distinction, and thus he can only fulfill the promise in giving any horse without distinction. If he promises a universal thing, the position is gained. If a concept, this is not true, since he promises a true thing. Likewise, he would then fulfill the promise, not in giving some real horse, but only some concept.

This cavil would not be offered here, except that some thinking themselves to know logic ponder such juvenile matters, because of which they maintain many absurdities concerning the supposition of terms. But to treat this would be much too prolix and tedious. Hence I dismiss it; and I say that he promises a true singular thing, since in this proposition, "He promises a horse to the other," the "horse" supposits personally for singular horses. Whence he would never fulfill the promise if he gave something universal, but only if he gave some particular horse. Whence, just as one who in saying "I promise you a particular horse" promises a singular, so does one in saying "I promise you a horse." And when it is said that he no more promises one singular thing than another, and therefore he promises none at all or any without distinction, that does not follow; but it is a fallacy of the figure of speech, changing one mode of supposition into another. This is just as if one should argue, "Every man is a singular man, but no more one singular man than another; therefore, every man is any singular man without distinction or else none at all," since in the first, "singular man" has merely confused supposition, and in the second, it has confused and distributive supposition. So it is in what is proposed. In this proposition "I promise you a horse," the "horse" has merely confused supposition, or some such, since it does not have confused and distributive supposition; and any singular without distinction is inferred under the disjunction, so that the consequence is of a disjoined predicate, and not a disjunctive proposition. For this follows validly: "I promise you a horse, therefore I promise you this horse or that one, and so for all present and future." But a disjunctive does not follow, for this does not follow: "I promise you a horse, therefore, I promise you this horse or I promise you that horse, and so for others." Just so, this follows validly: "Every man is an animal, therefore every man is this animal or that animal and so for each"; but the disjunctive does not follow: "Every man is an animal, therefore every man is this animal, or every man is that animal, and so for many other such." For often the term predicated has merely confused supposition, or something similar so far as predicates are concerned, with a distributive sign preceeding. But whether from the force of the term it has merely confused supposition or not, I do not for the present care. And hence these points are omitted, since they pertain to logicians. But ignorance of them makes many difficulties, both in theology and in other real sciences, which difficulties would be truly easy if these and other juvenile matters were perfectly known.

⌃ • •

QUESTION 6

On the same subject, I ask thirdly, *whether anything exists in reality outside the soul which is universal and univocal, and distinct from an individual by the nature of the thing, although not really distinct.* It seems that this is so, since the nature of man is "this," and yet it is not of itself "this," since then it could not have existence in another. Therefore it is "this" through something added to it, and yet not through what is really distinct, since by the same argument the nature of whiteness would be "this" through something added and really distinct, and then this whiteness would be really composite, which seems false. Therefore a nature is "this" through something added which is formally distinct. For the opposite: no nature which is really individual is really universal. Therefore, if this nature is really this individual, it is not really universal.

In reply to this question, it is said that in reality outside the soul there is the nature really the same with but formally distinct from a differentia contracting to a determinate individual, which nature of itself is neither universal nor particular, but is incompletely universal in the thing and completely so according to its being in the intellect. And since this opinion is, as I believe, the opinion of the Subtle Doctor, who excelled others in the subtlety of his judgment, I wish to recite here in one place and without changing his words what he maintained scattered about in various places. And it is the position of this doctor that outside of numerical unity there is a real unity less than numerical unity, which belongs to that nature which in some way is universal. And hence the contractible nature can first be compared to a singular. Secondly, it can be compared to numerical unity. Thirdly, it can be compared to universal being. Fourthly, to a unity less than numerical unity. If it is compared to a singular, this opinion holds first that a nature is not of itself "this," but through something added. And second, it holds that what is added is not negation (Book II, dist. iii, q. 2), nor any accident (q. 4), nor accidental existence (q. 3), nor matter (q. 5). Third, that what is added belongs to the genus of substance and is intrinsic to an individual. Fourth, that the nature is naturally prior to that which contracts. Whence he says that every entity whether whole or part of some genus is of itself indifferent to this entity or that one, so that as a quidditative entity it is naturally prior to that entity as it is "this." And as it is naturally prior, just as it does not belong to it from itself that it is "this," so the opposite is not repugnant to it from its own character. And just as a composite does not include that entity which is this composite, so matter just as matter does not include that entity which is this matter, and the same for form. This entity is thus not matter nor form nor the composite insofar as any of these is the nature; but it is the ultimate reality of the being which is matter, and the being which is form, and the being which is the composite, such that anything common is yet determinable. To this degree, however much a thing is one, it can be distinguished into several formally distinct realities, of which this is formally not that, and this is formally the singular entity and that is formally the entity of a common nature. . . .

Against this opinion there is a two-fold argument. First, that it is impossible for creatures to differ formally unless they are really distinguished. Therefore, if the nature is distinguished in some way from that contracting difference, it is necessary that they be distinguished as thing and thing, or as conceptual being and conceptual being, or as real and conceptual being. But the first is denied by him and likewise the second. Therefore, it is necessary that the third be adopted. Therefore, whatever way the nature is distinguished from an individual, it is only a conceptual being. The antecedent is obvious, since if the nature and that contracting difference are not the same in all ways, then something can truly be affirmed of one and denied of the rest; but the same cannot truly be affirmed and truly denied of the same thing among creatures. Therefore, they are not one thing. The minor is obvious, since if that were so, every way for proving a distinction of things among creatures would perish, since contradiction is the most effective way for proving the distinction of things. . . . This is confirmed, since all contradictories have equal repugnance, but such is the repugnance between being and not being that if A exists and B does not, it follows that B is not A. Therefore, such is the case for any contradictories whatever. If it is said that this is true for primary contradictories, since it is through them that one proves real non-identity, but not through other contradictories, the reply is that the syllogistic form holds equally well in every matter. Therefore, this is a good syllogism: "Every A is B. C is not B. Therefore, C is not A." And consequently, the following is true for A and not-A: if this is A and this is not-A, this is not this, just as if this exists and this does not, then this is not this. Therefore, it is likewise in what is proposed. If every individual difference is of itself proper to some individual, and a nature is not of itself proper to any individual, it follows that the nature is not the individual difference and "this" in reality. . . .

Hence I reply otherwise to the question, and first I set forth the conclusion that any singular thing is in itself singular. And I offer this persuasion: singularity immediately belongs to that which has it. Therefore, it cannot belong to that through something else. Therefore, if anything is singular, it is singular in itself.

Besides, just as that which is singular is disposed to singular being, so that which is universal is disposed to universal being. Therefore, just as that which is singular cannot be made universal or common through something added to it, so that which is common cannot be made singular by something added to it. Therefore, whatever is singular through nothing added, is singular in itself.

The second conclusion is that every thing outside the soul is really singular, and one in number, since every thing outside the soul either is simple or composite. If it is simple, it does not include many things; but every thing not including many things is one in number, for every such thing and another similar thing are precisely two things. Therefore, each of them is one in number. Therefore, every simple thing is one in number. If the thing is composite, it is still necessary to arrive at a certain number of parts, and consequently the whole composed from them will be one in number, or else it will be one aggregatively. . . .

From these it follows that any thing whatever outside the soul is singular in itself, so that without any addition it is that which is immediately denominated by a singular intention. Nor are there any possibles whatever on the part of the thing distinct in any way at all, of which one is more indifferent than the rest, or of which one is more one in number than the rest, unless perchance one is more perfect than another, as this angel is more perfect than this ass. And thus anything at all outside the soul will be "this" in itself, nor should any cause of individuation be sought, unless perhaps the extrinsic and intrinsic causes when an individual is composed; but the cause more to be sought is how it is possible for something to be common and universal.

I reply, therefore, to the form of the question, that that which is universal and univocal is not anything in reality on the part of the thing, formally distinct from the individual.

· · ·

Book II (*Reportatio*)

QUESTION 15 *Whether a Higher Angel Knows Through Fewer Species than a Lower?*

The affirmative is proved, since according to the Philosopher in the *De Caelo et Mundo,* the more perfect a nature is, the fewer means it requires for its operation. therefore, etc. For the opposite: things distinctly known require distinct reasons for knowing; for anything at all, therefore, the superior requires just as many reasons as the inferior.

TO THE QUESTIONS

Here I first suppose that a species is that which goes before the act of knowing and can persist before and after knowing, even with the thing absent. And consequently, it is distinguished from a habit, since a habit of the intellect follows the act of knowing; but a species precedes the act as well as the habit.

Translated by James J. Walsh for this volume from the text established by Philotheus Böhner, O.F.M., in "The Notitia Intuitiva of Non-Existents According to William of Ockham," *Traditio,* I (1943), 223–275.

THE COMMON OPINION ON THE FIRST QUESTION

On this assumption, and extending the first Question to our intellect as well as the angelic, there is an opinion which maintains that it is necessary to posit a species impressed on the intellect in order that it should know. . . .

THE OPINION OF ST. THOMAS ON THE SECOND QUESTION

As to the second Question it is proved that the superior angel knows through fewer and more universal species than the inferior, since God, who is at the limit of intelligences, knows everything through one, that is, through his essence, and every intellectual nature outside of God knows what is diverse through what is diverse. But the closer a nature is to God in perfection, the fewer it requires for knowing. But the nature of a superior angel is closer to God than that of an inferior. Therefore, etc. . . .

The Subtle Doctor holds this opinion regarding the first conclusion, and he proves it through different arguments. Look in John (Duns Scotus). But he does not hold the second conclusion.

As far as the first part of this opinion goes, it cannot evidently be disproved through natural reasons, and yet it seems to me that the opposite part is more probable; and this is because plurality should not be posited without necessity. But everything which is preserved with a species can be preserved without a species. Therefore, there is no necessity for positing it.

CONCERNING INTUITIVE AND ABSTRACTIVE COGNITION

Hence, concerning this question, I first offer certain distinctions. One is that some cognition is intuitive, and some, abstractive. The intuitive is that by means of which a thing is known to exist when it exists and not to exist when it does not exist. For when I perfectly apprehend any extremes intuitively, I can at once form the complex, that those extremes are united or are not united, and assent or dissent. For instance, if I should intuitively see a body and whiteness, the intellect can at once form this complex: "The body is white," or, "The body is not white"; and, these complexes having been formed, the intellect at once assents. And this is by virtue of the intuitive cognition which it has of the extremes, just as, having apprehended the terms of some principle, for instance, "Every whole, etc.," and the complex having been formed through the apprehensive intellect, at once the intellect assents by virtue of the apprehension of the terms.

But it should be known that although, given intuitive cognition through the senses as well as the intellect with respect to some incomplexes, the intellect can form a complex from those incomplexes intuitively known in the aforesaid way, and assent to such a complex, still, neither the formation of the complex nor the act of assenting to the complex is intuitive cognition. For each of these is complex cognition, and intuitive cognition is incomplex. And if these two, "abstractive" and "intuitive," were to divide all cognition, complex as well as incomplex, then these cognitions would be called abstractive cognitions, as would every complex cognition, whether in the presence of the thing, with intuitive cognition of the extremes given, or in the absence of the thing, and intuitive cognition not given. And then according to this it could be conceded that intuitive cognition, through the intellect as well as the senses, is a partial cause of abstractive cognition, which is had in the aforesaid way. And this is because every effect sufficiently depends on its essential causes which, when posited, the effect can be posited, and when they are not posited, it cannot be naturally posited; and it depends on no other, as is frequently said. But the cognition by which I evidently assent to this complex: "This body is white," whose extremes I know intuitively, cannot naturally exist unless each cognition is given, since if the thing is absent and the intuitive cognition is corrupted, the intellect does not evidently assent that the body which it previously saw is white, since it does not know whether it is or not. But with respect to apprehensive cognition, through which I form a complex, it is not intuitive cognition, with neither a sensitive nor an intellective partial cause. For any complex which can be formed with them can be formed without them—in absence as well as presence. So, therefore, it is obvious that through intuitive cognition we judge a thing to exist when it exists, and this generally, whether the intuitive cognition is naturally caused or supernaturally, by God alone. For if it is naturally caused, then it cannot be unless the object exists and is present in the required proximity, since there can be such a distance between the object and the power that the power cannot naturally intuit such an object. And when the object is thus present and in proximity in such a way, the intellect through the act of assenting can judge that the thing exists, in the aforesaid way. But if it is supernatural, for instance, if God should cause in me the intuitive cognition of some object existing at Rome, immediately upon the possession of the intuitive cognition of it I can judge that that which I intuit and see exists, just as well as if that cognition were had naturally.

If you say that the object is not present in this way, nor in the required proximity, I reply that although intuitive cognition cannot be naturally caused except when the object is present in the required proximity, still, it could be supernaturally. And hence the differences which John (Duns Scotus) gives between intuitive and abstractive cognition—that intuitive cognition is of what is present and existent as it is present and existent—are understood of intuitive cognition naturally caused, but not when it is supernaturally caused. Whence, speaking absolutely, no other presence is necessarily required for intuitive cognition than that which can terminate the intuitive act. And it is consistent with this that the object should be nothing, or that it should be distant by the greatest distance; and however far away the intuitively known object may be, I can by virtue of it judge at once that it exists, if it is in the aforesaid way. But still, since intuitive cognition is not naturally caused nor conserved unless the object is in the required way existing in proximity at a certain distance, I cannot judge that which is naturally intuitively known unless the object is present. In the same way, I can judge through intuitive cognition that a thing does not exist when it does not. But this cognition cannot be natural, since such cognition never is nor is conserved naturally unless with the object present and existent. And hence this natural intuitive cognition is also corrupted through the absence of the object; and on the assumption that it persists after the destruction of the object, then it is supernatural with regard to conservation, although not with regard to causation. And hence, etc. Moreover, it is necessary that the intuitive cognition by which I know that a thing does not exist when it does not, should be supernatural with regard to causation or conservation or both. For instance, if God should cause in me the intuitive cognition of some non-existent object and should conserve that cognition in me, by means of that cognition I can judge that the thing does not exist, since I see that thing intuitively; and having formed this complex: "This object does not exist," the intellect at once assents to this complex and dissents from its opposite by virtue of the intuitive cognition, so that the intuitive cognition is the partial cause of that assent, as was said before about natural intuition. And so, consequently, the intellect assents that that which I intuit is a pure nothing with regard to supernatural conservation, and not causation. The case is this: if at first the intuitive cognition of some object is caused naturally, and after the destruction of the object God conserves the previously caused intuitive cognition, then it is natural cognition with regard to causation, and supernatural with regard to conservation. Then the same should be said here for all, just as if that cognition were supernaturally caused, since through it I can judge that a thing exists when it does, no matter how far away the object known may be, and that it does not exist when it does not, given that the object is destroyed. And so in a certain way it can be conceded that through natural intuitive cognition I judge that a thing does not exist when it does not, since it is through cognition naturally caused although supernaturally conserved. So, therefore, it is obvious that intuitive cognition is that through which I know that a thing exists when it does and that it does not when it does not.

But we do not judge through abstractive cognition that a thing exists when it does and that it does not when it does not, whether natural or supernatural. . . .

CONCERNING THE REASON FOR KNOWING

Another distinction concerns the reason for knowing, which in one way is taken for all that which goes before the act of knowing; and so any partial cause of knowledge, the intellect as well as the object, and even God, is called the reason for knowing. In another way it is taken as what is distinguished from the possible intellect, so that it is the efficient cause of knowing; and thus knowledge of a principle is the reason for knowing a conclusion. In a third way it is taken as distinguished from the agent and possible intellect, which is still necessarily required for knowing, just as much as a principle.

CONCLUSIONS

These having been seen, I prove some conclusions.

FIRST CONCLUSION

The first is that for having intuitive cognition it is not neceessary to posit anything outside the intellect and the thing known, and most of all, no species. This is proved, since it is in vain to do through many what can equally well be done through fewer; but intuitive cognition can be accomplished through the intellect and the thing seen, without any species. Therefore, etc. The assumption is proved, since given a sufficient agent and patient in proximity, the effect can be posited without anything else; but the agent intellect with the object are sufficient agents with respect to the cognition of it; and the possible intellect is a sufficient patient. Therefore, etc.

Again: Nothing should be posited as naturally necessarily required for some effect unless certain experience or a certain argument from what is self-evident leads to that; but neither of these leads to the positing of a species. Therefore, etc. The assumption is proved: Experience does not lead to that, because it includes intuitive knowledge, so that if one experienced some thing to be white, he would see whiteness to be in it. But no one sees a species intuitively. Therefore, experience does not lead to that.

If you say that in sensitive powers other than sight, interior as well as exterior, there is experiential cognition but not intuitive, I reply that in any sense at all which has some cognition by virtue of which it can know that a thing exists when it does and does not when it does not, there is intuitive as well as experiential cognition, since intuitive cognition is that through which I know that a thing exists or does not exist. And hence I concede that in every sense, interior as well as exterior, there is intuitive cognition, that is, cognition such that by virtue of it one can in the aforesaid way know that a thing exists or does not, even though it is not visual intuitive cognition. And in this many are deceived, for they believe that there is only visual intuitive cognition, which is false. Nor does any argument from what is self-evident lead to that, since no argument can prove that a species is required unless because it has efficent causality. For every effect sufficiently depends on its essential causes, according to John (Duns Scotus). But that anything created is an efficient cause cannot be proved demonstratively, but only through experience, that is, through the fact that in its presence the effect follows, and in its absence, not. But now, without any species, on the presence of the object with the intellect, there follows the act of knowing, just as well as with the species. Therefore, etc.

Again: If a species were posited as necessarily required for intuitive cognition, as the efficient cause of it, then, since the species could be preserved in the absence of the object, it could naturally cause intuitive cognition in the absence of the thing, which is false and against experience.

SECOND CONCLUSION

The second conclusion is that in order to have abstractive cognition it is necessary to posit something previous outside of the object and the intellect. This is proved:

For every power which can now perform some act which previously it could not, with the object and the power persisting equally now as before, has now something which it did not have before. But the intellect having intuitive knowledge can perform abstractive cognition, and not having it, cannot—and this with the object persisting in itself after the intuitive knowledge as well as before. Therefore, something is left in the intellect by reason of which it can perform abstractive cognition and could not before. Thus outside of the object and the power it is necessary to posit something else in order to have abstractive cognition. . . .

THIRD CONCLUSION

The third conclusion is that what is left is not a species, but a habit. This is proved:

For that which remains from acts, follows the act; but a species does not follow, it rather precedes. Therefore, etc.

Again: When something is in an accidental power with respect to cognition, it is not necessary to posit another than that through which it is in the accidental power for eliciting the act. But given a habit in the intellect, inclining toward some cognition, the intellect is in the accidental power. Thus it is not necessary to posit anything else in the intellect outside of the habit. The assumption is obvious according to the Philosopher in Book Three of the *De Anima*, where he says that for the intellect to be in a power is different before learning or discovering from after, since before, it is in the essential power, and after, when through some act some habit is left, it is in the accidental power to a similar act. Thus, through the habit generated from an act, the intellect is in the accidental power. Whence only after the act of knowing does one experience himself as being in an accidental power with regard to cognition. For were a thousand species posited previous to the act of intellect, if the intellect had no act, it would no more experience itself as being in the accidental power than if there were no species there, and if not a single species were posited in the intellect. And yet, if the act of knowing is given, the intellect at once experiences itself as being in the accidental power with respect to a further cognition. And this can only be through a habit left in the intellect from the first act.

Again: Everything which can be preserved through a species can be preserved through a habit; therefore, a habit is required and a species is superfluous.

But it is obvious that a habit is necessarily required for knowing some object. For were it not required, and a species should suffice, then, if the species were corrupted after many acts of knowledge, I could not know the object whose species it is, any more than I could before any act of knowledge at all. For a habit is not posited and the species is corrupted. This conclusion seems absurd.

If you say that the species is strengthened through many cognitions, the reply is that then through such strengthening of the species the intellect is always more inclined to knowing; and consequently, the habit, which is posited by everyone, would be superfluous. And so, either the species or the habit is posited superfluously. Therefore, since the habit, and not the species, is posited by everyone, it seems that the species is superfluous.

Again: The species is only posited because of assimilation, or the causation of the act of knowledge, or the representation of the object, or the determination of the power, or the union of the mover and the moved. The species is posited most of all because of these; but it is not necessary to posit it because of any of these. Therefore, it should not be posited.

Not because of assimilation: Because that assimilation is either in the intellectual essence and nature through which the object known is assimilated, or else it is the assimilation of effect to cause. Not the first way, since if the intellect should know a substance, it would be more assimilated to the object in its own nature, which is substance, than through a species, which is an accident. For an accident is less assimilated to a substance than is a substance to a substance. Nor in the second way, since the assimilation of patient to agent is through the fact that it receives some effect caused by the agent; but in this way the intellect is sufficiently assimilated through the act of knowledge caused by the object and received in the intellect. Therefore, a species is not required. . . .

Nor ought a species be posited because of representation, since in intuitive knowledge nothing representative is required other than the object and the act, as is obvious above. And therefore neither is anything other than the object and the act required in abstractive, which immediately follows intuitive. The consequence is obvious, since just as the object sufficiently represents itself in the one cognition, so in the other which immediately follows intuitive.

Again: What is represented has to be previously known; otherwise, what represents would never lead to the cognition of what is represented as in a likeness. For example, a statue of Hercules would never lead me to the cognition of Hercules unless I had previously seen Hercules, nor could I otherwise know whether the statue is like him or not. But according to those positing a species, it is something previous to any act of knowing the object. Therefore, it cannot be posited because of the representation of the object. . . .

Nor ought a species be posited because of the causation of the act of knowledge. According to them, the corporeal and material cannot act on the spiritual; hence it is necessary to posit such a species in the intellect. But against this: Just as what is corporeal and material cannot be an immediate partial cause with respect to the act of knowing, which is received in what is spiritual—since it is in the possible intellect and is a spiritual quality—so neither can what is material be a partial cause concurring with the agent intellect in producing the species— which is spiritual in the possible intellect, which is also spiritual. Or, if you hold that what is corporeal can be a partial cause in causing a species in what is spiritual, so I hold that what is corporeal is a partial cause in causing the act of knowledge in what is spiritual.

If you say that the intellectual nature requires what is material in order to produce the species, I say the same concerning the act of knowledge.

Nor ought a species be posited because of the determination of the power, since every passive power is sufficiently determined by the sufficient agent, most of all when that power itself is active; but the sufficient agent is the object and the intellect, as has been proved. Therefore, etc.

Nor ought it be posited because of the union of the object with the power as mover and moved, since I would then argue in the same way that another species must be posited before that one. For in order that the object should be able to cause the first species in the intellect, it is required that it be united with it, just as a union is required in order that it should cause the act of knowledge. And this will be through another species, and so on to infinity.

In this way, therefore, it is obvious that because of experience, a habit and not a species should be posited.

TO THE FIRST QUESTION

These seen, I say to the first question, speaking of natural intuitive cognition, that an angel and our own intellect know what is other than themselves, not through their species nor through their own essence, but through the essence of the things known, and this as through the said circumstance of the efficient cause. So the reason for knowing, as it is distinguished from the power, is the essence itself of the thing known. . . .

TO THE SECOND QUESTION

To the second question: If it is understood as concerning species properly so-called, a superior angel knows neither through a greater nor a lesser number, since it knows through none at all. But if the question is understood as concerning species as reasons for knowing, it does not know in this way through universal species, for instance, through the concepts of things, but it knows through diverse reasons, that is, diverse things known. And this is speaking about intuitive cognition naturally acquired, since in this case the reason for knowing as distinguished from the power, is the object. . . .

Against these there are several doubts.

I. First, it seems that the intellect cannot have intuitive knowledge with respect to a singular, since the intellect abstracts from material conditions, for instance, from existing here and now; but neither singular nor intuitive cognition abstract from the aforesaid conditions. Therefore, etc. . . .

V. Again. Against the position that a species is not posited in the intellect, but a habit. . . .

3. The intellect has not only the essential power for the cognition of complexes, but also of incomplexes; but that which reduces the intellect from an essential power to an accidental one cannot be a habit. This is, first, because it presupposes the act and, consequently, it presupposes the intellect reduced from the essential power and second, because the habit is only with respect to complexes. And, consequently, if a habit could reduce the intellect from the essential to the accidental power with respect to cognition of a complex, it still would not do so with respect to cognition of an incomplex, for which a habit is not posited. . . .

TO THE DOUBTS

To I. To the first of these, I say that the intellect at first knows the singular intuitively. This is because the intellect knows intuitively what exists in reality, but nothing is such unless it is singular, and because this belongs to an inferior power, namely sense, and is a perfection. Therefore, etc.

Again: That which knows something as it is here and in this place and in this "now" and so for other circumstances, knows more perfectly and has a more perfect nature than that which does not know in this way. Thus, if sense should know in this way and intellect not, intellect would be less perfect than sense. . . .

To V, 3. To another I say that a habit should be posited with respect to the incomplex in the same way and for the same cause. But it is necessary to have recourse to experience for when it exists and when not, since when someone is more inclined to knowing, whether complex or incomplex, after rather than before a frequently elicited act concerning such, then a habit should be posited with respect to it; and when not, a habit should not be posited. Whence, just as not every incomplex knowledge is generative of a habit for the incomplex, so neither is every complex knowledge generative of a habit for the complex. For example, intuitive cognition—taking intuitive and abstractive cognition in the way mentioned above, as occurring together—is not generative of a habit for the incomplex, even though it is incomplex knowledge. And this is because no one experiences himself to be more inclined to knowing something intuitively after having frequently had intuition, than before. . . .

TO THE ARGUMENTS FOR THE FIRST OPINION

To the third. To another I say that there is not required before the act of knowing, any previous assimilation which is accomplished through a species; but the assimilation suffices which is accomplished through the act of knowing, which is a likeness to the thing known. For according to Augustine in the Fifteenth Book of *On the Trinity,* when something is known as it is in itself, then the act of knowing will be quite similar to the thing, and a likeness other than the act of knowing is not required. . . .

TO THE ARGUMENTS OF SCOTUS, OXON. I. 1, d. 3, q. 6, OMITTED ABOVE

To the argument I therefore reply that a species alone in the imagination does not suffice for the cognition of any thing; but just as for corporeal intuitive cognition there is required the power and the object, without any species, so for intellectual intuitive cognition the object together with the intellect suffices. And for the first abstractive knowledge, which stands together with intuitive, intuitive knowledge together with the intellect suffices; but for the second, a habit is required, as was said above. Nor does the imagination unconditionally accomplish anything necessary for intuitive or abstractive cognition, but only incidentally, given our present condition. For the separated soul can see intuitively things present to it, without any phantasm. But the Philosopher only sees things and their concourse for our present condition; hence he speaks well for that present condition, which does require a phantasm.

To another, I say that there are not two representable characteristics in reality, of which one is represented to the imagination and the other to the intellect, since there are no two such in reality, namely, a contracted nature and a contracting property. For whatever is in reality, is singular. . . .

If you say that the agent intellect makes a universal because it makes a species which indifferently represents many—Against: Then I would say that in the same way the sense makes a universal because it makes a species indifferently representing many. The assumption is obvious, since when there are things that are very similar, nothing can be a likeness or representative of one unless it is a likeness and representative of the other. For example, if a Socrates existing here and another at Rome are very similar, there could not be any image in the likeness of the Socrates here which would be representative of him, which would not through everything be similar to the Socrates existing at Rome and representative of him. Therefore, in the same way, if there were two very similar whitenesses, no species in sense could be a likeness or representative of one which would not equally be a likeness and representative of the other. And consequently, a sensible species can represent many just as an intelligible one can; and so the action of a sense would terminate in a universal just as the action of the intellect.

Moreover, I say that the action of the intellect is real, because it terminates in real intuitive or abstractive cognition in the aforesaid way.

And when it is said that the agent intellect makes a universal in act, that is true, in that it makes a certain fictive being and produces a certain concept in objective being, which terminates its act. But this has only objective being, and in no way, subjective being. And in this way it makes a universal, as was said elsewhere. . . .

And when the Commentator says that if the quiddities of things were abstracted from matter, as Plato held, then we would not need an agent intellect; and therefore, the agent intellect does abstract—I reply that abstraction by the agent intellect is two-fold. One is partially to cause an intuitive or abstractive act of knowledge, together with the object or habit in the aforesaid way, which act of knowledge is altogether abstracted from matter, since it is immaterial in itself and has its being in what is immaterial. Another is the abstraction through which it produces a universal, or universal concept of a thing, in objective being, as was said elsewhere.

• • •

Book I (*Ordinatio*), Dist. XXX

QUESTION I

In the thirtieth Distinction, the Master treats of the relational names pertaining to creatures and to God. Concerning which, it should be asked whether God, really or according to reason, is referred to a creature. But since the question presupposes what a relation is, I inquire first concerning relation, and I ask:

Whether, with all authority of the faith or of any of the philosophers whatsoever excluded, it can be more easily denied than maintained that every relation is something on the side of the thing in some way or other distinct from every absolute or absolutes? . . .

Concerning this question it should first be understood that for the intellect it is not a question as to what should be maintained according to the truth, but as to what one would maintain who wishes only to be supported by the reason possible in this present condition, and who does not wish to accept any doctrine or authority, just as one who wished to be supported only by the reason possible to him and who did not wish to accept any authority whatsover would say that it is impossible for three persons distinct in reality to be one supremely simple thing. Likewise, such a one would say that God is not man, and much else which according to the truth of the matter is false. Understanding the question so, there are various opinions. One is that not only because of authorities, but also because of rational arguments, it should be maintained that a relation is a thing other than any absolute thing or things, so that just as substance and quality are distinct things of which neither belongs to the essence of the other, so also substance and relation are in reality distinct things, and neither belongs to the essence of the other.

There are several arguments for this opinion. The first is this: Nothing is in reality the same as A without which A can exist in reality without contradiction. Many relations are such that without them their foundations can exist without contradiction. Therefore, etc. The major is proved in many ways, which I omit, since I reckon them to be conclusive. The minor is apparent in all relations of which the foundations can exist without the terms, as it is in all relations of equivalence, such as "similar," "equal," and so forth. For if this white exists and that white does not, this white is without similarity; and if another white is made, there is similarity in white. Therefore, it can exist without as well as with this. Likewise, for many relations of nonequivalence, just as a master can exist without mastership, and he can be a master upon the acquisition of slaves.

Besides, unless the aforesaid opinion is maintained, many inconveniences follow. The first is that every composition in beings will be denied, since if A and B compose AB, and the union of these parts is nothing in addition to those absolutes A and B separated, then the total reality which belongs to A and B when

Translated by James J. Walsh for this volume from Guillelmus De Occam, O.F.M., *Super 4 Libros Sententiarum,* Vol. III, *Opera Plurima,* Lyon, 1494–1496, *Réimpression en fac-similé,* London: The Gregg Press Limited, 1962.

united persists when they are separated. And then A and B separated remain really united, and so the composite persists when the component parts are separated. And so the composite is not composite, since when a composite persists with the component parts separated, it is not composed of them. For nothing would then be, except an aggregation. The second inconvenience that would follow is that all causality of causes will be denied, since what is caused by various second causes requires a due proportion and proximity in them in order that it be caused by them. But if this proximity and proportion are nothing except these very absolutes, then these are really causative of this effect when they are not in proximity; and so when they are in proximity they can in reality cause nothing which they cannot even when they are not in proximity. For without something else given in reality, a thing cannot cause what it could not previously cause. From these it can be argued so: If A and B when separate do not compose AB, then neither do they when united; since just as the same thing, without anything else added in reality, cannot now cause what it previously could not, so neither can the same things, without anything else in reality, compose something which they previously could not. . . .

And if it is said that a relation is not another thing, since it is not a thing but is only in the intellect, it is argued against this, first, that this destroys the unity of the universe, second, that it destroys all substantial and accidental composition in the universe, third, that it destroys all causality of second causes. . . .

The first is proved, since the unity of the universe is in the order of the parts to one another and in the order to the first, just as the unity of an army is in the order of the parts of the army to one another and to the leader. And hence, against those denying that a relation is a thing outside an act of the intellect, it can be said in the words of the Philosopher in the Twelfth Book of the *Metaphysics,* that those who speak thus undo the substantial connection of the universe.

The second is proved, since nothing is composed without the union of component parts, so that with the parts separated, the composite does not remain. But nothing real depends on what is merely a reason, and especially a reason caused through an act of our intellect, at least such a real which is not merely artificial. Therefore, since a relation is nothing except a conceptual being, no whole will be really natural, since it necessarily requires a relation for its existence.

The third is proved, since the causation of a real effect does not require a conceptual entity in the cause. But second causes cannot cause unless they are proportionate and in proximity. Therefore, if this approximation is merely a conceptual entity, causes will not be able to cause anything real under this kind of approximation. For without this approximation they cannot cause, and according to this opinion this approximation, which is a relation, is no thing. Therefore, a second cause contributes nothing to what is possibly caused. . . .

However much these arguments seem difficult and apparent for proving that a relation is a thing other than absolutes, still, it seems to me that there are more difficult and evident arguments for the other side. And hence I argue against this opinion in general as well as more specifically concerning the various relations which are posited.

First, then, I argue thus: Every thing distinct in reality from another thing can be understood without that other thing being understood, and most of all, if neither is a part of the other. But it is impossible for some thing which is a relation to be understood without any other thing. Therefore, etc. The major seems manifest, since the understanding of one thing totally disparate from another does not seem to depend on the other, any more than the understanding of an effect depends on the understanding of its essential cause. But there is no inconvenience, nor does it include a contradiction, for that which is an effect to be understood without its cause having been understood.

Therefore, in the same way, if similarity or another such relation were a thing different from absolutes and from the corresponding relation, it would not be repugnant to it to be understood with no absolute and no other relation understood. I prove the minor, since if anyone understands the similarity of Socrates to Socrates without the corresponding similarity, he will be able to know that Socrates is similar and still doubt whether he is similar to anything else; and in the same way, one will be able to know that someone is a father, and yet not know whether he has a son, rather, one can also not know whether he could have a son. . . .

Hence, I reply otherwise to the question, that whatever the truth may be, one wishing to be supported by reason, so far as it is possible for a man to judge from what is purely natural, in this present condition, would more easily deny that any relation of the genus of relation is a different thing, as previously expounded, than maintain the opposite. And this is because the more difficult arguments are for this side rather than the other. Indeed, I also say that the arguments for proving such a thing which are not supported by Scripture and the sayings of the saints are in no case fundamentally efficacious. And hence I say that just as one who would wish to follow reason alone and not accept the authority of Sacred Scripture would say that in God there cannot be three persons with a unity of nature, so one who would wish to be supported only by the reason possible for us in this present condition would equally have to hold that a relation is not any such thing in reality as many imagine. For no inconvenience for the negative side follows from principles known from what is purely natural, and not taken on faith. Nor can it be shown through reason that not every thing really distinct from another is thus an absolute thing as the other is, however much not every thing is thus a perfect absolute thing, on the ground that if one thing is really and totally distinct from another, it is not truly a thing absolute in itself, as whiteness is a thing absolute in itself. Either this is because the one thing essentially depends on the other, or because it necessarily co-requires the other, so that it cannot exist without the other, and vice versa. It is not because of the first, since an effect essentially depends on its cause, and yet the cause is totally extrinsic to the effect, and vice versa. Nor is it because of the second, since man necessarily co-requires God in order that he should exist; indeed, it is a contradiction that men should exist and not God. And yet man is truly an absolute thing. And if it is said that neither of the relateds can exist without the other, and hence each is relative, this does not suffice. For, following natural reason, it ought to be said that an accident cannot exist without a subject, nor a subject without an accident; and yet each is truly an absolute. And in this way I should equally easily say that whiteness is a certain relation to something else, just as I should about any other imaginable thing. Nor does it seem that, following natural reason alone, it cannot be said that when there are two things distinct in place and subject, so that each is totally extrinsic to the other and one is no more of the essence of the other than whiteness is of the essence of blackness nor accident of subject, then it is necessary that each of those things is a thing in itself and for itself and has its own nature in itself, just as whiteness is a thing for itself, however much it necessarily co-requires another thing to exist, and just as an accident necessarily co-requires a subject in order to exist. Nor is it more repugnant to such a thing to be understood through itself, without another thing totally extrinsic and distinct in place and subject (and this I say insofar as it is from its nature), than it is repugnant to whiteness to be understood through itself without a subject. Nor is it more repugnant to such a thing to be signified by some name which does not signify or consignify another totally distinct thing than it is repugnant to whiteness. And so, just as whiteness is not said with respect to another according to this name "whiteness," however much it necessarily belongs to its subject according to those holding that an accident cannot exist without a subject (as philosophers following only natural reason hold), so one name could be imposed which would signify just that thing which they say is paternity, and which would not consignify nor connote anything imaginable, however much it might necessarily co-require something else. And so according to that, the name would no more be said of another than is whiteness. And so it does not seem that it would not be one thing in and for itself, everything else set aside by the intellect, just as whiteness is. And if you say that from its nature it is a relative thing, this would not suffice, following natural reason. For with equal ease one would say that in this way whiteness is not an absolute thing, but is a certain relation to a subject, since it necessarily co-requires a subject. And with equal ease one would say that whiteness cannot be understood without a subject, or not unless it is ordered to a subject. In the same way one would say about science that it is not something absolute, but only a certain relation, since it necessarily is of something else; and so for many others. Therefore, those wishing to be supported by natural reason would say, or would have to say speaking in consequence if they were not deceived by some sophisma or did not adhere to certain propositions, wishing to say the opposite rather than because of true, efficacious, and conclusive argument, that in reality, nothing is imaginable except an absolute or absolutes. For all that, a relation is either a name or a word or a concept or an intention, since I reckon that among philosophers an intention is what we call a concept. Such as I call relational convey two extremes existing at once, and this in speaking of certain relative names, since which are such and which are not will be obvious in the following question. For example, the similarity which is said of Socrates with regard to Plato conveys nothing except that Socrates is white and Plato likewise, or that each is black, or that they have qualities of the same character. In the same way, that this is double and that half only conveys that this is of such a quantity and that of such. Whence he who could understand Socrates and Plato and their whiteness, with nothing else understood, would say at once that Socrates is similar to Plato. Whence even skilled laymen understanding little or nothing about such relations still say promptly and without doubt that two whites are similar, just as they say that they are white. This would not be true if those could only be similar because of certain other things outside of whitness added to those whites.

The opposing arguments are reckoned quite easy to resolve.

To the first they would say that the major is true, since if A exists and B does not, it follows that they are not really the same. To the minor, when it is said that there are many relations without which the foundations can exist, they would say that speaking properly and from the force of the term, this is true. For relations do not exist except as intentions or concepts in the mind, and these certainly are not the same as external things; and hence they do not establish that there are extremes really distinct. And if it is said that this white can exist although it is not similar, and still it can be made similar, and so it then has something which it did not have when it was not similar, they would easily reply that this white which at one time is not similar can be made similar, not through the advent of any such thing to it, but only through another white being made. For in order that it should be similar and was not before, no more is required than that something should now be white which was not white before. And if it is said that similarity is in this white, and that other white is not in this white, and therefore, similarity expresses something other than this white and that white, to this I say that speaking properly and from the force of the term, it should not be conceded that similarity is in this white. For speaking properly, similarity does not exist except as a certain concept or intention or name which conveys several whites. Just so, others have to say that causality is not really in God, however much God really is causative. Or, given an abstraction corresponding to the created just as creativity corresponds to the creative, and given that it is creation, then it is not true to say that creation is really in God, since God would then have something in himself which he did not have before. For before the creation of the world, this was false: creation is God, or vice versa. In the same way, I say that speaking properly, this similarity is not in this white; for just as it is conceded that God really is creative or creating, however much creation is not really in God, so it ought to be conceded that this white really is similar, however much similarity is not in this white. Whence, that argument proves equally that creation is a thing different from God and from creature, since this white can be similar without similarity no less than God can be creating without creation; and so God really is creating and is capable of not creating, just as this white really is similar and is capable of not being similar. . . .

To the first confirming argument about composition, perhaps it can be said that composition does not express two absolutes alone, for instance matter and form, but it expresses also that nothing corporeal intervenes; and hence perhaps it should be said that it is not possible for form to exist and matter to exist and that nothing corporeal intervenes, and still that the composite does not exist. This response will be further clarified in what follows.

In the same vein they would reply to the second that approximation does not merely convey the two absolutes, but it also conveys that no impediment intervenes. And hence, when no impediment intervenes between what can be impeded, and they exist, then one will be able to act in the rest. But when there is some intervening impediment, then it is not necessary that one should act in the rest. And so this argument is against those others. For I take something luminous and something illuminable; if some opaque body is interposed, it surely does not act. But with the body removed, without anything acquired by the luminous or the illuminable, it will be able to illuminate. Therefore, it is possible that some two are so disposed that one acts in the other only because of the change of place of one or the other, or rather, only because of the corruption of something in something else, for instance, if the opacity in the opaque body were corrupted. And still nothing new is added to either. So I propose that when in proximity to the other, it can act in it, and when not in proximity, it cannot.

This is not from the fact that when approximated it has some true thing formally in itself which it did not have when it was not approximated; but this is because when it is in proximity, no impediment intervenes. But when it is not in proximity, some impedient intervenes; for even a great quantity of air can sometimes be an impediment if it intervenes.

Through this argument I say further that just as causes can cause something which they could not previously, without any other thing formally added to any of those causes, but only because of the removal of an intervening impediment, so, according to them, parts can sometimes compose without anything formally added to either of those causes, but only because nothing now intervenes between matter and form. They would also say that it is not possible for such parts of a different character sometimes to compose and sometimes not to compose what is intrinsically one, with all the parts still persisting.

To the next, I concede the major; but I say to the minor that the foundation neither simultaneously nor successively contains such relations through identity. For this is false: "Socrates is really similarity," and likewise, "Socrates is really dissimilarity." And hence I do not hold that a relation is really the same as the foundation. But I say that a relation is not a foundation, but rather an intention and concept in the soul conveying many absolutes. Or else it is many absolutes, just as a people is many men, and no man is a people. Which of these propositions is more in accordance with the property of the term pertains more to a discussion in logic than theology.

In the same vein I concede the major to the next; but I say to the minor that this is simply false: "Several relations are really in the same foundation," just as this is simply false: "Several similarities are really the same foundation." The reason for this is that similarity so posited in the abstract can only stand either for an intention in the soul or for many things, of which any one is similar, as "people" can only stand for many. And hence, just as each of these is false: "Many intentions or concepts in the soul are really in the same foundations," and likewise, "The many things of which any one is similar are really in the same foundation," so this is simply false: "Many relations or many similarities are really in the same subject." And if it is said that every relation is founded in some foundation, I say that if being founded is taken for inherence in reality and not for denomination in predication, then this is simply false. But otherwise it is true. . . .

To the other arguments against one way of holding that a relation is not a different thing but is rather in the intellect, I say that it should not be imagined that according to this opinion a relation is in the intellect in such a way that nothing is truly such except because of an act of the intellect or something caused in the intellect. For example, that Socrates is only similar to Plato because of an act of the intellect, just as Socrates can only be called a subject or predicate because of an act of the intellect. But it should be imagined that the intellect contributes no more to the fact that Socrates is similar than to the fact that Socrates is white. Indeed, from this itself, that Socrates is white, and that Plato is white, Socrates is similar to Plato, with everything else imaginable set aside. And so, nothing exists in reality outside of absolutes. Since there are many absolutes in reality, the intellect can express them in diverse ways: in one way expressing only that Socrates is white, and then it only has absolute concepts;

in another way, that Plato is white; and in a third way, expressing that Socrates as well as Plato is white. And this can be accomplished through a relational concept or intention, in saying that Socrates is similar to Plato with regard to whiteness. For it is altogether the same which is conveyed through these propositions: "Socrates as well as Plato is white," and "Socrates is similar to Plato with regard to whiteness." And hence it should be conceded without qualification that the intellect contributes nothing to the fact that the universe is one or that a whole is composite or that causes cause when in proximity or that a triangle has three, etc. And so it contributes no more concerning the others than to the fact that Socrates is white or that fire is hot or water, cold.

In the same vein I say to the proof of the first inconvenience which was adduced that according to the understanding of the Philosopher it ought to be conceded that the unity of the universe is the order of the parts to one another. For he understands nothing other than that for the universe to be one is for the parts to be so ordered—not that the order or unity is something distinct in reality from every part and all parts of the universe, for so would be to proceed to infinity. For that thing would be ordered to the others, and consequently, by the very same argument, there would be another thing outside of that and the others, which would be their order; and there would be an infinite sequence. Nor does it avail to say that there is a stop at the second step, since with equal ease a stop can be posited at the first; and plurality should never be posited without necessity. And hence according to the opinion of the Philosopher, there is nothing outside of those absolute parts, since the opinion of the Philosopher was that every imaginable thing is absolute. Still, this intention or concept in the soul, namely, "unity" or "order" is relational, even though without that concept nothing is any less one or ordered. Just so, this concept or intention "every" is syncategorematic in the soul; and although without this concept every man is capable of laughter, because every man is capable of laughter without any concept, we can only express this through a syncategorematic concept.

Through the same, I say to the second that nothing is composed without a union of component parts, taking "union" for those united parts, since thus, this is valid: "Nothing is composed without parts really united and unseparated." But if the "union" supposits for a concept expressing the thing just as it is, it should be conceded that it can be composed without the union of component parts. For just as every man is capable of laughter without this distributive sign "every," so here. But the first sense is more usual among writers, whether it is more in accordance with the property of the term or not.

Through the same, to the third: that second causes cannot cause unless they are in proximity; and yet they do not require a conceptual entity in order to cause. And hence they are well able to cause without that intention in the soul which is "approximation." Still, if "approximation" should stand for the things themselves in proximity, then they could not cause without approximation, since then this is valid: "They cannot cause unless they are approximate."

To the fourth, I concede that metaphysical affections are relative or relational. Yet it does not follow because of this that the reality of the metaphysical sciences is destroyed, since for the reality of a science it is not required that the extremes of a known proposition should be realities; but it suffices that they supposit for realities, as is made clear above. And hence, however much the metaphysical affections may be intentions or concepts in the soul, just as the affections of other sciences invented by man, still they supposit and stand for true things. And hence those are real sciences.

So, therefore, I say that the arguments against this opinion are in no case conclusive.

. . .

DE SUCCESSIVIS

That motion is not a thing other than permanent things.

With these points seen regarding change, it should be argued that no motion is a kind of thing different in itself from permanent things. This is shown first for motion in general, and second, for each type of motion.

For motion in general I argue first thus: change does not bespeak a kind of thing different in itself from permanent things; therefore, by the same reasoning, neither does motion, since the argument is not more valid of change than of motion; and the antecedent is obvious from what has been said.

Besides, if motion were a different thing, either it would be simple or composite. It is not simple, for then it would not differ from instantaneous change. Nor is it composite, for in that case I ask whether its parts exist or do not. If they exist, then many parts of a motion exist at once, which is against the very character of motion, since motion has one part after another. If the parts of motion do not exist, then motion is not a composite thing, since that which does not exist is not the part of any thing. The Philosopher also makes this argument regarding time, in the chapter on time, which we shall see more of below.

Secondly, the same conclusion is shown for the special types of motion, and the first is local motion. If local motion is a different thing, I ask, is it an absolute or a relational thing? It is not an absolute thing, since then it would be quantity, quality or substance. But it is none of these, as is obvious inductively. For if it were, it would follow that everything moved locally would have new substance or new quality or new quantity, which is manifestly false. Also, because local motion would be just as perfect or more perfect than its terminus. Nor can it be said that it is a relational thing, for every thing is an absolute thing; there is no relational thing that is not absolute. . . .

Thirdly, I show that the motion of alteration is not a different thing, and so forth, since sometimes there is alteration without the taking on of any new thing, as when something is altered in continuously losing part after part of a form it had. Then that is continuously moved and yet it takes on nothing in itself, but only loses. Thus by the same reasoning, when something acquires part after part of a form, it is not required that it should have anything outside of that form and its part.

Fourthly, the same is clear for augmentation and diminution, since in such motion it suffices that quantity alone is gained or lost, without anything else; therefor it is vain to posit anything else there outside of quantity and other permanents.

Translated by James J. Walsh for this volume from *The Tractatus De Successivis attributed to William Ockham,* ed. P. Boehner, St. Bonaventure: The Franciscan Institute, 1944.

Hence it should be said that motion is not any such thing completely different in itself from the permanent thing. For it is pointless to do with more what can be done with less. But we can explain motion and all that is said about motion without any such thing; therefore such an extra thing is pointless. That we can indeed explain motion and all that is said about it without such an additional thing is clear in working through the types of motion.

This is clear regarding local motion. For we truly have local motion when a body is in one place and afterwards in another place, going on in this way without any rest or anything intervening between the body and what moves it. Therefore it is pointless to posit such a different thing.

If it is said that body and place do not sufficiently explain local motion, because then whenever there were body and place there would then be motion, and thus a body would always be in motion, the reply is that body and place do not sufficiently account for the fact that motion exists. Thus the following is not a formal implication: "Body and place exist, therefore there is motion." Even so, nothing else outside of body and place is needed. What is needed is that the body was first in one place and afterwards in another place, and so on continuously, so that never in the entire time does it rest in any place. And it is clear that outside of all these, nothing different from permanent things is assumed. Thus nothing different from A is called for merely by a body being at first in A, and likewise, merely by it being at first not in B is anything different from B and the body assumed. And again, merely by the body being next in B is anything other than the body and B assumed. And in going on in this way it is evidently clear that one does not need to lay down any other thing beyond the body and places and other permanent things. What must be laid down is that the body be at some time in a particular place and sometime not. And this is what it is to be moved locally: at first to have one place, and with no other thing called for, afterward to have another place without any intervening rest and without anything outside of place and body and other permanents, and so going on continuously. And so, there is no other thing outside of those permanent things, but one only needs to add that the body is not in those places at the same time, and that it does not rest in them. And such negative requirements do not call for anything outside of permanent things. As a result, the entire nature of motion can be explained by a body being in distinct places successively and not resting in any of them, without any other thing whatsoever.

It is also clear for the motion of alteration that it does not require a thing different from permanent things. For merely from the parts of a form being acquired by a subject one before another, and not at once, one has the motion of alteration. Thus one does not have to assume any thing other than the subject and the parts of the form; it is enough to set out the subject and the parts of the form, with the further requirement that they are not acquired all at once. But not being acquired at once does not assume anything different from the parts of the form, but rather that certain parts of the form exist at a certain time and not together. Therefore, it is not that some other thing is assumed on account of this, but rather that some thing is denied: not any particular one, but the simultaneity of many parts.

And if it is said that this non-simultaneity of parts is something, when this is asserted, "The parts do not exist all at once," this should be the reply: Such a fiction of abstract nouns taken from adverbs, conjunctions, prepositions, verbs, syncategorematic terms, makes for many troubles, and leads many people into mistakes. For they imagine that just as there are distinct names, so there are distinct things corresponding to them, with the result that there is just as much of a distinction among things signified as among names signifying. This just is not true. Sometimes it is the same things that are signified, but there is diversity in the logical or grammatical way of signifying. Hence non-simultaneity is not some thing different from the things which can exist at the same time, but it signifies that those things do not exist at the same time. And so in these modern times, because of errors born from the use of such abstractions, it would be better in philosophy because of those simple-minded ones, not to make use of such abstractions, but only the verbs, adverbs, conjunctions, prepositions, and syncategorematic terms as they were initially set up rather than forming and using such abstractions. Indeed, if it were not for the use of such abstractions: "motion", "mutation", "mutability", "simultaneity", "succession", "rest" and such as these, there would be little difficulty concerning motion, mutation, time and instants and such as these.

It is also clear for the motion of augmentation and diminution that nothing else is there than permanent things, for the motion there can be explained on these grounds alone, that there is a greater and greater quantity, or less and less quantity, and not at once. But in order to say that there is greater and greater quantity, one need not posit a thing different from permanent things; unless perchance someone might wish to make up an abstraction from this conjunction "and", saying that "andness" or "andeity" is a thing different from those parts of quantity, which is thoroughly silly. Therefore, in the case of greater and greater, or less and less quantity, one need not posit a thing different from permanent things—permanent things are sufficient, so long as the same thing is at first of a certain quantity and afterwards not, and going on in that way. And in this vein I have said elsewhere that motion is compounded from negations and affirmations— that is, that in order that there should be motion it suffices that permanent things or parts should be, but not at once, so that for the truth of the proposition "There is motion" certain affirmatives and certain negatives are enough. And neither through these affirmatives nor negatives is any thing other than the permanent things laid down or indicated to exist. But in the motion of alteration it is enough that at first there is one thing and not another, and afterward the other thing is and not still another, and going on in this way without anything different from a permanent thing. . . .

As for the manner of speaking, in placing this noun "motion" in a sentence, we should note the same kind of thing that was remarked for the noun "mutation", that sometimes "motion" has supposition for the verb "to be moved" and for its moods and tenses, sometimes it has supposition for the thing itself which is moved, sometimes for the end reached or thing acquired when something is moved. Sometimes it is given in place of such an expression as "that it is moved" or "when it is moved", or some such. Likewise, what are added to this noun "motion" in one position or the other of a sentence, are to be analyzed in different ways. For instance, "Motion exists in time" should be expounded thus: "When something is moved, it does not gain or lose all that it loses or gains at once, but one after another." In this way it is clear that these nouns "motion" and "time", like other such abstractions, are invented for the sake of brevity, so that, namely, all that is conveyed through the long expression "What is moved does not gain or lose all that it gains or loses at once, but one after another" is conveyed through the brief expression "Motion exists in time." Likewise, the proposition "Motion is in what is moved" ought to be expounded thus: "What is moved gains or loses something." Many other cases can be handled in the same way. Other propositions, however, should be expounded differently. . . .

COMMENTARY ON THE SENTENCES

Book II *(Reportatio)*

QUESTION 26

... It should also be noted that with respect to the movement of a projectile there is a serious difficulty concerning the causally moving principle of that movement. For it cannot be the projector, since that can be destroyed with the movement still going on. Nor can it be the air, since that can be moved with a contrary movement, as if an arrow should meet an oncoming stone. Nor can it be a power in the stone, for I ask by what that power is caused? It is not caused by the projector, for a natural agent brought to what it works on in the same way, always causes its effect in the same way; but the projector, whether with regard to anything absolute or relational in it, can be brought to a stone as when it moves it and yet not move it. For my hand can be brought to some body slowly, and then it will not move it in place: it can also be moved swiftly and with force, and then it is brought to it as before. And then it will cause motion, whereas previously it did not. Therefore this power which you propose is not caused by anything absolute or relational in the projector, nor by the movement in place of that projector. For movement in place does nothing to the effect unless the active agent is brought to what it works on as was said above. But everything posited in the projector is brought to the projectile in the same way through slow movement as through swift.

Hence I say that in such movement after the separation of the projectile from the initial projector, what does the moving is that very thing moved in itself; the moving is not through some power in it, whether absolute or relational, so that the mover and the moved are totally indistinct. If you say that movement in place is a new effect and a new effect has some cause, I reply that movement in place is not a new effect, whether absolute or relational. I say this while denying (the reality of) location. For local motion is not anything other than that the moveable thing coexists with various parts of space, such that it coexists with no single one for such a time that two contradictories are verified of it. Whence, although any part of space which the moving thing crosses is new with respect to that crossing thing, seeing that the moving thing is now crossing through those parts and previously was not, still that part is not new without qualification. This has already been pointed out. Indeed, it would be remarkable if my hand should cause some power in a stone merely by touching the stone through local motion.

Translated by James J. Walsh for this volume from Guillelmus De Occam, O.F.M., *Super 4 Libros Sententiarun*, Vol. IV, *Opera Plurima*, Lyon, 1494–1496, *Reimpression en fac-simile*, London: The Gregg Press Limited, 1962.

SEVEN QUODLIBETS

Quodlibet IV

QUESTION 1. *Whether, Whatever the Effect, It Has a Final Cause Distinct from the Efficient?*

And at first, it seems not, since God is the efficient and final cause of the same effect. Therefore, the final cause is not always distinguished from the efficient.

To the contrary: if not, then the causes would not be distinct.

Concerning this question, it should first be seen what an end is. Secondly, I shall reply to the question.

With regard to the first, I say that the causality of an end is not other than being effectively loved and desired by an agent, because of which, what is loved is effected. Just as the causality of matter is only being informed, and the causality of form is only informing, so the causality of an end is not other than being effectively loved and desired, without which love and desire the effect would not be accomplished.

From these, it is obvious that the final and efficient cause are distinguished by reason, that is, the definitions expressing their nominal meaning are diverse. For the definition of the final cause is to be effectively loved and desired by an agent, because of which, what is loved is effected. The definition of the efficient cause is to be that at whose existence or presence something follows. And sometimes one of these definitions belongs to one thing and the other, to another; sometimes they can pertain to the same.

From which it is further obvious that sometimes an end is a cause when it does not exist, since sometimes an end is desired when it does not exist. For to be a final cause is not other than being desired or loved in the aforesaid way. Whence this is peculiar to the final cause, that it can cause when it does not exist. Just as if a form could inform when it did not exist, it could be a cause when it did not exist, so from the fact that an end can be desired when it does not exist, it can be a cause when it does not exist.

If you say that that which does not exist is not the cause of anything, I say, that is false; but one must add that it does not exist, nor is it loved, nor desired. And then indeed it does follow that it is not a cause. But an end can be loved or desired now however much it does not exist. And hence it can be a final cause when it does not exist.

Concerning the second, it should be remarked that one should speak differently according to the truth of faith and if one should accept no authority. For speaking in the first way, I say that according to the truth of faith it is not the case that whatever the effect, it has a final cause distinct from the efficient. For sometimes

Translated for this volume by James J. Walsh from Guillelmus De Occam, O.F.M., *Quodlibeta Septem*, Strasbourg, 1491.

the same is both the final and the efficient cause, as when God is the efficient cause and the end of many effects; at least, according to right reason he ought always be the final cause. But speaking in the second way, if I should accept no authority, I would say that it cannot be proved, either from what is self-evident or through experience, that whatever the effect, it has a final cause distinct from the efficient. For it cannot be sufficiently proved that whatever the effect, it has any final cause.

And if you ask whether the causality of a final cause is distinct from the causality of an efficient cause, I reply that some causality is distinct from the causality of an efficient, and some is not. For when the same is end as well as efficient, then they are not distinguished; but when they are diverse, then the causalities are distinguished. Still, writers understand that these causalities are distinguished, since from the fact that something is an efficient cause it does not follow that it is an end, nor vice versa.

But there are doubts here.

The first is that it seems that the description of the final cause is not well given.

First, because someone can hate someone, because of which hate he does something, for instance, he strikes him on the jaw; and the final cause of this effect is the hated one alone. Therefore, the causality of the final cause is for something to be hated, because of which it exists.

Second, someone can love something without it being necessary that he accomplishes any effect because of what is loved.

Third, either an end causes through its own reality—and this does not, since the effect is caused when the end does not exist—or else it causes through something taking its place, for instance, through love. And this is efficient causality.

Fourth, because natural agents and likewise agents acting from what is proposed in primary cognition and primary volition act for the sake of an end; and yet they do not act because of any previously loved or desired end.

Fifth, because the final cause is more noble than other causes; but that which is loved and desired, because of which an agent acts, is not always more noble. Therefore, etc.

The second doubt is that it seems that on the ground of natural reason, one must hold that whatever the effect, it has a final cause, since through a final cause reply is made to the question, because of what cause an effect is done— as, if it were asked why these men fight, and the reply is, so that they might govern. And then, because otherwise it cannot be explained why anyone goes anew from potency to act. And then, because otherwise, all other agents would act by chance, since natural agents act through determined means, just as an effect is inherently accomplished. And then, because otherwise there would be error in the action of nature, since one is no more intended than the rest.

To the first of these doubts I say that this description is well given. To the proof I say that the final cause of the hate is the hater himself, since he loves himself, and it is because of what is loved that he hates the adversary. But the final cause of the blow is the affliction of the adversary, whom the striker hates. For he would not strike unless he desired his affliction. And so the causality of an end is always being loved, and not being hated, since that hated one is not the final cause.

To the next, I say that the causality of an end is being loved effectively, also for the reason that one never loves in this way if he would not accomplish the effect unless he were impeded. But if it is love under a condition, then it is not efficacious love.

To the third, I say that an end in this way causes through its own reality, since its own reality is desired. Nor it is necessary that the reality exist when the effect is caused, as was said.

To the fourth, I say that natural agents and those acting from what is proposed in primary cognition and volition do not have a final cause previously established by a created will; but they only have the end previously established by God, who is the agent.

To the fifth, I say that that which is the final cause according to right reason is more noble than the others, or at least equally noble; but in fact it is not so. Otherwise it could be said that the end is always more noble than other causes, either in reality, or in reputation, or in the estimation of the will.

But you say that an effect is sufficiently produced through the power of the agent and the patient, and therefore another cause is superfluous. I reply that the existence of an end is not required in order that an effect be produced, yet in agents acting from what is proposed it is required that the end be loved and desired efficaciously.

To the second doubt I say that all the arguments of the Philosopher are conclusive only with regard to an agent who can sin and fail without the variation of concurrent agents and patients and other dispositions. This is a free agent alone, because he can desire and sin in his action, however much everything else is uniformly disposed. They do not conclude that other agents have a final cause. Whence, to the first opposing argument it should be said following reason that this question only has a place for voluntary agents, because it does not have a place for natural actions. For it would be said that there is no question, for what reason fire is generated. And hence it is well asked, for what reason these men fight; so that they might govern. And it can be proved evidently and through experience, and not otherwise, that a free agent acts because of an end; and in such actions sometimes the effect has a final cause distinct from the efficient, and sometimes it does not have an end distinct from the efficient.

To the next, I say that natural agents do not go anew from inactivity to act unless some impediment is now removed, as if fire should now be brought into proximity with wood and previously it was not. But a free agent goes anew from inactivity to act because now he intends an end and previously he did not. To the next, I say that it is conclusive for a free agent, because he is no more inclined from his nature to one effect than to another. It is not conclusive for a natural agent, since such an agent from its nature is inclined to one determined effect, so that it cannot cause the opposite effect, as is obvious concerning fire with respect to heat.

To the next, I say that they act thus through determined means from their nature, since nature necessarily requires this.

To the last, I say that it is conclusive for a free agent, to whose action error properly pertains, and not for a natural agent, since nothing is intended by such an agent. Hence, whatever happens naturally, happens; and there will not be error.

To the principal argument, I say that the four causes are spoken of distinctly because they are frequently distinct, although not always. And also, since from the fact that something is a final cause it does not follow that it is an efficient, nor does the opposite follow, etc.

COMMENTARY ON THE SENTENCES

Book III (*Reportatio*)

QUESTION 12. *Whether the Virtues Are Connected?*

Concerning this question, four things should be done. First, some conclusions necessary to the position should be offered. Second, some distinctions. Third, the reply to the question should be made. Fourth, there are some doubts to be raised and resolved. . . .

The third conclusion is that some act is necessarily and intrinsically virtuous. This is proved, since it is impossible that some contingently virtuous act, that is, one which can indifferently be called vicious and virtuous, should be made determinately virtuous because of the advent of some act not necessarily virtuous. For through nothing contingent in the said way is another act either made or denominated virtuous. For if so, either that second act, which is contingently virtuous, is necessarily virtuous through another act, or else it is contingently virtuous through that act. If the first, then for the same reason there will be a stop at the first; also then the position is had, namely, that in man there is some act which is necessarily virtuous. If the second, there will be an infinite sequence, or else it will stop at some necessarily virtuous act and thus the position is had. But exterior human acts as well as interior—for instance, to understand and to will—according to which any act is indifferent, are contingently virtuous. For instance, to go to church because of an obligatory end is a virtuous act; and given the same, to go to church because of an evil end is vicious; and consequently, it is contingently virtuous. It is the same for understanding and contemplation. At first, because of an obligatory end, the understanding will be virtuous; and after, given the same act and intellect, with an altered intention, that is, that such an act should continue because of a forbidden end, that contemplation will be vicious. Consequently, that contemplation will be contingently virtuous. Hence I say that some primarily and necessarily virtuous act is to be given, which act is praiseworthy and perfectly circumstanced, because it is so virtuous that it cannot be made vicious, just as to do something because it is divinely commanded is an act so virtuous that it cannot be made vicious while the divine command stands. And from such an act is generated the virtue concerning which the saints say than no one can make a bad use of virtue.

The fourth conclusion is that the act primarily and principally virtuous is the act of will. This is obvious, first, because that alone is primarily praiseworthy and blameworthy. But others are so only secondarily and by a certain extrinsic

Translated by James J. Walsh for this volume from Guillelmus De Occam, O.F.M., *Super 4 Libros Sententiarum*, Vol. IV, *Opera Plurima*, Lyon, 1494–1496, *Réimpression en fac-similé*, London: The Gregg Press Limited, 1962.

denomination, for instance, through the fact that they are elicited in conformity with an act of will. Besides, any act other than the act of will can, while remaining the same, be vicious and virtuous; but it alone is virtuous such that it cannot be made vicious, as is obvious in the third conclusion. . . .

Concerning the second article, the first distinction is: that prudence is taken in four ways. In one way, it is taken for every knowledge which is directive with respect to anything which can be done, mediate or immediate, as Augustine takes prudence in the First (Book) of *On Free Will*. And in this way, it includes the evident knowledge of any universal proposition evidently known through teaching, since the proposition proceeds from self-evident propositions—which scientific knowledge is properly moral science. And it also includes evident knowledge of a universal proposition which is only evidently known through experience—which experience is also moral science and prudence. An example of the first is: "Every benefactor should be benefited." An example of the second is: "An angry man should be mollified with fair words."

In another way, it is taken for evident knowledge immediately directive with regard to something particular which can be done; and this is for the knowledge of some particular proposition which follows evidently from a universal proposition as a major, whether self-evident or known through teaching. An example is: "This one here should be so benefited," which follows evidently from this one: "Every benefactor, etc."

In the third way, it is taken for immediate directives accepted through right experience alone of something which can be done. An example is: "This angry man should be mollified through fair words." And this knowledge is accepted through right experience alone of some particular proposition known through experience; and this seems to be prudence properly so-called, according to the intention of the Philosopher, as it is distinguished from moral science.

In the fourth, it is taken for any aggregate of immediately directive knowledge, whether had through teaching or through experience, concerning everything a human being is required to do in order absolutely to live well. And in this way, prudence is not one knowledge; but it includes as many knowledges as there are moral virtues required in order absolutely to live well, because whatever the moral virtue, it has its own prudence and directive knowledge. . . .

The third distinction is that justice, and any other moral virtue, according to which there is no other virtue, neither formally nor equivalently, has five grades, not indeed of the same species, but of distinct species. The first grade is when someone wishes to perform just deeds, conforming to right reason dictating that such deeds should be done, according to determined circumstances respecting that object alone, because of the honorableness of that deed, just as for the sake of an end. For instance, the intellect orders that every such deed should be done at such a place and such a time because of the honorableness of the deed itself or for the sake of peace or another such; and the will elicits the act of willing such deeds in conformity with the command of the intellect. The second grade is when the will wishes to perform just deeds following the aforesaid right command and because of it, with the intention that such deeds should in no way be abandoned for anything against right reason, including death, if right reason should command that such a deed should not be abandoned in the face of death. For instance, if a man should wish so to honor his father at a time and place, etc., following the aforesaid right command, with the intention and will of not abandoning him even if death should impend. The third grade is when someone wishes to perform such a deed following the aforesaid right reason, with the intention that, etc.; and because of this he wishes to perform such a deed according to the aforesaid circumstances and once only, since it is so commanded by right reason. The fourth grade is when he wishes to do that according to all the aforesaid conditions and circumstances, and more than this, just because of the love of God, for instance, since it is so commanded by the intellect that such deeds should be performed just because of the love of God; and universally such is the perfect and true moral virtue that saints talk about. . . .

Hence I reply to this article, and let this be the first conclusion: that all the general virtues are connected in certain universal principles, for instance, that everything honorable should be done, that every good should be loved, that everything dictated by right reason should be done. And these can be major and minor premises in a practical syllogism concluding with a particular conclusion, the knowledge of which is prudence immediately directive in a virtuous act. And a principle numerically the same can be the major premise with diverse minor premises accepted, in order to draw diverse particular conclusions, the knowledge of which is prudence directive in diverse virtuous acts. . . .

As to the fourth article of this third article, this is the first conclusion: Moral virtues in the first three grades do not necessarily require theological virtues, whether narrowly or widely accepted. This is obvious, since theological virtues cannot be had without cognition of the end in particular, in the way by which it is known in this present condition, in a concept proper to it. But moral virtues in the aforesaid grades can be acquired without such cognition of the end, as is obvious in a simple pagan who can do such things according to right reason without investigation for having the proper concept concerning the character of the end. . . .

The fourth conclusion is that moral virtue in the fourth grade requires theological virtues, and this according to the ordained power of God. This is obvious, since one cannot love for the sake of God a creature or anything created unless he loves God above everything, since it is for the sake of some one thing, etc. But by the ordained power of God such love cannot exist nor be acquired in any way without (divinely) infused faith, hope, and charity. . . .

As to the fourth article of this third argument, here is the first conclusion: No moral virtue nor virtuous act is possible without any prudence, since no act is virtuous unless it conforms to right reason. For right reason is posited in the definition of virtue, in the Second (Book) of the *Ethics*. Therefore, whatever the virtuous act and habit, it necessarily requires some prudence. And if you ask whether, after the generation of virtue, a virtuous act can be elicited without an act of prudence, I reply that it cannot, since no one acts virtuously unless he acts knowingly and from freedom. And hence, if such an act of the will were at some time elicited from such a habit without an act of prudence, it would neither be nor be called virtuous, but rather, vicious, just as an act of the habituated sensitive appetite among the foolish. It is obvious that some wish what they previously wished virtuously, because of a habit remaining in the will, which inclined to virtuous acts when it was in a good condition; but now the act is not virtuous, since such a one is not praiseworthy nor blameworthy because of his acts. And the reason is that he does not know what he does, in that he does not have prudence or right reason. If you ask in what type of cause the act of prudence is disposed to the virtuous act, from the fact that it is necessarily required, and an effect sufficiently depends on its essential causes, etc., I reply that it is an efficient cause necessarily required for a virtuous act, without which it is impossible for an act to be virtuous, given the divine ordination which now exists. So that, for a virtuous act there is necessarily required the activity of an act of prudence and the activity of the will, so that these two causes are partial causes together with God, with respect to a virtuous act. . . .

The sixth conclusion is that whatever the moral virtue, it can exist without prudence in the first and second aforesaid ways. For in order that a virtuous act be elicited, it is not required that the immediately directive knowledge be caused through the self-evident propositions by which prudence in the second aforesaid way is caused. The same knowledge can be caused through propositions known self-evidently or through experiences, and being caused in either of these ways is sufficient. For instance, in order that I should virtuously benefit this man it is not required that the proposition, "This man should be benefited," follow from this one, "Every friend should be benefited, etc." But it suffices that I should evidently assent to the former, since I have seen or have otherwise experienced that this man benefited me. But in order that a virtuous act be elicited, prudence in the second or third aforesaid way is necessarily required. Likewise, prudence in the first aforesaid way is not required for moral virtue, since, as is obvious, immediately directive particular knowledge of whatever kind can be had through experience, which does not require the knowledge of any universal. Yet if evident knowledge of some particular cannot be had through experience, the virtue of which that particular would be directive necessarily requires prudence in the first and second ways, but not the third way.

Against the fourth article there are some doubts to be raised.

The first is, whether any act of the will is indifferent, so that at first it is indifferent regarding good and bad, and afterwards, the same is made good or bad. It seems that this is so, since every act elicited conforming to right reason is unqualifiedly virtuous; but someone can at first elicit an indifferent act without right reason, and after, continue the same with right reason. Therefore, etc. And in the same way it can be proved that an act at first intrinsically good can be made intrinsically bad, since if at first it is elicited conforming to right reason, and afterwards is continued against right reason, and finally is continued according to right reason, it will at first be intrinsically good, and afterwards, intrinsically bad, and finally, intrinsically good again. Therefore, etc.

The second doubt is that it does not seem that right reason, the end, the place, the time, etc., are secondary and partial objects of the virtuous act. First, because these are circumstances of such an act; therefore, they are not objects of that act, since the same cannot be object and circumstance. Second, because then the same act would be an act of negative and of positive volition, since someone can hate and refuse and detest sin because of God, as because of an end. But this act as it is terminated toward God cannot be an act of hating and refusing, since it is a virtuous act and no one virtuously hates God. Therefore, as it is terminated, it is an act of positive volition; but as it is terminated toward sin, it is an act of negative volition. Therefore, etc. . . .

To the first of these John (Duns Scotus) replies, . . . and he says that a habit as well as an act of will can be indifferent, as in the case of a generated habit of abstinence as customarily exists in nature, the act of which is only a natural act; afterwards, through the coexistence of an act of prudence, it can be intrinsically good. . . . Third, he says . . . that sin or deformity in the act of sinning is only the lack of rectitude, not indeed that which is in the act nor which was at some time in it. For the act is the same and, consequently, is not altered from opposite into opposite. But it is only the lack of rectitude which ought to be in every such act, which rectitude the will is bound to give to it.

Against the first: it is impossible that from being non-virtuous, an act should be made virtuous through any purely natural act which is in no way in the power of the will, since no one is praised or blamed because of a natural act alone. But according to him and the truth, the act of prudence is only a natural act, and in no way in our power, any more than is the act of seeing. Therefore, it is impossible that an indifferent and non-virtuous act of will should be made virtuous through the coexistence of prudence alone. . . .

Hence I say with regard to this doubt that an act can be called virtuous intrinsically or extrinsically. In the first way, it is impossible that an indifferent act should be made morally good through the coexistence of an act of prudence, since it is impossible that any non-virtuous act should be made virtuous through what is merely natural. In the second way, it well can be; but this will not only be through the coexistence of prudence, but through a new volition together with it. Take as an example someone who wishes to study. Setting aside every circumstance, this act is generically good. And after, the intellect dictates that this act of willing should be continued, according to all the required circumstances, and the will wills the first act to continue according to the dictate of right reason. This second is perfectly virtuous, since it conforms to right reason dictating completely; and it is intrinsically virtuous. The first is only nominally virtuous, through an extrinsic denomination, in that it is conformed to the second act; and the second act is distinct from the first, which is obvious from their separability and the distinction of their objects. For the second has right reason for object, and the first does not. Whence, if there were only the first act, it would not be deliberate; and hence, this first act is not otherwise good than is an exterior act of the apprehensive or executive powers. . . . Still, an act of prudence would not be called intrinsically virtuous nor extrinsically good unless because it is conformed to some intrinsically good act which is not an act of prudence but only an act of will, as is obvious from what has been said. And when it is argued from an act at first intrinsically good and afterwards, bad, I say that this case is impossible. For these reasons are contrary, since the first dictates that such an act be elicited and continued, and the second dictates that the act not be continued. For it is impossible that these reasons should stand together in the intellect because of their formal repugnance; and just as these reasons are repugnant, so are the volitions elicited in conformity with these reasons. For to wish to study according to right reason and to refuse to study against reason are opposite volitions concerning the same object, because of the opposite reasons which are the objects of these volitions. And likewise, the first virtuous act of willing could not be naturally elicited nor continued without right reason, which is the formal cause of it in eliciting as well as in conserving. And hence, with the destruction of that right reason there is destroyed that act of willing; but that reason is destroyed when the opposite act is elicited. Therefore, etc. And hence an intrinsically good act cannot be afterwards made intrinsically bad, nor an indifferent, nor an intrinsically bad, nor vice versa. . . .

As to the third which he says, I say that deformity or sin in an act is not the lack of rectitude which ought to be in the act, which is called sin because of the reason previously mentioned. But it is the lack of rectitude which ought to be in the will, which is to say nothing other than that the will is obliged to elicit some act following the divine precept, which act it does not elicit, and so it sins with the sin of omission. And so rectitude whether absolute or respective is nothing other than that very act which ought to be elicited according to right reason and the will of God. And from this it is obvious that the imagination of John (Duns Scotus) and others is false, that rectitude is a respect of conformity to circumstances, as to right reason, for the reasons previously mentioned. And this seems to follow from his remarks. For he says that deformity is not the lack of rectitude which at some time was in the act and now is not, because that act, since it is the same and is unqualifiedly simple, cannot be altered from opposite to opposite. Then I argue so: deformity cannot be the lack of rectitude which was in it and now is not, because of that transition from a contradictory. Therefore, in the same way it cannot be the lack of rectitude which is now in it and previously was not, for the same reason. And consequently, it is also impossible according to him that an act of will should at first be indifferent . . . and afterwards, the same act should be made intrinsically virtuous. Whence all these imaginations which say that rectitude in an act adds something over and above the absolute or respective act are false, because it is nothing other than the very act itself. And hence to lack rectitude in an act is to lack such an act; and likewise, should the will elicit some act of friendship which it is bound not to elicit because it is against right reason and the divine command, it sins thus with the sin of commission, even if the will is not bound to the opposite act, if it were possible to find it somewhere. And then the deformity would not be the lack of any rectitude which ought to be in it, nor in that act, nor in the will, through what is posited; but it would be the very act itself elicted against the command of God, and would be a lack of nothing. And from this it is obvious that it is not well said that the positive act is what is material in sin and the lack of the justice which ought to be in it is what is formal, since there is either a sin of commission or omission in the will, or both at once. If the first alone, for instance if the will should elicit some act against right reason and the divine command, and it were not bound to elicit the opposite act, then there is in the will only the act of sinning without any lack of rectitude or of justice which ought to be in it, and consequently, the lack is not what is formal to it. If the second alone is in the will, for instance, should the will be bound to elicit some act which it does not elicit, then there is only that lack of rectitude without any material and without any elicited act. If the third is given, for instance that the will elicits some act against the command of God while it is bound to the opposite, then there is here a two-fold sin of commission and omission. The sin of commission is that positive act alone. That of omission is the lack of the other act which ought to be in it, which consequently is nothing other than to say that in the sin there are two such of what is material and formal, and that the sin committed is material and that omitted is formal. And consequently, where there is only a sin of omission, it will not do to assign two such, and imagine that is true. For if it is imagined that the lack of rectitude and justice is what is formal in sin, such that that rectitude is something positive, absolute or respective, inherent or possible, existing in the act through which that act of sin would be made virtuous, and this because of the right act which the will is bound to elicit, the imagination is impossible, as has previously been proved. From this it is obvious in what way sin is said to be privation, since a sin of omission is formally a privation. And some sin, namely, of commission, is not called privation; but it is a positive act which the will is bound not to elicit, and hence it is the sin. Nevertheless, if along with this sin there is always a sin of omission, then there is a privation with every sin, because that is a sin. But not every sin is a privation, because only a sin of omission is a privation.

And from this it is obvious what is the efficient cause of sin, since in a sin of omission there is no positive cause, because it is nothing positive; but yet it has a defective cause, and that is the will which is bound to elicit the act opposite to the one lacking, and does not elicit it. But if we speak in this way of the sin of commisssion, the created will is not alone the efficient cause of that act, but God himself, who causes immediately every act, just as any secondary cause whatever. And so He is the positive cause of the deformity in such an act, just as of the substance itself of the act. For as was said, deformity in an act of commission is only the very act itself elicited against the divine command, and expresses nothing else at all. And if you say that God would then sin in causing such a deformed act, just as the created will sins when it causes such an act, I reply that God is under obligation to no one; and hence He is neither bound to cause that act, nor the opposite act, nor not to cause it. And hence He does not sin, however much He may cause that act. But the created will is bound through the divine command not to cause that act; and consequently, in causing that act, it sins, since it does what it ought not do. Whence, if the created will were not obligated to cause that act or the opposite, it would never sin no matter how much it caused it, just as God does not. . . .

To the second doubt I say that the end as well as right reason and all other circumstances are secondary partial objects of the virtuous act. The reason for this is that, given the divine ordination which now exists, there is some act of the will which is intrinsically and necessarily virtuous and is in no way contingently virtuous. But now if those which are called circumstances are not objects of the virtuous act, no act of the will would be necessarily and intrinsically virtuous, but only extrinsically and contingently, the opposite of which has already been proved. The assumption is obvious, since every act of will remaining altogether the same can be continued and conserved, given only the apprehension and presentation of the object of that act. For no more seems to be required for the causing of that act than God, the will itself, and the apprehension of the object; and these suffice for causing every act of willing as partial causes which do not require anything other than the object in real existence. Therefore, these suffice for conserving such an act without anything else positive in real existence. Therefore, if right reason, or the act of assenting which is called right reason, were not the object of the virtuous act, for instance an act of temperance, but were only a circumstance, and food were the object of such an act, it would follow that upon the apprehension of the food, without right reason, rather perhaps with erroneous reason, the will could elicit a perfectly virtuous act. And just as on this hypothesis it could cause a virtuous act without right reason, so it could without right reason conserve an act that had been elicited with right reason. And so, that act would at first be virtuous, and later, not virtuous, or vicious, and so, contingently and not necessarily. If you say that the act of prudence is required as an essential and partial cause for the virtuous act, following John (Duns Scotus) and this opinion, but still it does not have to occur as an object—just as God and the apprehension of the object concur as partial causes for causing the virtuous act, but yet are not objects—against this: If right reason were required only as a partial and essential cause in the aforesaid manner, then, since God can furnish the entire causality of a second cause, if God should furnish the causality of right reason, given the causality of the will and of apprehension, that act could be perfectly virtuous without the act of prudence. This is manifestly false, since given the ordination which now exists, no act is perfectly virtuous unless it is elicited in conformity with an actually inhering right reason. Hence I say that right reason is an object of the virtuous act, and from this, that it is required for a virtuous act just as much as an object in real existence. It follows that right reason has effective causality with respect to the virtuous act, according to the frequently alleged principle, "An effect sufficiently depends, etc." For if it were not required as much as an object in real existence, then it seems that its presence alone, and that of the object of the virtuous act, together with the will, could cause the virtuous act, just as it can cause any other kind of act. This is confirmed since no act is perfectly virtuous unless the will through that act wishes what is dictated by right reason just because it is dictated by right reason. For if the will should wish what is dictated by right reason, not because it is dictated, but because it is delightful, or because of something else, it would wish what is dictated merely upon its being shown, because of the apprehension, and without right reason. And consequently, that act would not be virtuous, because it would not be elicited in conformity with right reason. For this is what it is to elicit in conformity with right reason: to wish what is dictated by right reason because of the fact that it is dictated. But now it is impossible that someone should wish something because of something else unless he wishes that other, since if he refuses or does not wish that other, he already wishes the something more because of itself than because of that other. Therefore, in order that I should virtuously wish what is dictated by right reason, I must necessarily wish right reason through the same act and not through another.

SELECTED BIBLIOGRAPHY

BIBLIOGRAPHIES

Heynck, V., "Ockham-literatur 1919–1949," *Franziskaner Studien*, XXXII (1950), 164–183.

Reilly, Jr., J., "Ockham Bibliography: 1950–1967," *Franciscan Studies*, XXVIII (1968), 197–214.

TRANSLATIONS

Adams, M. and Kretzmann, N., William Ockham, *Predestination, God's Foreknowledge, and Future Contingents*, Indianapolis, 1969.

Boehner, P., ed. and trans., *Ockham, Philosophical Writings*, Edinburgh, 1957. (English translation only in paperback edition, Indianapolis, 1964.)

Kluge, E., "William of Ockham's Commentary on Porphyry: Introduction and English Translation," *Franciscan Studies*, XXXIII (1973), 171–254, XXXIV (1974), 306–382.

Freddoso, A. and H. Schuurman, trans., *Ockham's Theory of Propositions: Part II of the Summa Logicae*, Notre Dame, 1980.

Loux, M., trans., *Ockham's Theory of Terms: Part I of the Summa Logicae*, Notre Dame, 1974.

Lerner, R., and M. Mahdi, eds., *Medieval Political Philosophy: A Sourcebook*, New York, 1963.

McKeon, R., ed. and trans., *Selections from Medieval Philosophers, II: Roger Bacon to William of Ockham*, New York, 1930.

Tornay, S., ed. and trans., *Ockham, Studies and Selections*, LaSalle, Ill., 1938.

STUDIES

Adams, M., "Intuitive Cognition, Certainty, and Scepticism in William Ockham," *Traditio*, XXVI (1970), 389–398.

Adams, M., "Ockham on Identity and Distinction," *Franciscan Studies*, XXXVI (1976), 5–74.

Adams, M., "Ockham's Theory of Natural Signification," *The Monist*, LXI (1978), 444–459.

Adams, M., "What Does Ockham mean by *supposition?*" *Notre Dame Journal of Formal Logic*, XVII (1976), 375–391.

Baudry, L., *Guillaume d'Occam*, Paris, 1949.

Baudry, L., "Les rapports de Guillaume d'Occam et de Walter Burleigh," *Archives d'histoire doctrinale et littéraire du moyen âge*, LX (1934), 155–173.

Baudry, L., *Lexique philosophique de Guillaume d'Ockham*, Paris, 1958.

Boehner, P., *Collected Articles on Ockham*, St. Bonaventure, N.Y., 1958.

Boler, J., "Ockham on Evident Cognition," *Franciscan Studies*, XXXVI (1976), 85–98.

Boler, J., "Ockham on Intuitive Cognition," *Journal of the History of Philosophy*, XI (1973), 95–106.

Clark, D., "Voluntarism and Rationalism in the Ethics of Ockham," *Franciscan Studies*, XXXI (1971), 72–87.

Clark, D., "William of Ockham on Right Reason," *Speculum*, XLVIII (1973), 13–36.

Davis, L., "The Intuitive Knowledge of Non-Existents and the Problem of Late Medieval Skepticism," *The New Scholasticism*, XLIX (1975), 410–430.

Day, S., *Intuitive Cognition. A Key to the Significance of the Later Scholastics*, St. Bonaventure, N.Y., 1947.

de Lagarde, G., *La naissance de l'esprit laïque au déclin du moyen âge*, IV–VI, 1942, 1946.

Garvens, A., "Die Grundlagen der Ethik Wilhelms von Ockham," *Franziskanische Studien*, XXI (1934), 243–273, 360–408.

Geach, P., "Nominalism," *Sophia*, III (1964), 3–14.

Guelluy, R., *Philosophie et théologie chez Guillaume d'Ockham*, Louvain, 1947.

Hochstetter, F., *Studien zur Metaphysik und Erkenntnislehre Wilhelms von Ockham*, Berlin, 1927.

Klocker, H., "Ockham and Efficient Causality," *The Thomist*, XXIII (1960), 106–123.

Klocker, H., "Ockham and the Divine Ideas," *The Modern Schoolman*, LVII (1980), 348–360.

Leff, G., *William of Ockham: The Metamorphosis of Scholastic Discourse*, Manchester, 1975.

Loux, M., "*Significatio* and *Suppositio*," *The New Scholasticism*, LIII (1979), 407–427.

Mathews, G., "Ockham's Supposition Theory and Modern Logic," *Philosophical Review*, LXXII (1964), 91–99.

Maurer, A., "Method in Ockham's Nominalism," *The Monist*, LXI (1978), 426–443.

Maurer, A., "Ockham on the Possibility of a Better World," *Mediaeval Studies*, XXXVIII (1976), 391–412.

Maurer, A., "Ockham's Conception of the Unity of Science," *Mediaeval Studies*, XX (1958), 98–112.

McGrade, A., *The Political Thought of William of Ockham*, London-New York 1974.

Menges, M., *The Concept of Univocity regarding the Predication of God and Creature according to William Ockham*, St. Bonaventure, N.Y., 1952.

Moody, E., "Empiricism and Metaphysics in Medieval Philosophy," *Philosophical Review*, LXVII (1958), 145–163.

Moody, E., "Ockham, Buridan, and Nicholas of Autrecourt," *Franciscan Studies*, VII (1947), 113–146.

Moody, E., *The Logic of William of Ockham*, New York, 1935.

Moody, E., *Truth and Consequence in Mediaeval Logic*, Amsterdam, 1953.

Pegis, A., "Some Recent Interpretations of Ockham," *Speculum*, XXIII (1948), 458–463.

Read, S., "The Objective Being of Ockham's *ficta,*" *Philosophical Quarterly*, XXVII (1977), 14–31.

Richards, R., "Ockham and Scepticism," *New Scholasticism*, XLII (1968), 345–363.

Scott, T., "Ockham on Evidence, Necessity, and Intuition," *Journal of the History of Philosophy*, VI (1969), 27–49.

Shapiro, H., *Motion, Time and Place According to William Ockham*, St. Bonaventure, N.Y., 1957.

Spade, P., "Ockham's Distinctions between Absolute and Connotative Terms," *Vivarium,* XIII (1975), 55–76.

Spade, P., "Ockham's Rule of Supposition: Two Conflicts in His Theory," *Vivarium,* XII (1974), 63–73.

Streveler, P., "Ockham and His Critics on Intuitive Cognition," *Franciscan Studies,* XXXV (1975), 223–236.

Swiniarski, J., "A New Presentation of Ockham's Theory of Supposition, with an Evaluation of some Contemporary Criticism," *Franciscan Studies,* XXX (1970), 181–217.

Urban, L., "William of Ockham's Theological Ethics," *Franciscan Studies,* XXXIII (1973), 310–350.

Vignaux, P., "Nominalisme," *Dictionnaire de théologie catholique,* XI (1931), 733–784.

Webering, D., *Theory of Demonstration According to William of Ockham,* St. Bonaventure, N.Y., 1953.

Weisheipl, J., "Ockham and some Mertonians," *Mediaeval Studies,* III (1968), 163–213.

Woods, E., "Ockham on Nature and God," *The Thomist,* (1973), XXXVII, 69–87.

NICHOLAS
OF AUTRECOURT

ca. 1 3 0 0 – ?

IF ANSELM OF CANTERBURY represents the medieval high-water mark in the claims made for reason, Nicholas of Autrecourt must come very close to representing the low-water mark. It is not only the dogmas of the faith which he finds to be indemonstrable, including the existence of God, but also the very foundational doctrines of philosophy itself. In his professed intentions, Autrecourt can be grouped with the old Christian antiphilosophical tradition that counts Tertullian and Peter Damian among its best-known advocates. Men spend their lives uselessly, he said, studying Aristotle and his Commentator, when they could be studying the good of the community instead. It is said that there are a thousand or more demonstrated truths in Aristotle and his followers; but Autrecourt can scarcely find one—and, what is worse, scarcely one that is even probable. Unlike those who merely denounced the illusory wisdom of the philosophers, however, Autrecourt enforced his rejection by an epistemological critique powerful enough to win him a modern characterization as "the medieval Hume." But he adds a dimension unknown to Hume in supplementing his critique with a probabilistic metaphysics including such exotic (for the medieval world) theses as atomism and the eternity of things.

From one point of view, then, Autrecourt fits into the critical movement of the later Middle Ages, bringing to a climax the dialectical scrupulousness of Duns Scotus and the various devices of William of Ockham. With Autrecourt, this movement achieves its simplest and clearest principle: the only evidence is that which is reducible to the law of noncontradiction, the "first principle," as it was called. He seems to suppose that the certainty of the senses and of our acts is established by this principle. But the principle requires that in all valid inferences, no matter how many steps may be involved, the consequent must be identical with the antecedent, or a part of it. The surprising result of this stringency is that arguments from qualities to substances and from effects to causes are invalid. Of course, if one *means* by "quality," "quality-of-a-substance," or by "effect," "effect-of-a-cause," then

7o3

such arguments are not invalid. But then, the characterization of what we sense as qualities or effects is not certain. Furthermore, on the ground that a probable inference must pertain to conjunctions of which we have at some time had evident knowledge, inferences to substances and causes cannot even be probable. Somewhat surprisingly, in view of the fact that the concept of the final cause is included in this critique, the first principle for his probabilistic metaphysics is that things are for the sake of the good. Thus, if it is better for things to be eternal than not to be so, we must say that it is more probable that they are than that they are not.

Nicholas of Autrecourt was born in Autrecourt, in the diocese of Verdun, about 1300. It is interesting to note that James of Metz and John of Mirecourt, two other critical and censured philosophers roughly from the same epoch, came from the same region. Autrecourt was at the Sorbonne from 1320 to 1327, presumably completing the arts program. He eventually added a bachelor's degree in laws and became a licentiate in theology. He thus must have completed a commentary on the *Sentences,* and there is evidence that he also lectured on the *Politics*. In 1338, he was made a canon of the cathedral of Metz, which would amount to a subsidy for advanced studies. By this time he had apparently composed the nine letters to Bernard of Arezzo, of which we have two, and certain other items of this kind of public correspondence, of which we have one letter to a man named Giles. There is some question as to whether his treatise *Order Requires (Satis ordo exigit)* was composed before 1338 or as late as 1345. In 1339, the University of Paris issued a statute directed against those who "dogmatized" the doctrines of William of Ockham and held secret meetings about them. This was followed in 1340 by one directed against "pernicious subtleties" stemming from arguing against "famous propositions" taken in their literal sense alone, and repeating the strictures against dogmatizing Ockhamism. This latter statute seems to have Autrecourt in mind among others, and hence it is often assumed that the former did as well. But Ockham did not confine his interpretations to the literal sense; and on the crucial topics of universals and the divine power, Autrecourt differs radically from Ockham. He denied that a universal is only a mental sign, holding that a quality is both individual and universal; and he denied that one could legitimately invoke the distinction between a miracle and the normal course of nature. It may be a mistake, then, to classify him as an Ockhamist. Regardless of philosophical affiliations, he was summoned to Avignon for questioning in 1340. The death of the Pope delayed the investigation, but in 1342 it was taken up again. The report of the investigation is usually called, after the man who conducted it, *The Articles of Cardinal Curti*. On May 19, 1346, Nicholas of Autrecourt was sentenced to burn his writings at Paris. He may before this have fled from Avignon, but he complied with the sentence on November 25, 1347. His degrees were rescinded and he was declared ineligible for the mastership in theology. However, on August 6, 1350, he became dean of Metz, and is then described as a licentiate in theology. Nothing more is known of him.

The following selections contain the two surviving letters to Bernard of Arezzo. They have as their point of departure the burning issue of the times concerning the intuitive cognition of non-existents, that is, whether there is any philosophical limit to skepticism about the existence of objects. In them, Autrecourt presents his theory of evidence and its critical consequences for much of the philosophy of Aristotle.

Although Pierre d'Ailly, a prominent theologian of Nominalist sympathies who flourished at the turn of the fifteenth century, said that Autrecourt had been condemned out of jealousy, we must not suppose that his extreme views, however persuasive or repellent they may be to us, dominated the Nominalist or any other school during the later Middle Ages. Some of his arguments were used, and the rejection of Aristotle in the name of a practical concern for salvation or man's natural welfare was to become an increasingly important attitude. What is interesting about Nicholas of Autrecourt is not that he epitomizes the collapse of reason in the later Middle Ages, but rather that in his thought medieval commonplaces received, as it were, an internal critique. For he did not come at the philosophy of the schools from an alien background. As Hume did with a later tradition, he simply showed what follows if one insists on consistency to a professed principle.

LETTERS TO BERNARD OF AREZZO

I. First Letter to Bernard

With all the reverence which I am obligated to show to you, most amiable Father Bernard, by reason of the worthiness of the Friars, I wish in this present communication to explain some doubts—indeed, as it seems to some of us, some obvious contradictions—which appear to follow from the things you say, so that, by their resolution, the truth may be more clearly revealed to me and to others. For I read, in a certain book on which you lectured in the Franciscian school, the following propositions which you conceded, to whomever wished to uphold them, as true. The first, which is set forth by you in the first book of the *Sentences*, Dist. 3, Qu. 4, is this: *"Clear intuitive cognition is that by which we judge a thing to exist, whether it exists or does not exist.* Your second proposition, which is set forth in the same place as above, is of this sort: *The inference, 'An object does not exist, therefore it is not seen' is not valid; nor does this hold, 'This is seen, therefore this exists'; indeed both are invalid, just as these inferences, 'Caesar is thought of, therefore Caesar exists,' 'Caesar does not*

Translation by Ernest A. Moody, University of California at Los Angeles, printed with his permission. The translation is from the text edited by J. Lappe, *Beiträge zur Geschichte der Philosophie des Mittelalters.* Bd. VI, Hft. 2, Münster i.-W. 1908, pp. 2–14 and used in Ernest A. Moody, trans., *Medieval Philosophy,* ed. H. Shapiro, New York: The Modern Library, 1964.

exist, therefore he is not thought of.' The third proposition, stated in that same place, is this: *Intuitive cognition does not necessarily require the existing thing."*

From these propositions I infer a fourth, that every awareness which we have of the existence of objects outside our minds, can be false; since, according to you it [the awareness] can exist whether or not the object exists. And I infer another fifth proposition, which is this: By natural cognitive means [*in lumine naturali*] we cannot be certain when our awareness of the existence of external objects is true or false; because, as you say, it represents the thing as existing, whether or not it exists. And thus, since whoever admits the antecedent must concede the consequent which is inferred from that antecedent by a formal consequence, it follows that you do not have evident certitude of the existence of external objects. And likewise you must concede all the things which follow from this. But it is clear that you do not have evident certitude of the existence of objects of the senses, because no one has certitude of any consequent through an inference which manifestly involves a fallacy. But such is the case here; for according to you, this is a fallacy, "whiteness is seen, therefore whiteness exists."

But you will perhaps say, as I think you wished to suggest in a certain disputation over at the Preaching Friars', that although from the fact of seeing it cannot be inferred, when that seeing is produced or conserved by a supernatural cause, that the seen object exists, nevertheless when it is produced precisely by natural causes—with only the general concurrence of the First Agent—then it can be inferred.

But to the contrary: When from some antecedent, if produced by some agent, a certain consequent cannot be inferred by a formal and evident inference, then from that antecedent, no matter by what thing it be produced, that consequent cannot be inferred. This proposition is clear, by example and by reason. By example in this way: If, whiteness being posited as existing by the agency of A, it could not be formally inferred "Whiteness exists, therefore color exists," then this could not be inferred no matter by what agency the whiteness be posited as existing. It is also clear by reason, because the antecedent is not in itself modified by whatever it is that causes it to be—nor is the fact which is signified by that antecedent.

Further, since from that antecedent it cannot be inferred evidently by way of intuitive cognition, "therefore whiteness exists," we must then add something to that antecedent—namely, what you suggested above, that the [vision of] whiteness is not produced or conserved in existence supernaturally. But from this my contention is clearly established. For when a person is not certain of some consequent, unless in virtue of some antecedent of which he is not evidently certain whether or not the case is as it states it to be—because it is not known by the meaning of its terms, nor by experience, nor is it inferred from such knowledge, but is only believed—such a person is not evidently certain of the consequent. It is clear that this is so, if that antecedent is considered together with its condition; therefore etc. On the other hand, according to your position, whoever makes the inference from that antecedent without adding that condition, makes an invalid inference—as was the case with the philosophers, and Aristotle, and other people who did not add this condition to the antecedent, because they did not believe that God could impede the effects of natural causes.

Again, I ask you if you are acquainted with all natural causes, and know which of them exist and which are possible, and how much they can do. And

I ask how you know evidently, by evidence reducible to that of the law of contradiction, that there is anything such that its coming to pass does not involve contradiction and which nevertheless can only be brought to pass by God? On these questions I would gladly be given certitude of the kind indicated.

Again, you say that an imperfect intuitive cognition can be had in a natural manner, of a non-existent thing. I now ask how you are certain (with the certitude defined above) when your intuitive cognition is of a sufficiently perfect degree such that it cannot naturally be of a non-existent thing. And I would gladly be instructed about this.

Thus, it is clear, it seems to me, that as a consequence of your statements you have to say that you are not certain of the existence of the objects of the five senses. But what is even harder to uphold, you must say that you are not certain of your own actions—e.g., that you are seeing, or hearing—indeed you must say that you are not sure that anything is perceived by you, or has been perceived by you. For, in the *Sentences, Book I, Dist.* 3, in the place above cited, you say that your intellect does not have intuitive cognition of your actions. And you prove it by this argument: Every intuitive cognition is clear; but the cognition which your intellect has of your acts, is not clear; therefore etc. Now, on this assumption, I argue thus: The intellect which is not certain of the existence of things of which it has the clearest cognition, will not be certain concerning those things of which it has a less clear cogniton. But, as was said, you are not certain of the existence of objects of which you have a clearer cognition than you have of your own acts; therefore etc.

And if you say that sometimes some abstractive cognition is as clear as an intuitive cognition—e.g., that every whole is greater than its part—this will not help you, because you explicitly say that the cognition which we have of our own acts is not as clear as intuitive cognition; and yet intuitive cognition, at least that which is imperfect, is not naturally of evident certainty. This is clear from what you say. And thus it follows evidently, that you are not certain of what appears evident to you, and consequently you are not certain whether anything appears to you.

And it also follows that you are not certain whether any proposition is true or false, because you are not evidently certain whether any proposition exists, or has existed. Indeed it follows that if you were asked whether or not you believed some articles of the Faith, you would have to say, "I do not know," because, according to your position, you could not be certain of your own act of believing. And I confirm this, because, if you were certain of your act of believing, this would either be from that very act itself, in which case the direct and reflective act would be identical—which you will not admit—or else it would be by some other act, and in that case, according to your position, you would in the same way be uncertain, because there would then be no more contradiction than that the seeing of whiteness existed and the whiteness did not exist, etc.

And so, bringing all these statements together, it seems that you must say that you are not certain of those things which are outside of you. And thus you do not know if you are in the heavens or on the earth, in fire or in water; and consequently you do not know whether today's sky is the same one as yesterday's, because you do not know whether the sky exists. Just as you do not know whether the Chancellor or the Pope exists, and whether, if they exist, they are different in each moment of time. Similarly, you do not know the things within you—as, whether or not you have a beard, a head, hair, and so forth. And *a fortiori* it follows from this that you are not certain of the things which occurred in the past—as, whether you have been reading, or seeing, or hearing. Further, your position seems to lead to the destruction of social and political affairs, because if witnesses testify of what they have seen, it does not follow, "We have seen it, therefore it happened." Again, I ask how, on this view, the Apostles were certain that Christ suffered on the cross, and that He rose from the dead, and so with all the rest.

I wish that your mind would express itself on all these questions, and I wonder very much how you can say that you are evidently certain of various conclusions which are more obscure—such as concern the existence of the Prime Mover, and the like—when you are not certain about these things which I have mentioned. Again, it is strange how, on your assumptions, you believe that you have shown that a cognition is distinct from what is cognized, when you are not certain, according to your position, that any cognition exists or that any propositions exist, and consequently that any contradictory propositions exist; since, as I have shown, you do not have certainty of the existence of your own acts, or of your own mind, and do not know whether it exists. And, as it seems to me, the absurdities which follow on the position of the Academics, follow on your position. And so, in order to avoid such absurdities, I maintained in my disputation at the Sorbonne, that I am evidently certain of the objects of the five senses, and of my own acts.

I think of these objections, and of so many others, that there is no end to them, against what you say. I pray you, Father, to instruct me who, however stupid, am nevertheless desirous of reaching knowledge of the truth. May you abide in Him, who is the light, and in whom there is no darkness.

II. The Second Letter of Nicolaus of Autrecourt to Bernard of Arezzo

Reverend Father Bernard, the depth of your subtlety would truly bring forth the admiration of my mind, if I were to know that you possess evident knowledge of the separated substances—the more so if I know this, but even if I had in my mind a slight belief. And not only, if I should think that you possess true cognition of the separated substances, but even of those conjoined to matter. And so to you, Father, who assert that you have evident cognition of such lofty objects of knowledge, I wish to lay bare my doubtful and anxious mind, so that you may have the materials for leading me and other people toward acquaintance with such great things.

And the first point is, that at the foundation of discourse this principle is primary: Contradictories cannot be simultaneously true. And with respect to this, two things hold: the first is, that this is the first principle, taken negatively as that than which nothing is more primary. The second is, that this is first, taken positively, as that which is prior to every other principle.

These two statements are proved by argument, as follows: Every certitude possessed by us reduces to this principle, and it in turn is not reduced to any other in the way that a conclusion is reduced to its premise; it therefore follows that this principle is first, with the twofold primacy indicated. This consequence is known from the meaning of the term "first," according to each of the expositions given. The antecedent is proved with respect to both of its parts. And first, with respect to its first part, namely that every certitude possessed by us, short of this certitude, reduces to this principle of which you say you are certain, I set forth this consequence: It is possible, without any contradiction being implied, that something will appear to you to be so, and yet that it will not be so; therefore you are not evidently certain that it is so. It is clear to me that if I were to admit this antecedent to be true, I would concede the consequent to be true; and therefore I would not be evidently and unqualifiedly certain of that of which I was saying that I was certain.

From this it is clear that every one of our certitudes is resolved into our said principle, and that it is not resolved into another, as a conclusion into its premise. From this it is plain that all certitudes are resolved into this one, as was said, and that this consequence is valid: If this is prior to everything other than itself, then nothing is prior to it. And thus it is first, with the twofold primacy above stated.

The third point is, that a contradiction is the affirmation and negation of the same (predicate) of the same (subject), etc., as is commonly said.

From these things I infer a corollary—namely, that the certitude of evidence which we have in the natural light, is certitude in the unqualified sense; for it is the certitude which is possessed in virtue of the first principle, which neither is nor can be contradicted by any true law. And hence whatever is demonstrated in the natural light of reason, is demonstrated without qualification; and, just as there is no power which can make contradictories simultaneously true, so there is no power by which it can come to pass that the opposite of the consequent is compatible with the antecedent.

The second corollary which I infer, with regard to this, is that the certitude of evidence has no degrees. Thus, if there are two conclusions, of each of which we are evidently certain, we are not more certain of one than of the other. For as was said, every certitude is resolved into the same first principle. Either, then, those first conclusions are reduced with equal immediacy to the same first principle—in which case there is no ground for our being more certain of one than of the other; or else one is reduced mediately, and the other immediately. But this makes no difference, because, once the reduction to the first principle has been made, we are certain of the one equally with the other—just as the geometrician says that he is as certain of a second conclusion as of the first, and similarly of the third and so on, even though in his first consideration, because of the plurality of the deductions, he cannot be as certain of the fourth or third as of the first.

The third corollary which I infer, in connection with what has been said, is that with the exception of the certitude of faith, there is no other certitude except the certitude of the first principle, or the certitude which can be resolved into the first principle. For there is no certitude except that in which there is no falsity; because, if there were any in which falsity could exist, let it be supposed that falsity does exist in it—then, since the certitude itself remains, it follows that someone is certain of something whose contradictory is true, without contradiction.

The fourth corollary is this: that a syllogistic form is immediately reducible to the first principle; because, by its demonstration, the conclusion is either immediately reduced (in which case the thesis holds), or else mediately; and if mediately, then either the regress will be infinite, or else it must arrive at some conclusion which reduces immediately to the first principle.

The fifth corollary: In every consequence which reduces immediately to the first principle, the consequent, and the antecedent either as a whole or in part, are really identical; because, if this were not so, then it would not be immediately evident that the antecedent and the opposite of the consequent cannot both be true.

The sixth corollary is this: In every evident consequence reducible to the first principle by as many intermediates as you please, the consequent is really identical with the antecedent or with part of what is signified by the antecedent. This is shown because, if we suppose some conclusion to be reduced to the certitude of the first principle by three intermediates, the consequent will be really identical with its (immediate) antecedent or with part of what is signified by that antecedent, by the fifth corollary; and similarly in the second consequence, by the same reason; and thus, since in the first consequence the consequent is really identical with the antecedent or with part of what is signified by the antecedent, and likewise in the second one, and likewise in the third, it follows that in these consequences, ordered from first to last, the last consequent will be really identical with the first antecedent or with a part of what is signified by that antecedent.

On the basis of these statements, I laid down, along with other conclusions, one which was this: From the fact that some thing is known to exist, it cannot be evidently inferred, by evidence reduced to the first principle or to the certitude of the first principle, that some other thing exists.

Aside from many other arguments, I brought forth this argument. In such a consequence, in which from one thing another thing is inferred, the consequent would not be really identical with the antecedent or with part of what is signified by the antecedent; therefore it follows that such a consequence would not be evidently known with the said evidence of the first principle. The antecedent is conceded and posited by my opponent; the consequence is plain from the description of "contradiction," which is affirmation and negation of the same of the same, etc. Since therefore in this case the consequent is not really identical with the antecedent or its part, it is evident that if the opposite of the consequent, and the antecedent, be simultaneously true, this would not be a case of one thing being affirmed and denied of the same thing, etc.

But Bernard replies, saying that although in this case there is not a formal contradiction, for the reason given, yet there is a virtual contradiction; he calls a contradiction virtual, however, if from it a formal contradiction can be evidently inferred.

But against this we can argue manifestly, from the fifth and sixth of the above corollaries. For it has been shown that in every consequence reducible either immediately or mediately to the certitude of the first principle, it is necessary that the consequent—whether the first one or the last—be really identical with the first antecedent or with a part of it.

Again, we may argue conclusively from another premise. For he says that, although in a consequence in which from one thing another thing is inferred, there is not a formal contradiction, there is nevertheless a virtual one from which a formal one can be evidently inferred. Then let there be, for example, the following consequence propounded: "A exists, therefore B exists." If, then, from the propositions, "A exists," "B does not exist," a formal contradiction could be evidently inferred, this would be through a consequent of one of these propositions, or through a consequent of each of them. But whichever way it is, the thesis is not established. For these consequents would either be really identical with their antecedents, or they would not. If identical, then there will not be a formal contradiction between those consequents, since there will not then be an affirmation and a negation of the same predicate of the same subject, and hence not between the antecedents either. Just as it is not a formal contradiction to say that a rational animal exists and that a neighing animal does not exist; and for the same reason. But if it be said that these consequents differ from their antecedents, we argue the same way as before, that this is not a consequence evidently reduced to the certitude of the first principle, since the opposite of the consequent is compatible with whatever is signified by the antecedent, without contradiction. And if it be said that there is a virtual contradiction, from which a formal one can be inferred, we argue as before, either there is a regress without end, or else we must say that in a consequence evident without qualification the consequent is identical in its signification with the antecedent, or with part of what is signified by the antecedent.

And it is true that the reverend Father has said, with regard to this question, that it would not be true to say that in a consequence evident without qualification it is required that the opposite of the consequent, and the antecedent, cannot simultaneously be false, and that they are therefore not opposed as contradictories. But in actual fact this does not in any way prevent what I am maintaining. For I do not wish to say that the opposite of the consequent must be the contradictory of the antecedent—for in many consequences the antecedent can signify more than does the consequent, though the consequent signifies a part of what is signified by the antecedent—as in this consequence, "A house exists, therefore a wall exists." And on this account the opposite of the consequent, and the antecedent, can both be false. But I wish to say that in an evident consequence the opposite of the consequent, and the antecedent or a part of what it signifies, are opposed as contradictories. It is plain that this is the case in every valid syllogism; for since no term occurs in the conclusion which did not occur in the premises, the opposite of the conclusion, and something signified by the premises, are opposed as contradictories. And so it must be in every valid inference, because an enthymeme is only valid in virtue of a proposition presupposed—so that it is a kind of incomplete syllogism.

Further, I offer this argument for my main conclusion: Never, in virtue of any inference, can there be inferred a greater identity of the extreme term, than that which is between the extreme term and the middle term, because the former is only inferred in virtue of the latter. But the opposite of this will occur, if from the fact that one thing is a being, it could evidently be inferred that something else is a being; because the predicate of the conclusion, and the subject, signify what is really identical, whereas they are not really identical with the middle term which is posited as another thing.

But Bernard objects to this proposed rule, because it follows evidently, with an evidence reduced to the certitude of the first principle, "Whiteness exists, therefore something else exists"—because whiteness cannot exist unless some subject maintains it in existence. Likewise it follows, "Whiteness is not a being in the primary sense, therefore some other thing exists." Or likewise, "Fire is brought into contact with the fuel, and there is no impediment, therefore there will be heat."

To these objections I have elsewhere given many answers. But for the present I say that if a thousand such objections were adduced, either it must be said that they are irrelevant, or, if relevant, that they conclude nothing against my position. Because in these consequences which he states, if the consequent is really identical in its signification with the antecedent as a whole or with a part of the antecedent, then the argument is not to the point, because in that case I would concede the consequences to be evident, and nothing against my position would be adduced. But if it be said that the consequent is not identical with the antecedent or part of it, then, if I concede the opposite of the consequent, and the antecedent, to be simultaneously true, it is plain that I am not conceding them to be contradictories, since contradictories are of the same predicate of the same subject, etc. And thus such a consequence is not evident by the evidence of the first principle, because the evidence of the first principle was understood to be had when, if it were conceded that the opposite of the consequent is compatible with the antecedent, contradictories would be admitted as simultaneously true. For though one might concede, with respect to this consequence "A house exists, therefore a wall exists," that a house exists and a wall does not exist, he does not thereby concede contradictories to be simultaneously true, because these propositions are not contradictories, "A house exists," "A wall does not exist," since both of them may be false; yet he does concede contradictories on another ground, because to signify that a house exists is to signify that a wall exists, and then it is a contradiction that a house exists and that a wall does not exist.

From this rule, so explained to anyone having the grasp of it, I infer that Aristotle never possessed an evident cognition concerning any substance other than his own soul—taking "substance" as a thing other than the objects of the five senses, and other than our formal experiences. And this is so, because he would have had a cognition of such a thing prior to every inference—which is not true, since they (substances) are not perceived intuitively, and since (if they were) rustics would know that such things exist; nor are they known by inference, namely as inferred from things perceived to exist antecedently to discursive thought—because from one thing it cannot be inferred that another thing exists, as the above conclusion states.

And if he did not have evident cognition of conjoined (material) substances, much less did he have it of abstract substances. From which it follows, whether you like it or not, and not because I make it so but because reason determines it, that Aristotle in his whole natural philosophy and metaphysics had such certitude of scarcely two conclusions, and perhaps not even of one. And Father Bernard, who is not greater than Aristotle, has an equal amount of certitudes, or much less.

And not only did Aristotle not have evident cognition (of these things)—indeed, though I do not assert this, I have an argument which I cannot refute, to prove that he did not have probable knowledge. For a person does not have probable knowledge of any consequent, in virtue of some antecedent, when he is not evidently certain whether the consequent will at some time be true together with the antecedent. For let anyone really consider well the nature of probable knowledge—as for example that because it was at one time evident to me that when I put my hand in the fire I was hot, therefore it is probable to me that if I should put it there now I would be hot. But from the rule stated above, it follows that it was never evident to anyone that, given these things which are apparent without inference, there would exist certain other things—namely those others which are called substances. It therefore follows that of their existence we do not have probable knowledge. I do not assert this conclusion; but let this argument be resolved, for a solution will surely occur.

And that we do not possess certitude concerning any substance conjoined to matter, other than our own soul, is plain—because, pointing to a piece of wood, or a stone, this conclusion will be most clearly deduced from a belief accepted at the same time. For by the divine power it can happen, with these things which appear prior to all inference, that no substance is there; therefore in the natural light of reason it is not evidently inferred from these appearances that a substance is there. This consequence is plain from what we explained above. For it was said that a consequence is evident only if it is a contradiction for it to occur, through any power, that the opposite of the consequent is true along with the antecedent. And if it is said that the consequence is evident, if to the antecedent we add "God is not performing a miracle," this is disproved by what we have said on this point in our first letter to Bernard.

I ask, Father, that you take up these doubts and give counsel to my stupidity; and I promise that I will not be stubborn in evading the truth, to which I adhere with all my strength.

SELECTED BIBLIOGRAPHY

TRANSLATIONS

Kennedy, L., *et al., The Universal Treatise of Nicholas of Autrecourt*, Milwaukee, 1971.

STUDIES

Copleston, F., "The Logical Empiricism of Nicholas of Autrecourt," *Proceedings of the Aristotelian Society*, LXXIV (1973–1974), 249–262.

Moody, E., "Ockham, Buridan, and Nicholas of Autrecourt," *Franciscan Studies*, VII (1947), 113–146.

O'Donnell, J., "The Philosophy of Nicholas of Autrecourt and his Appraisal of Aristotle," *Mediaeval Studies*, IV (1942), 97–125.

Rashdall, H., "Nicholas de Ultricuria, a Medieval Hume," *Proceedings of the Aristotelian Society*, VIII (1907), 1–27.

Scott, T., "Nicholas of Autrecourt, Buridan, and Ockhamism," *Journal of the History of Philosophy*, IX (1971), 15–41.

Weinberg, J., *Nicolaus of Autrecourt*, Princeton, 1948.

Wolfson, H., "Nicholas of Autrecourt and Ghazali's Argument against Causality," *Speculum*, XLIV (1969), 234–238.

MARSILIUS OF PADUA

Between 1275 and 1280 – ca. 1342

WHEN, ABOUT 1260, William of Moerbeke translated Aristotle's *Politics* into Latin from the Greek, new political speculations arose under the impact of the work. Stimulated by Aristotle's doctrines, political philosophers investigated afresh the nature of the state, the source of its authority, the function of its parts, and its role in the production of happiness here on earth. But just as in the theoretical sciences the reintroduction of Aristotle's works produced moderates who, while philosophers, displayed theological interests, and secularists who studied philosophy apart from any theological concerns (see p. 490), so in politics, the appearance of Aristotle's work produced Aristotelians of the same two kinds. Both derived their political theories from Aristotelian principles, but whereas the moderates recognized some ultimate superiority of the Church, the secularists held that the state in temporal matters rules supreme. In political thought, Marsilius of Padua was the most articulate spokesman for the secularist view.

But to see Marsilius merely as a political philosopher who was a secular Aristotelian is to do an injustice to his intention and the complexity of his thought. As he explicitly states, it was his aim to free the state from discord and from strife which had resulted from the temporal uses of ecclesiastical power. The very title of his major work, *The Defender of Peace,* suggests that he wanted to restore to the state the peace which it had lost through clerical interference. Living in the fourteenth century, Marsilius could hardly hope to accomplish this task without considering the long tradition of political writings devoted to the demarkation of areas of secular and ecclesiastical power. Nor could he ignore the persistent struggles between popes and secular rulers over whose authority should be supreme. Hence to understand Marsilius requires at least a cursory glance at some of the doctrines and historical events which form the backgrounds of his views.

How religious and secular authority are related was an issue as old as Christianity itself. Already the first Christian teachers had to instruct their followers how to meet demands for civil obedience made by the Roman state. Since Christianity, in its beginning, was a religion without political power or ambitions, their counsel was "obey the secular rulers." Jesus had advocated to render unto Caesar what was his (Matthew 22:21) and, in a much-to-be-quoted text, the Apostle Paul had stated:

Let every soul be subject unto the higher powers. For there is no power but of God: the powers that be are ordained of God. . . . For he [the ruler] is the minister of God to thee for good. . . . Render therefore to all their dues: tribute to whom tribute is due; custom to whom custom; fear to whom fear; honor to whom honor (Romans 13:1, 4, 7).

While passages such as these leave little doubt about the political teachings of the early Church, there were others which could be used in support of ecclesiastical temporal claims. Jesus had said to Peter:

And I will give unto thee the keys of the kingdom of heaven: and whatsoever thou shalt bind on earth shall be bound in heaven: and whatsoever thou shalt loose on earth shall be loosed in heaven (Matthew 16:19).

And Paul had written to the Corinthians:

Know ye not that we shall judge angels? how much more things that pertain to this life? (I Corinthians 6:3)

These passages and others like them were in Marsilius' mind when he developed his own political views.

As the organization of the Church developed, as its power grew, and as the Roman Empire became Christian, Christian thinkers had to re-examine the nature of the Church's temporal claims. In the west, Latin Fathers, chief among them Augustine (see p. 17), developed their political views and even though they differed in emphasis and detail, a consensus began to emerge. The orientation of the Fathers was theological and hence they viewed the state primarily as a corrective for the vices resulting from the fallen nature of man. Men, according to the Fathers, were created free and equal, and political institutions exist among them by convention. Christian society is to be governed by two authorities, the jurisdiction of each of which is to be distinct. There is the Church which cares for man's eternal salvation, and there is the state which, by preserving order, justice, and peace, ministers to his temporal needs. Between the two authorities a spirit of helpfulness and respect is to prevail, but at the same time the authority of the Church is ultimately supreme. These patristic teachings found their authoritative formulation in the doctrine of the two powers or the "two swords" (Luke 22:38) which Pope Gelasius I (end of the fifth century) expressed when he wrote to Anastasius, emperor in the east:

There are, then, august Emperor, two powers by which the world is chiefly ruled, the sacred power of the prelates and the royal power. But of these, the *burden of the priests is the heavier, for they will have to give account in the divine judgment even for the kings of men . . .**

While the Gelasian doctrine was to remain the foundation of political theory in the west, it was vague and required interpretation. Defenders of secular claims pointed out that Gelasius had spoken of the independence of the temporal power, while proponents of the ecclesiastical cause emphasized that he had affirmed the final superiority of the Church. But whatever the theoretical differences, the implementation of the doctrine depended on how much power state or Church could muster. Though churchmen took an active part in political processes, until the end of the eleventh century the secular power generally ruled supreme. Yet from the ninth century on, forces were at work which helped to strengthen the position of the Church. There were the Pseudo-Isidorean Decretals. Forgeries of the ninth century, they denied to secular rulers the right to confiscate the property of bishops, and they placed bishops under the jurisdiction of their own councils and, ultimately, under the jurisdiction of the pope. The Decretals also incorporated an earlier forgery known as the "Donation of Constantine" according to which Constantine gave the western portion of the Empire to Pope Sylvester I, in gratitude for having cured him of leprosy. In their own days the Decretals had little effect, but in the skillful hands of canon lawyers later on they became powerful weapons in the arsenal of papal claims. Then there were the Cluniac reforms. By refusing to render feudal service for land received, by combatting ecclesiastical abuses such as simony and clerical marriage, and by securing the transfer of papal elections from secular authorities to the College of Cardinals, the reformers helped to build a Church which, spiritual in its orientation, possessed a strong, centralized administration.

However much these developments increased ecclesiastical power, the Church was unable to enforce its claim until it found a strong champion in Pope Gregory VII and a cause in the Investiture Controversy. In 1075, Gregory decreed that henceforth bishops were to be appointed by the Church, not by the secular ruler. Emperor Henry IV ignored the decree and Gregory excommunicated him, at the same time relieving his vassals of their feudal oath. Because of political conditions, Henry was forced to submit, though later on the victory was his. This phase of the controversy was settled by the Concordat of Mainz (1122), a compromise which left the secular ruler a voice in the election of bishops. Though Gregory in the end did not prevail, he had provided an example of how the Church could use its power.

Under the impact of the Investiture Controversy, papalists and imperialists began to explicate the details of their respective claims. Both parties accepted the Gelasian doctrine of the two swords, but for papalists it came to mean that both powers were entrusted to the pope and that the emperor receives his by delegation, while for imperialists it came to mean that the secular ruler receives his power directly from God. In the twelfth century the papalist posi-

---

* Gelasius I, *Letters,* XII, 2. Cited in R. Carlyle and A. Carlyle, *A History of Medieval Political Theory in the West,* 6 vols., London, 1903–1936, Vol. I, p. 191.

tion found an exponent in John of Salisbury (see p. 166) who, while respecting the lawful exercise of power by the secular ruler, wrote in a famous passage:

. . . the prince receives the [secular] sword from the hand of the Church. . . . For the Church also possesses it, but it uses it through the hand of the prince. . . . The prince, therefore, is indeed the minister of the sacred power (minister sacerdotii) and he exercises that part of the sacred offices which seems to be unworthy of the hands of the sacred power. For every office [pertaining to] the sacred laws is religious and holy; however, that is inferior which is exercised in the punishment of crimes and which appears to be represented by the figure of the executioner.*

By contrast, the imperialist position found its expression in the somewhat earlier (*ca.* 1100) *York Tracts,* the product of an investiture controversy in England. According to the *Tracts,* the power of the king is higher than that of bishops, though the Church possesses the right to invest bishops with the symbols of their spiritual authority. In sentiments foreshadowing those of Marsilius, the author of the *Tracts* asserts that, in spiritual matters, all bishops are equal, denying concurrently the supremacy of the bishop of Rome. At the same time, the renewed study of Roman law and its development provided the imperialists with support, for now civilian jurists set forth the legal basis of royal authority and the details of royal claims.

In the first half of the thirteenth century the Church reached the zenith of its political power under such skilled and powerful popes as Innocent III, Gregory IX, and Innocent IV. The Empire and the papacy were now at war. The papacy used military force, alliances, diplomatic pressures, and economic aid to enforce its temporal goals. Innocent III, for example, decided the election of Otto and Frederick II as emperors, and in controversies with the kings of France and England he forced the two rulers to submit. Though the struggle ended in the defeat of the Empire, the papacy itself was eventually greatly weakened. Innocent III strengthened the papacy through a system of papal legates through which even outlying districts came under his effective control. Regular taxes imposed on the clergy as well as levies and "gifts" on special occasions became important sources of papal economic power. At the same time, canon lawyers, though theoretically committed to the doctrine of the two swords, defined wider and wider areas of papal authority. According to their teachings, the pope had the right to judge the fitness of elected candidates, to confirm treaties between secular rulers, and to supervise the administration of justice. Their claims culminated in the doctrine of the "papal plentitude of power" according to which the pope, as vicar of Christ, possesses full power in both secular and spiritual affairs. The Gelasian doctrine had come a long way.

In the light of these backgrounds, the impact of Aristotle's *Politics* can now be more fully understood. Most political philosophers retained the

---

* *Policraticus* IV, 3. Cited in Carlyle and Carlyle, *op. cit.,* Vol. IV, p. 333.

doctrine of the two swords, but Aristotle's well-developed political teachings required a revised understanding of the nature and function of the state. Whereas for the Fathers the state existed by convention as a corrective for the transgressions of fallen man, for Aristotle it existed by nature for man's moral education and for the production of happiness here on earth. Christian thinkers, to be sure, had to allow for man's supernatural salvation and for the temporal Church, but at the same time they found it possible to examine the state in its own terms. Imperialists, papalists, and moderate papalists alike turned to Aristotle for support of their views.

The shift in political thought is well illustrated by Aquinas, who was a moderate papalist. For Aquinas, the definition of papal and imperial power is no longer the overriding issue, but it becomes part of a political philosophy at large. As a theologian, Aquinas sees the state as part of a hierarchically ordered universe created and governed by God, but as an Aristotelian, he sees it as a human institution required to bring man to that natural end which, without the collaborative efforts of others, he could never attain. It is significant that Aquinas finds in the well-ordered state a contributing factor even for the ultimate salvation of man. Perhaps the central theme of Aquinas' political thought is his philosophy of law (see p. 569). Law for him is an "ordinance of reason" which in the form of natural and human law becomes the instrument for the moral and political training of man. Even the ruler is ultimately subject to law. Speaking of the form that government should take, Aquinas strikes a balance between what is best in itself, and what is best, given men as they are. Absolutely, monarchy is best; but relatively, a mixed government (which seems to be a limited monarchy) is preferable. Aquinas' view is similarly balanced when he speaks of secular and ecclesiastical power. The pope, he holds, is ultimately supreme and he has the right to interfere in political affairs; but as long as the secular ruler exercises his power within his proper sphere, it is unjust for the ecclesiastical authorities to interfere.

Whereas Aquinas adopted a moderate position, Dante, some fifty years later, defended the imperialist cause. But the Empire of which Dante spoke did not exist in his day. Using Aristotelian principles, Dante undertook to show that the attainment of man's natural end requires peace and that this peace can only be guaranteed by a universal empire governed by a single ruler. From these theoretical foundations, he went on to argue that the Roman Empire was the providentially ordained state for providing the required temporal unity. And finally he turned to Scripture and the decrees of early councils to demonstrate that the emperor received his power directly from God and that, hence, he is not subject to any superior human power.

While Aquinas' and Dante's expositions were rather theoretical, the set of political writings next to be considered were occasioned by renewed conflicts between Church and state. This time the issue was taxation and the antagonists were Pope Boniface VIII (1294–1303) and Philip the Fair, King of France (1285–1314). Political power had shifted from the emperor to national rulers and a feeling of national loyalty had grown. When Philip imposed taxes on the French clergy to finance a war, Boniface issued the bull *Clericis laicos* which forbade the clergy to pay. This bull was followed later (1302) by the famous *Unam sanctam* which contained the most extreme statement of papal claims. In this bull, Boniface declared that subjection to the pope is necessary for salvation and that both swords belong to the Church, the king using his "at the command and with the permission of the priests." But this time the papacy could not enforce its claims. The French clergy, imbued with nationalist feelings, paid willingly. The controversy ended with the "Babylonian Captivity," during which Avignon was the papal seat.

Once again tracts appeared in support of both sides. On the papalist side, Egidius Romanus was the major spokesman. Invoking philosophic arguments, scriptural passages, and historical precedents, he developed a position in which the temporal ruler is the vassal of the pope, and which is well summarized in the following passage:

> *As in the universe itself corporeal substance is ruled by spiritual . . . so among Christians all temporal lords and all earthly power ought to be governed and ruled by spiritual and ecclesiastical authority, and especially by the pope. . . .**

The royalist position was presented by John of Paris. Holding that, though the priest is superior in dignity to the secular ruler, the king, nevertheless, receives his power directly from God, John writes:

> *. . . secular power is greater than spiritual power in certain matters, namely, temporal matters; and with respect to this it is not subject to it in anything, because it does not stem from it. Rather, both powers stem directly from one supreme power, namely divine power.†*

We now come to the time of Marsilius, once again a time of political controversy. The pope was John XXII (1316–1334), the emperor, Louis of Bavaria (1314–1347), the occasion an imperial election. Marsilius took the emperor's part. The defense of secular power, as we have seen, was nothing new; but whereas earlier imperialists granted some superior power to the pope, Marsilius proposed a more radical solution. A secularist in politics, and following a secular interpretation of Aristotle, Marsilius set out to show that the clergy possesses no right to temporal power, and that its proper role is to instruct and admonish. Moreover, he attacked papal claims by showing that in spiritual matters all priests are equal. To establish these doctrines he first developed a secular theory of the state and then, as many another reformer, he re-examined the religious texts.

Marsilius begins with an analysis of the state. Invoking a biological analogy, he shows that the state is like an animate being and that its health (which is peace) consists in the orderly functioning of its parts. There are

---

* *On Ecclesiastical Power,* I, 5. Cited in G. Sabine, *A History of Political Theory,* 3rd ed., New York, 1961, p. 174.

† *On Papal and Royal Power,* chap. 5. See R. Lerner and M. Mahdi, *Medieval Political Philosophy: A Sourcebook,* New York, 1963, p. 414.

six classes within the state of which the clergy is one. It follows then that the clergy is one class among many and that its political role (such as it is) is determined by the secular ruler. Marsilius emphasizes, moreover, that though the clergy is quite properly concerned with man's well-being in the life to come, the good life here on earth is the prerogative of the state.

Marsilius' secularist position becomes still more explicit in his analysis of law. Unlike Aquinas, for whom the various kinds of law form parts of a well-ordered whole, Marsilius distinguishes sharply between divine and human law. The latter possesses coercive force here on earth, the former does not. Moreover, Marsilius displays great interest in the efficient cause of the law. In a statement which is central to his thought, he affirms that legislative power rests "with the people, or the whole body of citizens, or the weightier part thereof" and, for him, the people or their delegates are the source of judicial and executive power. These doctrines make Marsilius an important precursor of modern political thought.

Not satisfied with investigating the relation of Church and state, Marsilius also examines the internal structure of the Church. Though he could hardly deny the reality of the Church as a temporal organization, he tries to redefine its structure. To that end he affirms the equality of all priests in their spiritual function and the Church, for him, is ultimately the whole body of Christian believers. Claims for papal plenitude he counters by advocating that matters of doctrine be settled by a general ecclesiastical council rather than by the pope.

Marsilius dei Mainardi was born in Padua, sometime between 1275 and 1280. Son of a notary at the University, he seems to have considered the study of law, but instead turned to medicine and natural philosophy. From December 1312 until March 1313 he was rector of the University of Paris. There he came in contact with "secular Aristotelians." In 1316, Pope John XXII promised him a canonry in Padua, and two years later a benefice. Marsilius' interests were not only academic, but also political. We hear, in a letter dated 1319, that Can Grande della Scala and Matteo Visconti had sent him to Count Charles of La Marche to offer him the captaincy of the Ghibelline League. The mission failed and he returned to Paris. At this time he seems to have become acquainted with some Spiritual Franciscans, among them Michael of Cesena, who defended the doctrine of evangelical poverty (see p. 651). This doctrine played a significant role in Marsilius' thought. During the years at Paris he worked on the *Defender of Peace* which he finished on June 24, 1324. When the authorship of the work became known, Marsilius, together with John of Jandun, was forced to flee Paris and went to the court of Louis of Bavaria. In Louis they found a defender, since he also was at odds with the pope, who had refused to confirm his election. In 1327 Louis undertook an expedition to Italy to secure the imperial crown. He conquered Rome and, in accordance with Marsilius' doctrines, he was crowned in 1328 by Sciarra Colonna as delegate of the people. Marsilius was appointed spiritual vicar of the city. However, when the people became disaffected, Louis, and with him Marsilius, had to leave Rome. Marsilius spent the remainder of his life at Louis' court where there were also Spiritual Franciscans, among them William of Ockham. In 1342, Marsilius composed a summary of his major work, entitled *Defensor Minor,* part of which is a treatise *Concerning the Jurisdiction of the Emperor in Matrimonial Cases.* He died shortly thereafter.

All the following selections are taken from the *Defender of Peace.* The first describes the purpose of the state and its division into parts. It is in this section that Marsilius discusses the political function of the clergy. The next two sections contain his account of the law and of the legislator. The last two sections, which contain much analysis of religious texts, deal with ecclesiastical claims of temporal power and with the claim for "papal plenitude."

THE DEFENDER OF PEACE

Discourse I

CHAPTER IV. *On the Final Cause of the State and of Its Civil Requirements, and the Differentiation in General of Its Parts*

The state, according to Aristotle in the *Politics,* Book I, Chapter 1, is "the perfect community having the full limit of self-sufficiency, which came into existence for the sake of living, but exists for the sake of living well." This phrase of Aristotle—"came into existence for the sake of living, but exists for the sake of living well"—signifies the perfect final cause of the state, since those who live a civil life not only live, which beasts or slaves do too, but live well, having leisure for those liberal functions in which are exercised the virtues of both the practical and the theoretic soul.

2. Having thus determined the end of the state to be living and living well, we must treat first of living and its modes. For this, as we have said, is the purpose for the sake of which the state was established, and which necessitates all the things which exist in the state and are done by the association of men in it. Let us therefore lay this down as the principle of all the things which are to be demonstrated here, a principle naturally held, believed, and freely granted by all: that all men not deformed or otherwise impeded naturally desire a sufficient life, and avoid and flee what is harmful thereto. This has been acknowledged not only with regard to man but also with regard to every genus of animals, according to Tully in his treatise *On Duties,* Book I, Chapter III, where he says: "It is an original endowment which nature has bestowed upon every genus of living things, that it preserves itself, its body, and its life, that

From Marsilius of Padua, *The Defender of Peace,* trans. A. Gewirth, Vol. II, New York: Columbia University Press, 1956. Reprinted by permission.

it avoids those things which seem harmful, and that it seeks and obtains all those things which are necessary for living." This principle can also be clearly grasped by everyone through sense induction.

3. But the living and living well which are appropriate to men fall into two kinds, of which one is temporal or earthly, while the other is usually called eternal or heavenly. However, this latter kind of living, the eternal, the whole body of philosophers were unable to prove by demonstration, nor was it self-evident, and therefore they did not concern themselves with the means thereto. But as to the first kind of living and living well or good life, that is, the earthly, and its necessary means, this the glorious philosophers comprehended almost completely through demonstration. Hence for its attainment they concluded the necessity of the civil community, without which this sufficient life cannot be obtained. Thus the foremost of the philosophers, Aristotle, said in his *Politics,* Book I, Chapter 1: "All men are driven toward such an association by a natural impulse." Although sense experience teaches this, we wish to bring out more distinctly that cause of it which we have indicated, as follows: Man is born composed of contrary elements, because of whose contrary actions and passions some of his substance is continually being destroyed; moreover, he is born "bare and unprotected" from excess of the surrounding air and other elements, capable of suffering and of destruction, as has been said in the science of nature. As a consequence, he needed arts of diverse genera and species to avoid the afore-mentioned harms. But since these arts can be exercised only by a large number of men, and can be had only through their association with one another, men had to assemble together in order to attain what was beneficial through these arts and to avoid what was harmful.

4. But since among men thus assembled there arise disputes and quarrels which, if not regulated by a norm of justice, would cause men to fight and separate and thus finally would bring about the destruction of the state, there had to be established in this association a standard of justice and a guardian or maker thereof. And since this guardian has to restrain excessive wrongdoers as well as other individuals both within and outside the state who disturb or attempt to oppress the community, the state had to have within it something by which to resist these. Again, since the community needs various conveniences, repairs, and protection of certain common things, and different things in time of peace and in time of war, it was necessary that there be in the community men to take care of such matters, in order that the common necessity might be relieved when it was expedient or needful. But beside the things which we have so far mentioned, which relieve only the necessities of the present life, there is something else which men associated in a civil community need for the status of the future world promised to the human race through God's supernatural revelation, and which is useful also for the status of the present life. This is the worship and honoring of God, and the giving of thanks both for benefits received in this world and for those to be received in the future one. For the teaching of these things and for the directing of men in them, the state had to designate certain teachers. The nature and qualities of all these and the other matters mentioned above will be treated in detail in the subsequent discussions.

5. Men, then, were assembled for the sake of the sufficient life, being able to seek out for themselves the necessaries enumerated above, and exchanging them with one another. This assemblage, thus perfect and having the limit of self-

sufficiency, is called the state, whose final cause as well as that of its many parts has already been indicated by us in some measure, and will be more fully distinguished below. For since diverse things are necessary to men who desire a sufficient life, things which cannot be supplied by men of one order or office, there had to be diverse orders or offices of men in this association, exercising or supplying such diverse things which men need for sufficiency of life. But these diverse orders or offices of men are none other than the many and distinct parts of the state.

Let it suffice, then, to have covered thus in outline what the state is, why there came about such an association, and the number and division of its parts.

CHAPTER V. *On the Differentiation of the Parts of the State, and the Necessity of Their Separate Existence for an End Discoverable by Man*

We have now completely listed the parts of the state, in whose perfect action and intercommunication, without external impediment, we have said that the tranquillity of the state consists. But we must now continue our discussion of them, since the fuller determination of these parts, with respect both to their functions or ends and to their other appropriate causes, will make more manifest the causes of tranquillity and of its opposite. Let us say, then, that the parts or offices of the state are of six kinds, as Aristotle said in the *Politics,* Book VII, Chapter 7: the agricultural, the artisan, the military, the financial, the priestly, and the judicial or deliberative. Three of these, the priestly, the warrior, and the judicial, are in the strict sense parts of the state, and in civil communities they are usually called the honorable class (*honorabilitatem*). The others are called parts only in the broad sense of the term, because they are offices necessary to the state according to the doctrine of Aristotle in the *Politics,* Book VII, Chapter 7. And the multitude belonging to these offices are usually called the common mass (*vulgaris*). These, then, are the more familiar parts of the city or state, to which all the others can appropriately be reduced.

2. Although the necessity of these parts has been indicated in the preceding chapter, we wish to indicate it again more distinctly, assuming this proposition as having been previously demonstrated from what is self-evident, namely, that the state is a community established for the sake of the living and living well of the men in it. Of this "living" we have previously distinguished two kinds: one, the life or living of this world, that is, earthly; the other, the life or living of the other or future world. From these kinds of living, desired by man as ends, we shall indicate the necessity for the differentiation of the parts of the civil community. The first kind of human living, the earthly, is sometimes taken to mean the being of living things, as in Book II of the treatise *On the Soul:* "For living things, living is their being"; in which sense life is nothing other than soul. At other times, "living" is taken to mean the act, the action or passion, of the soul or of life. Again, each of these meanings is used in two ways, with reference either to the numerically same being or to the similar being, which is said to be that of the species. And although each of these kinds of living, both as proper to man and as common to him and to the other animate things, depends upon natural causes, yet we are not at present considering it insofar as it comes from these causes; the natural science of plants and animals deals with this. Rather, our present concern is with these causes insofar as they re-

ceive fulfillment "through art and reason," whereby "the human race lives."

3. Hence, we must note that if man is to live and to live well, it is necessary that his actions be done and be done well; and not only his actions but also his passions. By "well" I mean in proper proportion. And since we do not receive entirely perfect from nature the means whereby these proportions are fulfilled, it was necessary for man to go beyond natural causes to form through reason some means whereby to effect and preserve his actions and passions in body and soul. And these means are the various kinds of functions and products deriving from the virtues and arts both practical and theoretic.

4. Of human actions and passions, some come from natural causes apart from knowledge. Such are those which are effected by the contrariety of the elements composing our bodies, through their intermixture. In this class can properly be placed the actions of the nutritive faculty. Under this head also come actions effected by the elements surrounding our body through the alteration of their qualities; of this kind also are the alterations effected by things entering human bodies, such as food, drink, medicines, poisons, and other similar things. But there are other actions or passions which are performed by us or occur in us through our cognitive and appetitive powers. Of these some are called "immanent" because they do not cross over (*non transeunt*) into a subject other than the doer, nor are they exercised through any external organs or locomotive members; of this kind are the thoughts and desires or affections of men. But there are other actions and passions which are called "transient" because they are opposed in either or in both respects to the kind which we have just described.

5. In order to proportion all these actions and passions, and to fulfill them in that to which nature could not lead, there were discovered the various kinds of arts and other virtues, as we said above, and men of various offices were established to exercise these for the purpose of supplying human needs. These orders are none other than the parts of the state enumerated above. For in order to proportion and preserve the acts of the nutritive part of the soul, whose cessation would mean the complete destruction of the animal both individually and as a species, agriculture and animal husbandry were established. To these may properly be reduced all kinds of hunting of land, sea, and air animals, and all other arts whereby food is acquired by some exchange or is prepared for eating, so that what is lost from the substance of our body may thereby be restored, and the body be continued in its immortal being so far as nature has permitted this to man.

6. In order to moderate the actions and passions of our body caused by the impressions of the elements which externally surround us, there was discovered the general class of mechanics, which Aristotle in the *Politics,* Book VII, Chapter 6, calls the "arts." To this class belong spinning, leathermaking, shoemaking, all species of housebuilding, and in general all the other mechanic arts which subserve the other offices of the state directly or indirectly, and which moderate not only men's touch or taste but also the other senses. These latter arts are more for pleasure and for living well than for the necessity of life, such as the painter's art and others similar to it, concerning which Aristotle says in the *Politics,* Book IV, Chapter 3: "Of these arts some must exist from necessity, and others are for pleasure and living well." Under this class is also placed the practice of medicine, which is in some way architectonic to many of the above-mentioned arts.

7. In order to moderate the excesses of the acts deriving from the locomotive powers through knowledge and desire, which we have called transient acts and which can be done for the benefit or for the harm or injury of someone other than the doer for the status of the present world, there was necessarily established in the state a part or office by which the excesses of such acts are corrected and reduced to equality or due proportion. For without such correction the excesses of these acts would cause fighting and hence the separation of the citizens, and finally the destruction of the state and loss of the sufficient life. This part of the state, together with its subsidiaries, is called by Aristotle the "judicial" or "ruling" and "deliberative" part, and its function is to regulate matters of justice and the common benefit.

8. In addition, since the sufficient life cannot be led by citizens who are oppressed or cast into slavery by external oppressors, and also since the sentences of the judges against injurious and rebellious men within the state must be executed by coercive force, it was necessary to set up in the state a military or warrior part, which many of the mechanics also subserve. For the state was established for the sake of living and living well, as was said in the preceding chapter; but this is impossible for citizens cast into slavery. For Aristotle the preeminent said that slavery is contrary to the nature of the state. Hence, indicating the necessity for this part, he said in the *Politics,* Book IV, Chapter 3: "There is a fifth class, that of the warriors, which is not less necessary than the others, if the citizens are not to be slaves of invaders. For nothing is more truly impossible than for that which is by nature slavish to be worthy of the name 'state'; for a state is self-sufficient, but a slave is not self-sufficient." The necessity for this class because of internal rebels is treated by Aristotle in the *Politics,* Book VII, Chapter 6. We have omitted the quotation of this passage here for the sake of brevity, and because we shall quote it in Chapter XIV of this discourse, paragraph 8.

9. Again, since in some years on earth the harvests are large, and in others small; and the state is sometimes at peace with its neighbors, and sometimes not; and it is in need of various common services such as the construction and repair of roads, bridges, and other edifices, and similar things whose enumeration here would be neither appropriate nor brief—to provide all these things at the proper time it was necessary to establish in the state a treasure-keeping part, which Aristotle called the "money class." This part gathers and saves monies, coins, wines, oils, and other necessaries; it procures from all places things needed for the common benefit, and it seeks to relieve future necessities; it is also subserved by some of the other parts of the state. Aristotle called this the "money" part, since the saver of monies seems to be the treasurer of all things; for all things are exchanged for money.

10. It remains for us to discuss the necessity of the priestly part. All men have not thought so harmoniously about this as they have about the necessity of the other parts of the state. The cause of this difference was that the true and primary necessity of this part could not be comprehended through demonstration, nor was it self-evident. All nations, however, agreed that it was appropriate to establish the priesthood for the worship and honoring of God, and for the benefit resulting therefrom for the status of the present or the future world. For most laws or religions promise that in the future world God will distribute rewards to those who do good and punishment to doers of evil.

11. However, besides these causes of the laying down of religious laws, causes which are believed without demonstration, the philosophers, including Hesiod, Pythagoras, and several others of the ancients, noted appropriately a quite different cause or purpose for the setting forth of divine laws or religions—a purpose which was in some sense necessary for the status of this world. This was to ensure the goodness of human acts both individual and civil, on which depend almost completely the quiet or tranquillity of communities and finally the sufficient life in the present world. For although some of the philosophers who founded such laws or religions did not accept or believe in human resurrection and that life which is called eternal, they nevertheless feigned and persuaded others that it exists and that in it pleasures and pains are in accordance with the qualities of human deeds in this mortal life, in order that they might thereby induce in men reverence and fear of God, and a desire to flee the vices and to cultivate the virtues. For there are certain acts which the legislator cannot regulate by human law, that is, those acts which cannot be proved to be present or absent to someone, but which nevertheless cannot be concealed from God, whom these philosophers feigned to be the maker of such laws and the commander of their observance, under the threat or promise of eternal reward for doers of good and punishment for doers of evil. Hence, they said of the variously virtuous men in this world that they were placed in the heavenly firmament; and from this were perhaps derived the names of certain stars and constellations. These philosophers said that the souls of men who acted wrongly entered the bodies of various brutes; for example, the souls of men who had been intemperate eaters entered the bodies of pigs, those who were intemperate in embracing and making love entered the bodies of goats, and so on, according to the proportions of human vices to their condemnable properties. So too the philosophers assigned various kinds of torments to wrongdoers, like perpetual thirst and hunger for intemperate Tantalus: water and fruit were to be near him, but he was unable to drink or handle these, for they were always fleeing faster than he could pursue them. The philosophers also said that the infernal regions, the place of these torments, were deep and dark; and they painted all sorts of terrible and gloomy pictures of them. From fear of these, men eschewed wrongdoing, were instigated to perform virtuous works of piety and mercy, and were well disposed both in themselves and toward others. As a consequence, many disputes and injuries ceased in communities. Hence too the peace or tranquillity of states and the sufficient life of men for the status of the present world were preserved with less difficulty; which was the end intended by these wise men in laying down such laws or religions.

12. Such, then, were the precepts handed down by the gentile priests; and for the teaching of them they established in their communities temples in which their gods were worshiped. They also appointed teachers of these laws or doctrines, whom they called priests (*sacerdotes*), because they handled the sacred objects of the temples, like the books, vases, and other such things subserving divine worship.

13. These affairs they arranged fittingly in accordance with their beliefs and rites. For as priests they appointed not anyone at all, but only virtuous and esteemed citizens who had held military, judicial, or deliberative office, and who had retired from secular affairs, being excused from civil burdens and offices because of age. For by such men, removed from passions, and in whose words

greater credence was placed because of their age and moral dignity, it was fitting that the gods should be honored and their sacred objects handled, not by artisans or mercenaries who had exercised lowly and defiling offices. Whence it is said in the *Politics,* Book VII, Chapter 7: "Neither a farmer nor an artisan should be made a priest."

14. Now correct views concerning God were not held by the gentile laws or religions and by all the other religions which are or were outside the catholic Christian faith or outside the Mosaic law which preceded it or the beliefs of the holy fathers which in turn preceded this—and, in general, by all those doctrines which are outside the tradition of what is contained in the sacred canon called the Bible. For they followed the human mind or false prophets or teachers of errors. Hence too they did not have a correct view about the future life and its happiness or misery, nor about the true priesthood established for its sake. We have, nevertheless, spoken of their rites in order to make more manifest their difference from the true priesthood, that of the Christians, and the necessity for the priestly part in communities.

CHAPTER X: *On the Distinction of the Meanings of the Term "Law," and on the Meaning Which Is Most Proper and Intended by Us*

Since we have said that election is the more perfect and better method of establishing governments, we shall do well to inquire as to its efficient cause, wherefrom it has to emerge in its full value; for from this will appear the cause not only of the elected government but also of the other parts of the polity. Now a government has to regulate civil human acts (as we demonstrated in Chapter V of this discourse) and according to a standard (*regulam*) which is and ought to be the form of the ruler, as such. We must, consequently, inquire into this standard, as to whether it exists, what it is, and why. For the efficient cause of this standard is perhaps the same as that of the ruler.

2. The existence of this standard, which is called a "statute" or "custom" and by the common term "law," we assume as almost self-evident by induction in all perfect communities. We shall show first, then, what law is; next we shall indicate its final cause or necessity; and finally we shall demonstrate by what person or persons and by what kind of action the law should be established; which will be to inquire into its legislator or efficient cause, to whom we think it also pertains to elect the government, as we shall show subsequently by demonstration. From these points there will also appear the matter or subject of the aforesaid standard which we have called law. For this matter is the ruling part, whose function it is to regulate the political or civil acts of men according to the law.

3. Following this procedure, then, we must first distinguish the meanings or intentions of this term "law," in order that its many senses may not lead to confusion. For in one sense it means a natural sensitive inclination toward some action or passion. This is the way the Apostle used it when he said in the seventh chapter of the epistle to the Romans: "I see another law in my members, fighting against the law of my mind." In another sense this term "law" means any productive habit and in general every form, existing in the mind, of a producible thing, from which as from an exemplar or measure there emerge the forms of things made by art. This is the way in which the term was used in the forty-third chapter of Ezekiel: "This is the law of the house . . . And these are the

measurements of the altar." In a third sense "law" means the standard containing admonitions for voluntary human acts according as these are ordered toward glory or punishment in the future world. In this sense the Mosaic law was in part called a law, just as the evangelical law in its entirety is called a law. Hence the Apostle said of these in his epistle to the Hebrews: "Since the priesthood has been changed, it is necessary that there be a change of the law also." In this sense "law" was also used for the evangelic discipline in the first chapter of James: "He who has looked into the perfect law of liberty, and has continued therein . . . this man shall be blessed in his deeds." In this sense of the term law all religions, such as that of Mohammed or of the Persians, are called laws in whole or in part, although among these only the Mosaic and the evangelic, that is, the Christian, contain the truth. So too Aristotle called religions "laws" when he said, in the second book of his *Philosophy:* "The laws show how great is the power of custom"; and also in the twelfth book of the same work: "The other doctrines were added as myths to persuade men to obey the laws, and for the sake of expediency." In its fourth and most familiar sense, this term "law" means the science or doctrine or universal judgment of matters of civil justice and benefit, and of their opposites.

4. Taken in this last sense, law may be considered in two ways. In one way it may be considered in itself, as it only shows what is just or unjust, beneficial or harmful; and as such it is called the science or doctrine of right (*juris*). In another way it may be considered according as with regard to its observance there is given a command coercive through punishment or reward to be distributed in the present world, or according as it is handed down by way of such a command; and considered in this way it most properly is called, and is, a law. It was in this sense that Aristotle also defined it in the last book of the *Ethics,* Chapter 8, when he said: "Law has coercive force, for it is discourse emerging from prudence and understanding." Law, then, is a "discourse" or statement "emerging from prudence and" political "understanding," that is, it is an ordinance made by political prudence, concerning matters of justice and benefit and their opposites, and having "coercive force," that is, concerning whose observance there is given a command which one is compelled to observe, or which is made by way of such a command.

5. Hence not all true cognitions of matters of civil justice and benefit are laws unless a coercive command has been given concerning their observance, or they have been made by way of a command, although such true cognition is necessarily required for a perfect law. Indeed, sometimes false cognitions of the just and the beneficial become laws, when there is given a command to observe them, or they are made by way of a command. An example of this is found in the regions of certain barbarians who cause it to be observed as just that a murderer be absolved of civil guilt and punishment on payment of a fine. This, however, is absolutely unjust, and consequently the laws of such barbarians are not absolutely perfect. For although they have the proper form, that is, a coercive command of observance, they lack a proper condition, that is, the proper and true ordering of justice.

6. Under this sense of law are included all standards of civil justice and benefit established by human authority, such as customs, statutes, plebiscites, decretals, and all similar rules which are based upon human authority as we have said.

7. We must not overlook, however, that both the evangelical law and the

Mosaic, and perhaps the other religions as well, may be considered and compared in different ways in whole or in part, in relation to human acts for the status of the present or the future world. For they sometimes come, or have hitherto come, or will come, under the third sense of law, and sometimes under the last, as will be shown more fully in Chapters VIII and IX of Discourse II. Moreover, some of these laws are true, while others are false fancies and empty promises.

It is now clear, then, that there exists a standard or law of human civil acts, and what this is.

CHAPTER XII: *On the Demonstrable Efficient Cause of Human Laws, and also on That Cause Which Cannot Be Proved by Demonstration: Which Is To Inquire into the Legislator. Whence It Appears also That Whatever Is Established by Election Derives Its Authority from Election Alone Apart from Any Other Confirmation*

We must next discuss that efficient cause of the laws which is capable of demonstration. For I do not intend to deal here with that method of establishing laws which can be effected by the immediate act or oracle of God apart from the human will, or which has been so effected in the past. It was by this latter method, as we have said, that the Mosaic law was established; but I shall not deal with it here even insofar as it contains commands with regard to civil acts for the status of the present world. I shall discuss the establishment of only those laws and governments which emerge immediately from the decision of the human mind.

2. Let us say, to begin with, that it can pertain to any citizen to discover the law taken materially and in its third sense, as the science of civil justice and benefit. Such inquiry, however, can be carried on more appropriately and be completed better by those men who are able to have leisure, who are older and experienced in practical affairs, and who are called "prudent men," than by the mechanics who must bend all their efforts to acquiring the necessities of life. But it must be remembered that the true knowledge or discovery of the just and the beneficial, and of their opposites, is not law taken in its last and most proper sense, whereby it is the measure of human civil acts, unless there is given a coercive command as to its observance, or it is made by way of such a command, by someone through whose authority its transgressors must and can be punished. Hence, we must now say to whom belongs the authority to make such a command and to punish its transgressors. This, indeed, is to inquire into the legislator or the maker of the law.

3. Let us say, then, in accordance with the truth and the counsel of Aristotle in the *Politics,* Book III, Chapter 6, that the legislator, or the primary and proper efficient cause of the law, is the people or the whole body of citizens, or the weightier part thereof, through its election or will expressed by words in the general assembly of the citizens, commanding or determining that something be done or omitted with regard to human civil acts, under a temporal pain or punishment. By the "weightier part" I mean to take into consideration the quantity and the quality of the persons in that community over which the law is made. The aforesaid whole body of citizens or the weightier part thereof is the legislator regardless of whether it makes the law directly by itself or

entrusts the making of it to some person or persons, who are not and cannot be the legislator in the absolute sense, but only in a relative sense and for a particular time and in accordance with the authority of the primary legislator. And I say further that the laws and anything else established through election must receive their necessary approval by that same primary authority and no other, whatever be the case with regard to certain ceremonies or solemnities, which are required not for the being of the matters elected but for their well-being, since the election would be no less valid even if these ceremonies were not performed. Moreover, by the same authority must the laws and other things established through election undergo addition, subtraction, complete change, interpretation, or suspension, insofar as the exigencies of time or place or other circumstances make any such action opportune for the common benefit. And by the same authority, also, must the laws be promulgated or proclaimed after their enactment, so that no citizen or alien who is delinquent in observing them may be excused because of ignorance.

4. A citizen I define in accordance with Aristotle in the *Politics*, Book III, Chapters 1, 3, and 7, as one who participates in the civil community in the government or the deliberative or judicial function according to his rank. By this definition, children, slaves, aliens, and women are distinguished from citizens, although in different ways. For the sons of citizens are citizens in proximate potentiality, lacking only in years. The weightier part of the citizens should be viewed in accordance with the honorable custom of polities, or else it should be determined in accordance with the doctrine of Aristotle in the *Politics*, Book VI, Chapter 2.

5. Having thus defined the citizen and the weightier part of the citizens, let us return to our proposed objective, namely, to demonstrate that the human authority to make laws belongs only to the whole body of the citizens or to the weightier part thereof. Our first proof is as follows. The absolutely primary human authority to make or establish human laws belongs only to those men from whom alone the best laws can emerge. But these are the whole body of the citizens, or the weightier part thereof, which represents that whole body; since it is difficult or impossible for all persons to agree upon one decision, because some men have a deformed nature, disagreeing with the common decision through singular malice or ignorance. The common benefit should not, however, be impeded or neglected because of the unreasonable protest or opposition of these men. The authority to make or establish laws, therefore, belongs only to the whole body of the citizens or to the weightier part thereof.

The first proposition of this demonstration is very close to self-evident, although its force and its ultimate certainty can be grasped from Chapter V of this discourse. The second proposition, that the best law is made only through the hearing and command of the entire multitude, I prove by assuming with Aristotle in the *Politics*, Book III, Chapter 7, that the best law is that which is made for the common benefit of the citizens. As Aristotle said: "That is presumably right," that is, in the laws, "which is for the common benefit of the state and the citizens." But that this is best achieved only by the whole body of the citizens or by the weightier part thereof, which is assumed to be the same thing, I show as follows: That at which the entire body of the citizens aims intellectually and emotionally is more certainly judged as to its truth and more diligently noted as to its common utility. For a defect in some proposed law can be better noted by the greater number than by any part thereof, since every whole, or at least every corporeal whole, is greater in mass and in virtue than any part of it taken separately. Moreover, the common utility of a law is better noted by the entire multitude, because no one knowingly harms himself. Anyone can look to see whether a proposed law leans toward the benefit of one or a few persons more than of the others or of the community, and can protest against it. Such, however, would not be the case were the law made by one or a few persons, considering their own private benefit rather than that of the community. This position is also supported by the arguments which we advanced in Chapter XI of this discourse with regard to the necessity of having laws.

6. Another argument to the principal conclusion is as follows. The authority to make the law belongs only to those men whose making of it will cause the law to be better observed or observed at all. Only the whole body of the citizens are such men. To them, therefore, belongs the authority to make the law. The first proposition of this demonstration is very close to self-evident, for a law would be useless unless it were observed. Hence Aristotle said in the *Politics,* Book IV, Chapter 6: "Laws are not well ordered when they are well made but not obeyed." He also said in Book VI, Chapter 5: "Nothing is accomplished by forming opinions about justice and not carrying them out." The second proposition I prove as follows. That law is better observed by every citizen which each one seems to have imposed upon himself. But such is the law which is made through the hearing and command of the entire multitude of the citizens. The first proposition of this prosyllogism is almost self-evident; for since "the state is a community of free men," as is written in the *Politics,* Book III, Chapter 4, every citizen must be free, and not undergo another's despotism, that is, slavish dominion. But this would not be the case if one or a few of the citizens by their own authority made the law over the whole body of citizens. For those who thus made the law would be despots over the others, and hence such a law, however good it was, would be endured only with reluctance, or not at all, by the rest of the citizens, the more ample part. Having suffered contempt, they would protest against it, and not having been called upon to make it, they would not observe it. On the other hand, a law made by the hearing or consent of the whole multitude, even though it were less useful, would be readily observed and endured by every one of the citizens, because then each would seem to have set the law upon himself, and hence would have no protest against it, but would rather tolerate it with equanimity. The second proposition of the first syllogism I also prove in another way, as follows. The power to cause the laws to be observed belongs only to those men to whom belongs coercive force over the transgressors of the laws. But these men are the whole body of citizens or the weightier part thereof. Therefore, to them alone belongs the authority to make the laws.

7. The principal conclusion is also proved as follows. That practical matter whose proper establishment is of greatest importance for the common sufficiency of the citizens in this life, and whose poor establishment threatens harm for the community, must be established only by the whole body of the citizens. But such a matter is the law. Therefore, the establishment of the law pertains only to the whole body of the citizens. The major premise of this demonstration is almost self-evident, and is grounded in the immediate truths which were set forth in Chapters IV and V of this discourse. For men came together to the

civil community in order to attain what was beneficial for sufficiency of life, and to avoid the opposite. Those matters, therefore, which can affect the benefit and harm of all ought to be known and heard by all, in order that they may be able to attain the beneficial and to avoid the opposite. Such matters are the laws, as was assumed in the minor premise. For in the laws being rightly made consists a large part of the whole common sufficiency of men, while under bad laws there arise unbearable slavery, oppression, and misery of the citizens, the final result of which is that the polity is destroyed.

8. Again, and this is an abbreviation and summary of the previous demonstrations: The authority to make laws belongs only to the whole body of the citizens, as we have said, or else it belongs to one or a few men. But it cannot belong to one man alone for the reasons given in Chapter XI and in the first demonstration adduced in the present chapter; for through ignorance or malice or both, this one man could make a bad law, looking more to his own private benefit than to that of the community, so that the law would be tyrannical. For the same reason, the authority to make laws cannot belong to a few; for they too could sin, as above, in making the law for the benefit of a certain few and not for the common benefit, as can be seen in oligarchies. The authority to make the laws belongs, therefore, to the whole body of citizens or to the weightier part thereof, for precisely the opposite reason. For since all the citizens must be measured by the law according to due proportion, and no one knowingly harms or wishes injustice to himself, it follows that all or most wish a law conducing to the common benefit of the citizens.

9. From these same demonstrations it can also be proved, merely by changing the minor term, that the approval, interpretation, and suspension of the laws, and the other matters set forth in paragraph 3 of this chapter, pertain to the authority of the legislator alone. And the same must be thought of everything else which is established by election. For the authority to approve or disapprove rests with those who have the primary authority to elect, or with those to whom they have granted this authority of election. For otherwise, if the part could dissolve by its own authority what had been established by the whole, the part would be greater than the whole, or at least equal to it.

The method of coming together to make the laws will be described in the following chapter.

Discourse II

CHAPTER IV: *On the Canonic Scriptures, the Commands, Counsels, and Examples of Christ and of the Saints and Approved Doctors Who Expounded the Evangelic Law, Whereby It Is Clearly Demonstrated That the Roman or Any Other Bishop or Priest, or Clergyman, Can by Virtue of the Words of Scripture Claim or Ascribe to Himself No Coercive Rulership or Contentious Jurisdiction, Let Alone the Supreme Jurisdiction over Any Clergyman or Layman; and That, by Christ's Counsel and Example, They .Ought To Refuse Such Rulership, Especially in Communities of the Faithful, if It Is Offered to Them or Bestowed on Them by Someone Having the Authority To Do So; and Again, That All Bishops, and Generally All Persons Now Called Clergymen, Must Be Subject to the Coercive Judgment or Rulership*

of Him Who Governs by the Authority of the Human Legislator,
Especially Where this Legislator Is Christian

We now wish from the opposite side to adduce the truths of the holy Scripture in both its literal and its mystical sense, in accordance with the interpretations of the saints and the expositions of other approved doctors of the Christian faith, which explicitly command or counsel that neither the Roman bishop called pope, nor any other bishop or priest, or deacon, has or ought to have any ruler-ship or coercive judgment or jurisdiction over any priest or non-priest, ruler, community, group, or individual of whatever condition; understanding by "co-ercive judgment" that which we said in Chapter II of this discourse to be the third sense of "judge" or "judgment."

2. The more clearly to carry out this aim, we must not overlook that in this inquiry it is not asked what power and authority is or was had in this world by Christ, who was true God and true man, nor what or how much of this power he was able to bestow on St. Peter and the other apostles and their suc-cessors, the bishops or priests; for Christian believers have no doubts on these points. But we wish to and ought to inquire what power and authority, to be exercised in this world, Christ wanted to bestow and in fact (*de facto*) did bestow on them, and from what he excluded and prohibited them by counsel or command. For we are bound to believe that they had from Christ only such power and authority as we can prove to have been given to them through the words of Scripture, no other. For it is certain to all the Christian believers that Christ, who was true God and true man, was able to bestow, not only on the apostles but also on any other men, coercive authority or jurisdiction over all rulers or governments and over all the other individuals in this world; and even more perhaps, as for example the power to create things, to destroy or repair heaven and earth and the things therein, and even to be in complete command of angels; but these powers Christ neither bestowed nor determined to bestow on them. Hence Augustine, in the tenth sermon *On the Words of the Lord in Matthew,* wrote the following: " 'Learn of me' not how to make a world, not how to create all visible and invisible things, nor how to do miracles in the world and revive the dead; but: 'because I am meek and humble of heart.' "

3. Therefore for the present purpose it suffices to show, and I shall first show, that Christ himself came into the world not to dominate men, nor to judge them by judgment in the third sense, nor to wield temporal rule, but rather to be subject as regards the status of the present life; and moreover, that he wanted to and did exclude himself, his apostles and disciples, and their successors, the bishops or priests, from all such coercive authority or worldly rule, both by his example and by his words of counsel or command. I shall also show that the leading apostles, as Christ's true imitators, did this same thing and taught their successors to do likewise; and moreover, that both Christ and the apostles wanted to be and were continuously subject in property and in person to the coercive jurisdiction of secular rulers, and that they taught and commanded all others, to whom they preached or wrote the law of truth, to do likewise, under pain of eternal damnation. Then I shall write a chapter on the power or author-ity of the keys which Christ gave to the apostles and their successors in office, bishops and priests, so that it may be clear what is the nature, quality, and extent

of such power, both of the Roman bishop and of the others. For ignorance on this point has hitherto been and still is the source of many questions and damnable controversies among the Christian faithful, as was mentioned in the first chapter of this discourse.

4. And so in pursuit of these aims we wish to show that Christ, in his purposes or intentions, words, and deeds, wished to exclude and did exclude himself and the apostles from every office of rulership, contentious jurisdiction, government, or coercive judgment in this world. This is first shown clearly beyond any doubt by the passage in the eighteenth chapter of the gospel of John. For when Christ was brought before Pontius Pilate, vicar of the Roman ruler in Judaea, and accused of having called himself king of the Jews, Pontius asked him whether he had said this, or whether he did call himself a king, and Christ's reply included these words, among others: "My kingdom is not of this world," that is, I have not come to reign by temporal rule or dominion, in the way in which worldly kings reign. And proof of this was given by Christ himself through an evident sign when he said: "If my kingdom were of this world, my servants would certainly fight, that I should not be delivered to the Jews," as if to argue as follows: If I had come into this world to reign by worldly or coercive rule, I would have ministers for this rule, namely, men to fight and to coerce transgressors, as the other kings have; but I do not have such ministers, as you can clearly see. Hence the interlinear gloss: "It is clear that no one defends him." And this is what Christ reiterates: "But now my kingdom is not from hence," that is, the kingdom about which I have come to teach.

5. Expounding these evangelic truths, the saints and doctors write as follows, and first St. Augustine:

> If he had answered Pilate's question directly, he would have seemed to be answering not the Jews but only the Gentiles who thought this of him. But after answering Pilate, he answered the Jews and the Gentiles more opportunely and fitly, as if to say: Hear ye, Jews and Gentiles, I do not impede your rule in this world. What more do you want? Through faith approach ye the kingdom which is not of this world. For what is his kingdom but those who believe in him?

This, then, is the kingdom concerning which he came to teach and order, a kingdom which consists in the acts whereby the eternal kingdom is attained, that is, the acts of faith and the other theological virtues; not, however, by coercing anyone thereto, as will be made clear below. For when there are two coercive dominions in respect of the same multitude, and neither is subordinated to the other, they impede one another, as was shown in Chapter XVII of Discourse I. But Christ had not come to impede such dominion, as Augustine said. Hence on the passage in the same chapter of John: "Thy own nation and the chief priests have delivered thee up to me. What hast thou done?" Augustine wrote: "He sufficiently shows that the act is looked upon as a crime, as if to say: If you deny you are a king, what then have you done to be delivered up to me; as if it would not be strange if he who called himself king were delivered up to the judge to be punished." So, then, Augustine thought that it would be nothing strange if Christ had been punished, had he called himself secular king, especially before those who did not know he was God; and that he denied he would be a king of such a kingdom or with such authority, namely, to coerce transgressors of the law. Hence on the words in the same chapter of John: "Sayest thou this thing of thyself, or did others tell it thee of me?" Theophylact wrote: "Christ spoke to Pilate as if to say: If you say this on your own, show the signs of my rebellion, but if you have heard it from others, then make the ordinary inquiry." But if the opinion of our adversaries were correct, Christ should never have said what Theophylact states, namely, that Pilate should make the ordinary inquiry about him; indeed, were they correct, he should rather have said that it did not pertain to Pilate to make this inquiry, inasmuch as he, Christ, of right (*de jure*) was not and did not wish to be subject to him in jurisdiction or coercive judgment.

6. Again, on the words, "my kingdom is not from hence," Chrysostom says: "He does not deprive the world of his providence and leadership, but he shows that his kingdom is not human or corruptible." But every kingdom which is coercive over anyone in this world is human and corruptible. Moreover, on the words in the same chapter of John: "Thou sayest that I am a king," Augustine wrote: "He spoke in this manner not because he feared to admit that he was king, but so that he might neither deny he was a king nor affirm that he was such a king whose kingdom is thought to be of this world. For he said, 'Thou sayest,' as if to say: You, a carnal man, speak carnally," that is, about carnal rule over contentious and carnal temporal acts, taking "temporal" in its third sense; for the Apostle called such acts "carnal" in the first epistle to the Corinthians, Chapter 3.

From the above it appears, therefore, that Christ came into the world to dispose not about carnal or temporal rule or coercive judgment, but about the spiritual or heavenly kingdom; for almost always it was only about this latter that he spoke and preached, as is plain from the gospel in both its literal and its mystical sense. And hence we most often read that he said: "Like is the kingdom of heaven," etc., but very rarely did he speak of the earthly kingdom, and if he did, he taught that it should be spurned. For he promised that in the heavenly kingdom he would give rewards and punishments according to the merits or demerits of the agents, but never did he promise to do such things in this world, but rather he does the contrary of what the rulers of this world do. For he most often afflicts or permits the affliction of the just and the doers of good, and thus he leads them to the reward of his kingdom. For "all that have pleased God passed through many tribulations," as it is written in the eighth chapter of Judith. But the rulers of this world, the judges of the worldly kingdom, do and ought to do the contrary, maintaining justice; for when they distribute rewards in this world to those who observe the laws, and punishments to perpetrators of evil, they act rightly; whereas if they did the contrary they would sin against human and divine law.

7. Let us return to the principal question through what Christ showed by deed or example. For in the sixth chapter of John we read that "when Jesus therefore knew that they would come to take him by force and make him king, he fled again into the mountain, himself alone." Whereon the interlinear gloss: "From this he descended to care for the multitude, teaching men to avoid the good fortunes of this world and to pray for strength to withstand them." It is certain, therefore, that Christ avoided rulership, or else he would have taught us nothing by his example. This view is supported by the expositions of St. Augustine, who wrote that "the Christian faithful are his kingdom, which is now cultivated, now redeemed, by the blood of Christ. But his kingdom will be manifest when the clarity of his saints will be revealed after the judgment made by him. But

the disciples and the crowds, believing in him, thought he had come to reign." So, then, the saints never understood, by Christ's kingdom in this world, temporal dominion or judgment over contentious acts and its execution by coercive power against transgressors of the laws in this world; but by his kingdom and governance in this world they understood, rather, the teaching of the faith, and governance in accordance with it toward the heavenly kingdom. This "kingdom," says Augustine, will indeed be "manifest after his judgment" in the other world. He repeatedly states that to think Christ then reigned as the crowds thought was to "ravish him," that is, to have a wrong assumption and opinion of him. Whereon Chrysostom also: "And the prophet," that is, Christ, "was now among them, and they wanted to enthrone him as king," that is, because he had fed them. "But Christ fled, teaching us to despise worldly honors."

8. Moreover, the same is shown very evidently by Christ's words and example in the following passage of the twelfth chapter of Luke: "And one of the multitude said to him, Master, speak to my brother, that he divide the inheritance with me. But he," that is, Christ, "said to him, Man, who hath appointed me judge or divider over you?" As if to say: I did not come to exercise this office, nor was I sent for this, that is, to settle civil disputes through judgment; but this, however, is undoubtedly the most proper function of secular rulers or judges. Now this passage from the gospel contains and demonstrates our proposition much more clearly than do the glosses of the saints, because the latter assume that the literal meaning, such as we have said, is manifest, and have devoted themselves more to the allegorical or mystical meaning. Nevertheless, we shall now quote from the glosses for a stronger confirmation of our proposition, and so that we may not be accused of expounding Scripture rashly. These words of Christ, then, are expounded by St. Ambrose as follows: "Well does he who descended for the sake of the divine avoid the earthly, and does not deign to be judge over disputes and appraiser of wealth, being the judge of the living and the dead and the appraiser of their merits." And a little below he adds: "Hence not undeservedly is this brother rebuffed, who wanted the dispenser of the heavenly to concern himself with the corruptible." See, then, what Ambrose thinks about Christ's office in this world; for he says that "well does he avoid the earthly," that is, the judgment of contentious acts, "who descended for the sake of the divine," that is, to teach and minister the spiritual; in this he designated Christ's office and that of his successors, namely, to dispense the heavenly or spiritual; that spiritual of which Ambrose spoke in his gloss on the first epistle to the Corinthians, Chapter 9, which we quoted in Chapter II of this discourse under the third meaning of this word "spiritual."

9. It now remains to show that not only did Christ himself refuse rulership or coercive judgment in this world, whereby he furnished an example for his apostles and disciples and their successors to do likewise, but also he taught by words and showed by example that all men, both priests and non-priests, should be subject in property and in person to the coercive judgment of the rulers of this world. By his word and example, then, Christ showed this first with respect to property, by what is written in the twenty-second chapter of Matthew. For when the Jews asked him: "Tell us therefore, what dost thou think? Is it lawful to give tribute to Caesar, or not?" Christ, after looking at the coin and its inscription, replied: "Render therefore to Caesar the things that are Caesar's, and to God the things that are God's." Whereon the interlinear gloss says, "that

is, tribute and money." And on the words: "Whose image and inscription is this?" Ambrose wrote as follows: "Just as Caesar demanded the imprinting of his image, so too does God demand that the soul be stamped with the light of his countenance." Note, therefore, what it was that Christ came into the world to demand. Furthermore, Chrysostom writes as follows: "When you hear: 'Render to Caesar the things that are Caesar's,' know that he means only those things which are not harmul to piety, for if they were, the tribute would be not to Caesar but to the devil." So, then, we ought to be subject to Caesar in all things, so long only as they are not contrary to piety, that is, to divine worship or commandment. Therefore, Christ wanted us to be subject in property to the secular ruler. This too was plainly the doctrine of St. Ambrose, based upon this doctrine of Christ, for in his epistle against Valentinian, entitled *To the People,* he wrote: "We pay to Caesar the things that are Caesar's, and to God the things that are God's. That the tribute is Caesar's is not denied."

10. The same is again shown from the seventeenth chapter of Matthew, where it is written as follows: "They that received the didrachmas came to Peter, and said, Doth not your master pay the didrachmas?" and then, a little below, is written what Christ said to Peter: "But that we may not scandalize them, go to the sea and cast in a hook, and that fish which shalt first come up, take: and when thou hast opened its mouth, thou shalt find a piece of money: take that, and give it to them for me and thee." Nor did the Lord say only, "Give it to them," but he said, "Give it to them for me and thee." And Jerome on this passage says: "Our Lord was in flesh and in spirit the son of a king, whether we consider him to have been generated from the seed of David or the word of the Almighty Father. Therefore, being the son of kings, he did not owe tribute." And below he adds: "Therefore, although he was exempt, yet he had to fulfill all the demands of justice, because he had assumed the humility of the flesh." Moreover, Origen on the words of Christ: "That we may not scandalize them," spoke more to the point and in greater conformity to the meaning of the evangelist, as follows: "It is to be understood," that is, from Christ's words, "that while men sometimes appear who through injustice seize our earthly goods, the kings of this earth send men to exact from us what is theirs. And by his example the Lord prohibits the doing of any offense, even to such men, either so that they may no longer sin, or so that they may be saved. For the son of God, who did no servile work, gave the tribute money, having the guise of a servant which he assumed for the sake of man."

How, then, is it possible, on the strength of the words of the evangelic Scripture, that the bishops and priests be exempt from this tribute, and from the jurisdiction of rulers generally, unless by the rulers' own gratuitous grant, when Christ and Peter, setting an example for others, paid such tribute? And although Christ, being of royal stock in flesh, was perhaps not obliged to do this, yet Peter, not being of royal stock, had no such reason to be exempt, just as he wanted none. But if Christ had thought it improper for his successors in the priestly office to pay tribute and for their temporal goods to be subject to the secular rulers, then without setting a bad example, that is, without subjecting the priesthood to the jurisdiction of secular rulers, he could have ordained otherwise and have made some arrangement about those tax collectors, such as removing from them the intention of asking for such tribute, or in some other appropriate way. But he did not think it proper to do so, rather he wanted to pay;

and from among the apostles, as the one who was to pay with him the tribute, he chose Peter, despite the fact that Peter was to be the foremost teacher and pastor of the church, as will be said in Chapter XVI of this discourse, in order that by such an example none of the others would refuse to do likewise.

11. The passage of Scripture which we quoted above from the seventeenth chapter of Matthew is interpreted in the way we have said by St. Ambrose in the epistle entitled *On Handing Over the Basilica,* where he writes as follows: "He," that is, the emperor, "demands tribute, it is not denied. The fields of the church pay tribute." And a little further on he says, more to the point: "We pay to Caesar the things that are Caesar's, and to God the things that are God's. The tribute is Caesar's, it is not denied." Expressing more fully this which we have called the meaning of the above-quoted passage of Scripture, St. Bernard in an epistle to the archbishop of Sens wrote as follows: "This is what is done by these men," namely, those who suggested that subjects rebel against their superiors. "But Christ ordered and acted otherwise. 'Render,' he said, 'to Caesar the things that are Caesar's, and to God the things that are God's.' What he spoke by word of mouth, he soon took care to carry out in deed. The institutor of Caesar did not hesitate to pay the tax to Caesar. For he thus gave you the example that you should do likewise. How, then, could he deny the reverence due to the priests of God, when he took care to show it even for the secular powers?"

And we must note what Bernard said, that Christ, in taking care to pay the tax to the secular powers, showed "due," and therefore not coerced, "reverence." For everyone owes such tax and tribute to the rulers, as we shall show in the following chapter from the words of the Apostle in the thirteenth chapter of the epistle to the Romans, and the glosses thereon of the saints and doctors; although perhaps not every tax is owed everywhere by everyone, such as the entry tax which was not owed by the inhabitants, although the custodians or collectors sometimes wrongly demanded and exacted it from simple inhabitants or natives, such as were the apostles. And therefore, in agreement with Origen, who I believed grasped the meaning of the evangelist on this point better than did Jerome, I say that it seemed customary and was perhaps commonly established in states, especially in Judaea, that entry taxes were not to be paid by inhabitants or natives, but only by aliens. And hence Christ said to Peter: "Of whom do the kings of the earth receive tribute?" etc., by "tribute" meaning that entry tax which the tax collectors were demanding. For Christ did not deny that the children of the earth, that is, natives, owe "tribute," taking the word as a common name for every tax; on the contrary, he later said of it, excepting no one: "Render to Caesar the things that are Caesar's"; and this was also expressed by the Apostle in agreement with Christ, when he said, in the thirteenth chapter of the epistle to the Romans: "For this cause also you pay tribute," that is, to rulers, "for they are the ministers of God." By "children," therefore, Christ meant the children of kingdoms, that is, persons born or raised therein, and not the children of kings by blood; otherwise his words would not seem to have been pertinent, for very often he spoke in the plural both for himself and for Peter, who was certainly not the child of such kings as those discussed by Jerome. Moreover, if Christ was of David's stock in flesh, so too were very many other Jews, although not perhaps Peter. Again, the tribute was not then being exacted by David or by anyone of his blood; why, therefore, should Christ have said, "The kings of the land . . . then the children are free," saying nothing about the heavenly king? But it is certain that neither Christ nor Peter was a child of Caesar, either in flesh or in spirit. Moreover, why should Christ have asked the above question? For everyone certainly knows that the children of kings by blood do not pay tribute to their parents. Jerome's exposition, therefore, does not seem to have been as much in agreement with Scripture as was Origen's. But the above words of Scripture show that Christ wanted to pay even undue tribute in certain places and at certain times, and to teach the Apostle and his successors to do likewise, rather than to fight over such things. For this was the justice of counsel and not of command which Christ, in the humility of the flesh which he had assumed, wanted to fulfill and to teach others to fulfill. And the Apostle, like Christ, also taught that this should be done. Hence, in the first epistle to the Corinthians, Chapter 6: "Why do ye not rather take wrong? why do yet not rather suffer yourselves to be defrauded?" than to quarrel with one another, as he had said before.

12. Moreover, not only with respect to property did Christ show that he was subject to the coercive jurisdiction of the secular ruler, but also with respect to his own person, than which no greater jurisdiction could be had by the ruler over him or over anyone else, for which reason it is called "capital jurisdiction" (*merum imperium*) by the Roman legislator. That Christ was thus subject can be clearly shown from the twenty-seventh chapter of Matthew; for there it is written that Christ allowed himself to be seized and brought before Pilate, who was the vicar of the Roman emperor, and he suffered himself to be judged and given the extreme penalty by Pilate as judge with coercive power; nor did Christ protest against him as not being a judge, although he perhaps indicated that he was suffering an unjust punishment. But it is certain that he could have undergone such judgment and punishment at the hands of priests, had he so desired, and had he deemed it improper for his successors to be subject to the secular rulers and to be judged by them.

But since this view is borne out at great length in the nineteenth chapter of John, I shall here adduce what is written there. When Christ had been brought before Pilate, vicar of Caesar, to be judged, and was accused of having called himself king of the Jews and son of God, he was asked by Pilate: "Whence art thou?" But having no reply from Jesus, Pilate spoke to him the following words, which are quite pertinent to our subject; here is the passage: "Pilate therefore saith to him, Speakest thou not to me? Knowest thou not that I have power to crucify thee, and I have power to release thee? Jesus answered: Thou shouldst not have any power against me, unless it were given thee from above." See, then, Jesus did not deny that Pilate had the power to judge him and to execute his judgment against him; nor did he say: This does not pertain to you of right (*de jure*) but you do this only in fact (*de facto*). But Christ added that Pilate had this power "from above." How from above? Augustine answers: "Let us therefore learn what he," that is, Christ, "said, and what he taught the Apostle," that is, Paul, in the epistle to the Romans, Chapter 13. What, then, did Christ say? What did he teach the Apostle? "That there is no power," that is, authority of jurisdiction, "except from God," whatever be the case with respect to the act of him who badly uses the power. "And that he who from malice hands over an innocent man to the power to be killed, sins more than does the power itself if it kills the man from fear of another's greater power. But God had certainly given to him," that is, Pilate, "power in such manner that he was under the power of Caesar."

The coercive judicial power of Pilate over the person of Christ, therefore, was from God, as Christ openly avowed, and Augustine plainly showed, and Bernard clearly said in his epistle to the archbishop of Sens: "For," as he wrote, "Christ avows that the Roman ruler's power over him is ordained of heaven," speaking of Pilate's power and with reference to this passage of Scripture. If, then, the coercive judiciary power of Pilate over Christ was from God, how much more so over Christ's temporal or carnal goods, if he had possessed or owned any? And if over Christ's person and temporal goods, how much more over the persons and temporal goods of all the apostles, and of their successors, all the bishops or priests?

Not only was this shown by Christ's words, but it was confirmed by the consummation of the deed. For the capital sentence was pronounced upon Christ by the same Pilate, sitting in the judgment seat, and by his authority that sentence was executed. Hence in the same chapter of John this passage is found: "Now when Pilate had heard these words, he brought Jesus forth, and sat down in the judgment seat"; and a little below is added: "Then therefore he delivered him," that is, Jesus, "to them to be crucified." Such was the Apostle's view regarding Christ, when he said in the third chapter of the epistle to the Galatians: "But when the fulness of the time was come, God sent his son, made of a woman, made under the law," and therefore also under the judge whose function it was to judge and command in accordance with the law, but who was not, however, a bishop or a priest.

13. Not only did Christ wish to exclude himself from secular rulership or coercive judicial power, but he also excluded it from his apostles, both among themselves and with respect to others. Hence in the twentieth chapter of Matthew and the twenty-second chapter of Luke this passage is found: "And there was also a strife among them," that is, the apostles, "which of them should seem to be the greater. And he," Christ, "said to them, The kings of the Gentiles lord it over them, and they that have power over them are called beneficent." (But in Matthew this clause is written as follows: "And they that are the greater exercise power upon them.") "But you not so: but he that is the greater among you, let him become as the younger; and he that is the leader, as he that serveth." "But whosoever will be the greater among you, let him be your minister. And he that will be first among you shall be your servant: even as the Son of man is not come to be ministered unto, but to minister," that is, to be a servant in the temporal realm, not to lord it or rule, for in spiritual ministry he was first, and not a servant among the apostles. Whereon Origen comments: "'You know that the princes of the Gentiles lord it over them,' that is, they are not content merely to rule their subjects, but try to exercise violent lordship over them," that is, by coercive force if necessary. "But those of you who are mine will not be so; for just as all carnal things are based upon necessity, but spiritual things upon the will, so too should the rulership of those who are spiritual rulers," prelates, "be based upon love and not upon fear." And Chrysostom writes, among other remarks, these pertinent words:

The rulers of the world exist in order to lord it over their subjects, to cast them into slavery and to despoil them [namely, if they deserve it] and to use them even unto death for their [that is, the rulers'] own advantage and glory. But the rulers [that is, prelates] of the church are appointed in order to serve their subjects and to minister to them whatever they have received from Christ, so that they neglect their own advantage and seek to benefit their subjects, and do not refuse to die for their salvation. To desire the leadership of the church is neither just nor useful. For what wise man is there who wants to subject himself of his own accord to such servitude and peril, as to be responsible for the whole church? Only he perhaps who does not fear the judgment of God and abuses his ecclesiastic leadership for secular purposes, so as to change it into secular leadership.

Why, then, do priests have to interfere with coercive secular judgments? for their duty is not to exercise temporal lordship, but rather to serve, by the example and command of Christ. Hence Jerome: "Finally he," that is, Christ, "sets forth his own example, so that if they," the apostles, "do not respect his words they may at least be ashamed of their deeds," that is, wielding temporal lordship. Hence Origen on the words: "And to give his life a redemption for many," wrote as follows:

The rulers of the church should therefore imitate Christ, who was approachable, and spoke to women, and placed his hands upon the children, and washed the feet of his disciples, so that they might do the same for their brethren. But we are such [he is speaking of the prelates of his day] that we seem to exceed even the worldly rulers in pride, either misunderstanding or despising the commandment of Christ, and we demand fierce, powerful armies, just as do kings.

But since to do these things is to despise or be ignorant of Christ's commandment, the prelates must first be warned about it, which is what we shall do in this treatise, by showing what authority belongs to them; then, if they disregard this, they must be compelled and forced by the secular rulers to correct their ways, lest they corrupt the morals of others. These, then, are the comments made on the passage in Matthew. On Luke, Basil writes: "It is fitting that those who preside should offer bodily service, following the example of the Lord who washed the feet of his disciples."

Christ, then, said: "The kings of the Gentiles lord it over them. But you," that is, the apostles, "not so." So Christ, king of kings and lord of lords, did not give them the power to exercise the secular judgments of rulers, nor coercive power over anyone, but he clearly prohibited this to them, when he said: "But you not so." And the same must consequently be held with respect to all the successors of the apostles, the bishops or priests. This too is what St. Bernard clearly wrote to Eugene, *On Consideration,* Book II, Chapter IV, discussing the above words of Christ: "The kings of the Gentiles lord it over them," etc. For Bernard wrote, among other things:

What the apostle [Peter] has, this did he give, namely, the guardianship, as I have said, of the churches. But not lordship? Hear him. "Neither as lording it over the clergy," he says, "but being made a pattern of the flock." And lest you think he spoke only from humility, but not with truth, the voice of the Lord is in the gospel: "The kings of the Gentiles lord it over them, and they that have power over them are called beneficent." And he adds: "But you not so." It is quite plain, then, that lordship is forbidden to the apostles. Go, then, if you dare, and usurp either the apostolate if you are a lord or lordship if you are an apostle. You are plainly forbidden to have both. If you wish to have both at once, you shall lose both. In any case, do not think you are excepted from the number of those about whom God complains in these words: "They have reigned, but not by me: they have been princes, and I knew not."

And so from the evangelic truths which we have adduced, and the interpretations of them made by the saints and other approved teachers, it should be clearly apparent to all that both in word and in deed Christ excluded and wished to exclude himself from all worldly rulership of governance, judgment, or coercive power, and that he wished to be subject to the secular rulers and powers in coercive jurisdiction.

CHAPTER XXIII: *On the Modes of Plenitude of Power, and the Manner and Order of Their Assumption by the Roman Bishop, Together with a General Statement of How He Has Used and Still Uses Them*

The nature and extent of the priestly powers was determined in Chapters VI, VII, IX, and XI of this discourse; the equality or inequality of the priests in power and dignity was examined in Chapters XV and XVI of this discourse; and in the preceding chapter we discussed the proper and expedient priority or leadership of one bishop, church, or clerical college over all others, and the origin and development of this primacy, its secret and gradual transition into an improper form and species of priority, extending to so grave and unbearable an excess as the seizure of secular power, and the immoderate and completely intolerable desire of the Roman bishops for rulership, to which desire they have already given vocal expression.

2. In all the seizures of secular power and rulership which the Roman bishops have perpetrated in the past, and which, as everyone can plainly see, they are still striving with all their might, although wrongly, to perpetrate, no small role has been played in the past, and will be played in the future, by that sophistical line of argument whereby these bishops ascribe to themselves the title of "plenitude of power." This sophistry is also the source of the misreasoning whereby they try to prove that all kings, rulers, and individuals are subject to them in coercive jurisdiction. Hence it will be well to examine this plenitude of power, first by separating or distinguishing its various modes; next by inquiring whether in any one or more of these modes plenitude of power belongs to the Roman pontiff or to any other bishop; then, by showing which meaning of this title the Roman bishop first claimed for himself; and finally by examining how this was transferred into other forms (would that they were not frauds!) harmful to all rulers and subjects living a civil life, and what use the Roman pontiff has hitherto made, and still makes, and unless he is prevented will most likely continue to make, of these forms of the title of plenitude of power.

3. Inasmuch as plenitude of power seems to imply a certain universality, and it is our purpose to deal only with voluntary powers, we must differentiate plenitude of power into its various modes or senses, according to the different kinds of universal voluntary power.

[*i*] In one sense, then, plenitude of power is and can be truly understood to mean, in accordance with the significance or force of the words themselves, the unlimited power to perform every possible act and to make anything at will. This power seems to belong only to Christ from among all men. Whence in Matthew, last chapter, it is written: "All power is given unto me in heaven and in earth."

[*ii*] In a second sense, more pertinently, plenitude of power can be understood to mean that whereby a man is allowed to perform any voluntary controlled act upon any other man and upon any external thing which is in men's power or

can be put to their use; or again, plenitude of power can be understood to mean that whereby a man is allowed to perform every act aforesaid, but not upon every other man or everything subject to human power; or, furthermore, plenitude of power can be understood as that whereby a man is allowed to perform not every act, but only a determinate kind or species of act, and yet following every impulse of the will, and upon every other man and everything subject to human power.

[*iii*] In a third sense, plenitude of power can be understood as the power of supreme coercive jurisdiction over all the governments, peoples, communities, groups, and individuals in the world; or again, over only some of these, but yet following every impulse of the will.

[*iv*] In a fourth sense, plenitude of power can be understood to mean the kind of power defined above, but over all clergymen only, and including the power to appoint them all to church offices, to deprive them thereof or depose them, and to distribute ecclesiastic temporal goods or benefices.

[*v*] In a fifth sense, it can be understood as the power whereby priests can in every way bind and loose men from guilt and punishment, and excommunicate them, lay them under interdict, and reconcile them to the church, all of which was discussed in Chapters VI and VII of this discourse.

[*vi*] In a sixth sense, it can be understood to mean the power of the priests to lay their hands on all men so as to receive them into ecclesiastic orders, and the power to bestow or prohibit ecclesiastic sacraments, which was discussed in Chapters XVI and XVII of this discourse.

[*vii*] In a seventh sense, it can be understood as the power to interpret the meanings of Scripture, especially on matters which are necessary for salvation; and the power to distinguish the true meanings from the false, the sound from the unsound; and the power to regulate all church ritual, and to make a general coercive command ordering the observance of such regulations under penalty of anathematization.

[*viii*] In an eighth sense, and the last so far as our purposes are concerned, plenitude of power can be understood to mean a general pastoral cure of souls, extending to all the peoples and provinces in the world, which was discussed in Chapters IX and XXII of this discourse.

Plenitude of power might also be understood, in each of the senses given above, as that power which is limited by no law, so that non-plenary power would be that which is limited by the laws human or divine, under which right reason can also properly be placed. There are perhaps other modes and combinations of plenitude of power, but I think that we have enumerated all those which are pertinent for our purposes.

4. And so, having thus distinguished these modes of plenary power, I say that plenitude of power in the first two senses given above does not belong to the Roman bishop, to any other priest, or to anyone else except Christ or God. Because this fact is so evident, and is certified by divine and human wisdom and all moral science, I omit to discuss it, and also for the sake of brevity.

As to the third and fourth modes of plenary power, we have shown by demonstration in Chapter XV of Discourse I, and more fully confirmed by the infailible testimony of the sacred Scripture in Chapters IV, V, and VII of this discourse, and most firmly corroborated in Chapters XV, XVI, XVII, and XXI of this discourse, that in no way at all, let alone with plenitude, do these powers belong by divine law to any priest or bishop, as such, over any clergyman or layman. But as to whether human law has granted such plenitude of power to any clergyman, bishop or priest, or to any layman, in any way in which such power is capable of being granted and of being revoked by the judgment of the human legislator for a reasonable cause, this must be ascertained from the human laws and the rescripts or privileges of the human legislator.

As to the fifth and sixth modes of plenary power, it has been shown in Chapters VI and VII of this discourse that the power to bind men to and loose them from guilt and punishment, and publicly to anathematize or excommunicate anyone, has not been granted to the priest absolutely or with plenitude, but rather this power has been so delimited by divine law that the priest cannot damn the innocent or loose the guilty with God. Also, the power of any bishop or priest publicly to excommunicate someone, and especially to lay a ruler or community under interdict, must properly be delimited by human enactment, as has been shown in Chapters VI, VII, and XXI of this discourse. Moreover, in Chapter XVII of this discourse it has been shown that the power to appoint ministers of the church by laying on hands, and to teach and preach, and to minister the ecclesiastic sacraments in communities of believers, does not belong to bishops or priests with plenitude, since the proper way to use these powers has been determined for bishops and priests by divine and human law.

As to the remaining modes of plenitude of power, the seventh and eighth, it has been shown in Chapters XX, XXI, and XXII of this discourse that they belong to no bishop or priest with plenitude, but in accordance with the determination of both divine and human law. Therefore, plenitude of power does not belong to the Roman bishop or to any other priest, as such, unless perhaps they mean by plenitude of power the priority or leadership which we have shown, in Chapter XXII of this discourse, to belong to the Roman bishop and his church over all other priests and churches, by authority of the faithful human legislator.

5. Now we must discuss what was the source of the Roman pontiff's original ascription to himself of the title of plenitude of power, and which mode of this title he first assumed, although such plenary power truly belongs to him in none of the senses given above. But this title seems to have been first assumed by the Roman pontiff in its eighth sense, and the original source wherefrom this title appeared to belong to him seems to have been the statement of Christ to St. Peter, in John, Chapter 21: "Feed my sheep"; and also the words in Matthew, Chapter 16, spoken to Peter alone: "And I will give unto thee the keys of the kingdom of heaven"; also the passage in John, Chapter 18: "Put up thy sword into the sheath"; and again the reply of the disciples to Christ: "Behold, here are two swords." These passages are interpreted by some men as meaning that the whole body of sheep, that is, the Christian believers in the whole world, has been entrusted to Peter alone, and thus to every Roman pontiff as the particular vicar of St. Peter; and that the other apostles and the bishops who succeeded them were not entrusted with the guidance of all the sheep throughout the whole world, but to each of them was entrusted a particular determinate flock and province. St. Bernard, thus interpreting the words of Christ which we quoted above from John, Chapter 21, writes in his treatise addressed to the Roman pope Eugene *On Consideration,* Book II, as follows: "You are the one universal shepherd, not only of the sheep, but also of the shepherds. How do I prove this, you ask? By the word of the Lord. For to which, I will not say of the bishops, but even of the apostles, were all the sheep entrusted so absolutely and without differentiation?

'If you love me, Peter, feed my sheep.' Where no distinctions are made, no exceptions are made." And a little below, Bernard adds: "Hence, to each of the other apostles, who knew the sacrament, was allotted a particular flock. And thereupon James, 'who seemed to be a pillar' of the church, was content to serve only in Jerusalem, yielding to Peter the care of the whole." And then Bernard draws this pertinent inference: "According to your canons, therefore, the others have been called to take care of a part, while you have been called to plenitude of power." At the beginning, then, plenitude of power was understood to mean the general administration or care of all souls.

6. While such was the meaning of this title when the Roman bishop first assumed it for himself, although it was not in harmony with the true sense of Scripture, as will be sufficiently proved in Chapter XXVIII of this discourse, this meaning was presumptuously transformed by him into a different one, perhaps for the sake of gain or other advantage, or in order to usurp preeminence over others. By this transformation, the Roman bishop claimed and publicly declared that he alone, by his own pronouncement or by the imposition of any this-worldly satisfaction which he might care to demand, could completely absolve sinners and exempt them from the penalties which they would be obliged to pay or suffer for the status of the future world in accordance with the demerits of their sins.

7. Having thus assumed these powers under a guise of piety and mercy (piety, that they might seem to have care and solicitude for all men by the motivation of charity; mercy, that they might be thought to have the power and the desire to take pity upon all men), the Roman bishops, supported by the privileges and grants of rulers, and especially when the imperial seat was vacant, then extended this title: first they made it apply to the regulation of church ritual by making certain laws over clergymen, which from the beginning were called "decrees"; and then they persuaded laymen to accept certain regulations which were made in the form of requests or exhortations, imposing fasts and abstinences from certain foods at fixed periods, for the purpose of obtaining divine suffrage and mercy so that the epidemics and the atmospheric tempests which then plagued men might be averted. All this is to be seen from the history of St. Gregory and of certain other saints.

8. When the laymen in their devoutness voluntarily accepted and observed these regulations or requests, and such observance became an established custom, the Roman bishops began to proclaim them in the form of commands, and thus ventured, without leave by the human legislator, to frighten their transgressors with vocal threats of anathematization or excommunication—but all this under the guise of piety or divine worship.

9. But then the desire of the Roman bishops for domination grew even stronger. Seeing that devout believers, because of their foolishness and their ignorance of divine law, were frightened by such pronouncements, and that, from fear of eternal damnation, they believed they were obliged to obey the proclamations of the priests, the Roman bishops with their coterie of clergymen had the presumption to issue certain oligarchic edicts or ordinances concerning civil acts, declaring that they and the clerical order or office, wherein they also included any mere laymen they chose, were exempt from public burdens; and they promoted to the clerical order even married laymen, who readily joined in order to enjoy immunity from public burdens. In this way they have subjected to themselves a not

inconsiderable part of the civil multitude, removing them from the power of the rulers. And again, desiring further to lessen the rulers' power, they have issued other edicts imposing the penalty of anthema upon those who have inflicted any personal injuries on men who were enrolled in a clerical group; similarly, they publicly defame them in their temples by excommunicating them, nonetheless demanding that such culprits be given the punishments fixed by human laws.

10. But here is a still more detestable act, truly execrable in the priestly office: in order to expand their jurisdiction and thereby to increase their shameful gains, in open contempt of God and to the patent harm of rulers, the Roman and other bishops excommunicate and exclude from the ecclesiastic sacraments laymen and clergymen who neglect or are unable to pay certain pecuniary debts which it had been their civil obligation to discharge at the end of a certain time. Christ and the holy apostles had brought these men into the church by means of many exhortations, hardships, and exertions, and finally through martyrdom and the spilling of their precious blood. For he who was "made all things to all men," in order that he might win over all men, did not act in the way these bishops do, but rather he wished that only grave crimes should cause sinners to be cut off from the company of the other believers, as we have shown from I Corinthians, Chapter 5, in Chapter VI of this discourse.

11. Not content even with these acts, but seeking the highest degree of secular power, contrary to the command or counsel of Christ and the apostles, these bishops have rushed forth to make laws distinct from those of the whole body of citizens, decreeing that all clergymen are exempt from the civil laws and thus bringing on civil schism and a plurality of supreme governments, the incompatibility of which with the peace of men we demonstrated in Chapter XVII of Discourse I, adducing the sure testimony of experience. For this is the root and origin of the pestilence besetting the state of Italy; from it all scandals have germinated and grown, and so long as it continues, civil discord in Italy will never cease. For the Roman bishop fears that this power into which he has gradually stolen through sly deception, and which custom (or rather abuse) has enabled him to retain, will be revoked by the ruler (which revocation he would richly deserve because of the excesses he has committed); and so by all kinds of malicious devices he prevents the appointment and inauguration of the Roman ruler. And a certain bishop has finally gone so far in his audacity as to issue edicts proclaiming that the Roman ruler is bound to him by an "oath of fealty," as being subject to him in coercive jurisdiction this assertion can be found plainly expressed, by anyone who reads the document entitled *On the Sentence and the Thing Judged,* which is in the seventh ridiculous and despicable part of the statements which they call "decretals."

12. Because Henry VII, of happy and divine memory, who occupies a position of preeminence among the rulers of all ages, places, and conditions, refused to bow down before such headstrong rashness, this most Christian emperor and man of all the virtues is called a transgressor "who pretends to have forgotten" his sworn oath, in a certain document called a "decretal," which is as false as it is rash, entitled *On Oaths,* although its title might more appropriately be: on the wrongful injuries and insults inflicted upon the divine emperor, and upon all his successors, relatives, and allies. For this prince is defamed as a perjurer by the so-called "founders of the canons," who strive to blacken his fair memory (if it could be stained by the words or writings of such calumniators).

13. Not daring to call these oligarchic ordinances "laws," the Roman bishops and their cardinals gave them the name "decretals" instead, although, like human legislators, they intend them to be binding on men for the status of the present world, with penalties to be inflicted for their transgression. From the very beginning they were afraid explicitly to express this intention by using the word "laws," for they feared resistance and correction by the human legislator, since by making such ordinances they committed the crime of treason against rulers and legislators; and so from the beginning they called these ordinances "canonic rights," in order that by the coloring of the phrase (although it was used with impiety) they might better lead the faithful to regard such ordinances as valid and thus more fully to believe, respect, and obey them.

In this way, then, to conclude, the Roman bishops have gradually and secretly accomplished this transformation, and now openly claim for themselves plenitude of power in the last six senses, thereby committing very many monstrous crimes in the civil order against divine and human law and against the right judgment of every rational being. Of some of these crimes, although not all, we have made individual mention in the preceding chapter.

SELECTED BIBLIOGRAPHY

TRANSLATIONS

Gewirth, A., trans., *Marsilius of Padua, The Defender of Peace*, II: *The Defensor Pacis*, New York, 1956.

Lerner, R., and M. Mahdi, eds., *Medieval Political Philosophy: A Sourcebook*, New York, 1963.

STUDIES

Emerton, E., *The Defensor Pacis of Marsiglio of Padua*, Cambridge, Mass., 1920.

Gewirth, A., *Marsilius of Padua, The Defender of Peace*, I: *Marsilius of Padua and Medieval Political Philosophy*, New York, 1951.

Kates, P., *The Two Swords: A Study of the Union of Church and State*, Washington, 1928.

de Lagarde, G., "Marsile de Padoue et Guillaume d'Ockham," *Revue des sciences religieuse*, XVII (1937), 168–185, 428–454.

de Lagarde, G., *La naissance de l'esprit laïque*, II: *Marsile de Padoue théoricien de l'état laïque*, 2nd ed., Paris, 1948.

de Lagarde, G., *La naissance de l'esprit laïque, au declin du moyen âge*, III: *Le Defensor pacis*, Louvain, 1970.

Previté-Orton, C., "Marsiglio of Padua, Doctrine," *English Historical Review*, XXXVIII (1923), 1–21.

Previtée-Orton, C., "Marsilius of Padua," *Proceedings of the British Academy*, XXI (1935), 137–183.

Quillet, J., *La philosophie politique de Marsile de Padoue*, Paris, 1970.

Scholz, R., "Marsilius von Padua und die Genesis des modernen Staatsbewusstseins,' *Historische Zeitschrift*, CLVI (1936), 88–103.

Stieglitz, L., *Die Staatslehre des Marsilius von Padua*, Leipzig, 1914.

Tosel, A., "Nature de la politique chez Marsile de Padoue," *Réseaux*, XXIV–XXV (1975), 101–121.

JOHN BURIDAN

ca. 1300 – ca. 1358

"THE INFLUENCE of Buridan went far beyond what we can imagine." Thus speaks Etienne Gilson, a most eminent historian—and one unsympathetic to Buridan's philosophical orientation—in his *History of Christian Philosophy in the Middle Ages*. His estimate is confirmed by the range of remaining manuscripts from Poland to Italy, by the assignment of Buridan's works as texts at various times in the fourteenth and fifteenth centuries from Scotland to Austria, and by printed editions from every century from the fifteenth through the eighteenth. Buridan clearly was one of the great teachers of the late medieval and early modern periods. As modern scholars explore this unusually popular body of work, they find physical theories with some claim to have influenced and even anticipated Galileo, and semantic investigations sufficiently precise and subtle to prove instructive for modern logicians. Thus Buridan is known today as much for his theory of impetus and his treatment of the paradoxes of self-reference as for the legendary example of the ass placed between two equally appetizing bundles of hay.

Buridan was a Nominalist, and is sometimes dismissed simply as the leader of the Parisian Ockhamists. But this classification does not do him justice, especially if the skeptical and disintegrative potentialities of Ockham's thought are emphasized. Buridan is firm in rejecting universals as extra-mental entities; but he is equally firm in rejecting skepticism, and he develops ingenious qualifications to blunt the force of the disintegrative argument from divine omnipotence which was cutting such a swath at the time. One might say that in his hands the Nominalist methods were not put to a polemical use dominated by moral or religious zeal, but rather were used to clarify problems and eliminate controversy. "I believe that the controversy sprang from a lack of logic" is one of his characteristic remarks. This temperament may have something to do with the fact that he was one of the rare medieval philosophers who did not go on to theology, and also perhaps with the fact that he was a secular priest and thus not committed to the official doctrine of one of the religious orders. Indeed, it has been suggested that his attitude toward theology was akin to that of the so-called "Averroists," and that he avoided trouble only by extreme circumspection.

He once pointed out that like all arts masters, he had taken a vow not to touch upon purely theological matters and to refute philosophical positions contrary to the faith. But he also said that it pertains to philosophy to consider what can be concluded beyond given premises, whether possible or impossible, and to do this for moral as well as natural terms. This suggests the rather independent attitude that as a logician he has the right to criticize the validity of arguments in whatever field they may be employed. But for the most part Buridan is more interested in detailed questions of logic, ethics, and what he calls "natural science" than in the large metaphysical issues most relevant to theology. In this close focus, in his scientific and semantic interests, and in his persistent resolution of issues by means of logical analysis, Buridan strikes many of his readers as an unusually "modern" philosopher; and it may be fitting to end this anthology with a figure whose modes of thought may be familiar to the student, thus emphasizing the continuity of the history of philosophy by helping to dispel the illusion of a great gap between the later Middle Ages and the beginnings of modern philosophy in the seventeenth century.

As a widely known teacher, Buridan became the subject of legends—such as the one that has him dally with the Queen of France and tossed into the Seine sewed up in a sack. Beyond these legends little is known of his life. He is first mentioned as rector of the University of Paris in 1328, which presumably indicates that he was born before 1300. His birthplace is traditionally put at Bethune, in the diocese of Arras. Sometime between 1316 and 1334, he journeyed to Avignon where he climbed Mont Ventoux considerably before Petrarch, for the significantly different purpose of making scientific observations. In 1340 he was rector again, and seems to have been a prominent mediator in university disputes. In this role he signed a statute prohibiting the "dogmatizing" of Ockhamism, but it has been convincingly argued that the main burden of this statute is directed against Nicholas of Autrecourt rather than Ockham. Buridan accumulated benefices and by 1349 seems to have been prosperous. The last direct record of him comes from 1358. He appears to have left a considerable bequest, including a house, to the university. There is a story, rejected by most modern scholars, that he helped found the University of Vienna in 1366.

Buridan left the works one would expect of a master of arts of more than thirty years' teaching experience. His logical works include the *Sum of Dialectic (Summulae de dialectica), Consequences (Consequentiae)*, and an advanced work on logical problems, *Sophismata*. The bulk of his work consists of literal commentaries and collections of Questions on the works of Aristotle, including the *Physics, De caelo, De anima,* and *Metaphysics,* and Questions alone on the *Ethics, Politics,* and *Rhetoric.* There are various other works on minor or pseudo-Aristotelian treatises, and a few treatments of specific topics. Questions of chronology have little meaning for such a corpus, since he no doubt lectured on many of these topics concurrently.

However, there is some evidence that the *Summulae* is among his earliest published works, and the *Questions on the Ethics,* among the latest.

The selections which follow show Buridan more as a philosopher than as a logician or natural scientist, and they deal with topics which look back over much covered elsewhere in this anthology. In the first selection Buridan deals with skeptical implications of the argument from divine omnipotence and replies to Nicholas of Autrecourt. He concedes that induction is not a formally valid type of inference, but attempts to defend natural science from skepticism by elaborating a conception of degrees of evidence. He says here that he speaks only of "complexes," or propositions, and that he has spoken of "simples" elsewhere. This must refer to Question 4, Book I of the *Questions on Aristotle's Physics,* where he says that neither in the abstraction of concepts from perception, nor in the formation of propositions from concepts is there any argument from one proposition to another. And only in such an argument is there any application of the principle of non-contradiction so devastatingly invoked by Nicholas. The next selection gives very straightforwardly the Nominalist objections to the modified Platonism perpetuated by the doctrine of essences. It also gives an example of intramural Nominalist controversy—in this case, whether scientific laws are categorical or hypothetical in logical force. He mentions here the rejection of a real distinction between essence and existence, which is taken up in the following selection. There he criticizes the other major interpretation of the distinction of essence from existence as a distinction of reason, and presents his own rather peculiar solution of the problem. The next selections on motion contrast with those by his supposed fellow nominalist, Ockham, and have led to controversy concerning the extent to which these medieval thinkers may have anticipated such later scientific concepts as inertia. In the final selection concerning ethics, as well as in previous selections, one can find the crucial employment of the distinction between absolute and connotative reference. In view of his often alleged dependence on Ockham, it is worth noting that he presents a traditional teleological ethics, revealing very little of Ockham's deontological authoritarianism. It is also interesting to notice that he pays inordinate attention to Cicero and Seneca—which suggests that it is not only in climbing Mont Ventoux that he should be linked with Petrarch. Even though he associates "moral logic" with rhetoric and poetics, he presents here a prime example of the analysis of terms which the later Nominalists proclaimed as one of their defining characteristics (see p. 649). Buridan seems here to go beyond his earlier view that since natural science is based on relative rather than absolute evidence, it is not subject to arguments from divine omnipotence. Here he seems to say that because ethical terms are connotative, they are only applicable when the natural network of connotations is fulfilled. Arguments from divine omnipotence would thus seem to remove the very conditions for significant discourse, and hence are irrelevant to ethics. Here we have a Nominalism that is the very reverse of skeptical and disintegrative.

In these selections, the infinitive-with-accusative construction (e.g., *rosam esse*) is translated by the expression "X-exists" (rose-exists) rather than by the awkward "for an X to exist."

QUESTIONS ON ARISTOTLE'S METAPHYSICS

Book II

QUESTION I

On the second Book it is asked *whether comprehension of the truth of things is possible for us*. It is argued that it is not: . . .

Again, the senses can be deluded, as is commonly said, and sensible species can surely be conserved in the organs of sense with the sensible things absent, as it says in the *De Somno et Vigilia*. And then we judge about what does not exist as if it existed; hence we err through the senses. And the difficulty is greatly augmented in that we believe from the Faith that God can form the species of sensible things in our senses without the sensible things being present, and He can conserve them for a long time; and then we judge as if the sensible things were present. Further, since God can do this and even greater things, and you do not know whether He wishes to do this, you do not have certitude and evidence whether you are awake and there are men before you, or whether you are asleep. For in your sleep, God could produce sensible species as clear as, or rather, a hundred times clearer than could be produced by sensible objects. And you would then judge formally that there are sensible things before you, just as you now judge. Hence, since you know nothing about the will of God, you cannot be certain of anything.

Then on the side of the intellect, it is argued that our intellect depends on the senses in knowing. Hence if we do not have certitude through the senses, as was said, it follows that neither do we through the intellect. . . .

Again, regarding principles, it is argued that they are known through experiences, and experiences are deceptive, as is obvious through Hippocrates. Second, it is proved that they are fallacious, for experiences only have the force of establishing a universal principle by way of induction from many cases; and a universal proposition never follows from an induction unless the induction includes every singular of that universal, which is impossible. Indeed, consider that whenever you have touched fire, you have sensed it to be hot, and so through experience you judge this fire which you have never touched to be hot, and so on. At length you judge every fire to be hot. Let us assume, therefore, that from the will of God, whenever you have sensed iron, you have sensed it to be hot. It is sure that by the same reasoning you would judge the iron which you see and

Translated by James J. Walsh for this volume from Joannes Buridanus, *In Metaphysicen Aristotelis Quaestiones*, Paris, 1588. Reprinted by Minerva G.M.B.H., Frankfurt a.M., 1964.

which in fact is cold, to be hot, and all iron to be hot. And in that case there would be false judgments, however much you would then have as much experience of iron as you now in fact have of fire. . . .

Again, neither a conclusion nor an effect can be known through a cause, nor a cause through an effect, since a cause is neither essentially nor virtually contained in its effect; nor is an effect known through a cause, since causes are less well known to us. And if you say that they are more known by nature, that is not to the point, since we are inquiring about our learning and not about nature's. Moreover, it seems that we can never have evidence of one thing through another, since there is no evidence except according to a reduction to the first principle, which is founded in contradiction. But we can never have a contradiction concerning two diverse things. Let us posit that they are A and B. It will be no contradiction for A to exist and B not to exist, or for A to be white and B not to be white. Hence there never will be an evident series concluding that B exists from the fact that A exists, and so for the others. . . .

The opposite is argued through Aristotle, who says it is in one way easy and in another, hard; and so he assumes it to be possible. And the Commentator argues thus: that for which we have a natural desire is possible, since nothing founded in nature is vain. As Aristotle says in the beginning, we have a natural desire to know, and consequently, the certain comprehension of the truth is possible for us.

To clarify the question, the terms should be expounded in some way. More is said concerning incomplex truth in other books. But for the present, I only intend the complex truth by which a proposition is called true, and no care should be taken for vocal or written propositions, since they are only called true or false because of true or false mental propositions which they represent, just as urine is called healthy or ill because it signifies the health or illness of the animal.

And further, I presume for the present that the truth of a mental proposition is not anything other than the very mental proposition which is true, however much these names "true" and "truth" connote that this kind of mental proposition is conformed to the things signified, in the way mentioned elsewhere. Then we must see what we should understand by the comprehension of truth, and it is already obvious according to what was said that the comprehension of truth is nothing other than the comprehension of a true proposition. Now the comprehension of truth can be taken in three ways. In one, the comprehension of truth is nothing other than the formation or the existence of a proposition in the mind, and again, the comprehension of a true proposition is nothing other than that very true proposition itself. It is obvious that this is possible, and hence it should be concluded that the comprehension of truth is possible in us. In another way, the comprehension of truth is the same as the understanding of a true proposition as an object of the mind, such that we know the proposition just as we comprehend or know a stone. And this surely is still possible for us, since we understand both terms and propositions, and hence we know how to say a great deal about them. And so it should also be concluded that in this way the comprehension of truth is possible for us.

In yet another way, the comprehension of truth is taken for the adhesion or assent through which we assent or adhere to a true proposition, and this surely is still possible for us. Indeed, we can assent not only to true propositions, we also often assent to false ones, as when we are stubborn in false opinions. So it should be concluded that in this way still the comprehension of truth is possible for us. But the arguments made raise a doubt as to whether such assent to the truth is possible for us with certitude. And then we should note that in order to assent to the truth with certitude, firmness of truth and firmness of assent are required. Now firmness of truth is possible. In one way, absolutely, as in this proposition, "God exists," since in no case can it be falsified; but also there is firmness of truth on the assumption of the common course of nature. And thus it would be a firm truth that the heaven is moved, that fire is hot, and so for other propositions and conclusions of natural science, notwithstanding that God could make fire be cold, and so the proposition "All fire is hot" would be falsified. In this way, then, it is obvious that firmness of truth is possible. But firmness of assent is that by which we adhere and assent to a proposition without fear for the opposite. And this can exist in three ways: in one, from the will or natural appetite, and so Christians assent and adhere firmly to the articles of the Catholic faith, and some heretics also adhere to their false opinions so much that they wish to die before denying them, and such is the experience of the saints who wished to die for the Christian faith. It is manifest that in this way, firmness of assent is possible for us.

In a second way, firmness comes to us from natural appearances by way of certain arguments, and in this way it is still possible that we can firmly assent, not only to the truth, but also to falsehood; for many having false opinions believe that they have firm knowledge, as Aristotle says in Book VII of the *Ethics,* where he says that many adhere to what they opine no less than to what they know. In the third way, firmness of assent comes from evidence, and the evidence of a proposition is termed absolute or unqualified when from the nature of sense or intellect, a man is disposed without necessity to assent to the proposition, so that he cannot dissent. And according to Aristotle, this kind of evidence belongs to the first complex principle, as is obvious in Book IV of this work. But in another way, evidence is taken as relative (*secundum quid*) or on the assumption, as was previously mentioned, that it would be observed among beings in the common course of nature; and so it would be evidence for us that all fire is hot and that the heaven is moved, even though the contrary is possible through the power of God. And this kind of evidence suffices for the principles and conclusions of natural science. Indeed, there is still another weaker evidence which suffices for acting morally well, for when all circumstances have been regarded and inquired into which a man can inquire into with diligence in judging according to the exigencies of this kind of circumstance, the judgment will be evident with evidence sufficient for acting morally well, even though the judgment should be false because of the invincible ignorance of some circumstance. For instance, it is possible that a magistrate should act well and meritoriously in hanging a saintly man because through witnesses and other documents in accordance with the law it appeared sufficiently to him that the good man was guilty of homicide. Hence the conclusion is reached which certain wicked ones wishing to destroy the natural and moral sciences proclaim, that in many of the principles and conclusions of those sciences there is no simple evidence, but they can be falsified through cases supernaturally possible. But absolute evidence is not required for such sciences; the previously mentioned relative evidence or evidence on assumption suffices. Hence Aristotle well says in Book II of this work that mathematical exactitude is not to be sought in all sciences. And since it has appeared that in all the aforesaid ways firmness of truth and firmness of assent are possible to us, the question should be answered that the comprehension of truth with certitude is possible for us. . . .

To the next objection, I say that if the senses are naturally deluded, the intellect has the ability to inquire when a man is and when he is not deluded, and it has the ability to correct illusory judgments. But if God operates simply miraculously, it should be concluded that He can; and so this is only evidence on an assumption, and as was previously said, it is sufficient for natural science.

To the next, I concede that the intellect in its simple and first apprehension depends on sense. But afterwards, the intellect can compound and divide, and discern beyond sense. . . .

To the next, which says that experience is not valid for concluding to a universal principle, I say that this is not an inference by grace of the form (of inference); but the intellect, predisposed by its natural inclination to truth, assents to a universal principle through experiences. And it can be conceded that such experiences are not valid for absolute evidence; but they are valid for the evidence which suffices for natural science. And with this there are also other principles from the inclusion or repugnance of terms or propositions, which do not require experiences, just as is the case for the first principle. Indeed, it is evidently true that a chimera exists or does not exist, that a goat-stag exists or does not exist, and that man is an animal, if the signification of the terms is known.

To the next, I say that effects are known through their cause by an adequate ground (*propter quid*), since the cause is better known to us as the reason why (*propter quid*) the effect exists. Likewise, a cause is known through the effect as to the fact that it exists (*quia est*), since the effect bears a certain similarity to the cause; hence it can represent the cause, together with the natural inclination of the intellect to truth. When it is also said that one thing cannot be conclusively known through another, I deny this, and I say that there are an almost infinite number of principles known self-evidently or known through sense or through experience or through the inclusion of terms, without requiring to be demonstrated through the first principle.

QUESTIONS ON THE TEN BOOKS OF THE NICOMACHEAN ETHICS OF ARISTOTLE

Book VI

QUESTION 6. *Whether Everything Knowable Is Eternal?*

It is argued that the answer is no: . . .

Again, natural science is had of hail-storms and rains, of plants and animals, and universally of what can be generated and destroyed; and these are not eternal. Therefore, etc.

The opposite is apparent through Aristotle in Book VI of this work, where he says:

Translated by James J. Walsh for this volume from *Johannis Buridani Quaestiones in decem libros ethicorum Aristotelis ad Nicomachum*, Oxford, 1637. The text has been checked against the Paris edition of 1513 and *Ms. Bibl. Nat. Lat. 16128.*

Now what scientific knowledge is, if we are to speak exactly and not follow mere similarities, is plain from what follows. We all suppose that what we know is not even capable of being otherwise; of things capable of being otherwise we do not know, when they have passed outside our observation, whether they exist or not. Therefore the object of scientific knowledge is of necessity. Therefore it is eternal: for things that are of necessity in the unqualified sense are all eternal; and things that are eternal are ungenerated and imperishable.*

The same is had from Book I of the *Posterior Analytics*.

Again, "Science is a firm habit and always determined to the truth, and cannot be turned into error nor removed from the intellect, except perhaps through oblivion." But these would not be true unless the knowable were eternal, since, as is said in the *Categories,* when the knowable is removed, so is the science. For if the knowable does not exist, neither does the science.

It should be noted that "the knowable" can be taken in two ways. In one way, for the demonstrable conclusion. In the other, for the thing or things signified by the terms of the conclusion, or for that or those things for which the terms of the conclusion supposit. For this conclusion, "Every man is capable of laughter," is knowable since it is demonstrable, and in knowing it we have science about all men and everything capable of laughter.

If the question is asked concerning the knowable as a demonstrable conclusion, then again a distinction should be made, since a conclusion is taken with regard to its reality or with regard to its truth. If with regard to its reality, then no conclusion ought to be called eternal or necessary, any more than asses or horses or colors or tastes, since we form conclusions afresh in writing as well as in voice or in the mind. And so they begin and cease to exist, just as do colors and tastes. But if a conclusion is taken with regard to its truth, then it can still be understood in two ways that a conclusion is eternal or necessary, or that it cannot possibly be otherwise. In one way, because the conclusion is always true, speaking categorically and unqualifiedly; and in this way a conclusion is no more necessary or eternal with regard to its truth than with regard to its reality. For whenever it does not exist, it is not true. In another way, speaking hypothetically, because every such conclusion is true whenever it is propounded, so that it cannot be false. And propositions are called necessary and perpetual and impossible to be otherwise in this way or in an equipollent sense—and not in the other way, whether they are written propositions or uttered, or formed in our mind.

It is in this way, then, that everything knowable (speaking of scientific knowledge proper) should be said to be eternal, necessary, impossible to be otherwise, ungenerated, and incorruptible. And this can be clarified by the difference between science, sense, and opinion. Although sense and science judge of the truth and falsity of different propositions, they differ further in that sense only judges with certitude of what is sensibly present. But through the habit of science the intellect judges truly in the absence as well as in the presence of what is intelligible. Science differs from opinion because, although both can judge in the absence of intelligible things, opinion does not judge with certainty, but with fear, and science judges with certainty and without fear. And all this ought to be assumed from the meaning of the terms "science" and "opinion." But surely it is impossible to judge of the truth of a proposition with certainty in the absence of the things

* (1139b 18–25, Ross translation.)

signified by the terms. If a proposition can be false, then a knowable proposition cannot be false. And this is the argument Aristotle intended in the text, "if we are to speak exactly and not follow similarities, we all suppose that what we know is not capable of being otherwise; of things capable of being otherwise, we do not know, when they have passed beyond our observation," etc. And all this seems self-evident to me.

But if we speak of the knowable as the thing or things signified by the terms of the conclusion, or that for which the terms of the conclusion supposit, there are diverse opinions on the proposed question.

One distinguishes between existence (*esse*) and essence, for we see that names and definitions signify the essences of things, which do not signify the things to exist nor not to exist, as is had in the *Posterior Analytics*. This opinion, however, maintains that things persist eternally according to their essences or quiddities, although they do not persist according to existence; for essences, they say, remain the same, and receive existence through generation and lose it through destruction.

They say, therefore, that there can be science of things in two ways. In one way, with regard to essence. In another way, with regard to existence (*esse*). That is, since a definition expresses essence only, and neither existence nor non-existence, things are known only with regard to essence; and so it is for demonstrative science, where an attribute intrinsically following upon the essence of a thing is demonstrated of its subject through its definition. But a demonstration answering the question, does it exist? makes the thing known with regard to existence. They say, therefore, that as things are knowable, so they are eternal. For if they were knowable with regard to existence, it would be necessary that they be eternal in existence; but if they are knowable as to essence only, it is not necessary that they be eternal as to existence.

I do not like this opinion. First, because I do not think that existence and essence are distinguished in the thing itself outside the soul, which you should look up in Book IV of the *Metaphysics*.

Second, because it seems to me dangerous in the faith to say that anything is eternal which is not God.

Third, because it seems to me to imply the contradiction that essence persists and existence does not, since what persists, is, and has existence.

Fourth, because if persisting essence takes on existence and non-existence, no other matter need be posited, since that essence will be capable of undergoing change and bearing the limits of change while itself remaining the same.

Fifth, because it seems to me that this name "essence" is only the abstract of this concrete "existence" (*esse*), just as "entity" is of this concrete "being" (*ens*), and "quiddity" of this concrete "what" (*quid*), and "reality" of this concrete "thing" (*res*); and hence, just as a thing is called white by whiteness, so it is called existence by essence and being by entity and what by quiddity. And many other difficulties can be adduced against this opinion; but I pass over them, since our present concern is not primarily speculative. . . .

Others distinguish between universal and singular, not only according to concept, but also in external reality, to such an extent that they say that a universal as an external thing is neither generable nor destructible. Singulars, however, they say, are generable and destructible. Therefore, they say, science is not of singulars, but universals; and so they say that the knowable is perpetual, although the singulars of them are destructible.

But I think that a universal does not exist outside the soul distinct from singulars, which for the present I assume from Book VII of the *Metaphysics*; and even if it were distinct, it could persist with all its singulars destroyed only if it were a separated Idea. And yet it is acknowledged, as it seems to me, that if all roses were now destroyed, so that they did not exist in any way, or if there were no thunders nor comets nor eclipses of the sun and moon, still, the doctor would not on that account lose the science which he has of the rose, nor the astronomer, the science which he has of eclipses, nor you, the science which you have from the book of *Meteorology* about thunders and comets. Indeed, you could teach me the science of the *Meteorology* just as if there were a thousand thunders. Hence even if such a distinction between universal and singular in reality were conceded, it would be worth nothing for the proposed position.

Others, however, holding universals to be distinct from singulars only through the operation of the soul (as Aristotle and the Commentator, I think, seem to wish), say that the knowable as external reality ought to be eternal in that there always is some thing or things for which the terms of the knowable conclusion supposit. For this it is not required that any of those knowable things is itself perpetual, but it suffices that individuals of the same species perpetually succeed one another through generation, so that to take horses and asses as examples, it is never true to say "There is no horse; there is no ass."

But I still do not think that is necessary, since, as was said, a doctor need not lose his science of roses if there are no roses, etc. I therefore believe that the knowable things for which the terms of a knowable conclusion supposit do not have to be perpetual in any of the aforesaid ways. But it is possible for them to be capable of destruction out of existence altogether, because it is sometimes true to say that no such thing exists; for instance, I believe that I have true science about thunders and comets even though just now there are no thunders and comets. Nor is this strange, for if it has been demonstrated to me that every triangle has three angles, etc., I do not through this demonstration have scientific knowledge only of the triangles which now exist, but also of past and future ones. Otherwise, it would follow that if a new triangle were made tomorrow, I would not then know that every triangle has three angles, unless a demonstration containing that new triangle were repeated to me, which is absurd. Therefore, I say that through the book of *Meteorology* I have scientific knowledge of all thunders, past, present, and future, if any are present; and if none are present, then I have scientific knowledge of past and future ones alone.

But then a doubt occurs, since scientific knowledge requires conformity or adequation to knowable things, since science requires the conclusion to be true. And truth consists in the adequation of the intellect to the thing known. But when the things known do not exist, there is no adequation to them, for nothing is adequated to what is nothing. Therefore, science cannot be had of things which do not exist.

Some reply to this that science can be had of things existing or not existing, or even impossible, with regard to propositions of perpetual truth which can be formed about them, namely, propositions which cannot be false. Thus they say first that concerning things which do not and even cannot exist, propositions of perpetual truth can be formed which are categorical but negative, as that a vacuum is nothing. And so I have negative science about a vacuum. For the adequation required for the truth of a proposition is preserved in this case, since it is not required that some thing exist which is equal to the intellect, but only that as the intellect understands the thing to exist or not, so in reality it exists or not. Therefore, that understanding is true by which I understand a vacuum not to exist, since it is so in reality that a vacuum does not exist.

Second, they say that concerning things which do not exist, propositions of perpetual truth can be formed which are affirmative, but hypothetical, such as "If a vacuum exists, a vacuum is a place," or "If thunder exists, it is sound in the clouds." And in this way affirmative science can be had of non-entities, for in the said propositions adequation of the intellect to the thing sufficient for truth is preserved. For the intellect does not understand that a vacuum is a place, but that if it existed, it would be a place; and so even though in reality a vacuum is not a place, still, if there were a vacuum in reality, it would be a place.

Third, they say that concerning things which do not exist, no true categorical affirmative proposition can be formed, at least of inherence and with a verb of present tense. For if there were no thunder, this would not be true: "Thunder is sound in the clouds," since what does not exist is not sound in the clouds, and since according to the rules of logic, an affirmative proposition is true in that the terms supposit for the same. But what does not exist is the same as nothing. Hence they say that in the science of such things we ought not understand the propositions categorically, even though they are propounded categorically for the sake of brevity. Rather, we ought to understand them hypothetically. For instance, in the book of *Meteorology* I should not understand the proposition "Thunder is sound in the clouds" categorically, since thus it would not be knowable, but rather, hypothetically, namely that if thunder exists, or whenever it does, it is sound in the clouds.

And I myself believe that such a great controversy between those holding these opinions sprang from a lack of logic. For it seems to me that names which signify things and do not consignify any determinate time, signify present, past, and future things indifferently. Nor is that strange, since I can understand a thing without co-understanding a determinate time. So I can form a composite in the intellect from the concept of a thing and the concept of a time, past or future as well as present, such as in saying "Caesar was; Caesar will be." And so it is not unsuitable for a term sometimes to supposit for past and future things just as for present ones.

For according to the older logicians, the supposition of a common term is two-fold, namely, natural and accidental. It is accidental when the term only supposits for its supposita at some determinate time; it is natural when it supposits for all its supposita indifferently, whether they are present, past, or future. And the demonstrative sciences use this latter supposition. Otherwise, we would not have scientific knowledge of future triangles through a demonstration showing that a triangle has three angles, etc., which is unsuitable, as was said. And Aristotle in Book I of the *Posterior Analytics* gives the understanding of the general proposition, where the terms have the said natural supposition, that animal is predicated of every man; for if it is true to call something man, it is true to call it animal. And if one is true, so is the other, that is to say, this proposition "Man is an animal" or "Every man is an animal," is general according to natural supposition if whatever it is true to call man and whenever it is true to call it man, then it is also true to call it animal. And this is true in that way, "Thunder is sound in the clouds," referring singulars to singulars.

But someone will immediately say, Master, you coincide with the preceding opinion, since you assign a hypothetical sense to knowable propositions; and the others conceded that such hypothetical propositions are necessary and knowable. I reply that perhaps this opinion and that other one intend the same science, but they differ logically in the manner of speaking. For the former does not concede in these matters that the proposition is categorical, with a categorical sense. But I concede it to be true according to natural supposition. Nor is it necessary that a proposition be hypothetical merely because its sense is clarified through a hypothetical. For in this way, every proposition would be hypothetical. For the sense of this proposition, "A man runs," can be explicated through this hypothetical, "Socrates runs, or Plato runs, and so for each"; and the sense of this one, "Every man runs," can be explicated through this one, "Socrates runs and Plato runs and so for each." Nor are the two arguments they adduced conclusive.

To the first, when it is said, what is not (does not exist) is not sound in the clouds; there is no thunder; therefore, no thunder is sound in the clouds, it should be replied that if there is no thunder, the major and minor premises are true, since the terms in both are drawn to accidental supposition, that is, for present supposita alone, by virtue of this verb "is" occurring without a further predicate. Hence the conclusion is well inferred, understanding the terms in it to have accidental supposition just as in the premises, but not understanding that they have natural supposition. Rather, that would be the fallacy of figure of speech from the variation in supposition.

To the next, when it is said that in a true affirmative proposition, the terms ought to supposit for the same, I concede, for the same present, past, or future. For it is true in this way to say that some animal was in Noah's ark, since then there was some animal being in Noah's ark. And I would yet concede with the aforesaid opinion that if the terms of a proposition, or one of them, should supposit for nothing, neither present, past, nor future, the affirmative categorical proposition could not be true. For instance, this is false: "Vacuum is place not filled with body," if "vacuum" is taken significatively. For then the terms cannot supposit for the same, since one or the other or both supposit for nothing. But that proposition should be conceded if "vacuum" is taken according to material supposition, and the proposition is predicative of a definition giving the nominal meaning of the defined term. For this is the difference between nominal and real definition, that a real definition is verified of a defined term having personal supposition, as in "Man is the rational animal." But a nominal definition is verified of a defined term having material supposition. In this sense, vacuum is place not filled with body, that is, this name "vacuum" signifies "place not filled with body." And it is a true affirmative categorical proposition and each of the terms supposits for a true being. But all this, since it does not belong to ethics, is said in abbreviated form here, and you can find it more explicitly investigated, if you wish, in my writing on the *Summulae*, where there is a treatise on suppositions. . . .

To the opposing arguments: To the first it should be said that if "eternal" is taken in the most proper way, nothing is eternal except God alone; hence we do not say that everything knowable is eternal in that way, but rather in the aforesaid way.

The other opposing arguments go their ways, and the Question is finished.

QUESTIONS ON ARISTOTLE'S METAPHYSICS

Book IV

QUESTION 8

The eighth question is *whether existence (esse) and essence are the same in anything whatsoever* and by "essence" I understand the thing itself. And so the question is whether rose is the same as rose-exists (*rosam esse*), man and man-exists, and so for others. First it is argued that the answer is no: For I understand rose or thunder even when I do not understand that a rose or thunder exists. Hence they are not the same. Likewise, I have scientific knowledge about rose and thunder and still am ignorant as to whether a rose exists or whether thunder exists. Therefore, if this is known by me and that is not, it follows that this is not the same as that.

Again, names and definitions signify essences and they neither signify existence nor non-existence, as is had from Book I of the *Posterior Analytics*; and this is because they signify without a time. Therefore, existence is not the same as essence. Again, the question, if something is, differs greatly from the question, what it is, as is clear from Book II of the *Posterior Analytics*; and they differ only because of the difference between existence and essence. For the question, *what* something is, is asked concerning the essence or quiddity; but the question, *if* something is, is asked concerning the existence of the thing. Again, the same does not happen to itself, but existence happens to a thing, for it happens to a rose that it exists or does not, since a rose can exist and it can also not exist. Therefore, rose and rose-exists are not the same. . . .

The Commentator says that the opposite is the intention of Aristotle in this Book IV, where he says that man is the same as being man (*ens homo*) and one man. By "being man," Aristotle seems to understand the existence of man (*esse hominis*).

And you ought to know that the older philosophers, including St. Thomas, held that in every being other than God there was a composition from essence and existence. And so it would be necessary to distinguish essence from existence in some way, because only God was unqualifiedly simple. Others also said that existence and non-existence are in some way diverse accidents happening to essence, so that essence takes on existence through generation and non-existence through destruction. And so some held that the essences of things are perpetual, however much these diverse modes are successively attributed to them, as we sometimes say that rose exists and sometimes that it does not. And thus they conceded that quidditative predications are true even though the things do not exist. And perhaps that cardinal was of this opinion who sent the Bull proclaiming that this proposition, "Man is animal," or even this proposition, "Horse

Translated by James J. Walsh for this volume from Joannes Buridanus, *In Metaphysicen Aristotelis Quaestiones*, Paris, 1588. Reprinted by Minerva G.M.B.H., Frankfurt a.M., 1964.

is animal" is necessary because of the inclusion of terms and would be true even though God should annihilate all horses. But on Book II of the *Posterior Analytics,* Grosseteste (*Lincolniensis*) seems to be of the contrary opinion. For he says that everything predicated of God predicates or signifies the simple essence of God, but to be predicated of something different from God predicates or signifies the dependence of that upon God. And this dependence, he says, does not make for multiplicity in the dependent thing. And I say with Grosseteste and the Commentator that in each and every thing, the thing and the thing-exists are the same, so that essence does not differ from existence, nor existence from essence. This can be proved thus: rose can only be said to differ from its existence by saying that existence is a mode added to it and acquired by it through generation, and by saying that the quiddity or essence is eternal, just as that opinion maintains. But all this is impossible; therefore. And the major seems manifest, since the arguments made in the beginning seem to argue for this and nothing else, and it is because of these that men were moved to posit the difference between existence and essence. But the minor is proved, namely, that it is impossible to speak thus. First, because it would follow that we do not need to posit prime matter, for that is only posited because it is necessary that the subject undergoing transmutation persists through both limits of the change; and that subject would be posited to be the quiddity or essence, and then (the limits would be) existence and non-existence. Hence it would not be necessary to posit matter. Second, it would follow that humanity would persist in a corpse, and it is by humanity that the thing is man, just as it is by whiteness that a thing is white. Hence the corpse would still be man, which is to utter a falsehood. And the first consequence is proved, since humanity can be nothing other than the essence or quiddity of man which persists when the man is destroyed, and it either persists separately or it persists in the matter of the corpse. If it persists in the matter of the corpse, the proposed position is had. If it is said that it persists separate from the matter, this will be to posit the Ideas of Plato, which Aristotle later disproved. And this argument which I have made about man and humanity can be made about horse and horseness or stone and its quiddity, and so for others. Arguing from them, one is led into the difficulty more obviously than in arguing from man, since we concede that the human soul is separable, and perhaps some would say that it is the quiddity of man. And again, such added modes of being would be posited altogether in vain, since if existence is a mode added to the thing, for instance, to rose, and acquired through substantial generation, at once all the same difficulties which arose concerning rose come back concerning that existence. For just as rose can exist and can not exist, so that mode can exist and can not exist; and I could understand that mode without understanding it to exist, and perhaps I would understand it not to exist. For I could understand that to exist or to have existed which Aristotle was when he was; and yet whatever he was, I understand this, that he does not exist. Hence it appears that such an added mode does nothing toward preserving definitions. . . .

But because of the solutions of the arguments, it seems that what should be said about that question is that essence and existence, or rose and rose-exists differ according to reason. For this name "rose" is imposed from a different concept than this name or expression "rose-exists." Therefore, when it is said that I understand rose when I do not understand it to exist, I concede that; but it does not follow that therefore, rose-exists differs from rose. But it only follows that there are diverse concepts or reasons according to which a rose is understood through this name "rose" and through this expression "rose-exists." But you argue thus through an expository syllogism: I know this rose; this rose is that one which exists; therefore, I know the rose exists. I concede the entire syllogism. And so I concede that it is impossible, given that that rose is the rose you know, and which you also know does not exist. But this does not follow: the rose which exists, I know; therefore, I know the rose exists. Whence you should know that since we cognize, know, or understand a thing according to determinate and distinct reasons, we also can know the thing according to one reason and be ignorant of it according to another. Hence the terms following the verbs "understand" or "know" connote the reasons according to which they are imposed, and they do not thus connote them if they precede those verbs. Because of this you have it from Aristotle that this consequence is not valid: I know Choriscus; Choriscus is coming; therefore, I know the one coming. For to know the one coming is to know that thing according to the concept according to which it is called the one coming. Now, however much I know Choriscus, still, even though he is the one coming, it does not follow that I know him under that concept according to which I know he is coming. But this would a good expository syllogism: I know Choriscus; Choriscus is coming; therefore, I know the one coming. So, therefore, in the proposed position: I know a rose, and yet I do not know that the rose exists. But the rose which exists, I know. In the same way to the other argument: I concede that I may have scientific knowledge concerning rose or thunder through many conclusions and yet I may not have scientific knowledge of rose or thunder with regard to the conclusion that rose exists or that thunder exists.

Again, to the next argument, it can be conceded concerning signification just as concerning knowledge, because of the fact that names are imposed for signifying by means of the understandings of things. Hence this name "rose" signifies rose, and it does not signify that a rose exists; and still it signifies this rose and the rose which exists. And so concerning definition.

Again, I say that rose-exists does not happen to (*accidit*) rose; but this predicate "exists" indeed accrues to (*accidit*) this subject "rose." Hence the proposition "Rose exists" is contingent and can be false; but so it is also concerning the proposition "Rose is rose," for it would be false if no rose existed. And when it is also said that rose can not exist, I concede that also rose can not be rose. So that when rose does not exist, its quiddity does not exist, nor does it persist.

To the next, I say that God is most of all simple, since He is not composed of parts, nor can He be composed of anything.

· · ·

QUESTION 9

The ninth question is, *Whether existence (esse) and essence differ according to reason?*

It is argued that they do not, since it follows that if they differ according to reason, then they differ. And it further follows that if they differ, then existence is not essence, which is against what was said in the other question.

Again, existence and essence do not differ according to the thing, as was decided in the preceding question; therefore, they do not differ according to reason, or else that reason would be in vain or false. For those reasons in the intellect are fictitious and false which do not have a correspondence on the part of the thing. Now, it is unsuitable to say that this kind of reason is fictitious. Therefore, it well follows that they do not differ according to reason.

Again, just as the same thing is named by these two names "existence" and "essence," so I am called by two names, namely, "John" and "Buridan." Let us assume, then, that I have two different asses; we should never because of this say that John and Buridan are different according to ass or asses. By the same reasoning, therefore, even though that thing which is existence and essence should have two different reasons in the intellect, it should never because of this be said that existence and essence differ according to reason or reasons. . . .

Yet Aristotle and the Commentator conclude the opposite, nor can the arguments which were made in the other two questions be refuted: if existence and essence, and also being and one, were altogether the same, according to the thing as well as according to reason, those names would be synonymous. First, you can assume some logical conclusions, namely, that existence and essence differ or are not the same, namely, my existence and your essence. Then also, existence and essence are the same and do not differ, namely, my existence and my essence. For those conclusions are indefinite and subcontraries and hence they can well be true simultaneously. Then also I say that existence does not differ from essence, indeed, no existence differs from essence and no essence differs from existence. For every existence is essence and every essence is existence, as is obvious through the preceding Question. Yet it is conceded that existence differs from essence and essence differs from existence. And we have all this through logic because of the negation implicit in this verb "differs." But I come more to the point and I posit the conclusion that my existence and my essence do not differ according to reason, nor does a stone and its existence, since it is impossible that the same should differ from itself, whether according to the thing or reason or anything else. Hence if my essence is the same as my existence, it is impossible that my essence should differ from my existence, whether according to reason or anything else. Thus I also say that these words "my essence" and "my existence" do not differ according to reason, since they differ from themselves formally and intrinsically, and setting such reasons aside altogether, they still differ. And hence it appears that such "reasons" of Aristotle and others are improper, in that if they were true, they would not be true according to the proper sense of the terms, but rather according to some other sense. I speak of such propositions as "Being and one differ according to reason," or "Existence and essence," or "Man and animal," and so for others. But such propositions as this are still conceded: "Existence and essence are the same according to the thing, but they differ according to reason." They are conceded, that is, for the senses which I use. For when I say that existence and essence are the same according to the thing, the sense is that existence and essence are the same thing. But when I say that existence and essence differ according to reason, the sense is that the reason by which this name "existence" is imposed is different from that by which this name "essence" is imposed, or else those names would be altogether synonymous. And so should it be said for all other similar propositions.

But then there remains a great difficulty, since that difference of reasons should not be called fictitious. Whence such a difference of reasons comes originally from on the side of the thing, and on this there were quite diverse opinions. One opinion was that existence is attributed to a thing according to a singular concept, and essence, according to a universal concept; hence, because sense senses singularly, it judges everything which it senses to exist. And because generations are also of singulars, we therefore say that generation terminates in the existence of the thing. But this opinion is not valid, since this name "Socrates," which is a singular name imposed for signifying according to a singular concept, signifies an essence and does not signify that the thing exists. Again, it is certain that "existence" signifies not only singularly, but also universally. I judge universally and I know that every being exists, that every man exists; therefore, etc. Hence even though demonstrative science does not descend to singular concepts, Aristotle raises the question if it is demonstratively knowable. Another opinion, held by Grosseteste, is that all things are called existence and essence because of their dependence on God. For according as things were in God in the exemplary mode, so they are called essences and quiddities; and from that it was said that quiddities are eternal, since God is the exemplar of all things from eternity. But Grosseteste did not understand that it is absolutely true that quiddities or the essence of things are eternal, but he intended that their reflections in the divine intellect are from eternity, and such reflections are not the simple divine essence. But insofar as things depend on God as bringing them about or conserving them, they are said to exist. Hence no one says that things exist from eternity, since God was not bringing things about from eternity. But that opinion still does not suffice for the proposed position, since just as stone and stone-exists differ according to reason in the previously mentioned sense, so one must say that in a similar sense, God and God-exists differ; and the remarks of Grosseteste do not bear on such a difference. Again, we form those different reasons, namely understanding rose and rose-exists, without understanding anything about God —indeed, children know roses to exist without perceiving any connection between them and God. And so Aristotle and the grammarians seem to solve the difficulty straight off, for names signify without a time. Since things are conceived without any given time being understood, they can also be understood without a determinate time in which they exist or co-exist being understood. And so verbs are imposed for signifying with a time. Therefore, the same thing is called essence according to a simple concept, that is, as absolute, without the connotation of a time, and it is said to exist or to have existed or to be going to exist according to a concept connoting a time. But without doubt, even though these remarks seem at first glance to be clear, they contain a great difficulty. First of all, it is true that even if there were no time, God would still exist and would know Himself to exist. Indeed, we posit through divine power that, with everything quiet and without movement, God conserves us without any movement; the visual image would remain in my eye according to which I see you, and I would still judge you to exist, and it would also be true that you exist. Hence it does not seem to be because of the apprehension of time that this judgment is proper, even if the proposition "John exists" connotes the present time and would not be true if there were no present time because it is falsified from the lack of what is connoted. For since "white" supposits for man and connotes whiteness, take whiteness away and 'Man is white" would be false. And yet it is sure that if there were no time, as there would be none if everything were conserved in utter quiet, it would be no less true that things exist. And so it seems difficult (to find) where the concept by which we judge a thing to exist comes from. And what seems to me should be said is that things are perceived and judged to exist according as they are perceived as in the prospect of the knower.

Whence you do not judge anything to exist unless it is in the prospect of sense; and so if Socrates recedes from the prospect of sense, then you do not know whether it is true that he exists. Yet we judge something to exist by reasoning, but this is by referring to things which were in the prospect of sense. For instance, even though the stars are not in the prospect of the knower, the intellect judges them to exist, because we have seen stars in the prospect of sense, and by reasoning, the intellect concludes that they are indestructible. Again, the intellect judges by arguments that everything moved is moved by a mover, and the first moved thing by the first mover. Some motion appears to us in the prospect of sense, and hence we judge that a mover exists, and indeed, that the first mover exists. And so, turning again to the aforesaid opinion of Aristotle and the grammarians, it seems to me that this verb "to exist" connotes presence, which "essence" or this name "stone" do not connote, even though it does not connote a temporal and successive present, but rather, presence just as you are present to me. Even if all things were motionless, it would still be true that "to be going to exist" or "to have existed" necessarily connote succession; and if succession had never appeared because all things which now are had been perpetually without motion or succession, I believe that we never would have judged anything to have existed or to be going to exist. But we would have judged those things to exist which appeared to us in the prospect of sense. And perhaps we do apply the connotation of such a presence to the presence of time in order to distinguish between "to exist," "to be going to exist," and "to have existed," however much in order to know that a thing exists, it is not required that a time be co-understood, but only that the thing be apprehended through the mode of presentness in the prospect of the knower—even though there is no succession nor is it imagined. But when through the intellect we detach the concept of a thing from the concept of such presence and from the concept of the connection of the thing to such presence, then we impose those names "essence," "man," "stone" for signifying the thing. And all the arguments which were made are conceded according to these remarks, since it has been conceded that according to the proper sense of the terms, my existence and my essence do not differ according to reason, etc.

QUESTIONS ON THE EIGHT BOOKS OF THE PHYSICS OF ARISTOTLE

Book III

QUESTION 7. *Seventh, it is asked whether local motion is a thing distinct from place and from that which is locally moved.*

It is argued that it is not, since if everything can be explained without a thing in addition to what is moved and place, those additions would be pointless and hence improper. But everything can be explained without such addition. The proof is that there would be local motion if the moved thing should continuously be in one and another part of space even though nothing else were held to exist. And succession and priority and posteriority would be explained by means of different parts of space which have order and position according to location with any addition set aside.

Again, it follows that God could separate and separately conserve motion without what is moved and without place, or rather, even with these annihilated. This seems improper, for then there would be motion and nothing to be moved. . . .

The opposed argument is that neither the being of place nor of the moved thing consists in becoming. Rather, each of these is completely achieved *(perfecte factum)*, unless it is eternal; but the being of local motion or of time consists in becoming, one (part) after another. Therefore the being of motion is not the being of place nor of that which is moved. Thus it is not of the essence of any of these nor, in consequence, is it any of them. The consequence is valid because the same is the being of man, the essence of man, and man, as ought to be manifest from *Metaphysics*, Book IV.

Again, the moved thing as well as place is by nature permanent; motion is not, but is by nature successive. . . .

. The older thinkers did not doubt concerning this question, but with one voice they conceded that local motion is a thing other than the thing moved and place. But now the later moderns claim on account of the aforesaid arguments that motion is not a thing other than the thing moved. To look into this one must assume the meaning of the word *(quid nominis)*, since without this one cannot argue, as is clear from *Metaphysics*, Book IV, the *Posterior Analytics* and the *De Sensu*, where it is said that the meaning of the word is the beginning of instruction. Thus everyone concedes that local motion is some kind of change *(mutatio)* and that to be moved is to be changed. But in Book V, Aristotle says, and it is self-evident, that to change is first to be disposed one way and later, another, or at least it is at first to be disposed in some way and later not to be disposed in that way or vice versa. Whence

Translated by James J. Walsh for this volume from *Johannis Buridani subtilissime questiones super octo physicorum libros Aristotelis*, Paris, 1509. Reprinted by Minerva G.M.B.H., Frankfurt a.M., 1964.

Aristotle says that since every change is from some condition into some condition; the name at the least makes clear that something is different, and what is at first is manifestly different later. And the Commentator says this is manifest in itself, since while a thing is in the same disposition, then there will be no change *(transmutatio)*.

Therefore I lay down some conclusions. The first conclusion is that it would be possible for the outermost sphere to be moved by a motion in which it is moved without place. This is proved so: If the outermost sphere and the others were through the divine power a single continuum, so that the entire world were one continuous body, then there would be no place, according to Aristotle. For there would be no surface of a containing body touching what is divided from it. Whence Aristotle holds that the world as a whole does not have a place, except by reason of parts of which one places another because it contains and is divided from it and touches it. For this is required in order that there should be place. And so if God should annihilate all bodies outside of this stone, this stone would no longer be in a place. Yet given this case, it would still be possible that God should move the entire world at one time in a circle. I prove this through a certain condemned Parisian Article which says that God cannot move the entire world at the same time with rectilinear motion. This is in error. And there is no reason why He should move it more with rectangular motion than with circular motion. Again, just as in the daily motion He moves all the heavenly spheres at the same time with the outermost sphere, so He could revolve all the others, that is, the lower ones, at the same time and by Himself. He can revolve everything at the same time now, while they are discontinuous from one another; he could do this no less if they were to be made a single continuum. Therefore He could move the entire world even if there were no place. . . .

The fourth conclusion is that the motion of the outermost sphere is not that sphere nor its place. Manifestly it is not its place, since it is possible that it should be moved even though it did not have a place, as was said above, and since if it has a place, still that is divided from it. But its motion is not divided from it, since it is said that the sphere itself is disposed one way and another intrinsically. But neither is that motion the very sphere, since as was said in the Question on the distinction of figure from what has the figure, it is not imaginable nor possible that something should be disposed otherwise than it was disposed before, unless this is with regard to something extrinsic or unless this is because of something existing which did not exist before, or ceasing to exist which existed before. But the two first ways are not pertinent to the motion of the outermost sphere, as is obvious from the remarks. Therefore the third way has to be conceded. And still, so far as the substance of the outermost sphere is concerned, there is nothing which would not have existence before, and nothing existed before which does not do so now. Therefore, what did not exist before or vice versa is other than the sphere, and this is only motion or its parts. Therefore, etc. . . .

The fifth conclusion is that the motion of the outermost sphere is distinct from that sphere and its place, if it should have a place, since it does exist and it is not the one nor the other. . . .

And then, in reply to the arguments: To the first, it is manifest that without an added disposition it cannot be explained how the outermost sphere should be intrinsically disposed one way and another as it is so disposed.

To the second I say that I do not deem it more improper that there should be motion and nothing moved or changed, than that there should be whiteness and nothing should be white. Neither is possible naturally and each is possible supernaturally. Concerning this it is said that for local motion to exist and place not to exist implies a contradiction. I say that the motion of the outermost sphere or a ship in a river is not called local because according to that, place has to be altered, but because according to the common course of nature, everything which is moved by that motion in fact changes local residence or situation with respect to something else. And all that motion which we call local could be not local, since no place nor location would be changed with respect to any other thing. But then we could not perceive it. It is not, therefore, called local because place is necessary for it, but because it could not be perceived unless a change of the place or location of the thing with respect to another were apparent. Whence those on ships in the sea moved at the same time with equal speed do not perceive that they are in motion.

Book VIII

QUESTION 12.   *Twelfth, it is asked whether a projectile, after leaving the hand of the projector, is moved by the air, or by what it is moved.*

It is argued that it is not moved by the air, for the air seems rather to resist, since it has to be divided. Again, if you say that in the beginning the projector moves the projectile and the adjacent air with it, and that the moved air moves the projectile further to whatever the distance, the doubt returns as to what that air is moved by after the projector ceases to move it. There is just as much difficulty about this as about the thrown stone. . . .

In my judgment this question is indeed difficult, for it seems to me that Aristotle did not resolve it. He treats of two opinions. The first is called "antiperistasis". According to it the projectile leaves swiftly the place in which it was, and nature, not allowing a vacuum, swiftly sends air after it to refill that place. The air thus swiftly moved, upon reaching the projectile, propels it further, and this goes on continuously for some distance. Aristotle rejects this conclusion, saying in Book VIII of this work that antiperistasis makes everything both move and be moved at once. This seems to be understood thus: if some way other than the said antiperistasis is not put forward, it requires that all bodies follow after the projectile, and even the heavens. For just as the projectile leaves the place in which it was, the body behind has to follow; and thus that following body leaves the place in which it was, and so it is required again that another body again follow, and so on always . . . . it seems to me that this proposal is worth nothing, because of several observations.

The first concerns a wheel or a millstone, which are moved for a long time and do not leave a place, so that air is not required to follow in order to refill the place from which they left. Therefore, a wheel and millstone are moved in such a way that it cannot be said to be according to that fashion.

The second observation is that if a lance having a rear as sharply pointed as the front were projected, it would be moved no less than if its rear were not sharp; yet the following air could not push the sharp end since it would be easily divided by the sharpness.

The third observation is of a ship in a river drawn swiftly even against the current. It cannot be said to pause, but with the pulling stopped it is moved for a long time, yet a sailor up top does not feel air pushing from behind, but he only feels air resisting from the front. . . .

The other opinion, which Aristotle seems to approve, is that along with the projectile the projector moves the adjacent air, and that swiftly moved air has the power of moving the projectile. It should not be understood that the same air is moved from the place of the projector up to the place at which the projectile stops, but that the air joined to the projector is moved by the projector, and that moved air moves another next to it and that other, up to a certain distance. Thus the first air moves the projectile to the second air and the second to the third and so on. Hence Aristotle says that there is not one mover, but many, one after another. Hence he also says that the motion is not continuous, but consequently of contiguous beings.

But it seems to me without a doubt that this fashion is just as impossible as the preceding one, for using this way it could not be said by what the wheel or millstone is turned once the hand is removed. If you should keep the adjacent air away from the millstone with a cloth all around it, the millstone would not stop moving because of that, but it would be moved for a long time. Therefore it is not moved by that air. . . .

Besides, however rapidly air is moved, it is easily divisible; thus it is not obvious how it would sustain a stone weighing a thousand pounds projected from a sling or mechanical device.

Again, you could move the adjacent air just as swiftly or more swiftly with your hand if you held nothing in the hand than if you held a stone in your hand which you wished to hurl. Therefore, if that air from the speed of its motion were of such a force that it could move that stone swiftly, it would seem that if I should push the air against you equally swiftly, that air ought to push you forcefully and truly noticeably, and we do not perceive this.

Again it would follow that you would project a feather farther than a stone, the less heavy farther than the more heavy, with the sizes and shapes the same; and this is observed to be false. The consequence is manifest, since the moved air should sustain or bear or move a feather more easily than a stone, the lighter more easily than the heavier. . . .

And so it seems to me that what should be said is that the mover in moving what is moved impresses upon it a certain impetus or force that moves the moved thing in the direction the mover moved it, whether up or down, laterally or in a circle. And the more swiftly the mover moves the moved thing, the stronger the impetus it impresses on it. The stone is moved by that impetus after the projector ceases to move, but the impetus is continuously diminished by the resisting air and by the gravity of the stone inclining it against the direction the impetus inherently moves it. Hence the motion of that stone is made continuously slower, and finally the impetus is so diminished or corrupted that the gravity of the stone prevails over it and moves the stone down to its natural place. This manner seems to me to be maintained in that the others do not seem true; also all the appearances are consonant with this way.

For if someone should ask how it is that I hurl a stone farther than a feather, and a hand-sized iron ball farther than the same sized wooden one, I reply that the reception of all natural forms and dispositions is in matter and by reason of the matter. Hence, howevermuch more there is of matter, by that much more can a body take on the impetus more intensely. Now other things being equal, there is more prime matter in a dense and heavy body than in a rarified and light one; hence the dense and heavy one receives more from that impetus and more intensely, just as iron can receive more from heat than wood or water of the same quantity. A feather, however, receives such an impetus so sparsely that such an impetus is at once corrupted by the resisting air. And so even if a light piece of wood and a heavy piece of iron of the same size and shape should be moved equally swiftly by the projector, the iron would be moved farther because the impetus would be impressed more intensely in it. This impetus would not be corrupted as rapidly as would a less intense impetus. This is also the reason why it is more difficult to stop a swiftly moved large millstone than a small one, since, other things being equal, there is more impetus in the large one. . . . And from this also appears the cause whereby the natural downward motion of a heavy thing is continuously speeded up, for at first only gravity moved it and so it moved more slowly; but in moving, impetus is impressed on that heavy thing, which impetus then moves it along with the gravity. Hence the motion becomes swift, and the swifter it goes, the more intense the impetus becomes. Hence the movement appears to become continuously swifter. . . . Also, since it does not appear from the Bible that there are intelligences to whom it pertains to move the heavenly bodies, one could say that there seems no need to posit such intelligences. For it might be said that when God created the world He moved each of the celestial orbs however He pleased; and in moving them He impressed an impetus which moves them without His moving them any more, except in the way of the general influence, just as He concurs in co-acting in everything which is done. For He rested on the seventh day from every work He had achieved by committing to others their reciprocal actions and passions. And those impetuses impressed upon the heavenly bodies were not afterwards lessened or corrupted because there was no inclination of the heavenly bodies to other motions nor was there the resistance which would corrupt or restrain that impetus. But I do not assert this; I request the theologians to teach me how these things can be done.

Still, there are serious difficulties concerning this opinion. . . .

The second difficulty is: what kind of a thing is that impetus? Is it the motion itself or a different thing? And if it is a different thing, is it a purely successive thing like motion, or is it a thing of a permanent nature? Whatever the answer, the arguments to the contrary seem difficult.

To the second problem, which is indeed difficult, it seems to me one should respond by laying down three conclusions.

The first is that that impetus is not the local motion by which the projectile is moved, since the impetus moves the projectile and the mover makes the motion; therefore the impetus makes the motion, and the same thing does not make itself. Therefore, etc.

Again, since every motion is from a mover present and existing at the same time as that which is moved, if that impetus were the motion, one would have to assign a different mover for that motion, and the chief difficulty would recur. Hence nothing would be gained by positing such an impetus.

But some would quibble, saying that the prior part of the motion which accomplishes the projection makes the next following part of the motion and that the next and so on up till the entire motion stops. But this not probable, since what is making something ought to exist while that is done, but the prior part of the motion does not exist while the later does, as was remarked elsewhere. Thus the prior does not exist when the posterior does, and the obvious consequence from this, which is remarked elsewhere, is that for motion to be is nothing other than for it to become or be corrupted; whence motion does not exist when it is achieved, but when it is taking place.

The second conclusion is that impetus is not a purely successive thing, since such a thing is motion, and the definition of motion pertains to it, as was said elsewhere. And it was just now said that impetus is not local motion.

Again, since a purely successive thing is continuously made and corrupted, it requires a continuous maker, and no maker of that impetus could be given which would exist at the same time as it does.

The third conclusion is that impetus is a thing of permanent nature distinct from the local motion by which the projectile is moved. This is apparent from the aforesaid two conclusions and the preceding ones. And it is likely that impetus is a quality whose nature it is to move the body on which it is impressed, just as a quality is said to be impressed on iron by a magnet which moves iron to the magnet. It is also likely that just as that quality is impressed on what is moved by the mover along with the motion, so is it lessened or corrupted or impeded by resistance or contrary inclination just as the motion is. . . .

This is what I have to say on this question, and I would rejoice if anyone should find a more probable way with it.

QUESTIONS ON THE TEN BOOKS OF THE NICOMACHEAN ETHICS OF ARISTOTLE

Book X

QUESTION 4. *In What Act or Acts Does Human Happiness Consist, and the Question Can Be Asked in This Form: Whether Human Happiness Consists in One Act or Several?*

It is argued that it consists in one, through the saying of Aristotle that "the good of man," that is, happiness, "is the operation of the soul according to the most perfect virtue," but if there should be several virtues, "according to the best and most perfect." And he does not say "operations" nor "according to virtues," but "operation" and "according to one virtue, and the most perfect and best." And he says the same and clarifies it further in Book X. . . .

Again, in Book I of this work, Aristotle calls that the end of human operations which we wish for its own sake, and the others for the sake of it. He calls it the good and best, and by that he intends human happiness. And this cannot belong to two human acts, since just as there is no disorder in the greater world, so should there be none in man. But there would be disorder in human acts if two were best and equally final, of which neither was ordered to the other as its end. Therefore, such an end must be single, and that is happiness.

Again, intellectual contemplation is one act, not two, and Aristotle concludes in Book X of this work that happiness is a certain kind of intellectual contemplation.

Translated by James J. Walsh for this volume from *Iohannis Buridani Quaestiones in decem libros ethicorum Aristotelis ad Nicomachum,* Oxford, 1637. The text has been checked against the Paris edition of 1513 and *Ms. Bibl. Nat. Lat. 16128.*

Again, Seneca does not cease proclaiming in his letters that the good of man is single, and that it is reason most perfect. Hence he concludes in his letter *Inimicitias* that "only perfect reason makes man blessed." Therefore, happiness seems to consist in one act and not in several.

Those believing otherwise argue for the opposite with many authorities and arguments, since all who say that human happiness consists in one act, say that this is either the act of intellect, such as the vision or contemplation of God, or in the act of will, such as the love of God, whichever of these is most perfect and best. But it is claimed that this is impossible, whichever of these you pick. For if you say that the most noble act possible to man is the clear vision of God, then I prove that this is not essentially happiness. For with that act remaining and other acts removed, as they can be removed by the absolute power of God— as some theologians say—a man would then still be happy, just as a stone would be white if whiteness remained in it and all other accidents were removed. And yet the consequent is false, namely, that a man clearly seeing God without delight and without the love of God would be called happy. For it is necessary that happiness be most delightful, as Aristotle says. Therefore, etc. And this is more strongly confirmed, since those theologians say that together with the clear vision of God, God could form intense sadness in the soul of Socrates, without delight, and hatred of God without love. Would he then be happy? I myself surely would not want such happiness.

Again, every human power can be made happy whose work is inherently to attain the beatifying object, which is God. But the vegetative power is not such, nor the sensitive, nor the power of local movement, nor the sensitive appetites. It is intellect and will that are such, for through the intellect we know God and through the will we love Him. Therefore, man can truly be made happy according to both those powers. Therefore, if he were made happy according to only one of those powers, he would not be perfectly nor totally happy, but partially and in a diminished way, which should not be said, since nothing diminished should be attributed to happiness. Thus in Book X of this work it says that nothing imperfect belongs to that of which happiness consists. Happiness, therefore, must be a whole made up essentially of the acts of those powers, and must not be the single act of only one of them.

Again, happiness is held to consist in the perfect contemplation of God; but the perfect contemplation of God does not exist without love, nor does love without knowledge. But happiness is constituted from both.

Again, happiness is held to be that which is most self-sufficient; and no single act is most self-sufficient.

Again, Aristotle says in Book I of this work, "He who is extremely ugly or ignoble, or alone and without issue," and how would this be true if happiness consisted in one act, whether of the intellect or the will? . . .

Indeed, other moralists and Holy Scriptures seem to intend the same. For many authoritative texts of Holy Scripture seem clearly to say that human happiness consists in the vision of God, and many others, in the love of God. This is because it is not merely in this or in that, but in both conjointly and together.

And the same seems to come from Seneca and Cicero, for they say now one thing and now the other. For instance, in his paradoxes, Cicero says, "All the wise are free, and the foolish, servile." And so freedom and thus happiness are attributed to wisdom, which is an intellectual habit. But in the same book he also asks, "For what is freedom?" And he replies, "It is the power of living as you wish." And so he attributes happiness to the will.

Likewise, Seneca often attributes happiness to wisdom and right reason, and also often to the moral virtues. For instance, in the letter *Agnosco,* he says of the highest good, and hence of happiness, that "it cannot exist unless the science of things obtains, and art, through which divine as well as human things are known." And in the letter which begins *Epistola tua,* he says, "those goods are true which reason holds for genuine," etc. Moreover, he later says that "nothing is stronger than reason." And in the following letter: "What is the best in man? this very right reason, which completes the highest happiness." Further, he concludes afterwards that only perfect reason makes one blessed; and thus it is manifest that in that letter, Seneca holds that happiness consists in reason and wisdom.

But you at once would say that all these texts of Seneca and the arguments on which they are founded conclude the opposite of what I wish to prove. For I intend to conclude that it is not only in an act of the intellect, such as are wisdom, science, and reason, that human happiness consists, but rather in a composite from the act of intellect and the act of will. And the texts adduced say expressly that it is in the act of intellect alone. For Seneca says, "only perfect reason makes one blessed;" and one who saw all his books would say that he proclaims and extols wisdom above all human goods.

But the reply is that if one looks very carefully into Seneca's intention or opinion, it will appear that he knew quite well how to distinguish between the moral virtues (which we call virtues of appetite or the will) on the one hand, and prudence (which we call the virtue of the practical intellect) on the other— as is obvious from that most beautiful little book of his called *De quattuor virtutibus cardinalibus.* And he calls both kinds virtues or types of virtue in that little book, the former, the virtues of our soul as it is called the practical appetite, and the latter, the virtues of the same soul as it is called the practical intellect. But he does not call either taken alone the virtue of the human soul absolutely, as it is simply called the human soul, since virtue should be the perfect disposition of that of which it is called the virtue, by the characteristic for which it is called its virtue. But none of these taken separately is the perfect disposition of the human soul according to that for which it is called the human soul, nor even of human practice according to that for which it is called human practice. . . .

And so, reasoning according to the aforesaid arguments, it seems that the virtue of the active soul, according to which it is called active, is the aggregation of mo a virtue and prudence, and neither one taken separately. . . .

If we say, therefore, that in the collection of moral virtue and prudence, the principal virtue of the active soul is prudence, it follows according to the denomination of a collection from its principal member that every virtue of man insofar as he is active is prudence. This is what Seneca intended by "reason" and even by "wisdom," since he always spoke about practical happiness, in which connection prudence is called "wisdom." In this way Seneca also calls all the virtues of the soul "reasons," and courage he says is "science." . . .

Socrates also should be regarded as having used this way of speaking and his intent when he said that all virtues are reasons and prudences, as Aristotle tells in Book VI of the *Ethics.* Nor does Aristotle seem there to reject those remarks taken with that intent; but he rejects the words, just as he rejects Socrates' words when he says "Man is the intellect."

From all these, it seems that what should be said is that practical happiness, which is what these philosophers mostly talk about, is neither the act of intellect according to prudence nor the act of will according to moral virtue taken separately, but an act compounded from those acts according to perfect virtue, and compounded from those partial virtues. In this collection the most principal, noble, and best member is prudence and its act, according to the clarification of the intention of those previously cited philosophers.

And it seems that proportional remarks should be made regarding contemplative happiness and the act of the contemplative intellect, so far as that is called the happiness of the human soul as it is and is called contemplative. Whence I think that in Heaven there corresponds to clear vision, which properly and with regard to itself ought not be called practical, a love which also ought not be called practical, but rather contemplative.

I myself believe that it is not possible to disprove this way of speaking with arguments having much force, nor do I think that Aristotle rejected this way in the aforesaid sense. Nonetheless, another way of speaking can be given, namely, that since that should be called happiness which is the best and most perfect of what is inherently capable of being happy according to virtue, the best of what is in man can be considered in two ways: in one, by the way of composition or aggregation and in another, by the way of division or resolution; and so in either of these ways it can be called human happiness.

By the way of composition, then, the "best" in man is the collection of all the virtues, operations, and dispositions which inherently belong to man and pertain to his betterment, according to the soul and each of its powers and also the body and each of the parts pertaining to its integrity. In this way, the name "happiness" would supposit for such a collection, at the same time connoting the possession of extrinsic goods sufficient for a man to be able effectively to perform the single operations suitable to him according to the virtues both of the soul and the body. And this is the happiness described by Boethius and which is the perfect condition through the aggregation of all goods; and so nothing imperfect belongs to what is included in happiness, as it says in Book X of this work. And so one would say that he who had a limb cut off, or was confined because of illness, or was imprisoned, or unfortunate, or lacked external goods, was not a happy man, as was noted in Book I. And philosophers lacking the Catholic faith and spiritual and supernatural revelation assign this kind of happiness to this life.

But by the way of resolution, what is called "best" in man is that disposition or act or whatever is named by the name, which would be best in that collection when resolved into its parts, and to which each of the other members is ordered as its end—not that the resolution is made by a real removal of the parts from one another, but by reason considering all the parts distinctly.

Therefore, if we say that what is best is the act of speculation concerning the divine essence, we should say that that will be human happiness, so that this name "human happiness" supposits precisely for the act, but yet not absolutely and without connotations. Rather, it connotes everything required for the effective operation of that act of speculation, and also what is naturally consequent or annexed to it. And thus it connotes first of all the love of God, as naturally following from that speculation, and, if this is right and perfect, delight, which is naturally annexed to these acts. Then it also connotes the virtue of wisdom, of which that speculation is the perfection. Consequently, it connotes prudence, and the moral virtues preparing the way for wisdom, as was said in Book VI. And then, the liveliness of the senses serving the intellect for speculation. And finally, the virtues of the body and exterior goods, as was sufficiently deduced in Question 16 of Book I.

And it is sure that Aristotle held to this way of speaking; and the previous arguments do not prevail against it, for they are easily met.

To the first: we posit that the clear vision of God is human happiness in heaven; you argue that then a man would be happy if he should clearly see God without delight, but rather with sadness and hatred of God. I deny this. Indeed, he would instead be unhappy, since then that clear vision would not be happiness, because of a lack of what is connoted—just as snubness which, although it supposits for a curve, still connotes the nose. And if the magnitude and curve of the nose which are snubness were removed from the nose and put in stone, that would no longer be snubness, because of a lack of what is connoted. And thus, although Aristotle held happiness to be the act of speculating, still he says in Book VII of this work that "those who say that the victim on the rack or the man who falls into great misfortunes is happy if he is good are, whether they mean to or not, saying nothing." And similarly in Book I of this work. And what is said about whiteness is not to the point, since "whiteness" signifies that for which it supposits without the connotation of other things. . . .

When it is said that happiness is the perfect contemplation of God, I can concede that. This contemplation is speculation or the vision of God, but still the name "contemplation" connotes, just as does the name "happiness," the presence of love and delight naturally connected to that speculation or vision.

And you say that vision is perfect contemplation. I say that is true, adding to it love and delight; but if they were not present, that would not be perfect contemplation nor perfect vision. For the vision might well be perfect in its essential perfection, but it does not follow that it is perfect with the perfection inherently added to it—just as a man without moral and intellectual virtues would not be an absolutely or unqualifiedly perfect man, even if he were perfect according to his essential perfection.

• • •

SELECTED BIBLIOGRAPHY

TRANSLATIONS

Clagett, M., ed., *The Science of Mechanics in the Middle Ages,* Madison, 1959.

Scott, T., trans., *John Buridan: Sophisms on Meaning and Truth,* New York, 1966.

STUDIES

Duhem, P., *Le système du monde: histoire des doctrines cosmologiques de Platon à Copernic,* 10 vols., Paris, 1913–1959.

Faral, E., "Jean Buridan. Notes sur les manuscrits, les éditions et le contenu de ses ouvrages," *Archives d'histoire doctrinale et littéraire du moyen âge*, XV (1946), 1–55.

Faral, E., "Jean Buridan: Maître de l'Université de Paris," *Histoire littéraire de la France*, XXVIII (1949), 462–605.

Geach, P., *Reference and Generality: An Examination of Some Medieval and Modern Theories*, Ithaca, 1962.

Korolec, J., "Les principes de la philosophie morale de Jean Buridan," *Mediaevalia Philosophia Polonorum*, XXI (1975), 53–71.

Maier, A., "Philosophy of Nature at the End of the Middle Ages," *Philosophy Today* (Summer, 1961), 92–107.

Michalski, K., "Le criticisme et le scepticisme dans la philosophie du XIVe siècle," *Bulletin international de l'Académie polonaise des sciences et des lettres* (1925), 41–122.

Michalski, K., "Les courants critiques et sceptiques dans la philosophie du XIVe siècle," *Bulletin international de l'Académie polonaise des sciences et des lettres* (1927), 202–209.

Michalski, K., "Le problème de la volonté à Oxford et à Paris au XIVe siècle," *Studia Philosophica*, II (1937), 233–365.

Monahan, E., "Human Liberty and Free Will according to John Buridan," *Mediaeval Studies*, XVI (1954), 72–86.

Moody, E., "Buridan and a Dilemma of Nominalism," *Harry Austryn Wolfson Jubilee Volume*, Jerusalem, 1965, 577–596.

Moody, E., "Ockham, Buridan and Nicholas of Autrecourt," *Franciscan Studies*, VII (1947), 113–146.

Moody, E., *Truth and Consequence in Medieval Logic*, Amsterdam, 1953.

Pinborg, J., ed., *The Logic of John Buridan*, Copenhagen, 1976.

Prior, A., "Some Problems of Self-Reference in John Buridan," *Proceedings of the British Academy*, XLVIII (1962), 281–296.

Rescher, N., "Choice without Preference: a Study of the History and the Logic of the Problem of 'Buridan's Ass,' " *Kant-Studien*, LI (1959–1960), 142–175.

Scott, T., "John Buridan on the Objects of Demonstrative Science," *Speculum*, XL (1965), 654–673.

Walsh, J., "Buridan and Seneca," *Journal of the History of Ideas*, XXVII (1966), 23–40.

Walsh, J., "Is Buridan a sceptic about free will?" *Vivarium*, II (1964), 50–61.

Walsh, J., "Nominalism and the Ethics: Some Remarks about Buridan's Commentary," *Journal of the History of Philosophy*, IV (1966), 1–13.

Walsh, J., "Teleology in the Ethics of Buridan," *Journal of the History of Philosophy*, XVIII (1980), 265–286.

Selected Bibliography

This BIBLIOGRAPHY is intended as an introduction to the rich scholarly literature concerning medieval philosophy. For more exhaustive reports, the reader should consult the works with an asterisk below, and the bibliographies mentioned at the end of the reading selections. Preference has been given to works in English; but important works in French and German have been included, especially concerning the Islamic and Jewish traditions, where research has been less intensively pursued than in the Christian tradition. References to the translations of texts have been limited throughout to those in English, but it should be noted that important translations, particularly of works from the Islamic and Jewish traditions, exist in other European languages.

HISTORIES OF MEDIEVAL PHILOSOPHY

Altmann, A., "Jewish Philosophy," *History of Philosophy, Eastern and Western*, ed. S. Radhakrishnan, London, 1953. (Reprinted in *Philosophy A to Z*, ed. J. Gutmann, New York, 1963.)

Armstrong, A., ed., *The Cambridge History of Later Greek and Early Medieval Philosophy*, Cambridge, 1967.

Badawī, A., *Histoire de la philosophie en Islam*, 2 vols., Paris, 1972.

Brehier, E., *The History of Philosophy: The Middle Ages and the Renaissance*, trans. W. Baskin, Chicago, 1965.

Burch, G., *Early Medieval Philosophy*, New York, 1951.

Carra de Vaux, B., *Les penseurs de l'Islam*, 5 vols., Paris, 1921–1926.

Copleston, F., *A History of Philosophy*, London. Vol. II, *From Augustine to Scotus*, 1950. Vol. III, *From Ockham to Suarez*, 1953.

De Boer, T., *The History of Philosophy in Islam*, trans. E. Jones, London, 1903.

*De Wulf, M., *Histoire de la philosophie médiévale*, 6th ed., 3 vols., Louvain, 1934, 1936, 1947. *History of Medieval Philosophy*, 3rd ed., first 2 vols., trans. E. Messenger, London, 1935, 1937.

Fakhry, M., *A History of Islamic Philosophy*, New York-London, 1970.

*Forest, A., F. Van Steenberghen, and M. de Gandillac, *Le mouvement doctrinal du XIe au XIVe siècle*. Vol. 13 of *Histoire de l'église*, fondée par A. Fliche et V. Martin. [No city on title page], 1951.

*Gilson, E., *History of Christian Philosophy in the Middle Ages*, New York, 1955.

*Guttmann, Julius, *Philosophies of Judaism*, trans. D. Silverman, Philadelphia, 1964.

Hawkins, D., *A Sketch of Medieval Philosophy*, New York, 1968.

*Husik, I., *A History of Medieval Jewish Philosophy*, Philadelphia, 1916.

Horten, M., *Die Philosophie des Islam*, München, 1924.

Hyman, A., "Philosophy, Jewish," *Encyclopedia Judaica*, Jerusalem, 1972, XIII, 421–465.

Katz, S., *Jewish Philosophers*, Jerusalem, 1975.

*Kenny, A., N. Kretzmann, J. Pinborg, eds., *The Cambridge History of Later Medieval Philosophy*, Cambridge, 1982.

Knowles, D., *The Evolution of Medieval Thought*, London, 1962.

Leff, G., *Medieval Thought*, Harmondsworth, 1958.

*Maurer, A., *Medieval Philosophy*, 2d ed., Toronto, 1982.

McInerny, R., *A History of Western Philosophy*, Vol. II: *Philosophy from St. Augustine to Ockham*, Notre Dame, 1970.

Munk, S., *Mélanges de philosophie juive et arabe*, Paris, 1859. (Reprinted, 1956.)

Quadri, G., *La philosophie arabe dans l'Europe médiévale des origines à Averroès*, trans. R. Huret, Paris, 1947.

Sharif, M., ed., *A History of Muslim Philosophy*, 2 vols., Wiesbaden, 1963–66.

*Überweg, F., *Grundriss der Geschichte der Philosophie*. Vol. 2, B. Geyer, *Die Patristische und Scholastische Philosophie*, 11th ed., Berlin, 1928. (Reprinted, Graz, 1951.)

*Vajda, G., *Introduction à la pensée juive du moyen âge*, Paris, 1947.

Vignaux, P., *Philosophy in the Middle Ages: An Introdutcion,* trans. E. Hall, New York, 1959.

Walzer, R., "Islamic Philosophy," *History of Philosophy, Eastern and Western,* ed. S. Radhakrishnan, London, 1953. (Reprinted in R. Walzer, *Greek into Arabic,* Oxford, 1962,

and in *Philosophy A to Z,* ed. J. Gutmann, New York, 1963.)

Watt, W., *Islamic Philosophy and Theology,* Edinburgh, 1962.

Weinberg, J., *A Short History of Medieval Philosophy,* Princeton, 1964.

BIBLIOGRAPHIES

Ashworth, E., *The Tradition of Medieval Logic and Speculative Grammar from Anselm to the End of the Seventeenth Century: A Bibliography from 1836 Onwards,* Toronto, 1978.

Berman, L., "Medieval Jewish Religious Philosophy," *Bibliographic Essays in Medieval Jewish Studies,* New York, 1976.

Brockelmann, O., *Geschichte der Arabischen Literatur,* 2 vols., Weimar, 1898; 1902. Supplementary vols. 1–3, Leiden, 1937–1942.

Bulletin Analytique: Philosophie, Paris.

De Brie, G., *Bibliographia Philosophica, 1934–1945,* 2 vols., Brussels and Antwerp, 1950, 1954.

De Menasce, P., *Arabische Philosophie.* Vol. 6 of *Bibliographische Einführungen in das Studium der Philosophie,* Bern, 1948.

Farrar, C., and A. Evans, *Bibliography of English Translations from Medieval Sources,* New York, 1946.

Joel, I. and others, *Reshimat Ma'amarim be-Maddæi ha-Yahadut* (Index of Articles on Jewish Studies), Jerusalem, 1966—(ongoing, section VI deals with publications on Jewish Philosophy in Hebrew and European languages).

Kirjath Sefer, Jerusalem.

Pearson, J., *Index Islamicus* 1906–55. Cambridge, 1958; *Supplement* 1956–60. Cambridge, 1962. *Second Supplement 1961–1965,* Cambridge, 1967; *Third Supplement 1966–1970,* London, 1972; *Fourth Supplement (Part I) 1971–1972,* London, 1973; *Fourth Supplement (Part II) 1972–1973,* London, 1973; *Fourth Supplement (Part III)*

1973–1974, London 1975 (ongoing).

Progress of Medieval and Renaissance Studies in the United States and Canada, Boulder.

Repertoire bibliographique de la philosophie, supplement to *Revue néoscolastique de philosophie.* (Since 1946, *Revue philosophique de Louvain.*)

Spade, P., *The Medieval Liar: A Catalogue of Insolubilia Literature,* Toronto, 1975.

Steinschneider, M., *Die Arabischen Übersetzungen aus dem Griechischen,* Leipzig, 1897. (Reprinted, Graz, 1960.)

Steinschneider, M., *Die hebräischen Übersetzungen des Mittelalters und die Juden als Dolmetscher,* Berlin, 1893. (Reprinted, Graz, 1956.)

Vajda, G., *Jüdische Philosophie.* Vol. 19 of *Bibliographische Einführungen in das Studium der Philosophie,* Bern, 1950.

Vajda, G., "Les études de philosophie juive du moyen âge depuis le synthèse de Julius Guttmann," *Hebrew Union College Annual,* XLIII (1972), 125–147 and XLV (1974), 205–242.

Vajda, G., "Les études de philosophie juive du moyen âge 1950–1960," *Die Metaphysik im Mittelalter,* ed. P. Wilpert, Berlin, 1963, 127–135.

Van Steenberghen, F., *La bibliothèque du philosophie médiéviste,* Louvain–Paris, 1974.

Van Steenberghen, F., *Philosophie des Mittelalters.* Vol. 17 of *Bibliographische Einführungen in das Studium der Philosophie,* Bern, 1950.

PERIODICALS

Al Andalus

Archives d'histoire doctrinale et littéraire du moyen âge

Augustinian Studies

Beiträge zur Geschichte der Philosophie des Mittelalters

Bulletin de la Société Internationale pour l'Étude de la Philosophie Médiévale

Bulletin de Philosophie Médiévale

Bulletin de théologie ancienne et médiévale

Franciscan Studies

Franziskanische Studien

Der Islam

Islamic Culture

Islamic Quarterly

The Jewish Quarterly Review

Journal Asiatique

Journal of Jewish Studies

Journal of the American Oriental Society
Journal of the History of Philosophy
Journal of the Royal Asiatic Society
Mediaeval Studies
The Modern Schoolman
Monatsschrift für Geschichte und Wissenschaft des Judentums (last issue, 1939; printed, 1963)
The Muslim World
The New Scholasticism
Oriens

Proceedings of the American Academy for Jewish Research
Recherches de théologie ancienne et médiévale
Revue des études Islamiques
Revue des études Juives
Revue philosophique de Louvain
Sefarad
Speculum
The Thomist
Traditio
Vivarium

STUDIES

Altmann, A., Studies in Religious Philosophy and Mysticism, Ithaca, N.Y., 1969.

Anawati, G., Études de philosophie musulmane, Paris, 1974.

Anawati, G., "Le Neoplatonism dans la pensée musulmane: état actuel des recherches," Plotino e il Neoplatonismo in Oriente e in Occidente (Accademia Nazionale dei Lincei, Roma), 1974, 339–405.

Arberry, A., An Introduction to the History of Sufism, New York, 1943.

Arberry, A., Revelation and Reason in Islam, London, 1957.

Arberry, A., Sufism, London, 1950.

Arnaldez, R., "L'histoire de la pensée greque vue par les Arabes," Bulletin de la Société Française de Philosophie, LXXII (1978), 117–168.

Bernand, M., "La critique de la notion de nature (Tab) par le Kalām," Studia Islamica, LI (1980), 59–105.

Bigongiari, D., Essays on Dante and Medieval Culture. Critical Studies in the thought and texts of Dante, St. Augustine, St. Thomas Aquinas, Marsilius of Padua, and others, Florence, 1964.

Bochenski, I., A History of Formal Logic, trans. I. Thomas, Notre Dame, Ind., 1961.

Boehner, P., Medieval Logic, Chicago, 1952.

Bouamrane, Le problème de la liberté humaine dans la pensée musulmane (solution mu'tazilite), Paris, 1978.

Bowman, L., "The Development of the Doctrine of the Agent Intellect in the Franciscan School of the Thirteenth Century," The Modern Schoolman, L (1972–73), 251–279.

Carlyle, R., and A. Carlyle, A History of Medieval Political Theory in the West, 6 vols., London, 1903–1936.

Carré, M., Realists and Nominalists, London, 1946.

Cayré, F., Manual of Patrology and of History of Theology, trans. H. Howitt, 2 vols., Paris, 1936. (4th French ed., Paris, 1945.)

Chenu, M., La théologie au XIIe siècle, Paris,

Chenu, M., La théologie comme science au XIIIe siècle, Paris, 1957.

Chenu, M., Nature, Man, and Society in the Twelfth Century. Essays on the New Theological Perspectives in the Latin West, with a preface by E. Gilson, ed. and trans. by J. Taylor and L. Little, Chicago–London, 1968.

Craig, W., The Kalām Cosmological Argument, New York, 1979.

Davidson, H., "The Active Intellect in the Cuzari and Hallevi's Theory of Causality," Revue des Études Juives, CXXX (1972), 351–396.

De Bruyne, E., The Esthetics of the Middle Ages, trans. E. Hennessy, New York, 1969.

de Ghellinck, J., Le mouvement théologique du XIIe siècle, 2nd ed., Bruges, 1948.

d'Entrèves, A., The Medieval Contribution to Political Thought, Oxford, 1939.

De Wulf, M., Philosophy and Civilization in the Middle Ages, Princeton, 1922.

Efros, I., Studies in Medieval Jewish Philosophy, New York–London, 1974.

Efros, I., The Problem of Space in Medieval Jewish Philosophy, New York, 1917.

Fakhry, M., Islamic Occasionalism, London, 1958.

Fortin, E., Dissidence et philosophie au moyen âge: Dante et ses antécédents. Vol. VI, Cahiers d'Études Médiévales, Montreal–Paris, 1981.

Frank, R., Beings and their Attributes. The Teachings of the Basrian School of the Mu'tazila in the Classical Period, Albany, 1978.

Frankl, P., Ein mu'tazilitischer Kalam aus dem 10. Jahrhundert, Wien, 1872.

Gardet, L., and M. Anawati, Introduction à la théologie musulmane. Vol. 37, Études de philosophie médiévale, Paris, 1948.

Gauthier, L., "Scolastique musulmane et scolastique chrétienne," Revue d'histoire de la philosophie, II (1928), 221–253, 333–365.

Gilson, E., "Les sources Gréco-Arabes de l'Agustinisme Avicennisant," Archives d'histoire doctrinale et littéraire du moyen âge, IV

(1929), 5–149.

Gilson, E., *Reason and Revelation in the Middle Ages*, New York, 1938.

Gilson, E., *The Spirit of Medieval Philosophy*, New York, 1948.

Glorieux, P., *La littérature quodlibetique*, 2 vols., Paris, 1925, 1935.

Goldziher, I., *Vorlesungen über den Islam*, 2nd ed., Heidelberg, 1925.

Grabmann, M., *Die Geschichte der Scholastischen Methode*, 2 vols., Freiburg, 1909, 1911. (Reprinted, Graz, 1956.)

Grabmann, M., *Mittelalterliches Geistesleben*, München, Vol. I, 1926; Vol. II, 1936; Vol. III, 1956.

Guillaume, A., "Philosophy and Theology," *The Legacy of Islam*, ed. T. Arnold and A. Guillaume, Oxford, 1931.

Guttmann, Jacob, *Das Verhältnis des Thomas von Aquino zum Judentum und zur Jüdischen Literatur*, Göttingen, 1891.

Guttmann, Jacob, *Die Scholastik des 13. Jahrhunderts in ihren Beziehungen zum Judentum und zur jüdischen Literatur*, Breslau, 1902.

Guttmann, Julius, "Das Verhältniss von Religion und Philosophie bei Jehuda Halewi," *Festschrift zu Israel Lewys 70. Geburtstag*, Breslau, 1911, 327–358.

Guttmann, Julius, "Zur Kritik der Offenbahrungslehre in der islamischen und jüdischen Philosophie," *Monatsschrift für Geschichte und Wissenschaft des Judentums*, LXXVIII (1934), 456–464.

Harnack, A., *History of Dogma*, trans. N. Buchanan, 7 vols., Boston, 1895–1900.

Hearnshaw, F., ed., *The Social and Political Ideas of some Great Medieval Thinkers*, London, 1923.

Henry, D., *Medieval Logic and Metaphysics. A Modern Introduction*, London, 1972.

Heinemann, I., *Die Lehre von der Zweckbestimmung des Menschen im griechisch-römischen Altertum und im jüdischen Mittelalter*, Breslau, 1926.

Horovitz, S., *Die Psychologie bei den jüdischen Religionsphilosophen des Mittelalters von Saadia bis Maimûni*, Breslau, 1898–1912.

Horten, M., *Philosophische Probleme der spekulativen Theologie im Islam*, Bonn, 1912.

Hourani, G., ed., *Essays on Islamic Philosophy and Science*, Albany, 1975.

Hourani, G., *Islamic Rationalism; The Ethics of Abd al-Jabbar*, Oxford, 1971.

Hyman, A., ed., *Essays in Medieval Jewish and Islamic Philosophy*, New York, 1977.

Hyman, A., "The Liberal Arts and Jewish Philosophy," *Arts libéraux et philosophie au moyen âge* (Actes du quatrième congrès international de philosophie médiévale), Montreal–Paris, 1969, 98–110.

Kantorowicz, E., *The King's Two Bodies*, Princeton, 1959.

Kaufmann, D., *Die Sinne: Beiträge zur Geschichte der Physiologie und Psychologie im Mittelalter*, Budapest, 1884.

Kaufmann, D., *Geschichte der Attributenlehre in der jüdischen Religionsphilosophie des Mittelalters von Saadia bis Maimûni*, Gotha, 1877.

Klibansky, R., *The Continuity of the Platonic Tradition*, London, 1939.

Kneale, W., and M. Kneale, *The Development of Logic*, Oxford, 1962.

Knuutila, S., ed., *Reforging the Great Chain of Being: Ancient and Medieval Modality*, Dordrecht–Boston, 1980.

Kraus, P., "Plotin chez les Arabes," *Bulletin de l'Institute d'Egypte*, XXIII (1941), Cairo.

Kretzmann, N., ed., *Medieval Philosophy in the Philosophy Curriculum*, San Francisco, 1981.

Lagarde, G., *La naissance de l'ésprit laïque au declin du moyen âge*, 6 vols., 3e éd., Louvain, 1956–1963.

Leff, G., *The Dissolution of the Medieval Outlook*, New York, 1976.

Lottin, O., *Psychologie et morale au XIIe et XIIIe siècles*, 4 vols., Louvain, 1942–1954; Vol. 5, Gembloux, 1959.

MacDonald, D., *Development of Muslim Theology, Jurisprudence, and Constitutional Theology*, London, 1903.

Madkour, I., *L'Organon d'Aristote dans le monde Arabe*, 2nd ed., Paris, 1969.

Marenbon, J., *From the Circle of Alcuin to the School of Auxerre*, Cambridge, 1981.

Massignon, L., *La passion d'al-Hallaj, martyr mystique de l'Islam*, Paris, 1922.

Maurer, A., "Some Aspects of Fourteenth Century Philosophy," *Medievalia et Humanistica*, VII (1976), 175–188.

McIlwain, C., *The Growth of Political Thought in the West*, New York, 1932.

McMullin, G., ed., *The Concept of Matter in Greek and Medieval Philosophy*, Notre Dame, 1963.

Modern Studies in Medieval Logic, Semantics, and Philosophy of Science, Synthese, XL (1979), Nr. 1.

Moody, E., *Studies in Medieval Philosophy, Science, and Logic*, Berkeley–Los Angeles–London, 1975.

Moody, E., *Truth and Consequence in Mediaeval Logic*, Amsterdam, 1953.

Morewedge, P., "Contemporary Scholarship in Near Eastern Philosophy," *The Philosophical Forum*, II (1970), 22-140.

Morewedge, P., ed., *Islamic Philosophical Theology*, Albany, 1979.

Morewedge, P., ed., *Studies in Islamic Philosophy and Science*, Albany, 1974.

Morrall, J., *Political Thought in Medieval*

Times, London, 1958.

Nader, A., *Le système philosophique des Muʿtazila,* Beirut, 1956.

O'Leary, D., *Arabic Thought and its Place in History,* London, 1922.

O'Leary, D., *How Greek Science Passed to the Arabs,* London, 1948.

Pegis, A., "Four Medieval Ways to God," *The Monist,* LIV (1970), 317–358.

Peters, F., *Aristotle and the Arabs;* The Aristotelian Tradition in Islam, New York, 1968.

Peters, F., *Aristoteles Arabus.* The Oriental Translations and Commentaries of the Aristotelian Corpus, Leiden, 1968.

Philosophical Forum, IV, 1 (Fall 1972) (Issue on Islamic Philosophy).

Pieper, J., *Scholasticism: Personalities and Problems of Medieval Philosophy,* tr. R. and C. Winston, New York, 1960.

Pines, S., "Aristotle's *Politics* in Arabic Philosophy," *Israel Oriental Studies,* V (1975), 150–160.

Pines, S., *Beiträge zur islamischen Atomenlehre,* Berlin, 1936.

Pines, S.,"Notes sur la doctrine de la prophétie et de la réhabilitation de la matière dans le Kuzari," *Mélanges de philosophie et literature Juives,* I–II (1956–1957), 253–260.

Pines, S., *Nouvelles études sur Awḥad al-Zamân Abuʾl-Barâkat al-Baghdâdi,* Paris, 1955.

Potts, T., *Conscience in Medieval Philosophy,* Cambridge, 1980.

Quasten, J., *Patrology,* 2 vols., Westminster, Md., 1950, 1953.

Rahman, F., *Prophecy in Islam,* London, 1958.

Renan, E., *Averroès et l'Averroisme,* 3rd ed., Paris, 1866. (Reprinted in *Oeuvres Complètes de Ernest Renan,* ed. H. Psichari, Vol. III, Paris, 1948.)

Rescher, N., *Studies in Arabic Philosophy,* Pittsburgh, 1967.

Rescher, N., *Studies in the History of Arabic Logic,* Pittsburgh, 1963.

Rescher, N., *The Development of Arabic Logic,* Pittsburgh, 1964.

Rosenthal, E., *Griechisches Erbe in der jüdischen Religionsphilosophie des Mittelalters,* Stuttgart, 1960.

Rosenthal, E., *Political Thought in Medieval Islam,* Cambridge, 1958.

Rosenthal, F., *Knowledge Triumphant. The Concept of Knowledge in Medieval Islam,* Leiden, 1970.

Rosenthal, F., "On the Knowledge of Plato's Philosophy in the Islamic World," *Islamic Culture,* XIV (1940), 387–422.

Rosenthal, F., "Plotinus in Islam: The Power of Anonymity," *Plotino e il Neoplatonismo in Oriente e in Occidente* (Accademia Nazionale dei Lincei, Roma), 1974, 437–448.

Ross, J., ed., *Inquiries into Medieval Philosophy,* Westport, Conn., 1971.

Sabine, G., *A History of Political Theory,* 3rd ed., New York, 1961.

Scholem, G., *Major Trends in Jewish Mysticism,* 2nd ed., New York, 1946.

Scholem, G., *On the Kabbalah and its Symbolism,* New York, 1965.

Schreiner, M., *Der Kalam in der jüdischen Literatur,* Berlin, 1895.

Seeberg, R., *Text-book of the History of Doctrines,* trans. C. Hay, Philadelphia, 1905. (Reprinted, 1956. 5th ed. of *Lehrbuch der Dogmengeschichte,* reprinted, Graz, 1953.)

Smalley, B., ed., *Trends in Medieval Political Thought,* New York, 1965.

Spade, P., "Recent Research on Medieval Logic," *Synthese,* XL (1979), 3–18.

Steinschneider, M., *Die arabische Literatur der Juden,* Frankfurt a.M., 1902.

Stern, S., ed., *Islamic Philosophy and the Classical Tradition: Essays Presented . . . to Richard Walzer. . . .* Columbia, S.C., 1972.

Strauss, L., *Persecution and the Art of Writing,* New York, 1952.

Strauss, L., *Philosophie und Gesetz,* Berlin, 1935.

Sur la place du Moyen Âge en histoire de la philosophie, Bulletin de la Société Française de Philosophie, LXVIII (1974), n. 1.

Sweetman, J., *Islam and Christian Theology,* London, 1945 sqq.

Synan, E., "Latin Philosophies of the Middle Ages," in J. Powell, ed., *Medieval Studies: an Introduction,* Syracuse, 1976, 277–311.

Touati, C., "La controverse de 1303–1306 autour des études philosophiques et scientifiques," *Revue des Études Juives,* MXXVII (1968), 21–37.

Ullman, W., *Medieval Political Thought,* Baltimore, 1976.

Vajda, G., *Isaac Albalag, Averroist juif, traducteur et annotateur d'Al-Ghazâli,* Paris, 1960.

Vajda, G., *L'amour de Dieu dans la pensée juive du moyen âge,* Paris, 1957.

Vajda, G., *La théologie ascétique de Bahya Ibn Paqûda.* Vol. VII, *Cahiers de la Société Asiatique,* Paris, 1947.

Vajda, G., "Le 'Kalam' dans la pensée religieuse juive du moyen âge," *Revue de l'Histoire des Religions,* MLXXXIII (1973), 143–160.

Vajda, G., "Le néoplatonisme dans la pensée juive du moyen âge," *Atti della Accademia Nazionale dei Lincei,* Rome, XXVI (1971), 309–324.

Vajda, G., *Recherches sur les relations entre la philosophie et la Kabbale dans la pensée juive du moyen âge,* Paris, 1962.

Van Steenberghen, F., *Aristotle in the West,* trans. L. Johnston, Louvain, 1955.

Van Steenberghen, F., ed., "Problèmes specifiques de méthode en histoire de la philosophie médiévale," *Revue de l'Université de Bruxelles*, 1973, n. 3–4, 398–410.

von Gierke, O., *Political Theories of the Middle Ages*, trans. F. Maitland, Cambridge, 1900.

von Grunebaum, G., ed., *Logic in Classical Islamic Culture*, Wiesbaden, 1970.

Wallace, W., *Causality and Scientific Explanation*, Vol. I, *Medieval and Early Classical Science*, Ann Arbor, 1972.

Walzer, R., *Greek into Arabic, Essays on Islamic Philosophy*, Oxford, 1962.

Watt, W., *Free Will and Predestination in Early Islam*, London, 1948.

Watt, W., *Islamic Political Thought, The Basic Concepts*, Edinburgh, 1968.

Wensinck, A., *The Muslim Creed; Its Genesis and Historical Development*, Cambridge, 1932.

Wippel, J., *The Metaphysical Thought of Godfrey of Fontaine*, Washington, 1981.

Wolfson, H., "Notes on Proofs of the Existence of God in Jewish Philosophy," *Hebrew Union College Annual*, I (1924), 575–596.

Wolfson, H., *Philo, Foundations of Religious Philosophy in Judaism, Christianity and Islam*, 2 vols., 2nd printing, rev., Cambridge, Mass., 1948.

Wolfson, H., *Repercussions of the Kalam in Jewish Philosophy*, Cambridge, Mass., 1979.

Wolfson, H. A., *Studies in the History of Philosophy and Religion*, ed. I. Twersky and G. Williams, vol. 1–2, Cambridge, Mass., 1973–77.

Wolfson, H., "The Amphibolous Terms in Aristotle, Arabic Philosophy and Maimonides," *Harvard Theological Review*, XXXI (1938), 151–173.

Wolfson, H., "The Classification of Sciences in Medieval Jewish Philosophy," *Hebrew Union College Jubilee Volume* (1925), 263–315. Additional notes, *Hebrew Union College Annual*, III (1926), 371–375.

Wolfson, H., "The Double Faith Theory in Clement, Saadia, Averroes and St. Thomas," *Jewish Quarterly Review*, N.S., XXXIII (1942), 213–264.

Wolfson, H., "The Internal Senses in Latin, Arabic and Hebrew Philosophical Texts," *Harvard Theological Review*, XXIX (1935), 69–133.

Wolfson, H., *The Philosophy of the Church Fathers*, Vol. I, Cambridge, Mass., 1956.

Wolfson, H., *The Philosophy of the Kalam*, Cambridge, Mass., 1976.

Wolfson, H., "The Veracity of Scripture in Philo, Halevi, Maimonides and Spinoza," *Alexander Marx Jubilee Volume*, 1950, 603–663. (Reprinted in *Religious Philosophy*, Cambridge, Mass., 1961.)

Zainaty, G., *La morale d'Avempace*. Vol. 22, *Études Musulmanes*, Paris, 1979.

ENCYCLOPEDIAS

Dictionnaire de théologie catholique, 1902–1950.

Dictionnaire d'histoire et de géographie ecclésiastique.

Encyclopedia Judaica, 10 vols. (A-Lyra), 1928–1934.

Encyclopedia Judaica, 16 vols., Jerusalem, 1972 (Yearbook, 1973, ongoing).

Encyclopedia of Islam, 1908–1936, supplement, 1938. New edition begun, 1954.

Encyclopedia of Philosophy, 8 vols., 1967.

Hasting's Encyclopedia of Religion and Ethics, 1908–1927.

Histoire littéraire de la France, 1733 sqq.

The Jewish Encyclopedia, 1901–1906.

The New Catholic Encyclopedia, 1967.

MEDIEVAL HISTORY, CULTURE AND LEARNING

Altmann, A., ed., *Jewish Medieval and Renaissance Studies*, Cambridge, Mass., 1967.

Artz, F., *The Mind of the Middle Ages: A.D. 200–1500*, New York, 1953.

Baldwin, J., *The Scholastic Culture of the Middle Ages, 1000–1300*, Lexington, Mass., 1971.

Baron, S., *A Social and Religious History of the Jews*, Philadelphia, 1952 sqq., especially Vol. VIII.

Barraclough, G., *The Medieval Papacy*, London, 1968.

Benson, R. and G. Constable, eds., *The Renaissance of the Twelfth Century*, Cambridge, Mass., 1982.

The Cambridge Economic History of Europe from the Decline of the Roman Empire, 2 vols., Cambridge, 1941–1952.

The Cambridge History of Islam, ed. by P. Holt and others, 2 vols., Cambridge, 1970 (esp. S. Pines, "Philosophy," II, 780–823).

The Cambridge Medieval History, 8 vols., Cambridge, 1913–1936.

Clagett, M., *Nicole Oresme and the Medieval Geometry of Qualities and Motions*, Madison, 1968.

Clagett, M., *Studies in Medieval Physics and*

Mathematics, London, 1979.

Cobban, A., *The Medieval Universities: Their Development and Organization*, London, 1975.

Crombie, A., *Medieval and Early Modern Science*, 2 vols., Garden City, N.Y., 1959.

Daly, L., *The Medieval University*, New York, 1961.

de Ghellinck, J., *L'essor de la littérature latine du XIIe siècle*, Paris, 1946.

de Ghellinck, J., *Littérature latine au moyen âge*, Paris, 1939.

Duhem, P., *Le système du monde*, 10 vols., Paris, 1913–1059.

Goitein, D., ed., *Religion in a Religious Age*, Cambridge, Mass., 1974.

Grant, E., ed., *A Source Book in Medieval Science*, Cambridge, Mass., 1974.

Grant, E., *Much Ado About Nothing: Theories of Space and Vacuum from the Middle Ages to the Scientific Revolution*, Cambridge, Mass., 1981.

Grant, E., *Physical Science in the Middle Ages*, New York, 1971.

Hale, J., Highfield and B. Smalley, eds., *Europe in the Late Middle Ages*, London, 1965.

Halphen, L., *Initiation aux études d'histoire du moyen âge*, 3e éd. par Y. Renouard, Paris, 1952.

Haskins, C., *Studies in Medieval Culture*, Oxford, 1929.

Haskins, C., *The Renaissance of the Twelfth Century*, Cambridge, Mass., 1939.

Haskins, C., *The Rise of Universities*, New York, 1923.

Heer, F., *The Medieval World*, trans. J. Sondheimer, New York, 1963.

Histoire de l'église depuis les origines jusqu'a nos jours, fondée par A. Fliche et V. Martin, 26 vols. (No city on title pages.) Especially vols. 4–14.

Histoire du moyen âge, 10 vols., Paris. Part of *Histoire générale*, fondée par Gustave Glotz.

Hitti, P., *The Arabs, A Short History*, 4th ed., London, 1960.

Huizinga, J., *The Waning of the Middle Ages*, trans. F. Hopman, London, 1924.

Ijsewijn, J. and J. Paquet, eds., *The Universities in the Late Middle Ages*, Leuven, 1978.

Knowles, D., *The Monastic Order in England*, Cambridge, 1940.

Knowles, D., *The Religious Orders in England*, Cambridge, 1948.

Kretzmann, N., ed., *Infinity and Continuity in Ancient and Medieval Thought*, Ithaca, 1982.

Langholm, O., *Price and Value in the Aristotelian Tradition*, Oslo, 1979.

Leff, G., *Heresy in the Later Middle Ages: The Relation of Heterodoxy to Dissent*, c. 1250–1450, 2 vols., Manchester–New York, 1967.

Leff, G., *Paris and Oxford Universities in the Thirteenth and Fourteenth Centuries. An Institutional and Intellectual History*, New York–London, 1968.

Lindberg, D., ed., *Science in the Middle Ages*, Chicago–London, 1978.

Lindberg, D., *Theories of Vision from al-Kindi to Kepler*, Chicago, 1976.

Maier, A., *An der Grenze von Scholastik und Naturwissenschaft*, 2nd ed., Roma, 1952.

Maier, A., *Die Vorlaüfer Galileis im 14. Jahrhundert*, Roma, 1949.

Maier, A., *Metaphysische Hintergründe der spätscholastischen Naturphilosophie*, Roma, 1955.

Maier, A., *Zwei Grundprobleme der scholastischen Naturphilosophie*, 2nd ed., Roma, 1951.

Margolis, M., and A. Marx, *A History of the Jewish People*, Philadelphia, 1945.

McEvedy, C., *The Penguin Atlas of Medieval History*, London, 1961.

McLaughlin, M., *Intellectual Freedom and its Limitations in the University of Paris in the Thirteenth and Fourteenth Centuries*, New York, 1977.

Mundy, J., *Europe in the High Middle Ages*, New York, 1973.

Munro, D., and G. Sellery, *Medieval Civilization*, New York, 1917.

Murdoch, O. and E. Sylla, eds., *The Cultural Context of Medieval Learning*, Dordrecht–Boston, 1975.

Murray, A., *Reason and Society in the Middle Ages*, Oxford, 1978.

Nasr, S., *An Introduction to Islamic Cosmological Doctrines*, rev. ed., London, 1978.

Nasr, H., *Ideals and Realities of Islam*, London, 1966.

Nasr, H., *Science and Civilization in Islam*, Cambridge, Mass., 1968.

Norton, A., *Readings in the History of Education: Medieval Universities*, Cambridge, 1909.

Oberman, H., *The Harvest of Medieval Theology*, Cambridge, 1963.

Origines du Christianisme et moyen âge, vols. 27–49, 2e section: *L'évolution de l'humanité*, dirigée par Henri Berr, 1920 sqq.

The Oxford History of England, ed. G. N. Clark, Oxford, 1934 sqq. Vols. II–VI cover the medieval period.

Paetow, L., *A Guide to the Study of Medieval History*, 2nd ed., New York, 1931.

Painter, S., *A History of the Middle Ages*, New York, 1953.

Paré, G., A. Brunet, and P. Tremblay, *La renaissance du XIIe siècle: les écoles et l'enseignement*, Paris, 1933.

Pirenne, H., *Economic and Social History of Medieval Europe*, trans. I. Clegg, New York, 1937.

Poole, R., *Illustrations of the History of Medie-*

val Thought, 2nd ed., London, 1920.

Rahman, F., *Islam*, 2nd ed., Chicago, 1979.

Rand, F., *The Founders of the Middle Ages*, Cambridge, 1928.

Rashdall, H., *The Universities of Europe in the Middle Ages*, new ed. by F. Powicke and A. Emden, 3 vols., Oxford, 1936.

Rosenthal, F., ed., *The Classical Heritage in Islam*, Berkeley, 1975.

Sarton, G., *Introduction to the History of Science*, 3 vols. in 5 parts, Baltimore, 1927, 1931, 1948.

Schacht, J. and C. Bosworth, eds., *The Legacy of Islam*, 2nd ed., Oxford, 1974.

The Shorter Cambridge Medieval History, 2 vols., Cambridge, 1952.

Smalley, B., *Historians in the Middle Ages*, London, 1974.

Smalley, B., *The Study of the Bible in the Middle Ages*, 2nd ed., New York, 1952.

Southern, R., *Medieval Humanism and other Studies*, Oxford, 1970.

Southern, R., *The Making of the Middle Ages*, New Haven, 1953.

Taylor, H., *The Classical Heritage of the Middle Ages*, 3rd ed., New York, 1911.

Thompson, J., *The Medieval Library*, Chicago, 1939. (Reprinted with supplementary review article by B. Boyer, New York, 1957.)

Taylor, H., *The Medieval Mind*, 4th ed., 2 vols., Cambridge, Mass., 1949.

Thorndike, L., *History of Magic and Experimental Science*, 6 vols., New York, 1923–1941.

Thorndike, L., *The History of Medieval Europe*, 3rd ed., Boston, 1949.

Ullmann, W., *Law and Politics in the Middle Ages*, Ithaca, 1975.

Ullmann, W., *The Growth of Papal Government in the Middle Ages*, London, 1955.

Ullman, W., *The Individual and Society in the Middle Ages*, Baltimore, 1966.

Vinogradoff, P., *Roman Law in Medieval Europe*, 2nd ed., London, 1929.

von Grunebaum, G., *Islam and Medieval Hellenism: Social and Cultural Perspectives*, London, 1976.

von Grunebaum, G., *Islam, Essays in the Nature and Growth of a Cultural Tradition*, London, 1969.

von Grunebaum, G., *Medieval Islam*, 2nd ed., Chicago, 1953.

Weisheipl, J., "Curriculum of the Faculty of Arts at Oxford in the Early Fourteenth Century," *Mediaeval Studies*, XXVI (1964), 143–185.

Wilks, J., *The Problem of Sovereignty in the Later Middle Ages*, Cambridge, 1964.

Wiornszowski, H., *The Medieval University*, Princeton, 1966.

Zimmermann, A., ed., *Die Auseinandersetzungen an der Pariser Universität im XIII. Jahrhundert*, Berlin–New York, 1976.

TEXTS IN TRANSLATION

A clearing house for philosophical texts in English translation has been established. For information, write to Professor Walter Scott, Department of Philosophy, Oklahoma State University, Stillwater, OK 74078.

Albo, Joseph, *Sefer ha-'kkarim (Book of Principles)*, ed. and trans. I. Husik, Philadelphia, 1929.

Al-Kindī's Metaphysics, A. Ivry, Albany, 1974.

"Al-Kindi's Treatise on the Intellect," R. McCarthy, ed. and trans., *Islamic Studies*, III (1964), 119–149.

Altmann, A., and S. Stern, *Isaac Israeli*, Oxford, 1958.

Ancient Christian Writers, ed. J. Quasten and J. Plumpe, Westminster, Md., 1946 sqq.

The *Ante-Nicene Christian Library*, 24 vols. plus supplementary vol., Edinburgh, 1866–1872, 1897.

Clagett, M., *The Science of Mechanics in the Middle Ages*, Madison, Wis., 1959.

Fairweather, E., *A Scholastic Miscellany: Anselm to Ockham*, Philadelphia, 1956.

Giles of Rome, *Giles of Rome: Errores Philosophorum*, trans. J. Riedl, ed. J. Koch, Milwaukee, 1944.

Halevi, Jehuda, *Kuzari: The Book of Proof and Argument*, abridged by I. Heinemann, Oxford, 1947. (Reprinted in *Three Jewish Philosophers*, New York, 1960.)

Halevi, Judah, *The Kuzari*, trans. H. Hirschfield, London, 1905.

Ibn Paquda, Bachya, *Duties of the Heart*, trans. M. Hyamson, 5 vols., New York, 1925–1945. (Reprinted in 2 vols., Jerusalem, 1962.)

Ibn Tufayl's Hayy Ibn Yaqzān, L. Goodman, trans., New York, 1972.

Katz, J., and R. Weingartner, eds., *Philosophy in the West*, New York, 1965.

Lerner, R., and M. Mahdi, eds., *Medieval Political Philosophy: A Sourcebook*, New York, 1963.

Lewis, E., *Medieval Political Ideas*, 2 vols., London, 1954.

The Library of Christian Classics, Philadelphia, 1953 sqq.

McKeon, R., ed. and trans., *Selections from*

Medieval Philosophers, 2 vols., New York, 1929, 1930.

Mediaeval Philosophical Texts in Translation, vols. 1–23, Milwaukee, 1942– .

Mediaeval Sources in Translation, Toronto.

Paul of Venice, *Logica Magna Prima Pars*, N. Kretzmann, trans., Oxford, 1979.

Paul of Venice, *Logica Magna Secunda Pars*, M. Adams, trans. and F. Del Punta, ed., Oxford, 1978.

Philo, trans. F. Colson, G. Whitaker, and Ralph Marcus, 10 vols., and 2 suppl. volumes, Cambridge, Mass., 1949 sqq.

Peter of Ailly: Concepts and Insolubles, P. Spade, trans., London, 1980.

A Select Library of Nicene and Post-Nicene Fathers of the Christian Church, 14 vols., 2nd series, New York, 1890–1900.

Shapiro, H., ed., *Medieval Philosophy*, New York, 1964.

Thorndike, L., *University Records and Life in the Middle Ages*, New York, 1944.

William of Sherwood's Introduction to Logic, N. Kretzmann, ed. and trans., Minneapolis, 1966.

Wippel, J. and A. Wolter, eds., *Medieval Philosophy: From St. Augustine to Nicholas of Cusa*, New York, 1969

Index